AMERICA'S CHALLENGE

AMERICA'S CHALLENGE

ENGAGING *a* RISING CHINA
in the TWENTY-FIRST CENTURY

MICHAEL D. SWAINE

CARNEGIE ENDOWMENT
FOR INTERNATIONAL PEACE
WASHINGTON DC ▪ MOSCOW ▪ BEIJING ▪ BEIRUT ▪ BRUSSELS

Carnegie Endowment for International Peace
1779 Massachusetts Avenue, N.W., Washington, DC 20036
Phone: + 202 483 7600   Fax: + 202 483 1840
CarnegieEndowment.org

The Carnegie Endowment does not take institutional positions on public policy issues; the views represented here are the author's own and do not necessarily reflect the views of the Endowment, its staff, or its trustees.

To order, contact Carnegie's distributor:
Hopkins Fulfillment Service
PO Box 50370, Baltimore, MD 21211-4370
Phone: + 1 800 537 5487 or + 410 516 6956   Fax: + 410 516 6998

Library of Congress Cataloging-in-Publication Data

Swaine, Michael D.
  America's challenge : engaging a rising China in the twenty-first century / Michael D. Swaine.
    p. cm.
  Includes bibliographical references and index.
  ISBN 978-0-87003-257-8 (pbk.) — ISBN 978-0-87003-258-5 (cloth) 1. United States—Foreign relations—China. 2. China—Foreign relations—United States. 3. China—Foreign relations—Asia. 4. Asia—Foreign relations—China. 5. United States—Foreign relations—Asia. 6. Asia—Foreign relations—United States. 7. China—Strategic aspects. 8. Asia—Strategic aspects. I. Title.

  JZ1480.A57C6 2011a
  327.73051—dc23

                          2011018889

Cover Design by Mission Media
Composition by Circle Graphics
Printed by United Book Press

MIX
Paper from
responsible sources
FSC® C010236

CONTENTS

ACKNOWLEDGMENTS

▼

This book began its life as a chapter I wrote in 2008 for a volume in the Strategic Asia series of annual monographs edited by my friend and colleague Ashley J. Tellis and published by the National Bureau of Asian Research (NBR). That chapter, "Managing China as a Strategic Challenge," in Ashley J. Tellis, Mercy Kuo, and Andrew Marble (eds), *Strategic Asia 2008–09: Challenges and Choices* (Seattle: National Bureau of Asian Research, 2008), 71–105, was the product of a considerably longer draft that the editors of Strategic Asia wisely rejected as "exceeding our space limitations." However, rather than let all that additional work go to waste (!), I resolved to turn the manuscript into a broader report on U.S. policy toward China, thinking such a task would require at most a few weeks or a couple of months. Three years later, here is that "report," more comprehensive, certainly more detailed, and hopefully more analytical and probing than originally anticipated. This more ambitious work emerged as it became apparent to myself and others that it had the potential to be the first extensive study of the many new and in some ways more daunting policy challenges that China poses for the United States in the twenty-first century. I hope that potential has been realized. But that is for the reader to judge.

An undertaking of this size would not have been possible without the steadfast efforts and prodigious talents of many individuals. First and foremost among them are a coterie of research assistants, beginning with Stephanie Renzi (formerly of the NBR), and extending through three tenures of Carnegie Junior Fellows associated with the China (now Asia) Program: Ali Wynne, Kevin Slaten, Tiffany Ng, Weilu Tan, and Rachel Esplin Odell. Usually serving for a one year period, each of these highly capable college graduates devoted many long hours and applied seemingly endless reservoirs of creative energies to what at times seemed like a never-ending effort. Their contributions involved locating and often summarizing thousands of sources, creating hundreds of footnotes, providing invaluable assistance for the seemingly endless updates required over a three year period, and offering countless suggestions for improvement in structure and content. Jessica Chen, an unpaid assistant during part of 2010, also provided important research support. I owe each of these talented individuals a huge debt of gratitude. I am particularly indebted to Tiffany and Rachel. The former was instrumental in the production of the first full rough draft and the latter provided invaluable assistance in producing the final, revised draft sent to the Carnegie Publications Department. The term "research assistant" does not adequately encompass their contribution. In many cases, they helped to shape my thoughts and analysis on many issues.

I am also indebted to several colleagues who read parts or all of the draft at various points in its production. Excellent comments and suggestions were pro–vided by three formal reviewers: Robert Sutter of Georgetown University, Alice Miller of the Hoover Institution at Stanford University, and Aaron Friedberg of Princeton University. Several colleagues read parts of the manuscript, in many cases applying their particular expertise to individual chapters. These included Kenneth Lieberthal, Philip Saunders, Dennis Blasko, Bernard Cole, Albert Keidel, Yukon Huang, Pieter Bottelier, and Mike Mochizuki. I incorporated their corrections, additions, and assessments wherever possible. Finally, I am deeply appreciative of the insights and observations provided by over fifty current and former U.S. policy practitioners whom I interviewed at various times during the course of my research, from 2008–2010. Their real-world experiences were invaluable to the analysis presented in chapter 9 in particular. In the end, however, I alone am responsible for what is contained herein.

Finally, I would like to thank Ilonka Oszvald, the senior manager of the Carnegie Publications Department, and her very able staff for expediting the production of this book.

ACRONYMS

ACD	Asia Cooperation Dialogue
AEC	Asian Economic Community
APEC	Asia-Pacific Economic Cooperation (forum)
APT	ASEAN Plus Three
ARF	ASEAN Regional Forum
ASEAN	Association of Southeast Asian Nations
C4I	Command, control, communications, computers, and intelligence
C4ISR	Command, control, communications, computers, intelligence, surveillance, and reconnaissance
CCP	Chinese Communist Party
CECC	Congressional-Executive Commission on China
CGWIC	China Great Wall Industries Company
China CDC	Chinese Center for Disease Control and Prevention
CO_2	Carbon dioxide
CTBT	Comprehensive Test Ban Treaty
DOE	Department of Energy (United States)
DPJ	Democratic Party of Japan

DPP	Democratic Progressive Party (Taiwan)
DPRK	Democratic People's Republic of Korea (North Korea)
EAC	East Asian Community
EAI	East Asia Informal
EAS	East Asia Summit
EIA	Energy Information Administration (United States)
EEZ	Exclusive economic zone
EPA	Environmental Protection Agency (United States)
ETIM	East Turkistan Islamic Movement
FTA	Free trade agreement
FTAAP	Free Trade Agreement of the Asia-Pacific
G-8	Group of Eight
G-20	Group of Twenty
GDP	Gross domestic product
H1N1	Influenza A (H1N1) virus, a.k.a. swine flu
H5N1	Influenza A (H5N1) virus, a.k.a. avian flu
IAEA	International Atomic Energy Agency
IEA	International Energy Agency
IMCAPI	International Ministerial Conference on Animal and Pandemic Influenza
IMF	International Monetary Fund
IPAPI	International Partnership on Avian and Pandemic Influenza
IPR	Intellectual property rights
JCCT	Joint Commission on Commerce and Trade
JSCC	(United States–Japan) Joint Security Consultative Committee
KMT	Kuomintang (Taiwan)
LDP	Liberal Democratic Party (Japan)
LNG	Liquefied natural gas
MOOTW	Military operations other than war
MTCR	Missile Technology Control Regime
NATO	North Atlantic Treaty Organization
NDPG	National Defense Program Guidelines (Japan)
NEC	National Energy Commission (China)
NFU	No-first-use
NORINCO	China North Industries Corporation
NPR	Nuclear Posture Review
NPT	Nuclear Non-Proliferation Treaty

NSC	National Security Council
NSG	Nuclear Suppliers Group
PACOM	U.S. Pacific Command
PKO	Peacekeeping operation
PLA	People's Liberation Army
PLAN	People's Liberation Army Navy
PRC	People's Republic of China
PSI	Proliferation Security Initiative
RMB	Renminbi
6PT	Six-Party Talks
S&ED	(U.S.-China) Strategic and Economic Dialogue
SARS	Severe acute respiratory syndrome
SCO	Shanghai Cooperation Organization
SED	(U.S.-China) Strategic Economic Dialogue
SEPA	State Environmental Protection Administration (China)
SIPRI	Stockholm International Peace Research Institute
(New) START	(New) Strategic Arms Reduction Treaty
TAC	Treaty of Amity and Cooperation
TIFA	Trade and investment framework agreement
TPP	Trans-Pacific Partnership (or Trans-Pacific Strategic Economic Partnership)
UNCLOS	United Nations Convention on the Law of the Sea
UNHRC	United Nations Human Rights Council
U.S. CDC	U.S. Centers for Disease Control and Prevention
WHO	World Health Organization
WMD	Weapons of mass destruction
WTO	World Trade Organization

FOREWORD

There is no shortage of studies examining the impact of China's rising power and influence. Since at least the early 1980s, numerous observers have tracked and assessed the political, economic, security, and social implications for the United States, Asia, and the world of everything from China's rapid growth and demand for external resources to its expanding military capabilities and deepening involvement in developing countries. But, until now, few if any studies—and no book-length volume—have examined and assessed U.S. relations with China in every major area of relevance, from great power interactions in Asia to human rights.

Indeed, this volume is unique in several respects. First and foremost, it is not a history or assessment of China's rise or of United States–China relations per se. It focuses primarily on American strategy and policies, drawing on an exhaustive set of primary and secondary sources and detailed interviews with over fifty U.S. policy practitioners, conducted by the author in 2008–2010. Such research provides the basis for a truly comprehensive examination of the beliefs, actions, and processes influencing U.S. policy toward China, and of the key trends shaping the future.

Second, this study attempts to capture what is new and different about the context within which U.S. policymakers must operate in the twenty-first century. It argues that three new sets of variables—China's growing power and global presence, the forces of economic and social globalization, and an array of nontraditional security threats—are fundamentally reshaping the strategic assumptions, policy priorities, and internal decision-making structures that have governed Washington's policy toward Beijing.

Michael Swaine draws what will almost certainly prove to be several controversial conclusions regarding future U.S. strategy. He argues that to successfully manage the growing number of challenges that China's emergence presents in the new century, U.S. policymakers need to reexamine some of their most fundamental beliefs regarding the role of American power in the Western Pacific, existing prohibitions on consulting with Beijing over arms sales to Taiwan, and the value of democracy promotion in the context of U.S. engagement with China.

Whether one agrees or disagrees with Swaine's policy assessments and recommendations, there is little doubt that he is asking the critical questions and that he has provided the most complete and detailed perspective available for answering them. This study will serve for years to come as an essential basis for understanding and shaping America's China policy in the new century.

—Jessica T. Mathews
President, Carnegie Endowment for International Peace

INTRODUCTION

Aside from the collapse of the Soviet Union, the emergence of the People's Republic of China on the global stage constitutes the most significant event for world politics since the end of World War II. China's physical size and population, rapid growth, geostrategic location, internal dynamism, and to some extent non–status quo attitude toward many political, economic, social, and military issues will likely enable it to play a major—perhaps decisive—role in reshaping the global distribution of power in this century. Of particular note, China's growing power will likely enable it to influence the handling of major issues confronting the international community in the new century, from climate change and the management of an increasingly globalized economy to the evolving security relationship between the advanced democracies and the major rapidly developing nations.

As the world's predominant political, economic, and military power, the United States faces a particularly tough challenge in responding to China's growing power and influence, especially in Asia. Beijing has of course played a significant role in Washington's foreign policy for at least the past thirty years, since the advent of its market-led reform policies and general economic and social opening in the late 1970s. However, the new century in many ways presents a new set of challenges related to China's rise, which will force the United States to not only develop more effective policies, but also perhaps fundamentally reassess its strategic assumptions and relationships. This book examines both these old and new challenges.

THE POLICY CHALLENGES OF THE REFORM ERA

Since at least the early 1980s, China has constituted a significant foreign policy issue for U.S. policymakers for three dynamic and interrelated reasons:

- China's obvious geostrategic significance as a large continental power in a region critical for U.S. security interests;
- China's growing economic and technological value (both globally and within Asia) as an enormous market, target of investment, supplier of goods, and competitor in many areas;
- China's image and behavior as a non-democratic, authoritarian polity with a decidedly non-Western approach to human rights and political development.

Together, these factors have posed enormous challenges and opportunities for American interests and policies. In the security realm, China first provided critical strategic leverage in managing the former Soviet Union and then, after the end of the Cold War, constituted a growing challenge as both a potential source of military confrontation (mostly because of the evolving Sino-American dispute over Taiwan) and a participant in destabilizing activities related to the proliferation of weapons of mass destruction (WMD). In this area, the primary policy challenge for Washington centered on how to beneficially influence or shape Beijing's security interests and capacities while discouraging or even preventing threatening behavior.

In the economic arena, since at least the late 1980s, China has been heralded as a new source of growth for the world economy and U.S. businesses and as a potential partner in managing an array of regional and global economic challenges. At the same time, it has generated deep anxiety and some hostility as a suspected "unfair" competitor and apparent usurper of American jobs. As in the security realm, this situation has produced a highly mixed set of imperatives for U.S. policymakers, involving efforts to jointly develop or refine bilateral and international mechanisms for strengthening the global economic order, while discouraging Chinese "mercantilist," predatory, or free riding behavior.

With regard to promoting human rights and democracy, China's one-party dictatorship has continuously presented concerns for the United States during the reform era, despite the undeniable expansion of social and economic freedoms for the vast majority of the Chinese citizenry. Beijing has continued to suppress many political freedoms at home, permit the abusive treatment of Chinese dissidents by security forces and local governments, and support or ignore the repressive behavior of many foreign governments. As a result, Washington policymakers have faced pressure to encourage the Chinese leadership to show more respect for human rights and promote a freer political realm while they seek to maintain bilateral cooperation and build the trust needed for managing a growing array of economic and security challenges.

Since at least the early 1980s, many scholars and former policy practitioners have examined these basic security, economic, and human rights issues, especially in the context of the evolving bilateral Sino-American relationship. Their studies have focused on core policy challenges confronting U.S. decision makers, including:

- the avoidance of a bilateral confrontation over the status of Taiwan;
- the management of Beijing's actual or alleged involvement in WMD proliferation;
- a variety of largely episodic trade disputes;
- the degree of China's adherence to international economic norms; and
- repeated rifts over Beijing's domestic and international approach to human rights.[1]

NEW CHALLENGES IN THE TWENTY-FIRST CENTURY

These three basic issues and the resulting five policy challenges are still obviously central concerns of American policymakers and will undoubtedly continue to draw the attention of U.S. leaders for many years to come. However, the twenty-first century has also witnessed the emergence of new forces, and a deepening of existing trends, that together have arguably led to a vastly different era in Sino-American relations involving significantly new policy issues. Three recent trends are particularly dynamic and important.

First and perhaps foremost, although still subject to enormous domestic and foreign constraints, China's capacity to influence the world has nonetheless expanded exponentially in the past decade, building upon nearly two generations of rapid economic growth and social change. While China's comparative economic standing improved dramatically in the 1980s and 1990s, since 2000 it has consolidated its ascendancy as a global economic powerhouse. Its gross domestic product (GDP) has grown from 1.7 percent of the world's GDP in 1980 ($189 billion) to 3.7 percent in 2000 ($1.2 trillion) and to 8.4 percent in 2009 ($4.9 trillion)—launching China from a position as the world's eleventh-largest economy to its sixth largest in 2000, third largest in 2009, and second largest in the summer of 2010, when China's GDP surpassed Japan's.

China's involvement in world trade has also burgeoned; its merchandise trade as a share of its GDP has grown from 20 percent in 1980 to 40 percent in 2000, and to 57 percent in 2008, when it became the world's largest exporter.[2] In particular, China has become increasingly important to the Asia-Pacific region, a reality exemplified by the dramatic increase in China's bilateral trade with the members of the Association of Southeast Asian Nations (ASEAN), which grew by over 640 percent from 2000 to 2010, as well as by the China–ASEAN Free Trade Agreement.[3] China's demand for global resources has similarly grown as its share of global consumption of oil has increased—from 2.8 percent in 1980 (1.77 million barrels a day) to 6.2 percent in 2000 (4.8 million) and to 9.8 percent in 2009 (8.2 million).[4] China's importance as a target of foreign direct investment (FDI) and a source of finished and semi-finished products has also increased dramatically, as its inflows of FDI have increased from 0.1 percent of global FDI in 1980 ($57 million) to 2.5 percent in 2000 ($38.4 billion) and to 8.1 percent in 2008 ($148 billion).[5] Financially, China has moved from a net debtor nation in the mid-1980s to the world's number one creditor nation, with its current account surplus having surpassed that of Japan in 2006.[6] With respect to the United States, China is now America's second-largest trading partner and third-largest export market, a major source of funds and consumer products, and a destination for U.S. capital and technology.[7]

The second key trend is that a more intertwined, global pattern of power distribution and interaction has emerged in three areas that critically affect the capacity of both the United States and China (as well as other nations) to solve problems and exercise influence on their own.

- The economic and financial systems of all major nations are now intimately linked to a global trade and finance network, thus drastically increasing their interdependence and need for collective action to maintain economic stability.[8]
- The information revolution has exponentially increased the speed, density, volume, and accessibility of information available to larger numbers of

citizens around the world, especially in more advanced and rapidly developing nations such as the United States and China, thus dramatically promoting the transfer and heightening the impact of various economic, political, and social ideas.[9]

- Larger numbers of citizens are moving around the globe in search of employment and amusement and as part of their jobs, thus expanding the scope and density of direct human contact and the speed of transfer of diseases.[10]

The third key trend is that nontraditional dangers such as terrorism, WMD proliferation, and climate change have emerged or intensified in the past two decades to pose far more serious threats to both individual nations and the global community. The advent of truly global networks of suicidal terrorists able and willing to utilize new information technologies, combined with the greater availability of know-how and materials related to nuclear weapons, have resulted in a particularly lethal new threat to many nations, including both the United States and China.[11] In addition, politically unstable and/or potentially threatening autocratic states such as North Korea, Iran, and Pakistan have acquired or now seek nuclear weapons, and could proliferate their new capabilities to other states. And although climate change also poses a serious global threat demanding a high level of cooperation among nations, this cooperation is proving extremely difficult to achieve, largely because the threat's gradual nature permits leaders and citizens alike to defer tough decisions, and because both citizens and nations argue over the threat's very existence and how to apportion responsibility among developed and developing nations.[12]

CHINA'S GROWING SIGNIFICANCE FOR THE UNITED STATES

As a result of these three highly dynamic trends, China's significance for America's most vital national interests has grown enormously, involving more problems, more participants at every policy level (domestic, bilateral, and international), and higher stakes to "get China policy right" on an ongoing basis. This impact can be seen in several major policy arenas.

In the political and security arena, as a result of its rapid economic growth and expanding regional and global involvement, China has increased its political, economic, and military capabilities, especially in the Asia-Pacific. This development is forcing the region's major powers—Japan, Russia, India, and South

Korea—to adjust their relations with one another, and with the United States, to cope with China's increasing power. For each country this response primarily involves making more concerted attempts to capitalize on China's growing political and economic clout while maximizing one's own leverage and strengthening Beijing's incentives to cooperate rather than compete politically, diplomatically, and in some cases strategically.

Closely related to this development, China's expanding involvement in a variety of regional and global forums and institutions, along with the growing international activism of other Asian powers and the broader globalization trends mentioned above, are leading to a much greater emphasis within Asia on a variety of multilateral efforts to integrate Beijing into a growing number of global and regional security and economic organizations. ASEAN is taking the lead in this effort, although others are also playing an increasingly important role.

In the realm of military security, China's growing ability to project power beyond its borders is now beginning to alter both U.S. security perceptions and the larger balance of power in Asia in ways that could (1) produce destabilizing security competition between China and other major nearby countries, such as Japan and India; (2) aggravate sensitive regional hotspots such as Taiwan, the Korean Peninsula, and the East and South China seas; and (3) in general challenge the United States' long-term ability to continue playing what it regards as a unique security role in the Asia-Pacific region. Most notably, China's growing military presence on its maritime periphery is challenging U.S. military predominance in the Western Pacific, thereby casting doubt on the future viability of a basic condition underlying America's strategy in this key region. This potential shift in relative power has been underscored in recent years by the growing possibility that America might confront the need to reduce its military power—both globally and in Asia—as a result of its ongoing economic difficulties, and by the concurrent rise of other regional power centers such as India.

In the economic arena, China's recent emergence as a major force in global trade, finance, and resource consumption, and its simultaneous integration with the world economy, have greatly raised its importance as a key player influencing both the world's economic stability and the growth and the vitality of the U.S. economy. In particular, China's economic behavior now exerts a great influence on the fortunes of major U.S. corporations (as investors, traders, and competitors in or with China), on the choices available to U.S. consumers, and on the quality and number of American jobs. China's significance as the second-largest economic power and its obvious importance to America's economic well-being place an unprecedented premium on the proper management of Sino-U.S. economic relations. As a result, China's economic views and actions must be taken into consideration by the leaders of other world powers, and especially by those in the United States, more than ever before.

With regard to nontraditional security threats, the emergence of a particularly virulent form of global terrorism, arguably worsening worldwide WMD proliferation, and the appearance of challenges such as climate change and pandemics similarly increase China's importance to the global community and particularly to the United States. Because China is a target of terrorism, a nuclear power with a checkered history of WMD proliferation, a major contributor to global warming, and a possible incubator of global epidemics (given its huge population and large stock of potential animal sources of disease), it has become a key player in any effort to cope with these problems. Indeed, without strong United States–China cooperation, such transnational threats will prove virtually impossible to manage.

Finally, the United States is facing significant new challenges to promoting democracy and advancing human rights brought on by China's rapidly expanding economic, social, and political influence on the nations of Asia, Africa, and Latin America; its close ties with several authoritarian regimes; and its recent emergence as a model for successful, nondemocratic economic and social development. This challenge has arguably grown significantly in the aftermath of the global economic recession, especially given China's contrasting success thus far vis-à-vis the United States in emerging from that catastrophe, along with the apparent structural deficiencies of the American economic system that it allegedly revealed. Moreover, in the domestic political sphere, Beijing has continued to show significant success in repressing a growing array of dissent and coopting potential opposition.

GENERAL IMPLICATIONS FOR U.S. POLICIES TOWARD CHINA

In all these issue areas, Beijing's expanding power and influence—often accompanied by deepening interdependence with the United States and the other major powers—are raising the stakes for Washington in its relationship with Beijing while increasing the interaction required to cope with and benefit from Beijing's growing capabilities. Increasingly, in many critical policy arenas, the past pattern of limited, somewhat ad hoc bilateral policy coordination has given way to a situation in which each side's foreign and domestic actions have a direct impact on those of the other. U.S. leaders, instead of "merely" reaching understandings or coordinating policies with Beijing (as they did to constrain Soviet behavior in the 1970s and 1980s), or avoiding disruptive trade disputes while promoting human rights (as they increasingly did in the 1980s and 1990s), must now develop carefully conceived strategies toward China to avoid adversely affecting a broad array of vital interests, many extending far beyond the bilateral relationship. In particular, such strategies can: fundamentally alter the strategic landscape in the Asia-Pacific region, significantly shape the future chances of severe political or military crises in Asia (possibly including a direct Sino-U.S. military clash); greatly impact America's and the world's economic well-being; and either successfully manage or seriously aggravate an array of global security threats, ranging from energy shortages to financial instability, global warming, conflicts over nuclear-armed powers such as North Korea and Iran, and global pandemics.[13]

Equally important, the new challenges facing U.S. policymakers in the twenty-first century will become more demanding as a result of the continuation of another long-standing feature of the Sino-American relationship: the two countries' contrasting political systems and strategic viewpoints, which have been exacerbated by their long history of mutual suspicion. These factors inject a strong element of deep-rooted uncertainty, distrust, and bilateral competition into many policy arenas. Indeed, during the past few years, this mutual suspicion has arguably worsened in the wake of various disputes, primarily involving the security of China's periphery, long-standing Chinese sovereignty claims, and China's overall growing "assertiveness." At the same time, China's expanding involvement with the United States–led global order, its strong desire for international respect, and its continued close attention to U.S. power and views suggest that Beijing will likely remain subject to Washington's influence for some time, even as China's own influence over the United States increases.

As this analysis implies, the most fundamental policy problem that U.S. leaders face in meeting these challenges is how to pursue a strategic approach to China that coordinates two basic objectives: on the one hand, efforts to maximize China's cooperation with (or at least acquiescence toward) those international and bilateral relationships and structures that best serve vital U.S. interests; and on the other hand, efforts to weaken or prevent any Chinese actions that could undermine those interests. These two goals are most commonly described on the basis of the policy approaches that advance them—either as cooperation-oriented engagement and deterrence or as shaping-oriented hedging or balancing. Moreover, both sets of approaches seek not only to influence Chinese incentives, but also to shape and in some cases even alter Chinese interests. They also imply that, in order to maintain an effective strategy overall, U.S. interests and incentives might also need to change as China's capabilities increase.

FACTORS INFLUENCING THE FUTURE
EFFICACY OF THE U.S. STRATEGY

Since the normalization of relations between Beijing and Washington in the 1970s, the United States has essentially pursued the twin strategic policy objectives of maximizing China's cooperation with vital U.S. interests and dissuading Chinese actions that could undermine these interests. However, in the twenty-first century, the emergence of the new and more intense challenges outlined above has significantly heightened this strategic problem. First, the policymaking process for addressing these challenges has become far more complicated and "messier," because it now involves coordinating an increasing number of domestic and international agencies and individuals with more complex, and often competing, interests. Equally important, the participants in this process now need a deeper level of understanding, expert knowledge, management capability, and restraint to craft and implement effective policies. Moreover, to work successfully, the twin objectives of U.S. policy must be more thoroughly integrated into a larger overall U.S. strategic approach toward China, Asia, and global issues such as climate change.

Ultimately, the United States' ability to develop and maintain an optimal strategy that maximizes Chinese incentives to cooperate on a growing array of challenging issues while shaping and deterring possible adverse Chinese behavior requires a tacit or explicit agreement or understanding between Beijing and Washington on two closely related sets of issues:

- the basic distribution of power within the international system—and especially across the Asia-Pacific—that best promotes stability and prosperity and advances each nation's interests; and
- the core values and norms that govern the activities of the nations, multilateral agreements, processes, and forums that make up the global and regional system.

Significantly divergent perceptions on such fundamental issues could lead each power to adopt largely zero-sum approaches in many areas, thus almost certainly creating an intense strategic rivalry.

The basic distribution of power centers on two factors: (1) the relative roles played by both the United States and China in the global and regional security architecture (and especially the future of U.S. military and political predominance in the Western Pacific); and (2) the dominant political and security relationships between both powers and with the other major powers in the system, especially in Asia. The core values and norms center on beliefs about such critical issues as free trade and open access to resources; the principles governing international agreements (on issues ranging from WMD counterproliferation to human rights); the definition of state sovereignty and humanitarian intervention in the domestic affairs of nation-states; the legal principles required to adjudicate various inter-state disputes; definitions of relevant social and political rights; and the proper relative levels of voting power in key international institutions held by China (and perhaps other developing nations) compared with the United States and Western democracies.

Another set of issues is of course closely related to the first set—that is, many norms governing the international system reflect the existing or passing distribution of power among nations, and highly revisionist norms will likely disrupt that distribution. Major changes in power distribution will likely lead to efforts to alter many existing norms. Therefore, if there is a high probability that Washington and Beijing can agree upon, or at least accept, each other's views on both sets of issues over time and in the face of dynamic change (including shifts in relative economic and military power), then it is likely that an effective balance between the two core elements of U.S. strategy (that is, cooperative engagement and security-oriented hedging) can be sustained well into the future. However, if, as China's power and influence grow, it increasingly comes to challenge American views in these two critical issue areas, or the United States increasingly demands more from China than it can deliver or refuses to revise its own views to accommodate Chinese requirements, then the continued viability of America's two-sided strategic approach will likely prove problematic. That is, Washington will be unable to elicit the necessary level of cooperation with China and exercise the level of deterrence toward China to maintain stability and manage the growing challenges facing both countries. Specifically, those issues identified above—including political relations among the major powers, the development of Asian regional institutions, China's growing ability to project military power beyond its borders, a large array of economic problems, future nontraditional security threats such as global warming and weapons proliferation, and U.S. promotion of democracy and human rights—will become far more difficult to handle.

This will by no means be an easy task. At the strategic level, there are many different possible approaches to engagement and hedging, and the two activities are highly interactive and subject to the influence of rapidly changing external events. In addition, individual functional policy arenas pose their own significant set of problems for U.S. policymakers, requiring a keen understanding of the issues involved and the relationships of the issues to each other and to the underlying U.S. strategy. In fact, these policy challenges, if improperly handled, would make it difficult if not impossible for Beijing and Washington to agree on the power relationships that should sustain the international system, and thus could fatally undermine any American strategy toward China. In other words, the strategy toward China on the one hand, and individual policy arenas on the other hand, influence and shape one another.

Taken together, the challenges identified here place a growing premium on the need for U.S. policymakers to implement an approach to China that is not only more farsighted but is also rooted in more finely grained assessments of (1) the likely strengths and weaknesses of Chinese and American power over time and across issue areas; (2) the adaptability of Chinese and American strategic views and national interests, especially in the face of rapidly evolving political, economic, and military circumstances; and (3) the changing views and capabilities of other major powers with a strong interest in both China and the United States. These requirements in turn suggest that U.S. leaders must first identify their own prerequisites for stability and prosperity within both the regional and global systems—not only in the sense of "hard power," but also with regard to "soft power," including predominant norms and values. They must also accurately understand the best means of influencing Chinese views and calculations, both at the strategic level and on individual issues.

ASSESSING THREE SETS OF VARIABLES FOR U.S. POLICY IN THE TWENTY-FIRST CENTURY

This study assesses the challenges described above by examining several key questions:

- What have been the key features of U.S. policy toward China during the first decade of the century, at both the strategic level and in specific policy arenas?
- How effectively has the United States been pursuing these policies during the past decade to influence Chinese behavior in the desired directions?
- What factors are likely to influence the effectiveness of U.S. policy during at least the current decade in each policy arena?
- What does this analysis say about the future effectiveness of the United States' approach to China? In particular, what needs to be changed or retained, regarding both America's strategic approach and individual

policies, to maximize the attainment of U.S. objectives over time in an ever-more-challenging power and policy environment?

- Should basic U.S. objectives or any underlying policy assumptions themselves change in response to changing circumstances?

In an effort to answer these questions, this study will examine three sets of closely interrelated variables. These include, first and foremost, U.S. policymakers' basic beliefs and underlying assumptions regarding those core interests and strategic goals of the United States that are at stake in its relationship with China, along with the implications that China's own strategic goals and actions (as perceived by U.S. policymakers) present for these beliefs and assumptions. At the most fundamental level, these notions include U.S. and Chinese leaders' requirements for continued peace, stability, and prosperity for each nation, both domestically and outwardly, throughout Asia and the world. The domestic requirements center on those capabilities needed for defending each country's territory against potential threats from the other power, and those bilateral and multilateral economic and security-related activities that affect each nation. The outward requirements center primarily on the respective roles played by American and Chinese political, economic, and military power and influence across the Asia-Pacific. Assumptions regarding both sets of requirements are obviously closely related to one another, since each country's broader posture in Asia has direct implications for its domestic defense strategy.

The second major category of variables consists of the recent legacy and logic of U.S. and Chinese policy practices in seven key policy areas: (1) the relations among key Asian powers; (2) bilateral and multilateral political and security structures and forums; (3) U.S. and Chinese military modernization programs and military-to-military activities; (4) economic development and assistance activities; (5) counterterrorism and counterproliferation challenges; (6) nontraditional security threats; and (7) efforts to promote human rights and democracy. Although the broader history of American and Chinese policies since the advent of China's reform era is obviously relevant, the policy experiences of the period since 2000 are most central to the analysis presented herein. Within these policy arenas, the combination of both past and present policy successes (as perceived by the George W. Bush and Barack Obama administrations) and simple policy inertia exert a particularly notable impact on the myriad individual contacts that make up most of America's day-to-day policy interactions with China.

The third and final set of variables consists of those possible factors that will have the most direct impact on the ability and willingness of a future U.S. administration to sustain or modify policy approaches to China. These include evolving economic and political factors, such as the cost and overall feasibility of maintaining superior U.S. military forces in the Western Pacific; the demands placed on U.S. policymakers by other issues and relationships (for example, those associated with the fight against terrorism); and the growing capabilities, expectations, and leverage of China and of those major powers that have an impact on Sino-U.S. relations and U.S. interests regarding Beijing. They also of course include the views and actions of domestic political leaders and interest groups, government agencies and shapers of public opinion, as well as the specific features of the U.S. policymaking process. As noted above, such variables are arguably becoming more important as China's power grows, as other powers with different agendas emerge in Asia and other regions, as the United States confronts political and human rights problems in other areas of the globe, and as the U.S. economy encounters new challenges.

Of course, there is no precise formula for predicting the evolution of these three sets of variables (that is, strategic assumptions, policy histories and precedents, and future features and trends), their relative importance at any particular moment, or how they might interact to influence U.S. policy toward China. To a great extent, their effect on U.S. policy is subject to the perceptions of individual leaders (particularly the U.S. president), the individuals they select to manage policy, and the policymaking process they establish to implement their decisions. Nonetheless, any U.S. political leader must operate within the parameters established by these variables.

THE IMPLICATIONS OF A FAILING CHINA

As the title of this book states, the analysis presented in this study largely assumes that despite significant challenges, China will continue to experience relatively high and constant rates of economic growth and enjoy reasonably stable social conditions for the next ten to fifteen years. As indicated in chapter 5 and elsewhere in this study, most analysts of China's situation tend to support this assumption. That said, it is certainly possible that China could lapse into a period of prolonged economic stagnation and social unrest—or even worse—over the longer term. Such a development would obviously pose a very different set of implications for U.S. policy than most of those considered in the pages that follow. In that case, Washington would likely need to cope with an insecure, unstable, and perhaps unpredictable Beijing, rather than dealing with China's challenges to U.S. military predominance in the Western Pacific and with its growing power as a far more influential and assertive global player. The challenges for the United

States in such a situation would depend very much on the form and severity of China's decline. However, they would probably not be as hugely consequential for overall U.S. interests as the challenge of a rising China examined herein—without a scenario of extreme political and social disarray or collapse.[14] In any event, the impact on U.S. policy of such longer-term possible alternative situations is beyond the scope of this study.

THE STRUCTURE OF THE STUDY

The following ten chapters examine the major features of the three sets of variables outlined above that influence U.S. policy toward China, assess their likely evolution during the current decade, and draw conclusions regarding the challenges and opportunities for U.S. policy. Chapter 1 identifies the major national interests and policy goals of the United States and China of greatest relevance to the seven core policy areas identified above and discusses possible variations in strategic approaches among the elites of both countries.

Chapters 2 through 8 analyze the policies that have been pursued to achieve U.S. objectives in each area, primarily during the George W. Bush and the Barack Obama administrations. Each chapter presents the major issues confronting U.S. policy in each area and summarizes the evolution of Bush and Obama administration policies. This discussion is combined with a summary of Chinese policy objectives and behavior during the same period. These descriptions provide the basis for an evaluation of the major challenges, successes, and apparent failures of U.S. policy. Each chapter ends with an examination of those key features that will most likely affect U.S. policy in each area during at least the current decade.

Chapter 9 augments the information on the historical record and future trends given in the preceding chapters by addressing two sets of general observations obtained primarily from interviews with more than 50 policy practitioners. These include (1) those key features of the U.S. policymaking process or domestic situation that facilitate or constrain U.S. actions; and (2) approaches to China that have had both positive and negative consequences for U.S. policy.

Chapter 10 utilizes the combined findings of the previous chapters to assess the future viability of America's current two-sided strategy toward China. It identifies the likely strategic and policy challenges and opportunities for future U.S. policymakers, and it presents recommendations relevant to both cooperative engagement and hedging, as well as to overall U.S. strategy.

MAJOR CONCLUSIONS

Barring the unlikely emergence of truly paradigm-altering changes affecting China's relation to the underlying interests of the United States (such as a Sino-American conflict over Taiwan or the collapse or democratization of the Chinese political system), U.S. policy toward China must continue to incorporate the two closely related approaches outlined above (cooperative engagement balanced with hedging) for many years to come. In the absence of significant changes, China will become neither a sworn enemy nor an ally or close and trusted friend of the United States. It will remain both an increasingly important partner or interlocutor and in many areas a difficult-to-manage competitor and potential adversary. As a result, America's leaders will need to continue to cope with the resulting uncertainties by judiciously balancing efforts to deepen cooperation with efforts to shape and deter threats. However, the new challenges of the twenty-first century, combined with many long-standing strategic and policy problems—often involving growing levels of mutual distrust—will place unprecedented demands on U.S. policymakers, requiring them to take a more proactive stance on many issues, adopt a longer-range perspective, and consider alternatives to the current emphasis on predominance in the Western Pacific as the basis of U.S. strategy toward China.

This study draws several conclusions and offers recommendations for the seven key policy arenas introduced here. Regarding political relations with the major Asian powers, even though recent events have brought Tokyo and Seoul closer to Washington, the United States risks undermining this advantage if it does not develop a more integrated strategic approach to working with both these allies, based on greater clarification of the long-term purpose and disposition of the two bilateral alliances and their relationship to one another and to China. Washington needs to resolve the basing issue in Tokyo (most likely by renegotiating the existing agreement), create a more regular and probing Track Two dialogue on the United States–Japan alliance, and work to develop a basis for stronger relations between Tokyo and Beijing.

Concerning Taiwan, Washington's largely hands-off stance toward the Beijing–Taipei relationship could prove unsustainable in light of China's growing military leverage vis-à-vis Taiwan and the unwillingness of either side to initiate serious security-oriented confidence-building measures. To avert a likely Sino-U.S. crisis over Taiwan, Washington should consider engaging in dialogue with Beijing to develop a more stable modus vivendi regarding deployments of the People's Liberation Army and U.S. arms sales and defense assistance to Taiwan, and link progress in this undertaking with the development of a political dialogue between the Chinese and Taiwanese governments.

The North Korean imbroglio is likely to become a source of growing distrust between Washington and Beijing, especially in the absence of an improvement in the broader strategic environment in Northeast Asia. Washington needs to coordinate its efforts to deepen cooperation with Seoul and Tokyo with a broader reassessment of the long-term security needs of all the major players in the region, including China. This must be a central part of more far-reaching strategic discussions, which should include a genuine Track Two strategic dialogue with Beijing that feeds directly into official negotiations.

During at least the past decade, Washington has largely failed to engage adequately with multilateral institutions in Asia to advance its objectives vis-à-vis China. Although the Obama administration has begun to reengage with these institutions, this effort needs to become more substantive. The United States needs to balance between strengthening alliances with Asian democratic governments and seeking to cooperate with China in broader regional security arrangements. Washington should make more careful and deliberate use of minilaterals and trilaterals to address a range of security issues, especially in Northeast Asia. Bilaterally, the Strategic and Economic Dialogue should involve more regular, ongoing working-level discussions.

In the military arena, for much of the past decade, the United States has largely failed to strike the right balance between deterrence and reassurance in its policies toward China. Though the U.S. military is still predominant across maritime Asia, as China's military continues to modernize and if the U.S. economy continues to stagnate, America's relative military position could diminish notably in the Western Pacific, in perception if not in reality. Such a dynamic could unnerve both friends and allies. This prospect is already producing a dangerous zero-sum mindset in the defense communities in both China and the United States, leading analysts and some U.S. officials to assert the need for the United States to maintain clear predominance over Beijing at whatever cost. But such a one-dimensional approach could prove self-defeating, especially given Washington's growing economic limitations, and possibly spur Chinese efforts to challenge U.S. military capabilities on issues such as Taiwan. Instead, Washington should undertake greater efforts to strengthen its military relationship with China, push back against hawkish voices in the defense community, and seek to enhance strategic dialogues at both the bilateral and multilateral level. At the same time, Washington should continue to strengthen its early warning and rapid deployment capabilities with regard to potential crisis areas in the Western Pacific, while examining alternatives, over the long term, to the current emphasis on U.S. military predominance.

In the increasingly important and complex economic arena, even though U.S. policy toward China has proven broadly successful, it has thus far failed to resolve or even ameliorate most problems, which could potentially result in a vicious circle of protectionism and economic nationalism. For the United States, the most important steps toward preventing this include efforts to strengthen its economy, reach free trade agreements with Asian nations (starting with ratification of the Korea–United States agreement), and seek broader multilateral cooperation on issues such as currency valuation and trade disputes.

With regard to counterterrorism, overall U.S. policy has secured cooperation with China in many areas, although there is still tension over fears that the Chinese are using counterterrorism as an excuse to repress Uighur Muslims. In the increasingly sensitive area of countering nuclear proliferation, although the United States has incorporated Beijing into the existing process, China remains a possible source of proliferation vis-à-vis Iran, North Korea, and Pakistan. This is partly due to China's lack of capacity to control proliferation activities by subordinate Chinese actors, and here Washington can help Beijing. However, U.S. policy has failed to gain sustained and sufficient levels of Chinese cooperation on Iran and North Korea due in large part to fundamental strategic disagreements, which again points to the need for a more intensive strategic dialogue, as well as more in-depth consideration of long-term U.S. strategic relations, in Northeast Asia and the Middle East.

On the environment, the United States and China have achieved substantial progress in bilateral cooperation on a wide range of issues, especially on joint projects related to capacity building and transparency in China. However, they have not been able to overcome fundamental disagreements on responsibility and burden sharing, and they have failed to work together in multilateral venues. Part of this is due to the United States' failure to reach a domestic consensus and lead internationally on this issue, which discourages Chinese cooperation. In the area of health and pandemics, although some very notable progress has been made, further advances will probably occur on the domestic front in China, involving local public health improvements and increased internal collaboration.

Finally, U.S. policy has clearly facilitated China's participation in international human rights organizations (which have to some extent improved individual rights in China) and has helped persuade China to cooperate in eliminating international rights abuses. However, U.S. policymakers have the least success vis-à-vis domestic human rights in China, partly because U.S. top-down pressure can be counterproductive. Instead, Washington should apply low-level pressure while encouraging China's participation in international rights organizations and providing aid to facilitate improvements in China's legal system, political and religious liberties, and minority and labor rights. However, China's democratization should not be a strategic objective of the United States or invoked as a standard in measuring the effectiveness of U.S. policies overall.

The formation of U.S. China policy needs to be governed by a strong central authority—most logically, the staff of the National Security Council—that can coordinate the many debating bureaucratic voices. In pursuing various approaches, U.S. policymakers should also implement the lessons learned from decades of interaction with Chinese officials. Thus, they should strive to understand China's national interests and how Beijing can be influenced by U.S. actions; develop closer personal relationships with Chinese officials through sustained dialogue; balance positive and negative inducements in leveraging the Chinese bureaucracy; and always recognize the critical importance of protocol, respect, and saving face. And to facilitate information sharing, trust building, and communication of the rationale for China policy, the National Security Council should hold regular briefings with members of Congress, congressional staff members, and key media representatives.

Effective ways of meeting these challenges will require more than just better management of each policy arena. On the strategic level, they will also likely require far more serious consideration of alternatives to U.S. predominance in the Western Pacific, including selective engagement (such as reduced levels of U.S. commitment elsewhere in the world to permit continued predominance in that vital region), offshore balancing (a withdrawal from the preponderant U.S. presence in Asia, combined with continued ties with allies), and variants of a genuine balance of power involving cooperative security structures that include China.

Each approach would confront major problems of implementation and may not be an adequate long-term means of advancing U.S. interests. That said, sustained progress in working together, both bilaterally and multilaterally, to address the growing array of challenges examined in this study could greatly increase both U.S. and Chinese incentives to overcome at least some obstacles to a transition beyond U.S. predominance. For the United States, these activities should involve efforts to develop common standards in many policy arenas that will vest Beijing more deeply into the regional and global systems. This will obviously also mean granting China more authority within these systems, and coordinating policies between the United States, other key Asian democratic powers, and the democracies of Europe.

Even in the absence of any decision by the United States to allow a transition toward an alternative to U.S. predominance, and assuming that China's capabilities continue to increase, America's strategy toward China will need to place a much greater emphasis on cooperation instead of rivalry and hedging, to enable the United States to maintain a productive relationship with China and thus attain its objectives in the Asia-Pacific region and beyond. In particular, more concerted efforts will be required to diminish—not merely manage—those Chinese territorial concerns that continue to exacerbate Sino-American mistrust.

The single most important action that U.S. leaders could take to improve America's strategic position and the management of individual policy issues is to enable the United States to recover from the current economic recession before it deepens into a prolonged period of economic stagnation, and to develop policies designed to sustain America's economic and technological prowess over the long term. Without a strong and growing economic capacity, Washington will find itself at an increasing disadvantage in maintaining a stabilizing presence in East Asia (whether based on predominance or any other strategic approach), shaping Beijing's strategic perceptions, and engaging with China and other nations on policy issues ranging from trade and finance to counterproliferation, climate change, and human rights.

01

INTERESTS, STRATEGIES, AND POLICY OBJECTIVES

Any evaluation of America's approach to China must first proceed from an understanding of the fundamental national interests and policy objectives that motivate and guide U.S. behavior, as well as Chinese interests and goals. These factors are not always clearly defined in great detail, nor are they consciously or deliberately applied to each element of policy or with regard to each policy decision. Indeed, several policymakers interviewed for this study acknowledged that many U.S. policy decisions regarding China (and particularly those formulated within individual agencies) are made with little if any conscious reference to larger strategic assumptions or beliefs, beyond a general desire to "engage" Beijing on the specific issue in question. Nonetheless, discussions with many U.S. officials, and the record of U.S. decisionmaking toward China, strongly suggest that basic assumptions about Washington's overall objectives vis-à-vis Beijing (and more broadly), and the relationship of these objectives to U.S. power and influence, are present in the thinking of most, if not all, senior U.S. policymakers. These notions are usually most clearly reflected in both the overall approach adopted toward China (for example, in the relative emphasis placed on cooperative engagement and deterrence- or shaping-oriented hedging) and in the basic tenets guiding the seven policy areas addressed in this study.

U.S. INTERESTS, GOALS, AND STRATEGY

At the most fundamental level of strategy, U.S. national objectives have centered on the defense of U.S. territory and the preservation of the physical safety, prosperity, and beliefs of the American people and the nation's core political and social institutions. Since at least the end of World War II, these goals have been attained by the protection and advancement of the United States–led global order and the material and value-based assets of the United States at home and abroad via political, diplomatic, military, and societal-cultural means. This global order consists of six key elements:

- United States–centered bilateral and multilateral political and military alliance relationships;
- a general commitment to a post–World War II norm against the unilateral use of force to alter national borders;
- a nonproliferation program for weapons of mass destruction (WMD) embodied in a range of formal institutions and informal practices, from the Nuclear Non-Proliferation Treaty to the Proliferation Security Initiative;
- a set of bilateral and multilateral institutions, forums, and agreements designed to promote capitalist market systems and global free trade, ranging from the World Trade Organization to the International Monetary Fund, the Group of Twenty, and various bilateral economic treaties;
- domestic governance norms (in the form of international treaties, statements, and bodies) designed to address basic humanitarian concerns and political or social issues related to corruption, the rule of law, and basic human rights; and
- a range of institutions, agreements, and activities designed to counter nontraditional security threats to all nations, from global terrorism to pandemics, illegal drug trafficking, environmental degradation, climate change, and financial/energy crises.

From the perspective of most, if not all, American policymakers, the preservation of this order and the protection of U.S. assets have relied on the maintenance of a global power structure in which the United States has enjoyed a preponderance of military power in certain key strategic regions, as well as significant (if not dominant) levels of political, diplomatic, moral, and economic presence and influence on critical issues, within key institutions, markets, and other related areas.[1] The Asia-Pacific region has long been regarded by U.S. policymakers as a vital component of this global power structure, given the region's proximity to the U.S. homeland, economic dynamism, political diversity, geostrategic relationship to other key regions, and presence of several major powers, notably China, Russia, India, and Japan.[2]

Throughout the post–World War II era, the United States has sought to protect or advance five key interests in this vital region:

- To prevent the emergence of a hostile power that could limit or exclude U.S. access to the region.
- To prevent the emergence or intensification of regional disputes or rivalries that could disrupt overall peace and economic development.[3]
- To ensure freedom of commerce, market access, and sea lines of communication throughout the region
- To defend and encourage democratic states and humanitarian processes and to discourage the expansion of nondemocratic movements or regimes hostile to the United States.
- To prevent the proliferation of weapons and weapons-related technologies and know-how across littoral Asia and to cope with nontraditional security threats, in particular global and regional terrorism, pandemics, and environmental degradation.[4]

The defense of these key interests has required a general strategy consisting of two elements. First and foremost, in the security arena, are the creation and maintenance of predominant American political and military influence across the vast reaches of maritime East Asia, extending from the West Coast of the United States to the Indian Ocean.[5] The United States has pursued this objective by maintaining the ability to project superior naval, air, and (to a lesser extent) land power into or near any areas within this region.[6] This has been facilitated by the maintenance of formal bilateral political and security alliances and military-basing arrangements with several key states in the region—including Japan, South Korea, Australia, Thailand, and the Philippines—along with the maintenance of close political and security relations with other significant Asian powers, such as India and Indonesia.[7]

The second core element of U.S. strategy in Asia has focused on the advancement and protection of those global and regional norms and institutions that support the above-noted interests, largely via close political, diplomatic, economic, and social interactions with a wide range of state actors and multilateral regional and international organizations, from the United Nations to the Association of Southeast Asian Nations (ASEAN) Regional Forum.[8]

During the Cold War, this overall strategic posture was largely oriented toward defending against the expansion into Asia of Communist influence originating from the former Soviet Union and Maoist China, and, secondarily, toward protecting or enlarging U.S. political and economic interests across the region. Since the collapse of the Soviet Union and the emergence of a more pragmatic, market-oriented economic system in China, America's grand strategy in Asia has primarily focused on strengthening its cooperative political, economic, and security relations with all the region's major powers while sustaining its political and military predominance in the maritime realm.

AMERICA'S BASIC APPROACH
TOWARD CHINA

The general implications of these broad objectives and approaches for overall U.S. policy goals toward China have been quite clear. As indicated in the introduction, since Beijing replaced the militant, anti-Western, anticapitalist rhetoric and policies of revolutionary Maoism with the pragmatic, open-door, and market-led approach of the reform era, Washington has pursued two broad sets of objectives toward China. On one hand, it has sought to sustain the Chinese leadership's emphasis on maintaining stability and prosperity within China, in Asia, and beyond by vesting Beijing in the maintenance and to some extent the protection of the existing global and Asian order and by augmenting its willingness and capacity to work with the United States and other Western powers in addressing a variety of bilateral, regional, and global issues and problems. On the other hand, Washington has increasingly sought to dissuade or deter Beijing from using its growing capabilities to undertake actions or acquire the level and type of power and intentions that could undermine global or regional stability, peace, and prosperity or directly threaten the above-noted vital U.S. capabilities and interests, both globally and in the Asia-Pacific.

Thus, U.S. policies toward China combine efforts to engage and enmesh Beijing in stability-inducing and problem-solving norms, structures, and processes[9] with attempts at realist-style balancing, deterrence, and interest shaping. The former often take the shape of external political-security cooperation among many Asian states. The latter often involve unilateral U.S. military modernization and force deployments.[10] As indicated in the introduction, in the twenty-first century, these dual efforts have intensified, become far more complex, and taken on a greater overall sense of significance and urgency, in response to the forces of globalization, the growing challenge posed by a range of nontraditional security threats such as terrorism and climate change, and the rapid expansion of China's overall international presence and capability.

These two basic objectives and strategic approaches (that is, cooperative engagement and hedging or balancing) obviously exist in some tension with one another, although they are certainly not mutually exclusive. Actions and signals designed to encourage or facilitate cooperation and accommodation in some areas can weaken those designed to deter or dissuade problematic behavior in other areas, and vice versa. For example, excessively strong, energetic, and confrontational hedging efforts by Washington can alarm Beijing and provoke it into greater efforts to reduce its vulnerability to a possible future U.S. shift toward containment by seeking more potent power projection capabilities or more competitive political strategies than it might otherwise pursue.[11] Conversely, an excessive emphasis on cooperation and mutual gains at the expense of efforts to deter and dissuade can lead to dangerous miscalculations and even confrontations, if, for example, such an emphasis leads either party to incorrectly conclude that it can neglect or downplay serious differences of interest between the two sides.[12]

These dynamics are obviously highly interactive, with each country's actions and responses influencing the relative emphasis placed by the other side on cooperative engagement as opposed to hedging and competitive policies. The greatest danger, of course, is that the emergence of the sort of negative dynamic mentioned above could eventually propel the two sides into an otherwise avoidable focus on relative gains and mutual deterrence rather than on the search for positive-sum outcomes and mutual reassurance. This could produce highly destabilizing consequences, including reduced incentives to cooperate in solving the increasingly complex bilateral, regional, and global challenges and problems cited above; a greater propensity to exaggerate the threat to key interests presented by relatively small disputes; and a much greater level of security competition overall that could increase the likelihood of arms races, infuse virtually every issue with tension, and alarm other nations. In particular, the emergence of an adversarial United States–China relationship could vastly complicate, if not undermine altogether, efforts to achieve American objectives in all the policy areas noted above.

In general, the cooperative side of America's strategic approach to China has usually been emphasized in the public statements of U.S. officials during most of the reform era.[13] However, American political and military deterrence and dissuasion actions and influential alliance relationships have been present since at least the early 1990s, and they sometimes come to the fore in U.S. statements, especially during times of tensions about specific issues such as Taiwan or when addressing the larger deterrence role of U.S. forces in Asia. Beyond such specific strategic political-military objectives, U.S. efforts to advance democracy and human rights vis-à-vis China also generate significant tensions. Though to some extent serving strategic ends, such endeavors, if improperly handled, could also undermine U.S. attempts to deepen certain types of cooperation or to solve important problems with China.

In recent years, U.S. administrations have tried, through the use of strings of adjectives and qualifiers in their statements, to accentuate the positive in the bilateral relationship without ignoring the uncertainties and suspicions. For example, during the George W. Bush administration, America's overall policy approach toward China was often described as involving the search for a "constructive, cooperative, and candid" relationship with China that included strategic actions designed to shape Chinese actions and in some cases deter Chinese threats.[14] During the Barack Obama administration, the key adjectives used to describe the Sino-U.S. relationship have been "positive, cooperative, and comprehensive."[15] However, this arguably more upbeat description is qualified by an explicit recognition of the continued need to hedge against uncertainty, and to seek more concrete indications of so-called strategic reassurance from Beijing, while also providing such assurance to China (also see chapter 2).[16]

America's Policy Objectives in Seven Key Arenas

The broad, dual engagement- and hedging-oriented U.S. approaches toward China described above have heavily influenced Washington's basic approach toward the seven policy arenas outlined in the introduction: (1) relations among key Asian powers, (2) bilateral and multilateral political and security structures and forums, (3) U.S. and Chinese military modernization programs and military-to-military activities, (4) economic development and assistance activities, (5) counterterrorism and counterproliferation challenges, (6) nontraditional security threats, and (7) human rights and democracy promotion efforts. Some of the current policies in these arenas emerged at the beginning of China's reform era in the late 1970s, and others are of more recent vintage. But all have evolved over time in response to changing external and domestic conditions.

Regarding the Asian political and security environment, the United States has pursued a wide variety of basic objectives toward China since at least the end of the Cold War:

- To prevent the emergence of a full-blown strategic rivalry with China centered on bilateral (or larger regional) arms races and a zero-sum approach to political and security relationships across the Asia-Pacific region.
- To deter China's use of force against Taiwan while maximizing the conditions for a peaceful resolution of the Beijing/Taipei standoff.

- To elicit Chinese cooperation in preventing conflict on the Korean Peninsula, eliminating North Korea's nuclear weapons capability, and advancing the ultimate objective of denuclearization and the creation of a peaceful peninsula.
- To support the peaceful resolution of outstanding territorial and resource disputes between China and nearby states, especially Japan, India, and several countries belonging to ASEAN.
- To strengthen the United States–Japan alliance and advance Tokyo's willingness and ability to play a larger security role in Asia—partly to reduce the possibility of a Sino-Japanese rivalry emerging but also to counter balance China's growing regional power.
- To develop closer political, economic, and military relations with rising powers such as India, partly to increase strategic leverage against China.
- To reassure both smaller and larger Asian nations that China's rise will not result in either a diminished U.S. presence in Asia or a new cold war.
- To elicit Chinese support for U.S. positions on critical security issues beyond the Asia-Pacific region, such as the Iranian nuclear imbroglio.

As chapters 2 through 8 explain, these goals have required an array of political, diplomatic, and military policies and actions toward China. First, in the area of political and security relations with key Asian powers, U.S. policy has focused primarily on strengthening and enlarging the alliance with Japan while supporting improvements in Sino-Japanese relations, developing a new strategic relationship with India, maintaining stability in the Taiwan Strait, and working with Beijing to denuclearize and stabilize the Korean Peninsula. Second, more broadly, the United States has to varying degrees sought to integrate China more fully into the United States–led regional security environment in Asia by strengthening cooperation via the development of multilateral security-related forums and institutions—without, however, undermining U.S. bilateral alliances or overall U.S. influence. This obviously calls for something of a balancing act for U.S. policy, as discussed in chapter 3. Third, in the military arena, Washington has striven to reassure its allies, shape Chinese security perceptions, and hedge against uncertainties regarding China's future strategic posture by augmenting its air, naval, and space capabilities and enhancing its military-to-military relationships with Beijing and other major Asian powers.

In the economic arena, U.S. policy toward China has focused on achieving three key, interrelated objectives, as discussed in chapter 5. First, on the broadest level, Washington has encouraged Beijing to contribute more actively to the maintenance and improvement of the global economic order by supporting the efficient operation of capitalist market systems and global free and fair trade, especially in vital strategic commodities such as energy and natural resources. Second, the United States has tried to maximize the benefits, while minimizing the damage, that economic engagement with China can produce for U.S. employment and corporate profits as well as for the overall health and well-being of the U.S. consumer. Third, the United States has sought to contribute to the stability, openness, and productivity of the Chinese economy, especially as these factors relate to China's domestic social order and the broader impact of China on Asia and on U.S. allies in the region.

Regarding terrorism, U.S. policies toward China have centered primarily on both bilateral and multilateral (and often UN-backed) efforts to elicit Beijing's support and assistance in detecting, pursuing, and interdicting or arresting terrorists or terrorist-related materials in the Asia-Pacific region in particular and especially within or near China (that is, in Southeast, South, and Central Asia). Chapter 6 also discusses the related area of counterproliferation, where U.S. policies focus on attempts to deter or prevent Chinese involvement in the transmission of WMD-related materials, in part by enhancing China's nuclear safeguards and export controls. Additionally, the United States has sought to obtain China's support for economic sanctions and other unilateral and multilateral measures deemed necessary to curb the acquisition or proliferation of WMD-related items by third-party countries, especially those with which China might possess some significant leverage or influence, such as Iran and North Korea, and to enhance Sino-U.S. cooperation in preventing weak and/or failing states like Pakistan and Bangladesh from becoming breeding grounds for terrorism.[17]

As chapter 7 indicates, primary U.S. objectives in combating nontraditional security threats such as pandemics and climate change have included the full integration of China into international initiatives that address such issues and the expansion of bilateral and multilateral mechanisms and activities for dialogue, information sharing, and the provision of assistance. They have also included attempts to develop coordinated or joint actions (both bilaterally and with other countries) to cope with specific crises or incidents, such as pandemics and maritime piracy. In all these cases, the goal of U.S. policy has been to strengthen the capacity and willingness of China to work with the United States and the international community to address these arguably growing challenges to the international system.

Finally, as chapter 8 shows, in the area of human rights and democracy promotion, U.S. policies have aimed at encouraging or (at times) pressuring China by a variety of bilateral and multilateral means, to provide greater support for human rights both within and beyond its own borders and especially in the two critical areas of political and religious freedom. These have included efforts to achieve some degree of understanding, if not agreement, with Beijing regarding the definition of human rights and how these rights should be protected, both within China and abroad. In the former area, the United States has focused its efforts on encouraging China's evolution toward a more politically tolerant, open, and diverse society, primarily via expanded contacts with Western democracies and steady movement toward economic liberalization. In fact, as discussed in chapter 8, to varying degrees, this objective—that is, democracy promotion within China—has been cited by many observers, including senior U.S. officials,[18] as a primary or important goal underlying efforts at cooperative engagement with China since at least the early 1990s.[19]

Differing Strategic Approaches

U.S. political leaders and analysts, along with important segments of the American public, do not entirely agree on what overall regional and global approach and specific policies are required to achieve the strategic objectives and policy goals outlined above. From a strategic perspective, at the core of this issue is the question of how the United States should utilize both its key alliance relationships with Japan and South Korea and its broader relations with other Asian nations and the major European democracies. Should the United States constrain potentially adverse Chinese behavior and encourage Chinese cooperation by basing its approach to Beijing first and foremost on its bilateral alliance relationships in Asia? In other words, can Washington best influence Beijing's behavior by placing a priority on enhancing its cooperative relations and security ties with key allies such as Tokyo while treating Beijing as an important but not necessarily central interlocutor and partner? This approach would place a premium on downplaying differences with allies while working to deepen defense cooperation and (in the case of Japan and possibly other allies) expand security roles and missions in Asia and beyond. It would also emphasize building ties among other (especially democratic) friends and allies across the Asia-Pacific region, in part to deny China the ability to play other countries against the United States for leverage.

From this perspective, the United States would regard China as a growing regional power with which it could cooperate on some issues but not on others, and as a power that must be approached from a position of strength, with a clear and consistent message regarding where Washington agrees and disagrees with Beijing (for example, regarding Taiwan). This would not be a containment strategy. It would combine attempts to shape and engage in many political, economic, military, and social areas with unambiguous efforts to constrain and oppose where necessary, in large part through a heavy reliance on a strong, asser-tive U.S. presence in Asia and deepening political and defense ties with Japan and other nations. In short, this approach would emphasize the deterrence elements of U.S. strategy in dealing with China as a likely strategic adversary.

An alternative approach would place a lesser emphasis on working with and through existing bilateral alliances to shape and control China while plac-ing a greater focus on working directly with Beijing to reduce misperceptions and expand the overall boundaries of cooperation. To avoid unduly alarming China, this generally "cooperative security"–type approach would deempha-size America's building ever stronger bilateral defense relationships with Japan and other democracies. It would instead emphasize the search for positive-sum approaches to China in many issue areas as a major component of America's overall Asia strategy, building on the search for solutions to common problems and the strengthening of convergent interests. In this effort, Washington would work both bilaterally and via international and multilateral forums and institu-tions whenever possible. This approach would certainly not neglect America's bilateral relations with its democratic allies and friends. To the contrary, it would greatly emphasize working with them, but not so much to strengthen deterrence efforts toward Beijing as to increase common incentives for cooperation, as part of the effort to build a more inclusive multilateral political, economic, and—perhaps eventually—security mechanism in Asia. To some extent, this approach would view China not only as the most important new power player in Asia (and most likely globally) but also as a power that has many reasons to deepen coop-eration with the United States and few reasons to openly oppose it, as long as Washington does not engage in provocative behavior. Equally important, this approach also tends to view Japan as a relatively weaker or declining power that will likely prove increasingly unable or unwilling to play a vital security role alongside the United States in Asia or beyond, and hence cannot be relied upon to "balance" China politically or militarily.

Other, more radical regional and global approaches to China are possible, of course. On one extreme is an approach that moves significantly toward a zero-sum strategy by seeking to create a grand coalition of democracies explicitly designed to counter what, according to it, is a growing Chinese challenge to the United States and all democratic nations. This approach views Beijing as delib-erately attempting to undermine the West by promoting a potent countermodel to democracy that combines an authoritarian political apparatus with a neomer-cantilist economic order. And this approach clearly assumes that the forces driv-ing competition and confrontation between China and the United States will increasingly predominate over those forces driving cooperation. In response, it calls for the United States to lead in the formation and steady expansion of a political–security–economic consortium of democracies. It also calls for a major increase in the capacity of the United States and its allies to deter China from using its growing military power to fundamentally alter the existing distribution of military power globally, and especially in the Asia-Pacific region, largely through major increases in military spending designed to sustain U.S. military predominance in the Western Pacific.

At the opposite extreme from this approach that would move toward a zero-sum strategy is an approach that almost entirely rejects the supposedly obsolete great power politics of the past in favor of more inclusive, positive-sum, cooperative undertakings that build on the forces driving globalization and seek to address the emergence of an increasing range of nontraditional security threats to all powers (for example, environmental degradation and global inequality). This approach also includes some voices that point to the declining relative economic power of the United States as a major change necessitating its repudiation of many elements of the post–World War II status quo (for example, wholesale support for the United States–created post–Bretton Woods economic order) in favor of a new diplomatic and economic strategy. Overall, this approach emphasizes greater compromises by the United States vis-à-vis most nations (including China), more U.S. sacrifices at home, and a greatly lessened U.S. emphasis on the promotion of democracy in favor of pragmatic policies centered on economic development, especially among developing nations. This approach thus largely rejects attempts to induce China to accept variants of the status quo in favor of common, virtually coequal management of the regional and perhaps even the global order. It also downplays efforts to maintain U.S. military predominance in the Western Pacific, in favor of a new security architecture that is less dependent on American military power and more oriented toward cooperative or collective security systems.

These latter two approaches are both extreme because they do not share many of the assumptions underlying America's current strategic objectives and policy goals outlined above—in particular, both the uncertainties and the convergence of interests that reside in the Sino-U.S. relationship—and the resulting preference to strike a balance between engagement and hedging. Thus, it is likely that the former two approaches will continue to constitute the mainstream, paradigmatic alternatives for U.S. security strategy for some time to come, barring a major shift in those underlying assumptions (precipitated, for example, by a military conflict with China or a democratic revolution in China). Nonetheless, all four of these approaches clearly imply that any effective security strategy toward China must address—indeed, must be embedded within—a larger U.S. strategy toward Asia and the world.[20]

CHINA'S BASIC INTERESTS, GOALS, AND STRATEGY

One cannot understand, much less evaluate, America's policies toward China without first understanding China's national interests and strategic approach to the world.[21] As in the case of the United States, China's fundamental approach to foreign relations derives from several core national interests and related objectives, including the defense of Chinese sovereignty and territorial integrity and, to varying degrees, the preservation of the physical safety, prosperity, and beliefs of both the Chinese populace and the nation's core institutions, the most important of which is the Chinese Communist Party (CCP). Since the advent of economic reform and opening and the transition away from Maoist ideology in the late 1970s, China's leadership has sought to achieve these basic national goals through a largely pragmatic strategy designed to maintain, above all else, high levels of undistracted economic growth.

Such growth is viewed as essential to the achievement of several key national goals, including the maintenance of domestic social order and development, which is viewed as critical to the preservation of the Chinese state's power and stability;[22] the acquisition of military and other means deemed essential to the defense of China against foreign threats to its territory and sovereignty, including threats to the eventual reunification of Taiwan with the Mainland and the resolution of other claimed territories; and the eventual attainment of high levels of international power and prestige commensurate with China's historical status as a great power. Moreover, from the viewpoint of the senior PRC leadership, the CCP's survival is regarded as both the essential precondition for and an essential by-product of the attainment of all these goals.[23]

To achieve this fundamental strategic objective, Beijing has repeatedly and emphatically enunciated an overall foreign policy of peace, cooperation, and goodwill toward all states, which is often described by Chinese officials as the search for a "mutually beneficial, win–win cooperative pattern" (huli shuangying de hezuo geju, 互利双赢的合作格局).[24] Specifically, with regard to concrete political and diplomatic policies, China is pursuing an overall approach marked, in the areas of both multilateral and bilateral state-to-state interactions, by the search for mutually beneficial outcomes, the maintenance of amicable ties with virtually all nations and institutions, and the deepening of those types of relationships that are most conducive to economic development.[25]

Under President Hu Jintao, this approach has been conveyed, at the rhetorical level, via the two interrelated concepts of China's peaceful development (heping fazhan, 和平发展), and its support for the creation of a harmonious world (hexie shijie, 和谐世界). The former concept seeks to rebut the notion that China's rise will disrupt Asian and global stability, by stressing Beijing's current and future dependence on commercial and technological globalization, its primary reliance on nonmilitary forms of contact and influence, and its historical aversion to hegemonic and expansionist behavior. The latter concept stresses China's support for multilateralism, international institutions, forums, and initiatives; its increasing contribution to global humanitarian and developmental assistance programs; its respect for diverse political cultures and economic systems; its defense of the principle of national sovereignty; and the overall development of friendly relations on the basis of the 1950s notion of the Five Principles of Peaceful Coexistence.[26] Domestically, the concept of a harmonious world is reflected in the ideal of a harmonious society (hexie shehui, 和谐社会), which reflects a strong desire to overcome a variety of serious internal problems—from a widening income gap to rampant corruption and a deteriorating ecosystem—through a more coordinated approach among different Chinese groups and interests.[27]

In addition, during the past two years, Hu has also extended the concepts of peace and development as guidelines for the entire international community. Specifically, he has recommended four ways in which the international community can implement such guidelines:

- "First, we should view security in a broader perspective and safeguard world peace and stability."
- "Second, we should take a more holistic approach to development and promote common prosperity."
- "Third, we should pursue cooperation with a more open mind and work for mutual benefit and common progress."
- "Fourth, we should be more tolerant to one another and live together in harmony."[28]

Hu has also emphasized, for the first time, the need for China to focus on so-called domain diplomacy, meaning various global issues and functional topics associated with globalization, such as the financial crisis, energy security, and climate change.[29]

Regarding bilateral interstate relations, China has been pursuing policies designed to reinforce and supplement the general political-security objectives outlined above. It has acted on several fronts (political, diplomatic, economic, military-to-military, cultural, people-to-people) primarily to strengthen relations with all major Asian nations (for example, South Korea, Japan, the

ASEAN members, India, Russia, Indonesia, and most Central Asian states) while also establishing closer political and economic relations with key countries in Africa, Latin America, South America, and Europe.[30] At the same time, Beijing insists that its search for positive-sum relationships with other powers must not come at the expense of efforts to advance or protect its most vital interests, including the protection of China's sovereignty and territorial integrity (discussed further below).[31]

CHINA'S BASIC APPROACH TOWARD THE UNITED STATES

In advancing and protecting its interests in the international system, Beijing has placed a primary emphasis on its relationship with Washington. At a minimum, Beijing has required stable—if not affable—relations with Washington for a variety of reasons: to continue rapid economic growth, to maintain regional stability, to address common (and in many cases increasingly urgent) international problems, to achieve greater power and influence in the Asia-Pacific region, to minimize efforts to constrain China's emergence, and to avoid a conflict over Taiwan. As a result, it has sought to sustain cooperation with Washington and to manage problems via dialogue and negotiation to the greatest extent possible, both bilaterally and multilaterally. It has not thus far pursued a zero-sum strategic rivalry with Washington across various policy arenas, nor sought to displace the United States as a global superpower.[32]

At the same time, Beijing remains highly suspicious of Washington's intentions and actions in the international arena and with regard to China in particular, especially in the context of Beijing's growing regional and global power and influence. Such suspicion derives in part not only from the long history of mutual tension and (at times) conflict that has plagued relations between the PRC and the United States, but also from the basic antagonism created by the contrasting nature of the two countries' political systems, and China's overall frustration and resentment toward the West in general (and Japan). The latter derives from its modern history of supposed victimization at the hands of imperialist powers and its long-held desire to reclaim its rightful place as a major Asian nation. Chinese leaders to some extent view U.S. policies in many areas as aggressive, arrogant, and designed to defend or advance American values and to perpetuate dominant American power at the expense of the interests and needs of developing nations, including a rising China. Many Chinese do not accept the notion that the stability and prosperity of the international system are best ensured through the maintenance of a United States–dominated political, economic, and security order, and they view the U.S. stance toward international norms and values as excessively self-serving at best and hypocritical and rife with double standards at worst.[33] Many Chinese also fear that, as China's power and influence within the international order continue to expand, Washington will increasingly seek to constrain Beijing's freedom of action and resist any attempts to reorder the international system to better reflect the interests of China and other developing powers.[34]

Such fears have led Beijing to undertake a variety of political and diplomatic policies or actions in the bilateral, multilateral, and international spheres to reduce U.S. and international concerns about China's growing power and reach, and to hedge against the ability or willingness of the United States (and other nations) to create and sustain policies designed to frustrate the expansion of China's capabilities, status, and influence.[35] Most recently, the hedging effort has included an attempt to lay down a marker regarding the need for the United States and other countries to respect China's position on certain issues, especially with regard to sovereignty and territorial integrity. This has taken the form of deliberate efforts to more clearly define and vigorously promote the concept of China's "core interests" (hexin liyi, 核心利益).[36]

As a result of these mixed incentives and concerns, as with Washington, Beijing has also pursued a two-sided set of basic policy approaches during this period, seeking to enhance those cooperative interactions that facilitate China's economic development and extend its international influence, while also striving to minimize the ability of other nations (particularly the United States) to limit its growing power and influence.

China's Key U.S. and Other Policy Objectives

As in the case of the United States, China's dual objectives of cooperating with Washington while hedging against adverse U.S. behavior have influenced Beijing's basic strategic approach toward the seven policy arenas outlined above. In the political and security realm, on the broadest level, China has sought to advance its definitions of the concepts of peace, development, and harmony through the enunciation of approaches such as the so-called New Security Concept (xin anquan guan, 新安全观), unveiled in 1997, along with the notion of establishing bilateral "strategic partnerships" (zhanlue huoban guanxi, 战略伙伴关系) with nations along China's periphery (for example, Russia, the ASEAN states, Japan, and South Korea) and in other strategically important regions. Both the New Security Concept and the strategic partnership idea were initially intended to offer a potential alternative to the concept of bilateral security alliances (and in particular the United States–centered "hub-and-spokes" security structure of formal alliances and forward-deployed military forces in the Asia-Pacific region), as well as the broader notion of United States–led, unilateral or non-UN-sanctioned military interventions.[37]

These concepts serve a clear strategic purpose for Beijing by presenting, in a systematic and consistent fashion, an overall argument as to why China's rise will contribute greatly to—rather than threaten or undermine—regional and global stability, peace, and prosperity, thus comporting with U.S. interests in Asia. However, they are also designed to advance the notion that U.S. strategic dominance in general, and any type of United States–led opposition to China's rise in particular, is unnecessary and potentially destabilizing for the region. In addition, these concepts also play to the fears that some nations harbor about America's unilateralism and intervention in their domestic affairs.

Aside from such general approaches, in Beijing's political and security relations with other Asian powers, it has also particularly emphasized preventing or discouraging the United States from undertaking the following actions: (1) providing greater support for Taiwanese independence; (2) promoting what Beijing views as destabilizing military and diplomatic actions on the Korean Peninsula; (3) increasing greatly or making permanent the U.S. military presence in South Asia; and (4) intervening politically, and perhaps militarily, in territorial or resource disputes between China and other Asian powers, such as India, Japan, and countries in Southeast Asia. As subsequent chapters explain, in all these areas, China often shares similar goals with the United States (such as long-term peace and stability), while differing to varying degrees over how to achieve them.

As this list of concerns suggests, China's policies toward territorial and resource disputes constitute a contentious and critical issue in its relations with many Asian powers along its periphery that in turn directly affects U.S. interests in regional peace and stability. In this case, Beijing's policy goals largely reinforce Washington's by focusing on the desire to resolve peacefully or defer most if not all major territorial disputes and avoid the use of force if at all possible, while also preventing nearby states from combining to oppose Chinese territorial claims. Beijing's strategy has resulted in a two-pronged approach in this area.

First, if the territorial dispute in question is both intrinsically trivial and marginal to China's larger interests, Beijing has sought to resolve it amicably in order to pursue its larger goals. Its border disputes with Russia, for example, are evidence of this approach, whereby Beijing's overarching interest in improving its political relationship with Moscow and securing access to Russian military technology resulted in quick, hopefully permanent, solutions to the Ussuri River dispute.

Second, if the territorial dispute is significant but cannot be resolved to China's advantage by peaceful means, it has advocated indefinitely postponing consideration of the basic issue. This tactic has been adopted, for example, for the disputes with India, Japan, and the ASEAN states.[38] The basic logic underlying this approach has been to steadfastly avoid conceding Chinese claims with respect to the dispute, while simultaneously seeking to prevent the dispute from undermining the pacific environment that China needs to successfully complete its internal transformation. In some instances, this led in the 1990s to an increased reliance on multilateral organizations to settle territorial disputes and increase border security (even though Beijing prefers to negotiate such disputes on a bilateral basis to maximize its strategic leverage).[39]

Among these disputes, the one of greatest concern to the United States has arguably been what Beijing insists is a purely internal matter: the continued separation of Taiwan from Mainland China. Even in this case, however, China's basic stance does not clash with that of the United States, since Beijing would prefer to resolve the issue peacefully through gradual movement toward a negotiated reunification settlement rather than to employ force. As discussed in detail in chapter 2, to achieve this objective, Beijing pursues a multifaceted policy, including efforts to increase its economic and cultural pull on Taiwan while avoiding any actions that might generate alarm; to politically isolate strongly proindependence political elements, in part by deepening direct contacts with all other political forces on Taiwan, particularly (at present) the government of Ma Ying-jeou; to strengthen support for China's position regarding Taiwan among all relevant powers (and especially nearby Asian states); to severely limit Taiwan's ability to participate in international organizations and forums; and to avoid a confrontation with Washington over the issue while maintaining strong objections to American arms sales and official contact with Taiwan. On the negative side, the last two elements of Beijing's policy—opposition to international representation and U.S. arms sales— serve as sources of significant and possibly growing tension with Washington, by reinforcing Chinese suspicions that U.S. policies are ultimately designed to perpetuate a permanent separation of the two sides.

More broadly, China's views on peace, development, and harmony and its pursuit of strategic partnerships and espousal of the New Security Concept have also provided the rhetorical foundation for its policy of expansive involvement in and support for international and multilateral political and security-related organizations, initiatives, and forums, as well as an increasing number of economic-related structures (mentioned below).[40] Through such extensive and deepening involvement in the international system, Beijing has sought to project and maintain its image as a constructive member of the international community, to more effectively manage its growing international challenges, and to advance collaborative solutions to common problems at a minimal cost to itself. It has also shown a desire to use such organizations and initiatives to reassure other nations that its growing power and influence do not threaten (and indeed, could benefit) their economic and security interests, and in general to shape regional and global views and actions in ways that advance Chinese interests.[41]

In the political and security realm, the United States–oriented, hedging and deterrence side of China's basic strategy has also contained an increasingly prominent military component, involving a systematic, increasingly well-funded, and focused program of force modernization marked by growing power projection capabilities. This undertaking was originally motivated by China's desire to bring its military forces up to more modern levels commensurate with those of an aspiring great power. It subsequently gained focus and momentum as a result of growing Chinese fears that Taiwan was moving toward independence, possibly with U.S. backing, and in response to a growing awareness of the vastly superior technical capabilities of the U.S. military, as demonstrated during the Gulf wars and the Kosovo conflict. However, in recent years, and from the broadest, most long-term perspective, this effort has also become increasingly oriented toward strengthening China's capacity to augment its diplomatic and political leverage abroad and to protect its expanding foreign economic assets and interests while generally reducing its vulnerability to future threats to its territory or populace by other nations, including the United States.[42] In particular, many Chinese increasingly regard the PRC military as an essential instrument in defending against possible future U.S. efforts to constrain, harass, or intimidate a rising China.

In the economic policy realm, China's leaders have been pursuing a highly pragmatic, market-led economic development program—albeit with significant state intervention and administrative controls in certain areas—involving increasing integration into a wide variety of bilateral, regional, and global economic and financial institutions and forums. Beijing's overseas economic activities are primarily designed to maximize China's access to overseas markets; to acquire ample, steady supplies of foreign products (including reliable, affordable, and efficient sources of energy), technologies, and investment capital through a combination of profit-driven and strategically oriented commercial and state-directed organizations and individual actions; and, increasingly, to facilitate its economic goals (and augment its political influence) via the use of official development assistance.[43] In some cases, such activities have emphasized the acquisition of overseas equity assets and long-term contracts designed to shield China from sudden price fluctuations or adverse political shifts. In most cases, China has pursued these objectives with little concern for the political makeup or orientation of its overseas economic partners or suppliers. At home, this strategy has manifested itself in high levels of infrastructure investment, high savings rates, and an increasing attention to the adverse environmental consequences of rapid growth.[44]

With regard to the United States, these Chinese interests and goals have resulted in strong incentives to cooperate with Washington in maximizing mutual economic benefits at the national and enterprise levels, while at the same time preventing or minimizing what are viewed as United States–led attempts to constrain China's domestic and global trade, currency, investment, technology, and energy policies. China's relative success (compared with more developed economies) in weathering the global financial crisis has arguably contributed to a greater level of assertiveness in some economic areas—as reflected, for example, in calls for a move away from the dollar standard (discussed in chapter 5).

Beijing's basic strategy toward terrorism is largely derived from its core national objectives, including, on the one hand, its concern with domestic stability and central control and, and on the other, its desire to cooperate with the United States and other powers in combating international terrorism. The former goals translate into a primary focus on eliminating internal terrorist groups that are largely associated with separatist movements among China's large populations of ethnic and religious minorities located in the western and northwestern border areas of Tibet and Xinjiang. The latter goal has resulted in Chinese support for international efforts to locate and eliminate both regional and global terrorists through a variety of means discussed in detail in chapter 6. The two goals are related in the sense that, while resisting any effort to "internationalize" its domestic counterterrorist or counterinsurgency activities, Beijing nonetheless seeks international acceptance of these actions as part of the global war on terrorism. Though generally supportive of international counterterrorist activities, China's leaders resist those actions that might undermine the principle of national sovereignty or circumvent the authority of international organizations such as the United Nations. In fact, the Chinese take the position that leadership in the global war on terrorism should reside within the UN and not with any single nation.[45]

In the realm of WMD counterproliferation and arms control, since the advent of the reform era, China has by and large cooperated in the advancement of the overall objectives of the Western-led international order to prevent the production or transfer of WMD and weapons-related materials and technologies to non-nuclear states or groups, and to move toward a nuclear-free world. China has officially stated that it supports, as the ultimate goal of disarmament, the complete prohibition and thorough destruction of all nuclear weapons and other WMD.[46]

Beijing also repeatedly declares that it opposes arms races of whatever type and any use of WMD or threats to use WMD against other states. In line with this overall position, China is a party to or supports (that is, it has at least acceded to, if not ratified) most of the major international agreements concerning the control and/or abolition of nuclear, chemical, and biological weapons, including the Nuclear Non-Proliferation Treaty, the Comprehensive Test Ban Treaty, the Geneva Protocol, the Biological Weapons Convention, and the Chemical Weapons Convention.[47]

At the same time, Chinese leaders believe that, given the continued presence of WMD in the international community along with China's general historical experience in the modern era, it remains essential for China to possess a small, retaliatory, second-strike WMD capability, to deter superpower blackmail and threats, to reduce the likelihood of instability and war, and generally to heighten China's regional and global status and political influence.[48] Nuclear weapons are of particular importance in this effort.[49] Given the small size of China's strategic nuclear arsenal compared with the arsenals of both the United States and Russia, China has been unwilling to participate in strategic arms limitation discussions with either or both powers. Moreover, the small, defensive nature of China's nuclear force and China's general opposition to nuclear blackmail and intimidation are reinforced by the public enunciation of a supposed commitment never to use nuclear weapons first in a conflict and never to use or threaten to use nuclear weapons against non-nuclear states or nuclear free zones.[50] Such a strategy is often described by the Chinese as following the general principle of "houfa zhiren" (后发制人, to gain mastery by striking only after the enemy has struck first).[51] In more technical terms, this so-called minimum deterrence doctrine generally assumes that China would absorb an initial nuclear attack rather than undertake a launch under attack or a launch on warning.[52] Perhaps most important, Beijing also relies for its deterrent effectiveness on the inability of an adversary to destroy all its nuclear facilities in a first strike. However, its basic stance toward WMD does not totally exclude the possibility that Chinese leaders might be the first to use such weapons in a crisis, especially within a limited military theater;[53] nor does it mean that China's leaders would never transfer nuclear, biological, or chemical weapons or related technologies to other powers. These points are discussed in greater detail in chapter 6.

Similar to counterterrorism and counterproliferation, China's strategic approach to nontraditional security threats derives from its desire to support international norms and activities and defend against direct and indirect threats to its national security, while at the same time sustaining high levels of economic growth and protecting its national freedom and independence or the prerogatives of the CCP regime. Moreover, as in the economic arena, in advancing or protecting such interests, PRC leaders portray China as a developing country with limited (albeit expanding) capabilities and yet an increasing involvement in, dependence upon, and responsibility toward the international system. Indeed, as discussed in detail in chapter 7, the principle of "common but differentiated responsibility" is often invoked in handling many such international threats such as environmental degradation, often resulting in policy deadlocks with the United States and the West.

These two sets of goals and attitudes exist in some tension with one another, depending on the specific nontraditional threat involved. For example, efforts to combat environmental degradation could threaten rapid growth and/or the interests of key leaders or organizations committed to this growth, and attempts to disseminate accurate information concerning rapidly spreading diseases could threaten the social order or challenge the vested interests of secrecy-prone political leaders at the central and local levels. China's leaders have therefore sought to strike a balance between these two goals by pursuing a strategy designed to enhance the country's national and international capabilities through both unilateral efforts and greater participation in various bilateral and multilateral organizations and processes on the one hand, along with attempts to minimize costly commitments or avoid undertakings that could weaken domestic state (including local government) capacities on the other hand. This balancing act requires constant attention, particularly on the part of the central government, both internally and in contacts with foreign entities, including the United States. However, in many cases, the requirements of economic growth and stability usually win out, and China's strategy often appears to place a stronger emphasis on "declarations of intent" than on more costly and difficult efforts at implementation, given insufficient funding, staff, authority, and experience among responsible agencies. These issues are discussed in further detail in chapter 7.

Finally, China's basic strategy toward human rights and democracy promotion also reflects the often crosscutting or conflicting interests and objectives evident in other policy arenas. Beijing rejects the notion that it does not support human rights or even democracy, as defined by its own concepts and principles. It supports global efforts to advance human rights, taken primarily as the right to individual and collective security, health, and economic prosperity, and it thus has acceded to most international agreements designed to advance such goals. It also rhetorically supports the ability of individual citizens to express their political preferences (albeit not necessarily via Western-style liberal democratic institutions), and it has theoretically legalized certain basic freedoms, such as the freedom of religion and speech. And it advocates a

degree of "vertical democracy" *within* the CCP, in order to optimize its organization and effectiveness. However, Chinese leaders usually assert that the welfare
of the collective should supersede individual rights when the two are in conflict,
and that a strong and stable government is necessary to protect human rights,
thereby placing limits on "excessive individual freedom" for the public good. This
emphasis on so-called second-generation human rights (that is, those that focus
on economic, cultural, and social issues) often identifies poverty and inequality
as far more deserving of attention than political independence and competition.

Internationally, Beijing argues that a universal "one-size-fits-all" definition
of human rights should not apply among nations, given economic, cultural, and
political differences. It nonetheless also argues that democratic principles should
apply in many cases to relations among individual nation-states; that is, that they
should interact whenever possible on the basis of principles that treat each country as an equal actor in the international system. As in other areas, China's leadership also places limits on its actions in advancing human rights and democracy overseas, on the basis of its limited capabilities as a developing nation, its
commitment to the defense of the principle of national sovereignty and nonintervention, and its resistance to what it regards as the hypocritical and potentially chaos-producing prodemocracy stance espoused by many democratic governments, especially the United States. As in the area of nontraditional security
threats, Beijing also to a great extent views human rights and democracy promotion as secondary to the requirements of economic growth and the preservation
of amicable and stable political relations with strategically important nations on
its periphery and elsewhere.

Differing Strategic Approaches

The summary of Chinese national objectives, interests, and basic policy orienta-
tions given above suggests that Beijing, along with Washington, pursues a strategy containing both cooperative and hedging elements. And as in the case of
the United States, these elements generate potential tensions within Beijing's
overall approach and reflect domestic political differences about specific strategies and policies. In particular, the Chinese leadership is confronted with the
need to strike the right balance between encouraging and facilitating cooperation with the United States and other powers on the one hand, and sending clear
signals, via words and actions, that it has the capability and will to deter or prevent attempts to undermine its growth or challenge its core interests regarding
issues such as Taiwan on the other hand. Too great an emphasis on the latter
area can obviously undermine efforts in the former area. Conversely, an exces-

sive focus or concern with the former area can arguably compromise or weaken China's defense of its vital interests, at least in the view of some of its leaders and segments of the public.

These tensions and related domestic differences result in efforts to influence Chinese policy by both leaders and, increasingly it seems, some elements of the public. At the broadest level, the balance struck between cooperation and hedging, and the specific policy approaches adopted in each of the seven policy arenas, are to some extent subject to the differing outlooks and agendas of so-called hard-liners and those more moderate elements within the leadership. The former apparently believe that the United States—and perhaps other Western powers—view China's emergence as a major threat to be countered, and therefore seek not only to restrain Chinese power in many areas but to undermine and perhaps precipitate the collapse of the PRC regime altogether. Hence, hard-liners advocate policy approaches designed to weaken U.S. influence and counter or confront U.S. pressure in critical areas such as regional security and human rights. This viewpoint is arguably supported, intentionally or otherwise, by some elements of the Chinese public, who view the U.S. government as an arrogant, overbearing, and hypocritical entity that at times seeks to humiliate China and constrain its emergence as a great power.[54]

Moderates, conversely, emphasize the growing need for the United States to cooperate with China in many areas and to avoid a confrontation over issues such as Taiwan. They argue that China's expanding power and influence, the emergence of a growing number of serious global problems requiring Sino-American cooperation, and the fact that the United States is heavily distracted by events in Iraq and Afghanistan and the global economic recession together present Beijing with a golden opportunity to reduce U.S. incentives to challenge Chinese power by promoting policies that emphasize the positive-sum aspects of bilateral relations while avoiding any overt confrontations with the United States. Advocates of this viewpoint do not argue for reductions in Chinese military power. However, they believe that China's strategic goals can best be served by efforts to create a set of positive incentives for the United States and other Western nations to work with China, as well as a set of relationships and arrangements in global and regional institutions that increasingly limit the ability of these nations to challenge China.[55]

Within the Chinese political spectrum, it is hard to identify which individuals or groups hold which of these views. Some outside observers associate hard-line views on overall strategy and specific security policies with the Chinese military and propaganda apparatus and more moderate views with the civilian foreign policy establishment, along with newly emergent organizations associated with international initiatives (for example, in the areas of nuclear counterproliferation and environmental protection). In truth, one can find hard-liners and moderates within most of these institutions. Moreover, in general, it remains extremely difficult to determine how specific institutions and individuals influence the formulation and implementation of Chinese strategies and policies. As a result, it is very hard to identify exactly how domestic political factors have exerted influence over the PRC's strategy and policies in the past. (The issue of possible military departures from civilian policy is discussed further in chapter 4.)

Although moderate views have usually tended to prevail on most policy issues—given China's overall strategic need to deepen cooperation, avoid confrontation, and work with other major powers to develop positive-sum solutions to a growing number of problems—it has generally been safer politically within the Chinese leadership (and often among the Chinese public) to take a hard-line (or at least strongly suspicious) view toward the United States on many issues. This is especially the case when a foreign policy crisis emerges or Washington appears to be pressuring or openly confronting Beijing about an important matter. The persistence of such hard-line views is largely due to the presence, noted above, of deep-seated, historically based distrust toward American motives, resulting from bilateral confrontations and conflicts that have occurred since the 1940s and the basic animosity generated by the contrast between China's undemocratic political system and America's support for democracies and democratization. Moreover, it is most likely at such times that popular attitudes exert an influence over Chinese policies toward the United States. For historical and cultural reasons, the Chinese government wants very much to avoid appearing weak and compromising in the face of apparent U.S. slights to Chinese honor or apparent attempts to suppress or deny Chinese power and interests or to exert overt pressure on the Chinese government. Hence, Chinese leaders could conceivably toughen their stance on individual policy issues and during specific policy-related crises to improve their political standing with the public or to appear more patriotic than potential political rivals.[56]

Finally, China's policy community likely contains different views about the extent of the leadership role that China should play in the foreign policy arena. Some Chinese observers see growing opportunities for China to shape and even lead or create various international organizations and forums.[57] Others advocate a circumscribed and cautious approach, largely due to fears that China could be drawn into playing a deeper, more activist role in many foreign policy areas that could potentially limit its options, expose it to increasing levels of international scrutiny, undermine efforts to sustain its image among smaller countries as a non-superpower, and generally challenge its ability to keep a low profile.[58] Still others adopt a middle ground, calling for a more active role for China in the world (reflecting in part both China's rise and a perception of American decline), while stressing the importance of sensitivity, wisdom, and caution in order not to frighten or offend other countries.[59] These differences do not easily translate into contrasting or contending domestic political interests. However, they probably influence leadership debates over specific policy issues.[60]

IMPLICATIONS FOR U.S. POLICIES

The analysis given above of U.S. and Chinese key interests, strategic objectives, policy goals, and the major domestic variations in viewpoints and assumptions that influence policymaking lead to three general observations of central relevance for America's future policies toward China. First, there is no doubt that China and the United States share a significant number of basic interests and objectives, both regionally and globally. Most important, they are both committed to maintaining stability, peace, and prosperity in Asia through largely cooperative interstate relations, a strong reliance on the use of market mechanisms, and a general restraint in the use of force in the Asia-Pacific region. At present, Washington and Beijing are not pursuing any fundamentally incompatible strategic objectives in Asia or beyond of a structural nature. That is, they are not advocating incompatible territorial claims, holding wide-ranging and fundamentally conflicting beliefs regarding regional and global institutional or regime norms, presiding over competing alliance structures or spheres of influence, or confronting basic economic disputes about resources or access to markets that appear unmanageable outside acceptable bilateral or multilateral market mechanisms or market-based agreements.

Moreover, the above-noted strategic interests and assumptions strongly suggest that neither side is *at present* committed to a *fundamental* reordering of the balance of power in the Asia-Pacific region or a basic reversal of existing political, economic, and military trends. Specifically, the United States does not seek, as a primary element of its strategic outlook, to neutralize, severely weaken, or contain China's core capabilities as an Asian continental power (possessing very large ground forces), or as a robust and growing economic power with expanding political influence in the region and beyond. To the contrary, Washington by and large encourages Beijing's economic development and its expanding involvement in the international system and it desires China to be stable and secure. Similarly, Beijing does not deliberately seek, as part of its *current* grand strategy, to neutralize Washington's predominant capabilities as a naval power throughout the Western Pacific and as a key political and economic player and security guarantor for many nations. In short, *at present*, neither power pursues interests and objectives that require significant reductions in the core capabilities in Asia (or beyond) of the other power in order to satisfy its own basic national interests. A focus on relative gains is not central to the strategic mindset of either power.

Second, on several policy issues, many of the current differences between Beijing and Washington center primarily on the means used to achieve specific, shared ends. For example, as suggested above (and as discussed in detail in subsequent chapters), U.S. leaders believe that nations have a right, under certain conditions, to intervene in the internal affairs of other nations or to attach stringent conditions to foreign assistance, in order to address gross abuses of human rights or to encourage more open and democratic political systems. In contrast, Chinese leaders generally believe that such interventions—and many other international actions taken by the United States and other major industrial, democratic powers—should only occur under international auspices, with the consent of the government involved, and only if the targeted behavior clearly violates international norms or has a major impact on other nations. As discussed in chapter 10, many of these issues have implications for international norms, especially those involving issues of national sovereignty. Chinese leaders also believe that developed nations should in some instances shoulder greater responsibilities and make greater sacrifices than China and other developing countries in advancing international political, security, and especially economic norms and conditions. This is particularly evident with regard to policies toward climate change, as discussed in chapter 7.

In the security arena, as noted above, Chinese leaders do not believe that the best way to preserve stability and prosperity in Asia over the long term is through a strong, United States–led bilateral alliance system and significant numbers of deployed U.S. forces. As the New Security Concept suggests, Beijing prefers a multipolar system in which several major powers interact cooperatively to ensure security, in place of formal bilateral alliances. At the same time, Beijing has stated publicly and officially that it "welcomes the United States as an Asia-Pacific nation that contributes to peace, stability and prosperity in the region."[61] More narrowly, as discussed in chapters 4 and 10, China also does not share America's interpretations of some international laws or agreements that impinge directly on security issues (such as the UN Convention on the Law of the Sea).[62]

Such contrasting approaches to some extent reflect differing perceptions of the proper role of nation-states in the international system that derive from the very different historical experiences of the United States and China in the modern era. In this respect, the United States is a long-standing global economic and military power with far-flung interests, considerable self-confidence, and a record of foreign policy successes, most notably those associated with the containment and demise of Soviet Communism. Conversely, China is a relatively weak yet rapidly growing and highly nationalistic power with a recent memory of subjugation at the hands of more advanced nations, severe economic deprivation, internal division, and social unrest. However, as noted above and in the introduction, such contrasting general approaches also reflect, arguably to an even greater degree, the presence of deeply rooted mutual suspicions, resulting primarily from the sharply contrasting U.S. and PRC political systems, along with the history of tension and conflict that have at times marked the Sino-U.S. relationship since the establishment of the PRC in 1949.[63]

These mutual suspicions often lead one or both sides to focus on uncertainties about (or to cast doubt upon) each other's motives and to utilize basic policy means that are partly designed to protect or advance one's interests vis-à-vis the other's. More broadly, these sentiments considerably reinforce each country's tendency to hedge against the other through efforts to avoid or minimize possible attempts to weaken, constrain, or undermine its own position. Moreover, on China's side, this outlook is reinforced by its desire to present itself to weaker nations as a nonpredatory developing nation, in contrast to what it regards as the hegemonic and interventionist behavior of the United States and other traditional great powers. On the U.S. side, this outlook is strengthened by the notion that America is uniquely endowed, both morally and politically, to advance liberal democracy and oppose autocratic regimes. As we have seen above, such sentiments fuel the arguments of hard-liners in both countries.

Such differences can and, as we shall see, often do create tensions between China and the United States that sometimes result in competitive and even confrontational behavior. Indeed, as outlined above and discussed in detail in subsequent chapters, Beijing has arguably become more assertive toward Washington and other powers in various foreign policy areas (ranging from bilateral and multilateral economic relations to an array of territorial issues) since roughly mid-2008, apparently at least partly in response to China's growing power and its relative success in weathering the global financial crisis.[64] However, such tensions thus far have not led to a fundamental revision of either side's grand strategy or produced a clear pattern of strategic rivalry, in which, for example, China deliberately attempts to challenge the United States–led alliance system or other core U.S. interests. To the contrary, as suggested above, Beijing has indicated at times that it is willing to accept Washington's power (and, by implication, its leadership role in many areas) as long as this power is not directed at containing Beijing or weakening its development.[65]

And yet, as discussed in detail in chapter 10, the potential certainly exists for deeply rooted mutual suspicions to produce deep misunderstandings, misperceptions, and worst casing of motives and actions that can in turn seriously weaken the ability of one or both sides to avoid or manage tense situations or crises. This potential deficiency is reinforced by both nations' tendency to place a high priority on showing resolve and maintaining the initiative in political-military crises. And both nations have also historically shown little reticence in employing military threats or force to implement such supposed "crisis management" techniques.[66] All these factors clearly increase the dangers confronting stable and productive United States–China relations, especially in the context of the broader dynamic changes occurring in the new century that are identified in the introduction.

Third, in some policy areas, the differences and resulting tensions between Washington and Beijing go beyond the above-noted general assumptions, perceptions, inclinations, and suspicions to involve more tangible and vital interests associated with specific structural factors, such as China's growing military capabilities and influence abroad and the maintenance of the perception and reality of U.S. military predominance in the Western Pacific. Perhaps the most important such difference is over Taiwan. Although both countries support a peaceful resolution of the problem, there is little doubt that China views the United States as illegitimately intervening in the resolution of a domestic conflict that can and should be resolved solely by the Chinese themselves. Moreover, many Chinese (both political leaders and ordinary citizens) believe that Washington holds a hypocritical stance on the Taiwan issue by, on the one hand, acknowledging Beijing's claim to Taiwan while, on the other hand, continuing to block a peaceful resolution by providing arms to Taiwan and maintaining quasi-official government relations with the island. For many Chinese, Washington is persevering in this obstructionist stance because it serves the strategic interests of the United States to keep China divided and distracted about the issue. The United States of course rejects this argument and views its relations with and support for Taiwan as contributing to a peaceful resolution of the situation and the protection of the rights and liberties of the island's citizens, in part by protecting Taipei from coercion. Moreover, the United States remains deeply involved in the Taiwan issue in part to sustain its credibility as a great power and (in recent decades) to support a democratic friend. As discussed further in chapter 2, this basic difference in outlook and interests (between the forces of nationalism on the one hand and the credibility and support of a democratic global power on the other hand) has the potential to produce sharp confrontation and even conflict between the United States and China, given the lack of basic trust between the two powers, and Beijing's steady acquisition in recent years of significant coercive and war-fighting military capabilities. However, it has not done so, in large part because of the many above-outlined incentives that exist in both Beijing and Washington to cooperate in many areas, and the likely hugely adverse consequences that would result from a resort to force.

In the longer term, the most fundamental divergent strategic interest between the United States and China arguably derives from the potential for a rising China and a predominant United States to enter into a deliberate security competition that leads to a focus on relative gains in virtually every area of foreign and defense policy, especially in Asia. As stated above, at present, neither power is pursuing goals and policies that are designed primarily to reduce the influence of the other and undermine the other's basic strategic approach and required capabilities. The primary objective of policies on both sides is to avoid conflict, reduce suspicion, deter threatening behavior, enhance cooperation where possible, and induce the other side to either accept, or at least not oppose, its own core interests. As suggested, this overall strategic orientation infuses the specific approaches that each nation takes within each of the seven policy arenas examined in this study. Conversely, developments in each policy arena (particularly those related to security) can also affect overall strategy by driving the two sides toward an emphasis on security competition over cooperation, as noted in the introduction and discussed in detail in chapter 10.

To what extent the primarily nonconflicting objectives and strategic approaches of the United States and China outlined above can be sustained during the medium and long terms remains an open question, given the suspicions, uncertainties, competing domestic political interests and viewpoints, and changing capabilities that influence the relationship and, potentially, each side's definition of what constitutes a "core" interest. These factors are—and will likely remain—capable of intensifying the hedging elements of each side's strategic approach toward the other in major ways. However, among these factors, arguably the most important potential source of long-term strategic competition and conflict between Washington and Beijing derives from the interplay between two sets of basic security views: (1) the deeply held assumption, among many U.S. political and military leaders, that American interests in Asia (and to some extent beyond) require the maintenance of an unambiguous level of military and political predominance in the maritime Western Pacific; and (2) the deeply held belief, among many Chinese political and military leaders, that Beijing must reduce its vulnerability to any possible future U.S. attempt to constrain China's continued growth or undermine the stability of the PRC regime. Under some conditions, assuming continued Chinese growth, the latter Chinese imperative (that is, efforts to reduce key vulnerabilities) might result in what most U.S. leaders would regard as unambiguous threats to the former U.S. imperative (that is, efforts to retain predominance). For some U.S. observers, as discussed in chapter 4, such threats are already emerging in a de facto sense, if not deliberately, as a result of China's growing power projection capabilities in Asia.

Hence, for current U.S. policymakers, any attempt to balance cooperation with hedging and to develop appropriate persuasion, dissuasion, and enmeshment approaches in each of the seven policy arenas examined in subsequent chapters should aim not only to solve specific problems and deter threats but also to maximize Chinese incentives to deepen cooperation. This two-sided effort should center on attempts to appeal to the arguments of Chinese moderates supportive of cooperation while minimizing or denying political leverage to those who advocate hard-line positions oriented toward the hedging (or worse, confrontational) elements of Chinese policy. This is no easy task, given the Sino-U.S. relationship's high (and arguably growing) level of mutual suspicion, the lack of detailed knowledge regarding the PRC's policymaking process and the domestic political dynamics influencing China's external policies, and the presence on both sides of political forces whose interests might be served by pushing policy toward more hard-line positions. (The influence of domestic political forces on America's policy toward China is examined in subsequent chapters, particularly chapter 9.) It is also complicated by the simple fact that China's size and growing resource base create new levels of military, political, and economic power and influence that potentially limit America's leverage in many areas, and could alter each side's respective approach to relative gains. However, on the positive side, the outline given above of strategic goals and policy objectives suggests that the United States possesses strong incentives and enormous capabilities that can facilitate the implementation of successful policies in most areas. And as demonstrated above, Washington and Beijing share significant objectives in many areas and face a growing number of common problems in this new century that demand cooperative solutions, thus reinforcing incentives on both sides to avoid worst case outcomes.

The following seven chapters examine in detail the record of America's policies and actions toward China taken during the past decade in each of seven core policy arenas identified in the introduction, as well as China's actions and reactions in each arena. Each chapter begins with a brief assessment of the major issues and questions that influence policy in the particular arena, especially with regard to U.S. and Chinese interests and objectives. The main features of specific U.S. and Chinese policies during the George W. Bush and Barack Obama administrations are then summarized and evaluated, largely in light of America's stated goals toward China, both with regard to the specific arena in question and in the larger context of overall U.S. strategy. Each chapter ends with an assessment of the impact of likely future trends on U.S. policy. As indicated in the introduction, the purpose of this undertaking is to provide a basis for assessing the present and likely future effectiveness of U.S. policies in addressing the major challenges confronting the United States in each arena, and the continued viability of the larger U.S. strategy toward China during the current decade and beyond. These issues are discussed in detail in the final, concluding chapter.

02

POLITICAL AND
SECURITY RELATIONS
WITH KEY ASIAN POWERS

▾

Despite its steadily expanding global involvement, China's major political and security concerns remain primarily focused on Asia. This is due to both the turbulent and to some degree uncertain nature of Beijing's regional environment and its limited capability to exercise significant political and security-related influence globally. Thus, it is little surprise that U.S. political and security policy toward China is largely directed toward the Asia-Pacific region. Ideally, American efforts to both deter (or caution) and cooperate with (or reassure) China on a host of political and security-related issues involving Asia should reflect the objectives and approaches of a much larger U.S. regional (and even global) political-military security strategy. As suggested in chapter 1, fundamental issues such as the relative capabilities, role, and disposition of U.S. forces across the region, and the nature of Washington's political and diplomatic relations with major regional powers or involvement in regional multilateral structures, should support (indeed, facilitate or ensure) its overall political and security agenda toward Beijing. Most importantly, regional political and security policies—involving the nature, extent, and durability of American maritime predominance in the Western Pacific; the larger structure and function of the alliance relationship with Japan; relations with other major or important powers such as India, Russia, and the two Koreas; the management of the Taiwan issue; and Washington's role in leading or supporting key emergent security-related forums and processes—should inform, if not determine, the basic forms and levels of cooperative engagement and reassurance—along with efforts at dissuasion and deterrence—adopted toward China on *all* major policy issues, from economics and trade to human rights and democracy promotion.

This chapter focuses primarily on the most important non-military and bilateral components of U.S. regional policies—that is, Washington's political-security approach toward the major powers in Asia—as they affect China and U.S. China policy, as well as Chinese policies toward these powers. (Chapter 3 examines U.S. and Chinese policies toward the most important multilateral and related bilateral structures and processes influencing America's China policy, and chapter 4 examines the military dimensions of Washington's China-related policies in Asia.) This analysis is preceded by an overview of those larger changes in the U.S. strategic approach toward Asia and China that have shaped specific policies toward the key powers of the region.

THE LARGER STRATEGIC APPROACH UNDER BUSH AND OBAMA

Unsurprisingly, for much of the reform era, the linkage between America's larger security policies and objectives in Asia and its stance toward China has often been unclear and inconsistent over time, reflecting the vicissitudes of domestic political calculations, a general lack of clarity in some key elements of overall U.S. strategy, or variations among officials and administrations in the emphasis placed upon key regional actors such as Japan. These problems were and remain to some extent unavoidable, given the democratic nature of the U.S. political process and the frequency of leadership changes at senior levels of the U.S. bureaucracy. However, the extent to which such structural factors are allowed to influence policy is certainly subject to some control. During the transition into the twenty-first century (that is, from the 1990s onward), the historical record suggests that such problems were particularly evident during parts of the Bill Clinton and, especially, the George W. Bush eras, but have been less evident thus far during the Barack Obama administration.

In the early years of the Clinton and Bush administrations, both leaders promoted a more adversarial overall relationship with Beijing upon entering office, focusing strongly on Beijing's dismal human rights record (in the case of Clinton) or its supposed status as a strategic competitor and potential threat to the United

States (in the case of Bush). These stances had an impact on specific policies for a time—resulting, for example, in Clinton's efforts to link Beijing's progress in meeting specific human rights goals with the granting of most-favored-nation trade status, and in Bush's public labeling of Beijing as a "strategic competitor" and his approval of Taiwan's request to provide it with a range of previously off-limits weapons systems.[1]

To a large extent, these hard-line positions derived from each administration's perceived political need to strike a clear contrast with what it saw as the excessively conciliatory China policies of the preceding administration (of the other political party). In the case of Bush's first term in office, this position was reinforced to some extent by the strategic views of ideological neoconservatives and some senior officials in the Pentagon,[2] who viewed China as a potentially hostile strategic adversary engaged in a largely zero-sum competition with the United States for influence and power in Asia. These individuals reportedly desired to use the supposedly long-term strategic threat posed by China (along with the allegedly more imminent threat presented by Saddam Hussein in Iraq) as the basic organizing principles of the Bush administration's foreign policy.[3]

However, during both the Clinton and Bush administrations, some of the most extreme rhetorical and policy aspects of these views were eventually dropped, resulting in a shift toward a far more balanced overall approach to Beijing. This shift largely resulted from a combination of policy failures (for example, the ineffectiveness of the human rights–most-favored-nation trading status linkage during the Clinton era) and a general recognition of the growing need, in the new century, to develop and sustain good working relations with China in order to protect and advance an expanding number of core U.S. interests, ranging from economic prosperity to a non-nuclear Korean Peninsula.

As noted in the introduction, the United States' substantive need to work with China to address a range of common concerns was hugely reinforced by the consequences of the terrorist attacks of September 11, 2001, and the subsequent wars in Afghanistan and Iraq. These events placed the war on terrorism (and related issues such as the proliferation of weapons of mass destruction) front and center in U.S. foreign policy, and consequently made it imperative for Washington to avoid new crises and confrontations with China and other major powers, while striving to work more effectively with Beijing to solve a growing number of common regional and global problems. As one insider interviewee stated, describing the president's view at the time: "Bush didn't want to hear any more from those who wanted to focus on China as the enemy. He wanted friends and coalitions, not distractions."[4] One should add that, according to many former Bush administration officials, relatively few individuals in the administration advocated a strong hard-line stance toward China in any event, and these did not include many, if any, in the White House or the State Department.[5]

Thus, even though some internal differences remained in the Bush administration regarding specific policies toward China (as are discussed in subsequent chapters), the basic, overall cooperative thrust of Washington's approach to Beijing had been clearly established by late 2001, and in fact shared some strong similarities with the more cooperative Clinton strategy of the initial "post–most-favored-nation–human rights linkage" period.

An "Inside-Out" Approach to the Asian Region

That said, some knowledgeable observers believe that the Bush administration's strategy toward China during at least the remainder of its first term exhibited one key difference with the Clinton administration. While holding a common desire to expand Japan's security role in Asia and beyond, the Bush strategy initially allegedly placed the improvement of political, military, and diplomatic relations with Tokyo *and* with other Asian democracies (such as India, discussed below) more toward the center of its Asia strategy, and it deliberately sought to avoid treating China as *the* key power in the region or to give it more deference and consideration than it deserved.[6]

Specifically, this approach incorporated three central elements: first, efforts to downplay economic and other policy differences with Japan in order to strengthen political ties and advance common security goals; second, a clearer and tougher approach toward Beijing regarding those issues about which the United States and China might disagree; and third, efforts to nonetheless avoid needlessly provoking or confronting Beijing over sensitive core national security issues such as Tibet and Taiwan, human and political rights, and domestic stability.[7] As indicated in the introduction, this Bush strategy also recognized the need, in the new century, to vest China more solidly in the existing international system by working hard to support its entrance into various regimes such as the World Trade Organization and to shape its behavior in those regimes, once admitted.[8]

In sum, the combination of a strong, alliance-based approach to the region, greater clarity and toughness regarding the defense of U.S. interests, alongside enhanced efforts to bring China more fully into the international system while avoiding provocative actions formed the basis of a what was regarded as an effective set of balanced, cooperative/hedging-oriented policies toward China. Thus, for the proponents of this strategy, the focus on Asian alliance relationships did not simply constitute a hedge against possible adverse Chinese actions. It was also seen as a means of encouraging China to "emerge in a benign way," according to one respondent. During the first term of the Bush administration, this general undertaking was the centerpiece of the so-called inside-out approach to the overall Asian security environment, which emphasized the primacy of developing coordinated security roles and policies with Asian democratic allies over sustaining or improving cooperative relations with China as the key to the advancement of U.S. regional security objectives.[9]

Whether the Bush administration was able to enforce and effectively implement such a strategy over time is another matter, of course. Some observers (including some of those interviewed for this book) argue that core elements of this strategy either atrophied or were poorly implemented during at least the second Bush term, resulting in less attention paid to Japan and an excessively deferential stance toward Beijing, best exemplified by the unprecedented high-profile, multiagency Strategic Economic Dialogue with China inaugurated by Treasury Secretary Henry Paulson in 2006 and the supposedly excessive focus placed on working with Beijing to manage the North Korean nuclear issue (both points are discussed in detail below and in other chapters). Some associate this shift with the departure from the administration of key senior-level proponents of the "inside-out," alliance-centered strategy, such as Richard Armitage, Michael Green, and Torkel Patterson.[10]

Responsible Stakeholdership

However, other inside observers argue that the above-mentioned Bush administration's emphases on the United States–Japan alliance and toughness toward China were, in reality, not as pronounced from the start and that the administration's basic overall approach was best reflected in the "responsible stakeholder" concept unveiled by former deputy secretary of state Robert Zoellick in 2005. This concept focused on reducing potential sources of confrontation and encouraging Beijing to play a more active role in the maintenance and protection of the international system via in-depth discussions with Washington, while nonetheless continuing to hedge against uncertainty. It assumed that (1) China is already well integrated into the international system; (2) a growing number of global problems require Chinese cooperation to resolve; and (3) such cooperation is probably possible in many areas—that is, Beijing and Washington share a sufficient number of interests, or are at least close enough in outlook on many vital issues, to permit a constructive dialogue aimed at reducing misunderstandings and developing concrete solutions for both regional and global problems.

In other words, the "responsible stakeholder" concept—and the associated Senior Dialogue, Security Dialogue, and Strategic Economic Dialogue of the

Bush era (which are discussed in the following chapter)—viewed China as a potential partner in achieving common ends, not as a threat to be contained, and thus rejected the pessimistic assumptions of those who assume that China's rise will inevitably result in a prolonged Cold War in Asia.[11] At the same time, this approach did not ignore potential problems stemming from China's military modernization program and apparently "mercantilist" approach to foreign economic relations that required both dialogue and hedging.[12]

Although the Zoellick "responsible stakeholder" approach was clearly relevant to overall United States–China relations in a global context, it posed direct implications for U.S. political and security policies in Asia. Indeed, some observers insist that, at bottom, it represented an alternative, "China-centered" security strategy toward Asia to the earlier, so-called Japan-centered Armitage approach outlined above.[13] In truth, there is little doubt that the responsible stakeholder approach to China at the very least recognized China's growing importance to U.S. global and regional interests and therefore placed an increased emphasis, within overall U.S. strategy, on relations with Beijing. Whether this shifting emphasis occurred at the expense of U.S. relations with Japan (or Japanese interests) is unclear. As many interview respondents confirmed, Zoellick's concept was at least partly motivated by his past experience in dealing with Tokyo. He personally viewed Japan as a somewhat difficult and frustrating partner, often unable or unwilling to undertake responsible actions in the international system or to engage the United States in meaningful dialogue. To some extent, the responsible stakeholder concept offered a possible template for the kind of cooperative relationship that Zoellick desired with Tokyo, while perhaps reflecting his optimism that China could eventually (and possibly more easily?) play a constructive role in many areas.

That said, the concept of "responsible stakeholder" was not entirely incompatible with the so-called Japan-centered Armitage approach toward China. Both views fully endorsed the need to pursue cooperative and hedging policies with regard to Beijing, and both views certainly had precedents in U.S. policy before the George W. Bush administration. The key difference, *vis-à-vis overall security policy toward China*, perhaps lay in the degree of emphasis that each placed on political engagement versus military-political hedging within the overall policy. The Armitage approach sought to bring China along by shaping its larger security environment in Asia through a deepening of the United States–Japan alliance, whereas the Zoellick approach sought to emphasize dealing directly and deeply with Beijing through expanding dialogue and other bilateral activities both in and outside the region.

As suggested above, the former view, often strongly supported by Japan specialists in the Bush administration, reflected a long-standing concern that "attention paid to China had come at the expense of the United States–Japan relationship and the alliance."[14] Hence, this approach strongly emphasized the continued "reinvigoration" and deepening of the United States–Japan security partnership, largely regardless of Chinese reactions, and at times resulted in tactics and statements that seemed to give strong consideration to Tokyo's concerns on many China related issues.[15] The latter view, often supported by China specialists, focused significantly on the notion that Beijing's growing power and influence within the global and regional order were steadily increasing its leverage within that order relative to any other major power, including Japan. Indeed, some proponents of this view argued that Japan was in many ways a declining and reluctant power and unable to serve as Washington's key political and security ally in the region. Hence, this approach stressed the need for Washington to more deeply understand and effectively adapt to Beijing's rise through dialogue and other actions and at times appeared to address Beijing's concerns above those of other powers.

Obviously, both then and now, it is the case that any effective China policy must contain strong elements of both indirect shaping through strengthened relationships with key Asian powers and direct dialogue and interaction with Beijing. The trick is to modulate each aspect so that they together optimize the attainment of an agreed-upon set of policy objectives vis-à-vis China. However, the greater, related challenge posed by these two approaches arguably lay in their apparent implications for the United States' overall political and security strategy toward Asia and beyond. The Armitage approach seemed to aim at the eventual transformation of the United States–Japan alliance into a regional and perhaps global strategic partnership to protect and advance the United States–led international order. In contrast, the Zoellick approach seemed to imply that China could play an increasingly important role in shaping and perhaps even directing, as a partner, the future international order through a deepening of cooperation with Washington. In other words, from Zoellick's perspective, the stability, peace, and prosperity of Asia and the international system would result in large part from the enhancement of trust and cooperation between China and the United States— involving a process of mutual accommodation, where necessary—and not primarily through the strengthening and expansion of an existing alliance system.

It is also important to note that at least one former senior U.S. official has expressed the belief that "Zoellick's formulation was not clear about the kind of voice [the Bush administration] was prepared to give China. It is clear what they wanted China to do but it is less clear whether they were ready to accept China having a more active role." However, other interview respondents made it clear that, although not publicly stated, the Zoellick approach certainly anticipated some level of U.S. accommodation to Chinese interests. The question of the degree to which Washington is able to accommodate to Chinese wishes in the political and security arena is of course critical to any assessment of the viability of the Zoellick (or any other) approach. This issue is discussed in chapter 4 and the conclusion in particular.

The Obama Approach

Obama and his senior administration officials speak of the need to bolster alliance relationships and engage more broadly with Asian countries in general, as part of an overall effort to enhance America's political, diplomatic, economic, and security involvement with the entire Asia-Pacific region. However, thus far, it is clear that the Obama administration has not adopted the larger, and highly ambitious, objectives of the "inside-out" Japan-centric Armitage approach to advancing U.S. security objectives in Asia.

Indeed, as indicated below and in subsequent chapters, to a great extent, the Obama administration has significantly increased U.S. political and diplomatic engagement in Asia, both bilaterally and among multilateral structures and forums. This effort, which is partly intended to counterbalance growing Chinese power and assertiveness, certainly includes the maintenance of the United States' security alliance with Japan.[16] However, for both conceptual and practical reasons (discussed in greater detail below), the basic Obama security approach apparently does not view a deepened and expanded United States–Japan security alliance as the *primary* key to managing China and ensuring the Asia-Pacific region's long-term order. It does not place a strong emphasis on the need to expand Japan's security capabilities and military roles well beyond the home islands. To the contrary, the Obama administration strikes many of the same themes and uses much of the same logic found in the "responsible stakeholder" approach toward China. This includes a strong emphasis on deepening bilateral cooperation with Beijing in handling a wide array of regional and global problems, including many in the security realm, such as counterproliferation.[17]

On a broader level, this approach also reflects the generally pragmatic, basically nonideological approach adopted by the Obama administration in its overall Asia policy.[18] At the same time, in the security realm, the Obama administration has also placed a particular emphasis on the need for China to provide "strategic reassurance" toward the United States and other powers by taking concrete actions that clearly demonstrate a commitment to positive-sum approaches and outcomes, in order to facilitate the avoidance of an overall pattern of bilateral security competition.[19]

Although notable for being singled out as an explicit element of Sino-U.S. security policy, the notion of providing strategic reassurance through concrete means is inherent in the "responsible stakeholder" concept. That is, Zoellick also emphasized the need for China to affirm its commitment to global norms and to clarify or correct the impression that it was engaged in competitive or zero-sum policy behaviors.[20] The Obama administration has merely placed a particular emphasis on the need for Beijing to provide concrete examples of such reassurance in the broad strategic sense, apparently to show that it recognizes the continuing uncertainties accompanying China's growing power and influence, and the associated need to resolve certain troubling aspects of China's behavior (more on this point below).[21]

Taken as a whole, these contrasting emphases evident in America's overall security approach toward both Asia and China in particular clearly illustrate the challenges involved in integrating political-military policies toward China into a larger strategic vision that rejects the simplistic notion of Washington's "balancing" (or choosing) between Beijing and Tokyo in favor of a broader, more comprehensive set of regional policies and objectives. Such integration requires a clear notion of how America's alliance relationship with Japan, as well as its relations with the other major Asian powers, should relate to its China policy. This in turn requires a clear understanding of the role that these other powers are willing and able to play in supporting American political and security policies toward China, and the degree of mutual accommodation that the United States and China are willing to make to each other's interests. These issues are discussed in greater detail in the conclusion.

With this larger strategic context as a backdrop, the remainder of this chapter examines in greater detail the specific political and defense policies that the Bush and Obama administrations have pursued with regard to the major Asian powers, as well as Chinese policies toward each power. As noted above, chapter 3 will examine U.S. bilateral and multilateral political and security interactions in Asia as they relate to China and then assess Chinese interactions. And chapter 4 will round out the examination of U.S. political and security policies by assessing the purely military dimensions of U.S. policy toward China, followed by an examination of Chinese military policies and actions. In each chapter, these policy histories are followed by an evaluation and discussion of possible future trends.

RELATIONS WITH
KEY ASIAN POWERS

Within the Asia Pacific, the sub-region of Northeast Asia is without doubt the most critical to U.S. interests and policies with regard to China. That area contains Washington's two most important and influential regional allies (Japan and South Korea), as well as the two most volatile security-related locations confronting the Sino-U.S. relationship: Taiwan and North Korea. The following analysis examines the China-relevant dimension of U.S. policies toward each of these entities in turn (Japan, South Korea, Taiwan, and North Korea), as well as Chinese policies and interactions of significance to the United States.

Japan

Since the end of the Second World War, Japan has been the linchpin of U.S. diplomatic, economic, and security policies in Asia, and a major regional political and economic player on its own. For these reasons, as indicated above, the development of effective U.S. policies toward China during the new century will depend to a very great extent on Washington's ability to fully coordinate and integrate its policies toward Japan with those toward China and the larger region. Close, well-coordinated political, economic, and security policies with Tokyo can enormously strengthen the effectiveness of U.S. policies toward China. At the same time, an excessive or poorly managed U.S. reliance on Japan as a deliberate strategic counter-balance to China, and/or the emergence of unstable, tension-laden relations between Tokyo and Beijing can significantly undermine overall U.S. objectives vis-à-vis China and more broadly.

U.S. Policies

As suggested above, during the past ten to fifteen years, U.S. administrations have placed a strong emphasis on strengthening America's overall alliance relationships with its key democratic allies in Asia. This effort has focused in particular on improving political and defense relations with Tokyo, in order to facilitate Japan's emergence as a more active political-military ally that is capable of addressing a wide range of potential traditional and nontraditional security issues within Asia and beyond, from peacekeeping and involvement in the Iraq War to the provision of extensive levels of support for U.S. military deployments in a possible future Taiwan crisis. Such actions have thus included support for Japan's ongoing military modernization and expansion program, involving the sale of new platforms, cooperation in missile defense, and the attainment of greater coordination regarding United States–Japan air and naval operations. Together, these military and political efforts were largely intended to move the bilateral relationship with Japan from "burden sharing" to limited "power sharing," with obvious implications for China. This shift did not, however, succeed to the extent anticipated by many, as discussed below.

This undertaking was foreshadowed during the Ronald Reagan administration by the so-called pan-Asian policy of then–secretary of state George Shultz and continued during the George H. W. Bush and Clinton administrations.[22] However, it developed its greatest momentum and focus, as both a core element of China policy and with regard to military-security factors, after Bush took office, and it formed a central part of the "inside-out" Japan-centric regional security strategy outlined above.[23] It also fit into a larger Bush strategy—contained in the 2001 Quadrennial Defense Review, Bush's June 2002 speech at West Point, and the September 2002 and February 2006 publications of the National Security Strategy—that placed a heavy reliance on a limited number of U.S. bases in a few "bedrock" allied states, such as Japan, as part of an effort to transform the U.S. military into a more agile and flexible global force.[24]

In the military arena, although Japanese defense modernization had already been under way for several years, it arguably witnessed its greatest successes during the prime ministerships of Junichiro Koizumi and Shinzo Abe, from April 2001 to September 2007, in large part because it dovetailed with these Japanese leaders' concerted efforts to strengthen the capabilities of the Japanese military and enhance the alliance with Washington. With U.S. support, and despite an overall small decline in total defense spending (see more on this point below), Koizumi intensified a program of military modernization in late 2001 that included the acquisition of new air and naval platforms of significant relevance to Japan's ability to deploy military power beyond its borders. Key elements of this program included:

- A shift in emphasis toward limited power projection rather than simple territorial defense, using "multifunctional, flexible, and effective" forces with mobile and rapid-reaction capabilities.
- Maritime Self-Defense Force procurement of Aegis-type frigates and destroyers, light carriers, amphibious craft, and patrol aircraft to expand their range in the Asia Pacific and well beyond.
- Major steps toward the deployment of Aegis-based and PAC-1 ballistic missile defenses, with PAC-3 terminal-phase interceptor batteries already in operation.
- Air Self-Defense Force procurement of the F-2 fighter bomber, in-flight refueling capability, joint direct attack munitions, and more sophisticated

defense and cruise missile detection systems, enabling greater power projection beyond Japanese territory.[25]

- The launch of intelligence-gathering satellites with monitoring capabilities.
- Enhanced real-time coordination between military forces, the introduction of unmanned aerial vehicles, and joint triservice operations.
- Increased Ground Self-Defense Force mobility for counterinsurgency and overseas operations, with lighter vehicles resistant to rocket-propelled grenades and improvised explosive devices and additional ballistic protection for transport helicopters.
- The establishment of a Central Readiness Group intended as a rapid-reaction force for coordinating nationwide mobile operations; for responding to domestic terrorism, to guerrilla incursions, and to threats of nuclear, biological, and chemical warfare; and for training personnel for overseas deployment.[26]

The conceptual foundation for Japan's more ambitious military role was presented in the National Defense Program Guidelines (NDPG) of 2004, which were issued by the Japan Defense Agency (upgraded to the Ministry of Defense in 2007). Although this document continued to advocate a "defensive defense policy," it also supported movement toward an array of new security roles that reflected an expanding definition of those regional and global conditions that might threaten Japanese security, including, potentially, China's rise.[27] According to T. J. Pempel, it emphasized the importance of peacekeeping operations and "the creation of a multifunctional military capability with a centralized [Self-Defense Force] command and a rapid reaction force." Even more important, the NDPG specifically highlighted North Korea and China as the most likely future security threats to Japan.[28]

Regarding defense relations with Washington, Tokyo at this time committed Japan to the U.S. ballistic missile defense system, permitted deployment to Japan of the U.S. missile defense destroyer USS *Shiloh*, and enhanced interoperability between Japanese and U.S. weapons systems. In addition, Washington and Tokyo continued the United States–Japan Joint Security Consultative Committee (JSCC) (the so-called two-plus-two meeting of foreign and defense secretaries) and initiated the Trilateral Security Dialogue among the United States, Japan, and Australia. In the February 19, 2005, joint statement of the JSCC, Tokyo and Washington specified, among many other things, that a peaceful resolution of the Taiwan situation through dialogue constituted a common strategic objective.[29]

Thus the JSCC statement, along with the NDPG of 2004, marked a clear evolution toward the identification of China—and the Taiwan situation in particular—

as security concerns for the United States–Japan alliance, a process that arguably began in the mid-1990s, with the April 1996 U.S.-Japan Joint Declaration on Security and the subsequent Revised Defense Guidelines of 1997. The declaration spoke of the importance of defense cooperation between Washington and Tokyo in "situations in the areas surrounding Japan."[30]

By mid-2007, the United States and Japan had completed a formal dialogue on alliance transformation that placed a stronger emphasis on power projection, amphibious capabilities, force transformation, and improved command and control. Tokyo had also established new areas of technological cooperation with Washington on cyberspace defense operations, surveillance and reconnaissance, integrated disaster relief planning and response, and shared intelligence, among other areas. In addition, in a shift that strengthened Japan's role in the U.S. global military strategy, Tokyo allowed the transfer of U.S. Army I Corps command functions from Fort Lewis, Washington, to Camp Zama. And in September 2007, Japan joined with the United States, Australia, Singapore, and India to conduct a multinational naval exercise in the area west of the Malacca Straits.[31]

Finally, U.S. policies also supported an active Japanese role in an expanding number of security-related regional multilateral forums and mechanisms, including long-standing organizations such as the Asia-Pacific Economic Cooperation forum and the Association of Southeast Asian Nations (ASEAN) Regional Forum (ARF), as well as more recent bodies such as the East Asia Summit (EAS) and ASEAN+3 (APT)—the latter of which does not include the United States.[32] Indeed, the 1996 U.S.-Japanese Joint Declaration on Security asserted that the two states would cooperate with each other and other states to promote multilateral bodies such as ARF, while the 2004 NDPG stressed that the U.S. alliance should facilitate the promotion of multilateral security cooperation and dialogue. In addition, Japan has been one of the most consistent supporters of ARF—particularly active in both Track I and Track II dialogues.[33] Tokyo was also initially a major backer of the EAS and advocated expanding its membership to include the democratic Asian states of India, Australia, and New Zealand. This move was taken in part to provide a potential counterweight to China's influence within a genuinely regionwide organization that did not include the United States (although the United States will be joining the EAS as a full member in 2011).[34]

Needless to say, these military and political activities were not all connected with or directed against China. Indeed, some of Japan's actions in support for Asia-wide security dialogues were partly intended to bring China more fully into such regional interactions and to reassure the Asia-Pacific region about Japan's strategic intentions. In addition, while supporting a larger redefinition of U.S. strategy, greater military cooperation with the United States also served

Koizumi's push for constitutional revision in the direction of a more "normal" security posture for the Japanese state. Indeed, many of the above-mentioned actions were undertaken at the behest of the Koizumi and Abe governments, although Japan's embrace of multilateralism in the security realm predates Koizumi. Moreover, Abe placed a greater focus on improving relations with Beijing after the tensions of the Koizumi era (see below). Nonetheless, such bilateral United States–Japan activities certainly formed an important part of the Bush administration's efforts to maintain regional stability by explicitly counterbalancing growing Chinese political and military influence. This aspect of the alliance had been intentionally downplayed during the Clinton administration. According to some former Clinton officials, Washington at that time deliberately sought to avoid casting the improvements it undertook in the United States–Japan security relationship as being directed at China because the primary regional focus of such activities was North Korea.[35] That said, the Taiwan Strait crisis of 1995–1996 undoubtedly facilitated those above-mentioned increases in United States–Japan defense cooperation occurring in the years 1996–1997.

Conversely, Bush administration political and defense initiatives toward Tokyo, especially in the second term, were also partly intended to *discourage* Sino-Japanese strategic competition by providing Tokyo with a strong reassurance that it need not be overly concerned with Beijing's rising military power, given Washington's strong commitment to the maintenance of peace and stability in the region. As is discussed in greater detail below, the prospect of Sino-Japanese strategic rivalry had become particularly acute by 2005, as relations between Tokyo and Beijing worsened due to disputes over historical issues associated with World War II, Koizumi's repeated trips to the Yasukuni Shrine, competing resource-oriented territorial claims in the East China Sea, and Tokyo's concerns over Beijing's growing air and naval capabilities along China's maritime periphery. The Bush administration recognized that it was not in the interests of the United States for Asia's two most powerful and influential nations to be locked in an emotionally charged, deteriorating relationship. Such a dispute could disrupt regional growth and stability and even increase the chances of a new Cold War emerging in the region. Washington therefore sought to combine improvements in bilateral defense relations with Japan with efforts to encourage an improvement in Sino-Japanese relations.[36]

A New Era in Japan and a Changing Alliance

The above-outlined political and defense-related interactions with Tokyo did not constitute an unqualified success for the Bush administration, however. As the above discussion of overall U.S. Asia strategy indicates, efforts to continue strengthening the United States–Japan security relationship arguably lost momentum in the second Bush term, as a result not only of the departure of some U.S. officials but also because major political changes occurred within Japan— specifically, the end of the Koizumi and Abe administrations and the emergence of what will likely prove to be a prolonged period of political upheaval and some policy uncertainty in Tokyo. The latter development was reflected most notably, during the initial months of the Obama administration, by the replacement in mid-2009 of the conservative Liberal Democratic Party (LDP) that has ruled Japan since not long after the end of World War II (with one brief exception) by a political coalition led by the inexperienced opposition Democratic Party of Japan (DPJ).[37]

The DPJ and its coalition partners initially signaled a strong desire to reassess and perhaps restructure basic aspects of the United States–Japan security relationship and Japan's larger security role in Asia (and beyond) in ways that could have a significant impact on U.S. policies toward China. Specifically, in 2009 and early 2010, officials within the DPJ-led government, including the new DPJ Premier Yukio Hatoyama, expressed support for a more "equal" security partnership with Washington that could provide Tokyo with more flexibility and freedom of action to pursue more autonomous security policies, albeit still within the overall context of the alliance. These could include further reductions in support of both security deployments beyond the home islands and the overall development of a more jointly operational security partnership.

In addition, more broadly, some DPJ leaders initially indicated a desire for Japan to focus its overall policies more on Asia and the development of an East Asian Community that *apparently* did not include the United States (a notion that was not well received in Washington—see below). Equally important, some senior figures associated with the DPJ showed a strong desire to cultivate closer ties with Beijing, partly in response to what was regarded as the excessively anti-China actions of the Koizumi period, as well as Japan's growing economic dependence on China and a general desire to maximize Tokyo's diplomatic leverage.[38] Moreover, continuing DPJ support for a reexamination of burden sharing within the Status of Forces Agreement, protracted problems regarding the repositioning of U.S. forces in Japan, and other highly sensitive alliance-management issues also produced additional tensions between Washington and Tokyo that could affect efforts to develop coordinated bilateral policies toward Beijing.[39]

This initial DPJ-led shift in attitudes toward the alliance and Japan's security posture in Asia and vis-à-vis China changed notably beginning in late 2010, however, largely as a result of highly tense maritime incidents with Beijing and broader Japanese concerns over China's greater assertiveness in the Western Pacific (discussed below). In the aftermath of these developments, DPJ leaders have more recently expressed stronger support for the alliance and a greater desire to move closer to the United States strategically, have attempted to defuse tensions over the basing of U.S. forces in Japan, and have enunciated a new 2010 NDPG more oriented toward addressing the growing potential threat from China to Japanese territories in the south. Many Japanese are also becoming more concerned about Japan's continued economic dependence on China, and the ongoing economic malaise affecting both Tokyo and Washington.[40]

Taken as a whole, and despite the recent shift back toward closer security ties with the United States, the Japanese political scene nonetheless continues to exhibit great turbulence, involving a significant transition in Japanese perceptions toward the United States, China, and the overall security environment in Asia. In particular, as suggested above, this transition is marked by movement away from the strong, alliance-based perspective of the past and toward a more independent, Asia-oriented, and Japan-centered foreign policy and considerable hedging against a more pronounced shift in the balance of forces in Asia between Washington and Beijing. This shift has precipitated an internal debate in Japan over how to position the country strategically between a rising China and a United States that many in Japan and elsewhere view as seriously struggling, if not in decline. This overall transition in Japan's strategic position will undoubtedly require many years to run its course, and it will likely be marked by ongoing debates involving those favoring a continued emphasis on the alliance; those seeking a more independent role for Japan in the trilateral relationship with the United States and China (without, however, abandoning the alliance); and other perspectives.[41] The United States will undoubtedly play a major role in this transition—both directly, via its handling of the alliance, and indirectly, via its policies toward China and its overall political, economic, and military posture in the Asia-Pacific region and beyond.[42]

In addition to such fundamental political shifts, prolonged economic stagnation (accompanied by a very large and growing government budget deficit) and demographic aging (which will result in much greater public spending on social welfare) have reinforced long-standing postwar prejudices against funding the military. The principal social barrier to Japan's remilitarization has been and remains its Constitution.[43] Past efforts to reexamine and liberalize interpretations of the Japanese Constitution have lost impetus in recent years for domestic political reasons, including, most recently, the emergence of the more pacifist-oriented, DPJ-led government. In fact, support for constitutional revision among the Japanese public appears to be declining.[44]

Thus, despite major advances in Japanese military capabilities and an expansion in Japan's role as a security actor in Asia and beyond, in the view of many observers, Tokyo has never shown an ability or willingness to achieve the level of interoperability with U.S. forces or more active security role in Asia that many U.S. officials arguably desire, and it has also resisted an explicit commitment to collective defense. As T. J. Pempel states:

> [Tokyo continues] to limit SDF dispatch to non-combat functions, underscoring Japan's contention that such actions are predicated not on the bilateral alliance but on specific UN resolutions. In these ways, Japanese policymakers have retained legal safeguards that limit the country's participation in military operations that are not sanctioned by the UN and have avoided setting precedents that, under the bilateral security treaty, might commit Japan to specific actions in any future East Asian conflicts.[45]

As a result of these factors, Japanese spending on new weapons systems has declined since the departure of the Koizumi and Abe governments, as part of an overall decline in defense spending.[46] According to the Stockholm International Peace Research Institute, Tokyo's 2009 defense spending was close to $47 billion (0.9 percent of gross domestic product), up $500 million from 2008 but down $2 billion from its peak in 2003.[47] All three branches of Japan's armed services face the prospect of further cutbacks under a DPJ government. The amounts available within this tightening defense budget for the procurement of new weapons systems are also under severe pressure. An increasing proportion of budgetary funds are directed toward personnel and provisions, with a declining proportion going toward equipment acquisition.[48] These developments have occurred despite growing concern among many Japanese defense analysts over China's military developments and actions, as noted above.[49]

United States–Japan relations have also encountered problems in recent years regarding critical regional security issues. Washington's shift toward a negotiated settlement of the North Korean nuclear issue (discussed below) has resulted in growing Japanese concerns that the United States might (1) press for a final agreement at the expense of the abductees issue; and (2) permit Pyongyang to retain some nuclear weapons-related material, thereby "risking regional nuclear proliferation, causing the collapse of the already weakened [Nuclear Non-Proliferation Treaty], and lowering Japan's confidence in U.S. defense commitments, including extended deterrence. In the view of some observers, this scenario could even eventually push Japan to begin exploring the country's own nuclear options."[50]

In addition, in recent years, some Japanese officials (and in particular some senior military officers) have shown increasing concern that what they view as

America's growing dependence on cooperative relations with China to resolve the North Korean nuclear issue and manage the rapidly expanding United States–China economic relationship, along with its overall focus on problems in the Middle East, will lead Washington to downplay the importance of relations with Japan and underestimate the security implications of China's growing regional influence. Japanese observers were perplexed by what they regarded as the lukewarm response by the Bush administration to Japan's attempt to initiate a quadrilateral security dialogue among Japan, the United States, Australia, and India as part of a larger "arc of freedom and prosperity." Some Japanese suspected that Washington's response was largely due to a desire to avoid angering Beijing. Indeed, in the view of some analysts, the fear of a U.S. tilt toward China "lies at the heart of Japanese insecurity today."[51] Such fears have arguably intensified as a result of increased tensions between Beijing and Tokyo, and despite a subsequent tightening of the United States–Japan alliance.

Conversely, other Japanese and outside observers have raised concerns over the potential adverse impact that Tokyo's involvement in multilateral security-related institutions might have on the viability of the United States–Japan alliance over time. They argue that such forums might weaken the robustness of the United States–Japan alliance by raising false expectations of their ability to provide an alternative security option for Tokyo. In this regard, they are seen as potentially increasing the likelihood of U.S. abandonment, one of the two cardinal fears of Japanese leaders and security analysts regarding the United States–Japan alliance.[52]

The Obama administration has attempted to address several of the above-mentioned issues of relevance to China policy. Both before and during President Obama's visit to Japan in November 2009, Washington undertook actions designed to show the new administration's firm commitment to the alliance and U.S. security pledges in particular, even as it has also sought to strengthen the Sino-U.S. relationship in political-military and other areas. Such actions have included substantive improvements in the U.S. military presence in the Asia-Pacific region (discussed in detail in chapter 4), as well as repeated assurances, conveyed in person and via public and private statements, that the United States remains fully committed to nuclear deterrence and extended deterrence toward its allies in Asia (especially Japan), while also expressing greater support for the DPJ government's goal of reducing the role of nuclear weapons in global politics. In addition, regarding key regional security issues, the Obama administration has sought to reassure Tokyo that it will not accept a nuclear North Korea, and it has reiterated Bush's statements of support for continued improvements in Sino-Japanese relations.[53] And with regard to the highly sensitive issue of the relocation of U.S. forces in Japan, after some initial toughness, Washington indicated in early 2011 that it would follow Tokyo's lead in working with local residents to develop an acceptable solution to the problem.[54]

Despite such actions, as suggested above, the overall turbulence and transformation of Japan's political scene, accompanied by the statements described above from the new DPJ government in 2009 and early 2010, and the emergence of the above-mentioned Japanese debate over Tokyo's future strategic orientation, continue to cause concerns among outside analysts and also within the Obama administration—regarding Japan's security role as an alliance partner and regional-global actor. As a result, at that time, some observers concluded that both Tokyo's and Washington's core expectations toward the alliance were not being met and would unlikely be met under existing conditions. Moreover, President Obama's trip to Tokyo in November 2009, as part of a larger visit to Southeast Asia, Japan, China, and South Korea, did not significantly resolve these emerging problems in the United States–Japan relationship.[55] Although such concerns have abated somewhat today, in the aftermath of improved U.S.-Japan relations, they continue to present a challenge. One significant current symbol of this problem is the continued inability of the two sides to resolve the above-mentioned U.S. forces relocation issue, despite assurances from DPJ leaders, in response to U.S. secretary of defense Robert Gates and Obama, that Tokyo will follow through on its existing agreements, and despite the softer tone adopted by U.S. officials in recent months, as noted in the previous paragraph.[56]

In light of these realities, old approaches—such as the Armitage "inside-out" vision of a U.S. regional security strategy that incorporates a tight, well-coordinated, and expansive United States–Japan security partnership—seem less likely during this decade.[57] Moreover, the above difficulties and uncertainties are causing a seemingly increasing number of observers to emphasize the need for Tokyo and Washington to engage in a fundamental strategic dialogue about the future of their alliance and its relationship to the security challenges facing both countries, including the rise of China. Thus, both sides need to clarify their own positions and better understand those of the other, in order to determine how convergent or divergent Japanese and American interests, preferences, and priorities will be with regard to a rising China.[58] This is arguably the most important priority facing America's regional political and security relationships in Asia.

Chinese Policies

The role of Japan in U.S. political-security policies toward China is also a function of the state of Sino-Japanese relations. As suggested above, Washington regards peaceful, stable, and cooperative relations between Beijing and Tokyo as highly conducive to its overall objectives in Asia and vis-à-vis China in particular. However, the Sino-Japanese relationship has experienced enormous fluctuations during the past ten to fifteen years. Within this dynamic bilateral relationship, China's policies and outlook toward Japan are of particular importance to the analysis here, as an indicator of the impact of U.S. policies.

Partly in response to the strengthening of the United States–Japan security relationship outlined above, and more broadly as part of its overall security strategy, Beijing has attempted, with varying success, to stabilize and enhance its relationship with Tokyo since at least 2000. Nonetheless, Beijing's actions and policies toward Tokyo have included both positive diplomatic, political, and economic initiatives and responses and intensely negative political and military moves, in part in reaction to domestic public pressure and Japanese behavior.

As indicated above, after a period of ups and downs, Sino-Japanese relations began to deteriorate significantly in 2002, as Beijing began to protest (in an increasingly emphatic manner) Prime Minister Koizumi's annual trips to the Yasukuni Shrine, became involved in a dispute with Tokyo over the construction of natural gas drilling rigs in contested territorial waters in the East China Sea, and responded negatively to the above-mentioned inclusion of China as a potential security threat in Japan's 2004 NDPG.[59] In addition, a Chinese nuclear submarine and maritime research vessel violated Japanese territorial waters during this period, and popular anger toward Japan manifested itself at the Asia Cup soccer games in August 2004. In 2005, China actively lobbied against Japan's unsuccessful bid to join the UN Security Council, and it responded with anger when the American and Japanese defense chiefs and foreign ministers for the first time publicly identified the peaceful resolution of the Taiwan issue as a shared strategic objective.[60]

These developments, along with Japanese actions, contributed to a sharp decline in the bilateral relationship in 2005 and early to middle 2006. During this period, tens of thousands of Chinese took part in anti-Japanese demonstrations in several major cities, and senior Chinese officials canceled meetings and suspended planned trips to Japan in response to Koizumi's continued visits to the Yasukuni Shrine and Tokyo's approval of controversial new history textbooks that many Chinese believe are part of an attempt to whitewash Japan's wartime atrocities.[61]

At this time, Beijing apparently sought to use regional concerns over Japan's stance toward such history-related issues—along with its disputes with Tokyo over territorial issues, competition for foreign energy supplies, Japan's growing military role in the United States–Japan alliance, and its search for a permanent seat in the UN Security Council—to isolate Tokyo from the rest of the

Asia-Pacific region. This did not have the desired effect, however, as Asian governments resisted Chinese pressures to downgrade their links with Tokyo and refused to side with China against Japan on most of these issues. Moreover, as one observer noted, Chinese pressure appeared to undercut "[Beijing's] efforts to foster a benign and accommodating image in the Asia-Pacific" and "energized Japanese efforts to work with the United States, Australia, India, and other powers and to use multilateral groupings and Japan's substantial economic, trade, and aid interactions to foster an Asia-Pacific order where China would not be in a position to dominate Japan."[62]

Beginning in late 2006, Beijing moved (in tandem with Tokyo) to improve the bilateral relationship, partly in response to the change in leadership in Japan from Koizumi to Shinzo Abe, but also because of the above-noted costs incurred by its attempts to isolate or constrain Japan in the region. Officials on both sides initiated a series of strategic dialogues that resulted in private understandings regarding the Yasukuni issue and other matters and paved the way for an exchange of high-level official visits and meetings, marked by an "ice-breaking" trip to China by Abe in October 2006 and the return visit of Premier Wen Jiabao to Japan in April 2007.[63] These visits in turn paved the way for the regularization of mutual visits between Chinese and Japanese leaders (marked by Prime Minister Yasuo Fukuda's trip to China in December 2007), helped to improve public opinion on both sides, and led to a joint commitment to advance relations in a wide variety of areas, as affirmed by the Japan–China joint press statements issued at the end of Abe and Wen's official visits. In addition, bilateral trade and investment have continued to increase, with the number of Chinese visitors to Japan exceeding the number of Americans for the first time in 2007 and with China ousting the United States as Japan's top trading partner for the first time in that year.[64]

Beijing continued to seek better diplomatic and political relations with Japan in 2008 and 2009, facilitated initially by the rise of the relatively pro-China Yasuo Fukuda to serve as Japan's prime minister, and most recently by the advent of the more pacifist-oriented DPJ government. During this period, Beijing agreed with Tokyo to provide mutual prior notification for entry into each side's claimed exclusive economic zone and made some limited progress toward realizing the joint development of disputed seabed resources in the East China Sea. Moreover, on the diplomatic front, Hu Jintao hosted a state banquet for Prime Minister Fukuda (the first such banquet for a Japanese prime minister since the Nakasone visit in 1986) and visited Japan in May 2008. Hu's trip to Japan was the first such state visit in ten years and only the second time a Chinese head of state ever visited Japan. The Hu–Fukuda summit produced a joint statement in which both sides agreed to promote mutually beneficial strategic ties, "squarely face history," and deepen bilateral cooperation and exchange. Authoritative Chinese media gave the summit very positive treatment, noting a "warm spring" in Sino-Japanese ties and seeing the trip as a signal for further improvements in bilateral ties.[65]

At the same time, both Chinese and Japanese media commentary also suggested that little substantive progress was made on the contentious core issues in the bilateral relationship, including the disputed East China Sea, growing Chinese military activity in the waters surrounding Japan, tainted Chinese food exports, and human rights. Although they welcomed the joint statement, the Japanese media had a more negative overall assessment of the trip, giving prominent coverage to the unresolved bilateral issues, and especially to the thousands of pro-Tibet Japanese demonstrators who took to the streets during Hu's visit. The Japanese public was similarly ambivalent about the summit, and Fukuda's domestic approval rating sank to 23 percent the week after Hu's visit.[66] However, Sino-Japanese relations were bolstered in mid-2008 by the significant levels of assistance that Japan provided to China in the wake of a powerful 7.8 magnitude earthquake that rocked Sichuan in mid-May, just days after Hu's departure from Japan. Weeks later, Japan and China reached an agreement on a "joint development zone" of gas fields in the East China Sea. This announcement was supposed to reduce significantly, if not end, a five-year dispute over the boundaries of each country's respective exclusive economic zone.[67]

In late 2008 and early 2009, efforts by both sides to build on recent improvements in the bilateral relationship were jolted by disagreements over Chinese maritime activities near the disputed Senkaku/Diaoyu Islands, reports of increased Chinese naval activity in waters near Japan, Chinese drilling in the Kashi/Tianwaitan gas field in the disputed East China Sea (which Tokyo protested as a violation of the joint development agreement reached in June 2008; Beijing argued that the gas fields were part of China's exclusive economic zone and not subject to the agreement), China's apparent plans to begin construction of aircraft carriers, and further significant increases in Chinese defense spending in fiscal year 2008. In addition, the Obama administration arguably contributed to tensions in the Sino-Japanese relationship in the spring of 2009, when, to Beijing's dismay, it reaffirmed the Bush administration's stance that the United States–Japan Security Treaty includes the disputed Senkaku/Diaoyu Islands.[68]

However, under the DPJ government, the bilateral relationship initially showed signs of significant improvement. In May 2010, Beijing and Tokyo reached several agreements on issues ranging from maritime security to food safety and opened the door to formal talks on a treaty for the joint development of gas resources in contested waters. Chinese and Japanese leaders also agreed to establish a maritime crisis management mechanism between their defense agencies and urged the active use of a leadership "hotline" that had been established in 2008.[69] Yet despite such further advances, in September 2010, Sino-Japanese relations again deteriorated significantly as a result of a new dispute over an incident near the Senkaku/Diaoyu Islands resulting from a collision between a Chinese fishing vessel and Japanese coast guard vessels.[70]

All in all, Beijing's strategic relationship with Tokyo thus remains subject to enormous instability, fed by growing military capabilities on both sides, the enhancement of Japan's role as a security actor in the Asia-Pacific region, unresolved territorial disputes, and the presence of strong negative emotions toward the other side, especially in China. Improvements in the United States–Japan defense relationship have to some degree contributed to this negative dynamic. As indicated above, in recent years, Beijing has expressed strong concerns over the strengthening of the United States–Japan alliance, Japan's past pursuit of constitutional revision and the right of collective self-defense, the growing external deployment of Japan's military strength, and the reorientation of its forces away from Russia and toward China in the 2010 NDPG. It also strongly criticized the above-mentioned Japanese-sponsored quadrilateral security dialogue and related "arc of freedom and prosperity."[71] And Beijing took a very aggressive diplomatic stance toward Tokyo as a result of the latter's arrest of a Chinese fishing boat captain on suspicion of intentionally ramming his vessel into Japan Coast Guard ships near the Senkaku/Diaoyu Islands in September 2010, noted above.[72]

That said, on balance, Beijing quite possibly regards the DPJ government as a net plus, particularly in the security realm. Despite recent movement by Japan toward a closer security relationship with Washington, and growing concerns over China's foreign policy in Asia, the rise to power of the DPJ appears to "lock in," for the next several years at least (and perhaps much longer), those trends toward reduced (or more likely stagnant) defense spending and a less ambitious vision of Japan's role as a regional and global security partner with the United States that emerged after the departure of Koizumi and Abe from power and the advent of a period of Japanese economic stagnation and (most recently) recession. In addition, an economically weakened Japan's growing dependence on the Chinese economy, along with the DPJ government's apparent desire to strengthen ties with Beijing by avoiding trips to the Yasukuni Shrine and enhancing bilateral cooperation via (among other moves) the formation of an East Asian Community, together reinforce a continued desire, among at least some Japanese political leaders, to forge a more cooperative China policy in Japan. All these developments provide the Chinese leadership with reasons to expect that Tokyo's political-security policies during this decade at best will frustrate further possible attempts by the United States to utilize its alliance with Japan as a key means of counterbalancing or constraining China's rise and at worst will ensure a continued period of uncertainty in Japanese security policies in Asia.[73]

And yet, the above-noted concerns regarding China's expanding military capabilities expressed by Japanese defense circles and analysts remain strong, and indeed have perhaps deepened as a result of the rise to power of the apparently more "pacifist" DPJ government, along with recent diplomatic confrontations with Beijing over territorial issues in the East China Sea. More broadly, Japanese elite and public sentiment regarding China has also become far more negative as a result of the confrontations with China in 2009 and 2010.[74] Indeed, as indicated above, the September 2010 incident has had a catalytic effect on many Japanese, increasing concerns over China's strategic intentions while drawing Tokyo closer to Washington and their alliance. Taken together, these developments raise the possibility of growing internal Japanese tensions over how to manage China and, by implication, how to view the United States–Japan alliance and U.S. security policies toward Beijing.[75] In short, while committed to the alliance, Japan's security posture in general, and toward both Washington and Beijing, remains very much in flux.

South Korea

America's relations with South Korea, its other major ally in Northeast Asia, are arguably not as critical to the Japan-related strategic issues involving China that have been described above. Nonetheless, U.S. political and security relations with South Korea are indirectly important to America's China policies in at least two ways. First, given the U.S. military presence on the Korean Peninsula and the existing closeness and level of coordination between Seoul and Washington on regional security matters (for example, involving Taiwan or the role of U.S. and South Korean forces in the Western Pacific), the United States–Japan–South Korea relationship obviously influences China's regional security perceptions and actions, as well as U.S. leverage vis-à-vis Beijing. In particular, China's leaders would presumably prefer to see a relatively loose security relationship between the three democratic allies, involving low levels of coordination regarding any effort to contain China's emerging influence in the region. Second, and perhaps more important, Seoul's relationship with Washington has a major impact on the latter's handling of the slow-motion crisis over North Korea's developing nuclear weapons program, a major issue in U.S. and allied relations with Beijing.

U.S. Policies

The historical record indicates that, in partial contrast to the qualified successes achieved with Japan, until quite recently, U.S. administrations have by and large failed to strengthen security relations and increase coordination with South Korea in the security realm. For many years during the George W. Bush administration, Washington and Seoul experienced a rocky relationship, especially following the election of Roh Moo-hyun in late 2002 and the emergence of serious differences over the handling of the North Korean nuclear issue. President Roh "explicitly devalued relations with the United States" for a variety of reasons and pursued major changes in defense policy in the direction of long-term military self-sufficiency and an independent security strategy.[76]

Most notably, Roh sought a "balancer" role for South Korea in East Asia that involved disassociation from the United States–Japan alliance and noninvolvement in Washington's attempts to include Seoul in regional contingency plans. Equally important, upon entering office, the Bush administration adopted a highly confrontational approach toward North Korea (involving efforts to stigmatize and isolate Pyongyang while avoiding any genuine negotiation over its nuclear weapons program) that contrasted enormously with Roh's desire to deepen engagement with the North through a continuation of the so-called Sunshine Policy enunciated by his predecessor Kim Dae-jung. Roh's search for greater reconciliation with North Korea culminated in an October 2007 visit to Pyongyang at the end of his term in office. The Bush administration alienated many South Koreans by openly criticizing Seoul's more accommodating approach to North Korea and showing thinly veiled contempt toward both the Kim Dae-jung and Roh Moo-hyun governments, epitomized by Bush's harsh treatment of the former South Korean leader during the bilateral summit of early 2001.[77]

However, relations between Washington and Seoul improved significantly following the election of a more right-leaning, proalliance politician, Lee Myung-bak, to South Korea's presidency in December 2007 and the acceptance by the Bush administration of a more flexible, coordinated strategy of negotiation and engagement with Pyongyang regarding the ongoing nuclear issue. Improvements in the U.S.–South Korean relationship have continued during the Obama administration. In June 2009, Obama and Lee issued a joint vision statement regarding the bilateral alliance during the latter's state visit to Washington. In that document, the two governments affirmed the intent to "build a comprehensive strategic alliance of bilateral, regional and global scope, based on common values and mutual trust." In press remarks accompanying the issuance of this statement, Lee described the alliance as "upgrading to a new plateau," while Obama characterized it as "a sustained strategic partnership . . . on the full range of global challenges, . . . from economic development to our support for democracy and human rights, from nonproliferation to counterterrorism and peacekeeping." Obama also reaffirmed the "firm commitment" of the United States to ensuring the security of South Korea through extended deterrence, and the two sides reiterated their continued support for the denuclearization of the Korean Peninsula and the "robust" implementation of UN Security Council Resolution 1874 relevant to that issue.[78]

Most recently, U.S. ties with South Korea were further strengthened by the unexpected apparent sinking by North Korea of a South Korean warship in a disputed area of the Yellow Sea in March 2010 and the shelling of South Korea's Yeonpyeong Island in November 2010, resulting in several deaths. These incidents brought Washington and Seoul even closer together in the application of a tough approach to dealing with Pyongyang, including the holding of joint military exercises near the Korean Peninsula, the passage of a UN Security Council presidential statement, and the postponement of the transfer of U.S. operational control over South Korean forces in wartime to Seoul.[79]

President Lee has also shown an increased South Korean desire to enhance security cooperation with another close American ally in the region: Australia. During a March 2009 trip to New Zealand, Indonesia, and Australia intended, in part, to demonstrate the broadening of South Korean foreign policy beyond issues associated with the peninsula, Lee issued a joint statement on security cooperation with Australian prime minister Kevin Rudd. The statement specifically confirmed "the strategic importance of [the two nations'] respective alliance partnerships with the United States" and provided the basis for enhanced security cooperation in a variety of areas. Although not specifically directed at China, the document affirmed the shared interests of both countries regarding the security environment "in Northeast Asia, the Asia-Pacific, and beyond," and in accompanying press remarks, Lee specifically pointed to China's high level of military spending as a security issue.[80]

Despite such improvements in U.S.-South Korean relations and Seoul's expanding efforts to player a broader security role in the Asia-Pacific region, one must note that long-standing political and social tensions and animosities between Seoul and Tokyo have complicated past U.S. efforts to coordinate regional security policies toward China among the three democratic allies.[81] Washington is apparently attempting to improve this situation by reviving trilateral security consultations among the three powers. These talks, begun in October 2008, mark the revival and expansion of a similar dialogue (the Trilateral Coordination and Oversight Group) that existed between 1999 and 2003. This group focused on enhancing coordination among the three governments regarding the North Korean nuclear issue and became inactive due to the emergence of differences over how to deal with Pyongyang.

In contrast, the new trilateral dialogue has addressed a broader agenda, including how to handle Northeast Asian regional cooperation, the wars in Iraq and Afghanistan, and other global security issues. Several weeks after the revival of this senior-level dialogue, the United States, South Korea, and Japan agreed to increase military exchanges and to participate in joint exercises organized by the U.S. Pacific Command. After defense officials met to discuss humanitarian assistance and international peacekeeping operations, they also confirmed plans to continue holding such tripartite security talks on a regular basis. Close consultation has since gone up to the highest levels, as when the three heads of defense pledged cooperation on dealing with North Korea when they met on the sidelines of a security forum in May 2009. Tripartite security-related cooperation increased still further in the aftermath of North Korea's armed provocations in 2010, as noted above. Those events greatly stimulated closer security ties between Seoul and Tokyo, a development strongly encouraged by Washington. They also increased South Korean public support for the United States and the bilateral alliance.[82]

Finally, the emergence of a South Korean government and public that are more supportive of the United States–led alliance system, combined with the rise to power in Japan of a DPJ-led government, will likely facilitate further improvements in the Washington–Tokyo–Seoul security relationship. The DPJ is viewed in South Korea as more flexible than the LDP toward contentious historical and other bilateral issues, and is generally seen as being relatively "pro–South Korea."[83] Thus, overall, in recent years, an opportunity has emerged to deepen strategic cooperation between the three democracies in ways that might benefit U.S. policies toward China, if handled properly. The basic challenge for Washington will be to make use of such growing ties in order to increase common incentives to enhance cooperation on issues such as the North Korea nuclear crisis while avoiding the creation of a strategic rift with Beijing that results in greater levels of security competition.

Chinese Policies

In part to provide it with greater strategic leverage in Northeast Asia and to augment its economic ties throughout the region, Beijing has for many years sought to deepen and expand its relations with Seoul. Since the normalization of Sino-South Korean relations in 1992, bilateral relations have moved forward in four key areas identified by both sides: political communication and understanding,

economics, cultural communication and understanding, and security cooperation. Key activities have included annual summits of the prime ministers; a bilateral strategic dialogue; deepening economic cooperation in investment, logistics,
finance, and energy; a rapidly expanding trade relationship; increasing numbers
of students and tourists; and coordination of approaches to handling the North
Korean nuclear issue, as part of the Six-Party Talks (discussed below).[84]

By 2008, the Sino-South Korean relationship had developed into a "strategic
partnership" involving expanded political, economic, social, and diplomatic ties.
In late 2009, China's vice president, Xi Jinping, received head-of-state treatment
during a visit to South Korea and announced a four-point proposal to deepen
bilateral relations, including efforts to expand high-level contacts, deepen trade
and economic cooperation, increase personnel exchanges, and strengthen coordination in multilateral forums. The two countries have signed an economic
cooperation agreement that seeks to increase bilateral trade to $300 billion by
2015 and to strengthen cooperation on other bilateral and global efforts.[85]

On the negative side, significant tensions and concerns in bilateral relations
have also been evident since at least 2005–2006, involving disputes over historical issues such as the relative "Chineseness" of the ancient kingdom of Koguryo,
Beijing's treatment of refugees from North Korea, and China's stance toward the
North Korean nuclear issue. According to Robert Sutter, these disputes have
caused many South Korean officials to become more wary of China and to suspect
that Beijing seeks to sustain an independent North Korean state under Chinese
influence, in contrast to Seoul's efforts to achieve peaceful reunification under
South Korean influence.[86] More recently, such suspicions have been reinforced
by the fact that a growing number of South Koreans now view China as an economic threat, especially in key areas such as information technology and electronics.[87] Perhaps of equal importance, Beijing's repeated refusal to acknowledge publicly that North Korea had sunk the above-mentioned South Korean
warship in March 2010, and its efforts to prevent the UN from explicitly blaming
Pyongyang for the incident, further damaged Beijing's ties with Seoul.[88] After the
November 2010 bombardment of Yeonpyeong Island, China apparently induced
North Korea to avoid further armed provocations (for which it received considerable praise), but only after South Korean and U.S. officials had expressed dismay at China's initially weak response.[89]

Such developments suggest that, despite ongoing improvements in relations
between Seoul and Beijing, South Korea appears more inclined than it was during the Kim and Roh eras to align itself more closely with United States (and
Japanese) regional security priorities.[90] If this trend continues, Beijing's ability to
leverage its relations with Seoul in order to advance its interests with Washington

on a wide range of policy issues, from North Korea to Taiwan and multilateral defense ties, could diminish appreciably in the years ahead.[91] That said, it remains far from certain that Seoul will fully coordinate its future regional security strategy with those of Washington and Tokyo, particularly as it relates to Beijing. For example, although Seoul finally agreed in May 2009 (following North Korea's second nuclear weapons test) to fully participate in the United States–backed Proliferation Security Initiative, it continues to resist signing onto a United States–backed regional ballistic missile defense plan that is opposed by Beijing.

Evaluation and Future Trends: The U.S. Alliance Relationship with Tokyo and Seoul

What trends and events of relevance to the United States' relations with its two major Asian allies will likely most influence the future of Washington's security policies toward Beijing? It is arguably the case that the strengthening of the United States–Japan defense relationship in particular—combined with Washington's growing attention to regional security structures and its increased military deployments and more forward-leaning regional security activities, as outlined in the next two chapters—have to some extent encouraged Beijing to cooperate more closely with other Asian nations and to become more integrated into the Asian system overall.[92]

Conversely, as suggested above, future U.S. efforts to enhance Japan's security role and military capabilities in Asia and beyond could also prove counterproductive by heightening anxieties in China, and perhaps elsewhere, in ways that fuel rather than dampen security competition and that undermine incentives for cooperation and confidence building. Nonetheless, some U.S. officials contend that various beliefs and structural factors applicable to Japan limit Tokyo's ability and willingness to acquire the type of military capabilities and undertake the sort of missions that would seriously alarm China or other Asian nations, regardless of U.S. efforts to push in that direction.[93] According to this viewpoint, there is, in effect, no practical upper limit to how far the United States should push to enhance Japanese military capabilities and missions in the context of the United States–Japan alliance.

In any event, recent developments in both Japan and South Korea suggest that U.S. leaders will probably not be able to test this proposition, even if the desire to do so were to emerge. Clear limits will likely persist—at least over the short to medium terms—on the ability and willingness of either leadership to align its regional security strategies with one another in support of a more ambitious, integrated United States–led and military-centered trilateral approach toward China.

In the political and economic arenas, Tokyo recognizes that Beijing is rapidly increasing its importance in East Asia as a key economic partner and could become the overall center of gravity for trade and investment activity in the region. In the face of this development, Japan will almost certainly seek to maintain its long-standing position of importance in Asian economic and financial affairs through deepening contacts with Northeast, Southeast, and South Asia *while to some degree accommodating China's regional rise*. The apparent overall desire of the DPJ to focus more attention on Japan's relations with the Asia-Pacific region arguably reflects this impulse.[94]

Nonetheless, in the security arena, in addition to the direct threat to Japanese territory (including disputed islands) and the broader coercive capacities presented by the growing air and naval capabilities of the People's Liberation Army (PLA), many Japanese worry that the military balance across the Taiwan Strait is decisively tilting toward China, and that the PLA navy and air force could at some point in the future block access to the Malacca Strait and perhaps even deny the U.S. Pacific Command access to the East Asian region. More broadly, some influential Japanese defense strategists fear that China's growing military capabilities could significantly degrade—if not neutralize entirely—the ability of the U.S. military to perform vital deterrence and reassurance functions in the Western Pacific.[95]

Equally worrisome, as indicated above, these Japanese strategists and other observers have expressed uncertainty as to whether or not the United States will remain committed to the security of the Asia-Pacific region in the face of China's rise and the growing array of economic and social problems and constraints faced by the United States. Worse yet, as also indicated above, an apparently growing number of Japanese fear that China's expanding capabilities and influence, combined with Washington's growing need to gain Chinese cooperation to handle many of its problems, will increasingly compel the United States to accede to Chinese preferences and neglect Japanese interests in a variety of areas. In particular, some Japanese believe that the United States has shown reluctance to sell advanced F-22 aircraft to Japan and is avoiding placing greater pressure on North Korea on many issues (from Pyongyang's possible covert uranium facilities to its inventory of nuclear weapons, and the Japanese abductee issue) largely in deference to Chinese interests.[96]

It is unlikely that such concerns will dissipate significantly during the current decade. At the same time, and equally important, current and likely future trends within Japan suggest that Tokyo will almost certainly lack the kind of sustained political unity and will required to undertake new and more energetic efforts to address such concerns, by either (1) expanding significantly Japan's military capabilities and missions within (or outside) the United States–Japan alliance, or (2) adopting innovative, confidence-building multilateral or bilateral approaches toward China. Such domestic trends include an increasingly fractured domestic political process and a high turnover rate among political leaders that will likely result in a continuing succession of divided or weak and cautious governments; a weak economy rocked by the global economic crisis and the devastating March 2011 earthquake and tsunami; and continued strong pacifist sentiments among the public that resist more expansive reinterpretations of the Japanese Constitution toward "collective self-defense."[97] At best, according to some analysts, Japan might be able to continue to exert significant economic influence within Asia, given its deep experience and strong relationships and financial and trade ties across the region, thereby indirectly influencing the dynamics of regional integration.[98]

Other observers, in contrast, emphasize the need for Japan to become far more activist if it is to assist in efforts by the United States and others in the region to maintain stability and prosperity in the face of a rising China.[99] As indicated, this is probably unlikely during the current decade, given the types of systemic constraints and features discussed here. In general, Japan's likely future political circumstances could significantly constrain U.S. options in managing China via the United States–Japan alliance and broader multilateral forums or structures. Although this could perhaps to some degree dampen security competition between Tokyo and Beijing, it could also complicate or obstruct efforts to improve Sino-Japanese relations. The emergence of an official United States–China–Japan dialogue could significantly assist U.S. policy toward China by reducing mutual distrust in many areas and advancing efforts to address growing nontraditional security concerns, but this will undoubtedly be a slow and uncertain process. Thus, in all, Japan's domestic political situation currently places a strong obstacle in the way of any accelerated movement toward greater Japanese military capabilities and more expansive roles and missions in the region and beyond. This is not necessarily bad for U.S. policy toward China, however, because a more militarized and diplomatically assertive Japan could significantly worsen Sino-Japanese relations and fuel strategic distrust between Washington and Beijing.

Although South Korea is apparently committed to enhancing its power projection capabilities and acquiring broader regional security missions, it by and large does not regard China as the primary object of such efforts. In addition, recently revived tripartite security activities have assiduously avoided appearing to be aimed at Beijing. And of course neither Seoul nor Tokyo currently shows much inclination to undertake actions that might put at risk its rapidly growing economic relationship with China.

As a result of these trends, Washington will likely confront significant challenges in developing approaches toward Beijing that rely on the formation of a robust, security-oriented "alliance of democracies" in Asia or a heavy emphasis on building ever stronger bilateral defense alliance relationships centered on counterbalancing growing Chinese power. The current political and security dynamics in both Tokyo and Seoul argue in favor of Washington's continued emphasis on maximizing incentives to cooperate with Beijing. That said, some negative perceptions evident in both Japan and South Korea could also obstruct efforts to implement even a more restrained U.S. approach to leveraging alliance relationships vis-à-vis China. For example, Japanese anxieties over both the extent of the U.S. political and defense commitments to the alliance and Washington's alleged lack of attention to the implications of China's rise for Tokyo could increase significantly over time. If improperly handled, this could result in Tokyo undertaking efforts to hedge against a perceived weakening of its security position by either moving closer to Beijing than Washington might like, or, conversely, by adopting military capabilities and/or policies that could greatly alarm Beijing and destabilize the region. For its part, Seoul could again move toward a more independent security posture and perhaps even lean more toward Beijing, despite recent domestic political shifts in favor of the alliance, depending in large part on future domestic political developments.

Such developments are by no means likely in the foreseeable future. However, the factors that underlie them, and the larger features outlined above, point to the need for Washington to be highly attentive to the growing complexity of the United States–China–Japan–South Korea strategic relationship and the potential difficulties confronting U.S. efforts to leverage alliance relations vis-à-vis China. In particular, this scenario leaves unanswered two vital questions: (1) Militarily, to what extent are Washington, Tokyo, and Seoul prepared, and willing, if necessary, to transition to a security approach toward China and the region that is less reliant on U.S. military predominance in the Western Pacific (as discussed in chapter 1)? And (2) politically, how will Washington deepen its relationship with Beijing (as is clearly desired by the Obama administration, for a host of reasons) without alarming Japan?[100] The former will require a serious examination of the sustainability of U.S. military predominance and the relationship between possible future U.S. military postures in Asia and the military capabilities and preferences of Japan and South Korea. The latter will require a serious examination of the future of the United States–Japan and United States–South Korea alliances in a broader Asian context.

Another variable to consider will be Beijing's behavior toward both Tokyo and Seoul. If Beijing continues to take actions that alienate significant portions of the publics and elites in both Tokyo and Seoul (as in the case of the September 2010 ship collision near the Senkaku/Diaoyu Islands and the March 2010 sinking by North Korea of a South Korean warship), both Tokyo and Seoul might shift less ambiguously toward policies designed to balance against a rising China, in part through an increased reliance on a stronger security relationship with Washington. Such a shift could significantly polarize East Asia and considerably undermine U.S. efforts to strengthen cooperation with Beijing, especially if a much stronger Beijing concludes that Washington is deliberately seeking to create an anti-China alliance with the two Asian powers. Finally, one cannot dismiss the possibility that a significant worsening in Sino-Japanese relations could precipitate a military clash or a crisis over disputed maritime territories that might draw Washington into an unwanted confrontation with Beijing. All of these uncertainties will almost certainly increase significantly the challenges confronting Washington's political and security strategy in Asia in the years ahead.

Taiwan

Washington's military and diplomatic policy toward Taiwan is of immediate and direct relevance to China's strategic position in Asia and America's security stance toward China and the region. U.S. and Chinese policies regarding this issue have constituted a major source of contention between the two powers since the 1950s. Indeed, a major confrontation between Beijing and Washington over the island could escalate into direct military conflict or severely damage overall bilateral political-diplomatic relations, posing extremely negative consequences for U.S. interests and stability across the entire Asia-Pacific region. Hence, the effective management of the Taiwan issue is arguably the sine qua non for the maintenance and development of stable and productive U.S. relations with China.

U.S. Policies

In general, since at least the early 1980s, U.S. political and diplomatic policies toward Taiwan have focused on preventing a conflictual outcome (and buying time for an eventual peaceful resolution of the issue) by: reassuring Beijing that Washington remains committed to the "One China" policy; reassuring Taipei that the United States will neither pressure it into negotiating a final resolution nor strike a deal with China at its expense; and deterring both sides from undertaking unilateral actions that would greatly increase the chance of a major crisis or military conflict.[101]

Taken together, these policies have required Washington to walk a fine line between, on the one hand, the legal obligation to provide Taiwan with the means to defend itself against Chinese coercion and to remain militarily prepared to come to Taiwan's assistance if necessary, and, on the other hand, the need to sustain Beijing's belief that the United States does not support Taiwan's independence and remains open to the possibility of a peaceful reunification. Leaning too far to one side or the other could entice or compel either Taipei or Beijing to undertake provocative actions, in the form of movement by Taiwan toward de jure independence or efforts by China to employ military coercion or outright force to resolve the situation on its terms.[102]

This tightrope walk has become increasingly challenging for the United States in recent years, largely as a result of the growth of a separate Taiwan identity and accompanying pro-independence political movement on the island, and the acquisition and deployment by China of the potent military capabilities summarized in chapter 4, many of which can be used to coerce or attack the island. During the early years of the George W. Bush administration, these developments resulted in U.S. policies that stressed the military deterrence side of the U.S. approach to Taiwan, in order to enhance the expression of American resolve, to reduce the possibility of miscalculation in the face of China's military buildup, and to differentiate itself from what U.S. officials regarded as the overly accommodating stance toward Beijing on this issue taken by the Clinton administration. This policy shift was implemented not only via enhanced force deployments and defense assistance but also by a public presidential statement that Washington would "do whatever it takes" to assist Taiwan if China were to employ force against the island. In other words, even though Washington continued to caution Taipei against undertaking provocative actions, it placed a high priority on reducing the ambiguity that had existed in U.S. policy regarding whether and to what extent the United States would intervene militarily if China were to employ force against the island.[103]

In more recent years, however, Washington has increasingly addressed the political deterrence and reassurance side of the equation (while continuing efforts at military deterrence), largely in response to events occurring in Taiwan. The election to the presidency in 2000 of a strongly pro-independence politician, Chen Shui-bian, resulted in a series of steadily provocative actions by Taipei that threatened to generate a dangerous crisis with China in the Taiwan Strait. These actions included public policy statements and attempts to approve island-wide referenda and constitutional revisions that sought to establish Taiwan's de jure status as a sovereign, independent state. Washington responded by privately—and at times pointedly and emphatically—urging Taipei to exercise restraint and, when these efforts failed, by publicly rebuking Chen for threatening to unilaterally alter the status quo and thereby threaten peace and stability in the region.[104]

The Bush administration also increasingly criticized the Taiwan government for failing to enhance its military capabilities in the face of a steady buildup of Chinese forces on the other side of the Taiwan Strait. In tandem with these actions, Washington also sought to reassure Beijing by repeatedly affirming the "One China" policy in high-level talks with the Chinese leadership. As one knowledgeable former official stated, "Washington needed to reassure and calm China during this period, sometimes by dispatching U.S. officials to Beijing for private discussions." Washington's "dual deterrence and reassurance" approach was assisted by the growing domestic unpopularity of the Chen Shui-bian government and the fact that Beijing arguably displayed an increasing degree of political restraint toward Taipei's provocative actions.[105]

With the overwhelming defeat of pro-independence political forces on Taiwan in the legislative and presidential elections of early 2008, tensions over the island abated considerably and the prospect emerged of a more stable cross-Strait situation over the longer term. The current government, which is dominated by the Kuomintang (KMT), led by President Ma Ying-jeou, has stressed the need to improve relations with both Beijing and Washington through increased official and unofficial dialogue and consultation, deeper contacts, no "surprises" directed at either Washington or Beijing, and various cross-Strait social, economic, and cultural agreements. Direct cross-strait plane flights, transportation links, and postal ties (the "three links," or *san tong* 三通) were established on December 15, 2008. In 2010, Taipei and Beijing concluded several understandings designed to expand and regularize a variety of cross-Strait links and to increase trade and investment, including the signing of a comprehensive economic pact known as the Economic Cooperation Framework Agreement. And Beijing has also finally permitted Taiwan to join the World Health Organization as an observer.[106]

At the same time, the Ma government has also avoided undertaking any notable advances in political contacts with Beijing (such as efforts to develop military confidence-building measures or to lay other foundations for a cross-Strait peace accord), largely to defend itself—during a period of sagging popularity—against charges by the opposition led by the Democratic Progressive Party (DPP) that it is too "pro-China" and is involved in somehow "selling out" Taiwan's interests.[107] In line with this approach, Ma has pledged not to enter into any discussions with Beijing on political unification during his term in office, as part of an overall "three no's" policy toward cross-Strait issues—no unification, no independence, and no use of force during his presidency.[108] In addition, to bolster its standing at home and in dealings with Beijing, the KMT government has also sought improved political relations with Washington and signaled a strong desire to enhance Taiwan's military capabilities, in part via additional arms sales and closer defense relations with the United States.[109]

Despite these improvements in the cross-Strait situation, Beijing's acquisition of military capabilities of high relevance to a possible future Taiwan conflict continues virtually unabated. In response, the Bush administration eventually decided (in late 2008, just before leaving office) to sell additional arms to Taipei. (Beijing's reaction was highly negative. It canceled several planned military-to-military activities and lodged formal protests.) In addition, as outlined in chapter 4, Washington has also worked for some years to strengthen its own force deployments in the Western Pacific, partly in an attempt to improve its overall ability to deter future Chinese miscalculations regarding the Taiwan issue.[110]

The Obama administration has by and large continued the balancing act that is at the center of U.S. policy toward Taiwan, reiterating the standard mantra involving support for the three communiqués with Beijing, the Taiwan Relations Act, and opposition to any unilateral changes in the status quo while publicly encouraging the overall trend toward better cross-Strait relations under the KMT government in Taipei. In addition, while signaling continued "unofficial" political support for Taiwan (and arguably for the Ma government in particular), the Obama administration has also followed in the footsteps of previous administrations by offering new weapons sales to Taipei, in this instance worth more than $6 billion (including 114 Patriot missiles, 60 Black Hawk helicopters, Harpoon missiles, and mine-hunting ships), and by deepening the bilateral defense relationship. Such actions have again provoked a strong reaction from Beijing, including an unprecedented direct threat to sanction any U.S. defense companies involved in a likely sale. In response, the Obama administration has stood firm, reiterating the U.S. policy stance, including its commitment to the long-standing U.S. position on arms sales to Taiwan.[111]

Thus, while cross-Strait economic and cultural ties continue to deepen, few signs have emerged thus far of a significant improvement in cross-Strait military tensions. And yet the ability of the Ma government to significantly strengthen its military capabilities against China remains in some doubt, especially given Taiwan's ongoing economic constraints and the existence of significant levels of domestic resistance to a continued military buildup while Taipei works to improve cross-Strait ties.[112]

Chinese Policies

Beijing's policies regarding Taiwan during this tumultuous period also witnessed changes in emphasis, from military deterrence and pressure to a search for greater cooperation with Washington and renewed contacts with Taipei. This changing emphasis reflects an evolution in Beijing's basic stance toward Taiwan that took place largely during the Bush administration: from growing concern in 2000–2001, to genuine alarm (involving a firm determination to deter independence while contemplating a "deadline" for reunification) in 2002–2004, to reduced concern and somewhat greater confidence regarding the eventual peaceful resolution of the issue on favorable terms, beginning roughly in 2006 and deepening considerably after the 2008 Taiwan elections. The most notable recent expression of this recent shift in Beijing's overall stance was provided by Hu Jintao's famous speech of December 31, 2008, in which he conveyed support for military confidence-building measures across the Strait and the opening of political discussions on the basis of pragmatic considerations.[113]

Beijing's current confidence results from several developments, including (1) an increasing military capacity to deter or oppose movement by Taipei toward de jure independence; (2) ever greater levels of social contact and economic integration between Taiwan and Mainland China (marked by increasing volumes of Taiwan trade and investment, the movement of large numbers of Taiwanese citizens to China for economic and other reasons, and growing public support on Taiwan for even closer economic ties, stimulated in part by Taiwan's overall economic malaise); (3) the establishment of constructive political contacts between Beijing and various anti-independence elements on Taiwan (such as the KMT and People's First parties); (4) the passage of an Anti-Secession Law by the Chinese National People's Congress in March 2005, which is viewed by Beijing as strengthening the credibility of China's willingness to employ "nonpeaceful measures" to prevent Taipei from achieving de jure independence while also confirming a primary emphasis on peaceful efforts at reunification; (5) the growing success of China's long-standing efforts to limit Taiwan's international presence and influence; (6) the results of the 2008 Taiwan legislative and presidential elections, which greatly strengthened the political position of the KMT; and (7) the emergence of more credible (from Beijing's viewpoint) U.S. efforts to restrain the pro-independence activities of the Chen Shui-bian government.[114]

The last point resulted in large part from the emergence of a Chinese belief that the United States has no desire to facilitate or permit potentially crisis-inducing actions regarding Taiwan. This belief emerged as a result not only of the above-outlined reassurance efforts undertaken by the Bush administration but also from the conviction that Washington could not afford a foreign policy crisis over Taiwan, given its heavy involvement in combating global terrorism and managing ongoing crises and conflicts in Iraq, Afghanistan, and Pakistan, as well as its arguably growing need to address an array of domestic political and economic problems.[115]

It is also likely that the recent shift in Beijing's overall approach to Taiwan reflects the personal influence of Hu Jintao. According to many observers, Hu has largely rejected Jiang Zemin's hard-line approach to Taiwan in favor of a flexible stance that emphasizes positive incentives toward Taipei while maintaining China's military buildup.[116]

Evaluation and Future Trends

Taken as a whole, the political, diplomatic, and economic aspects of U.S. policy toward Taiwan described above have served to counterbalance, to some degree, the destabilizing effects of the escalating cross-Strait military dynamic outlined here and to reduce considerably, during at least the short term, the likelihood that Beijing will be tempted to resolve what is essentially a political problem using coercive military means. In fact, the emergence of a KMT-dominated government in Taiwan has opened the prospect for not only a significant reduction in cross-Strait tensions but also a new modus vivendi between Taipei and Beijing that could lead to a period of peace and stability over the long term.

In the absence of such a modus vivendi, however, the Taiwan situation will continue to present a major challenge for U.S. policy toward China, because of the potential for confrontation and possibly conflict between Beijing and Washington resulting from the ongoing interaction between three sets of factors: (1) China's claim to sovereign authority over the island, combined with its increasing political, economic, and military ability to press this claim; (2) Taiwan's refusal to accept China's claim or to be intimidated by Beijing's growing capabilities; and (3) America's commitment to ensuring that any resolution of the Taiwan imbroglio will occur peacefully and with the uncoerced consent of the people of Taiwan, in part via the provision of military assistance to the island, as well as a limited amount of political support, both of which Beijing strongly opposes. This fundamental dynamic has remained unaltered, despite recent improvements in both cross-Strait and United States–China relations.

It is highly unlikely that any of these three factors will change over the foreseeable future in ways that will permit a final resolution of the Taiwan situation and its removal as a major potentially disruptive element in U.S. policy toward China. Beijing shows no signs of reducing its claim to Taiwan, and no current trends suggest that it will do so in the foreseeable future. To the contrary, as long as China continues to increase its economic and military capabilities and remains politically stable and unified, it is not unreasonable to assume that Chinese nationalist sentiments (and Chinese self-confidence in handling the issue) will grow, and that Beijing's claim over Taiwan will at the very least remain steadfast. At the same time, it is unlikely that Taiwan will suddenly accept Beijing's offer of a "one country, two systems" relationship across the Strait or otherwise significantly reduce its pragmatic, generally cautious support for the status quo (defined, since the failure of Chen Shui-bian's disastrous pro-independence efforts, as support for policies that maximize Taiwan's economic prosperity and political freedoms while avoiding any actions that might either provoke Chinese aggression or reduce U.S. support). And it is also extremely unlikely, barring the emergence of a full-blown strategic rivalry or conflict between the United States and China, that Washington will significantly alter its balanced policy approach to handling the Taiwan issue. This approach is widely viewed by U.S. policymakers as fundamentally sound in principle and is likely to remain so for some time, despite calls from some quarters for its revision.[117]

That said, despite the low likelihood that these basic stances will change in the foreseeable future, it is possible that various elements of them could alter in ways that either increase or decrease the challenge presented to U.S. policy in managing the Taiwan situation. First and perhaps foremost, there is a danger that China could become more assertive over time with regard to its claim to Taiwan. Such increasing Chinese assertiveness is not terribly likely in the short term (that is, during the Hu Jintao era).[118] However, it could become increasingly likely in the medium to long term, if (1) contacts and political relations across the Taiwan Strait deteriorate significantly or stagnate, thus reducing movement toward some future modus vivendi or resolution of the issue; (2) Sino-U.S. relations deteriorate badly, thus increasing the likelihood that Taiwan will become a source of strategic rivalry between the two governments; and (3) China achieves a level of military capability with regard to potential Taiwan-related contingencies—along with increased political and economic leverage with Washington—that appears to Beijing to lower the risks involved in pursuing a more coercive approach toward the island. These three possible trends are obviously mutually influential.

During at least the near to medium term, it seems unlikely that both cross-Strait relations and Sino-U.S. relations will deteriorate significantly. As indicated above, under the Ma Ying-jeou government, Taipei's relations with Beijing (and Washington) have improved greatly, and most analysts expect to see a continuation of this trend throughout at least Ma's first term in office (that is, until 2012), and perhaps during a second term as well (if one occurs), thus presenting China with the prospect of eventual movement toward some level of peaceful reconciliation in the longer term.[119] And despite the continued presence of many potentially conflictual issues, Beijing's relations with Washington are not expected to decline markedly during at least this time frame, as this study and others suggest.[120]

At the same time, China is expected to steadily improve its ability to project military force against Taiwan, and to pose an increasingly credible threat against any U.S. forces that might seek to intervene in a future Taiwan conflict. As a result, in less than a decade, China might have the capability to overwhelm Taiwan's defenses more quickly than the United States could respond to the attack, or to force Taiwan to fight alone for at least a short period, as discussed further in chapter 4.[121] If not adequately counterbalanced by Taipei and/or Washington, such a military trend might also lead to the psychological intimidation of Taiwan's leaders and citizens in ways that could result in coercion or political-social instability on the island. In addition, some analysts fear that China's growing economic strength and deepening economic and social ties with Taiwan could reinforce the potential intimidating leverage that might result from China's growing military capabilities.[122]

Over time, these military, economic, and social trends could arguably lower the threshold at which Beijing might apply coercion against Taipei or otherwise increase the possibility that China's leaders could react aggressively to future adverse political occurrences involving Taiwan.[123] Nonetheless, many analysts believe that *in the absence of a precipitous decline in both the cross-Strait political situation and in the overall Sino-U.S. relationship*, it is highly unlikely that Beijing will attempt to employ its growing capabilities in an effort to coerce Taiwan into submission, much less to seize it outright. This is because, despite likely increases in Chinese military capabilities vis-à-vis Taiwan, such an undertaking will remain highly problematic at best, and whether successful or not, would almost certainly place at risk China's entire strategy of peaceful, market-led development through extensive political and economic ties with the United States and other major powers.[124]

It is of course quite possible that the cross-Strait relationship could again decline, as a result of one or more factors, including the replacement of Ma Ying-jeou by a pro-independence member of the opposition in the presidential election of 2012, a rapid decline in economic and other relations across the Strait, or the unexpected occurrence of one or more provocative incidents between the two sides. Regarding the first possibility, it is obvious that the Ma government (indeed, any Taiwan government) faces major challenges in maintaining Taiwan's prosperity and freedoms within both an unstable external environment marked by a variety of threats from China and a highly divisive domestic situation centered on a continuous debate over the island's political and social identity. To maximize his chances of serving a second term (and to minimize the chance of a future pro-independence or anti-China leader replacing him), Ma must simultaneously (1) convince a majority of Taiwan's public that his policies offer the best means of providing for their security, freedom, international dignity, and economic well-being; (2) convince Beijing that his domestic and foreign policies offer the best means of avoiding a return to a pro-independence government while laying the foundation for eventual movement toward some form of cross-Strait political reconciliation; and (3) assure Washington that he will neither undermine the current status quo (primarily by drawing the United States into a confrontation with China through military weakness or provocative political actions) nor threaten the long-term U.S. interest in an eventual peaceful, uncoerced resolution of the issue.

Such policies require a delicate balancing act, involving effective efforts to: strengthen Taiwan's defenses against a steadily rising Chinese military threat while advancing cross-Strait political relations; maximize Taiwan's economic growth while avoiding becoming overly dependent on the Mainland; strengthen Taiwan's international reputation and presence without excessively provoking Beijing; and repair and advance Taipei's political and defense relations with Washington without either provoking Beijing or raising significant suspicions in Taiwan that Ma is pandering to American and Taiwanese defense corporations. As indicated above, Ma has thus far managed to advance relations with Beijing, and many analysts express cautious optimism that cross-Strait relations will continue to improve during his current term in office.[125]

While advancing relations with Beijing, Ma has also unveiled ambitious plans to strengthen and streamline Taiwan's military, centering on major improvements in passive and active defense capabilities (as opposed to long-range, offensive deterrence and preemptive forces), further reductions in personnel, and the transition to an all-volunteer force.[126] This initiative is partly motivated by an awareness of the need to show Washington, the Taiwan public, and members of the Legislative Yuan that the Ma government is committed to bolstering Taiwan's military capabilities in a prudent and effective manner—that is, without unduly provoking Beijing or spending excessive amounts of scarce public funds and in ways that strengthen deterrence across the Strait. For the United States, this will likely remain a critical issue in United States–China–Taiwan relations, especially given the ongoing Chinese military buildup and the uncertainties of the cross-Strait relationship in the medium and long terms. As indicated above, U.S. defense officials and analysts have been concerned for some time that Taiwan has not been adequately strengthening its military capabilities, not only to maintain deterrence against potential Chinese coercion and attack but also to strengthen Taipei's overall political and diplomatic hand in interacting with Beijing. Nonetheless, it remains unclear whether Ma's ambitious plan will prove feasible (given domestic financial and political constraints on significant defense spending) and, if implemented, will sufficiently reassure Washington both militarily and politically.[127]

Beyond such considerations of feasibility and sufficiency, any U.S. assessment of the utility and effectiveness of Taiwan's future defense plans will also depend on the current state of political relations between Beijing, Taipei, and Washington over the current decade, and not simply the military balance across the Strait. As long as Ma continues to improve relations with both Beijing and Washington, most analysts believe there is little chance that future increases in Taiwan's defense capabilities—if successful—will destabilize the cross-Strait situation, at least in the medium term. Indeed, such actions might strengthen stability and encourage Taiwan to engage Beijing more deeply.

However, one significant potential source of political problems concerns U.S. arms sales to Taiwan. Beijing continues to press Washington to end such sales, while Taipei is publicly and privately requesting more weapons, especially those likely to provoke Beijing's ire, such as advanced C/D versions of F-16 fighter aircraft.[128] The Obama administration has thus far resisted approving such major weapons sales, because Taiwan has shown a limited ability to absorb many already-approved weapons systems, and because the Pentagon has not yet assessed whether specific weapons such as the advanced F-16s are militarily necessary at this time. Some analysts assert that U.S. restraint also derives from a concern that major arms sales to Taiwan might destabilize the Sino-U.S. relationship just when Washington faces a growing need to deepen cooperation with Beijing in managing a variety of other critical challenges, such as the global economic recession and climate change. In any event, whether and when to approve further major arms sales to Taiwan will almost certainly remain a major factor in U.S. policy toward Taiwan and China, despite the improvements in cross-Strait and United States–Taiwan relations noted above.[129]

Short of a major breakthrough leading to some degree of significant political reconciliation across the Taiwan Strait, there is little doubt that Washington will continue to see a strong need to attempt to maintain some level of credible Taiwanese and American deterrent capability against a Chinese use of force, at the very least in order to prevent a miscalculation by Beijing.[130] In fact, it is quite possible that, unless Beijing significantly reduces the size and scope of its growing military threat to Taiwan (for example, in the context of a cross-Strait peace accord), Washington will eventually be compelled to approve major weapons sales to Taipei within the next several years, for example, during a second Obama administration or a new Republican one. Such a U.S. decision could not only have an adverse impact on other areas of United States–China relations but more generally contribute to an increasingly dangerous arms buildup across the Strait.[131]

Indeed, the Chinese leadership is likely to make any decision to provide significant arms to Taiwan increasingly costly for Washington as Beijing's power and influence grow vis-à-vis issues of importance to the United States, thus possibly presenting U.S. leaders with potentially serious trade-offs.[132]

Such a prospect places a high premium on Taipei and Beijing making significant progress toward the reduction of cross-Strait military tensions *sooner* rather than later, perhaps in the context of a cross-Strait peace accord. Yet the attainment of such an objective still confronts considerable difficulties, despite the significant advances that have occurred in the overall China–Taiwan relationship since early 2008. Although apparently supportive of military confidence-building measures, the Chinese leaders insist that any significant reduction in tensions must occur as part of a larger negotiating process involving tangible concessions by both sides, and they have hinted that such negotiations should also involve some type of political talks, presumably regarding Taiwan's status. In addition, Beijing has also hinted that such talks can only begin on the basis of a more explicit recognition by Taiwan of the notion that the island is a part of China.[133]

The Ma government will not agree to such conditions. Moreover, Ma's precarious political standing at home will likely continue to prevent him from engaging in even the lowest-level, semiofficial Track Two confidence-building discussions with Beijing. According to senior Taiwan officials, this situation will almost certainly continue unless Ma's political fortunes improve, most likely as a result of a further significant advance in Taiwan's economic situation. For some observers, any positive movement by Taipei toward serious military confidence-building measures will likely also require clearer signs of support from Washington, in the form of closer political and military contacts. And this requirement is reinforced by the fear among some Taiwanese and U.S. observers that U.S. support for the island is declining as Washington confronts a growing need to deepen cooperation and avoid potential crises with Beijing on many critical policy issues.[134]

Largely as a result of such concerns, U.S. policy toward Taiwan remains a subject of some debate in Washington, despite recent improvements in China–Taiwan–United States relations. Some observers advocate much closer U.S. political and security relations with Taiwan to counterbalance growing Chinese military and political leverage. In fact, a small minority of observers call for an end to Washington's long-standing "One China" policy, in favor of unambiguous support for Taiwan's de facto independent status.[135] In the absence of a major deterioration in Sino–U.S. relations, however, such arguments will continue to receive scant attention among policymakers, largely because such a fundamental change in U.S. policy could result in a direct military confrontation, or even conflict, between Beijing and Washington, and almost certainly severely damage overall Sino-U.S. relations.

In addition, some outside analysts, along with many Chinese and Taiwanese observers, believe that it is in the U.S. interest to discourage or prevent Beijing and Taipei from reaching a level of political accommodation that would remove the Taiwan issue as a major Chinese distraction or—worse yet, in their view—result in Beijing's employment of the island as a strategic political and military asset.[136] In truth, although the resolution of the cross-Strait situation on terms favorable to Beijing is undoubtedly of some concern among a few outside U.S. political commentators and perhaps some mid-level officials and military analysts within the Pentagon, according to interviews, senior U.S. officials regard such a development as a highly remote possibility at best, and of little pressing threat to U.S. interests in any event. It does not drive U.S. policy moves toward China on this issue. In the absence of a major deterioration in Sino-U.S. relations, Washington will almost certainly have no incentive to obstruct or undermine future improvements in cross-Strait relations in the foreseeable future.[137]

In Taiwan's domestic political arena, even though the highly moderate and restrained Ma government is improving relations with both Beijing and Washington, it is possible that domestic factors could limit President Ma to a single term and perhaps even lead to his replacement by a proponent of Taiwan's independence. Such outcomes will depend in large part on whether the Pan-Green opposition is able to produce a strong challenger to Ma who is supportive of independence, whether Taiwan's economy continues to improve markedly in the wake of recent advances in cross-Strait economic links, whether the Ma government is able to continue improving the cross-Strait relationship, and whether the ruling KMT is not tainted by a major new political scandal. Current trends and features are largely indeterminate regarding such variables.

The Pan-Green opposition has been in a state of internal crisis and disarray since revelations emerged in 2007 of the likely involvement of Chen Shui-bian, his wife, and other relatives and advisers in several serious financial scandals. These developments, along with the policy failures of the Chen administration and steadily worsening relations with both Beijing and Washington, resulted not only in major defeats for the DPP in the presidential and legislative elections of 2008 but also in increased levels of factional and personal infighting, and a general decline in public support.[138]

In mid-2010, the DPP concentrated on grassroots organizing and protesting KMT policies, such as the Economic Cooperation Framework Agreement with the Mainland, and as a result it became more effective in providing opposition to the ruling party, which is currently plagued by its own problems. However, an ongoing debate within the opposition apparently exists over whether the movement should remain focused on a pro-independence set of objectives or should restructure its policies to emphasize a variety of domestic political reforms and the maintenance of maximum levels of flexibility in the face of a rising China and deepening cross-Strait relations. No political figure has yet emerged to pull the opposition together and present the kind of clear, unified national policy platform that could offer the prospect of garnering significant levels of public support above the usual 30 to 40 percent they receive in polls and elections. In the absence of such a development, the likelihood of the opposition regaining and building power during the current decade is not very great. That said, one can never say "never" with regard to Taiwan politics. Even a relatively weak and divided opposition might defeat Ma Ying-jeou and achieve major political gains if the Taiwan economy falters and Ma's energetic engagement policies toward Beijing come to be viewed by most of the public as threats to Taiwan's freedom.[139]

Many analysts seem to agree that Taiwan's ability to sustain reasonably high growth rates and continued increases in living standards for most citizens in the coming years will depend in large part on its future economic relationship with China. As indicated above, the Ma government has made major advances since early 2008 in cross-Strait shipping, air transportation, mutual investments, and various trade arrangements, and further such advances are no doubt planned.[140] Such developments, in the larger context of overall improvements in the global economy and the beginnings of China's recovery, are contributing to a major improvement in Taiwan's economic situation.[141] This bodes well for the KMT government, assuming that Ma is able to prevent closer cross-Strait economic ties from producing strong public concern over a possible increase in Beijing's political leverage vis-à-vis the island. In addition, even if for some reason (for example, an unexpected scandal) the opposition is able to regain power in the coming years, broad public attitudes on Taiwan associated with generational change suggest that future Taiwan political leaders and parties will find it increasingly difficult to advance their position by espousing strong independence or unification agendas in the absence of any clear shift in external conditions (that is, those involving China and the United States) toward one outcome or the other. And this, in turn, could mitigate the polarized conflict over national identity, at least in the short term, while sustaining support for some version of the status quo. In particular, a variety of polls and surveys strongly suggest that Taiwan's younger generation is less serious about politics, more pragmatic and optimistic, and therefore less committed in principle to achieving either independence or unification with Mainland China than was the more ideological and alienated generation of the 1940s and 1950s. Many Taiwan youth are focused primarily on maintaining or expanding their standard of living and preserving their freedom and are thus potentially open to a variety of cross-Strait relationships that could serve those ends.[142]

That said, despite the likely presence of a weak political opposition, a strong preference among the Taiwanese public for pragmatic and cautious policy approaches toward Beijing and Washington, and the likely prospect of an improved economic situation associated with deepening cross-Strait ties, basic divisions will remain within Taiwanese society over the island's political identity, and many citizens will no doubt continue to support energetic efforts to preserve or enlarge Taiwan's freedom of action and to expand its international presence.[143] Moreover, any cross-Strait dialogue and intensification of contacts will likely continue to confront strong opposition from the most committed pro-independence elements of the Pan-Green alliance. In general, possible future political scandals, economic difficulties, and the basic zero-sum mindset of many Pan-Blue and Pan-Green political activists will almost certainly ensure that Taiwan politics will remain unstable and subject to shifts in directions that Beijing or Washington might regard as provocative, at least in the near to medium terms. And such provocations will likely prove particularly dangerous as long as Beijing continues to develop and deploy military capabilities of direct relevance to Taiwan, and the United States continues to acquire and deploy capabilities designed to deter any Chinese use of force and to sell arms to Taipei. Whether Beijing can trust Washington to maintain controls on Taipei (thereby obviating the necessity for Beijing to do so via coercive means) will depend a great deal on whether the U.S. government can maintain the delicate balance between deterrence and reassurance toward Beijing that is required to sustain stability in the Taiwan Strait.

North Korea

Other than the Taiwan issue, developments connected with the ongoing multilateral effort to prevent political-military crises or conflict between North and South Korea and to pressure or entice Pyongyang to abandon its nuclear weapons program arguably constitute the most significant potential source of security-related tension between the United States and China. Although both nations want a stable and non-nuclear Korean Peninsula, each holds significantly different views toward the best means for achieving such ends; and each power views the problem from a significantly different strategic vantage point.[144]

U.S. Policies

Over the past ten to fifteen years, U.S. policy interactions with China regarding the slow motion North Korean nuclear crisis have witnessed even more significant shifts in approach and emphasis than have taken place regarding the Taiwan issue. During the first term of the George W. Bush administration, Washington held largely to a hard-line position toward Pyongyang that favored pressure and isolation (including strong sanctions), tough talk (for example, the public inclusion of North Korea in an "Axis of Evil" of rogue states), and a rejection of South Korea's previous "Sunshine Policy" of engaging and encouraging the North in favor of up-front demands that Pyongyang dismantle its nuclear weapons infrastructure and fully disclose all nuclear activities before Washington would consider tension reductions or compensation of any type.[145]

U.S. policy during the Bush era was also highly critical of the Agreed Framework that was reached between Pyongyang and Washington during the Clinton era. As part of the early Bush approach, Washington would at times criticize Beijing for not using what it regarded as China's considerable economic and political leverage upon North Korea to elicit greater compliance for commonly held denuclearization objectives, and likewise Washington would reject Beijing's frequent calls for it to negotiate with Pyongyang on a direct, bilateral basis. These stances produced frequent finger-pointing and recrimination on both sides, but little if any progress toward the common Sino-American objective of a stable Korean Peninsula without nuclear weapons.[146]

However, heightened tensions with Pyongyang, along with some U.S. pressure and persuasion directed at Beijing, as well as independent Chinese reassessments of the worsening situation in North Korea, eventually resulted in the emergence of a multilateral approach that in turn led in mid-2003 to the creation of the Six-Party Talks (6PT)—involving North Korea, the United States, China, Russia, South Korea, and Japan—along with frequent bilateral "sideline" discussions between Washington and Pyongyang.[147]

In this 6PT process, China came to play an increasingly important role as host, facilitator, and on some occasions motivator of the North Korean regime. This high-profile role emerged in part as a result of a specific U.S. decision, made at the end of the Bush administration's first term, to regard Beijing as its primary interlocutor in the engagement process.[148] Equally important, the U.S. desire to cooperate with China in advancing efforts to denuclearize the Korean Peninsula deepened during the Bush administration's second term, especially in the aftermath of North Korea's ballistic missile test and first nuclear detonation in 2006.

As a result, during this period, the Bush administration completely abandoned its long-standing opposition to bilateral engagement and a phased, quid pro quo approach toward North Korea and began working much more closely with China to implement a coordinated carrots-and-sticks negotiating strategy. Indeed, Washington came to regard Beijing as a vital partner in managing the North Korea issue.[149]

This basic approach has carried through to the Obama administration. Indeed, in recent years, Washington has arguably developed an extremely close relationship with (and, some would argue, dependence upon) Beijing in handling Pyongyang, largely in response to a further series of major setbacks beginning in 2009, centered on a second round of North Korean missile launches and a nuclear weapons test in the spring, and the North's announcement that it would no longer uphold any of its agreements, would reverse the nuclear disablement process, and must henceforth be treated as a nuclear power.[150] These setbacks were compounded by the above-mentioned sinking of a South Korean warship and Pyongyang's shelling of a South Korean island, as well as Pyongyang's disclosure of a uranium enrichment facility and light water reactor, all occurring in 2010.[151]

Throughout this tumultuous two-year period, Washington has consulted frequently and extensively with Beijing in an effort to bring Pyongyang back to the negotiating table and (hopefully) reinstate the denuclearization process, to compel Pyongyang to end its armed attacks on South Korea, and to express private and public concern over Pyongyang's uranium enrichment program. In 2009, the two powers worked together with Seoul, Tokyo, and Moscow to institute further UN sanctions and condemnations of North Korea for its nuclear provocations.[152] Washington also relied on Beijing to pressure North Korea to stand down after its bombardment of Yeonpyeong Island in late 2010.[153] And after some persistent and lengthy efforts, the Obama administration eventually elicited Beijing's support for a joint public expression of concern over the North's uranium enrichment facility.[154]

In addition, Beijing took the lead in an effort to entice, pressure, and persuade North Korea to participate in some form of talks with (at a minimum) the United States, if not the other four parties of the original 6PT.[155] The Obama administration supports such efforts to resume talks with Pyongyang.[156] However, Washington has also rejected the notion of talking for the sake of talking, and remains steadfast in its insistence that Pyongyang must return to the denuclearization process as agreed upon in earlier years, and not receive any rewards for doing so.[157] This position has remained consistent in the aftermath of the above-mentioned North Korean armed provocations and the discovery of Pyongyang's uranium enrichment program during 2010. Washington is willing to return to the negotiating table, but only if Pyongyang avoids further provocations and first meets bilaterally with Seoul.[158]

Chinese Policies

As with Washington, Beijing's political and diplomatic stance has also evolved considerably in recent years, from an insistence that the United States make significant concessions in purely bilateral negotiations with Pyongyang and a strong reluctance to place any pressure on the North Korean regime to forgo its nascent nuclear weapons capability, to active leadership of the 6PT, accompanied by attempts to convince North Korea (through greater pressure and enticements) to cooperate and comply with agreements reached, and barely concealed disgust with the North's repeated provocations and prevarications during the negotiation process. As examples of this changed stance, Beijing has

- Opposed Pyongyang's withdrawal from the Nuclear Non-Proliferation Treaty and repeatedly called for a nuclear-free Korean Peninsula.
- Temporarily cut off supplies of oil to the North.
- Privately informed outside observers that Pyongyang has become more of a liability than an asset to China.
- Publicly rebuked North Korea after it fired ballistic missiles in July 2006 and April 2009 and supported UN resolutions containing tough language and limited military and economic sanctions following Pyongyang's explosion of a nuclear device in October 2006 and May 2009.
- Intercepted shipments to North Korea of chemicals relevant to the production of weapons-grade plutonium.
- Repeatedly contributed to efforts to bring North Korea back to the negotiating table.[159]

China's transition from reluctant observer to active participant in the slow-motion North Korean nuclear crisis occurred because of: the Bush administration's constant prodding and persuasion; Beijing's fear that the Bush administration would take preemptive coercive actions or perform a "surgical strike" to bring about regime change in North Korea, as it did with Iraq; and Beijing's heightened sense of crisis following North Korea's provocations in 2006, 2009, and 2010.[160]

This transition also gained momentum because of the change in the U.S. position noted above. At the same time, one must emphasize that, throughout the course of the North Korean crisis, Beijing has strenuously and repeatedly sought to express official caution and, whenever possible, an evenhanded and balanced approach to managing the issue, at times frustrating and angering Washington. Specifically, Beijing has continuously placed a primary emphasis, over all other goals and means, on the need to preserve peace and stability on the Korean Peninsula via the persistent application of dialogue and consultations, and the avoidance of actions by any side that might provoke conflict, including extreme pressure on Pyongyang (for example, by entirely cutting off or severely reducing its long-standing and arguably vital supplies of food and oil to the impoverished regime) or any type of military solution to the imbroglio. In this effort, it has consistently presented itself as a mediator seeking to sustain or resume dialogue between the six parties (and especially the United States and North Korea), while also working with the other members of the 6PT to achieve the ultimate goal of denuclearization and the maintenance of the international nonproliferation system.[161]

In support of this primary objective, Beijing has also sought on many occasions to counterbalance its expression of displeasure toward Pyongyang with public, often official, affirmations of Sino-North Korean comity and friendship, along with fairly steady increases in the scope and depth of bilateral commercial economic ties and assistance. One prominent example of this behavior occurred in October 2009, when Pyongyang apparently agreed to come back to the negotiating table in return for further Chinese economic assistance and pledges of mutual support, as part of a deal apparently struck during Prime Minister Wen Jiabao's visit to North Korea at that time.[162] In line with this stance, Beijing has also avoided blaming Pyongyang for the alleged sinking of a South Korean warship in March 2010, and avoided condemning it for the November 2010 shelling of a South Korean island, arguably at some cost to its relationship with Seoul.[163] In addition, it has apparently worked to block a UN panel report that condemns North Korea for reneging on its commitments and violating UN sanctions through its uranium enrichment program and development of a light-water reactor, despite its public statement of concern regarding such activities, mentioned above.[164]

Evaluation and Future Trends

The North Korean nuclear issue has become a major example of success in Washington's strategic interactions with Beijing, despite its many difficulties. However, the potential for this situation to generate significant problems between the United States and China certainly remains. Future bilateral (or multilateral) tensions (or worse) precipitated, for example, by a prolonged inability to bring North Korea back to the denuclearization process, further nuclear and/or ballistic missile tests or armed provocations, the development by North Korea of a nuclear-armed ballistic missile capable of reaching Japan or U.S. territory, or the outbreak of a domestic political crisis in Pyongyang are very possible, especially given enduring suspicions and related differences that exist among the actors concerned over the possible use of sanctions or other pressure against Pyongyang and the relative importance each leadership places on eventual regime change versus the maintenance of the existing political status quo on the peninsula. These possibilities speak to the continued strong need for Washington to plan for future negative shifts that could generate both bilateral and broader regional instability. There are some signs that serious military contingency planning involving North Korea is taking place, as part of the Pentagon's 2010 Quadrennial Defense Review.[165]

However, it is unclear whether such planning is coordinated fully with any larger political, economic, or strategic assessments that might be under way in other agencies of the U.S. government. More important, Washington has yet to engage with the Chinese in any serious, in-depth government-to-government discussion of possible Korean crisis contingencies (involving, for example, the breakup of the North Korean regime) and their potential impact. There are still significant obstacles to conducting such discussions, deriving partly from a strong Chinese concern over possible North Korean reactions, along with strong Chinese suspicions that such discussions could reinforce the position of those in the United States who wish to see the Pyongyang regime collapse. More broadly, for China's leadership, all the plausible alternatives to its current cautious, even-handed stance toward the North Korean problem (including a high-pressure policy of isolation and containment, along with more subtle efforts to undermine the Pyongyang regime, or a commitment to follow Washington's lead in handling the problem) pose far more serious risks and dangers, given the high stakes and deep uncertainties China confronts.

Beijing's conservative stance toward the North Korea issue reflects a range of strategic, political, and military concerns and priorities associated with its overall need to maintain peace and stability along its periphery, along with various suspicions regarding the calculations under varying circumstances of both Pyongyang and Washington.[166] These factors are unlikely to change for the foreseeable future. Nonetheless, for Beijing, the maintenance of stability on the Korean Peninsula and the prevention of Pyongyang's emergence as a full-fledged nuclear power will continue to constitute critical strategic objectives requiring close cooperation with Washington. Moreover, from a purely bilateral perspective, China desires to retain its value to the United States as an indispensable mediator and participant in the negotiating process with North Korea.

In addition to such bilateral issues and concerns, Washington needs to address whether and how the United States, Japan, South Korea, and China can improve policy coordination toward the North Korean problem, not only to avoid future crises on the peninsula but also as a foundation for a larger effort designed to facilitate discussions about other security issues in East Asia and the overall regional security environment. Such U.S.-led efforts (which amount to a multilateral examination of the region's future strategic landscape) are especially important, given the above-outlined differences in outlook and resulting concerns among some circles in Tokyo and Seoul regarding Washington's stance toward the North Korean nuclear issue, the regional security environment, and China's growing power and influence in Asia.

India

Over the past ten to fifteen years, the gradual emergence of India as a more significant regional and global economic power, its resulting expanding strategic ambitions, and significant advances in both Indo-American and Indo-Chinese bilateral relations have made New Delhi an increasingly important factor in U.S. policy calculations toward China. Indeed, to an important degree, concerns over Beijing's growing strategic influence motivate U.S. policies toward India, contributing to the formation of a more complex trilateral strategic relationship.

U.S. Policies

Washington's growing cooperation with New Delhi in several political, economic, and military-related areas is part of a larger effort to encourage the evolution of a more friendly, cooperative, secure, and strong India via an array of unprecedented interactions mostly begun during the George W. Bush administration but foreshadowed by President Clinton's historic visit to India in 2000. These interactions include a civilian nuclear technology cooperation agreement; closer political, economic, military, and diplomatic ties; and enhanced cooperation in addressing a variety of common global and regional problems. The ultimate objective of this undertaking is to facilitate India's stable emergence as a new strategic actor in the Asia-Pacific region that is broadly supportive of U.S. interests and goals, as part of the implementation of a larger "balance-of-power" strategy among China, India, and Russia. According to Ashley Tellis, a scholar who was deeply involved in this initiative, this strategy "seeks to prevent any one of these [countries] from effectively threatening the security of another [or that of the United States] while simultaneously preventing any combination of these [entities] from 'bandwagoning' to undercut critical U.S. strategic interests in Asia."[167]

Thus, though not congruent with the requirements of a containment strategy, this approach is presumably designed *in part* to improve Washington's ability to counterbalance Beijing's growing power through a limited version of "offshore balancing" involving shifting relationships among other increasingly more capable major Asian powers.[168]

Aside from such relatively narrow balance-of-power considerations, the Bush administration's opening to India was also designed to shape Indian views, interests, and behavior in ways that enhance the resolution of common political, economic, and security problems and issues facing the United States, China, and India. These include global warming, counterproliferation, terrorism (especially in Central Asian states such as Pakistan and Afghanistan), and the Asian and global economic recession.[169] These policies and objectives have by and large continued during the Obama administration. U.S. defense secretary Robert Gates has described New Delhi as "a partner and net provider of security in the Indian Ocean and beyond."[170]

Such enhanced political and security-related cooperation has included an unprecedented level of intelligence sharing, major sales of U.S. civilian and military-related hardware (including maritime reconnaissance aircraft and possible fighter jets), various meetings and agreements designed to enhance economic and commercial ties (including a Bilateral Investment Treaty, a memorandum of understanding designed to facilitate foreign direct investment between the two powers, and the intention to create a United States–India Economic and Financial Partnership as well as a free trade agreement), and a doubling of bilateral trade since 2004.[171]

During Prime Minister Manmohan Singh's state visit to Washington in November 2009 (the first state visit by a foreign leader during the new administration), President Obama stated that Washington and New Delhi are "natural allies," and that the United States "welcomes and encourages India's leadership role in helping to shape the rise of a stable, peaceful and prosperous Asia." He also pledged to "fully implement" the 2005 nuclear accord, as well as a clean-energy initiative.[172]

In addition, besides signing a memo of understanding on "Advancing Global Security and Countering Terrorism," the two sides signed pacts covering education and development, health cooperation, economic trade and agriculture, and green partnerships. Obama and Singh also affirmed their commitment to work together to prevent the spread of weapons of mass destruction and missile-related technology, and to realize their "shared vision" of a world free of nuclear weapons.[173] Singh's visit to Washington (on the heels of Obama's trip to East Asia), along with such positive bilateral statements and cooperative agreements, were in part designed to counterbalance the notion, expressed by many Indian observers, that the Obama administration was tilting more toward Beijing and downplaying ties with India than was the case during the Bush administration.[174]

In general, the Obama administration has arguably sought to downplay the China-related "balance-of-power" aspects of its India policy, in favor of a greater overall stress on either cooperative bilateral U.S.-Indian relations or the positive-sum aspects of multilateral relations involving both India and China. As William Burns, the U.S. undersecretary of state for political affairs and a key administration official in relations with India has stated, "Few relationships matter more to our collective future, or hold greater promise for constructive action on the challenges that matter most for us, than the partnership between the U.S. and India."[175]

In line with this effort at balancing between the three powers, Washington held the first-ever Strategic Dialogue with India in the spring of 2010, in many respects duplicating the dialogues held with China. Topics covered a wide variety of issues, from science and technology to security issues. But the main strategic focus of the discussion was East Asia, and especially the growing power and influence of China. Likewise, Obama's state visit to Mumbai and New Delhi in November 2010 sought to reinforce United States–India ties and indirectly reassure India in the face of China's rise. During that visit, Obama also expressed support for India's permanent membership on the UN Security Council.[176]

Chinese Policies

India's improving ties with the United States are of course being watched carefully—and likely with considerable concern—by China. To some extent, the burgeoning Indo-American strategic relationship has provided a stimulus to rapid developments in Sino-Indian relations. Indeed, the often tumultuous Sino-Indian bilateral relationship has improved enormously since at least 2000—characterized by frequent high-level visits by civilian and military leaders; increasing cooperation on bilateral, regional, and international issues (involving the formation of myriad agreements, memorandums, and working groups on issues such as the long-standing border dispute, defense exchanges, and economic cooperation in areas such as energy, agriculture, education, and technology); an annual strategic dialogue;[177] completed or planned joint military exercises in the fields of search and rescue; antipiracy and counterterrorism; port calls; and expanding levels of bilateral trade (from $5 billion in 2000 to over $60 billion in 2010 and a target of $100 billion by 2015).[178]

Moreover, Beijing has sought to reassure New Delhi about its defense ties with Pakistan, has declared its support for India's aspiration for a seat on the UN Security Council, and has adopted a neutral stance with regard to the Indo-Pakistani dispute over Kashmir. For its part, New Delhi has reassured Beijing that it will not participate in any "axis of democracy" that seeks to restrain Chinese power and has declared its adherence to Beijing's "One China" policy regarding Taiwan. India has also echoed China's long-standing support for an open and inclusive international system that promotes the "democratization" of international relations and multilateralism as core objectives. Both sides have also pledged that their territorial dispute will not be allowed to undermine the positive development of bilateral relations; indeed, during recent years, there has been episodic progress on sensitive border talks.[179]

Most recently, the two countries have held frequent meetings between senior political and military officials to build greater trust, especially regarding simmering border disputes, as well as regular trilateral foreign ministerial meetings with Russia. The latter three-way dialogues have most recently produced a Joint Communiqué pledging cooperation on a variety of issues, from enhancing the Group of Twenty to fighting terrorism. India has also stepped up its involvement in the Shanghai Cooperation Organization (SCO), sending the prime minister to lead the Indian delegation at the SCO Summit for the first time in 2009. China has also voiced support for India's measures to curb emissions and fight climate change.[180] Such developments clearly suggest that both countries wish to avoid a destabilizing security competition, which is obviously beneficial to the larger regional order.[181]

Conversely, Beijing's concerted effort to improve its security relationship with New Delhi remains subject to significant limitations, given the continued high levels of mutual distrust and suspicion between the two rising powers— which stem from historical tensions and border disputes, China's close strategic relationship with Pakistan, and the overall dynamics of the security dilemma. As Jing-dong Yuan states:

> India has watched China's phenomenal growth in economic and military areas with both envy and alarm. Likewise, China is paying close attention to India's growing military power and its nuclear and missile developments. Beijing is wary of New Delhi's eastward strategy of developing greater economic and military ties with Japan and the countries of the Association of Southeast Asian Nations. Moreover, unresolved territorial disputes continue to be a key obstacle to the full normalization of bilateral relations.[182]

Analysts also cite growing bilateral economic and trade tensions, continued military deployments on both sides of the Sino-Indian border, growing attention by both nations to naval power, and apparently competitive political moves toward surrounding smaller states as confirmation of an emerging pattern of strategic rivalry.[183]

It must be noted that much of the commentary on the presumed growing strategic rivalry between New Delhi and Beijing is stoked by inaccurate and misleading statements, for example, regarding Chinese activities in nations or oceans close to India or the state of the border dispute. One common myth asserts that China is engaged in building a line of strategic bases or ports (a so-called string of pearls) along the northern seaboard of the Indian Ocean in Sittwe, Burma; Chittagong, Bangladesh; Hambantota, Sri Lanka; and Gwadar, Pakistan. Another argues that the long-simmering Sino-Indian border dispute is steadily escalating toward ever greater levels of tension and potential conflict.[184]

Nonetheless, there is little doubt that the two powers are becoming increasingly wary of one another, despite their efforts to enhance cooperation in many areas. In recent months, India has become more alarmed by the potential threat of a rising China, largely in response to China's growing presence and influence in South Asia and overall increasing assertiveness on maritime issues (as noted above and discussed in chapter 4). For its part, Beijing has become more suspicious toward deepening U.S. and Japanese political and military contacts with New Delhi and the strategic intent behind India's so-called Look-East policy.[185]

Evaluation and Future Trends

The developments described above have resulted in the emergence of a nascent China–India–United States strategic triangle in which leaders in each capital are increasingly attentive to the effects of policies in the other two capitals (and with regard to other states such as Pakistan) upon their own political and security interests. Thus far, this dynamic has on balance served to maximize the search for positive-sum outcomes by each party, which certainly serves U.S. interests. Conversely, it also suggests that there are definite limits to the extent that Washington can utilize its burgeoning relations with India to support any possible future effort to counterbalance Chinese power, particularly in the absence of a major downturn in Sino-Indian relations. New Delhi is likely to continue to strengthen its positive relations with both Washington and Beijing in order to maximize its strategic leverage. In addition, U.S. efforts to facilitate the acceptance of India into the international community as a stable and responsible nuclear power could generate serious tensions between Beijing and both Washington and New Delhi, given the former's concern over India's growing nuclear weapons capabilities and the overall level of distrust that will almost certainly persist (indeed, could deepen) in Sino-Indian relations.

Moreover, U.S. nuclear initiatives toward India also arguably provide Beijing with an excuse to enhance its nuclear assistance to Pakistan, while recent U.S. efforts to elicit greater Chinese support for Washington's counterterrorism policies in both Afghanistan and Pakistan potentially threaten to disrupt the improving United States–India–China relationship. Overall, U.S. policy toward India is becoming increasingly interconnected with its policies toward China, and will thus require a high level of attention and considerable sophistication to manage successfully.

Russia

After many years of declining strategic importance following the collapse of the Soviet Union, Russia is again becoming a more important player for both the United States and China. As a source of advanced weaponry and technologies, a large energy producer and consumer, a major nuclear power, a source of past tension and confrontation with both Washington and Beijing, and a long-standing strategic player on the Eurasian continent, Russia should form a significant component of the U.S. calculus toward China in the new century.

U.S. Policies

U.S. policies toward Russia during the Bush administration for the most part operated independently of policies toward China, although some actions certainly posed significant implications for Sino-U.S. relations or required some coordination of actions toward Moscow and Beijing, especially in Central Asia. In general, during the Bush administration, Washington sought to maintain good relations with Moscow, not only to manage global issues and problems regarding terrorism, economic development, and nuclear proliferation and to reduce adverse Russian responses to the expansion of NATO eastward and southward, but also to minimize Russian incentives to strengthen strategic and defense cooperation with China in ways that might threaten Western interests (for example, via the activities of the SCO or Sino-Russian military cooperation). Washington also sought to elicit Russian support for U.S. goals in the China-sponsored 6PT concerning North Korea and with regard to the effort to prevent Iran from acquiring nuclear weapons (which also deeply involve Beijing). Perhaps the most direct U.S. actions of relevance to Beijing have involved efforts to restrain Russian arms sales to China.[186]

Unfortunately, these and other efforts by Bush to influence Russia, for whatever ends, met with little concrete success in many cases, largely due to the somewhat steady decline in overall U.S.-Russian relations that took place starting in the early years of the Bush administration.[187] This occurred largely as a result of tensions over Bush's strong support for the expansion of NATO into several former client states and Soviet republics, its withdrawal from the Anti–Ballistic Missile Treaty, Russian opposition to the war in Iraq, and, most notably, the Russian invasion of the former Soviet republic (now democratic state) of Georgia, in response to the latter's attack on the breakaway regions of South Ossetia and Abkhazia.[188]

The deterioration in U.S. relations with Russia was also intensified by Moscow's growing political and diplomatic confidence during the later years of the Bush administration, propelled in large part by the rise of former KGB intelligence officer Vladimir Putin to the Russian presidency and an oil-driven, rebounding economy.[189]

Efforts to influence Russia in ways that could benefit U.S. security policies toward China also largely failed during the Bush era because of the significant incentives Moscow and Beijing had (and still have) to cooperate on issues of concern to Washington. The most notable areas of cooperation include major Russian arms sales and military-related technology transfers in key areas of great relevance to China's military buildup opposite Taiwan, and the development of greater levels of security cooperation during the past several years, involving joint military exercises, collaboration in the development of the SCO, and closer military-to-military relations. These military activities form part of an overall attempt to promote a Sino-Russian strategic partnership that is designed, in part, to maintain a stable environment for the strategic development of both countries, and, to some extent, to counterbalance U.S. and Western influence in Asia and beyond.[190]

Since entering office, the Obama administration has focused considerable efforts on improving U.S. ties with Russia, in order to resolve common problems and increase its strategic leverage vis-à-vis a variety of issues, some of great importance to United States–China relations. The latter include the Iran and North Korean nuclear imbroglios, the future of the global arms control regime, energy policy, stability in Central Asia, and China's military modernization program. Thus far, this effort to "reset" the United States–Russia relationship has shown some limited results, especially following President Obama's visit to Russia in July 2009. Most notably, as discussed in greater detail in chapter 6, the Obama administration signed a follow-on agreement for the Strategic Arms Reduction Treaty (known as New START) in April 2010 (ratified by the U.S. Senate and the Russian Duma in December 2010 and January 2011, respectively) and concluded the Nuclear Non-Proliferation Treaty Review Conference with Moscow in May 2010. This more constructive approach also contributed to the breaking of a long deadlock on a work plan in the Conference on Disarmament in Geneva, whose members include China and Russia. This conference agreed in June 2009 to enter into discussions on nuclear disarmament, the prevention of an arms race in outer space, and assurances that non–nuclear-weapon states will not be attacked with nuclear weapons.[191] The Obama administration is also working through the Conference on Disarmament to facilitate negotiations on a verifiable fissile material cutoff treaty.[192] Such improvements in Washington's arms control relationship with Russia could facilitate efforts to engage China on such issues.[193]

Second, Obama's September 2009 decision not to deploy a ballistic missile defense system in Poland and the Czech Republic (to which Moscow strenuously objected) also gave incentives for Russia to express increased support for U.S. efforts to eliminate Iran's suspected nuclear weapons program.[194] Such advances arguably put greater pressure on China to also support U.S. efforts. Indeed, in early 2010, Russia shifted its position on Iran to support further sanctions on that country. This shift contributed, in part, to China's support for a fourth round of sanctions in June 2010.[195]

For its part, China has also increased cooperation with Russia regarding energy and economic issues. In March 2007, for example, the two countries signed a joint statement pledging to boost cooperation in the oil, gas, and power sectors in order to consolidate "the comprehensive and long-term strategic collaborative relations in energy and resources." In 2008, Moscow and Beijing signed a three-year agreement that emphasized cooperation in astronautics, nanometer technology, shipbuilding, auto manufacturing, oil, and natural gas, and in February 2009 they signed a $25 billion energy-cooperation agreement.[196]

Conversely, Sino-Russian security-related activities and the objective of opposing "American hegemony" in general have remained severely limited by many factors, including (1) the continued presence of strong levels of mutual distrust; (2) the ongoing weak strategic position of Russia in the Asia-Pacific region; (3) the potentially threatening nature of China's growing power, geopolitical presence, and economic dynamism (including, for some Russians, the "creeping colonization" by China of Russia's Far East and Beijing's growing challenge to Moscow's traditional position of diplomatic and economic dominance in Central Asia); (4) disputes over energy pipelines and prices (in which Russia needs high energy prices while China would like to see them fall); and, perhaps most important, (5) the fact that Beijing in particular ultimately values the maintenance of a constructive relationship with the United States above the development of a genuine anti–United States strategic alliance with Russia. Moreover, in recent years, one strong basis for the Sino-Russian relationship—arms sales to Beijing—has declined significantly, in part because of Chinese demands for transfers of more sophisticated Russian military technologies. The two powers have also differed notably in their approach toward the crisis over Georgia. Beijing resisted endorsing Russia's actions, choosing instead to counsel restraint and negotiations. China's leadership apparently fears that Moscow's desire to recognize the breakaway regions of South Ossetia and Abkhazia might embolden nationalism in Tibet and Taiwan. In addition, Beijing does not want to antagonize Washington (and possibly other Western democracies) by taking sides with Russia on such a potentially volatile issue.[197]

Evaluation and Future Trends

Russia has not figured prominently in U.S. policies toward China during the Bush and Obama administrations. Moscow has not enjoyed significant leverage with either Beijing or Washington in ways that could greatly affect United States–China relations or key U.S. policies toward Beijing. In particular, despite achieving some notable level of cooperation in various areas, Beijing has for the most part been unwilling or unable to establish the sort of alliance with Moscow that could seriously undermine core U.S. interests or degrade the United States–China relationship. However, this situation could change in the future, if U.S.-Russian relations again deteriorate, resulting in a major rift and confrontation. Such a development could produce significant pressure on Beijing by one or both nations to choose sides or otherwise alter its behavior in ways that pose serious implications for U.S. policies toward China.

Fortunately, such a scenario seems unlikely at present and for at least the next several years, given the above-outlined U.S. shift toward a more constructive relationship with Moscow under Obama and persistent strategic mistrust between Russia and China. Indeed, continued improvements in U.S. relations with Russia on specific issues such as Iran and nuclear disarmament are more likely to provide Washington with a greater ability to leverage Beijing in these areas. But much will depend on the durability and depth of the current U.S.-Russian rapprochement on the one hand, and the future incentives for more or less cooperation between Moscow and Beijing on the other hand.

CONCLUSION

This chapter's analysis of U.S. and Chinese policies toward the major powers in Asia clearly confirms the highly dynamic nature of the key political relationships in that region and the growing challenges that such a situation presents for U.S. policymakers as they grapple with the impact of China's growing influence. U.S. policies toward Japan, Taiwan, and both Koreas in particular confront new or rapidly changing problems that will almost certainly directly influence Washington's capacity to sustain its overall two-sided strategic approach to China during the current decade and beyond. As we have seen, in many cases, the assumptions underlying U.S. policies are increasingly being cast into doubt by developments within and among these powers, pointing to the possible need for a basic reassessment by U.S. leaders of existing approaches and priorities.

In addition, the ability of the United States to manage relations with the major Asian powers, as part of its overall strategy toward China, is increasingly linked to larger, multilateral and bilateral arrangements and dialogues that encompass the political, economic, and security views of many powers. The next chapter examines this increasingly important dimension of U.S. policy toward China.

03

MULTILATERAL INTERACTIONS, BILATERAL DIALOGUES, AND ASIAN PERCEPTIONS

As indicated in the previous chapters, during the past ten to fifteen years, U.S. policymakers have at times attempted, to varying degrees, to utilize bilateral interactions with smaller powers, most notably in key areas such as Southeast Asia, and in several multilateral political, economic, and security-related venues, to augment and support Washington's overall approach to China. This effort has taken place in large part to reassure the region that the United States remains fully engaged on all fronts and seeks to work with a rising China to maximize cooperation and to integrate an increasingly active Beijing into various international regimes and forums, while also sustaining the ability to hedge against adverse developments in the Sino-U.S. relationship. In addition, Washington has initiated direct, bilateral dialogues with China to support these larger strategic goals and to address a variety of issues related to political, security, and economic policy. Taken as a whole, these dialogues and interactions are arguably playing an increasingly important role in U.S. policy toward China. Hence, they deserve treatment separately from the political and security relationships with major Asian powers discussed in the previous chapter.

U.S. MULTILATERAL REGIONAL INTERACTIONS

During the past ten to fifteen years, Asia has witnessed an unprecedented expansion in the number, size, and type of multilateral interactions of relevance to U.S. policy toward China. These include a diverse array of new region-wide and sub-regional (that is, Northeast Asian, East Asian, Southeast Asian, and Central Asian) political, economic, and security-related dialogues, structures, and forums, as well as a growing number of military-related interactions. Additional new types of multilateral activities are also under consideration. Such phenomena have in no way superseded the bilateral relationship between the United States, China, and other major powers in Asia as core channels of policy influence, especially in the political and security arenas. However, multilateral regional venues are increasingly becoming an important potential means of shaping the larger regional environment to serve Washington's objectives toward Beijing, from the resolution of specific regional and global problems to the shaping of China's views and influence regarding international norms and values.

Asian and Southeast Asian Multilateral Forums

During the George W. Bush era, Washington focused its multilateral engagement in Asia on the Association of Southeast Asian Nations (ASEAN) Regional Forum (ARF) and the Asia-Pacific Economic Cooperation (APEC) forum in particular, continuing past policy priorities. During the Bush administration, every meeting of APEC and almost every ARF meeting were attended, respectively, by President Bush and the sitting secretary of state. However, U.S. interactions with the ARF (and ASEAN in general) during the Bush administration were almost entirely focused on counterterrorism and nonproliferation measures from the events of 9/11 until approximately 2005–2006. They only expanded somewhat thereafter, to include nontraditional security issues such as international crime, disaster management, and emergency response.[1]

Moreover, diplomatic efforts to confront the economic and social conditions of local populations were largely absent from Bush policy toward Southeast Asia. Also, Secretary of State Condoleezza Rice's skipping of the ASEAN foreign ministers' meeting and the ARF in 2005 was perceived as showing a lack of American interest in the region, while the Bush administration's focus on counterterrorism activities in Muslim Asian nations seemed to anger moderate Muslims by conveying the impression that Washington was engaged in a struggle against Islam.[2]

In general, as one observer remarked, there was a perception in Southeast Asia that the Bush administration, and perhaps also earlier U.S. administrations, regarded ASEAN as a rather ineffective "talk shop" that was unable to produce truly beneficial results. For many regional observers, this reflected a U.S. failure to appreciate or understand the role that ASEAN has played as the region's facilitator, convener, and peacemaker.[3]

Despite these criticisms, the Bush administration did attempt to escalate engagement with ASEAN, particularly toward the end of its tenure. In 2002, President Bush began to use the annual APEC leaders' summit to engage in multilateral meetings with seven of the attending ASEAN leaders, and at the 2005 APEC summit in Busan, South Korea, he worked with other leaders to launch the ASEAN–U.S. Enhanced Partnership. This forum was intended to deepen cooperation in a broad range of economic, political, and security areas, as stipulated in a five-year plan of action. Under this new plan, U.S. security engagement with ASEAN primarily related to weapons proliferation, transnational crime, and terrorism. And in 2008, the United States also appointed an ambassador to ASEAN, the first country to do so.[4]

Toward the end of the Bush administration, its officials also seemed to acknowledge that the United States' neglect of the Asia-Pacific region was disadvantaging America's economic position in Asia.[5] As a result, in September 2008, U.S. trade representative Susan C. Schwab announced that the United States would negotiate accession to the Trans-Pacific Strategic Economic Partnership Agreement among the Pacific Four trading bloc of Chile, New Zealand, Singapore, and Brunei.[6] Despite announcing this plan, however, no negotiations were held before Bush left office.

Also toward the end of President Bush's tenure, administration officials voiced some support for the idea of developing the current Six-Party Talks (6PT) concerning North Korea into a permanent security forum in Northeast Asia (often referred to as the "Northeast Asian peace and security mechanism"), and they considered dealing with emergent multilateral groupings such as the ASEAN-led East Asia Summit (EAS), inaugurated in December 2005 and attended by sixteen countries (the ten nations belonging to ASEAN, plus China, Japan, South Korea, India, Australia, and New Zealand). The former concept was being addressed by a working group within the 6PT led by Russia.[7] However, little real progress was made toward the realization of a Northeast Asia security forum, and discussion of the forum was largely placed in abeyance following the suspension of the 6PT in the aftermath of North Korea's second round of missile and nuclear weapons tests in mid-2009. The forum's future establishment is largely viewed by the United States, and probably also other nations, as primarily dependent upon the prior resolution of the North Korean nuclear crisis, and this crisis is arguably nowhere near resolution, as we have seen.[8]

The EAS, which usually meets after the annual ASEAN leaders' gatherings, was established as a forum for dialogue and community building on broad strategic, political, and especially economic issues of common interest and concern, ostensibly with the aim of promoting peace, stability, and prosperity in East Asia. However, from its inception, many ASEAN participants viewed the EAS as a possible pathway toward the eventual establishment of an East Asian Community (EAC) along the lines of the European Union (a notion endorsed by former Japanese prime minister Yukio Hatoyama and reiterated at the October 2009 EAS, with several leaders calling at that time for the creation, variously, of an Asia Pacific Community or an East Asian Community).[9] Thus, even though the EAS has at times discussed such issues as energy security and cooperation, responses to the avian flu, counterterrorism, the denuclearization of the Korean Peninsula, and maritime security, it has primarily focused on enhancing regional economic cooperation. Overall, the EAS has thus far achieved few concrete results since its establishment in late 2005.[10]

In addition, the Bush administration did not become a member of the EAS (having refused to join the Treaty of Amity and Cooperation, a precondition for membership), and in general adopted a lukewarm attitude toward it, merely watching how it developed, while placing a greater emphasis on the ARF as a regional, security-oriented multilateral venue (despite its limitations).[11]

The Obama administration has taken a more positive and activist stance toward these Asian and Southeast Asian multilateral forums, as part of an overall effort to show, in supposed contrast to the Bush era, that Washington is again fully engaged in the region in the political, cultural, economic, and security realms.[12] The administration has continued the ASEAN–U.S. Enhanced Partnership, including the negotiation of a second five-year plan of action, and it has expressed its intention to "elevate [the] partnership to a strategic level."[13] In July 2009, Secretary of State Hillary Clinton signed the Treaty of Amity and Cooperation and attended the ARF in Phuket, Thailand, and was the first secretary of state to visit the ASEAN regional headquarters in Jakarta. And President Obama attended the first ever U.S. presidential meeting with the heads of state and government of the ASEAN member nations in Singapore in November 2009, along with a second annual leaders' summit in September 2010.[14]

Before the Singapore meeting, while in Tokyo, the president also stated that Washington now regards multilateral organizations as potential contributors to regional security and prosperity and will actively support such structures. He particularly singled out APEC as central to the promotion of regional commerce and prosperity, and he mentioned ASEAN as a "catalyst for Southeast Asian dialogue, cooperation, and security." Perhaps most notably, he also stated: "As an Asia Pacific nation, the United States expects to be involved in the discussions that shape the future of this region, and to participate fully in appropriate organizations as they are established and evolve."[15] This remark signaled that the United States intends to join the EAS and to be included in any major regional groupings in the security, political, and economic realms.[16] In fact, following Obama's speech in Tokyo, senior U.S. officials, including Secretary of State Clinton and Assistant Secretary for East Asian and Pacific Affairs Kurt Campbell, announced Washington's plans to engage with the EAS, with Secretary Clinton attending the 2010 EAS Summit as a guest of the chair and Obama attending the 2011 EAS Summit as a full participant.[17]

Negotiations regarding a Trans-Pacific Partnership also regained momentum in 2010, after having stalled during the first year of the Obama administration, and six formal rounds of negotiations for a revamped and broader trade agreement had been held as of April 2011. Several senior administration officials, including U.S. trade representative Ron Kirk, Secretary Clinton, and President Obama himself, placed an emphasis on advancing the Trans-Pacific Partnership as a key part of broader U.S. engagement in Asia.[18] Clinton also attended the ARF in Hanoi in July 2010 and delivered a major speech that addressed regional security issues, including the United States' interest in the peaceful resolution of territorial disputes in the South China Sea (this point is also discussed in chapter 4).[19] When Clinton attended the October 2010 East Asia Summit in Hanoi, she reiterated the U.S. commitment to the EAS and other multilateral institutions in the Asia-Pacific region and specifically highlighted the role the EAS should play in issues that have an impact on regional security, "including nuclear proliferation, the increase in conventional arms, maritime security, climate change, and the promotion of shared values and civil society."[20]

Central Asia and the Shanghai Cooperation Organization

Another multilateral structure of relevance to United States–China relations is the Shanghai Cooperation Organization (SCO). The SCO was formally established in June 2001 on the basis of the Shanghai Five Organization of 1996, which included China, Russia, Kazakhstan, Kyrgyzstan, and Tajikistan. With the establishment of the SCO, a sixth member, Uzbekistan, joined the group, and since that time, India, Iran, Mongolia, and Pakistan have become observers. The SCO marks the first time in the history of the People's Republic of China that Beijing has taken the lead in the creation of a multilateral security-related organization. The organization is primarily focused on (1) working out extant border disputes peacefully; (2) instituting military confidence-building measures among the respective armed forces in the border regions; and (3) coordinating and cooperating in handling cross-border security issues such as terrorism, separatism, and criminal activities such as drug trafficking. Among these activities, the SCO has arguably worked hardest to combat the new threats of "terrorism, separatism, and extremism" (in the Chinese lexicon, the "three forces"), along with universal problems such as drug trafficking, cybersabotage, and aspects of the proliferation of weapons of mass destruction.[21]

Although the SCO is not a formal military alliance or bloc directed against other states or regions, it can conceivably serve as a mechanism for resisting (or supporting) U.S. influence in Central Asia. Washington has generally avoided commenting on, much less disdaining, the SCO, with the exception of its negative response to the SCO's 2005 Astana Declaration that called for a deadline for U.S. troop withdrawals from Central Asia. Indeed, U.S. policy toward the SCO is largely subsumed beneath overall U.S. policy toward Central Asia, which has in turn been heavily influenced by the wars in Iraq and Afghanistan and the general struggle against terrorism. Specifically, U.S. goals and actions have focused primarily on such issues as sustaining political, economic, and especially military access to Central Asia, the Middle East, and (to a lesser extent) Southeast Asia; increasing access to oil and gas; improving trade and transportation infrastructures; expanding bilateral and multilateral military cooperation on counternarcotics and counterterrorism efforts; and generally supporting Central Asian development. In all these areas, U.S. policy during the Bush administration sought to elicit Chinese support or, at the very least, minimize or avoid Chinese opposition, whether undertaken unilaterally or via the SCO.[22] But China was only one of many regional players in these issue areas, and not the primary focus of U.S. policy. Indeed, as one former Bush era interview respondent stated: "The Chinese were paranoid about U.S. activities in Central Asia and often thought such activities were directed at themselves, but they were not."

Some observers have argued that overall U.S. influence and connections in Central Asia have declined in recent years. Matthew Oresman points out that China has surpassed the United States in every measure of economic contact with the region, including aid, foreign direct investment, and trade, and that it "now possesses resources and influence in Central Asia that rival those of the United States." According to this view, this development underscores the point that Beijing's involvement in Central Asia is organic and long term, while Washington's contact is subject to constant modification based on the changing policy priorities of the U.S. government. And both powers must also contend with the continued strong aspirations of Russia to enhance its political and economic influence over the region.[23]

Military Interactions in the Asia-Pacific Region

In addition to these largely civilian political and security-related interactions, the U.S. Pacific Command (PACOM) has also engaged in a wide variety of multilateral interactions with Asian militaries and governments during recent U.S. administrations (beginning at least with Bill Clinton), under a succession of highly activist PACOM commanders, from Admiral Dennis Blair to Admiral Robert Willard. At a more senior level, most recently, U.S. secretary of defense Robert Gates attended the inaugural ASEAN Defense Ministers Meeting-Plus in Hanoi on October 12, 2010, along with the defense ministers from the ten ASEAN countries, China, Japan, South Korea, India, Russia, Australia, and New Zealand.[24] The general purpose of such activities has been to reassure other powers that the U.S. military remains strongly engaged in the region in the midst of rapid change and to strengthen or foster cooperation on a wide range of military- and security-related issues, from disaster relief to nuclear counterproliferation. Nonetheless, as in the civilian sphere, most such military multilateral activities have focused primarily on enhancing cooperation in countering transnational crime, terrorism, and disaster preparation and relief,[25] with some notable exceptions, such as the biannual Rim of the Pacific exercise (known as RIMPAC).[26] As part of these efforts, Washington has demonstrated to smaller powers its superior capabilities in responding to large-scale, nontraditional security threats such as the 2004 Southeast Asian tsunami disaster.[27]

However, despite such multilateral activities, in general, the United States has conducted most of its security-related activities in Southeast Asia and with smaller Asian nations on a bilateral or trilateral basis. In recent years, Washington has paid particular attention to advancing security ties with allies such as Australia, the Philippines, and Thailand, as well as Indonesia and Vietnam, and Kazakhstan in Central Asia. These efforts include training, the provision of military assistance and equipment, security consultations, and diplomacy.[28] Moreover, in 2003 the Bush administration granted the Philippines and Thailand "major non-NATO ally" status (a designation already applied in the region to Australia, New Zealand, Pakistan, Japan, and South Korea).[29] As with the above-mentioned multilateral activities, most of this bilateral security assistance has been closely related to the war on terrorism. Moreover, such support has not generally translated into enhanced relative U.S. political influence vis-à-vis China, given the desire of most of these countries to continue deepening their close relationships with Beijing.[30]

Overall, the situation described above suggests that, for most of the past decade, the U.S. Defense Department and PACOM in particular have exhibited the most sustained interest in and worked the most energetically with multilateral structures and forums to advance U.S. political and security-related objectives in Asia, especially in Southeast Asia. In contrast, the State Department under Bush only episodically engaged in such activities, preferring instead to focus on bilateral interactions, especially with the major powers. In addition, as noted above, during the Bush administration, Washington often focused the bulk of its attention in these interactions on enhancing cooperation in combating terrorism over other political, economic, and security issues of interest to Asian nations.[31]

CHINESE MULTILATERAL REGIONAL INTERACTIONS

In at least partial contrast to this record of U.S. activities, China has in general been extremely active in recent years in both promoting and initiating bilateral and especially multilateral security-related interactions, statements, and forums among its neighboring Asian states. Chinese involvement in such security-related activities actually began to deepen and expand in 1996 and 1997. This shift in part reflected a broader decision by Beijing to press more deliberately for a cooperative security approach internationally, and especially in Asia, as expressed in notions such as the New Security Concept. As noted in chapter 2, China's promotion of cooperative security approaches was designed in part to present an alternative to the United States–led bilateral alliance structure in Asia and to make it more difficult for Washington to obtain regional support for future pressures against Beijing, and also to signal to other Asian nations that Beijing supports cooperative, multilateral approaches to regional security issues.[32] Indeed, to some extent, Beijing's approach seeks to take advantage of what is perceived by many observers as "a growing regional momentum toward cooperative security."[33]

At the same time, this approach also emerged from Beijing's recognition that many Asian (and particularly Southeast Asian) states were increasingly concerned about China's growing national power and perceived regional aspirations and thus required reassurance. In addition, such undertakings also derived from a desire to address specific common nontraditional security problems in sensitive border areas such as Central Asia.

In this effort, China has focused primarily on bilateral and multilateral economic, security, and diplomatic undertakings that emphasize confidence building, mutual benefits, and noninterference in internal affairs. Examples of this aspect of China's regional behavior include:

- a huge increase in the number of official delegations and state visits by senior and midranking Chinese civilian and military officials to the region—to consult on matters of mutual concern, to reassure neighbors that China's economic growth and military modernization do not threaten them, to extract support for China's policies, to develop joint initiatives, and to form trade agreements;
- the dispatch of People's Liberation Army (PLA) personnel to attend security conferences and forums across much of the Asia-Pacific region;
- involvement with other Asian states in search-and-rescue and counter-terrorism operations;
- the receipt of Asian militaries to observe (and participate in) some PLA exercises;
- the establishment of bilateral strategic partnerships with most states along the Chinese periphery (for example, ASEAN, Russia, Japan, South Korea, and India);
- greater involvement in rulemaking and new initiatives regarding APEC, the ARF, the ASEAN Plus Three (APT), the EAS, the Asia Cooperation Dialogue, and initiatives to form a "New Security Policy Conference" in 2003;[34]
- the signing of a "Declaration of Conduct" with ASEAN regarding territorial claims and military activities in Southeast Asia and an agreement on the voluntary notification of any joint/combined exercises conducted in the South China Sea, with limited progress toward negotiation of a more binding "Code of Conduct";[35]
- the completion of a Joint Declaration on Non-Traditional Security Concerns (piracy, antiterrorism, and so on), as part of the ASEAN Plus China and APT forums;
- the signing of agreements endorsing common principles of equality, mutual respect, and development (such as the China ASEAN Joint Declaration on Strategic Partnership for Peace and Prosperity and ASEAN's Treaty of Amity and Cooperation);

- strong support for "on-the-side" summit-level meetings with Japan and South Korea during APT meetings; and
- significant involvement in the formation or development of new multilateral security-related organizations, such as the 6PT and the SCO.

In addition to (and partly as a result of) such political and security-oriented undertakings, Beijing has also worked energetically to facilitate the expansion of trade and investment with many Southeast Asian nations in particular. In 2009, China became ASEAN's largest trading partner, and in 2010, ASEAN became China's third-largest trading partner after the European Union and the United States and ahead of Japan, with total annual bilateral trade reaching nearly $300 billion. Moreover, beginning in January 2010, large levels of China–ASEAN trade became duty free, as part of the unfolding China–ASEAN Free Trade Area. The flow of foreign direct investment to and from ASEAN has also continued to increase significantly in recent years. (See chapter 5 for further discussion of the increasing economic interlinkages between China and ASEAN.)[36]

Those Chinese multilateral activities of greatest significance for U.S. political and security policies arguably include Beijing's involvement in the SCO, the EAS, and the APT, none of which included the United States until it became engaged in the EAS in 2010 and 2011. Although the SCO is not a military alliance, some of its members, including China, have engaged in joint military exercises, and Uzbekistan, Kyrgyzstan, and Tajikistan (supported by China and Russia) called for the United States to set a deadline for troop withdrawal from Central Asia at an SCO meeting in 2005, as mentioned above.[37] Moreover, China supposedly supported Uzbekistan's subsequent expulsion of U.S. forces, and some statements made at past SCO summits have been "viewed as thinly veiled swipes at Washington."[38]

In addition, Washington was denied a request for observer status to the SCO in 2005. Finally, the SCO signaled its desire to include Iran in its multilateral framework by inviting Iranian president Mahmoud Ahmadinejad to its Shanghai summit in 2006. Though it is unclear whether China initiated this invitation, China's leadership role on the SCO would have allowed it to weigh in on the decision.[39] Such actions have caused some observers to believe that the SCO has developed into an anti–United States coalition.[40]

In reality, as suggested above, the SCO has thus far primarily been a discussion forum with rather poorly defined security and economic elements. The joint military exercises and other-military-related activities of SCO members are more symbolic than a genuine demonstration of a shared capacity and commitment to address common military threats, and they have declined in size and scope in recent years. In general, on most critical issues, SCO members act more on an individual basis, in accord with their respective national interests, than collectively via the SCO, with many smaller members (and Central Asian states in general) viewing China as a useful counterweight to overbearing Russian influence. In addition, China wants the SCO to play a much stronger economic role, whereas Russia wishes to use it to augment its security role, reflecting these two countries' comparative advantages in Central Asia. These competing objectives have clashed in recent meetings. Moreover, some observers see the SCO as a declining organization, in light of its failure to support Russia's stance on the Georgia issue and the growing emphasis among its members on bilateral arrangements in many areas.[41]

Although Beijing has arguably worked quietly at times (with uncertain results) to undermine any long-term U.S. military presence in the region, it has thus far avoided directly challenging that presence. China's primary focus in Central Asia and within the SCO has been on other issues, particularly counterterrorism, separatism, and the search for stable, long-term energy resources.[42]

East Asian Regionalism

China was originally a strong proponent of the EAS concept, probably to some extent viewing it as a mechanism for the eventual creation of a regional community of purely Asian nations—exclusive of the United States—within which Beijing could exercise significant (if not decisive) leadership. Such an intention sought to build upon the momentum that emerged after the Asian financial crisis of 1997–1998 in favor of organizations such as the APT.[43]

However, as suggested above, the EAS undertaking has not evolved in such a direction. ASEAN has thus far successfully established itself as the lead organizer and host of the EAS, and competition between Beijing and Tokyo over the summit's composition and role has led to the inclusion of Asian democracies (that is, India, Australia, and New Zealand), as well as the United States and Russia starting in 2011, that arguably dilute Beijing's influence. China remains a supporter of the EAS, publicly endorses ASEAN's dominant role within it, and disavows any intention of seizing its leadership. Conversely, the organization has thus far failed to establish itself as the primary mechanism or framework for East Asian community building.

Partly as a result of this development, Beijing has increased its support for the APT as the primary mechanism for the enhancement of a multifaceted Asian dialogue, along with the construction of some type of East Asian community that can together promote greater cooperation on political, security, and economic issues.⁴⁴ China is arguably more active in the APT than it is in any other multilateral Asian organization, and it is the most active member of the group. Beijing reportedly places primary emphasis on the APT because its membership, subject areas, processes, and practical successes thus far clearly indicate that it has a greater potential than any other regional forum or process to become the key mechanism for building a purely East Asian community within which China can exercise a significant role.⁴⁵

In addition, China more generally places a high importance on deepening relations with ASEAN, as reflected in an array of further measures announced by Beijing in the spring of 2009 (including setting up a $10 billion China–ASEAN Fund on Investment Cooperation, extending $15 billion in credit support for ASEAN nations in the next three to five years, and providing a RMB 270 million special aid fund to underdeveloped ASEAN nations) and the proposals for cooperation presented at the annual ASEAN–China (that is, 10+1) leaders' meetings, the most recent of which was held in Vietnam in late October 2010.⁴⁶

At least one Chinese analyst believes that the APT might play a large role in dealing with nontraditional security issues in Asia and eventually perhaps address more "hard security" issues in the region as well, including nonproliferation, peacekeeping, and maritime security. At the same time, Beijing has sought to downplay any fears that it might ultimately "seize the initiative" or "pursue privilege" through the APT, and it has more broadly affirmed its opposition to turning the East Asian region into "an enclosed and exclusive bloc."⁴⁷

Indeed, according to at least one senior Obama administration official, Beijing has conveyed to Washington the notion that "any fundamental dialogue in Asia has to include the United States."⁴⁸ Although one might argue about what exactly constitutes a regional "dialogue" as opposed to a forum or mechanism, such a Chinese stance nonetheless suggests that Beijing is not spearheading efforts to exclude the United States from such regional activities.⁴⁹ Moreover, the U.S.-China Joint Statement issued after President Obama's trip to China in November 2009 expressed the position that "China welcomes the United States as an Asia-Pacific nation that contributes to peace, stability and prosperity in the region," indicating formal Chinese acceptance of the U.S. presence in Asia.⁵⁰ The joint statement issued during President Hu Jintao's state visit to Washington in January 2011 reiterated this language and also affirmed each side's commitment "to work together with other Asia-Pacific countries, including through multilateral institutions, to promote peace, stability, and prosperity," acknowledging the U.S. role in Asian multilateral forums.⁵¹

At the same time, Beijing has indicated publicly that it will work with Tokyo to develop an East Asian Community (EAC) that, as noted above, some observers model on the European Union, thus echoing the concept proposed by former Japanese prime minister Hatoyama. It is possible that such support may have arisen because China supported the preference initially expressed by Hatoyama for a community that does not necessarily include the United States. However, China has not explicitly endorsed the notion that such a community should exclude the United States. It has only indicated that it would want the grouping to promote regional cooperation in energy and the environment.[52]

Moreover, since the time when Hatoyama first presented the idea for an EAC, Japanese officials, including Prime Minister Naoto Kan and former foreign minister Seiji Maehara, have altered the Japanese position, expressing support for U.S. participation in a future EAC.[53] Chinese support for working with Tokyo to develop a regional community to some extent seems to represent a shift from competition with Japan on this issue. In the view of some analysts, this change might reflect a diminution in Beijing's enthusiasm for ASEAN as a leader in regional community building.[54] But the nature and extent of Beijing's relationship to the Japanese proposal remains unclear at this point, given China's ongoing involvement with ASEAN and continued support for the APT (as noted above), and the fact that official Chinese media articles are often critical or cool toward it. Beijing probably regards the regional community-building concept as a worthwhile long-term objective requiring considerable study.

EVALUATION

During the course of at least the past decade, a strong impression emerged among many observers that Beijing had in general been far more active and successful than Washington in promoting and developing both bilateral and multilateral political, economic, and security-related interactions, processes, and forums among smaller Asian states, especially in Southeast and Central Asia. This incongruence developed in the late 1990s, and it was amplified during the George W. Bush administration. However, this trend was partially reversed beginning in 2009 and throughout 2010, when the Obama administration reasserted the U.S. presence in Asia and the Chinese committed a series of political and diplomatic blunders (especially in the South China and East China seas) that unnerved its neighbors.

Before this more recent shift, China was viewed in particular as more successful in taking advantage of a general regional trend toward greater levels of interstate cooperation and the formation of Asia-wide structures and processes that offer the prospect of reducing security competition and enhancing the ability to solve common security problems, while in general addressing those economic, political, and social issues that most concern the region's governments and populations. Some have associated these trends with the emergence of a new Asian order that is less deferential to the power and preferences of "outside" powers such as the United States.

Specifically, the United States was viewed by many as excessively focused, during the Bush administration in particular, on narrower, parochial concerns connected with counterterrorism and counterproliferation, and in general wedded more to Cold War–era bilateral alliance relationships than to the advancement or creation of those existing or new multilateral forums that can best address regional political, economic, and social trends. As a result, for some observers, Beijing was seen as having gained greater influence among such powers relative to Washington, while in general conveying a basic impression that it was gradually emerging as the dominant power in the Western Pacific.[55]

The overview given above of U.S. and Chinese policies and actions in this arena in the first several years of the twenty-first century suggests that there is some truth to the notion that Beijing was able to increase its influence relative to Washington among smaller states and within multilateral venues through a very extensive set of activities centered on promoting positive-sum political, economic, and defense interactions and efforts to reassure other states of China's overall benign intentions. To some extent, such activism, combined with Washington's distractions and focus on combating terrorism, caused many Asian and outside observers to conclude that the United States was "out of step" with many trends in the region and generally "outmaneuvered" by Beijing.[56] The global financial crisis that struck in 2008 also heightened concerns in Asian nations that the United States would become mired in domestic political and economic troubles and could not be relied upon as a growth engine in Asia.[57]

However, this overview also suggests that, in the past few years, U.S. policies in this area in support of multilateral political and security-related forums and institutions have demonstrated greater sensitivity and adaptability, presumably in part under pressure from China's successes and in response to the preferences of other Asian states. As indicated above, the Obama administration in particular is taking a more active, broad-based stance toward the region. More important, it is incorrect to conclude that China is in some sense overtaking or displacing the United States or otherwise undermining vital U.S. interests as a result of its actions in this area. There is little evidence of such a fundamental shift.

Moreover, even during the Bush administration, despite signs of neglect or misplaced emphases, the United States generally sustained a high level of political and security-related involvement in the region on a bilateral basis, especially in the area of defense relations. Also, as Robert Sutter convincingly argues, the United States maintains an enormous presence in the Asia-Pacific region through many nongovernmental groups and, equally important, continues to be regarded by most Asian elites as highly influential and critical to their most vital interests. They view a continued high level of U.S. political, economic, and security engagement in Asia as largely indispensable for their security and prosperity, particularly in light of China's growing global presence. At the same time, most Asian leaders would like Washington to deal with Beijing as a responsible stakeholder and not as an adversary, and they would not welcome any effort to force smaller powers to take sides or to play China off against other larger regional powers such as India.[58]

While expressing concern about Washington's relative neglect of multilateral forums and excessive emphasis on terrorism, many Asian elites have also continued to recognize that the American military presence, and U.S. bilateral security alliances in particular, continue to serve essential "hard" security functions that cannot be provided by multilateral forums of any type. In addition, as Sutter points out, despite a rapidly expanding level of involvement in Asian meetings and forums and the issuance of numerous agreements and statements, China has "remained reluctant to undertake significant costs, risks, or commitments in dealing with difficult regional issues."[59]

These views accord with the view of a strong majority of those current and former officials interviewed for this study. These individuals view multilateral interactions as reinforcing channels and structures to a foundation centered on U.S. bilateral security alliances. For them, multilateral interactions provide a sense of inclusiveness and help build habits of trust and cooperation in many areas, especially regarding common problems such as economic instability and nontraditional security threats. But they cannot replace bilateral alliances, which provide "hard" security assurances that allow both allies and other smaller countries to engage in multilateral interactions with confidence while forgoing recourse to expensive and destabilizing external balancing efforts.

Conversely, Beijing's increasingly active role in developing multilateral structures and processes in Central and East Asia arguably reduces the likelihood that Asian states will support any future efforts by the United States or others to contain China's growing political, economic, and security presence in the region. In fact, on balance, it is possible that some states view China as more actively contributing to positive-sum approaches to regional stability and security than the United States. Indeed, to *optimistic* observers both in and outside Asia, China's growing

involvement in multilateral venues suggests Beijing's acceptance of cooperative security norms, confidence-building measures, enhanced transparency, and
preventive diplomacy as a means of constraining power rivalries and potential
crises in that region and maximizing the conditions for mutual economic growth.
Thus, for many such observers, Beijing's increasingly collaborative interactions
with the region (and particularly with close U.S. friends and allies) demonstrate
that China is at present a status-quo-oriented power and an increasingly responsible strategic actor.[60]

Yet China has not given up its extensive claim to islands and waters in the
South China Sea also claimed by several Southeast Asia nations, it has not legally
bound itself never to use force to resolve these disputes, and it is opposed to
efforts by outside states to interfere directly in the issue. And the same holds
true for China's disputes with Japan and South Korea in the East China Sea and
elsewhere.[61] Indeed, in 2009 and 2010, China became more assertive toward its
claims in virtually all these areas, and it conducted extensive military exercises,
thus promoting significant levels of concern among many of the region's states,
and also the United States. (See chapter 4 for the details on this greater assertiveness, and a more detailed overall discussion of China's claims in Southeast
and East Asia, from a military security perspective.) Moreover, although Beijing
has undertaken a wide variety of positive actions toward East Asia, the potential
for strategic rivalry or confrontation over the region (and especially regarding
Southeast Asia) with India, Japan, and the United States doubtless remains. As
Evan Medeiros argues, China's overall diplomacy toward the region has produced mixed success at best in reassuring the region about its long-term intentions, and in some cases (for example, with regard to territorial disputes in
the South China Sea and the East China Sea) has produced new concerns and
tensions.[62]

In addition, China almost certainly continues to regard multilateral, security-
related forums as *potential* mechanisms for reducing the region's reliance on the
United States–centered bilateral alliance system and a possible means of establishing an intra-Asian community that is less subject to U.S. influence.[63] That said,
China also realizes that it would likely threaten its gains in the region if it were
to attempt to compel multilateral forums and individual Asian states to weaken
their political or security arrangements with the United States, and recently it
has in fact backed away from such apparent efforts. Whether such a calculation
will prevail over the long term if China acquires much greater leverage over these
states is impossible to say at present. But this overall situation clearly suggests
the need for Washington to focus more closely on political and security-related
multilateral activities in Asia.

UNITED STATES–CHINA BILATERAL POLITICAL AND SECURITY-RELATED DISCUSSIONS

During several administrations, the United States has utilized a variety of official and semiofficial dialogues, forums, and working groups to exchange views and discuss solutions to common problems with China on important policy-related issues, in both security and non-security-related fields. However, the George W. Bush and Obama administrations have arguably conducted the largest number and most extensive, regular, and authoritative exchanges with China to date. By the end of the Bush administration, Washington had approximately sixty discussions under way with Beijing, covering subjects ranging from aviation to counterterrorism to food safety to nonproliferation and including senior Cabinet officials, diplomats and military officers, and working-level technical experts.[64]

In the areas of political and security affairs, the most important exchange during the Bush administration was the Senior Dialogue. This regular discussion—initiated in mid-2005 between U.S. Deputy Secretary of State Robert Zoellick and Chinese Executive Vice Foreign Minister Dai Bingguo—was designed to provide a forum for the exchange of views on short-, medium-, and long-term political and security issues that bear on the functioning of the global system, including energy security, pandemic disease and terrorism, the political and security situations in Iraq and Afghanistan, United Nations reform, and nuclear weapons proliferation with regard to Iran and North Korea. Such discussions focused not only on how to improve bilateral interactions in these and other areas but also on how to develop common approaches to those regional and global problems that confront many nations in regions such as Africa, Latin America, and East, South, and Central Asia. In January 2008, military officials were involved in the discussions for the first time, and military-political security matters were a primary topic.

As part of this effort, the Senior Dialogue during the Bush era included regular subdialogues between Washington's regional assistant secretaries of state and China's assistant foreign ministers. Closely related to the Senior Dialogue was a vice ministerial–level United States–China Security Dialogue that focused on strategic security, nonproliferation, arms control, and international and regional security issues. Under Bush, this dialogue was led on the U.S. side by the undersecretary for arms control and international security at the Department of State and included both diplomatic and military representatives. A second strategic-oriented dialogue involved military officials on both sides and focused solely on nuclear strategy. It was initiated by the U.S. side and announced by President Bush and President Hu in April 2006. The goal of this dialogue was to increase

understanding of each other's nuclear doctrines, including the roles and capabilities of both offensive and defensive strategic systems. However, it appears
that only one such dialogue was ever held, in April 2008.[65]

From the U.S. perspective, these dialogues, and the Senior Dialogue in particular, were part of a broader effort to enhance cooperation, reduce misunderstandings, build trust, and generally advance China's role as a "responsible stakeholder"
in the global order.[66] Taking these functions in turn, during the Bush administration, the subdialogues of the Senior Dialogue reportedly improved cooperation between Beijing and Washington in handling a variety of common problems
and issues of concern, including Iran, Burma, Sudan, and energy security. And
the defense-oriented Security Dialogue arguably strengthened cooperation in
countering the global threat of nuclear proliferation, while in general it focused
on identifying areas of cooperation and reducing misunderstandings.[67] Arguably,
the most significant accomplishment of the "responsible stakeholder" concept
as envisioned during the Bush era is that it reconfigured the terms of the U.S.
policy debate about China, from a focus on how to deal with Beijing as a potential strategic competitor, to a focus on how to reduce distrust and enhance bilateral cooperation, in part via a process of mutual accommodation. The Bush era
bilateral dialogues certainly supported such a reconfiguration. In addition, the
Senior Dialogue under Bush contributed to some specific achievements, including greater Chinese controls over weapons sales to Iran; the dispatch of PLA
engineering troops to Darfur to build housing, roads, and other infrastructure;
and greater mutual understanding regarding sensitive issues such as Taiwan.[68]

During the final years of the Bush administration, the Senior Dialogue arguably diminished in importance, following Deputy Secretary Zoellick's departure
from the U.S. government. It was to some extent eclipsed by the more complex
and ambitious Strategic Economic Dialogue (SED) with China, led on the U.S.
side by Treasury Secretary Henry Paulson (as an economic activity, the SED
is discussed further in chapter 5). In addition, as indicated in chapter 2, some
knowledgeable observers believe that the "responsible stakeholder" concept and
the accompanying strong emphasis of the Bush administration on bilateral dialogues with China led to an excessive prioritization within the U.S. government
of developing and maintaining cooperative relations with China, at the possible
expense of maintaining strong levels of consultation and trust with close allies
such as Japan. Nonetheless, it seems clear that, at the very least, the Bush strategic dialogues with China created a formal, regularized, high-level channel of
communication between the two nations that provided a groundwork for avoiding future strategic confrontation and enhancing cooperation in resolving critical bilateral and multilateral problems.

During the Obama administration, the Senior Dialogue was merged with the SED and renamed the strategic component of an overall Strategic and Economic Dialogue (S&ED) that is now jointly run by both the State and Treasury departments and convenes, at the leadership level, on an annual basis, and not semiannually, as occurred during the Bush administration.[69] The overall purpose of the S&ED remains essentially the same as the two separate dialogues held during the Bush era (again, the economic track of the S&ED is discussed in chapter 5). The strategic track continues to cover a broad range of political, security, and global issues, as described above.[70] Moreover, the strategic track dialogue again includes a large number of relevant cabinet and subcabinet level officials as well as several working groups on specific topics.[71] However, its leadership has been raised from the deputy secretary of state level (as was the case during the Bush era) to the level of the secretary of state. And it has taken over one major issue that was previously lodged within the SED: the dialogue on energy and climate. It was originally hoped that these changes would ostensibly deepen the attention given to the strategic dialogue within the U.S. government and raise the priority of the energy and climate issue in particular within the larger United States–China relationship.[72] However, contrary to the predictions of at least some U.S. officials, the climate change issue has not yet penetrated the upper reaches of high-level diplomacy at a strategic level.[73]

The first meeting of the S&ED was held in Washington in July 2009, and the second round was held in Beijing in May 2010. In the security arena, the topics covered included primarily the North Korea and Iran nuclear issues, the Afghanistan-Pakistan situation, the ongoing conflict in Sudan, Taiwan, and a variety of topics related to clean energy and climate change. Although representatives of the military were present, there was little substantive discussion of defense-related issues. Moreover, the level of military presence was highly lopsided, with Beijing sending a one-star rear admiral and Washington sending the head of the Pacific Command (a four-star admiral). The United States will reportedly push for a higher level of PLA representation at the next S&ED. (See chapter 4 for a more in-depth discussion of United States–China military-to-military relations.)

Much of the first session was devoted to establishing good working relations and clarifying each side's policies and views, so there were few concrete policy achievements.[74] Nonetheless, it was viewed as a good first step by both sides toward the creation of a comprehensive, regularized mechanism for strategic discussion. This reflects the continuation, under Obama, of the notion that "strategic engagement with China is part of the solution to many of the daunting global and bilateral political and economic challenges."[75] As Secretary Clinton noted in her closing remarks at the 2009 S&ED, "What has taken place over the past two days is unprecedented in United States–China relations. The meetings we have just concluded represent the largest gathering ever of top leaders from our two countries. The range of issues covered was unparalleled. And the result is that we have laid the foundation for a positive, cooperative and comprehensive relationship for the 21st century."[76] The second S&ED focused, in the security arena, primarily on nuclear and energy security issues and produced mainly verbal agreements to cooperate further.[77]

On the negative side, as suggested above, a broadened and arguably higher priority strategic dialogue could convey the impression to U.S. allies and friends (such as Japan and India) that Washington is placing primary emphasis on relations with Beijing (that is, forming a primary "strategic partnership") to address a host of regional and global issues. In addition, the reduction in frequency of the S&ED to an annual event could reduce the effectiveness of the enterprise, unless the dialogue's subordinate working groups are able to maintain momentum and create more productive agendas.[78] Also, the perceived success of the S&ED might decrease the possibility that China will take actual steps to constructively cooperate. As with much of Chinese diplomacy, the high-profile nature of the dialogue might become an end to itself in some respects and thereby give the Chinese less incentive to work toward tangible outcomes. This view is apparently held by some former U.S. officials.

FUTURE TRENDS

The capacity of the United States to sustain or expand its multilateral, China-related political and security relations in Asia and elsewhere, as with its overall regional profile, will depend on a wide variety of factors. Among these, the most important are arguably bilateral and multilateral economic trends; the likely evolution of regional political, economic, and security-related institutions; the future capabilities and views of major regional powers such as Japan; and the overall attractiveness of China's "soft power." The following discussion attempts to assess the likely future trends that could emerge in each of these critical areas.

China's Growing Economic Influence and the "Beijing Consensus"

From a broad economic perspective, there is little doubt that intraregional trade and investment patterns are growing steadily across Asia. Intra-Asian trade has now reached $1 trillion annually and accounts for over 50 percent of Asia's total trade, making it one of the world's most economically integrated regions. As explained in chapter 5, a complex production network accounts for much of this growing interlinkage.[79]

This trend is likely to continue during the current decade. Indeed, the current global economic slowdown could accelerate it, as declines in Western demand for Asian imports compel regional powers to trade and invest more with one another.[80] According to HSBC, Asia's intraregional trade during this decade is projected to increase at a rate that is two-thirds higher than its trade growth with the United States. The implementation of various regional free trade areas throughout Asia in the next several years will probably also reinforce this trend.[81]

In contrast, some analysts argue that the recession induced drop in Western demand for Asian exports will inevitably lead to "excess industrial capacity, financial difficulties for businesses, and rising unemployment throughout Asia" unless Asian leaders act vigorously in the near to medium term to "reduce trade imbalances, promote domestic consumption, and develop social safety nets."[82]

However, this view apparently remains in the minority, because few signs have emerged thus far to suggest that Asia is taking such a downward path. Indeed, it is possible that China's relatively rapid and (thus far) durable recovery from the recession (see chapter 5) is facilitating a transition by the rest of the region toward greater levels of intraregional trade and investment. Thus, as indicated above, if current trends continue, many observers believe that the global economic center of gravity will shift decisively toward Asia.[83]

Even more important, China's significance as both an economic and political power within the region is expected to increase commensurately as a central part of this shift. As Ikenberry states: "China's extraordinary economic growth and active diplomacy are already transforming East Asia, and future decades will see even greater increases in Chinese power and influence."[84]

Overall, a majority of so-called strategic elites in nine Asia-Pacific nations (the United States, Japan, South Korea, China, Thailand, Indonesia, India, Australia, and Singapore) polled in late 2008 stated that China will be the strongest nation in overall power in the Asian region in ten years and would become the most important country to their nation by that time.[85] As a result of such expectations, some observers believe that U.S. regional influence relative to China will probably decline steadily during at least the medium term, although not necessarily in absolute levels.[86]

Some analysts are concerned that China's growing regional and global economic capabilities and presence, its particular approach to economic and social development, its "no-strings-attached" foreign policy, and the significant problems encountered in capitalist democracies as a result of the global recession will combine to strengthen China's appeal across Asia and elsewhere as a specific model for future governance. Some observers have termed China's so-called development model the "Beijing Consensus," in contrast to the "Washington Consensus" concept that has defined the dominant approach to national political, economic, and social development in the post–World War II era.[87]

According to the original proponent of the concept, the Beijing Consensus is characterized by a highly pragmatic, flexible, incremental, and growth-oriented yet equitable approach to economic development that makes little distinction between theory and practice and is "defined by a ruthless willingness to innovate and experiment, by a lively defense of national borders and interests, and by the increasingly thoughtful accumulation of tools of asymmetric power projection."[88]

Others view the Beijing Consensus more narrowly, in largely economic and social terms as the "promotion of economies in which public ownership remains dominant; gradual reform is preferred to 'shock therapy'; the country is open to foreign trade but remains largely self-reliant; and large-scale market reform takes place first, followed later by political and cultural change."[89] One Chinese analyst identifies features of China's "successful" development path that resemble elements of the Beijing Consensus, including the prioritization of economic over political rights; tight state control; a long-term, holistic, and strategic approach to development; and performance-based legitimacy.[90]

The Beijing Consensus is thus seen as rejecting the emphasis of the Washington Consensus on "fiscal discipline, public spending on primary education and health care infrastructure, an increasing tax base, market-based interest rates, exchange rate and trade liberalization, privatization of state enterprises, deregulation, and protection of property rights."[91] In short, it is interpreted as an authoritarian-based economic reform and development approach, standing in opposition to free trade, neoliberal concepts, and U.S. economic and cultural hegemony in general, which is thus a central component of Chinese "soft power."[92] If clearly defined and understood, such a development model could thus increase incentives to resist democratic political reforms in many developing states in Asia and elsewhere while reducing respect for the United States and its economic and diplomatic policies in general, especially in comparison with those promoted by China.[93]

However, many analysts argue that it is far from clear that the so-called Beijing Consensus has much real content or actual influence on other states. In fact, some insist that no such model exists as a coherent, integrated approach to social and economic development.[94] Others argue that China's authoritarian and repressive political system will limit its external influence as a model, regardless of how successful its economic policies prove to be.[95] Some experts have even challenged whether the more statist elements of China's development approach have actually been the source of its rapid development, and question whether they will prove sustainable. A study by MIT professor Yasheng Huang concluded that "China has performed the best when it has pursued liberalizing, market-oriented economic reforms, as well as conducted modest political reform, and moved away from statist policies."[96] And some Chinese argue that China should not and does not advocate the adoption by other countries of the Chinese approach to development; these observers maintain instead that "every country has the right to build and work out its own state system and development path in accordance with its own national conditions and in the light of advanced international experience."[97] And yet, as Chestnut and Johnston observe, the concept nonetheless serves a useful purpose for Chinese nationalists hoping to claim a difference between U.S. hegemony and China's rise—one reactionary, one progressive—without seriously examining the precise degree of this alleged difference.[98]

Moreover, other observers argue that, from a global perspective if not within parts of Asia, the United States will almost certainly remain a major model of successful development and, in combination with other democracies, maintain a clear level of political and economic predominance for some time to come, given its substantial material, human, and other resources and advantages. As Heinrich Kreft states: "The geographical dimensions of the United States, its material resources and human capital, its military strength and economic competitiveness as well as its liberal political and economic traditions, are the ingredients of superiority. It has the capacity to heal its own wounds like no other country."[99]

In fact, some polling suggests that most Asian publics regard the United States as far stronger than any other Asian nation in terms of "soft power." As Minxin Pei observes, according to a poll of soft power in Asia conducted in early 2008 by the Chicago Council on Global Affairs, "only 10 percent of Japanese, 21 percent of South Koreans, and 27 percent of Indonesians said they would be comfortable with China being the future leader of Asia." Even Chinese respondents demonstrated consistently positive attitudes toward U.S. influence in Asia. And there are few indications that this attitude is expected to change during this decade, especially relative to China.[100] It is also important to note that Chinese observers tend to overestimate China's global image and influence. One study found that a much larger percentage of Chinese regard China's role in the world more positively than do the citizens of most other countries.[101] These public opinion trends have persisted despite the difficulties imposed by the global financial crisis, which arguably has had a larger negative impact on the United States economy than the Chinese economy.[102]

Thus, in general, there is no clear evidence that current trends will result in China becoming an alternative developmental model to the Western democracies. Moreover, there is little if any indication that Beijing is actively promoting the notion of the so-called Beijing Consensus as such an alternative.[103] In fact, Chinese officials reject the idea that China's development approach constitutes a specific model for other nations to emulate, and they seek instead to emphasize the need for each country to develop its own independent and innovative approach to social and economic growth.[104]

Many Asian strategic elites believe that the United States will remain the greatest force for peace in Asia for the indefinite future, despite expectations of a steady shift of power and influence toward China, as noted above.[105] Equally important, some U.S. analysts believe that China's growing regional influence will not necessarily threaten U.S. interests, at least during the medium term.[106] And yet a significant proportion of strategic elites in Asia also believe that China will be the most likely threat to peace and security in the region in ten years, even though others view China as a growing force for peace in the region.[107] Many analysts also express the concern that America's *relative* ability vis-à-vis China to shape events in Asia will diminish during the current decade and beyond, to the detriment of U.S. policy.[108] This belief has arguably increased significantly as a result of the global financial crisis, given Washington's relative failure to rebound from that event, especially in contrast to China's rather rapid recovery. And as indicated elsewhere is this study, most Asian observers want the United States to remain actively engaged in the region, as an economic and political partner and a principal security guarantor and counterweight to a rising China. At the same time, they do not want Washington to confront and contain Beijing.[109]

All in all, though current trends suggest that China's presence and influence in Asia will certainly rise in the context of growing intraregional contacts, there is considerable ambivalence regarding its impact during at least the current decade, and a significant desire and expectation among most U.S. allies that Washington will continue to remain the dominant political (and military) force across the Asia-Pacific region. These sentiments have increased notably in the aftermath of China's increased assertiveness about maritime territorial issues in 2009 and 2010, thus pushing many states closer to the United States. Nonetheless, as Asia—and China in particular—rise in importance both politically and economically, and as Beijing's military capabilities increase, the possibility remains that regional powers could encounter increasing pressures or incentives to establish or alter bilateral or multilateral relationships in ways that might disadvantage the United States and favor China.[110]

Moreover, in the political and economic realms, some observers believe that an increasingly capable Beijing will seek to reshape the rules and institutions of the existing Asian (and larger global) order to more effectively serve its interests, thus creating growing levels of tension and insecurity among other countries. This, in turn, could lead many governments to cooperate to balance against China, or to individually "choose sides" between Beijing and Washington, thus encouraging the emergence of a genuinely adversarial bipolar system in Asia. As we have seen, few, if any governments in Asia desire such an outcome.

Asian Economic Regionalism

The evolution of Asian regionalism, and its relationship to existing bilateral and multilateral political, economic, and security structures and alliances, will exert a significant influence on the relative abilities of the United States and China to shape the future Asian environment.[111] Many observers, including a significant number of Asian elites and officials, believe that there is significant momentum in the region in favor of greater levels of increasingly formal levels of both political and economic integration. This trend is driven not only by greater amounts of intra-Asian trade and investment but also by: the larger process of globalization outlined in the introduction; concerns about both the future impact of a rising China and America's continued political, economic, and security commitment to the region; a perceived lack of genuinely effective, policy-oriented multilateral regional political and economic structures following the Asian financial crisis of 1997–1998; and an overall quest for both security and (paradoxically) national autonomy in the face of uncertainty.[112]

These trends have led to strong expectations among a sizable number of elites regarding the formation of a variety of regional economic institutions by 2020, such as a pan-Asian free trade and investment area, an ASEAN or Asian Economic Community (AEC) (possibly associated with the emergence of a broader and more integrated ASEAN Economic Community or an expanded Trans-Pacific Partnership loosely associated with APEC), an Asian institution to promote financial stability, and a secretariat for economic policy cooperation.[113] In fact, the Asian Development Bank has stated that an economically integrated Asia is indeed possible by 2020, propelled in large part by continued intraregional growth and the activities of ASEAN-related forums.[114]

For some analysts, greater levels of economic interdependence and the associated process of regional economic integration could very likely stabilize the region by restraining the security competition associated with China's growing military and economic capabilities. This would clearly serve long-term U.S. interests in ensuring a secure and stable region.[115]

However, other observers argue that Beijing is already utilizing the trend toward greater economic integration to encourage, deliberately or not, the formation of multilateral political and economic relationships and structures that exclude the United States, weaken the United States–backed international economic order, and thereby generally diminish U.S. influence in Asian affairs. Some observers, such as Fred Bergsten, point to China's ongoing support for a variety of "hands-off, standards-free" foreign aid policies and intraregional economic agreements (such as the China–ASEAN Free Trade Agreement), which allegedly indicates a Chinese preference for more flexible and less demanding regional and bilateral understandings over more demanding, United States–backed international aid and trade agreements based on the WTO, the World Bank, the International Monetary Fund, or APEC.[116] Other observers point to China's strong support for the development of a more robust East Asian monetary fund (the Chiang Mai Initiative) in response to the global economic recession.[117] They suggest that such a fund challenges the United States–led economic order by constituting a more flexible alternative to IMF conditionality and standards, while supposedly providing Beijing with greater voting power over regional financial decisions than Japan.[118]

Moreover, in general, some observers argue that the various bilateral and multilateral regional free trade agreements that have emerged with increasing rapidity (many of which involve China) will increasingly place the United States at a major economic disadvantage in Asia, with eventual adverse implications for the U.S. economy and the willingness and ability of Americans to sustain a high political and security commitment to the region.[119] These analysts, including Evan Feigenbaum, contend that America's aloofness from Asian economic integration is as much or more to blame for this disadvantage as is Chinese economic assertiveness, given that the South Korea–United States Free Trade Agreement has long languished without ratification and the United States has failed to actively pursue trading arrangements in Asia to a sufficient level, despite its initial overtures toward the negotiation of a Trans-Pacific Partnership agreement.[120] However, Yukon Huang, a former World Bank country director for China, provides a caveat to this argument by suggesting that even if the United States does become more engaged in Asian trade agreements, broader economic forces—such as the increasing integration of the assembly trade in Asia—will, over time, continue to gradually lessen U.S. economic influence in the region.[121]

In contrast, some observers seriously doubt that Asia's proliferating agreements and forums can serve as an effective vehicle for enhancing China's regional influence over time, and particularly not at the expense of the United States.[122] In addition, many (though not all) Asian elites still regard the IMF and the WTO as key institutions for managing international financial crises and advancing free trade, respectively.[123] Moreover, if the Korea–United States Free Trade Agreement is ratified in 2011 and the Trans-Pacific Partnership continues to make rapid progress, the United States may be able to regain some lost ground in Asia. Indeed, many observers in both Asia and the United States view such potential agreements (which exclude China) as mechanisms to "balance" or "hedge" against China.[124] In short, there is no clear consensus, and in fact there is considerable doubt, regarding the notion that greater regional economic integration will benefit China over other nations, including the United States.

Asian Political and Security Regionalism

In the political-security sphere, there are currently no strong indicators of trends toward new types of regionalism that could enhance Chinese capabilities and influence at the expense of the United States. There are few signs of either a pan-Asian, inclusive regional structure that could supersede the existing system of "hard" United States–led bilateral security alliances and "soft" multilateral institutions and forums, or new types of Chinese-led alternative political-security structures. As indicated above, neither the APT nor the EAS has yet moved in this direction. And the SCO gives few signs of evolving into the type of cohesive security organization that might rival or undermine U.S. power.

Nonetheless, in response to persistent concerns about growing security competition and a variety of social issues, many Asian elites support the creation of an "East Asia Community" with a broad mandate to promote not only economic ties but also confidence and mutual understanding, conflict prevention and resolution, and universal norms in areas such as governance and human rights. Among the respondents to the 2008 poll by Bates Gill and others at the Center for Strategic and International Studies, Indians and South Koreans expressed the most enthusiasm for such a community, while "American elites demonstrated the least enthusiasm, but were still fairly close to the weighted average in expressing support."[125]

At the same time, some regional strategic elites do not foresee the emergence during this decade and beyond of the type of multilateral security structures that could defend their members against attacks or otherwise serve robust collective security functions. Elites in the largest military powers (the United States, India, and China) express the view that their own militaries would be most effective in preventing a direct attack, whereas Japanese and Korean elites "put far more emphasis on their alliance with the United States than on their own capabilities or regional or global institutions" in providing physical security against attack.[126]

Indeed, for many elites and analysts, United States–led, formal bilateral alliances will continue to serve vital functions for the Asian (and global) systems, especially in the context of a rising China. Among well-regarded national security analysts, G. John Ikenberry perhaps conveys most succinctly the current and likely future benefits of the American-led alliance system:

> First, the "hub and spoke" alliance system provides the political and geographical foundation for the projection of American influence into the region. . . . Second, the bilateral alliances bind the United States to the region, establishing fixed commitments and mechanisms that increase certainty and predictability about the exercise of American power. . . . Third, the alliance ties create channels of access for Japan and other security partners to Washington. . . . Finally, the U.S.-Japan alliance has played a more specific and crucial role—namely, it has allowed Japan to be secure without the necessity of becoming a traditional military power. Japan could be defended while remaining a "civilian power" and this meant that Japan could rebuild and reenter the region without triggering dangerous security dilemmas. . . . It is hard to envisage a wholly new logic of order for East Asia that is equally functional. It is difficult to imagine a peaceful and workable regional system without these bilateral security underpinnings and a continuing hegemonic presence by the United States.[127]

Nonetheless, some observers anticipate that further efforts might be undertaken during this decade to form new trilateral or quadrilateral security arrangements among the major democracies in Asia, including combinations of the United States, Japan, Australia, South Korea, and India.[128] However, the departure from political office of key advocates of the quadrilateral security dialogue in many of the capitals involved (for example, former Japanese prime minister Shinzo Abe), along with persistent concerns about the impact of such an undertaking on Beijing, and the general unwillingness of India to engage in such a security arrangement, make it problematic at best for the foreseeable future.[129] Nonetheless, the Obama administration has indicated a desire to create or expand other, smaller multilateral security structures with America's allies, such as the United States–Japan–Australia Trilateral Strategic Dialogue, and a United States–Japan–South Korea dialogue.[130]

In addition, some in Washington, Tokyo, Beijing, and some outside observers, favor the formation or deepening of one or more non-democracy-based multilateral confidence and security-building mechanisms between the United States, China, and Japan, or the United States, Russia, South Korea, Japan, and China (and possibly India). These institutions would be tasked with strengthening cooperation, increasing understanding, and reducing misperceptions and distrust so as to more effectively address common traditional and nontraditional security problems, such as, possibly, the North Korean nuclear issue, territorial disputes (for example, between China and Japan), energy issues, climate change, and natural disasters, and generally to avoid increasing levels of security competition.[131]

In particular, the Obama administration, in contrast to Bush-era officials, at one time supported Beijing and Tokyo in an effort to create a United States–Japan–China strategic dialogue at the policy planning level. This dialogue was intended to focus initially on coordinating approaches to common, nontraditional security issues such as clean energy and climate change, rather than more sensitive traditional national security issues such as North Korea's nuclear program or maritime territorial disputes.[132] It was envisioned by some as providing a potential basis for a more ambitious, five-party Northeast Asia grouping involving the United States, Japan, China, South Korea, and Russia. Nonetheless, its first meeting, originally planned for July 2009, was postponed due to increased Chinese concerns regarding the reaction of North Korea (following the missile and nuclear tests of spring 2009), along with persistent concerns voiced by South Korea.[133] Both nations apparently feared that the dialogue would inevitably address the North Korean nuclear issue.[134] After the collision of a Chinese fishing boat with a Japanese coast guard ship in fall 2010, the U.S. government again proposed the idea of such a trilateral dialogue. Beijing rebuffed this overture, likely because Washington had recently reiterated its commitment to defend Japan in the event of an armed conflict over the Senkaku/Diaoyu Islands.[135]

As this experience indicates, these so-called minilaterals confront many obstacles. On the one hand, as one former U.S. official has pointed out, they can easily become irrelevant if they do not address difficult and sensitive issues (such as competing Chinese and Japanese territorial claims or Chinese suspicions of the United States–Japan alliance) or do not include those parties that should necessarily participate in discussions of the larger regional security environment (for example, South Korea, Russia, and India). On the other hand, they can also create frustrations, suspicion, and increased tensions if they do attempt to address such tough issues.[136] As the same former U.S. official stated (in the case of the proposed United States–Japan–China dialogue): "Rather than creating yet another trilateral in search of purpose, converting an existing process into a forum that assembles the right players with a modest—but concrete—agenda for Northeast Asia, even if the discussion proves too hard, would have a better chance of producing lasting results."[137] In addition, some Chinese proponents argue that a United States–Japan–China trilateral dialogue can offer the prospect of enhancing security cooperation and mutual trust with Beijing only if the United States–Japan alliance is explicitly reoriented to become purely defensive, focused on nontraditional security issues, and acceptant of China as a cooperative partner—all somewhat unlikely scenarios.[138]

Thus, given the many variations put forth and the political complications accompanying each of them, many observers view the emergence of significant levels of Asian political and security—as opposed to economic—regionalism (that is, those involving multilateral mechanisms designed to deal with traditional or "hard" security problems) as highly uncertain at best, and most likely dependent on the evolution of key geostrategic variables, such as the future state of the Sino-Japanese and Sino-U.S. relationships and the fate of the Taiwan and Korean imbroglios.[139]

If both the latter regional problems were peacefully resolved, and Beijing and Tokyo were to reach a more stable and durable understanding, then it is conceivable that the need or desire for the United States to continue to play a decisive regional role as alliance partner and overall balancer might dissipate in favor of more meaningful types of genuinely broad-based regional security structures. In particular, significant movement toward the handling of the North Korea nuclear issue could facilitate the emergence of a five-power Northeast Asia Security Mechanism. But in the absence of such changes, it is more likely that multilateral dialogues or mechanisms dealing with a variety of "soft," nontraditional security issues will emerge during this decade. For example, in this area, it seems that the United States–China–Japan trilateral dialogue might prove to be the most productive in addressing issues such as climate change, despite its initial false start.

Nonetheless, even with such successes, it is highly possible that enduring variations in the interests and hence the future visions toward the Asia-Pacific region held by the United States, China, and Japan will continue to complicate or even prevent any efforts to develop genuinely cooperative, inclusive security structures. It is quite possible that such undertakings, and the multilateral mechanisms that could conceivably result from them, will simply become further avenues for maneuvering among and between these and other lesser powers.

Thus, in the absence of fundamental changes in the East Asian security environment (and none seem likely at this point), it is almost certain that China's continued rise will pose significant challenges to the United States' effort to encourage greater political and security cooperation across the Asia-Pacific region while maintaining adequate levels of stability through bilateral alliances and a strong regional presence. In particular, the forces driving greater levels of regional economic integration and movement toward more diverse and inclusive types of "soft" political and security-oriented community building will likely interact with (1) U.S. and allied efforts to sustain the vitality of the American-led "hard" security-oriented alliance system and (2) Chinese attempts to create a more favorable (and perhaps deferential) regional economic and political order designed to bring about continued adjustments (including, in some cases, possible weakenings) in both multilateral structures and bilateral alliances.

Reinforcing this potentially conflictual dynamic are the likely contrasting visions held by the United States and China regarding the type of power distributions and architecture that can best maintain peace, stability, and prosperity in the region over the long term. Although, as indicated in chapter 1, the two countries certainly aspire toward many of the same goals for the region and beyond—that is, they both favor cooperative political and diplomatic relations among the major powers, growing levels of largely capitalist-oriented economic interaction, and a variety of confidence-building security dialogues and contacts—they also to some extent hold divergent assumptions and expectations regarding the best means to achieve these goals. In particular, despite official public statements that suggest otherwise, China remains highly suspicious of (if not opposed to) the United States' commitment to the maintenance of its predominant military and political positions and relationships in the Western Pacific. At the same time, according to many Chinese and non-Chinese analysts alike, Beijing is likely to remain highly focused on a growing array of domestic challenges that will serve to moderate its approach to a new security architecture in Asia.[140]

04

MILITARY DEPLOYMENTS AND RELATIONS

<hr>

The United States regards military power as an essential element of its national strategy, as was indicated in the introduction and chapter 1. Moreover, since the end of World War II, Washington has viewed the maintenance of its predominant military power in maritime Asia as key to the attainment of its objectives in that critical region of the globe. With regard to China in particular (and, most important in the twenty-first century, a rising China with growing power projection capabilities), U.S. military instruments serve several crucial purposes: to facilitate Beijing's integration into cooperative security-oriented processes and behaviors that are compatible with overall American interests (for example, via military deployments, diplomacy, and dialogues); to reassure the other Asian powers (and in particular America's essential Asian allies and partners) that the United States has the capability and will to protect and advance its political, economic, and security interests and commitments; and to deter Beijing from attempting to use coercive military force to adversely shape or resolve specific disputes with neighboring territories and states, such as Taiwan. In all these areas, U.S. military instruments ideally must complement and support other political, economic, social, and diplomatic instruments of U.S. policy, and thus strike the optimal balance between cooperative engagement and deterrence.

POLICY APPROACHES

Obviously, a wide range of potential U.S. defense-centered policies and behaviors could be employed to address these military-related objectives toward China, involving varying configurations of military systems and different military or diplomatic strategies. Indeed, within U.S. policy circles, there is significant discussion and debate about priorities, emphases, and approaches, both at the broad military strategic level and with regard to specific policies and tactics. However, much of this debate involves elements of two alternative strategic approaches: a hard-line realist approach, and a more moderate approach.

A Hard-line, Zero-Sum Strategy

For some U.S. policy observers and participants—including some analysts and decisionmakers in the U.S. military, in the intelligence community, and in private (often conservative) research institutes and defense industry corporations—the deterrence side of U.S. security policy should constitute the core of a basic military approach that treats China as an actual or likely adversary. These individuals point to China's ambitious military modernization program, along with its supposed efforts to reduce U.S. influence in various regional multilateral forums and organizations, as providing prima facie evidence of Beijing's intent to achieve military and political predominance in the Asia-Pacific region, at the expense of the United States. For these observers, China is thus fully engaged in an intense zero-sum strategic competition that directly challenges American interests.[1]

This argument rests on—or is reinforced by—two basic assumptions. The first is that the United States must continue to convey both the perception and the reality that it possesses the ability to deter or defeat, through clearly superior military capabilities, any conceivable attempt by China to (1) threaten or employ force against other Asian powers deemed strategically significant by the United States; or (2) more generally undertake military actions that appear to call into question or eclipse U.S. military predominance. The second assumption flows directly from the preceding one: The capabilities of the People's Liberation Army (PLA) that are designed to reduce or eliminate China's vulnerability to America's most potent weapons systems in Asia (for example, carrier battle groups, long-range aircraft, space-based intelligence, surveillance, and reconnaissance platforms, and information warfare capabilities) convey an *offensive intention* behind China's strategy, and hence are not designed merely to achieve more limited deterrence objectives, such as preventing U.S. support for Taiwan independence, or to counter direct threats to the Chinese homeland. Thus, not only are "worst case" motives (for example, regional dominance) imputed to China, but also potential "worst case" military behavior (conflict), which could lead "worst case" outcomes (U.S. defeat) to be placed front and center as the standard for America's response to China's military buildup. Hence, this viewpoint implies that China's acquisition of military capabilities (again, primarily maritime, air, and space) must be neutralized by whatever means necessary, presumably short of outright war.

In some instances, such assumptions regarding Chinese intentions are reinforced by references to the authoritarian nature of the government of the PRC. Given its political makeup (and the confrontational history of Sino-American relations during much of the Cold War), the Chinese government is viewed by these advocates as essentially hostile to the United States as a democratic power, and discontent with anything less than the attainment of a position of predominance in the Asia-Pacific region. Some observers will also invoke Chinese history to support this argument, asserting that, whether democratic or not, China will seek to reestablish its alleged historical position as a hegemonic imperial power exercising control over the region.[2]

Several conclusions are usually drawn from these hard-line arguments regarding U.S. defense policy toward China. First, advocates in this camp argue that it is naive and dangerous for the U.S. government to think that it can persuade or entice Beijing to give up its pursuit of strategic predominance in the Asia-Pacific region. As has been indicated, from this perspective, China is a rising imperial power that will settle for nothing less than military and political preeminence in Asia and perhaps globally as well. Hence, this viewpoint either assumes that the Chinese are not interested in any meaningful discussion aimed at averting an increasingly confrontational strategic rivalry through mutual accommodation or insists that such a dialogue has already been attempted and failed, largely because Beijing has thus far refused to engage meaningfully on the issue. Indeed, some observers believe that attempts to soften or eliminate China's presumed strategic objectives through such efforts are dangerous because they will produce a false sense of security and potentially cause the United States to avoid undertaking the necessary military and political responses to the growing threat.

Second, proponents of this viewpoint argue that the most effective means of addressing China's military buildup are, first and foremost, to increase U.S. defense spending and/or force deployments in Asia significantly beyond current or planned levels; to encourage or pressure America's allies to strengthen their military capacity to counter China; to adopt reinforcing political and diplomatic strategies designed to raise concerns among other countries about China's destabilizing behavior; and to undertake economic and other measures designed to weaken China's capacity to acquire or deploy a more capable military. In other words, Washington's security strategy toward Beijing should focus almost entirely on enhancing deterrence and undermining Chinese power through a variety of military and nonmilitary means. This viewpoint presupposes a process of intensifying the strategic rivalry between the United States and China that can only be effectively managed through a primary reliance on Cold War–style approaches.

From this perspective, approaches that center on military dialogue, confidence-building measures, and an overall attempt to deepen cooperation in order to solve problems and reduce distrust or "worst case" thinking are usually viewed as, at best, of secondary or tertiary importance to deterrence-based countermeasures. At times, proponents of this viewpoint will acknowledge that the pace and scope of China's military buildup might be ameliorated through dialogue and positive incentives. However, such actions are often viewed as being effective only on the margins. Though they might avert a major conflict, they will not avoid an intensifying process of strategic confrontation leading to a virtually inevitable cold war and perhaps eventually military conflict, unless there is a major change in the military and political behavior and makeup of the PRC regime.[3] Indeed, many proponents of this viewpoint assume that the United States is already in a de facto cold war–type situation with China in the military-security arena. Hence, for many advocates, intensifying Sino-U.S. strategic rivalry can be avoided only if China falls into serious internal political and social disarray, or is defeated in combat.

A Moderate Strategy of Engagement

Although this hard-line perspective is certainly present in some quarters of the U.S. government, interviews and other research conducted by the author suggest that it does not predominate among senior civilian (and many, if not most, military) decisionmakers. As America's overall strategy clearly indicates, most U.S. leaders reject the notion that Beijing and Washington are already deeply engaged in a purely zero-sum strategic rivalry centered on political-military moves and countermoves in the Asia-Pacific region and beyond. They do not assume that Beijing is determined to eject the United States from the region, and they appear to recognize that both nations—not just the Chinese—could create a self-fulfilling hostile relationship through their own actions. To the contrary, they believe that the Chinese leadership recognizes the huge cost to China's national goals that will result from efforts to confront the U.S. militarily (and otherwise), and thus has strong incentives to resolve problems through negotiation. Hence, advocates of a moderate approach recognize the need to maximize incentives on both sides to cooperate while retaining the ability to counter possible aggressive military and political actions by Beijing. In short, they grasp the highly contingent nature of current strategic relations between America and China, as reflected in the two-sided objectives behind America's grand strategy explained in chapter 1.[4]

Equally important, many supporters of this perspective also to some extent remain confident that both U.S. military and political predominance in maritime Asia is not being fundamentally eroded by China (more on this point below).[5] This attitude reflects the findings of U.S. public opinion polls, which seem to suggest that, though many Americans regard the PRC government with considerable coolness or suspicion (and perhaps some hostility), a clear and steady majority have for many years supported cooperation and constructive engagement with China rather than any efforts at containment.[6] As a result of this prevailing moderate perspective, U.S. administrations have attempted to utilize military deployments, exercises, and diplomatic relations to strike the proper balance between cooperative engagement and deterrence or dissuasion in attaining America's objectives vis-à-vis China. That said, the proponents of the hard-line approach outlined above remain an important force in some U.S. policy circles. Indeed, their influence is possibly growing in some quarters, perhaps partly in response to the contrasting images of a militarily growing China and an economically troubled America.

U.S. MILITARY DEPLOYMENTS AND STRATEGIC POSTURE

During the past ten to fifteen years, as a central part of its effort to achieve its strategic goals of deterrence and reassurance, the United States has systematically and steadily enhanced its overall military capabilities and influence in the Asia-Pacific region.[7] This effort has centered on the deployment of additional naval and air weapons platforms to the region, the holding of regular exercises and patrols (often with allies and friends), some diversification of the U.S. structure of military bases, an overall strengthening of military alliances and partnership cooperation, and the enhancement of long-range strike capabilities into and within the region. These actions have occurred alongside an effort to realign the U.S. forward military presence in Asia to stress capability over manpower levels and to reduce the U.S. footprint in urban areas.[8] The most notable examples of such activities during this period include

- the permanent deployment to Guam and/or Pearl Harbor of additional attack submarines (including Virginia-class submarines that specialize in shallow water and near-shore operations), long-range strike aircraft and bombers, and Marine units;

- the addition of an aircraft carrier to the Pacific Fleet (now totaling six, more than half the entire U.S. fleet);
- the holding of large-scale military exercises (involving, in some instances, several carriers and the militaries of other Asian nations);
- the deployment to the Pacific of all the U.S. Navy's SM-3 equipped Aegis ships and plans to develop a long-range penetrating bomber with a range beyond those of offshore-based cruise missiles;
- the refitting of some nuclear-armed ballistic missile submarines with long-range conventional cruise missiles (known as submersible, ship, guided, nuclear submarines, that is, SSGNs);
- the improvement of U.S. satellite-based communication, reconnaissance, and surveillance systems;
- support for Japan's ongoing military modernization and expansion program (including the sale of new platforms, cooperation in missile defense, and the attainment of greater coordination regarding U.S.-Japanese air and naval operations);
- plans to augment or replace fixed bases with more flexible access arrangements and forward operating bases;
- new levels of cooperation with India regarding space, dual-use technologies, advanced military equipment, joint military exercises, and missile defense (as part of a larger strategic shift toward closer relations with New Delhi);
- the rejuvenation of the U.S.-Philippine alliance and the development of a quasi-alliance with Singapore (including increased ship visits and the location of a naval logistics command);
- revived military-to-military ties with Indonesia and closer security-oriented relations with Malaysia and Thailand (facilitated by cooperation against global terrorism);
- increased military cooperation with Vietnam, including joint military exercises, high-level exchanges, and an annual U.S.-Vietnamese Political, Security, and Defense Dialogue;
- the establishment of a new military command for cyberspace (known as CYBERCOM), to conduct both offensive and defensive computer warfare, presumably including potential operations against nations that possess or are developing robust cyberwarfare capabilities, including China; and
- researching and developing several prompt global strike capabilities (including the X-37 unmanned spacecraft) that could enable the United

States to deliver conventional weapons anywhere in the world within one hour, thus posing clear implications for China.[9]

Some of these capabilities (for example, in the areas of cyberwarfare, enhanced surveillance, and long-range precision strikes) are presumably supportive of a larger Pentagon effort to develop a so-called air-sea battle concept, designed to deter or defeat adversaries equipped with sophisticated antiaccess and area-denial capabilities.[10]

Beyond these largely region-oriented military efforts, the United States has also increased its overall level of military assistance to Taiwan in particular, via increased arms sales (such as those announced in January 2010 worth $6.4 billion—including 114 Patriot missiles, 60 Black Hawk helicopters, Harpoon missiles, and mine-hunting ships), offers to provide unprecedented weapons systems such as submarines, and greater levels of military consultation and advice. The George W. Bush administration steadily increased the level and status of defense contacts with the Taiwanese military and provided more in-depth and systematic assistance in a wide variety of areas, including so-called software assistance related to military organizational and procedural reforms. The Barack Obama administration has also provided additional arms to Taiwan and has repeatedly insisted that it will sustain military assistance to Taipei in the face of Beijing's ongoing military buildup across the Taiwan Strait.[11]

In addition, in the strategic military arena, Washington is undertaking and considering several moves that could affect Beijing's plans and assumptions regarding nuclear deterrence and crisis stability. Specifically, the Obama administration supports significant reductions in the size of the U.S. nuclear arsenal and the role of nuclear weapons in the overall U.S. national security strategy. This move has been connected by Obama to a larger process leading to the eventual elimination of all nuclear weapons worldwide, although few analysts in the West (or China) believe that Washington will make significant and concrete steps in that direction anytime soon.[12] As part of this effort, Washington has signed and ratified a New Strategic Arms Reduction Treaty (START) with Russia to replace the one signed and ratified under President George H. W. Bush.[13] The Obama administration's position also provided the foundation for the most recent Nuclear Posture Review, the quadrennial process that establishes the United States' nuclear policy, strategy, capabilities, and force posture for the next five to ten years. In line with New START, the 2010 review seeks to maintain strategic deterrence and stability with fewer deployed nuclear forces and reaffirms America's desire to pursue high-level bilateral dialogues with China and Russia aimed at developing more stable and transparent strategic relationships.[14]

In addition, the Pentagon conducted its first-ever Ballistic Missile Defense Review in February 2010 to lay out the appropriate role of ballistic missile defense in the national security and military strategies of the United States, provide a strategic context for current and future missile defense program and budgetary decisions, and align the U.S. force structure with national priorities and strategic realities. The review stated that "the threat from short-, medium-, and intermediate-range ballistic missiles (SRBMs, MRBMs, and IRBMs) in regions where the United States deploys forces and maintains security relationships is growing steadily." In response to this trend, the review concluded that "the United States will work with allies and partners to strengthen regional deterrence architectures, pursue a phased adaptive approach to missile defense within each region that is tailored to the threats and circumstances unique to that region, and develop capabilities that are mobile and re-locatable." Regarding China, the review stated a desire to "seek further dialogue on strategic issues of interest to both nations, including missile defense," while announcing increased funding for regional missile defense systems, and for the protection of U.S. forces and U.S. allies and partners such as Japan.[15]

Another U.S. move of relevance to China is the Obama administration's enunciation of a new U.S. National Space Policy in June 2010, along with the completion of the first-ever Space Posture Review, conducted by the Department of Defense and the intelligence community as mandated by the FY09 Defense Authorization Act, which resulted in a new National Security Space Strategy in January 2011. Alongside commitments to expand cooperation and transparency in undertaking a wide variety of space activities, Obama's space policy reiterates the long-standing U.S. intent to utilize space to enhance the ability to "identify and characterize threats" and to "deter, defend, and if necessary defeat efforts to interfere with or attack U.S. or allied space systems." However, both the president's space policy and the space strategy apparently indicate a greater willingness than expressed during previous U.S. administrations to consider space-related arms control accords. Both documents state that the United States "will consider proposals and concepts for arms control measures if they are equitable, effectively verifiable, and enhance the national security of the United States and its allies." This is a modest step in the direction of future discussions with China and other space-faring powers on possible limits on the use of space for military purposes. Yet as some observers attest, Washington is more likely to explore possible confidence-building measures in this area than a treaty banning weapons in space.[16]

These developments pose several issues of direct and indirect relevance to China, involving (1) changes in U.S. nuclear doctrine away from the pre-Obama stance of "calculated ambiguity" regarding the use of nuclear weapons, and toward some version of a Chinese-style no-first-use policy; (2) likely increased efforts to bring China into future nuclear arms reductions talks; (3) an increasing emphasis on regional and national ballistic missile defense systems for the United States and its allies; and (4) a greater willingness to consider possible international agreements or understandings on the military use of space. The first change arguably provides some level of reassurance to Beijing regarding Washington's disinclination to level nuclear threats at China during a crisis. The second change portends possible future pressure on Beijing to become more transparent regarding its nuclear weapons program. The third change could exacerbate Chinese concerns regarding the impact of U.S. missile defense activities on China's strategic deterrent vis-à-vis the United States and Japan.[17] And the fourth change could encourage some Chinese observers to think that Washington might engage in a future dialogue regarding the banning of weapons in space, as advocated by the PRC government.[18]

Military-to-Military Relations and Technology Transfers

While recent U.S. administrations have been increasing military engagement, deterrence, and reassurance capabilities in Asia, they have also at times sought to enhance direct interaction with the Chinese government and military. During the George W. Bush and Obama administrations, this has primarily consisted of efforts:

- To increase the scope and tempo of Sino-U.S. military-to-military contacts, including several Defense Consultative Talks (the top-level defense interactions between the U.S. and Chinese militaries), Defense Policy Coordination Talks, and coordination under the Military Maritime Consultative Agreement,[19] as well as reciprocal visits by high-level defense officials and officers, and functional contacts in the areas of military medicine, officer exchanges, and policy and operational dialogues.[20]
- To engage China in direct joint military exercises involving such issues such as humanitarian aid and disaster relief.
- To publish regular Defense Department reports assessing PRC military capabilities, strategy, and doctrines.
- To repeatedly emphasize the need for Beijing to be more transparent about the motives, pace, directions, and ultimate purpose of its military buildup.[21]

Washington has also undertaken strong efforts to control or curtail specific types of military-to-military contacts, along with the sale or transfer to China of many types of advanced weapons, military technologies, and dual-use products by both U.S. and foreign corporations and some foreign governments, especially items that could significantly affect military stability across the Taiwan Strait. The former effort has included legal proscriptions by the U.S. Congress on the discussion of defense strategies, weapons systems, and other relevant military topics with members of the Chinese military, as expressed primarily in the 2000 Defense Authorization Act.[22] The latter effort has at times involved very tense political interactions with potential or actual military suppliers to China such as the members of the European Union and the Russian government.[23] It has also generated intense debate in the United States about technology transfers. In this debate, there are basically two camps, "those that want to liberalize controls in order to promote exports and grow economic opportunity, and those who believe that further liberalization may compromise national security goals."[24]

Finally, it should be noted that both Washington and Beijing have at times suspended military-to-military contacts in response to severe disruptions in the overall relationship, beginning with the U.S. suspension in contacts following the Tiananmen Square incident in 1989.[25] Chinese officials have also at times enumerated obstacles to the development of a strong military-to-military relationship between the United States and China.[26] Recent efforts undertaken to strengthen that relationship are presumably partly intended to reduce if not eliminate such disruptions.

CHINA'S MILITARY DEPLOYMENTS AND STRATEGIC POSTURE

These U.S. military activities have taken place partly in response to Chinese actions and as part of the overall U.S. desire to shape the security environment in the Asia-Pacific region. Since at least the mid-1990s, Beijing has undertaken a systematic, well-funded, and focused program of force modernization. As indicated in chapter 1, this effort is directed at strengthening China's capacity to augment its diplomatic and political leverage abroad (in part by building trust with other militaries), to enhance its overall power and image as a great nation, and to protect its expanding foreign economic assets and interests, while generally reducing its vulnerability to future threats to its territory or populace by other nations. Under this strategy, the pace and scope of China's military modernization were originally intended to be gradual, incremental, and focused primarily on overcoming the general obsolescence of the PLA, reflecting the Chinese leadership's view that a major war was unlikely and that Chinese development required a primary emphasis on civilian over military growth.

Since the later 1990s, however, the tempo of China's force modernization program has increased significantly and its focus has sharpened, largely as a result of concerns about increasing U.S. military capabilities (as demonstrated in the two Gulf wars and the Kosovo conflict) and growing tensions over the Taiwan issue.[27] This has included greater efforts to acquire the military wherewithal to deter or if necessary defeat Taiwanese efforts to attain independence, possibly with U.S. support. Most recently, China's force modernization effort has also begun to place a greater emphasis on acquiring more ambitious power projection capabilities beyond Taiwan, apparently for the purpose of conducting various types of area denial and extended presence missions along the littoral of the Western Pacific, and to exert greater influence over disputed territories in areas such as the East China and South China seas (more on these latter points below).[28]

Among these gains, perhaps the most notable systemic advances include

- the downsizing and reorganization of the overall force structure;
- the professionalization of the officer corps;
- the promulgation of new doctrinal regulations that respond to the challenges posed by high-technology warfare;
- the development of more expansive and realistic training regimens;
- the holding of more realistic, complex, and large-scale military exercises (involving "integrated joint operations");
- improvements in logistics, and especially command, control, communications, computers, and intelligence (C4I) capabilities;
- the emergence—after considerable effort and much delay—of a far more capable defense industrial complex possessing research and development and production capabilities; and
- the deployment of increasingly advanced short- and medium-range ground, air, and naval weapons systems.[29]

Regarding the last area, PLA deployments of particular concern to the United States include

- medium-range fourth-generation fighter/interceptors;
- intermediate-range ballistic missiles with high levels of accuracy and sophisticated defense countermeasures;

- sophisticated, largely Soviet-designed antiaircraft missiles with ranges extending well past China's shoreline;
- a large and growing number of conventional attack submarines and (to a lesser extent) surface combatants;
- Improved C4I and carrier detection systems involving ground, naval, air, and space-based assets;
- growing amphibious capabilities and improvements in special operation and reconnaissance forces;
- more sophisticated antisatellite, cyberwarfare, and electronic warfare capabilities; and
- long-range, standoff, antiship weapons, including cruise missiles and anti-carrier torpedoes.[30]

In addition, there is now some evidence that China is moving forward with the development of one or more midsized aircraft carriers and the acquisition of a new range of conventional, offensive-oriented capabilities, including

- a multiregimental military air- and sea-lift capacity;
- a multiregimental amphibious attack capability;
- a demonstrated offshore, medium-range bomber or strike aircraft capability;
- a fifth-generation stealth fighter (that is, the J-XX line, including the Chengdu J-20);[31]
- an operational, inflight refueling capacity for at least 100 aircraft (approximately four regiments);
- the demonstrated ability to mount sustained naval operations;
- the demonstrated ability to deploy special operations force and Marine units beyond China's borders, probably totaling several brigades; and
- the capability to undertake true joint operations or coordinated deployments across military regions.[32]

One should note that, though the above clearly indicates that the PLA has acquired and is attempting to acquire a wide range of conventional military capabilities, it also continues to confront some major obstacles in translating these capabilities into a genuine capacity to conduct warfare against not only a sophisticated opponent such as the United States but also capable U.S. allies such as Japan. First, the PLA has never engaged in combat against an adversary armed with modern weaponry; indeed, it has not conducted a significant military operation of any kind since the Sino-Vietnamese clash of 1979. Only a very few senior PLA officers have combat experience. Second, the PLA enunciated a sophisticated joint warfare doctrine in about 1999 that requires it to conduct military operations of a level of complexity that it has never attempted in the past—that is, mastering this ambitious doctrine involves a very steep learning curve. Indeed, by its own admission, the PLA is still experimenting in training efforts designed to implement its new joint doctrine; some outside observers believe that such efforts are still at the rudimentary stage. Third, the timeline that the PLA has set for attaining its modernization objectives is 2049, thus indicating an awareness of the major challenges it confronts.[33]

In the strategic realm, Beijing has been steadily improving the survivability and potency of its small, retaliatory "countervalue" deterrent nuclear force, largely by developing more reliable, accurate, and road-mobile medium-, intermediate-, and intercontinental-range nuclear-capable ballistic missiles. Some of these missiles are being deployed aboard a new class of nuclear-armed submarines (that is, nuclear strategic ballistic missile submarines, SSBNs). And Beijing is also developing methods to counter ballistic missile defenses. According to many analysts, future Chinese intercontinental ballistic missiles probably will include some with multiple independently targetable reentry vehicles, and the number of nuclear warheads capable of reaching the United States could increase to more than 100 within the next fifteen years.[34] Already in 2002, a monograph published by the RAND Corporation argued that China was close to achieving a much more secure (that is, credible) level of minimal deterrence capability with regard to the continental United States.[35]

An Apparent Antiaccess Strategy and Efforts to Assert Greater Influence over Claimed Territory

In doctrinal terms, from a combat perspective, the weapons systems, resources, and capabilities described above appear, from a U.S. perspective, to be largely oriented toward the acquisition of key elements of a so-called antiaccess/area-denial capability. According to many observers, such a capability presumably includes the eventual ability to conduct integrated offshore offensive and defensive military operations along the littoral of the Western Pacific (presumably extending out approximately 1,500 nautical miles to the so-called first island chain, which includes the Kuril Islands, the main Japanese islands, the Ryukyu Islands, Taiwan, the Philippines, and Indonesia, along with much of the Yellow Sea, the East China Sea, and the South China Sea), strategic deterrence and counterattacks, and long-range precision strikes and sustained operations in distant waters.[36]

This also includes the ability to defend Chinese claims over its territorial waters and within the 200-nautical-mile exclusive economic zone (EEZ). Beijing holds a different interpretation from the United States regarding several provisions of the United Nations Convention on the Law of the Sea (UNCLOS), including those governing "the right to draw straight baselines from which the breadth of the territorial sea is measured, the right to exercise innocent passage through the territorial sea by warships, and the right to conduct military surveillance activities in the . . . EEZ of the coastal state."[37] Most notably, the Chinese government argues that foreign military vessels must provide prior notification before entering an EEZ and that foreign military activities involving hydrography, surveys, and intelligence gathering within the EEZ are illegal because they signify hostile intent and thus violate the "peaceful purposes" provisions of UNCLOS. The United States and an apparent majority of other nations do not accept this interpretation, however, arguing instead that such activities are not hostile and hence are not prohibited under UNCLOS.[38] Unfortunately, the United States remains at a disadvantage in asserting, defending, and interpreting the meaning of UNCLOS for military (and commercial) activities in the EEZ, as well as other maritime issues because the U.S. Congress has thus far failed to ratify UNCLOS.[39]

In addition, some Chinese defense analysts argue, *unofficially*, for China's need to acquire so-called far sea defense (yuanhai fangyu, 远海防御) capabilities emphasizing multidimensional precision attacks beyond the first island chain and operations outside China's EEZ, to defend the PRC's national interests, thereby adding a layer of strategic depth within which to defend China's coastline.[40] Similarly, some Chinese military analysts even express the need for China to reassess its long-standing prohibition on the deployment of combat forces overseas (for purposes beyond so-called "military operations other than war") and the establishment of overseas military bases.[41] And at least some Chinese observers explicitly argue (again, *unofficially*) that China must acquire these capabilities specifically to counter U.S. maritime strategy as it pertains to the Western Pacific. For these analysts, U.S. strategy is not only designed to sustain Washington's conventional maritime hegemony in the region but also to prohibit or restrain China's "core interests" (hexin liyi, 核心利益), including "reunification with Taiwan, assertion of sovereignty over disputed islands, and ultimately some form of sea-lane security and regional maritime influence."[42]

On an *official level*, Beijing has defined its so-called core interests more generally (and vaguely) as comprising three components: (1) the protection of the basic system and national security of the PRC state (维护基本制度和国家安全); (2) the preservation of China's national sovereignty and territorial integrity

(国家主权和领土完整); and (3) the continued stable development of China's economy and society (经济社会的持续稳定发展).[43] Yet Chinese officials and official PRC statements or commentary have not explicitly connected either the concept of China's core interests or the PLA's formal maritime strategy with sea-lane security and the assertion of Chinese sovereignty over disputed islands beyond Taiwan.[44] Nonetheless, whether driven by a notion of core interests or formally included in its maritime strategy, Beijing has certainly given clear signs that it intends to employ its growing offshore military capabilities to support or defend its position vis-à-vis disputed maritime territories in the East China and South China seas and more generally to expand its military presence in the Western Pacific. In recent years, Beijing has shown a greater willingness to assert its claims over territories and waters in the South China Sea, through both diplomatic and military means, including the imposition of an annual unilateral fishing ban (in the northern part of the area), more numerous and regular maritime security patrols (primarily conducted by the Chinese Fisheries Administration), various forms of political and diplomatic pressure (including the detention of Vietnamese fishermen), and the holding of scientific activities and extensive naval exercises in the vicinity.[45] It has also recently increased the tempo and expanded the routes of PLA Navy vessels operating in or near disputed areas of the East China Sea.[46]

In recent years, Chinese officials and military officers have also been more vocal in expressing opposition to U.S. and allied military exercises in nearby seas *outside* China's EEZ. For example, in the summer and fall of 2010, Beijing repeatedly criticized military exercises (involving a U.S. carrier battle group) held by Washington and Seoul in the Yellow Sea between China and the Korean Peninsula, despite the fact that such exercises occurred in international waters, and have been held in the past. The exercises were criticized for several reasons, including (1) their possibly provocative effect on North Korea (which was the announced target of the exercises); (2) the close proximity of the exercises to key Chinese strategic assets and population centers; (3) the potential for the United States to conduct reconnaissance that might infringe upon China's "security interests"; and (4) the intense historical sensitivity of the area for the Chinese, as a former "gateway" for the invasion of China by foreign powers such as Japan.[47] After North Korea shelled South Korea's Yeonpyeong Island in November 2010, the Chinese government appeared to take a more moderate position on the issue, protesting only exercises conducted within China's EEZ, but the persistent indignation expressed by many Chinese observers about U.S. exercises in the area—despite North Korea's belligerence—angered many U.S. observers.[48]

An Expanding PLA Mandate

While the PLA is acquiring greater levels of combat-oriented power projection capabilities, it is also expanding its knowledge and strengths in another increasingly important area noted above: military operations other than war, abbreviated in numerous Chinese publications as MOOTW. Domestically, these operations include an array of security and assistance activities associated with natural disasters, pandemics, and social unrest. Beyond China's borders, MOOTW encompass overseas noncombat missions such as counterpiracy operations, disaster response, and humanitarian relief efforts, as well as steady increases in China's contribution to international, noncombat peacekeeping activities.[49] Two notable examples are Beijing's unprecedented deployment of warships to the Gulf of Aden and Horn of Africa to participate with other navies in an international effort to combat maritime piracy, along with its operations to evacuate Chinese nationals from Libya in early 2011. These undertakings mark a significant step forward in the PLA's ability to conduct sustained military operations relatively far from China's shores.[50]

The conceptual rationale and motivation for all these missions was presented by Hu Jintao in a speech to the Chinese Communist Party's Central Military Commission delivered on December 24, 2004—as well as subsequent remarks to PLA delegations attending the National People's Congress in 2005 and 2006—on the so-called four historic missions (lishi shi ming, 历史使命) of the PLA. In these speeches, Hu identified a set of four broad, ambitious objectives for the Chinese military. These included two long-standing "traditional" missions and tasks (the defense of the Chinese Communist Party; and countering threats presented by land and maritime border issues, Taiwan separatism, ethnic separatism in Xinjiang and Tibet, terrorism, and domestic social stability) and two more recent and future tasks (the protection of China's expanding national interests, particularly in maritime, space, and cyberspace environments; and support for MOOTW, especially international peacekeeping and humanitarian operations).[51] In the political or psychological realms, the PLA has also enunciated a concept of "Three Warfares" (三种战) to define the major noncombat roles and missions of the Chinese military in the current era. This notion stresses the need for the political apparatus of the PLA to join the overall effort to establish integrated joint military operations by becoming more adept at conducting media, psychological, and legal forms of struggle.[52]

To make such advances and goals possible, Beijing has steadily increased its level of defense spending for nearly twenty years, and especially during the past decade. From 2000 to 2009, the average annual increase in China's official defense expenditures was 11.8 percent, while the average annual growth in

GDP was 9.6 percent and that of the state's total expenditures was 18.9 percent. China's official 2010 defense budget was about $78 billion, but the Stockholm International Peace Research Institute estimates that China actually spent $114.3 billion on its military in 2010, which accounts for slightly more than 2 percent of its GDP.[53] China's annual military expenditures are now the second-largest in the world behind the United States, although U.S. spending remains far ahead of that of all other powers by a wide margin—in 2010, America accounted for 43 percent of total global military spending.[54]

EVALUATION

These U.S. and Chinese policies and actions in the area of military security suggest several conclusions of relevance to U.S. policy. First, the United States has thus far shown no signs of reducing its commitment to the maintenance of very strong maritime capabilities in the Western Pacific, in support of the kinds of reassurance and deterrence objectives discussed in this study. These activities are not solely directed at China by any means. Washington associates overall regional stability with a strong military presence, as was made clear in chapter 1. Nonetheless, there is little doubt that a significant portion of the military activities described above are designed to send a strong signal to Beijing that Washington intends to retain a qualitative edge in specific military capabilities of relevance to the Taiwan situation and other potential sources of military conflict between the two powers (such as various territorial and maritime claims), and to reassure other Asian nations that China's growing power projection capabilities will not drastically alter the overall security environment.

Cross-Strait Dynamics and the Regional Security Balance

That said, there is also little doubt that China's improving military prowess, made possible in part by annual defense budget increases of between 10 and 20 percent since the early 1990s, have direct relevance to the long-term ability of the United States to maintain a strong deterrent capability in the Taiwan Strait and to preserve its position as the predominant political and military power in the maritime Western Pacific and the security guarantor for close allies and friends. Regarding the former issue (Taiwan deterrence), many U.S. observers are increasingly concerned that the PLA is acquiring capabilities that permit it (1) to rapidly weaken or destroy Taiwan's capacity to resist a future attack (especially given what is viewed in some U.S. defense circles as Taiwan's rather anemic attempt to strengthen its defense capabilities); and (2) severely complicate (or in some cases prevent) U.S. efforts to come to the assistance of Taiwan in a timely and effective manner, should the need arise. U.S. observers worry that the attainment of such capabilities (or a Chinese belief that they possess such capabilities) could lead to dangerous attempts to apply coercion or force against Taipei by lowering China's threshold for taking military action.[55]

Regarding the latter issue (the larger regional security situation), some U.S. (and Asian) strategists are concerned that China's military buildup is increasingly oriented toward the projection of power beyond Taiwan and China's immediate maritime periphery in ways that could eventually destabilize the region's security environment, for example, by compelling costly arms races and/or dangerous confrontations over specific maritime territorial disputes with Japan and some states belonging to the Association of Southeast Asian Nations, by intensifying overall military-oriented hedging toward China among Asian powers such as India and Japan, and by generally weakening the perceived capacity of the United States to provide security to its allies and to serve the larger "public good" by protecting the sea lanes of commercial transportation.[56]

Regardless of the accuracy or inaccuracy of specific assessments regarding Chinese intentions, taken together, and despite the obvious limitations noted above, concerns about the PLA's growing power projection capabilities along its periphery and beyond raise to a more tangible level the question of whether Washington can sustain its predominant military position in the Western Pacific in the medium to long terms—especially when considered against the current backdrop of a declining U.S. economy and the demands placed on U.S. resources and energies by ongoing crises in the Middle East and South and Central Asia. Equally important, the dynamic portrayed above—involving significant regional military acquisitions and deployments by both the United States and China— arguably increases the danger that military hedging will become a more pronounced element of overall strategy on both sides and thereby contribute to the emergence of an increasingly zero-sum mentality in assessing each other's future actions, thus possibly raising the likelihood of future miscalculations and conflict.

In this regard, despite the continued robustness of the U.S. military presence in the Western Pacific, China shows little signs of being significantly deterred from developing greater capabilities in critical areas of direct relevance to Taiwan and the larger regional balance (see the discussion of future trends below). It also shows little indication of being deterred from asserting its interpretation of UNCLOS provisions regarding the EEZ and disputed territorial waters in areas such as the East China and South China seas.[57] To the contrary, as China's military and economic capabilities increase in at least absolute (and possibly, in some areas, relative) terms, Beijing could become more, not less, willing to use military means (in the form of increased presence, implied or actual pressure on other states, or perhaps even direct attacks) to defend its perceived security interests, especially if Beijing sees itself as acting in response to provocations by other states.

Thus, this issue constitutes a significant source of confrontation between China and the United States, reflecting a larger clash between China's objective of increasing its control over its maritime periphery and the United States' geostrategic interest in maintaining the freedom of navigation on which the vitality and stability of the global maritime commons presumably rely, and which are essential to support U.S. security guarantees in East Asia.[58] In fact, since 2000, Chinese naval vessels and aircraft have aggressively confronted U.S. military surveillance ships and aircraft operating in the waters and airspace of China's EEZ, resulting in at least one collision (the so-called EP-3 incident in April 2001) and several near collisions or close-by harassment (including the so-called USNS *Impeccable* and USNS *Victorious* incidents in March and May 2009) and in each case generating serious political crises.[59] Despite some signs of restraint following each incident, the two powers continue to hold fundamentally different positions regarding the conditions under which military (and especially surveillance) craft can enter the EEZ.

In addition, in recent years, China's military aircraft and naval vessels, along with its civilian fisheries and law enforcement vessels, have also increased their presence in the waters that it disputes with Japan, South Korea, and several Southeast Asian nations, as part of an apparent effort to assert Chinese claims and oppose intrusive actions taken by other claimants. Beijing has also undertaken more vigorous legal and diplomatic efforts to support its position.[60] This has resulted in growing concerns expressed by several of these states regarding China's possible willingness to increase its use of military, diplomatic, and economic pressure to advance such claims. Many of these states are close U.S. allies and friends. Such connections, along with the larger U.S. interest in maintaining peace and stability in the region, have resulted in heightened efforts by Washington to deter all parties, and most notably Beijing, from engaging in various forms of military coercion, while reasserting its support for the prevailing interpretation of UNCLOS and the right to freedom of navigation in international waters.[61] This effort has elicited a strong, sometimes angry, reaction from China.[62] As China's military capabilities and overall national confidence grow, it is very likely that this issue will serve as the basis for (and perhaps the primary focus of) future confrontations between Washington and Beijing.[63]

One additional aspect of this issue that serves to complicate U.S. efforts to manage it is the possibility that both the U.S. and Chinese militaries might exercise some level of independence from civilian oversight in conducting their activities (such as surveillance, attempts at interdicting surveillance, and field tests of new capabilities), thus increasing the likelihood of unexpected or undesired incidents or crises. This is a particular concern with regard to the PLA, given the lack in the Chinese policy apparatus of an interagency vetting process for military-related operations that includes officials in the foreign affairs system and other relevant senior civilian officials charged with managing relations with other nations. Indeed, some Western observers (including some U.S. officials) suspect that incidents such as those discussed in the previous paragraphs in many cases occurred because local or central PLA leaders undertook specific "tactical" actions without the knowledge or consent of the senior civilian (and perhaps military) leadership. Some observers even fear that the PLA undertakes broader policy actions independently (and perhaps in defiance) of the civilian leadership. The latter (that is, broader policy independence) seems highly unlikely, given the existence of strong Communist Party and security apparatus controls over the Chinese military, the general onus against major military "freelancing" that pervades the party-state system, and the weak presence of senior PLA officers within the party's most senior decisionmaking structures; however, the former (that is, "tactical" independence) is quite possible. This points to the need for greater military-to-military dialogues on crisis avoidance and crisis management issues, as well as greater efforts to understand the nature of the Chinese decisionmaking system involving defense-related matters.[64]

The United States–China Strategic Balance

In the nuclear arena, despite the above-outlined improvements that have taken place in the size, diversity, and sophistication of its nuclear forces, Beijing's nuclear capabilities remain vastly inferior to those of Washington, and there are no signs that China is attempting to "catch up" with the United States numerically. China also remains wedded, in its official statements, to the no-first-use (NFU) concept and to its commitment not to employ nuclear weapons against non-nuclear states. Moreover, China's nuclear deployment posture (keeping its land-based warheads separate from their delivery systems) and its lack of a real-time launch-on-warning capability confirm its continued commitment to a second-strike retaliatory nuclear doctrine.[65]

Nonetheless, some analysts have become concerned about the stability of strategic deterrence between Beijing and Washington in a future major political-military crisis given the combination of a number of factors—including signs of apparent debates within Chinese strategic circles about the continued viability of the NFU concept in the face of continued advances in U.S. conventional, long-range, precision-strike capabilities; the development by China of new classes and types of dual-use (both nuclear and conventional) ballistic and cruise missiles; the likely operational deployment of a new class of SSBNs with mated nuclear weapons and missiles; and the possible deployment by the United States of a credible theater and national ballistic missile defense capability (associated with Chinese fears of U.S. attempts to establish "nuclear primacy"). Specifically, these developments could produce confused signaling and overreactions in a crisis, resulting in inadvertent escalation and even conflict.[66]

In addition, significant reductions in the U.S. nuclear arsenal—though unlikely at this point, as indicated above—could increase pressures to engage Beijing in future arms reductions negotiations, a development that Beijing would almost certainly resist, whereas further U.S. movement toward an NFU policy would have major implications for those U.S. Asian allies with concerns about China's growing power, such as Japan and perhaps South Korea.[67] Most important (given its arguably higher probability and more direct relevance to China), a U.S. decision to devote more resources and effort to the creation of larger and more effective regional and national ballistic missile defense systems than those anticipated by Beijing could have a significant impact on the size and sophistication of the Chinese nuclear force, along with its nascent ballistic missile defense program.

These present and potential future issues and problems point to the importance of the military-political elements of U.S. policy toward China and the region, as critical means of providing reassurance, resolving disputes, and encouraging cooperation and positive-sum perspectives toward issues. Many of these elements are connected with the United States' stance toward Japan, South Korea, and other key regional actors, as well as with basic U.S. efforts to encourage mutual "strategic reassurance" dialogues with Chinese politicians and diplomats, as discussed in chapters 2 and 3.[68]

Military-to-Military Relations

In terms of bilateral military relations, however, efforts to reduce potential tensions over both strategic and conventional military developments relate most directly to U.S.-Chinese military-to-military contacts. As indicated above, this policy has generated a considerable amount of debate and opposition among some U.S. observers and policy officials both past and present, in part because the Chinese military has clearly not adopted norms of strict reciprocity and transparency in its contacts with the U.S. military. The main debate is about whether military-to-military relations with China actually advance U.S. interests (such as the advancement of mutual understanding, reductions in tension, and deterrence) or whether contacts have contributed, instead, to the PLA's war-fighting capabilities by revealing sensitive information. Over time, and as often-sensational and at times inaccurate reports on Chinese military-related espionage appeared in the U.S. media, the U.S. government (through both executive branch policies and congressional legislation) has tightened controls over the scope and form of military-to-military contacts, in an effort to increase transparency and reciprocity and to prevent the transmission of militarily sensitive information to the PLA. These provisions have led to the placement of strong limits on the ability of the Defense Department to learn about China's military modernization by holding discussions with PLA personnel on strategic issues, defense doctrines, and war-fighting capabilities.[69] In addition, as indicated above, America's military-to-military ties with China have been highly vulnerable to shifts in the political winds in both countries, as well as ups and downs in the U.S.-Chinese relationship. They are thus the first bilateral contacts to be suspended in the event of a serious rift between Beijing and Washington.[70]

However, most knowledgeable current and former U.S. officials and military officers interviewed by the author believe that such contacts have raised mutual understanding and obtained extremely important information from PRC military circles. They argue that existing controls are excessive and restrict the ability of the U.S. government to obtain benefits from contact with the PLA.[71] Furthermore, as Secretary of Defense Robert Gates has contended, such contacts, especially if they involve both civilian and military leaders, could help facilitate improved civilian–military coordination in China, thereby further improving communication and preventing miscalculations.[72]

Finally, efforts by the United States and other nations to encourage China to provide more information about its military strategy and force modernization program have arguably produced some positive results, in the form of more detailed PRC defense white papers and other publications and the occasional granting of greater access by U.S. military personnel to some PLA facilities. But much more can and should be provided. For its part, the U.S. Defense Department's official reports on China's military (along with other documents) have shown that the U.S. government actually knows quite a lot about the PLA's intentions and capabilities, even though the "hard data" on Chinese forces and doctrine presented in such reports are often combined with inaccurate and politically motivated statements and assessments. In this regard, in the worst instances, the Defense Department's reports and statements by its personnel at times provide an incomplete and (worse yet) overly alarmist assessment of Chinese military modernization. Such information and statements can undermine efforts to reassure and deter China (and other states) by conveying the impression that the U.S. government (or perhaps the Pentagon alone) deliberately hypes the threat posed by Beijing in order to encourage confrontation, to justify higher levels of defense spending on advanced armaments, or to intimidate other powers into adopting a more belligerent policy toward China.

FUTURE TRENDS

The analysis given above suggests that two major issues lie at the center of any effort to assess the future of Washington's military and defense policies and capabilities vis-à-vis China: first, the economic and financial capacity of the United States to sustain what policymakers would regard as necessary levels of deterrence, reassurance, and war-fighting capabilities in the Western Pacific; and second, the likely economic capacity of the Chinese leadership to continue deploying a growing array of power projection capabilities that potentially challenge U.S. capabilities, and the specific challenges that future PLA deployments will pose for core U.S. military missions.

Economic Trends

The major economic variables influencing these future capabilities center on the scope and structure of U.S. and Chinese defense spending. As noted above and elsewhere, dynamic changes are occurring in this area that could exert a critical influence on the future tenor and viability of U.S. security policies toward Beijing.

U.S. Defense Spending
As indicated in chapter 1, U.S. security policy toward China largely assumes that the future stability and prosperity of Asia relies to a considerable extent on the ability and willingness of Washington to maintain or, if necessary, expand its military predominance in the Western Pacific in the face of Beijing's growing capabilities. However, many analysts and observers of the U.S. defense budget point to a variety of factors that could constrain future levels of U.S. military spending, with potentially adverse consequences for the U.S. military posture in Asia.[73] These include the already extremely high level of defense spending that emerged during the George W. Bush era, the high cost of maintaining troops and/or supporting security forces or operations in Iraq, Afghanistan, and other hotspots

during at least the next several years, the likely adverse impact of the current global economic recession and Washington's exploding fiscal deficit on U.S. government spending levels and priorities in general, and growing structural problems associated with the defense budgeting process.

Analysts of American global power such as Paul Kennedy maintain that such factors, and especially the global economic recession, will greatly intensify over time the difficulties confronting the United States' efforts to sustain its already-taxed overseas commitments and deployments, resulting in "imperial over-stretch."[74] Other analysts argue, more broadly and ominously, that, over the long term, the financial crisis could permanently damage the overall economic capacity of the United States, primarily by creating huge, increasingly-difficult-to-manage budget and current account deficits and weakening enormously the dollar and its role as the international reserve currency. These developments would raise the cost of maintaining a strong overseas military presence and generally diminish America's overall global political influence and prestige.[75] And prudent and balanced observers of the U.S. posture in Asia (and former policymakers) such as Richard Armitage and Joseph Nye express strong doubts about Washington's fiscal and military capacity to operate effectively in the region by 2020.[76]

In addition, some experts on the U.S. defense budgeting process express strong concerns that persistent and deep-rooted problems in U.S. national security planning, programming, and budgeting will force significant "trade-offs between major increases in the budget and current force plans."[77] All these factors could constrain American popular and elite support for existing or new levels of overall defense spending of relevance to China.[78]

That said, such concerns have not resulted in the emergence of any consensus among analysts regarding the future of U.S. defense spending during the next five to ten years or beyond. In other words, even though there is considerable agreement that defense spending faces many (and some new) challenges, there is no agreement that such challenges will reduce defense spending overall, much less affect spending and deployment patterns in Asia or the overall capacity of the United States as a global power (the latter point is discussed in greater detail in chapter 5).

Some observers argue that the end of the conflict in Iraq (or a decrease in the U.S. presence there) and a concentration on domestic spending will necessitate significantly less overall defense spending in the future.[79] However, many analysts argue that, from a purely financial perspective, the United States can afford to sustain, or even expand, its current level of defense spending. They point to the fact that, in most recent years, the United States has spent less on defense (often about 3 to 4 percent of GDP) than during any other period since World

War II and has about 2 million fewer active duty personnel today than in the 1950s. (Defense spending did increase significantly in 2009, to nearly 5 percent of GDP, and it remained at that level in 2010 and 2011, but it is still below Cold War levels.)[80] Such analysts often argue that domestic spending, not defense spending, is the true source of America's ballooning deficits and mounting debt. This argument directly refutes the "imperial overstretch" argument of Kennedy and others.[81] Others take a middle-of-the-road position, arguing that it is too early to say whether the United States will be forced to constrain its global and regional military, political, and economic presence.[82]

Actually, the Obama administration has expressed the clear intention to eventually at least level off, if not decrease, defense spending during the remainder of its term in office, even though it has most recently increased defense spending in both absolute and relative terms (in light of problems in Afghanistan and the troop surge). Such reductions are expected to come from lowered defense spending in Iraq and the elimination of some high-priced major weapons systems programs.[83] Even before the current global economic recession, many experts were actually predicting that overall U.S. defense spending on hard military capabilities during the current decade or so will decline quite significantly, largely because of increases in spending on mandatory programs such as Medicare, Medicaid, and Social Security, and increased defense costs associated with personnel, operations, and maintenance.[84] The likely continuation of America's economic problems (marked by low growth rates, high unemployment, and a massive budget deficit) will almost certainly intensify such trends, by reducing tax revenues and enormously expanding U.S. deficit spending (and interest payments).[85]

In partial anticipation of such growing pressures, in April 2009, Defense Secretary Gates unveiled an ambitious plan to reorder U.S. defense priorities and rebalance weapons programs. Though not reducing overall defense spending appreciably in the next few years, Gates nonetheless announced a broad range of cuts or limitations to specific major weapons systems, including national missile defense, the advanced F-22 fighter, and a new, advanced Zumwalt-class destroyer, as well as a likely slowdown in the production of new antisubmarine aircraft and improvements in the aerial tanker fleet.[86] More recently, Gates has also questioned the future financial feasibility and strategic logic of investing huge sums of money into a declining number of ever more sophisticated military weapons systems, especially when U.S. high-technology military capabilities will continue to vastly exceed those of any likely adversary by a significant magnitude.[87]

Gates has thus asserted that, "before making claims of requirements not being met or alleged gaps—in ships, tactical fighters, personnel, or anything else—we need to evaluate the criteria upon which requirements are based and the wider real world context." As a result, he has directed those relevant Pentagon agencies involved in preparing the 2012 defense budget "to take a hard, unsparing look at how they operate—in substance and style alike. The goal is to cut our overhead costs and to transfer those savings to force structure and modernization within the programmed budget."[88] These and other proposed changes reflect efforts to eliminate wasteful weapons programs and procurement processes and ensure future funding for rapidly growing personnel, maintenance, and operations costs.

These proposed recalibrations also reflected, at least to some degree, a shift in U.S. defense planning away from possible but less likely conflicts with major powers such as Russia and China and toward less conventional threats from irregular forces and nonstate actors such as terrorists, along with smaller but potent powers such as Iran and North Korea. However, Gates at least partially reversed such a shift in early January 2011, when he announced decisions to fund a new generation of long-range nuclear bombers, new electronic jammers and radar, and other items that could have great relevance to potential threats from China and Russia.[89]

Nonetheless, some analysts believe that, despite Gates's partial reversal, these emerging trends in defense spending and weapons programs could erode U.S. deterrence and reassurance capabilities vis-à-vis China during the current decade. In particular, they argue that reductions in antisubmarine warfare platforms, advanced fighters (especially the F-22), advanced destroyers, and other systems, along with a failure to increase the number and aircraft strike range of U.S. carrier battle groups, could make a large difference in a future confrontation with a militarily stronger China over Taiwan.[90] Even more ominously, some experts argue that, assuming continued economic constraints and worldwide mission demands, and under existing development trends, the U.S. Navy is steadily losing its capacity to operate as a globally dominant force. As a result, these experts maintain, unless it makes some fundamental choices among alternative deployment strategies, the U.S. Navy will likely lose its ability to maintain the combat credibility necessary to deter potential adversaries such as China, and to reassure America's maritime allies and partners in Asia and elsewhere.[91]

However, a systematic and detailed assessment of U.S. security strategy in Asia by a wide range of scholars and former officials argues that economic pressures will probably not adversely affect the U.S. force posture in the Western Pacific during at least the current decade.[92] Moreover, U.S. officials, including Gates and former head of the U.S. Pacific Command Timothy Keating, as well as official U.S. statements such as the Quadrennial Defense Review, have repeatedly claimed in recent years that Washington has neither the intention nor the desire to reduce the U.S. military presence in the Asia Pacific. Indeed, Washington intends to maintain its current predominance as Beijing acquires greater antiaccess and area-denial capabilities in the region.[93] And influential nongovernmental defense think tanks such as the Center for Strategic and Budgetary Assessments will undoubtedly seek to reinforce and deepen such a U.S. intention, through the continued advocacy of highly ambitious (and likely very costly) strategic concepts such as the above-mentioned air-sea battle.[94] Yet if the United States does not recover its economic footing, such intentions will likely come up against stark economic realities in the next ten to fifteen years.

Chinese Defense Spending

Above and beyond potential U.S. economic and policy constraints, the activities of the Chinese military will probably exert the greatest impact on Washington's ability to maintain its existing roles and missions in the Western Pacific. From an economic perspective, almost all analysts expect that China will sustain its past double-digit increases in annual defense spending and continue to deploy advanced military platforms and technologies of concern to the United States during at least the current decade.

Moreover, China is only in the early stages of developing a sophisticated military-industrial complex. It will thus continue improving its indigenous defense procurement capabilities, and most likely transition away from foreign procurement, as its defense industry advances in complexity and sophistication, thus contributing to its status as a major military power.[95] At the same time, most analysts expect that Chinese military spending will probably remain relatively constant as a proportion of (increasing) government spending and GDP for the foreseeable future. Moreover, overall PLA spending will almost certainly continue to be overshadowed by U.S. defense budgets. The Pentagon estimate for China's total defense spending in 2009 (more than $150 billion) was less than the 2010 budget for the U.S. Navy alone ($171.7 billion).[96]

Despite expectations of sustained double-digit increases in annual defense spending levels during the next five to ten years at least, China is expected to continue to lag significantly behind overall U.S. conventional military capabilities in most critical measures, especially with regard to power projection beyond its immediate periphery, and its overall experience in conducting actual military combat operations. Leading analysts agree that most Chinese air and naval firepower is far behind the standards seen in the United States, Russia, or Japan. Even China's military leadership and domestic Chinese military publications have acknowledged that China will need decades before it can attain world-ranked military standards in most areas.[97] The Defense Department assesses that the

PLA will not be able to "project and sustain large forces in high-intensity combat operations far from China" until about 2025.[98] On the sea, China's navy does not approach the ability to control waters out to 1,000 kilometers. Moreover, some analysts (for example, Taylor Fravel) believe that spending on potentially provocative capabilities such as maritime denial and control and overall regional force projection will likely to some extent remain constrained by Chinese concerns about exacerbating the security dilemma.[99] More broadly, and from a longer-term perspective, it is possible that fundamental structural problems (and in particular demographic trends) will increasingly constrain China's growth rate and thus its ability to devote significant resources to ambitious military modernization programs.[100]

Military Trends

Even though China will likely remain inferior overall to the United States in many key aspects of power projection, it is expected to continue making significant strides in some specific areas that have great applicability to U.S. interests in Asia. In particular, expanding Chinese military capabilities of relevance to Taiwan and, secondarily, to other areas of the Western Pacific are expected to generate the greatest security concerns for the U.S. military (and other Asian nations) during the next ten to fifteen years.

Implications for Taiwan

Regarding the Taiwan situation, as suggested above, many analysts expect that, given current trends, by approximately 2012–2017, the People's Liberation Army Navy (PLAN) will possess the capability to conduct a range of activities—centered on air and missile attacks and coordinated air, naval, and space-based antiaccess and area-denial operations—that could overwhelm Taiwan's defenses in a short period and complicate or even prevent any effective U.S. military response. Of particular note, among these capabilities, are PLA and Second Artillery Corps weapons systems designed to strike U.S. surface warships (including carriers), along with military bases in Taiwan, Japan, Guam, and elsewhere, primarily with short-, medium-, and intermediate-range ballistic missiles; improvements in the numbers and sophistication of PLAN submarines capable of operating on all sides of Taiwan and to Guam and beyond; larger numbers of more sophisticated strike aircraft capable of operating on the open ocean; highly potent, long-range, land-based antiaircraft missiles; an increasingly robust sea mine capability; a space-based surveillance architecture, and the apparent adoption of operational principles that emphasize preemption and surprise.[101]

In fact, some analysts have concluded from these developments that China has already acquired capabilities that make it impossible for the United States to credibly guarantee the security of Taiwan, and that this trend will simply deepen during the next several years, in the absence of major new increases in U.S. and Taiwanese capabilities, including potentially destabilizing forces directed at China's land-based military bases and infrastructure.[102]

However, other analysts, including this author, assert that current trends in the PLA's modernization do not unambiguously confirm a shift in the overall balance of power across the Taiwan Strait (including available American forces) in Beijing's favor within the current decade, given both the PLA's lack of war-fighting experience and the numerous uncertainties it would confront in any Taiwan crisis or conflict. Regardless of the specific, relative force-on-force calculations of the cross-Strait military balance (and the larger antiaccess capabilities of the PLA vis-à-vis U.S. forces), China will continue for a long time to face daunting challenges in coercing or subduing Taiwan, especially in any attempt to seize the island via an all-out invasion. In particular, it cannot be assured of *sustained* air superiority or of the success of a naval blockade of the island in any foreseeable time frame. The former is essential to the success of a wide range of contingencies. Moreover, China does not currently possess the amphibious and airborne forces required for a major attack, and it does not appear to be focusing its efforts on acquiring such capabilities in the future.[103]

That said, there is little doubt that China is acquiring new and enlarged military capabilities in specific areas (and thus apparently narrowing the gap vis-à-vis both Taiwan and the United States) in ways that could, over time, weaken deterrence and thereby severely destabilize the cross-Strait military balance. In particular, future advances in *specific* PLA air and naval capabilities (those most applicable to antiaccess and area-denial operations), integration of a joint warfare doctrine that maximizes available assets, growing asymmetrical options in areas such as information operations, as well as an expanding arsenal of short-range ballistic missiles, might together lead the Chinese leadership to regard certain "lesser-order" military options—such as panic-inducing air and missile attacks or a rapid decapitation strike involving preemptive attacks and a variety of special operations force and fifth-column actions—as possibly worth undertaking under *extreme* circumstances. Such an option would gain credibility if Chinese leaders were to believe that they could quickly establish a military fait accompli that the United States would find difficult to reverse without a major escalation of the conflict. Under such circumstances, China's leaders might conclude that they would enjoy a distinct advantage over the United States, given their apparent belief that Washington would have less resolve than Beijing in a major crisis concerning Taiwan and thus would seek to avoid a prolonged or intense conflict.[104]

Such concerns could also arguably increase Taiwan's incentives to attempt to acquire a nuclear deterrent (despite official statements to the contrary), and increase pressure within Taiwan to develop the capability and doctrine to undertake potentially destabilizing, tactically offensive counterforce operations, including preemptive strikes.[105] These possibilities underscore the importance for Washington of developing a strategy toward the Taiwan issue that minimizes the incentives for Beijing to resort to coercive options, not only via effective military deterrence but also (and arguably more important) via policies designed to deepen political, diplomatic, and economic reassurance and cooperation across the Strait, as suggested in chapter 2. But beyond this, China's growing military capabilities vis-à-vis Taiwan also suggest the need for Washington to seriously reassess its historical aversion to discussing Taiwan-related military issues with Beijing—in consultation with Taipei. (This point is discussed in chapter 10.)

Technological Advances toward a Long-Range Military Capability

Of likely equal or greater importance during the medium to long terms (that is, for eight to ten years and beyond), China's growing military capabilities also have potential consequences for the PLA's ability to project power across and even beyond the East Asian littoral.[106] In this regard, most analysts point to the growing size and prowess of the PLAN's missile and torpedo-armed conventional and nuclear-powered submarine fleet, its rapidly expanding fleet of increasingly sophisticated surface combatants, and its growing cyberwarfare and antisatellite warfare capabilities, along with Beijing's increasing number of regional ballistic missiles. Specifically, China now has more submarines than Russia, and many of its new classes of submarines are domestically built—like the Jin-class ballistic missile submarines. Also, as indicated above, a growing number of sources suggest that China will likely acquire its first aircraft carrier soon, probably by 2012. By 2016, the PLAN is expected to be three times its present size, dominating—in numbers, if not necessarily in capability—any other East Asian navy, with the possible exception of Japan's Maritime Self-Defense Force.[107]

Partly in response to such projections, the 2006 U.S. Quadrennial Defense Review called for 60 percent of attack submarines to be based in the Pacific and 40 percent in the Atlantic by 2010, thus reversing the ratio of Pacific-versus-Atlantic submarine deployments that existed during the height of the Cold War.[108] Some analysts (including many in the U.S. government) argue that, within a decade, China is expected to acquire a credible threat to hold surface warships, including U.S. carriers, at risk not only in the vicinity of Taiwan but also within approximately 2,000 nautical miles of its entire coastline, through a combination of conventionally armed antiship ballistic missiles; command, control, communications, computers, intelligence, surveillance, and reconnaissance (C4ISR), for geolocation and the tracking of targets; and onboard guidance systems, for terminal homing to strike surface ships. The Pentagon believes that such a capability "would have particular significance, as it would provide China with preemptive and coercive options in a regional crisis."[109] In addition, China is expected to create an arsenal of short- and medium-range ballistic missiles, ground-launched land-attack cruise missiles, special operations forces, and computer network attack capabilities that could pose a credible threat to U.S. and allied bases in Asia, along with logistics and support infrastructures.[110]

Also, Pentagon analysts believe that China could even acquire the capability to compete in a major way for air superiority in areas along its periphery, and, perhaps, further afield, through continuing advances in the development and deployment of advanced surface-to-air missiles, Russian-built and domestic fourth-generation combat aircraft (including, perhaps, carrier-based aircraft), fifth-generation stealth aircraft, more sophisticated air refueling platforms, and long-range unmanned aerial vehicles.[111]

Some U.S. analysts are concerned about China's likely significant future gains in the areas of information warfare and computer network operations, including cyberattacks. Many analysts also believe that China will soon have (or might already possess) the C4ISR support for campaigns of up to 2,000 kilometers from the Chinese coast. Such capabilities, if successfully employed and defended, could significantly degrade U.S. military deployments, logistical sustainment, and combat operations in the Asia-Pacific region.[112]

The development of many of these capabilities together suggests that China will likely attain some type of fairly long-range, blue-water naval capability during the next ten to fifteen years.[113] The PLAN has already shown the capability to operate a small number of warships and aircraft at a significant distance from its shores, with the dispatch in December 2008 of a naval flotilla to the Gulf of Aden to participate in antipiracy operations and the deployment in February and March 2011 of a missile frigate and four military transport aircraft to evacuate Chinese citizens from Libya. This capability will likely only expand.[114] More broadly (and ominously), senior Pentagon officials have publicly stated that China's growing military capabilities pose an increasing potential threat to the ability of the United States to project power and assist its allies in the Pacific.[115]

China's Strategic Intentions in the Pacific

However, as suggested at the beginning of this chapter, there is considerable debate among analysts and observers about the ultimate strategic intent of such developments and their overall security implications for the United States beyond Taiwan. Some analysts assert that China's expanding power projection capabilities pose a direct and deliberate challenge to U.S. military (including space-based) and commercial dominance in maritime East Asia, and perhaps beyond. As indicated above, many such analysts claim that Beijing has the explicit intention of displacing the United States as the predominant maritime power in the Western Pacific and encouraging or forcing the eventual withdrawal of the U.S. military from the region.[116] Some observers also argue that China's growing maritime capabilities indicate an intent to protect energy sources and sea lanes not only within *but also beyond* East Asia.[117] As indicated above, some analysts point to China's apparent decision to deploy one or more midsized carriers as confirmation of such an intent.[118]

Conversely, many analysts contend that China's navy is likely to remain regionally defensive and focused almost exclusively on area-denial missions, not the acquisition of preponderant regional, much less global, power projection capabilities for the foreseeable future. In particular, they point out that many aspects of the PLAN's current and emerging force structure are most consistent with peripheral defense operations against foreign navies in waters near China and particularly with regard to Taiwan. For example, China's new conventional submarines have missile range limits, stealth characteristics, speed constraints, and operational restraints that suggest that China's submarine force will be used for such purposes.[119] The PLAN's new SSBNs will remain hugely outnumbered by the U.S. submarine fleet for many years to come, and they have yet to conduct a single strategic deterrence patrol, according to one observer.[120]

Rather than focusing exclusively on potential threats, still other analysts emphasize the opportunities for cooperation that emerge from a Chinese blue-water navy. China's interests in secure sea lanes are in line with U.S. interests in many cases. As noted above, Beijing has already joined Washington and other naval powers in dispatching naval forces to undertake unprecedented antipiracy operations in the Gulf of Aden.[121] And the PLAN's growing ability to provide disaster and humanitarian relief will almost certainly reinforce the impression that China seeks to perform the duties of a responsible stakeholder in the international system. In fact, as noted, official PRC policy documents such as China's defense white paper and other government statements are placing an increasing emphasis on the use of the PLA for MOOTW.[122]

In this regard, the acquisition of Chinese aircraft carriers is viewed by many analysts as motivated at least as much by the desire to enhance MOOTW capabilities (and national prestige) as by any conceivable combat mission, given the potential benefits that carriers offer in the realm of disaster relief and other nontraditional security missions.[123] And in most instances, any potential future combat mission for a PLAN carrier is defined by many analysts as being directed primarily against powers other than the United States—for example, those Southeast Asian nations with which China has territorial disputes over islands in the South China Sea.

The Future of Space

China's capability to support an ambitious space program, along with ground-based antisatellite systems, is also developing rapidly. This includes an expanding number and variety of indigenous satellites (including microsatellites), an enhanced space launch capability, a new launch center in Hainan Province, plans to put people on the moon within the next fifteen years (as well as Mars and Sun missions), and the development of land-launched, kinetic, antisatellite ballistic missile attack capabilities, ground-based lasers, and jammers.[124] Moreover, some senior PLA officers have also reportedly asserted that China will eventually deploy spaced-based weapons, although official Chinese policy stands opposed to such a move.[125] At the very least, Beijing's rapidly expanding space capabilities present a potential security challenge to Washington's ability to freely employ satellites for military purposes such as communication, reconnaissance, remote sensing, surveillance, and electronic surveillance, thus posing implications for PLA power projection regarding Taiwan and beyond.[126]

Some observers assert that the potential space threat from China will inevitably grow and cannot be controlled via bilateral or multilateral arms control efforts, and must therefore be countered through the acquisition of ever more vigorous U.S. counterspace capabilities. In other words, these observers believe that Washington is fated to engage in an arms race in space with Beijing, which it thus should prepare to win, to ensure America's continued military predominance, especially in the Western Pacific.[127]

Other analysts hold less pessimistic views of the implications of China's space capabilities for U.S. security, arguing that various commercial and other factors are increasing mutual incentives to avoid a space arms race.[128] Indeed, some observers argue that the United States might obtain some notable security-related gains from Beijing if it were to pursue an agreement to prohibit the weaponization of space.[129]

Taking a middle ground in this debate, many analysts argue that, rather than trying to achieve strategic parity (much less dominance) in space capabilities with Washington, Beijing is instead viewed (as in many other areas) as adopting a defensive, reactive stance. This stance is centered on efforts to prevent total U.S. space dominance, given China's growing interest in and likely involvement in space, and the increasing importance of space-based, military-related assets for communication and surveillance. These analysts argue that future efforts by Washington to maintain space dominance will likely result in greater asymmetrical efforts by Beijing to offset U.S. space advantages.[130]

Nonetheless, and despite the fact that the United States will likely remain the preeminent space power overall for the next twenty to thirty years, such lesser-order, "active" defensive-oriented Chinese space activities pose potential threats to vital U.S. capabilities and raise the serious question for U.S. policy of "what kind of feasible and stable space regime best serves U.S. long-term security interests."[131] In other words, at the very least, the debate about U.S.-PRC space capabilities and intentions suggests that there is a strong need for Washington to carefully consider, from an overall policy perspective, its security objectives in space, the long-term implications for these objectives of existing trends in China's space program, and the feasibility and implications of various alternative approaches to managing the emerging challenge.[132]

The Nuclear Balance

Finally, in the strategic arena, most analysts believe that, even though the Chinese nuclear arsenal increased by 25 percent between 2005 and 2008 to approximately 240 total warheads, Beijing will continue to remain massively inferior in nuclear capability to the United States, in the absence of a huge reduction in Washington's nuclear inventory as a result of arms control negotiations with Russia—an unlikely outcome in any foreseeable time frame.[133]

In addition, China's nuclear weapons program (and associated debates over the continued viability of the NFU concept) will almost certainly remain largely defensive and reactionary, driven to a large degree by actions taken by the United States. In particular, four aspects of U.S. policy will remain critical: (1) the overall strategic orientation of U.S. doctrine, nuclear posture, and nuclear weapons use, especially as they affect crisis stability involving Taiwan; (2) the possible development of new types of nuclear weapons with the apparent capacity to penetrate hardened underground facilities and thus reduce the nuclear threshold; (3) any U.S. missile defense deployments in East Asia that might threaten China's strategic deterrence capabilities; (4) and the future development of U.S. conventional, long-range, precision-guided weapons that could support a disarming non-nuclear first strike against China.[134]

In this regard, as in the aerospace arena, the likely continued importance of U.S. actions as an independent variable in the nuclear equation with China suggests a critical need to examine (or reexamine) the assumptions driving U.S. nuclear weapons policy in all the areas described above, especially in light of existing U.S. plans to modernize the nuclear arsenal and deploy more capable ballistic missile systems of relevance to China.

An Overall Assessment

On balance, there is very little, if any, evidence to suggest that Beijing is seriously considering (or will likely begin considering during the next few years) altering its current "peace and development"–oriented grand strategy and associated defense policy priorities (defined in chapter 1) toward a more assertive overall strategy that is deliberately designed both to challenge the United States and to supplant it as the dominant maritime power in the Western Pacific. Indeed, from a purely logical point of view, such efforts would directly undermine, if not altogether destroy, Beijing's capacity to maintain the larger environment of peace, stability, and prosperity upon which it relies to achieve its long-term national goals and remain in power.[135]

Nonetheless, there are apparently debates among PRC military and political strategists over how a rising China can best achieve its existing goals and avoid conflict with the United States (and other powers such as Japan) in the face of continued U.S. regional deployments and strategic developments. In these debates, as indicated above, some analysts argue in favor of very ambitious new strategies that envision steadily expanding power projection capabilities beyond China's territory and immediate periphery, to include expanses of the Western Pacific, space, and the cybersphere.[136]

However, as the 2009 Pentagon report on China's military power states, most of these debates "appear to remain largely on the margins" and are unlikely to generate a basic shift in approach during the next decade.[137] Conversely, as this report points out, "China's thinking appears to be gradually moving toward a strategic concept that considers defense of maritime interests, in addition to defense of homeland, as drivers for force modernization."[138]

Moreover, despite the uncertain intent behind Beijing's expanding conventional military capabilities, some analysts believe that existing overall trends in naval and air power projection could precipitate an arms race in Asia between India, China, Japan, the United States, and perhaps other powers.[139] In addition, it is possible, and indeed likely, that efforts by China and other powers (such as Russia) to improve their space-based military support systems and to explore asymmetrical ways to neutralize U.S. advantages in this area, along with Washington's continued resistance to any international attempts to restrict its access to or use of space, could increase pressures to militarize space and contribute to Sino-U.S. security competition.[140]

Equally important, the acquisition by China of credible, robust conventional area-denial capabilities in the Western Pacific could lead key U.S. allies such as Japan and South Korea to doubt the ability of Washington to prevail against Beijing in a military standoff or conflict in the region. Such doubts could significantly weaken American security commitments to those nations and lead to more pronounced hedging by them and others. Hence, the basic value of U.S. extended deterrence to such nations could be undermined.

On a more positive note, a fairly recent, thorough review of the implications of Asian (and especially Chinese) military modernization for U.S. (and Western) maritime predominance by Geoffrey Till offers a less pessimistic assessment of the changing security environment in the Western Pacific over the long term. Though acknowledging that China's military gains will likely "challenge the strategic primacy of the United States in a geographic area hitherto dominated by American naval power," Till argues that "the U.S. Navy is still far ahead of all others in its size, technological sophistication and global reach." More important, he also concludes that "it will be many years before this commanding global lead in deployable naval power is seriously compromised."[141] This conclusion is further buttressed by the observation that, "of the world's next 20 fleets in aggregate tonnage terms, no less than 18 are either formal allies of the United States . . . or friendly towards it."

Although this observation does not decisively resolve the concerns of those, including those who fret over the eroding ability of the United States to apply superior force against the PLA *at vital points* in the Western Pacific within a *very short time frame*,[142] it does suggest that Washington will likely retain the capacity to prevail over Beijing in a military contest if given enough time to prepare and react. In other words, in a crisis, U.S. predominance might hinge to a great extent on warning times and deployment capabilities, rather than force-on-force estimates. Nonetheless, the continued viability of at least some aspects of U.S. predominance in the Western Pacific—as viewed by the United States, China, and other Asian powers—is very likely to become an increasingly serious issue. This problem is discussed further in chapter 10.

05

ECONOMIC RELATIONS AND DEVELOPMENT ASSISTANCE

--- ▼ ---

U.S. economic policies toward China have both responded to and shaped the enormous changes in Chinese economic and aid behavior during the past three decades. Among these changes, the most notable include: domestic economic behavior of direct relevance to Chinese stability and prosperity and to external economic policies; bilateral (especially Sino-U.S.) and multilateral trade, technology, and investment patterns; and activities related to external resources.

In recent decades, China's policy of rapid economic growth has featured high levels of investment in physical inputs to production and relatively weaker efforts to foster innovation, entrepreneurship, and the development of competitive markets. This has resulted in an economic model that is extremely energy and capital intensive, with a very high savings rate, high levels of domestic infrastructure investment, and a relatively weak (but expanding) social welfare infrastructure.

These economic characteristics pose significant implications for China's pattern of economic involvement with (and impact upon) the outside world, and the United States in particular. Indeed, as indicated in the introduction to this book, in the twenty-first century, Beijing's economic behavior is posing a much more diverse and far-reaching set of challenges for Washington's policymakers.

Thus, any assessment of U.S. economic policies toward China must begin with an overview of the most significant current features of Chinese economic behavior.

THE MAIN FEATURES OF CHINA'S DOMESTIC ECONOMY AND GLOBAL ECONOMIC ENGAGEMENT

China's domestic economy and global economic engagement contain seven features of central relevance to the interests of the United States. These are its global interdependence, defense spending, economic relations with other major powers, large current account surplus, thirst for energy, ties with developing countries, and official economic aid and other assistance.

Global Interdependence

First, although to a great extent driven by domestic investment patterns, China's economic growth is nonetheless increasingly dependent on trade, investment, and technology ties with the world. For example, between 1980 and 2006, China's trade as a proportion of its gross domestic product (GDP) grew from 22 to 71 percent, and the ratio of its imports to GDP soared from 11 percent in 1980 to 32 percent in 2007. In addition, its net exports of goods and services have increased hugely, both absolutely and as a share of GDP.[1]

As a result of this foreign economic involvement, China has become an increasingly active participant in international economic institutions and forums, including the World Bank, International Monetary Fund, World Trade Organization (WTO), Asian Development Bank, Association of Southeast Asian Nations (ASEAN) Plus Three (APT), and Group of Twenty (G-20), the forum for finance ministers and central bank governors from 20 major developed and developing economies.[2]

China has also been promoting a variety of trade and other economic agreements across Asia and beyond. Most notably, these include seven free trade agreements (FTAs), two closer economic partnership agreements, and one economic cooperation framework agreement, with a total of seventeen countries (including Taiwan) and two special administrative regions.

Beijing is currently negotiating six additional FTAs and conducting feasibility studies on several more. Sixteen of China's nineteen trade agreement partners are in the broader Asia-Pacific region (including the ASEAN countries, Pakistan,

New Zealand, Hong Kong, Macao, and Taiwan), and the other three are Latin American countries. The FTAs began in the early 2000s with the China–ASEAN FTA and have accelerated since 2005. The China–ASEAN FTA, inaugurated in January 2010, is perhaps the best known among them.[3]

China's participation in these institutions and arrangements has greatly assisted its economy and to some degree is helping to build international confidence in its commitment to peaceful development and support for the basic norms of the international system.[4] But this participation has also raised concerns in the United States and elsewhere over how China's growing leverage within international economic decision-making circles will be exercised as its financial and trade power increase.[5] Some observers charge that China is using both multilateral and bilateral mechanisms (such as ASEAN, the APT, and bilateral agreements with powers such as India) to move toward the creation of an Asian trading bloc that excludes the United States and other "non-Asian" powers, while reducing support for broader trade initiatives such as the WTO.[6] Other observers are also concerned that the growing web of intra-Asian economic agreements are placing the United States at a distinct economic disadvantage, which in turn undermines Washington's overall position in the region and hence vis-à-vis Beijing.[7]

Defense Spending

Second, China's sustained pattern of rapid economic growth and technology innovation and acquisition also provide the wherewithal for high levels of defense spending and an ambitious program of military modernization. For the past decade, as described in chapter 4, China's official defense expenditures have increased at an average annual rate of around 12 percent. In 2010, according to the Stockholm International Peace Research Institute (SIPRI), China spent around $114.3 billion on its military, which made up 2.2 percent of its GDP.[8] Clearly, without Beijing's dynamic economic development, the expanding size and composition of China's naval, air, and ground forces would almost certainly not produce the kind of concern currently found in U.S. defense circles. Hence, the question of the scope, makeup, and vulnerability (to U.S. influence) of China's economy as it pertains to military capabilities constitutes an important issue for U.S. policymakers. To achieve its military modernization goals, Beijing has steadily increased its level of defense spending for nearly twenty years, and especially during the past decade. China has become the world's second-biggest military spender behind the United States, although overall U.S. defense spending remains far ahead of all other powers by a wide margin.

Economic Relations with Other Major Powers

Third, China's increasing reliance on foreign trade, investment, and expertise to maintain its rapid growth has posed significant consequences for the economies of other major powers. For example, in 2002, China surpassed the United States to become the world's largest recipient of foreign direct investment. And in 2009, China surpassed Germany to become the world's second-largest trading nation after the United States and the world's largest exporter, while the European Union as a whole surpassed the United States as the largest recipient of Chinese exports. Indeed, the EU and China are becoming increasingly interdependent economically. Finally, in the summer of 2010, China edged past Japan to become the world's second-largest economy in terms of GDP.[9]

Much of China's foreign economic activity is concentrated in Asia, an increasingly critical region for U.S. prosperity. Moreover, since 2002, China has become a vital, perhaps indispensable, economic partner for key U.S. friends and allies such as Japan and South Korea. These Asian economies are part of an elaborate production network, wherein multinational firms based in many countries coordinate a multi-stage processing trade among these and other separate economies. This network makes Asia (particularly East and Southeast Asia) one of the most economically integrated regions in the world. Equally important, the United States and Europe now constitute the primary ultimate export destinations for China's goods, and China has become a major destination of U.S. exports during the past decade.[10]

Large Current Account Surplus

Fourth, in recent years, China's trade performance has resulted in the accumulation of a very large current account surplus—$306.2 billion in 2010.[11] This factor, combined with high levels of inward foreign direct investment and large inflows of speculative capital, generated nearly $2.85 trillion in foreign exchange reserves by the end of 2010, approximately seventeen times the level in 2000. These are predominantly dollar-denominated assets, including more than $1 trillion in U.S. Treasury notes and other U.S.-dollar-denominated paper.[12] In theory, China could significantly influence the value of the dollar if it were to rapidly divest itself of a large amount of these reserves and holdings or simply stop buying them for an appreciable period of time. Most analysts believe that such an action is highly unlikely, however, because it would likely cause significant damage to the Chinese economy (see below for more on this issue).[13]

Nonetheless, senior leaders of the PRC have publicly expressed concern over the "safety" of China's huge investment in U.S. government debt and have urged the Barack Obama administration to provide assurances that these holdings will maintain their value.[14] And China is opting for increasingly large acquisitions of foreign companies in various industries such as financial services, mining and oil, electronics, and telecommunications. For some observers, this partial shift represents China's desire to diversify its investment portfolio and accelerate the integration of the global economy more on its own terms.[15] In addition, Chinese financial officials have proposed the idea of creating a new international reserve currency system controlled by the IMF, even though Beijing understands that "there is no alternative to the dollar in the short term and may not be for many years."[16] Beijing is also taking actions to facilitate the use of the renminbi as a settlement currency for trade and other current account transactions in Asia and beyond, making it easier for China to promote exports and to protect its exporters from exchange risk. As of January 2011, China had signed $122 billion (RMB 803 billion) in currency-swap agreements with eight monetary authorities, beginning with South Korea in December 2008. And the MICEX exchange in Moscow began offering yuan-ruble trading on December 15, 2010, marking the first time the renminbi has been directly traded abroad.[17]

Whether credible or not, this issue exerts an influence over U.S. public and elite perceptions and feeds concerns about future potential Chinese leverage. It also fuels Chinese concerns about the value of Beijing's U.S. dollar holdings, prompting calls in some quarters for greater government pressure on the United States to undertake actions to prevent further depreciation (for example, via an inflation of the U.S. currency) or more diversification of China's financial investments.[18]

For some observers, China's currency and monetary policies, including its exchange rate policy and foreign exchange reserves, are a source of significant imbalance within the Chinese economy and a growing strain on the international economic system. Many analysts believe that China's currency policy adversely affects global trade balances, and especially the huge United States–China trade imbalance.[19] Other observers believe that the aftereffects of the global economic crisis will provide Beijing with greater economic and possibly political leverage over Washington, given the likelihood that the United States will become increasingly dependent on Chinese purchases of U.S. Treasury notes to fund the massive levels of U.S. fiscal deficits. And such concerns are bolstered by the fact that China is weathering the global economic crisis far better than any other major power.[20]

Finally, some analysts expect Beijing to become increasingly assertive (and Washington to lose negotiating leverage) regarding many bilateral economic issues of contention, as a result of Beijing's apparent strengths and successes and Washington's significant, and continuing, economic problems.[21] Indeed, Chinese officials vigorously assert that Beijing has done its part in boosting domestic demand and rebalancing the Chinese economy during and since the global recession.[22] Moreover, though cognizant of the need to increase domestic consumption,[23] Chinese officials do not regard global structural economic imbalances as a key cause of the recent global recession. They point instead to lax financial supervision in developed economies and among organizations such as the IMF, resulting in "very risky levels of leverage and too much speculation." PRC leaders have also complained that U.S. monetary policies aimed at stimulating the American economy (for example, so-called "quantitative easing") threaten to destabilize a weak world economy and send volatile "hot money" flowing into developing countries.[24]

Some analysts argue that China could significantly assist regional and global economies (and thereby itself and the United States) by injecting large amounts of its huge foreign exchange reserves into the IMF, World Bank, and/or the Asian Development Bank. However, despite China's enjoying increased voting shares in these organizations, Chinese officials have made it clear that they cannot take a major role in leading them, or in assisting other countries to recover from the global economic recession. China still views itself as a developing country in many respects, and thus it does not feel responsible for or capable of leading efforts to find a global solution to the economic crisis. Instead, it is fiercely focused on its own economy.[25]

Thirst for Energy

Fifth, to sustain its energy- and capital-intensive growth, China is increasingly dependent on foreign raw materials and commodities, including steel, oil, iron ore and other base metals, plastics, and chemicals.[26] According to the International Energy Agency (IEA), China surpassed the United States as the world's largest energy consumer in 2009, and it has also become the world's largest emitter of carbon dioxide in recent years.[27] China has also displaced the United States to become the world's greatest consumer of copper, nickel, iron ore, lead, and other base metals, and it is second to the United States in oil consumption. China contributed 20 percent to the total global increase in oil demand from 2002 to 2005 and is part of the reason for the prerecession increase in world oil prices. Moreover, the "trade value" of China's energy imports and exports increased by an amazing 330.5 percent between 2001 and 2006, from $23.27 billion to $100.19 billion.[28] Imported crude oil constituted 55 percent of China's total oil consumption in 2010. China accounted for 17 percent of global energy demand in 2009 and is forecast to contribute half of the growth in world oil demand from 2011 to 2015, according to the IEA.[29]

To address its growing energy challenge, China has adopted a multipronged market- and non-market-based approach that includes the diversification of supply sources; the use of long-term energy contracts and the formation of close political and economic relationships in energy-producing areas (in Asia, the Middle East, South America, and parts of Africa); equity ownership of some overseas production or refining facilities; a greater use of domestic coal, nuclear power, and natural gas; increases in energy efficiency and conservation; and additions to China's strategic oil reserves. However, it remains unclear whether these activities reflect the workings of a coordinated, comprehensive global energy security strategy. Although foreign-oriented activities are often associated with a so-called go-abroad (走出去) energy strategy, many knowledgeable observers assert that separate (and sometimes competing) bureaucratic and commercial interests often complicate China's search for energy security overseas. Indeed, until recently, some experts have described China's energy policymaking apparatus as "fractured" and its so-called strategy as "a collection of ad hoc initiatives."[30] In an apparent response to this situation in January 2010, Beijing announced the establishment of a new "super ministry" for energy, the National Energy Commission, to better coordinate, integrate, and control energy policies and activities.[31] Some analysts believe that this move will also result in a more hawkish or aggressive effort to address China's exploding energy demands, given the inclusion in the commission of senior military intelligence, foreign affairs, and military figures.[32]

Overall, the size and pace of China's imports of these basic goods have led some observers to suggest that China's demand is shaping global prices. According to at least one knowledgeable observer, China's growing appetite for energy resources and basic commodities will likely reduce, if not eliminate, the West's ability to determine international policy with respect to many of these products.[33] In addition, as indicated in chapter 4, other observers conjecture that Beijing might develop its naval and air forces to secure greater access to energy markets and to protect its sea lines of communication, posing significant implications for security perceptions in Asia and the United States. And some argue that China regards the creation of a large, state-owned tanker fleet as essential to this effort.[34]

Ties with Developing Countries

Sixth, Beijing's search for more expansive and reliable sources of raw materials, trade goods, and energy is resulting in deeper Chinese ties with countries in Africa, the Middle East, Latin America, and Central and Southeast Asia. For example, during the past decade, China has focused on expanding economic relations with Africa, through a variety of commercial and government-to-government arrangements, including duty-free treatment of some imports and exports, resource exploration and production arrangements, and the provision of export credits for PRC investment and business activities in areas such as infrastructure and utilities.[35]

In the Middle East, China is increasingly dependent upon oil from Saudi Arabia and Iran and is striking a variety of energy, trade, and investment arrangements with these and other local powers. Since the mid-1990s, the region has consistently been the largest source of China's oil imports, providing 2 million barrels per day in 2009, or about 50 percent. Saudi Arabia and Iran (along with Angola) have consistently been among the top three sources of oil imports for the past several years. Saudi Arabia provided about 20 percent of China's oil imports in 2009, and Iran is a major partner in large energy and commercial projects. In addition, in 2009 China overtook the United States as the world's largest exporter to the Middle East. Its exports to the region have increased to approximately $60 billion from just $4 billion a decade ago, as Chinese manufacturers have increasingly focused on the Middle East while buyers in Europe and the United States have reduced their spending.[36]

In much of Latin America, China's economic presence remains relatively small compared with that of the United States. However, in Brazil and the Southern Cone countries, China has already surpassed the United States economically. China is now the largest trading partner of both Brazil and Chile, and the largest trading partner of Argentina and Paraguay after Brazil. China has also become the largest source of new foreign direct investment flows to Brazil. And throughout Latin America, China is using its large supply of U.S. dollar reserves to provide significant levels of investment and aid. It is also acquiring resources and raw materials (mainly oil, iron ore, soybeans, and copper) and exporting manufactures and other products in growing amounts. The level of China–Latin American trade expanded nearly fifteen times (from a very low base) between 2000 and 2008, from $10 billion to $140 billion, reflecting the expansion of commodity exports to China from Brazil and the Southern Cone countries, and a broad-based penetration by China into Latin American product markets.[37]

In Central Asia, Beijing has become an increasingly important presence in the areas of trade and energy, providing substantial levels of investment and making deals for oil and gas supplies and mineral extraction. In the energy sector alone, China has invested approximately $6 billion in firms and has provided more than $14 billion in loans for the development of resources. Conversely, thus far the region provides a relatively small proportion (about 10–15 percent) of China's overall oil imports. But this number is expected to grow, especially as China seeks to diversify its energy sources away from the Middle East and as the 10,000 km-long China–Central Asia gas pipeline reaches its full capacity by 2012 or 2013. Throughout the 1990s, China held a very modest position in the Central Asian states' foreign trade. However, during the period 2000–2007, annual Sino-Central Asian trade grew very rapidly, increasing on average more than fifteen times compared with the 1990s. At the end of 2007, China's share of Central Asian trade reached about 14 percent.[38]

In Southeast Asia, China has become a very significant economic presence during the past twenty years. China became ASEAN's largest trading partner in 2009, and in 2010, ASEAN surpassed Japan to become Beijing's third-largest trading partner after the European Union and the United States. The growth rate of China's trade with ASEAN averaged 23 percent a year during the period 2000–2010. On the investment front, by 2008, the ASEAN nations had $52 billion in accumulated investment in China, led by Singapore, Malaysia, and Thailand, while China's accumulated direct investment in the ASEAN nations had reached $11.8 billion by the end of 2006. On January 1, 2010, China and ASEAN established a free trade zone to strengthen trade cooperation and liberalize two-way investment, based on a Framework Agreement on Comprehensive Economic Cooperation signed in November 2002. The China–ASEAN FTA, covering a combined population of 1.9 billion and a combined GDP of close to $6 trillion, is now the world's third-largest free trade area, incorporating China and Brunei, Cambodia, Indonesia, Laos, Malaysia, Myanmar, the Philippines, Singapore, Thailand, and Vietnam.[39] These developments have generally benefited both China and the ASEAN nations considerably, enabling them to serve as complements to each other within a regional production network. Although China's development has also presented a threat of competition to Southeast Asia, that danger is arguably diminishing as China moves up the production value chain and instead competes more with higher-income countries.[40]

Beijing's policies and actions in many of these regions are raising a variety of concerns in the United States and other Western countries, ranging from the proliferation of weapons of mass destruction and counterterrorism to human rights. For example, China's search for more stable energy supplies and other resource extraction and trading relationships in Africa have led Beijing to strengthen its political relations with authoritarian regimes in Sudan and elsewhere while downplaying or ignoring the involvement of these regimes in human rights abuses. And Beijing's increasingly close economic and political relationship with Tehran is contributing to China's resistance to cooperating with Western countries in putting pressure on Iran about its nascent nuclear weapons program.

In addition, more broadly, China's steady economic expansion in many regions throws doubt on the credibility of its oft-repeated commitment to not interfere in other nations' internal affairs.[41]

In the economic realm, some outside observers fear that China is pursuing "mercantilist" economic policies designed to establish strategic footholds and lock up resources in many of these regions, thereby distorting market forces and eventually destabilizing local social and political relationships. Compounding this situation, in some cases, are tensions between local workers and the many Chinese laborers being sent to work on overseas economic projects.[42]

Official Economic Aid and Other Assistance

Seventh, and closely related to Beijing's ties with developing countries, its official economic aid and other assistance to various developing countries have also expanded significantly in recent years, especially in Africa and Latin America. China's official foreign aid white paper states that China had provided $38.83 billion in total cumulative aid by the end of 2009, including about $16 billion in grants, $11 billion in interest-free loans, and $11 billion in concessional loans. Unofficial estimates of China's pledged foreign aid range much higher, and "according to one study using unofficial reports of both actual and *pledged* aid, the PRC promised a total of $31 billion in economic assistance to Southeast Asian, Latin American, and African countries in 2007, a threefold increase compared to 2005 and 20 times greater than 2003."[43]

Beyond traditional aid and interest-free or concessional loans, much of China's foreign assistance is in the form of government-sponsored investment and debt forgiveness, as well as aid packages with trade and investment agreements for areas such as infrastructure and national resource development, especially energy (grants, by contrast, are only a small portion of assistance). One study estimated that China's total foreign aid to Africa, Latin America, and Southeast Asia in 2007 was as high as $25 billion when factoring in loans, government investment, and other aid.[44]

To some observers, when all these types of assistance are included, China ranks as one of the largest bilateral aid donors in some African and Southeast Asian countries. However, the composition of this assistance indicates that China is not a provider of large amounts of official development assistance—that is, aid that is at least 25 percent gratis.[45] As Deborah Brautigam explains, China's overall aid to Africa remains limited compared with that given by "traditional donors" from the developed world.[46]

Moreover, as the PRC foreign aid white paper states, "China's foreign aid has emerged as a model with its own characteristics" that does not impose "any political conditions on recipient countries." For many U.S. officials and other outside observers, this refusal to link economic assistance to the behavior of recipient countries in areas such as human rights, the environment, and good governance has negative implications for the long-standing conditional aid policies promoted by the World Bank and other international lending agencies and backed by the United States.[47] Others are concerned that China's aid serves the interests of local elites and Chinese state and business entities far more than it does local businesses, the local citizenry, and overall national development. And China's generous foreign assistance has been criticized for being rife with corruption and shrouded in secrecy.[48]

U.S. ECONOMIC POLICY TOWARD CHINA

The most basic challenge that U.S. policymakers face in the economic and aid areas is how to formulate an approach to China that will significantly advance three primary U.S. economic policy goals—supporting the global and Asian economic order, U.S. jobs and prosperity, and China's stable development—without generating serious domestic political upheaval or damaging the overall Sino-U.S. relationship. Every U.S. policy approach will likely confront serious pressures from, or result in serious consequences for, elements of the international community, U.S. domestic political entities, and the Chinese leadership and populace. In particular, each approach will be shaped by several key issues—the relative political, social, and economic strengths and weaknesses of the two powers; the costs and benefits of collective (that is, international) versus unilateral action in addressing Chinese economic behavior; and the influence over U.S. policymakers exerted by domestic political factors. These issues have thus far generated three general potential policy approaches for the United States that are applicable to each economic issue area.

Policy Approaches

For the United States, one extreme approach to China would emphasize pressure and inducements, seeking to extract Chinese economic concessions or compromises (or any type of beneficial change) through the threat of unilateral or multilateral tariffs, boycotts, or sanctions, targeted at individual entities or the PRC government as a whole. The assumptions underlying this approach would likely include a belief that the size, scope, and strength of the U.S. economy, along with the possible influence of international economic institutions or groups of like-minded countries, are sufficient to induce Chinese leaders to comply with demands rather than to risk the negative consequences of noncompliance. This, in turn, assumes that Chinese economic and political leverage is probably inadequate to deter such pressures—for example, through threats of retaliation—and also that the Chinese leadership generally responds best to clear demands conveyed from a position of strength.

An opposite approach by the United States to China would eschew pressure and threats in favor of nonconfrontational negotiation and dialogue aimed at producing positive-sum outcomes through mutual compromises and trade-offs. This approach largely assumes that the United States—and other advanced economies—does not enjoy a clear preponderance of leverage over China on most economic issues, and that the Chinese leadership does not usually comply with external demands, especially ones that might generate significant domestic political or social discontent. In addition, it largely views China as increasingly able to retaliate in significant ways to punitive, zero-sum approaches from the United States in the economic arena. And it tends to favor multilateral approaches to dealing with what are viewed as increasingly global or regional economic issues involving China and the United States.

Between these two extremes, a range of other possible intermediate approaches by the United States to China combine varying amounts of public and private pressure, compromise, and mutual accommodation via both bilateral and multilateral contacts. In general, these approaches assume that the economic policy arena is too dynamic to justify a single approach; that pressure, persuasion, and dissuasion are all appropriate at times; and that U.S. political leaders must therefore constantly adapt their approach to changing circumstances. These approaches tend to assume that the United States remains strong (and thus enjoys considerable leverage) in some areas at certain points in time, but they also recognize that Chinese leaders are both increasingly able to retaliate in many areas if pressed too hard and are to a significant extent amenable to persuasion and inducements.

Policy History

In confronting these challenges and opportunities presented by China's dynamic economic growth, Washington has largely pursued a variety of intermediate approaches, especially in recent years. In the arena of international economics, the George W. Bush administration built on earlier efforts to bring China into the global economic order by actively supporting China's admission to all the major bilateral and multilateral economic institutions. This was done in order to reinforce the major norms of these structures, to promote China's economic liberalization, and thereby over time to encourage Beijing to become a major supporter and even shaper of the global economic system. This concept was arguably expressed most completely and systematically during Bush's second term by Robert Zoellick in his public remarks on China's role as a "responsible stakeholder,"[49] but it was implicit in Bush's (and Bill Clinton's) policies from early on.

The most important policy initiatives in this area were the Bush administration's endorsement of permanent normal trade relations with China and its strong support for Beijing's entry into the World Trade Organization, following years of accession negotiations.[50] Although U.S. officials recognized that China's entry into the WTO would be challenging—especially in the areas of agriculture, financial services, intellectual property rights (IPR) enforcement, and exchange rates—they nonetheless expected that the benefits of economic liberalization would strengthen China's stable economic growth; increase the overall balance, efficiency, and openness of its economy; and possibly expand human rights and other basic freedoms within Chinese society. Equally important, the Bush administration, in similar fashion to the Clinton administration, believed that China's entrance into the WTO would not only benefit the U.S. economy but would also constitute the single most important action that could be taken to deepen Beijing's commitment to the norms of the global economic system.[51]

Accordingly, facilitating China's smooth entrance into the WTO and subsequently monitoring and enforcing China's implementation of its WTO obligations constituted a centerpiece of the Bush administration's economic policy toward China.[52] Sino-U.S. negotiations had constituted the centerpiece of China's efforts to meet WTO requirements—that is, the achievement of a bilateral WTO agreement between Beijing and Washington would greatly increase the likelihood that China would be admitted to the WTO by opening the door to the subsequent completion of similar bilateral agreements with more than 40 other WTO member nations.

The Clinton administration eventually achieved a basic bilateral agreement with Beijing in November 1999, after overcoming considerable fits and starts precipitated largely by avoidable U.S. domestic issues.[53] The agreement contained far-reaching Chinese concessions in agriculture, services (especially financial services), telecommunications, and overall market access that facilitated a subsequent series of bilateral WTO agreements, including a critical agreement with the European Union in May 2000 that included several additional Chinese compromises. However, before China's final accession to the WTO could take place, the United States and other countries also needed to negotiate an agreement with Beijing on documents explaining in detail how it would implement its WTO commitments. The Clinton administration was unable to move these multilateral negotiations forward appreciably before it left office (largely because of domestic bureaucratic obstacles), and hence final discussions took place during the initial months of the Bush administration. Of greatest concern to U.S. officials were Chinese agricultural domestic subsidies and trading rights (that is, the rights to import and export).[54] Washington and Beijing reached a consensus on these and other remaining bilateral concerns in early June 2001, and both countries subsequently worked closely together to complete China's WTO accession. The Bush administration was thus strongly supportive when China became a WTO member in December 2001.[55]

By Bush's second term in office, however, Washington was expressing a growing sense of frustration with China's rate of progress on complying with the WTO's requirements, along with other economic matters (for example, the U.S. trade deficit with China had exploded to more than $250 billion by 2007).[56] As a result, U.S. officials made increasingly forceful calls for the revaluation of the renminbi (RMB), the protection of IPR, and an end to what the United States viewed as mercantilist economic practices, particularly regarding China's increasingly intensive quest for secure sources of energy. U.S. officials encouraged Beijing to realize that "the best way for it to pursue its energy security is to help strengthen global markets, not to seek preferential equity deals with irresponsible and, ultimately, unstable regimes."[57] They also asserted that Beijing needed to make much more progress in liberalizing its industrial policies, reducing import and export restrictions, reversing discriminatory regulations and prohibited subsidies, protecting IPR, and limiting government intervention in the market. Along with this rhetorical and diplomatic pressure, the Office of the U.S. Trade Representative initiated its first WTO dispute settlement case against China in March 2004, which was followed by another suit in 2006 and five more in 2007 and 2008. These complaints addressed specific violations of China's WTO commitments involving its discriminatory tax and subsidy laws and lax IPR protection efforts.[58] Some U.S. politicians also criticized China's use of its sovereign wealth fund to support strategic domestic industries in areas such as telecommunications, transportation, and energy as a form of state subsidization.[59]

As the U.S. economy has weakened during the latter Bush and Obama eras and the trade deficit with Beijing has exploded, Americans have become less enthralled with globalization and more skeptical of China. Public pressure has exerted a growing influence over the Sino-U.S. economic relationship, manifested in demands to prevent or discourage Chinese investment in U.S. strategic sectors, such as ports, oil companies, potential dual-use technologies, and high-technology product areas. Moreover, public outrage about tainted human and animal food and dangerous consumer products from China (ranging from toxic toothpaste to hazardous highchairs and baby toys), has resulted in strong criticism of China's internal oversight mechanism and demands for enforcement of country-of-origin labeling. Such criticism was in many cases largely one-sided, with the Chinese government and Chinese companies bearing the brunt of the criticism, and U.S. companies deflecting blame. As a response, the U.S. House and Senate have both taken measures to reform the Consumer Product Safety Act.[60]

Partly as a result of such public sentiments, the U.S. Congress has remained a vocal critic of China's economic practices. It has threatened to label Beijing a "currency manipulator" (although the U.S. Treasury has not done so since 1994), blamed China's currency rate and trade practices for U.S. unemployment, and threatened to impose punitive tariffs on Chinese goods, arguing that China's exports are excessively underpriced across a range of industries (wood products, computers, steel, and so on) and have thereby adversely affected small and medium-sized American businesses trying to compete.[61]

The Bush administration generally discouraged such confrontational (and sometimes purely symbolic) actions, however, favoring low-key, businesslike dialogues and negotiations. For example, the former undersecretary for international affairs at the Department of the Treasury, David McCormick, stated:

> China and the United States must be careful not to derail this reform through protectionist actions on either side that risk disrupting this relationship. And the leadership and the interest of the U.S. Congress on China's currency reform, and China's economic reform more broadly, is both needed and welcomed. But, it's especially important now during this time of turmoil in global markets that we remain steadfast in our commitment to an open and expanding trade and investment relationship between the United States and China.[62]

The Obama administration has generally taken the same stance, even though it has also at times been quite critical of China's currency policies privately while publicly suggesting that China is increasingly using protectionist measures and export subsidies, for goods ranging from textiles and refrigerators to beer and peanuts. It has also imposed special safeguards on imports of low-end Chinese-made tires—a measure the Bush administration avoided—despite the fact that the United States is not a significant manufacturer of tires.[63] The Office of the U.S. Trade Representative under Ron Kirk has launched four additional complaints against China before the WTO, one in 2009 and three in 2010, one of which resulted from a high-profile investigation of China's "indigenous innovation" policies in the clean energy sector in response to a 5,800-page petition submitted by the United Steelworkers Union in September 2010 (just before the 2010 midterm elections in America).[64] Indeed, concerns over both Chinese policies toward indigenous innovation and IPR violations have been increasingly stressed by the Obama administration and various analysts.[65]

Methods of Economic Engagement

Despite these continued tensions, the main thrust of U.S. policy in both the Bush and Obama administrations has continued to focus on managing economic differences through bilateral negotiations via such mechanisms as the annual Joint Commission on Commerce and Trade (JCCT) and the Treasury-led U.S.-China Strategic Economic Dialogue (SED) (now part of the combined Strategic and Economic Dialogue—S&ED—led by the State and Treasury departments).[66] And most recently, in January 2011 the Obama administration reaffirmed a public commitment to work with Beijing to strengthen macroeconomic communication and cooperation.[67]

The Joint Commission on Commerce and Trade

The JCCT continues to be billed as "the main forum for addressing bilateral trade matters and promoting commercial opportunities between the United States and China."[68] It was initially founded in 1983 and was strengthened in 1994 with the establishment of several working groups that operate year-round on a range of issues, including IPR, agriculture, textiles, commercial law, and trade remedies. The Bush administration further strengthened the JCCT in 2003, designating the secretary of commerce and the U.S. trade representative as cochairs on the U.S. side (a vice premier serves as the Chinese chair). Trade and industry groups, as well as specific companies, often seek to utilize the JCCT as a platform for resolving complaints about Chinese trade practices and addressing obstacles to operating in China. As a result, JCCT outcomes generally address specific issues affecting American industry (such as PRC government policies relating to, for example, indigenous innovation, government procurement, and IPR), rather than broader macroeconomic concerns.[69]

The Strategic and Economic Dialogue

Given the relatively narrow focus of the JCCT, Bush administration officials led by Secretary of the Treasury Henry Paulson perceived the need for a higher-level dialogue that would address broader, more strategic economic matters. As a result, the SED was established in September 2006 as an interagency effort designed to address a broad range of bilateral economic issues and their impact on various domestic and international conditions (for example, environment, health care, and education).[70]

The SED's original intent was to develop long-term, strategic solutions or approaches, while also addressing economic issues of pressing concern. The methodology was to define and discuss each side's strategic objectives, produce a course of concrete action designed to improve cooperation or avoid confrontation, and reduce misunderstandings via extensive dialogue. In addition, each dialogue session was to follow up on previous agreements reached in an attempt to maintain progress and resolve any problems.[71] These features have largely remained the same during the Obama era. However, the specific focus of the discussions has understandably increasingly shifted to issues related to the ongoing global recession and contributing factors basic to the United States–China economic relationship. For example, the SED originally focused on macroeconomic policy (including Chinese currency reforms and market access); innovation and IPR protection, energy, and the environment; and services trade and investment. But the S&ED has more recently settled on a framework for economic cooperation based on four pillars: (1) sustainable and balanced growth; (2) promoting resilient, open, and market-oriented financial systems; (3) strengthening trade and investment; and (4) strengthening the international financial architecture.[72]

Given the growing number of significant problems confronting the United States–China economic relationship, it is not surprising that the search for concrete solutions to pressing economic issues has often taken precedence over longer-term strategic discussions in both the SED and the S&ED. In particular, during the SED, Washington attempted to accelerate the pace of China's currency reform; expand market access for financial and nonfinancial services (beyond Beijing's WTO accession commitments); take steps to boost China's domestic consumption; improve the business climate in China; and address high-priority U.S. trade issues such as beef import restrictions, IPR protection, and product health and safety. During the first and second rounds of the economic track of the S&ED (held in mid-2009 and mid-2010), the United States agreed to work on shrinking its fiscal deficit, sustaining growth in its private savings rates, and providing stronger regulation and supervision of its financial system. China made its own commitments to boost domestic consumption, liberalize access to its financial sector, improve the business climate for foreign investors, reassess its policy favoring indigenous innovation (which some observers believe amounts to de facto protectionism), and accelerate the pace of its currency reform. Bilateral discussions also addressed reforming the international financial architecture in order to better engage and represent developing countries such as China, as well as barriers to foreign investment and financial and regulatory system reform. At the same time, the U.S. Treasury secretary, first Henry Paulson and now Timothy

Geithner, has also sought to engage Beijing in longer-range strategic discussions involving issues such as energy security and the environment.[73]

This set of ambitious objectives creates a multitude of challenges for the U.S. policymaking process, given the significant number of agencies and interests involved in these areas, the complexity of the issues being considered, and the growing political pressure exerted by Congress and the public. In response to these challenges, Paulson originally devised a highly ambitious approach toward the SED that combined intra-agency and interagency tasking and coordination with extensive interactions with Chinese counterparts at all levels, along with well-timed publicity for SED meetings and their results.[74]

In all these areas, the pressure on the SED and S&ED to attain concrete results (or "deliverables") in the economic arena has been considerable, and some successes have been achieved thus far. For example, in May 2007, agreements were reached to allow foreign banks in China to issue RMB-denominated bank cards, double the number of U.S. passenger flights to China by 2012, and lower barriers for bilateral trade in environmental goods and services. The December 2007 SED session produced memorandums of understanding to increase coop-eration on illegal logging, food and feed, drugs and medical products, and bio-fuels. Beijing also agreed to allow foreign companies in China to issue RMB-denominated stocks and bonds, while the United States agreed to permit mutual funds administered by Chinese banks to invest in the U.S. stock market. The June 2008 SED session resulted in a range of agreements on energy and the environ-ment, bilateral investment, financial sector reform, trade and competitiveness, and product safety and quality. However, the SEDs arguably did not result in any significant actions by Beijing to increase the value of the RMB or reduce China's growing trade imbalance with America.[75] Although the 2009 S&ED arguably produced few tangible results in the economic realm, it did generate a mem-orandum of understanding on climate change, energy, and the environment. The memo established a mechanism for enhancing dialogue and cooperation between the United States and China on transitioning to low-carbon economies, sharing technologies, and capacity building.[76] The 2010 S&ED resulted in sev-eral agreements that mostly dealt with clean or renewable energy and nuclear cooperation. However, these negotiations took place on the strategic track, not the economic one.

Some observers also claim that U.S. pressure in the SED and other forums has played a role in motivating Beijing to allow the RMB to appreciate more than 25 percent since 2005. Paulson in fact claimed that such currency reval-uation was one measure of the SED's success.[77] However, many other analysts insist that the RMB is increasing in value primarily for macroeconomic reasons associated with overall trends in the Chinese economy, and not because of U.S. pressure or encouragement.

International and Regional Trade and Financial Groupings

A second major set of interactions in the economic arena has focused on working within multilateral programs and forums. For example, Washington has increasingly used the WTO dispute resolution mechanism to raise complaints against China in a variety of areas—for example, imported automobile parts, industrial subsidies, export quotas, export duties (along with other restraints allegedly maintained by China on exporting key raw material inputs for which China is a leading world producer), and alleged discriminatory tax treatment regarding imported semiconductors. In many instances, such complaints have led to WTO rulings in favor of the United States or resulted in some type of satisfactory Chinese response.[78] For this reason, the WTO process is viewed by both the administration and some in Congress as a significant mechanism for resolving economic disputes with Beijing, and it can to some extent thus serve as a compromise between low-level negotiations and higher-pressure, higher-visibility criticisms of Chinese practices.[79]

Of course, the WTO dispute resolution mechanism can also serve China's interests, because the WTO might rule in Beijing's favor in some cases. Indeed, Beijing has asked the WTO to investigate U.S. duties on Chinese steel pipe, tires, and shrimp (among other products). In a particularly important case, the WTO Appellate Body in March 2011 issued a major ruling in favor of the PRC that will limit the type of tariffs China's trading partners can impose on Chinese products. China has also won a case against a U.S. ban of Chinese poultry and scored a partial victory in a case challenging the Chinese IPR regime.[80] On the positive side, China has passed many pieces of legislation related to its WTO obligations and has significantly improved its economic policies and behavior, though it continues to be challenged in the area of enforcement (see below for more on this point).[81]

In addition to these mechanisms, the Bush and Obama administrations have also supported efforts by the IMF, the Group of Eight (G-8, composed of advanced economies), and more recently the G-20 (including both advanced and developing economies) to address a variety of economic relations involving Beijing. For example, in the G-8 forum, Washington endorsed the Heiligendamm Process launched in the second half of 2007, which consisted of a high-level dialogue with China and four other important emerging economies covering four key areas: promoting and protecting innovation; strengthening the freedom of investment; determining joint responsibilities for development (especially in Africa); and improving joint access to know-how aimed at reducing carbon dioxide emissions. A final report on the results of this dialogue was presented at the 2009 G-8 summit. The G-8 leaders also issued statements on various issues of relevance to United States–China economic relations. For example, they urged countries with large and growing current account surpluses to adjust their exchange rates, and declared support for the promotion and protection of IPR, particularly through anticounterfeiting and antipiracy initiatives.[82]

Since the emergence and worsening of the global recession, the G-20 has become an increasingly important forum for addressing a variety of economic issues involving China, and thus it has largely eclipsed the G-8. However, both the tone of the proceedings and the specific topics covered have shifted decidedly away from direct or implicit criticism of Chinese economic practices and toward a general emphasis on collective economic action in critical areas such as financial reform, along with criticism of economic practices in the United States and other Western industrial nations. For the first time, China, the United States, and other G-20 members agreed to a United States–backed plan to submit their policies to a "peer review" from other governments. They also identified key economic indicators, including public and private debt and external imbalances (composed of trade balances, net investment flows, and exchange rates), that the IMF would monitor for signs of possible future crises—though they have not yet agreed upon any numerical targets for those indicators. The G-20 has also agreed to give China and other Asian nations a bigger share of the vote at the IMF and the World Bank, even though these moves have created friction between the United States and Europe. However, in general, the G-20 has also served to highlight the significant differences between the United States, China (and other major developing nations), and Europe on the core problems facing the global economy. All this makes it very problematic for Washington to use the larger, more diverse G-20 forum to advance its economic objectives vis-à-vis China, especially in the midst of a severe economic recession during which many past U.S. practices have become targets of attack.[83] In addition, Chinese officials have repeatedly rejected U.S. calls to revalue the RMB more rapidly and have (along with Germany) resisted Secretary Geithner's proposal to numerically limit current account balances as a percentage of GDP as a means to reduce global imbalances.[84]

Finally, as indicated in chapter 3, in recent years, Washington has also sought to deepen its involvement in economic structures and agreements in the Asia-Pacific region. These include a wide range of activities associated with the Asia-Pacific Economic Cooperation forum (APEC) and ASEAN, the establishment of FTAs, and negotiations regarding the Trans-Pacific Strategic Economic Partnership (TPP). In 2006, the Bush administration and ASEAN signed a Trade and Investment Framework Agreement (TIFA). That same year, at the APEC leaders' meeting in Hanoi, Washington put forth a proposal for a Free Trade Agreement of the Asia-Pacific (FTAAP) that would include all 21 APEC economies. But this idea failed to gain traction, and although feasibility studies for such an arrangement have been conducted, no formal FTAAP negotiations have taken place.[85] Due to the lack of movement on the FTAAP, Bush administration officials shifted their attention in 2008 toward membership in the Pacific-4 Agreement, also known as the TPP.[86] After some delay in moving forward with the TPP, President Obama expressed a renewed U.S. commitment to it in late 2009.[87] In addition, the Bush administration signed a Korea–United States FTA with South Korea on June 30, 2007.

On the negative side, the U.S. Congress has yet to ratify the Korea–United States FTA, and this has been a source of serious concern for Asian nations concerned about America's future economic presence in the region.[88] Overall, even though Washington has thus far enacted FTAs with seventeen countries worldwide, only two of them are in Asia (Australia and Singapore). Moreover, although six rounds of negotiations regarding the TPP had taken place as of April 2011, most observers believe it will be a long time before a substantive, regionwide pact emerges—if ever.[89]

Continuing Areas of Concern

Despite the above undertakings and achievements, there is little doubt that more substantial, long-term successes in United States–China economic relations are necessary to resolve growing frictions between Beijing and Washington over financial services, trade and protectionism, currency policy, IPR, and several other economic issues. Moreover, the global recession has not only lent greater urgency to the resolution of many of these long-standing problems but has also made them more difficult to manage from a U.S. perspective, given the widespread perception that American political and economic leverage is declining both globally and vis-à-vis China. The global financial crisis and America's continued economic stagnation, huge fiscal deficits, and high unemployment suggest that it might become virtually impossible for the United States to play the kind of leadership role and enjoy the kind of prestige and influence on economic matters that it has enjoyed in the past.[90]

Moreover, some U.S. analysts also stress that both Chinese stability and future improvements in the United States–China economic relationship are threatened by the alleged fact that the overall pace of China's economic reform remains slow.[91] Other analysts strongly disagree. The most optimistic analysts argue that China's reform program—combined with its admission into the WTO—have created high annual growth rates of more than 10 percent since 2001 and will likely continue to produce rapid growth for several more decades.[92] Regardless, U.S. officials certainly believe that China needs to implement more fundamental structural reforms to reduce Chinese savings and increase domestic consumption, and thereby not only lower the huge U.S. trade deficit with China but also create a more stable overall economic relationship.

Finally, beyond such bilateral issues, Chinese trade, investment, and aid policies toward developing regions such as Africa and Latin America have also become an unresolved issue of growing concern for U.S. policymakers in recent years, as indicated above.[93] U.S. government agencies often observe that China is not transparent regarding the level and type of official assistance it provides to other countries.[94]

EVALUATION

Given China's continued rapid overall growth, increasingly heavy involvement in the global economy and in all major global regions, and extensive trade and investment relationship with the United States, there is little doubt that the economic policy arena will remain a central component of U.S. policy toward China. Indeed, the Sino-American economic relationship has become critical to the economic health and vitality of both nations. As scholar and former U.S. official Thomas Christensen has noted, this relationship "has opened China's economy to quality U.S. products and services, has helped educate and inspire a generation of Chinese entrepreneurs, engineers, and officials, and has contributed to keeping inflation low in the United States by lowering prices on a wide range of consumer goods and inputs to U.S. production."[95] In addition, China has become a major market for American exports, thus generating and sustaining a large amount of jobs. It is also funding a large portion of American debt and in general is contributing to the economic stability and prosperity of the Asia-Pacific region.

Conversely, despite common American and Chinese support for regional and global economic prosperity and growing levels of mutual economic dependence, this policy arena will continue to witness significant, perhaps growing, friction in this decade and beyond with respect to a very wide range of issues. These issues will likely include bilateral trade balances, foreign energy and resource acquisition policies, product safety, IPR, Chinese attempts to acquire U.S. companies in so-called strategic sectors of the U.S. economy (oil and natural gas, high-technology products, and port facilities), the pace and scope of China's economic liberalization effort, potentially contrasting approaches to emerging global challenges such as climate change and the international financial crisis, Beijing's expanding role in and views toward a wide array of international economic institutions and forums, and U.S. concerns regarding China's record in implementing its WTO commitments. All these potential problems will almost certainly generate significant domestic political attention in both the United States and China, thereby potentially complicating efforts to craft effective policies in both countries. This is all the more likely given the pressures created by the ongoing economic problems confronting Washington. And these pressures in turn could lead to increased demands to confront Beijing as a "source" of many of America's economic ills.

However, given the obviously growing importance of China's economy to both the United States and world economies and its growing role within multilateral economic forums and institutions such as the G-20 and the IMF, it is becoming increasingly clear that the days are gone when Washington could effectively apply unilateral pressure or otherwise threaten Beijing to obtain economic benefits, whether bilateral or in broader venues. Today, and for the foreseeable future, such actions cannot be taken without exposing the United States to very significant and potentially damaging retaliations from China, or other consequences, such as damage to the overall economic environment.[96] In short, Washington will need to cooperate more closely with—and in some instances accommodate more to the views of—other nations, including China and other developing economics, to manage its most vital economic concerns, and to reorder the governing structures and procedures of the international economic order.[97]

This policy history also suggests that Washington has been able to achieve significant results with Beijing by relying on dialogue and negotiation rather than confrontation and threats. Despite a lack of major concrete "deliverables," the SED and S&ED in particular have made slow but notable progress in encouraging China to address both specific improvements and comprehensive economic reforms and thereby have arguably reduced America's temptation to take more provocative actions. These efforts have strengthened mutual trust and have gradually drawn China into playing a fuller, more supportive role in a range of multilateral and bilateral economic institutions.[98] Perhaps equally important, the SED and S&ED have also arguably mitigated U.S. domestic pressures to take more forceful action against China on economic and other disputes. At the same time, the S&ED has also given the appearance of becoming more oriented toward the holding of a massive public event once a year, to highlight important issues and announce agreements or specific actions. This has, arguably, led to a deemphasis on sustaining an ongoing, interactive problem-solving and longer-range strategic planning process throughout the rest of the year, according to some observers.

In addition, although China has not fully complied with all its WTO obligations and is unlikely to make rapid progress in this regard, it is fair to say that the Bush and Obama administrations have succeeded in continuing to make this a priority for Beijing. China's increasing reliance on the WTO dispute settlement mechanism arguably shows the United States and other powers that Beijing supports a major, internationally accepted process to resolve economic disputes.[99] Moreover, the use of this mechanism helps significantly in diffusing bilateral political tensions over economic disputes, although the process remains beset with many pressures and uncertainties. As Chad Bown, a senior economist at the World Bank, states:

> In order for the WTO dispute process to "work," both the United States and China need to act and react with political savvy and have an underlying, long-term commitment to the process and WTO system. . . . Missteps by either side through careless mismanagement of the politics of the dispute resolution process could lead to stalemates and both sides becoming disenchanted with the current rules-based trading system. Such an outcome would have serious consequences, as the WTO system needs both the United States and China to be confident and invested in the future of the institution.[100]

Although some might view Beijing's proliferation of WTO-related economic reform legislation as a mere rhetorical gesture, it is important to assess these activities in light of the Chinese governance structure. Despite Western perceptions of the omnipotence of the Chinese central government, it is not a monolith able to enforce its will over all subordinate entities. In fact, it without doubt cannot ensure immediate implementation and enforcement of economic reforms at the local level. Thus, slow progress on WTO issues does not necessarily signal that the Bush and Obama administrations' overtures to China have been ignored. Rather, slow progress is partly a function of the Chinese system.[101]

As indicated above, perhaps the greatest area where the Bush and Obama administrations have succeeded is by channeling potentially volatile U.S. economic concerns into nonconfrontational arenas, via both the WTO dispute settlement mechanism and the S&ED. If handled incorrectly, public and/or congressional outrage over China's currency policy, the country's lack of effective product safety oversight, and the huge bilateral trade deficit could spawn a trade war and perhaps even set overall relations back significantly. Given this possibility, Washington has done a decent job of keeping United States–China economic relations on a positive footing, despite growing domestic economic pressures largely resulting from the global recession. Nonetheless, managing American public opinion and perceptions in the economic area will remain a very challenging task during this decade and well beyond.[102]

In addition to such accomplishments, the SED/S&ED process has also established a possible model for interacting with China that can be applied to other areas of the relationship. In particular, it offers a mechanism for undertaking the kind of interagency consultation, coordination, and formulation regarding complex policy issues that is increasingly required to handle the rapidly expanding organizations and interests involved on both sides in the bilateral relationship. Conversely, the dialogue process is also extremely demanding in time and resources and has been highly dependent for its success on the energy, commitment, and personal relationships (with the president and other senior U.S. and Chinese officials) of Cabinet-level officials such as Paulson, Geithner, and Secretary of State Hillary Clinton.

Some knowledgeable observers of the S&ED process believe that the limited concrete successes attained through the dialogue thus far do not justify the level of energy and resources required. On the other hand, the S&ED has arguably empowered parts of the U.S. economic bureaucracy and given them more clout than they might otherwise enjoy in the China policy arena. And by interacting with the Chinese side at a sufficiently high (that is, vice premier) level, it has also provided an unprecedented structure for overcoming bureaucratic stovepiping and foot-dragging within the PRC governmental apparatus. However, some observers believe that the Chinese system remains unable to deal effectively both internally and with the United States in the S&ED on complex issues such as energy, climate change, and environmental policy, due to structural and organizational constraints. Some knowledgeable observers also believe that the S&ED should include discussions of domestic, long-term, macroeconomic issues that affect both countries, such as health care costs and infrastructure. Finally, several observers believe that the overall S&ED process needs to focus more than it currently does on maintaining an array of continuous, working-level, in-depth dialogues rather than on convening a single annual high-level event keyed to a few public deliverables. Hence, overall, many observers believe that the S&ED is a valuable yet still limited exercise that has not realized its full potential.[103]

Concerning China's economic behavior (trade, investment, and assistance) in relation to other countries in regions such as Southeast Asia, Africa, and Latin America, there is little doubt that Beijing is becoming highly active as an economic partner and to some extent as a leader of economic cooperation initiatives in organizations such as ASEAN, the Shanghai Cooperation Organization, and the APT. It is also making significant economic gains in establishing an apparently growing number of FTAs with various key Asian countries and subregions, such as Southeast Asia. Nonetheless, many observers tend to exaggerate the level of economic influence exerted by Beijing as a result of these activities, along with the level of concern expressed by U.S. officials regarding China's behavior. As Robert Sutter has shown, thus far, the scope and composition of China's economic involvement in Asia have been less impressive than many observers believe.[104] And other analysts and U.S. officials point out that, even though China's economic and political presence in Latin America has increased rapidly from a low base in a few short years—especially in Brazil and the Southern Cone countries— the United States still retains a dominant economic position vis-à-vis China in Mexico, Central America, and the northern countries of South America.[105]

At the same time, in the aftermath of the global financial crisis, most Asian countries are increasingly concerned about America's ability to provide the sort of economic growth stimulus it clearly generated for them in past decades, and as a result, many are looking toward China. As some knowledgeable observers assert, the United States must more actively deepen its involvement in the growing web of regional economic agreements described above if it hopes to sustain its credibility and influence across the region—an essential precondition to any effective strategy toward China.[106]

In addition, many observers assert that China's influence in Africa, though growing, does not constitute a threat to U.S. interests and thus by implication should not motivate U.S. counterpolicies.[107] To the contrary, for some knowledgeable analysts and officials, China's growing economic involvement in such developing regions of the world, and the fact that its involvement generates both positive and negative consequences, provide the United States with an opportunity to draw Chinese entities into relevant international economic structures and to enhance economic cooperation among the United States, China, and regional states.[108]

That said, there is little doubt that China's overall stress on its "noninterference" in the internal affairs of many developing countries where it is heavily involved economically, and its resulting willingness to work closely with and sometimes support tyrannical regimes, remains a potential area of strong contention between Washington and Beijing. This issue is discussed further below.

FUTURE TRENDS

It is likely that the economic relationship between the United States and China will continue to deepen and expand during this decade, thus posing significant challenges and opportunities for the management of U.S. policy issues relating not only to bilateral relations but also to larger regional and global economic issues. China's economy is expected to continue growing at a much more rapid pace than the U.S. economy—through a combination of high levels of domestic investment and expanding foreign trade—and will almost certainly become the world's largest economy (in aggregate size) by 2040 at the latest. Moreover, the many bilateral issues discussed above will likely continue as major topics of Sino-U.S. negotiation, while China's growing power as a creditor nation with enormous reserves, and its general impact on the global economy, will increasingly present the United States with a host of important issues to manage.[109]

Perhaps the three most pressing issues for consideration by U.S. policymakers are (1) the impact of the global economic downturn on the Chinese economy and the activities of United States and other foreign economic entities in China, (2) the relative position and influence of Beijing and Washington in the global and regional economic order, and (3) the ability of both countries to cooperate in addressing the economic challenges associated with the global economic recession. It is useful to briefly consider these and related issues.

Economic Recovery and Global Rebalancing

From a broad perspective, there is some debate about the likely impact of the global recession on long-term Chinese economic growth rates and the structural stability of the Chinese economy and society during the decade.[110] In 2008 and early 2009, many analysts, including those at the IMF and the Organization for Economic Cooperation and Development, expected China's growth rate to decline from approximately 11 percent to 6 or 7 percent through 2010 and perhaps beyond, precipitated largely by huge decreases in foreign trade and the collapse of a real estate bubble that had emerged in the past decade.[111] Such fears led to concerns about excessive unemployment and a weakening of the legitimacy and stability of the PRC regime. Moreover, the latter concerns were fueled by severe ethnic-based violence in Tibet and Xinjiang in 2008 and 2009.[112]

Yet, by the second half of 2009, it became clear that China had led the world out of the global downturn, with growth rates increasing from virtually zero in late 2008 to an estimated 17 percent annualized growth by the second quarter of 2009, driven largely by a nearly $600 billion fiscal stimulus (including an investment plan, a set of funding mechanisms, and a series of industrial policies) and a massive program of government-directed bank lending. By the end of 2009, China had attained an annual growth rate of 8.7 percent, and its 2010 growth rate climbed to 10.3 percent.[113] In the summer of 2010, China edged past Japan to become the world's second-largest economy in terms of GDP.[114] Many experts have also observed that China's recovery has significantly assisted the global recovery, and particularly the recoveries of other Asian economies.[115]

Nonetheless, some analysts have expressed concerns that China's recovery is unsustainable over the long term and/or will exacerbate future friction in United States–China economic relations. In particular, regarding the former point, some observers argue that China's large (and in some cases increasing) reliance on exports, fixed infrastructure investment, a rapid growth of the state sector, and huge amounts of subsidized bank lending (that is, "soft" loans) to achieve economic recovery will likely spur inflation and asset price bubbles, raise government debt to dangerously high levels, sustain a large trade surplus, and prevent a stable transition to a more consumption-driven economy. Therefore, rebalancing away from excessive production toward higher consumption is viewed by many analysts (and U.S. officials) as essential to China's long-term economic stability and high growth rates, and to more stable relations with major trade and investment partners such as the United States.[116]

In particular, with regard to the global economy, some analysts have expressed the fear that domestic consumption in China (and other countries) cannot increase rapidly enough and to sufficient levels to balance the current significant drop in U.S. consumption, thus eventually creating a global "downward spiral of unstable adjustment" marked by low growth (and continued massive deficits) in many economies, and accompanying trade frictions.[117]

This danger results from the so-called global capital-flow paradox, whereby developing countries such as China became net capital exporters to developed current account-deficit countries such as the United States, largely via huge reserve holdings in the form of U.S. Treasury securities. Thus, any amelioration of this problem over time will supposedly require significant levels of consumer saving and public spending in the United States (and elsewhere) and much greater levels of Chinese consumer spending (and a lower reliance on net exports), to avoid a prolonged global economic slowdown. In other words, from this perspective, long-term stability will require major, likely wrenching changes in both the U.S. and Chinese economies.[118] For Beijing, a shift away from an emphasis on domestic infrastructure and industrial investment and exports to an economy centered on services and consumer products will require a paradigm shift in Chinese policies, structures, and institutions involving difficult economic and political choices. This is unlikely to occur in short order, if at all.[119] If such adjustments are not implemented, analysts such as Michael Pettis argue that China could enter a prolonged period of economic stagnation similar to that of Japan during its post-1980s "lost decades."[120]

However, other analysts are far less pessimistic about the strength and sustainability of China's recovery from the stimulus, and its implications for global imbalances, the American and Chinese economies, and their economic relations. They argue that Beijing has been addressing some of the structural impediments to long-term, stable growth by increasing investments in social safety nets, creating a bond market, further opening its capital markets, introducing modestly leveraged investible instruments (for example, a rudimentary secondary mortgage market), conducting expanding experiments in a greater role for the Chinese currency in trade and investment, gradually raising interest rates, and expanding consumer lending of various sorts.[121] And some observers stress that China's deep and long-term investment in low-income housing, rural infrastructure, utilities, transportation, education, and the environment (among other sectors) will encourage stability domestically by mitigating unemployment and boosting consumption. Such developments can also serve as the basis for future long-term Chinese growth.[122]

Moreover, some analysts argue that the current global imbalance was caused primarily by excess liquidity in the U.S. economy, which had been essentially fueled by financial deregulation during the period 1992–2006. This created a spending surge that greatly accelerated Chinese exports to the United States, resulting in huge bilateral trade and current account deficits and the buildup of China's U.S. dollar reserves. Hence, such issues are best addressed by putting the U.S. economic house in order, rather than by pressing Beijing to increase domestic consumption or appreciate its currency.[123] In addition, many analysts argue that the best way for China to increase domestic consumption levels is to enhance its relatively low capital stocks by continuing to invest heavily in production-enhancing infrastructure.[124] However, other analysts challenge the very notion that China is underconsuming, and they argue that, in any event, China's consumption growth will catch up with its investment and export growth in the medium and long terms.[125]

Despite these differences among analysts about China's long-term economic stability and its relationship to global imbalances, most observers agree that continuing economic problems resulting in part from the global recession could lead to serious levels of protectionism in the Sino-U.S. relationship (as part of a global trend), thus generating major tensions in bilateral economic relations in the near to medium terms at least. If U.S. unemployment deepens or remains high through 2011 and beyond, political leaders in Washington might experience increasing pressures to strengthen trade barriers or generally retaliate against China's "excessive" trade surplus. And, to maintain high growth rates, China might push exports through import substitution and other subsidies. In fact, the Chinese stimulus and recovery program is strongly favoring large government-controlled enterprises over private small and midsize firms and is reinforcing an effort to favor domestic over foreign companies in a wide range of product areas. A deepening of this trend could augment fears of both rising protectionism and economic nationalism. Governments have met on several occasions throughout the crisis to call for resistance against such potential protectionist measures, including at regular summits of the G-20, APEC, and the World Economic Forum. In addition, both President Obama and President Hu Jintao have spoken out against protectionism in public. Washington must remain particularly attentive to such dangers.[126]

Chinese Holdings of U.S. Debt

U.S. attempts to address the current recession through stimulus packages funded by extremely high levels of deficit spending have also highlighted the apparent dangers of relying on China's continued large-scale purchase of U.S. debt. As indicated above, some analysts fear that Beijing might (1) reduce its large dollar holdings for economic reasons and thereby significantly aggravate the U.S. recession by forcing an increase in interest rates; and/or (2) seek to use its holdings to pressure Washington in a variety of policy areas.[127]

Whether or not China would stop buying or even begin selling off dollar reserves *at significant levels* due to a faltering U.S. economy is a contentious issue among analysts, however. Some argue that a sell-off of dollar-denominated securities by Beijing is particularly likely during the current economic downturn when the value of the dollar is relatively high. That is, if China—and other foreign holders—expect the dollar to decline significantly in the near to medium terms as a result of aggressive U.S. deficit spending, then they might decide to diversify away from the dollar in the near term. Indeed, as noted above, many ordinary Chinese citizens are criticizing Beijing for purchasing huge amounts of what they view as a declining asset. Some even charge that Washington deliberately sought to dupe Beijing into acquiring ever larger amounts of depreciating dollar holdings.[128]

But many other analysts contend that it is not in China's interest to sell off dollar reserves, because to do so would almost certainly reduce the value of whatever dollar-denominated assets China might still hold, and add to the severity of the U.S. recession, thereby reducing Sino-U.S. trade and investment levels and damaging the PRC economy. Specifically, a drop in the dollar's value would decrease the ability of Americans to buy Chinese goods, thus having profound adverse effects on Chinese exporters. The Chinese government's concern about falling demand in the United States is signified by its recent efforts to prop up its export sector and halt job losses. China's unemployment problem would only be exacerbated, then, by a weaker dollar. In addition, given both the role of the U.S.

dollar as a global reserve currency and the relative confidence that most nations have in America, with its highly stable political and economic systems, as a safe haven during economic crises, it makes little sense for China to divest its dollar holdings under current conditions and for the foreseeable future.[129] Apparently, Beijing agrees with this perspective, because Chinese finance officials have indicated that they have little choice but to continue purchasing U.S. Treasuries.[130]

However, as also noted above, China has called for the reform of the current, United States–based global monetary system and has specifically urged the creation of an alternative international reserve currency to the U.S. dollar, utilizing the IMF's Special Drawing Rights associated with a combination of freely convertible currencies and managed by the IMF. The goal, according to Zhou Xiaochuan, head of the People's Bank of China, would be to create a "super-sovereign reserve currency . . . that is disconnected from individual nations and is able to remain stable in the long run, thus removing the inherent deficiencies caused by using credit-based national currencies."[131] Although the implications of such a move for the United States are a source of debate, it could produce significant instability in the U.S. economy in the short to medium terms if it were poorly implemented by other nations.[132]

In any event, most analysts do not believe that the global monetary system can be significantly moved away from the current United States–based system any time in the foreseeable future, given the relatively large size of the U.S. economy compared with other economies and the likely continuation of the United States as a safe haven for investments. But China's concerns (backed by similar concerns expressed by other nations) do suggest that Washington must maintain the stability of the dollar and remain highly attentive to Beijing's growing willingness to press for changes in United States–centered global financial practices. Such challenges could indeed grow over time, as China's global economic imprint deepens.[133]

Currency Frictions

As noted above, the global economic recession and its aftermath have also had an impact on the friction between Washington and Beijing over the value of the renminbi. The recession intensified Washington's own efforts to engage in monetary practices that result in a de facto "manipulation" of the dollar. This development, combined with the fact that the RMB had appreciated by roughly 20 percent between 2005 and 2008, eased U.S. criticism in some quarters that Beijing was artificially manipulating its currency to maintain its trade surplus.[134] However, Beijing halted this trend and again pegged the RMB to the dollar in mid 2008, in an effort to ease the damage to China's export industries caused by the global recession. Some analysts asserted at the time that this was a sign of things to come, as long as China remained dependent on exports for continued high rates of growth. Indeed, if China had maintained this peg indefinitely, the RMB's value would likely have again become a major source of contention between Washington and Beijing.[135] Such a dispute would be particularly dangerous because it is not amenable to WTO resolution, and thus could facilitate extreme calls for economic sanctions, which in turn could trigger a trade war.[136]

Fortunately, in mid-2010 Beijing again reversed course and allowed a gradual appreciation of the RMB, as a result of its decision to resume using a flexible exchange rate. This move was obviously welcomed by Washington. However, the rate of RMB appreciation is expected to remain relatively low in the next several years, and thus this issue will remain a source of tension.[137] That said, it is possible that the real exchange rate could appreciate more rapidly than the nominal exchange rate.[138]

And yet a cheaper RMB arguably benefits U.S. consumers of Chinese exports. Moreover, U.S. exports to China have grown almost five times faster than U.S. exports to the rest of the world since China joined the WTO in 2001, suggesting that engagement and dialogue coupled with transparent, rule-based trade measures have worked better than threatening unilateral sanctions and tariffs. As a result, many analysts believe that the best way to address trade disputes with China is to increase U.S. exports, not protect U.S. markets or sanction China for having an undervalued currency.[139] Nonetheless, China's managed exchange rate and resulting undervalued currency arguably contribute significantly to economic adjustment problems in many other countries, again pointing to the need for Beijing to expand domestic demand.[140]

In the medium to long terms (that is, five to fifteen years), China is expected to continue to slowly appreciate its currency and loosen capital controls. And, as suggested above, according to many analysts, the long-term pressure to appreciate the RMB is more likely to emanate from within China than from the United States or any other foreign power. This is in part because China's growing consumer class will demand more buying power to purchase both domestic and imported goods. And, perhaps more important, domestic firms will be less competitive abroad as prices within China rise without a commensurate appreciation in the RMB relative to foreign currencies.[141] In addition, the gradual emergence of a larger and more affluent middle class, spurred in part by Beijing's efforts to stimulate domestic consumption in response to the global economic recession,[142] could benefit the United States. Indeed, China is the fastest-growing market for U.S. exports, and America is China's third-largest source of imports.

Despite the global recession, U.S. exports to China in 2009 remained relatively constant, even though overall U.S. exports declined nearly 18 percent. According to the U.S.-China Business Council, during the period 2000–2009, nearly 400 U.S. congressional districts witnessed triple-digit growth in their exports to China. And East Asia's share of the U.S. trade deficit actually declined from 1998 to 2007 (from 75 to 49 percent), as many East Asian nations shifted their exports toward China and their trade deficits with the United States decreased as a result. Rising Chinese consumption will likely continue that trend. Overall, U.S. manufacturers—and the U.S. trade deficit—could gain significantly from the growth of China's domestic demand.[143]

Relative Economic Power

Another possible long-term trend resulting in part from the global recession involves changes in relative U.S. and Chinese growth rates and their impact on the relative power relationship between the two nations, including military power. Before the crisis, China was growing approximately three times faster than the United States. If U.S. growth stagnates at an average of about 2.5 percent during the next three to five years, and even if China's rate drops to 7 or 8 percent, then China could still grow at least three times faster than the United States. When one also considers the fact that China has little debt and enormous reserves while the United States will probably be struggling to overcome a massive debt burden incurred by the current economic crisis (and growing government costs associated with entitlement programs such as Medicare), it is possible that China's GDP could exceed that of the United States by 2030 or even earlier, and could grow to double the size of the U.S. economy by 2050.[144]

One broad assessment of relative U.S. and Chinese growth rates argues that even worst case scenarios involving a very slow and tortuous U.S. recovery would not result in a genuine power transition in the international system in the near term. However, this analysis is less consistently optimistic about the medium and long terms, arguing that America could lose its global predominance if the U.S. economy remains plagued by high unemployment, low savings rates, and massive current account and budget deficits for many years to come. Such problems could lead to significant budgetary constraints, limits on the expansion of military and nonmilitary capital stocks, a significant drop in dollar prices, and the loss of the dollar's status as the international reserve currency stemming from a loss of confidence in the dollar and dollar-backed securities by foreign investors.[145] In addition, some analysts believe that the United States' advantage over China in many areas of high-skilled labor will narrow significantly within ten years and almost entirely disappear by 2025 as Chinese investments in education, nutrition, and health care come to fruition and many wealthy, skilled Chinese return to China from the United States.[146]

Such doomsday scenarios reinforce the need for the United States to vigorously address its economic problems, in order to enhance its ability to deal not only with the prospect of a power transition vis-à-vis China but also with many of the other bilateral economic issues outlined above. However, regardless of the scenarios one might examine, some serious analysts conclude that the U.S. will likely continue to increase, not decrease, its overall economic size and capabilities relative to China's for several more years before Beijing begins to catch up.[147]

If it indeed occurs, China's long-term emergence as the world's largest economy will undoubtedly hold many implications for U.S. policy. In the realm of global economic governance, China will become more deeply involved and perhaps more assertive on many issues, ranging from international financial institutions to trade, investment, and technology programs. Some analysts believe that China, along with India, will become "the new arbiters of the global economy's direction."[148] However, many other observers are far more cautious in predicting such a basic transformation in the global economic order. Some point to the fact that, though large in aggregate terms, the economies of China (and India) will continue to both lag behind the West and Japan in per capita income for decades and also face a variety of serious domestic developmental problems, including pollution and climate change, regional economic disparities, inadequate technological and managerial capabilities, and growing demographic imbalances, marked by a rapidly aging population and a chronic scarcity of females. As a result, China's rapid ascent to global power cannot be viewed as certain, and the attention of China's leaders will likely remain primarily fixed on preserving domestic social order and extending prosperity gains.[149] Moreover, China's size and influence likely will not surpass the combined weight of the United States and other Western democratic powers during the next several decades. Therefore, for some analysts, such as G. John Ikenberry, the capitalist democratic world will constitute a powerful constituency for the preservation and extension of the existing international order.[150] This, of course, assumes that the Western democratic order will cooperate in countering any challenges to the existing order that China might pose.

Overall, despite the extensive diversification that is occurring in Beijing's economic interactions with the world,[151] many analysts believe that the U.S. and Chinese economies will remain structurally interdependent in many ways for many years to come, and increasingly tied to larger global economic issues that require their cooperation to address, thus reducing the likelihood that bilateral economic disputes will lead to major, prolonged confrontations or disruptions of the global economic system.[152] Such complex and growing interdependence makes even less likely the possibility that bilateral economic disputes between the United States and China will result in military conflict.

Energy Security

There is little doubt that the supply of energy from overseas sources will continue to be an important issue in China's development strategy, given the growing importance of imported energy for its continued rapid growth, the presence of significant fluctuations in the global price of oil and gas in recent years, and the obvious desire of the Chinese government to increase the security of its energy supplies. Therefore, China's efforts to strengthen its energy security will remain a concern to the United States, and might even become an increasingly important issue in the bilateral relationship, involving an array of economic, military, and international human rights aspects.

All analysts agree that China's overall demand for energy—specifically in oil, gas, and coal—will continue to rise rapidly in the foreseeable future in order to support its fast-paced economic growth. According to the International Energy Agency, China's energy demands will increase by more than 75 percent between 2011 and 2035. An increasing proportion of these energy supplies will come from overseas. Even in coal—the PRC's most abundant resource, on which it is most dependent—the country is now a net importer.[153] And China is expected to have a growing oil deficit in the years ahead. By 2035, the U.S. Energy Information Administration expects the PRC to consume 17 million barrels of liquid fuels per day and depend on imports for 72 percent of its crude oil.[154]

Some analysts believe that China's growing dependence on energy imports will require it to develop the military capability to defend its sea-based lines of transport, to develop a large tanker fleet, and to deepen its political and economic relationships with authoritarian energy-producing regimes in Africa, Latin America, and especially the Middle East and Central Asia, possibly to the detriment of U.S. interests and (in some cases) the local economy. Some observers also believe that China will increasingly distort the normal functioning of the global energy market by pursuing "mercantilist" energy policies and overall efforts to "lock up" supplies of oil and other resources, such as the rare earth elements used in high-technology products.[155]

However, such observations and predictions are often not based on solid evidence of existing trends, overstate the potential dangers involved, or entirely misstate the likely implications of such behavior for U.S. interests. As indicated in chapter 4, even though China is certainly developing more potent naval and air power projection capabilities of potential use beyond the Asian littoral, there is no clear evidence—despite occasional writings by Chinese scholars and analysts—that it is officially committed to an effort to build sophisticated blue water naval capabilities that could "secure" its energy supply lines against highly capable navies of the type maintained by the United States or even Japan and India. Current trends in force acquisitions certainly do not preclude movement in that direction. However, they also do not confirm it. In fact, the challenges confronting any nation—even the United States—in acquiring such a capability are enormous and will likely remain so.[156]

In addition, China's likely future completion of long-term contracts with energy producers and refiners and its attempts to increase equity holdings in various overseas energy sectors will not necessarily constitute a clear threat to the workings of the global energy market or to U.S. interests in particular. Many observers believe that Chinese companies are primarily motivated to acquire equity holdings in the energy sector for commercial, not security, reasons. For example, the operations of the state-owned China National Petroleum Corporation in Sudan are arguably the most commercially successful of any overseas projects undertaken by China's national oil corporations.[157] And the commercial motivation behind China's activities in developing regions such as Africa and Latin America is strongly suggested by the fact that many Chinese enterprises and government arrangements are reducing their profile in response to falling commodity prices during the global recession. Moreover, China's overall economic involvement in these regions is arguably becoming more controversial within those countries over time.[158] It also appears that concerns about China's energy-driven forays into African nations such as Nigeria and Angola are overblown. The major Western oil corporations remain the leading foreign energy actors in both countries, dominating production and holding the majority of reserves. This situation is unlikely to change greatly during the current decade.[159] Moreover, the United States' economic involvement in many parts of Latin America—including oil-rich Venezuela—is expected to remain far higher than China's for the foreseeable future.[160]

This pattern of behavior derives from the strong, profit-driven, market-oriented attitude of China's energy companies; the inability of the Chinese government's energy bureaucracy to provide controls for such entities; and the ad hoc, uncoordinated nature of China's overall energy security policies. These uncoordinated policies could change as a result of the formation of the National Energy

Commission, as noted above. However, there is little evidence thus far that the overall situation described in the preceding paragraphs is changing. Moreover, projections of China's future demand for imported energy suggest that Beijing will not be able to fully compensate for possible interruptions in oil and gas imports or sudden fluctuations in price by relying primarily on its overseas equity holdings or long-term contracts. Even if Beijing could compel its overseas corporations to provide it with oil and gas supplies exclusively at below existing market prices, the resulting amounts would fall far short of its projected needs, forcing a continued reliance to some significant degree on the open market. In the long term, a strategy of selling to China at artificially low prices would also deny Chinese energy corporations the opportunity to take advantage of higher prices, which could provide funds for investment in other oil exploration and development projects.[161]

Equally important, even if China were able to "lock up" a certain portion of overseas energy supplies either in normal times or during a crisis, it is unlikely that such a development would threaten the supplies of other nations. The vast majority of global oil and gas supplies are under the control of foreign governments, are largely subject to global market demand, and will likely remain so.[162] Hence, other energy-consuming countries would arguably gain access to a larger portion of such market-based supplies if China were to choose to rely heavily on its own equity energy assets. Moreover, it is by no means clear that a growing Chinese reliance on equity oil in unstable states such as Sudan and Libya would prove more secure than oil purchased on the open market, because internal political and social unrest in such countries could threaten Chinese holdings.[163] These facts have contributed to a debate within policy circles and among industry specialists in China over whether the foreign investments of the PRC's energy corporations actually enhance the security of China's oil supply.[164]

All in all, some very knowledgeable observers believe that, although sizable foreign equity energy holdings might provide some level of psychological comfort and might even provide some secure supplies in the unlikely event that the global market for oil disappears, the level of security provided to Beijing will prove to be marginal at best and could in some cases even weaken China's energy security. More important, there is little evidence that China's energy policies will pose a growing economic threat to the United States and other energy importing nations during any foreseeable time frame (that is, in the next ten to twenty years).

Perhaps the greatest future concern that emerges from China's overseas energy policies derives from the political implications that Beijing's growing energy-based ties with authoritarian states such as Iran, Sudan, Libya, Myanmar, Uzbekistan, Venezuela, and Cuba will have for U.S. counterproliferation and human rights policies. According to some observers, China is increasingly being forced to deal with such "unsavory" governments because the best overseas energy assets to foreign investment have already been taken by the major international oil companies, and Chinese energy corporations are generally unable to compete in certain areas (for example, deepwater drilling) with well-established Western energy conglomerates such as ExxonMobil, Royal Dutch/Shell and ConocoPhillips in mainstream markets located in the Middle East and the Caspian Sea region. Also, more than three-quarters of the world's oil reserves are controlled by national oil companies and thus closed to foreign equity investment, which further reduces China's energy investment options.[165]

As indicated in chapter 8, China has resisted attempts to place high levels of pressure on states such as Sudan, Iran, and Myanmar, in part for economic reasons.[166] This type of resistance is likely to continue in many cases, given the high stakes involved for China in the development of energy (and other economic) arrangements with such governments. However, Beijing's support for such governments is by no means absolute. On several occasions, China's leaders have agreed to support sanctions and other pressure tactics against Iran and other powers. In each case, it must balance those economic and political incentives that resist such high pressure policies against its clear desire to avoid highly destabilizing regional developments (such as Iran's acquisition of nuclear weapons or prolonged social instability in important oil producing countries such as Libya) along with serious human rights or nuclear counterproliferation confrontations with the United States, other major powers, or the United Nations. This calculus is unlikely to change in any major way in the foreseeable future.[167]

CONCLUSION

This chapter's analysis suggests that the United States' policymakers are confronting a growing number of increasingly complex challenges in advancing its three basic economic policy objectives vis-à-vis China—supporting the global and Asian economic order, U.S. jobs and prosperity, and China's stable development. On balance, the intermediate strategy adopted by the Bush and Obama administrations (combining varying degrees of public and private pressure, compromise, and mutual accommodation via both bilateral and multilateral means) has produced some significant successes, especially in supporting or advancing China's stable development, the Asian economic order, the profits of many major

U.S. corporations, and the choices available to American consumers. At the same time, the global economic recession has highlighted the significant structural imbalances between the U.S. and Chinese economies, and has arguably exacerbated many bilateral trade and financial problems. Moreover, future trends regarding global rebalancing, relative economic power, and energy security all suggest that U.S. economic policies toward China will have an increasing impact on the stability and vibrancy of America's economy and global influence. Taken together, these growing challenges place a very high premium on the need for U.S. policymakers to develop more integrated strategies that address both the Sino-U.S. and the larger U.S. economic situation.

06

GLOBAL TERRORISM AND
WMD PROLIFERATION

Although U.S. policies for combating terrorism and for limiting or eliminating the proliferation of weapons of mass destruction (WMD) are treated as separate in many ways, in fact they are increasingly interrelated, given the growing fear in many U.S. government circles that global terrorists might obtain WMD capabilities from existing or aspiring nuclear powers.[1] Hence, U.S. policies toward China must address terrorism and WMD proliferation both as distinct issues and as interrelated problems.

U.S. and Chinese objectives in the arenas of counterterrorism and counterproliferation, along with the features of each country's domestic political environment, raise several basic issues for U.S. policymakers. First, with respect to counterterrorism, how can the United States enhance cooperation with China in combating terrorism without indirectly assisting Beijing in repressing domestic political dissidents? In particular, should the United States provide intelligence and material assistance to Beijing that could potentially be used against both terrorists and dissidents? More broadly, to what degree and in what ways should the United States cooperate with China in sharing intelligence, technologies, and approaches to combating terrorism? And regarding counterproliferation, how much influence does Beijing actually possess vis-à-vis potential WMD proliferators such as

Iran, Pakistan, and North Korea, and what combination of carrots and sticks will best induce Chinese leaders to support U.S. policy goals toward these states? More broadly, what kinds of quid pro quos, if any, should the United States be prepared to offer to advance its goals in this important policy arena? Finally, to what extent can and should the United States rely on international agreements as opposed to bilateral contacts to advance its objectives in both these arenas?

POLICY APPROACHES

As in the previously noted policy arenas, alternative U.S. approaches would likely place different emphases on an array of coercive, cooperative, or mixed strategies, depending on the assumptions that policymakers hold regarding relative U.S. and Chinese bilateral and multilateral leverage, Chinese interests in this arena, the overall compatibility between the objectives of the two countries, and the role played by domestic political factors. In this arena, a predominantly coercive approach would probably minimize U.S. assistance to China in combating terrorism, might seek to pressure Beijing through a variety of means—possibly including threats of various sorts—to end its economic and political assistance to both North Korea and Iran and to restrain Pakistan's existing nuclear-weapons program, and would possibly link U.S. cooperation in other policy arenas with Chinese compliance in this arena. Such an approach would obviously assume that (1) Beijing does not genuinely support U.S. objectives in this arena (or at least not to a significant extent), (2) is subject to strong U.S. (and perhaps multilateral) pressure, and (3) cannot retaliate significantly in ways that would seriously damage U.S. interests. This approach might also assume that domestic political views of terrorism and especially proliferation would largely support— and indeed, might necessitate—such a tough posture toward Beijing.

As in the economic arena, the opposite approach would reject confrontation and pressure in favor of cooperation, negotiation, and dialogue aimed at producing positive-sum outcomes, based on assumptions that would largely be the opposite of those underlying the coercive approach. In particular, this approach would recognize that, despite the possible existence of differences about the definition of key concepts such as terrorism and WMD proliferation, the United States and China do genuinely share a desire to combat terrorists; support the strengthening of international efforts to prevent nuclear, chemical, and biological weapons proliferation; want Pakistan to remain stable and its government to keep control of its nuclear weapons; and basically oppose the acquisition or development of WMD capabilities by Iran and North Korea.

This cooperative approach would also assume that Beijing has strong incentives to engage in mutual compromises with Washington and other powers in dealing with sensitive issues such as nuclear proliferation. It also often assumes that Beijing possesses the ability to retaliate significantly against excessive outside confrontational pressure. Moreover, this approach would emphasize America's need to work with other countries in approaching China, would assume that Chinese cooperation is necessary to strengthen international agreements regarding both counterterrorism and counterproliferation, and would regard such agreements as essential to attaining U.S. objectives in this arena. Finally, this approach would likely assume that U.S. domestic political interests can be persuaded to support such an approach.

Again, as in the economic arena, mixed strategies would reflect a basic belief that the complexity and dynamism of this policy arena requires a combination of coercive and cooperative tactics toward China, varied on the basis of timing, circumstance, and the features of the specific issue confronted. This approach would also likely assume that the majority of the public and political interests in America do not usually drive or heavily influence U.S. policy toward China in both policy arenas and hence can be utilized or neutralized as necessary.

POLICY HISTORY

U.S. and Chinese policies with regard to terrorism and WMD proliferation cover a wide array of activities and approaches. The major elements include policies to combat terrorism and counter proliferation; national policies regarding the use and transmission of WMD; and policies toward the major nation-state-based challenges to those international counterterrorism and counterproliferation efforts that heavily involve both Washington and Beijing: Iran and North Korea. The following policy history will cover these areas in turn.

U.S. Counterterrorism Policies

The George W. Bush administration placed an extremely strong emphasis on counterterrorism activities in Asia and elsewhere.[2] These efforts came to dominate U.S. foreign and security policies in most regions of the world and, equally important, were brought into close association with U.S. counterproliferation activities following the terrorist attacks on the USS *Cole* in Yemen in 2000 and the September 11, 2001, attacks in the United States. Attempts to combat terrorist activities in general and to prevent terrorists and present or past terrorist-supporting states such as Iran and North Korea from obtaining nuclear weapons and ballistic missiles (and their related equipment and technologies) became a key component of U.S. foreign policy. As part of this combined undertaking, the Bush administration intensified efforts to work with Beijing in all these arenas, especially given the latter's close relationships with Pyongyang and Tehran and its strong interest in combating Islamic terrorism within and near Chinese territory.

Specifically, the Bush administration asked China to share intelligence information on terrorist networks and to join the international coalition against terrorism, and it repeatedly stressed that combating terrorism is a shared interest with China. In support of these goals, Washington and Beijing began a U.S.-China Counterterrorism Sub-Dialogue in 2001, led by the U.S. coordinator for counterterrorism on the U.S. side and the director-general of either the Department of International Organizations and Conferences or the Department of External Security Affairs within the Ministry of Foreign Affairs on the Chinese side.[3]

This dialogue, which met six times during the Bush administration between 2001 and 2008, has served as a regular forum for discussing a wide variety of counterterrorism issues of interest to both countries, including their experiences and assessments of domestic, regional, and international counterterrorism efforts and the terrorist situation in Afghanistan and in such regions as Central Asia, South Asia, and Southeast Asia. In May 2002, experts from the United States and China held the first semiannual meeting at the working-group level to exchange views on how to prevent and combat terrorist financing. Beijing and Washington have since alternated serving as hosts of future meetings. In addition, in 2002, following China's provision of information about terrorist activities against U.S. government assets in Central Asia, the United States designated the East Turkistan Islamic Movement as a terrorist organization.[4]

The Barack Obama administration has generally continued the basic approach followed by the Bush administration in combating terrorism worldwide.[5] More important, it has also continued the activities of the Bush approach toward China in this policy arena while seeking to erase the impression, conveyed during the Bush era, that Washington's Asia policies are focused primarily on counterterrorism to the detriment of most other concerns. For example, it has continued to hold the U.S.-China Counterterrorism Sub-Dialogue but has also attempted to elicit greater Chinese support in managing two closely connected terrorist-related issues: the fight against growing Taliban influence in Afghanistan, and the effort to get Pakistan to take stronger measures against terrorist elements operating within its borders, including Afghan Taliban groups. With respect to the former issue, Washington has encouraged Beijing to contribute more to stabilizing Afghanistan by deepening its assistance for mine clearing, police training, counternarcotics, and humanitarian assistance, while also expanding its extensive economic investments. With respect to the latter issue, Washington wants Beijing to utilize its long-standing close relationships in Pakistani military and intelligence circles to convince Islamabad to devote more resources to attacking those terrorists operating in Pakistan's western tribal areas adjacent to Afghanistan. These undertakings became a high priority for Washington after the Taliban began to regain significant parts of Afghanistan and Pakistan-based terrorists attacked a hotel in Mumbai in 2008. At the Strategic and Economic Dialogue in July 2009, the United States and China "pledged to increase coordination to jointly promote stability and development in Afghanistan and Pakistan." However, since 2009, negotiations over such issues as access routes for logistical support to troops have stalled. Chinese officials have reportedly refused to consider U.S. proposals for a cooperation program in Pakistan and the Ministry of Foreign Affairs has not acted on a proposed U.S.-China plan for cooperation in Afghanistan.[6]

U.S. Counterproliferation Efforts

The United States' efforts to engage China on WMD nonproliferation topics have a long history. For many years, Washington used a variety of tools to induce Beijing to become a more responsible exporter of sensitive materials and technologies. The Bill Clinton administration used a mix of incentives (for example, technology cooperation) and disincentives (the threat of and imposition of sanctions) to prod China to change its behavior and limit its sensitive WMD-related exports. Washington also succeeded in linking improvements in the overall United States–China relationship to advances in Beijing's proliferation behavior, a linkage that China "ultimately, but grudgingly, accepted."[7] The United States also pushed China to improve its bureaucratic capabilities to carry out its growing number of nonproliferation commitments; and as China's capacity improved, its illicit exports also declined. Beijing thus improved many aspects of its proliferation behavior during the Clinton era.[8]

Partly as a result of these achievements, the Bush and Obama administrations have been able to focus their efforts on a narrower range of counterproliferation issues involving China. These have included attempts to further limit the PRC's assistance to the missile programs of Iran and Pakistan and the provision of dual-use items to North Korea. In this regard, a major U.S. policy challenge has involved both helping and pressuring China to improve its ability to stop its illicit exports, along with Washington's efforts to induce Beijing to apply its nonproliferation commitments to its technical assistance programs for both Pakistan and Iran. In these and other related areas, the Bush administration often followed a largely punitive, confrontational approach toward China. Thus, it targeted China's weak export controls and imposed sanctions many times on more than 30 unspecific PRC "entities" for transfers to several countries (including Pakistan, North Korea, Iran, and Libya) of various items related to missiles and chemical weapons.[9]

In addition, the Bush administration initiated the use of financial sanctions, implemented through the Treasury Department, to achieve many of its nonproliferation goals vis-à-vis China. For example, Washington threatened to sanction Chinese banks that were facilitating proliferation in Iran. During the first Bush term alone, the U.S. government sanctioned Chinese entities a total of 62 times, as opposed to 8 times during the two terms of the Clinton administration.[10] Moreover, as of April 2011, China was designated as the country of residence or incorporation for 135 entities on the U.S. Treasury Department's "Specially Designated Nationals" list, which consists of organizations and individuals that are restricted from doing business with the United States, American companies, or Americans. Thirty-three of these entities are sanctioned as "Weapons of Mass Destruction Proliferators and Their Supporters," and 23 additional entities are sanctioned for engaging in commercial transactions with Iran.[11]

Beyond such China-centered proliferation issues, both the Bush and Obama administrations have sought at various intervals to compel, persuade, or entice Beijing to support the United States' approach toward eliminating Iran's and North Korea's nuclear-weapons programs.[12] As noted in chapter 2, the Bush administration's approach to China regarding North Korea changed appreciably over time, from a largely unilateral emphasis on pressuring Beijing to apply greater pressure on Pyongyang to working cooperatively with China in the context of the Six-Party Talks (6PT). The United States also engaged Beijing in an ongoing dialogue to elicit Chinese recognition of the danger posed by Iran's nuclear program and to secure its active support for efforts to pressure Tehran to abandon that program. In addition, the Bush administration also urged Beijing to become an active participant in the Proliferation Security Initiative (PSI)— announced by President Bush in 2003—and to support Washington's attempts to apply PSI actions against possible North Korean proliferation activities.[13]

The Obama administration has by and large adopted a similar approach in attempting to elicit Chinese support for its counterproliferation policies toward North Korea and Iran. It has continued to work closely with Beijing to bring Pyongyang back into the denuclearization negotiating process following a second round of North Korean missile and nuclear-weapons tests in 2009 and the suspension of the 6PT. This effort has involved extensive bilateral and multilateral interactions with Chinese officials using several U.S. channels, including the special U.S. envoy to North Korea, Stephen Bosworth. Unfortunately, the sinking of a South Korean frigate (the *Cheonan*) in disputed waters near the Korean Peninsula on March 26, 2010, almost certainly by North Korea, along with the North Korean bombardment of South Korea's Yeonpyeong Island on November 23, 2010, presented new challenges to Washington's ability to elicit Beijing's cooperation in dealing with Pyongyang's nuclear-weapons program (as discussed below).

Regarding Iran, Obama administration officials have met on numerous occasions with their Chinese counterparts—both bilaterally in Beijing, New York, and Washington and as part of the UN-led multilateral process—to discuss and convey information, explore options, and at times exhort Beijing to support greater international pressure on Tehran, including additional United Nations Security Council sanctions.[14] Although Washington was ultimately successful in getting Beijing to back further sanctions against Tehran in June 2010, it has continued to struggle to elicit the full cooperation of Beijing and/or various Chinese companies to comply with those measures. Moreover, Beijing has criticized Washington for subsequently adopting unilateral sanctions against Tehran.[15]

On a broader level, however, Obama has arguably given more emphasis, both rhetorically and substantively, to efforts to strengthen nonproliferation efforts and reduce the size and utility of America's nuclear arsenal than the Bush administration did. These have included

- successful efforts to negotiate the New Strategic Arms Reduction Treaty (START) with Russia in the spring of 2010;
- enhanced attempts to ratify the Comprehensive Test Ban Treaty and reinforce a global ban on nuclear testing;
- a commitment to review and strengthen the Nuclear Non-Proliferation Treaty (NPT) as a basis for international cooperation;
- a commitment to the passage of a verifiable Fissile Material Cut-Off Treaty;
- the promulgation of a revised Nuclear Posture Review (NPR) with language intended to strengthen global adherence to the NPT and narrow significantly the conditions under which the United States would consider using nuclear weapons;
- increased efforts to secure all vulnerable nuclear materials around the world, marked by the holding of a Global Summit on Nuclear Security in Washington in April 2010; and
- an intention to transform efforts such as the PSI and the Global Initiative to Combat Nuclear Terrorism (discussed below) into more durable international institutions.[16]

If successful, such efforts could increase the ability of the United States to work with other nations, including China, to prevent and reduce WMD proliferation through more effective monitoring, engagement, and sanctions.

U.S. Nuclear-Weapons Policies

During the Bush era, Beijing was deeply concerned that more countries would be pressured to attempt to acquire nuclear deterrence options and thereby also increase their proliferation behavior because of a number of aspects of U.S. policy—including Washington's apparent reliance on both strategic and tactical nuclear weapons for deterrence and war-fighting purposes (combined with its refusal to commit to a no-first-use principle), the existence of continued support in the U.S. policy community for the further modernization of America's nuclear arsenal, Washington's overwhelming superiority in conventional long-range precision-strike capabilities, its efforts to acquire more robust theater and national missile defense systems, and its possible continued observance of preemptive strike doctrines aimed at those it deemed to be "rogue regimes."[17] Some analysts (and the Chinese government) therefore argued strongly in favor of greater efforts by all nuclear powers to abolish nuclear weapons, as a means of reducing proliferation and preventing nuclear terrorism.[18]

The Obama administration has arguably addressed some of these Chinese concerns by negotiating New START with Russia to reduce the size of the U.S. nuclear arsenal (with further reductions possible in the future); offering public expressions of support for the eventual elimination of nuclear weapons; pledging in the NPR not to develop new classes of nuclear weapons; and, perhaps most important, emphasizing in the NPR the deterrence versus war-fighting or preemptive functions of nuclear weapons, especially with regard to those nations, such as China, that are deemed compliant with the nonproliferation obligations of the NPT.[19] Obama has also downgraded the Bush administration's emphasis on preemptive strikes and unilateral undertakings.

Chinese Counterterrorism Policies

Taken as a whole, the above-described U.S. policy efforts have both caused and facilitated significant Chinese actions during the Bush and Obama administrations, presenting both challenges and significant strategic opportunities for China. In the counterterrorism arena, during the past nine years, Beijing has used the global war on terrorism to deepen its cooperative relations with many nations along its periphery and to enhance its value to the West, and to the United States in particular. On September 20, 2001, Beijing responded to Washington's request for assistance by offering America "unconditional support" in fighting terrorism. On September 28, 2001, China voted with all the other members of the UN Security Council for Resolution 1373, which reaffirmed the need to combat terrorism. Since then, Beijing has worked with Washington and other nations in a variety of areas to fight terrorism or terrorist-related activities, both bilaterally and multilaterally. For example, Beijing has participated in many UN-sponsored conferences on counterterrorism and has held several antiterrorism military exercises in recent years, both as part of the Shanghai Cooperation Organization and together with other countries such as India. China also joined the Global Initiative to Combat Nuclear Terrorism, announced in July 2006 by U.S. president Bush and Russian president Vladimir Putin with the intention of deepening international efforts to prevent, protect against, and respond comprehensively to the nuclear terrorist threat. More broadly, the Chinese government has assisted in the United States–led reconstruction of post-Taliban Afghanistan and supported Pakistan's close cooperation with the United States in combating both the Taliban and al-Qaeda.[20]

One of the areas that Beijing has cooperated most effectively with the United States and the international community is in combating money laundering and terrorist financing—though "the government has yet to develop an asset freezing and confiscation regime that meets international standards or that adequately implements" related UN Security Council resolutions.[21] Beijing has provided intelligence on possible terrorist activities and networks related to money laundering within or near China, while also seeking to strengthen its domestic capacity to prevent terrorist financing. Chinese entities such as the Financial Intelligence Unit (established by the People's Bank of China in 2004 to collect, analyze, and disseminate suspicious transaction reports) have also worked closely with the Financial Crimes Enforcement Network in the United States to develop its capabilities.[22] In 2006, Beijing adopted a new Anti–Money Laundering Law, which strengthens efforts to record customer information and report suspicious transactions that could be associated with illicit financing. In the following year, China expanded its role in international efforts on this front by becoming a full member of the Financial Action Task Force, an intergovernmental body whose purpose is to develop and promote policies to combat such activities. Several additional regulatory and judicial measures were adopted in 2009 to further strengthen Beijing's regime for combating money laundering and the financing of terrorism.[23]

Beijing has also engaged with Washington to improve cooperation in counterterrorism investigations and strengthen port security. In 2002, the Chinese government permitted the U.S. Federal Bureau of Investigation to open its Legal Attaché Office in Beijing to strengthen Sino-U.S. cooperation on counterterrorism investigations. This joint United States–China effort was designed to improve both countries' capability to target and prescreen cargo containers to protect containerized shipping from exploitation by terrorists. In 2009, Beijing engaged in various bilateral capacity-building activities with the Federal Bureau of Investigations on both Track-I and Track-II levels. According to the U.S. State Department, "China has provided substantive intelligence in some counterterrorism cases, but more work remained to be done" to strengthen its overall responsiveness to U.S. requests.[24] In early 2006, China also permitted the establishment of a U.S. Coast Guard Liaison Office in Beijing to facilitate United States–China exchanges designed to enhance port security in both countries. China also became a member of the Megaports Initiative and the Container Security Initiative, which allows U.S. inspection of containers bound for the United States to detect and interdict illicit nuclear and radiological materials. As part of these arrangements, U.S. Customs and Border Protection inspectors are stationed in the ports of Shanghai and Shenzhen. And prior to the 2008 Beijing Olympics, the U.S. Energy Department sent a Nuclear Emergency Support Team to China to assist in searching for possible nuclear weapons.[25]

Moreover, China has obtained support from the United States in its efforts to combat terrorism through U.S. sales of counterterrorism-related equipment and expertise. In 2005, according to the Congressional Research Service, "the Bush administration reportedly approved the export of sensitive equipment and expertise to PRC security and PLA forces. . . . The equipment included that used to detect explosives and radiation."[26]

On the negative side, the Chinese have been deeply concerned about possible U.S. counterterrorism measures that might impinge on their sovereignty or undermine the general principle of nonintervention in China's domestic affairs. Thus, they have rejected some U.S. requests to utilize Chinese airspace in counterterrorist activities. In addition, Beijing did not provide military cooperation for the United States' Operation Enduring Freedom in Afghanistan, and the counterterrorism intelligence it has offered has been regarded by some observers as insufficiently detailed.[27]

Washington has criticized Beijing for not exerting enough of its influence to convince Pakistan to cooperate with Washington in the global war on terrorism. In particular, as noted above, progress in U.S.-China cooperation in the Afghanistan–Pakistan conflict has stalled since 2009. U.S. observers characterized China's approach to the situation in the region as "defending a relatively narrowly conceived set of bilateral interests" rather than a broader, coordinated attempt to pursue international objectives.[28] China has resisted pressuring Pakistan to exert greater efforts against Afghan Taliban elements operating within its borders in large part because it does not want to significantly jeopardize or strain its long-standing privileged political-strategic relationship with Islamabad or to weaken Pakistan's role as a strategic counterweight to India by compelling it to divert resources and energies from the Indian border.[29]

Overall, it is likely that Beijing's level of cooperation with the United States during both the Bush and Obama administrations has been limited at various times by several concerns, including Washington's supposedly "unilateralist" and "interventionist" approach to prosecuting the global war on terrorism; the development during the Bush era of new military doctrines in favor of preventive warfare, which in Beijing's view reinforced Washington's penchant for armed interventions in other countries in the absence of any international authorization; disagreements about the definition of terrorism and terrorists; related concerns about Washington's apparent refusal to repatriate what Beijing regards as Uyghur terrorists confined at the Guantánamo Bay detention facility; and China's larger geostrategic interests in Central and South Asia.[30]

Moreover, Beijing's support for the global war on terrorism has undoubtedly permitted it to gain some international backing for its efforts to control nonterrorist dissident groups.[31] This development is of obvious concern to U.S. officials, especially given the support that Washington has provided to Chinese efforts to combat foreign connected Islamic terrorist groups, via the 2002 designation of the East Turkistan Islamic Movement (ETIM) as a terrorist group.[32] This issue has produced domestic debates over U.S. support for Chinese counterterrorism activities within the PRC, congressional criticism of Chinese policies, and expressions of judicial doubt regarding the link between the ETIM and outside terrorist groups. And this controversy, in turn, has created tensions between Beijing and Washington over the latter's refusal to return to China the twenty-two Uyghurs detained at Guantánamo Bay.[33] Nonetheless, on balance, the overall level and scope of Chinese assistance in the global war on terrorism have been beneficial to U.S. interests, according to many U.S. officials interviewed for this study.

Chinese Counterproliferation Efforts

In the arena of counterproliferation, China's counterterrorism activities in recent years reinforced and gave added momentum to preexisting policy trends within the PRC toward the enactment of greater internal controls over activities related to WMD proliferation and have stimulated efforts to "make cooperation on nonproliferation issues a positive aspect of bilateral relations."[34] Thus, in general, the terrorism–proliferation linkage provided China with a means to use the post-9/11 environment to improve relations with the United States and to put the two nations' relationship on a longer-term, more stable footing.[35]

To be sure, the gradual improvements in Chinese nonproliferation behavior emerged in the late 1980s and early 1990s as a result of U.S. pressure and inducements, image concerns, and a growing recognition of the threats posed by the proliferation of WMD. Since that time, China has signed or joined most major international nonproliferation agreements, significantly reduced its involvement in the transfer of WMD-related equipment and technologies (including delivery systems such as ballistic missiles), formulated new domestic laws and regulations to govern the exporting and importing of dual-use and WMD-related items, and promised to improve the government's enforcement of these controls and regulations. In addition, although China has yet to ratify the Comprehensive Test Ban Treaty, it nonetheless maintains a moratorium on testing and calls for restraints on the research and development of new types of nuclear weapons and a reduction of their role in national security strategy. Beijing also reportedly stopped producing weapons-grade fissile materials in the early 1990s, and it supports the negotiation of a legally binding Fissile Materials Cutoff Treaty. But China has not committed to a certified moratorium on the production of fissile materials, apparently due to concerns about a possible future need to increase their production in response to U.S. missile defense plans, concerns about the future weaponization of space, and the possibility of a growing gap in conventional capabilities with the United States.[36]

In addition, the geographic distribution of Chinese proliferation-relevant exports has narrowed from almost a dozen countries to three—Iran, Pakistan, and, to a lesser extent, North Korea. Also, the character of China's exports has similarly narrowed from a broad range of nuclear materials and equipment (much of it unsafeguarded) and complete missile systems in the past, to exports of dual-use nuclear, missile, and chemical technologies in the 1990s, to a point where such dual-use exports are now also covered by Beijing's WMD export control regime. However, despite the progress China has made in the implementation of export controls, the enforcement of those controls has been less successful.[37]

During the Bush administration, China took a variety of significant steps in these areas. In August 2002, Beijing published regulations and a control list governing exports related to ballistic missiles that were intended to show compliance with the Missile Technology Control Regime (MTCR). In October 2002, the PRC issued regulations for export controls over dual-use biological agents and related technology. China is also a member of the International Atomic Energy Agency's (IAEA's) Additional Protocol, which entered into force in 2002.

In December 2003, China issued a white paper on nonproliferation, which stated that its control lists are almost the same as those of the Zangger Committee, the Nuclear Suppliers Group (NSG), the Chemical Weapons Convention, the Australia Group, and the MTCR. In May 2004, China applied to join the NSG, and it was subsequently admitted. In June 2004, it applied to join the MTCR, but it has not yet been accepted as a member. And it did not join 93 other countries in signing the International Code of Conduct Against Ballistic Missile Proliferation in The Hague in November 2002. Nonetheless, it no longer exports MTCR-class missiles. In September 2005, it issued another white paper titled "Endeavors for Arms Control, Disarmament, and Non-Proliferation," which reaffirms its commitment to nonproliferation and arms control. Moreover, since 2006, Washington has been training Chinese Customs officers in how to interdict illicit shipments of WMD-related "dual-use," strategic commodities.[38]

Since Barack Obama came into office, Beijing has restated its firm opposition to proliferation of WMD and their means of delivery while emphasizing a commitment to "the attainment of the nonproliferation goal through political and diplomatic means."[39] It has also restated its long standing position that "international cooperative action in whatever form should abide by the UN Charter and international laws and should not result in a negative impact upon regional peace and security."[40] In other words, Beijing has reaffirmed its support for nonproliferation efforts using primarily peaceful means and its adherence to international laws and organizations. In line with this position, it has recently expressed support for the intention behind the Proliferation Security Initiative, but it has also thus far refused to join that effort, citing concerns that the interdiction activities taken by PSI participants might "go beyond the international law."[41] Specifically, Beijing fears that the PSI could undermine the principle of state sovereignty and produce uncertainty and instability among nations. Nonetheless, the United States continues to consult with China regarding the PSI, and there is some evidence that China conducts its own PSI-like interdiction efforts along its coastline.[42]

China's Actions Regarding Iran[43]

In addition to these activities, China has also provided notable support for international efforts to prevent Iran from acquiring nuclear weapons. As early as the late 1990s, Washington and Beijing agreed that Tehran was developing a nuclear-weapons program that posed dangers to international nonproliferation efforts and regional security in the Middle East. In February 2006, China supported the IAEA's decision to report Iran's noncompliance with the UN Security Council, a position it resisted for years. Despite its original objections to sanctions, China then relaxed its stance and supported four UN sanctions resolutions on Iran, beginning in late 2006, and most recently in June 2010. China also endorsed a more stringent freeze on assets already in place. In addition, in November 2009, Beijing supported the board of the IAEA when the latter issued a strong rebuke of Tehran for its continued defiance of UN resolutions that demand a halt to activities that many outside observers believe are part of an effort to acquire nuclear weapons.[44]

These Chinese actions (and in particular the June 2010 sanction resolution) were apparently taken with some reluctance and only after the United States and other powers exerted considerable persuasion. Such efforts apparently included: (1) a U.S.-EU guarantee that Chinese companies would be exempted from any follow-on sanctions; (2) intense lobbying by Israeli officials—including possible discussion about Israeli air strikes on Iran; (3) the desire to avoid an implied threat of diplomatic isolation, given Russia's shift in support of limited sanctions; and possibly (4) an agreement by Saudi Arabia to increase its oil exports to China in compensation for Beijing's support.[45]

Beijing's reluctance to support sanctions stems in part from concerns expressed by Chinese officials that punitive sanctions could undercut ongoing efforts to resolve the Iranian nuclear issue through peaceful negotiations by likely provoking a military confrontation. Indeed, some Chinese apparently continue to suspect that Washington seeks to use sanctions to eventually topple the Iranian regime.[46] Moreover, many observers have expressed concerns about China's failure to adequately enforce these sanctions, which they allege have been violated by state-owned Chinese oil companies that continue to do business with Iran.[47]

Beijing's cautious balancing act toward the issue of Iran's nuclear trajectory reflects several crosscutting interests that it seeks to address simultaneously. On the one hand, China's leaders have a strong desire to maintain its political connections and growing commercial ties with Iran, which is an important source of their oil and gas supplies and a major current and (especially) future geostrategic player in the Middle East; moreover, few Chinese view a nuclear Iran as a direct threat to their interests. On the other hand, Beijing does not want to seriously aggravate its ties with the United States and other Western powers over the issue of Iran, or to undermine its growing relationship with Saudi Arabia, another major oil supplier and an opponent of the Tehran regime.[48]

The Six-Party Talks and North Korea[49]

China has adopted a similar balancing act in its policies toward North Korea's nuclear-weapons program. On the one hand, Beijing has played an increasingly important role in efforts to achieve the complete, verifiable, and irreversible dismantlement of Pyongyang's nuclear-weapons program—and especially in preventing the volatile North Korean nuclear issue from degenerating into a major crisis—through its involvement in the Six-Party Talks, support for various UN resolutions, and direct bilateral discussions with Pyongyang. For example, in October 2006, Beijing voted with all the other members of the UN Security Council for Resolution 1718, following Pyongyang's initial detonation of a nuclear device and test launch of several long-range ballistic missiles.[50]

Although China's leaders resisted applying further sanctions to North Korea (and a second UN resolution) following its second missile test in mid-2009, they did support the issuance of a (less significant) Security Council presidential statement condemning Pyongyang's launch as a violation of Resolution 1718 and calling for strengthening the punitive measures specified in that resolution.[51] Moreover, following North Korea's second nuclear test, Beijing supported UN Security Council Resolution 1874 condemning "in the strongest terms" North Korea's second nuclear test and imposing new sanctions in the form of cargo inspections, while resisting stronger, punitive measures.[52]

On the other hand, as in the case of Iran, the Chinese government has repeatedly sought to express official caution and, whenever possible, what it regards as an even-handed and balanced approach to managing the North Korea problem, urging all parties to "to stay cool and restrained, stop all moves that may . . . increase . . . tensions, and be resolved in settling the issue peacefully through consultation and dialogue." Such a sentiment has at times led Beijing to dilute sanctions proposed by Washington and to resist U.S. urgings to do more to encourage Pyongyang to return to the negotiating table. Overall, Beijing has consistently presented itself as a mediator on the North Korea issue, seeking to sustain or resume dialogue between the members of the Six-Party Talks (especially the United States and North Korea), while also working with the other members of the 6PT to achieve the ultimate goal of both peninsula stability and the maintenance of the international nonproliferation system.[53]

Current and former U.S. officials interviewed for this study generally speak in positive terms of China's efforts to manage the North Korea nuclear issue, while remaining cognizant of the differences between American and Chinese interests in some areas. At the same time, some observers in and out of the U.S. government also criticize Beijing for not pressuring Pyongyang enough,[54] and in some instances argue for the United States to reduce its reliance on Chinese mediation.

The gap between U.S. and Chinese assessments of how best to manage the North Korean nuclear crisis was most recently made clear by the negotiation process and other events following the sinking of the Cheonan in March 2010. Although Washington (and Seoul) exerted considerable efforts to elicit Chinese support for an unambiguous UN statement condemning Pyongyang as the party responsible for the sinking, Beijing would not even examine the results of the international investigation into the incident, much less directly identify North Korea as the guilty party. The Chinese also criticized U.S. and South Korean plans to conduct joint deterrence-oriented military exercises in the Yellow Sea between China and the Korean Peninsula. This stance reflected Beijing's persistent desire to avoid actions that might severely provoke Pyongyang and thereby undermine stability on the peninsula, in contrast to Washington's desire both to deter violent behavior and compel North Korea's return to the denuclearization process through a strong show of unified resolve.[55]

Beijing's cautious attitude, and Washington's patience with the Chinese approach, were both tested further when the North Koreans escalated the tense situation by shelling South Korea's Yeonpyeong Island on November 23, 2010, killing two Marines and two civilians and wounding several others. In the same month, Pyongyang also revealed a new uranium enrichment facility, thus escalating concerns that it was expanding its nuclear-weapons program in violation of earlier commitments. Eventually, after several rounds of discussions among U.S., Chinese, South Korean, Japanese, and other officials of the concerned countries—perhaps also involving coordinated U.S., South Korean, and Japanese pressure on China—Beijing apparently took actions to prevent further North Korean provocations and to facilitate movement toward diplomatic contacts with Pyongyang.[56]

These episodes arguably tightened the U.S.-South Korean security relationship and clarified, in the minds of both powers, the limited nature of China's willingness to pressure the North Korean regime (as discussed in chapter 2). However, criticisms of Chinese actions have not appreciably altered the United States' commitment to work with, and in many cases through, China and to avoid undue pressure on Beijing. This might be because there is no clear evidence to suggest that the survival of the North Korean regime is decisively dependent on Chinese assistance and, more importantly, that Pyongyang would become compliant, as opposed to more desperate and defiant, in response to strong Chinese pressure. Moreover, as knowledgeable observers point out, the North Korean government has already shown enormous resilience in the face of considerable diplomatic, political, financial, and economic pressure.[57]

China's Involvement in Weapons Proliferation and the Arms Trade

Although China has often declared that it does not advocate or encourage nuclear proliferation and does not help other countries to develop nuclear weapons,[58] it has probably, on at least one occasion, been willing to engage in limited levels of nuclear proliferation to serve what are regarded as critical strategic objectives.[59] Moreover, as in the arena of counterterrorism, China's support for counter-proliferation activities is also subject to constraints arising from its commitment to the principle of national sovereignty, noninterference, and a reliance on international norms and procedures to combat proliferation. However, China's record of proliferation behavior in recent years has shown notable improvements, along with some continuing problems. According to U.S. officials, several major Chinese firms sanctioned for proliferation-related activities connected with both North Korea and Iran expressed an interest in taking actions that might result in the lifting of such sanctions because of damage incurred to their reputations and business. In fact, the United States began working in 2007 with various entities such as the China North Industries Corporation (NORINCO) and the China Great Wall Industries Company (CGWIC) to implement policies to prevent inadvertent transactions to such countries.[60] As a result of this effort, U.S. sanctions against NORINCO and CGWIC were officially lifted, in 2007 and 2008, respectively.[61]

At the same time, Beijing's record in this area during the past decade is by no means pristine. China's assistance to Pakistan, Iran, and perhaps other nations has at times aggravated global trends in WMD proliferation by providing "ambiguous technical aid, more indigenous capabilities, longer-range missiles, and secondary (retransferred) proliferation."[62] Most of this activity has involved dual-use or alleged weapons technologies, primarily applicable to missiles and chemical weapons. In many such instances, Chinese suppliers were most likely profit-driven commercial firms acting independently of the PRC government. But in other instances, Beijing might have intentionally permitted shipments of items opposed by the United States.[63]

In any event, the U.S. government has imposed sanctions on more than 30 such PRC "entities" for transfers related to missiles and chemical weapons. These have included repeated sanctions on some "serial proliferators." More ominously, some U.S. officials have stated that some PRC entities are also involved with both missile and possibly *nuclear-weapons* programs in Pakistan and Iran, and have implied that the Chinese government has knowledge of at least some of these relationships, according to Congressional Research Service analyst Shirley Kan.[64] And Beijing apparently continues to provide support for Pakistan's civilian nuclear program, despite repeated U.S. urgings to stop.[65]

Most recently, China has agreed to provide two additional civilian nuclear reactors to Pakistan, thus again drawing the criticism of the United States and outside observers.[66] For many observers, China's action violates the nonbinding guidelines of the Nuclear Suppliers Group that prohibit nuclear assistance to non-IAEA-compliant states such as Pakistan. Beijing is going ahead with the deal, reportedly claiming that the sale is "grandfathered" because it was being pursued before Beijing joined the NSG in 2004 and, according to nuclear expert Mark Hibbs, that there are "compelling political reasons concerning the stability of South Asia to justify the exports."[67] It might also expect that Washington should ultimately accept the sale because China did not object to the civilian nuclear-sharing agreement between the United States and India in 2008. Indeed, for some observers, America's opposition is viewed as morally weak in this case, given its success in apparently bending the rules of both the NSG and the Nuclear Non-Proliferation Treaty to reach its deal with India, another state that has developed nuclear weapons in defiance of the international community.[68]

Finally, during the past two decades at least, China has also allegedly transferred to countries such as Burma, Cuba, Iran, Libya, Iraq, Sudan, and Syria a wide variety of conventional-weapons-related materials and technologies or missile-related items that Washington believed (or in some cases still believes) could be used to threaten regional stability and international security and undermine U.S. military dominance in certain areas, such as with regard to offensive air interdiction. Some (but not all) of China's weapons sales to such nations have been conducted by commercial entities in apparent violation of Chinese export controls and official UN monitoring.[69]

On one hand, none of these activities are banned under existing international agreements or any of China's bilateral commitments. Yet Washington is particularly concerned about China's delivery of conventional weapons and military services to Iran despite UN Security Council resolutions, because some of these weapons apparently are being transferred to Shi'i militants and Hizbollah.[70] On the other hand, Beijing has reportedly "demonstrated sensitivity to growing international concerns about recipients of some of its arms sales, notably Sudan."[71] Indeed, in some cases (Iraq), such weapons sales have either diminished notably or ended altogether in recent years, while in other cases (Burma and Cuba) they apparently continue.[72] Some U.S. officials have also expressed concern that high-technology, defense-related items that China has received from Russia for many years—such as advanced fighter aircraft, submarines, torpedoes, surface ships, and military-technical cooperation—could lead to improvements in the technologies and weapons systems that Chinese commercial entities sell abroad.[73]

Conflicting Views and Interests

In addition, even though Beijing might share Washington's concerns about global WMD proliferation and (in some instances) conventional arms sales, it has often expressed reservations about the utility of sanctions and the credibility of some U.S. intelligence involving Iran, North Korea, and Pakistan, thus strongly implying that it does not agree entirely with Washington's position and approach in the counterproliferation and arms control arenas. Moreover, Beijing obviously has significant political and economic relations with such states that undoubtedly make it very cautious and circumspect when assessing U.S. calls to undertake actions that might put such relationships at risk. For example, thus far Beijing has multi-billion-dollar energy agreements and significant trade relations with Iran but few if any equity investments in it, although this could be changing.[74] Beijing also has a long-standing and close relationship with Pakistan involving extensive defense assistance, several billion dollars in trade and investment (and pledges of much more to come), and a long-term plan to develop an energy corridor for the overland shipment to China of Middle Eastern oil supplies. And although Beijing is arguably not nearly as politically committed to North Korea as it once was, it continues to provide vital oil and food supplies to Pyongyang and certainly does not want to see the current regime collapse (or lash out) under pressure.[75]

Overall, Beijing has been far less critical of Tehran than Washington would like, has not scaled back non-defense-related economic ties with Tehran to the extent that Washington would prefer, and has favored the handling of the Iranian nuclear issue by negotiation rather than through highly punitive UN Security Council actions. Moreover, Beijing has arguably not been as supportive and energetic as Washington would like in handling Pyongyang. Although Beijing is apparently committed to the denuclearization of the Korean Peninsula, it has at times worked to soften sanctions against Pyongyang. Moreover, Beijing has not joined the Proliferation Security Initiative, along with Indonesia, India, and a few other powers.[76] Finally, the United States remains concerned about the continued gap "between declared Chinese policy and continued noncompliance by certain Chinese entities," and it thus continues to display doubts about Beijing's willingness to enforce its nonproliferation commitments and fulfill its obligations.[77]

EVALUATION

The dual global security challenges of preventing the spread of WMD and countering global terrorism became major priorities in United States–China relations at the beginning of the last decade. Whereas, in past years, these issues either had been a source of conflict, in the case of proliferation, or had simply not been on the bilateral agenda, in the case of terrorism, they now became areas of limited cooperation. Moreover, the two policy areas became more directly interconnected during this period. This shift in the U.S. agenda, the resulting growing level of bilateral Sino-American cooperation, and the consequent changes in Chinese behavior were collectively driven by the United States' recognition that it needed China to manage these issues more effectively. This change was also motivated by a corresponding recognition by China that its foreign policy interests had become more global and that it possessed some leverage to manage these security challenges.

On balance, U.S. policy has played a major—but not exclusive—role in facilitating many of the above-described positive developments in China's approach to counterterrorism and counterproliferation. Washington has alternately encouraged, supported, prodded, and persuaded Beijing to undertake actions supportive of U.S. interests in both areas, with some notable success. In this effort, as in many other cooperative areas of Sino-U.S. relations, Washington's ability to influence Beijing's behavior has thus depended significantly on its ability to pursue policies that serve not only U.S. but also specific Chinese interests, as well as facilitate international cooperation in general.

In the case of the global war on terrorism, China was already significantly inclined to provide notable assistance, for a host of political and strategic reasons.[78] The primary challenge for U.S. policy has been not only to deepen the level of Chinese support but, equally important, to ensure that Sino-U.S. cooperation in this area does not facilitate Beijing's repression of nonterrorist domestic dissidents. The Bush administration was moderately successful in this undertaking when it responded to Chinese concerns and identified areas where the two countries could exchange information of mutual benefit. But its ability to deepen Chinese support for the global war on terrorism in general arguably remained constrained by the limited value to the United States of bilateral cooperation on this issue (given Washington's primary focus on the Middle East and Islamic Asia), along with the excessive emphasis that the Bush administration placed on military (and largely unilateral) means in combating terrorism, as opposed to nonmilitary (and multilateral or international) means designed to address the root causes of the problem, such as weak governance, corruption, and poor economic conditions. This approach limited the support of some nations, including China, for the Bush policies in this area.[79]

Although the Obama administration has arguably downplayed the emphasis on military and unilateral approaches to the terrorist threat—in rhetorical terms at least—it has certainly not (yet) discarded the heavy U.S. reliance on military approaches to the problem in Iraq and Afghanistan.[80] Moreover, in any event, it remains far from certain that much stronger Sino-U.S. cooperation in combating terrorism would result from a major "demilitarization" of the U.S. approach, given the general levels of mutual suspicion between the two countries.

In the counterproliferation area, U.S. policy success has often derived from changes in Chinese national security priorities, growing Chinese concerns about the regional security and economic implications of proliferation in East Asia, South Asia, and the Middle East, the provocative behaviors of North Korea and Iran, and an effort to put the United States–China relationship on a more strategic footing. Conversely, U.S. policy failures in the international arena partly result from U.S. approaches that appear unilateral and highly coercive to China, force China to make tough trade-offs in its relationships with North Korea and Iran, and are seen as hypocritically inconsistent with other U.S. policy goals. Chinese leaders have been particularly suspicious of what they regard as U.S. attempts to "use WMD proliferation as a pretext for domestic inference in states of proliferation concern" and "promote regime change through international pressure and military operations."[81]

Moreover, to a much greater extent than for counterterrorism, the bilateral United States–China nonproliferation agenda (regarding both agreements and disagreements) is more complex and long-standing, resulting in a variety of issues that have yet to be resolved. The highly punitive approach of the Bush administration (centered on the successive imposition of sanctions against PRC "entities") achieved some positive initial results (vis-à-vis firms such as NORINCO) but nonetheless served to frustrate the Chinese government and arguably reduced U.S. leverage overall, according to some observers interviewed by the author. In part, this was because U.S. policy never specified the conditions under which sanctions would be lifted or even the evidence for the sanctions' imposition in the first place. For some knowledgeable observers, much of China's improved behavior with respect to proliferation can be attributed to internal factors, such as a gradual acceptance, for national security and other reasons, of the importance of international counterproliferation measures, improvements in China's bureaucratic capabilities that permitted genuine advances in its export control infrastructure, and declining support for money-making WMD-related foreign business deals as China became wealthier.

This suggests that U.S. policy can work best when it supports domestic Chinese forces for change, and when U.S. officials strive to coordinate their approach with potential domestic "allies," such as China's growing community of counterproliferation specialists. Overall, much more can and should be done to increase Beijing's willingness and ability to support U.S. counterproliferation objectives, particularly for implementation and enforcement. For some observers, incapacity, insufficient infrastructure, and a lack of outreach continue to obstruct Chinese progress in these areas, along with growing decentralization and an explosion in the number of private and semiprivate entities potentially involved in proliferation activities. Nonetheless, it is important to recognize that, for developmental, political, and strategic reasons, the PRC will probably never bring its policies fully into line with those of the United States.[82]

FUTURE TRENDS

Beijing and Washington share a variety of interests and objectives in the two closely related policy arenas of counterterrorism and counterproliferation, and they have achieved some notable successes in cooperating to advance their respective policy goals. Several major trends will likely influence the future effectiveness of U.S. policy toward China in both arenas.

First, from the broadest perspective, Washington's ability to work more effectively with Beijing will depend on a variety of international factors associated with the overall evolution of the counterproliferation, arms control, and counterterrorism movements. In this regard, many analysts point to several current and likely trends that will probably increase significantly the challenges facing both the United States and China in (1) attempting to control WMD proliferation in general, and (2) keeping WMD-related materials out of the hands of unstable or threatening governments and terrorists in particular:

- The continued existence (and perhaps expansion) of organized terrorist movements (or activists identifying themselves as jihadists) with the desire to detonate chemical, biological, and nuclear weapons or conventional weapons containing highly lethal radioactive materials (so-called dirty bombs) in the United States and elsewhere.
- The continued activities of nations (such as Iran) that are willing to sponsor certain types of terrorists to advance key national security and foreign policy interests, including efforts to counter U.S. and Western influence.
- The growing desire of many governments to acquire or expand domestic nuclear power facilities (that is, the so-called nuclear renaissance that has emerged in the wake of the global recession and growing concerns over global warming), thereby gaining potential access to nuclear-weapons-usable fissile material;[83] and to use advances in biology and chemistry to develop new chemical warfare agents or improve existing ones.
- Growing indications of lax and inconsistent compliance among many nations with the rules and regulations of international nuclear nonproliferation efforts, partly as a result of the failure to fully enforce existing procedures involving the IAEA's Board of Governors, the Nuclear Suppliers

Group, the parties to the Nuclear Non-Proliferation Treaty, and the UN Security Council.

- The rapidly growing ability (through globalization and other trends) of both state and nonstate actors to transmit WMD-related technologies and other information across borders via the Internet and other means, as witnessed by the former activities of the A. Q. Khan network based in Pakistan.
- Growing concerns among some observers regarding the continued credibility of Washington's extended deterrence commitments to Tokyo and Seoul in the face of Pyongyang's acquisition of nuclear weapons, thus prompting some governments to consider acquiring independent nuclear capabilities.
- The possible development by the United States (and other powers) of new types of nuclear weapons that might blur the distinction between conventional and nuclear weapons, that might thus lower the threshold for the use of nuclear weapons, and that might thereby encourage nations to acquire nuclear deterrents.[84]
- The arguably increasing danger of a loss of control over nuclear weapons or weapons-usable materials as a result of the deterioration of domestic order in Pakistan and North Korea.
- The potential negative impact on nonproliferation efforts of the international community's de facto acceptance of the acquisition of nuclear weapons by Pakistan, India, and Israel, and the apparently intensifying efforts of Iran and North Korea to develop nuclear weapons.[85]

Of course, in the closely related areas of counterproliferation and arms control, such challenges confront not only Washington and Beijing but also all five nuclear-weapons states and the entire international community, including the specific agreements and mechanisms established to control WMD proliferation—especially the IAEA, the UN Security Council, the NSG, the NPT, the global Fissile Material Cutoff Treaty. But cooperation between the largest nuclear-weapons power, the United States, and arguably the most rapidly expanding nuclear-weapons power, China, will become increasingly essential to the effective management of most, if not all, of these trends.

For example, ratification of the Comprehensive Test Ban Treaty (CTBT) by both nations would constitute a dramatic move toward strengthening counterproliferation efforts and even provide an indication of the willingness of the nuclear powers to begin movement toward their disarmament obligations under Article VI of the NPT. As one analyst states, "Ratification would create significant momentum for the CTBT's entry into force, helping to strengthen support for the NPT and for nonproliferation actions by the NPT's many non-nuclear-weapon states."[86]

However, Beijing's willingness to ratify the CTBT will continue to remain dependent to a large extent on what Washington does, not only with regard to the CTBT directly but also regarding space weaponization and ballistic missile defense. The Chinese leadership would likely regard any significant expansion of American capabilities in such areas as threatening to China's retaliatory-based, minimum-deterrent strategic capability. Such a conclusion could induce Beijing to enhance its deterrent capability by developing more sophisticated and larger numbers of nuclear weapons, which thus would require more fissile materials and additional nuclear tests.[87]

Factors Affecting United States–China Cooperation

Several factors will undoubtedly continue to influence the ability of the United States and China to cooperate in addressing the above-noted major trends influencing future U.S. policies in the arenas of counterterrorism and counterproliferation.

Chinese Suspicion of U.S. Intentions

Despite some apparent improvements undertaken during the Obama administration, Beijing will likely remain suspicious about what it regards as Washington's tendency to rely on unilateral measures or ad hoc coalitions (rather than international bodies) to advance its objectives regarding counterproliferation, counterterrorism, and arms control. Beijing will remain particularly concerned that the United States will attempt to utilize WMD proliferation as a pretext for what it would regard as excessive interference in the domestic affairs of possible proliferator states or to bring about regime change. As we have seen above, such concerns play a role in China's stance toward the Iran and North Korea nuclear issues.[88]

With regard to nuclear-weapons development, despite the Obama administration's efforts to adopt a nuclear policy that advocates a reduction of the U.S. nuclear arsenal and various other measures, few Chinese (or Western) analysts believe that the United States will make significant strides toward nuclear disarmament in the foreseeable future, nor renounce tactical nuclear-weapons research, rely fully on international (versus unilateral or ad hoc) approaches to dealing with WMD proliferation threats, or entirely cease the development of a national ballistic missile defense system.[89] Beijing will probably continue to resist entering into any discussions with the United States (or Russia) regarding significant nuclear-weapons reductions until both powers decrease the number of existing weapons in their respective inventories significantly beyond the levels projected in New START.[90] Moreover, the fact that China is continuing to modernize its nuclear arsenal much more than any other nuclear power certainly does not facilitate movement toward greater counterproliferation efforts.[91]

Hence, as a result of the absence of serious movement toward major reductions in nuclear arsenals (much less the abolition of nuclear weapons), non-nuclear-weapons states could become increasingly resistant to safeguards "ensuring that civilian nuclear facilities are not used for military purposes, and . . . refuse to accept constraints on their access to nuclear technology."[92]

Some observers believe that Washington can and should undertake further actions (beyond those thus far taken by the Obama administration) to significantly increase the perception by China and other countries that the United States is reducing the importance of nuclear weapons, thereby lowering pressures toward greater proliferation. According to some observers, once such action would be for Washington to explicitly state that its nuclear weapons are "solely" for deterrence purposes.[93] The Obama Nuclear Posture Review eschewed such a statement, apparently believing that it would erode U.S. extended deterrence pledges to allies and excessively limit U.S. flexibility in dealing with massive conventional attacks.[94]

Developments in Pakistan, North Korea, and Iran

Efforts to advance U.S. policy goals toward China in the arenas of counterterrorism and counterproliferation will undoubtedly be affected by developments in three countries of vital concern: Pakistan, North Korea, and Iran.

In the counterproliferation area, there is no clear evidence to indicate that Beijing's ongoing support for Pakistan's civil nuclear program is benefiting Islamabad's unsafeguarded nuclear-weapons program, as some observers have suggested. Nonetheless, U.S. officials have expressed concern that Pakistan's desire for increased PRC assistance in this area could result in the proliferation of weapons-related materials or technologies to Pakistan from China by individual entities on an unauthorized basis.[95] At the same time, efforts to strengthen stability in Pakistan—and thereby not only ensure greater control over nuclear weapons and related materials by the Pakistani government but also strengthen efforts to combat terrorism in Central Asia—could doubtless benefit from greater cooperation between Beijing and Washington, given the close relations and strong interests that both nations possess regarding Islamabad.[96]

Unfortunately, there are few indications that Beijing is moving to work together actively with Washington and the international community to deal with the ongoing domestic problems in Islamabad.[97] Beijing has historically kept a low profile regarding its close relations with Islamabad. Nonetheless, Obama administration officials have met with PRC officials to encourage more direct cooperation, and some observers believe that the Chinese might begin moving in that direction, given Beijing's growing concern about developments within Pakistan.[98] At the very least, Beijing appears to be working on its own to strengthen cooperation with Pakistan in combating terrorism.[99]

In the case of North Korea, developments in 2009 and 2010 have increased China's willingness to support more assertive United States–led international actions against Pyongyang, including stronger resolutions of condemnation, tougher sanctions, and perhaps greater support for interdiction activities against North Korean ships that might contain WMD-related materials.[100] Beijing is apparently angry at Pyongyang for walking away from the China-brokered Six-Party Talks and ignoring its warnings not to detonate a nuclear device and conduct further missiles tests in 2009. It is also deeply concerned that Pyongyang's actions could trigger closer defense interactions between Washington, Seoul, and Tokyo and perhaps increase support among the latter two nations for the development of a nuclear deterrent.[101] Indeed, as indicated above, the aftermath of the *Cheonan* incident of March 2010 and the bombardment of Yeonpyeong Island in November of the same year has likely deepened such Chinese concerns.

How far China is willing to go to punish and contain Pyongyang in the future remains unclear, however, and is probably under constant debate in Chinese leadership circles. Beijing is extremely unlikely to fully align its policies with Washington's regarding both sanctions and counterproliferation measures. Its basic interest in a stable Korean Peninsula, and hence its desire to avoid provoking North Korea into military action and to focus instead on negotiations and dialogue over pressure and confrontation, will almost certainly continue to remain Beijing's top priority. Although the Chinese leadership might support actions designed to strengthen the position of more moderate leaders within the North Korean elite (if indeed such individuals exist), they will remain opposed to policies specifically designed to eliminate the North Korean regime and reunify the peninsula. One must add that there is some uncertainty about the degree to which domestic succession issues and other factors unrelated to the positions of China, the United States, and other powers are driving North Korean provocations. From Beijing's perspective, such uncertainties also argue in favor of continued caution in approaching the issue. That said, Beijing might eventually accept Korean reunification if such an outcome could be achieved in a stable and peaceful manner, and would not result in a Korea–United States–Japan military alliance.[102] However, at the very least, Beijing would require greater clarity and assurances regarding the goals of U.S. strategy toward Pyongyang (and the Korean Peninsula) before it would consider committing to much deeper levels of cooperation with Washington in handling the nuclear problem.[103]

Moreover, it is possible that China's approach to the North Korean crisis could become more supportive of pressure against Pyongyang, or generally more activist, if (1) Japan or South Korea were to radically shift their current policies and become clearly receptive to taking more aggressive responses (including the possible adoption of nuclear weapons), and/or (?) if Pyongyang were clearly on the verge of deploying a ballistic missile with a nuclear warhead capable of striking Tokyo or (worse yet) Washington. Such a dynamic highlights the importance of gauging broader regional security trends as key variables influencing this particular WMD proliferation issue. The activities of Tokyo and Seoul, along with the possible future unraveling of Pyongyang, also suggest the need for Beijing and Washington to initiate serious discussions about future contingencies in this extremely unpredictable situation.[104]

Regarding Iran, current trends suggest that Washington could face greater challenges in cooperating with Beijing than it will face in dealing with North Korea. Although Obama's initial shift away from the Bush policy of pressure and isolation toward a policy of tough-minded engagement with Tehran was viewed as reassuring by China's leaders,[105] Washington's limited success in this approach and its continued reliance on economic sanctions have generated little enthusiasm in Beijing. Moreover, Beijing's rapidly growing economic and political ties with Tehran, combined with its continued commitment to nonintervention in the domestic affairs of sovereign states and its overall strong support for stability in the Middle East, together suggest that it will continue to resist any U.S. policies that fail to receive the full backing of the international community, and it will likewise probably remain very suspicious of U.S. political motives toward Tehran. In particular, in the aftermath of the turbulent Iranian presidential election of 2009, and in the midst of the popular protest movements that have emerged across much of the Middle East and North Africa in early 2011, Beijing is probably becoming increasingly concerned that Washington might destabilize Iran by attempting to manipulate rifts in the Iranian polity to encourage a so-called color revolution.[106] Moreover, Tehran sees the obvious strategic advantage of strengthening its ties with both Beijing and Moscow and will undoubtedly continue to strike lucrative economic deals with both countries.[107]

Conversely, China will want to avoid antagonizing its other key friends and economic partners in the Middle East, such as Saudi Arabia and Israel—both of which are implacably opposed to Iran and any Iranian nuclear-weapons program.[108] In addition, Beijing has shown that it is willing to support sanctions toward Tehran when they are fully endorsed by the international community and are combined with strong diplomatic efforts. And it will doubtless remain opposed to Iran's efforts to acquire a nuclear-weapons capability, which could destabilize the region and perhaps increase the chances of weapons-related technologies getting into the hands of Uyghur terrorists.[109]

Despite this, it is unlikely that Beijing will support a "sanctions-centered" policy that threatens to neutralize or entirely cut off its increasingly important economic ties with Tehran, unless Moscow and the rest of the international community clearly press for such an approach—an unlikely possibility. At best, it might move slowly in implementing many of its ongoing energy-related agreements with Tehran, until the nuclear issue is resolved or at least brought under greater control.[110] In general, it will favor limited sanctions combined with persistent efforts at negotiation.[111] Clearly, this issue will continue to pose a major challenge to Washington, despite the progress made in summer 2010 in achieving greater international cooperation in managing it.

The Shanghai Cooperation Organization

A final factor that could enhance cooperation between the United States and China in the international sphere regarding both counterterrorism and counterproliferation is Beijing's role in the Shanghai Cooperation Organization (SCO). Although it was originally created largely to manage a variety of border issues affecting its member states, over time, the SCO has also increasingly addressed terrorism and proliferation issues.[112] According to one 2008 source, "Talks are under way to amend the [SCO's] mission statement to include, among other things, increased military cooperation, intelligence sharing, and counterterrorism drills."[113]

The United States is of course not a member or observer of the SCO. And in the view of most analysts, it is very unlikely that this situation will change in the foreseeable future, given the apparent strong interest of China (and perhaps other members) in keeping the SCO a non-Western entity.[114] However, even without U.S. participation, the SCO could become an important mechanism in advancing China's support for counterterrorism and counterproliferation in areas of interest to the United States, given China's strong commitment to utilizing the SCO to combat "terrorism, separatism, and extremism." And yet it is by no means a foregone conclusion that the SCO will serve U.S. interests regarding counterterrorism and counterproliferation. It could facilitate Chinese efforts to suppress legitimate domestic dissent in the name of a larger, SCO-backed campaign against regional counterterrorism. Moreover, as suggested in chapter 3, there are indications that China might not embrace giving the SCO an increased emphasis on security issues (because such an emphasis might disadvantage China vis-à-vis Russia within the organization) and would instead prefer giving it a stronger economic role.[115]

Curbing Chinese Proliferation

Aside from the issue of controlling international WMD proliferation and terrorism, U.S. policy must also address the issue of China as a proliferator. U.S. policy has played a significant role in encouraging and pressuring Beijing to alter its actions in this area in ways that have significantly benefited U.S. interests. There is little doubt that future U.S. success in reducing Chinese proliferation of WMD-related materials, technologies, and know-how will continue to depend on

- Beijing's overall assessment (based on national security requirements, international image concerns, and other reasons) of the importance of achieving common counterproliferation goals.
- The continued improvement of China's export control infrastructure.
- Lessening support within the PRC government and among Chinese corporations for WMD-related foreign business deals.

These factors will doubtlessly remain subject to the influence of China's internal factors associated with the central, regional, and local governments' commitment to and control over the rapidly increasing number of entities potentially involved in proliferation activities. For example, the continued decentralization of economic authority into the hands of regional and local governments and individual public and private entities will likely sustain proliferation activities.[116] Some analysts also point to the need to increase civilian control over the Chinese military in order to strengthen the country's compliance with domestic WMD-related proliferation controls.[117] However, most experienced observers insist that the military does not play a highly significant role in WMD-related proliferation activities.[118]

Some of these internal factors are undoubtedly amenable to international and U.S. influence, both directly and indirectly. In particular, the United States can do more to help improve China's domestic incapacity, insufficient infrastructure, and lack of outreach to the outside world. Nonetheless, it is likely that, even though Beijing will probably exert greater efforts in the future to strengthen its overall counterproliferation efforts both unilaterally and in cooperation with Washington and other powers, in at least the near to medium terms, Chinese entities will doubtlessly continue to provide sensitive WMD- and ballistic-missile-related technologies and components to Pakistan and perhaps Iran and several other countries.[119]

Domestic "Terrorists"/Dissidents in China

Concerning the domestic dimension of China's counterterrorism efforts, current trends suggest that Beijing will almost certainly continue to use the repression of alleged internal terrorists (centered largely in Xinjiang and Tibet) to justify its repression of nonterrorist dissidents. This is all the more true in the aftermath of the domestic unrest occurring in both regions in 2008 and 2009. And the U.S. government will no doubt remain highly sensitive to such issues. As some analysts observed in 2005 (and the point remains true today):

> Washington and Beijing will continue to differ over how China chooses to treat the [terrorism] issue domestically. This issue will be particularly difficult given strong political support in the United States for the legitimate political expression of ethnic minorities in China such as the Uyghurs and Tibetans. Chinese authorities will take a far more narrow view of what kind of "political expression" can and cannot be tolerated, and has shown little reticence to crack down on and label as "terrorism" the political activities of groups in Xinjiang, Tibet, and elsewhere.[120]

Moreover, some Western analysts believe that the Chinese government is steadily increasing its ability to fight terrorism within Chinese areas such as Xinjiang through a variety of sophisticated economic, social, and military measures that do not essentially rely on outside assistance or benefit from the country's foreign counterterrorism activities. These include enhanced efforts at economic development, the gradual introduction of Han Chinese into the population of such areas, and the advantages that accrue to a population that is willing to accept extremely repressive measures from the state in order to maintain domestic stability.[121]

To the extent that Beijing is able to insulate its domestic approach to terrorism from international (and in particular U.S.) influence and expands its attacks on political dissidents in the name of counterterrorism, Washington will be faced with a growing challenge in balancing its opposition to Beijing's domestic actions against its desire for greater Chinese support in combating international terrorism.

CONCLUSION

The summary and analysis given above of U.S. and Chinese policies in the increasingly important and troublesome policy arenas of counterterrorism and counterproliferation clearly indicate that a mixed carrots-and-sticks strategy toward Beijing has constituted the mainstream U.S. approach, and is almost certainly still called for during the second decade of this century and beyond. In particular, the potential certainly exists for Beijing and Washington to increase their cooperation in combating both WMD proliferation and terrorism, given their common interests, the presence of supportive specialist communities in both countries, and China's arguably growing capacity to address both issues. At the same time, U.S. policies in the counterproliferation arena will face a growing array of severe challenges, many associated with the larger strategic problems confronting the Sino-U.S. relationship—for example, with regard to Iran and North Korea. Specifically, Beijing will likely continue to resist bringing its approach to Pyongyang more fully into line with those of Washington, Tokyo, and Seoul, as long as it continues to harbor suspicion toward Washington's motives and as long as it continues to believe that the best chance for Pyongyang to evolve in a more moderate direction is via noncoercive negotiations.

07

NONTRADITIONAL SECURITY THREATS: CLIMATE CHANGE AND PANDEMICS

━━━━━━━━━━━━━━━ ▼ ━━━━━━━━━━━━━━━

Although nontraditional security threats such as environmental pollution and disease have existed for centuries, their intensity and scope have grown rapidly only in recent decades, largely as a result of technological change, economic development, and the emergence of a truly interconnected regional and global order. Thus these problems increasingly pose a national security threat to many nations through their ability to undermine economic growth rates, increase health care costs, and exacerbate domestic and regional tensions and strife.[1]

From a U.S. perspective, China is of particular significance to this policy arena with regard to the two security threats of environmental degradation and pandemics, largely because of the size of its pollution problems (including the production of carbon emissions relevant to climate change), its rapid rate of growth, and its recent involvement in the outbreak of serious pandemics such as severe acute respiratory syndrome and the avian flu.[2] Hence, these two threats constitute the focus of this chapter.

POLICY APPROACHES

Transnational problems such as environmental degradation—especially including climate change—and pandemics present a somewhat narrower range of alternative approaches than those evident for the policy arenas discussed in previous chapters. There is little doubt that the United States and China largely agree on the need to strengthen both bilateral and international cooperation in handling these nontraditional security threats.

Two primary challenges confront the United States in this policy arena. The first one is how to strengthen public support for committing increasing levels of public and private resources, during extremely difficult economic times, and with regard to either the controversial and gradually emerging problem of climate change,[3] or the episodic and hard-to-predict problem of pandemic diseases. This is essentially a domestic political and educational issue for U.S. leaders, requiring more determined and effective political and public outreach programs. These efforts must extend far beyond policies toward China and cannot be examined in any detail in this study.

The second primary challenge, however, does directly concern U.S. relations with China: how to draw China more fully into cooperative bilateral and international efforts to address climate change and pandemics in ways that truly contribute to reducing these threats while also addressing the concerns of domestic interest groups, and, to some extent, U.S. security interests. In this regard, key issues and questions include political constraints on information sharing between the Chinese government and Chinese society and between Chinese and foreign entities, the general willingness and ability of both governments to undertake mutually agreed upon (and costly) commitments to reduce environmental damage, the potential security limitations involved in developing joint civilian and military operations to combat nontraditional threats, and the overall capability of Chinese government and quasi-governmental agencies to interact effectively with more advanced international and U.S. agencies.

Concerns about these and other issues affecting U.S. objectives in this arena do not easily fall into alternative overarching policy approaches *toward China*, however. This is largely because these nontraditional security threats are essentially complex, global problems, involving several international agencies, and usually many different countries, not just China. As a result, some approaches place a strong emphasis on working with and through international agencies and a variety of nations to deal with potential global threats such as pandemics and environmental degradation. Few observers would advocate a heavy reliance on bilateral Sino-American interactions in managing these threats, given the prominent role played by existing global organizations such as the United Nations and the World Health Organization (WHO).

Moreover, there is little logical basis for arguing that Washington should adopt unilateral, high-pressure tactics to compel Beijing to share information regarding pandemics or to reduce China's pollution levels. These threats obviously require multilateral, cooperative action. That said, bilateral agreement on some issues, such as climate change, could arguably influence other nations to cooperate in developing international solutions. Perhaps the greatest variation in approach toward Beijing thus centers on the extent to which Washington should (1) rely on some level of prior bilateral understanding to influence multilateral negotiations, (2) rely on governmental agencies versus private commercial mechanisms to assist Beijing in improving its ability to cope with these threats, and (3) permit joint operations between U.S. and Chinese military forces or other security entities (for example, in the area of disaster relief) to address a sudden or gradually emerging crisis.

POLICY HISTORY: ENVIRONMENTAL DEGRADATION

Regarding climate change, on a per capita basis, and in cumulative historical terms, China's contribution to environmental degradation worldwide does not yet approach that of developed nations in some key areas, at least according to senior Chinese officials.[4] Nonetheless, China's absolute and relative adverse impact on the environment continues to increase at a high rate. It has already overtaken the United States in total greenhouse gas emissions, and it accounts for 90 percent of the huge increase in worldwide coal consumption during the past few years, largely as a result of steeply rising demand for electricity that is mostly generated by coal-fired power plants.[5]

U.S. Environmental Policies and Activity

The George W. Bush administration adopted a variety of policies and actions to address environmental issues involving China. From a global and regional perspective, during the Bush era, Washington promoted common participation in multilateral organizations and forums such as the Group of Twenty (G-20) leadership summit, the Asia-Pacific Partnership on Clean Development and Climate, the Energy Working Group of the Asia-Pacific Economic Cooperation forum, the Carbon Sequestration Leadership Forum, the Partnership for the

Hydrogen Economy, and the Methane to Markets Partnership. Most of these entities are designed to improve energy security and efficiency and to address climate change. But some, such as the G-20, have a much broader agenda that includes environmental issues.[6]

The Bush administration also commenced annual bilateral dialogues with Beijing such as the Energy Policy Dialogue with the U.S. Department of Energy (DOE) and the U.S.-China Global Issues Forum. The DOE dialogue was originally focused on assessing industrial efficiency in an effort to assist China in reaching its energy conservation goal of a 20 percent reduction in energy consumption per unit of gross domestic product (GDP) by 2010. The annual Global Issues Forum was inaugurated in April 2005 to "identify ways to strengthen cooperation between the United States and China on transnational issues and to explore new avenues of joint work on a global basis." Thus far, it has focused on topics relating to energy security, clean energy, environmental conservation, and sustainable development, as well as public health, humanitarian assistance, international development cooperation, and human trafficking.[7]

Under Bush, the U.S. Environmental Protection Agency (EPA) also became deeply involved with China in this area. The EPA and the U.S. Department of Agriculture began collaborating with Beijing to advance biofuel technology.[8] The EPA also formed a partnership with the China State Environmental Protection Administration (SEPA) to improve hazardous-waste management and to help Beijing develop programs to clean up large areas of contaminated land and turn them into commercially viable new developments.[9] It also supported two pilot projects in China to introduce alternative energy technologies into rural homes and schools and reduce the indoor air pollution from burning biomass and coal.[10]

Of equal significance with these dialogues and initiatives, the EPA also began working with its Chinese counterparts to create six regional environmental protection offices in China in order to improve the ability of the Ministry of Environmental Protection (and, before 2008, SEPA) to monitor and enforce air pollution control laws.[11] This initiative addresses a top U.S. policy priority: the improvement of China's enforcement of its environmental laws and regulations at subnational levels, where provincial and local governments play a major role. And yet, too many such entities often avoid their responsibilities by focusing instead on sustaining rapid growth over all else.[12] SEPA (and now the Ministry of Environmental Protection) has also historically lacked the staff, regulatory powers, and subnational presence to overcome this problem and enable the enforcement of existing laws. The six regional centers are expected to improve oversight and serve as platforms for better enforcement at the provincial and local levels.[13]

Finally, in the overall context of bilateral, government-to-government relations, the Strategic Economic Dialogue during the Bush administration produced the formal Framework for Ten-Year Cooperation on Energy and Environment. According to then—U.S. Treasury secretary Henry Paulson, the framework focuses on "shared objectives, including energy security, lower greenhouse gas emissions, clean water, clean air, and preservation of wild and beautiful places," laying out action plans in these areas. Paulson also noted that the private sector will play a role in creating a "green" economy in both countries, particularly as it develops advanced technologies. As part of this initiative, the two countries conducted a joint economic study that identified cost-effective approaches to saving energy and controlling emissions from the power generation sectors in both countries, which produced a set of recommendations on energy saving and pollution abatement for policymakers in both Beijing and Washington.[14]

In addition to these governmental activities, during the Bush era, nearly 60 U.S. nongovernmental organizations, professional societies, think tanks, and universities became involved in energy and environmental projects with China, ranging from developing energy conservation incentives to improving water management. For example, the Natural Resources Defense Council and the China–U.S. Energy Efficiency Alliance worked together to link the Jiangsu Provincial Economic and Trade Commission, the California Public Utilities Commission, and the California Energy Commission in an effort to establish energy efficiency programs in Jiangsu Province. Then and now, other entities involved in United States–China environmental and climate change cooperation include the Carnegie Endowment for International Peace, the Brookings Institution, the World Resources Institute, Harvard University, Columbia University, Stanford University, the China Center for International Economic Exchanges, and Beijing University. Such nongovernmental organizations have served an important function in this policy area as mediators and facilitators among Chinese government agencies, local governments, the nongovernmental community, and U.S. public and private interests.[15]

On the negative side, during the Bush administration, many of the above-mentioned bilateral U.S. government programs with China—and especially those focused on the energy sector—were undersized and underfunded.[16] More broadly, Washington under Bush did not do much to set a larger example for China by contributing significantly to international efforts to address environmental degradation, including global warming. The Bush administration failed to ratify the Kyoto Protocol and, in the view of many experts, also generally failed to take the lead in seriously confronting the greatest cause of adverse global climate change: carbon emissions. During the Bush era, bilateral collaboration in support of a major effort to address global climate change consisted largely of verbal affirmations and little concrete significant action.[17]

Since taking office, the Barack Obama administration has adopted a much more active stance toward this issue overall than the Bush administration, pushing for so-called cap-and-trade legislation in the U.S. Congress and international agreements to reduce carbon emissions and increase investments in clean energy technologies.[18] President Obama also launched the Major Economies Forum on Energy and Climate in April 2009 as a new dialogue among developed and emerging economies to combat climate change and promote clean energy.[19] He has given several strong speeches emphasizing the criticality of the issue,[20] and he made a major personal effort to reach a binding international agreement on climate issues at the international climate change summit held in Copenhagen in December 2009, although the resulting Copenhagen Accord was a mere twelve-paragraph statement of intentions rather than a binding pledge.[21]

With regard to China, under Obama, Washington has also considerably increased its efforts at bilateral dialogue and cooperation in a variety of areas relevant to climate change. For example, during the restructured Strategic and Economic Dialogue that first took place in July 2009, Washington and Beijing signed a "Memorandum of Understanding on Enhancing Cooperation on Climate Change, Energy, and the Environment." This memorandum elevated climate change as a top priority in the bilateral relationship, recommitted the two countries to reaching a successful international agreement on this issue, and deepened their individual and cooperative efforts to "respond vigorously to the challenges of energy security, climate change and environmental protection through ambitious domestic action and international cooperation." The memorandum also established an ongoing dialogue between Beijing and Washington on what both countries are doing to reduce emissions and to advance international climate change measures, and it laid a foundation for expanded cooperation in addressing climate change and promoting energy efficiency, renewable energy, smart grid technologies, electric vehicles, carbon capture and sequestration, joint research and development, clean air and water, and the protection of natural resources. In addition, the two sides recognized the ongoing importance of the Framework for Ten-Year Cooperation on Energy and Environment in facilitating practical cooperation between the two countries in the areas of energy and the environment.[22]

Also in mid-2009, the U.S. DOE joined with China's Ministry of Science and Technology and the National Energy Administration (formed in mid-2008) to establish a U.S.-China Clean Energy Research Center to "facilitate joint research and development on clean energy by teams of scientists and engineers. . . ." The center, to be located in existing facilities in both the United States and China, will initially focus on energy efficiency, clean coal—including carbon capture and storage—and clean vehicles. Beijing and Washington originally pledged $15 million to support the center's activities. Then, in April 2010, DOE announced that it would contribute $37.5 million in U.S. funding during the next five years to support the center, with matching funding to be provided by the grantees.[23]

Building on these advances, during Obama's state visit to China in November 2009, several additional cooperative endeavors in this policy area were announced. These included the establishment of a U.S.-China Clean Energy Research Center and a U.S.-China Energy Cooperation Program and the launch of the U.S.-China Electric Vehicles Initiative. The two nations also established new initiatives such as the U.S.-China Energy Efficiency Action Plan, the U.S.-China Renewable Energy Partnership, the U.S.-China Shale Gas Resource Initiative, and a pledge to promote cooperation on cleaner uses of coal, including large-scale carbon capture and storage demonstration projects.[24] Funding for many of these initiatives was not immediately available, but in some cases commenced in 2010.[25]

During the second round of the Strategic and Economic Dialogue in May 2010, the Obama administration also announced several notable achievements with China, including progress in implementing the above-outlined memorandum of understanding and the publication of all seven action plans associated with the Framework for Ten-Year Cooperation on Energy and Environment, and it announced the holding of several bilateral dialogues on energy-related issues in late 2010, as well as the first U.S.-China Renewable Energy Forum and Advanced Biofuels Forum.[26] In September 2010, the U.S. DOE also announced the formation of two new bilateral consortia to develop clean vehicles and clean coal technologies, with shared funding of $100 million. The consortiums will combine universities, car companies, national laboratories, electric utilities, and think tanks.[27]

Despite this clear shift in policy direction and effort, however, President Obama has thus far been unable to achieve any significant breakthrough on this issue, either domestically or internationally.[28] In part, this is because the U.S. Congress has yet to enact climate and energy legislation that would establish binding targets for domestic carbon emissions, especially as evidenced by the Senate's inability to act on cap-and-trade legislation. Washington's failure in this regard has arguably provided Beijing with cover to avoid making more serious changes and has thus undermined efforts at greater collaboration, both bilaterally and through multilateral venues.[29] Conversely, U.S. leaders point to China's repeated failure to enact specific, binding emission objectives and timelines as a reason for not passing its own laws, arguing that, without corresponding

Chinese action, such moves would place the United States at a decided economic disadvantage. Some critics also accuse Beijing of providing unfair subsidies to China's commercial clean energy sector.[30]

More broadly, the United States and other Western governments are also restrained by strong sentiment in favor of China making major cuts in greenhouse gas emissions, along with popular opposition to providing funds for developing countries to assist them in adapting to climate change. In recent years, public opinion in the United States has also resisted more government action in this area, perhaps reflecting what appears to be a growing disbelief in the existence of human-caused climate change, along with concerns that greater investments in costly clean energy programs will threaten attempts to recover from America's economic problems in the aftermath of the global recession. China takes the opposite stance on both these issues, arguing that the United States and other developed industrial societies must make the largest effort to curb their carbon emissions, given their much longer history of polluting the environment, and thus also should provide substantial assistance to developing countries, including China.[31] As a result, bilateral collaboration to address global climate change by significantly reducing carbon emissions worldwide has thus far largely consisted of verbal statements, voluntary pledges, and little significant, binding action. Unfortunately, a larger effort in this area is unlikely to succeed without such concrete Sino-American action.[32]

Chinese Environmental Policies and Activity

China has begun working with the United States, other countries, and various international bodies to reduce its exploding level of carbon emissions, increase energy efficiency, limit or reduce air and water pollution levels, and develop alternative, less polluting sources of energy. It is also initiating positive unilateral actions in some areas. For example, the Chinese government established a national climate change leading group in 2007, headed by Premier Wen Jiabao. In June 2007, Beijing unveiled a 62-page climate change plan, after two years of preparation by seventeen government ministries. The plan promised to put climate change at the center of its energy policies and repeated a commitment to reduce energy use per unit of GDP by a fifth before 2010 and increase the amount of renewable energy it produces by some 10 percent.[33] In January 2011, Beijing claimed to have met this goal.[34] Also, the above-mentioned National Energy Administration was established in 2008.[35] The Chinese central government has also become more serious in holding local governments and companies accountable for meeting the national energy intensity standard. For example, the State-

Owned Assets Supervisory and Administration Commission has released interim measures on energy consumption and emissions monitoring.[36]

In addition, China has set fuel economy requirements for new cars that are more stringent than those of the United States (but less stringent than those in the European Union) and has begun requiring power companies to invest in larger coal-fired power plants instead of smaller power plants, which tend to require more coal per kilowatt-hour generated. China has also taken a leading position in the development of several green technologies, eliminating subsidies for high-energy consumption enterprises and implementing a variety of financial incentives to encourage energy-saving investments. In fact, as part of the country's 4 trillion yuan ($586 billion) economic stimulus package enacted in 2009 in response to the global financial crisis, Beijing announced that the National Development and Reform Commission would invest $30 billion in green projects as part of an effort to double the nation's 2007 output of alternative energy by 2020. In 2010, investment in China's clean energy sector was 60 percent higher than in the United States' ($54.4 billion versus $34 billion, respectively). China exceeded the United States in five-year growth rates of energy investment between 2005 and 2010 (88 percent versus 61 percent for the United States). And in 2009, China surpassed the United States in total installed clean energy production capacity.[37]

More broadly, China has adopted a target of having renewable fuels account for 10 percent of its total energy consumption by 2010 and 15 percent by 2020. And China has adopted important policy mechanisms to encourage clean energy, including a fixed-rate feed-in tariff supporting wind energy investment, as well as ambitious nationwide renewable targets (the United States has none) calling for 300 gigawatts from hydropower, 150 gigawatts from wind, 30 gigawatts from biomass, and 20 gigawatts from solar energy by 2020. China has established a leading position in clean energy manufacturing, particularly in solar and wind energy, and it now accounts for 50 percent of global exports of wind turbine and solar modules. Beijing is also greatly increasing its nuclear energy production, with plans to build enough additional nuclear reactors to provide 6 to 10 percent of the country's total power capacity by 2020 (up from the current 1.9 percent).[38] Overall, China is now regarded by many analysts as a leading force in the promotion of clean energy.[39]

In addition, in 2009, Beijing became more willing to agree to specific targets for carbon emissions, largely in response to what it views as the more "responsible" approach toward climate change adopted by the Obama administration.[40] For example, although China's official negotiating position is unchanged, in September 2009 President Hu Jintao announced four basic steps of significance: a reduction in the amount of carbon dioxide that China will emit per unit of GDP by a "notable margin" by 2020 compared with 2005 levels, an increase in the size of forests by 40 million hectares (about 98.8 million acres), increases in the level of nuclear or nonfossil fuels to 15 percent of power by 2020, and more concerted efforts to develop a green economy.[41] The National Energy Administration has finalized a ten-year new energy development plan (with an investment of $740 billion) to help China realize its goals of achieving 15 percent of its primary energy mix from nonfossil sources and also to reduce its carbon intensity by 40 to 50 percent by 2020.[42] Also, as part of its Twelfth Five-Year Plan, China announced in 2010 that it is studying plans to adopt a domestic carbon trading market to help meet its carbon emissions reduction targets.[43] Moreover, despite the many shortcomings of the Copenhagen Accord, Beijing nonetheless publicly announced a specific numerical target of improving its carbon intensity, and it initially agreed to join an international system for biannually reporting national emissions that could facilitate a future move toward independent examination.[44] And at the Cancún climate change talks at the end of 2010, Beijing adopted a somewhat more positive and cooperative stance, reiterating its commitment to biannual emissions reporting and softening its overall message.[45]

On the negative side, Beijing has yet to indicate any willingness to submit to *internationally* legally binding emissions targets rather than targets governed by domestic law, a stance it reaffirmed at Cancún in late 2010.[46] Also, though Obama indicated in late 2009 that the United States intends to reduce its greenhouse gas emissions from 2005 levels by approximately 17 percent by 2020 and 83 percent by 2050, Chinese officials only speak of reductions in carbon dioxide emissions as a percentage of GDP units, meaning that China's total emissions could (and almost certainly will) still grow in absolute terms, but possibly at a slower rate. Beijing refuses to commit to any absolute reduction in carbon emissions, "arguing that environmental concerns must be balanced with economic growth and that developed countries must first demonstrate a significant commitment to reducing emissions."[47]

More broadly, as suggested above, Beijing has also insisted that developed countries have an "unshirkable responsibility" to take the lead on cutting greenhouse gas emissions, in line with the notion of the "common but differentiated responsibility" principle enunciated by past international agreements such as the Kyoto Protocol. Many Chinese also apparently believe that the United States uses climate change as a vehicle to inhibit China's rise. Specifically, during 2009, some argued that Washington intended to enmesh Beijing in pledging to meet international targets but would subsequently retreat from meeting its own targets because of an inability to get domestic legislation passed—a suspicion exacerbated by the United States' failure to pass cap-and-trade legislation in 2010. Some Chinese also believe that United States–China energy-related interactions are intentionally structured in such a way that Washington generally enjoys the clean, high-value part of the trade (design, research, marketing, sales, service) while Beijing only produces the low value, highly polluting elements. Washington is then blamed by many Chinese for employing moral and other arguments about Beijing's pollution in order to constrain its options and growth.[48] Many Chinese also charge that Washington and the West in general hypocritically criticize Beijing for establishing subsidies to support clean energy industries while employing such subsidies themselves, and refusing to help developing countries foster competitive industries.[49]

Another challenge to improving China's environmental policies is evident in its 2007 climate change plan, which stressed that technology and costs remain major barriers to achieving domestic energy efficiency, and noted that it will be difficult to reduce the nation's dependency on coal in the short term.[50] Although the above-noted advances are promising overall, Beijing has thus far failed to meet many of its environmental targets and continues to confront many major funding, staffing, and enforcement problems. In particular, many local governments continue to shield local industries from central regulations regarding clean energy issues, and the Ministry of Environmental Protection remains understaffed and underfunded.[51]

Moreover, after the Copenhagen talks in December 2009, some observers expressed concern that Beijing was equivocating on its commitment to submit biannual emission reports to the United Nations Framework Convention on Climate Change.[52] China's position was clarified to a degree at the Cancún climate talks a year later, when Beijing affirmed a compromise deal wherein developing countries agreed to submit reports on emissions every four years, with biannual updates that would be subject to international consultation and analysis—in contrast to the more formalized and binding measurement, reporting, and verification process required of developed nations. However, the details of how that international consultation and analysis mechanism would operate remained unclear, and the commitments made at Copenhagen and elaborated in Cancún are likely to ultimately depend upon individual national governments rather than binding, rigorous international verification.[53]

POLICY HISTORY: PANDEMICS

The United States' and the international community's attention to the acute danger that an outbreak of a pandemic disease could pose to national security in the modern era, and China's likely relationship to such a danger, were triggered most significantly by the appearance of the new, highly contagious disease called severe acute respiratory syndrome (SARS) in southern China in late 2002.[54] The newness, lethality, and speed of transmission of SARS, combined with the fact that local Chinese authorities initially attempted to suppress information about its outbreak and spread within China, were of great concern not only to the U.S. government but also to other governments and health organizations worldwide. Such concern was buttressed by the occurrence in China in 2003 of cases of avian influenza, and again in 2009 with the outbreak of the H1N1 virus (swine flu) in the West, which made its way to China in May of the same year.[55]

U.S. Policy on Pandemics

With regard to communicable diseases, the Bush and Obama administrations have promoted a variety of multilateral initiatives involving China. These have included the International Partnership on Avian and Pandemic Influenza (IPAPI), announced by President Bush at the UN General Assembly in September 2005.[56] The IPAPI has held several global conferences since its inception, in Washington, Beijing, Vienna, Bamako, New Delhi, and Sharm el-Sheikh. It is now known as the International Ministerial Conference on Animal and Pandemic Influenza (IMCAPI) Process. The seventh IMCAPI Process conference, which took place in April 2010 in Hanoi, examined how to combat pandemic influenza and bring greater attention to the interconnection between animal and human health.[57] Washington has also worked with Beijing to establish a Global Disease Detection Center in China as part of its overall effort to expand the network of such centers around the world.[58]

On a bilateral level, Washington has encouraged Beijing to adopt more transparent reporting and sharing of health information and to work more effectively with both the WHO and the U.S. Centers for Disease Control and Prevention (U.S. CDC), along with other agencies, to address mounting health crises. In November 2005, the United States and China announced a joint initiative to combat avian influenza through cooperative actions at the bilateral, global, and regional levels.[59] Also in 2005, the China Ministry of Health and the U.S. Department of Health and Human Services signed a memorandum of understanding to establish the China–U.S. Collaborative Program on Emerging and Reemerging Infectious Diseases. This memorandum was renewed during the second U.S.-China Strategic and Economic Dialogue in May 2010.[60] The Chinese Center for Disease Control and Prevention (China CDC) and the U.S. CDC now collaborate closely in training field epidemiologists to detect and respond to disease outbreaks. During the height of the H1N1 influenza pandemic, the United States and China exchanged technology and information to improve the quality and speed of the public health response in both countries.[61] U.S. government scientists have also assisted with onsite investigations in China of outbreaks of avian viruses that could generate pandemics, providing laboratory diagnosis, identification of disease risk factors, and analyses of clusters of diseases to determine whether human-to-human transmission was occurring.[62]

After the outbreak of the swine flu pandemic in 2009, Washington and Beijing institutionalized interagency health discussions following the first round of the Strategic and Economic Dialogue in July 2009.[63] During his visit to China in November 2009, President Obama promised closer collaboration with China on joint research on pandemics, on prevention, on surveillance, and on reporting and controlling swine flu, avian influenza, and other diseases.[64] China's Ministry of Health and the U.S. Department of Health and Human Services also pledged to improve collaboration in the public health sector, at a China–U.S. Health Policy Forum held in Beijing in June 2010.[65]

Also, Washington now actively funds HIV/AIDS programs in China bilaterally through the U.S. Agency for International Development, the Global AIDS Program of the U.S. CDC, the National Institutes of Health, and the Department of Labor, as well as through multilateral organizations such as the UN and the Global Fund to Fight AIDS, Tuberculosis, and Malaria. Since 2006, all bilateral HIV/AIDS-related programs funded by the U.S. government in China have been integrated into the President's Emergency Plan for AIDS Relief in order to improve coordination and management. These U.S. government programs are coordinated by the Office of the U.S. Global AIDS Coordinator (within the U.S. Department of State).[66] In this regard, a partnership of the U.S. CDC with China's Ministry of Health and the China CDC is now introducing innovative HIV detection and prevention strategies and infection control practices in hospitals. And the U.S. CDC supports clinics in fifteen provinces around China to strengthen HIV/AIDS prevention.[67]

Yet despite these cooperative efforts, as in the environmental policy area, Washington also needs to provide a better example for China (and other Asian nations) in the general area of government-sponsored health programs. According to knowledgeable experts, although the Bush administration significantly increased spending on global HIV/AIDS relief, it also underfunded other global health efforts and did not focus much attention on long-term prevention through the creation of strong health systems. Nearly all U.S. programs were heavily earmarked, and they contained little if any funding designated for general health threats or health systems management and support.[68] This situation might be improving, however. In an effort to deepen global health promotion, President Obama announced the launch of a U.S. Global Health Initiative in

December 2009 "as a new effort to develop a comprehensive U.S. government strategy for global health by proposing $63 billion over six years ([fiscal years] 2009–2014)." This initiative would build on and go beyond the above-mentioned Bush administration's President's Emergency Plan for AIDS Relief to combat diseases in developing countries, strengthen health systems overall, and leverage cooperation with key partners, including China.[69] Also, regarding pandemics, in June 2009, Obama requested $1.5 billion in supplemental funding for U.S. domestic and international pandemic preparedness and response activities. During that month, the 2009 Supplemental Appropriations bill (HR 2346) was also approved. The bill commits $50 million for U.S. Agency for International Development pandemic preparedness activities and $200 million to the U.S. CDC for domestic and international H1N1 activities.[70] Despite these positive trends, however, the congressional debates over the 2011 and 2012 budgets will likely result in reduced funding for global health activities, and could result in the underfunding of the Global Health Initiative.[71]

Chinese Policy on Pandemics

Such U.S. efforts, along with the hard lessons conveyed by the poor handling of the SARS epidemic, have undoubtedly contributed to China's overall efforts in recent years to improve its ability to detect, contain, and eradicate pandemic diseases. Since the SARS outbreak in 2003, the China CDC and the Ministry of Health have established a nationwide rapid information network for nearly 20 communicable diseases that reportedly covers 100 percent of economically developed provinces in the eastern part of the country and has reached 75 percent of townships throughout the whole country. By mid-2005, all of China's counties had direct Internet connections to the Ministry of Agriculture's monitoring system for avian influenza. A total of 93 percent of counties or higher-level hospitals and 43 percent of township hospitals have direct links to the China CDC's disease reporting system. This network is reportedly the world's largest nationally coordinated, real-time biosurveillance system. It has improved the accuracy of disease reporting, facilitated containment, and resulted in an overall improvement in infectious disease management. In addition, specialized training courses stressing the diagnosis and reporting of infectious diseases are now provided annually in China for all health care workers. Guangdong Province has invested more than 10 billion yuan ($1.46 billion) in infrastructure for disease control, medical resuscitation, and public health surveillance. In addition, the WHO is working closely with Beijing to strengthen China's capabilities in many areas, including surveillance, laboratory diagnosis, and reporting.[72]

Following the outbreak of the H1N1 influenza in 2009, China not only increased its examination and disinfection capabilities nationwide but also invested 5 billion yuan ($725 million) in flu prevention and control, stepped up research of vaccines and medicines, provided financial and technical support for countries and regions that needed assistance, and tightened the monitoring of pig farms, slaughterhouses, and livestock markets.[73] In early September 2009, China became the first country to mass produce a vaccine against the H1N1 pandemic. In addition, Beijing's more rapid, forthright, and energetic response to the H1N1 outbreak (compared with its response to the SARS epidemic) probably contributed significantly to the successful management of the disease. No H1N1-caused fatalities were reported until early October 2009.[74]

China has also opened several new laboratories to research virology and disease prevention and control, including a world-class avian flu laboratory in Wuhan.[75] Moreover, in a sign that it is serious about improving its image, in 2006 China nominated Margaret Chan—an expert on avian influenza and SARS from Hong Kong who had been openly critical of Beijing for its role in the SARS outbreak—as the director of the WHO.[76]

In addition to these domestic activities, China has also increased its level of cooperation with other nations, on both bilateral and multilateral levels. In particular, since receiving strong criticism from many quarters during the SARS outbreak, China has become far more willing to share important public health-related information with the international community. Since 2003, much information on veterinary epidemics has no longer been regarded as a state secret, and China has established high-level dialogue mechanisms with the Association of Southeast Asian Nations (ASEAN), the United States, Russia, the United Kingdom, and Japan. The annual U.S.-China Global Issues Forum (as noted above) also provides a platform for discussing issues such as humanitarian assistance, public health, human trafficking, environmental conservation, and sustainable development.[77]

Beijing is also a member of the Mekong Basin Disease Surveillance Network, a collaboration with Cambodia, Laos, Myanmar, Thailand, and Vietnam that links public health workers to share information, provide training, and develop protocols on handling infectious disease. This network is reportedly a proven model for collaboration that is being replicated in other regions of the globe.[78] And China is one of sixteen Asian nations that signed the East Asia Summit Declaration on Avian Influenza Prevention, Control, and Response in December 2005, and it is involved in several ASEAN-based disease control programs.[79]

In particular, ASEAN's members and three of their dialogue partners—Japan, South Korea, and China—agreed in 2009 to implement common national pandemic

preparedness plans, surveillance approaches, and responses to avoid social disruptions from a possible H1N1 pandemic. Such measures include the continuous implementation of national pandemic-preparedness plans; improved surveillance and responses; and effective public communication to avoid panic and social
disruption.[80]

At the same time, China still has significant weaknesses in the areas of early
warning and surveillance, accurate reporting, medical services, and its overall
public health infrastructure and medical finance system, especially at the grass-
roots level. It lacks detailed risk assessments and integrated strategic plans at
both the national and local levels. It also depends on only two national agencies, the Ministry of Agriculture and the Ministry of Health, to prepare for and
respond to the avian flu and pandemic flu. Moreover, though some local public
health departments and a few local governments have released their own preparation and response plans for the pandemic flu, most of these plans still exist
only on paper. More important, China lacks specific implementation plans under
its overall preparation and response strategy for the pandemic flu.[81]

Moreover, according to one analyst, "the bifurcation of services between the
public-health-oriented CDCs and the market driven hospital system have proven
a significant challenge for infectious disease control, including HIV/AIDS treatment."[82] And outbreaks of hand, foot, and mouth disease in rural areas of China in
the spring of 2010 highlighted continued problems with poor hygiene and medical care and the overall low level of health awareness outside the major cities.[83]
Also, despite recent efforts by the Chinese central government to become more
transparent in reporting on disease incidents, concerns remain regarding the
willingness and ability of both local and central agencies to support disease surveillance outside official, state-controlled channels.[84] Similarly, although China in
2005 accepted the "universal application" principle in revising the International
Health Regulations following its initial mishandling of the SARS outbreak, it subsequently resisted the use of this concept when it became an issue in Taiwan's
diplomatic campaign for formal participation in the WHO's activities.[85]

Perhaps most important, China reportedly lacks a single, unified vision for
health care and disease prevention and alleviation that connects its national
interests, long-term goals, and strategies for attaining these goals with broader
global health efforts. Rather, as one analyst observed in 2009, "Chinese initiatives
up to now have been overwhelmingly crisis driven, reactive, ad hoc, and fragmented. Internal discussions are reportedly under way on developing a long-term
strategic approach, but these efforts remain at an early stage."[86]

Finally, at least one knowledgeable observer asserts that regional cooperative mechanisms are greatly underfunded and constitute little more than decla-

rations of intent.[87] According to another analyst, China's and ASEAN's common espousal of the nonintervention principle, along with ASEAN's fear of being dominated by its huge and rapidly growing neighbor, together limit cooperation between them on disease management to forums, declarations, and dialogues. This basic lack of trust thus inhibits common efforts to develop vaccines or share samples, for example.[88]

EVALUATION

The U.S. government has been far more active in cooperating with China to address the two major nontraditional security threats facing both countries than most outside observers might realize. U.S. officials at both senior and, especially, working levels have launched long-term initiatives in a fairly wide variety of areas with their Chinese counterparts, and in collaboration with various nongovernmental organizations and international organizations. These actions have certainly had some effect, largely by enhancing Chinese (and U.S.) capabilities in many areas; encouraging greater dialogue, transparency, and a general sharing of information; possibly building a basis for future broader-based bilateral and multilateral agreements; and adding a greater impetus to many existing Chinese undertakings. But overall, U.S. policy actions have thus far placed a strong emphasis on bilateral and multilateral dialogues, the establishment of plans and frameworks, and cooperative projects in specific, somewhat narrow, areas.

This has been especially true regarding environment-related policies. Although some progress has occurred (largely under President Obama) in this policy arena, results-oriented, concrete programs designed to tackle major problems remain inadequate and underfunded. Those areas requiring greater collaborative effort and financial support include research and development, the demonstration of carbon capture and storage, renewable energy, energy storage, and energy efficiency technologies.[89] In addition, according to one knowledgeable observer, bilateral negotiations in this policy arena are made more difficult by the fact that there is a major imbalance between the responsibilities and authorities of the lead negotiators on each side. Whereas China's top official (currently Xie Zhenhua) is both chief climate negotiator and plays a major role in moving China toward a less carbon-intensive path, the top U.S. official (currently Todd Stern) is strictly a negotiator.[90] Also, each side does not adequately appreciate those key structural constraints or pressures under which the other side operates.[91] Even more important, Washington's ability to improve Beijing's performance on the environment will remain limited as long as America fails to provide a good model for other countries and Washington is unable to reach an understanding with Beijing on how to determine the increased level of responsibility and improvements that each country must achieve. As we have seen, this issue is bound up with both U.S. domestic political conflict over the reality and urgency of climate change, and debates about the standards that should be applied to developing versus developed countries. It also reflects broader suspicions in both countries regarding the other side's allegedly perfidious motives and intentions. For some (perhaps many) observers, neither side is likely to compromise on the arguments each is advancing, thus posing a major obstacle to the conclusion of a binding carbon emissions treaty, for example.[92]

Yet this could change, if the Obama administration continues to push hard for an agreement with China and other major developing states on this issue. This appears unlikely in the near term, but certainly cannot be ruled out over the course of the decade or longer. China is still developing its approach to negotiations and diplomacy and shaping public opinion on climate issues. As Rob Bradley, founder of the Institute for Energy Research, states:

> Like all countries, [China's] motivations reflect an evolving understanding of national interest on a complex set of interrelated issues. These issues range from concerns about ensuring future energy security and economic growth to efforts to reduce domestic pollution and establish itself as a key global player in the green energy business sector. Clearly understanding these motivations—many of which are shared by the United States—will be key to identifying areas of both potential conflict and mutual benefit.[93]

Currently, both the United States and China continue to increase their energy consumption and carbon dioxide (CO_2) emissions at unsustainable rates, despite the recent global economic downturn. There is little doubt that technical and economic cooperation between the two countries will be central to ensuring energy security and reducing global emissions.[94] In the absence of a breakthrough on the production side of environmental pollution, U.S. and Chinese policy thus must and arguably can do more on both the production and consumption sides not only by increasing funding for existing or new government initiatives at all levels but also by encouraging or facilitating the efforts of commercial and nongovernmental entities to improve energy efficiency, reduce demand, and generally reduce the production of environmentally damaging pollutants in both countries.[95]

Regarding policies to prevent and combat pandemics, until recently, U.S. efforts toward China had also been significantly underfunded, and some doubt remains as to whether Washington provides a good example for China and other nations of a major power that is fully committed to detecting and responding to the outbreak of a future pandemic. It is probably true that no amount of U.S. funds, incentives, or pressure will fully guarantee desired levels of Chinese transparency in reporting outbreaks and sharing information or vastly more effective efforts to implement existing plans and regulations. China continues to suffer from inadequate enforcement mechanisms in its overall public health care system, with many local officials still stressing economic gain at the expense of public health.[96] But much more can be achieved through the application of greater resources and closer efforts to work with both international agencies and Chinese counterparts.

FUTURE TRENDS

Nontraditional security threats and concerns constitute an increasingly important dimension of Sino-American relations and will likely continue to do so for the foreseeable future. Indeed, some analysts believe that such issues will most likely become some of the most critical areas for cooperation or friction between Washington and Beijing during this decade, thus exerting a central influence on the tenor of the entire bilateral relationship. This is largely because (1) China and/or the United States are expected to become increasingly major (and in some cases primary) contributors to or sources of various nontraditional threats; and (2) the impact of such threats is expected to take on an increasingly global significance, thus demanding very high levels of attention by both Washington and Beijing.

In particular, various studies have estimated that China could become a source of serious nontraditional security threats in four areas. First, environmental problems such as toxic water supplies, air pollution, and water shortages are likely to worsen in China and to extend beyond its borders. Second, though likely mild in its impact, transnational crime based in China is likely to continue. Third, pandemics are likely to occur in or near China, especially in high-density areas where humans and animals are in close proximity and pose a serious risk to many other countries. Fourth, climate-related crises could severely affect the economies and social stability of China, the United States, and many other countries in the long term. Such climate-related risks threaten the sustainability of China's most densely populated regions.[97]

Environmental Issues

Of the four areas noted above, the related issues of environmental degradation and climate change will arguably produce the farthest-reaching and most serious challenges to overall Sino-U.S. cooperation during this decade. China has surpassed the United States as the top emitter of energy-related carbon (CO_2) emissions, largely because of its huge dependence on coal as an energy source. Over 70 percent of Chinese energy is provided by coal, and 80 percent of Chinese greenhouse gas emissions come from coal. In 2009, China consumed an estimated 3.5 billion tons of coal, constituting over 46 percent of the world's total and a 180 percent increase since 2000. China is likely to continue using more coal in the future due to domestic pressure to deliver rapid growth. Between 2007 and 2035, the International Energy Agency predicts that China will maintain a 2.7 percent average annual growth rate in energy-related CO_2 emissions. By 2035, CO_2 emissions from China are expected to account for 31 percent of total world emissions. During the same period, the United States is still expected to be the largest source of *petroleum-related* CO_2 emissions, with projected emissions of 2.6 billion metric tons in 2035—only slightly above the corresponding projection for China of 2.2 billion metric tons.[98] All these statistics indicate that China and the United States will remain the two most pivotal nations in addressing the growing problems produced by global pollution and climate change.[99]

In addition, the success or failure of China's efforts to significantly reduce its CO_2 footprint will probably exert a strong influence on the behavior of other developing nations. Specifically, if China does not change its composition of energy sources, then other developing countries may see this as a reason to continue their own carbon-intensive path. Alternatively, if China invests heavily in reducing its energy pollution, this may strengthen the normative argument for other countries to do the same.[100]

Indeed, trends in China's environmental trajectory will depend largely on its ability to reduce the energy intensity of its development model, which, in its emphasis on investment-oriented growth, is heavily resource dependent. For example, the industrial sector accounted for 50 percent of China's energy consumption in 2007, compared with 20 percent in the United States and slightly more than 30 percent in India, Russia, and Japan.[101] Because China consumes very low levels of energy on a per capita basis, most analysts believe that it is not going to scale back its absolute energy consumption levels for the sake of global warming and will likely continue consuming at rising rates. Despite such likely increases, however, some experts conclude that, if China's GDP continues to grow rapidly, Beijing might manage to meet its stated carbon intensity targets for 2020 of a 40 to 45 percent reduction *per unit of GDP* without altering its current practices (that is, largely via "business-as-usual").[102]

China's efforts to reduce its CO_2 emissions will thus probably focus more on the composition and efficiency of its energy consumption. Therefore, most experts assert that Beijing's areas for cooperation with Washington (and other powers) will likely involve agreements to limit carbon production, share clean and renewable energy technologies and best practices (involving both private- and public-sector cooperation), incentivize clean energy, and reduce barriers to clean energy development.[103]

In pursuing these objectives, China and the United States both offer major assets. As U.S. senator Maria Cantwell, chair of the Energy Subcommittee of the Senate's Energy and Natural Resource Committee and a leading voices on energy and climate, has stated:

> Generally speaking, the U.S. enjoys a lead in terms of basic science research, high-tech manufacturing and an established process for commercialization of the research and for breakthroughs. . . . China has its own substantial technological capabilities and a better understanding of what technologies work in the developing world. And China can often manufacture products more rapidly and cheaply than the United States. But a robust U.S.-China partnership has the potential to catalyze development and drive down the costs of a diverse array of clean energy technologies. . . . Rather than competing with China for an ever-shrinking foreign energy reserve, we could combine our market opportunity and turbocharge promising, nascent clean energy technologies.[104]

Current and likely future trends in Chinese behavior indicate both growing incentives and barriers to clean energy and greater energy efficiency. Beijing has recently established regulations aimed at lowering energy intensity and promoting cleaner types of energy. At the same time, China still faces significant financial, regulatory, procedural, tax, and local governmental barriers to clean energy, and current trends suggest that, even though some of these barriers are weakening, most will remain serious problems during at least the remainder of this decade.[105]

Moreover, some analysts argue that China will likely face growing financial and soft power incentives to develop and market cheap coal-fired technologies to the developing world, at lower costs than clean energy technologies offered by the West and Japan. This could strengthen even further China's existing strong interest in continuing its emphasis on coal-based energy production. As many specialists have pointed out, slowing or halting climate change will become a near impossibility if most of the new energy production in the next twenty-five years comes from high-carbon sources.[106]

At the same time, until very recently (when some indications of a counter-trend have emerged in the United States, as noted above), public and elite support had been increasing in both China and the United States for making greater efforts to address both climate change and global pollution issues. Yet while some Americans have been demanding carbon controls to stave off the ill effects of climate change in general, many ordinary Chinese remain primarily concerned with the quality of the air they breathe each day. Despite this difference, some observers believe that domestic political concerns will enable an alignment of clean energy interests at the national level that is likely to grow over time, assuming that the U.S. public again becomes more supportive of such efforts.[107]

However, significant challenges remain to enhancing Sino-U.S. cooperation regarding both climate change and pollution controls, beyond some of the technology-sharing and incentivizing methods. Despite expected huge increases in annual CO_2 emissions in the coming decades, China's per capita emissions are still projected to be only slightly more than half those of the United States in 2035, thus suggesting that it will continue to be extremely difficult to convince Beijing to agree to the same type of mandatory limits that richer, more developed countries might observe.[108]

Chinese officials have repeatedly stated that the United States can and should do more than what has already been done by the Obama administration regarding future goals for the reduction of greenhouse gas emissions.[109] Future congressional legislation on climate change, including a proposed cap-and-trade system, faces considerable opposition and debate. Indeed, congressional action seems dead in the water, in part because the lead Republican negotiator on climate legislation, Senator Lindsay Graham, withdrew his support for the Kerry-Graham-Lieberman climate bill in April 2010 in protest against efforts by the Democrats to place a higher priority on immigration legislation. The likelihood of passing a cap-and-trade bill diminished even further after the Republicans regained control of the U.S. House in the 2010 midterm elections and increased their presence in the Senate.[110]

At the same time, the U.S. Supreme Court has significantly increased the likelihood of forward movement on controlling future emissions by ruling in April 2007 that the Environmental Protection Agency is permitted to regulate CO_2 and other greenhouse gases, and by concluding that CO_2 fits the Clean Air Act's definition of an "air pollutant."[111] In addition, some observers believe that Beijing will likely become more willing to set firm targets for absolute carbon emissions in the years ahead, in response to both domestic and international pressures.[112] As Rosen and Houser state:

> Ultimately, to have any hope of stabilizing global CO_2 levels, the world will need to deal with both US consumers and Chinese industry. . . . The current politics of

energy in China makes it highly unlikely that Beijing will be able to significantly alter its carbon future alone, and Beijing will see absolutely no reason to take this challenge on if America hasn't done so first. Therefore the United States' leadership is required, both to address its own environmental footprint, and to help change the economics of doing so elsewhere in the world.[113]

Pandemics

There is little doubt among specialists that the danger of a serious pandemic will remain, and could indeed worsen, during the current decade and beyond. Global outbreaks of fatal diseases usually occur every twenty-five to thirty years, and influenza pandemics occur approximately every forty years. However, the accelerating movement of humans around the globe—together with continued population growth, greater population density, global warming, and the loss of greenbelts and uninhabited land—increase the likelihood that such diseases might occur more frequently and spread more rapidly from their point of origin. Moreover, the majority of the world's population (that is, those under the age of forty years) has no protective immunity to the type of influenza viruses that circulated between 1957 and 1968, but these viruses are still held in many laboratory freezers, thus posing the possibility of accidental leakage and reinfection of populations. The cost of a future pandemic in both human lives and economic growth could be very large.[114]

Of more importance for this study, there is a high likelihood that a significant number of future pandemics will originate in or near China, given the close proximity of large numbers of humans in China and Southeast Asia to a wide variety of potential animal sources of future pandemic viruses, such as birds and pigs.[115] Moreover, the danger presented by this situation is compounded by the fact that, despite some improvements in recent years, two key obstacles to reporting and controlling an outbreak in China are likely to remain: the propensity of officials and farmers to limit the flow of information regarding large-scale threats to society (mostly for political and economic reasons), and the relatively poor state of the public health infrastructure and finance system in some parts of the country.[116]

By all accounts, Beijing has improved its ability to detect and counter an emerging pandemic, and to cooperate with outside entities in doing so. However, the description given above clearly indicates that much more can and should be done to improve China's ability to prevent, minimize, and combat future pandemics, in collaboration with the United States and other countries.

CONCLUSION

The analysis given above suggests that, perhaps even more than counterterrorism and counterproliferation, the policy arena of nontraditional security threats certainly has the potential to serve as a major catalyst for enhanced cooperation between the United States and China. Climate change in particular presents a huge and likely growing challenge for both countries that cannot be ignored, especially given their economies' critical impact on global carbon emissions. More important, truly effective action in this arena likely will require far higher levels of mutual assistance and cooperation between Beijing and Washington if the potentially disastrous consequences of global warming are to be avoided. Over time, this cooperation could in turn provide a solid basis for both countries to build stronger strategic trust in their bilateral relationship. Nonetheless, overcoming the significant hurdles to greater cooperation will probably require new approaches, involving the development of better incentives on both sides to encourage them to cooperate.

08

HUMAN RIGHTS AND
DEMOCRACY PROMOTION

Human rights and democracy promotion has been an important element of U.S. policy toward China since the Chinese Communist Party came to power in 1949. American advocacy of a Chinese regime that defends the rights of the individual (both within China and abroad) against arbitrary, oppressive, or unjust governmental actions, and whose legitimacy is based on some form of popular representation rests largely on two notions: first, that the U.S. government and its populace have a general moral duty to oppose, or seek to correct, oppressive and undemocratic political behavior by other governments; and second, that a regime which accords greater respect for the rights of the individual, has limited powers, and is representative of the views of its citizenry through some approximation of "free and fair" elections will not only prove more politically and socially stable, but also advocate policies more in line with those of the United States and other democratic nations. Such notions and objectives are quite understandable and possibly even correct, to some degree. However, translating them into effective policies that serve the overall interests of the United States over time and under varying conditions is an entirely different matter.

Indeed, this policy arena presents a wide range of issues and questions for U.S. policymakers, and could potentially generate several alternative policy approaches, given its sensitivity and the level of attention it receives in both countries. The most fundamental question facing U.S. policy makers in this policy arena is how the United States can advance democracy and human rights within China substantively without significantly threatening its other strategic and policy objectives, or producing major Chinese domestic political problems that could lead to severe chaos or worse. As with the other policy arenas examined in this study, any answer to this question must flow from a clear sense of the trade-offs involved for U.S. interests in pursuing a variety of different approaches. This, in turn, requires some sense of the relative importance of democracy and human rights promotion as compared with other core U.S. objectives, the attainment of which in many cases requires significant cooperation with China's existing government. The pursuit of certain types of changes in this arena, using certain methods, could put this cooperation, and at times even various goals within the arena of human rights or democracy promotion, at risk. In addition, U.S. policymakers must assess the degree to which the United States or any foreign government can actually alter China's political system and human rights conditions, regardless of the approach taken. This requires a clear understanding of the attitude of the Chinese leadership toward human rights and democracy, its ability and ultimate willingness to promote or prevent change in these areas, and the types of actions that could result in genuine change for the better.

POLICY APPROACHES

As with most of the policy arenas examined in previous chapters, there are several possible approaches, involving two extreme alternatives and a range of mixed strategies. One approach would place the advancement of human rights and democracy very high among U.S. policy objectives toward China and hence be willing to put other policy objectives at risk. Indeed, some advocates of this approach might argue that cooperative engagement with China is largely justifiable only if it can produce significant progress in this policy arena. Moreover, this approach would tend to define its objectives in largely maximalist terms— for example, as significant movement toward attaining free and fair elections and granting individual political rights such as the freedom of speech and assembly. A variety of tactics might be employed to achieve such results, including

- efforts to link U.S. cooperation with (or benefits granted to) China in other policy areas with specific improvements in political freedoms and human rights within China or in China's approach to such rights and freedoms overseas;

- efforts to work with other countries to build international coalitions designed to compel China to improve its policies in this arena;
- direct unilateral warnings intended to shame and criticize Beijing publicly; and
- sanctions against the Chinese government or other restrictions of Chinese interests if certain pertinent improvements are not made.

As in the economic arena, such a high-pressure, maximalist approach assumes that the United States enjoys considerable leverage to alter the behavior of the Chinese government and that Beijing is unwilling or unable to retaliate in ways that could deter Washington from applying such leverage or otherwise severely damage U.S. interests.

The opposite approach would avoid applying strong and direct pressure to China to achieve maximalist objectives, on the assumption that the United States and other nations have limited leverage with China and that such an approach would likely produce serious retaliation in other areas. Instead, this approach would favor the pursuit of gradual, indirect changes that could contribute over time to the emergence of a more open and politically tolerant polity and society. These would include efforts to encourage greater Chinese respect for the rule of law and individual rights, notions of limited government, and support for common international standards of human social and political rights. It would involve calm and positive discussions behind the scenes, not public confrontations, with an emphasis on universal standards and mutual benefits, as well as some U.S. self-criticism. This approach would reject the application of rigid criteria or timelines to Chinese behavior, instead favoring an open-ended process of indirect change via education, dialogue, and expansive bilateral and multilateral social, political, and economic contacts with democratic societies. Hence, this approach would not be based on the assumption that significant improvements in China's human and political rights performance constitute an urgent, high-priority U.S. interest. And it would certainly not accept the viewpoint that the advancement of democracy and human rights in China constitutes the primary rationale for the entire policy of engagement.

Several types of mixed strategies could also potentially exist in this arena, reflecting a general belief that both direct pressure and indirect, incremental changes via unilateral and multilateral actions can produce the most useful improvements in Chinese behavior over time. As with other policy arenas, the selection of tactics would vary according to the issue, time, and circumstances involved. In particular, this approach would assume that U.S. leverage and the need to place a higher priority on achievements in this arena would be greatly influenced by variations in the political salience of this issue within U.S. society. Overall, this approach would regard the promotion of human rights and democracy as an important but not top priority for the U.S. government.

U.S. POLICY TOWARD CHINA

Since the normalization of bilateral relations in the 1970s, every U.S. administration has sought to varying degrees to improve the human rights record of the PRC government. These efforts have focused on both China's domestic situation and its behavior toward other nations, especially other authoritarian regimes. In addition, the U.S. government has also at times attempted to encourage the development within China of various structures, processes, and beliefs that might promote the emergence of a more open, tolerant, and democratic political system as an aspect of China's modernization and opening to the outside world. Indeed, to a significant extent, America's engagement with China has been justified by many policymakers on the basis of its putative ability to advance such goals, both directly and indirectly.

However, in reality, every U.S. administration has been forced to balance the obvious moral and political benefits that might result from the active pursuit of these objectives against the potential damage that could be done to U.S. interests by an overly aggressive stance, along with a clear-headed assessment of the basic feasibility of various approaches. In many such instances, Washington has confronted (1) the practical limitations on its ability to compel or entice the political and social liberalization of an authoritarian regime that is intensely sensitive toward any perceived threats to its monopoly on power; (2) the restraining influence over U.S. policy in this arena exercised by important U.S. and foreign commercial and other interests involved in China; and (3) the obvious need to maintain close bilateral cooperation with Beijing to achieve vital or more pressing U.S. policy goals in other areas, such as regional security, counterproliferation, and economic development.[1]

The Bush Administration's Approach

As with earlier administrations, the presidency of George W. Bush, in many of its formal policy statements, placed a relatively high priority on the advancement of human rights and democracy within China, and it engaged in a variety of activities designed to achieve this objective. Its approach was reportedly founded on two basic principles, which had also been common to previous U.S. administrations: "that international pressure can over time encourage China to take steps to bring its human rights practices into compliance with international standards and that there are opportunities to support those within China who see structural reform in China's best interests."[2]

Capacity-Building Programs

Upon entering office, President Bush continued the official bilateral U.S.-China Human Rights Dialogue that had existed, on and off, since the Tiananmen Square incident of June 1989. However, the administration soon suspended this dialogue—and did not resume it for six years—reportedly due to a lack of solid progress and Beijing's reactions to subsequent efforts by Washington to pressure it internationally. The dialogue only resumed in May 2008 after lengthy discussions between the two sides.[3] Washington was also an active participant in the Bern Process meetings, a gathering to discuss China's human rights record with other governments that hold similar human rights dialogues with Beijing.[4]

In addition to promoting dialogues on human rights, the U.S. State Department's Bureau of Democracy, Human Rights, and Labor has also funded projects to promote China's development of the institutional and social foundations for a more just and representative polity, including the rule of law, public participation in the political process, and civil society, and to support those in China working on reform. It has, for example, funded projects designed to provide legal technical assistance, assist efforts to reform the country's criminal law, strengthen legal education, support judicial independence, and enable average citizens to find the information necessary to seek protection under the law. It has also "offered training for elected village officials and deputies to local legislatures. U.S. officials have also participated in election observation missions, and U.S. programs have provided technical assistance to ministries and legislative bodies charged with drafting local election regulations and to those experimenting with legislative oversight, budget reform, and public participation in government decision-making." Washington has also encouraged the development of civil society in China by supporting projects that "increase the capacity of independent NGOs [nongovernmental organizations] to address societal needs, expand access for marginalized citizens to legal services, and enable citizens to either individually or collectively provide input into public decisions."[5] The U.S. Embassy in Beijing also awards small grants to members of China's NGO movement in support of democratic values. During the Bush administration, these programs were funded at annual levels of between $10 million and $20 million.[6]

Moreover, for many years, Washington has attempted to encourage progressive views among Chinese elites through a variety of public diplomacy programs, including educational and cultural exchanges such as the Fulbright Scholarship, the Humphrey Fellowship, and the U.S. International Visitor Leadership Program. In fact, according to the State Department, almost half of all Chinese citizens involved in such programs are participating in activities related to democracy, human rights, and religious freedom.[7]

Specific Actions
Aside from such largely indirect, capacity-building programs, the Bush administration at times also advocated or applied pressure or took other actions directly intended to promote democracy and human rights in China. For example, in 2004, it introduced a motion at the 60th session of the UN Commission on Human Rights condemning China's human rights practices, citing its failure to meet commitments made at the December 2002 dialogue and to follow through on its stated intention to expand cooperation on human rights in 2003, along with "backsliding on key human rights issues."[8] In addition, from 2002 to 2008, the Bush administration suspended funding for the United Nations Population Fund because of its involvement in China, where the State Department asserted that coercive family planning practices had occurred.[9]

The U.S. government has also "funded programs to help Internet users in China circumvent censorship, established a task force to deal with Internet freedom issues, and called upon both the PRC government and U.S. Internet companies that have entered the Chinese market to promote human rights. The Broadcasting Board of Governors' International Broadcasting Bureau supports counter-censorship technologies (approximately $2 million per year) that help enable Internet users in China, Iran, and other countries to access Voice of America [VOA] and other censored U.S. governmental and non-governmental websites and to receive VOA e-mail newsletters."[10]

In October 2008, the Bush administration also supported the creation of a quasi-governmental effort, the Global Network Initiative, to evaluate and respond to the challenges confronting the Internet in countries such as China. This initiative is a voluntary, multistakeholder forum, including representatives of industry, investors, nonprofits, and academic institutions. Its members have accepted a set of guiding principles on human rights, including protecting "the freedom of expression rights of their users when confronted with government demands, laws and regulations to suppress freedom of expression, remove content or otherwise limit access to information and ideas." The initiative has also created evaluation and accountability mechanisms for judging companies' participation.[11]

The Bush administration also reportedly helped political prisoners gain early release from prison or improved treatment, and publicly and privately urged the government not to use the war on terrorism in Northwest China or domestic protests in Tibet as a pretext for ignoring legal rights or suppressing peaceful political dissent. It also repeatedly called on Beijing to honor its international commitments and its own Constitution in respecting religious freedom. Washington also strove to monitor compliance with the 1992 U.S.-China Memorandum of Understanding and the 1994 Statement of Cooperation on Prison Labor and to investigate allegations of forced child labor. And at various meetings with senior Chinese leaders, senior U.S. officials, including President Bush, publicly emphasized America's interest in human rights and religious freedom in China.

It needs to be added that just before President Bush took office, Congress created the Congressional-Executive Commission on China (CECC) with the legislative mandate to monitor human rights and the development of the rule of law in China, and to submit an annual report with recommendations to the president and the Congress. The CECC consists of nine senators, nine members of the House of Representatives, and five senior administration officials appointed by the president, and has a staff of ten. According to a Congressional Research Service report, the CECC "provides human-rights-related news and analysis, keeps track of pertinent PRC laws and regulations, and maintains a database of political prisoners," all presented on its website. In addition, with an annual budget of approximately $2 million, the CECC has held more than 80 public hearings and roundtables on "rights-related topics, including the following: the Beijing Olympics, rule of law development, social unrest, religious freedom, ethnic minorities, political reform, labor conditions, mass media, property rights, and the Internet in China."[12]

China and Third-Party Concerns

Internationally, the Bush administration also undertook efforts to improve China's handling of issues related to human rights in third-party states, especially Burma and Sudan. With respect to Burma, Washington repeatedly sought to press Beijing, largely through private discussions at both the middle and senior levels, to support UN Security Council statements on the situation there and to exercise its influence on the Burmese government in order to permit visits by the UN special adviser, to secure the release of detainees, and to initiate a genuine dialogue between the regime and prodemocracy leaders and ethnic minority representatives. With respect to Sudan, Washington similarly pressed Beijing—at times employing public criticism—to support the efforts of the African Union and the UN to establish and maintain a stable peace between the government and rebel forces, to end its arms trade with the government, to send in peacekeepers, and to encourage the Sudanese government to accept the African Union's and UN's peacekeeping efforts and to prevent further attacks on innocent civilians in Darfur.[13]

However, in 2003, the Bush administration had declined to sponsor a resolution criticizing China's human rights record at the annual meeting of the UN Human Rights Commission in Geneva, despite the apparent deterioration in Beijing's behavior on many human rights issues, and in contrast to the annual U.S. sponsorship during the Bill Clinton era. Washington stated that such a departure was a response to Chinese assurances that human rights cooperation would "get back on track," and that it reflected a good faith effort by the United States to find a new way forward in this policy area.[14] Yet many outsiders criticized the move, and some speculated that it had resulted from a desire to consolidate Chinese support for U.S. efforts in Iraq.[15] (As noted above, Washington did advance such a resolution the following year.)

In addition, the Bush administration arguably undermined its ability to hold the moral high ground in assessing China's human rights record by giving the impression that it condoned the use of torture against suspected terrorists and by withdrawing its support for the establishment of the UN Human Rights Council in 2006.[16]

The Obama Administration's Approach

The Barack Obama administration has by and large continued most of the above-described long-standing U.S. programs and approaches to encouraging human rights and democracy in China. For example, it has continued the official bilateral U.S.-China Human Rights Dialogue that was resumed in May 2008 during the last months of the Bush administration.[17]

There have been some exceptions to this trend of continuity, for Obama basically reversed the stance of the Bush administration with regard to the UN Human Rights Council, and America became a council member in May 2009.[18] In addition, Washington restored funding for the United Nations Population Fund, although Congress stipulated, via the Omnibus Appropriations Act of 2009, that none of those funds may be used for any country program in China.[19] And it has reinvigorated the Global Internet Freedom Task Force as a forum for addressing threats to Internet freedom and is urging U.S. media companies to take a more active role in challenging foreign governments' demands for censorship and surveillance.[20]

Despite these actions, however, the Obama administration's rhetoric has been less confrontational, and its activities in this policy area have arguably been less energetically pushed, than during the Bush era. Especially in its first two years, the Obama administration did not place the advancement of human rights at or near the top of its overall China policy agenda, out of a desire to emphasize other highly urgent issues facing both nations that require extensive bilateral cooperation. This was strongly suggested by the fact that, soon after taking office and just before arriving in China, Secretary of State Hillary Clinton had said that in dealing with China, human rights issues should not interfere with other policy priorities, such as the global financial crisis, climate change, and the North Korean nuclear issue. Although Clinton's remark was subsequently "clarified" to indicate a continued willingness to speak out on human rights issues, the impression lingered that Obama would not attempt to exert significant direct pressure on Beijing, especially in ways that might endanger presumably more urgent policy priorities.[21]

Indeed, one senior Obama China specialist stressed the administration's desire to advance human rights and democracy within China by "leading through example" and generally by enhancing the "soft power" attraction of the United States, while also employing one-to-one conversations between the president and senior Chinese leaders on U.S. values, democracy, and human rights.[22] This position reflects the general stance taken by the Obama administration toward human rights promotion. In line with its overall stress on finding common approaches to global problems, repairing relations with foreign governments, and rebuilding multilateral institutions, the Obama administration is focusing on direct dialogues, setting a better example, and building practical working relationships in areas such as business development, science education, women's and children's health, and student exchanges, not human rights and political empowerment.[23] This stance was evident in the restrained language about human rights issues in the U.S.-China Joint Statement that was issued during Obama's state visit to China in November 2009.[24]

At the same time, Obama was the first president to challenge censorship of the Internet while on Chinese territory, and he raised the issue of the treatment of Tibet and the Dalai Lama during a joint television appearance with President Hu Jintao.[25] He also met with the Dalai Lama in February 2010, despite vociferous opposition from Beijing, and he was one of the first world leaders to publicly call for the release of the Chinese prodemocracy dissident Liu Xiaobo after Liu was awarded the Nobel Peace Prize in October 2010.[26] The Obama administration also urged Beijing to undertake a thorough examination of the Google issue regarding Internet security and freedom (discussed in greater detail below).[27]

Moreover, in part responding to criticism for being soft on human rights, the Obama administration adopted a slightly strengthened stance on the issue leading up to President Hu's January 2011 state visit to Washington. Secretary Clinton discussed human rights concerns in China at length in a speech just before the visit,[28] and Obama also invited human rights advocacy groups for a meeting at the White House before Hu's arrival.[29] Obama called for respect for "universal rights" in his welcome address, and he raised the issue in private conversations with Hu. However, his comments were described as more of a "gentle reminder" than a rebuke. Though the language of the U.S.-China Joint Statement issued at the end of Hu's visit was stronger on human rights than that of the November 2009 statement, on the whole, the engagement reflected continuity with past Obama policy, given that trade and security concerns dominated the visit.[30] Finally, one strong proponent of human rights issues in the Obama administration was former U.S. ambassador to China Jon Huntsman. In his public statements, Huntsman took a very energetic stance in this policy arena.[31]

CHINA'S HUMAN RIGHTS RECORD

Despite the above-noted U.S. actions, China's activities in the area of domestic and international human rights have not fundamentally improved during the Bush and Obama administrations, despite some notable advances. This is especially true in areas related to political speech and the formation of organizations independent of the state. Indeed, in some respects, the Chinese government's repression in these areas has become more severe in recent years.[32]

Areas of Domestic Suppression

Beijing's internal human rights policies and behavior are designed to monitor and control a wide variety of activities, from political organizations to Internet statements. In many areas, the level and type of suppression has increased considerably as Chinese society has become more engaged with the outside world.

Political, Religious, and Legal Activities

Internally, both Beijing and China's local governments continue to deny or severely restrict freedom of political expression, freedom of association, and freedom of religion, using extensive police and state security apparatus controls and strict political controls over courts and judges.[33] These controls include professional, commercial, and administrative measures; limitations on foreign travel and domestic movement; monitoring of Internet and telephone communications; the frequent use of abduction and confinement incommunicado; and unofficial house arrests. Overall, the central government continues to "monitor, harass, detain, arrest, and imprison journalists, writers, dissidents, activists, petitioners, and defense lawyers and their families, many of whom sought to exercise their rights under law." Beijing and/or the local governments also continue to engage in "extrajudicial killings, executions without due process, torture, and coerced confessions of prisoners, and the use of forced labor, including prison labor."[34]

Recent examples of such behavior include the systematic arrest and jailing of many members of a network of more than 300 political activists, writers, and lawyers who signed a December 2008 political manifesto entitled Charter 08 calling for democracy and the rule of law in China and the end of one-party rule. This group modeled itself after the famous Charter 77 dissident group formed in Cold War Czechoslovakia. According to the Congressional Research Service, Charter 08 was "eventually signed by over 8,000 citizens representing a cross-section of Chinese society, including not only dissidents and public intellectuals but also workers, farmers, entrepreneurs, professionals, local officials, and others."[35]

More broadly, since spring 2008 and accelerating since February 2011, China's central and local governments have taken many measures (including jailing and harassment) to discourage lawyers from challenging the government in any significant manner and to deter political dissidents from inspiring popular uprisings.[36] Beijing has tried and imprisoned several prominent activists, including some associated with Charter 08 (such as Liu Xiaobo), and has charged them with subversion. Others have been imprisoned for investigating and writing about apparent government corruption and malfeasance involving the deaths of thousands of children in the massive Sichuan earthquake of 2008, apparently as a result of shoddy building construction. Even after release from imprisonment, many lawyers and activists have been the target of ongoing government persecution, such as torture, house arrests, and forced disappearances.

The awarding of the Nobel Peace Prize to Liu Xiaobo in October 2010 triggered a vicious response from Beijing, including threats against any foreign government that might send officials to attend the awards ceremony and verbal attacks against the West in general for allegedly orchestrating the granting of the award. Domestically, China increased house arrests, censorship, surveillance, and detentions in the wake of the Nobel Prize announcement, including placing Liu's wife, Liu Xia, under house arrest and preventing dozens of his family members and friends from leaving the country before the awards ceremony.[37]

As indicated above, such imprisonments and extrajudicial persecution accelerated in spring 2011 in response to the widespread uprisings in North Africa and the Middle East and the attendant call issued online for peaceful protests in China as part of a "jasmine revolution." Hundreds of activists and dissidents were detained, jailed, placed under house arrest, or beaten, including Ai Weiwei, an internationally famous artist and codesigner of the Bird's Nest Olympic stadium in Beijing who has been openly critical of the PRC government.[38]

In addition to Liu Xiaobo and Ai Weiwei, individuals whose plights have been prominently highlighted by senior U.S. officials include Chen Guangcheng, a blind lawyer who has advocated for reproductive rights in opposition to strict population controls and forced abortions, Gao Zhisheng, a lawyer who has defended the religious freedoms of Falun Gong members and underground Christians, and Xue Feng, a U.S. citizen and geologist who was convicted for allegedly stealing state secrets.[39] In most cases, protests by the United States and other nations over such repression have been ignored or curtly dismissed by Beijing.[40]

The Chinese government also continues to severely restrict the activities of both local and international NGOs and maintains strong controls over the cultural and religious activities of ethnic minorities such as Uyghurs and Tibetans.[41] Also, the outbreak of violent protests and rioting in Tibet and other nearby areas within China in March 2008, along with violent incidents between local Han Chinese and Uyghurs in Urumqi, Xinjiang, in July 2009, have resulted in Chinese attempts to tighten security and enforce an even tougher stance toward human rights activities in both areas. In both cases, Beijing blamed "separatists" and exile groups for planning the protests and riots and vowed to maintain stability and punish those responsible.[42] This repression has continued despite the passage of many new laws and regulations in recent years that were allegedly designed to strengthen the rule of law in China and despite Beijing's assurance that hosting the 2008 Olympic Games would advance the country's human rights progress.[43] On the contrary, there was a systematic crackdown before the Olympics, as noted above.[44] And as it did on a large scale before the Olympics, the Chinese government continues to engage in the forced relocation of residents to make way for various types of construction.[45]

Finally, in the area of press freedoms, in March 2011, Beijing reversed progress it had made when it reinstated regulations that require foreign correspondents to seek authorization from government authorities before conducting interviews or reporting. This move was part of Beijing's broader crackdown after the 2011 Arab uprisings.[46]

Internet Censorship

Beijing has also increased its attempts to control or prohibit, as well as shape, the flow of information on the Internet, by proposing the installation of censoring software (which is called Green Dam Youth Escort) on all computers produced by or sold in China after July 1, 2009; by increasing vigorous restrictions on foreign search engines operating in China, such as Google; by building new types of firewalls and requiring Internet bloggers to register their real identities; and by strengthening efforts to "guide public opinion."

The attempt to install censoring software (presented by the government as an effort to protect youth from online pornography) failed, in part due to strong domestic resistance from both consumers and commercial entities, as well as foreign governments and computer makers.[47] The attempt to restrict foreign search engines along with a severe hacking attack from unknown (but most likely PRC government) sources, resulted in Google's decision to move its China operations to Hong Kong (and automatically redirect Chinese users to its sister site in that city), which triggered a strong official defense by the PRC of its efforts to control the Internet.[48] This defense included criticism of the United States for allegedly employing Internet social networking media such as Twitter and YouTube to foment unrest in Iran and possibly Xinjiang, and generally promoting the concept of "Internet freedom" and social networking sites as a foreign policy tool. Beijing's concerns about such sites deepened after the 2011 Arab uprisings, in which protestors in Egypt and elsewhere used Facebook and other online social media tools to organize their movements. Beijing has subsequently stepped up the monitoring and censoring of such sites.[49] In addition, more broadly, the effort to control public opinion involves employing huge numbers of low-paid commentators "to monitor blogs and chat rooms for sensitive issues, then spin online comment in the government's favor."[50] Finally, according to some observers, commercial entities with close ties to the Chinese government are also acting as de facto censors of business customers and suppliers, thus adding to the overall level of repression and intimidation.[51]

Improvements in China's Human Rights Behavior

On the positive side, there is no doubt that, as the State Department observes, China's economic development and reform policies since 1978 have "dramatically improved the lives of hundreds of millions of Chinese, increased social mobility, and expanded the scope of personal freedom. This has meant substantially greater freedom of travel, employment opportunities, educational and cultural pursuits, job and housing choices, and access to information."[52]

Indeed, Beijing's definition of human rights places a strong emphasis on such nonpolitical freedoms and security over classic notions of individual political liberties.[53] Also, China has passed new criminal and civil laws in recent years that provide more protections to its citizens, and its courts are arguably responding more responsibly to complaints and suits while judging cases more on the basis of legal procedures rather than applying purely political criteria dictated by the local or central authorities.[54] Beijing has also drafted laws that would limit the scope of crimes eligible for capital punishment, a move that has been well received by human rights groups but is viewed as likely to have little practical significance for reducing the number of executions.[55]

Equally important, the Chinese government is becoming increasingly transparent with regard to information, in large part to improve efficiency, fight corruption, and enhance its international reputation. In 2008, the State Council issued regulations requiring the disclosure of a growing array of statistics and other data on health, education, budgets, economic programs, and urban planning. These same regulations allow citizens to request the release of information from the government. For some observers, this move "represents a major political shift," albeit one motivated by strategic calculations rather than support for democratic principles.[56]

International Actions

Internationally, China has continued to pursue an overall pattern of interaction with foreign governments and groups that often ignores, downplays, or resists calls by outside entities such as international human rights organizations and foreign nations to assist in improving conditions in localities where it has a significant presence.[57] More broadly, Beijing also uses its seats on the UN Security Council and UN Human Rights Commission and its participation in other international human rights efforts to push a restrictive interpretation of international norms and treaties, stressing the importance of economic development, social stability, and collective rights over individual political rights.[58]

At various times, the Chinese government has undertaken energetic campaigns to avoid international censure of its human rights record by instead pressing countries to engage in bilateral dialogues, or by offering development assistance and trade advantages to nations that support its position.[59] China also in many cases disburses economic assistance without regard to human rights or other conditions that are typically taken into account in making loans and grants. For many observers, such actions undercut the ability of the World Bank, the Organization for Economic Cooperation and Development, and Western donor countries to restrict access to their funds as an incentive for prospective recipients in Africa and South and Southeast Asia to improve their human rights protections and otherwise reform their economic and governance systems.[60]

To some extent, Beijing defends such actions by citing the need to uphold what it regards as the sacred principle of state sovereignty against arbitrary or excessive interference, the highly limited utility of external pressures (such as sanctions) on sovereign governments to make them alter their behavior, the inherently limited nature of China's influence on a particular regime or situation, and the relatively superior results attained by private dialogue and positive incentives.[61] In this regard, academic research sponsored at high levels of the Chinese government and government-linked NGOs like the China Society for Human Rights Studies has made an increasingly sophisticated case on Beijing's behalf to the Chinese public as well as to foreign governments and international civil society organizations such as the UN Conference of NGOs.[62]

Nonetheless, Beijing also recognizes that humanitarian crises or other local problems occurring in so-called areas of instability (from the Chinese perspective) or failed states (from a Western perspective) can pose serious political, diplomatic, and economic threats to other nations, including China. Additionally, the Chinese leadership agrees with many other nations that although it is important to diagnose the underlying, long-term problems that cause such local instability, this overall objective should not prevent short-term actions necessary to deal with emerging and immediate humanitarian and other threats. For many observers, China's increasing willingness to act under such conditions marks a dramatic shift in its strategic priorities.[63] A recent example of such changing behavior was provided by Beijing's willingness to permit UN-backed, NATO-led military intervention in Libya to prevent the killing of innocent civilians by the Gaddafi dictatorship.[64]

A more broad-based and assertive example of China's changing stance is provided by its growing participation in the deployment of UN peacekeeping forces. Since 1990, China has contributed 17,390 personnel to nineteen UN peacekeeping operation (PKO) missions, and it had approximately 2,000 peacekeeping troops deployed as of December 2010. Beijing is now the UN's 15th largest contributor to PKOs and the greatest contributor among the Security Council's permanent five members. Beijing clearly receives certain geostrategic benefits from participating in PKOs, such as increased local influence, improvements in its international reputation, and an expanded global presence. Its involvement in PKOs also enhances the professionalism and overseas experience of its military and security forces, especially with regard to noncombat missions and military operations other than war—such as counterpiracy, disaster response, and humanitarian relief. These kinds of missions have become a major component of its military doctrine, and are in line with Hu Jintao's call for the People's Liberation Army to perform "new historic missions" in the twenty-first century.[65]

Moreover, in international organizations since the early 1980s, China has signed or acceded to many of the major human rights conventions and organizations— such as the UN's International Covenant on Economic, Social, and Cultural Rights, signed in 1997 and ratified in 2001; and the International Covenant on Civil and Political Rights, signed in 1998 (but not yet ratified).[66] Beijing arguably joined these organizations primarily in an effort to bolster its international status, despite the challenge they posed—at least in theory—to its principle of national sovereignty. And its adherence to the norms embodied in these human rights agreements has often been weak at best. Nonetheless, according to observers such as Ann Kent, China's mere membership in these organizations has led it to redefine its interests and institute positive domestic reforms. For example, many of its labor laws were improved in the mid-1990s as a result of its participation in the International Labor Organization. It also instituted a series of legislative acts in the mid-1990s aimed at bolstering the rule of law domestically and protecting individual rights.[67]

Yet at the same time, Beijing often continues to resist outside pressure and demands to do more in this policy area because it regards the criticisms related to human rights that are leveled against it and other nondemocratic regimes by foreign organizations and governments as hypocritical and self-serving. It also sometimes does not want to endanger its growing and increasingly important economic and political relationships with particular regimes by applying strong pressure on them to improve their human rights records. In other words, it cares more about advancing its national economic development interests than observing moral principles, and it holds a rather cynical view of the stance taken by the Western powers on this issue. In this regard, the most notable examples of its recent behavior have involved its relations with Sudan and Burma. In both countries, China has at times resisted the United States' and other nations' urgings that it utilize its allegedly decisive political and economic influence with the ruling elite to compel desired humanitarian changes.[68]

Conversely, while blocking international efforts to impose serious sanctions, Beijing has nonetheless increasingly taken more significant steps to help address the human rights crises in both countries. Thus, in Darfur, Sudan, it has strongly urged Sudanese president Omar Hassn al-Bashir to cooperate with the United Nations in the development of a peace settlement (and used its leverage to gain acceptance by Khartoum of UN Security Council Resolution 1769), it has appointed a full-time envoy to assist in resolving the crisis, and it has contributed peacekeeping troops. Yet much of this activity has occurred behind the scenes and is not well known to outside observers.[69] Some observers contend that Beijing will likely continue to play a stabilizing role as the country transitions toward partition after southern Sudan's vote for independence in an early 2011 referendum.[70]

In Burma, China has also undertaken positive, albeit more limited, actions in response to the repressive acts of the military government witnessed in August and September 2007. Most notably, China has supported the establishment of a UN special envoy (Ibrahim Gambari) and the activities of UN secretary-general Ban Ki-moon in attempting to mediate the country's domestic political unrest, as part of a general effort to provide constructive assistance to resolve the situation. In October 2007, China also allowed a UN resolution condemning Burma's crackdown to pass the UN Human Rights Council by consensus. In addition, Beijing has made positive statements about the need for reconciliation and in the process has commented on Burma's domestic politics. In the spring of 2008, it assisted in enabling a U.S. C-130 aircraft to land in Burma as part of the relief effort following a devastating cyclone. Moreover, Beijing has come to serve as a broker in negotiations between the government in Naypyidaw and various Burmese ethnic groups, particularly after military actions in August 2009 resulted in 30,000 Burmese refugees fleeing into China's southern Yunnan province. A report by the International Crisis Group stated that Beijing has "invested considerable diplomatic resources to facilitate negotiations between the military government and the ethnic groups," though its objectives in Burma remain focused on a gradual approach that seeks primarily to protect China's own interests rather than to pursue Western objectives toward the country.[71]

Such positive actions by Beijing have taken place in response to growing international dialogue and pressure by the United States and other nations (and many NGOs), a fear that worsening violence will threaten China's future economic interests in the region involved, and image concerns linked to a greater recognition of the need for Beijing to take a more active role in supporting international efforts to counter highly public and major human rights violations by other nations.[72]

Some observers believe that Beijing at bottom is deliberately challenging the very idea of internationally binding human rights standards. They argue that, with its actions in Africa, Southeast Asia, and other regions, the Chinese leadership is increasingly promoting the notion of administered economic growth under authoritarian rule as a new regime paradigm designed to counter the "capitalism under democracy" model promoted by the United States and other democratic nations, thereby providing support for "enlightened" dictators worldwide.[73] The economic dimensions of this allegedly alternative governance paradigm (which some observers have labeled the "Beijing Consensus") are discussed in some detail in chapter 3.

In reality, however, there is very little evidence that Beijing is deliberately and actively promoting its political-economic experience as an alternative model to democratic development. It has clearly used its experience to encourage highly closed, backward, and authoritarian regimes such as North Korea and

Burma to adopt more enlightened policies centered on economic openness and reform. But it has done this for largely political and economic, not ideological, reasons, to promote orderly development in two unstable neighboring states, and to some extent to avoid international censure. In general, China's leaders seem to believe that, though other developing nations can learn from its experience, no single model—whether democratic or authoritarian—can work for all nations to ensure the combination of economic progress and stability that Beijing prizes above all else. Thus, China tends to place more emphasis on pragmatism, competent management, and adapting to local conditions than on the overall attributes of any particular political system.[74]

The Chinese also believe that some types of political reforms are necessary to sustain growth, although they certainly do not believe that such reform is part of a single, linear process of development toward Western-style liberal democracy. In general, China's leaders apparently place a much greater emphasis on promoting the image of China as a peace-loving, culturally attractive nation than as an alternative model for political development to liberal, democratic nations. One method Beijing has adopted in an attempt to cultivate its "soft power" has been the promotion of so-called Confucian Institutes and other culture-oriented activities around the world.[75]

EVALUATION

The above-described U.S. actions convey an impression of significant activity on the part of both the Bush and Obama administrations in the arena of human rights and democracy promotion vis-à-vis China. However, as a recent Congressional Research Service report states, "there has been little sign that the U.S. position on human rights has affected PRC policies."[76] Moreover, as the six-year hiatus in the official bilateral dialogue on human rights issues during the Bush era suggests, for most of the past decade U.S. human rights policy has not focused on engaging senior levels of the Chinese government. Much activity instead took place at lower levels and often through indirect, long-term programs aimed at capacity building in a variety of areas. In addition, the level of funding for such U.S. efforts has not been particularly high, thus limiting their impact. Also, as with many past U.S. presidents, Bush's willingness to place a high priority on China's domestic human rights behavior and to engage Beijing energetically on the issue arguably declined over time, as a result of the Iraq and Afghanistan conflicts and the growing need for closer Sino-American cooperation to address a host of critical problems, ranging from counterterrorism to North Korea and trade. In other words, progress in addressing Beijing's human rights record was usually subordinated to more pressing U.S. economic and strategic interests.

Perhaps of equal importance with the above factors, the Bush administration's ability to influence China's behavior in this policy arena also arguably suffered as a result of its failure to present itself to the world community as a strong defender of human rights, both domestically and overseas. Specifically, America's support for the death penalty (despite strong opposition from most other industrial democracies), passage of antiterrorism laws that appeared to erode individual liberties, apparent acceptance of certain forms of torture as interrogation techniques for suspected terrorists, and long-standing failure to sign or ratify several international human rights treaties together undermined its ability to pressure China on a host of human rights issues.

Since taking office, President Obama has arguably improved the U.S. record on some of these issues, in line with his desire to influence Chinese human rights practices by enabling the United States to serve as a more positive role model. And he has placed a greater emphasis on engaging the senior Chinese leadership directly on human right issues. However, this effort has certainly not produced any significant successes regarding China's domestic human rights policies. Indeed, in the view of some human rights activists, Obama is on balance doing far less to promote human rights in China than other recent presidents.

In the international arena, as we have seen, Washington has arguably achieved somewhat greater results in specific cases, such as Sudan and Burma. This has been done largely through private interactions, and by working closely with other nations and international organizations. But U.S. policies are merely one of several factors that can explain what limited Chinese improvements have occurred in this area. As in the case of domestic human rights issues, Washington can in most instances maximize its influence by working patiently, and often privately, with others to persuade and to apply pressure.

FUTURE TRENDS

Assessing the variables that will likely influence future U.S. policy toward China in this arena is a complex and challenging task. Any such assessment must include not only those internal and external factors that could encourage an evolution toward greater levels of human rights and democracy within the Chinese state and society but also the capacity of the Chinese government to deflect or coopt such factors.

In addition, it must also examine those trends and attitudes that influence China's behavior within the international arena. These factors are examined in turn.

Factors Affecting the Future of Democracy

Washington's future ability to significantly affect Beijing's stance vis-à-vis the issues of human rights and democracy promotion, both domestically and in its foreign relations, will likely depend on a wide array of factors, most already evident but some new. Five factors are of particular importance. The first will be Washington's willingness to devote significant levels of time, energy, and resources to advancing these issues in China. As we have seen, the management of other urgent issues such as climate change, the global recession, and the nuclear ambitions of Iran and North Korea all require increased cooperation with Beijing. Attempts to compel changes in China's domestic human rights practices through direct official pressure at the national level could undermine efforts to move forward in these and other high-priority areas. In this context, the significant, albeit limited, successes attained thus far via indirect, low-profile approaches involving the promotion of the rule of law and democratic values are arguably more likely to enjoy continued progress over the foreseeable future.

A second, equally important factor will be the willingness of both the Chinese elite and citizenry in general to bring about the kind of changes that Washington desires in this area. This will depend in large part on the future impact of a wide variety of political, social, and economic variables on the continuing ability of China's authoritarian, one-party political system to maintain domestic order and address the growing needs of an increasingly complex society. In recent decades, there have been huge changes in these areas, which most Western (and some Chinese) analysts identify as key drivers of democratization and the expansion of human rights. For example, the pressures of demographics and the likely need to shift China's economic model toward a more service-oriented, knowledge-based economy built upon the free flow of ideas could hasten a shift toward democratic reform.[77] That said, as indicated above, the Chinese state has been increasingly repressive in recent years, and may continue to exhibit such behavior.

Some analysts assert that there is a correlation between the formation in developing societies of a large middle class, as measured by the attainment of per capita levels of gross domestic product of between $3,000 and $10,000, and the transition to some form of democratic polity. In recent years, China's per capita gross domestic product has already reached this level, particularly when estimated in terms of purchasing power parity. As for actual individual incomes, China's rapid economic growth has produced a sizable middle class that was virtually nonexistent twenty years ago; some predict that this class will consist of 670 million people by 2021.[78]

Recent decades have also witnessed an explosion in the availability of information in China, which in 2007 already had more than 2,000 newspapers, more than 8,000 magazines, 282 radio stations, and 374 television stations (according to official Chinese estimates), all reporting on an increasingly diverse range of formerly taboo topics, ranging from official corruption to industrial accidents.[79] And of course, the Internet and cellphones have become ubiquitous in urban China, permitting a level of rapid access to and transmission of information that did not exist even ten years ago. Accompanying this trend has been the rapid and unprecedented expansion of direct contacts between a growing number of Chinese citizens and democratic societies, primarily through educational, social, political, and cultural exchange programs and visits.

The third factor is the emergence of civil society groups and lawyers and signs of a greater willingness by China's judges to take on cases and pass verdicts that are unfavorable or embarrassing to government officials. As of mid-2009, China had approximately 280,000 registered civil society groups, including 6,000 foreign-affiliated NGOs. And the number of registered lawyers and law school students has also increased dramatically.[80]

The fourth related factor is the steady improvement of corporate governance practices that presumably inculcate "democratic habits" involving greater transparency, stronger and more independent boards of directors, and management by mutually agreed-on rules. The expansion of such habits among China's business elite and senior government officials who sit on the boards of state-owned enterprises presumably will increase their receptivity to the creation of genuinely independent, publicly accountable political and economic groupings.

The fifth and final factor is the passing of the original generation of powerful and dictatorial revolutionary figures such as Mao Zedong and Deng Xiaoping and the emergence of new generations of political and social leaders who rule largely through a process of consensus building, more institutionalized procedural rules, and checks and balances among political coalitions. Currently, some individual Chinese leaders even seem to express support for key features of Western democracy, including judicial independence and supervision based on formal checks and balances.[81] In addition, in the intellectual realm, according to at least some Chinese analysts, a notion of "soft authoritarianism" is emerging that increasingly accepts the validity of some democratic concepts. For some analysts, these include, most fundamentally, the notion of a limited state and "the accommodation and coordination of diverse social interests in a political process predicated in the dualism of state and society."[82]

Differing Theories About China's Democratization

There is every reason to expect that most if not all these trends will continue to unfold throughout this decade and beyond, as long as China's economy maintains reasonably high growth levels through market-led and open-door approaches to trade, investment, technology development, and social progress.[83] Some analysts believe that such continued development could bring about fundamental democratic changes and greater respect for individual human rights in China within the next few decades at most, and perhaps much sooner, presumably regardless of what the U.S. government does.[84]

However, for what appears to the author to include a majority of observers, in recent decades, the PRC regime has displayed a remarkable ability to adapt to the above-noted changes and many others in ways that have often weakened, blunted, or otherwise neutralized movement toward what some would regard as true democratic and human rights change in China.[85] For example, despite considerable corruption and a growing income gap in many areas, rapid economic growth is structured to convey benefits to large numbers of ordinary citizens, not just the political elite and a tiny handful of business entrepreneurs. Moreover, the middle class and many businesspeople have been permitted to join the Chinese Communist Party (CCP) and in some cases have a significant influence on policy decisions. Rather than pushing for more freedom and autonomy, they have in many instances become strong supporters of a more "enlightened" and business-oriented yet still autocratic system. They often favor policies designed to increase profits and raise living standards and the quality of their family's life over the attainment of any basic political power objectives.[86]

More broadly, by expanding its membership among a wide range of China's citizenry and focusing more on practical issues of day-to-day concern among them, the CCP has made itself more relevant and useful to Chinese society. As one observer states: "The party has largely transformed itself 'from a mass organisation designed for mass mobilisation and ideological campaigns, into a technocratic leadership corps.'"[87] As part of this effort, the CCP has strengthened its ties with intellectuals and professionals to solicit their policy advice. It is also improving its ability to gauge and influence public sentiment through a greater reliance on more scientifically based focus groups, opinion polls, and public hearings involving peasants, workers, students, and professionals. It is also increasingly utilizing the Internet to monitor, control, and respond to the views and concerns of ordinary citizens.[88]

The CCP has also enabled its officials to become more professional and has begun to allow for greater internal debate and dissent in many areas, as well as some criticism from the outside. And petty interference by the state at all levels has diminished significantly, especially for the urban middle class. At the same time, the PRC regime continues to crack down quickly and in many cases ruthlessly on clear challenges by intellectuals and others to the CCP's monopoly position. Equally important, as part of its effort to show its integrity and responsiveness to public concerns, the CCP regime has become increasingly attentive to reducing both the appearance and the reality of corruption in many respects, by rotating officials and by making examples of relatively senior officials who have been convicted of corrupt practices by conveying harsh punishments, including the death sentence. It has also introduced local-level elections that are not entirely controlled by the CCP authorities and has permitted the public and elements of the media to pursue sensitive issues and even to challenge the decisions of governments at various levels. Alongside these efforts, the CCP has also undertaken initiatives to strengthen an atrophying party apparatus in many localities.[89]

In addition, the PRC regime engages in sophisticated propaganda designed to appeal to the growing sense of nationalism felt by many Chinese by extolling with great pride China's accomplishments and the resulting prestige that it is achieving worldwide. This strengthens the government's legitimacy to some degree, although it also arguably leaves it more exposed to criticism and pressure if the authorities do not adequately address public expectations and demands in the international arena, for example, involving the defense of sovereignty and China's reputation. In addition, Beijing also sometimes attempts to utilize popular nationalism in its negotiations with foreign powers—for example, by arguing that certain policies or options are rooted in popular sentiments, thus requiring foreign "understanding."[90]

Finally, Beijing has been particularly adept at preventing the international community from joining together to compel or entice improvements in its domestic human rights practices. Such efforts include mobilizing its propaganda machine to neutralize Western criticism, advancing compromises that do not threaten its core interests, and offering commercial incentives to key nations in order to prevent unified Western policies. It also uses market-based business incentives to effectively suppress news and undesirable political information.[91]

In many instances, these mechanisms and approaches are arguably a means of coopting opposition and obscuring the serious human rights failings of the Chinese government. In fact, abuses, corruption, vigorous repression, and the commitment of the CCP's elite to maintaining ultimate power and preventing the emergence of truly autonomous movements or groups all persist.[92] And yet these practices, reinforced and facilitated by China's continued economic success, have led many analysts to conclude that the vast majority of the Chinese elite, *and many ordinary Chinese citizens*, are and will likely remain for some time committed to an administrative or guided form of political rule that rejects the type of open competition among autonomous political associations and genuine checks and balances between agencies of the government (including a fully independent judiciary) that are viewed as basic to Western liberal democratic systems.[93] Instead, this CCP-led system relies on the apparently widely accepted notion that only strong centralized oversight by party and state organs can safeguard the rights of all citizens and prevent excessive corruption and abuse by executive officials and the judiciary at all levels. The CCP regime also promotes a definition of "human rights" that focuses on the provision of better living standards and greater physical security for the community as a whole. Thus, in this context, "movement toward democracy" and "the advancement of human rights" in China, as viewed by many elites and ordinary citizens alike, consist of steady improvements in efficiency and responsiveness by the existing one-party state; the inclusion of ever-larger numbers of individuals and groups within the CCP-led decisionmaking process; continued advances in living standards and security for most citizens; and steady reductions in corruption and abuse by those charged with formulating, implementing, and enforcing public policy at all levels.[94]

Many analysts cite polls that ostensibly reveal strong support among the Chinese populace for "democracy" as a form of government.[95] This leads many observers to conclude that there is an adversarial relationship between the Chinese government and Chinese society on this issue, thus justifying the efforts of those who argue in favor of external human rights pressure designed to liberate the suppressed Chinese populace from a repressive Communist regime. However, as the above suggests, and Denny Roy states:

> Most Chinese . . . do not cheer this criticism of their government. Rather, they rally to the CCP's positions that China has made historically unprecedented progress in socioeconomic human rights by raising the living standards of tens of millions of its people, that immediate introduction of Western-style civil and political liberties would create chaos that could threaten China's recent gains, and that this pressure for political liberalisation from the West is largely driven by groups that want to embarrass rather than help China.[96]

Expert analysts of Chinese nationalism and democratization such as Chu Yun-han, Larry Diamond, Andrew Nathan, and Doh Chull Shin point out that, for most Chinese, "democracy" does not denote a Western-style system of competitive political pluralism but rather the concept of a just government in which the rulers are responsive to the desires of the people. Overall, "for many Chinese, a paternalistic government that denies political competition is consistent with their conception of democracy, and the increase in freedom they have enjoyed since the start of the post-Mao reforms marks a real step from the past toward what they see as democracy."[97] And hence, senior PRC leaders such as Hu Jintao are not inciting popular frustration and resentment when they often speak of a desire to develop a type of socialist democracy that largely equates to the administrative, guided form of democracy outlined above, rather than to a classic multi-party system with an independent judiciary and a free press.[98]

From this situation, many analysts have concluded that, as long as China's economy continues to expand and provide improved standards of living for most citizens and its political system is able to avoid major scandals that convey the impression that the senior elite can abuse the ordinary populace with impunity, the above-described approach to political rule and the protection of human rights will likely continue to enjoy significantly more elite and public support within China than any Western-style alternatives.[99] It is certainly difficult to see how the emergence of a larger middle class could fundamentally change the heretofore generally successful process of continual adaptation carried out by China's one-party state apparatus.[100] Moreover, the recent economic failings of capitalist democracies have arguably reaffirmed the advantages of the Chinese approach.[101]

In a variant of this arguably mainstream viewpoint, a minority of observers see the possibility that the CCP's system will eventually accept increasing levels of intraparty democracy that could evolve into a form of explicit and open competition among a variety of political factions over political posts and policy approaches, along with increasingly more humane government practices.[102] But few see this process as leading to a genuinely multiparty system in the absence of a potentially wrenching political crisis or revolution. However, other analysts believe that an "enlightened" and effective bureaucratic approach to political participation has existed only in theory and rarely in practice, due largely to the extremely deep-seated nature of corruption in the CCP's political system and the fundamental conservatism of the ruling CCP elite. Moreover, they see little reason for such dysfunctional features to change during at least the current decade. In fact, some predict a growing degree of regime "ossification," leading to increasing political paralysis and policy dysfunction over time.[103]

Still other analysts view the CCP regime as unremittingly oppressive and abusive toward the political rights of its own citizens, as incapable of evolutionary change under either internal or external pressure, and therefore as extremely weak and defensive politically, predatory and aggressive toward both Chinese society and other nations, and changeable only via its wholesale replacement by some version of a liberal democratic order.[104] And one version of this viewpoint predicts the wholesale systemic collapse of the regime under the weight of corruption, abuse, inefficiency, and a prolonged inability to adapt.[105]

Evaluating Trends in China's Democratization

Unfortunately, no existing theory of political development or democratic change will allow an analyst to predict with any degree of certainty which of these scenarios or some other assessment of the prospects for democratization and the advancement of human rights in China will prove correct. Perhaps of more importance, few observers of the above-described situation regarding the development of democracy and human rights in China believe that U.S. policies toward China will prove decisive in promoting such changes. At the same time, current trends have clearly shown that economic development and a vastly greater level of exposure to the outside world have enormously raised the quality of life of the vast majority of China's citizens. If human rights are measured in terms of many more physical comforts, greater freedom of movement, less reliance on torture and capital punishment, and access to a much wider variety of political, social, and economic ideas, then U.S. engagement policies during the last three decades, as important contributors to this process, have undoubtedly improved China's human rights, and such policies will continue to do so.

And yet the continued suppression of many basic political freedoms and features central to liberal democracies, and the demonstrated ability of the CCP regime to adapt to and weaken both internal and external pressures or incentives favoring such basic changes, suggest that U.S. policies have not necessarily moved China toward greater political freedoms and individual human rights as defined in the West. The PRC regime remains a one-party dictatorship that represses any unsanctioned, autonomous activities and political opinions that are viewed by the authorities as potentially threatening to its rule. This situation is unlikely to change fundamentally during at least the current decade and probably for years beyond—and almost certainly not as a result of any U.S. policies. Indeed, the overview given above of the major factors influencing domestic democratization and human rights advances in China suggests that Washington will probably see few benefits resulting from a public, top-down, confrontational effort to pressure or cajole Beijing in this area, especially if done independently of other nations. In fact, such an approach could over time become more likely to produce adverse consequences, given the fact that the Chinese elite is likely to become more resistant to such obvious attempts to apply outside pressure as its power and confidence grow in dealing with the United States and other major nations.

Moreover, as some Chinese analysts point out, although the idea of human rights matters in Western policy, it has seldom prevailed over economic considerations or concerns about national security. Western governments have not committed as many resources to engaging Beijing on human rights as to other issues, and, according to one analyst, the differing degrees of commitment to foreign policies related to human rights explain why Japan, Western Europe, and the United States, in that order, have gradually retreated from confronting China on human rights issues.[106] Barring a largely unpredictable and undesired (by both Washington and Beijing) systemic crisis, the process of attaining U.S. goals within China regarding human rights and democracy is likely to remain incremental, based primarily on nonconfrontational actions and coordination with other nations.

Human Rights in an International Context

In the area of foreign policy, China has generally pursued a policy of non-interference in the internal affairs of other nations, especially in the realms of democracy promotion and human rights advancement. The largely realpolitik logic underlying this approach derives from Beijing's fundamental interest in sustaining economic growth and international stability through the promotion of positive relations with all powers and in portraying itself as a strong political supporter of and economic partner with developing countries (regardless of their sociopolitical system) and as a general opponent of "great power chauvinism" and interference in the domestic affairs of sovereign nations. In addition, one might speculate that China's leaders do not want to promote international intervention against any state's repressive behavior that could set a precedent for future actions against their own domestic policies.[107]

Some observers believe that Beijing goes beyond its basic noninterference policy to assist nondemocratic developing nations in strengthening their ability to resist democratization and human rights, via training and education programs for media and Internet workers, law enforcement officials, local leaders, and members of the judiciary; the provision of military weapons; and overall developmental assistance, some of which is allegedly used for antidemocratic activities. China is also charged with providing "extensive diplomatic protection and support to the authoritarian rulers of countries like Burma, Sudan, Uzbekistan, and Zimbabwe."[108]

In reality, however, the dominant trends and features of China's foreign policy behavior in the area of democracy and human rights are not as simple as some might think. As suggested above, there is little hard evidence to suggest that China is actively engaged in a deliberate effort to prevent the emergence of (or much less overthrow) democratic governments in developing countries. Of course, given its basic long-term interests and objectives, China will probably continue to resist endorsing or otherwise falling in line with U.S. or Western-led efforts to promote democratization and the advancement of individual human rights practices, either as a general principle or with regard to individual states. It will almost certainly continue to place a primary emphasis on policies that promote the above-outlined Chinese definition of these concepts. At the same time, it is also highly likely that China's growing involvement in the world, its desire to be viewed by other nations as a responsible and admirable power, and, perhaps somewhat paradoxically, its overall realist inclinations toward international relations will increasingly pose challenges to its traditional noninterference approach.[109]

Some analysts observe that globalization and the general emergence of a wide range of social, economic, and security issues that span and erode national boundaries are contributing to the creation of so-called post-Westphalian norms, which emphasize "the right (and indeed the obligation) of the international community to infringe on the autonomy of the nation-state to protect or advance other considerations."[110] If such norms gain greater support, especially among major developing countries (and democracies) such as India, Brazil, and Indonesia, Beijing could encounter increasing pressure to support more interventionist policies, including those intended to advance a stronger, more inclusive, and individual-oriented definition of human rights, if not liberal democratic reforms. As one U.S.-China specialist points out, the promotion of such broadly accepted norms of international behavior could enhance China's soft power and also legitimate its development and use of harder forms of power.[111] In fact, as noted above, Beijing has already shown signs of accepting internationally endorsed interventions in other countries, in some cases for reasons associated with the protection of human rights (for example, in Libya, Sudan, Burma, and Zimbabwe). As two analysts state, "The debates in Beijing have moved on from how to defend the principle of noninterference to the conditions under which intervention is justified."[112]

In an increasing number of cases, Beijing will probably be forced to strike a balance between adhering to international norms (or avoiding appearing to be an outlier on a specific issue), preserving or advancing specific political and especially economic interests with the governments involved, and generally preserving respect for the principle of state sovereignty and nonintervention as much as possible. Each case will almost certainly present a unique combination of factors influencing Beijing's stance. And of course the United States will itself continue to balance its own objectives in advancing democracy and human rights against its other interests. This task will probably become more challenging as Chinese society becomes more complex, the economic power of the Chinese state increases, and Beijing's international presence expands. Yet the ability of U.S. leaders to decisively shape, much less direct, China's human rights behavior will almost certainly remain highly limited.

09

THE INFLUENCE OF
STRUCTURE, STRATEGY,
AND TACTICS

The direct experience of current and former U.S. policymakers, along with both scholarly and nonscholarly assessments of the overall U.S. national security policymaking process, offer a wealth of insights for U.S. policy toward China. In many instances, outside analyses of Washington's China policy either downplay or omit altogether such vital sources of information. As a result, policy recommendations can lack "real-world" relevance or prove unfeasible within the context of the U.S. policymaking process or political environment.

In an effort to avoid such problems, and to augment our understanding of the historical record, the author interviewed more than 50 current and former middle- and senior-level U.S. officials centrally involved in formulating and/or implementing policy toward China and Asia during the past twenty years or so (that is, primarily during the Clinton, Bush, and Obama periods).[1] In conducting these interviews, observations and analysis relevant to two specific areas were of particular significance: (1) those features of the U.S. policymaking process or domestic situation that facilitate or constrain U.S. actions; and (2) those specific tactical, diplomatic approaches to China that elicit either positive or negative consequences for U.S. policy.[2]

THE U.S. POLICYMAKING PROCESS

Both interview subjects and the general literature on U.S. foreign policymaking identify a wide array of broad, largely process-related features that can influence, in some cases decisively, the utility and effectiveness of U.S. policy in defining, protecting, and advancing American interests with regard to China. These include highly subjective variables (such as the personal views and capabilities of policy makers), bureaucratic relationships (such as those within the executive branch and between the executive branch and Congress), and the role of key political and social interests (such as political parties, interest groups, the public, and the media). These are examined in turn.

The Importance of Compatible Personal Views and Cooperative Personal Relationships

In general, previous studies of United States–China relations have pointed out, and this study's interview respondents have strongly confirmed, that, as in other policy areas, the role of personalities, personal relationships, and personal outlooks constitutes a hugely important aspect of the U.S. policymaking process toward China. In particular, the motives and personalities of executive branch officials, and their relationships with one another, members of Congress (and their senior staff), *and their counterparts within the Chinese government* or other relevant governments can significantly influence the policymaking process. And of course relationships outside of the U.S. government (for example, within the business and human rights communities), and between government and nongovernmental figures, can also influence policy in important ways.[3] As one respondent pointed out, with reference to the U.S. government: "Strategic guidance is formalized and written down, policies are developed and disseminated, and the policy process is regulated and policies corrected on the basis of personal relationships."

These are of course truisms for any policy arena, and perhaps for any type of government. But America's policy toward China has particularly confirmed the importance of personalities in the policymaking process, and in managing relations with Beijing, according to many respondents.[4] One key example of the importance of personalities was provided by Henry Paulson, the secretary of the Treasury during the last two years of the George W. Bush administration. Paulson was able to develop and implement the Strategic Economic Dialogue and in general establish himself as a dominant figure in making China policy during that period in large part because of his excellent relationship with the president, as well as his strong reputation among and good relations with senior Chinese officials. However, for some respondents, Paulson's supposedly dominant position within the China policymaking process was viewed as somewhat dysfunctional, largely because it allegedly resulted in an excessive emphasis on economic factors—and especially America's growing financial dependence on Beijing—in U.S. policy calculations.

Several respondents confirmed that the personal expertise and orientation of individual sub-Cabinet and midlevel officials responsible for Asia policy can also influence decisions notably. As mentioned in chapter 2, Japan specialists tend to regard the United States–Japan alliance as the key independent variable that should shape Asia and China policy, whereas China specialists often stress the Sino-U.S. relationship as pivotal. And few American officials have deep experience and knowledge of both countries and their relationship to the larger regional context. This is particularly true at the senior levels. Such personal viewpoints can undermine the ability of a U.S. administration to develop and sustain an overarching Asia strategy, according to some interviewees. For example, although Deputy Secretary of State Richard Armitage put forth a regional strategy centered on a particular vision of the United States–Japan alliance (as discussed in chapter 2), this outlook did not survive his departure from office at the end of the first Bush term.[5]

For many interview respondents, the lesson to be drawn from this basic feature of the policymaking process is that those individuals responsible for critical policy functions must work well together and trust one another in order to increase the likelihood that the various organizational problems associated with the process (discussed below) will be handled with minimum disruption. Such problems will also be more manageable if senior officials hold roughly compatible views of their objectives within the process. This understandably begins with the president and his relationships with relevant Cabinet-level officials, but it extends far beyond those individuals to much lower levels of the government.[6]

A Clear Need to Manage Growing Organizational Complexity and Interagency Rivalry

A second related requirement for an effective China policy concerns the ability to manage well the increasingly complex U.S. government bureaucracy, and likewise to understand and influence China's bureaucracy. Virtually all interview respondents emphasized the importance of bureaucratic behavior in the U.S. policymaking process toward China, particularly involving differing interagency viewpoints and rivalries. A few interviewees stressed that some level of interagency debate and competition is necessary to flesh out the pros and cons of different policy approaches and to introduce new ideas into the political system. This is no doubt true. However, many interviewees also pointed to the potential problems that emerge as a result of bureaucratic behavior. Many of these problems derive from the contrasting functional, domestic political, bilateral, and regional perspectives and interests that are associated with governmental organizations.

Again, as in the case of the personality factor, this feature of the U.S. policy-making process is by no means unique to China policy. To varying degrees, it affects the entire national security and foreign policy arena.[7] However, in the case of America's policy toward China, such problems are compounded by the fact that, over time, the increasing complexity and diversity of the Sino-U.S. relationship has resulted in a rapid expansion in the number of executive branch agencies and congressional committees involved in China policy and a deepening of their interest in and commitment to various policy approaches. As a result, growing bureaucratic competition over turf issues, policy priorities, and other matters has frequently emerged to undermine the formulation and implementation of overall policy, thus placing an increasing premium on effective bureaucratic oversight and coordination. For example, the existence of many U.S. executive branch agencies that have a desire to speak authoritatively on matters of concern to them can create a highly inconsistent U.S. policy message, resulting in poor signaling, Chinese and U.S. miscalculations, lost leverage, and missed opportunities to influence Beijing.[8]

A second potential problem cited by interviewees emerged from the fact that many agencies differ in the emphasis they place on aspects of cooperation versus competition with Beijing. The contrast in perspectives between the State and Defense departments was at times cited as a primary example of this potential problem. Specifically, China's growing military capabilities and past bilateral tensions over Taiwan have at times exacerbated the latent interagency friction that exists regarding the relative emphasis placed in China policy on engagement activities (often stressed by State) and deterrence and shaping activities (often stressed by Defense). For example, one respondent argued that some at State privately express concern over the apparent fact that many in the Pentagon appear to be "preparing for fighting war at the expense of advancing understanding and dialogue with the PLA [People's Liberation Army]." Others at State reportedly express concern that the Pentagon has yet to determine what level and type of Chinese military capabilities the United States can accept. In general, several respondents observed that State and Defense usually coordinate their approaches only at the working level, regarding specific policies, and not at the larger grand strategic level (see below).[9]

Moreover, according to a few respondents, bureaucratic coordination is also hampered by the fact that the U.S. military is usually able to develop and execute plans faster than the State Department and other civilian executive branch agencies. Such a situation can create an environment in which the military elements of policy are implemented faster than the diplomatic elements, thereby creating the impression that the Pentagon is driving or leading overall China policymaking efforts. Even more disturbing, a few interviewees expressed the view that military officials will at times distort vital information on the U.S. military's moves regarding China or conceal it from officials at State and the National Security Council (NSC), claiming a need to protect the confidentiality of military operations. One well-placed respondent also pointed out that State and Defense hold different views regarding the metrics for success and the time frame applied to policy performance. Whereas State tends to focus primarily on short-term or immediate issues and recent successes or failures, the Pentagon often adopts a longer-term perspective, involving the evolution of relative military capabilities between Beijing and Washington (see below for more on this point).

It is also important to note, in light of the above observations, that for some respondents, bureaucratic tensions are in many cases due at least as much to the views and personalities of senior U.S. officials as to any objective structural features of the policymaking process. A primary example of this was the ongoing dispute between the State and Defense departments about the resumption of meaningful military-to-military relations with China during George W. Bush's first term. Secretary of Defense Donald Rumsfeld repeatedly ignored arguments by those at State and elsewhere to resume such relations, largely because of his anger over Chinese behavior during the EP-3 incident of April 2001 (see chapter 4) and his apparent belief that the United States had little to gain from contacts with the PLA. Rumsfeld continued to resist resuming military-to-military ties with Beijing even after President Bush essentially ordered him to do so, but he eventually gave in. Moreover, in general, Rumsfeld largely rejected guidance or direction from the NSC regarding China policy or many other foreign policy issues, according to several knowledgeable informants.

Also, according to some respondents, within the defense establishment, there are natural differences between the Pentagon (and in particular the Office of the Secretary of Defense and the Joint Chiefs of Staff) and the U.S. Pacific Command (PACOM) over a variety of military-related issues involving China. These include, for example, the relative emphasis placed on deterrence and military competition versus the search for more cooperative, trust-building, and positive-sum interactions with the Chinese military, and the degree to which the larger goals of the United States–China relationship should shape defense interactions with both Beijing and Taipei. Such differences understandably reflect the somewhat contrasting policy priorities and primary responsibilities of the two organizations, as well as the political calculations and strategic views of individual senior officials.

For example, the Pentagon is arguably more influenced than is PACOM by the political winds that blow in Washington regarding the Chinese military and the larger bilateral relationship, as well as the arguments and pressures exerted by defense contractors (for example, with regard to U.S. arms sales to Taiwan or types of weapons systems needed to maintain U.S. military predominance in the Western Pacific). In addition, the Joint Chiefs of Staff and the Office of the Secretary of Defense have primary responsibility for the development of long-term global and regional strategies to counter actual and potential threats to U.S. national security. This naturally includes assessments of whether and in what sense China constitutes a strategic threat to the United States. In partial contrast, a large part of the PACOM commander's responsibility is to build trust among the major militaries in the Asia-Pacific region, in order to minimize the potential for security competition, facilitate the handling of a variety of traditional and nontraditional security problems, and strengthen the position of the U.S. military as an "honest broker" and security guarantor. Moreover, even though PACOM develops specific war plans to deal with Asian-Pacific contingencies in response to Pentagon directives, as the "spear point" in closest contact with the region and the PLA, it is perhaps most appreciative of the consequences of implementing these plans; and this naturally creates a significant level of prudence in assessing the Chinese threat.[10]

As a result of these contrasting priorities and perspectives, the U.S. military has at times produced public documents or undertaken actions that seem to vary significantly in the emphasis placed on the cooperative versus competitive aspect of relations with the PLA, according to some interviewees. Although such differences are to a great extent to be expected, given the size and complexity of the Defense Department's mission regarding China, they can nonetheless result in sending confusing messages to outsiders, including Chinese observers, or can lead to attempts by Beijing to manipulate contrasting Defense perspectives.[11]

According to several respondents, the above-noted bureaucratic features of the policymaking process place a further premium on the need to provide effective direction and coordination for the key policymaking agencies and their leaders. Without such coordination and leadership, individual agencies will pursue their own vested interests vis-à-vis China rather than a broader set of strategic priorities.

A Problematic Relationship between
the Executive Branch and Congress

Several respondents also stressed a second organizational challenge posed by the U.S. policymaking process of particular relevance: the often dysfunctional nature of executive branch–congressional relations regarding China policy. One interviewee strongly criticized past attempts at manipulation and deception of Congress and the public by the executive branch and the overall high level of secrecy, control, and compartmentalization often demanded by senior administration officials when dealing with Beijing.[12] This type of behavior allegedly creates enormous suspicion within Congress and produces greater attempts to intervene in China policymaking than might otherwise occur. It also undermines the basic right of the public to know how China policy is being formulated and implemented, according to this respondent. Several other respondents did not agree with this viewpoint, however.[13]

Most of those who addressed this issue seemed to think that the executive branch must communicate with and inform Congress when necessary while adopting strategies designed to limit its potentially disruptive influence over policy, especially in the area of national security.[14] This view is derived in part from the apparent presumption that Congress's actions toward China are often based on its individual members' narrow domestic calculations or interests, not the overall national interest. This viewpoint is also reportedly based on a fear of congressional attempts to constrain the overall foreign policy authority of the executive branch.[15]

In particular, some respondents confirmed that members of Congress at times engage in symbolic actions and/or statements toward China that are designed primarily to curry political favor with their constituents or the U.S. public at large, not to improve U.S. policy. Indeed, in some cases, members produce bills or threaten actions with the expectation that they will not become law or otherwise influence U.S. policy (termed by some observers as "fire and forget" legislation). In other words, they are often carried out (or threatened) purely for political effect, or to place pressure on Beijing, in support of a "good cop, bad cop" approach (further discussed below). Some respondents also pointed out that Congress tends to rely on negative inducements when dealing with China because it has relatively few carrots in its arsenal. Moreover, public attention— and hence congressional attention—is often most significantly stimulated by negative economic, military, and human rights behavior (actual or alleged) on the part of China, thus prompting calls for some form of retaliation or pressure on Beijing. Taken as a whole, these factors naturally orient Congress toward a punitive approach when dealing with China.

Conversely, some knowledgeable interviewees pointed out that those members of Congress who have a stake in or concern about U.S.-PRC relations or China's impact on important regional or global issues will often attempt to exert "adult supervision" over such parochial congressional reactions. This is often done by asserting different types of legislative power—for example, to conduct committee hearings, to extract concessions regarding a bill or resolution before it can be submitted to the floor of the House or Senate, and to deepen or expand staff work on an issue. On balance, however, most respondents viewed executive–congressional relations regarding China policy as a potential problem to be managed, rather than an asset of the policymaking process.

In addition, some respondents stressed the importance of the *political* relationship between the president and Congress as a sometimes decisive factor influencing China policy decisions. There are many examples of this, including President Bill Clinton's decision to grant a visa to Lee Teng-hui to visit the United States in 1995, which precipitated the U.S.-PRC Taiwan Strait crisis of 1995–1996, and Clinton's decision to back away from an agreement with China regarding its entrance into the World Trade Organization in 1998. Both moves were prompted in large part by a presidential desire to avoid a confrontation with Congress.

Significant Partisan Differences on China Policy, Combined with Growing Complexity

Differences in attitudes toward China between the two political parties also play a role in the U.S. policymaking process, especially given the highly partisan nature of congressional politics. However, the significance and meaning of such distinctions is changing notably in the new century. Though some aspects of China policy continue to exhibit long-standing partisan fault lines, many China-related issues are becoming so multifaceted and complex that an attempt to divide legislators into partisan camps, or to argue that there is a distinctly "Republican" or "Democrat" approach to China policy writ large, oversimplifies the competing, crosscutting interests and concerns that politicians face.

In the economic arena, one can arguably generalize, based on the historical record, that Republicans usually tend to favor probusiness China policies and to emphasize negotiating guarantees and concessions from China on commercial issues such as intellectual property rights protection, national treatment in government procurement, and expanded market access for U.S. companies. In contrast, Democrats are usually more likely to focus on the allegedly adverse impact of Chinese economic practices and U.S. trade and investment policies on American jobs and the U.S. manufacturing sector. That said, such general distinctions are usually most often reflected in political and, especially, campaign rhetoric among the two parties and less in actual policies. For example, as was shown in chapter 5, both Bush and Obama have in general resisted adopting economic policies toward China designed primarily to protect or create American jobs, instead favoring free trade and more indirect job-creating trade and investment policies.

And of even more importance, as the Sino-American economic relationship has become more complex, and extreme political groups on the right and the left have become more vocal and sometimes more influential in U.S. politics, such clear partisan ideological divides regarding China policy have become much more blurred, with regard to not only political rhetoric but also policy advocacy. For example, although Democratic Party campaign ads attacked Republicans during the 2010 midterm elections for encouraging trade policies and tax incentives that have allegedly facilitated the outsourcing of jobs to China, many libertarians and Tea Party conservatives pointed to Chinese holdings of U.S. Treasury bonds as evidence of the potential dangers of deficit spending—a concern that traditional probusiness Republicans tend to downplay.[16] In general, in the aftermath of the global financial crisis, Republicans and Democrats alike tend to use China as a rhetorical tool to project their various messages, ranging from the need to revitalize America's economy to the pressure to raise protectionist barriers to the call to reduce government debt. Moreover, the postures of legislators on both sides of the aisle increasingly tend to reflect the more complex China-related interests of the congressional districts or states they represent.

On noneconomic issues, over many years, Republicans have developed a reputation in China and among some U.S. and other observers as proponents of a more pragmatic and realist perspective toward Beijing that stresses strategic deal making and the maintenance of cooperative bilateral political relations over confrontation and pressure, particularly with regard to human rights issues and the authoritarian nature of the Chinese political system. In reality, even though Republicans have perhaps historically downplayed human rights somewhat both rhetorically and with regard to specific policies, in recent years, Democrats have done the same. As noted in chapter 8, President Obama has arguably adopted a more restrained and targeted approach to human rights issues than did his predecessor. Moreover, at least some conservatives and liberals find common cause in their criticisms of China's human rights record, its lack of progress toward democratization, and its persecution of dissidents and rights activists. In general, Republicans tend to emphasize its lack of religious liberties and its strict controls on reproduction rights, while Democrats focus on its poor labor and environmental protections.[17] But overall, this issue often takes a backseat to economic concerns—especially for Republicans.

In the security arena, in recent years, Republicans, and the extreme right in particular, have arguably been marginally more inclined, at least rhetorically, to cast China as an adversary and a potential future military threat and to emphasize enhanced ties with Asian democracies and allies.[18] In contrast, many Democrats have argued for enhanced engagement in multilateral institutions in Asia and the development of collective security mechanisms, emphasizing that China's rise need not be zero-sum.[19] Yet again, as in the economic sphere, such partisan divisions are not set in stone and often break down, especially in practice, because lawmakers on both sides are usually more concerned with economic ties with China. Indeed, during the past decade, Congress has generally subordinated China-related security issues to economic and trade concerns, instead focusing its military-related deliberations on terrorism and the Middle East.

Whether positive or negative in its ultimate effect, the potential for Congress to play a major role in China policymaking also places a premium on the need for any U.S. administration to manage the executive–congressional relationship more effectively by establishing high levels of trust, communication, and coordination of moves toward Beijing—by no means an easy task.

The Increasingly Complex Roles of Interest Groups, Public Opinion, and the Media[20]

Along with (and as a part of) managing the relationship with Congress, executive branch officials must to some extent play a two-level game in formulating and implementing policy toward China: They must address both national and broad functional interests along with the sometimes narrower or parochial views, complaints, and demands of diverse interest groups, the media, and the public.

Interest Groups

Interest groups (or key individuals representing such groups) can sometimes exert notable influence over specific policies or actions at particular points in time. These interest groups can include business interests (including specific companies and industries, as well as broader trade associations such as the U.S.-China Business Council and the U.S. Chamber of Commerce), labor advocates, human rights and democracy activists, pro-Taiwan groups, pro-China immigrant groups, and the defense industry establishment. One clear and notable example is the role of American business in discouraging the United States' attempts to employ trade or investment with China as a diplomatic or political weapon to attain goals in other areas, such as human rights.[21] More broadly, during the past twenty-five years or so, U.S. business interests have arguably played a strong role in support of efforts to deepen engagement with China overall, and to liberalize its trade, investment, and technology practices.

However, as indicated above, in recent years, as the Sino-U.S. relationship has become more complex and diversified, business interests, including labor interests, have increasingly taken a variety of different positions on a range of specific social and economic policy stances. Moreover, many other groups and viewpoints have also entered the China policy arena, making it far more difficult to generalize about the impact of such social groups on Washington's policy toward Beijing. Many significant business groups and working populations within most congressional districts now have a strong stake in expanding economic ties with China; at the same time, small businesses in some key sectors, along with less globally competitive working populations, increasingly see China as a threat and demand more protection or more aggressive efforts to increase U.S. exports to China or to limit the "loss" of U.S. jobs to China. This at times creates crosscutting pressures on both members of Congress and executive branch policymakers, as suggested above. In some cases, the need to acquire political support in key parts of the country can even influence strategic decisions regarding, for example, the development or acquisition of weapons systems relevant to China or the China–Taiwan situation.[22]

Given the significant number of American citizens who stress the importance of human rights issues regarding China,[23] it is no surprise that human rights groups also often play a role in maintaining U.S. attention on this policy arena. However, the influence of these groups is perhaps most often expressed through Congress, and to a lesser extent through specific offices of the State Department— as opposed to the White House and other executive branch offices—and is arguably increasingly diluted, given the fact that so many other issues now vie for attention within these two bodies and with respect to overall U.S. China policy. The nongovernmental defense establishment (consisting largely of defense industry corporations and private defense-oriented research and advocacy groups) can at times play a more critical role in specific security policy realms, especially as both an advocate of arms sales to Taiwan and of new or improved U.S. (and possibly allied) weapons systems designed to counterbalance China's growing military capabilities. Indeed, in the view of some interviewees, U.S. defense corporations (and their allies in foreign governments) exert *excessive* influence over specific major U.S. policy decisions, for example, with regard to arms sales to Taiwan.

Overall, however, several interviewees remarked that it is easy to overstate the influence that most interest groups have over major U.S. policy decisions. As the above discussion indicates, their influence is most often episodic, sometime operates at cross purposes, and rarely proves decisive.[24]

Public Opinion and the Media

The broader public and the media can also play an important role in the China policymaking process, particularly as they affect the views of members of Congress. On perhaps the broadest level, during the past decade at least, the American public has increasingly viewed China as an economic power, and most recently as a growing economic threat. At the same time, a rather consistent majority of the U.S. public does not view China as a serious strategic or military threat and favors continued efforts to deepen cooperation with it whenever possible as opposed to any efforts to limit its economic growth, much less to engage in military confrontation.[25] Such views arguably reinforce existing incentives for U.S. leaders to deepen engagement with China in ways that strengthen America's economic position in important areas while avoiding actions that exacerbate strategic distrust.

At the same time, certain influential social and political groups, such as elements of the U.S. mass media and congressional staff members, can potentially shape both public and elite views toward China on an ongoing basis. Specifically, media characterizations of Chinese motives and policies, United States–China relations, and individual issues affecting U.S. policy toward China (such as North Korea and Taiwan) can distract, shape, encourage, and perhaps even deter U.S. officials at times from undertaking specific policy actions. However, in some cases, the views of members of the media, Congress, and many congressional staff members can diverge significantly from those of the general public or important interest groups (such as business elites), thus again creating crosscutting pressures on policymakers.[26]

Perhaps in part because of such crosscutting pressures, along with the general pro-engagement stance of the public, according to many of the officials interviewed for this study, major policy decisions toward China are not usually made in response to the specific views of the media, interest groups, or even members of Congress.[27] Although the views of such entities can and should play an important role in shaping a basic policy approach—and in some cases can prove decisive with regard to specific, usually narrow policy actions—they usually do not *dictate* broad policy, much less strategic decisions.

As long as the public remains committed to the pursuit of cooperative relations with China, generally unsupportive of attempts to treat China as a Cold War–style strategic adversary or enemy, and focused largely on growing economic concerns, U.S. policymakers will have considerable leeway to formulate and implement general policies toward Beijing, while remaining highly attentive to group and public views on economic issues in the relationship.

COORDINATION (OR THE LACK THEREOF) VIA THE NATIONAL SECURITY COUNCIL SYSTEM

In addition to the above broad, process-oriented factors influencing U.S. policy toward Beijing, interview respondents and the literature on U.S. decision making stress the primary importance of the NSC system as the key structure overseeing the entire policymaking process. The centrality of this system to the structure of U.S. policy toward China merits its discussion as a separate set of issues and challenges.

The Key Players

The presence in China policy of the interagency or intra-agency and executive branch/congressional differences described above places a premium on the need to strongly coordinate the entire policymaking process (including relations with Congress), despite the huge challenges involved in doing so.[28] Historically, as in other areas of foreign policy, the president's National Security Council has been the primary agency of the executive branch responsible for coordinating policies among various relevant departments and advising or assisting the president on national security and foreign policy matters.[29] However, under most normal circumstances, and on a day-to-day basis, the NSC's staff members, under the direction of the assistant to the president for national security affairs (that is, the national security adviser) are responsible for (1) coordinating—and to some extent directing—all relevant executive departments and agencies involved in national security and foreign policy issues; (2) resolving any interagency problems that might emerge that would concern the president; and (3) generally advising the president on national security and foreign policy, including policy toward China.[30]

In addition, as in other policy areas, under the direction of the NSC and via the coordination of the national security adviser, the NSC Principals Committee, the NSC Deputies Committee, and various regional and functional policy committees serve as mechanisms for reviewing, coordinating, and monitoring the development and implementation of China-related national security policies at the Cabinet, senior sub-Cabinet, and subordinate department or office levels, respectively. The regional and functional policy coordination committees were by and large created by the George W. Bush administration in place of the NSC interagency working groups that existed under President Clinton. In the Obama administration, these groups have been rebranded as "interagency policy committees." They tend to be formed or convened to manage a specific issue within China policy, for example, human rights.[31]

In addition to this formal interagency process, beginning during the Ronald Reagan administration, the most important senior officials responsible for East Asia–related policy issues would meet informally on a weekly basis. This meeting, termed the East Asia Informal (EAI), was chaired by the assistant secretary of state for East Asia and began with the relevant officials within the NSC and the State and Defense departments. By the time of the George W. Bush administration, the EAI had expanded to include officials from the NSC, State, Defense, the national intelligence officer for East Asia, the Office of the Vice President, and the Joint Chiefs of Staff. According to interviewees, the EAI is mainly a coordination mechanism for providing guidance, updating calendars, establishing or maintaining consistency in policy messages, and sometimes resolving disputes, and it generally deals with specific issues on a real-time basis, in support of the formal interagency process.[32]

The most important executive branch agencies involved in the interagency system coordinated by the NSC are the State Department, the Department of Defense, the Office of the Director of National Intelligence, the Joint Chiefs of Staff, the Department of the Treasury, and the Department of Commerce. During the George W. Bush administration, the Treasury Department became a particularly important player in this process, as a result of the emergence of the Strategic Economic Dialogue and the overall deepening of bilateral economic and financial relations. And the Office of the Vice President also played an important role at times, largely via its National Security Office. Within the defense establishment, on Asia and China policy, both the U.S. Pacific Command in Honolulu and the Joint Chiefs of Staff have at times constituted important voices in the policymaking process, alongside the Office of the Secretary of Defense. However, during the Obama administration, both the State Department and the NSC have arguably played dominant roles in the process, in part as a result of the presence of strong and knowledgeable senior officials in both agencies.

Basic Obstacles within the NSC Process

The NSC system described above can provide satisfactory levels of guidance, coordination, and control for the China policymaking process when it is operating well. This was confirmed by several respondents. However, historically, the system has not always functioned as intended. In general terms, as outside analysts have observed, the NSC system, as with the larger policymaking process, often exhibits four basic structural, political, and personality-related features that can impede the formulation and implementation of policy.

First, as indicated above, the system is quite complex, involving different functions associated with policy formulation, coordination, and implementation; many organizations, each with their own missions and cultures; and a range of individuals from across the executive branch, many of whom form and alter or disband different types of coalitions over time as the policymaking process unfolds.

Second, the formal structure is strongly influenced by informal dynamics, including personal relationships, the competing interests of involved organizations and individuals, the lack of familiarity that some participants might have with one another, and the specific conditions under which a decision is occurring (for example, crisis versus noncrisis environments).

Third, power within the entire process is significantly fragmented, with no one individual or organization possessing the ability to determine outcomes with certainty. Moreover, power among the players in the system varies greatly by level and type, on the basis of experience, expertise, access to information, and a player's relationships to other powerful entities both within and outside the system.

Fourth and finally, the entire NSC process is often highly political, involving political appointees, bureaucratic interests, and external political pressures and requirements posed by Congress, the public, the media, and foreign entities.[33]

Key Issues and Problems Affecting China Policy

Interview informants and the literature on the NSC system identify several specific features that usually prove most decisive in influencing policy toward China. These include the quality of the national security adviser, the internal structure, process, and interests of the NSC system, the basic mindset under which the NSC operates, and the NSC's relationship to the president.

The Quality of the National Security Adviser

Regarding the general features described above, many respondents singled out the fact that the national security adviser sometimes lacked the experience, personal authority, and bureaucratic acumen to effectively coordinate (much less direct) the interagency process, enforce discipline, and resolve disputes or develop effective policy proposals. According to some interviewees, this was a particularly notable problem during the George W. Bush administration, in part because of the personal limitations of the adviser (Condoleezza Rice and, to a lesser extent, Stephen Hadley) in managing the bureaucracy and Bush's unwillingness to intervene when this situation resulted in interagency disputes. Conversely, some respondents pointed out that a strong and "in-command" adviser has at times used the president's authority to cut relevant agencies and individuals out of the policymaking process, thus resulting in poor overall coordination and policies that excessively emphasize narrower national security issues or reflect the adviser's personal predilections.

Informal Processes, Small Staffs, and Entrenched Interests

On a more specific level, a few interviewees asserted that the formal interagency process regarding China policy can be similarly bypassed or undermined by the use of narrow, informal groupings. According to one formerly well-placed respondent, such groupings often tend to include like-minded China specialists and exclude those nonspecialist functional officials from relevant agencies who would normally be involved in the formal process. Such a situation allegedly creates an excessive bias within the policymaking process toward the need to cooperate with China as opposed to the need to pressure or confront Beijing as a means of advancing U.S. interests. However, several other respondents rejected this argument, asserting that the formal, broadly integrative aspects of the policymaking process have usually been observed, thus permitting functional officials to play an important role as needed.[34]

Another problem cited by several respondents was the fact that the growing complexity of the U.S.-PRC relationship places severe pressures on the small staffs of many key agencies responsible for China policy, thus compounding the time and resource constraints confronting most officials and agencies. For example, the size of the China Desk at the State Department has not increased appreciably in over twenty years, despite the explosive growth in the size and complexity of that agency's interactions with Beijing that has occurred during that period. More broadly, as one scholarly observer has remarked, "the functional departments at the U.S. Department of State have proliferated to the point that a secretary of state's span of control is too broad, which in turn creates the ever present dangers of policy inattention, perpetual bureaucratic wrangling, and sending mixed messages to governments abroad and to Congress."[35] However, some respondents added the caveat that coordinating offices such as the Asia directorship within the NSC should maintain small staffs in order to preserve the ability of these oversight agencies to maintain a comprehensive approach to China policy and avoid the kind of fragmentation in outlook that would likely result from the creation of a large number of functionaries.[36]

A few respondents also stressed that the formal procedures involved in obtaining approval for a proposal, revising existing policy, or simply getting the president to make a telephone call to a Chinese leader can create enormous obstacles within the policymaking process. As suggested above, with respect to China policy, as in other areas, the effects of bureaucratic routine, tradition, personal biases, vested interests, and other factors can significantly slow down the procedural process and constrain outcomes. According to one interviewee, some large bureaucracies such as the State and Defense departments have developed offices with strong commitments to defending a specific position on a very particular issue or problem. Therefore, such offices can resist efforts to drastically alter or even eliminate those issues or problems and related policies, even if doing so would arguably serve the overall national interest.[37]

A Reactive, Short-Term Mindset

The bureaucratic rivalries and deficiencies, personality issues, and other problems or shortcomings noted above can contribute to what some interviewees regarded as an overall weakness of the NSC system: its limited ability to formulate overarching strategies for Asia and China that inform and guide individual agency policies and approaches. As one respondent pointed out, the absence of clear and sufficiently detailed strategic guidance for individual agencies—especially when accompanied by an interagency system that is ineffective at directing, coordinating, and monitoring implementation—results in a situation whereby individual agencies pursue their own interests and justify them by citing poorly defined or vague strategic objectives.[38]

Even under the best of conditions, the interagency process is usually driven more by breaking or unfolding issues of a narrow nature than by broader strategic problems or concerns, according to several respondents. Understandably, as with most governments, this is due in no small part to the fact that the president and other key senior decisionmakers and their senior staffs have neither the time nor, in some cases, the experience to fully grasp the long-term complexities of an issue or craft a nuanced, strategic approach to a growing problem.[39] As a result, NSC principals and deputies meetings tend to be more reactive than proactive, with meetings convened to deal with specific issues of the moment. Thus, most meetings tend to reaffirm the existing strategy (as spelled out in both public and classified documents and official statements) and not to reassess, revise, or challenge its basic assumptions in light of new developments.[40]

According to some respondents, this phenomenon is reinforced by the absence in the current policymaking process of an interagency mechanism for crafting and revising policies on the basis of long-term strategic plans, reflected in the lack of a true strategic planning entity within the White House or State Department.[41]

The president or the national security adviser usually issues national security policy documents to provide guidance to the appropriate agencies and departments for the execution and formulation of major national security policy issues (see below for more on the role of the president). Some of these memos and directives address specific China-related issues. However, such documents often do not provide a detailed, overall interagency China strategy, according to respondents. Although policy planning offices exist within the State and Defense departments, their focus and level of influence can vary enormously, due to personality issues, the emphasis placed upon them by senior officials, and other factors. Moreover, though such offices routinely supposedly engage in long-term planning and thinking, in the view of several respondents, they actually rarely reexamine the basic strategic assumptions driving U.S. policy, or craft long-term, comprehensive strategies, for example, toward the Asia-Pacific region.

In contrast, most respondents asserted that the policymaking process often functions quite well in coordinating or implementing policy responses to relatively narrow short- to medium-term issues and problems involving several countries or regions. Here the assistant and deputy assistant secretaries for East Asian policy within the State and Defense departments, as well as the NSC's senior director for Asia, play particularly important roles, given both (1) their responsibility for managing such policies from an Asiawide perspective, and (2) the often critical functions they perform in guiding and supporting policy discussions within the principals and deputies meetings. However, as suggested above, most respondents also agreed that the U.S. policymaking process does a fairly poor job of making clear, consistent connections between overarching global national security policy objectives, regional objectives, and policies regarding key Asian states, as well as of operationalizing these connections.

The Importance of Presidential Oversight

In addressing how to reduce the problems examined above and to strengthen the effectiveness of the U.S. policymaking process, many respondents stressed the necessity for the president to actively oversee America's China policy, in order to provide authoritative guidance on goals and approaches, set strategic directions and priorities, and reconcile interagency competition and conflicts. In addition, many interviewees pointed out that the ability of the president to perform these roles depends in turn on the existence of (1) a strong NSC with a demonstrative ability to coordinate the interagency process, conduct strategic planning, and authoritatively convey the views and preferences of the president to all responsible agencies; and (2) smooth working relationships among the major agencies involved in formulating and implementing policies. Moreover, several respondents stressed that, on any major policy issue, senior U.S. officials, and ideally the president himself, need to appear to be involved in or at least clearly supportive of a position in order to generate serious interest on the Chinese side. This is one reason why senior-level dialogues can be so important for the Chinese—they confirm direct, high-level U.S. interest and support.

However, a few interviewees insisted that the national security adviser did not necessarily need to take the lead in this process, as long as someone at a sufficiently high level was clearly designated to speak and/or act on behalf of the president and perform the role as the "guardian" of the Sino-U.S. relationship within the overall governmental process. Moreover, most respondents disagreed with the notion, raised by some observers, that China policy had become so important and challenging that it requires a special envoy or czar outside the normal policy apparatus to coordinate and direct decisionmaking. According to several respondents, such an individual would likely generate enormous resentment among existing officials and lead to demands for the establishment of similar czars to direct policy regarding other important nations or functional areas. Also, it is difficult to see how a China czar could manage such a complex and extensive relationship and be taken seriously. Finally, the presence of such a figure could also reinforce the notion that China policy is controlled by a small conclave of like-minded individuals.

STRATEGY AND TACTICS

In addition to the internal aspects of the policymaking process described above that can constrain or facilitate effective policies toward China, interview respondents also identified a basic strategic approach and a range of tactics for handling Beijing that can make a huge difference in the success or failure of U.S. policies.

Continued U.S. Maritime Predominance?

From a very broad perspective, some observers stressed the notion that a militarily strong, influential, and capable-looking America with growing ties internationally could induce Beijing to be more cooperative and less obstructionist regarding both bilateral and third-party issues. Presumably, the logic of this argument rests on the notion that Beijing is compelled to counter the potential threat posed by a more potent and influential Washington by improving its relationships with other states and by reassuring them (and Washington) that it does not pose a threat that requires increasingly assertive U.S. actions.

This of course raises the key question presented at the beginning of this study: How much assertiveness, and how much military predominance, are "necessary" to serve U.S. interests? And more specifically, at what point does a strong, assertive, and capable Washington induce a sense of threat in Beijing that will prompt it to make deliberate and competitive attempts to counterbalance or undermine Washington's power and influence, instead of trying to cooperate with it and other capitals?

The majority of those interviewed for this study agreed with the proposition that U.S. interests in Asia—and with regard to China in particular—are best served by the maintenance of a predominant level of American maritime power and political influence in Asia and globally. In fact, many respondents regarded such predominance as axiomatic and thus as accepted without question by most U.S. and foreign observers. For such interviewees, the notion of a genuine balance of power in Asia in which U.S. military capabilities and political influence are regarded as roughly coequal to those of China and/or other major powers is a recipe for enhanced regional rivalry, a widespread arms race, and general instability. Hence, for some of these individuals, any actions that degrade U.S. power and influence relative to China (or any other rising major power) will probably undermine U.S. interests and should therefore be resisted.

At the same time, most respondents also stressed that American predominance is best employed by keeping it largely muted, in support of a very active program of military, political, and diplomatic engagement with China and other Asian powers. Regarding the last point, many emphasized the importance of exercising American predominance in close consultation with and to some extent via U.S. allies and U.S.-allied military actions.[42] For some interviewees, this notion is closely associated with the "Japan-centric" approach discussed in chapter 2; that is, America's predominance is sustained and wielded most effectively—and China is best managed—through a primary reliance on an enhanced United States–Japan security alliance. Yet for other respondents, this notion implies the need for Washington to avoid a unilateralist approach to wielding power and influence.

In general, most respondents emphasized the need to combine America's predominance with efforts to establish and maintain a strong, positive relationship with Beijing, in order to allay fears that Washington seeks to undermine Beijing's power and influence or to obstruct its efforts to achieve its core objectives.[43] Thus, any attempt by Washington to indirectly encourage Beijing's cooperation by acting more assertively in Asia and toward other states must at least be balanced by equal or stronger efforts to maintain positive, cooperative relations with Beijing. In fact, for some respondents, in the absence of any clear confirmation of a shift in Beijing's strategy toward a zero-sum strategic rivalry with Washington, the latter undertaking should clearly take precedence over the former, in order to minimize worst casing by all parties concerned and thereby lower any impetus toward security competition.

A few respondents (both current and former U.S. officials) nonetheless argued that it is dangerous for America's leaders to assume that U.S. predominance in the Western Pacific can be sustained indefinitely. These individuals insisted that most Asian nations view such predominance as (in the words of one respondent) "a historical anomaly, the sustainability and rationale for which will inevitably go away." They emphasized the need for Washington to consider the implications for U.S. interests of the loss of military and political predominance in maritime Asia, and to develop strategies for dealing with such a shift. Some respondents stressed that the U.S. government does not think enough, if at all, about such possibilities.

Finally, some respondents argued that the United States should discard its preference for military predominance in favor of a strategy of "selective engagement" across Asia that drops overt references to hedging in U.S. policy statements; places a greater emphasis on diplomatic consultation, cooperative security arrangements, and regional community building; and in general adopts a more constrained and contingent approach to the deployment and use of U.S. military assets, both globally and in the Asia-Pacific region. With regard to China, this viewpoint stresses military and political actions that deter Chinese hegemonic behavior rather than those keyed to preserving U.S. predominance per se. It implies an "economy of presence" for U.S. forces, centered on "the maintenance of force structures, deployment patterns, and capabilities that are linked to actual defense challenges as they occur, as opposed to what the U.S. economy can bear or a mythical 'peer competitor.' "[44]

Clearly, the issue of U.S. predominance, and its possible alternatives, relates to the broader question of overall U.S. strategy toward China, Asia, and perhaps the world. This issue is discussed in some further detail in chapter 10.

The Need to Understand China's National Interests

The interviewees for this study almost unanimously asserted that any effective U.S. approach toward China must be based on an accurate understanding of the national interests motivating Chinese behavior and, equally important, an assessment of how to shape and influence these interests. For current and former U.S. officials, Beijing's foreign policy behavior is indeed most closely correlated to its perception of its national interest. Equally important, they also believe that

Beijing can be made or encouraged to alter its behavior or avoid certain types of actions in response to external influence, when doing so would serve its interests. Indeed, according to many interviewees, U.S. officials have on many occasions influenced, sometimes decisively, how the Chinese have viewed their interests and conducted policy. In fact, most respondents stated that Beijing has become more receptive to outside influence and more accepting of international norms and procedures over time. At the same time, some respondents point out that China is also deepening its understanding of the international system, is becoming more confident, and is acquiring the capacity to influence other countries—including the United States—through a growing variety of means, thus creating a growing challenge, and opportunity, for American policymakers.

Therefore, according to most respondents, the primary policy challenge for the United States has often been to identify Chinese interests in a given situation and to apply a set of tactics and approaches that can best shape these interests and the resulting actions in accord with U.S. goals. In this regard, most interviewees believe that the U.S. government has been quite successful in the past in identifying China's interests on most issues, through a careful parsing of Chinese public statements and actions, intensive diplomatic discussions, and a close reading of intelligence reports.[45] However, some interviewees added that it was often extremely difficult to determine how the PRC leadership (and especially military leaders) might differ among themselves on an issue (such as how to attain a particular policy goal) and which leaders had ultimate decisionmaking authority over an issue. In contrast, some interviewees stated that it was usually not difficult to determine which policy options would generate problems for PRC officials and which, if properly handled, would result in rewards for them.

Despite such challenges, most interviewees also asserted that U.S. officials have been able to shape Chinese actions most effectively through the use of several specific approaches: direct dialogue, positive and negative inducements (with very limited use of sanctions), and giving China "face." It is useful to briefly examine each of these tactics.

Direct Dialogue

In understanding Chinese interests and influencing Chinese actions, respondents overwhelmingly stressed the importance of direct dialogue with Chinese leaders and officials. Moreover, for most interviewees, the core of any bilateral dialogue should involve both an explanation of America's (or regional or global) interests and perspectives and an argument as to how both U.S. and Chinese interests can be served through a particular course of action. Many respondents stressed that such a dialogue should not involve "telling the Chinese what they should do,

or where their best interests lie." The Chinese do not like being lectured to or tutored in such a direct manner. Any dialogue should properly involve shaping the situation that surrounds a policy issue in a positive direction through both words and actions designed to (1) identify both common and disparate or conflicting interests, (2) present sets of options that could produce mutually beneficial outcomes, and (3) repeatedly reassure Chinese leaders that their worst fears will not be realized if they support or acquiesce in a position favored by the United States. And this entire approach, in turn, on most issues requires a certain level of trust and confidence in the notion that, as one respondent with extensive China experience stated, "We have common interests and we will find them."[46]

In this regard, many interviewees asserted that Chinese interlocutors had a good chance of obtaining higher-level approval of a particular course of action or policy change if these interlocutors could internally present arguments in favor of such a change as originating from a foreign source—that is, some other government, not themselves. Such foreign sourcing of new ideas and initiatives provides deniability for Chinese officials and reduces their exposure to criticism for advancing a creative policy approach within what is in fact a very conservative government system that does not generally encourage innovative thinking.[47] Some interviewees also responded that the views of PRC officials were particularly prone to shaping when such officials seemed somewhat uncertain about how to manage a particular situation. In some instances, Chinese interlocutors would even ask for advice from U.S. officials or request alternatives to China's official "party line" stance that they were required to espouse, according to one experienced respondent.[48]

And in most if not all instances, establishing personal relationships with Chinese counterparts was viewed as particularly useful. Many interviewees cited the personal relationships established at the presidential level between George H. W. Bush and Deng Xiaoping, between Bill Clinton and Jiang Zemin, and between George W. Bush and Hu Jintao, as well as relations between Cabinet-level officials such as Treasury Secretary Henry Paulson and his counterparts (noted above), as having a major impact on specific Chinese policy decisions. But even the cultivation of personal relations at lower levels has produced significant benefits for U.S. interests, according to many respondents.[49]

A good example of the positive effects of persuasion and dialogue offered by some interviewees was China's acceptance of the Chemical and Biological Weapons Convention. Although initially opposed to signing this convention, China's leaders were reportedly persuaded by an extremely effective presentation delivered in Beijing by the head of the U.S. Arms Control and Disarmament Agency, according to a highly knowledgeable and experienced interviewee. The

presentation apparently convinced China's civilian leadership to override the opposition of the Chinese military, in part by presenting them with convincing counterarguments to the military's position.[50]

Another example provided by a very knowledgeable former official consisted of direct dialogues with both Beijing and Taipei regarding preferred reactions by both governments to actions taken by Washington on the Taiwan issue. At such encounters, U.S. officials would explain in significant detail the logic and reasoning behind the U.S. decision, or the larger U.S. position on the issue in question. Such private, low-key dialogues reportedly exerted a significant influence at times on both capitals by moderating their response or otherwise bringing it more into line with U.S. preferences.[51]

A third example provided by respondents involved the introduction of the Peace Corps into China. Beijing initially intensely resisted this U.S. proposal because of the residual effects of hard-line, ideological thinking from the Cold War and Cultural Revolution eras. However, Washington was able to gain acceptance of its proposal by arguing that Beijing's approval would have a very positive effect on U.S. public opinion toward China, and thus help ensure successful visits by senior PRC officials.

These efforts at interest-based dialogue and persuasion seem very logical and perhaps to some observers both obvious and unobjectionable. And in many cases, they confirm observations made many years ago by specialists such as Richard Solomon and Lucian Pye.[52] It is important to stress their utility, however, because some critics of Chinese behavior—and of the policy of America's engagement with China—argue that Beijing is extremely rigid and unyielding in its treatment of most policy issues, that it can only be influenced by threats and coercive behavior, or that its officials are extremely duplicitous and deceiving in their interactions with foreign—and especially American—officials. The interviews conducted for this report by and large did not confirm such a perspective. No current or former U.S. official interviewed for this study argued that Chinese officials negotiate in bad faith, intentionally betray their commitments, or adhere to rigid ideological positions.[53]

Of course, none of this is meant to imply that China's officials are not at times highly suspicious of U.S. statements and actions, do not resist altering their behavior if it does not accord with their view of Chinese interests (despite U.S. arguments to the contrary), do not negotiate tenaciously, or never utter misleading or confusing statements. It suggests, as indicated above, that China's officials, as with the officials of many other countries, seek to serve their nation's interests above all else; are open to logical, well-reasoned arguments; and can be persuaded to alter their behavior at times.

Moreover, some knowledgeable interviewees assert that not only U.S. diplomats and executive branch officials but also members of Congress are increasingly able to influence Chinese behavior in positive directions. As one interviewee stated, the Chinese have been influenced by credible appeals from members of Congress, such as a letter from senior senators. And U.S. policy has been served at times when Congress has played the role of a "bad cop" (see below). Conversely, the Chinese continue to display some misunderstanding of how power in Congress operates by focusing their attention solely on its senior members or by using private channels. They do not sufficiently understand that even junior members can block (or precipitate) actions by the entire Congress, depending on the issue involved. As one interviewee states, "a little bit of poisoned dog food manufactured in China can go a long way in getting unanimous congressional support for a resolution proposed by a junior member."

Another area in which Sino-U.S. dialogue has produced positive results is military-to-military relations. Most interviewees with direct experience in this area stressed the importance of sustained high-level dialogue with the leadership of the People's Liberation Army. Invariably, respondents confirmed that Washington has obtained extremely valuable insights and information from such discussions, while also increasing a much needed sense of familiarity and perhaps even some greater level of trust between the two sides.[54] Dialogue with lower-level functionaries was also regarded by some interviewees as useful and important, as long as the bar is not set too high and the U.S. side knows what it wants out of the exchange and who it must meet with.

In short, several interviewees argued that, as long as classified information is protected through adequate preparations (including detailed briefings of American senior officers in contact with PLA officers), a well-planned, sustained, long-term military-to-military relationship can produce real value for the U.S. side over time and should be protected as a major U.S. asset.[55]

Providing Positive and Negative Inducements

A second, closely related approach deemed effective by many interviewees involved deliberate efforts to provide both positive and negative inducements to the Chinese side, as part of the U.S. approach. In some cases, U.S. officials have managed to influence Chinese behavior by substituting one Chinese interest for a more vital Chinese interest, such as the stability of the Sino-U.S. relationship.[56] A key example was provided by China's sale of silkworm missiles to Iran in the late 1980s. Such sales derived from China's interest in both strengthening its ties with Iran and supporting its emergent missile export industry. U.S. officials eventually convinced the Chinese that such behavior constituted a serious threat to vital U.S. interests and could severely damage the U.S.-PRC relationship. Washington reinforced its stance by freezing a process of export control liberalization with Beijing involving defense-related technologies. Beijing ended the sales to Tehran because it valued its relationship with Washington more than the economic and political benefits it was receiving from its relationship with Iran. In return, the United States resumed the export control liberalization process.[57]

This "inducement"-oriented approach could also involve efforts to structure Beijing's incentives by maximizing the benefits that might accrue from taking the course favored by the United States while minimizing (or eliminating) the benefits—or increasing the difficulties—that might result from other less favored options.[58]

A more hard-line, punitive version of this tactic favored by some interviewees involves taking away something of value to the Chinese, and then negotiating with them to restore it, in return for something favored by the U.S. side. This is usually deemed more effective when carried out in response to a failure by China to reciprocate a U.S. gesture or concession of some kind, however.[59] At times, this has involved elements of a "good cop, bad cop" approach that would juxtapose positive incentives from the executive branch against the threat of punitive congressional action. Whether done intentionally or (more likely) unintentionally by U.S. officials, several respondents affirmed that such an approach has produced positive results on many occasions in the past, especially in the economic policy arena.[60]

However, a few respondents expressed vehement opposition to this approach as a deliberate tactic, arguing that it creates the impression that decisions made by the most senior leadership of the U.S. government are not authoritative or can be reversed without much warning—that is, that the executive branch is weak. Moreover, the "good cop, bad cop" approach was generally viewed as becoming less and less effective, given Beijing's increasing understanding of the U.S. political system (and the significance, or lack thereof, of various congressional threats), and its growing ability to engage Congress directly.

In general, respondents indicated that positive inducements, as part of an overall win–win approach on an issue, or a mixture of positive and negative inducements, usually had the best chance of producing a good outcome for the United States. However, efforts to trade concessions in one policy arena for those in another one were not regarded as particularly useful by most interviewees, because such actions could be used by Beijing to pressure Washington on a sensitive issue such as Taiwan.[61] In addition, any "deals" struck with Beijing to trade concessions in one policy area for those in another runs a great risk of being leaked, according to some respondents.[62]

The Limits of Sanctions

Similarly, "blanket" or broad-based sanctions designed to punish Beijing almost never work, according to many respondents familiar with the history of U.S. efforts in this area. Sanctions usually work best when they (1) are formulated to address a specific, clearly defined problem as part of a negotiation process; (2) are proportional to the size and scope of the behavior one is seeking to change; (3) are compatible with the existing policy interests or preferences of at least some of the Chinese leadership; (4) can be coordinated with other relevant nations; (5) do not appear to publicly embarrass Beijing or make it look as if it is giving in to public (and especially U.S.) demands; (6) occur during a period when Beijing has increasing incentives overall to cooperate with Washington; (7) provide a clear road map of what is required to lift the sanctions; and (8) ideally, in some way accord with international norms or rules. In addition, one respondent stressed that it is important to realize that even the best-crafted sanctions seldom produce immediate results. Generating a positive response usually requires a long, complex process.

Overall, sanctions have arguably been most effective with regard to trade disputes and, to a lesser extent, alleged proliferation practices related to weapons of mass destruction, where the objectives are clear, international norms appear to apply, and some Chinese inclination to adopt actions that are in line with U.S. interests is already evident. In contrast, according to some very knowledgeable respondents, the human rights policy arena is least amenable to the application of sanctions.[63]

But even under the best of conditions, sanctions should be applied sparingly and carefully, according to most interviewees, and with an understanding of what entity within the PRC government is being squeezed. In some cases, the threat of specific sanctions can be more effective than their actual application, given the difficulties involved in implementing and assessing them over time. In many instances, once applied, they can become part of the strategic landscape and acquire vested interests within the U.S. bureaucracy and thus prove difficult to undo. As one respondent pointed out, in many cases, the negotiations that result in sanctions lead to another set of negotiations on how to end the sanctions; and the latter often results in a situation whereby one agency of the U.S. government ends up negotiating with another U.S. agency more than with the Chinese.

Finally, many interviewees stated that the utility of sanctions has declined significantly in recent years, given China's arguably increasing ability to retaliate by threatening credible countermeasures against Washington or evade them by dealing with other countries or entities. At least one former high-level official expressed a concern that most major economic sanctions would likely cause more damage to the United States than to China today. This situation could lead to scenarios whereby Washington threatens sanctions, attempts to apply them in response to Chinese obduracy, and then backs down when it realizes that they cannot be applied effectively or would have excessive costs for the United States. Invariably, interviewees stressed that such a scenario could seriously damage America's credibility and undermine its policy toward China.[64]

Giving China "Face"

A third approach that often generated positive outcomes for U.S. interests involved the trading of some type of concession or inducement regarding Chinese "face" or preferences in the area of protocol and appearances, or an acceptance of general principles on an issue, for some level of policy substance. As many interviewees asserted, Beijing is often extremely concerned about its public reputation—both overseas and at home—and in the past, individual Chinese leaders have placed a strong emphasis on receiving what they would regard as proper public treatment from the U.S. government, especially during state visits.[65] This has particularly been the case when China's national reputation has been in decline, for example, following the Tiananmen Square incident in June 1989 or in the aftermath of serious confrontations in the 1980s with Southeast Asian nations over disputed territories in the South China Sea. In partial contrast, American officials are relatively more concerned with what they would view as concrete matters of substance—that is, policy-related outcomes. In addition, as many experienced observers of Chinese negotiating behavior have pointed out, Beijing is very focused on gaining acceptance by foreigners of what it regards as general principles regarding an issue, such as the need to protect the sovereignty of nation-states. As a result of all these factors, on many occasions in the past, Beijing has been willing to provide policy concessions in return for specific types of desired treatment by Washington, or when a particular arrangement or concession can be made to appear to conform to a cherished principle, concept, or terminology favored by China.[66] Conversely, several interviewees pointed out that Washington has sometimes lost leverage when it has refused to provide Beijing with a largely symbolic event, such as a state visit or a formal signing ceremony.

Although some observers might disagree, one interviewee cited the understanding reached between Washington and Beijing about Taipei at the time of U.S.-PRC diplomatic recognition as an example of the success of such an approach. Though the United States provided an "acknowledgment" of China's position regarding Taiwan's status, the Chinese largely accepted some form of ongoing U.S. political and military ties with Taiwan in return. Others stated that

Chinese concessions on issues such as the North Korean nuclear weapons crisis have been obtained as a price for the United States granting a state visit to the PRC's president.

One of the most significant, clear-cut examples of this approach relates to the area of military-to-military relations. According to a very well-informed observer, a past superintendent of West Point was given unprecedented access and new information on military issues during a visit to China primarily because he had been a strong supporter of Chinese visits to West Point, a largely symbolic event. Similarly, the Defense Department enjoyed increased access to the PLA following President Clinton's June 1998 summit visit to China, largely because the Chinese greatly appreciated the fact that Clinton's visit had constituted the lengthiest overseas state visit by a sitting U.S. president in history.[67] In contrast, one interviewee pointed out that Defense Secretary Donald Rumsfeld gave up a potentially important point of leverage with the PLA in military-to-military relations by refusing to hold a signing ceremony for an agreed-upon program of future relations, as Beijing strongly desired.[68]

At the same time, many interviewees believe that China is increasingly less willing to trade form for substance in the Sino-U.S. relationship, largely because its leadership is becoming more self-confident, is less concerned with gaining respect, and believes it enjoys growing leverage on many issues, especially in the economic arena. Nonetheless, a few interviewees also stressed that Washington must keep in mind that depriving the Chinese of respect (that is, face) on an issue of significance will likely remain very costly. Beijing's intense concern with its public image has also at times permitted Washington to influence its behavior by portraying Beijing as being out of step with international norms or in danger of being labeled as a global pariah on an issue, according to several interviewees.[69] Such "shaming" of Beijing has at times been particularly useful because it has allowed Washington to present a favored course of action as also supported by third parties and not simply by the United States. Several interviewees stressed that Beijing is often more likely to change its policies if it can plausibly be viewed as agreeing with the international community, rather than as conceding to the United States.

Playing the Chinese Bureaucracy?

A few other approaches or tactics were also noted by interviewees. However, these enjoyed less of a consensus or were not raised as frequently. For example, some respondents mentioned that past attempts to play on China's image concerns, along with other approaches, have often been buttressed by efforts to influence China's various individual bureaucracies or relations among these bureaucracies. Such efforts were arguably most useful with regard to economics issues, where the players and internal debates were more clearly understood, U.S. officials had extensive access to a relatively wide range of PRC officials, and there were potential "allies" for a particular U.S. stance. However, one respondent pointed out that U.S. officials are steadily less able to successfully influence Chinese bureaucratic behavior in this area because PRC officials and agencies are arguably losing influence over economic policy to nongovernmental or quasi-governmental actors and becoming more like regulators. Moreover, a few respondents cautioned that many U.S. officials have a natural tendency to create "mirror images" of bureaucratic politics in China, which results in misunderstandings regarding many issues, ranging from the formulation of Beijing's interests to the effectiveness of sanctions. In short, considerable care must be taken when attempting to "play" the Chinese bureaucracy to serve U.S. policy interests, even in the economics arena.

CONCLUSION

The observations and analyses given above provide a wealth of insights applicable to the formulation and implementation of America's policy toward China in the years ahead. Most notably, on the negative side, the U.S. policymaking process exhibits a range of (sometimes growing) structural and other problems that can greatly inhibit effective policy coordination and direction, suggesting the need for strong presidential oversight, a highly competent and engaged Asia director for the National Security Council, improved executive branch–congressional relations, and a more effective long-range strategic planning process. Regarding America's basic strategy, most U.S. officials do not seem disposed to examine the future viability of the common assumption that America's predominance in the Asia-Pacific region must continue to provide the basis for regional order and stability-inducing policies toward China. However, on the positive side, U.S. officials seem to be highly attuned to an array of tactical approaches that often generate positive reactions from Chinese officials.

10

CONCLUDING
OBSERVATIONS AND
RECOMMENDATIONS

▼

The analysis presented in the preceding chapters clearly confirms that in the new century, Washington policymakers will confront an increasingly challenging and vital task in developing effective strategies and policies to contend with a rising China. In many ways, America's future security and prosperity will depend to a significant extent on its ability to fashion greatly improved (or in some cases entirely new) means of working with Beijing to address a growing array of regional and global problems while diminishing the forces that drive increasing levels of strategic distrust and rivalry on both sides. On the strategic level, this will require not only a reaffirmation and adjustment of Washington's two-sided cooperative engagement and hedging approach to China, but also a fundamental reexamination of the larger regional and global strategic context within which that approach operates. This effort should center on a consideration of two key factors influencing the future strategic relationship between Washington and Beijing: regional and global power distribution and attitudes toward international norms and values. On the policy level, deepening levels of cooperation and reduced levels of strategic distrust will likely require an array of new or improved concepts and activities in virtually every policy arena examined in this study, from great power relationships in Asia to human rights and democracy promotion.

THE CONTINUED RELEVANCE OF AN
ENGAGEMENT AND HEDGING APPROACH

At the strategic level, this study's analysis clearly indicates that the optimal strategy for the United States to pursue—in concert with other nations—in order to achieve the twenty-first-century goal of facilitating the emergence of China as "a responsible stakeholder" in the international system is to continue some form of cooperative engagement with Beijing, while maintaining a strong military, political, and economic presence in Asia and a high level of influence within the major policy arenas examined in this study. Any *radical* shift toward an alternative strategy designed primarily either to expansively appease or to rigidly contain or actively weaken Chinese power and influence abroad would not serve U.S. interests under current and foreseeable future conditions for six main reasons.

First, Washington's continued cooperation with Beijing will remain critical because, at the broad strategic level, maintaining the ability to work with China and to avoid a zero-sum strategic competition is essential to keeping Asia stable, open, prosperous, and receptive to the U.S. presence—all critical U.S. interests that will only become more important as the century progresses. Equally important, as this study abundantly shows, such a cooperative relationship is also essential to the management or resolution of the challenges inherent in all seven policy arenas examined in this book: (1) Asian major power relations; (2) bilateral and multilateral political and security interactions; (3) military modernization programs and military-to-military activities; (4) economic development and assistance activities; (5) counterterrorism and counterproliferation challenges; (6) nontraditional security threats; and (7) efforts to promote human rights and democracy. As chapters 2 through 8 indicate, all these policy arenas are important on their own terms, given the often-growing significance of the underlying issues they address. However, they are arguably most important because, as discussed in the introduction, the success or failure of U.S. efforts to maximize China's incentives to cooperate while avoiding severe, sustained confrontations with the United States in these functional areas (and especially in the security and economic realms) will in large part determine the overall strategic situation America confronts in the initial decades of the twenty-first century.[1]

Second, alternative strategic approaches and policies that place a heavy or sole emphasis on either cooperation or containment will likely remain infeasible during the remainder of the current decade and probably beyond, in light of the considerable uncertainty that exists regarding China's strategic intentions.

This uncertainty implies that Beijing has not clearly shown a desire either to align itself with or unambiguously oppose U.S. policy on many critical issues and especially regarding the Asian security environment. Indeed, as indicated in the analysis of Chinese policy behavior found in several chapters, there are ongoing debates within China about national goals and the proper level of cooperation or resistance that Beijing should adopt toward Washington's overall power in Asia and with regard to many of the seven functional policy arenas examined in this study. For many Chinese, the need to maintain, and in some cases strengthen, cooperation with the United States and other Western powers is viewed as essential to the advancement of Chinese interests, not only at present but for many years to come.[2] The United States must not undermine such views by adopting policies that assume deepening Chinese hostility and rivalry.

Third, and more important, despite clear differences over some tactics and approaches, this study suggests that China's practical incentives to cooperate with the United States and other Western powers have certainly increased during the reform era, in some policy arenas. Moreover, a significant level of cooperation has been attained and will likely continue and perhaps even deepen during the current decade and beyond. This is especially evident in policy arenas related to economic development and trade, counterproliferation of weapons of mass destruction, counterterrorism, climate change, and pandemics. At the same time, in other areas, China is acquiring capabilities and acting in ways that directly or indirectly challenge specific U.S. policies or in some cases potentially threaten U.S. capabilities and interests. This is most evident in issues such as military deployments, human rights, and, to a lesser extent, counterproliferation, counterterrorism, and economics. In many of these areas, the need is clearly growing for Washington and Beijing to increase mutual understanding and develop more effective means of reducing distrust and building cooperation.

Fourth, as this study has shown, neither China's existing grand strategy nor public PRC policy documents, statements, and formal policy actions provide conclusive evidence of such *fundamental* strategic hostility or any accompanying commitment to undermine or replace U.S. power. Those who argue that China's behavior with respect to the potentially threatening issues identified above proves its implacable and extreme hostility to the United States and therefore justifies a policy of hostility and containment toward Beijing are either extrapolating from broader theories regarding state behavior in general and the actions of rising powers in particular or are engaging in mind-reading exercises directed at the Chinese leadership. The adoption of such an assumption as a guiding principle of American foreign policy would almost certainly end efforts at cooperation with Beijing while greatly increasing the costs and risks involved in pursuing U.S. policy in Asia and in many other policy areas.[3]

Fifth, none of the major powers in Asia and elsewhere would likely favor an American transition to a clear policy of either alliance-style alignment with or Cold War–style opposition to China. As chapters 2 and 3 indicate, the leaders of Asia's major powers and its multilateral forums and mechanisms, as well as the publics and elites in many Asian countries, are simultaneously benefiting economically from yet also concerned about the political, economic, and security implications of China's rapid rise to power. As a result, these third parties do not want a new cold war to emerge in the region. Nor do they want the United States to end its efforts to deter and shape Chinese behavior through the maintenance of a strong political, economic, and military presence in the region. Indeed, U.S. efforts to appease China by ending most hedging practices could lead many Asian nations to assume that the United States is withdrawing from Asia, which could in turn lead these nations to attempt to bandwagon with Beijing or to counterbalance Chinese power through the acquisition of potent military capabilities, possibly including nuclear weapons. In addition, such a radical shift, especially if undertaken over a short time frame, could prompt Beijing to establish its dominance over much of Asia, and thereby exclude or minimize U.S. access to the region. In the absence of a major crisis (such as a Sino-U.S. conflict over Taiwan), such Asian calculations and proclivities are unlikely to change during the current decade at least, especially given China's growing economic integration with and military activities in the region.

Sixth and finally, as the discussion in chapter 5 indicates, without an unambiguously aggressive Chinese challenge to vital American interests in Asia and across the major functional policy arenas discussed in this study, it is uncertain whether America has either the resources or will to adopt a policy of strategic containment of China. The economic and political costs of such a strategy would likely prove enormous, involving unsustainably burdensome increases in defense spending beyond already high levels, adverse effects on American trade and investment in China and many other nations, a weakening of efforts to build multilateral economic and security structures, severe strains on America's political relations with its allies and other key countries in Asia and beyond, and an overall decline in the capacity of either the United States or China to solve the other major challenges of the twenty-first century discussed in this study, ranging from climate change to nuclear proliferation and human rights. Moreover, as indicated in chapter 9, Americans by and large do not support a policy of treating China as an adversary in the absence of any clear confirmation that China poses a threat to vital U.S. interests.

The Viability of Engagement and Hedging: Future Agreement on Power Distribution and Norms?

Despite the likely continued need for some type of balanced strategic approach toward China, it is by no means clear that the United States will manage to sustain such an approach in the increasingly dynamic environment of the future or will discover the right balance to strike between cooperative engagement and hedging. Assessing the future viability of any engagement and hedging effort by America toward China requires, first and foremost, an evaluation of the ability of the United States and China to maintain or reach a tacit or explicit agreement or understanding regarding (1) the overall distribution of power that best promotes stability and prosperity and advances each nation's own interests (both globally and especially in Asia); and (2) the core values and norms that govern the activities of the nations, multilateral initiatives, processes, and forums that make up the international system. This study (and the larger scholarly literature) suggests that, although prevailing U.S. and Chinese assumptions and views regarding both power and norms remain largely compatible, or at least nonconflicting, this situation might not persist throughout the current decade and beyond. Most notably, basic U.S. assumptions regarding both U.S. predominance in the Western Pacific and related norms affecting the rights and responsibilities of both coastal states and foreign military forces operating in that region might come under increasing, and perhaps intolerable, pressure for a variety of reasons.

Continuing Assumptions of American Predominance

The analysis of national interests and grand strategy, U.S. military actions, and the views of U.S. policymakers presented in this study all suggest that Washington will almost certainly retain a commitment to the maintenance of America's maritime predominance, along with close allied political and military relationships with key powers such as Japan and South Korea, as a critical means of maximizing China's incentives to cooperate with the United States and other nations in the Asia-Pacific region while deterring possible adverse Chinese behavior. As suggested in chapter 9, some U.S. decisionmakers apparently prefer to downplay, in public statements and diplomacy, the role of predominant U.S. military power in maritime Asia as part of Washington's overall policy stance toward China and the region. However, most of these individuals nonetheless assume that this power must continue as a requirement for the stability that is deemed as necessary for continued openness and prosperity in Asia and globally. Without such clear predominance and the deterrence and reassurance that it conveys, they believe, regional rivalries will sharpen, attention and resources will turn more to dealing with potential and actual security threats than to economic growth and social advancement, and sensitive security issues related to America's overall credibility in the eyes of allies and friends—such as North Korea, Taiwan, and various disputes over maritime issues including territorial claims in the East China and South China seas—could become far more volatile. In particular (although rarely stated), some officials apparently believe that, in the absence of American predominance, China could be tempted to adopt more exclusionary stances toward the United States in Asia and generally seek to dominate the region, to the detriment of U.S. interests.

Moreover, such a view is bolstered, in the minds of many officials and outside observers, and as reflected in much of the analysis presented in this study, by the belief that there are no viable alternatives to U.S. maritime predominance and allied political and basing relationships, either now or in the foreseeable future. As chapter 2 suggests, although some degree of greater strategic leverage vis-à-vis China might be attainable through the development of closer security and political relations with Tokyo, Seoul, and perhaps New Delhi, these powers are viewed as unlikely to take up a major part of the burden of providing regional maritime security in the defense of common interests or of balancing against growing Chinese power, at least during the current decade. In fact, as indicated in the preceding chapters and discussed in greater detail below, Japan seems increasingly less likely to take on the kind of expanded security role in Asia that former U.S. officials such as Richard Armitage once envisioned for it; and India is far from attaining the capabilities to play such a role, even if it wanted to do so. In addition, the possibility of transitioning to a multilateral, cooperative, or collective security architecture that includes all the major powers seems even less likely *during the current decade*. As indicated in chapter 3, and as most U.S. policymakers apparently believe, no major Asian leaders think that such structures can take over the "hard" security functions performed by either the United States–led alliance system or individual national defense establishments.

Emerging Challenges to American Predominance

Despite the likely continued prevalence, in the minds of both U.S. policymakers and many Asian leaders, of the above-noted assumptions regarding America's relative power and the United States–led pattern of allied political relationships in Asia, this study also suggests that two closely related factors have emerged in the twenty-first century to cast doubt on the viability of such long-standing, bedrock notions underlying U.S. policy in Asia and toward China. First, in the twenty-first century, the United States might not have the economic capacity to sustain what will likely be required to maintain its maritime military predominance *in the Western Pacific and especially along China's periphery.* And second, China might not continue to accept this predominance.

Regarding the first factor, as presented in chapters 4 and 5, both the existing situation and assessments of likely future trends indicate that, even under worst case assumptions regarding America's future economic capacity, it seems unlikely that economic factors will prevent the United States from maintaining an extremely potent military force in the Western Pacific well into the twenty-first century. But will an economically constrained force still be viewed as predominant? If not, is something less than clear predominance sufficient to manage China and, more broadly, to ensure regional stability and prosperity and to protect overall U.S. interests in Asia?

The analysis presented in chapters 2, 3, and 4 suggests that, during the current decade at least, the United States will probably continue to be perceived as the predominant maritime power in the Western Pacific. However, it is also possible, although by no means certain, that the combination of continued high levels of Chinese defense spending and expanding military deployments relevant to the Western Pacific, alongside a prolonged period of U.S. economic malaise (and growing demands for the application of U.S. resources to non-defense-related areas), might result in both a perceived and actual loss of unambiguous U.S. military superiority *in specific, key areas,* perhaps within the decade. In fact, as this study has shown, a growing number of defense analysts believe that America's ability to prevail in a Sino–U.S. military conflict over Taiwan is already in considerable doubt, and will increasingly depend on both future warning time and out-of-area deployment capabilities under most plausible crisis scenarios, barring a major change in existing force trajectories.

The uncertainties accompanying such assessments highlight the critical importance of subjective judgments (as opposed to simple force-on-force comparisons) in measuring the presence or absence of U.S. military predominance in maritime Asia, and hence the utility of such predominance for U.S. strategy toward China. Such judgments involve perceptions of relative leverage and the ability to press for political advantages in ways that might demonstrate either growing influence (in the case of China) or declining influence (in the case of the United States). Thus, the question must be asked: What constitutes American predominance, in the minds of not only U.S. and Chinese leaders but also (and perhaps more important) in the minds of Asian and other world leaders? Is this measured in terms of deployed numbers of weapons systems? In terms of displays of specific operational capabilities (for example, a Chinese demonstration of the ability to sink a large, maneuvering carrier-like ship on the open ocean using a ballistic missile)? In terms of types and levels of naval and air presence within the first island chain? Or in terms of the comparative ability of China and the United States to compel (using, partly or entirely, political and military means) other nations to shift their stance on important security issues such as Taiwan or other territorial disputes with China? These kinds of questions are perhaps unanswerable in any final, definitive manner, in the absence of an actual Sino-American military conflict or test of political influence. But they point to the complexities involved in sustaining American predominance into the twenty-first century. This study suggests that over time, these complexities, and hence the challenges involved in managing them, will likely increase, not diminish.

These questions also bring us to the second factor influencing American predominance as a critical element of U.S. strategy toward China: Chinese calculations and behavior. Overall, as suggested above, the examination of PRC grand strategy and of Chinese military modernization presented in chapters 1 and 4 confirms the conclusions of knowledgeable analysts of China's security behavior such as Iain Johnston that Beijing is not actively engaged in deliberate efforts to counterbalance or replace U.S. military power in Asia and elsewhere.[4] Also, as noted in chapter 1, the Chinese have formally stated, in both the November 2009 and January 2011 joint Obama-Hu statements, that they "welcome the United States as an Asian-Pacific nation that contributes to peace, stability, and prosperity in the region."

However, such statements, and the apparent absence of present-day attempts to counterbalance U.S. power on the strategic level, do not amount to an open-ended Chinese acceptance of continued U.S. military predominance in the Western Pacific and the United States–centered alliance structure that supports it. Indeed, as we have seen, notions such as the New Security Concept, along with Beijing's general support for a multipolar global power structure, together suggest that, in Beijing's view, such predominance does not serve the interests of global and regional peace and stability *over the long term*. Therefore, as indicated in the introduction and chapter 1, as China's overseas power and influence grow, it could increasingly oppose efforts by the United States to maintain its predominance in the Western Pacific, in order to reduce its own vulnerability to possible future American efforts to limit Chinese power and to facilitate the attainment of key Chinese security objectives, such as the absorption of Taiwan and the creation of a strong security buffer out to the first island chain. This could become particularly likely if serious Sino-American crises emerge over Taiwan or other territorial issues in that region (thus greatly aggravating mutual suspicion and hence overall strategic distrust), and if there continues to be a significant perception gap, in the minds of not only U.S. and Chinese observers but also other powers, between a stagnating or declining America and a dynamic, fast-growing China, further weakening the notion of U.S. predominance.

Convergence and Divergence Regarding Norms and Values

Beyond such primarily military issues, the larger distribution of political and economic power in Asia and beyond—and hence Washington's ability to sustain its existing strategic approach to Beijing—could also be severely affected by Beijing's future approach to international norms and values. This is particularly true in the security realm, regarding those international norms that relate to sovereignty and territorial issues.

Overall, the assessment of China's grand strategy and policies in the various functional areas examined in this study largely confirms the findings of several scholarly studies of China's relationship to international norms and values during the entire reform era. Thus far in the twenty-first century, Beijing, partly in response to Washington's policies but also for its own independent reasons, has on balance deepened and expanded its formal commitments to many international norms, especially in areas such as free trade, nuclear nonproliferation, human rights, and the management of nontraditional security threats such as pandemics and climate change. In all these areas, China has repeatedly to varying degrees upheld, accepted, or adapted to prevailing norms, while giving few if any clear signs of attempts to radically revise or eliminate most norms.[5]

In fact, as Iain Johnston points out, since at least the mid-1990s, China's increasing support for and involvement in international organizations has derived in significant part from its recognition of the positive domestic impact of globalization and multilateralism, two increasingly important trends. This reflects not only China's acceptance of the material benefits that these phenomena produce vis-à-vis its economic development but also its broader affirmation of the advantages that result from its behaving as a "responsible major power" supportive of existing international economic and security institutions.[6] However, its behavior apparently also stems from at least a partial acceptance of the collectivist logic and values underlying many international norms—that is, a recognition of the limits placed upon nations as a result of growing interdependence and an awareness of the need to accept specific costs in order to obtain common benefits.[7] In other words, China has supported these international initiatives and their underlying norms for a mixture of motives, including pragmatic considerations associated with its narrow economic and domestic interests, image concerns, and the maintenance of its strategic independence, as well as for broader reasons reflecting some level of internalization of international values.

At the same time, this study and other scholarly analyses indicate that, though Beijing generally supports the structures and norms of the international system (for various reasons), it has also sought to qualify or resisted implementing those international practices that it believes excessively infringe on its sovereignty or might pose serious domestic political or social problems.[8] More important for the present analysis, China has also indicated a desire to *alter* some international norms, including those that are directly related to the existing distribution of global and Asian power. As indicated in the preceding chapters, this revisionist tendency has usually been expressed via China's affirmation of the concepts of national self-determination, state sovereignty (including state control over economic activities), and nonintervention in the internal affairs of nations, as enshrined in the Five Principles of Peaceful Coexistence and the New Security Concept.

As indicated in chapter 8, this approach is particularly evident in the area of human rights, where Beijing advocates a restrictive interpretation of international norms and treaties that emphasizes the significance of economic development, social stability, and collective rights over individual political rights.[9] It is also seen in Beijing's attitudes toward developmental assistance, which it views more as the moral and legal *responsibility* of developed nations than as a "dispensation of favor."[10] And it is reflected in Beijing's support for greater representation and voting power by developing nations in international bodies such as the World Bank. As both Ann Kent and Iain Johnston have observed, in many of these cases, China's views are often intended to supplement rather than replace existing norms and laws. Moreover, in many instances, China's support for more radical levels of change (such as the concept of multipolarity in general) has usually been largely rhetorical and has been compromised when confronted with more urgent needs. For example, as Kent points out, Beijing generally remains silent when an expansion of developing nations' power would directly weaken its own power.[11]

But perhaps most notably for this discussion of American predominance, as was shown in chapter 4, China's revisionist views lead it to defend its territorial integrity and espouse weaker nations' right to freedom from intimidation by more powerful states, which in turn lead it to attempt to obtain international approval for coastal nations' expanded rights to control the air and seas adjacent to their territorial waters and airspace. China's position regarding this control provides the most notable example of its willingness to reinterpret international norms in ways that directly challenge the status quo regarding U.S. military power and, indirectly, Washington's political influence. As indicated in chapters 3 and 4, in recent years, Beijing has shown a willingness to both speak and act in support of new or revised norms that directly or indirectly challenge Washington's existing interests in freedom of the oceans and the ability to conduct surveillance and military operations in what America and most of the international community would regard as open international waters.[12]

Overall, this mixed picture of China's adherence to many international norms, combined with its penchant to reinterpret or avoid implementing norms that conflict with its core domestic interests, perhaps differs more in degree than in kind from the behavior of other major powers. However, China is the only major power that potentially could challenge basic U.S. norms regarding the exercise of American military—and ultimately political—power in the Western Pacific. And yet, as we have seen, China's stance toward the activities of foreign powers in nearby waters and airspace does not ipso facto validate the existence of a broad-based, principled, and concerted Chinese opposition to the U.S. position in Asia, especially given China's apparently strong adherence to many other international norms that apply to the larger distribution of power and the actions of other major powers in the economic, political, and even military realms. In other words, it is by no means a foregone conclusion that China will espouse, as a matter of national necessity, alternative *norms* for the international system that directly challenge U.S. maritime predominance across the entire Asia Pacific, or that it will undertake actions in support of such a goal.

A Need to Consider Alternatives?

Nonetheless, the observations made above regarding the sustainability of American predominance and possible changes in China's approach to at least some key norms that directly impact such predominance indicate that the core strategic question for U.S. policymakers during the coming decades of the twenty-first century, and perhaps even during the current decade, will be whether and how to maintain clear U.S. military superiority in the Western Pacific and the current pattern of allied political and security relations that support it, or whether to consider (perhaps out of growing necessity) alternative power structures or security architectures as a basis for a new U.S. strategy toward China. And closely related to this question is the issue of whether and how to modify those norms relevant to military activities along the Asian littoral that relate most directly to American predominance.

As indicated in chapter 9, some U.S. policymakers recognize this fundamental issue and are beginning to assess the future of American predominance, but few have offered any specifics. Within the academic world, an arguably growing number of analysts are discussing possible alternative U.S. global and regional security architectures for the long term, including variants of so-called selective engagement, offshore balancing, and cooperative security structures. These will each be discussed in turn.

Selective engagement. Some analysts believe that U.S. military predominance in Asia—or at least some type of effective military counterbalance to China's growing power—can be maintained only if Washington significantly reduces its assertive political and military presence in most other areas of the world, and then uses the political and economic resources saved through such a readjustment to sustain or expand its current positions in the Western Pacific and other vital regions such as Europe and the Middle East. At the global level, such a strategy would obviously require a significant readjustment in America's military and diplomatic stance, likely involving the closure of many U.S. military bases around the world and a reduced willingness (and perhaps ability) to intervene globally in security disputes and political-military crises. Assessing the logic and feasibility of such a strategy lies beyond the scope of this study. But it does suggest that, as also increasingly in other areas, America's ability to develop an effective, long-term security strategy toward China is closely linked to larger strategic decisions.[13]

One extreme variant of this selective engagement approach would involve the creation in the Asia-Pacific region of a United States–led coalition to balance China that includes all the other major Asian powers—India, Japan, Russia, South Korea, Indonesia, Australia, and Vietnam.[14] Within Asia, such a strategy would equate to a variant of the hard-line realpolitik containment policy toward China outlined in chapter 4, which would require a wholesale rejection of the two-sided cooperative engagement/hedging approach. Even if economically feasible, such an option poses an array of severe dangers, as discussed above and as indicated in most of the analysis presented in other parts of this study. In the absence of any clear confirmation of Beijing's desire to displace Washington as the new regional maritime hegemon in the Asia-Pacific region, Washington can ill afford to pre-emptively and unilaterally discard efforts to work with Beijing to resolve a growing array of bilateral, regional, and global problems. Moreover, as many observers have noted, such a containment strategy would virtually guarantee the emergence of a new cold war in Asia that would likely prove highly detrimental to stable economic growth and increase, not decrease, the chances of conflict over issues such as Taiwan.[15] For some realist analysts, such a severe polarization will be inevitable as long as China continues to grow at a rapid rate. But as has been indicated throughout this study, there is no hard evidence to substantiate this assessment. Instead, this dire conclusion usually derives from controversial theoretical or historical analogies regarding the behavior of rising and dominant powers.

Offshore balancing. One alternative to the maintenance of a clear-cut level of American predominance in maritime Asia (with or without an explicit anti-China containment policy) is some version of an offshore balancing strategy applied to Asia. As suggested by its name, this strategy involves maintaining a local power balance from a distance by developing and manipulating shifting power relationships among key regional states. In most cases, these efforts primarily aim to prevent the emergence of a regional hegemon. Historically, such a strategy has required the ability to strengthen or diminish local states and to shift alliances when needed, primarily in order to project decisive power into a region and then to withdraw afterward.[16]

With respect to the Asia-Pacific region and the rise of China, this offshore balancing strategy confronts certain obvious difficulties. It would likely require a major withdrawal of U.S. military forces from the region, the strengthening of the U.S. ability to deploy significant forces into the region (or to conduct long-range precision strikes from outside the region), and the replacement of existing bilateral security alliances with largely independent, militarily self-sufficient power centers. As part of this process, Tokyo might choose or be driven to acquire a nuclear deterrent or at least a far more robust conventional military and to take a more "normal," expansive approach to the use of military power, to counterbalance Beijing's growing regional power in Northeast Asia. Moreover, Seoul would probably need to acquire a more independent capacity to deter Pyongyang. And such developments would likely accompany an abrogation or severe diminution of America's security treaties with both countries.

It is unclear how such a fundamental transition in the region's power structure could be managed without precipitating arms races and severe political instability or even conflict. Some analysts argue that this transition could be achieved if the pertinent changes were to occur only incrementally, as part of a process of close consultation among all the major powers involved. Some also assert that Washington would need (1) to maintain its close military contacts with Japan and South Korea and assist both powers in developing an independent military capability through arms sales and technology transfers; (2) to establish military access arrangements with both powers, and others if necessary, to facilitate the reinsertion of American power when needed; and (3) to significantly reduce the likelihood of military conflict with a rising China by abandoning its commitment to Taiwan and clearly disclaiming any intention to intervene in domestic Chinese affairs or to promote democratic change in China.[17]

Although such changes might be logical from a purely theoretical, realist perspective, it is extremely difficult to envision how America could abandon Taiwan, how Japan could acquire nuclear weapons and more "normal" conventional forces, and how South Korea could adopt a largely independent deterrent capacity without at least producing massive political upheavals in all the concerned capitals. Why would political leaders run such risks, without some sort of major precipitating event? More important, how would Washington ensure that—even if undertaken incrementally—such changes would not greatly increase the chances of military conflict, for example, by enticing Beijing to preemptively seize Taiwan militarily before the island acquires an independent (probably nuclear-based) capacity to defend itself, or by precipitating equally dangerous military initiatives on the Korean Peninsula? It would likely prove extremely difficult politically for the United States to stand by passively if authoritarian Beijing were to attempt to militarily coerce democratic Taiwan into submission or if a conflict were to suddenly erupt between Seoul and Pyongyang. In either case, a detached U.S. stance would almost certainly severely undermine Japan's confidence in America's ability and willingness to intervene militarily in a confrontation with China. This in turn would likely reduce Washington's overall influence in the region, and perhaps would encourage Beijing to undertake coercive measures against powers other than Taiwan. It is difficult to see how Washington could deter or minimize the impact of such developments from afar.

More broadly, it is likely that the type of limited U.S. withdrawal from Asia envisioned under this offshore balancing strategy, even if managed peacefully and incrementally, would lead many powers in Asia to increase their military capabilities and alter their political and economic ties in ways that could severely damage U.S. interests—for example, by developing more exclusivist intraregional economic blocs and by leaning more heavily toward Beijing, on the assumption that the United States was largely abandoning the region. Even in the absence of such adverse behavior, the likely militarization of Asia that would result from these changes could prove highly destabilizing and detrimental to regional economic development. Preventing such highly negative outcomes, if at all possible, would require extremely sophisticated diplomacy and enormous restraint on the parts of all players.[18]

Cooperative security structures. A second alternative to American predominance that nonetheless involves its continued presence in the region consists of some type of cooperative balance among the major powers of the Asia-Pacific region, including the United States. For some analysts, this amounts to a variant of the Quintuple Alliance or concert of powers that characterized the power structure in Europe during most of the nineteenth century. In Asia, this would presumably involve an assertive but lessened U.S. presence, along with the maintenance of very close ties with current U.S. allies such as Japan and South Korea. However, this approach would also emphasize far deeper, more balanced levels of both formal and informal cooperative security interactions among all the key powers in the region, including the United States, China, Japan, India, and Russia.

These cooperative interactions would presumably require a clear, common understanding of each nation's most vital security interests; agreements on standards of military-security behavior that would reassure all members that their vital interests were being protected; and agreed-upon sanctions and enforcement mechanisms to guard against unacceptable behavior by any members. This structure would necessarily develop only gradually, most likely initially through frequent, informal meetings to "identify major security challenges and coordinate solutions," and through the development of increasingly ambitious levels of security interaction, beginning with less sensitive or provocative activities such as the management of common nontraditional security threats, and gradually developing toward "harder" security functions.[19] This process would presumably become more formal over time, however, partly through the creation of new, more formal multilateral security structures.[20]

Although perhaps laudable as a vision of the future, such cooperative security structures also pose two serious problems both conceptually and with regard to the Asia-Pacific security environment. First, how does the system transition from building stronger habits of cooperative interaction through the management of less sensitive, nontraditional security issues to the creation of a structure that can effectively address the more sensitive "hard" security requirements of all members, especially in the context of dynamic changes in relative power among the major powers? Specifically, in the Asian context, through what process can the existing United States–centered, bilateral alliance structure peacefully and stably transition to a genuinely coequal, inclusive security structure that enables each member to feel protected as formal bilateral security commitments are removed? And if such bilateral security commitments are not removed, how might they complement, rather than undermine, a cooperative security structure involving China?[21]

Second, how can such a system manage the potentially destabilizing combination of changes in relative power among key actors and the existence of potentially conflictual security views regarding important "hard" security issues such as sovereignty and territorial disputes? As we have seen, such disputes are particularly relevant in Asia. For such a system to work, all powers must be willing to cede to "the cooperative" both decisionmaking and enforcement powers regarding the accepted disposition of such potential security disputes, or at least reject any recourse to force a resolution of such disputes, even when there are significant variations in the coercive capability of the parties involved.[22] In addition, would all members take full responsibility (or have the capacity) to enforce such sensitive cases? If not, the major powers in such a structure would need to cooperate in enforcement.[23] This, in turn, would almost certainly mean that these powers (in Asia, most notably the United States and China) would need to sustain a high level of mutual strategic trust and have few fundamental differences over the accepted means of resolving any security disputes. This is clearly not the case with Washington and Beijing today, as this study has abundantly shown.[24]

In short, the creation of a cooperative security-type structure to replace the current one—centered on U.S. maritime predominance—would at least necessitate the creation of a much higher level of mutual strategic trust among the major participants.[25] Creating this trust would require not only deeper understanding by each side of both its own and other powers' security requirements over time and under changing conditions but also significant changes in behavior to defuse the most potentially volatile suspicions. Such actions would likely demand more extensive bilateral and multilateral military-to-military and other security-related forms of cooperation among the major Asian powers, "through which China and the regional powers could signal restraint and register commitments to the peaceful settlement of issues."[26]

These forms of security-related cooperation would also require more intensive and frank discussions of all parties' concerns under various changing relative power conditions, along with concrete bilateral and multilateral assurances to enhance mutual respect and provide a more stable basis for managing the major powers' most potentially explosive concerns. For China and the United States, these concerns would *first and foremost center on Taiwan, then North Korea, and then the sovereignty disputes in the East China and South China seas.* Another precondition for the peaceful transition to such a cooperative security structure would include a deeper understanding among all the involved powers of the most important norms of the nascent international order and the best means of resolving disputes.

Obviously, creating a level of strategic trust among the United States, China, and other key Asian powers sufficient to permit a transition toward a genuinely cooperative security structure would not be an easy task. But would it prove impossible? Perhaps the greatest obstacle on the U.S. side to the creation of such a structure would likely be the unwillingness of senior political and military leaders to accept that (1) U.S. maritime predominance *in the Western Pacific* is probably unsustainable over the long term, assuming that China's rapid pace of economic development continues; and (2) attempts to sustain this predominance in the face of continued regional increases in Chinese power are likely to prove more destabilizing than the alternatives to this predominance, especially in the absence of any resolution of the key security tensions that plague the Sino-U.S. relationship in the Western Pacific.

On the Chinese side, the greatest obstacle to efforts to create an effective cooperative security structure would likely be the unwillingness of senior PRC civilian and military leaders to genuinely accept that (1) U.S. leaders would willingly give up predominance in favor of a more balanced security structure, preferring instead to maintain limits on Chinese power through some variant of American predominance; and (2) China would not need to ensure against the destabilizing behavior that allegedly might result from the presumed thrashes of a U.S. giant in decline by seeking to replace American predominance with a variant of Chinese predominance in the Western Pacific.

Great powers rarely if ever undertake major changes in their existing security policies based on anticipations of possible (yet uncertain) long-term trends that suggest the need for a significant level of accommodation—or worse yet, reductions in relative power—with regard to potential rivals. More likely, such change is forced upon these powers by external events. That said, sustained progress by Washington and Beijing in working together bilaterally and multilaterally to address the growing array of regional and global social, economic, and security challenges examined in this study could greatly increase both U.S. and Chinese incentives to overcome at least some of the above-mentioned obstacles to a cooperative security approach. For the United States, such activities should involve deliberate efforts to not merely avoid or solve problems but to also develop genuinely common norms in many policy arenas, thereby vesting Beijing more deeply into the regional and global orders. This will obviously require—or accompany—the granting to China of greater authority within the regional and global systems. It will also require close coordination of political and economic policies between the United States, the other key Asian democratic powers, and the democracies of Europe.

Perhaps more important, even in the absence of any decision to transition toward an alternative to U.S. predominance, there is little doubt—in the view of this analyst at least—that the maintenance of a stable and productive U.S. relationship with China and hence the successful attainment of American goals in the Asia-Pacific region and beyond will require a much greater emphasis on cooperation over hedging in America's overall strategy toward China. In particular, there must be more concerted efforts to significantly diminish—not merely manage—those Chinese sovereignty and territorial concerns that play a critical role in sustaining Sino-American strategic distrust in the Western Pacific. Specifically, the United States must devote greater thought to developing ways of establishing a more stable, long-term modus vivendi with China with regard to Taiwan, territorial disputes in the East China and South China seas, and the use of exclusive economic zones and international waters along China's coastline.[27]

On a broader level, an increased emphasis on cooperation over hedging could be facilitated by the creation of new integrative conceptual frameworks, such as the concept of a Pacific community advocated (most recently) by analysts such as Henry Kissinger. For such a concept to work, some type of "consultative mechanism" must be created that "permits the elaboration of common long-term objectives and coordinates the positions of the two countries at international conferences. The aim should be to create a tradition of respect and cooperation so that the successors of leaders meeting now continue to see it in their interest to build an emerging world order as a joint enterprise."[28]

Ultimately, any assessment of alternatives to U.S. predominance in the Western Pacific hinges on the answer to three interrelated questions. First and foremost, does the United States have the political will to maintain the economic and technological means to sustain its predominance *in the Western Pacific* well into the current century, by recovering in relatively short order from its current economic malaise? If the answer to this question is uncertain at best, then one must ask: Can U.S. and Asian political leaders envision and accept an alternative to American predominance in the Western Pacific? And a third closely related question is: What measures, if any, might induce China's political leaders to tolerate or accept U.S. predominance in the Western Pacific, or, failing that, to assist in creating an alternative, stable security system and set of norms in Asia that protect both U.S. and Chinese core interests?

The First Step: A Genuine Strategic Dialogue

Any attempt to answer these three questions will require, at a minimum, for American leaders to engage in a much more probing, comprehensive, and far-reaching strategic dialogue with Chinese leaders than has yet occurred. Such a bilateral strategic dialogue would need to connect separate global, regional, and functional policy issues with a larger discussion of Chinese and American grand strategic objectives and interests over time, in the context of several alternative possible changes in the structural environment facing both countries. In more concrete terms, such a dialogue would (1) connect long-term alternative possible projections of political, economic, and military trends and developments with perceived core and secondary national interests as they relate to global, regional, and bilateral security issues; (2) identify and explain those trends and activities that would most likely create significant security concerns on either side over particular time frames; and (3) discuss what is likely required by each side, in terms of bilateral, multilateral, or other interactions, to avert growing security competition and worst casing, including, if necessary, changes in anticipated military force structures and deployments, new or more intense types of cooperative and trust-building exchanges, and other forms of reassurance, avoidance, and the like.

This type of strategic dialogue would obviously require detailed and frank discussions regarding a range of expectations, fears, and intentions, connected to or contained within a broad set of assumptions about global and regional objectives and trends. It would not necessarily involve straight-line projections from current trends but instead would seek to develop and assess alternative futures along a possible spectrum. And it would obviously involve imaginative thinking regarding how different types of evolving cooperative, competitive, and even confrontational policies might interact over time. Such a dialogue would thus require the application of genuine expertise regarding a variety of political, economic, and military phenomena and combine scholarly analytical approaches with a very practical, policy-oriented understanding of both countries' current and likely future needs.

Equally important, any such dialogue would need to be preceded by an internal U.S. effort to reach some clarity regarding long-term American goals toward China, and with regard to Asia in particular. Such an examination would need to aim at achieving a more coherent understanding within the U.S. political elite and policy community of both the likely future constraints on U.S. resources and the likely future security-related ambitions, fears, and capabilities of the region's other major powers under varying conditions, especially Japan. As suggested above, this discussion would require a reassessment of the viability of current U.S. assumptions regarding military predominance, existing interstate (including allied) political relations, and other foundations for America's strategy toward China, under a range of possible "what if" future conditions. This discussion would also need to be coordinated with parallel bilateral dialogues with U.S. allies.

Given their sensitivity and, to some extent, speculative nature, such dialogues could only occur on a Track II level, involving knowledgeable and experienced former officials and policy analysts as well as a wide range of relevant political, economic, and military experts. However, to have any conceivable impact on policy, such dialogues would also need to enjoy the strong support of the U.S. (and in the case of the Sino-U.S. dialogue, the Chinese) government, and be well informed (although not directed) by government views. As indicated in chapter 9, the U.S. policymaking process is not well structured and U.S. policymakers are not highly motivated (and do not have the time) to engage in such long-range, conceptual, and sensitive conversations. Moreover, such dialogues would require a level of candor that is virtually impossible for serving officials in any government to convey. That said, as also suggested in chapter 9, such deficiencies suggest the need for a governmental strategic—rather than policy—planning entity, housed within the White House or State Department, that could oversee an interagency mechanism for crafting and revising policies on the basis of long-term strategic plans.

Beyond Dialogues: A Need for the United States to Put Its House in Order

Of course, strategic dialogues alone cannot provide final answers to the above-described challenges that will confront U.S. policymakers in the current decade and beyond. At best, they can clarify obstacles and opportunities on the road ahead, strengthen strategic trust, and identify policy approaches for increasing cooperation and avoiding conflict. In a more practical sense, Washington must also sustain the capacity necessary to maintain its credibility and influence vis-à-vis Beijing and other key powers in Asia and elsewhere in the face of dynamic Chinese growth. This will require, first and foremost, concerted efforts (a) to recover from the current economic recession and exploding national deficit before they result in a prolonged period of economic stagnation; and (b) to develop long-range policies designed to sustain America's economic and technological prowess over the long term. Such actions are necessary whether the United States seeks to sustain its predominance in East Asia or begin the transition to an alternative security architecture.

ASSESSING THE SEVEN KEY POLICY CHALLENGES FOR THE CURRENT DECADE AND BEYOND

America's efforts to respond to the challenges described above will also depend in large part on its ability to successfully manage, for the mutual benefit of the United States and China, the core issues contained in the seven policy arenas examined in this study. In other words, the successful management of these policy challenges is essential not only to resolve the problems they present for U.S., allied, and global interests but also to create the underlying conditions necessary to maintain a stable distribution of power and mutually acceptable set of norms for the international system and, hopefully, to strengthen habits of cooperation and mutual trust between the United States and China. This study has produced several key recommendations for each of those policy arenas: political and security relations with major Asian powers, multilateral and bilateral security interactions, military balance and military-to-military relations, economic development and assistance, counterterrorism and counterproliferation, climate change and pandemics, and human rights and democracy.

Political and Security Relations
with the Major Asian Powers

By far the most important policy issues that will influence America's overall strategy toward China during the current decade and beyond center, first, on Washington's political and security relations with its two most critical East Asian allies, Japan and South Korea; and, second, on the Taiwan problem. As suggested in chapter 2, in both areas, dynamic changes have occurred during the transition to the twenty-first century that are of enormous relevance to America's China policy and especially to any efforts to maintain U.S. predominance in Asia.

The Critical East Asian Allies

Regarding Washington's political and security relations with its two most critical East Asian allies, a more fluid political and security stance has emerged in both Tokyo and Seoul in recent years that combines a continued formal commitment to the alliance with greatly increased economic dependence on China; a more determined effort to strengthen political, diplomatic, and economic ties with other nearby powers; and, in the case of Japan, an arguably lessened ability and willingness to play an expansive security role in Asia. In addition, though Japan and South Korea are also in some ways moving closer to Washington as a result of recent concerns about China's more assertive behavior regarding territorial disputes, its continued support for Pyongyang, and other issues, such a development, if mismanaged, could undermine Washington's efforts to reduce distrust and strengthen cooperation with Beijing. Moreover, despite such recent developments, some policy elites in Tokyo remain concerned about the possibility that Washington might improve relations with Beijing in ways that place Tokyo at a disadvantage over the long run. In short, both Tokyo and Seoul are subject to crosscutting pressures—apparently in some instances aggravated by perceived mixed signals from Washington—that together serve to deepen internal tensions and ambiguities over how to manage relations with Beijing and, by implication, how to view alliance relations with Washington and U.S. security policies toward Beijing.

This situation suggests that, even though America's policy has by and large succeeded in sustaining its political and defense positions with both allies, it has arguably failed, thus far, to establish a coherent, compelling, and unified long-term strategy for advancing mutual U.S. and allied interests in Asia, and hence for managing China's rise. This in part reflects the larger failure of the United States to establish a clear strategy for sustaining, over the long term, its two-sided cooperative engagement/hedging approach to Beijing in the face of adverse economic changes and growing Chinese challenges to U.S. predominance in the

Western Pacific. Three closely related requirements thus confront Washington with respect to both Tokyo and Seoul, all of direct relevance to U.S. China policy. The first is the need to clarify the relationship between possible future U.S. military and political postures in Asia and the military capabilities and political preferences of Tokyo and Seoul. The second is the need to clarify the future structure and function of the United States–Japan and United States–South Korea alliances vis-à-vis China. And the third is the need to examine more closely the relationship between both alliances and the possible creation or enhancement of broader security mechanisms for the region.

In addressing these three challenges, perhaps the most urgent, near-term need is for Washington to work with Tokyo to resolve the ongoing problem of American military bases in Japan, centered on the Futenma dispute, in order to pave the way for a larger strategic dialogue on the long-term structure and purposes of the bilateral alliance, especially with regard to China. As suggested in chapter 2, there are still fundamental political obstacles in Japan to any effective implementation of existing agreements for the repositioning of U.S. forces. It is quite possible that Washington will eventually need to renegotiate an entirely new agreement with Tokyo on this issue.

Second, as mentioned above, Washington should support the creation of a Track II dialogue on the future of the bilateral United States–Japan alliance in a regional security context, possibly involving other allies such as South Korea. Such a dialogue should explore regional allied views of the future political, military, and economic requirements for the maintenance of stability and prosperity in the Asian region under a variety of assumptions—especially as they relate to U.S. and Chinese power—and the resulting implications of such an analysis for the existing United States–centered hub-and-spokes security architecture. This dialogue should directly feed into the larger internal U.S. strategic dialogue that should be undertaken within U.S. policy circles, as discussed above. As indicated, official government talks are unlikely to produce the level of candor and the thorough exploration of alternative objectives that will likely be required in such a dialogue.

Aside from such initiatives with its key East Asian allies, Washington should also make every effort to strengthen relations between Tokyo and Beijing. It is clearly in Washington's interest to encourage greater cooperation and reconciliation between Tokyo and Beijing with respect to all areas of contention, including territorial disputes, economic rivalries, and the history issue. A confrontational Sino-Japanese relationship would obstruct Washington's efforts to work with Beijing in a wide variety of areas, and under some circumstances (for example, a conflict over East China Sea resources) could even draw Washington into a military confrontation with Beijing. The U.S. government thus should consider advancing its interests through the promotion of a United States–China–Japan forum, as suggested above and in chapter 2.[29]

Taiwan

Regarding Washington's political and security relations with Taiwan, as indicated in chapter 2, despite significant improvements in the cross-Strait situation, U.S. policy toward the island has essentially remained unchanged since the early 1980s. And yet, as has been clearly shown, underlying conditions have evolved enormously since that time, in some areas (for example, in the military realm and regarding the largely zero-sum nature of domestic politics on Taiwan) in decidedly negative ways.

In particular, since the mid-1990s, when China began building up its military capabilities vis-à-vis Taiwan, Washington's security-related position toward the resulting growing cross-Strait military imbalance has remained largely limited to telling Beijing that it must reduce its military presence in order to give Taipei the confidence to engage in cross-Strait talks, while making clear that it will sell more arms to Taipei and increase U.S. surveillance and military deployments relevant to a Taiwan conflict as long as Beijing refuses to comply. Though it has worked thus far, the problem with this position is that it is founded on the assumption that the United States will retain the capacity and will to deter Beijing indefinitely from adopting more assertive means toward the island, despite the fact that China's economic, political, and military capabilities will likely grow steadily along its periphery, and that the United States might continue to experience serious economic problems that could affect its ability to maintain its military predominance in the Western Pacific.

Under such circumstances, avoiding future escalating Sino-American crises over People's Liberation Army (PLA) deployments and arms sales will probably depend almost entirely on the ability of Taipei and Beijing to reach a strong political understanding that permits mutual restraint in the military realm. And yet such an understanding is unlikely without some level of credible prior understanding between Beijing and Washington regarding both arms sales and larger political calculations. As indicated in chapter 2, in the very likely absence of far more domestic political unity on Taiwan in favor of cross-Strait political talks, Beijing will probably maintain if not substantially increase its military deployments relevant to Taiwan during the current decade, regardless of how much progress occurs in advancing cross-Strait economic and social links, thus almost certainly provoking further significant U.S. arms sales to the island. Most important, assuming that China continues to grow in power and confidence, Beijing will also likely attempt to make any future major U.S. arms sale decisions increasingly costly for Washington, thus greatly feeding mutual security suspicions and undermining U.S. attempts to maintain or enhance both strategic reassurance and deterrence.[30] Such a situation could ultimately prove disastrous for the Sino-U.S. relationship, greatly increasing the risk of confrontation and even armed conflict.

In this context, a continued U.S. commitment to its long-standing, essentially "hands-off" approach to the cross-Strait political process, including a refusal to engage in discussions with Beijing over each side's respective military deployments and U.S. arms sales to Taiwan, will become increasingly counterproductive for stability in the Western Pacific. Only the United States can alter China's calculus toward Taiwan in ways that would facilitate a military drawdown and genuine movement toward a more stable cross-Strait modus vivendi through political dialogue. Therefore, Washington policymakers should consider negotiating directly with Beijing, in consultation with Taipei, a set of mutual assurances regarding PLA force levels and deployments on the one hand, and major U.S. arms sales and defense assistance to Taiwan on the other hand, that are linked to the opening of a cross-Strait political dialogue.[31]

Such an agreement would need to be designed as a combined military and political confidence-building measure, intended to create some level of trust that each side would stop directly threatening the other with military deployments specifically aimed at the Taiwan situation, while providing a basis for an open-ended (and almost inevitably long-lasting) political dialogue. It would not need to require either Washington or Beijing to give up its military deployments in other areas.[32]

The feasibility and parameters of such an agreement could be initially explored via an authorized Track II dialogue, given its many obvious sensitivities. Indeed, any such approach would confront three major problems for the United States. First and foremost, some politicians and pundits in both the United States and Taiwan (and perhaps also in Japan) would attempt to label any effort by Washington to negotiate with Beijing, even in consultation with Taipei, as a "sell-out" of Taiwan's interests that could result in China eventually coercing or seizing the island and, more broadly, in irreparable damage to America's credibility and strategic position in Asia and perhaps beyond. Second, both the United States and China might face considerable difficulties in defining what constitutes a reasonable exchange of forces, deployments, and arms sales to Taiwan. A third consideration, often voiced by some observers of the Taiwan situation, is that any such U.S. attempt to intervene in the cross-Strait imbroglio could easily expose Washington to manipulation by both Taipei and Beijing while possibly increasing the chances of a miscalculation by all three parties.

The first objection is the most serious because it is directly related to the domestic political environments in the United States and Taiwan—arguably the most serious obstacles to a resolution of the Taiwan problem. There is no doubt that those in both places who want Washington to treat Beijing as a mortal enemy and Taiwan as an independent, sovereign nation entirely separate from China would highlight (and in some instances distort or exaggerate) the dangers confronting such an approach. In fact, while pursuing such an option, Washington would obviously also need to enhance its larger security posture in Asia, partly in support of its basic commitment to an uncoerced and peaceful resolution of the Taiwan issue. Also, in this regard, one should not assume that Taipei would inevitably regard Washington's efforts to negotiate with Beijing as a form of coercion toward the island. Taiwan's objections to opening a cross-Strait dialogue could be reduced considerably if this dialogue were presented as seeking, with a more active U.S. role, higher levels of cross-Strait economic interdependence; negotiated Chinese commitments to more political, economic, and personal freedoms than those currently contained within the "one country, two systems" formula; and significant, tangible reductions in Beijing's capacity to launch a rapid attack on the island.

Also, it is by no means clear that other Asian nations would regard Washington's efforts to negotiate with Beijing about the Taiwan problem as an unambiguous indication of America's weakness or as a loss of its credibility, as some would argue. Most Asian nations would doubtless prefer for the issue to be addressed through some form of direct talks designed to place it on a more stable long-term footing. It is also possible that many Americans would support U.S. efforts to negotiate with China to stabilize, if not resolve, the Taiwan issue. This is suggested by the fact that most U.S. citizens view Taiwan as the least critical threat to U.S. vital interests out of a litany of threats. Moreover, a vast majority of Americans are opposed to using U.S. troops to prevent China from invading Taiwan.[33]

The second objection would obviously be addressed through negotiations and consultations between Washington and both Beijing and Taipei and is not on the face of it unsolvable. Some observers disagree, asserting that Beijing would need to severely limit or destroy most if not all of its more advanced power projection capabilities to provide significant assurances to Washington and Taipei as part of any negotiations—a highly unlikely possibility. Others argue that the United States could not in any event conclusively verify Chinese commitments to limit or destroy military capabilities such as ballistic missiles. In this author's view, neither objection is convincing. Some PLA capabilities, such as short-range ballistic missiles and amphibious attack platforms, are really only relevant (and critical) to Taiwan-based scenarios. Beijing would thus not be sacrificing its capabilities in other areas by limiting such forces as part of a Taiwan agreement. Other PLA capabilities of relevance to Taiwan—such as deployments of certain levels of air or naval forces to bases or ports within rapid striking distance of the island—could also be subject to limitation without arguably affecting China's other security interests. Given the potentially significant benefits for China of reaching a stable agreement on this matter, it is also not inconceivable that Beijing would permit or provide convincing levels of verification.

The third objection—that U.S. efforts in this arena could backfire and hurt America's interests—highlights the need for considerable caution and much skill on the part of U.S. negotiators, but again should not prevent a serious consideration of this option. In truth, the United States would inevitably play a major role in the calculations of both China and Taiwan in any cross-Strait discussion. Hence, it is misleading and potentially dangerous to pretend otherwise by asserting that the Taiwan problem can only be solved by direct discussions between the two sides of the Strait without U.S. involvement. The question is: What role should the United States play in encouraging the creation of a more stable modus vivendi between Taipei and Beijing? As stated, the current U.S. stance is probably not sustainable.

Overall, none of these three objections should deter Washington from taking a serious look at the long-term strategic implications of the negative security trends involving Taiwan outlined in this study and the possible benefits that could result from a more active U.S. policy stance aimed at creating a more stable political understanding across the Taiwan Strait. The Taiwan problem remains by far the most serious obstacle to defusing the arguably worsening strategic distrust between Washington and Beijing, and it is wrong to blithely assume that recent improvements in cross-Strait economic and social ties will inevitably create the basis for a more enduring modus vivendi, especially in the face of significant conflicting political and security trends. Ultimately, it is in America's long-term interest to get ahead of the curve on this issue by more closely examining the relative importance of the political versus strategic considerations influencing the Taiwan problem and by exploring alternatives to its current hands-off stance that might open a pathway to a more stable Sino-U.S. relationship.

In the absence of any new U.S. initiative along the above-described lines, Washington has no viable alternative to continuing its long-standing policy of "dual deterrence and reassurance" regarding Taiwan, in order to maintain stability across the Taiwan Strait and to sustain the growing prospects for an improvement in Taipei–Beijing relations.[34] As part of this ongoing effort, Washington should continue to strengthen, where possible, its ability to detect and rapidly respond to a possible Chinese use of force. Toward Taipei, it should deemphasize the provision of new "big ticket" weapons systems and focus on providing the essential infrastructure, logistics, ordnance, and other materials that will better operationalize Taiwan's defensive capacity. Washington should also strongly oppose any attempt by Taipei to acquire an offensive deterrent of any kind. Finally, Washington should continue to discourage or prevent Beijing's acquisition of military capabilities or related technologies that could directly challenge U.S. military superiority in critical areas relevant to Taiwan. To maintain advantages in these areas, the United States should maintain its arms embargo and export controls and should encourage the European Union to do likewise. But it should focus such efforts on the most advanced and "high-impact" technologies and weapons systems.

The North Korea Nuclear Crisis

The North Korea nuclear crisis is a third issue that will exert a major influence on Washington's ability to prevent a negative spiral in security perceptions vis-à-vis Beijing. As indicated in chapter 2, as with the Taiwan issue, many of the underlying negative dynamics driving this volatile issue have not lessened appreciably, despite more coordinated efforts between Beijing, Washington, and the other involved powers to manage it during the past decade and longer. Indeed, in some ways the situation on the Korean Peninsula has notably worsened, given the collapse of the Six-Party Talks process in the aftermath of two sets of nuclear weapons and missile tests by Pyongyang, and recent North Korean attacks such as the sinking of a South Korean corvette (the *Cheonan*) and the bombing of Yeonpyeong Island, all of which have led to greater friction between Beijing and both Seoul and Washington. In other words, this policy issue is also in danger of becoming yet another source of greater mutual Sino-U.S. distrust and an obstacle to overall cooperation between America and China in many other areas.

Thus far, U.S. policy toward North Korea has clearly failed to bring China fully into a coordinated carrots-and-sticks strategy among the concerned powers that holds a decent prospect of achieving the aim of denuclearizing the Korean Peninsula, reducing the chances of conflict, and establishing a basis for long-term stability and growth. As with the above-described policy challenges presented by Japan and South Korea, a more successful U.S. policy approach in this area will require more effective efforts to alter Beijing's basically conservative stance toward change on the peninsula, especially its suspicious calculus toward U.S. motives in Northeast Asia. And yet China's calculus will probably not change significantly in the absence of a larger agreement or alignment of interests regarding the overall long-term security environment in East Asia, which in turn will require prior agreement with Tokyo and Seoul regarding the three major issues identified above (that is, coordinating U.S. Asia policy with the policy preferences of Japan and South Korea; clarifying the purpose of the United States–Japan and United States–South Korea alliances vis-à-vis China; and examining the relationship between both alliances and possible broader regional security mechanisms). Therefore, U.S. policy in this area will depend greatly on the evolution of the larger strategic environment. Washington needs to coordinate its efforts to deepen cooperation with Seoul and Tokyo with a broader reassessment of the long-term security needs of all the major players in the region, including China. This again points to the urgent need for a deeper multilateral exploration of strategic trends in Northeast Asia, especially as they affect the United States and China.

India, Russia, and Other Key Emerging Powers

With regard to the two remaining major Asian powers, India and Russia, U.S. policy has also achieved mixed results at best vis-à-vis relations with China. In recent years, Washington has succeeded in improving relations with both powers, thereby reducing the likelihood of bilateral confrontations over a range of issues, from the proliferation of weapons of mass destruction to the geopolitical situation in Central Asia, while also assisting U.S. economic interests in both countries. However, such U.S. successes have arguably not greatly benefited U.S.-PRC relations or otherwise served U.S. objectives toward Beijing in any major way. Although improved U.S. political and security ties with Russia and especially India have perhaps increased Chinese incentives to cooperate with both powers and to some extent limited Chinese incentives to directly counterbalance U.S. power, they have not greatly augmented U.S. strategic leverage vis-à-vis Beijing in any clear manner, and are unlikely to do so during the current decade, barring a major deterioration of Sino-Indian and Sino-Russian relations.

Washington's overtures to New Delhi in particular have added greatly to Beijing's fears of U.S. encirclement and have almost certainly aggravated security competition in South Asia and perhaps beyond. Washington's actions have also arguably given Beijing more room to assist Islamabad's nuclear program and have weakened the international nuclear nonproliferation regime. And improvements in U.S.-Russian relations have had little demonstrable positive impact on Washington's relations with Beijing. Indeed, America's ability to utilize its relations with Russia is subject to the larger forces affecting U.S.-Russian and Sino-Russian relations.

Thus, overall, as chapter 2 indicates, the United States confronts strong limits on its ability to utilize its relations with both India and Russia as a means of managing the larger strategic relationship with China, given both countries' desires to maximize their strategic leverage with both Beijing and Washington by playing the roles of pivots in an emerging United States–China–India–Russia strategic relationship. All this suggests that, although Washington has thus far succeeded in striking a balance between improving relations with New Delhi and Moscow while avoiding unduly provoking Beijing, this undertaking will likely become increasingly difficult over time. Moreover, while U.S. policymakers continue their efforts to deepen strategic ties with both countries, they should also keep in mind that neither power is likely to supersede *China's* importance to the United States, at least during this decade.

Of even more importance in this context, the rise of India, along with the resurgence of Russia and the emergence onto regional and global stages of other major powers such as Brazil and Iran, herald the advent of a more genuinely multipolar global power structure with major implications for the current United States–led order and American military predominance overall. In other words, the significance for the United States of India and Russia extend far beyond their questionable utility in any effort to counterbalance rising Chinese power. The United States needs to base its approach to both powers in a larger strategic framework that addresses the new challenges to strategic stability and global governance presented by an increasingly multipolar order. This will require not only a greater stress on more inclusive multilateral strategic interactions (for example, between the United States, China, and India) but also a fundamental reassessment of the U.S. role in the world.[35]

Multilateral and Bilateral Security Interactions

As was described in chapter 3, multilateral interactions of various sizes and types are clearly becoming more prominent in the new century as a means of addressing a range of issues critical to U.S. interests, from general bilateral strategic distrust to specific political and economic problems and issues. Until recently, Washington was extremely hesitant to become actively involved in major forums such as the Association of Southeast Asian Nations (ASEAN) Regional Forum and the East Asia Summit, regarding them as largely ineffective or irrelevant in performing both "hard" and "soft" security functions. As a result, U.S. policies toward multilateral security structures and interactions in Asia have thus far had a very limited, if any, impact on strategic relations with China. But as the discussion in chapter 3 demonstrated, this situation is probably changing. On the broadest strategic level, multilateralism could become an increasingly important tool for the United States as it seeks to maintain the Asia-Pacific region's confidence in its continued capacity to balance cooperative engagement and hedging in its relations with Beijing and generally to avoid a zero-sum regional competition with China. Such interactions could also serve to lay the foundations, over the long term, for a more ambitious multilateral cooperative security structure, as discussed above.

In the near to medium terms, probably the most significant function that multilateral forums can perform in the security area is as mechanisms for discussing both norms and approaches for handling territorial disputes among Asian powers (most of which involve China), along with differences regarding the use of coastal waters and airspace. These issues are becoming the most significant security problems in Asia, aside from those involving Taiwan and North Korea. The United States arguably moved toward using one major multilateral forum in this manner at the 2010 ASEAN Regional Forum meeting in Hanoi, when it promoted efforts by several member nations to address the growing tensions over rival claims to islands in the South China Sea. However, the obvious danger presented by such actions is that they could damage relations with China and turn multilateral forums into objects of interstate (and especially U.S.-PRC) rivalry. A multilateral approach to territorial disputes directly challenges Beijing's strong preference for managing such issues in a bilateral manner. Indeed, Beijing viewed Washington's actions in Hanoi as a direct U.S. effort to organize other states to pressure China. Nonetheless, reaching a common understanding among all the relevant powers on how to address such disputes should become a major objective of future forums.

A probably more feasible alternative security function that large-scale, multilateral forums might serve over the near to medium term is simply to build trust via more discussion of less sensitive topics, such as transnational crime, terrorism, and disaster preparation and relief. This would largely amount to the continuation of long-standing efforts to expand potential agreements among the region's states—a very useful but much more limited endeavor than any effort to tackle territorial disputes.

The United States also needs to examine more closely the potential role of smaller multilateral venues (so-called minilaterals) in addressing subregional or narrower security problems involving China. Such forums could serve to strengthen policy coordination on a range of "soft" security issues, especially among the democratic Asian nations, such as the United States–Japan–Australia Trilateral Strategic Dialogue and a United States–Japan–South Korea dialogue. However, some "hard" security issues involving China could also be addressed through different types of trilateral discussions, for example, (1) between the United States, Japan, and China, regarding issues that relate to Sino-Japanese tensions, such as territorial and resource disputes;[36] (2) between the United States, China, and South Korea, regarding the future of the Korean Peninsula; and (3) between the United States, China, and India, regarding opportunities and concerns that affect this newly emerging strategic triangle.

In considering the value of such trilateral dialogues, Washington must assess their possible impact on key alliance partners such as Tokyo and Canberra, and their relationship to other possible broader dialogues. Indeed, the minilateral with the greatest potential for reducing strategic rivalry and distrust is probably some type of Northeast Asia security mechanism including the powers involved in efforts to negotiate the denuclearization of the Korean Peninsula.[37] But the specific agenda for and possible practical results of such an undertaking should be clearly discussed and agreed upon by all parties early in the formation process. Moreover, progress toward such a development will almost certainly depend on first resolving the North Korea imbroglio, as mentioned in chapter 3.

In the area of bilateral contacts with China, again from a broad strategic and security perspective, the Strategic and Economic Dialogue (S&ED) has significant potential to serve as a tool to increase understanding and decrease distrust. However, the S&ED's structure and process remain constraining. As suggested in chapter 3, the S&ED needs to become a more comprehensive, in-depth, and regularized mechanism for strategic discussion about U.S.-PRC interests and intentions in a highly dynamic environment.

Overall, the primary challenge for U.S. policymakers in this arena is twofold. First, Washington must more effectively coordinate between efforts to strengthen contacts with Asian democratic governments as a way of shaping or managing China's role in Asia on the one hand, and attempts to develop various forums that *include* China, such as a United States–Japan–China dialogue, on the other hand. The former approach obviously runs a risk of further exacerbating strategy rivalry if not handled properly (which would undermine the success of more inclusive forums), whereas the latter might precipitate greater attempts by the United States, China, and other powers to manipulate or control multilateral forums in general, especially in the absence of greater levels of mutual trust. Second, Washington must also integrate its overall approach to security-oriented multilateral forums with the existing United States–centered, bilateral alliance-based hub-and-spokes security architecture. As suggested above, maintaining a productive balance between these two types of undertakings will require a higher level of clarity regarding America's overall strategic design in Asia, especially given the changes being wrought by China's growing influence in the region.

The Sino-U.S. Military Balance and Military-to-Military Relations

As indicated in chapter 4, the purpose of America's military deployments in Asia and its military-to-military relations with China is to maintain both regional stability and an overall focus on economic development over security competition, despite an expanding PLA presence. This objective can primarily be accomplished by maintaining a clear U.S. capacity to deter attempts at military coercion or aggression by any major power, and especially China, and to build general trust by deepening cooperation in the military realm. In other words, the U.S. military clearly performs a vital two-sided function—that is, both military deterrence through deployments and military-based trust building through greater contacts—reflecting the two-sided nature of America's overall strategy toward China. However, as explained in previous chapters, these two functions exist in considerable tension with one another.

As noted above, the primary U.S. policy challenge in this arena is presented by China's growing capacity and presence in the Western Pacific and its accompanying willingness to confront the United States on issues relating to the U.S. military's presence along China's maritime periphery. Whether intentional or not, both actions pose direct challenges to overall U.S. military predominance and Washington's specific ability to deter and reassure both China and other states regarding issues such as Taiwan and to maintain the confidence of U.S. allies, particularly Japan. Such a development suggests that, if current trends continue, the perception, if not the material reality, that the United States is losing its military predominance in the Western Pacific—and especially with regard to the critical Taiwan issue—could emerge and deepen during the coming decades of the twenty-first century. And this will especially be the case if U.S. defense spending and deployments are adversely affected by a prolonged period of U.S. economic stagnation.

As explained in chapter 4, both Pentagon analysts and outside defense specialists are increasingly focusing on the threat posed by PLA capabilities, thus contributing to the creation of an overall mindset that increasingly regards U.S. and Chinese military activities as part of a zero-sum pattern of Sino-U.S. strategic rivalry. In this context, China's likely continued acquisition of what many Western defense analysts define as antiaccess and area-denial-oriented military capabilities, combined with a more aggressive stance toward territorial and political disputes in East Asia, could increasingly prompt U.S. defense analysts and perhaps some U.S. political leaders to conclude that China does in fact seek not only to negate the United States' predominance but also to eject it from the Western Pacific. In fact, there is already a dynamic whereby both sides perceive the need to push back or directly confront what are often viewed as efforts by the other side to test its resolve.

If such a mindset were allowed to spread within the U.S. policy community, it could greatly weaken the desire of U.S. policymakers to undertake dialogues and actions in the military and other realms that are designed to build trust or develop habits of cooperation. And military-to-military relations in particular would likely weaken and become even more subject to disruption as a result of political or other bilateral disputes.[38] More ominously, this situation could eventually result in deliberate Chinese efforts to undermine the overall U.S. position in the region.

Such trends are threatening to produce a vicious circle that would become increasingly difficult to break and could eventually overwhelm other, more positive aspects of the Sino-U.S. relationship. The existence (and, arguably, intensification) of this negative dynamic suggests that U.S. policy has largely failed to strike the right balance between deterrence and reassurance in its military policies toward China. As noted in chapter 4, the United States has clearly failed to deter greater PLA deployments relevant to Taiwan and U.S. capabilities in the Western Pacific, or to reassure Beijing that it does not need to deploy such capabilities. To the contrary, China is arguably becoming more militarily active not only with regard to Taiwan but also in other areas along its maritime periphery that potentially threaten U.S. interests or capacities. This outcome has occurred in part because the United States has failed to engage the PLA in effective confidence-building measures, either through direct bilateral or multilateral participation in joint military activities or via a deepened process of military-to-military interaction among officers and soldiers on both sides.

Such policy failures have to some extent been unavoidable because of the overall pattern of distrust between Beijing and Washington in the political and security arenas and the suspicious and secretive mindset that predominates within the Chinese elite, and especially the PLA. However, the United States, as by far the stronger power in the bilateral relationship, has the primary responsibility and arguably the greater capacity to initiate the kind of changes that are required to avert a fundamental strategic crisis later in this century. In particular, Washington could manage this problem more effectively by addressing the sources of strategic distrust between the two sides, partly by making more concerted efforts to both downplay (if not actively suppress) the increasingly loud calls for push back in the U.S. defense community, while also working more aggressively with other nations to bring the PLA more fully into a regionwide (not simply U.S.-PRC) pattern of military-to-military engagement—including exercises and other operational activities—and to effectively engage China and other Asian nations in clarifying norms regarding Asian territorial issues. Regarding the latter point, Washington must ratify the UN Convention on the Law of the Sea as soon as possible. As indicated in chapter 4, the United States will remain at a significant disadvantage in maintaining or revising such norms if it does not have a seat at the table. In addition, Washington needs to reexamine its long-term security objectives for outer space, the long-term implications for these objectives of trends in China's space program, and the feasibility of various alternative approaches for managing the emerging challenge posed by Beijing's potential military use of space.

Washington should also deepen its bilateral military-to-military interactions and exercises with China. The primary purpose of military-to-military relations should be for both sides to gain a better understanding, both professionally and on a personal level, of how the other party thinks about the role of military force in national strategy and with regard to individual policies. The secondary purpose, which should flow from the primary one, should be to develop a more accurate and finely grained appreciation by both sides of the potential for both cooperation and competition between them and what motivates behavior in either direction. The tertiary purpose should be to strengthen the incentives and abilities of both militaries to cooperate, bilaterally and otherwise, while minimizing the use of worst case assumptions toward one another. This type of relationship requires real communication, frequent contact (on both the personal and functional or operational levels), and as much candor as possible.

Establishing this type of military-to-military relationship requires a very different approach to reciprocity and transparency in the relationship than the United States has heretofore pursued. As military specialists have observed, transparency should be viewed from a very long-term perspective, not on a one-year basis. Each bilateral visit should thus be treated as one element of a long-term service-to-service relationship rather than as an isolated entity. In general, military-to-military discussions should focus on gaining a clearer understanding of how each side looks at the use of military power as part of overall national strategy, and in fairly broad terms, as part of a larger political-military strategic dialogue, and not with regard to specific weapons systems.

Again, the above-outlined U.S.-PRC strategic dialogue should directly contribute to the development of such communication, as well as narrower military dialogues of a similar type. The ongoing results of such a Track II effort should feed into a quasi-governmental Track I+ dialogue in the military realm, involving discussions of national and military strategy and doctrine among both government and nongovernment participants. In addition, to facilitate such a fundamental restructuring and expansion of the military-to-military relationship, Washington should also press for a revision or elimination of many of the provisions of the 2000 Defense Authorization Act that unreasonably prohibit the activities of the U.S. military in this area. It should be left to the executive branch, involving consultations between the Department of Defense, the Department of

State, and the White House—and not Congress—to determine the specific content and approaches to be employed in America's military-to-military relationship with China. That said, senior officials in the executive branch should not only keep Congress fully apprised of developments in this area, but also seek the views and suggestions of its members.

Finally, on a more concrete level, as analysts of this issue such as Lyle Goldstein have observed, "a systematic approach that actually institutionalises the habit of military cooperation is required at all levels and, in particular, at the junior-officer and staff levels." Moreover, cooperative efforts should be focused on the maritime domain specifically, involving enhanced activities in areas such as "confidence-building and crisis management; search and rescue; disaster relief; environmental stewardship; regional maritime security; and sea-lane security."[39]

Economic Development and Assistance

From a broad, structural perspective, U.S. policy has experienced major successes in facilitating China's full entrance into the global economy, as marked most notably by the success of the negotiations that led to China's joining the World Trade Organization (WTO). Such policies have undoubtedly assisted U.S. corporations seeking access to China's market (for both trade and investment purposes), as well as U.S. consumers seeking a wide range of quality-made, reasonably priced products. And equally important for the long term, such policies have also undoubtedly encouraged China's acceptance of international economic norms.

That said, U.S. policy has experienced a much more mixed track record regarding specific, narrower economic goals, including expanded market access, strengthened protection of intellectual property rights, and the liberalization of trade and financial practices. On the positive side, the S&ED process has arguably increased understanding on both sides regarding the complex array of interests, obstacles, and opportunities for cooperation in the economic realm. As noted in chapter 5, the S&ED has increased coordination both within and between the plethora of economic agencies involved on both sides and has prevented domestic politics from disrupting an increasingly well-established process of negotiating differences. And important concessions in specific areas have been obtained through both the S&ED and the Joint Commission on Commerce and Trade. U.S. policy has also arguably succeeded in keeping Beijing focused on meeting its WTO obligations while vesting Beijing more deeply in the WTO process.

However, on the negative side, U.S. economic policy in the twenty-first century has thus far failed to resolve, or even to significantly ameliorate, most of the concrete problems that confront the relationship. This challenge is greatly exacerbated by America's continued domestic economic problems, which have undermined its leadership role in economic affairs and cast doubt on the veracity and authority of the free market norms that it supports. This situation has also been exacerbated by China's failure to implement more far-reaching structural economic reforms, especially for finance and investment practices, as noted in chapter 5.

As in the case of military issues, this situation also threatens to create a vicious circle, in which reduced U.S. capacity and influence and Chinese deficiencies in the economic realm undermine the ability of both sides to reach the mutual accommodation required to resolve specific problems. This in turn aggravates public opinion in both countries and weakens the willingness and ability of both sides to make the hard choices necessary to improve their economic interaction. The result is a threat of rising protectionism and economic nationalism.

One major way to avoid such outcomes is for U.S. political leaders to overcome their excessively partisan differences to resolve America's deeply rooted domestic economic and financial problems. In particular, as suggested in chapter 5, Washington must shrink the size of the U.S. deficit (most likely through a combination of decreased federal spending and increased taxation), raise the U.S. savings rate, establish a more fiscally responsible pattern of domestic consumption, strengthen the U.S. educational system, and invest more in technological innovation in order to enhance American competitiveness. In addition, the United States must strengthen its overall economic position in East Asia through more concerted efforts to develop free trade agreements and other arrangements that sustain access by U.S. corporations to Asian markets on a strong, competitive footing. In particular, the U.S. Congress should overcome internal issues and ratify the Korea–United States Free Trade Agreement and the Obama administration should continue to place a high priority on the successful conclusion of the Trans-Pacific Partnership negotiations. As indicated in chapter 5, the United States is in danger of losing its political and economic credibility and influence in the Asia-Pacific region by failing to more assertively pursue such pacts.[40] Many of the problems that some Americans lay at the doorstep of Beijing are actually due—in part at least—to America's mismanagement or neglect of these and other economic and trade-related issues.[41]

Equally important, while striving to address such economic ills, U.S. political leaders and policymakers must work harder to strengthen multilateral coordination with other countries in addressing many of the problems in the U.S.-PRC economic relationship, including the currency dispute. Such problems are increasingly regional and global, and thus cannot be addressed on a purely bilateral basis. The U.S. Congress in particular needs to recognize, when addressing many of Washington's economic and trade concerns with Beijing, that integrating China into the global economy and eliciting its greater acceptance of international norms are multilateral challenges, requiring consultation and coordination with many nations in the international community.[42] Adopting a purely unilateral or protectionist approach to such issues is unlikely to produce positive results and could prove counterproductive.

On specific bilateral economic and trade issues, Washington should continue to stress persistent, low-key dialogue and negotiation rather than public, confrontational pressure. Such an approach, if properly timed and gauged to appeal to specific interests within the Chinese bureaucracy and economy, usually produces more positive outcomes than do public threats, finger-pointing, and cajoling. As indicated above, a confrontational approach is more likely to produce credible counterthreats from the Chinese side than compromise or accommodation, given China's growing economic leverage and influence within the global economy and in the bilateral Sino-U.S. economic relationship. Washington should also utilize the WTO's dispute settlement mechanism more systematically to achieve greater Chinese compliance with its obligations as a WTO member, and likewise should eschew actions that would "punish China in a manner that would violate [U.S.] WTO obligations or would benefit a few litigious industries at the expense of broader economic interests."[43]

Finally, the United States should continue to encourage China to realize that the best way for it to pursue its interests in the energy sector is to work through market mechanisms and help strengthen global markets overall, not to seek preferential equity deals with unstable regimes or to acquire deep water, long-range military power projection capabilities. Unfortunately, this effort has enjoyed only sporadic support in Washington and has at times been undermined by actions taken by other branches of the U.S. government—for example, when Congress has strongly opposed the sale of U.S. oil companies to Chinese firms or various types of energy-related investments by Chinese entities in the U.S. domestic market. Such moves short-circuit established procedures for vetting sensitive economic transactions and arguably weaken the attempt to encourage China to base its energy policies on market-based criteria. In addition, from a broader perspective, attempts to generally discourage Chinese investment in the United States limit the creation of the kind of mutually beneficial economic interdependence that can reduce overall economic disputes.[44]

In all, this policy arena confronts enormous challenges that, if improperly handled, could obstruct America's attempt to recover its economic footing and thereby more effectively manage the larger strategic challenges outlined above. In contrast, if the U.S.-PRC economic relationship is successfully managed, many of the problems confronting the U.S. economy, as well as many regional and global issues vital to U.S. interests, will become far easier to manage, thus providing a stabilizing ballast to the larger strategic relationship.

Counterterrorism and Weapons Counterproliferation

U.S. policy has produced very notable successes in the policy arena of counterterrorism and weapons counterproliferation, especially in facilitating both bilateral and multilateral cooperation in combating global terrorism and Beijing's participation in the nuclear nonproliferation regime (as described in detail in chapter 6). However, in the latter area, U.S. policy has also arguably fallen short in strengthening China's capacity and incentive to improve both the implementation and enforcement of controls over various types of proliferation practices, and to reduce its willingness to provide various forms of unacceptable assistance to countries of concern, most notably North Korea, Iran, and Pakistan. Equally important, the United States has failed to generate significant Chinese support for U.S. counterterrorist objectives in Central Asia, and especially in Afghanistan.

To some extent, the former failure has been largely unavoidable, given the inherent limits on Washington's ability to improve China's basic structural deficiencies in infrastructure and the apparent incapacity, in some areas, of the PRC's central government to enforce controls over the disparate local entities involved in activities related to weapons proliferation. At the same time, Washington has shown a capacity to influence such factors through a combination of dialogues, public and private pressures and inducements, persistent efforts at coordination with other nations, strong support for international initiatives, and highly targeted and low-key sanctions against specific violating entities.

With regard to the three countries of particular concern—North Korea, Iran, and Pakistan—Washington's failure has arguably resulted from an approach that has appeared excessively unilateral and militarily coercive to Beijing and (in the case of Iran and North Korea) motivated by efforts to induce regime change. Overall, as indicated in chapter 6, U.S. policy failures in working with China to combat terrorism have also stemmed from an inability to separate the PRC's efforts to combat terrorism from the repression of domestic political dissidents, along with a lack of U.S. attention to many of those underlying factors driving terrorist behavior that are often stressed by Beijing, including weak governance, corruption, and poor economic conditions.

Perhaps most important, Washington's failure in both policy areas has also stemmed from its fundamental inability to significantly influence Beijing's strategic calculus toward Islamabad, Pyongyang, and Tehran. Although Washington's ability to affect Beijing's strategic interests with regard to all three states will remain limited, more positive outcomes could result from attempts to engage Beijing in more intensive dialogues about possible contingencies regarding each country and the preferred changes that Beijing and Washington might favor in the larger regional security environment.

Finally, in the general area of nuclear weapons proliferation, Washington should continue to assist China in the development of controls over the transfer of dual-use items, in part by providing expanded technical assistance to Beijing in strengthening its export and border control capabilities. At the same time, Washington should reexamine its entire approach to controlling the exporting of advanced and dual-use products and technologies to China. The sheer number and complexity of U.S. regulations governing such exports have grown over many years, thus generating criticism among many businesses, experts, and foreign observers that they have become excessively complicated, inconsistent, and unwieldy.

Climate Change and Pandemics

U.S. policymakers have made notable progress in encouraging dialogue, transparency, and a general sharing of information on issues in the policy arenas of climate change and pandemics, possibly thereby building a basis for broader-based bilateral and multilateral agreements. Washington has also arguably contributed to producing a greater impetus to many existing Chinese undertakings in both areas.

Overall, in the area of climate change, U.S. policy has achieved its greatest successes in developing or encouraging cooperative programs with Chinese government and nongovernment entities to develop specific technologies and incentivizing practices that can reduce emissions. However, U.S. policymakers have thus far proven unable to bridge the divide between the two nations over how to apportion responsibility for environmental damage and hence levels and types of corrective measures. This problem is of course not limited to bilateral relations and to some extent can only be addressed in a multilateral setting. But the obvious failure of the 2009 Copenhagen summit suggests that such very large-scale, coordinated efforts to attack the problem will probably not succeed.

Equally important, Washington has also failed to create a strong consensus within U.S. society regarding the need to address climate change through concerted government action. As noted in chapter 7, the United States does not serve as a model for China and the rest of the world in confronting this issue. This failure has drastically affected China's willingness to make strong commitments. For the United States, the problem is in large part one of domestic education, partisan politics, and the political influence exerted by an extremely strong oil industry lobby. In other words, as with economic policy, a major part of the U.S. problem in this area is the result of domestic factors.

Thus, greater leadership is required by America, both to address its own environmental footprint and to help change the economics of doing so elsewhere in the world. In particular, Washington still needs to develop a coherent set of priorities in this area, given China's size and the Chinese government's low capacity for addressing this problem. One possible approach is to focus on strengthening the legal system with regard to environmental protection or the promotion of energy efficiency in China. However, to produce any genuine results, as in so many other areas, the United States must first exhibit overall leadership on environmental issues, as indicated in chapter 7.

With regard to the prevention, detection, and treatment of pandemic diseases, America and other nations together have arguably achieved greater policy successes in encouraging China's increasing transparency and overall conformance with international norms. Much more can be done, but many of the solutions reside within China, requiring improvements in the center–local relationship and more effective efforts to overcome the general penchant of governments at whatever level to avoid publishing facts that could create social disorder. The problem also stems from the preferences of local governments to stress economic gain over public health and the overall relatively poor state of the public health infrastructure and finance system in many parts of the country.

Human Rights and Democracy

As the discussion of norms above indicates, U.S. policy has arguably contributed to Beijing's participation in many of the major international human rights organizations and initiatives. Washington has also perhaps been modestly successful in encouraging Beijing's greater willingness to support international efforts to discourage or oppose gross human rights abuses in various countries of concern around the world, such as Sudan. Moreover, Washington has contributed to advances in Chinese laws that provide greater legal protection of individual rights.

However, in more concrete terms, and especially regarding Chinese domestic human rights activities, the policy arena of human rights and democracy has witnessed the least success for U.S. policymakers. U.S. policy has been sporadic and limited in providing funds, energy, and attention to human rights, for a variety of reasons noted in chapter 8. At the same time, few observers of this policy arena's development in China believe that U.S. policies toward China will prove decisive in promoting positive change in Chinese behavior. Washington will likely see few benefits resulting from public, top-down efforts to pressure or cajole Beijing in this area, especially if this pressure is applied independently of other nations. In fact, such an approach could more likely produce adverse consequences, given the fact that Chinese elites are likely to become more resistant to such obvious attempts to apply outside pressure as their power and confidence grow in dealing with the United States and other major nations.

U.S. policies should continue to encourage improvements in Chinese human rights policies and practices, both at home and abroad, by assisting efforts to promote structural prerequisites for the creation of a more humane and just society. In particular, Washington should increase its efforts to encourage Beijing to respect international norms for human rights, including not only political liberty and religious freedom but also labor and economic rights already contained in PRC laws. As part of this undertaking, Washington should provide greater public support and allocate increased funding for U.S. and international organizations that promote legal reform, institutional capacity, minority rights, and other civil society goals in China. It should also promote Chinese labor standards through greater support for social responsibility programs among U.S. businesses operating in China. In addition, Washington should continue to utilize a low-key but persistent approach to improve Chinese policies toward human rights violations in areas where Beijing has a considerable presence, such as Sudan and Burma. China's ability and willingness to bring about significant change in such countries will remain limited. However, again, America will obviously be most effective if it can coordinate its policy efforts with the international community. Moreover, Washington should deepen its dialogue with Beijing and other international donors on the issues of development assistance, poverty alleviation programs, lending by the multilateral development banks, and debt sustainability in Africa and other developing countries.[45]

That said, transforming China into a *democracy* should not be a strategic objective of the United States. As indicated in chapter 8, some observers have argued that this goal has constituted the underlying rationale for America's cooperative engagement with China since the 1970s and that the alleged failure to achieve it, or even to mark any notable progress, constitutes a refutation of the overall engagement approach. In its place, many proponents of this view argue for a more "realist"-oriented strategy of pressure, counterbalancing, and, if necessary, containment to either limit Chinese growth or simply compel more acceptable Chinese behavior. In truth, although the democratization of China has at times been presented by U.S. officials as a public rationale for the pursuit of cooperative policies with an authoritarian China, Washington does not need to employ such an argument to justify engaging Beijing, unless one assumes that an authoritarian China will inevitably seek to undermine America's most vital interests in Asia and beyond, or that the U.S. public will reject any other rationale for U.S. policy. As this study argues, there is no conclusive evidence indicating that China is fated to undermine America's most vital interests, and Americans apparently do not support engaging China solely or primarily in order to democratize it.

Equally important, as stated above, the United States will likely find it virtually impossible to manage many of the most critical policy challenges of the twenty-first century and to avoid a destabilizing security competition with China without cooperatively engaging China, regardless of the extent to which it democratizes. In other words, the key strategic objective of the United States toward China—to facilitate China's integration into the international system as a supportive and productive nation—does not require the destruction or fundamental transformation of the Chinese Communist Party's authoritarian regime.

TACTICS AND APPROACHES

Achieving further advances and resolving problems in all the policy arenas reviewed above will also depend to a significant degree on the ability of the U.S. leadership to reinforce or, in some cases, correct a range of structural and procedural features of the U.S. policymaking process, along with various tactical approaches employed in America's relations with China.

As discussed in chapter 9, the U.S. policymaking process toward China more and more requires the creation and maintenance of a strong central authority to provide coordination, control, and strategic direction over an increasingly complex, fragmented, and often competitive or contentious organizational structure. Such an authority should most logically reside within the executive branch in the National Security Council (NSC), under the close supervision of the president. In other words, the president must select highly capable, active individuals as NSC adviser and Asia director, each with a keen ability to coordinate and guide the U.S. organizational structure with regard to China, and remain closely engaged with such individuals in directing China policy. In addition, effective coordination and control over the disparate elements of the U.S. policymaking process also require the maintenance of cooperative personal relationships among the national security adviser and the leaders of the major agencies involved in China policy, ranging from the Department of State and the Department of Defense to the Department of the Treasury and the Office of the U.S. Trade Representative.

Equally important, such qualities, along with the ability to conduct frank dialogues, must also be present in relations between the executive branch and Congress. As noted in chapter 9, the relationship between these two entities remains problematic in many areas with regard to China. One way the NSC should work to address this problem is to hold *regular* off-the-record meetings on China policy with members of Congress and/or congressional staff members to facilitate trust building and information sharing. Such off-the-record briefings could also be conducted with key members of the media to help communicate the rationale for China policy and clear up misperceptions that might otherwise take on a life of their own.

Again, the president's role is critical. He or she must ensure that the executive branch's agency heads can work together effectively and are willing to receive guidance and coordination from the NSC. It is particularly important that the president and other senior officials actively engage in China policymaking at a high level on important issues, including paying regular bilateral visits to countries in the Asia-Pacific region and attending key Asian multilateral summits.

Finally, as chapter 9 clearly indicates, in engaging China in all the policy arenas analyzed in this study, U.S. policymakers should incorporate the key lessons and experiences of the past, including these needs:

- To understand China's national interests and to identify—to the extent possible—where these interests might be subject to influence by the United States or other global powers.
- To engage in direct and sustained dialogue with Chinese civilian and military officials, and in the process develop and sustain long-standing personal relationships with Chinese officials.
- To judiciously balance both positive and negative inducements vis-à-vis China through a keen understanding of both the limits and benefits of sanctions and other pressures and the leverage that can result from utilizing differences in interests and approaches within the Chinese bureaucracy.
- To recognize the critical importance of protocol, respect, and "face" in interactions with Chinese officials, and to utilize such factors to build greater trust and understanding in specific policy areas.[46]

Although these needs are largely well known to many experienced China diplomats and officials, they should nevertheless be disseminated more widely and kept firmly in mind by future policymakers and politicians. More broadly, these observations and most of the other insights provided by the vast majority of current and former U.S. officials interviewed for this study clearly indicate that effective diplomacy, founded on a deep understanding of Chinese interests and sensibilities and combined with a more far-sighted, strategic reassessment of the strengths and limits of U.S. power and influence in Asia over the current decade and beyond, can contribute enormously to blunting the sharpest edges of Sino-U.S. security competition. Such diplomacy can facilitate a process of mutual understanding and accommodation based on the notion that national interests and specific policy approaches in both countries are subject to significant adjustment over time and under changing circumstances.

FINAL THOUGHTS

America's leaders face a growing array of increasingly challenging issues as they attempt to protect and advance the nation's interests in the new century. In this overall effort—and particularly in America's engagement with a rising China—success will increasingly require willingness to significantly reduce strategic distrust through greater dialogue, to create new types of interstate relationships and multilateral forums, and to resolve major domestic economic problems. This will require thinking in more farsighted ways, making hard choices, and sometimes even abandoning long-standing policy beliefs and assumptions. None of this is beyond the grasp of U.S. leaders. But their success will almost certainly depend on recognizing that, in dealing with China in the twenty-first century, the status quo will not suffice.

APPENDIX
INTERVIEW SUBJECTS

▼

Over roughly a two year period, from early 2008 to early 2010, over fifty current and former American officials were interviewed to obtain first-hand accounts of the U.S. policy process and aspects of U.S. strategy and tactics toward China. Although the interviews were conducted on a "non-attribution" basis, most subjects agreed to have their names listed below. A small number of subjects insisted on anonymity.[1]

Richard Armitage: Deputy secretary of state (2001–2005); assistant secretary of defense for international security affairs (1983–1989)

Jeffrey Bader: Senior director for Asian affairs, National Security Council (2009–2011); assistant U.S. trade representative for China affairs (2001–2002); director of Asian affairs, National Security Council (1997–1999)

---

[1] Many of these officials also have non-government experience that is relevant to the U.S. policymaking process, China, and Asia more broadly; however, this list only mentions official government positions. Moreover, the listing of positions is not necessarily comprehensive; rather, it only includes select positions that are representative of the interviewees' experiences and are of greatest relevance to U.S. policy toward China.

Douglas Bereuter:	Member of the U.S. House of Representatives (R-NE) (1979–2004)
Dennis Blair:	Commander, U.S. Pacific Command (1999–2002); director of national intelligence (2009–2010)
Daniel Blumenthal:	Commissioner (2006-present) and vice chairman (2007), U.S.-China Economic and Security Review Commission; senior country director for China, Taiwan, Hong Kong, and Mongolia, country director for China and Taiwan, Office for International Security Affairs, Office of the Secretary of Defense (2002–2004)
Richard Bush:	Chairman, American Institute in Taiwan (1997–2002); national intelligence officer for East Asia (1995–1997); director for minority liaison, U.S. House Committee on International Relations (1995); director for committee liaison, U.S. House Committee on Foreign Affairs (1994).
Kurt Campbell:	Assistant secretary of state for East Asian and Pacific Affairs (2009-present); deputy assistant secretary of defense for Asia and the Pacific (1995–2000)
Thomas Christensen:	Deputy assistant secretary of state for East Asian and Pacific affairs with responsibility for relations with China, Taiwan, and Mongolia (2006–2008)
Christopher Clarke:	China analyst and chief of the China division in the Bureau of Intelligence and Research at the U.S. Department of State (1984–2009)
Evan Feigenbaum:	Deputy assistant secretary of state for South Asia (2007–2009); deputy assistant secretary of state for Central Asia (2006–2007); member of the secretary of state's policy planning staff for East Asia and the Pacific (2001–2006)
David Finkelstein:	Director of Asian Studies (J-8) for the chairman of the Joint Staff (1997–1998); assistant defense intelligence officer for East Asia and the Pacific (1993–1997); U.S. Army China foreign area officer (1984–1988)
Chas W. Freeman, Jr:	Assistant secretary of defense, international security affairs (1993–1994); deputy chief of mission at the U.S. Embassy in China (1981–1984; director, Chinese and Mongolian affairs, U.S. Department of State (1979–1981)

James Green:	State Department policy planning staff for East Asia; China Desk, U.S. Department of State (2002–2003); China director, National Security Council
Michael Green:	Senior director for Asian affairs at the National Security Council (2004–2005), director of Asian affairs on the National Security Council with responsibility for Japan, Korea, and Australia/New Zealand (2001–2004)
Paul Heer:	National intelligence officer for East Asia (2007-present); member of the Senior Analytic Service in the Directorate of Intelligence at the Central Intelligence Agency (2000–present)
Richard Holbrooke:	Special representative for Afghanistan and Pakistan (2009–2010); assistant secretary of state for East Asian and Pacific affairs (1977–1981)
Frank Jannuzi:	Policy director, East Asia and Pacific Affairs, Senate Foreign Relations Committee (1997–present); East Asia analyst, Bureau of Intelligence and Research, U.S. Department of State (1989–1997)
Roy Kamphausen:	Country director for China-Taiwan-Mongolia affairs, Office of the Secretary of Defense (2003–2004); China branch chief in the Directorate for Strategic Plans and Policy (J-5) (2001–2003); intelligence analyst, the Joint Staff (1996–1997)
James Kelly:	Assistant secretary of state for East Asian and Pacific Affairs (2001–2005); special assistant for National Security Affairs and senior director for Asian Affairs, National Security Council (1986–1989)
Anthony Lake:	National security adviser (1993–1997); director of policy planning, U.S. Department of State (1977–1981); special assistant to the national security adviser (1969–1970)
Kenneth Lieberthal:	Special assistant to the president for national security affairs and senior director for Asian affairs, National Security Council (1998–2000)
James Lilley:	Assistant secretary of defense for international security affairs (1991–1993); U.S. ambassador to China (1989–1991); U.S. ambassador to South Korea (1986–1989); deputy assistant secretary of state for East Asian affairs (1985)

Thomas Mahnken:	Deputy assistant secretary of defense for policy planning, Office of the Secretary of Defense (2006–2009)
Michael McDevitt:	Director for strategy, war plans, and policy (J-5) for the commander-in-chief, Pacific Command (1993–1995); director, East Asia Policy, Office of the Secretary of Defense (1990–1992)
Evan Medeiros:	Director for Asian Affairs, National Security Council (2009–present)
Frank Miller:	Defense intelligence officer for East Asia, Defense Intelligence Agency (2010–present); director, Northeast Asia Division, Joint Staff Strategic Plans and Policy Directorate (J-5) (2007–2010); army attaché, U.S. Embassy in Beijing, China (2003–2006)
Joseph Nye:	Assistant secretary of defense for International Security Affairs (1994–1995); chairman of the National Intelligence Council (1993–1994)
Douglas Paal:	Director of the American Institute in Taiwan (2002–2006); senior director of Asian affairs and director of Asian affairs, National Security Council (1986–1993)
Torkel Patterson:	Senior director of Asian affairs, National Security Council (2001–2002); director of Asian affairs, National Security Council (1991–1993); senior country director for Japan in the Office of the Assistant Secretary of Defence (1988–1993)
William Pendley:	Deputy assistant secretary of defense for East Asia and Pacific Affairs (1992–1993); acting assistant secretary of defense for International Security Affairs (1993)
Joseph Prueher:	U.S. ambassador to China (1999–2001); commander, United States Pacific Command (1996–1999)
James Przystup:	Director for regional security strategies on the policy planning staff, Office of the Secretary of Defense (1991–1993); policy planning staff, U.S. Department of State (1987–1991); staff of the U.S. House of Representatives Subcommittee on Asian and Pacific Affairs (1977–1981)
Alan Romberg:	Principal deputy director of policy planning, U.S. Department of State (1994–1998), deputy spokesman, U.S. Department of State (1981–1985); director of the Office of Japanese affairs (1978–1980) and member

	of the policy planning staff for East Asia, U.S. Department of State (1977–1978)
J. Stapleton Roy:	U.S. ambassador to China (1991–1995); assistant secretary of state for intelligence and research (1999–2000); U.S. ambassador to Indonesia (1996–1999)
James Sasser:	U.S. ambassador to China (1995–1999); U.S. senator (D-TN) (1977–1995)
Stephen Schlaikjer:	Senior adviser to the U.S.-China Economic and Security Review Commission (2002–2004); foreign policy adviser to the chief of naval operations (2000–2002); director, Office of Chinese and Mongolian Affairs, U.S. Department of State (1998–2000)
David Sedney:	Deputy assistant secretary of defense for Afghanistan, Pakistan, and Central Asia (2009–present); deputy assistant secretary of defense for East Asia (2007–2009); deputy chief of mission, U.S. Embassy in Beijing (2004–2007); deputy director, Office of Chinese and Mongolian affairs, U.S. Department of State (1999–2001)
James Shinn:	Assistant secretary of defense for Asian and Pacific security affairs (2006–2008); national intelligence officer for East Asia (2004–2006)
Randall Schriver:	Deputy assistant secretary of state for East Asian and Pacific affairs (2003–2005); chief of staff and senior policy adviser to Deputy Secretary of State Richard Armitage (2001–2002); senior country director for the PRC, Taiwan, and Mongolia in the Office of the Secretary of Defense (1997–1998)
Richard Solomon:	Assistant secretary of state for East Asian and Pacific affairs (1989–1992); director of policy planning, U.S. Department of State (1986–1989)
James Steinberg:	Deputy secretary of state (2009–2011); deputy national security adviser (1996–2001); director of policy planning, U.S. Department of State (1994–1996)
Robert Sutter:	National intelligence officer for East Asia and the Pacific, U.S. National Intelligence Council (1999–2001); senior specialist and director, Foreign Affairs and National Defense Division, Congressional

Research Service, Library of Congress (1988–1999); China division director, Bureau of Intelligence and Research, U.S. Department of State (1997–1998)

Dennis Wilder: Senior director for East Asian Affairs, National Security Council (2005–2009); chief of China analytic studies in the Office of East Asian and Pacific Affairs, Directorate of Intelligence, Central Intelligence Agency (1995–2005)

Stephen Yates: Deputy assistant to the vice president for national security affairs (2001–2005)

Philip Zelikow: Counselor, U.S. Department of State (2005–2007); executive director, 9/11 Commission (2002–2004); National Security Council staff (1989–1991)

NOTES

INTRODUCTION

1. For some of the general works on the relationship and (in some cases) U.S. policy during the 1970s, 1980s, and 1990s, see Robert L. Suettinger, *Beyond Tiananmen: The Politics of U.S.-China Relations 1989–2000* (Washington, D.C.: Brookings Institution Press, 2003); David Lampton, *Same Bed, Different Dreams: Managing U.S.-China Relations, 1989–2000* (Berkeley, Calif.: University of California Press, 2001); Elizabeth Economy and Michel Oksenberg, eds., *China Joins the World: Progress and Prospects* (New York: Council on Foreign Relations Press, 1999); Robert S. Ross, *After the Cold War: Domestic Factors and U.S.-China Relations* (Armonk, N.Y.: M. E. Sharpe, 1998); Wang Jisi, "The Role of the United States as a Global and Pacific Power: A View from China," *Pacific Review*, vol. 10, no. 1 (1997): 1–18; Ezra F. Vogel, ed., *Living with China: U.S.-China Relations in the Twenty-first Century* (New York: W. W. Norton, 1997); James Shinn, ed., *Weaving the Net: Conditional Engagement With China* (New York: Council on Foreign Relations, 1996); Robert S. Ross, *Negotiating Cooperation: The United States and China, 1969–1989* (Stanford, Calif.: Stanford University Press, 1995); David M. Lampton and Alfred Wilhelm, eds., *United States and China: Relations at a Crossroads* (Lanham, Md.: University Press of America, 1995); Yoichi Funabashi, Michel Oksenberg, and Heinrich Weiss, *An Emerging China in a World of Interdependence* (New York: Trilateral Commission, 1994); A. Doak Barnett, *U.S.-China Relations: Time for a New Beginning—Again*, pamphlet based on James and Margaret Loe Memorial Lecture (Washington, D.C.: Johns Hopkins University, School for Advanced International Studies, 1994); and Harry Harding, *A Fragile Relationship: The U.S. and China Since 1972* (New Haven, Conn.: Yale University Press, 1984).

For studies that specifically examine China's adherence to international norms, see Ann Kent, *Beyond Compliance: China, International Organizations, and Global Security*, East-West Center Studies in Asian Security (Stanford, Calif.: Stanford University Press, 2007); Alastair Iain Johnston, "Is China a Status Quo Power?" *International Security*, vol. 27, no. 4 (Spring 2003): 5–56; and Ann Kent, "China's International Socialization: The Role of International Organization," *Global Governance*, vol. 8, no. 3 (July-Sept 2002): 343–64.

For examinations of the security aspects of bilateral relations, see Shirley Kan, *China and Proliferation of Weapons of Mass Destruction and Missiles: Policy Issues*, Congressional Research Service Report RL31555 (Washington, D.C.: Library of Congress, January 31, 2006); Evan Medeiros, *Reluctant Restraint: The Evolution of China's Nonproliferation Policies and Practices, 1980–2000* (Stanford, Calif.: Stanford University Press, 2007); Steven M. Goldstein and Randall Schriver, "An Uncertain Relationship: The United States, Taiwan and the Taiwan Relations Act," in *Taiwan in the Twentieth Century*, edited by Richard Louis Edmonds and Steven Goldstein (Cambridge: Cambridge University Press, 2001); Thomas J. Christensen, *New Challenges and Opportunities in the Taiwan Strait: Defining America's Role* (New York: National Committee on U.S.-China Relations, November 2003); Alan D. Romberg, *Rein In at the Brink of the Precipice: American Policy Toward Taiwan and U.S.-PRC Relations* (Washington, D.C.: The Henry L. Stimson Center, 2003); Michael D. Swaine and Ashley J. Tellis, *Interpreting China's Grand Strategy: Past, Present, and Future* (Santa Monica, Calif.: RAND Corporation, 2000); David Shlapak, David Orletsky, and Barry Wilson, *Dire Strait? Military Aspects of the China-Taiwan Confrontation and Options for US Policy* (Santa Monica, Calif.: RAND Corporation, 2000); Thomas J. Christensen, "China, the U.S.-Japan Alliance, and the Security Dilemma in East Asia," *International Security*, vol. 23, no. 4 (Spring 1999): 49–80; John W. Garver, *Face Off: China, the United States, and Taiwan's Democratization* (Seattle, Wash.: University of Washington, 1997); Andrew J. Nathan and Robert J. Ross, *The Great Wall and the Empty Fortress: China's Search for Security* (New York: W. W. Norton, 1997); Martin L. Lasater, *The Taiwan Issue in Sino-American Strategic Relations* (Boulder, Colo.: Westview Press, 1984); A. Doak Barnett, *U.S. Arms Sales: The China-Taiwan Tangle* (Washington, D.C.: Brookings Institution Press, 1982).

For general studies of the economic issues in the Sino-U.S. relationship, see Chad P. Bown, "U.S.-China Trade Conflicts and the Future of the WTO," *Fletcher Forum of World Affairs*, vol. 33, no. 1 (Winter/Spring 2009): 27–48; Wayne Morrison, *China-U.S. Trade Issues*, Congressional Research Service Issue Brief IB91121 (Washington, D.C.: Library of Congress, May 15, 2006); Gary Clyde Hufbauer, Yee Wong, and Ketki Sheth, *U.S.-China Trade Disputes: Rising Tide, Rising Stakes* (Washington, D.C.: Institute for International Economics, 2006); Dale Copeland, "Economic Interdependence and the Future of U.S.-China Relations," in *International Relations Theory and the Asia-Pacific*, edited by G. John Ikenberry and Michael Mastundono (New York: Columbia University Press, 2003), 323–52; Nicholas Lardy, *Integrating China Into the Global Economy* (Washington, D.C.: Brookings Institution Press, 2002); Council on Foreign Relations, *Beginning the Journey: China, the United States, and the WTO*, Robert D. Hormats, Chair, Elizabeth Economy and Kevin Nealer, Project Directors (New York: Council on Foreign Relations Press, 2001); K. C. Fung and Lawrence J. Lau, *The China-United States Bilateral Trade Balance: How Big Is It Really?* (Stanford, Calif.: Asia/Pacific Research Center, 1996); James R. Lilley and Wendell L. Willkie II, eds., *Beyond MFN: Trade with China and American Interests* (Washington, D.C.: American Enterprise Institute, 1994); Nicholas Lardy, *Foreign Trade and Economic Reform in China* (New York: Cambridge University Press, 1992); Eugene Lawson, ed., *U.S.-China Trade: Problems and Prospects* (New

York: Praeger, 1988); and A. Doak Barnett, *China's Economy in Global Perspective* (Washington, D.C.: Brookings Institution Press, 1981).

For studies of the human rights dimension in Sino-American relations, see Michael A. Santoro, *Profits and Principles: Global Capitalism and Human Rights in China* (Ithaca, N.Y.: Cornell University Press, 2000); Rosemary Foot, *Rights Beyond Borders: The Global Community and the Struggle Over Human Rights in China* (Oxford; New York: Oxford University Press, 2000); Ann Kent, *China, the United Nations, and Human Rights* (Philadelphia, Pa.: University of Pennsylvania Press, 1999); Paul J. Smith, ed., *Human Smuggling: Chinese Migrant Trafficking and the Challenge to America's Immigration Tradition* (Washington, D.C.: Center for Strategic and International Studies, 1997); Melvyn C. Goldstein, *The Snow Lion and the Dragon: Tibet, China and the Dalai Lama* (Berkeley, Calif.: University of California Press, 1997); Tibet Information Network, Human Rights Watch/Asia, *Cutting Off the Serpent's Head: Tightening Control in Tibet, 1994–1995* (New York: Human Rights Watch, 1996); and R. Randle Edwards, Louis Henkin, Andrew J. Nathan, *Human Rights in Contemporary China* (New York: Columbia University Press, 1986).

2. China's merchandise trade as a share of GDP decreased to 45 percent in 2009, primarily as a result of contractions in trade during the global financial crisis. This reflected the worldwide decrease in merchandise trade as a proportion of world GDP from 53 percent in 2008 to 41 percent in 2009. World Development Indicators, World Bank, data.worldbank.org/indicator.

3. Ding Ying, "FTA Driving ASEAN Growth," *Beijing Review*, no. 4, January 22, 2011, www.bjreview.com.cn/world/txt/2011-01/23/content_327879.htm; International Monetary Fund Direction of Trade Statistics, www2.imfstatistics.org/DOT.

4. U.S. Energy Information Association, International Energy Statistics, http://tonto.eia.doe.gov.

5. Similar to merchandise trade, FDI flows plummeted worldwide in 2009 as a result of the financial crisis, and China was no exception as its FDI inflows dropped to $78 billion, or 7 percent of global FDI flows. World Development Indicators, World Bank, data.worldbank.org/indicator.

6. International Monetary Fund, www.imf.org/external/data.htm.

7. U.S. Census Bureau, www.census.gov/foreign-trade; U.S. International Trade Administration, trade.gov.

8. See Jagdish Bhagwati, *In Defense of Globalization* (New York: Oxford University Press, 2004); Joseph E. Stiglitz, *Globalization and Its Discontents* (New York: W. W. Norton & Company, 2003); Martin Wolf, *Why Globalization Works* (New Haven, Conn.: Yale University Press, 2005); Benjamin J. Cohen, "Containing Backlash: Foreign Economic Policy in an Age of Globalization," in *Eagle Rules?: Foreign Policy and American Primacy in the Twenty-First Century*, edited by Robert J. Lieber (Princeton, N.J.: Princeton Hall, 2002), 299–323.

Richard L. Kugler and Ellen L. Frost, eds., *The Global Century: Globalization and National Security* (Washington, D.C.: National Defense University Press, 2001); Banning Garrett, "U.S.-China Relations in the Era of Globalization and Terror: A Framework for Analysis," *Journal of Contemporary China*, vol. 15 no. 48 (August 2006): 389–415.

9. See Robert W. McChesney, *Communication Revolution: Critical Junctures and the Future of Media* (New York, NY: The New Press, 2007); John Micklethwait and Adrian Wooldridge, *A Future Perfect: The Challenge and Promise of Globalization* (Toronto, Canada: Random House Trade, 2003); Moisés Naím, "The Five Wars of Globalization," *Foreign Policy*, (Jan/Feb 2003): 36–41; Charles A. Kupchan, *The End of an American Era: U.S. Foreign Policy and the Geopolitics*

of the Twenty-First Century (New York: Alfred A. Knopf, 2002); Monroe E. Price, *Media and Sovereignty: the Global Information Revolution and its Challenge to State Power* (Cambridge, Mass.: MIT Press, 2002); Frank Webster, *Culture and Politics in the Information Age: A New Politics?* (New York: Routledge, 2001); and David J. Rothkopf, "Foreign Policy in the Information Age," in *The Global Century: Globalization and National Security*, edited by Richard L. Kugler and Ellen L. Frost (Washington, D.C.: National Defense University Press, 2001).

10. See Ian Goldin, *Globalization for Development: Trade, Finance, Aid, Migration, and Policy* (New York: Palgrave Macmillan, 2007); Ichiro Kawachi and Sarah Wamala, eds., *Globalization and Health* (New York: Oxford University Press, 2006); Moisés Naím, "The Five Wars of Globalization," *Foreign Policy* (January/February 2003): 36–41; Paul Kennedy, "Global Challenges at the Beginning of the Twenty-First Century," in *Global Trends and Global Governance*, edited by Paul Kennedy, Dirk Messner, and Franz Nuscheler (London: Pluto Press, 2002), "Globalization and Disease," *NPR*, March 2001, www.npr.org/programs/atc/features/2001/mar/010309.disease.html; James Mittelman, *The Globalization Syndrome: Transformation and Resistance* (Princeton, N.J.: Princeton University Press, 2000); and "A World in Motion: The Global Movement of People, Products, Pathogens, and Power," in *The Impact of Globalization on Infectious Disease Emergence and Control: Exploring the Consequences and Opportunities*, edited by Stacey Knobler, Adel Mahmoud, Stanley Lemon, and Leslie Pray (Washington, D.C.: National Academies Press, 2006), 21–48.

11. See Richard Haass, "Good Policies for Great Countries," Project Syndicate, May 18, 2010, www.projectsyndicate.org/commentary/haass31/English; Eben Kaplan, "Terrorists and the Internet," *Council on Foreign Relations*, January 8, 2009, www.cfr.org/publication/10005/terrorists_and_the_internet.html; Jaideep Saikia and Ekaterina Stepanova, eds., *Terrorism: Patterns of Internationalization* (Thousand Oaks, Calif.: SAGE, 2009); Bob Graham and Jim Talent, eds., *World at Risk: The Report of the Commission on the Prevention of WMD Proliferation and Terrorism* (New York: Vintage Books, 2008); Charles D. Ferguson, William C. Potter, Amy Sands, Leonard S. Spector, and Fred L. Wehling, eds., *Four Faces of Nuclear Terrorism* (New York: Routledge, 2005); and Richard L. Kugler and Ellen L. Frost, eds., *The Global Century: Globalization and National Security* (Washington, D.C.: National Defense University Press, 2001).

12. *Climatic Cataclysm: The Foreign Policy and National Security Implications of Climate Change*, edited by Kurt M. Campbell (Washington, D.C.: Brookings Institution Press, 2008); Ernesto Zedillo, *Global Warming: Looking Beyond Kyoto* (Washington, D.C.: Brookings Institution Press, 2008); "Booming nations 'threaten earth,'" *BBC News*, January 12, 2006, http://news.bbc.co.uk/2/hi/science/nature/4604556.stm; Eugene Linden, *The Winds of Change: Climate, Weather, and the Destruction of Civilizations* (New York: Simon and Schuster, 2006); Andrew E. Dessler and Edward A. Parson, *The Science and Politics of Global Climate Change: A Guide to the Debate* (New York: Cambridge University Press, 2006); Emma Duncan, "A Survey of Climate Change: The Heat Is On," *Economist*, September 7, 2006, www.economist.com/node/7852924; Tim Flannery, *The Weather Makers: How Man is Changing the Climate and What it Means for Life on Earth* (New York: Atlantic Monthly Press, 2006); Henry N. Pollack, *Uncertain Science . . . Uncertain World* (New York: Cambridge University Press, 2003); and Robert Jackson, *The Earth Remains Forever: Generations at a Crossroads* (Austin, Tex.: University of Texas Press, 2002).

13. For various major assessments of the new changes affecting China and the Sino-U.S. relationship in the late nineties and early years of the new century, see Robert Sutter, *U.S.-Chinese Relations: Perilous Past, Pragmatic Present* (Lanham, Md.: Rowman and Littlefield, 2010); David Shambaugh, "A New China Requires a New US Strategy," *Current*

History (September 2010): 219–26; David Lampton, "Power Constrained: Sources of
Mutual Strategic Suspicion in U.S.-China Relations," NBR Analysis 93rd Issue (Seattle,
Wash.: National Bureau of Asian Research, June 2010), www.nbr.org/publications/
analysis/pdf/2010_U.S._China.pdf; Robert Ross and Zhu Feng, eds., *China's Ascent: Power,
Security, and the Future of International Politics* (Ithaca, N.Y.: Cornell University Press,
2008); Zhao Suisheng, ed., *China-U.S. Relations Transformed: Perspectives and Strategic
Interactions* (New York: Routledge, 2008); Bates Gill, *Rising Star: China's New Security
Diplomacy* (Washington, D.C.: Brookings Institution Press, 2007); Michael Mastanduno,
"Rivals or Partners?: Globalization and U.S. China Relations," *Harvard International
Review*, vol. 39, no. 3 (Fall 2007): 42–46; Council on Foreign Relations, *U.S.-China
Relations: An Affirmative Agenda, Responsible Course*, Independent Task Force Report
no. 59, Carla A. Hills and Dennis C. Blair, Chairs, Frank Sampson Jannuzi, Project Director
(New York: Council on Foreign Relations, 2007); Alastair Iain Johnston and Robert S. Ross,
eds., *New Directions in the Study of China's Foreign Policy* (Stanford, Calif.: Stanford University
Press, 2006); Robert Sutter, *China's Rise: Implications for U.S. Leadership in Asia* (Washington,
D.C.: East-West Center, 2006); David Shambaugh, ed., *Power Shift: China and Asia's New
Dynamics* (Berkeley, Calif.: University of California Press, 2005); Aaron Friedberg, "The
Future of U.S.-China Relations: Is Conflict Inevitable?" *International Security*, vol. 30, no. 2
(2005): 7–45; Wang Jisi, "China's Search for Stability With America," *Foreign Affairs*, vol. 84,
no. 5 (September-October 2005): 39–48; Thomas J. Christensen, "Posing Problems Without
Catching Up: China's Rise and Challenges for U.S. Security Policy," *International Security*,
vol. 25 no. 4 (spring 2001): 5–40; Robert G. Sutter, *Chinese Policy Priorities and Their
Implications for the United States* (Lanham, Md.: Rowman and Littlefield, 2000); Zalmay M.
Khalilzad, et al., *The United States and a Rising China: Strategic and Military Implications* (Santa
Monica, Calif.: RAND Corporation, 1999); Bruce Cummings, *Parallax Visions: Making Sense of
American-East Asian Relations on the Eve of the Twenty-First Century* (Raleigh-Durham, N.C.:
Duke University Press, 1999); Robert G. Sutter, *U.S. Policy Toward China: An Introduction to
the Role of Interest Groups* (Lanham, Md.: Rowman and Littlefield, 1998); and Yan Xuetong,
Wang Zaibang, Li Zhongcheng, and Hou Roushi, *Zhongguojueqi: Guojihuanjingpinggu*
[International Environment for China's Rise] (Tianjin: Renmin Chubanshe, 1998).

14. Some observers challenge such an assertion, arguing that an unstable, conflicted
Chinese leadership would resort to highly aggressive external actions to unify the
country or defeat domestic political challengers, thus posing major challenges for
U.S. policy. Yet quantitative research has demonstrated no systematic relationship
between past episodes of domestic economic-induced unrest in China and involvement
in militarized interstate disputes. Historically, as Iain Johnston and other specialists
on China's external use of force have observed, the Chinese leadership has mobilized
society in response to external challenges that questioned their domestic credibility
as leaders, not in response to domestic discontent from which attention needed to be
deflected. In fact, with regard to such sensitive issues as territorial disputes, in the past,
regime insecurity at home most often caused China to make major concessions abroad.
See M. Taylor Fravel, "International Relations Theory and China's Rise: Assessing
China's Potential for Territorial Expansion," *International Studies Review*, vol. 12, no. 4
(December 2010): 505–32; M. Taylor Fravel, *Strong Borders, Secure Nation* (Princeton,
N.J.: Princeton University Press, 2008); and Alastair Iain Johnston, "China's Militarized
Interstate Dispute Behavior, 1949–1992: A First Cut at the Data," *China Quarterly*, no. 153
(March 1998): 1–30.

CHAPTER 1

1. For a discussion of overall U.S. strategic objectives, see Christopher P. Twomey, "Missing Strategic Opportunity in U.S. China Policy Since 9/11," *Asian Survey*, vol. 47, no. 4 (July–August 2007). Also see Barry R. Posen, "Command of the Commons: The Military Foundation of U.S. Hegemony," *International Security*, vol. 28, no. 1 (Summer 2003). As Posen states, "Today, there is little dispute within the U.S. foreign policy elite about the fact of great U.S. power, or the wisdom of an essentially hegemonic foreign policy." See Andrew J. Bacevich, *The Limits of Power: The End of American Exceptionalism* (New York: Metropolitan Books, 2008), 40–41; and William C. Wohlforth, "The Stability of a Unipolar World," *International Security*, vol. 24, no. 1 (Summer 1999): 5–41.

2. For an affirmation of this perspective, see Robert M. Gates, "America's Security Role in the Asia-Pacific," remarks delivered at the Eighth International Institute for Strategic Studies Asia Security Summit, Shangri-La Dialogue, Singapore, May 30, 2009, www.iiss.org/conferences/the-shangri-la-dialogue/shangri-la-dialogue-2009/plenary-session-speeches-2009/first-plenary-session/dr-robert-gates. Defense Secretary Gates stated: "It is hard to avoid the conclusion that few, if any, of the world's problems can be solved without the support and ideas of the nations of the Pacific Rim."

3. As Derek Mitchell states, "with the U.S. acting as security guarantor, regional states have been able to channel their resources into confidence-building and internal development rather than arms races and competing blocs." See Derek Mitchell, "Reduce, Maintain, Enhance: U.S. Force Structure Changes in the Asia-Pacific Region," in *America's Role in Asia: Asian and American Views*, Michael Armacost, J. Stapleton Roy, Han Sung-Joo, Tommy Koh, C. Raja Mohan, project chairs (San Francisco: Asia Foundation, 2008), 159.

4. For a recent statement by a senior U.S. official of many of these interests, see Secretary of Defense Robert M. Gates, remarks at ASEAN Defense Ministers Meeting Plus, October 12, 2010, U.S. Department of Defense news transcript, www.defense.gov/Transcripts/Transcript.aspx?TranscriptID=4700.

5. For example, see Secretary of Defense Robert M. Gates, remarks at Keio University, Tokyo, January 14, 2011, www.globalsecurity.org/military/library/news/2011/01/mil-110114-dod02.htm.

6. As Derek Mitchell states: "For decades, it has been axiomatic among American and most East Asian strategists that the U.S. military presence in East Asia has served an essential role in preserving regional stability." Mitchell, "Reduce, Maintain, Enhance," 159. That such presence essentially equates to military predominance in specific naval and air capabilities was largely confirmed by the current and former senior officials whom the author interviewed for this study. It is also reflected in the periodic reports and strategy statements issued by the Department of Defense and the Pacific Command. Also see Donna Miles, "Keating Passes PACOM Torch to Willard," American Forces Press Service, October 19, 2009, www.pacom.mil/web/Site_Pages/Media/News%20200910/20091019-ChangeOfCommand1.shtml; "U.S. Military Presence in Asia Appreciated, Says Pacific Commander," remarks by Admiral Keating at East West Center Policy Seminar, July 22, 2009, www.eastwestcenter.org/news-center/east-west-wire/us-military-presence-in-asia-appreciated-says-pacific-commander; Ashley J. Tellis, "Preserving Hegemony: The Strategic Tasks Facing the United States," in *Strategic Asia 2008–09: Challenges and Choices*, edited by Ashley J. Tellis, Mercy Kuo, and Andrew Marble (Seattle: National Bureau of Asian Research, 2008), 3–40; Admiral

Timothy J. Keating, commander, U.S. Pacific Command, statement before the U.S. House Armed Services Committee on U.S. Pacific Command posture, March 12, 2008, www. pacom.mil/web/pacom_resources/pdf/2008%20PACOM%20HASC%20Posture%20 Statement_12%20Mar%2008.pdf; "Gates Says U.S. Interest in Asia Pacific Remains Strong," Channel News Asia, May 31, 2008, www.iiss.org/whats-new/iiss-in-the-press/ press-coverage-2008/may-2008/gates-says-us-interest-in-asia-pacific-remains-strong; and Evan S. Medeiros, "Strategic Hedging and the Future of Asia-Pacific Stability," *Washington Quarterly*, vol. 29, no. 1 (Winter 2005–2006): 145–67.

7. Moreover, many Asian leaders agree with the U.S. position that America serves as an essential guarantor of security for the region. For a recent reference to this viewpoint, see Robert Sutter, "Trust Our Resiliency," *Asia Policy*, no. 7 (January 2009): 12–14. Sutter has conducted extensive interviews with Asian security analysts and elites in recent years. In this source, he writes: "Washington . . . wants stability and in contrast with the inability or reluctance of Beijing and other powers to undertake major risks and commitments— continues the massive expenditure of, and major risks associated with, a U.S. military presence in the Asia-Pacific region. This role is broadly viewed by Asian government officials as essential in stabilizing the often uncertain security relationships among Asian governments."

8. Jin H. Pak, "China's Pragmatic Rise and U.S. Interests in East Asia," *Military Review*, vol. 87, no. 6 (November–December 2007); James J. Przystup, "The United States and the Asia-Pacific Region: National Interests and Strategic Imperatives," *Strategic Forum*, no. 239 (April 2009): 1–5; Bruce Vaughn, "U.S. Strategic and Defense Relationships in the Asia-Pacific Region," Congressional Research Service Report for Congress, January 22, 2007.

9. It is important to point out that such norms, structures, and processes include what many observers regard as the "moral" or ethical dimension of U.S. objectives toward China, such as the protection and advancement of human rights. As indicated above, America's five core strategic interests include the defense and advancement of democratic and humanitarian beliefs, organizations, and processes. Although such an interest is regarded by many Americans as a good in itself, it also serves specific national goals by encouraging the emergence of political systems and international actions that are deemed convergent with broader U.S. attitudes toward state and interstate behavior. Thus, America's efforts to engage and enmesh are intended, in part, to advance democratic and humanitarian goals, including, eventually, the possible democratization of China.

10. See Medeiros, "Strategic Hedging"; Condoleezza Rice, "Our Asia Strategy," *Wall Street Journal*, October 24, 2003.

11. Similarly, on the Chinese side, excessive attempts by Beijing to neutralize virtually all potential avenues to containment that the United States might employ in the future and thereby weaken U.S. influence in critical areas could provoke Washington to treat China as a strategic adversary and resist efforts at greater cooperation.

12. As Twomey has written: "When not well integrated, these separate strategies can lead to unintended consequences: efforts at overwhelming deterrence can provoke fears of aggressive intent, a classic security dilemma. This undermines the prospects for an enmeshing strategy to shape the adversary's interests in benign directions." Twomey, "Missing Strategic Opportunities," 539.

13. An example from 2007: "Our vision is a China that is more open, transparent, and democratic, and a China that will join us in actions that strengthen and support a global system that has provided peace, security, and prosperity to America, China, and the

rest of the world. Encouraging China to move in that direction continues to be the foundation of our policy. . . . A strong U.S. regional presence combined with constructive and candid diplomatic engagement should serve to deepen areas of cooperation and reduce the likelihood of backsliding in the relationship." Thomas J. Christensen, deputy assistant secretary of state for East Asian and Pacific affairs, "The State of U.S.-China Diplomacy," statement before the U.S.-China Economic and Security Review Commission, February 2, 2007. Also see Thomas J. Christensen, "China's Role in the World: Is China a Responsible Stakeholder?" remarks before the U.S.-China Economic and Security Review Commission, Washington, D.C., August 3, 2006, www.uscc.gov/hearings/2006hearings/written_testimonies/06_08_3_4wrts/06_08_3_4_christensen_thomas_statement.pdf; Condoleezza Rice, "Our Asia Strategy," *Wall Street Journal*, October 24, 2003; James A. Kelly, "U.S.-China Relations," testimony before the Senate Foreign Relations Committee, September 11, 2003, http://2001-2009.state.gov/p/eap/rls/rm/2003/24004.htm; and Colin L. Powell, "Interview on CCTV," transcript of television interview, Beijing, July 28, 2001, http://2001-2009.state.gov/secretary/former/powell/remarks/2001/4330.htm.

14. For example, see James A Kelly, "U.S. Policy on China and North Korea," remarks to the World Affairs Council, Washington, D.C., January 30, 2003, http://2001-2009.state.gov/p/eap/rls/rm/2003/17164.htm. In the early years of the George W. Bush presidency, the term "strategic competitor" was also employed to describe China, in contrast to the Clinton administration's term "strategic partner." This was largely done to convey the impression that Washington under Bush would take a more realistic, hard-nosed stance toward a rising China than the Clinton administration had done. The term was largely dropped during the latter years of the first Bush term, however, as Washington sought more cooperative relations with China.

15. This phrase was agreed upon by Obama and Hu Jintao in April 2009, when the two leaders met in London during the G-20 meeting, and has been repeated many times since then. For example, see "Chinese, U.S. Presidents Discuss Bilateral Ties," Xinhua, September 23, 2009.

16. U.S.-China Joint Statement, Beijing, China, November 17, 2009, www.whitehouse.gov/the-press-office/us-china-joint-statement; Office of the Press Secretary, White House, "Joint Press Statement by President Obama and President Hu of China," Great Hall, Beijing, China, November 17, 2009, www.whitehouse.gov/the-press-office/joint-press-statement-president-obama-and-president-hu-china; James B. Steinberg, "Administration's Vision of the U.S.-China Relationship," keynote address at Center for a New American Security, Washington, D.C., September 24, 2009, www.state.gov/s/d/2009/129686.htm. The U.S.-China Joint Statement issued during Hu Jintao's state visit to Washington in January 2011 also illustrates this "strategic reassurance" dynamic: "The United States reiterated that it welcomes a strong, prosperous, and successful China that plays a greater role in world affairs. China welcomes the United States as an Asia-Pacific nation that contributes to peace, stability and prosperity in the region. Working together, both leaders support efforts to build a more stable, peaceful, and prosperous Asia-Pacific region for the 21st century." U.S.-China Joint Statement, Washington, D.C., January 19, 2011, www.whitehouse.gov/the-press-office/2011/01/19/us-china-joint-statement. See also Michael Schiffer, deputy assistant secretary of defense for East Asia, "Building Greater Cooperation in the U.S.-China Military-to-Military Relationship in 2011," Institute for International Strategic Studies, Washington, D.C., January 6, 2011. Schiffer identifies the three pillars of the Obama administration's China policy as (1) strengthen bilateral engagement with China,

(2) strengthen relationships with allies and partners in the region, and (3) ensure that China abides by the norms of the existing global order.

17. See Banning Garrett, "U.S.-China Relations in the Era of Globalization and Terror: A Framework for Analysis," *Journal of Contemporary China*, vol. 15, no. 48 (August 2006): 389–415; and James J. Przystup, "The United States, Australia, and the Search for Order in East Asia and Beyond," in *The Other Special Relationship: The United States and Australia at the Start of the 21st Century*, edited by Jeffrey D. McCausland, Douglas T. Stuart, William Tow, and Michael Wesley (Carlisle, Pa.: Strategic Studies Institute, 2007). Also see Paul Richter, "U.S. Appeals to China to Help Stabilize Pakistan," *Los Angeles Times*, May 25, 2009, www.latimes.com/news/nationworld/nation/la-fg-us-china-pakistan25-2009may25,0,6047766.story.

18. For example, see Robert Zoellick, "Whither China? From Membership to Responsibility," remarks to the National Committee on U.S.-China Relations, September 21, 2005, www.ncuscr.org/files/Zoellick_remarks_notes06_winter_spring_0.pdf. In the last sentence of this well-known speech, the former deputy secretary of state states: "We can cooperate with the emerging China of today, even as we work for the democratic China of tomorrow."

19. As noted in chapter 8, such statements have arguably served as a source of suspicion and irritation among Chinese leaders.

20. These differing strategic approaches toward China are discussed to varying degrees in subsequent chapters, as part of the examination of specific U.S. policy arenas, and in chapter 9 as part of the examination of what has worked in U.S. policy in the past. Most importantly, in the conclusion, they are linked to an assessment of future alternative U.S. Asia strategies.

21. Some observers question whether China pursues a grand strategy in the international arena. Although not explicitly promulgated in an official document or formally labeled as a "grand strategy" per se, there is little doubt that Beijing pursues an explicit and very particular set of foreign and defense policies designed to achieve certain national goals; this is the definition of a "grand strategy."

22. Stability is particularly prized by the Chinese leadership not only because of China's long history of instability in the modern era but also because the reforms themselves threaten to generate enormous instability, as a result of (1) rapid economic growth; (2) the structural evolution of the Chinese economy and society from a closed, controlled, planned system to a more open, market-led system; and (3) the transformation of China's leadership system from a generation of charismatic leaders to one of technobureaucrats. See Jia Qingguo, "The Impact of 9-11 on Sino-U.S. Relations: A Preliminary Assessment," *International Relations of the Asia Pacific*, vol. 3, no. 2 (August 2003): 159–77.

23. Fei-Ling Wang defines Chinese goals as constituting a "three-P incentive structure": the political preservation of the CCP regime, China's economic prosperity, and Beijing's pursuit of power and prestige. See Fei-Ling Wang, "Preservation, Prosperity and Power: What Motivates China's Foreign Policy?" *Journal of Contemporary China*, vol. 14, no. 45 (November 2005): 669–94. For a clear official statement of China's emphasis on stability in particular, see "Resolutely Carry Out the Lofty Mission Entrusted by the Party and the People—Warmly Celebrating the 82nd Anniversary of the Founding of the Chinese People's Liberation Army," editorial in *Jiefangjun Bao Online*, August 1, 2009. For general statements of these basic goals, see Michael D. Swaine and Ashley J. Tellis, *Interpreting China's Grand Strategy: Past, Present, and Future* (Santa Monica, Calif.: RAND Corporation, 2000). The goal of achieving the

"great revival" of the nation by the middle of the twenty-first century through the creation of a "well-off society" was set by the Sixteenth Party Congress in November 2002. See Wang Jisi, *China's Changing Role in Asia*, Atlantic Council Occasional Paper (Washington, D.C.: Atlantic Council of the United States, 2004), 2–3. Also see Wang Yizhou, "China's Diplomacy: Ten Features," *Contemporary International Relations*, vol. 19, no. 1 (January–February 2009): 45–64; and Wang Yizhou, "Mianxiang ershiyishiji de zhongguo waijiao: Sanzhong xuqiu de xunqiu jiqi pingheng" (Chinese diplomacy in the twenty-first century: Achieving and balancing three needs), *Zhanlue yu Guanli* (Strategy and Management), no. 6 (1999): 18–27. In the latter (1999) source, Wang identifies three basic requirements or objectives for China's foreign and security policies during the 21st century: development; sovereignty; and responsibility (that is, becoming a superpower). In the former (2009) source, Wang states: "A salient feature of China's diplomacy since the reform and opening up is its flexibility in operating among a variety of international blocs of power, without confining the country to a single ideological status, thus winning itself strategic initiative and vast strategic space. . . . As a country with one fifth of the world's population, with its per capita income still behind the first one hundred places in the world, in the face of both domestic and international major events, China needs to devote undivided attention to building the country first and setting its own agenda without being disturbed by outside distractions." See also Thomas J. Christensen and Michael A. Glosny, "China: Sources of Stability in U.S.-China Security Relations," in *Strategic Asia 2003–2004: Fragility and Crisis*, edited by Richard Ellings, Aaron Friedberg, and Michael Wills (Seattle: National Bureau of Asian Research, 2003); and Thomas J. Christensen, "China," in *Strategic Asia 2003–2004*, ed. Ellings, Friedberg, and Wills.

24. For example, see "Address by Hu Jintao at the Opening Session of the Second Round of the U.S.-China Strategic and Economic Dialogue," Xinhua, May 24, 2010, http://politics.people.com.cn/GB/1024/11678677.html; Li Keqiang, "The World Should Not Fear a Growing China," *Financial Times*, January 9, 2011; and Dai Bingguo, "Stick to the Path of Peaceful Development," *Beijing Review*, December 21, 2010. Dai Bingguo writes: "The objective of China's development boils down to one sentence: to build a harmonious society at home and help build a harmonious world abroad."

25. Xiao Ren and Travis Tanner, "Roundtable: Chinese Foreign Policy and Domestic Decisionmaking," *Asia Policy*, no. 10 (July 2010): 43–101.

26. The best example of such rhetoric is given by Hu Jintao, "Building Towards a Harmonious World of Lasting Peace and Common Prosperity," speech at the United Nations, September 15, 2005, www.fmprc.gov.cn/eng/wjdt/zyjh/t213091.htm. Hu states: "China will, as always, abide by the purposes and principles of the UN Charter, actively participate in international affairs and fulfill its international obligations, and work with other countries in building towards a new international political and economic order that is fair and rational. The Chinese nation loves peace. China's development, instead of hurting or threatening anyone, can only serve peace, stability and common prosperity in the world." For more recent articulations of the "peaceful development" notion, see Dai Bingguo, "Stick to the Path"; Li Keqiang, "World Should Not Fear"; Yang Jiechi, "Carry Forward the Fine Tradition of New China's Diplomacy and Strive for Diplomatic Success Under New Circumstances," *Renmin Ribao Online*, September 4, 2009, OSC CPP20090905722012; Qian Tong, "The 11th Meeting of Chinese Diplomatic Envoys Convenes in Beijing; Hu Jintao Makes an Important Speech; Wu Bangguo, Jia Qinglin, Li Changchun, Xi Jinping, Li Keqiang, He Guoqiang, and Zhou Yongkang Attend; Wen Jiabao Makes a Speech,"

Xinhua Domestic Service, July 20, 2009, OSC CPP20090720005007. Also see the remarks of Liang Guanglie, defense minister of China, "PRC Defense Ministry Holds Reception to Mark 82nd Anniversary of PLA's Founding," Xinhua, July 31, 2009; Chen Xiangyang, "The Direction of China's Great Diplomacy in the New Period," *Liaowang*, July 27, 2009; Zheng Bijian, "China's Road for Peaceful Development and Revival of China's Civilization," *China Strategic Review*, vol. 9 (2006): 3; and Zheng Bijian, "China's 'Peaceful Rise' to Great-Power Status," *Foreign Affairs*, vol. 84, no. 5 (September–October 2005): 18. Zheng places China's external policies within an overall set of "three grand strategies—or 'three transcendences": (1) "Transcend the old model of industrialization to advance a new one . . . based on technology, economic efficiency, low consumption of natural resources relative to the size of its population, low environmental pollution, and optimal allocation of human resources"; (2) "transcend the traditional ways for great powers to emerge . . . to strive for peace, development, and cooperation with all countries of the world"; and (3) "transcend outdated modes of social control and to construct a harmonious socialist society." Also see Ye Zicheng, "Carrying Forward, Developing and Pondering Deng Xiaoping's Foreign Policy Thinking in the New Situation," *Beijing Shijie Jingji Yu Zhengzhi*, November 14, 2004, 8–14. One Chinese observer attributes Beijing's peaceful grand strategy to China's unique cultural heritage, which emphasizes Confucian beliefs such as "grace," "generosity," and "benevolence." Ni Jianmin, "China's Peaceful Development and Harmonious World," *China Strategic Review*, vol. 3 (2006): 3–4. For secondary sources, see Wang Yizhou, "China's Diplomacy." Wang argue that Hu's stress on building a harmonious world reflects a concern over the domestic bottlenecks produced by China's rapid growth, including: a widening income gap, worsening ecosystem degradation, rampant corruption, dwindling social ethics and rising pressure for political reform, as well as deep worries over the lack of dialogue and understanding in an international life replete with threats and violence. It amounts to a solemn commitment to solving disputes through constructive dialogue and cooperation." Also see Evan S. Medeiros, *China's International Behavior: Activism, Opportunism, and Diversification* (Santa Monica, Calif.: RAND Corporation, 2006); Australian Department of Defense, "Defending Australia in the Asia Pacific Century: Force 2030," 2009; Swaine and Tellis, *Interpreting China's Grand Strategy*; Michael Swaine, "China: Exploiting a Strategic Opening," in *Strategic Asia 2004–05: Confronting Terrorism in the Pursuit of Power*, edited by Ashley J. Tellis and Michael Wills (Seattle: National Bureau of Asian Research, 2004), 67–101; Bates Gill, *Rising Star: China's New Security Diplomacy* (Washington, D.C.: Brookings Institution Press, 2007); Zhang Yunling and Tang Shiping, "China's Regional Trade and Investment Profile," in *Power Shift: China and Asia's New Dynamics*, edited by David Shambaugh (Berkeley: University of California Press, 2005), 48–68; and Avery Goldstein, *Rising to the Challenge: China's Grand Strategy and International Security* (Stanford, Calif.: Stanford University Press, 2005), esp. 118 and chap. 6. Goldstein argues that Beijing began to emphasize China's peaceful development and the search for cooperative bilateral and multilateral relationships in mid-1996. Swaine and Tellis point out that key elements of this notion have been a part of China's reform era strategy since the early 1980s.

27. See Wang Yizhou, "China's Diplomacy."

28. See President Hu Jintao, "Unite as One and Work for a Bright Future," statement at the General Debate of the 64th Session of the UN General Assembly, New York, September

23, 2009, www.china-un.org/eng/hyyfy/t606150.htm. As Medeiros writes, for Hu Jintao, "a harmonious world is one in which states act in ways that respect each other's national sovereignty, tolerate diversity (in national political systems and values), and promote national development by equitably spreading economic benefits. Although these ideas are all long-standing principles in Chinese diplomacy, they reflect Hu Jintao's effort to define a distinctive approach to foreign policy." Medeiros, *China's International Behavior*, 48–49.

29. See Chen Xiangyang, "Direction of China's Great Diplomacy"; Medeiros, *China's International Behavior*, 48. Medeiros also points out that "Chinese leaders now talk about the trinity of 'peace, development, and cooperation' as the 'basic principles' (jiben yuanze 基本原则) of China's diplomacy. The addition of 'cooperation' is a Hu Jintao innovation, which is meant to underscore China's commitment to multilateral organizations." See below for more on this point.

30. As Medeiros argues, China's relations with its Asian neighbors in particular have been the focus of most of its international behavior. He writes: "This effort has been driven by several objectives: to expand China's access to markets and investment, to reassure regional nations that China's rise does not threaten them economically or militarily, to broaden access to natural resources and technologies for further development, and to undermine any and all efforts, U.S.-led and otherwise, to constrain China's economic, diplomatic, and military influence. In this sense, China's regional diplomacy in East Asia has arguably received pride of place in Beijing's overall international strategy in the last decade." Medeiros, *China's International Behavior*, 125–26.

31. For example, in his speech to the U.S.-China Business Council during his state visit to Washington in January 2011, Hu Jintao called for "active efforts to advance China-US cooperative partnership," but also emphasized that such a partnership must build upon mutual respect for each other's core interests: "A review of the history of our relations tells us that China-U.S. relations will enjoy smooth and steady growth when the two countries handle well issues involving each other's major interests. Otherwise, our relations will suffer constant trouble or even tension. Taiwan and Tibet-related issues concern China's sovereignty and territorial integrity, and they represent China's core interests. They touch upon the national sentiments of the 1.3 billion Chinese. We hope that the US side will honor its commitments and work with us to preserve the hard-won progress of our relations." Hu Jintao, president of the People's Republic of China, "Building a China-U.S. Cooperative Partnership Based on Mutual Respect and Mutual Benefit," address at the welcoming luncheon hosted by friendly organizations in the United States, Washington, D.C., January 20, 2011, www.fmprc.gov.cn/eng/wjdt/zyjh/t789956.htm.

32. Again, as Medeiros writes: "Chinese leaders do not want China to be a global power on par with the United States—a peer competitor. They view their domestic challenges as too great to assume the burdens associated with such a role, and they recognize that they lack currently the material resources to be able to project and sustain military and economic power all over the world. They also fear that playing such a role could deplete much needed resources and would likely foster a backlash against China. . . . Such a course correction would likely only come about in reaction to a dramatic change in China's external security environment—one that precipitated a complete reassessment by China's top leaders." Medeiros, *China's International Behavior*, 208–9. This statement remains true today, despite an increase in Chinese assertiveness in several policy areas, as mentioned below and discussed in greater detail in several chapters.

33. As Robert Sutter states: "Chinese officials see the United States as the dominant power in Asian and world affairs, and the main potential international danger that can confront and complicate China's development and rising power. . . . Under these circumstances, Chinese officials and specialists say they are determined that the United States not see China's rise as a challenge to America." See Robert Sutter, "Asia in the Balance: America and China's 'Peaceful Rise,' " *Current History*, September 2004, 284–89. Also see Kenneth Lieberthal, "The U.S.-China Agenda Goes Global," *Current History*, September 2009, 243–49; and Robert S. Ross, "China," in *Fighting Chance: Global Trends and Shocks in the National Security Environment*, edited by Neyla Arnas (Washington, D.C.: National Defense University Press, 2009), 185–96

34. See "PLA Major General Peng Guangqian: Be Ready to Deal with any New Troubles That the U.S. Creates," China Review News, December 17, 2010, trans. China Scope, http://chinascope.org/main/content/view/3169/103. Peng expressed this sentiment when he stated that "because it is worried about its hegemony, the U.S. has increased its involvement in the East so it can hold back China's development."

35. Medeiros writes: "A core Chinese objective is to hinder the U.S. ability to constrain China; that is, China seeks to maximize its freedom of action and leverage as means of countering perceived U.S. efforts to limit Chinese choices. China seeks political influence to increase the costs, for the United States and its allies, of constraining China. . . . In this sense, China's approach is more celestial than confrontational—pulling nations toward China rather than pushing away from the United States or each other." Medeiros, *China's International Behavior*, 209.

36. See Michael D. Swaine, "China's Assertive Behavior, Part One: On 'Core Interests,'" *China Leadership Monitor*, no. 34 (Winter 2011), http://media.hoover.org/sites/default/files/documents/CLM34MS.pdf. As described in this essay, in July 2009, State Councilor Dai Bingguo publicly defined the general elements of China's core interests as including three components: (1) preserving China's basic state system and national security (维护基本制度和国家安全); (2) national sovereignty and territorial integrity (国家主权和领土完整); and (3) the continued stable development of China's economy and society (经济社会的持续稳定发展). For a specific example of how China insists on defending its core interests, while not seeking to displace the United States, see "Growing Chinese Navy No Cause for Fear," editorial, *Global Times*, April 27, 2010, OSC CPP20100427722005. The editorial states, "China does not hold an intention to challenge the U.S. in the central Pacific or engage in a military clash with Japan in close waters, though it is willing to protect its core interests at any cost."

37. See Swaine, "China: Exploiting a Strategic Opening." The New Security Concept stresses the principles of state sovereignty, nonintervention in a country's internal affairs, mutually beneficial economic contacts, "and the importance of the United Nations in establishing world norms and as a check against unilateralism and power politics. The bilateral expression of these principles is contained in the concept of 'strategic partnerships' between China and major global and regional powers. . . . Initiated in April 1996, such partnerships emphasize a mutual desire to work together to attain common international objectives, and a mutual commitment to avoid confrontation." Also see David Finkelstein, "China's New Concept of Security" in *The People's Liberation Army and China in Transition*, edited by Stephen J. Flanagan and Michael E. Marti (Washington, D.C.: Center for the Study of Chinese Military Affairs,

2003); Robert Sutter, "China's Regional Strategy and America," in *Power Shift*, ed. Shambaugh, 289–305; and David Shambaugh, *Modernizing China's Military: Progress, Problems, and Prospects* (Berkeley: University of California Press, 2002), 293. Shambaugh argues that the New Security Concept is "designed to shield Beijing from outside pressure over its 'internal affairs,' while, at the same time, articulating a genuine vision of international relations and security—a vision intentionally distinct from the American view that emphasizes alliances, deterrence, and military force"; Gill, *Rising Star*, 4. Susan Shirk, *China: Fragile Superpower* (New York: Oxford University Press, 2007), 129. See also Zhang Yongxing, "Chinese Representative Explains China's New Concept of Security at Asian Security Conference," Xinhua, June 4, 2005. Regarding China's support for the principle of nonintervention in the internal affairs of sovereign nations, see Wang Yizhou, "China's Diplomacy." Wang states: "The principle of non-intervention China advocates has the following traits: respect for diversity and democratic consultations, for the free choice of nations in regard to their development path and model . . . limited forced international intervention based on the legitimacy granted by the UN Security Council resolutions and the approval of most UN member nations . . . international intervention of a primarily peaceful, cooperative and diplomatic nature. . . . Such international intervention should be put in the context of global peace and development."

38. This basic approach has remained in place despite recent indications of a greater Chinese willingness to employ political and military pressure with regard to territorial issues concerning Japan and Southeast Asia. As noted above, such greater Chinese assertiveness is discussed in subsequent chapters.

39. Swaine and Tellis, *Interpreting China's Grand Strategy*; Gill, *Rising Star*, chap. 2, esp. 36. Gill cites the Declaration on the Conduct of Parties in the South China, which came out of the November 2002 China–ASEAN summit, as an example. He points out that this agreement marked a decisive break with Chinese precedent, as Beijing's old approach to territorial disputes preferred bilateral as opposed to multilateral settlement. China's approach toward territorial disputes along its periphery is a part of its overall policy toward frontier defense. This policy includes three basic elements: (1) internal security and policing to counter separatist, terrorist, and rebellion struggles; (2) economic growth to mitigate social unrest and dissatisfaction; and (3) diplomatic efforts to resolve or neutralize territorial disputes. See M. Taylor Fravel, "Power Shifts and Escalation: Explaining China's Use of Force in Territorial Disputes," *International Security*, vol. 32, no. 3 (2007); and M. Taylor Fravel, "Securing Borders: China's Doctrine and Force Structure for Frontier Defense," *Journal of Strategic Studies*, vol. 30, nos. 4–5 (August–October 2007): 705–37.

40. Wang Yizhou, "China's Diplomacy"; Yang Jiechi, "Carry Forward the Fine Tradition of New China's Diplomacy and Strive for Diplomatic Success Under New Circumstances," *Renmin Ribao Online*, September 4, 2009, OSC CPP20090905722012; Gill, *Rising Star*; Medeiros, *China's International Behavior*; Goldstein, *Rising to the Challenge*, 24, 29–30, 102–3; Swaine, "China: Exploiting a Strategic Opening"; Swaine and Tellis, *Interpreting China's Grand Strategy*.

41. See Medeiros, *China's International Behavior*, esp. 52; Evan S. Medeiros and M. Taylor Fravel, "China's New Diplomacy," *Foreign Affairs*, vol. 82, no. 6 (November–December 2003): 25–27; David Shambaugh, "China Engages Asia: Reshaping the Regional Order," *International Security*, vol. 29, no. 3 (Winter 2004–2005): 69–70; Gill, *Rising Star*,

12–13; and Robert G. Sutter, *China's Rise: Implications for U.S. Leadership in Asia*, Policy Study 21 (Washington, D.C.: East-West Center, 2006), viii. Sutter argues that "China's Asian approach focuses on 'easy' things—the 'low-hanging fruit'—and avoids costly commitments or major risk."

42. As Medeiros writes: "Many Chinese argue that the United States is using its alliances in Asia and its regional military deployments to contain Chinese power. These deep concerns are most evident in Chinese commentaries about changes to the U.S.-Japan alliance, U.S. military interactions with Taiwan, the emerging U.S.-India strategic relationship, U.S. military deployments in Central Asia, and the U.S. military's force enhancements in the Western Pacific." Thus, China's diplomacy worldwide—but especially in Asia—seeks to forge political relationships that collectively create an environment in which the United States cannot use its diplomacy or military cooperation to constrain China's freedom of action and especially cannot work with other Asian states to balance or otherwise constrain China. Medeiros, *China's International Behavior*, 53–55. Also see Goldstein, *Rising to the Challenge*, esp. 24, 29–30, 102–3. Goldstein states that China's grand strategy is designed to ensure its national interests by increasing the perceived advantages of working with China while also underscoring the disadvantages of working against it (118). In this way, China hopes to offset fears about the so-called China threat and become a more instrumental player in the international system. Also see Evan S. Medeiros, "China's International Behavior: Activism, Opportunism, and Diversification," *Joint Forces Quarterly*, 4th quarter, 2007, 34–41. For other similar characterizations of China's overall strategy, see Swaine, "China: Exploiting a Strategic Opening"; Swaine and Tellis, *Interpreting China's Grand Strategy*; Jia Qingguo, "Learning to Live with the Hegemon," *Journal of Contemporary China*, vol. 14, no. (August 2005): 395–407; Sutter, *China's Rise*; Sutter, "China's Regional Strategy"; Gill, *Rising Star*, 10; Shirk, *China: Fragile Superpower*, esp. 25; Shi Yinhong, "Basic Trials and Essential 'Platforms' for China's Peaceful Rise," *Ta Kung Pao*, March 14, 2004; Joseph Y. S. Cheng and Zhang Wankun, "Patterns and Dynamics of China's International Strategic Behavior," *Journal of Contemporary China*, vol. 11, no. 31 (May 2002): 259; and Zhang Yunling and Tang Shiping, "China's Regional Trade and Investment Profile," in *Power Shift*, ed. Shambaugh, esp. 49.

43. China's overseas search for reliable energy sources at stable prices is viewed by Beijing as increasingly critical to the maintenance of Chinese growth and to improvements in China's huge and growing environmental problems. See chapters 5 and 7 for further discussion of these issues. For China, energy security is apparently defined as "sufficient energy to support economic growth and prevent debilitating energy shortfalls that could trigger social and political turbulence"; Daniel Yergin, "Ensuring Energy Security," *Foreign Affairs*, vol. 85, issue 2 (March–April 2006); See Erica Downs, *China*, Brookings Foreign Policy Studies, Energy Security Series (Washington, D.C.: Brookings Institution, 2006); Wang Jiacheng, "Chinese Energy Security: Demand and Supply" *China Strategic Review*, vol. 11, 2005; and Medeiros, *China's International Behavior*, 58.

44. John Fox and François Godement, "A Power Audit of EU–China Relations," European Council on Foreign Relations, April 2009, http://ecfr.3cdn.net/532cd91d0b5c9699ad_ozm6b9bz4.pdf; Wang Yizhou, "China's Diplomacy"; Medeiros, "China's International Behavior: Activism, Opportunism, and Diversification"; Medeiros, *China's International Behavior*; Swaine, "China: Exploiting a Strategic Opening"; Swaine and Tellis, *Interpreting China's Grand Strategy*; Gill, *Rising Star*; Goldstein, *Rising to the Challenge*.

45. Martin I. Wayne, "Five Lessons from China's War on Terror," *Joint Force Quarterly*, 4th quarter, 2007, 42–47; Shirley A. Kan, "U.S.-China Counterterrorism Cooperation: Issues for U.S. Policy," Congressional Research Service, May 7, 2009, 1–27; Bates Gill and Melissa Murphy, "China's Evolving Approach to Counterterrorism," *Harvard Asia Quarterly*, vol. 9, nos. 1–2 (Winter–Spring 2005); David M. Lampton and Richard Daniel Ewing, "The U.S.-China Relationship Facing International Security Crises: Three Case Studies in Post-9/11 Bilateral Relations," Nixon Center, 2003.

46. See, for example, Information Office of the State Council of the People's Republic of China, Beijing, "China: Arms Control and Disarmament," November 1995; and Information Office of the State Council of the People's Republic of China, "China's National Defense," July 1998. We should also point out that, for some Chinese, the complete prohibition of WMD would serve to increase the relative leverage exerted by China's large conventional forces in a political or military crisis near China's borders.

47. For a summary of China's participation in arms control regimes, see Michael D. Swaine and Alastair I. Johnston, "China and Arms Control Institutions," in *China Joins the World: Progress and Prospects*, edited by Elizabeth Economy and Michel Oksenberg (New York: Council on Foreign Relations, 1999), 90–135.

48. John Wilson Lewis and Xue Litai, *China Builds the Bomb* (Stanford, Calif.: Stanford University Press, 1988), 36. Also see Lieutenant General Li Jijun (vice president of the Academy of Military Science of the Chinese People's Liberation Army), "Traditional Military Thinking and the Defensive Strategy of China," address at U.S. Army War College, Letort Paper 1, August 29, 1997.

49. Indeed, some Chinese strategists apparently believe that nuclear weapons will become increasingly important for medium-sized nuclear states like China, given supposedly inherent contradictions between the interests of such states on the one hand and U.S. hegemony and its vision of a new world order on the other. See Alastair Iain Johnston, "China's New 'Old Thinking': The Concept of Limited Deterrence," *International Security*, vol. 20, no. 3 (Winter 1995–1996): 10.

50. For a standard official statement of China's stance regarding nuclear disarmament and nuclear use, see "The Peaceful Foundation of the Grand Military Parade," interview with Ministry of Defense spokesman Hu Changming, *Liaowang*, nos. 40–41 (October 5, 2009): 30–32, OSC CPP20091016710011. Hu Changming states: "From the day China first possessed nuclear weapons, it has always advocated a complete ban and destruction of nuclear weapons, China has adhered to a self-defensive nuclear strategy, China has always firmly abided by the policy of no first use of nuclear weapons ever or under any circumstances, and China has clearly pledged unconditionally not to use or threaten to use nuclear weapons against a country or area which does not have nuclear weapons. China is not a participant in a nuclear arms race in any form, and China keeps its own nuclear forces at the minimum level needed for China's national security." During his speech to the UN General Assembly in September 2009, Hu Jintao stated: "China has consistently stood for the complete prohibition and thorough destruction of nuclear weapons and a world without nuclear weapons. We call on the international community to take credible steps to push forward the nuclear disarmament process, eradicate the risks of nuclear weapons proliferation and promote peaceful use of nuclear energy and related international cooperation." See Hu Jintao, "Unite as One and Work for a Bright Future."

51. See Lewis and Xue, *China Builds the Bomb*, 216.

52. See "China's Nuclear Doctrine," from the database of the Center for Nonproliferation Studies, Monterey Institute of International Studies, http://cns.miis.edu.

53. The concept of preemptive military action within a limited theater (that is, at a substrategic level), to deter a major conventional attack or to prevent a major escalation of a lesser attack is usually applied by the Chinese to the conventional arena. Yet for some Chinese at least, this notion apparently has a potential application to the WMD arena as well. In particular, some Chinese strategists apparently believe that Beijing would contemplate the initial use of theater-oriented nuclear, biological, or chemical weapons in a crisis if the leadership believed that China was about to be attacked by such weapons. This possibility is made more likely by the fact that many Chinese apparently do not automatically accept that a limited nuclear conflict would escalate to a general nuclear war.

54. For example, see "China Needs Hawks to Safeguard Its National Interest," *Global Times*, April 9, 2009, http://chinascope.org/main/content/view/1489/92. Also see Yan Xuetong, "The Rise of China in Chinese Eyes," *Journal of Contemporary China*, vol. 10, no. 26 (2001): 33–39; Ta Yin, "The United States Is the Culprit who Started North Korea's Nuclear Crisis," *Ta Kung Pao*, December 21, 2006; Ren Weidong, "The DPRK-U.S. Relationship Is the Crucial Point in the Peninsula Issue," *Liaowang*, no. 26 (June 29, 2009): 58; and Yong Deng, "Hegemon on the Offensive: Chinese Perspectives on U.S. Global Strategy," *Political Science Quarterly*, vol. 116, no. 3 (Fall 2001): 343–67.

55. For a recent statement of official Chinese views stressing the need for deep cooperation, see "Chinese, U.S. Presidents Discuss Bilateral Ties," Xinhua, September 23, 2009; and Bonnie S. Glaser and Lyle Morris, "Chinese Perceptions of U.S. Decline and Power," *China Brief*, vol. 9, no. 14, www.jamestown.org/programs/chinabrief/single/?tx_ttnewstt_news=35241&tx_ttnewsbackPid=25&cHash=444d48ec32. Also see Niu Xinchun and Liu Quan, "China–U.S. Relations Facing with New Opportunities for Development," *Peace and Development*, no. 3 (June 2009): 73–80; Wang Zaibang, "China and Global Governance," *Contemporary International Relations*, vol. 17, no. 2 (March–April 2007); Wang Jisi, "China's Search for Stability with America," *Foreign Affairs*, vol. 84, no. 5 (September–October 2005); Zhu Feng, "Just Good Competitors?" *Guardian*, November 9, 2008; Wang Jisi, "China's Changing Role in Asia," in *The Rise of China and a Changing East Asian Order*, edited by Kokubun Ryosei and Wang Jisi (Tokyo: Japan Center for International Exchange, 2004), 3–21; and Yong Deng and Thomas G. Moore, "China Views Globalization: Toward a New Great-Power Politics?" *Washington Quarterly*, vol. 27, no. 3 (2004).

56. For example, see Jayshree Bajoria, "Nationalism in China," Council on Foreign Relations, April 23, 2008, www.cfr.org/publication/16079/nationalism_in_china.html; and Peter Hays Gries, *China's New Nationalism: Pride, Politics, and Diplomacy* (Berkeley: University of California Press, 2004), 4–8.

57. For example, see "Editorial: China Should Act as Regional Stabilizer," *Global Times*, October 20, 2009, OSC CPP20091020722002. The *Global Times* is a newspaper sponsored by the official CCP newspaper *People's Daily*.

58. For an examination of various current Chinese views on Beijing's growing role in foreign affairs, see Michael D. Swaine, "Perceptions of an Assertive China," *China Leadership Monitor*, no. 32 (May 11, 2010), www.hoover.org/publications/china-leadership-monitor/article/35436; and Medeiros, *China's International Behavior*. More recently, Medeiros has

written: "China's worldview and its international strategy produce a unique reluctance to be a global leader. China wants the status and influence associated with global activism but it fears the burdens of leadership." See Evan S. Medeiros, "Is Beijing Ready for Global Leadership?" *Current History*, vol. 108, no. 719 (September 2009): 250–56. Chinese fears in this regard are likely to be heightened as calls grow for China to shoulder global responsibilities. See, for example, An Ping, " 'Pragmatic' President Will Reach Out to China, Obama Asia Adviser Bader Says at Committee of 100's 18th Annual Conference," May 1, 2009, www.marketwire.com/press-release/Committee-of-100-983310.html; and James B. Steinberg, "East Asia and the Pacific," remarks at the National Bureau of Asian Research Conference, "Engaging Asia 2009: Strategies for Success," Washington, D.C., April 1, 2009, www.state.gov/s/d/2009/121564.htm. The imperative of keeping a low profile internationally was reportedly enunciated by Deng Xiaoping during the midst of the Soviet collapse in the late 1980s or early 1990s and is summarized in the famous phrase "tao guang yang hui you suo zuo wei" (韬光养晦, 有所作为; hide our capacities and bide our time, but also get some things done). However, various versions of this statement exist. One version, "Leng jing guan cha, zhan wen jiao gen, chen zhuo ying fu, tao guang yang hui, shan yu shou zhuo, jue bu dang tou" (observe calmly; secure our position; cope with affairs calmly; hide our capacities and bide our time; be good at maintaining a low profile; and never claim leadership), is contained in the Office of the Secretary of Defense, *Annual Report to Congress: Military Power of the People's Republic of China 2008* (Washington, D.C.: U.S. Government Printing Office, 2009), 8. It is possible that the statement combines several remarks made by Deng and other Chinese leaders at different times. Some observers believe that this phrase conveys the PRC leadership's intent to conceal its military capabilities until it grows strong enough to challenge the United States in an effort to achieve regional or global hegemony. No direct confirmation of this interpretation exists, based on any official PRC sources. More important, it is extremely uncertain that both the "tao guang yang hui" phrase and the larger statement in which it often appears are regarded by the Chinese leadership as a key guideline for China's grand strategy, especially its military strategy. Some very knowledgeable observers believe the phrase applies solely to China's diplomatic (as opposed to military) approach and is usually viewed by Chinese analysts as an admonition for China to remain modest and low key while building a positive image internationally and achieving specific (albeit limited) gains, in order to avoid suspicions, challenges, or commitments that might undermine Beijing's long-standing emphasis on domestic development.

59. For example, see Jin Canrong, "Chinese Growing Pains," *Beijing Review*, no. 1 (January 6, 2011).

60. See Shirk, *China: Fragile Superpower*, 106–9. Also see Fei-Ling Wang, "Preservation, Prosperity and Power," 675; and Wang Yizhou, "China's Diplomacy." Wang states: "The challenge is how to combine Deng Xiaoping's behest of practicing a 'low-profile,' non-confrontational diplomacy and accomplishing some diplomatic successes as the country is growing stronger in its peaceful development." Indeed, some observers believe that the two phrases "tao guang yang hui" and "you suo zuo hui" are the subject of an ongoing debate within Chinese policy circles over whether China should pursue a more versus less active foreign policy.

61. U.S.-China Joint Statement, January 19, 2011; U.S.-China Joint Statement, November 17, 2009.

62. Some observers might argue that China desires to achieve preeminence over *all* other powers in Asia (that is, a Sinocentric security system), although there is no substantial evidence for the existence of such an objective at present, based on PRC strategy and formal pronouncements, or Chinese actions.

63. As Kenneth Lieberthal writes, "the single biggest failure of 30 years of diplomatic ties between Washington and Beijing is that neither side, even today, trusts the long-term intentions of the other toward itself. Close observers of U.S.-China relations constantly hear evidence of this lack of trust as they listen to concerns voiced in each capital. . . . This distrust on both sides is deeply rooted. Moreover, because the distrust concerns long-term (that is, 10- to 20-year) intentions rather than immediate goals and policies, it is very difficult to change." Lieberthal, "U.S.-China Agenda Goes Global," 243–49.

64. Some Chinese observers are apparently now arguing that an overextended and weakened America should prompt China's leaders to play an increasingly more confident and assertive role internationally in ways that directly challenge U.S. interests. However, other observers, including many leading Chinese officials, strongly reject such arguments. See Swaine, "Perceptions of an Assertive China"; Glaser and Morris, "Chinese Perceptions"; and Liu Jianfei, "Chinese Foreign Strategy in Wake of the Financial Crisis," *Sousuo yu Zhengming*, vol. 3 (May 2009). For more recent examples of debate on this subject, see Canrong, "Chinese Growing Pains"; "Strategic Analysis of Sino–U.S. Relations," interviews by Yang Shilong with Wu Baiyi; Huang Renwei, and Xu Tao, *Liaowang*, no, 36 (September 6, 2010): 10–14, OSC CPP20100910704005; Wang Jisi, "It Will Be Difficult to Avoid a Major Strategic Trial of Strength Between China and the United States," *Guoji Xianqu Daobao Online*, August 9, 2010, OSC CPP20100830671002; "Scholar Calls for Nations to Face Up to Differences," Q&A with Yan Xuetong, *China Daily*, July 30, 2010; and Jin Canrong, "Future China–U.S. Ties Bright and Stable, Despite Rocky Roads," *China Daily*, July 30, 2010. For recent statements by Chinese government officials on this subject, see Li Keqiang, "World Should Not Fear"; Cui Tiankai, "China Will Never Seek Hegemony: Vice Foreign Minister," Xinhua, January 14, 2011; "U.S. Still Unbeatable: PRC Official [Le Yucheng]," Reuters, January 25, 2011; and Dai Bingguo, "Stick to the Path." Addressing this debate, State Councilor Dai Bingguo bluntly writes, "Some say China wants to replace the United States and dominate the world. That is simply a myth. . . . Some people misinterpret the Chinese idiom 'keep a low profile and make due contributions.' They take China's announcement of a peaceful development path as a smokescreen for its real intention before it gets strong enough. This is groundless suspicion." This important essay by Dai Bingguo was described by Jin Canrong of Renmin University as an effort to address debate within China over whether China should continue its "peaceful development" efforts. See Minnie Chan, "We Don't Want to Replace U.S., Says Dai Bingguo," *South China Morning Post*, December 8, 2010.

65. Whether China's current stance will prevail over the long term as and if its power and influence continue to grow, and America's clearly begins to decline, is at best uncertain and constitutes one major factor motivating efforts to shape Chinese views, as discussed in chapter 10. For a Chinese source espousing Beijing's historically induced inclination to work within the existing international order, see Wang Chuanxing, "On China's Foreign Policy," *Contemporary International Relations*, vol. 19, no. 4 (July–August 2009): 85–94.

66. Michael D. Swaine and Zhang Tuosheng with Danielle F. S. Cohen, eds. *Managing Sino-American Crises: Case Studies and Analysis* (Washington, D.C.: Carnegie Endowment for International Peace, 2006).

CHAPTER 2

1. For general discussions of these approaches, see David M. Lampton, *Same Bed, Different Dreams: Managing U.S.-China Relations, 1989–2000* (Berkeley: University of California Press, 2001); and Robert L. Suettinger, *Beyond Tiananmen: The Politics of U.S.-China Relations 1989–2000* (Washington, D.C.: Brookings Institution Press, 2004).

2. For a discussion of Bush's hawkish China policy on assuming office, see Robert S. Ross, "The Stability of Deterrence in the Taiwan Strait," *National Interest*, Fall 2001, 67–68.

3. Interviews with former U.S. officials.

4. See Michael Swaine, "China: Exploiting a Strategic Opening," in *Strategic Asia 2004–05: Confronting Terrorism in the Pursuit of Power*, edited by Ashley J. Tellis and Michael Wills (Seattle: National Bureau of Asian Research, 2004), 67–101. One interviewee also stressed that the negotiated resolution of the April 2001 EP-3 incident by the State Department and the U.S. embassy in Beijing further reduced the attractiveness of a confrontational approach to China by showing the effectiveness of dialogue and negotiation in managing crises.

5. Contrary to popular impression, Vice President Dick Cheney was not among the proponents of the "strategic adversary" approach to China, according to these officials.

6. As one interviewee stated, "It seeks to convey the view, without saying so explicitly, that 'we don't need you [that is, China] as much as you think we do.'" There is more on this point below.

7. As one very knowledgeable former official stated: "We didn't view U.S. relations with China and Japan as a balancing act. This is the key. We never denigrated China. We talked about the peaceful rise of China being as important as the rise of a united Germany or of the U.S. The best way to manage this was to have a very stable relationship with Beijing."

8. As one strong proponent of this approach (and former senior Bush administration official) stated: "We held the view that China worked better within organizations, and her behavior was more predictable within organizations."

9. See James J. Przystup and Phillip C. Saunders, "Visions of Order: Japan and China in U.S. Strategy," *Strategic Forum*, no. 220 (June 2006); and Victor Cha, "Winning Asia: Washington's Untold Success Story," *Foreign Affairs*, vol. 86, no. 6 (November–December 2007).

10. Richard Armitage was deputy secretary of state from March 2001 to February 2005. Michael Green served on the National Security Council as the director of Asian affairs for Japan, Korea, and Australia/New Zealand from April 2001 to January 2004 and then as the senior director for Asian affairs until his departure in December 2005. Torkel Patterson was senior director for Asian affairs on the National Security Council from 2001 to 2002.

11. Some former U.S. officials insist that the logic underlying the Zoellick approach has actually been a basic part of U.S. policy since at least the Clinton era, if not earlier. According to one knowledgeable former Bush official, Zoellick's understanding of the "responsible stakeholder" concept accepted neither of the assumptions of the "pure" engagement or "pure" containment viewpoints, that is, that "China is either a flawed

friend that requires some encouragement or a growing rival that requires vigorous counter-balancing. Instead, the concept assumed that China's path remains largely undetermined and that the Chinese themselves have made no decision about their long-term strategic orientation toward the U.S." This set of assumptions is congruent with mainstream U.S. policy views toward China since at least the Clinton administration. However, the need to put forth and define such a concept publicly as an explicit goal of U.S. policy arguably became more urgent during the Bush era, in response to both the growing importance of Beijing to a wide array of U.S. interests, and the increasingly polarized nature of the debate over what to do about a more influential China.

12. As one former Bush official stated: "It's not that the 'responsible stakeholder' concept eliminates the difference between engagement and hedging. What you have eliminated is the dichotomy between engagement and containment—this is an essential point. The conceptual premise of a containment policy is that China's power in the world needs to be limited. The conceptual premise of a responsible stakeholder policy can't be reconciled to this view. China is to be welcomed. But you can still hedge against the uncertainty that, candidly, continues to exist regarding China." Another former official added: "We were trying to get China to play a larger role on problems that concerned both our countries. We wanted China to do more to stabilize the international space. It makes it easier to deal with the bilateral relationship when it's couched in a global context—that is, you're dealing with global issues at the same time. You're constantly emphasizing that you have common interests." Also see Bates Gill and Michael Schiffer, "A Rising China's Rising Responsibilities," in *Powers and Principles*, edited by Michael Schiffer and David Schorr (Lanham, Md.: Lexington Books, 2009), 99–124.

13. This is from interviews. For the full statement of the Zoellick view, see Robert B. Zoellick, "Whither China: From Membership to Responsibility?" Remarks to the National Committee on U.S.-China Relations, New York, September 21, 2005, www.ncuscr.org/files/2005Gala_RobertZoellick_Whither_China1.pdf. For the Armitage view, see Richard L. Armitage and Joseph Nye, "The United States and Japan: Advancing Toward a Mature Partnership," Institute for National Strategic Studies, Special Report, October 11, 2000.

14. See, in particular, James J. Przystup and Phillip C. Saunders, "Visions of Order: Japan and China in U.S. Strategy," *Strategic Forum* (Institute for National Strategic Studies, National Defense University), no. 220 (June 2006).

15. For example, the original Armitage report that provided the basis for this approach during the Bush era "put the United States squarely on the side of Japan in its dispute with China over the Senkaku/Diaoyu Islands." See Przystup and Saunders, "Visions of Order."

16. In fact, Obama's Asia policy explicitly includes three core elements: (1) an emphasis on maintaining ". . . core traditional treaty alliances with Japan and South Korea, with Australia, Thailand and the Philippines;" (2) "building strong relationships with the new emerging powers and particularly, in East Asia with India and China and Indonesia;" and (3) "complementing these bilateral relationships with more effective and comprehensive multilateral cooperation." See James B. Steinberg, deputy secretary of state, "The Critical Relationship Between the United States and China," speech at Center for American Progress, Washington, D.C., December 7, 2010, transcript by Federal News Service. For a similar three-prong formulation, see Hillary Rodham Clinton, secretary of state, "America's Engagement in the Asia-Pacific," remarks at the

Kahala Hotel, Honolulu, HI, October 28, 2010, available at www.state.gov/secretary/rm/2010/10/150141.htm.

17. For example, see Phillip C. Saunders, "Managing Strategic Competition with China," *Strategic Forum* (Institute for National Strategic Studies, National Defense University), no. 242 (July 2009): 3. Saunders writes: "The Obama administration has not employed the responsible stakeholder language, but its focus on expanding the areas of U.S.-China cooperation and encouraging China to take on more responsibility in addressing global challenges appears compatible with this approach." Also see White House, Office of the Press Secretary, "Background Briefing by a Senior Administration Official on the President's Meeting with President Hu of China," press release, September 22, 2009; and "Chinese, U.S. Presidents Discuss Bilateral Ties," Xinhua, in English, September 23, 2009.

18. François Godement, "The United States and Asia in 2009: Public Diplomacy and Strategic Continuity," *Asian Survey*, vol. 50, no. 1 (January–February 2010): 8–24. As Godement states, the Obama approach to Asia seems to be "whatever works" to preserve security and get along.

19. James B. Steinberg, "Administration's Vision of the U.S.-China Relationship," keynote address at the Center for a New American Security, Washington, September 24, 2009. We should add that in these remarks, Steinberg also recognizes that Washington must provide strategic reassurance to Beijing as he states well: "Strategic reassurance rests on a core, if tacit, bargain. Just as we and our allies must make clear that we are prepared to welcome China's 'arrival,' as you all have so nicely put it, as a prosperous and successful power, China must reassure the rest of the world that its development and growing global role will not come at the expense of security and well-being of others."

20. And he also understood the need for Washington to provide assurances to Beijing as well, as indicated in a conversation with the author.

21. For a general discussion of the continuities between the Bush and Obama approaches to China, see Dennis Wilder, "The U.S.-China Strategic and Economic Dialogue: Continuity and Change in Obama's China Policy," *China Brief*, vol. 9, no. 10 (May 15, 2009).

22. See Jean A. Garrison, *Making China Policy: From Nixon to G. W. Bush* (Boulder, Colo.: Lynne Rienner, 2005); and Robert G. Sutter, *U.S.–Chinese Relations: Perilous Past, Pragmatic Present* (Lanham, Md.: Rowman & Littlefield, 2010). Sutter writes: "Some scholars discern an important shift in U.S. strategy toward China and in East Asia more broadly beginning in 1982. The reevaluation of U.S. policy toward China under Secretary of State George Shultz is seen to bring to power officials who opposed the high priority on China in U.S. strategy toward East Asia and the world, and who gave much greater importance to U.S. relations with Japan and other U.S. allies in securing U.S. interests amid prevailing conditions."

23. This viewpoint was presented most cogently by Armitage and Nye, "United States and Japan." As indicated above, Armitage and several Japan specialists associated with this report later became senior Bush administration officials. Also see T. J. Pempel, "What the President-Elect Should Know About Japan," in *Challenges and Choices, Strategic Asia 2008–09*, edited by Ashley J. Tellis, Mercy Kuo, and Andrew Marble (Seattle: National Bureau of Asian Research, 2008).

24. Pempel, "What the President-Elect Should Know"; also see Christopher W. Hughes, "Japanese Military Modernization: In Search of a 'Normal' Security Role," in *Strategic*

Asia 2005–06: Military Modernization in an Era of Uncertainty, edited by Ashley
J. Tellis and Michael Wills (Seattle: National Bureau of Asian Research, 2005), 105–34.

25. This is according to "Japan Still Keen on F-22 Despite U.S. Obstacles," *Japan Times*,
August 1, 2009, http://search.japantimes.co.jp/cgi-bin/nn20090801a7.html. Japan is still
interested in the F-22 despite the recently imposed U.S. ban.

26. Christopher W. Hughes, *Japan's Remilitarisation* (London: Routledge for International
Institute for Strategic Studies, 2009), 35–52; Emma Chanlett-Avery and Mary Beth
Nikitin, *Japan's Nuclear Future: Policy Debate, Prospects and U.S. Interests*, CRS Report
for Congress, May 9, 2008, www.fas.org/sgp/crs/nuke/RL34487.pdf; Paul J. Smith,
"China–Japan Relations and the Future Geopolitics of East Asia," *Asian Affairs: An
American Review*, vol. 35, no. 4 (Winter 2009): 230–56; Hughes, "Japanese Military
Modernization."

27. National Defense Program Guideline, FY 2005, Japanese Ministry of Defense,
Approved by the Security Council and the Cabinet on December 10, 2004 (Provisional
Translation), www.kantei.go.jp/foreign/policy/2004/1210taikou_e.html. See also
Japanese Defense Agency, *Defense of Japan: 2006* (Tokyo: Boeicho, 2006). Most recently,
this expanded security role has included the dispatch of Japanese warships and military
surveillance aircraft to participate in international antipiracy missions off the coast of
Somalia. See Mari Yamaguchi, "Japanese Destroyers Head to Somalia on Anti-Piracy
Mission," Associated Press, July 6, 2009.

28. Pempel, "What the President-Elect Should Know." Subsequent official Japanese defense
documents have continued to draw attention to the potential threat posed by China.
Most recently, see "Defense of Japan 2010," Japanese Ministry of Defense, September
10, 2010, OSC JPP20100914134001 and National Defense Program Guidelines for FY
2011 and beyond, Japanese Ministry of Defense, Approved by the Security Council
and the Cabinet on December 17, 2010, (Provisional Translation), www.mod.go.jp/e/
d_act/d_policy/pdf/guidelinesFY2011.pdf. See below for more on this point.

29. "Joint Statement of the U.S.-Japan Security Consultative Committee," Ministry of
Foreign Affairs of Japan, Washington, February 19, 2005, www.mofa.go.jp/region/
n-america/us/security/scc/joint0502.html. The relevant passage stated: "In the
region, common strategic objectives include:

- Ensure the security of Japan, strengthen peace and stability in the Asia-Pacific
region, and maintain the capability to address contingencies affecting the United
States and Japan.
- Support peaceful unification of the Korean Peninsula.
- Seek peaceful resolution of issues related to North Korea, including its nuclear
programs, ballistic missile activities, illicit activities, and humanitarian issues such
as the abduction of Japanese nationals by North Korea.
- Develop a cooperative relationship with China, welcoming the country to play a
responsible and constructive role regionally as well as globally.
- Encourage the peaceful resolution of issues concerning the Taiwan Strait through
dialogue.
- Encourage China to improve transparency of its military affairs.
- Encourage Russia's constructive engagement in the Asia-Pacific region.
- Fully normalize Japan–Russia relations through the resolution of the Northern
Territories issue.
- Promote a peaceful, stable, and vibrant Southeast Asia.

- Welcome the development of various forms of regional cooperation, while stressing the importance of open, inclusive, and transparent regional mechanisms.
- Discourage destabilizing sales and transfers of arms and military technology.
- Maintain the security of maritime traffic.

30. This phrasing elicited great concern in China at the time since it could theoretically include Taiwan. In fact, the Japanese government never explicitly rejected such a connection. See Soeya Yoshihide, "Taiwan in Japan's Security Considerations," *China Quarterly*, vol. 165 (March 2001): 141–44.

31. "Countering China's Military Modernization," Backgrounder, Council on Foreign Relations, February 4, 2009, www.cfr.org/publication/9052/countering_chinas_military_modernization.html?breadcrumb=/publication/publication_list percent3Ftype percent3Dbackgrounder; Pempel, "What the President-Elect Should Know"; Hughes, "Japanese Military Modernization"; Thomas A. Drohan, *American-Japanese Security Agreements, Past and Present* (Jefferson N.C.: McFarland, 2007), 174–75; Christopher W. Hughes and Akiko Fukushima, "U.S.-Japan Security Relations: Toward Bilateralism Plus?" in *Beyond Bilateralism: U.S.-Japan Relations in the New Asia-Pacific*, edited by Ellis S. Krauss and T. J. Pempel (Stanford, Calif.: Stanford University Press, 2004), 55–86.

32. Washington was probably at least initially not terribly supportive toward the APT, which had emerged in large part because of Asian irritation with the way the United States had handled the regional financial crisis of 1997–1998. However, once it emerged as a significant dialogue, Washington supported a strong Japanese role within it, given that the United States had been excluded from it. I am indebted to Mike Mochizuki for this observation.

33. Indeed, in the early 1990s, Japan had led the way in pushing for a regionwide security forum, an initiative that the United States at first greeted with some dismay. I am again indebted to Mochizuki for this observation.

34. Hughes and Fukushima, "U.S.-Japan Security Relations." For more on the EAS, see below.

35. This is from interviews. According to one interviewee, reportedly few if any discussions between security officials in Tokyo and Washington during the Clinton era dealt with China.

36. Several former senior U.S. officials stressed that Sino-Japanese tensions did not serve U.S. interests and were discouraged by Washington at various times. As one respondent remarked: "We're not smart enough to play that game [that is, manipulating Sino-Japanese tensions to serve U.S. interests]. Nobody but Kissinger is smart enough, and he had full control of the apparatus. Plus we don't have an interest in raised Sino-Japanese tension, and we don't want to get pulled into a conflict over the Senkakus."

37. I am especially indebted to Tiffany Ng for her invaluable assistance in preparing this discussion of the DPJ's stance toward China.

38. This development actually began under the LDP, during the Abe administration (see below), but it became most pronounced during the Hatoyama period. In March 2010, Katsuya Okada, former DPJ prime minister Hatoyama's foreign minister, stated that Japanese foreign policy under the more conservative Liberal Democratic Party followed the U.S. stance "too closely" and described the future as "the age of Asia." In December 2009, Ichiro Ozawa, a dominant figure in the DPJ, led a delegation of more than 600 Japanese to Beijing, including 143 parliamentarians. Moreover, when

Hu Jintao's presumed successor, Xi Jinping, visited Tokyo shortly afterward, he was granted an audience with the emperor. See Gideon Rachman, "Japan Edges from America Towards China," *Financial Times*, March 8, 2010. Okada has since rejected the notion (believed by many in Washington) that Japan is trying to develop closer relations with China while moving further from the United States. See Mure Dickie and David Pilling, "Tokyo Struggles to Solve US Marine Base Dispute: Minister Sees May Deadline Difficulty," *Financial Times*, April 19, 2010; Leif-Eric Easley, Tetsuo Kotani, and Aki Mori, "Electing a New Japanese Security Policy? Examining Foreign Policy Visions Within the Democratic Party of Japan," *Asia Policy* (National Bureau of Asian Research), no. 9 (January 2010), Weston S. Konishi, "The Democratic Party of Japan: Its Foreign Policy Position and Implications for U.S. Interests," Congressional Research Service, August 12, 2009, www.voltairenet.org/IMG/pdf/Democratic_Party_of_Japan.pdf.

39. Martin Fackler, "Japan Relents on U.S. Base on Okinawa," *New York Times*, May 23, 2010; Michael Werbowski, "Hatoyama's Resignation," WorldPress.org, June 11, 2010; Blaine Harden, "Japanese Prime Minister Yukio Hatoyama Resigns," *Washington Post*, June 2, 2010; "Japan PM Apologises for U.S. Bases in Okinawa," BBC News, June 23, 2010; George R Packard, "The United States–Japan Security Treaty at 50," *Foreign Affairs*, vol. 89, no. 2 (March–April 2010): 92–104; Weston S. Konishi, "The Democratic Party of Japan: Its Foreign Policy Position and Implications for U.S. Interests," CRS Report for Congress, August 12, 2009; Democratic Party of Japan, "Our Basic Philosophy," www.dpj.or.jp/english/about_us/philosophy.html; "Minshu, "Chi-i kyōtei kaitei mo   Gaikō seisaku gen-an ni moru" (Democratic Party, even revision of the Status of Forces Agreement—Included in the foreign policy draft plan), *Asahi Shimbun*, June 24, 2009, 4; William Pfaff, "A New Japan Confronts Its American Problem," September 1, 2009, www.williampfaff.com/modules/news/article.php?storyid=427; Mark Landler and Martin Fackler, "U.S. Is Seeing Policy Thorns in Japan Shift," *New York Times*, September 2, 2009; "Asia's Biggest Economies Promise Greater Cooperation," Associated Press, October 12, 2009; Martin Fackler, "Fresh Off Victory, Japanese Party Flexes Muscle," *New York Times*, September 3, 2009; "Japan's New Leader Vows More Equal U.S. Relationship," Associated Press, September 16, 2009; Takenori Noguchi, "Hatoyama Cabinet (Part 2)—Foreign Minister Katsuya Okada: 'Japan Should Assert What It Should Assert,' " interview with Foreign Minister Katsuya Okada, *Mainichi Shimbun*, September 20, 2009; Helene Cooper, "Japan Cools to America as It Prepares for Obama Visit," *New York Times*, November 12, 2009.

40. Planning for the 2010 NDPG was of course under way before the DPJ rose to power. The document connected growing concerns over China's military buildup and more active military presence in neighboring waters with a strategic shift southward and the development of a more "dynamic" defense posture involving more flexible, mobile, and sustainable Japanese force deployments. Privately, Japanese defense officials stated that the NDPG marked the beginning of a systematic effort to assess how best to strengthen Japan's capacity to meet the growing security challenge posed by China, especially in the East China Sea. See Japanese Ministry of Defense, "National Defense Program Guidelines for FY 2011 and Beyond," Approved by the Security Council and the Cabinet on December 17, 2010, (Provisional Translation), www.mod.go.jp/e/d_act/d_policy/pdf/guidelinesFY2011.pdf; Prime Minister Naoto Kan, "Opening Japan and Reinventing Kizuna," speech presented at the World Economic Forum, Davos, Switzerland, January 29, 2011, (Provisional Translation), www.kantei.go.jp/foreign/kan/statement/201101/29davos_e.html; "Press Conference by Prime Minister Naoto

Kan Following His Visit to the United States," September 24, 2010, www.kantei.go.jp/
foreign/kan/statement/201009/24un_naigai_e.html; "Q&A: Japanese Foreign Minister
Seiji Maehara on China, the Yen," *Wall Street Journal*, September 25, 2010, http://
online.wsj.com/article/SB10001424052748703793804575512543702131502.html; U.S.
secretary of state Hillary Clinton and Japanese foreign minister Maehara, Joint Press
Availability, U.S. Department of State, Office of the Spokesman, October 27, 2010,
Kahala Hotel and Resort, Honolulu, www.america.gov/st/texttrans-english/2010/October/
20101028123524su0.6718823.html#ixzz1CdUPlNsw; Seiji Maehara, speech at Center
for Strategic and International Studies, Washington, January 6, 2011, http://csis.org/
files/attachments/110106_maehara.pdf; Martin Fackler, "Japan Announces Defense
Policy to Counter China," *New York Times*, December 16, 2010; "Japanese Defence,"
Financial Times, Editorial, December 14, 2010, www.ft.com/cms/s/0/0a406b46-07bb-
11e0-a568-00144feabdc0.html#axzz18BhKtDUr; Martin Fackler, "Japan Plans Military
Shift to Focus More on China," *New York Times*, December 12, 2010, www.nytimes.
com/2010/12/13/world/asia/13japan.html?ref=world; Chico Harlan, "New Japanese
Defense Plan Emphasizes Threat of China," *Washington Post*, December 12, 2010,
www.washingtonpost.com/wp-dyn/content/article/2010/12/12/AR2010121203790.
html; Martin Fackler, "Japan Announces New Defense Policy to Counter China," *New
York Times*, December 16, 2010, www.nytimes.com/2010/12/17/world/asia/17japan.
html. Also see "Summary of National Defense Program Guidelines FY 2011," Japanese
Ministry of Defense, December 17, 2010, www.kantei.go.jp/foreign/kakugikettei/2010/
summary_ndpg_e.pdf.; Tomoko A. Hosaka, "China Surpasses Japan as World's No. 2
Economy," *Washington Post*, August 16, 2010; and Linda Sieg, "Analysis: Japan Dilemma
as Economic Dependence on China Grows," Reuters, September 2, 2010, www.reuters.
com/article/2010/09/02/us-japan-china-idUSTRE6810LQ20100902.

41. The position of the former group has been buttressed significantly in recent months as
a result of the above-mentioned Japanese diplomatic clashes with Beijing (see below
for further details). Narushige Michishita and Richard Samuels believe that this debate
largely involves four different groups in Japan: (1) "Autonomists," who want distance
from both the United States and China, and prefer that Japan acquire and sustain an
independent military capability; (2) "Bandwagoners," who advocate a China–Japan
economic condominium, discount the Chinese military threat, and emphasize the
benefits from a robust bilateral economic relationship with the new global economic
giant; (3) "Balancers," who are particularly attentive to direct military threats from
China and less enamored with the economic benefits to be derived from closer relations
with China; and (4) "Integrators," who believe that Japan can—and should—have it both
ways, that is, that better economic relations with Beijing need not be purchased at the
price of diminished relations with Washington. See Narushige Michishita and Richard
J. Samuels, "Hugging and Hedging: Japanese Grand Strategy in the 21st Century," paper
prepared for the project on "Worldviews of Major and Aspiring Powers: Exploring
Foreign Policy Debates Abroad," Sigur Center for Asian Studies, Elliot School of
International Affairs, George Washington University, forthcoming.

42. This is from interviews and discussions with former U.S. officials.

43. Article 9 is the legal basis for Japan's exclusively defense-oriented policy, its nonexercise
of the right of collective self-defense, and a range of antimilitaristic prohibitions. It
states: "Aspiring sincerely to an international peace based on justice and order, the

Japanese people forever renounce war as a sovereign right of the nation and the threat or use of force as means of settling international disputes.
(2) In order to accomplish the aim of the preceding paragraph, land, sea, and air forces, as well as other war potential, will never be maintained. The right of belligerency of the state will not be recognized."

44. In an *Asahi Shimbun* poll in 2004, 53 percent of respondents were in favor of revision—the first time a majority had been recorded since the newspaper began polling on the issue. According to the survey, 60 percent of respondents opposed revision of Article 9, a decline of 14 points from the previous survey in 2001. In 2008, the same poll suggested that public support had shifted significantly, with 59 percent opposed to constitutional revision overall, and 66 percent opposed to revision of Article 9, 23 percent in favor, and 11 percent undecided. Similarly, in April 2010, *Asahi Shimbun*'s poll indicated that 67 percent of Japanese opposed revision of Article 9, with only 24 percent in favor. Overall, 47 percent of respondents favored revision of the Constitution (39 percent opposed), but the reason respondents overwhelmingly (75 percent) identified was the need for a new system of rights, and *not* Article 9 (which was the reason for only 15 percent of constitutional revision advocates). *Asahi Shimbun*, April 2010 Regular Public Opinion Poll, released April 19, 2010, available in the Mansfield Asian Opinion Poll Database, www.mansfieldfdn.org/polls/2010/poll-10-12.htm.

45. T. J. Pempel, "Japan: Divided Government, Diminished Resources," in *Strategic Asia 2008–09*, ed. Tellis, Kuo, and Marble, 116; Richard J. Samuels, "Wing Walking: The U.S.-Japan Alliance," *Global Asia*, vol. 4, no. 1 (Spring 2009): 16–21.

46. "Defense Program and Budget of Japan: Overview of FY 2011 Budget Request," Japanese Ministry of Defense, August 2010, 35, www.mod.go.jp/e/d_budget/pdf/221020.pdf.

47. Stockholm International Peace Research Institute, Military Expenditures Database, http://milexdata.sipri.org. These military expenditure numbers are calculated in terms of constant 2008 U.S. dollars.

48. As Samuels stated (before the 2009 victory of the DPJ): "It is remarkable that after decades of cheap talk about how Tokyo is ready to provide global public goods, only 38 Japanese troops participate in just three UN peacekeeping operations today, compared to more than 2,000 Chinese soldiers in 11 peacekeeping operations. Its defense budget continues to decline (it is now less than 0.9 percent of GDP), host nation support for U.S. forces was temporarily suspended in 2008, and the Japanese government has abandoned its efforts to reinterpret the constitution to allow its military to protect allied forces under fire outside of Japanese territory. Japan today—even before the inevitable accession of the Democratic Party of Japan (DPJ) to power and despite paying more than $6 billion for the relocation of U.S. marines from Okinawa to Guam—is less able and less willing to support the U.S. than it was three years ago." Samuels, "Wing Walking."

49. For example, in 2005, Japan's Defense White Paper for the first time highlighted Tokyo's growing angst over China's increasing air and naval power capabilities. In January 2007, Japanese leaders and analysts were alarmed at China's test of an antisatellite system, which poses implications for U.S. military satellite capabilities and Japan's burgeoning military satellite program. Japanese officials have also taken note of Chinese submarine incursions into Japan's territorial waters: It detected the passage of a Chinese nuclear-powered submarine in its waters on November 10, 2004 (China

apologized and claimed the vessel had unintentionally veered off course), and claimed that a Chinese submarine entered its territorial waters in September 2008 (which China denied). In October 2008, for the first time, a Chinese flotilla of four naval ships sailed into the Pacific Ocean through the Tsugaru Strait between Honshu and Hokkaido, and then passed between Okinawa and Miyako islands in November; and a Chinese survey ship entered Japanese territorial waters near the Senkaku/Diaoyu islets in December 2008. In addition, Japan's Defense White Paper of 2008 highlighted concerns over the potentially adverse impact of continued PLA maritime and air modernization on Japan's security environment, stating that "Japan is apprehensive about how the military power of China will influence the regional state of affairs and the security of Japan." In particular, this statement reflects growing concerns within Japanese defense circles over the implications of China's growing maritime power projection capabilities for the continued defense of Japan's vital sea lines of communication and those outlying island territories disputed by Beijing and Tokyo. See Michael McDevitt et al., *Sino-Japanese Rivalry: Implications for U.S. Policy* (Washington, D.C.: Center for Naval Analyses, 2009).

50. Michael Finnegan, *Managing Unmet Expectations in the U.S.-Japan Alliance*, Special Report 17 (Seattle: National Bureau of Asian Research, 2009). Also see Pempel, "What the President-Elect Should Know"; Ralph A. Cossa, "U.S.-Japan Relations: What Should Washington Do?" in *America's Role in Asia: Asian and American Views*, Michael Armacost, J. Stapleton Roy, Han Sung-Joo, Tommy Koh, C. Raja Mohan, project chairs (San Francisco: Asia Foundation, 2008), 208–9; and Richard Halloran, "Japan Sliding," *Washington Times*, November 5, 2008, www.washingtontimes.com/news/2008/nov/05/japan-sliding. During Koizumi's state visit to Pyongyang in September 2002, Kim Jong-il admitted that North Korea had abducted Japanese citizens decades earlier. Pyongyang subsequently released only five of the abductees and claimed that the others had died under mysterious circumstances. This issue has strongly influenced the Japanese stance toward the North Korean nuclear issue, leading to strong public demands for an accounting of the Japanese abductees as part of any agreement with Pyongyang. Also see Cossa, "U.S.-Japan Relations," 209. While reaffirming Japan's strong concerns regarding the North Korean nuclear issue, officials of the DPJ government have not reiterated the above fears toward the United States in this area. In fact, the DPJ government has sent some signals that it might downplay the abductee issue, and strongly favors a greater emphasis on global denuclearization disarmament. See Minshu, "Chi-i kyōtei kaitei mo."

51. Finnegan, *Managing Unmet Expectations*. Finnegan cites the views of Japanese defense analysts and officials (participating in a National Bureau of Asian Research workshop on the alliance) that U.S. political leaders tend "to underestimate the Chinese military and downplay Japan's concerns regarding China's intentions." Some among this group also "conveyed dismay at how the United States often seems to defer to China at the United Nations and to underappreciate Japan's contributions in the same venue. This feeling has been exacerbated with recent comments regarding a U.S.-China 'Group of 2' (G-2)." Finnegan concludes that "the perception of a growing preference for China over Japan, though arguably not the case, contributes to a lessening of confidence in the U.S. commitment to Japan's most basic defense." Also see Cossa, "U.S.-Japan Relations," 208–9. The author adds that Japanese concerns toward the United States were also aggravated by Washington's supposed lack of enthusiasm for Tokyo's bid for

a permanent U.N. Security Council seat, the Honda Amendment calling on Japan to apologize to World War II comfort women, and the U.S. rejection of Japan's request for F-22 aircraft. Also see Richard Halloran, "Japan Sliding," *Washington Times*, November 5, 2008, www.washingtontimes.com/news/2008/nov/05/japan-sliding.

52. The other fear is entrapment. This essentially refers to the possibility that Japan could be pulled into a U.S.-designed and -dominated security posture that does not serve Japanese interests, for example, one that is sharply antagonistic toward China and thereby forces Tokyo to make a potentially costly choice between the two powers. For a discussion of both these concerns, see Hughes and Fukushima, "U.S.-Japan Security Relations."

53. White House, Office of the Press Secretary, "Remarks by President Barack Obama at Suntory Hall, Tokyo, Japan," November 14, 2009. In this address on U.S. policy in Asia, Obama stated: "America's alliances in Asia continue to provide the bedrock of security and stability that has allowed the nations and peoples of this region to pursue opportunity and prosperity that was unimaginable at the time of my first childhood visit to Japan. And even as American troops are engaged in two wars around the world, our commitment to Japan's security and to Asia's security is unshakeable [applause], and it can be seen in our deployments throughout the region. Also see Yoichi Kato, "U.S. Warm to Proposal to Reaffirm Security Pact," *Asahi Shimbun*, July 23, 2009, www.asahi.com/english/Herald-asahi/TKY200907230065.html; Kurt M. Campbell, "Press Availability in Beijing, China," Remarks in Beijing, October 14, 2009; James B. Steinberg, "East Asia and the Pacific," remarks at the National Bureau of Asian Research Conference, "Engaging Asia 2009: Strategies for Success," Washington, April 1, 2009, www.state.gov/s/d/2009/121564.htm. Moreover, Japanese prime minister Taro Aso was the first foreign head of government to visit Washington after Obama took office, and Japan was the site of Hillary Clinton's first foreign visit as secretary of state, before she headed to the 2009 ARF meeting. See also Robert M. Gates, secretary of defense, remarks at Keio University, Tokyo, January 14, 2011, www.defense.gov/Speeches/Speech.aspx?SpeechID=1529; in his remarks, Gates expressed that the U.S.-Japan "alliance is more necessary, more relevant, and more important than ever."

54. Joint Press Conference with U.S. secretary of defense Robert M. Gates and Japanese minister of defense Tosihimi Kitazawa, Tokyo, January 13, 2011, www.defense.gov/transcripts/transcript.aspx?transcriptid=4753; Sheila Smith, "Talking Strategy with Japan," blog post, Council on Foreign Relations, January 13, 2011, http://blogs.cfr.org/asia/2011/01/13/talking-strategy-with-japan; Martin Fackler and Elisabeth Bumiller, "U.S. Will Defer to Japan on Moving Okinawa Base," *New York Times*, January 13, 2011. In contrast to this more accommodating stance, in the fall of 2009, senior Obama defense officials such as Defense Secretary Robert Gates had communicated Washington's strong desire for the DPJ government to follow through with the agreed-upon U.S. forces relocation agreements and to continue to exercise "leadership in meeting global security challenges." See U.S. Department of Defense, "Joint Press Conference with Japanese Defense Minister Toshimi Kitazawa and Secretary of Defense Robert Gates," October 21, 2009.

55. Finnegan, *Managing Unmet Expectations*. Finnegan writes: "Japan is not meeting critical U.S. expectations to (1) build a more operationally capable alliance, one that is not only more capable of defending Japan but also includes an increasingly lead role for Japan, as well as to (2) transition this more capable alliance to one that is reliably

applicable to regional and global security contingencies. From the Japanese point of view, the United States is failing to fully meet primary expectations both to (1) sustain the proper capability for the defense of Japan in accordance with the basic functions of the alliance and the security treaty, and to (2) fulfill commitments to extended deterrence and nuclear nonproliferation that allow Japan to maintain its non-nuclear stance." Moreover, Finnegan asserts that "the failure of the allies to meet mutual expectations creates gaps in the respective security strategies of the two countries that make the alliance highly vulnerable to a significant shock should one of these areas of mismatched expectations be tested in a crisis. This shock would then potentially lead to a crisis of confidence by one or both partners, and to subsequent decisions to seek other options—perhaps beyond the alliance—in order to ensure their respective security." Also see Blaine Harden, "Japanese Premier at Odds over Air Station Negotiations; Hatoyama Says Talks, as Viewed by U.S., are 'meaningless,' " *Washington Post*, November 17, 2009; Masami Ito, "Hatoyama and Obama Put Off Hard Decisions," *Japan Times*, November 15, 2009; and Linda Sieg, "Japan, U.S. Ties Still Troubled After Summit," Reuters, November 15, 2009.

56. In May 2010, former prime minister Hatoyama reversed course and assured President Obama in a telephone conversation that Japan would abide by the existing relocation agreement. This assurance was reflected in the joint statement issued following the so-called Two-Plus-Two meeting of U.S. Defense Department and Japanese Foreign Ministry leaders on May 28, 2010. However, this Japanese concession precipitated Hatoyama's political demise, and the fate of the agreement remains in limbo. See "Joint Statement of the U.S.–Japan Security Consultative Committee," Office of the Spokesman, U.S. Department of State, Washington, May 27, 2010, www.state.gov/r/ pa/prs/ps/2010/05/142318.htm; Greg Chaffin, "Okinawa and the Changing U.S.-Japan Alliance," Foreign Policy in Focus, October 5, 2010, www.fpif.org/articles/okinawa_and_ the_changing_us-japan_alliance; Eric Talmadge, "Amid Island Rows, Japan, U.S. Affirm Security Ties," *Washington Post*, November 13, 2010, www.washingtonpost.com/wp-dyn/ content/article/2010/11/12/AR2010111207383.html; and Gavan McCormack, "The U.S.-Japan 'Alliance,' Okinawa, and Three Looming Elections," *Japan Focus*, September 13, 2010, www.foreignpolicyi.org/2010forum.

57. Gerald Curtis, "Obama and East Asia: No Room for Complacency," East Asia Forum, August 30, 2009, www.eastasiaforum.org/2009/08/30 obama-and-east-asia-no-room-for-complacency.

58. Mike Mochizuki stressed this point to the author in a private correspondence, and the author readily agrees with it. See also Smith, "Talking Strategy."

59. Although China began developing gas fields in disputed territory in the East China Sea in the mid-1990s, Japan did not object to such activities until after Koizumi came into office.

60. Beijing viewed this development as a breach by Japan of its "One China" commitments and an indication of Japanese willingness to join the United States in intervening in the defense of Taiwan in the event of a potential conflict over the island. See Kent E. Calder, "China and Japan's Simmering Rivalry," *Foreign Affairs*, vol. 85, no. 2 (March–April 2006): 129–39; Mike M. Mochizuki, "Japan's Long Transition: The Politics of Recalibrating Grand Strategy," in *Domestic Political Change and Grand Strategy*, edited by Ashley J. Tellis and Michael Wills (Seattle: National Bureau of Asian Research, 2007), 68–111; Michael M. Mochizuki, "China–Japan Relations: Downward Spiral or a New Equilibrium?" in *Power*

Shift: China and Asia's New Dynamics, edited by David Shambaugh (Berkeley: University of California Press, 2003); Robert G. Sutter, *China's Rise: Implications for U.S. Leadership in Asia*, Policy Study 21 (Washington, D.C.: East-West Center, 2006); "Asia: The Return of the Fukuda Doctrine; Japan's Foreign Policy," *Economist*, December 15, 2007; James J. Przystup, "Japan–China Relations: New Year, Old Problems, Hope for Wen," *Comparative Connections*, vol. 9, no. 1 (April 2007): 117–32; Mure Dickie, "Talks Signal Warming Japan-China Ties," FT.com, December 28, 2007; Michael Yahuda, "The Limits of Economic Interdependence: Sino-Japanese Relations," in *New Directions in the Study of China's Foreign Policy*, edited by Alastair Iain Johnston and Robert S. Ross (Stanford, Calif.: Stanford University Press, 2006), 162–85.

61. Many in Japan viewed the demonstrations as encouraged and orchestrated by the Chinese government.

62. See Robert G. Sutter, *The United States in Asia* (Lanham, Md.: Rowman & Littlefield, 2008), 268. Also see Calder, "China and Japan's Simmering Rivalry." See below for more discussion of multilateral regional initiatives.

63. Abe also met with Chinese president Hu Jintao at the sidelines of the Asia-Pacific Economic Conference in Vietnam and with Prime Minister Wen during the Association of Southeast Asian Nations 10+3 trilateral leaders' meeting in the Philippines; *China Daily*, November 18, 2006, and Xinhua, January 15.

64. In addition to pledging to build a "mutually beneficial relationship based on common strategic interest," both sides agreed to launch a high-level economic dialogue, strengthen existing dialogues in many other areas (including the Japan–China Security Dialogue, Japan–China Economic Partnership Consultation, consultations between Japan and China concerning UN reform, consultations between Japan and China concerning Africa, and the Japan–China Press Secretary consultations), increase defense contacts and ship visits, establish a "communication mechanism" between the two defense authorities, enhance a wide range of economic cooperation mechanisms, and pursue joint development of resources in contested areas (for example, the East China Sea) while putting aside the issue of territorial sovereignty. See the Japan–China Joint Press Statement of April 11, 2007, issued in Tokyo. In addition, Japan's Ministry of Economic Trade and Industry unveiled in summer 2006 a proposal for an East Asian Economic Partnership Agreement that includes China, as well as the ASEAN states, Japan, South Korea, Australia, New Zealand, and India. Mochizuki, "Japan's Long Transition," 103, 106.

65. "China, Japan Sign Joint Statement on Promoting Strategic, Mutually Beneficial Ties," Xinhua, May 8, 2008, http://news.xinhuanet.com/english/2008-05/08/content_8124331.htm.

66. Kazuyo Kato, "Fukuda-Hu Summitry: Mutual Interests, Not Mutual Trust?" *China Brief*, vol. 8, issue 11 (June 6, 2008). Reiji Yoshida, "Fukuda, Hu Put Focus on Future," *Japan Times*, May 8, 2008. Akio Yaita, "Tough Trip for President Hu, Protests Wherever He Went Over Human Rights, Food Poisoning," *Sankei Shimbun*, May 11, 2008, OSC JPP20080512034001. Takashi Sudo, Kenichi Narusawa, and Mayumi Otani, "Japan–China Diplomacy: Unstable 'Mutual Benefits,' Persistent Hard Line, Both Leaders Emphasize Achievement," *Mainichi Shimbun*, May 11, 2008, OSC JPP20080512026006. Ding Ying, "The Season of Regeneration," *Beijing Review*, no. 20 (May 15, 2008), OSC

CPP20080520715033. "President's 'Warm Spring' Visit to Japan a Complete Success: FM," Xinhua, May 10, 2008, OSC CPP20080510968106.

67. "China Accepts Japan Quake Rescue Team," Jiji Press, May 15, 2008, OSC JPP20080515969051; "Japan Announces Additional Relief Aid for China Over Quake," Xinhua, May 30, 2008, OSC CPP20080530968221; Kazuto Tsukamoto, "Japan, China Seal Deal On Gas Fields," *Asahi Shimbun*, June 18, 2008, OSC JPP20080618969105; "China and Japan Reach Principled Consensus on the East China Sea Issue," Xinhua, June 18, 2008, OSC CPP20080618172003.

68. James J. Przystup, "Japan–China Relations: Gyoza, Beans, and Aircraft Carriers," *Comparative Connections*, vol. 10, no. 4 (January 2009). Kenji Minemura, "PRC Steps Up Offensive on Territorial Dispute Over Senkaku Islands; Heated Exchange During Summit Meeting," *Asahi Shimbun Online*, December 13, 2008, OSC JPP20081215036002. "More on Aso Protesting to Wen Jiabao Over Chinese Ships Entering 'Japanese Waters,'" Kyodo World Service, December 13, 2008, OSC JPP20081213969045; Satoshi Ogawa, "Official U.S. View: Senkakus Fall Under the U.S.-Japan Security Treaty," *Yomiuri Shimbun*, March 5, 2009. James J. Przystup, "Japan–China Relations: New Year, Old Problems," *Comparative Connections*, vol. 11, no. 1 (April 2009). For the U.S. position on the disputed islands as expressed during the Bush administration, see Adam Ereli, deputy spokesman, U.S. Department of State, Daily Press Briefing, Washington, March 24, 2004, http://2001-2009.state.gov/r/pa/prs/dpb/2004/30743.htm. To quote: "Mr. Ereli: The Senkaku Islands have been under the administrative control of the Government of Japan since having been returned as part of the reversion of Okinawa in 1972. Article 5 of the 1960 U.S.-Japan Treaty of Mutual Cooperation and Security states that the treaty applies to the territories under the administration of Japan; thus, Article 5 of the Mutual Security Treaty applies to the Senkaku Islands. Sovereignty of the Senkaku Islands is disputed. The U.S. does not take a position on the question of the ultimate sovereignty of the Senkaku Diaoyu Islands. This has been our longstanding view. We expect the claimants will resolve this issue through peaceful means and we urge all claimants to exercise restraint."

69. Mure Dickie and Kathrin Hille, "Beijing Agrees to Start Gas Talks with Japan," *Financial Times*, May 31, 2010.

70. The Japanese government seized the Chinese ship and its crew, released them all but the captain, and then eventually released the captain after holding him for several days. This led to anti-Japanese protests in China (some allegedly encouraged by the Chinese government), suspension of high-level government-to-government contacts, and the postponement of joint development talks by Beijing. See Yoree Koh, "Boat Crash Fuels Beijing-Tokyo Row," *Wall Street Journal*, September 8, 2010; Austin Ramzy, China-Japan Tensions Grow After Shipping Collision,"*Time*, September 13, 2010.

71. Chinese observers interpreted such actions as rhetoric calling for the containment of China. Compounding the difficulties that resulted from these developments was Abe's denial that the Japanese government ever coerced the "comfort women" during World War II. See *People's Daily*, March 16, 2007. For overall assessments of the Sino-Japanese relationship, see Gerald L. Curtis, Ryosei Kokubun, and Wang Jisi, eds., *Getting the Triangle Straight: Managing China–Japan–U.S. Relations* (New York: Japan Center for International Exchange, 2010); Christopher M. Dent, *China, Japan and Regional Leadership in East Asia* (Northampton: Edward Elgar, 2008); Michael J.

Green and Nicolas Szechenyi, "Green Shoots in the U.S.-Japan Alliance," *CSIS Japan Chair Platform*, November 9, 2010, http://csis.org/files/publication/101109_Green_GreenShoots_JapanPlatform_formatted.pdf; Leszek Buszynski, "Sino-Japanese Relations: Interdependence, Rivalry and Regional Security," *Contemporary Southeast Asia: A Journal of International and Strategic Affairs*, vol. 31, no. 1 (2009): 143–71; Mochizuki, "Japan's Long Transition," 105; Wang Jisi, "China's Changing Role in Asia," in *The Rise of China and a Changing East Asian Order*, edited by Kokubun Ryosei and Wang Jisi (Tokyo: Asia Pacific Agenda Project, 2004), 3–20; and Richard J. Samuels, *Securing Japan: Tokyo's Grand Strategy and the Future of East Asia* (Ithaca, N.Y.: Cornell University Press, 2007); "Japan's military ambition," *China Daily*, December 20, 2010.

72. See Richard C. Bush III, "China–Japan Security Relations," Brookings Policy Brief Series, October 2010, Brookings Institution, www.brookings.edu/~/media/Files/rc/papers/2010/10_china_japan_bush/10_china_japan_bush.pdf; Elizabeth C. Economy, Joshua Kurlantzick, Sheila A. Smith, and Scott A. Snyder, "Checking China's Territorial Moves," October 21, 2010, Interview at Expert Roundup of Council on Foreign Relations, www.cfr.org/publication/23196/checking_chinas_territorial_moves.html; "China's Spat with Japan: Out but Not Over," *Economist*, September 24, 2010, www.economist.com/blogs/asiaview/2010/09/chinas_spat_japan?page=46; M. G. Koo, "The Senkaku/Diaoyu Dispute and Sino-Japanese Political-Economic Relations: Cold Politics and Hot Economics?" *Pacific Review*, vol. 22, no. 2 (2009): 205–32; and Krista Wiegand, "China's Strategy in the Senkaku/Diaoyu Islands Dispute: Issue Linkage and Coercive Diplomacy," *Asian Security*, vol. 5, no. 2 (2009): 170–93.

73. "Japan, China Agree to Enhance Defense Exchanges," Xinhua, November 27, 2009; Yang Xiao and Liu Cong, "The Democratic Party of Japan Sends Positive Signals in Policy Toward China—Experts' View," Beijing Qingnian Bao, August 31, 2009, OSC CPP20090831710009; Yang Bojiang, "Respond to Change to Guarantee Health, Stability of China–Japan Relations," Dangdai Shijie, September 5, 2009, OSC CPP20090923671011; He Degong, "After Hatoyama Administration Sets Sail: To Hold Political Power, Democratic Party Must Score Pragmatic Achievements to Win Trust of Vast Number of the People," *Liaowang*, no. 38 (September 21, 2009), OSC CPP20090930710007; Weston S. Konishi, "The Democratic Party of Japan: Its Foreign Policy Position and Implications for U.S. Interests," CRS Report for Congress, August 12, 2009; Democratic Party of Japan, "Our Basic Philosophy," www.dpj.or.jp/english/about_us/philosophy.html; "DPJ to Further Advance Japan-China Ties: Party Chief," Xinhua, August 11, 2009, OSC CPP20090811968310; Li Yang, "Chinese and Japanese Experts Interpret the Prospect of the Two Countries' Relations as Optimistic on the Whole, but a Breakthrough Is Difficult," Zhongguo Xinwen She, August 28, 2009, OSC CPP20090828704001; "Sino-Japanese Ties Under 'DPJ Government,'" "Oriental Horizon" Dong Fang Shi Kong, CCTV-13, July 21, 2009, OSC CPP20090722136001; Hitoshi Tanaka, "Japan Under the DPJ," *East Asia Insights*, vol. 4, no. 3 (September 2009); and "Japan, China to Work Together on Creating 'East Asia community,'" *Japan Times*, September 29, 2009.

74. For example, see "Japanese Who Feel Friendly Toward China Drop to Record Low 20 percent," Kyodo News, December 18, 2010, OSC JPP20101218969031.

75. Hiroyuki Akita, "Don't Take U.S. Ties for Granted, Hatoyama," Nikkei Telecom 21, September 4, 2009, OSC JPP20090904969064; "Analysis: Japan Defense Policy Incoherent, Even as China Looms," Nikkei Telecom 21, November 7, 2009, OSC JPP20091107038001; Kensuke Ebata, "China Strategy Should Be Worked Out Promptly," Komentoraina, September 2, 2009, OSC JPP20090901045003. According to one knowledgeable observer of Japanese security circles, a quiet debate has emerged in Tokyo on these issues, with the major division between those hawks who advocate a strategy of "competitive engagement with a hard edge" and doves who urge "cooperative engagement with a soft hedge."

76. Jonathan D. Pollack, "The Korean Peninsula in U.S. Strategy: Policy Issues for the Next President," in Strategic Asia 2008–09, ed. Tellis, Kuo, and Marble.

77. Pollack, September 2008. Also see Eric Heginbotham and Christopher P. Twomey, "America's Bismarckian Asia Policy," Current History, vol. 104, no. 683 (September 2005): 244, 247; Juergen Kleiner, "A Fragile Relationship: The United States and the Republic of Korea," Diplomacy and Statecraft, vol. 17, no. 2 (June 2006): 215–35; Hyeong Jung Park (Center for Northeast Asian Policy Studies), "Looking Back and Looking Forward: North Korea, Northeast Asia and the ROK-U.S. Alliance" (December 2007): 8–12, 18–23; and Jonathan D. Pollack, "The Strategic Futures and Military Capabilities of the Two Koreas," in Strategic Asia 2005–06, ed. Tellis and Wills, 136–72.

78. Joint Vision for the Alliance of the United States of America and the Republic of Korea, Washington, issued June 16, 2009, White House; and Remarks by President Obama and President Lee Myung-Bak of the Republic of Korea in Joint Press Availability, June 16, 2009, White House Rose Garden.

79. Mark McDonald, "Crisis Status in South Korea After North Shells Island," New York Times, November 23, 2010, www.nytimes.com/2010/11/24/world/asia/24korea.html?_ r=1; Chico Harlan and Colum Lynch, "U.N. Security Council Condemns Sinking of South Korean Warship," Washington Post, July 10, 2010; Kwang-Tae Kim, "S. Korea, U.S. to Hold War Games After Any UN Action," Associated Press, July 6, 2010, www.google. com/hostednews/ap/article/ALeqM5hP68wYc-SVkurz50Ez4sLGIfoV9wD9GPFCMO1; Greg Torode, "US Submarines Emerge in Show of Military Might," South China Morning Post, July 4, 2010, www.scmp.com/portal/site/SCMP/menuitem.2af62ecb329d3d773349 2d9253a0a0a0/?vgnextoid=6c48dbee25999210VgnVCM100000360a0a0aRCRD&ss=A sia+ percent26+World&s=News.

80. Ser Myo-ja, "Australia And Korea Reach Security Deal," JoongAng Ilbo, March 6, 2009, http://joongangdaily.joins.com/article/view.asp?aid=2901899. "Seoul, Canberra Sign Defence Pact," BBC News, March 5, 2009; Rob Taylor, "China Arms Spend Prompts South Korea Arms Race Warning," Reuters, March 5, 2009; "Australia, South Korea Agree On Security Pact, Free Trade," Agence France-Presse, March 5, 2009; "Lee, Rudd Agree On Security Cooperation," Chosun Ilbo, March 6, 2009, http://english.chosun. com/w21data/html/news/200903/200903060018.html.

81. Terence Roehrig, "Restructuring the U.S. Military Presence in Korea: Implications for Korean Security and the U.S.-ROK Alliance," Academic Paper Series on Korea 1 (2008): 132–49, www.keia.org/Publications/OnKorea/2008/08Roehrig.pdf. For discussions of the sporadic disturbances occurring in Japan-South Korea relations over a variety of issues—including Japanese history textbooks, the Dokdo (Takeshima) islets dispute, Japanese abductees, Japan's so-called sex slaves of World War II, and Koizumi's annual

visits to the Yasukuni Shrine—see Gilbert Rozman and Shin-wha Lee, "Unraveling the Japan-South Korea 'Virtual Alliance': Populism and Historical Revisionism in the Face of Conflicting Regional Strategies," *Asian Survey* (Berkeley), vol. 46, no. 5 (September–October 2006): 761–84; Onishi, Norimitsu, "Denial Reopens Wounds of Japan's Ex-Sex Slaves," *New York Times*, March 8, 2007; and Anonymous, "Asia: Change of Heart; South Korea," *Economist*, July 19, 2008. Some South Korean media and experts view the disputed islands issue as the biggest potential "stumbling block" to achieving comprehensive bilateral ties. See "Nuga han-il gwangye naggwanhaneunga" (Who is optimistic about Korea–Japan relations), *Chosun Ilbo*, August 31, 2009, cited in OSC KPF20090902117002; "Ilbon Jeong-gwon gyochewa hyanghu han-il gwangye" (Regime change in Japan: Japanese relations and the future), *Segye Ilbo*, August 31, 2009, cited in OSC KPF2009090211700; and "Korea Hopes for New Era in Japanese Relations," *JoongAng Daily*, September 1, 2009, cited in OSC KPP20090901971015.

82. See Michael Green, "The power of trilateralism," *JoongAng Daily*, March 7, 2011, http://joongangdaily.joins.com/article/view.asp?aid=2933075; Chico Harlan, "Japan, S. Korea Seek to Boost Military Relations," *Washington Post*, January 11, 2011; Lee Chi-dong, "S. Korea, U.S., Japan to Regularize High-Level Security Talks," *Yonhap*, October 9, 2008; Jin Dae-woong, "Trilateral Talks Underway in Tokyo," *Korea Herald*, October 29, 2008; "Korea, Japan, US to Step Up Joint Drills," *Choson Ilbo*, November 3, 2008; Kim Ji-hyun, "Korea, Japan, U.S. Reopen Security Dialogue," *Korea Herald*, November 6, 2008; Jung Sung-ki, "S. Korea, US, Japan to Hold Security Talks Regularly," *Korea Times*, November 9, 2008; Sam Kim, "S. Korea, US, Japan Pledge Joint Action Against N. Korea," *Yonhap*, May 31, 2009. Regarding South Korean public views toward the United States and the alliance, according to a late 2010/early 2011 BBC poll, 74 percent of South Koreans feel that America's influence in the world is "mainly positive," whereas only 19 percent believe the United States has a mainly negative influence. Such a strong positive majority placed South Korea among the countries most favorable toward the United States, with its positive ratings of America more than twice as high as Japan's (36 percent positive) and China's (33 percent positive). "Views of US Continue to Improve in 2011 BBC Country Rating Poll," BBC World Service/GlobeScan/PIPA, March 7, 2011, www.worldpublicopinion.org/pipa/pdf/mar11/BBCEvalsUS_Mar11_rpt.pdf. Furthermore, a large majority of South Koreans advocate continuing or even strengthening the U.S.–South Korea alliance. As of late November 2010, 48.6 percent of South Koreans advocate strengthening the alliance, with 30.5 percent in favor of continuing the status quo (only 18.1 percent support an "independent foreign policy"). These numbers reveal a more favorable attitude toward the alliance than in January 2010, before the Cheonan and Yeonpyeong bombings. However, even at that earlier date, 68.3 percent of respondents favored either continuing the status quo (33.6 percent) or strengthening the alliance (34.7 percent). Nae-young Lee and Han-wool Jeong, "The Impact of North Korea's Artillery Strike on Public Opinion in South Korea," Issue Briefing on Public Opinion No. 91, East Asia Institute, December 02, 2010, www.eai.or.kr/type/panelView.asp?bytag=p&catcode=&code=eng_report&idx=9638&. I appreciate the assistance of Rachel Esplin Odell for providing the information contained in this paragraph.

83. "Korea Hopes for New Era in Japan Relations," *JoongAng Ilbo*, September 1, 2009, OSC KPP20090901971015; "ROK President Wants 'Mature Partnership' with Japan," *Korea Times*, August 31, 2009, OSC KPP20090831971094. However, as this article states, some South Korean observers assert that the DPJ is divided on how to handle disputes with

Seoul over historical issues, suggesting that such issues won't be resolved as easily as South Korea hopes.

84. See Dennis Roy, "China–South Korea Relations: Elder Brother Wins Over Younger Brother," Special Assessment: Asia's Bilateral Relations, Asia-Pacific Center for Security Studies, October 2004, www.apcss.org/Publications/SAS/AsiaBilateralRelations/China-SouthKoreaRelationsRoy.pdf; and Jae Ho Chung, *Between Ally and Partner: Korea–China Relations and the United States* (New York: Columbia University Press, 2007).

85. Scott Snyder and See-won Byun, "China–Korea Relations: China Embraces South and North, but Differently," *Comparative Connections*, vol. 11, no. 4 (January 2010), http://csis.org/files/publication/0904qchina_korea.pdf.

86. Robert G. Sutter, *Chinese Foreign Relations: Power and Policy Since the Cold War* (Lanham, Md.: Rowman & Littlefield, 2008), 217–60; Also see Scott Snyder and See-won Byun, "China–Korea Relations: China Embraces South and North, but Differently," *Comparative Connections*, vol. 11, no. 4 (January 2010), http://csis.org/files/publication/0904qchina_korea.pdf; and Scott Snyder, "China–Korea Relations: Strategic Maneuvers for the 'Sandwich Economy,'" *Comparative Connections* vol. 9, no. 2 (July 2007): 121–26.

87. Scott Snyder and See-won Byun, "China-Korea Relations: China's Nuclear North Korea Fever," *Comparative Connections*, vol. 11, no. 3 (October 2009), http://csis.org/files/publication/0903qchina_korea.pdf.

88. Christian Oliver and Jonathan Soble, "China Refuses to Blame N Korea for Sinking Ship," *Financial Times*, May 31, 2010.

89. Ian Johnson and Helene Cooper, "China Seeks New Talks to Ease Korean Tension," *New York Times*, November 28, 2010; Kathrin Hille, "Beijing Helps Defuse Korean Crisis," *Financial Times*, December 29, 2010; Song Jung-a, "Seoul Reverses Stance on Talks with North," *Financial Times*, December 29, 2010, www.ft.com/cms/s/0/e4d82bd2-1327-11e0-a367-00144feabdc0.html#axzz19VlzfNAn; Michael Wines and Mark Landler, "U.S. Shifts Toward Talks on N. Korea," *New York Times*, January 6, 2011, www.nytimes.com/2011/01/07/world/asia/07korea.html?ref=world.

90. Martin Fackler, "Japan to Propose Closer Military Ties with South Korea," *New York Times*, January 4, 2011, www.nytimes.com/2011/01/05/world/asia/05japan.html.

91. See Scott Snyder, "Lee Myung-bak and the Future of Sino-South Korean Relations," *China Brief*, vol. 8, issue 4, February 15, 2008. Snyder writes: "A renewed South Korean focus on the security alliance with the United States serves both as a hedge and as a platform for more intensive economic and political engagement with China by providing South Korea leverage that it would not have on its own in dealings with China, while strategic over-dependence on China without the ROK-U.S. alliance would be accompanied by a loss of political leverage." Also see Kang Jun-young, "Outlook: Look Both Ways," *Joong Ang Ilbo*, trans. *Joong Ang Ilbo* staff, January 31, 2008, OSC KPP20080131971361.

92. This point most strongly argued, for example, by Thomas J. Christensen, See "Fostering Stability or Creating a Monster?" *International Security*, vol. 31, no. 1 (Summer 2006): 81–126. Of course, such an assertion is extremely difficult to substantiate empirically.

93. One former senior Bush administration official pointed out that the United States is largely unconcerned about the possible negative implications of Japan's military modernization efforts because (1) Japan is nowhere near achieving the kind of

capabilities and roles that could alarm most Asian nations; (2) Japan will not have the physical capacity to again become a major conventional military power with the ability to project ground forces far from home, for largely demographic and political reasons; and (3) Japan is highly vulnerable to any type of threat from weapons of mass destruction, given the concentration of its population in a few metropolitan areas. Thus, in this view, as long as Japan remains a non-nuclear power dependent on the United States for its ultimate security, it will remain incapable of posing the kind of existential threat to China or any other nation that some might fear. Interview. Also see Dick K. Nanto, "East Asian Regional Architecture: New Economic and Security Arrangements and U.S. Policy," CRS Report for Congress, January 4, 2008. Nanto states that "Japan's vision for East Asia is one in which the United States continues to provide a nuclear umbrella for the region and in which Tokyo relies on its economic power to exercise leadership. . . . Japan would like to bury its World War II history and be viewed as a peaceful nation and a force for betterment in Asia through economic progress."

94. For another similar view, see Nanto, "East Asian Regional Architecture."

95. In particular, see Tokyo Foundation, "New Security Strategy of Japan: Multilayered and Cooperative Security Strategy," October 8, 2008. This report was produced by a group of highly regarded, influential Japanese security specialists and advisers to the Japanese government. Shinichi Kitaoka (one of the leaders of the project that gave rise to this report) is a senior research fellow at the Tokyo Foundation and a professor in the Graduate School of Law and Politics at Tokyo University. He was Japan's ambassador to the UN from 2004 to 2006. Akihiko Tanaka (the other project leader) is chief research fellow at the Tokyo Foundation and a professor in the Graduate School of Interdisciplinary Information Studies at Tokyo University. The report states: "Chinese military modernization is generating new challenges for the defense of Japan and the Japan–U.S. alliance. Chinese navy and air force buildups may change the Japan–China military power balance in the East China Sea. If China's naval and air operational capability is extended beyond the first island chain in the East China Sea to the second island chain in the Western Pacific Ocean, its ability to block the access of U.S. Pacific Command will be enhanced, affecting the U.S. deterrence capability in the entire East Asian region. Also, with improved capability of medium- and long-range missiles, China has acquired increased potential to target major cities and facilities in Japan, U.S. bases in Japan, U.S. forces deployed in the Pacific, and even major cities in the continental U.S." Also see William Choong, "Flutter Over China's Naval Expansion," *Straits Times*, November 21, 2008.

96. Tokyo Foundation, "New Security Strategy of Japan." The authors state: "It is uncertain whether or not the U.S. will be committed, in the future, to the security of the Asia Pacific at the same level. Sooner, rather than later, we need to create a system that ensures the peace and stability of the region even when the capabilities and determination of the U.S. are weakened." Also see Aaron L. Friedberg, "Asia Rising," *American Interest*, vol. 6, no. 3 (Winter 2009): 53–61; and Samuels, "Wing Walking." Samuels writes: "There has been plenty of open discussion in Tokyo and Washington about 'abandonment,' 'opting out,' 'accommodation to China's rise,' 'erosion of the East Asian balance of power,' 'failure of extended deterrence,' the 'failure of the nonproliferation regime,' 'weak reassurance' and other uncoded indications of an enfeebled alliance."

97. See Hitoshi Tanaka, "Defining Normalcy: The Future Course of Japan's Foreign Policy," *East Asia Insights* (Japan Center for International Exchange), vol. 3, no. 1 (January 2008), www.jcie.org/researchpdfs/EAI/3-1.pdf. Tanaka was deputy minister for foreign affairs of Japan. He states: "Whatever its ultimate evolution, Japan is sure to pursue a foreign policy that is consistent with evolving global norms, embracing multilateralism and allowing the use of military force only in self-defense or with the explicit sanction of the international community." Also see Emma Chanlett-Avery and Bruce Vaughn, "Emerging Trends in the Security Architecture in Asia: Bilateral and Multilateral Ties Among the United States, Japan, Australia, and India," Congressional Research Service, January 7, 2008, www.fas.org/sgp/crs/row/RL34312.pdf. Regarding the "collective self-defense issue," the authors state: "Japan's approach to the principle of 'collective self-defense' has in the past been considered an obstacle to close defense cooperation. The term comes from Article 51 of the UN Charter, which provides that member nations may exercise the rights of both individual and collective self-defense if an armed attack occurs. A 1960 decision by Japan's Cabinet Legislation Bureau interpreted the Constitution to forbid collective actions because it would require considering the defense of other countries, not just the safety of Japan itself." Tobias Harris, "Japan's Leadership Deficit," March 20, 2009, available at www.feer.com/politics/2009/march53/exploring-japans-leadership-deficit; Mure Dickie, "Tough Times for Leaders Could Lead to Political Chaos," *Financial Times*, March 17, 2009, www.ft.com/cms/s/0/b95ec4d4-11b7-11de-87b1-0000779fd2ac.html.

98. For a particularly optimistic take on Japan's ability to thrive economically in Asia over the near to medium terms, see Jesper Koll, "Why I'm Bullish on Japan," *Far Eastern Economic Review*, March 26, 2009, www.feer.com/economics/2009/march58/Bullish-on-Japan. Koll states: "Make no mistake, the immediate future will be designed and invented in Japan, not China, nor elsewhere in Asia. . . . Japan's competitive edge may be hidden by the current gloomy cyclical news. But structurally Japan is in pole position—whether it's in the field of energy efficiency, medical devices, construction machinery, cars or electronic components, the world cannot do without Japanese suppliers. . . . In the end, public debt will have to be paid back by the people and by the returns generated on national assets. Japan's technology base and its powerful diligent workforce should bring high returns."

99. Takashi Inoguchi, Center for Strategic and International Studies, "Japan Desperately Needs Grand Strategy," *PacNet* (Center for Strategic and International Studies), no. 23, March 25, 2009, www.csis.org/media/csis/pubs/pac0923.pdf. "Japan should be globally proactive in the cause for peace. Islands of anarchy and disorder that are filled with injustices must be transformed into islands of peace and order backed by justice. The use of military force for UN-sanctioned operations must be approved by Japan as well."

100. This remains an issue, despite Japan's recent shift toward closer security ties with the United States and its growing suspicion of China, discussed above.

101. These deterrence and reassurance policies are rooted in several policy documents, including formal policy statements, the three joint communiqués signed with China in the 1970s and 1980s, the Taiwan Relations Act, and the so-called Six Assurances. See Taiwan Relations Act, Public Law 96-8, 96th Congress, January 1, 1979; "Joint Communiqué of the United States of America and the People's Republic of China (Shanghai Communiqué)," February 28, 1972, www.ait.org.tw/en/us-joint-communique-1972.html; "Joint Communiqué of the United States of America and the People's Republic of China (Normalization Communiqué)," January 1, 1979, www.ait.

org.tw/en/us-joint-communique-1979.html; "Joint Communiqué of the United States of America and the People's Republic of China (the 1982 Communiqué)," August 17, 1982, www.ait.org.tw/en/us-joint-communique-1982.html; and "The 'Six Assurances' to Taiwan," July 1982, www.taiwandocuments.org/assurances.htm.

102. Richard Bush, "The U.S. Policy of Dual Deterrence," in *If China Attacks Taiwan: Military Strategy, Politics, and Economics,* edited by Steve Tsang (New York: Routledge, 2006), 35–53; Thomas J. Christensen, "Fostering Stability or Creating a Monster?" *International Security* 31, no. 1 (Summer 2006): 81–126; Thomas Christensen, testimony before the Subcommittee on Asia, the Pacific, and the Global Environment of the House Foreign Affairs Committee, "U.S.-China Relations," March 27, 2007, Washington.

103. Alan D. Romberg, *Rein in at the Brink of the Precipice: American Policy Toward Taiwan and U.S.-PRC Relations,* (Washington, D.C.: Henry L. Stimson Center, 2003); Richard C. Bush, *Untying the Knot: Making Peace in the Taiwan Strait* (Washington, D.C.: Brookings Institution Press, 2005); Shirley Kan, "China/Taiwan: Evolution of the 'One China' Policy—Key Statements from Washington, Beijing, and Taipei," CRS Report for Congress, June 1, 2004; Michael Swaine, "China: Exploiting a Strategic Opening," in *Strategic Asia 2004–05,* ed. Tellis and Wills, 67–101; David M. Lampton, *Same Bed, Different Dreams: Managing U.S.-China Relations, 1989–2000* (Berkeley: University of California Press, 2001); Nancy Bernkopf Tucker, ed., *Dangerous Strait: The U.S., China, Taiwan Crisis* (New York: Columbia University Press, 2005).

104. Robert Sutter, "Is Taiwan 'Over'?—I Think Not," *PacNet* (Center for Strategic and International Studies), no. 19, March 17, 2008), www.csis.org/media/csis/pubs/pac0819.pdf. Also see Michael D. Swaine, "Trouble in Taiwan," *Foreign Affairs,* vol. 83, no. 2 (March–April 2004); and Michael D. Swaine, "Managing Relations with the United States," in *Presidential Politics in Taiwan: The Administration of Chen Shui-bian,* edited by Steven M. Goldstein and Julian Chang (Norwalk, Conn.: East Bridge, 2008). According to some interview respondents, the U.S. Congress largely cooperated with the Bush administration in restraining Chen Shui-bian during this tumultuous period. Many Members viewed Chen as uncooperative and his actions as a potential threat to overall U.S. interests in maintaining a stable, workable relationship with Beijing. According to one respondent, a very senior U.S. Senator directly informed Chen that "'if Taiwan provoked a military conflict with China, then I do not think Congress would support Taiwan. On the other hand, if Taiwan were attacked, then that would be quite a different thing.' He actually shocked Chen." Such congressional views resulted from many factors, including: a strong desire to avoid a crisis with China during the prosecution of the global war on terrorism, a growing need to cooperate with China in other areas, and a marked decline in the lobbying ability of the Taiwan government under Chen Shui-bian.

105. The dispatch of private emissaries to both Taipei and Beijing to counsel restraint and, if necessary, issue diplomatic warnings also occurred during earlier administrations. Also see Swaine, "Managing Relations."

106. An Economic Cooperation Framework Agreement was signed on June 29, 2010, as an agreement between Taiwan and the Mainland to reduce and remove tariffs on hundreds of products and promote trade between the two nations. However, it is simply a framework for an agreement that needs to be decided on in the following one or two years. See Ben Richardson and Mark Williams, "China Pulls Taiwan

Closer with Historic Trade Deal," *Bloomberg Businessweek*, June 29, 2010; Zhang Xiang, "Chinese Mainland, Taiwan Sign Landmark Economic Pact," Xinhua, June 29, 2010; and "Taiwan Signs Historic ECFA Trade Agreement with China," *Taiwan News*, June 30, 2010. For details on earlier advances in cross-Strait ties, see Robin Kwong, "A Delicate Detente," *Financial Times*, May 6, 2009, www.ft.com/cms/s/0/5f58b97a-3a72-11de-8a2d-00144feabdc0.html; John Pomfret, "China and Taiwan Get Snuggly," *PostGlobal*, April 29, 2009, http://newsweek.washingtonpost.com/postglobal/pomfretschina/2009/04/one_less_war_to_worry_about_as.html; Keith Bradsher, "Taiwan Takes Step Forward at U.N. Health Agency," *New York Times*, April 29, 2009, www.nytimes.com/2009/04/30/world/asia/30taiwan.html?_r=1&partner=rss&emc=rss; Chiang Chin-yeh and Y. F. Low, "Taiwan, China One Step Closer to Normalized Ties: Chief Negotiator," Central News Agency, April 28, 2009, www.chinapost.com.tw/china/national-news/2009/04/28/206043/Taiwan-China.htm; Alan D. Romberg, "Cross-Strait Relations: 'Ascend the Heights and Take a Long-Term Perspective,'" *China Leadership Monitor*, no. 27 (Winter 2009), http://media.hoover.org/documents/CLM27AR.pdf; Steven M. Goldstein, "China and Taiwan: Signs of Change in Cross-Strait Relations," *China Security*, vol. 5, no. 1 (Winter 2009): 67–72; "China, Taiwan in Direct Exchange," BBC News, July 27, 2009, http://news.bbc.co.uk/2/hi/asia-pacific/8170128.stm; and "Ko Shu-ling, Mo Yan-chihm Chen, and Chiang Sign Four Agreements," *Taipei Times*, November 5, 2008, www.taipeitimes.com/News/front/archives/2008/11/05/2003427809. "Taipei and Beijing inked four agreements yesterday, agreeing to drastically expand flights and allow shipping links across the Taiwan Strait. The four pacts addressed direct sea links, daily charter flights, direct postal service and food safety." "Mainland to Recognize More Taiwanese Court Decisions," Caijing, May 14, 2009, http://english.caijing.com.cn/2009-05-14/110165969.html. To get a sense of how rapidly Sino-Taiwanese economic exchanges have increased, see Robin Kwong, "A Delicate Detente," *Financial Times*, May 6, 2009, www.ft.com/cms/s/0/5f58b97a-3a72-11de-8a2d-00144feabdc0.html. See also "Reunification by Trade?" *Economist*, August 6, 2009, www.economist.com/world/asia/displaystory.cfm?story_id=14191252. Also see Ma Ying-jeou, "The Taiwan Relations Act: Turning a New Chapter," remarks at the Videoconference with the Center for Strategic and International Studies, April 22, 2009. At this event, Ma stated: "We have made significant strides in restoring America's trust in Taiwan. . . . In truth, the policies of my administration share the same common ideals as those embodied in the Taiwan Relations Act. This sentiment was echoed by American Institute in Taiwan chairman, Raymond Burghardt, who recently welcomed this 'new era of cross-Strait civility' as not only reducing the 'danger of miscalculations' but also creating 'real tangible economic benefits' for America and American businesses as a whole. The future prospects of Taiwan–U.S. relations will particularly focus on issues of low politics with an emphasis on pragmatism. We will work closely with our American friends."

107. Ma is not opposed in principle to undertaking such initiatives. However, Taipei views them as simply too risky politically. Moreover, the KMT government has presented a list of conditions that must precede such actions. See "How to Develop Cross-Strait Military Confidence-Building Measures?" *Biweekly on the Mainland Situation* (Kuomintang Policy Committee), no. 1561 (October 14, 2009): 1–5, OSC CPP20091016312003. This document states: "If China and Taiwan both have the will and wish to pragmatically work on building trust for each other, it is absolutely necessary for them to expand their political goodwill and political mutual trust. To this end, they have to remove the following

obstacles: (1) ending cross-Strait hostility and signing a peace agreement; (2) recognizing the legitimacy of each other's political domain; (3) renouncing the use of force on each other; (4) not to mess and meddle with the definition and recognition of the sovereignty of each other by means of symbols, words, or languages." President Ma Ying-jeou has publicly indicated that the Mainland must first remove the missiles trained at Taiwan before the two sides can start talking on building military mutual trust. However, Beijing has insisted that whether to remove the missiles is a matter for negotiation not a precondition. Furthermore, President Ma has also stressed that building cross-Strait military mutual trust is a very sensitive question in that it also involves Taiwan's relations with the United States. "Our major weapons and equipment all come from the United States. Therefore, we have to be very careful."

108. Alongside this basic policy stance, Ma has at the same time arguably expressed some openness to the possibility of undefined political talks with Beijing at some point in the future, after economic issues are resolved, as long as they are (1) "needed by the country"; (2) "supported by the people; and (3) "supervised by the national parliament." Western media interpreted this to mean he would initiate or permit political talks during a second term in office, but Ma has resisted such an interpretation, insisting that there would be no specific timetable for such potential talks. See President Ma Ying-jeou, Associated Press Interview, Office of the President, Taipei, Taiwan, October 19, 2010, http://udn.com/udnplus/Ma_english.pdf; Brian Carovillano and Peter Enav, "AP Interview: Taiwan's Ma moves ahead with China," Associated Press, October 19, 2010, www.boston.com/news/world/asia/articles/2010/10/19/ap_interview_taiwans_ma_moves_ahead_with_china; "Ma denies China political talks report," *China Post*, October 20, 2010, www.chinapost.com.tw/taiwan/national/national-news/2010/10/20/276800/Ma-denies.htm.

109. Alan D. Romberg, "Cross-Strait Relations: Weathering the Storm," *China Leadership Monitor*, vol. 30 (Fall 2009), http://media.hoover.org/documents/CLM30AR.pdf; Romberg, "Cross-Strait Relations: 'Ascend the Heights'"; Kathrin Hille, China Says Ready to Talk Peace with Taiwan, *Financial Times*, March 5, 2009; Cindy Sui, "Ma Goes Too Far, Too Fast for Taiwan," *Asia Times*, October 31, 2008; Luis Yu, "Ties with China Do Not Jeopardize Taiwan's Sovereignty: President," Central News Agency, December 28, 2008, http://english.cna.com.tw/SearchNews/doDetail.aspx?id=200812280012; "Ma Goes for a 'Hard' Taiwan," *Strait Times*, March 20, 2009, www.asianewsnet.net/news.php?id=4658&sec=3; Ma Ying-jeou, "A SMART Strategy for National Security," remarks given before the Association for the Promotion of National Security, February 26, 2008, www.taiwansecurity.org/TS/Ma-SMART.htm; Ko Shu-ling, Ma Urges U.S. to Sell Advanced Fighters, *Taipei Times*, May 29, 2009, www.taipeitimes.com/News/front/archives/2009/05/29/2003444820. Ma Ying-jeou has stated that Beijing must remove the ballistic missiles that are currently threatening Taiwan in increasing numbers before a future peace accord might occur and has asserted that "it's only when Taiwan is properly armed and defended that we have the confidence to make a deal with the Mainland." See Stuart Biggs and Stephen Engle, "PRC Must Remove Missiles, Ma Says," *Taipei Times*, August 1, 2009, www.taipeitimes.com/News/taiwan/archives/2009/08/01/2003450084.

110. The October 2008 U.S. weapons deal was worth $6.4 billion and included "the sale of components for upgrading E-2 Hawkeye early-warning aircraft, 30 Apache attack helicopters, the PAC-3 anti-missile system, 32 Harpoon missiles, spare parts for F16A/B, F5E/5F and C-130 aircraft as well as 182 Javelin anti-tank missiles."

Significantly however, the arms deal did not include 60 Black Hawk helicopters, eight diesel-electric submarines, and four Patriot air defense missile batteries. China's vice foreign minister, He Yafei, lodged a formal protest with the U.S. embassy at the time, and a Chinese spokesman said that the arms deal seriously harmed China's interests as well as Sino-U.S. relations. The Chinese statement said, "The U.S. has violated the three Sino-US communiqués, blatantly interfered in China's internal affairs and endangered China's national security. The Chinese side reserves the right to make further reaction." See Shirley Kan. "Taiwan: Major U.S. Arms Sales Since 1990," Congressional Research Service, August 4, 2008; Summary," *Earth Times*, October 4, 2008, www.earthtimes. org/articles/show/235378,taiwan-welcomes-us-arms-sale-china-protests—summary. html; and John Pomfret, "Taiwan Gets Its Weapons. . . . at Least Some of Them," *PostGlobal*, October 3, 2008, http://newsweek.washingtonpost.com/postglobal/ pomfretschina/2008/10/taiwan_gets_its_weaponsat_leas.html.

111. Alan D. Romberg, *U.S. Arms Sales to Taiwan: Beijing Reacts Sharply* (Washington, D.C.: Henry L. Stimson Center, 2010), www.stimson.org/pub.cfm?id= percent20927; Helene Cooper, "U.S. Approval of Taiwan Arms Sales Angers China," *New York Times*, January 30, 2010; Ben Blanchard and Paul Eckert, "U.S. Seeks Calm as China Fumes Over Taiwan Arms," Reuters, February 1, 2010; Kevin Brown, Kathrin Hille, and Daniel Dombey, "Aerospace Sector Fears China Sanctions," *Financial Times*, January 31, 2010; and Anthony Kuhn, "Nuclear Security Summit May Bring U.S., China Closer," *NPR: Morning Edition*, April 9, 2010. Also see Romberg, "Cross-Strait Relations: 'Ascend the Heights.' " Romberg, "Cross-Strait Relations: Weathering the Storm," cites an Obama official as stating: "That framework of the three U.S.-PRC joint communiqués and the Taiwan Relations Act is unalterable. We're not going to touch it. There will be nothing we say or do on the trip that will go in different directions." He also said: "Our policy on arms sales to Taiwan has not changed, and that will be evident over the course of our administration."

112. Michael S. Chase, "Taiwan's Defense Budget Dilemma: How Much Is Enough in an Era of Improving Cross-Strait Relations?" *China Brief*, vol. 8, issue 15 (July 17, 2008). As Chase states, improving cross-Strait relations under Ma "may suggest to some that there is no pressing need for Taiwan to approve further increases in defense spending, especially if it would risk derailing the Ma Ying-jeou administration's zealous attempts to improve China–Taiwan ties. Moreover, it may be difficult to build support for defense budget increases that could necessitate cutbacks in other parts of the government budget, particularly programs that are more closely tied to the electoral prospects of politicians and legislators, such as social welfare and infrastructure development projects." Also see Sutter, "Is Taiwan 'Over'?"

113. Hu Jintao, "Join Hands to Promote Peaceful Development of Cross-Strait Relations; Strive with Unity of Purpose for the Great Rejuvenation of the Chinese Nation–Speech at the Forum Marking the 30th Anniversary of the Issuance of 'Message to Compatriots in Taiwan,' " Xinhua Domestic Service, December 31, 2008, OSC CPP20081231005002.

114. Steve Tsang, "A Hungry Dragon," *Foreign Policy*, April 30, 2009, http://experts.foreignpolicy. com/posts/2009/04/30/a_hungry_dragon; Robin Kwong, "A Delicate Detente," *Financial Times*, May 6, 2009, www.ft.com/cms/s/0/5f58b97a-3a72-11de-8a2d-00144feabdc0.html; Pomfret, "China and Taiwan Get Snuggly"; Xin Qiang, "Mainland China's Taiwan Policy Adjustments," *China Security*, vol. 5, no. 1 (Winter 2009): 55–66; Steven M. Goldstein, "China and Taiwan: Signs of Change in Cross-Strait Relations," *China Security*, vol. 5, no. 1 (Winter 2009): 67–72; Yun-han Chu, "The Evolution of Beijing's Policy Toward

Taiwan During the Reform Era," in *China Rising: Power and Motivation in Chinese Foreign Policy*, edited by Yong Deng and Fei-ling Wang (Oxford: Rowman & Littlefield, 2005); Sutter, *China's Rise*, 37–38; John Q. Tian, *Government, Business, and the Politics of Interdependence and Conflict Across the Taiwan Strait* (New York: Palgrave Macmillan, 2006), Swaine, "China: Exploiting a Strategic Opening"; Michael D. Swaine and Oriana Skylar Mastro, "Assessing the Threat," in *Assessing the Threat: The Chinese Military and Taiwan's Security*, edited by Michael D. Swaine, Andrew N. D. Yang, Evan S. Medeiros, and Oriana Skylar Mastro (Washington, D.C.: Carnegie Endowment for International Peace, 2007), 219–41; Richard C. Bush and Michael E. O'Hanlon, *A War Like No Other: The Truth About China's Challenge to America* (New York: John Wiley & Sons, 2007); and T. J. Cheng, "China–Taiwan Economic Linkage: Between Insulation and Superconductivity," in *Dangerous Strait*, ed. Tucker.

115. Swaine, "China: Exploiting a Strategic Opening."

116. Chu Shulong and Guo Yuli, "Change: Mainland's Taiwan Policy," *China Security*, vol. 4, no. 1 (Winter 2008): 127–33; Xu Shiquan, "New Perspectives on the Chinese Mainland's Policy Toward Taiwan," *American Foreign Policy Interests*, vol. 28 (2006): 379–80; Chien-min Chao and Wu-yen Chang, "Managing Stability in the Taiwan Strait: Non-military Policy Towards Taiwan under Hu Jintao," paper delivered at the International Conference on Politics in the Hu Jintao Era: CCP's Adaptation to Domestic and Foreign Challenges, organized by Sciences-Po, Paris, June 27, 2008.

117. Interviews with current and former U.S. officials. For similar assessments, see Alan D. Romberg, "U.S.–Taiwan Relations: Looking Forward," remarks delivered at "U.S.-Taiwan Relations in a New Era: Looking Forward 30 Years after the Taiwan Relations Act," conference at the Center for Strategic and International Studies, Washington, April 22, 2009. Romberg states: "The hard fact is that unification not only is not on the table today, it will not be on the table for as far as the mind's eye can see." Also see Harry Harding, "China Risk," Eurasia Group, June 2006; and Larry Wortzel and Admiral Joseph W. Prueher, "Agenda 2008: A New Look at the U.S.-China Relationship," Center for the Study of the Presidency, 2008. This report stated: "U.S. policy toward Taiwan is sound and needs no comprehensive or strategic revision."

118. As Alan Romberg has stated: "So long as Taiwan is not moving in the direction of de jure independence and constitutional change, President Hu Jintao has introduced a strong element of patience into the equation. Indeed, his six-point proposal of last December 31 really only makes sense if one assumes that unification is not on the table now and that it will not be for a very long time to come." See Romberg, "U.S.-Taiwan Relations: Looking Forward."

119. That said, some analysts nonetheless cite potential problems even during the short term. For example, Phil Saunders points to the specific possibility that improving cross-Strait relations under the Ma Ying-jeou government could generate a crisis if Beijing develops heightened expectations for closer relations that are subsequently dashed by Taipei. See Saunders, "Managing Strategic Competition with China."

120. For example: "Deteriorations in cross-Strait relations and U.S.-China relations . . . are considered the lowest risk to the Asia Pacific regional outlook." Pacific Economic Cooperation Council, "Survey Results: Provisional Release," in *State of the Region Report 2008–2009* (Singapore: Pacific Economic Cooperation Council, 2008), www.pecc.org/sotr/papers/SOTR-2008-Survey-Results.pdf.

121. Swaine et al., *Assessing the Threat*. Some analysts believe that China already possesses this capability. See David A. Shlapak, David T. Orletsky, et al., *A Question of Balance: Political Context and Military Aspects of the China–Taiwan Dispute* (Santa Monica, Calif.: RAND Corporation, 2009).

122. See "Dismal Prospects," *China Economic Review*, February 2009, www.chinaeconomic review.com/cer/2009_02/Dismal_prospects.html; Collin Spears, "Taiwan: Identity Politics and Economic Free Fall in the Other China," *Brooks Foreign Policy Review*, April 13, 2009, http://brooksreview.wordpress.com/2009/04/13/taiwan-identity-politics-and-economic-free-fall-in-the-other-china; Avery Goldstein, *Rising to the Challenge: China's Grand Strategy and International Security* (Stanford, Calif.: Stanford University Press, 2005); Richard L. Armitage and Joseph S. Nye, *The U.S.-Japan Alliance: Getting Asia Right Through 2020* (Washington, D.C.: Center for Strategic and International Studies, 2007), 1–28; Morton Abramowitz and Stephen Bosworth, "America Confronts the Asian Century," *Current History*, vol. 105, no. 690 (April 2006): 147–52; and International Security Advisory Board, U.S. State Department, "China's Strategic Modernization," Wolfowitz ISAB Report, September 2008, http://video1. washingtontimes.com/video/ChinaStrategicPlan.pdf. For detailed examinations of the impact of growing cross-Strait economic ties on Beijing's coercive capacities, see Murray Scot Tanner, *Chinese Economic Coercion Against Taiwan: A Tricky Weapon to Use* (Santa Monica, Calif.: RAND Corporation, 2007); and Scott Kastner, *Political Conflict and Economic Interdependence Across the Taiwan Strait and Beyond*, Studies in East Asian Security Series of the East-West Center (Stanford, Calif.: Stanford University Press, 2009). Tanner and Kastner show that, though growing cross-Strait economic linkages can in some cases provide Beijing with mechanisms for possible coercion against Taiwan, many disincentives exist to utilizing them, most notably their possible impact on China's international economic relations.

123. Dan Blumenthal and Christopher Griffin, "China Looks Across the Strait," *Weekly Standard*, August 25, 2008, www.weeklystandard.com/Content/Public/ Articles/000/000/015/429gvayn.asp; Dan Blumenthal and Randall Schriver (American Enterprise Institute and Armitage International), "Strengthening Freedom in Asia: A Twenty-First Century Agenda for the U.S.–Taiwan Partnership," February 2008, www.aei.org/docLib/20080222_TaiwanreportEnglish.pdf. Also see Li Mingjiang, RSIS, "Taiwan Strait Relations: How Far Can It Go?" RSIS Commentaries, Rajaratnam School of International Studies, www.rsis.edu.sg/publications/ Perspective/RSIS0412008.pdf (March 31, 2008).

124. Swaine et al., *Assessing the Threat*; Phillip C. Saunders and Scott L. Kastner, "Bridge Over Troubled Water?" *International Security* 33, no. 4 (Spring 2009): 98; Ellen L. Frost, James J. Przystup, and Phillip C. Saunders (Institute for National Strategic Studies, National Defense University), "China's Rising Influence in Asia: Implications for U.S. Policy," *Strategic Forum*, no. 231 (April 2008); "Project on the Next East Asia Security Strategy: Workshop #4 Summary," Institute for National Strategic Studies, September 2008, 1–19; Ralph A. Cossa et al., "The United States and the Asia-Pacific Region: Security Strategy for the Obama Administration, 2008," Asia-Pacific Strategy Project, February 2009; Harding, "China Risk"; Council on Foreign Relations, *U.S.-China Relations: An Affirmative Agenda—A Responsible Course*, Report of an Independent Task Force sponsored by Council on Foreign Relations, Carla A. Hills and Dennis C. Blair, Co-Chairs, Task Force

Report 59, (Washington, D.C.: Council on Foreign Relations, 2007); and "Strait Dispute Unlikely to Spark War," *Financial Times*, May 26, 2004. The last source states: "It is evident that China will become an increasingly important player in the region and the world as the pace of globalization accelerates and trends toward regional integration rise. As the PRC now receives more overseas investment than any other country in the world and has moved into a role as 'the workshop of the world,' it would seem obvious that Beijing should continue to promote economic development and openness and as a long-term strategy endeavor to shake off the stereotype of an aggressive military power and instead focus on promoting herself as a benign regional hegemon. With this strategy in place, it is hard to imagine that the PRC authorities would seriously contemplate triggering a war in the Taiwan Strait."

125. Romberg, "Cross-Strait Relations: Weathering the Storm"; Romberg, "Cross-Strait Relations: 'Ascend the Heights'"; Tsang, "Hungry Dragon"; Joseph Miller, Carter Center, "One China?" June 19, 2008, www.chinaelections.net/newsinfo. asp?newsid=18089. Also see Ma Ying-jeou, "The Taiwan Relations Act: Turning a New Chapter," remarks at the Videoconference with the Center for Strategic and International Studies, April 22, 2009.

126. Michael M. Tsai, "An Assessment of Taiwan's Quadrennial Defense Review," *China Brief*, vol. 9, issue 8 (April 16, 2009); Republic of China, *Quadrennial Defense Review 2009*, March 16, 2009, http://merln.ndu.edu/whitepapers/Taiwan_EnglishQDR2009.pdf; Ma Ying-jeou, "SMART Strategy for National Security"; Ma Ying-jeou, "Taiwan Relations Act"; Rowan Callick, "Taiwan Army to Be Cut by 20%," *Australian*, March 18, 2009, www. theaustralian.news.com.au/story/0,25197,25202391-5013948,00.html; Julia M. Famularo, "The Taiwan Quadrennial Defense Review Implications for U.S.–Taiwan Relations," Project 2049 Institute, June 22, 2009, http://project2049.net/documents/the_taiwan_ quadrennial_defense_review_implications_for_US_taiwan_relations.pdf. According to Famularo, "The major themes of Taiwan's QDR are prevention and transformation. It is a defense-oriented strategy that aims to shape the regional security environment and deter conflict while overhauling the military into a leaner, more efficient fighting force with sustainable capabilities. It also has three major implications for the future of Taiwan's military including solidifying civilian control over the military, consolidating the country's strategic defense systems, and articulating Ma Ying-jeou's vision for future development of the armed forces and implementing reforms."

127. Romberg, "U.S.-Taiwan Relations: Looking Forward"; Tsang, "Hungry Dragon." Tsang writes: "The Ma administration . . . faces a delicate task: maintaining a degree of momentum in improving cross-Strait ties without putting Taiwan's own security at risk in the long term. Ironically, the easing of tension presents Taiwan with a security dilemma: As the threat from China appears to recede, it will be more difficult to procure desperately needed weapons systems without a clear enemy to justify them." For a standard U.S. argument on the benefits of arms for Taiwan that also attempts to convince Beijing that arms sales are in its interest as well, see the summary of remarks by U.S. assistant secretary of defense for Asian and Pacific security affairs, Wallace Gregson, in "U.S. Urges China Not to Be Afraid of 'a Strong Taiwan,'" by Jorge Liu and Y. F. Low, Central News Agency (Taiwan), September 29, 2009, OSC CPP20090929968234. Addressing the 2009 U.S.-Taiwan Defense Industry Conference held in Virginia, Gregson said that Washington believes that promoting a strong Taiwan will help ensure that

Taiwan is able to make choices that benefit both sides of the Taiwan Strait. Also, a strong Taiwan will be less susceptible to coercion or intimidation and better able to engage China with confidence, as well as being free to expand cross-Strait economic, cultural, and political ties without fear or reservation. "And therefore, everyone in the region—including the People's Republic of China—should view a strong Taiwan not as a threat but as a stabilizing factor in cross-Strait affairs, regional security and economic development."

128. "Taiwan Leader Seeks US Weapons," Agence France-Presse, April 22, 2009, www.google. com/hostednews/afp/article/ALeqM5hO746GACmcVrwQ6Bg88HjHP4UtWw. It should be noted, however, that some Taiwan officials have stated that the Ma government will consult with Washington before issuing another request to buy the F-16 C/D aircraft. "Taiwan to Reach Consensus with US Before Issuing Request for Modern F-16 Jets," *Taiwan News*, www.etaiwannews.com/etn/news_content.php?id=928285&lang=eng_ news&cate_img=logo_taiwan&cate_rss=TAIWAN_eng (April 23, 2009); Jim Wolf, "Taiwan Renews Push for U.S. F-16 fighters," Reuters, March 14, 2009, www.reuters.com/article/ newsOne/idUSTRE52E00F20090315; Siva Govindasamy, "Taiwan Tries to Expedite Black Hawk Purchase," Flight International, www.flightglobal.com/articles/2009/04/16/325150/ taiwan-tries-to-expedite-black-hawk-purchase.html; Ma Ying-jeou, "Taiwan Relations Act." Ma stated: "I urge the United States to not hesitate to provide Taiwan with the necessary defensive arms as stipulated in the TRA."

129. Swaine et al., *Assessing the Threat*.

130. Alan D. Romberg, "U.S.-Taiwan Relations: Looking Forward." Also see Robert Sutter, "Asia in the Balance: America and China's 'Peaceful Rise,'" *Current History*, September 2004, 284–89. As Sutter writes: "American security planners, like their Japanese counterparts, are unlikely to fully embrace Beijing's avowed peaceful intent until China reduces its strong military modernization efforts targeted at Taiwan and at U.S. forces that might intervene in a Taiwan contingency."

131. For example, see David Shambaugh, "Obama's Strategic Agenda," Spero News, April 9, 2009, www.speroforum.com/a/18813/Obamas-strategic-agenda-with-China. The administration will have to make a decision soon concerning this arms package, that is, whether it sends official notification to Congress of its intent to carry through on the Bush administration's October 2008 declaration of intent to sell.

132. As Aaron Friedberg states, "Among other matters crowding President Obama's Asian inbox will be the question of whether and how to help Taiwan preserve some semblance of a military balance with the Mainland. Renewed American arms sales will incur Beijing's wrath, but failure to act will leave Taiwan increasingly exposed and demoralized." Friedberg, "Asia Rising."

133. However, some reporting has indicated that Beijing might be willing to redeploy some short-range ballistic missiles facing Taiwan, as a unilateral goodwill gesture. See Xie Yu, "Mainland May Pull Some Missiles: Expert," *China Daily Online*, November 26, 2009, OSC CPP20091126968027. For an earlier assessment, also see Xin, "Mainland China's Taiwan Policy Adjustments"; he writes: "Even though the Mainland is considering the possible redeployment of missiles and planning to gradually decrease the number of [short-range ballistic missiles] targeting Taiwan, . . . it is believed that the decision is hard to make and consensus hard to reach, especially against the background of contrary gestures from Taiwan."

134. "China's National Defense Official Says Cross-Strait Military Mutual Trust Can Be Discussed," Central News Agency, October 28, 2009, as summarized in OSC CPP20091029100002. "No Timetable for Discussing Cross-Strait Confidence-Building Measures," Central News Agency, October 28, 2009. "Chairman Ma Takes Office— Cross-Strait Political Dialogue? Ma Ying-jeou: Timing Not Right Yet," *Tung-sen Hsin-wen Pao*, October 17, 2009, as summarized in OSC CPP20091018102001. David G. Brown, "China–Taiwan Relations: Moving Relations Toward a New Level," *Comparative Connections*, vol. 11, no. 2 (July 2009), http://csis.org/files/publication/0902qchina taiwan.pdf. Romberg, "Cross-Strait Relations: Weathering the Storm." Also, the various obstacles and opportunities confronting a possible cross-Strait peace accord are discussed by Saunders and Kastner, "Bridge Over Troubled Water?"

135. For example, see John J. Tkacik, ed., *Rethinking "One China"* (Washington, D.C.: Heritage Foundation, 2004).

136. For a typical Chinese argument as to why a continuation of the China–Taiwan imbroglio serves U.S. interests and is thus actively promoted by Washington, see Jian Junbo, "US Sees Devil in Cross-Strait Detente," *Asia Times*, April 2, 2009, www.atimes. com/atimes/China/KD02Ad01.html. "Apparently separating Taiwan from China— without granting it formal independence—is the status quo which best serves U.S. interests in the Asia-Pacific. A separate Taiwan hostile to Mainland China can be a card in the U.S.'s hands. Such a Taiwan is a natural ally of the U.S. that can help it expand its power in the Far East and feed the U.S. military-industrial complex. . . . The U.S. will never give up this card to contain China's rise, although the U.S. actually recognizes that China is a strong competitor or even a potential successor to its hegemony in the Asia-Pacific region." For a somewhat contrasting Chinese perspective on U.S. interests, see "The United States Should Gradually Withdraw from Cross-Strait Affairs," *Huanqiu Shibao*, April 24, 2009: "The withdrawal of the United States from cross-Strait affairs does not mean that China wants to drive the United States out of Asia or to hurt US interests in China or Asia. As long as 'Taiwan independence' and foreign forces do not make trouble, nobody wants to see people suffer. If the United States truly wants to see an Asia utterly different from that in the Cold War, if it is to adjust its Asian strategy and 'carefully and gradually turn its hegemonistic position into a self-sustaining international system' (in Brzezinski's words), then it must learn to phase itself out of cross-Strait affairs." For a discussion of some of the possible negative repercussions for U.S. interests that might result from Beijing's recovery of Taiwan, see Nancy Bernkopf Tucker, "If Taiwan Chooses Unification, Should the United States Care?" *Washington Quarterly*, vol. 25, no. 3 (2002): 15–28, http://taiwansecurity.org/IS/2002/tucker.pdf. Tucker concludes: "Manifestly, if China ultimately intends to drive the United States out of the western Pacific rather than coexist with it, then anything that helps China grow stronger, including unification with Taiwan, would not be in U.S. interests. . . . Yet, despite the potentially negative implications of peaceful unification, one benefit is overriding. The eradication of this flashpoint would instantly and overwhelmingly reduce friction and the risk of accidental clashes between Washington and Beijing. Unification would unquestionably affect some U.S. interests adversely, but not nearly as much as would war between China and the United States."

137. For a careful consideration and rejection of this viewpoint, see Romberg, "U.S.-Taiwan Relations: Looking Forward." As Romberg states: "I suppose if one wants to fantasize about all the theoretical possibilities of the PLA stationing forces in Taiwan, using

Taiwan's bases and harbors to project power, removing Taiwan from the list of true democracies, well, then yes perhaps that would cross some American 'red lines' and occasion a rethinking of U.S. policy. But no one is talking about that and no one who is serious is thinking about it. It won't happen."

138. Thomas B. Gold, "Taiwan in 2008: My Kingdom for a Horse," *Asian Survey*, vol. 49, no. 1 (January–February 2009): 88–97.

139. Romberg, "U.S.-Taiwan Relations: Looking Forward." Romberg writes: "We know, of course, that the fate of the economy will be the most important key to the success or failure of the current administration to remain in power. (One might note that Taiwan is not the only place where this is true.) But cross-Strait relations will likely be an important element in how the economy does—and whether resources and energy will have to be distracted from the basic tasks of recovery and revitalization or, on the other hand, Taipei's economic program will have an augmented effectiveness. And continuing close Taiwan–U.S. relations, based on trust and common interests, will be an important element, in turn, in helping to bring success to Taiwan's efforts to harness cross-Strait relations to the benefit of the people in Taiwan as well as of the rest of us." Also see "New Actors and Factors in Cross Strait Relations," panel discussion hosted by the Sigur Center for Asian Studies at George Washington University, Washington, January 29, 2009; David G. Brown, "China–Taiwan Relations: Moving Relations Toward a New Level," *Comparative Connections*, vol. 11, no. 2 (July 2009), http://csis.org/files/publication/0902qchina_taiwan.pdf; "Editorial: DPP Needs Coherent Policies to Win," *Taipei Times Online*, November 6, 2009, in OSC CPP20091106968010; and Alan M. Wachman, "Old Thinking Dominates 'New Thinking,' " *China Security*, vol. 5, no. 1 (Winter 2009): 73–79. Wachman writes: "Even now, Ma Ying-jeou confronts a daily barrage of brickbats lobbed by opponents who fear his openness to compromise with Beijing may one day be viewed as the ill-conceived blunder of a weak and naive leader." In addition, see Kwong, "Delicate Detente"; and Spears, "Taiwan: Identity Politics."

140. Jonathan Adams, "As Asia Builds Economic Ties, Taiwan Sidelined by China," *Christian Science Monitor*, April 12, 2009, www.csmonitor.com/2009/0412/p06s07-woap.html; Ma Ying-jeou, "Taiwan Relations Act"; Romberg, "Cross-Strait Relations: 'Ascend the Heights.' "

141. Alex Jiang, "Taiwan's Export Orders Unaffected by European Debt Crisis," *Taiwan News*, June 21, 2010; Chinmei Sung, "Taiwan's Exports Climb 47.8 percent, Sixth Monthly Increase," *Bloomberg Businessweek*, May 7, 2010; "Taiwan's Economy Sees 4th Straight Red Light Warning," *China Post*, May 28, 2010; Philip Liu, "Taiwan's Economy Will Grow 4.39 percent in 2010: DGBAS," China Economic News Service, November 27, 2009, http://news.cens.com/cens/html/en/news/news_inner_30245.html; Kevin Brown and Tim Johnston, "Taiwan Data Defy Regional Weakness," *Financial Times*, November 26, 2009; Anirban Nag, "Taiwan GDP Beats Forecasts, Outlook Healthy," Reuters, November 26, 2009. According to the Economist Intelligence Unit, real GDP growth is expected to recover to approximately 4 percent per annum levels by 2011 (just before the 2012 presidential election). See Economist Intelligence Unit, "Country Briefings: Taiwan," May 26, 2009, www.economist.com/countries/taiwan/profile.cfm?folder=Profile-Economic percent20Data.

142. Yun-han Chu, "Taiwan's National Identity Politics and the Prospect of Cross-Strait Relations," *Asian Survey*, vol. 44, no. 4 (2004): 484–512. "The existence of a large number

of noncommitted rationalists would, in the short run, mitigate the polarized conflict over national identity and could, over the long run, shift the political equilibrium in either direction, depending on whether external conditions become more favorable to unification or independence. As long as Taiwan's electorate keeps the future of cross-Strait relations open ended, the status quo should prevail over the scenarios for war or peaceful reconciliation." Also see Shelley Rigger, *Taiwan's Rising Rationalism: Generations, Politics, and "Taiwanese Nationalism,"* Policy Study 26 (Washington, D.C.: East-West Center, 2006), 1–74, www.eastwestcenter.org/fileadmin/stored/pdfs/PS026.pdf. As Rigger states: "As the third and fourth generations take positions of leadership in Taiwan, we can expect the island's politicians to behave less like Taiwan nationalists and more like pragmatic politicians. They will not jump at the chance to complete a unification deal, but they will not rush blindly toward independence either."

143. Ted Galen Carpenter, "Wild Card: A Democratic Taiwan," *China Security*, vol. 4, No. 1 (Winter 2008): 40–58. Carpenter writes: "But even a KMT government would likely find its options constrained by Taiwanese public opinion. True, most Taiwanese (outside the camp of pro-independence DPP hard-liners) are wary of going too far in provoking China. At the same time, support for asserting a distinct Taiwanese identity and gaining international recognition for Taiwan's status as a sovereign state has been steadily gaining traction." Also see Shelley Rigger, "Taiwan's Presidential and Legislative Elections," *Orbis*, vol. 52, no. 4 (September 2008): 689–700, www.fpri.org/orbis/5204/rigger.taiwanelections.pdf.

144. I am particularly indebted to Tiffany Ng for her invaluable assistance in preparing parts of this discussion of North Korea.

145. Jonathan D. Pollack, "The Korean Peninsula in U.S. Strategy: Policy Issues for the Next President," in *Strategic Asia 2008–09*, ed. Tellis, Kuo, and Marble.

146. See ibid.; and Swaine, "China: Exploiting a Strategic Opening."

147. One should also note that, according to one well-placed interview respondent, the U.S. shift toward a multilateral approach eventually took place because the leverage exerted by hardliners within the administration on the North Korea issue was undermined by the demands on U.S. resources and attention produced by the invasions of Afghanistan and Iraq. These events forced hardliners to "let the diplomats have freer rein over North Korea."

148. This is from interviews with U.S. officials. This decision resulted from the above developments, as well as changes in key senior U.S. personnel responsible for the Korean situation, including the emergence of Christopher R. Hill (then assistant secretary of state for East Asian and Pacific affairs) as the key negotiator on the North Korea issue.

149. As Thomas Christensen stated in early 2007: "The Chinese have played a very positive role in the Six-Party Process, hosting the talks, helping draft the September 19, 2005, Joint Statement, supporting strong measures in the United Nations, and urging Pyongyang to return to the negotiating table. It is imperative that China continue its efforts in this process. The Administration is committed to continuing to work closely with the Chinese to find ways to persuade North Korea to abandon completely, irreversibly, and verifiably its nuclear weapons program." In March 2008, Christensen stated that progress with North Korea through the Six-Party Talks would not have been possible "without China's support and will not continue to advance without

its active involvement." Thomas J. Christensen, "Shaping China's Global Choices through Diplomacy," statement before the U.S.-China Economic and Security Review Commission, Washington, March 18, 2008.

150. See "U.S. Secretary of State Praises China Relationship," Voice of America, November 15, 2009. Clinton stated: "The Chinese have stood with us in the sanctions against North Korea. . . . We are seeing signs of a cooperative relationship." Also see Kurt M. Campbell, "Press Availability in Beijing, China," remarks in Beijing, October 14, 2009; and Hillary Rodham Clinton, interview With David Gregory of *Meet the Press*, NBC Television, Washington, July 26, 2009. Clinton stated: "We have been extremely gratified by their forward-leaning commitment to sanctions and the private messages that they have conveyed to the North Koreans."

151. Regarding the uranium enrichment facility and light water reactor, see Siegfried S. Hecker, "A Return Trip to North Korea's Yongbyon Nuclear Complex," Center for International Security and Cooperation, Stanford University, November 20, 2010, http://iis-db.stanford.edu/pubs/23035/HeckerYongbyon.pdf. For the U.S. reaction, see Ambassador Glyn Davies, permanent US representative to the IAEA, "Application of Safeguards in the Democratic People's Republic of Korea: U.S. Statement," Agenda Item 4(b), IAEA Board of Governors Meeting, March 7–11, 2011, http://vienna.usmission. gov/110308dprk.html. Washington regards these activities as clear violations of North Korea's obligations under UN Security Council Resolutions 1718 and 1874, and contrary to its September 2005 Joint Statement commitments.

152. In June and July 2009, the United Nations Security Council unanimously adopted Resolution 1874, condemning "in the strongest terms" North Korea's second nuclear test, imposing new sanctions (permitting cargo inspection), "demanding that [North Korea] not conduct any further nuclear test or any launch using ballistic missile technology," and urging the isolated country to come back to the Six-Party Talks without preconditions. Beijing affirmed that China "will implement the resolution in an earnest way." See the transcript of Foreign Ministry spokesperson Qin Gang's regular press conference on June 16, 2009, www.fmprc.gov.cn/eng/xwfw/s2510/t568094.htm. For the text of the UN resolution, see Resolution 1874 (2009), United Nations Security Council, June 12, 2009, www.un.org/News/Press/docs/2009/sc9679.doc.htm.

153. See Mark Landler, "China's North Korea Shift Helps U.S. Relations," New York Times, December 23, 2010, www.nytimes.com/2010/12/24/world/asia/24diplo. html?ref=jamesbsteinberg.

154. Beijing initially attempted to avoid any open criticism of Pyongyang's uranium enrichment program by stating publicly that North Korea had a right to pursue such a (supposedly) peaceful, civilian nuclear program. See "Foreign Ministry Spokesperson Jiang Yu's Regular Press Conference on December 21, 2010," Ministry of Foreign Affairs of the People's Republic of China, December 22, 2010, www.mfa.gov.cn/eng/ xwfw/s2510/2511/t780909.htm; and "Foreign Ministry Spokesperson Jiang Yu's Regular Press Conference on December 30, 2010," Ministry of Foreign Affairs of the People's Republic of China, December 31, 2010, www.mfa.gov.cn/eng/xwfw/s2510/2511/t783080. htm. However, Beijing subsequently backed away from this stance, stating to South Korean diplomats that North Korea's right to the peaceful use of nuclear power would only be possible if Pyongyang abides by its international denuclearization obligations. See "China clarifies position on N. Korea's nuclear policy," Yonhap, December 24, 2010, http://english.yonhapnews.co.kr/national/2010/12/24/54/0301000000AEN2010122400

5800315F.HTML. The Chinese government then agreed to include in the January 2011 U.S.-China Joint Statement a statement that "expressed concern regarding the DPRK's claimed uranium enrichment program" and stated "Both sides oppose all activities inconsistent with the 2005 Joint Statement and relevant international obligations and commitments." See U.S.-China Joint Statement, January 19, 2011, Washington, D.C., www.whitehouse.gov/the-press-office/2011/01/19/us-china-joint-statement.

155. See Liao Lei and Li Zhongfa, "Qin Gang Says That the Chinese Side Is Willing to Make Incessant Efforts to Help the Korean Peninsula Nuclear Issue Return to the Track of Dialogue," Xinhua, June 25, 2009; Gu Zhenqiu, Bai Jie, and Wang Xiangjiang, "New UN Resolution Not All About Sanctions Against DPRK," Xinhua, June 12, 2009, http://news.xinhuanet.com/english/2009-06/13/content_11536115.htm.

156. Jeffrey Bader, "Obama Goes to Asia: Understanding the President's Trip," remarks at the Brookings Institution, Washington, November 6, 2009. Bader, who is Obama's senior director for Asia at the National Security Council, stated: "We are prepared to engage directly with the North Koreans. The Obama Administration believes it is better to hear directly from others, including adversaries, than to hear from them secondhand through a filter." Also see Campbell, "Press Availability."

157. See White House, Office of the Press Secretary, "Remarks by President Barack Obama at Suntory Hall." Obama stated: "Working in tandem with our partners—supported by direct diplomacy—the United States is prepared to offer North Korea a different future. Instead of an isolation that has compounded the horrific repression of its own people, North Korea could have a future of international integration. . . . So the path for North Korea to realize this future is clear: a return to the Six-Party Talks; upholding previous commitments, including a return to the Nuclear Non-Proliferation Treaty; and the full and verifiable denuclearization of the Korean Peninsula. And full normalization with its neighbors can also only come if Japanese families receive a full accounting of those who have been abducted." Also see Bader, "Obama Goes to Asia": "We are not interested in buying Yongbyon for a third time. We are not interested in indulging North Korea's dream of validation as a self-proclaimed nuclear power. We are ready to talk to North Korea in the context of the Six-Party Talks with the explicit goal of denuclearization and with recognition that its previous commitments to denuclearize and return to the Nuclear Non-Proliferation Treaty, notably those in 2005, remain valid." Defense Secretary Robert Gates reaffirmed the basic U.S. position on North Korea in late May of 2009: "The goal of the United States has not changed: Our goal is complete and verifiable denuclearization of the Korean Peninsula. We will not accept North Korea as a nuclear weapons state. North Korea's nuclear program and actions constitute a threat to regional peace and security. We unequivocally reaffirm our commitment to the defense of our allies in the region. The transfer of nuclear weapons or material by North Korea to states or non-state entities would be considered a grave threat to the United States and our allies. And we would hold North Korea fully accountable for the consequences of such action.'" See Robert M. Gates, "America's Security Role in the Asia-Pacific," remarks delivered at the Eighth International Institute for Strategic Studies Asia Security Summit, Shangri-La Dialogue, Singapore, May 30, 2009, www.iiss.org/conferences/the-shangri-la-dialogue/shangri-la-dialogue-2009/plenary-session-speeches-2009/first-plenary-session/dr-robert-gates.

158. Robert M. Gates, remarks at Keio University; John Pomfret, "North Korea Suggests Discarding One of Its Nuclear Arms Programs," Washington Post, November 23, 2010, www.

washingtonpost.com/wp-dyn/content/article/2010/11/22/AR2010112206747.html; Michael Wines and Mark Landler, "U.S. Shift Toward Talks on N. Korea," *New York Times*, January 6, 2011, www.nytimes.com/2011/01/07/world/asia/07korea.html. In his January 2011 speech at Keio University in Japan, U.S. secretary of defense Gates also expressed his concern that North Korea is becoming "a direct threat to the United States as a result of its nuclear and intercontinental ballistic missile programs. Stating that Pyongyang might develop a nuclear-armed missile within five years, he called for North Korea to place a moratorium on all missile and nuclear weapons tests, and he advocated a strengthened U.S.-Japanese partnership. See John Pomfret, "Defense Secretary Gates Says North Korean Ballistic Missiles Pose 'Direct Threat' to U.S.," *Washington Post*, January 11, 2011.

159. For a detailed assessment of China's stance toward North Korea, see Michael D. Swaine, "China's North Korea Dilemma," *China Leadership Monitor*, no. 30 (Fall 2009), http://media.hoover.org/documents/CLM30MS.pdf. Also see Bonnie S. Glaser, Scott Snyder, and John S. Park, *Keeping an Eye on an Unruly Neighbor: Chinese Views of Economic Reform and Stability in North Korea*, joint report by Center for Strategic and International Studies and U.S. Institute of Peace (Washington, D.C.: U.S. Institute of Peace Press, 2008); Bonnie S. Glaser, "China's Policy in the Wake of the Second DPRK Nuclear Test," *China Security*, vol. 5, no. 2 (2009): 1–11; and Ian Johnson and Helene Cooper, "China Seeks New Talks to Ease Korean Tension," *New York Times*, November 28, 2010.

160. Swaine, "China's North Korea Dilemma"; Shen Dingli, "North Korea's Strategic Significance to China," *China Security*, Autumn 2006, 19–34, www.wsichina.org/cs4_2.pdf; Ashton B. Carter and William J. Perry, "The Case for a Preemptive Strike on North Korea's Missiles," *Time*, July 8, 2006, www.time.com/time/world/article/0,8599,1211527,00.html; Harry Harding, "Where China Meets Korea: Chinese Interests in the Future of the Peninsula," paper presented at Korean Embassy, Washington, November 20, 2007; Stephanie Kleine-Ahlbrandt and Andrew Small, "China's New Dictatorship Diplomacy: Is Beijing Parting with Pariahs?" *Foreign Affairs*, January–February 2008. One former U.S. official stated to the author: "Sure, North Korea did its nuclear test, and that was a big factor in getting the Chinese to do more, but the diplomatic aspect was also really important—we convinced the Chinese of how serious a problem this was."

161. Swaine, "China's North Korea Dilemma."

162. See Choe Sang-hun, "Kim Secures a Pledge and a Deal for Survival: Chinese Minister's Visit Yields Breach in U.S.-Led Pressure Over Global Talks," *International Herald Tribune*, October 7, 2009.

163. "China Proposes Emergency Consultations for Heads of Six-Party Talks in Early December," Xinhua, November 28, 2010, http://news.xinhuanet.com/english2010/china/2010-11/28/c_13625768.htm; Martin Fackler, "China Sees New Talks to Ease Rising Korean Tensions," *New York Times*, November 28, 2010, www.ndtv.com/article/world/china-sees-new-talks-to-ease-rising-korean-tensions-69164. Also see Douglas H. Paal, "Crisis in the Koreas," Carnegie Endowment for International Peace, Q&A, June 7, 2010, www.carnegieendowment.org/publications/index.cfm?fa=view&id=40954.

164. See Louis Charbonneau, "China blocks U.N. report on N.Korea nuclear breaches," Reuters, February 17, 2011, www.reuters.com/article/2011/02/17/us-korea-north-china-idUSTRE71G75U20110217?pageNumber=1.

165. See: U.S. Department of Defense, *Quadrennial Defense Review Report* (Washington, D.C.: U.S. Government Printing Office, 2010), www.defense.gov/QDR/images/QDR_

as_of_12Feb10_1000.pdf. The chairman's report states: "I remain concerned about the nuclear ambitions and confrontational postures of Iran and North Korea. . . . The QDR addresses the need for investment in developing *appropriate counter-[weapons of mass destruction] measures and consequence management responses* [author's italics]. It also calls for expanding our capabilities to detect and secure uncontrolled weapons of mass destruction and related materials, as well as the need to enhance nuclear forensics— both of which are vital to our national interests." Also see Erin K. Fitzgerald and Anthony H. Cordesman, "The 2010 Quadrennial Defense Review: A+, F, or Dead on Arrival?" working draft, Center for Strategic and International Studies, August 27, 2009.

166. For a thorough discussion, see Swaine, "China's North Korea Dilemma."

167. Ashley J. Tellis, *India as a New Global Power: An Action Agenda for the United States* (Washington, D.C.: Carnegie Endowment for International Peace, 2005), 55, www. carnegieendowment.org/files/CEIP_India_strategy_2006.FINAL.pdf. Also see Zalmay Khalilzad, David Orletsky, Jonathan Pollack, Kevin Pollpeter, Angel Rabasa, David Shlapak, Abram Shulsky, and Ashley J. Tellis, *The United States and Asia: Toward a New U.S. Strategy and Force Posture* (Santa Monica, Calif.: RAND Corporation, 2001), 47.

168. Karl Inderfurth and David Shambaugh, "U.S.–India–China: Managing a Ménage à Trois," *International Herald Tribune*, July 19, 2005; John W. Garver, "The China–India– U.S. Triangle: Strategic Relations in the Post–Cold War Era," *NBR Analysis*, vol. 13, no. 5 (October 2002).

169. See Anand Giridharadas, "In Improving Ties with India, Bush Can Claim a Foreign Policy Success," *New York Times*, January 1, 2009; and David Frum, "Where Bush Was Right," *Newsweek*, December 31, 2008.

170. Gates, "America's Security Role."

171. Amy Kazmin and Edward Luce, "India Feels Chill as U.S. Courts China," *Financial Times*, November 23, 2009; William Cohen, "Obama's Chance to Cement Ties with India," *Financial Times*, May 27, 2009, www.ft.com/cms/s/0/860f20f2-4aeb-11de-87c2-00144feabdc0.html; Uttara Choudhury, "India Ready to Negotiate Free-Trade Pact with US," *Daily News & Analysis*, November 24, 2009; and White House, Office of the Press Secretary, "Fact Sheet: Stimulating Global Economic Revival—U.S.–India Cooperation in Economics, Trade, and Agriculture," press release, November 24, 2009, www.whitehouse.gov/sites/default/files/Economics_Trade_and_Agriculture_Fact_Sheet.pdf.

172. John Pomfret, "Obama Welcomes Singh, Hails India's 'Leadership Role' in Asia," *Washington Post*, November 25, 2009; Foster Klug, "Obama: U.S.-Indian Ties Help Define 21st Century," Associated Press, November 24, 2009.

173. White House, Office of the Press Secretary, "Joint Statement between Prime Minister Dr. Singh and President Obama," press release, November 24, 2009. Also see Ajay Kaul and Lalit K. Jha, "India, U.S. Sign Six Pacts During PM's State Visit," Press Trust of India, November 25, 2009.

174. Manoj Joshi, "Obama's Beijing Kowtow," *New Delhi Mail Today E-Paper*, November 20, 2009, in OSC SAP20091120534001; Lydia Polgreen, "China Gains in U.S. Eyes, and India Feels Slights," *New York Times*, November 24, 2009; Edward Luce, "Obama Must Prove His Love for India While Wooing China," *Financial Times*, November 24, 2009; Kazmin and Luce, "India Feels Chill." Many Indian analysts were highly agitated by the

reference in the joint statement issued by Obama and Hu Jintao during the former's visit to Beijing that both nations have a strong interest in stability in South Asia. Although this remark largely reflected Washington's effort to elicit greater Chinese support for its counterterrorism policy goals vis-à-vis Pakistan and Afghanistan, many Indians saw it as providing an opportunity for Beijing to increase its geostrategic influence in India's backyard.

175. Quoted by Kazmin and Luce, "India Feels Chill." Although the United States stressed the overall cooperative aspects of the United States–India relationship with no mention of China, Singh made some direct criticisms of Beijing during his visit to Washington, referring to "a certain amount of assertiveness on the part of the Chinese" over longtime border disputes between the two countries. Also, in referring to Beijing's emphasis on rapid economic growth, he stated: "I've always believed that there are other values which are important than the growth of the gross domestic product." Among them, he said, are "respect for fundamental human rights, the respect for the rule of law, the respect for multicultural, multiethnic, multi-religious rights." See Pomfret, "Obama Welcomes Singh."

176. Sheryl Gay Stolberg and Jim Yardley, "Countering China, Obama Backs India for U.N. Council," New York Times, November 8, 2010; Office of the Spokesman, U.S. Department of State, "U.S.-India Strategic Dialogue Joint Statement," Washington, June 3, 2010, www.state.gov/r/pa/prs/ps/2010/06/142645.htm. Also see Harsh Pant, "U.S.-India Strategic Dialogue: Move Beyond Symbolism," Rediff News, June 8, 2010; and Rajeswari Pillai Rajagopalan, "The Indo-U.S. Strategic Dialogue: Challenges Ahead," India & the World, article 3158, Institute of Peace & Conflict Studies, June 22, 2010, www.ipcs.org/article/india-the-world/the-indo-us-strategic-dialogue-challenges-ahead-3158.html.

177. In July 2010, senior Indian national security officials visited Beijing and discussed the possibility of deepening this strategic dialogue.

178. K. J. M. Varma, "India-China trade volume surpasses USD 60 billion target," PTI, January 27, 2011, http://in.news.yahoo.com/india-china-trade-volume-surpasses-usd-60-billion-20110126-235200-729.html; "India and China set $100bn trade target by 2015," BBC News, December 16, 2010, www.bbc.co.uk/news/world-south-asia-12006092; Kathrin Hill and James Lamont, "China Offers to Accelerate Trade Talks with India," Financial Times, April 3, 2010. In 2008, China became India's largest trading partner, at more than $50 billion in annual trade, as well as India's biggest overseas project contractor. See Valedictory Address by Shashi Tharoor, minister of state for external affairs at the international conference on the theme of "Emerging China: Prospects for Partnership in Asia," November 22, 2009, www.indianembassy.org.cn/newsDetails. aspx?NewsId=45.

179. "China, India conclude border talks to boost ties," Xinhua, November 30, 2010, www. chinadaily.com.cn/china/2010-11/30/content_11632416.htm.

180. Joint Communiqué of the Ninth Meeting of Foreign Ministers of India, Russia, and China, Bengaluru, India, October 27, 2009, www.indianembassy.org.cn/NewsDetails. aspx?NewsId=33&NAID=1; "China Backs India on Emissions Cut Stance," Xinhua, December 3, 2009; "Indian Defense Minister Meets with Chinese Military Delegation," Xinhua, December 4, 2009; Jing-dong Yuan, "The Dragon and the Elephant: Chinese–Indian Relations in the 21st Century," Washington Quarterly, vol. 30, no. 3 (Summer 2007): 131–44; Jing-dong Yuan, "Greater China: The Geometry of Sino-Indian Ties,"

Asia Times Online, November 22, 2006; Zhang Ge and Liu Runyuan, "Sino-Indian Relations Entering a New Stage of Comprehensive Development," *International Strategic Studies*, vol. 3 (2005): 57; Inderfurth and Shambaugh, "U.S.–India–China"; Michael Vatikiotis and Murray Hiebert, "India and China: Dancing Elephants," *Far Eastern Economic Review*, April 29, 2004; "China Conveys 'Understanding' for India's UN Bid," PTI News Agency, New Delhi, January 24, 2005; Jay Solomon, Charles Hutzler, and Zahid Hussain, "Beijing Plays Central Role in Pushing Negotiations with India, in Sign of Its Growing Clout," *Wall Street Journal*, December 8, 2003; John W. Garver, *Protracted Contest: Sino-Indian Rivalry in the Twentieth Century* (Seattle: University of Washington Press, 2001), Garver, "China India U.S. Triangle"; Jagannath P. Panda, "Assessing the Impact of the Sino-Indian Army Exercise on Bilateral Relations," *China Brief*, vol. 7, issue 15 (July 26, 2007); June Teufel Dreyer, "A New Era in Sino Indian Relations, or Déjà Vu All Over Again?" International Assessment and Strategy Center, January 19, 2008; "China, India Reinforce Growing Ties," UPI, January 14, 2008; Edward Lanfranco, "Sino-Indian Ties and the Chindian Vision," UPI, January 16, 2008.

181. In fact, one major Indian security strategist (formerly India's foreign secretary and now the national security advisor) has suggested that India and China, along with other major Asian powers (including the United States) should begin a discussion of a larger collective security arrangement to defend sea lines of communication and provide overall security for energy and trade flows from nontraditional security threats and local instability. See Shiv Shankar Menon, "The Maritime Imperatives of India's Foreign Policy," speech at National Maritime Foundation, New Delhi, September 11, 2009.

182. Jing dong Yuan, "Greater China." Also see James Lamont and Amy Kazmin, "Fear of Influence," *Financial Times*, July 12, 2009, www.ft.com/cms/s/0/84a13062-6f0c-11de-9109-00144feabdc0,dwp_uuid=9c33700c-4c86-11da-89df-0000779e2340.html; and Sutter, *China's Rise*, 47–48.

183. As a result, some Indian observers argue that New Delhi must move much closer to Washington, as a hedge against a rising China, a strategic shift that could create problems in the United States–India–China relationship. See those cited by Peter Wonacott, "China, India Stoke 21st-Century Rivalry," *Wall Street Journal*, October 26, 2009; and Jeff M. Smith, "The China–India Border Brawl, *Wall Street Journal Asia*, June 24, 2009, http://online.wsj.com/article/SB124578881101543463.html.

184. For example, see Robert D. Kaplan, "Center Stage for the 21st Century: Power Plays in the Indian Ocean," *Foreign Affairs*, March–April 2009; Smith, "China–India Border Brawl"; Lisa Curtis, "U.S.-India Relations: The China Factor," Heritage Foundation Backgrounder 2209, November 25, 2008, www.heritage.org/Research/AsiaandthePacific/bg2209.cfm; and Lamont and Kazmin, "Fear of Influence." In truth, according to very knowledgeable U.S. government and outside analysts, the Chinese military has established no bases or formal access agreements (for example, for use in an interstate military crisis) along the Indian Ocean, although it might be looking for "places" where PLAN ships could resupply or conduct repairs when deployed in support of various international missions in the future, such as the UN-backed antipiracy effort in the Gulf of Aden. The above port facilities primarily involve Chinese commercial entities engaged as contractors for local entities. The strategic nature of such activities most likely involves Chinese efforts to create more reliable or new economic routes for the transportation of energy products and other goods

into China. In addition, even though both New Delhi and Beijing have increased some deployments along their disputed border in recent years, the overall level of tension has not changed appreciably.

185. "India and China Eye Each Other Warily," *IISS Strategic Comments*, vol. 9, no. 27 (December 2010); "India and China: Pushing Back," *Economist*, December 16, 2010, www.economist.com/node/17732947; C. Raja Mohan, "East Asian Security: U.S. Wants Bigger Indian Role," RSIS Commentaries, Rajaratnam School of International Studies, no. 129/2010, October 12, 2010.

186. Stephen F. Cohen, "The Missing Debate," *Nation*, May 1, 2008, www.thenation.com/doc/20080519/cohen; Samantha Power, "A Question of Honor," *Time*, August 14, 2008, www.time.com/time/world/article/0,8599,1832701,00.html; Stephen Sestanovich (Council on Foreign Relations), "Russian-American Relations: Problems and Prospects," testimony before the House Foreign Affairs Committee, Washington, May 17, 2007, www.cfr.org/publication/13354/russianamerican_relations.html. For a relatively positive assessment of U.S.-Russian relations and U.S. policy at the end of the first Bush term, see Elizabeth Jones, "U.S.-Russia Relations in Putin's Second Term," testimony before the House International Relations Committee, Washington, March 18, 2004, www.state.gov/p/eur/rls/rm/30556.htm. For a broad overview of U.S. policy toward Russia during the second Bush term, including areas of cooperation and tension, see Daniel Fried, "Russia and U.S.-Russia Relations," remarks before the U.S. Senate Foreign Relations Committee, Washington, June 21, 2007, www.state.gov/p/eur/rls/rm/86990.htm.

187. This deterioration began during the Clinton administration, but gained significant momentum under Bush, after a brief period of positive U.S.-Russian relations following the terrorist attacks of September 11, 2001. Possible exceptions of relevance to China include successful coordination regarding the Six-Party Talks and to some extent Iran.

188. The Bush administration was a strong supporter of Georgia. It thus strongly condemned the Russian invasion and provided humanitarian assistance to the beleaguered nation. The resulting crisis that emerged between Washington and Moscow posed the prospect of damaging bilateral relations severely for many years. See Daniel Fried, "U.S.-Russia Relations in the Aftermath of the Georgia Crisis," testimony before the House Committee on Foreign Affairs, Washington, September 9, 2008, www.state.gov/p/eur/rls/rm/109363.htm; Dan Eggen and Karen DeYoung, "After Warnings to Moscow, U.S. Has Few Options," *Washington Post*, August 14, 2008; and Seumas Milne, "Georgia is the Graveyard of America's Unipolar World," *Guardian* (London), August 28 2008.

189. In fact, during that period, Russia leveraged its vast energy resources to counter American influence at times. For example, Moscow started limiting the operations of Western energy companies in Russia and halted natural gas shipments to the United States–backed Ukraine. See Sestanovich, "Russian-American Relations."

190. In 2005, Moscow and Beijing signed a statement in which they pledged to increase their strategic cooperation so as to counter the West's "monopoly in world affairs." See Marcel de Haas, "Russia–China Security Cooperation," Power and Interest News Report, November 27, 2006, available at www.pinr.com/report.php?ac=view_report&report_id=588&language_id=1; Sergei Blagov, "Arms, Energy and Commerce in Sino-Russian Relations," *China Brief*, vol. 7, no. 16 (August 8, 2007); Liu Long, "Russia's Revival and Sino-Russia Relations," *International Strategic Studies*, vol. 3 (2007): 30. For

recent joint military exercises, see Xie Rong and Gao Fan, "Guo Boxiong Meets Russian Defense Minister Anatoly Serdyukov Today," Xinhua, November 25, 2009, in OSC CPP20091125062003.

191. U.S. Department of State, "Secretary Clinton Outlines Nuclear Security Strategy in International Op-Ed," April 8, 2010, www.state.gov/r/pa/prs/ps/2010/04/139820. htm#op_ed; Dmitri Trenin and James Collins, "U.S.-Russian Relations: How Does Russia See the Reset?" remarks at the Carnegie Endowment for International Peace, Washington, October 28, 2009, www.carnegieendowment.org/ events/?fa=eventDetail&id=1474; James M. Goldgeier, "A Realistic Reset with Russia: Practical expectations for U.S.-Russian Relations," *Policy Review*, no. 156 (August–September 2009), www.hoover.org/publications/policyreview/51403357.html; Andrew C. Kuchins and Anders Åslund, "Pressing the 'Reset Button' on U.S.-Russia Relations," in *The Russia Balance Sheet*, edited by Andrew C. Kuchins and Anders Åslund (Washington, D.C.: Peterson Institute for International Economics, 2009), 139–63; Rebecca Johnson, "Enhanced Prospects for 2010: An Analysis of the Third PrepCom and the Outlook for the 2010 NPT Review Conference," *Arms Control Today*, no. 6 (June 2009), www.armscontrol.org/act/2009_6/Johnson; Cole Harvey, "U.S., Russia Continue Talks on START," *Arms Control Today*, no. 6 (June 2009), www.armscontrol. org/act/2009_6/START; Clifford J. Levy and Peter Baker, "U.S.-Russia Nuclear Agreement Is First Step in Broad Effort," *New York Times*, July 7, 2009, www.nytimes. com/2009/07/07/world/europe/07prexy.html; Cole Harvey, "CD Breaks Deadlock on Work Plan," *Arms Control Today*, no. 6 (June 2009), www.armscontrol.org/act/2009_6/ CD. Obama has vowed to ratify the long-stalled Comprehensive Test Ban Treaty, secure vulnerable nuclear materials around the world within four years, and hold a nonproliferation summit meeting in Washington in 2010.

192. Rose Gottemoeller, assistant secretary of state for arms control, verification and compliance, "The Way Forward After New START," remarks at Vilnius University, Vilnius, Lithuania, February 9, 2011, www.state.gov/t/avc/rls/156394.htm.

193. In the economic realm, the Obama administration has signaled support for Russia's accession to the World Trade Organization in 2011. Simon Shuster, "Russia to Join WTO Within a Year, Obama Aide Says," Associated Press, October 20, 2010.

194. See Oleg Shchedrov, "Russia Shifts Stance on Iran, Ahmadinejad Defiant," Reuters, December 1, 2009. Also see Trenin and Collins, "U.S.-Russian Relations." As Trenin and Collins state: "Neither Russia's interests, nor its basic approach regarding Iran have changed, but Moscow has concluded that they can do business with the Obama administration. The potential for a closer diplomatic alignment within the UN Security Council creates opportunities for a more effective approach toward Iran."

195. Michael D. Swaine, "Beijing's Tightrope Walk on Iran," *China Leadership Monitor*, no. 33 (Summer 2010).

196. "Chinese FM Praises Relations with Russia in 2009," ITAR-TASS, November 26, 2009, in OSC CEP20091126950225; "China–Russia Strategic Partnership of Coordination Reaches New High," Xinhua, October 15, 2009, in OSC CPP20091015968264. "China, Russia to Hash Out 3-Year Plan," *China Daily*, May 22, 2008, www.chinadaily.com.cn/ china/2008-05/22/content_6705467.htm.

197. Melinda Liu, Anna Nemtsova, and Owen Matthews, "The New Silk Road," *Newsweek*, April 30, 2010; Vyacheslav Leonov, "Chinese Miss Russian Weapons and Ask Dmitriy

Medvedev for Them," *Ros Biznes Konsalting Daily*, December 2, 2009, in OSC CEP20091202349007. Leonov states: "Russian–Chinese relations in military-technical cooperation have recently been characterized not only by dwindling volumes of orders but also by major scandals. In March [2009], the press got hold of information that Moscow was intending to refuse to sell Beijing a large consignment of Su-33 fighters out of fears that the Chinese would illegally copy this aircraft, the way they had earlier copied the Su-27." "Eastern Europe Politics: Russia: Losing Central Asia to China?" Economist Intelligence Unit, December 18, 2009. David Shambaugh, "When Giants Meet," *New York Times*, June 16, 2009. Tim Johnson, "Russian Economic Fall Hits Hard in China's Border Outpost," March 4, 2009, McClatchy Newspapers, www.mcclatchydc.com/117/story/64395.html. Bobo Lo, *Axis of Convenience: Moscow, Beijing, and the New Geopolitics* (Washington, D.C.: Brookings Institution Press, 2008); Bobo Lo (Centre for European Reform), "Ten Things Everyone Should Know About the Sino-Russian Relationship," December 2008, www.cer.org.uk/pdf/pb_china_bl_dec08.pdf. Lo offers what is probably a fairly common Chinese view of the relationship: "Internationally, engagement with Beijing is central to Moscow's pursuit of an 'independent,' assertive foreign policy. . . . By contrast, Beijing views Russia as a secondary bilateral partner—useful certainly, but not of the first importance. The bilateral relationship is merely one component in a larger foreign policy based on the principles of 'peaceful development' ('peaceful rise') and 'a harmonious world.' . . . There is Chinese interest in Russia as an expanding market for consumer and industrial goods, but Russia will remain of marginal importance compared to the huge markets in the West and the Asia-Pacific." See Rajan Menon, "The Limits of Chinese–Russian Partnership," Survival, vol. 51, no. 3 (June–July 2009): 99–130; Zhu Feng, "Russia–Georgia Military Conflict: Testing China's Responsibility?" Center for Strategic and International Studies Freeman Report, November 2008, http://csis.org/files/media/csis/pubs/fr08n11.pdf; Ian Bremmer, "Should We Be Worried About China and Russia Ganging Up on the West?" Slate, August 29, 2007, www.slate.com/id/2172874; Sutter, China's Rise; Robert G. Sutter, "Relations with Russia and Europe," in Chinese Foreign Relations; Sergei Blagov, "Arms, Energy and Commerce in Sino-Russian Relations," *China Brief*, vol. 7, no. 16 (August 8, 2007); Liu, "Russia's Revival"; Bhartendu Kumar Singh, "Hu's Visit to Russia and Sino-Russian Relations," Institute of Peace and Conflict Studies—India, April 3, 2007; Joyce Roque, "China Wrestles with Russia for Control of Central Asia," China Briefing News, April 14, 2008, www.china-briefing.com/news/2008/04/14/china-wrestles-with-russia-for-control-of-central-asia.html; and Viola Gienger and Dune Lawrence, "China's Georgia War Lesson: Today's Breakaway Bites Back Later," Bloomberg, August 19, 2008, www.bloomberg.com/apps/news?pid=20601080&sid=aRCR7u2eMans&refer=asia.

CHAPTER 3

1. U.S. Department of State, "PMC Joint Press Conference with ASEAN Foreign Ministers," August 1, 2002, www.state.gov/secretary/former/powell/remarks/2002/12410.htm; Association of Southeast Asian States, "2001 ASEAN Declaration on Joint Action to Counter Terrorism," www.aseansec.org/5318.htm; ASEAN Regional Forum, "ARF

Statement on Cooperation Against Piracy and Other Threats to Security," June 17, 2003, www.aseanregionalforum.org/PublicLibrary/ARFChairmansStatementsandReports/ ARFStatementonCooperationAgainstPiracyandOt/tabid/78/Default.aspx; Asia-Pacific Economic Cooperation forum, "2003 Leaders' Declaration," October 21, 2003, www.apec.org/apec/leaders__declarations/2003.html; ASEAN Regional Forum, "ASEAN Regional Forum Statement on Strengthening Transport Security Against International Terrorism," July 2, 2004, www. aseanregionalforum.org/PublicLibrary/ARFChairmansStatementsandReports/ ARFStatementonStrengtheningTransportSecurity/tabid/69/Default.aspx; U.S. Department of State, "ASEAN Post Ministerial Joint Press Briefing," July 27, 2006, www. state.gov/secretary/rm/2006/69599.htm; United Nations Security Council, "Resolution 1540," April 28, 2004, http://daccessdds.un.org/doc/UNDOC/GEN/N04/328/43/PDF/ N0432843.pdf?OpenElement; U.S. Department of State, "Remarks at ASEAN Post-Ministerial Conference," July 23, 2008, www.state.gov/secretary/rm/2008/07/107350. htm. Also see Brian McCartan, "U.S. Lifts Curb on Cambodia, Laos Trade," Asia Times, June 30, 2009, www.atimes.com/atimes/Southeast_Asia/KF30Ae01.html. As McCartan states: "Under the George W Bush administration, Washington was perceived by many to have downgraded its commitment to Southeast Asia while concentrating its resources on the so-called global war on terror. When America did engage with the region, it seemed to be focused primarily on counterterrorism." Also see Dick Nanto, *East Asian Regional Architecture: New Economic and Security Arrangements and US Policy*, Congressional Research Service Report 33653 (Washington, D.C.: Library of Congress, 2006); Robert G. Sutter, *China's Rise: Implications for U.S. Leadership in Asia*, Policy Study 21 (Washington, D.C.: East-West Center, 2006); Michael J. Green, "Organizing Asia: Politics, Trade, and the New Multilateralism," in *Global Forecast: the Top Security Challenges of 2008* (Washington, D.C.: Center for Strategic and International Studies, 2007), 25–26; and Renato Cruz De Castro, "U.S. War on Terror in East Asia: The Perils of Preemptive Defense in Waging a War of the Third Kind," *Asian Affairs: An American Review*, vol. 31, no. 4 (2005): 212–31.

2. See Diane K. Mauzy and Brian L. Job, "U.S. Policy in Southeast Asia: Limited Re-engagement after Years of Benign Neglect," *Asian Survey*, vol. 47, no. 4 (August 2007): 622–41.

3. Tommy Koh, "The United States and Southeast Asia," in *America's Role in Asia: Asian and American Views*, Michael Armacost, J. Stapleton Roy, Han Sung-Joo, Tommy Koh, C. Raja Mohan, project chairs (San Francisco: Asia Foundation, 2008), 42–45.

4. H. E. Ong Keng Yong, secretary-general of ASEAN, "The Future of ASEAN," address at the Singapore Institute of International Affairs, Singapore, March 22, 2003, www. aseansec.org/14689.htm; Susan Krause, "U.S., ASEAN Nations Establish Framework for Enhanced Partnership," Washington File, Bureau of International Information Programs, U.S. Department of State, July 31, 2006, www.america.gov/st/washfile-english/2006/July/20060731113613ASesuarK0.1748163.html#ixzz1HdSh7vbP; "Plan of Action to Implement the ASEAN–U.S. Enhanced Partnership," 2006, www. aseansec.org/18589.pdf; ASEAN Secretariat, "Secretary-General of ASEAN Welcomes Confirmation of First U.S. Ambassador to ASEAN," Press Release, May 2, 2008, www. ascansec.org/21496.htm. Scot Marciel, the deputy assistant secretary of state for Southeast Asia, was appointed to simultaneously serve as the first ambassador to ASEAN, based in Washington. See also U.S. Department of State, "The ASEAN–U.S.

Enhanced Partnership: Advancing Cooperation in Southeast Asia," July 26, 2006, http://2001–2009.state.gov/r/pa/scp/2006/69569.htm.

5. See Christopher A. Padilla, undersecretary of commerce for international trade, "Asian Economies in Transition: Will the United States Be Left Behind?" remarks at American Enterprise Institute, July 7, 2008, http://trade.gov/press/speeches/padilla_070708.asp.

6. See Office of the United States Trade Representative, "Trans-Pacific Partners and United States Launch FTA Negotiations," September 22, 2008, www.ustraderep.gov/Document_Library/Press_Releases/2008/September/Trans-Pacific_Partners_United_States_Launch_FTA_Negotiations.html. U.S. officials had already announced that they would be negotiating liberalization in investment and services with the Pacific Four countries earlier in 2008; see Padilla, "Asian Economies"; however, this September announcement signified U.S. intention to join the broader Trans-Pacific Partnership agreement. The original Trans-Pacific Strategic Economic Partnership was launched on the sidelines of a 2002 APEC summit, though it was not a formal APEC initiative, and was signed in 2005.

7. In early 2008, Chris Hill remarked that the forum might become a political-type dialogue that addresses dispute mechanisms. See Christopher R. Hill, assistant secretary of state for East Asian and Pacific affairs, "Remarks at Chulalongkorn University," Bangkok, February 29, 2008, http://bangkok.usembassy.gov/root/pdfs/ambhill022908.pdf.

8. See Christopher R. Hill, assistant secretary of state for East Asian and Pacific affairs, statement before the Senate Committee on Armed Services, July 31, 2008, www.ncnk.org/resources/publications/Amb_Hill_Testimony_SASC_July_08.pdf.

9. At the 2009 EAS, some level of discord apparently emerged about the scope and membership of the proposed "community" concept, with former Australian prime minister Kevin Rudd proposing an Asia-Pacific entity that would presumably include the United States and ultimately address a wide range of topics, from economics to politics and security. In contrast, former prime minister Hatoyama proposed a more limited, East Asian entity focused largely on economic issues. This point is discussed further below. See You Run Tim, "Dispute Over Future Regional Community Architecture in East Asia Pacific," *Lianhe Zaobao*, October 31, 2009, OSC SEP20091108004001; and "Leadership Aspirations Complicate Debate on East Asia Community," *Nikkei Telecom 21*, November 2, 2009, OSC JPP20091102969021. For more on Rudd's ambitious concept, see "Full Text of Kevin Rudd's Speech to the Asia Society Australasia," *Australian*, June 5, 2008, www.theaustralian.com.au/politics/full-text-of-kevin-rudds-speech/story-e6frgczf-1111116541962.

10. The EAS has convened five Leaders' Summits between December 2005 and October 2010. Several meetings are also held throughout each year at the ministerial level and below to facilitate EAS functions and prepare for the annual Leaders' Summits. It has thus far produced mainly nonbinding statements or launched study groups on a variety of topics, including avian influenza, East Asian economic development, climate change, disaster management, and perhaps most important, energy security. The EAS has also discussed a wide range of regional issues such as denuclearization of the Korean Peninsula and the global financial crisis and in 2009 had addressed the domestic political situation in Myanmar (which previously had been blocked by Myanmar). For the details, see "Chairman's Statement of the First East Asia Summit," Kuala Lumpur,

December 14, 2005, www.aseansec.org/18104.htm; "Chairman's Statement of the Second East Asia Summit," Cebu, Philippines, January 15, 2007, www.aseansec.org/19302.htm; "Chairman's Statement of the 3rd East Asia Summit," Singapore, November 21, 2007, www.aseansec.org/21127.htm; "Chairman's Statement of the 4th East Asia Summit," Cha-am Hua Hin, Thailand, October 25, 2009, www.aseansec.org/23609.htm; and "Chairman's Statement of the East Asia Summit (EAS)," Hanoi, October 30, 2010, www.aseansec.org/25490.htm. Also see John Ruwitch, "Q+A—What Is the East Asia Summit All About?" Reuters, October 24, 2009; Malcolm Cook, "The United States and the East Asia Summit: Finding the Proper Home," *Contemporary Southeast Asia*, vol. 30, no. 2 (August 2008): 293–312; Shulong Chu, "The East Asia Summit: Looking for an Identity," *Brookings Northeast Asia Commentary*, no. 6 (February 2007), www.brookings.edu/opinions/2007/02northeastasia_chu.aspx; Lu Jianren, "Stepping Up," *Beijing Review*, December 24, 2009, www.bjreview.com.cn/quotes/txt/2009-12/18/content_238581.htm; and C. S. Kuppuswamy, *East Asia Summit: Was It Just a Get-Together?* South Asia Analysis Group Paper 1648, December 19, 2005, www.southasiaanalysis.org/%5Cpapers17%5Cpaper1648.html.

11. See Christopher Hill, assistant secretary of state for East Asian and Pacific affairs, "The U.S. and Southeast Asia," Remarks to the Lee Kuan Yew School of Public Policy, Singapore, May 22, 2006, http://2001-2009.state.gov/p/eap/rls/rm/66646.htm. The Bush administration debated whether or not to sign the Treaty of Amity and Cooperation (TAC) but ultimately decided against doing so, for several reasons. These included (1) a concern that the TAC's emphasis on noninterference in domestic affairs would constrain U.S. freedom of action, especially with regard to possible efforts to penalize Burma for its human rights abuses; (2) a concern that the treaty would undermine U.S. security accords with Asian allies; (3) a view that acceding to the TAC would lend greater legitimacy to the Burmese junta; and (4) a belief that the TAC is an ineffectual, symbolic agreement. See Mark E. Manyin, Michael John Garcia, and Wayne M. Morrison, "U.S. Accession to the Association of Southeast Asian Nations' Treaty of Amity and Cooperation (TAC)," Congressional Research Service, October 26, 2009, http://fpc.state.gov/documents/organization/132306.pdf.

12. See Hillary Rodham Clinton, secretary of state, "Press Availability at the ASEAN Summit," Sheraton Grande Laguna, Laguna Phuket, Thailand, July 22, 2009, www.state.gov/secretary/rm/2009a/july/126320.htm. Clinton stated: "The United States is back in Southeast Asia. President Obama and I believe that this region is vital to global progress, peace, and prosperity, and we are fully engaged with our ASEAN partners on the wide range of challenges confronting us, from regional and global security to the economic crisis to human rights and climate change." Also see James B. Steinberg, deputy secretary of state, "East Asia and the Pacific," remarks at the National Bureau of Asian Research Conference "Engaging Asia 2009: Strategies for Success," Washington, D.C., April 1, 2009, www.state.gov/s/d/2009/121564.htm. Steinberg stated: "We recognize that the emerging regional architecture is an important part of how Asians see themselves and how the nations of the Asia-Pacific must set the norms for cooperation for decades to come."

13. Joint Statement of the 2nd U.S.-ASEAN Leaders Meeting, New York, September 24, 2010, www.whitehouse.gov/the-press-office/2010/09/24/joint-statement-2nd-us-asean-leaders-meeting. That said, despite such ambitious aspirations, according to at least one knowledgeable observer, the Enhanced Partnership concept, as a distinct entity, has

lost much of its steam since the Bush era, largely as a result of advances in the overall United States–ASEAN relationship. The entity is apparently more a formulation than a genuinely new substantive forum or mechanism. The U.S. government created it largely to demonstrate a desire for continued or greater engagement with the ASEAN member states, minus Burma, during a time when Washington was arguably sending mixed signals to ASEAN, in part due to its lack of contact with Rangoon for human rights reasons. The need for such a forum has thus arguably diminished during the Obama administration as a result of improvements in overall U.S.-ASEAN ties and the inauguration of a new engagement policy with Burma. Personal correspondence, Ernest Bower.

14. U.S. Department of State, "United States Accedes to the Treaty of Amity and Cooperation in Southeast Asia," July 22, 2009, www.state.gov/r/pa/prs/ps/2009/july/126294.htm. The State Department also announced that the United States ambassador to ASEAN will now be based in Jakarta at the ASEAN Secretariat headquarters. U.S.-ASEAN Leaders Joint Statement, "Enhanced Partnership for Enduring Peace and Prosperity," 1st ASEAN-U.S. Leaders' Meeting, Singapore, November 15, 2009, www.whitehouse.gov/the-press-office/us-asean-leaders-joint-statement; Joint Statement of the 2nd U.S.-ASEAN Leaders Meeting.

15. Jeffrey Bader, "Obama Goes to Asia: Understanding the President's Trip," remarks at the Brookings Institution, Washington, D.C., November 6, 2009. Office of the Press Secretary, White House, "Remarks by President Barack Obama at Suntory Hall, Tokyo, Japan," November 14, 2009, www.whitehouse.gov/the-press-office/remarks-president-barack-obama-suntory-hall. Also see Kurt M. Campbell, assistant secretary of state for East Asian and Pacific affairs, "Press Availability in Beijing, China," remarks in Beijing, October 14, 2009, www.state.gov/p/eap/rls/rm/2009/10/130578.htm. Campbell stated: "One of the most important is that we believe that critical dialogues that touch on security, economic, and commercial issues should involve the United States." And see Steinberg, "East Asia and the Pacific."

16. See Office of the Press Secretary, White House, "Remarks by President Barack Obama." Such U.S. signaling in support of participation in regional groupings was also in part a response to the former Japanese prime minister Hatoyama's proposal for an East Asian Community modeled after the EU that apparently would not necessarily include the United States. As indicated above, this proposal was not well received in Washington; nor, according to senior U.S. officials, by U.S. friends and allies in the region. In fact, former Australian prime minister Kevin Rudd had challenged Hatoyama's proposal at the time by offering a broader pan-Asian entity that explicitly includes the United States and focuses primarily on managing economic crises. See Jeremy Laurence, "Australia, Japan Pitch Rival Ideas for new Asia Bloc," Reuters, October 25, 2009. Laurence states: "Both the Japanese and Australian ideas would encompass Japan, China, South Korea, India, Australia and New Zealand, along with the 10-member Association of South-East Asian Nations (ASEAN). The key difference between the two is Rudd's plan definitely includes the United States while Hatoyama's doesn't." Meanwhile, ASEAN has endorsed the EAC concept, apparently in an effort to maintain an important, if not leadership, role in its creation and development. But it has avoided explicitly supporting any particular membership. See Martin Abbugao, "Asian Nations Jostle for Power in EU-Style Bloc," Agence France-Presse, October 26, 2009; and "ASEAN Leaders Back Japan's EAC," *Bangkok Post*, October 26, 2009. The title of the latter source is misleading. In addition, a survey of strategic elites conducted by the Center for Strategic and International

Studies confirmed the general level of regional opposition to excluding the United States from a future East Asian community. In fact, "80 percent of Chinese respondents said it was 'very important' or 'somewhat important' to have U.S. participation in East Asia community building. . . . That was the highest percentage of support Chinese respondents gave to any of the six international players in this question." See Bates Gill et al., *Strategic Views on Asian Regionalism: Survey Results and Analysis* (Center for Strategic and International Studies, February 2009), www.csis.org/media/csis/pubs/090217_gill_stratviews_web.pdf. Finally, it should be noted that at this point, the EAC concept is most often envisioned as an economic, not security, arrangement.

17. Hillary Rodham Clinton, secretary of state, "Remarks on United States Foreign Policy," Council on Foreign Relations, Washington, D.C., September 8, 2010, www.state.gov/secretary/rm/2010/09/146917.htm; Hillary Rodham Clinton, "Remarks on Regional Architecture in Asia: Principles and Priorities," Imin Center–Jefferson Hall, Honolulu, January 12, 2010, www.state.gov/secretary/rm/2010/01/135090.htm; Kurt M. Campbell, assistant secretary of state for East Asian and Pacific affairs, "Principles of U.S. Engagement in the Asia-Pacific," statement before the Subcommittee on East Asian and Pacific Affairs, Senate Foreign Relations Committee, Washington, D.C., January 21, 2010, www.state.gov/p/eap/rls/rm/2010/03/137754.htm; Kurt M. Campbell, "Regional Overview of East Asia and the Pacific," statement before the House Committee on Foreign Affairs Subcommittee on Asia, the Pacific, and the Global Environment, Washington, D.C., March 3, 2010, www.state.gov/p/eap/rls/rm/2010/03/137754.htm; Hillary Rodham Clinton, "Remarks at Press Availability," Hanoi, July 23, 2010, www.state.gov/secretary/rm/2010/07/145095.htm; and Kurt M. Campbell, "U.S.-Japan Relations for the 21st Century," statement before the House Armed Services Committee, Washington, D.C., July 27, 2010, www.state.gov/p/eap/rls/rm/2010/07/145191.htm. During his remarks before the House Armed Services Committee on United States–Japan relations, Campbell specifically expressed appreciation for Japan's support for U.S. participation and inclusion in the EAS, thus signaling that the post-Hatoyama Japanese government had corrected the impression that it was seeking to exclude the United States from the forum. Russia is also likely to join the EAS at the same time as the United States. See "U.S., Russia to Join East Asia Summit," Agence France-Presse, July 20, 2010.

18. The Trans-Pacific Partnership (TPP) is discussed further in chapter 5. See Office of the Press Secretary, White House, "Remarks by President Barack Obama to CEO Business Summit in Yokohama," November 12, 2010, www.whitehouse.gov/the-press-office/2010/11/12/remarks-president-ceo-business-summit-yokohama-japan; Hillary Rodham Clinton, secretary of state, "Inaugural Richard C. Holbrooke Lecture on a Broad Vision of U.S.-China Relations in the 21st Century," Benjamin Franklin Room, Washington, D.C., January 14, 2011, www.state.gov/secretary/rm/2011/01/154653.htm; Robert D. Hormats, undersecretary of state for economic, energy and agricultural affairs, "Engaging Asia: The Future of U.S. Leadership," National Bureau of Asian Research Engaging Asia 2010 Conference, Washington, D.C., September 17, 2010, www.state.gov/e/rls/rmk/2010/149393.htm; James Steinberg, deputy secretary of state, remarks at the Carnegie Endowment for International Peace, October 13, 2010, www.carnegieendowment.org/files/1013_transcript_steinberg_asia.pdf. In his remarks, Steinberg indicated that the TPP provided a "particularly important example . . . of how the building blocks created by APEC initiatives can positively shape the regional trade liberalization efforts and potentially be catapulted to even a broader level," and he linked

the TPP to an eventual Free Trade Area of the Asia Pacific. On the domestic front, the U.S. trade representative, Ron Kirk, conducted an ambitious outreach campaign across the United States in 2010 and 2011 to generate public support for the agreement. See Demetrios Marantis, deputy U.S. trade representative, "U.S. Trade Priorities in the Asia-Pacific: TPP and Beyond," remarks at the Center for Strategic and International Studies, Washington, D.C., January 28, 2010, www.ustr.gov/about-us/press-office/speeches/transcripts/2010/january/remarks-ambassador-demetrios-marantis-center. Ambassador Kirk expressed at a town hall in January 2011 that he hoped to conclude the bulk of the negotiations before the APEC Summit being hosted by the United States in Honolulu in November 2011. Tom Barkley, "USTR Kirk: Hope to Mostly Complete Asia-Pacific Trade Deal by Nov.," *Wall Street Journal*, January 21, 2011, http://online.wsj.com/article/BT-CO-20110121-710842.html.

19. Clinton, "Remarks at Press Availability." Secretary Clinton's speech was preceded by an American diplomatic courting of Southeast Asian nations, though it was also partly in response to Southeast Asian nations' overtures. Her remarks were interpreted by the Chinese as a deliberate attack, and Foreign Minister Yang Jiechi initially responded with an angry criticism of U.S. involvement and any departure from the status quo of bilateral management of territorial disputes in the region. "Chinese FM Refutes Fallacies on the South China Sea Issue," *China Daily*, July 25, 2010, www.chinadaily.com.cn/china/2010-07/25/content_11046054.htm; John Pomfret, "U.S. Takes a Tougher Tone with China," *Washington Post*, July 30, 2010; John Ruwitch and Ambika Ahuja, "China Ruffled at Security Forum Over Maritime Rows," Reuters, July 23, 2010; "ASEAN Acumen," *South China Morning Post*, July 28, 2010, OSC CPP20100728715008; "China Should Establish More Sovereign Presence on the Islands of the South China Sea," speech by and interview with Renmin University professor Shi Yinhong, Feng Huang Wang, transcript of Phoenix TV Century Forum broadcast, August 14, 2010, OSC CPP20100818705001.

20. Hillary Rodham Clinton, secretary of state, "Intervention at East Asia Summit," Hanoi, October 30, 2010, www.state.gov/secretary/rm/2010/10/150196.htm.

21. Andrew Scheineson, "The Shanghai Cooperation Organization," Backgrounder, Council on Foreign Relations, March 24, 2009, www.cfr.org/publication/10883/rise_of_the_shanghai_cooperation; Alyson J. K. Bailes, Pál Dunay, Pan Guang, and Mikhail Troitskiy, *The Shanghai Cooperation Organization as a Regional Security Institution*, SIPRI Policy Paper 17 (Stockholm: Stockholm International Peace Research Institute, 2007), 1–27, http://books.sipri.org/files/PP/SIPRIPP17.pdf; Bates Gill and Melissa Murphy, "China's Evolving Approach to Counterterrorism," *Harvard Asia Quarterly*, vol. 9, nos. 1–2 (Winter–Spring 2005): 21–32, www.csis.org/media/csis/press/050815_counterterrorism.pdf; Akihiro Iwashita, "The Shanghai Cooperation Organization and Japan: Moving Together to Reshape the Eurasian Community," March 14, 2008, www.brookings.edu/articles/2008/0128_asia_iwashita.aspx; Xu Tao, "The Course and Prospect for Shanghai Cooperation Organization's Regional Security Cooperation," *China Strategic Review*, no. 6 (2006): 9; Martha Brill Olcott, "The Shanghai Cooperation Organization: Changing the 'Playing Field' in Central Asia," testimony before the Helsinki Commission, Washington, D.C., September 26, 2006; Richard Giragosian, "The Strategic Central Asian Arena," *China and Eurasia Forum Quarterly*, vol. 4, no. 1 (2006): 133–53.

22. C. J. Chivers, "U.S. Policy Shifts in Central Asia," *International Herald Tribune*, February 3, 2008, www.iht.com/articles/2008/02/03/asia/uzbek.php; Olga Oliker and David A. Shlapak, "U.S. Interests in Central Asia: Policy Priorities and Military Roles," RAND Corporation, 2005, www.rand.org/pubs/monographs/2005/RAND_MG338.pdf, 32, 34.

23. See Matthew Oresman, "Reassessing the Fleeting Potential for U.S.-China Cooperation in Central Asia," *China and Eurasia Forum Quarterly*, vol. 6, no. 2 (2008): 5–13; Parag Khanna, *The Second World: Empires and Influence in the New Global Order* (New York: Random House, 2008), 65–115; Sascha Müller-Kraenner, *China's and India's Emerging Energy Foreign Policy*, Discussion Paper 15 (Bonn: German Development Institute, 2008), www.die-gdi.de/CMS-Homepage/openwebcms3.nsf/(ynDK_contentByKey)/ANES-7HJAZ8/$FILE/DP%2015.2008.pdf; Andreas Wenger, "U.S. Foreign Policy Under Bush: Balance Sheet and Outlook," *Center for Security Studies Analyses in Security Policy*, vol. 41, no. 3 (October 2008); and Robert Sutter, "Asia in the Balance: America and China's 'Peaceful Rise,'" *Current History*, September 2004, 284–89. Also see Gaël Raballand and Agnès Andrésy, "Why Should Trade Between Central Asia and China Continue to Expand?" *Asia Europe Journal*, vol. 5, no. 2 (June 2007): 235–52.

24. Chairman's Statement of the First ASEAN Defense Ministers' Meeting-Plus, "ADMM-Plus: Strategic Cooperation for Peace, Stability, and Development in the Region," ASEAN, Hanoi, October 12, 2010, www.aseansec.org/25352.htm. In addition to this meeting, the annual Shangri-La Dialogue first convened by the International Institute for Strategic Studies (IISS) in 2002 has also provided a "Track One" venue for defense ministers from 28 states in the Asia-Pacific region to discuss security and military concerns. See "IISS Asia Security Summit: The Shangri-La Dialogue—About," International Institute for Strategic Studies, www.iiss.org/conferences/the-shangri-la-dialogue/about.

25. Examples have included multilateral military exercises, such as the annual Malabar exercises, U.S.-Indian naval drills that in 2007 also involved participants from Singapore, Australia, and Japan, and in 2009 involved the United States, India, and Japan. Cobra Gold is a similar annual exercise hosted by Thailand, with participation from Japan, Indonesia, Singapore, South Korea, and the United States. Cobra Gold is principally aimed at drilling for multilateral peacekeeping operations and humanitarian and disaster responses. PACOM has also worked to improve multilateral information sharing with various regional states and has held conferences among Asia-Pacific intelligence chiefs. Moreover, PACOM has supported the activities of the Global Peace Operations Initiative (GPOI) by training (in the Asia-Pacific region) tactical peacekeepers, qualified staff officers, and trainers available for immediate deployment world-wide. Under the GPOI, PACOM has supported annual multinational peacekeeping training exercises in Asia, including Khaan Quest 2006 and 2007, hosted by Mongolia, Santi Dhoot 2008, hosted by Bangladesh, and Garuda Shield 2009, hosted by Indonesia. It has also supported the multilateral Center for Excellence in Disaster Management and Humanitarian Assistance, which educates civilian actors in the region in humanitarian response, peacekeeping, stability operations, and public health. Admiral Timothy J. Keating, commander, U.S. Pacific Command, statement before the U.S. House Armed Services Committee on U.S. Pacific Command posture, March 12, 2008, www.pacom.mil/web/pacom_resources/pdf/2008%20PACOM%20HASC%20Posture%20Statement_12%20Mar%2008.pdf; Matthew R. White, "U.S.,

India, and Japan Open Malabar 2009," Commander, U.S. Seventh Fleet, U.S. Navy, April 27, 2009, www.c7f.navy.mil/news/2009/04-April/18.htm; "US, Thailand Begin 6-Nation Military Exercise," Associated Press, February 1, 2010, http://abcnews. go.com/International/wireStory?id=9715520; Yuli Tri Suwarni, "20 Countries Join Peacekeeping Training," *Jakarta Post*, June 17, 2009, www.thejakartapost.com/ news/2009/06/17/20-countries-join-peacekeeping-training.html; April L. Dustin, "Khaan Quest 2006: Guard Teams Up with Mongolian Army," Oregon National Guard Public Affairs, October 16, 2006, www.nationalguard.com/mobile/news/2006/oct/16/ khaan-quest-2006-guard-teams-up-with-mongolian-army.

26. The RIMPAC exercise is oriented toward "regional maritime security" in general, not just nontraditional security threats. It was first held in 1971 and was most recently conducted—usually in waters near Hawaii—in 2010. It is the world's largest international maritime exercise, involving forces from the United States, Australia, Canada, Chile, Colombia, France, Indonesia, Japan, South Korea, Malaysia, the Netherlands, Peru, Singapore, and Thailand. (Brazil, India, and New Zealand are observer nations.). However, China does not participate. See Commander, U.S. Third Fleet Public Affairs Office, U.S. Navy, "About RIMPAC," July 30, 2010, www.c3f.navy.mil/ RIMPAC_About_Page.html.

27. Bruce A. Elleman, "Waves of Hope: The U.S. Navy's Response to the Tsunami in Northern Indonesia." *Naval War College Newport Papers*, February 2005. In addition, in 2006 and 2008, the U.S. Hospital Ship *Mercy* was deployed to Indonesia to provide humanitarian and disaster relief, and in 2007, the USS *Peleliu*, was sent to Indonesia and provided high-quality medical and dental care to more than 30,000 civilians.

28. In the military-to-military area, some specific examples include exercises such as Talisman Sabre, a biannual joint exercise with the Australian Defense Force inaugurated in 2005, Garuda Shield, an annual peacekeeping exercise with the Indonesian Armed Forces inaugurated in 2007, and Cope India, a series of airlift and airdrop drills in 2004, 2005, 2006, and 2009 focused on humanitarian assistance and disaster relief operations, which represent the largest bilateral air exercises with India in forty years. In 2007, U.S. Special Operations Command Pacific supported the Armed Forces of the Philippines in conducting continuous counterterrorism operations for eight months. Keating, statement on U.S. Pacific Command posture; Bruce Vaughn, "U.S. Strategic and Defense Relationships in the Asia-Pacific Region," Congressional Research Service, Report RL 33821, January 22, 2007; Genieve David, "Cope India Dubbed a Success," Thirteenth Air Force Public Affairs, October 28, 2009, www.af.mil/ news/story.asp?id=123174977.

29. Diane K. Mauzy and Brian L. Job, "U.S. Policy in Southeast Asia: Limited Re-engagement After Years of Benign Neglect," *Asian Survey*, vol. 47, no. 4 (August 2007): 622–41.

30. Robert G. Sutter, *Chinese Foreign Relations: Power and Policy Since the Cold War* (Lanham, Md.: Rowman & Littlefield, 2008); Daniel Twining, "America's Grand Design in Asia," *Washington Quarterly*, vol. 30, no. 3 (Summer 2007): 79–94; Vaughn, "U.S. Strategic and Defense Relationships," 22–25. With regard to Southeast Asia in particular, a good example of the past U.S. focus on bilateral interactions in the diplomatic sphere is contained in the 2003 remarks of Matthew Daley, deputy assistant secretary of state for East Asian and Pacific affairs, in his testimony to Congress, "U.S. Interests and Policy

Priorities in Southeast Asia," www.state.gov/p/eap/rls/rm/2003/19086.htm. In his remarks, Daley did not mention multilateral forums other than in passing. Instead, the speech was framed in the context of bilateral relations.

31. Christopher P. Twomey, "Missing Strategic Opportunity in U.S. China Policy Since 9/11," *Asian Survey*, vol. 47, no. 4 (July–August 2007): 536–59, 546; Toni Johnson, "And Now, Food Security, Too," Daily Analysis, Council on Foreign Relations, July 11, 2007, www.cfr.org/publication/13775/and_now_food_security_too.html.

32. Michael Swaine, "China: Exploiting a Strategic Opening," in *Strategic Asia 2004–05: Confronting Terrorism in the Pursuit of Power*, edited by Ashley J. Tellis and Michael Wills (Seattle: National Bureau of Asian Research, 2004), 67–101; Sutter, *Chinese Foreign Relations*; Sutter, "Asia in the Balance"; Rosemary Foot, "Chinese Strategies in a U.S.-Hegemonic Global Order: Accommodating and Hedging," *International Affairs*, vol. 82, no. 1 (2006): 77–94.

33. See Michael McDevitt, "Alliance Relationships," in *America's Role in Asia: Asian and American Views* (San Francisco: Asia Foundation, 2008), 170.

34. The Asia Cooperation Dialogue (ACD) was proposed by the Thai government in 2001, and the first ACD foreign ministers' meeting took place in June 2002 in Thailand. Seventeen Asian countries the ASEAN members (except Myanmar), China, Japan, South Korea, India, Pakistan, Bangladesh, Bahrain, and Qatar—participated in the meeting. As Shulong Chu observes, due to its pan-Asian character, it is difficult for the ACD process to produce meaningful regional economic and security cooperation, because West Asia and other parts of Asia are too far away from each other, and their problems are so different. "The members share little common ground from which to push for meaningful cooperation." Shulong, "East Asia Summit."

35. "Declaration on the Conduct of Parties in the South China Sea," November 4, 2002, www.aseansec.org/13163.htm. It is particularly important that the Declaration of Conduct has not yet been fully implemented. A working group operating under the auspices of the declaration has met several times to discuss its implementation; the fifth meeting of this working group was held in Kunming, China, in December 2010. The working group is also tasked with discussing a more legally binding Code of Conduct. Notably, this code is likely to only address conflict management rather than territorial dispute resolution, which Beijing prefers to manage on a bilateral basis. "China, ASEAN agree to follow South China Sea declaration," Xinhua, December 23, 2010, http://news.xinhuanet.com/english2010/china/2010-12/23/c_13662098.htm; Robert Sutter and Chin-Hao Huang, "China–Southeast Asia Relations: China Reassures Neighbors, Wary of U.S. Intention," *Comparative Connections*, vol. 12, no. 4 (January 2011), http://csis.org/files/publication/1004qchina_seasia.pdf; Ian Storey, "China's Missteps in Southeast Asia: Less Charm, More Offensive," *China Brief*, vol. 10, no. 25 (December 17, 2010), www.jamestown.org/uploads/media/cb_010_5447b0.pdf; "China, ASEAN Begin Discussion on Stronger Code of Conduct," Xinhua, September 30, 2010, www.chinadaily.com.cn/china/2010-09/30/content_11371512.htm; "China, ASEAN Gear Up for Spratlys Code of Conduct Meet," GMANews.TV, January 22, 2011, www.gmanews.tv/story/211244/china-asean-gear-up-for-spratlys-code-of-conduct-meet.

36. European Union Directorate General for Trade, "ASEAN Trade Statistics—EU Bilateral Trade and Trade with the World," January 18, 2011, http://trade.ec.europa.eu/doclib/docs/2006/september/tradoc_113471.pdf; "ASEAN surpasses Japan as

China's 3rd largest trading partner," *People's Daily Online*, June 18, 2010, http://english.
peopledaily.com.cn/90001/90778/90861/7030353.html; "ASEAN, China to work on
deepening strategic cooperation," *People's Daily Online*, March 3, 2011, http://english.
peopledaily.com.cn/90001/90776/90883/7306353.html; Ding Ying, "FTA Driving
ASEAN Growth," *Beijing Review*, no. 4, January 22, 2011, www.bjreview.com.cn/world/
txt/2011-01/23/content_327879.htm; International Monetary Fund, *Direction of Trade
Statistics*, June 2010; Wang Xinyuan, "Free Trade Agreement Boosts China-ASEAN
Investment," *Renmin Ribao*, July 27, 2010; "China-ASEAN Trade Grows Nearly 60%
Between Jan. and Apr.," *People's Daily*, June 11, 2010; ASEAN Secretariat, "ASEAN–
China Dialogue Relations," Association of Southeast Asian Nations, www.aseansec.
org/5874.htm; Robert Sutter and Chin-Hao Huang, "China–Southeast Asia Relations:
Trade Agreement Registers China's Prominence," *Comparative Connections*, vol. 12, no. 1
(April 2010), http://csis.org/files/publication/1001qchina_seasia.pdf; Brantly Womack,
"China and Southeast Asia: Asymmetry, Leadership and Normalcy," *Pacific Affairs*,
vol. 76, no. 3 (Winter 2003–2004): 529–48; Evan S. Medeiros, "China's International
Behavior: Activism, Opportunism, and Diversification," *Joint Forces Quarterly*, 4th
quarter 2007, 34–41; Sutter, *China's Rise*; Thomas Lum, Wayne M. Morrison, and
Bruce Vaughn, "China's 'Soft Power' in Southeast Asia," CRS Report for Congress,
January 4, 2008; "China, ASEAN Become 4th-Largest Trade Partners in 2007,"
Xinhua, February 29, 2008; U.S.-China Business Council, "Foreign Investment in
China: Forecast 2008;" Harnit Kang, *Maritime Issues in South China Sea: A Survey
of Literature*, IPCS Special Report 76 (New Delhi: Institute of Peace and Conflict
Studies, 2009), 1–8, www.ipcs.org/pdf_file/issue/SR76-Harneet-Final.pdf; Fu-kuo
Liu, "Beijing's Regional Strategy and China–ASEAN Economic Integration," *China
Brief*, vol. 8, no. 10 (May 13, 2008), www.jamestown.org/single/?no_cache=1&tx_
ttnews%5Btt_news%5D=4916; "China–ASEAN Trade Prospects Promising," Xinhua,
July 24, 2008, http://english.peopledaily.com.cn/90001/90780/91344/6458369.html;
Brian McCartan, "ASEAN Tightens Up to Ride China's Rise," *Asia Times*, December
17, 2008, www.atimes.com/atimes/Southeast_Asia/JL17Ae01.html; Qin Yaqing,
"China's Security Strategy with a Special Focus on East Asia," lecture given as part
of the Sasakawa Peace Foundation's "Asian Voices: Promoting Dialogue between the
U.S. and Asia" Seminar Program, July 7, 2004.

37. According to Iwashita, "The SCO decision on limiting the U.S. presence in Central Asia
was unexpectedly demanded by Uzbek President Islam Karimov, while Russia and
China both sought to tone down the terms of the declaration."

38. Joshua Kucera, "Shanghai Cooperation Organization Summiteers Take Shots at
U.S. Presence in Central Asia," Eurasianet, August 20, 2007, www.eurasianet.org/
departments/insight/articles/eav082007a.shtml.

39. John E. McLaughlin, "China, the United States and the Middle East," paper presented at
the Center for Strategic and International Studies, Washington, D.C., November 1, 2006;
Sanam Vakil, "Iran: Balancing East Against West," *Washington Quarterly*, vol. 29, no. 4
(Autumn 2006): 51–65.

40. Some observers assert that the SCO serves as a vehicle for Russia and China to enhance
their influence in Central Asia and curb U.S. access to the region's vast energy supplies.
Others speculate that an expanded and militarized SCO will essentially become a new
Organization of the Petroleum Exporting Countries with weapons. For a discussion of
these views, see Müller-Kraenner, *China's and India's Emerging Energy Foreign Policy*.

41. Scheineson, "The Shanghai Cooperation Organization"; "SCO Summit: 'Beast of the East' Appears to Have Lost Its Teeth," Radio Free Europe/Radio Liberty, June 16, 2009, www.rferl.org/articleprintview/1755390.html; A. Lukin, "Overview of Russia's SCO Presidency," *International Affairs: A Russian Journal of World Politics, Diplomacy, and International Relations*, vol. 55, no. 6 (2009): 58–71; "OSC Analysis: SCO Members Emphasize Organization's Growing Economic, Security Roles," Open Source Center, June 22, 2009, OSC CPF20090622554001; and "SCO's Tashkent Summit Cooks Up 'Thin Soup,' " June 11, 2010, EurasiaNet.org, www.eurasianet.org/node/61276.

42. As one Chinese analyst states: "From the Chinese perspective, it is of particular importance that China has been able, in the SCO framework, to count on the support of the other nine member and observer states in its campaign against [domestic terrorists such as the East Turkestan Islamic Movement, ETIM]." Bailes et al., *Shanghai Cooperation Organization*. Also see Scheineson, "The Shanghai Cooperation Organization"; Müller-Kraenner, "China's and India's Emerging Energy Foreign Policy; Iwashita, "The Shanghai Cooperation Organization and Japan"; Olcott, "The Shanghai Cooperation Organization"; Sutter, *China's Rise*; Medeiros, "China's International Behavior"; Michael R. Chambers, "Framing the Problem: China's Threat Environment and International Obligations," in *Right Sizing the People's Liberation Army: Exploring the Contours of China's Military*, edited by Roy Kamphausen and Andrew Scobell (Carlisle, Pa.: Strategic Studies Institute, 2007), 19–67; and Richard Weitz, "Averting a New Great Game in Central Asia," *Washington Quarterly*, vol. 29, no. 3 (Summer 2006): 155–67. According to Iwashita, "the SCO decision on limiting the U.S. presence in Central Asia was unexpectedly demanded by Uzbek president Islam Karimov, while Russia and China both sought to tone down the terms of the declaration."

43. Fu-Kuo Liu, "Asian Regionalism, Strategic Evolution, and U.S. Policy in Asia: Some Prospects for Cross-Strait Development," Brookings Institution Center for Northeast Asian Policy Studies, June 2008, www.brookings.edu/~/media/Files/rc/papers/2008/06_asian_regionalism_liu/06_asian_regionalism_liu.pdf; Ellen L. Frost, *Asia's New Regionalism* (Boulder, Colo.: Lynne Rienner, 2008). According to Frost, "Washington's passive response to the crisis drove Asian leaders to rely more on their own efforts, of which the integration movement is one."

44. Ellen L. Frost, "America's Role in Engaging with Asia's New Regionalism," in *America's Role in Asia*, 118–19; and Ellen L. Frost, James J. Przystup, and Phillip C. Saunders (Institute for National Strategic Studies, National Defense University), "China's Rising Influence in Asia: Implications for U.S. Policy," *Strategic Forum*, no. 231 (April 2008): 1–8. Thus far, Beijing regards the EAS as merely an important regional forum. See Feng Jian and Liao Lei, "Good-Neighborliness and Friendliness, Sincere and Mutual Assistance, Promote Cooperation, and Jointly Seek Common Development: Yang Jiechi Comments on Premier Wen Jiabao's Attendance at East Asian Leaders' Serial Meetings," Xinhua, October 25, 2009, OSC CPP20091026722001.

45. The APT's most significant achievement is the building of free trade agreements (FTAs), most notably the ASEAN–China FTA and several bilateral agreements. Unlike declarations by the EAS, APEC, the ARF, or ACD, these FTAs are in fact binding and obligate their members to uphold certain norms. Their importance for both China and the United States are discussed in chapter 5. Shulong, "East Asia Summit." Also see Sutter, *Chinese Foreign Relations*; Bates Gill, *Rising Star: China's New Security Diplomacy* (Washington, D.C.: Brookings Institution Press, 2007), 34; "3rd East Asia Summit

Held in Singapore, with Climate Change, Energy, Environmental Issues Topping Agenda," Xinhua, November 21, 2007, http://news.xinhuanet.com/english/2007-11/21/content_7120382.htm; Mark Beeson and Hidetaka Yoshimatsu, "Asia's Odd Men Out: Australia, Japan, and the Politics of Regionalism," *International Relations of the Asia-Pacific*, no. 7 (March 2007): 227–50; Edward Cody, "East Asian Summit Marked by Discord," *Washington Post*, December 14, 2005; Alan D. Romberg, "The East Asia Summit: Much Ado About Nothing—So Far," *Freeman Report* (Center for Strategic and International Studies), December 2005; Jonathan D. Pollack, "The Transformation of the Asian Security Order: Assessing China's Impact," in *Power Shift: China and Asia's New Dynamics*, edited by David Shambaugh (Berkeley: University of California Press, 2005).

46. At the 2010 10+1 meeting, Premier Wen Jiabao called for cooperation in six areas: (1) increase ASEAN–China trade to $500 billion by 2015 and establish bilateral economic and trade cooperation zones with each ASEAN member; (2) utilize the loans from the China–ASEAN Investment Cooperation Fund to strengthen ties; (3) advance financial and capital integration; (4) enhance regional agricultural cooperation; (5) strengthen sustainable development, including cooperation in climate change, poverty, and natural disasters; and (6) deepen cultural exchanges. In 2009, he had presented a similar six-point proposal that included efforts to realize the China–ASEAN Free Trade Area, accelerate the construction of infrastructural facilities, deepen agricultural and rural cooperation, encourage sustainable development, strengthen social and cultural exchanges, and promote regional cooperation at various levels. See Ministry of Foreign Affairs of the People's Republic of China, "Premier Wen Jiabao Addresses the 13th ASEAN–China Summit," October 29, 2010, www.fmprc.gov.cn/eng/wjdt/wshd/t765554.htm; Zhao Cheng and Liao Lei, "Chinese Premier Wen Jiabao Makes Six-Point Proposal on Cooperation with the ASEAN at the 12th ASEAN–China (10+1) Leaders' Meeting in Hua Hin, Thailand, on 24 October 2009," Xinhua, October 24, 2009, OSC CPP20091024172001.

47. Shulong, "East Asia Summit."

48. Campbell, "Press Availability in Beijing."

49. With regard to Southeast Asia in particular, some analysts argue that most Chinese do not regard the increased activism of the Obama administration toward the region as threatening to Beijing's interests, because "both countries have more important things to do such as tackling the economic crisis and global warming" and senior U.S. officials have espoused the desire to create a positive framework in working with Chinas in Southeast Asia. See Robert Sutter and Chin-Hao Huang, "China–Southeast Asia Relations: Myanmar, South China Sea Issues," *Comparative Connections*, vol. 11, no. 3 (October 2009), http://csis.org/files/publication/0903qchina_seasia.pdf.

50. U.S.-China Joint Statement, November 17, 2009, Beijing, http://beijing.usembassy-china.org.cn/111709.html. The inclusion of this statement was hailed as a major success, because, as Bonnie Glaser explains, "the last time a Chinese leader had commented on the subject was when former President Jiang Zemin told President Bush in October 2001 that China viewed the U.S. presence in the region as stabilizing and did not seek to expel U.S. military forces from the region." Bonnie Glaser, "Obama–Hu Summit: Success or Disappointment?" *Comparative Connections*, vol. 11, no. 4 (January 2010), http://csis.org/files/publication/0904qus_china.pdf.

51. U.S.-China Joint Statement, January 19, 2011, Washington, D.C., www.whitehouse.gov/the-press-office/2011/01/19/us-china-joint-statement.

52. "Japan, China to Work Together on Creating 'East Asia Community,' " *Japan Times*, September 29, 2009.

53. Ministry of Foreign Affairs of Japan, "Press Conference by the Deputy Press Secretary," October 7, 2010, www.mofa.go.jp/announce/press/2010/10/1007_01.html. Even Hatoyama was not in favor of leaving the United States out of the broader Asia-Pacific architecture. During his first press conference as prime minister on September 16, 2009, he stated, "I feel that to envisage a regional community in Asia, particularly in East Asia in the medium to long term is the correct path to take. . . . This idea certainly is not intended to exclude the U.S. dollar or the United States. Quite the contrary, as a step beyond this initiative I believe we should envisage an Asia-Pacific community, and I do not think that this could readily be achieved without the United States." "Press Conference by Prime Minister Yukio Hatoyama," Prime Minister of Japan and His Cabinet, September 16, 2009 (provisional translation), www.kantei.go.jp/foreign/hatoyama/statement/200909/16kaiken_e.html.

54. Naoto Kan, "Policy Speech by Prime Minister Naoto Kan at the 174th Session of the Diet," Prime Minister of Japan and His Cabinet, June 11, 2010, www.kantei.go.jp/foreign/kan/statement/201006/11syosin_e.html; Justin McCurry, "Japanese Prime Minister Naoto Kan Promises to Rebuild Country," June 4, 2010, www.guardian.co.uk/world/2010/jun/04/japan-prime-minister-naoto-kan; Sutter and Huang, "Myanmar, South China Sea Issues."

55. For an excellent description of this viewpoint, see Sutter, *Chinese Foreign Relations*; and Ralph A. Cossa et al., "The United States and the Asia-Pacific Region: Security Strategy for the Obama Administration," 2008 Asia-Pacific Strategy Project, February 2009. Also see Frost, "America's Role in Engaging with Asia's New Regionalism"; Joshua Kurlantzick, "Pax Asia-Pacifica? East Asian Integration and Its Implications for the United States," *Washington Quarterly*, vol. 30, no. 3 (Summer 2007): 67–77; Joshua Kurlantzick, *China's Charm: Implications of Chinese Soft Power*," Policy Brief 47 (Washington, D.C.: Carnegie Endowment for International Peace, 2006), 1–7; Joshua Kurlantzick, *China's Charm Offensive: How China's Soft Power is Transforming the World* (New Haven, Conn.: Yale University Press, 2007); and Greg Sheridan, "China Wins as 'U.S. Neglects Region,'" *Australian*, September 3, 2007.

56. As Mauzy and Job observe, Washington's historical lack of interest in multilateralism, along with China's primary multilateralist approach and vigorous engagement, have raised China's presence and status among Southeast Asian countries. Mauzy and Job, "U.S. Policy in Southeast Asia," 632–33. Also see Sutter, *China's Rise*, 38; and Jusuf Wanandi, "China and Asia-Pacific Regionalism," in *The Rise of China and a Changing East Asian Order*, edited by Kokubun Ryosei and Wang Jisi (Tokyo: Asia Pacific Agenda Project, 2004), 49–75.

57. Simon Tay, *Asia Alone: The Dangerous Post-Crisis Divide from America* (New York: John Wiley & Sons, 2010); Simon Tay, "South East Asian Views of the U.S.-China Relationship: Benefiting from Economic Cooperation, Suffering from Geopolitical Competition," remarks at the Woodrow Wilson International Center for Scholars, Conference on the "Impact of U.S.-China Relations in Asia: Regional Views," September 20, 2010. In his remarks at the Wilson Center, Tay explained that in the wake of the financial crisis, Asia is increasingly dependent upon China economically, and that Southeast Asians have lost hope in the U.S. economy to pull them along. At the same time, he conceded that it is an overstatement that China will become dominant in

Asia like the United States did after World War II. China has waged a "charm offensive," but nobody is in the pocket of China, and the ASEAN member nations are actually drawing nearer to the United States in terms of soft power.

58. Sutter, *Chinese Foreign Relations*; Also see Cossa et al., "United States and the Asia-Pacific Region"; Kang, *Maritime Issues*; Medeiros, "China's International Behavior"; Tommy Koh, "The United States and Southeast Asia," in *America's Role in Asia*, 42–45; and Evan S. Medeiros et al., *Pacific Currents: The Responses of U.S. Allies and Security Partners in East Asia to China's Rise* (Santa Monica, Calif.: RAND Corporation, 2008). Medeiros argues that America's East Asian allies and partners (Australia, Japan, the Philippines, Singapore, South Korea, and Thailand) are "seeking to maximize their maneuvering room by positioning themselves to benefit from ties with both China and the United States"; do not see China as a viable strategic alternative to a close reliance on the United States; and reject the idea of having to choose between Beijing and Washington.

59. Sutter, *Chinese Foreign Relations*. Also see Medeiros et al., *Pacific Currents*; and Victor Cha, "Winning Asia: Washington's Untold Success Story," *Foreign Affairs*, vol. 86, no. 6 (November–December 2007).

60. The Bush and Obama administrations seem to agree with this optimistic outlook, at least to some extent. As Thomas Christensen stated in March 2008: "In general we view China's greater participation and assertiveness in multilateral institutions as a positive signal that China intends to address its concerns through dialogue and building consensus within these institutions rather than outside of them. We believe that this approach has helped stabilize East Asia to the benefit of all, including the United States." See Thomas J. Christensen, "Shaping China's Global Choices through Diplomacy," statement before the U.S.-China Economic and Security Review Commission, Washington, D.C., March 18, 2008. The U.S.-China Joint Statement issued during Obama's trip to China stated: "The two sides stressed that they share broad common interests in the Asia-Pacific region and support the development and improvement of an open and inclusive regional cooperation framework that is beneficial to all." See U.S.-China Joint Statement, Beijing, November 17, 2009.

61. Greg Austin, *China's Ocean Frontier: International Law, Military Force, and National Development* (Sydney: Allen & Unwin, 1998); M. Taylor Fravel, *Strong Borders, Secure Nation: Cooperation and Conflict in China's Territorial Disputes* (Princeton, N.J.: Princeton University Press, 2008); and Mark J. Valencia, *China and the South China Seas Dispute*, Adelphi Paper (London: International Institute for Strategic Studies, 1995).

62. Evan S. Medeiros (RAND Corporation), "China's Diplomatic Rise: Assessing Chinese Influence in International Relations," paper prepared for a workshop on "Assessing China's Rise: Power and Influence in the 21st Century," Massachusetts Institute of Technology, Cambridge, Mass., February 27–28, 2009.

63. As Medeiros states: "China continues to probe for targets of opportunity to expand its military and security-related links with U.S. allies in East Asia, especially the smaller and weaker states." Medeiros, "China's Diplomatic Rise." Medeiros also argues that, on balance, China is gaining influence among America's closes allies and partners, but in a limited manner. He states: "These nations have become more sensitive to Chinese preferences and interests, often on sovereignty-related questions that already resonate. Also, many countries are more frequently self-censoring their China policy." See Medeiros et al., *Pacific Currents*.

64. Christensen, "Shaping China's Global Choices."

65. Wei Yan, "Cementing Military Bonds," *Beijing Review*, vol. 51, no. 6 (February 7, 2008): 13; Jing-dong Yuan, "Long March to Mutual Cooperation," *Asia Times Online*, June 26, 2007, www.atimes.com/atimes/China/IF26Ad01.html; Carla A. Hills, Dennis C. Blair, and Frank Sampson Jannuzi, *U.S.-China Relations: An Affirmative Agenda, a Responsible Course* (New York: Council on Foreign Relations, 2007); and Bonnie Glaser, "Chock-Full of Dialogue: SED, Human Rights, and Security." *Comparative Connections*, vol. 10, no. 2 (July 2008). During a January 2011 visit to Beijing, Defense Secretary Gates called for a new strategic dialogue that would address four subjects: nuclear, cyber, space, and ballistic missiles. The Chinese side indicated they would consider the proposal but did not immediately commit to such a dialogue. See "Secretary of Defense Robert M. Gates and Chinese Minister for National Defense General Liang Guanglie, Joint Press Conference," January 10, 2011, www.defense.gov/transcripts/transcript. aspx?transcriptid=4750.

66. As one former Bush official stated: "We always tell the Chinese, 'We want you do to well, we want you to do well economically, we want you to do well diplomatically, but the way to do well is to go in the same direction as the serious powers of the world.' "

67. In the case of the Security Dialogue, the exchanges seem to have consisted mostly of each side asserting their concern over security-related actions taken (or not taken) by the other side, for example, Beijing's lack of transparency about nuclear modernization, the January 2007 Chinese shooting-down of one of its defunct weather satellites, the U.S. military buildup at Guam, and U.S. cooperation with its Asian allies to deploy missile defense systems in the region. See Glaser, "Chock-Full of Dialogue."

68. Dennis Wilder, "The U.S.-China Strategic and Economic Dialogue: Continuity and Change in Obama's China Policy," *China Brief*, vol. 9, no. 10, www.jamestown.org/ programs/chinabrief/single/?tx_ttnews[tt_news]=34989&tx_ttnews[backPid]=25&cHas h=fb1545df57.

69. The Bush administration resisted describing the security-oriented Senior Dialogue as a "strategic" dialogue because the United States ostensibly held dialogues on security issues only with formal allies such as Japan and Australia. That said, the Chinese nonetheless always referred to the dialogue as a "Strategic Dialogue." The Obama administration has obviously dropped this distinction. I am especially indebted to Tiffany Ng for her assistance in preparing this discussion of the S&ED.

70. Hillary Rodham Clinton, "Toward a Deeper and Broader Relationship with China," remarks with Chinese foreign minister Yang Jiechi, Beijing, February 21, 2009, www. state.gov/secretary/rm/2009a/02/119432.htm.

71. David Shear, "Briefing on the U.S.-China Strategic and Economic Dialogue," State Department, July 27, 2009, www.state.gov/r/pa/prs/ps/2009/july/126525.htm.

72. Wilder, "U.S.-China Strategic and Economic Dialogue." Some observers originally thought that the transfer of the bilateral energy and climate dialogue to the State Department would create coordination problems within the U.S. government and with the Chinese side, given the heavily economic nature of this issue and the fact that the Chinese counterpart to Secretary Clinton (State Councilor Dai Bingguo) is not competent to engage on this issue. However, such problems have not occurred, at least thus far.

73. Kurt M. Campbell, Keynote Address at "Strategic Asia 2010–11 Book Launch Event: Asia's Rising Power and America's Continued Purpose," Paul H. Nitze School of

Advanced International Studies of Johns Hopkins University, Washington, D.C., September 29, 2010.

74. As Secretary Clinton stated: "We agreed that further cooperation and action is needed to achieve global economic recovery, to promote stability in Northeast Asia, resume the Six-Party Talks, and implement UN Security Council Resolution 1874 to address ongoing threats of violent extremism and nuclear proliferation, to encourage Iran to live up to its international obligations, and to work toward peace and stability in Afghanistan, Pakistan, and the Middle East." See Hillary Rodham Clinton, Timothy Geithner, Dai Bingguo, and Wang Qishan, "Closing Remarks for U.S.-China Strategic and Economic Dialogue," Eisenhower Executive Office Building, Washington, D.C., July 28, 2009, www.state.gov/secretary/rm/2009a/july/126599.htm. Also see U.S. Department of State, "Joint Press Release on the First Round of the U.S.-China Strategic and Economic Dialogue," July 28, 2009, www.state.gov/secretary/rm/2009a/july/126599.htm.

75. Wilder, "U.S.-China Strategic and Economic Dialogue."

76. Clinton et al., "Closing Remarks for U.S.-China Strategic and Economic Dialogue."

77. See U.S. Department of State, "U.S.-China Strategic and Economic Dialogue 2010 Outcomes of the Strategic Track," May 25, 2010, www.state.gov/r/pa/prs/ps/2010/05/142180.htm.

78. Wilder, "U.S.-China Strategic and Economic Dialogue."

79. Neel Chowdhury, "Global Trade's New Direction," Time, November 15, 2010, www.time.com/time/magazine/article/0,9171,2029401,00.html#ixzz1GzVNlVPO; Richard L. Armitage and Joseph S. Nye, "The U.S.-Japan Alliance: Getting Asia Right Through 2020," Center Strategic and International Studies, February 2007; Gill et al., Strategic Views; Sutter and Huang, "Myanmar, South China Sea Issues."

80. For this argument, see Pacific Economic Cooperation Council, "Impact of the Global Financial Crisis on the Asia Pacific Region and Economic Outlook," in State of the Region Report 2008–2009 (Singapore: Pacific Economic Cooperation Council, 2008), www.pecc.org/sotr/papers/SOTR-2008-Economic-Outlook.pdf. This report states: "The fall in energy and other commodity prices will sharply reduce the import bill of Asian economies, while the depreciation of their currencies [that is, Asian economies' currencies] relative to the U.S. dollar will improve the competitiveness of manufacturing exports. If anything, the recession in the United States will accelerate the pace of demand switching in Asia and of deeper regional integration and cooperation. Looking out five years, one of the likely consequences of the current financial crisis is that Asia will sell relatively more of its goods and services within the region, and less to the US and EU." Also, Keith Bradsher notes, Laura Tyson, chairwoman of the Council of Economic Advisers under President Clinton, has argued the current crisis will "accelerate the move of economic power to Asia. It was under way before, but this will accelerate it." Keith Bradsher, "China to Shun West's Finance Sector," New York Times, December 3, 2008.

81. HSBC cited in Neel Chowdhury, "APEC's Bonding Experience," November 16, 2009, www.time.com/time/magazine/article/0,9171,1934865,00.html#ixzz1GzZ5QJan. The share of Asia's exports going to the United States and Europe declined from 40 to 30 percent from 1998 to 2008; emerging Asia's intraregional exports increased from 46 to 54 percent during the same time period. HSBC predicts that this trend will accelerate,

with Asia's intraregional trade growing at an average annual rate of 12.2 until 2020 compared to 7.3 percent growth of trade with the United States. See also Ron Corben, "New ASEAN Free Trade Pact Viewed Positively," Voice of America, March 16, 2009, www.voanews.com/english/2009-03-16-voa11.cfm.

82. Brian P. Klein and Kenneth Neil Cukier, "Tamed Tigers, Distressed Dragon," *Foreign Affairs*, vol. 88, no. 4 (July–August 2009): 8–16.

83. See National Intelligence Council, *Global Trends 2025: A Transformed World* (Washington, D.C.: National Intelligence Council, November 2008), www.dni.gov/nic/ PDF_2025/2025_Global_Trends_Final_Report.pdf; National Intelligence Council, *Mapping the Global Future*, Report of the National Intelligence Council's 2020 Project (Washington, D.C.: National Intelligence Council, 2004). The 2020 NIC report states: "Asia looks set to displace Western countries as the focus for international economic dynamism—provided Asia's rapid economic growth continues." The 2025 report published in 2008 portrays a similar but somewhat more qualified picture: "The unprecedented shift in relative wealth and economic power roughly from West to East now under way will continue. The United States will remain the single most powerful country but will be less dominant." Also see Institute for National Strategic Studies, "Project on the Next East Asia Security Strategy: Workshop #4 Summary," September 2008, 1–19: "The balance of economic power in the Asia-Pacific region is shifting from the traditional 'West' to Asia."

84. G. John Ikenberry, "The Rise of China and the Future of the West: Can the Liberal System Survive?" *Foreign Affairs*, vol. 87, no. 1 (January–February 2008). Also see McCartan, "ASEAN Tightens Up"; China-ASEAN Trade Prospects Promising," Xinhua, July 24, 2008, http://english.peopledaily.com.cn/90001/90780/91344/6458369.html.

85. The survey targeted 150 "strategic elites" in each of nine Asia-Pacific nations, selected by an expert steering group. The total number of individuals actually interviewed was 313. Members were identified as nongovernmental experts who are influential in the debate on international and/or Asian regional affairs in their respective countries. Serving members of the legislative, judicial, or administrative branches of government or those with expertise outside of international relations and/or Asia were excluded from the group, as well as the members of the expert steering group. See Gill et al., *Strategic Views*. "In response to the question of which other country will be the strongest in overall national power in the Asian region in 10 years, a weighted average of 65.5 percent of respondents answered China, compared with the 31 percent for the United States, 5.5 percent for Japan, and 2.9 percent for India. . . . A weighted average of 59 percent said that China would be the most important country to their nation in 10 years, with 36 percent saying the United States would be most important."

86. Frost, Przystup, and Saunders, "China's Rising Influence." The authors state: "The balance of power in East Asia is stable, but the balance of influence is shifting in China's direction. The latter balance is not zero-sum. U.S. influence is declining relative to China, but not in absolute terms. The United States will remain the strongest power in Asia for the indefinite future." For a similar perspective, see Armitage and Nye, "U.S.-Japan Alliance."

87. John Williamson first coined the term "Washington consensus" in 1990 to describe a set of ten neoliberal policy prescriptions for development that Latin American countries would need to implement to "set their houses in order." John Williamson,

"What Washington Means by Policy Reform," in *Latin American Adjustment: How Much Has Happened?* edited by John Williamson (Washington, D.C.: Peterson Institute for International Economics, April 1990).

88. See Joshua Cooper Ramo, "The Beijing Consensus," Foreign Policy Centre, May 2004. According to Ramo, the Beijing Consensus is "already drawing a wake of new ideas that are very different from those coming from Washington," and "represents a fusion of Chinese thinking with lessons learned from the failure of globalisation culture in other places."

89. Ariana Eunjung Cha, "China Uses Global Crisis to Assert Its Influence," *Washington Post*, April 23, 2009, www.washingtonpost.com/wpdyn/content/article/2009/04/22/AR2009042203823.html.

90. Zhang Wei-wei, "Eight Ideas Behind China's Success," *International Herald Tribune*, October 1, 2009.

91. Sheena Chestnut and Alastair Iain Johnston, "Is China Rising?" in *Global Giant: Is China Changing the Rules of the Game?* edited by Eva Paus, Penelope Prime, and Jon Western (New York: Palgrave Macmillan, 2009). For the original articulation of these Washington Consensus policy principles, see Williamson, "What Washington Means."

92. Chestnut and Johnston, "Is China Rising?"; Andrew Leonard, "No Consensus on the Beijing Consensus," Salon, September 16, 2006, www.salon.com/tech/htww/2006/09/15/beijing_consensus.

93. For such arguments, see Institute for National Strategic Studies, "Project on the Next East Asia Security Strategy." Also see Alain Gresh, "Understanding the Beijing Consensus," *Le Monde diplomatique*, November 2008, http://mondediplo.com/2008/11/03beijingconsensus; and Arif Dirlik, "Beijing Consensus: Beijing 'Gongshi.' Who Recognizes Whom and to What End?" in *Globalization and Autonomy Online Compendium*, 2006, www.globalautonomy.ca/global1/servlet/Position2pdf?fn=PP_Dirlik_BeijingConsensus.

94. For a particularly powerful rebuttal of Ramo's argument, see Chestnut and Johnston, "Is China Rising?" As the author's state, "Ramos himself noted that the core of the Beijing Consensus model is that there is no model—each country chooses its own development route. Yet, it is hard to see how another state choosing its own development path translates into greater political influence for the PRC specifically."

95. David Shambaugh, "China's Soft Power: Fact or Fiction?" Rising Power Initiative's Worldviews of Aspiring Powers Project Lecture, Sigur Center for Asia Studies, George Washington University, Washington, D.C., September 8, 2010. See also the remarks by Bruce Gilley in *China's Soft Power Initiative*, edited by Esther Pan, (New York: Council on Foreign Relations, 2006), www.cfr.org/china/chinas-soft-power-initiative/p10715.

96. Yasheng Huang, "Rethinking the Beijing Consensus," *Asia Policy*, no. 11 (January 2011): 1–26.

97. See, for example, Wang Yusheng, "New Tasks Confronting China's Diplomacy," *Jiefang Ribao*, December 21, 2009, OSC CPP20091227001001.

98. See Chestnut and Johnston, "Is China Rising?" For more on the debate about the existence and influence (or lack thereof) of the Beijing Consensus, see Ariana Eunjung Cha, "China Uses Global Crisis to Assert Its Influence," *Washington Post*, April 23, 2009, www.washingtonpost.com/wp-dyn/content/article/2009/04/22/AR2009042203823.html.

99. Heinrich Kreft, "Indispensable World Power," *World Today*, February 2009, 11–13. Kreft adds that "thanks to immigration and a high birthrate, it has a young population compared to Europe, Japan, Russia as well as China. This makes the burden of providing for an ageing population far less onerous." For a similar point, see Ikenberry, "Rise of China": "Today's Western order, in short, is hard to overturn and easy to join. . . . Today, China can gain full access to and thrive within this system. And if it does, China will rise, but the Western order—if managed properly—will live on."

100. The poll by the Chicago Council on Global Affairs employed a random representative sample of populations within six countries: the United States, China, Japan, South Korea, Vietnam, and Indonesia to measure five indexes of soft power: economic, cultural, human capital, diplomatic, and political; these were combined to form a composite Soft Power Index. The results indicated that U.S. soft power scored surprisingly well across a series of indicators, while China's was surprisingly weak. A total of 69 percent of Chinese, 75 percent of Indonesians, 76 percent of South Koreans, and 79 percent of Japanese in the council's survey said that U.S. influence in Asia had risen over the past decade. See Christopher B. Whitney and David Shambaugh, "Soft Power in Asia: Results of a 2008 Multinational Survey of Public Opinion," Chicago Council on Global Affairs, April 2009, www.thechicagocouncil.org/UserFiles/File/POS_Topline%20Reports/Asia%20 Soft%20Power%202008/Soft%20Power%202008_full%20report.pdf. For summaries and assessments of the Chicago Council poll, see David Shambaugh, "China's Asia Strategy: Seven Questions for the United States Concerning China's Role in Asia," paper presented at the 3rd Berlin Conference on Asian Security, Berlin, September 17–19, 2008, www.swp-berlin.org/common/get_document.php?asset_id=5392. Shambaugh states: "While the survey found much respect for China's traditional culture and economy, there was very little respect for China's political system, rule of law, human rights, society, environment, popular culture, and educational system. The United States, by contrast, scored very well in each of these categories." Also see Minxin Pei, "Think Again: Asia's Rise," *Foreign Policy*, July–August 2009, 32–36; Gustaaf Geeraerts, "China: Soft Power-less in Asia," *Asia Briefing* (Brussels Institute of Contemporary China Studies), no. 33 (February 2009); and Daniel P. Mulhollan, "China's Foreign Policy and "Soft Power" in South America, Asia, and Africa," Congressional Research Service, April 2008, http://biden.senate.gov/imo/media/doc/ CRSChinaReport.pdf.

101. John Pomfret, "China's Far Too Rosy Self Image," *PostGlobal*, March 30, 2009, http:// newsweek.washingtonpost.com/postglobal/pomfretschina/2009/03/china_loves_itself_ more_than_the_world.html. As Pomfret observes, "This is the largest perception gap among the countries' polled. (And it's getting worse. Views about China have declined markedly over the last year.) . . . (Also China now ranks below the average of the U.S. in terms of positive influence for the first time since the poll was initiated five years ago.)"

102. A recent survey conducted in 27 countries between December 2010 and February 2011 found that respondents in six of the eight countries in Asia/Oceania polled (all except China and Pakistan) had a more positive impression of U.S. influence in the world than Chinese influence in the world. In some places, such as Japan, South Korea, and the Philippines, opinions of American influence were 25 to 30 percentage points more positive than attitudes toward Chinese influence. Moreover, far more Chinese (77 percent) viewed China's influence in the world positively than respondents in other Asian nations. "Views of US Continue to Improve in 2011 BBC Country Rating Poll," BBC

World Service/GlobeScan/PIPA, March 7, 2011, www.worldpublicopinion.org/pipa/pdf/mar11/BBCEvalsUS_Mar11_rpt.pdf.

103. Ariana Eunjung Cha, "China Uses Global Crisis to Assert Its Influence," *Washington Post*, April 23, 2009, www.washingtonpost.com/wp-dyn/content/article/2009/04/22/AR2009042203823.html; Chestnut and Johnston, "Is China Rising?"

104. For example, see "Full Text of Hu Jintao's Speech at the General Debate of the 64th Session of the UN General Assembly," Xinhua, September 23, 2009.

105. Gill et al., *Strategic Views*. Qualitative studies by other Asian specialists conclude that the United States will in fact "remain the strongest power in Asia for the indefinite future." See Frost, Przstup, and Saunders, "China's Rising Influence"; Armitage and Nye, "U.S.–Japan Alliance."

106. Frost, Przystup, and Saunders, "China's Rising Influence." The authors state: "China's economic openness, diplomatic flexibility, military restraint, and willingness to help deal with terrorism and other nontraditional threats contribute to peace and prosperity in the region." Also see Robert S. Ross, "Assessing the China Threat," *National Interest*, no. 81 (Fall 2005): 81–87.

107. Gill et al., *Strategic Views*. The authors state: "In every country other than China, China was listed as the most likely threat to peace and security in Asia in 10 years (among all respondents in the survey, 38 percent considered China the biggest threat, with North Korea the second-greatest threat with 21 percent and the United States third with 12.9 percent). . . . Interestingly, Japanese and Indians tended to see China as both the greatest threat to peace and as a potential force for peace at the same time, reflecting certainty about growing Chinese influence but lingering ambivalence about its impact." Also see Geeraerts, "China."

108. Armitage and Nye, "U.S.-Japan Alliance."

109. Medeiros et al., *Pacific Currents*. As Medeiros states: "All the countries we assessed support a robust role for the United States in regional security affairs. To varying degrees, they have strengthened their security relationships with the United States at the same time as they have engaged China—although often for reasons having little to do with China. . . . None of the six East Asian nations favor or expect China to supplant the United States as the predominant power in Asia. At the same time, none of them support an explicit or implicit U.S.-led effort to contain China's rise. None of these nations consider such a strategy desirable or feasible because it would precipitate unnecessary strategic rivalry. . . . U.S. policy remains a key variable in how these nations react to China's growing regional influence." For a related view, see Tay, *Asia Alone*; and Tay, "South East Asian Views." Tay argues that Southeast Asian nations prefer a China–U.S. relationship that is neither too hot nor too cold, and these nations prefer to maintain "equi-proximate" relationships with Beijing and Washington.

110. Indeed, as noted above, early signs of this were already emerging in the mid-2000s, in the view of some analysts. See Medeiros et al., *Pacific Currents*; and National Intelligence Council, *Mapping the Global Future*. "East Asian states are adapting to the advent of a more powerful China by forging closer economic and political ties with Beijing, potentially accommodating themselves to its preferences, particularly on sensitive issues like Taiwan. Japan, Taiwan, and various Southeast Asian nations, however, also may try to appeal to each other and the United States to counterbalance China's growing influence."

111. Frost, *Asia's New Regionalism*. As Frost states: "The Asian integration movement is an experiment reflecting far-reaching political and economic shifts. It is partly a natural outgrowth of globalization and partly an artificial construct reflecting conscious strategic judgments in key Asian capitals. On the surface it is all about Asian harmony, and it muffles numerous bilateral tensions with cottony rhetoric and backroom mediation. But it also shelters a trilogy of dramas—the resurgence of China, Asian reactions, and the future role of the United States. How Asia's new regionalism evolves will thus have huge bearing on regional stability and prosperity and may well have implications for the way the rest of the world governs itself."

112. Ibid. According to Frost, "many Asian leaders will look to the integration movement for opportunities to cope more successfully with shared domestic challenges—and thus to strengthen their national sovereignty, not to share it. This search is at the core of Asia's new regionalism, . . . pushed as much by a quest for security and national autonomy as by economic interdependence and a desire for efficiency." She also adds, however: "Handling the United States is a perpetual puzzle for Asians, who are never entirely sure about US commitments. The notion that U.S. priorities lie elsewhere arose during the Cold War and more recently during the Asian financial crisis."

113. See "Survey Results: Provisional Release," in *State of the Region Report 2008–2009*, www.pecc.org/sotr/papers/SOTR-2008-Survey-Results.pdf; McCartan, "ASEAN Tightens Up." Also see Armitage and Nye, "U.S.-Japan Alliance."

114. See Aditya Suharmoko, "An Integrated Asia Is Within Sight: ADB Chief," *Jakarta Post*, September 11, 2008, www.thejakartapost.com/news/2008/09/11/an-integrated-asia-within-sight adb chief.html. This article cites the Asian Development Bank's vision of an economically integrated Asia as containing these features: "(1) an integrated market free of restrictions on regional flows of goods, services, and capital; (2) deep and liquid financial markets open to cross-border financial flows and services, with high standards of oversight and strong protection for national and foreign investors; (3) effective frameworks to coordinate macroeconomic and exchange rate policies, taking into account global challenges and differing national circumstances; (4) collective efforts to address vital social issues, such as poverty, exclusion, income insecurity, migration, aging, and health and environmental threats; (5) a consistent and determined voice to effectively articulate the concerns of Asian economies in global policy forums and enhance responsible global governance; and (6) vibrant institutions, adequately and professionally staffed, to provide first-rate analytical and logistical support for these efforts." Also see Gill et al., *Strategic Views*. In this survey, 90 percent of respondents identified the establishment of a framework for trade and regional economic integration as "very important" or "somewhat important."

115. Mercy Kuo, Andrew D. Marble, David M. Lampton, Cheng Li, Pieter Bottelier, and Fenggang Yang, "Roundtable: China in the Year 2020," *Asia Policy*, no. 4 (July 2007): 1–52. Frost, *Asia's New Regionalism*. Frost states: "The integration movement engages a rising China and exerts collective pressure on both Japan and China to handle their quarrels with restraint."

116. C. Fred Bergsten et al., *China's Rise: Challenges and Opportunities* (Washington, D.C.: Peterson Institute for International Economics, 2008); C. Fred Bergsten, "A Partnership of Equals," *Foreign Affairs*, vol. 87, no. 4 (July–August 2008): 57–69. Also see Michael Hsiao, "Transformations in China's Soft Power Toward ASEAN," *China Brief*, vol. 8,

no. 22, (May 13, 2008), www.jamestown.org/programs/chinabrief/single/?tx_ttnews%5Btt_news%5D=34168&tx_ttnews%5BbackPid%5D=168&no_cache=1; and Fu-kuo Liu, "Beijing's Regional Strategy."

117. See Hyoung-kyu Chey, "The Changing Political Dynamics of East Asian Financial Cooperation: The Chiang Mai Initiative," *Asian Survey*, vol. 49, no. 3 (May–June 2009): 450–67.

118. Barry Eichengreen, "The Global Credit Crisis as History," University of California, Berkeley, December 2008, www.econ.berkeley.edu/~eichengr/global_credit_crisis_history_12-3-08.pdf. Eichengreen states: "Beijing prefers to see the creation of a more extensive financial support system within the region, while Tokyo resists this on the grounds that China would be the dominant party in that system. The Japanese government for its part would prefer recycling Asian reserves through the IMF, where it has twice the voting power of China and designates one of the deputy managing directors, whereas China, whose voting power in the Fund is roughly equivalent to that of Belgium, is understandably reluctant to go this route." Also see Gill et al., *Strategic Views*. The authors state: "The experience of the 1997 to 1998 financial crisis and subsequent intraregional debt-swapping arrangements through the Chiang Mai Initiative has given elites in the region increased confidence in regional versus international multilateral cooperation." The 2004 National Intelligence Council report states: "Asian finance ministers have considered establishing an Asian monetary fund that would operate along different lines from IMF, attaching fewer strings on currency swaps and giving Asian decision-makers more leeway from the 'Washington macro-economic consensus.' " See National Intelligence Council, *Mapping the Global Future*.

119. Evan A. Feigenbaum and Robert A. Manning, *The United States in the New Asia*, Council Special Report 50 (New York: Council on Foreign Relations Press, 2009); Cossa et al., "United States and the Asia-Pacific Region."

120. Evan A. Feigenbaum, "Challenge of a Changing Asia," *Business Standard*, September 6, 2010, www.business-standard.com/india/news/evanfeigenbaum-challengea-changing-asia/407057/. See also Arthur Lord, *Demystifying FTAs: A Comparative Analysis of American, Japanese, and Chinese Efforts to Shape the Future of Free Trade*, Asia-Pacific Policy Papers Series 10 (Washington, D.C.: Edwin O. Reischauer Center for East Asian Studies, Paul H. Nitze School of Advanced International Studies of Johns Hopkins University, 2010); and Padilla, "Asian Economies."

121. Yukon Huang, personal correspondence with the author, January 2011. See chapter 5 for further discussion of issues related to Asia's economic regionalism and U.S. economic policy in the region.

122. For a cogent example, see Richard Pomfret, "Asian Regionalism: Threat to the WTO-Based Trading System or Paper Tiger?" VoxEU, Centre for Economic Policy Research, June 22, 2007, www.voxeu.org/index.php?q=node/309. Pomfret states: "The recent East Asian regional agreements are less threatening to the world trade system than they may appear. They do not threaten the MFN tariff structure in a meaningful way, and if they can promote trade facilitation this will likely benefit Asia-traders from all countries." He adds that free trade agreements in particular "can be corrosive of regional integration, wasteful of policy-making capacities, sucking oxygen from reform momentum, and causing negative reactions which lead to poor dynamics."

123. Gill et al., *Strategic Views*.

124. See John Kerry, "Chairman Kerry Delivers A Speech on U.S.-China Relations," U.S. Senate Committee on Foreign Relations, December 7, 2010. In his speech, Kerry states: "Recent events on the Korean Peninsula and in the South China Sea reaffirm the importance of the alliances that came out of that conflict—and of forging new partnerships and strengthening regional institutions to maintain peace and stability. Two good places to start would be approving the new Free Trade Agreement with South Korea and fully funding the State Department's Lower Mekong Initiative. We should also negotiate the Trans-Pacific Partnership trade agreement to balance China's economic influence in the region. Some have called this intensified U.S. engagement in East Asia a 'hedging strategy'—insurance against the possible emergence of China as a regional hegemon. I don't care what we call it. I just want to see it done." See also Yang Danzhi, "APEC Faces TPP Challenge," *China Daily*, November 15, 2010, www.chinadaily.com.cn/cndy/2010-11/15/content_11547695.htm.

125. "A weighted average of 81 percent expressed support for the concept of building an East Asia Community, though only 37 percent within that number 'strongly favored' the idea." Gill et al., *Strategic Views*.

126. Gill et al., *Strategic Views*. The authors state: "While there is broad consensus across the region on the importance of establishing an East Asia Community and a high priority placed on confidence building and preventing conflict, regional strategic elites express relatively little confidence in the ability of regional multilateral institutions to actually prevent an attack on their country even in 10 years. On a weighted average, 43 percent consider their own militaries to still be the most effective for that purpose, followed by 25 percent that answered military alliances and 8 percent that answered the United Nations."

127. See G. John Ikenberry, "Asian Regionalism and the Future of U.S. Strategic Engagement," paper presented at the "China Net Assessment Seminar" at the Center for a New American Security in Washington, D.C., April 1, 2009. Also see Frost, *Asia's New Regionalism*. Frost states: "Asians need a robust U.S. presence and have no intention of expelling the United States from Asia. The combination of the U.S. market and U.S. security guarantees are so important to Asians that Americans will remain fully engaged, whether or not Washington has a seat at the table." Hitoshi Tanaka with Adam P. Liff state that "without U.S. involvement, no regional security institution has a realistic chance of success." Jusuf Wanandi and Tadashi Yamamoto, "The Strategic Rationale for East Community Building," in *East Asia at a Crossroads*, edited by Jusuf Wanandi and Tadashi Yamamoto (Tokyo: Japan Center for International Exchange, 2008), 90–104. Also see Michael Green, "American Aims: Realism Still Prevails Over Community Idealism," *Global Asia*, vol. 5, no. 1 (Spring 2010): 32–36.

128. For an argument in favor of a trilateral security dialogue between the United States, Japan, and South Korea, see Christopher Griffin and Michael Auslin, "Time for Trilateralism?" *AEI Outlook*, March 2008. For a brief but succinct assessment of the origins, rise, and decline of the concept of a United States–India–Japan–Australia quadrilateral security framework, see Rory Medcalf, "Chinese Ghost Story," *Diplomat* (Lowy Institute for International Policy), February–March 2008, 16–18.

129. For an excellent discussion of this problem, see Emma Chanlett-Avery and Bruce Vaughn, "Emerging Trends in the Security Architecture in Asia: Bilateral and Multilateral Ties Among the United States, Japan, Australia, and India," Congressional

Research Service, January 7, 2008, www.fas.org/sgp/crs/row/RL34312.pdf. The authors state: "Developing joint capabilities through enhanced defense partnerships with likeminded states may discourage China from asserting itself in ways that harm U.S. interests. On the other hand, it risks creating a dangerous cycle of mutual hedging, in which Beijing is tempted to exhibit more aggressive behavior. This atmosphere would not be conducive to engaging China more fully as a 'responsible stakeholder' in the international system. Developing multilateral groupings poses its own challenges, as all states must harmonize their approach to Beijing: at times, it may be difficult to reconcile a more conciliatory New Delhi or Canberra with a potentially more threatened Tokyo."

130. Steinberg, "East Asia and the Pacific." Steinberg added that future security arrangements should emerge as flexible groupings of nations with shared interests and relevant capabilities, in response to specific issues or problems, and not necessarily out of a desire to create new formal institutions per se.

131. For a proposal regarding the former trilateral United States–China–Japan mechanism, see David Fouse et al., *United States–China–Japan Working Group on Trilateral Confidence- and Security-Building Measures (CSBMs)*, Stanley Foundation Project Report (Muscatine, Iowa: Stanley Foundation, 2008). For a Chinese viewpoint on such a structure, see Zhang Tuosheng, "Time to Rethink Regional Security Cooperation," *China Daily*, March, 31, 2009, www.chinadaily.com.cn/opinion/2009-03/31/content_7632913.htm. For other discussions of this trilateral dialogue concept, see Shulong Chu, "A Mechanism to Stabilize U.S.–China–Japan Trilateral Relations in Asia," Brookings Institution, January 2008, www.brookings.edu/~/media/Files/rc/papers/2008/01_east_asia_chu/01_east_asia_chu.pdf; Morton Abramowitz, "The Globe's Most Important Relationship," *YaleGlobal*, http://yaleglobal.yale.edu/display.article?id=10161 (January 8, 2008); U.S. Institute of Peace, *"Trialogue": U.S.–Japan–China Relations and Asian-Pacific Stability*, Special Report 37 (Washington, D.C.: U.S. Institute of Peace Press, 1998), www.usip.org/pubs/specialreports/early/trilat/sr_trilat.html. Many U.S. observers believe that such a mechanism should also include South Korea. For a proposal in favor of an East Asian Security Institution involving the latter group of five powers, see G. John Ikenberry and Anne-Marie Slaughter (codirectors), "Forging a World of Liberty Under Law: U.S. National Security in the 21st Century," final paper of the Princeton Project on National Security, Woodrow Wilson School of Public and International Affairs, Princeton University, September 27, 2006. Similarly, Jonathan Holslag has suggested a concert of Asian powers similar to the Quintuple Alliance of nineteenth-century Europe that could address regional security concerns. Unlike the Ikenberry-Slaughter proposal, Holslag emphasizes incorporating India into this framework. See Jonathan Holslag, *Trapped Giant: China's Military Rise*, Adelphi Paper (London: International Institute for Strategic Studies, 2010). This concept is also discussed in the concluding chapter of this study.

132. See "U.S., Japan, China Plan Trilateral Powwow," *Japan Times*, June 7, 2009, http://search.japantimes.co.jp/cgi-bin/nn20090607a2.html.

133. "S. Korea's Influence Wanes in U.S.–China–Japan Relations," *Hankyoreh*, December 7, 2009, www.hani.co.kr/arti/english_edition/e_international/391907.html; Morton Abramowitz, "Triple Threat," *National Interest*, May 1, 2009, http://nationalinterest.org/article/triple-threat-3110.

134. Jungsoo Jang, "U.S. Initiative of Trilateral Talks Signals Danger for South Korea," *Hankyoreh*, March 30, 2009, http://english.hani.co.kr/arti/english_edition/e_opinion/346941.html.

135. "China: Trilateral talks merely U.S. wishful thinking," Xinhua, November 2, 2010, www.chinadaily.com.cn/china/2010-11/02/content_11491199.htm.

136. This was arguably seen in October 2010, when China quickly rebuffed Secretary of State Hillary Clinton's suggestion that Washington serve as a "mediator" in trilateral security talks on sensitive issues such as the disputed claims over the Diaoyu/Senkaku Islands. See Hillary Rodham Clinton, "Remarks with Vietnamese Foreign Minister Pham Gia Khiem," following signing ceremonies, Hanoi, October 30, 2010, www.state.gov/secretary/rm/2010/10/150189.htm; and "Foreign Ministry Spokesperson Ma Zhaoxu's Remarks," Ministry of Foreign Affairs of the People's Republic of China, November 2, 2010, www.mfa.gov.cn/eng/xwfw/s2510/2535/t766758.htm.

137. Personal correspondence. Also see Gerald Curtis, "Obama and East Asia: No Room for Complacency," East Asia Forum, August 30, 2009, www.eastasiaforum.org/2009/08/30/obama-and-east-asia-no-room-for-complacency. Curtis states, with regard to the United States–Japan–China dialogue: "There is a role for ad hoc trilateral consultations with China and Japan, but little to be gained from institutionalizing a consultative mechanism which would leave the South Koreans anxious about being left out, tempt China and Japan each to try to draw the U.S. to its side on controversial Sino-Japanese issues, and remove ASEAN as a useful neutral platform upon which these great powers can interact." Also see Susan Shirk, "American Hopes: An Agenda for Cooperation That Serves U.S. Interests," *Global Asia*, vol. 5, no. 1 (Spring 2010): 27–31. Shirk states: "We need to put relations between the U.S., Japan, China, and Russia at the core. The most feasible way to build a concert-like security architecture process is to embed it in a NE Asia security dialogue consisting of the 4 powers whose interests converge there, along with the two Koreas. . . . The U.S. should persuade China to start meeting together as an informal 6-country forum with an empty seat waiting for N. Korea—why allow NK to spoil it?"

138. For example, see Zhang Tuosheng, "Time to Rethink Regional Security Cooperation," *China Daily*, March, 31, 2009, www.chinadaily.com.cn/opinion/2009-03/31/content_7632913.htm. Also see Jian Junbo, "Doubts over U.S.–China–Japan talks," *Asian Times*, June 16, 2009, www.atimes.com/atimes/China/KF16Ad01.html.

139. For these points, see National Intelligence Council, *Global Trends 2025*. As the U.S. government authors of this study state: "Managing and adjusting to a transition to a reunified Korea could expand the Six-Party talks into a mechanism that features new levels of cooperation among the US, Japan, and China. Whether greater or lesser integration occurs also depends largely on the future character of Sino-Japanese ties. This is the first time in modern history that China and Japan have been major regional and global actors at the same time. A key question is whether they can transcend historical suspicions and compete peacefully. Peaceful resolution of the Korea and Taiwan disputes and a Franco-German type entente between China and Japan would sharply diminish the regional desire for a US 'offshore' balancer role."

140. For example, see Wang Yizhou, "China's Path: Learning and Growing," *Global Asia*, vol. 5, no. 1 (Spring 2010): 12–16; Weixing Hu, Gerald Chan, and Daojiong Zha, *China's International Relations in the 21st Century: Dynamics of Paradigm Shifts* (Lanham, Md.: University Press of America, 2000), 5. The authors write: "Outside-in perspectives

tend to underestimate the consequences of domestic politics and intellectual debate on foreign policy conceptualization within China." Also see Susan Shirk, *China: Fragile Superpower: How China's Internal Politics Could Derail Its Peaceful Rise* (Oxford: Oxford University Press, 2007).

CHAPTER 4

1. For one example of this argument, see Dick K. Nanto, "East Asian Regional Architecture: New Economic and Security Arrangements and U.S. Policy," CRS Report for Congress, January 4, 2008. Nanto states: "The United States and China both envision themselves as the preeminent country in the region. Economically, the United States wants to increase access for U.S. exports and companies through the WTO, APEC, FTAs, and other agreements" (pp. 30–31). "The U.S. vision for East Asia is roughly compatible with Japan's vision" (p. 32). "China would like to see U.S. influence decrease as its influence increases. Likewise, it would like to displace Japan as the economic leader of East Asia. As such, China prefers an exclusive East Asian regional organization that would keep the United States out and diminish Japan's leadership role" (p. 31). "China's vision for East Asia conflicts with the U.S. vision" (p. 32). Also see the discussion in chapter 3. For another example, see James A. Lyons (U.S. admiral, retired), "Countering China's Aggression: Communist Dictatorship Presents Trouble in Asia and Abroad," *Washington Times*, October 18, 2010. Lyons states, "Our message should be that the world's leading democracy will not be intimidated or bullied by another Communist threat. In addition to remaining militarily superior, the United States also can begin to organize multinational political and economic pressures that could help accelerate China's evolution from Communism. We led a similar campaign in the not-too-distant past."

2. A softer version of this general argument asserts that, even if China does not at present possess aggressive intentions toward the United States, the combination of the necessity to maintain complete U.S. military predominance in the Asia-Pacific region and China's desire to defend its increasingly expansive external interests as a regional—and nascent global—power will inevitably drive Beijing to acquire ever more threatening military capabilities and seek to displace the U.S. position in the region.

3. See Aaron L. Friedberg, "Asia Rising," *American Interest*, vol. 6, no. 3 (Winter 2009): 53–61: "If it is premature to declare engagement a failure, it is also far too early to be confident of its ultimate success. The fundamental character of the Chinese regime remains unchanged even as China grows richer and stronger, making the task of maintaining a favorable balance of power in Asia increasingly difficult and expensive. That is particularly the case in the military domain." Also see Arthur Waldron, "How Would Democracy Change China?" *Orbis*, vol. 48, no. 2 (Spring 2004): 247–61.

4. For a recent official statement of this view, see James B. Steinberg, "Administration's Vision of the U.S.-China Relationship," keynote address at the Center for a New American Security, Washington, D.C., September 24, 2009, www.state.gov/s/d/2009/129686.htm. As Steinberg notes, "In the face of uncertainty, policymakers in any government tend to prepare for the worst to focus on the potential threat down the road, and of course, some of that is necessary. But we also have to make sure that by preparing for the worst,

we don't foreclose positive outcomes; that we leave ourselves open to the positive, and avoid the trap of self-fulfilling fears."

5. Robert Sutter is probably the most notable proponent of this viewpoint among outside analysts. Sutter argues that "recent U.S. difficulties have not fundamentally undermined the main foundations of the leadership, power, and influence that the United States has exerted in the region for many years." Moreover, although China is certainly rising and probably will continue to do so, it "also has major limitations and weaknesses and has a long way to go to compete for regional leadership." Indeed, he compares Chinese strengths and weaknesses with U.S. strengths and weaknesses and concludes that "the power and interests of the United States and most Asia-Pacific governments work against China ever achieving dominance in the region." See Robert G. Sutter, *The United States in Asia* (Lanham, Md.: Rowman & Littlefield, 2008), 282.

6. For example, see Marshall M. Bouton, study chair, *Global Views 2010: Constrained Internationalism; Adapting to New Realities; Results of a 2010 National Survey of Public Opinion* (Chicago: Chicago Council on Global Affairs, 2010), www.thechicagocouncil. org/UserFiles/File/POS_Topline%20Reports/POS%202010/Global%20Views%202010. pdf; Marshall M. Bouton, study chair, *Global Views 2008: Anxious Americans Seek a New Direction in United States Foreign Policy: Results of a 2008 Survey of Public Opinion* (Chicago: Chicago Council on Global Affairs, 2008), www.thechicagocouncil.org/UserFiles/File/ POS_Topline%20Reports/POS%202008/2008%20Public%20Opinion%202008_US%20 Survey%20Results.pdf; and WorldPublicOpinion.org, "General Engagement with China," www.americans-world.org/digest/regional_issues/china/china3.cfm (2006). This reluctance to adopt a highly adversarial approach toward China policy reflects the fact that most Americans view China's challenge more in economic than security terms. In a January 2011 survey, 60 percent of U.S. respondents stated they were more concerned about China's economic strength than its military strength, while only 27 percent were relatively more concerned about its military strength. Furthermore, fully two-thirds of respondents identified the United States as the world's leading military power, while only 16 percent viewed China as such (in contrast, 47 percent of Americans view China as the world's leading economic power, compared to 31 percent who view the United States as such). Pew Research Center, "Strengthen Ties with China, But Get Tough on Trade," January 12, 2011, http://pewresearch.org/pubs/1855/china-poll-americans-want-closer-ties-but-tougher-trade-policy. I am indebted to Rachel Esplin Odell for contributing substantively to this footnote.

7. This undertaking has occurred alongside an overall massive increase in the U.S. defense budget. Between 2001 and 2010, U.S. defense spending has expanded by 81 percent, from $379 billion to more than $687 billion in constant 2009 dollars. See Stockholm International Peace Research Institute, "Background paper on SIPRI military expenditure data, 2010," April 11, 2011, www.sipri.org/research/ armaments/milex/factsheet2010; Stockholm International Peace Research Institute, Military Expenditures Database, http://milexdata.sipri.org; and Leonard Wong, "Living Perilously in a Bubble," Strategic Studies Institute, November 2008, www. strategicstudiesinstitute.army.mil/pdffiles/PUB898.pdf. President Obama's original proposed defense budget for 2011 was $708.2 billion, though $17 billion was reportedly cut from that number in the final budget passed by Congress. See "Leaner FY 2011 Defense Spending Bill Still Funds Top Committee Priorities," Newsroom of Congressman

Norm Dicks (D-Wash., ranking member of the House Appropriations Committee and the Defense Appropriations Subcommittee), April 15, 2011, www.house.gov/apps/list/speech/wa06_dicks/morenews1/defensefy11final.shtml; American Society of Military Comptrollers, "Congress ends FY2011 budget deadlock and approves funding for DoD and other federal agencies," April 16, 2011, www.asmconline.org/2011/04/congress-ends-fy2011-budget-deadlock-and-approves-funding-for-dod-and-other-federal-agencies; U.S. Department of Defense, "DoD News Briefing with Secretary Gates and Adm. Mullen from the Pentagon, February 1, 2010," www.defense.gov/Transcripts/Transcript.aspx?TranscriptID=4549; and Fred Kaplan, "Too Big to Fail?" *Slate*, February 1, 2010, www.slate.com/id/2243297. One analyst asserts that total U.S. defense-related spending (including programs within major U.S. agencies other than the Pentagon, such as the Department of Energy, the Department of State, and the Department of the Treasury) considerably exceeds $1 trillion per year. See Robert Higgs, "Defense Spending Is Much Greater Than You Think," posting on the Beacon Blog, Independent Institute, April 17, 2010, www.independent.org/blog/?p=5827.

8. See Derek Mitchell, "Reduce, Maintain, Enhance: U.S. Force Structure Changes in the Asia-Pacific Region," in *America's Role in Asia: Asian and American Views*, Michael Armacost, J. Stapleton Roy, Han Sung-Joo, Tommy Koh, C. Raja Mohan, project chairs (San Francisco: Asia Foundation, 2008), 163–64, 167; and Jeffrey Bader, "Obama Goes to Asia: Understanding the President's Trip," remarks at the Brookings Institution, Washington, November 6, 2009. Also see U.S. Navy, U.S. Marine Corps, and U.S. Coast Guard, *A Cooperative Strategy for 21st Century Seapower*, October 2007, www.navy.mil/maritime/MaritimeStrategy.pdf. This document states: "From now on, U.S. seapower will be concentrated in areas that have heightened tension or require the United States to fulfill commitments to allies. The United States will continue to deploy powerful operational forces in the Western Pacific, the Arabian Sea, and the Indian Ocean to protect U.S. and allied interest, and contain potential competitors." We should also note that, globally, the United States remains by far the largest military spender, with its expenditures increasing to $687 billion in 2010 and accounting for 43 percent of global military spending. These figures are stated in constant 2009 U.S. dollars, as reported in the Stockholm International Peace Research Institute Military Expenditures Database, http://milexdata.sipri.org; and Stockholm International Peace Research Institute, "World military spending reached $1.6 trillion in 2010, biggest increase in South America, fall in Europe according to new SIPRI data," April 11, 2010, available at www.sipri.org/media/pressreleases/milex. I am indebted to Rachel Esplin Odell for contributing substantively to this footnote.

9. Hillary Rodham Clinton, secretary of state, "America's Engagement in the Asia-Pacific," Kahala Hotel, Honolulu, October 28, 2010, www.state.gov/secretary/rm/2010/10/150141.htm; Robert M. Gates, "America's Security Role in the Asia-Pacific," remarks delivered at the 8th IISS Asia Security Summit, Shangri-La Dialogue, Singapore, May 30, 2009, www.iiss.org/conferences/the-shangri-la-dialogue/shangri-la-dialogue-2009/plenary-session-speeches-2009/first-plenary-session/dr-robert-gates; "COMSUBPAC Announces Changes of Homeport," Commander—Submarine Force U.S. Pacific Fleet (COMSUBPAC) Public Affairs, December 1, 2009, www.csp.navy.mil/releases/release_09064.shtml; Erik Slavin, "Submarine USS Hawaii First of Its Class to Enter Western Pacific," *Stars and Stripes*, September 7, 2010; International Institute for Strategic Studies, "North America," *The Military Balance 2010* (London: Routledge,

2010); Scot Marciel, "Maritime Issues and Sovereignty Disputes in East Asia," statement before the Subcommittee on East Asian and Pacific Affairs Committee in Washington, July 15, 2009; Mitchell, "Reduce, Maintain, Enhance," 159; David E. Sanger and Thom Shanker, "Pentagon Plans New Arm to Wage Wars in Cyberspace," *New York Times*, May 29, 2009, www.nytimes.com/2009/05/29/us/politics/29cyber.html; Daniel Wasserbly, "U.S. Forces Still Have Much to Do in Cyber War," *Jane's International Defence Review*, vol. 43 (August 2010): 5; U.S. Navy, U.S. Marine Corps, and U.S. Coast Guard, *Cooperative Strategy*; James J. Przystup, Japan–China Relations: New Year, Old Problems, Hope for Wen," *Comparative Connections*, vol. 9, no. 1 (April 2007): 117–32; Shirley Kan, "Taiwan: Major U.S. Arms Sales Since 1990," Congressional Research Service, August 4, 2008; Helene Cooper, "U.S. Approval of Taiwan Arms Sales Angers China," *New York Times*, January 30, 2010; Ben Blanchard and Paul Eckert, "U.S. Seeks Calm as China Fumes Over Taiwan Arms," Reuters, February 1, 2010; James J. Przystup, "The United States, Australia, and the Search for Order in East Asia and Beyond," in *The Other Special Relationship: The United States and Australia at the Start of the 21st Century*, edited by Jeffrey D. McCausland, Douglas T. Stuart, William Tow, and Michael Wesley (Carlisle, Pa.: Strategic Studies Institute, 2007), 261–78; Christopher P. Twomey, "Missing Strategic Opportunity in U.S. China Policy Since 9/11," *Asian Survey*, vol. 47, no. 4 (July–August 2007): 536–59; Ashley J. Tellis, "What Should We Expect from India as a Strategic Partner?" in *Gauging U.S. Indian Strategic Cooperation*, edited by Henry Sokolski (Carlisle, Pa: Strategic Studies Institute, 2007), 231–58; and William Cohen, "Obama's Chance to Cement Ties with India," *Financial Times*, May 27, 2009, www.ft.com/cms/s/0/860f20f2-4aeb-11de-87c2-00144feabdc0.html; Office of the Spokesman, U.S. Department of State, "Third U.S.–Vietnam Political, Security, and Defense Dialogue Yields Progress in Political-Military Cooperation," June 9, 2010, www.state.gov/r/pa/prs/ps/2010/06/142906.htm; "U.S., Vietnam Hold Talks Amid China Concerns," Agence France-Presse, August 17, 2010; General James E. Cartwright, Commander, U.S. Strategic Command, Statement Before the Strategic Forces Subcommittee Senate Armed Services Committee on Global Strike Plans and Programs," March 29, 2006, http://armed-services.senate.gov/statemnt/2006/March/Cartwright percent20SF percent2003-29-06.pdf; Caitlin Harrington, Sam LaGrone, and Daniel Wasserbly, "Silver Bullets: U.S. Seeks Conventional Weapons with a Global Reach," *Jane's International Defence Review*, vol. 43 (September 2010): 50–53; W. J. Hennigan, "X-37B Space Plane Returns to Earth After Seven Months in Orbit," *Los Angeles Times*, December 3, 2010, http://latimesblogs.latimes.com/technology/2010/12/x-37-space-plane-vandenberg.html.

10. See U.S. Department of Defense, *Quadrennial Defense Review Report* (Washington, D.C.: U.S. Government Printing Office, 2010), www.defense.gov/qdr/images/QDR_as_of_12Feb10_1000.pdf, 32. The report states: "The Air Force and Navy together are developing a new joint air-sea battle concept for defeating adversaries across the range of military operations, including adversaries equipped with sophisticated antiaccess and area-denial capabilities. The concept will address how air and naval forces will integrate capabilities across all operational domains—air, sea, land, space, and cyberspace—to counter growing challenges to U.S. freedom of action. The concept will also help guide the development of future capabilities needed for effective power projection operations."

11. Senior department official and senior official via teleconference, U.S. Department of State, "Background Briefing on Asian Security," January 29, 2010, www.state.gov/r/

pa/prs/ps/2010/01/136286.htm; David B. Shear, deputy assistant secretary, Bureau of East Asian and Pacific Affairs, U.S. Department of State, "Cross-Strait Relations in a New Era of Negotiation," remarks at the Carnegie Endowment for International Peace event, Washington, D.C., July 7, 2010, www.state.gov/p/eap/rls/rm/2010/07/144363.htm; Foster Klug, "U.S. Intel Chief Warns Against China–Taiwan Conflict," Associated Press, February 12, 2009; Michael D. Swaine and Oriana Skylar Mastro, "Assessing the Threat," in *Assessing the Threat: The Chinese Military and Taiwan's Security*, edited by Michael D. Swaine, Andrew N. D. Yang, Evan S. Medeiros, and Oriana Skylar Mastro (Washington, D.C.: Carnegie Endowment for International Peace, 2007); Michael D. Swaine and Roy D. Kamphausen, "Military Modernization in Taiwan," in *Strategic Asia 2005–06: Military Modernization in an Era of Uncertainty*, edited by Ashley J. Tellis and Michael Wills (Seattle, National Bureau of Asian Research, 2005); and Nancy Bernkopf Tucker, ed., *Dangerous Strait: The U.S.–Taiwan–China Crisis* (New York: Columbia University Press, 2005). See below for more on U.S. political relations with Taiwan. One former senior official during the George H. W. Bush administration stated that the U.S. position since the latter years of the Clinton era (and in the face of steadily increasing PLA capabilities) had become: "Don't do things that break the One China policy, but do everything we can to make Taiwan a more effective fighting force . . . that consumed a lot of time in the work of DOD."

12. President Barack Obama, remarks in Hradcany Square, Prague, Czech Republic, April 5, 2009, www.whitehouse.gov/the_press_office/Remarks-By-President-Barack-Obama-In-Prague-As-Delivered. However, Obama also promised that as long as nuclear weapons exist, the United States will maintain a safe, secure, and effective arsenal to deter any adversary, and guarantee that defense to U.S. allies. Also see "CNS Experts Welcome Release of Nuclear Posture Review," press release, James Martin Center for Nonproliferation Studies, Monterey Institute of International Studies, April 6, 2010, http://cns.miis.edu/activities/pdfs/100408_pr_npr.pdf; and Shi Weicheng, "Has American Nuclear Strategy Really Changed?" Zhongguo Wang, April 15, 2010, OSC CPP20100415787004.

13. See Office of the Press Secretary, White House, "Key Facts About the New START Treaty," press release, March 26, 2010, www.whitehouse.gov/the-press-office/key-facts-about-new-start-treaty. The new START binds the United States and Russia to bilateral and equal reductions in their nuclear forces, with an upper limit of 1,550 deployed warheads. Each side agrees to cut the number of its operationally deployed warheads and delivery vehicles (that is, bomber aircraft, nuclear submarines, and missiles). This is a 74 percent reduction below the limit of the 1991 START and a 30 percent reduction below the deployed strategic warhead limit of the 2002 Moscow Treaty. Also see Ellen Tauscher, "New START Treaty and the Obama Administration's Nonproliferation Agenda," U.S. Department of State, Washington, D.C., March 29, 2010, www.state.gov/t/us/139205.htm.

14. U.S. Department of Defense, "2010 Nuclear Posture Review (NPR) Fact Sheet," April 6, 2010, www.defense.gov/npr/docs/NPR%20FACT%20SHEET%20April%202010. pdf; Fred Kaplan, "Nuclear Dreams and Nightmares," *Slate*, April 6, 2010, www.slate. com/id/2249961. The former source states that the NPR also seeks to reinforce the fragile nonproliferation regime by reassuring non-nuclear states that the United States "will not use or threaten to use nuclear weapons against non-nuclear weapons states that are party to the Nuclear Non-Proliferation Treaty (NPT) and in compliance

with their nuclear nonproliferation obligations." Also see Anya Loukianova, "Issue Brief: The Nuclear Posture Review Debate," NTI/Monterey Institute, August 19, 2009; Department of Defense, "Nuclear Posture Review (NPR) Background," Fact Sheet, August 6, 2009; Department of Defense, "The NPR, Arms Control and Deterrence," Fact Sheet, August 6, 2009; and Marc Ambinder, "Debating Declaratory Policy On Nuclear Weapons," Politics blog, *Atlantic*, January 15, 2010.

15. Key areas of focus will include implementing a phased, adaptive approach for missile defense in Europe (see Office of the Press Secretary, White House, "Fact Sheet on U.S. Missile Defense Policy—A 'Phased, Adaptive Approach' for Missile Defense in Europe," September 17, 2009, http://geneva.usmission.gov/2009/09/17/missile-defense-policy); providing effective regional missile defenses for U.S. forces and allies against short-, medium-, intermediate-range missiles; providing effective defense of the United States against longer-range missiles; balancing ballistic missile defense capabilities and investments, accounting for near and long-term threats to the United States, its allies, and deployed forces; determining requirements for ballistic missile defense capabilities, as well as the execution and oversight of the U.S. ballistic missile defense program; and providing the objectives, requirements, and standards for ballistic missile defense program testing and evaluation. See Office of Public Affairs, U.S. Department of Defense, "2010 Ballistic Missile Defense Review (BMDR) Fact Sheet," March 3, 2010, www.defense.gov/bmdr/docs/BMDR%20FACT%20 SHEET%20March%202010%20_Final_.pdf; and U.S. Department of Defense, "2009 BMDR Terms of Reference," Fact Sheet, October 16, 2009. Also see Frank A. Rose, "U.S. Missile Defense and Regional Security," remarks at the First Annual Israel Multinational Ballistic Missile Defense Conference, Tel Aviv, May 5, 2010, www.state. gov/t/vci/rls/141673.htm.

16. U.S. Department of Defense and Office of the Director of National Intelligence, "National Security Space Strategy: Unclassified Summary," January 2011, www.dni. gov/reports/2011_nationalsecurityspacestrategy.pdf; "National Space Policy of the United States of America," June 28, 2010, www.whitehouse.gov/sites/default/files/ national_space_policy_6-28-10.pdf; Office of the Press Secretary, White House, "Fact Sheet: The National Space Policy," June 28, 2010, www.whitehouse.gov/ the-press-office/fact-sheet-national-space-policy; Jeff Foust, "A Change in Tone in National Space Policy," *Space Review*, July 6, 2010, www.thespacereview.com/ article/1660/1; Anna Newby, "Obama Administration Releases New Space Policy," Center for Strategic and International Studies, June 29, 2010, http://csis.org/blog/ obama-administration-releases-new-space-policy.

17. Regarding the last point, see U.S. Department of Defense, "Ballistic Missile Defense Review Report," February 2010, www.defense.gov/bmdr/docs/BMDR%20as%20of%20 26JAN10%200630_for%20web.pdf. The report states that the U.S. national missile defense system "does not have the capacity to cope with large-scale Russian or Chinese missile attacks, and is not intended to affect the strategic balance with those countries" (p. 13).

18. Whether Beijing is serious in advocating a ban of space weapons is of course another matter. See below for a discussion of this issue.

19. The Defense Consultative Talks (DCT) and Defense Policy Coordination Talks (DPCT) were first convened in 1997, and the Military Maritime Consultative Agreement

(MMCA) was completed in 1998. These were the first formal United States–China military-to-military interactions after the post–Tiananmen Incident downturn in United States–China relations. The DCT, held at the level of the undersecretary of defense, and the MMCA and DPCT, each convened at the level of deputy assistant secretary of defense, have continued during the Bush and Obama administrations, despite repeated interruptions and suspensions (see below). See the Department of Defense's annual reports to Congress, including U.S. Department of Defense, *Annual Report to Congress: Military and Security Developments Involving the People's Republic of China 2010* (Washington, D.C.: U.S. Government Printing Office, 2010), www.defense. gov/pubs/pdfs/2010_CMPR_Final.pdf. During his January 2011 visit to Beijing, U.S. defense secretary Robert Gates proposed a military-to-military Strategic Dialogue that would address four areas: nuclear, cyber, space, and ballistic missiles. General Liang Guanglie said he would consider the proposal, though no firm commitment was made to proceed with such a dialogue. See "Secretary of Defense Robert M. Gates and Chinese Minister for National Defense General Liang Guanglie, Joint Press Conference," January 10, 2011, www.defense.gov/transcripts/transcript. aspx?transcriptid=4750. I am indebted to Rachel Esplin Odell for researching and drafting this endnote.

20. According to one former senior official, the tensions and communications problems with Beijing evident during the EP-3 incident of 2001 precipitated an internal U.S. review of contacts with the Chinese government, in an effort to develop more effective means to improve discussions during a crisis. This undertaking contributed to subsequent efforts to make better use of the existing "hotline" between the civilian leaderships of the United States and China, and to establish a similar communication link between the two militaries. In November 2009, President Obama and President Hu Jintao reaffirmed the importance of military-to-military ties, stating that "they will take concrete steps to advance sustained and reliable military-to-military relations in the future." See U.S.-China Joint Statement, Beijing, China, November 17, 2009, www. whitehouse.gov/the-press-office/us-china-joint-statement. This agreement resulted in subsequent efforts to increase and deepen military-to-military relations.

21. One road map that has been enunciated to guide U.S.-China military-to-military relations developed when Secretary Gates hosted General Xu Caihou for a visit in Washington in October 2009 and they issued a statement identifying seven priority areas of cooperation: "[1] promoting high-level visits; . . . [2] enhancing cooperation in the area of humanitarian assistance and disaster relief; . . . [3] deepening military medical cooperation, particularly in the area of pandemic disease; . . . [4] expanding service-level exchanges between our two armies; [5] enhancing the program of mid-grade and junior officer exchanges; [6] promoting cultural and sports exchanges between the armed forces; [7] invigorating the existing diplomatic and consultative mechanisms in order to improve military maritime operational and tactical safety of the two armed forces when we operate near each other." U.S. Department of Defense, "Secretary Gates Hosts PRC Counterpart," press release 837-09, October 27, 2009, www.defense.gov/ Releases/Release.aspx?ReleaseID=13078. Both sides recommitted to "work to execute" these seven priority areas when Secretary Gates again visited Beijing in January just before Hu's state visit to Washington. See "Secretary of Defense Robert M. Gates and Chinese Minister for National Defense General Liang Guanglie, Joint Press Conference," January 10, 2011, www.defense.gov/transcripts/transcript.aspx?transcriptid=4750;

and Office of the Press Secretary, White House, "U.S.-China Joint Statement," January 19, 2011, www.whitehouse.gov/the-press-office/2011/01/19/us-china-joint-statement. See also Michèle Flournoy, undersecretary of defense for policy, "U.S. Department of Defense News Briefing," December 10, 2010, www.defense.gov/transcripts/transcript. aspx?transcriptid=4740; and Michael Schiffer, deputy assistant secretary of defense for East Asia, "Building Greater Cooperation in the U.S.-China Military-to-Military Relationship in 2011," Institute for International Strategic Studies, Washington, D.C., January 6, 2011, www.iiss.org/about-us/offices/washington/iiss-us-events/iiss-us-address building-cooperation-in-the-us-china-military-to-military-relationship. Schiffer identified a framework of six guiding principles for the military-to-military relationship, including mutual respect, mutual trust, reciprocity, mutual interest, continuous dialogue, and mutual risk reduction. These would help achieve the four primary goals of military-to-military relations, which he described as: (1) increased high-level communication, (2) improved safety of U.S. and Chinese military personnel, (3) greater insight into each other's intentions and capabilities to reduce misperceptions, and (4) more responsible participation by the PLA in the region.

22. See House of Representatives Committee on Armed Services, "National Defense Authorization Act for Fiscal Year 2000," 106th Congress, 1st Session, May 24, 1999, www. fas.org/man/congress/1999/hr1401commrept.htm. Section 1203 of this law establishes limits on the PLA "having access to advanced technologies and capabilities of the U.S. armed forces" and "prohibits U.S. armed forces from participating in contact that may endanger national interests."

23. Shirley A. Kan, "U.S.-China Military Contacts: Issues for Congress," Congressional Research Service, December 14, 2010, www.fas.org/sgp/crs/natsec/RL32496. pdf; Jonathan Pearlman, "Military Chiefs Woo China," *Age*, September 3, 2009; "Special Report: Kamphausen on U.S.-China Military-to-Military Cooperation," Asia Security Initiative blog, November 16, 2009, http://asiasecurity.macfound.org/blog/entry/111special_report_kamphausen_on_u.s.-china_military-to-military_cooperation; Derek Mitchell and Yuki Tatsumi, "U.S. Domestic Foreign Policy Process and Its Impact on China Policy," in *An Alliance for Engagement: Building Cooperation in Security Relations with China*, edited by Benjamin L. Self and Jeffrey W. Thompson (Washington, D.C.: Henry L. Stimson Center, 2002), 57–78; Kristin Archick, Richard F. Grimmett, and Shirley Kan, "European Union's Arms Embargo on China: Implications and Options for U.S. Policy," CRS Report for Congress, April 15, 2007; "China's Military Modernization and Export Controls," hearing before the U.S.-China Economic and Security Review Commission, Washington, D.C., March 16–17, 2006, www. uscc.gov/hearings/2006hearings/transcripts/march16_17/March_16-17_FINAL.pdf; Jeffrey Thomas, "Rice Describes EU Arms Embargo Discussion as 'Fruitful,'" State Department, Washington File, February 10, 2005. The Washington File is a product of the Bureau of International Information Programs, U.S. Department of State; see http://usinfo.state.gov. U.S. officials argue that China could easily sell dual-use technologies to less stable regions of the world or use them as tools of domestic political repression. Regarding the EU arms ban in particular, U.S. officials stressed that its lifting would have a negative effect on the U.S. force posture in the region and regional security overall. In response, some European officials have argued that the arms ban and U.S. regulations governing the transport of dual-use items are in many cases unnecessary, obsolete, weak, and inconsistent. Also see Andrew Rettman, "EU to Keep China

Arms Embargo Despite Massive Investments," *EU Observer*, January 5, 2011, http://euobserver.com/884/31592; "Mandelson Says EU Should Ease China Arms Embargo," Reuters, July 9, 2009, http://uk.reuters.com/article/idUKTRE5686EZ20090709; John M Doyle, Douglas Barrie, and Robert Wall, "China Syndrome," *Aviation Week & Space Technology*, February 20, 2006; and Richard A. Bitzinger, "A Prisoner's Dilemma: The EU's China Arms Embargo," *China Brief*, vol. 4, no. 13 (June 24, 2004).

24. Randy Forbes, "The Dual-Use Double-Edged Sword," *Military Information Technology*, August 25, 2005. Also see Peter Lichtenbaum, testimony before the U.S.-China Economic and Security Review Commission, Hearing on U.S.-China Trade Impacts on the U.S. Defense Industrial Base, June 23, 2005, www.uscc.gov/hearings/2005hearings/written_testimonies/05_06_21wrts/lichtenbaum_statement_wrts.pdf. One interview respondent with extensive experience regarding U.S. internal policy debates over China stated that disputes over export controls usually triggered the most intense arguments within the U.S. government over how best to balance between cooperation and hedging.

25. Other significant disruptions occurred following the U.S. bombing of the Chinese embassy in Belgrade in 1999, the EP-3 incident of 2001, and the announcement by the Obama administration of a decision to supply significant arms to Taiwan in January 2010.

26. In June 2010, General Ma Xiaotian identified the three obstacles to military-to-military exchanges between China and the United States as (1) arms sales to Taiwan, (2) U.S. reconnaissance in China's nearby waters, and (3) the 2000 National Defense Authorization Act and the DeLay Amendment. At the same conference, Secretary Gates criticized China for holding military-to-military contacts hostage to U.S. arms sales to Taiwan, calling for "sustained and reliable" military-to-military contacts that are not "repeatedly interrupted by and subject to the vagaries of political weather." See General Ma Xiaotian, deputy chief of General Staff, People's Liberation Army, China, "Remarks at the 9th IISS Asia Security Summit," Shangri-La Dialogue, Singapore, Second Plenary Session: New Dimensions of Security, Q&A, June 5, 2010, www.iiss.org/conferences/the-shangri-la-dialogue/shangri-la-dialogue-2010/plenary-session-speeches/second-plenary-session/copyof-ma-xiaotian; and Secretary of Defense Robert M. Gates, "Remarks at the 9th IISS Asia Security Summit," Shangri-La Dialogue, Singapore, June 5, 2010, www.defense.gov/speeches/speech.aspx?speechid=1483. See also Kan, "U.S.-China Military Contacts."

27. Michael R. Chambers, "Framing the Problem: China's Threat Environment and International Obligations," in *Right Sizing the People's Liberation Army: Exploring the Contours of China's Military*, edited by Roy Kamphausen and Andrew Scobell (Carlisle, Pa.: Strategic Studies Institute, 2007): 19–67; Michael D. Maples, "Current and Projected National Security Threats to the United States," Statement for the Record before the Senate Committee on Armed Services, February 27, 2008; Eric D. Hagt, "Chinese Military Modernization and its Impact on the United States and the Asia-Pacific," World Security Institute, March 30, 2007.

28. Roy D. Kamphausen, David Lai, and Andrew Scobell, eds., *The PLA at Home and Abroad: Assessing the Operational Capabilities of China's Military* (Carlisle, Pa.: Strategic Studies Institute, 2010); Dennis C. Blair, "Military Power Projection in Asia," in *Strategic Asia 2008–09: Challenges and Choices*, edited by Ashley J. Tellis, Mercy Kuo, et al. (Seattle: National Bureau of Asian Research, 2008), 416–17; Andrew S. Erickson, Lyle J. Goldstein, William S. Murray, and Andrew R. Wilson, *China's Future Nuclear Submarine Force* (Annapolis, Md.:

Naval Institute Press, 2007); Michael D. Swaine, "China's Regional Military Posture," in *Power Shift: China and Asia's New Dynamics*, edited by David Shambaugh (Berkeley: University of California Press, 2005); Loro Horta, "The PLAN Reaches the Atlantic: Assessing Chinese Navy's Recent Naval Exercises," Rajaratnam School of International Studies Commentaries, October 12, 2007; Roy Kamphausen, David Lai, and Andrew Scobell, eds., *Beyond the Strait: PLA Missions Other Than Taiwan* (Carlisle, Pa.: Strategic Studies Institute, 2009); Mark Cozad, "China's Regional Power Projection: Prospects for Future Missions in the South and East China Seas," in *Beyond the Strait*, 287–326; Marc Miller, "PLA Missions Beyond Taiwan," Colloquium Brief, Strategic Studies Institute, October 2008; Susan M. Puska, "Rough but Ready Force Projection: An Assessment of Recent PLA Training," in *China's Growing Military Power: Perspectives on Security, Ballistic Missiles, and Conventional Capabilities*, edited by Andrew Scobell and Larry M. Wortzel (Carlisle, Pa.: Strategic Studies Institute, 2002); Cliff, Roger. "The Implications of Chinese Military Modernization for U.S. Force Posture in a Taiwan Conflict," in *Assessing the Threat*, ed. Swaine et al., 285–310.

29. Dennis J. Blasko, *The Chinese Army Today: Tradition and Transformation for the 21st Century* (London: Routledge, 2006); David Shambaugh, *Modernizing China's Military: Progress, Problems, and Prospects* (Berkeley: University of California Press, 2002); David Shambaugh, "China's Military Modernization: Making Steady and Surprising Progress," in *Strategic Asia 2005–2006*, ed. Tellis and Wills; Jayshree Bajoria, "China's Military Power," Council on Foreign Relations Backgrounder, February 4, 2009, www.cfr.org/publication/18459; Andrew Scobell, Roy Kamphausen, Ellis Joffe, Michael R. Chambers, David M. Finkelstein, Cortez A. Cooper III, Dennis J. Blasko, Bernard D. Cole, Michael McDevitt, Phillip C. Saunders, Erik Quam, and Larry Wortzel, "Roundtable: Sizing the Chinese Military," *Asia Policy*, no. 4 (July 2007): 53–105; Harold Brown et al., *Chinese Military Power: Report of an Independent Task Force* (New York: Council on Foreign Relations, 2003); Michael McDevitt, "Asian Military Modernisation: Key Areas of Concern—Address to the IISS-JIIA Tokyo Conference," *Adelphi Series*, vol. 48, nos. 400–1 (October 2008): 125–32; Evan S. Medeiros, Roger Cliff, Keith Crane, and James C. Mulvenon, *A New Direction for China's Defense Industry* (Santa Monica, Calif.: RAND Corporation, 2005); Richard A. Bitzinger, "Reforming China's Defense Industry: Progress in Spite of Itself?" *Korean Journal of Defense Analysis*, vol. 19, no. 3 (Fall 2007): 99–118.

30. Yoichi Kato, "China's New Missile Capability Raises Tensions," *Asahi Shimbun*, January 27, 2011, www.asahi.com/english/TKY201101260340.html; Andrew Erickson, "China's Anti-Ship Ballistic Missile (ASBM) Reaches Equivalent of 'Initial Operational Capability' (IOC)—Where It's Going and What it Means," Andrew S. Erickson Blog, March 31, 2011, http://www.andrewerickson.com/2011/03/china%E2%80%99s-anti-ship-ballistic-missile-asbm-reaches-equivalent-of-%E2%80%9Cinitial-operational-capability%E2%80%9D-ioc%E2%80%94where-it%E2%80%99s-going-and-what-it-means; Fan Hangmu (pen name, which is a homophone for "antiaircraft carrier"), "Satellite-Missile Attack: Exploring a Model for Anti-Ship Ballistic Missile Combat Operations," *Xiandai Jianchuan* (Modern Ships), November 15–30, 2010, 30–33, OSC CPP20110118318001; Robert F. Willard, Statement Before the House Armed Services Committee on U.S. Pacific Command Posture, March 23, 2010, http://armed-services.senate.gov/statemnt/2010/03 percent20March/Willard percent2003-26-10.pdf; Dennis C. Blair, "Annual Threat Assessment of the US

Intelligence Community for the Senate Select Committee on Intelligence," Testimony Prepared for the Senate Select Committee on Intelligence, February 2, 2010, www.dni. gov/testimonies/20100202_testimony.pdf; Andrew S. Erickson, Lyle J. Goldstein, William S. Murray, and Andrew R. Wilson, *China's Future Nuclear Submarine Force* (Annapolis, Md.: Naval Institute Press, 2007); P. Gregory Metzler, "China in Space: Implications for U.S. Military Strategy," *Joint Forces Quarterly*, no. 47 (4th quarter 2007): 96–98; Dominic Descisciolo, "China's Space Development and Nuclear Strategy," in *China's Nuclear Force Modernization*, Naval War College Newport Papers 22, edited by Lyle J. Goldstein and Andrew S. Erickson (Newport: Naval War College, 2005), 49–64; Bruce W. MacDonald, "China, Space Weapons, and U.S. Security," Council on Foreign Relations, September 2008, Council Special Report 38; Michael D. Swaine, with Loren H. Runyon, "Ballistic Missiles and Missile Defense in Asia," *NBR Analysis*, vol. 13, no. 3 (June 2002); Bernard D. Cole, *The Great Wall at Sea: China's Navy Enters the Twenty-First Century* (Annapolis, Md.: Naval Institute Press, 2001); Ronald O'Rourke, "China Naval Modernization: Implications for U.S. Navy Capabilities—Background and Issues for Congress," CRS Report for Congress, February 3, 2011, www.fas.org/sgp/crs/row/RL33153.pdf.

31. Bill Sweetman, "Chinese J-20 Stealth Fighter in Taxi Tests," *Aviation Week*, January 3, 2011. Although U.S. secretary of defense Gates indicated in January 2011 that the development of the J-20 was further along than expected, many observers (including Gates) expressed doubts about the capabilities and stealth qualities of the aircraft. Some observers have also suggested that it might be as much as a decade before the aircraft is operational. See Greg Waldron, "Long March: China's Fifth-Generation Fighter Is Years Away," *Flight International*, January 4, 2011; Andrew Cockburn, "China Stealth Jet Is No Reason to Boost U.S. Defense Spending," op-ed, *Los Angeles Times*, January 12, 2011; Elisabeth Bumiller, "U.S. Will Counter Chinese Arms Buildup," *New York Times*, January 8, 2011. The first test flight of a prototype of the J-20 occurred on January 11, 2011, during a visit by Gates to Beijing, thus prompting some concern among U.S. officials that the timing was intended to send a confrontational signal to Washington. See John Pomfret, "China Tests Stealth Fighter Jet Just Before Gates, Hu Visit," *Washington Post*, January 11, 2011. The Chinese leadership denied being aware of the test, however, and Gates later suggested that it was most likely a bureaucratic miscommunication rather than a deliberate signal. Secretary of Defense Robert M. Gates, remarks at Keio University, Tokyo, January 14, 2011, www.globalsecurity.org/military/ library/news/2011/01/mil-110114-dod02.htm. Indeed, the test had likely been long scheduled, probably by lower-level officials and engineers. Michael Wines and Elisabeth Bumiller, "Test Unrelated to Gates Visit, China Says," *New York Times*, January 12, 2011. For a Chinese rebuttal, see Rear Admiral Yang Yi, "J-20 Makes Rumors Fly High," op-ed, *China Daily*, January 15, 2011.

32. Kathrin Hille, "China Reveals Aircraft Carrier Plans," *Financial Times*, December 17, 2010; Michael Forsythe, "Watching Beijing's Air Power Grow," *New York Times*, October 21, 2009; Ben Blanchard, "U.S. Says Watching China's Naval Expansion Closely," Reuters, April 19, 2009, www.reuters.com/article/topNews/idUSTRE53I 04R20090419?feedType=RSS&feedName=topNews; Chen Jun, "China's Aircraft Carrier: One Step Closer," News China, May 5, 2009; Larry M. Wortzel, "PLA 'Joint' Operational Contingencies in South Asia, Central Asia, and Korea," in *Beyond the Strait*, ed. Kamphausen, Lai, and Scobell, 327–90; Bernard D. Cole, "Right-Sizing the Navy: How Much Naval Force Will Beijing Deploy?" in *Right Sizing the People's Liberation*

Army, ed. Kamphausen and Scobell, esp. 523–56; Lyle J. Goldstein and William Murray, "Undersea Dragons: China's Maturing Submarine Force," *International Security*, vol. 28, no. 4 (Spring 2004): 161–96; Phillip C. Saunders and Erik R. Quam, "China's Air Force Modernization," *Joint Forces Quarterly*, no. 47 (4th quarter 2007): 28–33.

33. Indeed, China's self-assessment of its abilities and the pace of its modernization remains quite modest. For example, since at least January 2006, the official Chinese military and party media have repeatedly stated some variant of the following: "At present and for quite a long time to come, the main contradiction in our army building is still that the level of our modernization is incompatible with the demands of winning a local war under informationization conditions, and our military capability is incompatible with the demands of carrying out the army's historic missions in the new century and new age." See "New Year Message: Develop a New Situation in National Defense and Army Modernization, Guided by the 17th Party Congress Spirit," Jiefangjun Bao, January 1, 2008, OSC CPP20080101701001. I am indebted to Dennis Blasko for these observations.

34. Willard, Statement Before the House Armed Services Committee; National Air and Space Intelligence Center, "Ballistic and Cruise Missile Threat," NASIC Report 1031-0985-09, June 2009, www.fas.org/irp/threat/missile/naic/NASIC2009.pdf; Scarlet Kim and Alex Bollfrass, "Arms Control and Proliferation Profile: China," Fact Sheet, Arms Control Association, November 2007, www.armscontrol.org/factsheets/chinaprofile; Andrew S. Erickson and Michael Chase, "An Undersea Deterrent?" *Proceedings*, June 2009, 36–41; Larry M. Wortzel, *China's Nuclear Forces: Operations, Training, Doctrine, Command, Control, and Campaign Planning* (Carlisle, Pa.: Strategic Studies Institute, 2007); Mark Stokes, *China's Strategic Modernization: Implications for the United States* (Carlisle, Pa.: Strategic Studies Institute, 1999); Michael McDevitt, "The Strategic and Operational Context Driving PLA Navy Building," in *Right Sizing the People's Liberation Army*, ed. Kamphausen and Scobell, 481–522; Christopher McConnaughy, "China's Undersea Nuclear Deterrent: Will the U.S. Navy Be Ready?" in *China's Nuclear Force Modernization*, ed. Goldstein and Erickson, 23–47.

35. See Bates Gill, James Mulvenon, and Mark Stokes, "The Chinese Second Artillery Corps: Transition to Credible Deterrence," in *The People's Liberation Army as an Organization*, edited by James C. Mulvenon and Andrew N. D. Yang (Santa Monica, Calif.: RAND Corporation, 2002). The authors state: "At the present stage in the Second Artillery's modernization, China is nearing a historic convergence between doctrine and capability, allowing it to increasingly achieve a degree of *credible minimal deterrence* vis-à-vis the continental United States—a convergence of its doctrine and capability it has not confidently possessed since the weaponization of China's nuclear program in the mid-1960s." For a more recent analysis, see Erickson and Chase, "Undersea Deterrent?" The authors state: "With the introduction of the DF-31 and DF-31A road-mobile intercontinental ballistic missiles (ICBMs) and the JL-2 missiles on Jin SSBNs, China is thus on the verge of achieving a credible nuclear deterrent based on a survivable second-strike capability. . . . Many analysts have focused on the survivability issue as the main reason for China's decision to proceed with the development of the Jin and the JL-2."

36. See Robert F. Willard, Statement Before the House Armed Services Committee On U.S. Pacific Command Posture, March 23, 2010, http://armedservices.house.gov/pdfs/FC032510/Willard_Testimony032510.pdf; Blair, "Annual Threat Assessment"; Nan Li, "The Evolution of China's Naval Strategy and Capabilities: From 'Near Coast' and 'Near Seas' to 'Far Seas,'" *Asian Security*, vol. 5 (May 2009): 144–69; "China's Role in

Asia: Access and Anti-Access," Executive Summary of Conference hosted by National Defense University's Center for Technology and National Security Policy and Institute for National Strategic Studies, Washington, D.C., July 24–25, 2008, www.ndu.edu/CTNSP/docUploaded//TFX_China%20in%20Asia%20July%2008%20conf%20rep%20OPEN.pdf; David M. Finkelstein, "China's National Military Strategy: An Overview of the 'Military Strategic Guidelines,'" *Asia Policy*, no. 4 (July 2007): 67–72; Bates Gill, *Rising Star: China's New Security Diplomacy* (Washington, D.C.: Brookings Institution Press, 2007); Roger Cliff et al., *Entering the Dragon's Lair: Chinese Antiaccess Strategies and Their Implications for the United States* (Santa Monica, Calif.: RAND Corporation, 2007); U.S. Department of Defense, *Annual Report to Congress: Military Power of the People's Republic of China 2009* (Washington, D.C.: U.S. Government Printing Office, 2009), www.defenselink.mil/pubs/pdfs/China_Military_Power_Report_2009.pdf; and Cozad, "China's Regional Power Projection."

37. See Yann-Huei Song, "Declarations and Statements with Respect to the 1982 UNCLOS: Potential Legal Disputes between the United States and China after U.S. Accession to the Convention," *Ocean Development and International Law*, vol. 36 (2005): 261–89.

38. Ibid. Also see Ren Xiaofeng and Cheng Xizhong, "A Chinese Perspective," *Marine Policy*, vol. 29, no. 2 (2005): 139–46. The authors state: "Regarding the regime of military and intelligence gathering activities in the EEZ, China argues that the freedoms of navigation and overflight in the EEZ have certain restrictions including that the activity must be peaceful and not threaten to use force against the coastal State. [Such nonpeaceful activity allegedly] includes military surveys, military maneuvers, and military reconnaissance, which are a form of battlefield preparation. These activities are also subject to due regard for the rights of the coastal State. China also argues that there are serious shortcomings regarding the regime of marine scientific research in the EEZ and that marine surveys or military surveys carried out by MSR platforms require the consent of the coastal State." Washington does not accept the Chinese position on many of these issues. It asserts that, although coastal states are granted jurisdiction over environmental and economic resource-related activities within their EEZ, nothing in UNCLOS or state practice restricts military activities undertaken with due regard. See, for example, Peter Dutton and John Garofano, "High Seas Freedoms: China Undermines Maritime Law," *Far Eastern Economic Review*, April 3, 2009; Scot Marciel, "Maritime Issues and Sovereignty Disputes in East Asia," statement before the Subcommittee on East Asian and Pacific Affairs Committee in Washington, D.C., July 15, 2009; Peter Dutton, testimony before the U.S. Senate Committee on Foreign Relations, Hearing on Maritime Disputes and Sovereignty Issues in East Asia, July 15, 2009, http://foreign.senate.gov/testimony/2009/DuttonTestimony090715p.pdf; Peter A. Dutton, Testimony before the United States–China Economic and Security Review Commission Hearing on the Implications of China's Naval Modernization for the United States, June 11, 2009, www.uscc.gov/hearings/2009hearings/written_testimonies/09_06_11_wrts/09_06_11_dutton_statement.pdf; and Peter A. Dutton, "Through a Chinese Lens," *Proceedings*, vol. 136/4/1286 (April 2010): 24–29. Also see Raul (Pete) Pedrozo, "Responding to Ms. Zhang's Talking Points on the EEZ," *Chinese Journal of International Law*, vol. 10, no. 1 (2011): 207–23.

39. For an argument in favor of the urgent need for the United States to ratify UNCLOS, see Vern Clark and Thomas R. Pickering, "A Treaty That Lifts All Boats," *New York Times*, July 14, 2007.

40. According to the Pentagon, proponents of this strategy assert that "China requires a greater number of large- and medium-size warships, carrier-based aviation, improved C4ISR, and more long-range support vessels." U.S. Department of Defense, *Annual Report to Congress: Military Power of the People's Republic of China 2009*, 18. Some analysts also believe that the acquisition of such capabilities will also require the PLA to seek dominance in space. For references to discussions by PLA analysts of such a requirement, see Kamphausen, Lai, and Scobell, *Beyond the Strait*. Also see Nan Li, "Evolution of China's Naval Strategy." For a recent primary Chinese source, see the interview with Rear Admiral Zhang Huachen, deputy commander of the East Sea Fleet. Admiral Zhang stated: "With our naval strategy changing now, we are going from coastal defense to far sea defense. . . . With the expansion of the country's economic interests, the navy wants to better protect the country's transportation routes and the safety of our major sea lanes. . . . In order to achieve this, the Chinese Navy needs to develop along the lines of bigger vessels and with more comprehensive capabilities." (现在是海军战略发生变化, 由近海防御向远海防卫方向转变 . . . 随着国家经济利益的拓展, 海军如果想要更好的维护国家交通线, 主要航道的安全, 就必须要向大型化, 综合化的方向发展.) See "Donghai jiandui fusiling: Wo haijun xu xiang daxinghua zonghehua fazhan" (East Sea Fleet Deputy Commander: Navy Must Expand Large-Scale Integration), Xinhua, March 9, 2010, http://news.xinhuanet.com/mil/2010-03/09/content_13129335.htm. This interview was also cited in Edward Wong, "Chinese Military Seeks to Extend Its Naval Power," *New York Times*, April 23, 2010.

41. For example, see Gu Wei-Jun, "Need to Break Through China's Rigid Thinking: It's Unavoidable That China Will Use Military Forces Abroad" (Xu tupo jianghua siwei, zhongguo weilai haiwai yong bing bu ke bimian), *Huanqiu Shibao*, July 1, 2010, http://mil.huanqiu.com/Exclusive/2010-07/895638.html. AMS scholar Gu Weijun says that China needs to breakthrough the old ossified thinking that China should not deploy forces abroad or have bases abroad and suggests there should be more research on this issue. He gives five reasons for having the capacity to deploy forces abroad: (1) protecting China's territory and sovereignty in the Yellow, East and South seas; (2) protecting and extracting Chinese expatriates abroad; (3) counterterrorism activities abroad (for example, striking at East Turkestan lairs abroad); (4) deterrence patrols in order to express concern and indignation at some event that threatens China's interests; and (5) influencing/shaping some strategic situation by setting up military bases abroad.

42. Andrew Erickson, "Assessing the New U.S. Maritime Strategy: A Window into Chinese Thinking," *Naval War College Review*, vol. 61, no. 4 (Autumn 2008): 35–71.

43. State Councilor Dai Bingguo, Closing Remarks for U.S.-China Strategic and Economic Dialogue, Washington, D.C., July 28, 2009, www.state.gov/secretary/rm/2009a/july/126599.htm; "Shou Lun Zhongmei Jingji Duihua: Chu shang yue qiu wai zhuyao wenti jun yi tan ji," (First Round of China-U.S. Economic Dialogue: Everything Was Discussed Except Landing on the Moon) *Zhongguo Xinwen Wang*, July 29, 2009, www.chinanews.com.cn/gn/news/2009/07-29/1794984.shtml.

44. Michael D. Swaine, "China's Assertive Behavior—Part One: On 'Core Interests,'" *China Leadership Monitor*, no. 34 (Winter 2011). Also, the notion that China is developing a series of military bases or locations at critical points extending from Southeast Asia, across the Indian Ocean, to the Middle East (the so-called String of Pearls) is incorrect. This concept was developed in the West to explain China's apparent involvement in the

construction of port facilities in Pakistan, Bangladesh, and Myanmar, but when it was examined by the U.S. government and some scholars, the theory was found baseless. Although Beijing has assisted governments and countries in developing ports and other facilities in such locations with the help of Chinese companies, the assistance has primarily been designed to improve the abilities of the countries involved to operate as commercial entities and to establish infrastructure where resources—primarily energy supplies—can be shipped inland to China. Although probably of considerable benefit to China's economic development efforts, there is little—if any—evidence that the Chinese military is involved in such activities. For an analysis of these Chinese activities that misleadingly employs the term "String of Pearls" while largely confirming the above assessment, see Christopher J. Pehrson, "String of Pearls: Meeting the Challenge of China's Rising Power Across the Asian Littoral," Strategic Studies Institute, U.S. Army War College, July 2006, 3, 24, www.strategicstudiesinstitute.army.mil/pdffiles/PUB721. pdf. The author raises the possibility that China's activities in these locations could some day become more strategically significant from a military perspective. In the view of this analyst, such a view is pure conjecture, however, and not based on solid evidence.

45. Beijing has in recent years issued a unilateral ten-week moratorium on fishing in the South China Sea, ostensibly for purposes of conserving fish stocks, but it has been interpreted by the nations of the region as an effort to assert sovereignty over the disputed territories in the area. See STRATCOM Foreign Print Media Summary for PACOM, May 12–18, 2010, #202, OSC FBS20100525670630. In 2008, Beijing apparently pressured U.S. and other international oil firms to pull out of exploration deals with Hanoi in southern Vietnamese waters. Reuters, "U.S. Says S. China Sea Pacts in Its National Interest, Riling Beijing," South China Morning Post, July 24, 2010, CPP20100724718003. Also see Daniel Ten Kate, "U.S. Sees No 'Recent' China Pressure on Global Oil Companies in South Sea," Bloomberg, August 17, 2010, www.bloomberg. com/news/2010-08-18/u-s-sees-no-recent-china-pressure-on-global-oil-companies-in-south-sea.html. In addition to an increasing number of small-scale (and in many cases routine) military activities in the South China Sea, on March 18, 2010, China dispatched the Yuzheng 311, China's largest fishery patrol vessel, to the area, accompanied by a patrol vessel, apparently in response to complaints by Chinese fishing vessels of harassment by the Vietnamese coast guard. A Chinese news report specifically highlighted the presence of heavy machine guns on board the 311. In March and April 2010, the PLAN North Sea Fleet led a joint maneuver formation that traveled along China's territorial sea line, passing through the Bohai Sea, the Yellow Sea, the East China Sea, the Pacific Ocean, and the South China Sea. Also, on July 26, 2010, the PLA Navy engaged in a rare exercise in the South China Sea that involved all three fleets of the PLAN. Apparently, two members of the Central Military Commission supervised the exercises. See "China Plans to Build 36 Sea Surveillance Ships for Strengthened Monitoring in South China Sea," Asahi Shimbun, January 7, 2011; Wu Yuhua and Liu Wei, "Forging an Iron Fist by Riding the Waves and Throwing Themselves Into the Sea: An On-the-Spot Report of the Strengthening of Combat Capabilities by a Certain Destroyer Flotilla," Renmin Haijun, February 11, 2010, OSC CPP20100420478006; Zhang Guanghui, "Refrain from Acting According to Regular Ways, Practice More in Making Solid and Feasible Moves: A South Sea Fleet Speedboat Flotilla Carries Out Anti-Submarine Training That Exudes a Strong Smell of Gunpowder," Renmin Haijun, January 19, 2010, OSC CPP20100415090002; Chen Jin and Tan Wenwu, "A Certain Landing Ship Group:

Training Bids Farewell to 'Leaving Early, Returning Late,' " *Renmin Haijun*, February 24, 2010, OSC CPP20100419090005; Zhong Yan and Yang Bin, "South Sea Fleet Flying Regiment's Opposing Forces Training Has No 'Preheated' Training Events," *Renmin Haijun*, February 23, 2010, OSC CPP20100521090002; Jiangshan, "Pursuing Blue Dream in Normalized Manner," *Renmin Ribao*, May 14, 2010, OSC CPP20100514710003; U.S. Department of Defense, "China: PLA Activities Report 16-30 Apr 10," May 28, 2010, OSC CPP20100528563001; U.S. Department of Defense, "China: PLA Activities Report 01-15 Jun 10," July 12, 2010, OSC CPP20100712563001; "Military Report," *CCTV-7*, May 29, 2010, OSC CPP20100719017050; "Military Report," *CCTV-7*, June 27, 2010, OSC CPP20100627091002; Minnie Chan and Greg Torode, "Show of Force in PLA South China Sea Drill," *South China Morning Post*, July 30, 2010, OSC CPP20100730715008; and Russell Hsiao, "PLA Posturing for Conflict in the South China Sea?" *China Brief*, vol. 10, no. 16 (August 5, 2010), www.jamestown.org/uploads/media/cb_010_79.pdf. I am deeply indebted to Rachel Esplin Odell for conducting much of the research and drafting much of the text contained in this endnote.

46. PLAN warships have apparently entered and exited the East China Sea through Japanese-held narrow seas on at least six occasions since 2004. Three incidents were particularly noteworthy. In October 2008, a PLAN surface action group for the first time steamed through the Tsugaru Strait, circumnavigated Japan, and circled back to port by way of the international strait between Okinawa and the Miyako Islands. In June 2009, a Chinese naval flotilla visited waters near Okinotorishima through the same maritime strait. In April 2010, two Japan Maritime Self-Defense Force destroyers encountered eight PLAN warships and two submarines in international waters southwest of Okinawa, near the Ryukyus. The Chinese squadron transited the Miyako Strait before turning south toward Okinotorishima. According to some reports, this was the first time such a large number of Chinese warships had come so close to Japan. As the two Japanese destroyers shadowed the Chinese flotilla, one vessel was very closely approached by a Chinese helicopter, prompting a Japanese protest. See Toshi Yoshihara and James Holmes, "The Japanese Archipelago through Chinese Eyes," *China Brief*, vol. 10, no. 16 (August 5, 2010), www.jamestown.org/uploads/media/cb_010_79.pdf; "Chinese Submarines, Destroyers Spotted in High Seas Near Okinawa," *Kyodo News*, April 13, 2010, www.japantoday.com/category/national/view/chinese-submarines-destroyers-spotted-in-high-seas-near-okinawa; "Chinese Navy's New Strategy in Action," *Strategic Comments* (Institute for International Strategic Studies), vol. 16, no. 16 (May 2010); Abe Denmark, "China's Navy Gets Its Act Together, and Gets Aggressive," *Wired*, April 26, 2010, www.wired.com/dangerroom/2010/04/chinas-navy-gets-its-act-together-and-gets-aggressive/#ixzz0yO6DNodl; and Peter J Brown, "China's Navy Cruises into Pacific Ascendancy," *Asia Times*, April 22, 2010, www.atimes.com/atimes/China/LD22Ad01.html. I am deeply indebted to Rachel Esplin Odell for conducting much of the research and drafting much of the text contained in this endnote.

47. See Ministry of Foreign Affairs of the People's Republic of China, "Foreign Ministry Spokesperson Qin Gang's Regular Press Conference on July 15, 2010," July 16, 2010, www.mfa.gov.cn/eng/xwfw/s2510/2511/t717494.htm; "HK Phoenix TV: PLA Deputy Chief of Staff Opposes US-ROK Drill, Welcomes Gates' Visit," *Feng Huang Wei Shih Tzu Hsun Tai*, July 1, 2010, OSC CPP20100702572002; "Major General Luo Yuan Discusses the U.S.-ROK Joint Military Exercise in the Yellow Sea," *Renmin Wang*, July 13, 2010, OSC CPP20100713787008; Major General Luo Yuan, "U.S. Engaging in

Gunboat Diplomacy," *People's Daily*, August 13, 2010, OSC CPP20100813787009; Cary Huang, "PLA Ramped Up China's Stand on US-Korea Drill," *South China Morning Post*, August 6, 2010; Li Yang: "Sino-U.S. Relations Face Arduous Test as Curtains Lift on Large-Scale U.S.–ROK Military Exercise," *Zhongguo Xinwen She*, July 25, 2010, OSC CPP20100725138003; Wang Xiyi, "Chinese Government Takes 'Tough Line,' U.S. Carrier 'Turns Around,'" *Guangzhou Ribao*, July 17, 2010, OSC CPP20100725138004; "Major General Yin Zhuo, a Noted Military Expert, Comments on U.S.-South Korean Military Exercises," *Renmin Wang*, July 29, 2010, OSC CPP20100730787001.

48. "China opposes any military acts in exclusive economic zone without permission," Xinhua, November 26, 2010, http://news.xinhuanet.com/english2010/china/2010-11/26/c_13624036.htm; Jeremy Page, Jay Solomon, and Julian Barnes, "China Warns U.S. as Korea Tensions Rise," *Wall Street Journal*, November 26, 2010. In July 2010, the Chinese Ministry of Foreign Affairs condemned U.S. naval exercises in the Yellow Sea generally, but after the North Korean bombing of Yeonpyeong, it specified that "we oppose any party to take any military actions *in our exclusive economic zone* without permission" (emphasis added). See also Edward N. Luttwak, "Why North Korea Survives," *Wall Street Journal*, November 30, 2010; and Kan, "U.S.-China Military Contacts." I am indebted to Rachel Esplin Odell for conducting much of the research and drafting much of the text contained in this endnote.

49. See Andrew Scobell, "Discourse in 3-D: The PLA's Evolving Doctrine, Circa 2009," in *PLA at Home and Abroad*, ed. Kamphausen, Lai, and Scobell; Blair, "Annual Threat Assessment"; David S. Sedney, "China's Military and Security Activities Abroad," testimony before the U.S.-China Economic and Security Review Commission in Washington, D.C., March 4, 2009. Official PRC policy documents such as China's defense white paper and other government statements are placing an increasing emphasis on military operations other than war (MOOTW). And according to the white paper, over the past twenty years more than 11,000 Chinese individual peacekeepers have been deployed to eighteen UN operations. Today, China is the fourteenth-largest contributor to UN peacekeeping operations, ahead of other permanent members of the UN Security Council. See State Council of the People's Republic of China, *China's National Defense in 2008* (Beijing: Information Office of the State Council of the People's Republic of China, 2009). Also see Kamphausen, Lai, and Scobell, *Beyond the Strait*; Scobell et al., "Roundtable"; Erickson, "Assessing the New U.S. Maritime Strategy"; Gordon Fairclough, "Chinese Navy Might Get Role in Piracy Fight," *Wall Street Journal*, December 18, 2008; Andrew S. Erickson and Justin D. Mikolay, "Welcome China to the Fight Against Pirates," *Proceedings*, vol. 135, no. 3 (March 2009): 34–41; and Chin-Hao Huang, "China's Military and Security Activities Abroad," testimony before the U.S.-China Economic and Security Review Commission in Washington, D.C., March 4, 2009.

50. Gabe Collins, "China's Military Gets Expeditionary," *Diplomat*, April 15, 2011, http://the-diplomat.com/2011/04/15/china%E2%80%99s-military-gets-expeditionary; Alison A. Kaufman, "China's Participation in Anti-Piracy Operations off the Horn of Africa: Drivers and Implications," CNA China Studies, www.cna.org/documents/Piracy percent20conference percent20report.pdf; and Erickson and Mikolay, "Welcome China to the Fight."

51. For the purported Chinese text of Hu's December 2004 speech, see Hu Jintao, "Renqing Xinshiji Xinjieduan Wojun Lishi Shiming" (See Clearly Our Military's

Historic Missions in the New Period of the New Century), speech given to China's Central Military Commission, Beijing, December 24, 2004, http://gfjy.jiangxi.gov. cn/htmnew/11349.htm. Also see Information Office of the State Council, People's Republic of China, *China's National Defense in 2006*, available at www.chinadaily.com.cn/ china/2006-12/29/content_771191.htm; Jia Yong, Cao Zhi, and Li Xuanliang, "Advancing in Big Strides from a New Historical Starting Point: Record of Events on How the Party Central Committee and the Central Military Commission Promote Scientific Development in National Defense and Army Building," Xinhua, August 7, 2007, OSC CPP20070807338004; Carolyn Bartholomew and Larry M. Wortzel, *2009 Report to Congress of the US-China Economic and Security Review Commission* (Washington, D.C.. U.S. Government Printing Office, 2009); and Sun Kejia, Lin Peixiong, Liu Feng, and Liu Yang, eds., *Faithfully Implement Our Army's Historical Missions at the New Stage in the New Century* (Beijing: Haichao chubanshe, 2006), 55–91, 116–68, OSC CPP20081022325002. The last source describes the intent behind the latter two missions as "safeguarding world peace and promoting the common development of the world as well as seizing the strategic initiative in international military competition."

52. Psychological warfare is defined as efforts to undermine an enemy's ability to conduct combat operations through psychological activities aimed at deterring, shocking, and demoralizing enemy military personnel and supporting civilian populations. Media warfare aims as influencing domestic and international public opinion to build public and international support for China's military actions and to dissuade an adversary from pursuing policies viewed as adverse to China's interests. Legal warfare stresses the use of international and domestic laws to elicit international support and manage possible political repercussions of China's military actions. The concept was first approved by the Chinese Communist Party's Central Committee and the Central Military Commission in 2003. See "Chinese PLA Focusing on Media, Psychological, and Legal Warfare Training," *Wen Wei Po* (Internet Version), October 23, 2004, summarized in "Highlights: Chinese PLA's Military Theories, Informationization Efforts," *China–FBIS Report*, November 5, 2004, OSC CPP20041204000013; Blasko, *Chinese Army Today*, 164, 185; U.S. Department of Defense, *Annual Report to Congress: Military and Security Developments Involving the People's Republic of China 2010*, 26; Eric C. Anderson and Jeffrey G. Engstrom, "Capabilities of the Chinese People's Liberation Army to Carry Out Military Action in the Event of a Regional Military Conflict," Science Applications International Corporation, March 2009, prepared for the U.S.-China Economic and Security Review Commission, www.uscc.gov/researchpapers/2009/ SAIC%20–%20PLA%20Military%20Capabilities%20–%20Final%20Report%20 02June2009.pdf; and "PRC Book Excerpt: 'Under Informatized Conditions: Legal Warfare,' " *Military Science Press*, May 1, 2007, OSC CPP20090410623001. I am indebted to Rachel Esplin Odell for her assistance in preparing and drafting this endnote.

53. This number was calculated using a methodology developed by Shaoguang Wang of the China University of Hong Kong in a 1999 study; it incorporates elements of defense spending that are not figured into China's official numbers but are generally included in national defense budget totals. See Stockholm International Peace Research Institute (SIPRI), Military Expenditures Database, http://milexdata.sipri.org. The SIPRI figures for 2010 are reported in constant 2009 U.S. dollars. The author is grateful for the assistance of SIPRI senior researcher Sam Perlo-Freeman for his assistance in compiling this data. See also "China's defense spending to increase 7.5% in 2010: draft

budget," Xinhua, March 5, 2010, http://news.xinhuanet.com/english2010/china/2010-03/05/c_13198036.htm. China's official defense budget for 2011 is around $91.5 billion, a 12.7 percent increase in real terms over 2010. "China's defense budget to grow 12.7 pct in 2011: spokesman," Xinhua, March 4, 2011, http://news.xinhuanet.com/english2010/china/2011-03/04/c_13761030.htm.

Another estimate offered by the U.S. Department of Defense suggested China's defense spending was more than $150 billion in 2009, or more than 3 percent of its gross domestic product. However, it is unclear what methodology the Department of Defense used in calculating this estimate. U.S. Department of Defense, *Annual Report to Congress: Military and Security Developments Involving the People's Republic of China 2010*.

Both the SIPRI and the Department of Defense estimates are ultimately just educated guesses. As the United States–China Policy Foundation has stated, "We do not yet have enough information to make a reasonable estimate of the total amount of Chinese 'defense-related spending.' " Dennis J. Blasko, Charles W. Freeman, Jr., Stanley A. Horowitz, Evan S. Medeiros, and James C. Mulvenon, "Defense-Related Spending in China: A Preliminary Analysis and Comparison with American Equivalents," United States–China Policy Foundation, report based on November 2006 delegation, www.uscpf.org/v2/pdf/defensereport.pdf. I am indebted to Dennis Blasko for his assistance in preparing this note.

54. SIPRI, "World military spending."

55. See U.S. Department of Defense, "Ballistic Missile Defense Review Report, February 2010," www.defensemarket.com/wp-content/uploads/2010/01/BMDR percent2026JAN10.pdf; U.S. Department of Defense, *Annual Report to Congress: Military and Security Developments Involving the People's Republic of China 2010*; Swaine et al., *Assessing the Threat*; David A. Shlapak et al., *A Question of Balance: Political Context and Military Aspects of the China-Taiwan Dispute* (Santa Monica, Calif.: RAND Corporation, 2009; U.S. Department of Defense, *Annual Report to Congress: Military Power of the People's Republic of China 2009*; Thomas P. Ehrhard and Robert O. Work, "Range, Persistence, Stealth, and Networking: The Case For a Carrier-Based Unmanned Combat Air System," Center for Strategic and Budgetary Assessments, 2008; Cliff et al., *Entering the Dragon's Lair*; and Jim Yardley and Thom Shander, "Chinese Navy Buildup Gives Pentagon New Worries," *New York Times*, April 8, 2005. The authors assert that "the Pentagon now believes that China has purchased or built enough amphibious assault ships, submarines, fighter jets and short-range missiles to pose an immediate threat to Taiwan and to any American force that might come to Taiwan's aid." On the alleged insufficiency of Taiwan's defense efforts, see Larry M. Wortzel, "Resolving China and Taiwan's Differences," review of *Taiwan Security: History and Prospects*, by Bernard D. Cole, *Parameters*, Winter 2006–7, 108–27; Justin Logan and Ted Carpenter, *Taiwan's Defense Budget: How Taipei's Free Riding Risks War*, Cato Institute Policy Analysis 600, September 2007, www.cato.org/pubs/pas/PA600.pdf.

56. Andrew Krepinevich Jr., "The Pentagon's Wasting Assets: The Eroding Foundations of American Power," *Foreign Affairs*, vol. 88, no. 4 (July–August 2009): 18–33. The author states: "In East Asia, . . . the China's People's Liberation Army is aggressively developing capabilities and strategies to degrade the U.S. military's ability to project power into the region. . . . East Asian waters are slowly but surely becoming another

potential no-go zone for U.S. ships, particularly for aircraft carriers, which carry short-range strike aircraft that require them to operate well within the reach of the PLA's A2/AD systems if they want remain operationally relevant." Also Cozad, "China's Regional Power Projection"; Michael D. Maples, "Current and Projected National Security Threats to the United States," Statement for the Record before the Senate Committee on Armed Services, February 27, 2008. Defense Intelligence Agency director Maples states that China is "looking beyond a Taiwan contingency" and "pursuing capabilities needed to become a major regional power," and that Beijing desires "to prevail in regional conflicts and also counter traditional U.S. military advantages." Michael McDevitt argues that China's growing maritime capabilities are "beginning to upset the balance of power between continental and maritime powers that has been so successful in preserving stability in the region . . . Beijing's central wartime goal in securing its maritime frontier is to keep U.S. power at arms length, and to render the U.S. unable to intervene militarily. This could constrain U.S. access to the region which in turn worsens the security environment for Japan, Taiwan, and, potentially, South Korea." Dan Blumenthal has stated: "As China grows stronger and dedicates ever more resources to its military forces, Beijing wants to settle territorial disputes in its favor, push out its maritime periphery, and develop alternative pathways to break out into the open ocean. . . . Simply put, China wants to push the U.S. back further and further away from its shoreline and its claimed spheres of influence. . . . Our missile and fleet defenses are inadequate to the growing Chinese innovations in ballistic missile production and over-the-horizon targeting. Unfortunately, we have come to a point where, if we want to keep our forward deployed carriers relevant, we need to focus more on protecting them." Dan Blumenthal, testimony before the United States Senate Committee on Foreign Relations, Hearing on Maritime Disputes and Sovereignty Issues in East Asia, July 15, 2009, http://foreign.senate. gov/testimony/2009/BlumenthalTestimony090715p.pdf. Also see Michael McDevitt, "Alliance Relationships," in *America's Role in Asia*, 170; Michael McDevitt also argues— in *Right Sizing the People's Liberation Army*, ed. Kamphausen and Scobell—that China is constructing an aviation force aimed at deterring or preventing carrier-group operation, including seven regiments of planes (130–140 total) with cruise missiles, enough to attack a three-carrier force. However, McDevitt states that China retains a "defense-oriented maritime strategy" that employs Soviet-style distance-related "thresholds" as a model, indicated by the use of an "islands chain" defense perimeter concept. Also see David Lague, "U.S. Military Officials Wary of China's Expanding Fleet of Submarines," *International Herald Tribune*, February 7, 2008; and John Feffer, "Asia's Hidden Arms Race," *TomDispatch.com*, February 12, 2008. Goldstein and Murray, "Undersea Dragons," contend (p. 164) that "a dramatic shift in Chinese underwater aspirations and capabilities is under way, and that submarines are emerging as the centerpiece of an evolving Chinese quest to control the East Asian littoral." Former assistant secretary of defense Peter Rodman contends that China's military-related acquisitions suggest that Beijing is building capacities to go beyond a Taiwan scenario and "are intended to address other potential regional contingencies, such as a conflict over resources or territory. . . . China is at the very beginning stages of acquiring power projection capability." See "China's Military Modernization and Export Controls." For a particularly bombastic and alarmist interpretation of Chinese naval developments, see James Kraska, "China Set for Naval Hegemony," *Diplomat*, May 6, 2010.

57. As Peter Dutton states: "The Chinese . . . appear to be advocating revisionist legal interpretations [of UNCLOS] to apply operational pressure on U.S. naval activities in the South China Sea and perhaps to create sufficient friction to cause American national security decisionmakers to reduce the level of naval operations there. Additionally, by portraying this dispute as a struggle between developed powers (e.g., the United States) that seek to maintain power and developing states (e.g., China) that seek legal protections from naval aggression, some Chinese appear to believe they can undermine the perception of legitimacy with which American naval power is seen in the eyes of some regional states." Moreover, as Dutton continues, the failure of the United States to accede to UNCLOS " gives China unchallenged diplomatic space to attempt to shape law of the sea in its favor. This could have serious consequences for legal issues that are critical to America's global security interests. See Dutton, "Through a Chinese Lens."

58. For a strong statement of the U.S. position on this issue, see Dutton, Testimony before the United States–China Economic and Security Review Commission. Dutton states: "The Chinese approach to law of the sea is problematic on several levels. In a strictly legal sense, it is an attempt to carve out a regional exception to the traditional freedoms of access and rights of maritime communication that have long been protected by international law because they enhance global economic development and promote international political stability. Additionally, law is law, or not at all. In other words, an East Asian regional exception to a rule of international law undermines the applicability of the rule in all places. Increased maritime instability would be the logical and inevitable result of the universal application of interpretations of international law of the sea that remove the authority of all states to use non-sovereign maritime zones for traditional naval purposes. This is particularly problematic inasmuch as approximately 38 percent of the world's oceans are covered by the EEZ. Just as the lack of governance on land results in the disruptive spill-over effects of failed states, so too at sea would a removal of international authority to provide order result in increased zones of instability."

59. See Captain Raul Pedrozo, JAGC, U.S. Navy, "Close Encounters at Sea: The USNS Impeccable Incident," *Naval War College Review*, vol. 62, no. 3 (Summer 2009); Jim Garamone, "Chinese Vessels Shadow, Harass Unarmed U.S. Survey Ship," American Forces Press Service, March 9, 2009, www.defense.gov/news/newsarticle.aspx?id=53401; Li Xiaokun, "Chinese Fishing Vessels Confront U.S. Ship, *China Daily*, May 7, 2009, www1. chinadaily.com.cn/china/2009-05/07/content_7751489.htm; Eric Donnelly, "The United States–China EP-3 Incident: Legality and Realpolitik," *Journal of Conflict and Security Law*, vol. 9, no. 1 (2004): 25–42; and Trevor Hollingsbee, "Matters Behind the Mission: the Background to the EP-3 Affair," *Jane's Security*, April 10, 2001. Many such Chinese confrontations apparently took place in response to increased U.S. military surveillance operations within China's EEZ, according to some interviewed former officials.

60. For example, the PRC government submitted its formal opposition to the territorial claims of Vietnam and Malaysia in the South China Sea to the United Nations in May 2009, claiming that "China has indisputable sovereignty over the islands of the South China Sea and the adjacent waters, and enjoys sovereign rights and jurisdiction over the relevant waters as well as the seabed and subsoil thereof (see attached map)." See People's Republic of China, "Note Verbale to the Secretary General of the United Nations with Regard to the Joint Submission Made by Malaysia and Viet Nam to the Commission on the Limits of the Continental Shelf," May 7, 2009, CML/17/2009, www.un.org/Depts/los/clcs_new/submissions_files/mysvnm33_09/chn_2009re_mys_vnm_e.pdf. Similarly,

China has actively opposed Japan's claims in the East China Sea, submitting a "note verbale" to the UN in February 2009 that opposed Japan's claims over the Okinotori coral atoll on the grounds that they were rocks that could not independently sustain human habitation or economic life. The note insisted that all states should ensure their claims were "not subject to any illegal encroachment." See People's Republic of China, "Note Verbale to the Secretary General of the United Nations with Reference to Japan's Submission to the Commission on the Limits of the Continental Shelf," November 12, 2008, CML/2/2009, February 6, 2009, www.un.org/Depts/los/clcs_new/submissions_files/jpn08/chn_6feb09_e.pdf.

61. Washington chose to use the South China Sea disputes between China and several Southeast Asian nations to convey these policy messages. In May 2010, Admiral Robert Willard, commander of U.S. Pacific Command, stated in an interview: "There has been an assertiveness that has been growing over time, particularly in the South China Sea and in the East China Sea." Equally important, Willard singled out China, adding that Beijing's extensive claims to islands and waters in the region were "generating increasing concern broadly across the region and require address." See Kathrin Hille, "U.S. Warns Over Beijing's 'Assertiveness,' " *Financial Times*, May 25, 2010. In July 2010, Secretary of State Hillary Clinton signaled a more active U.S. stance toward the arguably worsening disputes over rival territorial claims in the South China Sea at a meeting of the Association of Southeast Asian Nations (ASEAN) Regional Forum held in Hanoi. Clinton stated that Washington has a "national interest" in the South China Sea region and that claims in the South China Sea "should be derived solely from legitimate claims to land features." She also reiterated U.S. support for the 2002 declaration of conduct but called for a more complete "code of conduct," suggesting that "the U.S. is prepared to facilitate initiatives and confidence building measures consistent with the declaration." Finally, Clinton urged "a collaborative diplomatic process by all claimants" and warned that the United States "oppose[s] the use or threat of force by any claimant." During the following month, Willard reiterated Secretary Clinton's remarks, stating that Washington will oppose any use "of force or any forms of coercion to stake these claims on the part of any single nation at the expense of the others." See Secretary of State Hillary Rodham Clinton, remarks at press availability, Hanoi, Vietnam, July 23, 2010, www.state.gov/secretary/rm/2010/07/145095.htm; and Jim Gomez, "US Opposes Use of Force in South China Sea dispute," Associated Press, August 18, 2010, www.boston.com/news/world/asia/articles/2010/08/18/us_opposes_use_of_force_in_south_china_sea_dispute.

62. Clinton's remarks at the above-mentioned meeting of the ASEAN Regional Forum in Hanoi elicited strong reactions from Chinese Foreign Minister Yang Jiechi. Yang accused the United States of orchestrating "an attack on China" that was a preconceived "scheme . . . to internationalize the South China Sea issue." See "Chinese FM Refutes Fallacies on the South China Sea Issue," *China Daily*, July 25, 2010, www.chinadaily.com.cn/china/2010-07/25/content_11046054.htm.

63. Captain Raul Pedrozo, JAGC, U.S. Navy, "Close Encounters at Sea: The USNS Impeccable Incident," *Naval War College Review*, vol. 62, no. 3 (Summer 2009); Clive Schofield and Ian Storey, *The South China Sea Dispute: Increasing Stakes and Rising Tensions* (Washington, D.C.: Jamestown Foundation, 2009); "United States Protests Chinese Interference with U.S. Naval Vessel, Vows Continued Operations," *American Journal of International Law*, vol. 103, no. 2 (April 2009): 349–51; Hans Kristensen,

"U.S.-Chinese Anti-Submarine Cat and Mouse Game in South China Sea," Posting on Federation of American Scientists Strategic Security Blog, March 10, 2009, www.fas. org/blog/ssp/2009/03/incident.php. For a particularly belligerent Chinese assessment of the EEZ issue, see Jin Wi, "United States Refuses to Stop Reconnaissance of China in Offshore Waters," Guoji Xianqu Daobao Online (Beijing), September 7, 2009, in CPP20090909072004. Also see Cai Penghong, "An Analysis of U.S. South China Sea Policy," *Xiandai Guoji Guanxi*, September 20, 2009, 1–7, 35, OSC CPP20091015671001; and Shirley A. Kan, "China–U.S. Aircraft Collision Incident of April 2001: Assessments and Policy Implications," CRS Report for Congress, October 10, 2001, http://fas.org/sgp/crs/row/RL30946.pdf; Donnelly, "United States–China EP-3 Incident"; Hollingsbee, "Matters Behind the Mission."

64. For the public indication of the thinking of at least some in the Pentagon regarding this issue, see Gates, remarks at Keio University. Gates stated: "This is an area where over the last several years we have seen some signs of—I guess I would call it a disconnect between the military and the civilian leadership. We think that the civilian leadership was not aware of the aggressive approach by Chinese ships to the U.S.'s Navy ship Impeccable two or three years ago. We think that—our information is that the civilian leadership may not have known about the antisatellite test that was conducted about three years ago. And as I indicated yesterday, there were pretty clear indications that they were unaware of the flight test of the F-35—of the J-20, rather. I think that part of this, based on my experience, very long experience in government, is—can be explained by bureaucratic mistakes. There have been more than a few occasions when the United States military was conducting an exercise or carrying out an activity, and not sensitive to the fact that a foreign visitor might be in Washington at the same time. But on the whole, I do think that this is something that is a worry. . . . I don't question the party's control of the PLA military or of the PLA. I have no doubts about the fact that President Hu Jintao is in command and in charge. But I just know from our own system at times there are disconnects between military information flowing to our civilian leaders." Also see Kan, "U.S.-China Military Contacts."

65. For example, see "China sticks to no-first-use of nuclear weapons: white paper," Xinhua, March 31, 2011; Robert S. Norris and Hans M. Kristensen, "Chinese Nuclear Forces, 2008," *Bulletin of the Atomic Scientists*, July–August 2008, 42–45; and Robert S. Ross, "Assessing the China Threat," *National Interest*, Fall 2005, 81–87.

66. Twomey, "Missing Strategic Opportunity"; and Keir A. Lieber and Daryl G. Press, "Superiority Complex," *Atlantic Online*, July–August 2007. Lieber and Press write: "American efforts to permanently secure nuclear primacy might encourage what defense experts call 'crisis instability' and increase the chance of an inadvertent escalation. If China doesn't redress its nuclear vulnerability in peacetime, it may feel great pressure to do so during a brewing crisis or conventional war—simply to protect its forces. But a Chinese decision to arm a portion of its ICBM force, or to disperse its shorter-range mobile nuclear missiles, might be misinterpreted by the U.S. as nuclear blackmail or preparation for a nuclear attack (for example, on American military bases in Asia). Such a step could trigger the preemptive attack that the Chinese action was meant to forestall." Also see Joshua Pollack, "Emerging Strategic Dilemmas in U.S.-Chinese Relations," *Bulletin of the Atomic Scientists*, July–August 2009, 53–63. In addition, according to some analysts, the emergence of credible U.S. ballistic missile defense systems, along with America's existing conventional long-range strike

capabilities, could increasingly pressure Chinese nuclear strategists to reinterpret concepts such as "active self-defense" and "counterattack in self-defense" into doctrines of preemption that would cast enormous doubt on the credibility of China's NFU doctrine in a crisis. For a discussion of this potential problem, see Linton Brooks, "The Sino-American Nuclear Balance: Its Future and Implications," in *China's Arrival: A Strategic Framework for a Global Relationship*, edited by Abraham Denmark and Nirav Patel (Washington, D.C.: Center for a New American Security, 2009), 59–76.

67. For an expression of strong skepticism that China will consider nuclear arms reductions in any foreseeable time frame (given the still significant nuclear arsenals of the United States and Russia), see Pan Zhenqiang, "Abolishing Nuclear Weapons: Why Not Outlaw Them First?" in *Abolishing Nuclear Weapons: A Debate*, edited by George Perkovich and James M. Acton (Washington, D.C.: Carnegie Endowment for International Peace, 2010), 249–63. Pan states that "although a reduction in the number of nuclear warheads would certainly be a positive development, China would still want to make sure that the quantitative reduction is not a way for the United States to disguise a qualitative upgrading of its nuclear weapons." Also see George Perkovich and James M. Acton, "Beyond U.S.-Russia Arms Control: Multilateral Reductions and the 'Low Numbers' Problem," Carnegie Endowment for International Peace, Abolition Debate Series, Part 4 of 8, April 14, 2010, www.carnegieendowment.org/publications/index. cfm?fa=view&id=40601; and Christopher P. Twomey, "Chinese-U.S. Strategic Affairs: Dangerous Dynamism," *Arms Control Today*, January–February 2009, www.armscontrol. org/act/2009_01-02/china_us_dangerous_dynamism.

68. James B. Steinberg, "Administration's Vision of the U.S.-China Relationship."

69. For further details on the impact of the 2000 Defense Authorization Act, see Kenneth Allen, "U.S.-China Military Relations: Not a One-Way Street," Henry L. Stimson Center, December 10, 1999, www.taiwansecurity.org/IS/Stimson-991210-US-China-Military-Relations.htm.

70. As one interview respondent commented, in describing U.S. leadership views toward military-to-military relations with China: "When the political winds said 'engage,' they couldn't do it fast enough. But . . . when the winds said 'this is bad,' then they turned off the PLA like a spigot."

71. One experienced former U.S. official remarked: "There were essentially three things we needed to accomplish: you wanted regular high-level contact between the U.S. and Chinese military, you wanted policy exchanges; and you wanted deep military dialogues at a high level. I'm much more interested in a high-level strategic transparency rather than trying to build a community between the U.S. and China. It is asking too much, is confusing, and creates uncertainties that aren't in our strategic interests. . . . You have to explain that reciprocity should not be what animates. You should have larger strategic goals in mind and recognize that because of the nature of our system and power there are bound to be inequities." See also Schiffer, "Building Greater Cooperation."

72. Gates, remarks at Keio University.

73. As Carl Conetta states: "The most costly peacetime function of the U.S. military in the post–Cold War era is something the 1997 U.S. Defense Review called 'environment shaping.' This encompasses America's worldwide military presence, its alliances and military-to-military contacts, and its arms transfers and military assistance programs." See Carl Conetta, "Forceful Engagement: Rethinking the Role of Military Power in U.S.

Global Policy," Project on Defense Alternatives, December 2008, www.comw.org/pda/fulltext/081201ForcefulEngagement.pdf.

74. Paul Kennedy, "American Power Is on the Wane," *Wall Street Journal*, January 14, 2009. For a similar take, see Ivan Eland, "Homeward Bound?" *National Interest*, July–August 2008.

75. For example, see Jeffrey Garten, "We Must Get Ready for a Weak-Dollar World," *Financial Times*, November 30, 2009; Niall Ferguson, "An Empire at Risk," *Newsweek*, November 28, 2009; and Ashley J. Tellis, "The Economic Crisis and the Future of U.S. Power," in *Strategic Asia 2009–10: Economic Meltdown and Geopolitical Stability*, edited by Ashley J. Tellis, Andrew Marble, and Travis Tanner (Seattle: National Bureau of Asian Research, 2009). Tellis states that "whether the U.S. can devise a non-inflationary exit from its vastly expanded deficit spending remains a key challenge."

76. Armitage and Nye state: "There are serious questions as to whether or not the United States will have the fiscal and military wherewithal to operate effectively in the region by 2020. Large budget deficits and a growing national debt, military overstretch, and the press of domestic requirements (everything from health care and social security for an aging population to the need to rehabilitate public education) all could impact U.S. capabilities for influencing Asia, irrespective of Washington's intentions." See Richard L. Armitage and Joseph S. Nye, "The U.S.-Japan Alliance: Getting Asia Right Through 2020," Center for Strategic and International Studies, February 2007. For a similar and more recent view, see James R. Holmes and Toshi Yoshihara, "Mahan's Lingering Ghost," *Proceedings*, vol. 135/12/1282 (December 2009). The authors argue, regarding the U.S. Navy, that "costs are escalating while acquisition budgets are stagnant. The result is inexorable downward pressure on the size of the Fleet. . . . Meanwhile, the Navy's most likely antagonist, China's People's Liberation Army Navy (PLAN), is on the opposite trajectory. . . . Few would claim that these assets equal their American counterparts on a one-to-one basis, but the Chinese fleet has the luxury of focusing on Asia, whereas the United States has commitments spanning the globe. Washington cannot apply maximum force to any single theater, however important. Quantity matters at vital points—as does proximity to the theater."

77. For example, see Anthony H. Cordesman, "A Poisoned Chalice? The Crisis in National Security Planning, Programming, and Budgeting," Center for Strategic and International Studies, June 18, 2008, http://csis.org/files/media/csis/pubs/080630_fy2009_poisoned_chalice.pdf.

78. See Leonard Wong, "Living Perilously in a Bubble," Strategic Studies Institute, November 2008, www.strategicstudiesinstitute.army.mil/pdffiles/PUB898.pdf. Wong cites a Gallup Poll taken in March 2008. "When asked about the amount of money the U.S. Government is spending for national defense, the percentage of Americans who responded [in the Gallup poll] that it was 'too much' rose from 19 percent in 2001 to 44 percent in 2008. Although a large majority of Americans—84 percent in 2007—still have a favorable view of the U.S. military, they are becoming increasingly reluctant to fund it, not to mention recommending it as a career for their sons or daughters." It should be pointed out, however, that such public attitudes probably reflect expenditures on the wars in Iraq and Afghanistan, and do not necessarily indicate a long-term trend. For more details on the Gallup poll, see Frank Newport, Gallup, "Almost Half of Americans Say Military Is Not Strong Enough," March 7, 2008, www.gallup.com/poll/104842/Almost-Half-Americans-Say-Military-Strong-Enough.aspx.

79. Wong, "Living Perilously."

80. Office of Management and Budget, "Table 15.5: Total Government Expenditures by Major Category of Expenditure as Percentages of GDP: 1948–2009," www.whitehouse. gov/omb/budget/Historicals. See also Deputy Secretary of Defense William J. Lynn, III, "Submitted Statement on the Budget Before the House Budget Committee," Washington, D.C., Thursday, March 4, 2010, www.defense.gov/speeches/speech. aspx?speechid=1429.

81. See Joseph S. Nye Jr., "The Future of American Power: Dominance and Decline in Perspective," *Foreign Affairs*, vol. 89, no. 6 (November–December 2010): 2–12. Nye writes: "Some argue that the United States suffers from 'imperial overstretch,' but so far, the facts do not fit that theory." Also see Robert Kagan, "The Price of Power," *Weekly Standard*, January 24, 2011; Alan W. Dowd, "Declinism," *Policy Review*, August–September 2007, 83 98. Dowd concludes: "In short, with a much larger economy, much larger population, and much smaller global footprint, the America of today is no more 'overstretched' than the America of 1950 or 1970 or 1990." Also see Fareed Zakaria, "The Future of American Power," *Foreign Affairs*, vol. 87, no. 3 (May–June 2008). Zakaria argues that "the Iraq war may be a tragedy or a noble endeavor, but either way, it will not bankrupt the United States. The price tag for Iraq and Afghanistan together—$125 billion a year—represents less than one percent of GDP. The war in Vietnam, by comparison, cost the equivalent of 1.6 percent of U.S. GDP in 1970, a large difference." And Cordesman states that even if a "worst case" assumption is made about future cost escalations in the defense budget, the burden on the GDP is likely to remain under 5 percent. See Cordesman, "Poisoned Chalice?"

82. Martin Wolf, "This Crisis Is a Moment, but May Not Be a Defining One," *Financial Times*, May 20, 2009. Tellis, "Economic Crisis."

83. See Craig Whitlock, "Pentagon to Cut Spending by $78 Billion, Reduce Troop Strength," *Washington Post*, January 7, 2011; Thom Shanker and Christopher Drew, "Pentagon Seeks Biggest Military Cuts Since Before 9/11," *New York Times*, January 6, 2011; and Dick K. Nanto, "Economics and National Security: Issues and Implications for U.S. Policy," Congressional Research Service, January 4, 2011. The Obama administration submitted a budget for 2012 that includes $553 billion of defense spending (excluding spending on Iraq and Afghanistan), an increase of less than 1 percent over what it requested for 2011. This is less than the $566 billion requested by the Pentagon. And the administration projects that increases in the defense budget will barely exceed inflation for the next several years and will level out by 2015–2016.

84. Greg Bruno, "The Fine Print on Defense Spending," February 26, 2009, CFR Backgrounder, www.cfr.org/publication/18624/fine_print_on_defense_spending.html#3. Bruno states that the Information Technology Association of America, a defense lobbyist, forecast in October 2008 that over the next decade, the base budget plus war-related costs will decrease from a high of $678 billion in the last year of the Bush administration to an estimated $531 billion by 2019. He also cites similar predictions by Robert Work, a defense budget analyst with the Center for Strategic and Budgetary Assessments.

85. Niall Ferguson argues: "As interest payments eat into the budget, something has to give—and that something is nearly always defense expenditure. According to the CBO, a significant decline in the relative share of national security in the federal budget is already baked into the cake. On the Pentagon's present plan, defense spending is set to

fall from above 4 percent now to 3.2 percent of GDP in 2015 and to 2.6 percent of GDP by 2028." See Niall Ferguson, "An Empire at Risk," *Newsweek*, November 28, 2009. See also Michael Mandelbaum, *The Frugal Superpower: America's Global Leadership in a Cash-Strapped Era* (New York: PublicAffairs, 2010); James Politi, "Record U.S. Budget Deficit Projected," *Financial Times*, January 26, 2011; Elisabeth Bumiller and Thom Shanker, "GOP Splits Over Plans to Cut Defense Budget," *New York Times*, January 26, 2011.

86. Robert M. Gates, "Defense Budget Recommendation Statement," speech delivered in Arlington, Va., April 6, 2009, available at www.defenselink.mil/speeches/speech. aspx?speechid=1341; Christopher Drew and Elisabeth Bumiller, "Military Budget Reflects a Shift in U.S. Strategy," *New York Times*, April 6, 2009, www.nytimes. com/2009/04/07/us/politics/07defense.html; Sylvia Pfeiffer and Demetri Sevastopulo, "Gates to Slash Top Military Projects, Defence Secretary to Rebalance Programmes," *Financial Times*, April 7, 2009; William Matthews, "2010 Budget: Men vs. Machines," *Defense News*, March 2, 2009, www.defensenews.com/story.php?i=3969091.

87. See Robert M. Gates, Remarks Delivered at the Navy League Sea-Air-Space Exposition, Navy Gaylord Convention Center, National Harbor, Md., May 3, 2010, www.defense. gov/speeches/speech.aspx?speechid=1460; and Robert M. Gates, Remarks at the Eisenhower Library, Abilene, Kan., May 8, 2010, www.defense.gov/speeches/speech. aspx?speechid=1467. Gates states: "At the end of the day, we have to ask whether the nation can really afford a Navy that relies on $3 to 6 billion destroyers, $7 billion submarines, and $11 billion carriers. . . . We simply cannot afford to perpetuate a status quo that heaps more and more expensive technologies onto fewer and fewer platforms—thereby risking a situation where some of our greatest capital expenditures go toward weapons and ships that could potentially become wasting assets. . . . Does the number of warships we have and are building really put America at risk when the U.S. battle fleet is larger than the next 13 navies combined, 11 of which belong to allies and partners? Is it a dire threat that by 2020 the United States will have only 20 times more advanced stealth fighters than China? Do we really need eleven carrier strike groups for another 30 years when no other country has more than one?"

88. Gates, Remarks at the Eisenhower Library, Abilene. In a speech outlining his approach to the 2012 budget debate, President Obama reaffirmed his intention to pursue further military spending cuts going forward, in addition to the $400 billion savings in current and future spending that Secretary Gates had already outlined. See Office of the Press Secretary, White House, "Remarks by the President on Fiscal Policy," George Washington University, Washington, D.C., April 13, 2011, www.whitehouse.gov/ the-press-office/2011/04/13/remarks-president-fiscal-policy.

89. Secretary of Defense Robert M. Gates, "Statement on Department Budget and Efficiencies," Pentagon, January 6, 2011, www.defense.gov/Speeches/Speech. aspx?SpeechID=1527. Also see Jim Garamone, "Gates Reveals Budget Efficiencies, Reinvestment Possibilities," American Forces Press Service, January 6, 2011, www. defense.gov/news/newsarticle.aspx?id=62351; Andrea Shalal-Esa, "Analysis: China Prism Focuses Pentagon Budget on New Weapons," Reuters, January 25, 2011.

90. Admiral (Retired) James A. Lyons, "Cruising for a Bruising?" *Washington Times*, May 18, 2010; Max Boot, "The Good and Bad of Gates' Agenda," *Commentary*, www. commentarymagazine.com/viewarticle.cfm/the-good-and-bad-of-bob-gates-s-agenda-15119. As Boot states: "I am worried that our fleet is getting dangerously small.

It's below 300 ships and we are projected under this plan to have only 10 carrier battle groups in the future. Those numbers seem inadequate to deal with all the threats we face, especially with China pursuing a breakneck military modernization program." Also see Dan Blumenthal and Michael Mazza, "The Lost Fighter," *Foreign Policy*, www.foreignpolicy.com/articles/2009/07/29/the_missing_fighter?page=0,0.

91. See Daniel Whiteneck, Michael Price, Neil Jenkins, and Peter Swartz, "The Navy at a Tipping Point: Maritime Dominance at Stake?" CNA Analysis and Solutions Report, February 2010, www.public.navy.mil/usff/Documents/navy_at_tipping_point.pdf. The authors state: "If the Navy refuses to choose an option, it faces the prospect of a long slow glide into the Shrinking Status Quo. This would be a navy 20 percent smaller than the one we have now, with the same balance of forces. It will fall through the capacity and capability necessary . . . to be constantly present overseas or to be dominant up and down the escalation ladder."

92. Ralph A. Cossa et al., "The United States and the Asia-Pacific Region: Security Strategy for the Obama Administration," 2008 Asia-Pacific Strategy Project, February 2009.

93. See Gates, remarks at Keio University. Gates stated: "In the United States we are engaged in a robust debate about the size, composition and cost of our military. Even as President Obama has committed the U.S. to a strategy of engagement and cooperation with special emphasis on Asia, we will continue to maintain the military strength necessary to protect our interests, defend our allies, and deter potential adversaries from acts of aggression and intimidation." Also see Donna Miles, "U.S. Will Stand by Deep Commitments in Asia, Gates Pledges," American Forces Press Service, May 31, 2008. Gates stated: "The security of all Asian countries—whether large or small—is strongly and positively enhanced by a strong U.S. presence." Michael McDevitt, "The 2010 QDR and Asia: Messages for the Region," PacNet no. 12, Pacific Forum, Center for Strategic and International Studies, March 15, 2010, http://csis.org/files/publication/pac1012. pdf. McDevitt states that "the QDR is quite explicit in stating that the U.S. possesses the military capability to 'deter, defend against and defeat aggression by potentially hostile nations-states. This capability is fundamental to the nation's ability to protect its interests and provide security in key regions.' This very explicit endorsement of the importance of U.S. military presence in East Asia is a significant signal to Asia that the U.S. has no intention of withdrawing from Asia in the face of growing Chinese military capability." For the text of the QDR, see U.S. Department of Defense, *Quadrennial Defense Review Report*. Also see Al Pessin, "U.S. Pacific Commander Sees No Major Changes Under President-Elect Obama," Voice of America, November 7, 2008; and U.S. Navy, U.S. Marine Corps, and U.S. Coast Guard, *Cooperative Strategy*. This report states: "The United States will continue to deploy powerful operational forces in the Western Pacific, the Arabian Sea, and the Indian Ocean to protect U.S. and allied interest, and contain potential competitors."

94. See Jan Van Tol, Mark Gunzinger, Andrew Krepinevich, and Jim Thomas, "AirSea Battle: A Point-of-Departure Operational Concept," Center for Strategic and Budgetary Assessment, 2010; Andrew F. Krepinevich, "Why AirSea Battle?" Center for Strategic and Budgetary Assesments, 2010, www.csbaonline.org/4Publications/ PubLibrary/R.20100219.Why_AirSea_Battle/R.20100219.Why_AirSea_Battle.pdf; and Andrew Krepinevich, "China's 'Finlandization' Strategy in the Pacific," *Wall Street Journal*, September 11, 2010.

95. Phillip C. Saunders, "China's Air Force Modernization," *Joint Forces Quarterly*, no. 47 (4th quarter 2007): 28–33; Bitzinger, "Reforming China's Defense Industry"; Medeiros et al., *New Direction for China's Defense Industry*. See also John Pomfret, "Military Strength Eludes China, Which Looks Overseas for Arms," *Washington Post*, December 25, 2010.

96. See U.S. Department of Defense, *Annual Report to Congress: Military and Security Developments Involving the People's Republic of China 2010*, 43; and U.S. Department of the Navy, "Highlights of the Department of the Navy FY 2010 Budget," May 2009, www.finance.hq.navy.mil/FMB/10pres/Highlights_book.pdf. Also see M. Taylor Fravel, "China's Search for Military Power," *Washington Quarterly*, Summer 2008, 125–41.

97. For example, the 2008 Chinese defense white paper states that the PLA "formulated in a scientific way strategic plans for national defense and armed forces building and strategies for the development of the services and arms, according to which it will lay a solid foundation by 2010, basically accomplish mechanization and make major progress in informationization by 2020, and by and large reach the goal of modernization of national defense and armed forces by the mid-21st century." See State Council of the People's Republic of China, *China's National Defense in 2008*. I am indebted to Dennis Blasko for providing this information.

98. U.S. Department of Defense, *Annual Report to Congress: Military and Security Developments Involving the People's Republic of China 2010*, 29.

99. Blasko, *Chinese Army Today*, 182; Bajoria, "China's Military Power." Bajoria provides a summary of the views of leading PLA analysts, stating that "experts say China is still decades away from challenging the U.S. military's preeminence. Its ground forces field 1980s vintage armor and suffer from significant shortcomings in command and control, air defense, logistics, and communications. Its air force, too, lags behind those of Western powers, though China flies about one hundred top-end Russian Su-27 warplanes and has contracted to purchase newer Su-33s, which are capable of carrier-based operations. China plans to build aircraft carriers domestically, but currently has none under construction." Also see M. Taylor Fravel, "China, Rising Power and Expansion: Can Conquest Pay?" 2008, unpublished manuscript, Massachusetts Institute of Technology. Fravel asserts that even if the PLA Air Force increases its number of heavy transports to almost 50 within the next decade (as expected), it will still possess just a fraction of the strategic airlift capacity of other major militaries such as Russia, much less the United States, and "be able to deploy only one or two fully-equipped battalions of mechanized infantry units up to 2,000 kilometers from its borders." Also see Larry M. Wortzel, "PLA 'Joint' Operational Contingencies in South Asia, Central Asia, and Korea," in *Beyond the Strait*, ed. Kamphausen, Lai, and Scobell, 327–90. Wortzel states: "We cannot expect to see dramatic changes in either the posture or the capabilities of the PLA to conduct joint contingency operations out of area, even in contiguous states, over the near term (say 5–10 years). Instead, observers will probably see an evolution of new operational doctrine and the equipment and forces to implement them over time." David Shambaugh states: "While some of the newest equipment in the PLA's ground force inventory is approaching world standards, . . . the bulk of the firepower still lags behind U.S., NATO, Russian, or even Japanese systems. . . . Unless the United States decided to engage in a direct conflict with China— particularly over Taiwan or on the Chinese Mainland—the improvements in PLA capabilities do not directly threaten U.S. capabilities or national security interests

in Asia, as U.S. forces remain in a league of their own." David Shambaugh, "Seven Questions for the United States Concerning China's Role in Asia," paper presented at the Third Berlin Asian Security Conference, Berlin, September 2008. Finally, the 2009 Pentagon assessment of the PLA points to several critical existing limitations on power projection capabilities, in the areas of joint operations, air and amphibious lift, at-sea replenishment, and aerial refueling/long-range air deployment. See U.S. Department of Defense, *Annual Report to Congress: Military Power of the People's Republic of China 2009*. The security dilemma refers to a situation in which actions taken by one or more states to strengthen security, such as increases in military strength, can prompt other states to respond similarly, thus resulting in growing tensions and even conflict, even though no party desires such an outcome. See Robert Jervis, "Cooperation under the Security Dilemma," *World Politics*, vol. 30, no. 2 (January 1978): 167–74.

100. For example, see Josef Joffe, "The Default Power: The False Prophecy of America's Decline," *Foreign Affairs*, vol. 88, no. 5 (September–October 2009): 21–35. Joffe states: "Even if China manages to avoid the pernicious dynamics of authoritarian modernization—war, revolution, and upheaval—that eventually befell imperial Germany, Japan, and Russia, it will face another challenge in its demographic deterioration. Essentially, China will grow old before becoming rich, as Mark Haas, a professor of political science at Duquesne University, has noted. According to Goldman Sachs, by 2050 the Chinese economy will long have overtaken the U.S. economy, with a GDP of $45 trillion, compared with the United States' $35 trillion. But by then, the median age in the United States will be the lowest of any of the world's large powers, except India. The United States' working-age population will have grown by about 30 percent, whereas China's will have dropped by three percent. The economic and strategic consequences will be enormous. China's aging population will require a shifting of resources from investment to welfare, thus reducing China's growth. And as the economic pie shrinks, a growing number of pensioners—329 million by 2050—will demand a larger slice. This will necessarily cut into the share for the People's Liberation Army. If China cannot dodge this double whammy, how can it be expected to unseat the United States as the greatest military power the world has ever seen?" For similar arguments, see Zhao Lingmin, "Optimistic View of Sino-U.S. Relations: Exclusive Interview with Professor Wang Jisi, Dean of the School of International Studies at Peking University," *Nanfeng Chuang*, October 8, 2008, 50–53, OSC CPP20081021066004; and David Lampton, "A Precarious Balance," in *The Three Faces of Chinese Power: Might, Money, and Minds*, by David Lampton (Berkeley: University of California Press, 2008), 207–51.

101. See U.S. Department of Defense, *Annual Report to Congress: Military Power of the People's Republic of China 2009*. This report states: "As part of its planning for a Taiwan contingency, China is prioritizing the development of measures to deter or counter third-party intervention in any future cross-Strait crisis. China's approach to dealing with this challenge appears to be reflected in a sustained effort to develop the capability to attack, at long ranges, military forces that might deploy (antiaccess) or operate (area-denial) within the western Pacific. In this context, China's antiaccess/area-denial forces increasingly overlap, providing multiple layers of offensive systems utilizing the sea, air, space, and cyber-space" (p. 20–21). Also see Cole, "Right-Sizing the Navy." Cole writes that PLA modernization is designed "to be able to maintain submarine deployments north, east, and southeast of Taiwan to impede U.S. intervention on behalf of Taiwan

and force Taiwan to fight alone for at least a short time and to establish a presence in the East China Sea and cope with Japanese naval forces. Submarine modernization will allow China to divide the East China Sea into operating areas patrolled by 24 subs armed with cruise missiles capable of submerged launch." He concludes that by 2016–2017, China's navy will be "capable of carrying out ambitious assigned missions," including denying control of the East and South China seas and possibly even commanding those seas for a short time. He adds that, based on present trends, in a decade the PLAN "will allow Beijing to exert *hegemonic leverage* [author's italics] in maritime East Asia." For similar assessments, see Andrew S. Erickson, Lyle J. Goldstein, and William S. Murray, *Chinese Mine Warfare: A PLA Navy 'Assassin's Mace' Capability*, Naval War College China Maritime Study (Newport: Naval War College, 2009); Scobell et al., "Roundtable"; Armitage and Nye, "U.S.-Japan Alliance"; Krepinevich, "Pentagon's Wasting Assets"; and Friedberg, "Asia Rising."

102. See, most notably, Shlapak et al., *Question of Balance*. Also see Ministry of National Defense, Republic of China, "Explanatory Statement of Ministry of National Defense on Recently Released RAND Corporation Report on Study of Military Situation Across Taiwan Strait," August 8, 2009. Regarding Taiwan's failure to enhance its own military capabilities at a pace and to a level that many U.S. analysts (including U.S. officials) might prefer, see Michael S. Chase, "Taiwan's Defense Budget Dilemma: How Much Is Enough in an Era of Improving Cross-Strait Relations?" *China Brief*, vol. 8, no. 15 (July 17, 2008), www.jamestown.org/programs/chinabrief/single/?tx_ttnews[tt_news]=5061&tx_ttnews[backPid]=168&no_cache=1. Chase concludes that even if the possibility of war with China appears to be declining, Taiwan must still make the investments required to strengthen its defense, in order to (1) reflect its commitment to its security and improve its strained relationship with the United States; (2) bolster its desire for greater international space; and (3) maintain a position of strength in any future negotiations with China.

103. Michael D. Swaine and Oriana Skylar Mastro, "Introduction" and "Assessing the Threat," in *Assessing the Threat*, ed. Swaine et al.; and Steve Tsang, ed., *If China Attacks Taiwan: Military Strategy, Politics and Economics* (New York: Routledge, 2006.).

104. Swaine et al., *Assessing the Threat*. The overall policy implications of these military trends for the stability of the overall Taiwan situation are discussed further in chapter 2.

105. "China and Weapons of Mass Destruction: Implications for the United States," conference sponsored by the National Intelligence Council, *Armed Forces Journal International*, and National Security Studies Program at Georgetown University, November 5, 1999, www.dni.gov/nic/confreports_chinawmd.html.

106. Bajoria, "China's Military Power"; Robert M. Gates, testimony given before the Senate Armed Services Committee, January 27, 2009, www.dod.mil/dodgc/olc/docs/testGates080206.pdf; "China's Role in Asia: Access and Anti-Access," Executive Summary of Conference hosted by National Defense University's Center for Technology and National Security Policy and Institute for National Strategic Studies. Also see Andrew Erickson and Lyle Goldstein, "Hoping for the Best, Preparing for the Worst: China's Response to U.S. Hegemony," paper presented at the annual meeting of the International Studies Association, San Diego, March 22, 2006; U.S. Department of Defense, *Annual Report to Congress: Military Power of the People's Republic of China 2009*. The authors conclude: "China continues to invest in military programs designed to improve extended-range power projection. Current trends in China's military

capabilities are a major factor in changing East Asian military balances, and could provide China with a force capable of conducting a range of military operations in Asia well beyond Taiwan. Given the apparent absence of direct threats from other nations, the purposes to which China's current and future military power will be applied remain uncertain. These capabilities will increase Beijing's options for military coercion to press diplomatic advantage, advance interests, or resolve disputes in its favor" (p. 28). O'Rourke, "China Naval Modernization"; and Australian Department of Defense, "Defending Australia in the Asia Pacific Century: Force 2030," 2009, www.defence.gov.au/whitepaper/docs/defence_white_paper_2009.pdf.

107. U.S. Department of Defense, *Annual Report to Congress. Military Power of the People's Republic of China 2009.* The report states: "Acquisition and development of the KILO, SONG, SHANG, and YUAN-class submarines illustrates the importance the PLA places on undersea warfare for sea denial. In the past ten years, China has deployed ten new classes of ships. The purchase of SOVREMENNYY II-class DDGs and indigenous production of the LUYANG I/LUYANG II DDGs equipped with long range ASCM and surface-to-air missile (SAM) systems, for example, demonstrate a continuing emphasis on improving antisurface warfare, combined with mobile, wide-area air control" (pp. 21–22). Also see Scobell et al., "Roundtable"; the authors write: "By 2016 China will have available as an instrument of national power a navy capable of carrying out assigned missions. The PLAN of 2016, at three times its present size, will dominate East Asian navies—with the possible exception of the Japan Maritime Self-Defense Force—and will offer a very serious challenge to the U.S. Navy when it operates in that region's waters." "Currently boasting the world's most formidable force of conventionally powered submarines, China has been building and deploying a new class of nuclear attack submarine and has launched a ship-building program that each year since 2000 has produced new ships designed to be multi-mission capable." David Lague, "U.S. Military Officials Wary of China's Expanding Fleet of Submarines," *International Herald Tribune,* February 7, 2008; William Choong, "Flutter Over China's Naval Expansion," *Straits Times,* November 21, 2008. Regarding a PLAN carrier, see Andrew Jacobs, "General Hints That China May Build Its First Aircraft Carrier," *International Herald Tribune,* November 18, 2008; O'Rourke, "China Naval Modernization"; and Andrew S. Erickson and Andrew R. Wilson, "China's Aircraft Carrier Dilemma," *Naval War College Review,* vol. 59, no. 4 (Fall 2006): 13–45. The authors state that potential roles for Chinese aircraft carriers include (1) supporting secondary missions, (2) complementing the submarine-centered PLAN, (3) "showing the flag" in regional power competition, and (4) collective maritime security (for example, sea-lane protection, counterpiracy. Some literature also suggests that Western helicopter "carriers" might be a more logical acquisition for the PLAN because they are smaller, simpler, easier to build/operate, and will better serve Chinese operational requirements in providing logistical support and even humanitarian missions. Another analyst argues that China's efforts to get an aircraft carrier are not based on objective calculations of national interest but instead on naval nationalism. See Robert S. Ross, "China's Naval Nationalism: Sources, Prospects, and the U.S. Response," *International Security,* vol. 34, no. 2 (Fall 2009): 46–81.

108. See William Cole, "Sub's Arrival Part of Pacific Plan," *Honolulu Advertiser,* May 4, 2009, www.honoluluadvertiser.com/article/20090504/NEWS08/905040350.

109. U.S. Department of Defense, *Annual Report to Congress: Military Power of the People's Republic of China 2009,* 21.

110. Ibid. Several analysts emphasize the serious potential threat to regional navies and the U.S. Navy in particular posed by China's emerging ASBM capability, combined with an integrated sensor network and supported by submarines and conventional naval aviation. See Mark Stokes, "China's Evolving Conventional Strategic Strike Capability: the Anti-Ship Ballistic Missile Challenge to U.S. Maritime Operations in the Western Pacific and beyond," Project 2049 Institute, September 14, 2009. Stokes concludes that an effective ASBM and persistent maritime surveillance capability could complicate the capacity of the United States to resist PRC use of force against Taiwan; diminish confidence in U.S. security guarantees in Taiwan and throughout the region; be used to enforce China's other regional sovereignty claims and ensure the security of SLOCs; diminish the effectiveness of carrier-based U.S. assets, such as the F/A-18 E/F, causing greater reliance on submarines, long range unmanned combat air platforms/prompt global strike assets, and hardening of U.S. military facilities throughout the region; generate pressure on the United States and Russia to revise/abandon arms control treaty on the elimination of intermediate- and short-range missiles, and possibly compelling others (Japan) to develop similar capabilities; harm counterproliferation efforts, as key technologies (especially those related to onboard guidance systems) could be sold to international customers of concern, such as North Korea and Iran; and in the long term, offer the Chinese Communist Party a flexible deterrent that could achieve strategic and operational effects against an enemy in a crisis. In short, for other analysts who agree with Stokes, Chinese ASBMs could be a "game changer," upsetting the strategic balance in the Western Pacific. See Andrew S. Erickson and David D. Yang, "On the Verge of a Game-Changer," *Proceedings*, vol. 135:5:1 (May 2009): 275; and Andrew S. Erickson and David D. Yang, "Using the Land to Control the Sea? Chinese Analysts Consider the Antiship Ballistic Missile," *Naval War College Review*, vol. 62, no. 4 (Autumn 2009): 53–86.

111. U.S. Department of Defense, *Annual Report to Congress: Military Power of the People's Republic of China 2009*. Also see Michael Forsythe, "Watching Beijing's Air Power Grow," *New York Times*, October 21, 2009.

112. See Bryan Krekel (Northrup Grumman Corporation), "Capability of the People's Republic of China to Conduct Cyber Warfare and Computer Network," report prepared for the U.S.-China Economic and Security Review Commission, October 9, 2009. The authors assert: "The Chinese have adopted a formal IW strategy called "Integrated Network Electronic Warfare" (INEW), which relies on a simultaneous application of electronic warfare and computer network operations against an adversary's C4ISR networks and other essential information systems. Analysis of this strategy suggests that computer network operations (CNO) tools will be widely employed in the earliest phases of a conflict, and possibly preemptively against an enemy's information systems and C4ISR systems." Also see Medeiros et al., *New Direction for China's Defense Industry*. "The PLA is very close to fielding a C4ISR architecture capable to support a campaign to about 2,000 kilometers out from the Chinese coast. To be able to maintain a competitive edge, the United States must continue to develop and stay ahead in the areas of kinetic and directed energy weapons, electronic warfare, and information warfare." Also see Bajoria, "China's Military Power"; Marc Miller, "*PLA Missions Beyond Taiwan*," Colloquium Brief, Strategic Studies Institute, October 2008; Scobell et al., "Roundtable"; and James Mulvernon, "PRC Information Operations: Myths, Trends, and New Opportunities," in *Assessing the Threat*, ed. Swaine et al.

113. Nan Li, "Evolution of China's Naval Strategy"; Choong, "Flutter"; National Intelligence Council, *Global Trends 2025: A Transformed World* (Washington, D.C.: National Intelligence Council, 2008). For Nan Li, China's naval modernization effort "clearly intends to transform the PLAN from a coastal defense navy to one capable of nearseas active defense. It also aims to lay the basis for further development of the PLAN into one capable of far-seas operations around the time of 2020."

114. See Collins, "China's Military Gets Expeditionary." Collins writes that the Libya operation "marked the first time China has deployed military assets to protect PRC citizens overseas." See also "Chinese navy begins landmark Somali piracy patrols," Agence France-Presse, January 6, 2009, www.channelnewsasia.com/stories/afp_asiapacific/view/400591/1/.html. This report states: "The naval task force, deploying two destroyers and a supply ship, marks China's first potential combat mission beyond its territorial waters in centuries. . . . The missile-armed destroyers DDG-171 Haikou and DDG-169 Wuhan, and the Weishanhu supply ship, are among China's most sophisticated and have all entered service this decade, Xinhua said previously." Also see "China: Navy Will Build Up Its Blue Water Capabilities," *Oxford Analytica*, February 9, 2009. "The deployment of two state-of-the-art Chinese destroyers and a supply ship to East African waters represents an important step forward in the Chinese navy's transformation from a coastal or 'brown-water' force into an ocean-going 'blue-water' navy." For a similar assessment of the significance of the Gulf of Aden deployment, see Bernard D. Cole, testimony before the U.S.-China Economic and Security Review Commission, Hearing on China's Military and Security Activities Abroad, March 4, 2009, www.uscc.gov/hearings/2009hearings/written_testimonies/09_03_04_wrts/09_03_04_cole_statement.pdf.

115. For example, see Secretary of Defense Robert M. Gates, Submitted Statement to the Senate Armed Services Committee, Washington, D.C., January 27, 2009, http://armed-services.senate.gov/statemnt/2009/January/Gates percent2001-27-09.pdf. Gates states: "China is modernizing across the whole of its armed forces. The areas of greatest concern are Chinese investments and growing capabilities in cyberwarfare and antisatellite warfare, antiair and antiship weaponry, submarines, and ballistic missiles. Modernization in these areas could threaten America's primary means of projecting power and helping allies in the Pacific: our bases, air and sea assets, and the networks that support them." Also see "China's Role in Asia: Access and Anti-Access," Executive Summary of Conference hosted by National Defense University's Center for Technology and National Security Policy and Institute for National Strategic Studies. The authors state: "Effective Chinese antiaccess capabilities may eventually threaten the ability of U.S. military forces to operate in the Western Pacific and weaken American security guarantees to allies in the region. This would have serious implications for U.S. allies and other nations that rely on the U.S. military presence to maintain regional stability."

116. See Friedberg, "Asia Rising." Friedberg states: "Beijing's buildup has greatly enhanced its ability to project power into the air and sea off its eastern shores and into the deep space above. As a result, China is far better equipped to threaten Taiwan than it was only a decade ago, and it is getting closer to the point where it will be able to pose a serious challenge to America's military preponderance in the western Pacific. . . . The PLA's recent modernization and expansion of its strategic nuclear missile force could weaken the credibility of regional U.S. security guarantees." Also see Choong, "Flutter";

Bajoria, "China's Military Power"; and O'Rourke, "China Naval Modernization." As O'Rourke writes: "In addition to the near-term focus on developing military options for addressing the situation with Taiwan, DOD and some other observers believe that broader or longer-term goals of China's military modernization, including naval modernization, include one or more of the following: asserting China's regional military leadership, displacing U.S. regional military influence, prevailing in regional rivalries, and encouraging eventual U.S. military withdrawal from the region."

117. For example, see David Pilling, "China Flexes New Economic Muscle at Sea," *Financial Times*, April 22, 2009, www.ft.com/cms/s/0/c467c848-2f63-11de-a8f6-00144feabdc0. html; and Armitage and Nye, "U.S.-Japan Alliance." The authors write: "[The PLA] is likely to place greater emphasis on the development of a blue-water navy. This flows in part from the perception that it needs to protect energy sources and sea lanes."

118. Michael Forsythe, "Watching Beijing's Air Power Grow," *New York Times*, October 21, 2009.

119. Fravel, "China's Search." Fravel states: "Although China is actively modernizing its navy, the emerging force structure is consistent with the pursuit of an area-denial capability or the ability to disrupt and complicate the operations of other navies in waters near China." Also see McDevitt, "Strategic and Operational Context." McDevitt argues that China is deploying "more modern, high-performance, conventionally-propelled submarines" that are limited in speed and time on station but quieter than nuclear subs—and as a result more appropriate for coastal defense. Also see Hans M. Kristensen, "Chinese Submarines Patrols Rebound in 2007, but Remain Limited," January 7, 2008, Federation of American Scientists, www.fas.org/blog/ssp/2008/01/chinese_submarine_patrols_rebo.php; and Hans M. Kristensen, "New Chinese SSBN Deploys to Hainan Island," FAS Strategic Security Blog, April 24, 2008, www.fas.org/blog/ssp/2008/04/new-chinese-ssbn-deploys-to-hainan-island-naval-base.php.

120. Kristensen, "Chinese Submarines Patrols Rebound in 2007." China's fleet of approximately 55 general-purpose submarines conducted a total of six patrols during 2007, compared to two patrols conducted in 2006 and zero conducted in 2005. Despite this increase, it is important to note that this is still only a fraction of the total number of patrols conducted by the U.S. Navy. None of China's ballistic missile submarines have ever conducted a deterrent patrol.

121. As Eckstein and Mikolay state: "China joined the international community to challenge piracy. It did not join the counter-piracy effort to challenge the international community. . . . The Chinese were careful to say that [the deployment] did not represent a shift in non-interventionist foreign policy . . . it does not constitute a commitment to further bluewater operations. See Erickson and Mikolay, "Welcome China to the Fight Against Pirates."

122. State Council of the People's Republic of China, *China's National Defense in 2010* (Beijing: Information Office of the State Council of the People's Republic of China, March 2011), http://news.xinhuanet.com/english2010/china/2011-03/31/c_13806851.htm; State Council of the People's Republic of China, *China's National Defense in 2008*. Also see Scobell et al., "Roundtable." The authors state: "While continuing to maintain a defensive strategy to protect China and its possessions, the PLAN will also deploy a force whose primary utility will be to provide peacetime presence, sea lane monitoring, and crisis response. Although this force will probably not be particularly valuable in case of a real war with the United States, such a war is not likely. This 'second-iteration navy'

[blue water?] not only will be useful to the PRC in furthering its own interests but will also demonstrate that China too can be a responsible stakeholder in a military sense." And see Erickson, "Assessing the New U.S. Maritime Strategy"; and Gordon Fairclough, "Chinese Navy Might Get Role in Piracy Fight," *Wall Street Journal*, December 18, 2008.

123. One analyst argues that China's naval modernization (beyond the Taiwan contingency) is driven primarily by "naval" nationalism and the pursuit of status, rather than any putative security objectives. See Ross, "China's Naval Nationalism." Ross views China as following in the footsteps of past continental powers (such as Russia) that sought naval power for primarily prestige reasons, given the focus of all such powers on the maintenance of a large ground force capability to ensure territorial security, as well as the prohibitive costs and steep learning curve involved in acquiring a blue water navy capable of defeating a major naval power such as the United States.

124. Gregory Kulacki, "A Space Race with China," *Harvard Asia Pacific Review*, Spring 2008, 12–15; Eric D. Hagt, "Chinese Military Modernization"; Erickson and Goldstein, "Hoping for the Best"; and MacDonald, "China, Space Weapons, and U.S. Security."

125. Stephen Chen and Greg Torode, "China 'to Put Weapons in Space,' " *South China Morning Post*, November 3, 2009, OSC CPP20091103715006. Also see Phil Stewart, "U.S. Eyes 'Intent' of China's Space Programs," Reuters, November 3, 2009.

126. Phillip C. Saunders and Charles D. Lutes, "China's ASAT Test: Motivations and Implications," Institute for National Strategic Studies Special Report, June 2007, www.ndu.edu/inss/Research/SRjun07.pdf; and Stewart, "U.S. Eyes 'Intent.' " In particular, some analysts argue that China will likely acquire the ability to destroy the U.S. Global Positioning System constellation, which is essential for guiding many "smart" weapons to their targets. For example, see Krepinevich, "Pentagon's Wasting Assets." The author states: "If China continues to develop and field antisatellite capabilities, the US satellite architecture may also become a wasting asset, one highly dependent on Chinese sufferance for its effective operation."

127. Ashley J. Tellis, "China's Military Space Strategy," *Survival*, vol. 49, no. 3 (Autumn 2007): 41–72. Tellis argues that Washington should not invest time, energy, and resources in attempting to negotiate space-control arrangements because such regimes are destined to be stillborn because the larger strategic logic conspires against them. Also see Erickson and Goldstein, "Hoping for the Best." The authors write: "Just as China was not dissuaded from submarine development in the recent past by American dominance in that area, Beijing also seems unwilling to cede aerospace dominance. As China's overall national power continues to rise, its aerospace capacities are likely to rise with it, with significant implications for Beijing's ability to manage its maritime periphery and challenge U.S. hegemony."

128. For criticisms of Tellis's argument, and Tellis's response, see "China's Military Space Strategy: An Exchange," in *Survival*, vol. 50, no. 1 (February–March 2008): 157–98.

129. Kenneth S. Blazejewski, "Space Weaponization and U.S.-China Relations," *Strategic Studies Quarterly*, Spring 2008, 33–55. The author suggests that the United States could expect to gain the following concessions from China in return for a commitment not to weaponize space: negotiations on the Fissile Material Cut-Off Treaty, which may facilitate corresponding commitments from India and Pakistan; greater support for the PSI; and greater transparency in Chinese military planning, especially with regard to ASAT and space-focused programs.

130. See, in particular, Nancy Gallagher and John D. Steinbruner, "Reconsidering the Rules for Space Security," American Academy of Arts and Sciences, 2008, www.amacad.org/publications/space_security.pdf. The authors state: "The more likely outcome of a sustained U.S. effort to dominate space for national military advantage is that incremental advances in U.S. capabilities will increase pressure on other countries to react by emulating, offsetting, or restraining the United States. So far, Russia and China have made the most visible moves related to these response options, simultaneously trying to improve their own space-based military support systems, to explore asymmetrical ways to neutralize advantages that the U.S. military gets or could gain from superior space capabilities, and to start PAROS [prevention of an arms race in outer space] negotiations." Also see Hagt, "Chinese Military Modernization." Hagt states: "China's ASAT test should not be interpreted as a direct threat to U.S. space power but a challenge to its ambitions for space control and dominance. . . . China has repeatedly said it will not enter a space race with the United States, certainly not in terms of achieving strategic parity (which it cannot afford)."

131. MacDonald, "China, Space Weapons, and U.S. Security." Also see Gallagher and Steinbruner, "Reconsidering the Rules." The authors state: "It is clear that military capabilities in space are advancing with no correspondingly serious effort to discuss, let alone to negotiate, how they should be used."

132. These difficult issues, among others, perhaps explain why the Obama administration took a relatively long time to complete its Space Posture Review. See Robert Haddick, "This Week at War: Star Wars in the Age of Obama," *Foreign Policy*, April 30, 2010, www.foreignpolicy.com/articles/2010/04/30/this_week_at_war_star_wars_in_the_age_of_obama; and John T. Bennet, " 'Rich Debate' Continues Over U.S. Space Policy," *Defense News*, May 13, 2010, www.defensenews.com/story.php?i=4624467&c=AIR&s=TOP.

133. For example, see Norris and Kristensen, "Chinese Nuclear Forces, 2008"; and Ross, "Assessing the China Threat."

134. Cristina Hansell and William C. Potter, eds., *Engaging China and Russia on Nuclear Disarmament*, Occasional Paper 15 (Monterey, Calif.: James Martin Center for Nonproliferation Studies, 2009), http://cns.miis.edu/opapers/op15/op15.pdf.

135. As Taylor Fravel states, at the very least, Chinese military assertiveness would risk an explosion in balancing behavior by other states in the region, and such nations would likely strengthen ties with the U.S. as a result. See Fravel, "China, Rising Power and Expansion."

136. U.S. Department of Defense, *Annual Report to Congress: Military Power of the People's Republic of China 2009*. For an example of a Chinese source arguing in favor of a more assertive naval strategy designed to heighten China's access to the Western Pacific, see "PRC Must Break Through 'Island Chain Encirclement,' Strengthen Naval Power," *Ta Kung Pao Online*, February 21, 2009.

137. U.S. Department of Defense, *Annual Report to Congress: Military Power of the People's Republic of China 2009*.

138. Ibid.

139. National Intelligence Council, *Global Trends 2025*. This report states: "A naval arms race in Asia may emerge in response to China's further development of naval power

projection. A naval arms race might also be spurred by 'antiaccess' capabilities—such as attack submarines and long-range antiship missiles—that become widely viewed as efforts by Beijing to extend its political influence in the region and to deter attempts to cut off China's seaborne energy supplies by threatening mutual disruption of sea trade."

140. Gallagher and Steinbruner, "Reconsidering the Rules."

141. See Geoffrey Till, "*Asia Rising and the Maritime Decline of the West: A Review of the Issues: IQPC/Asia Rising*," RSIS Working Paper 205 (Singapore: Rajaratnam School of International Studies, 2010), www.rsis.edu.sg/publications/Working_papers.html. In support of this conclusion, Till cites Sam Tangredi, *Futures of War: Towards a Consensus View of the Future Security Environment* (Newport: Alidade Press, 2008), 103, as follows: "The consensus of sources is that the size and level of operational experience of the U.S. Navy and Air Force make it nearly impossible for potential opponents to mount a serious challenge in the waters and air space over the world's oceans. This is likely to continue until 2035."

142. Such as Krepinevich, Holmes, and Yoshihara, as noted above.

CHAPTER 5

1. As a consequence of the global recession, China's global trade sharply decreased in 2008–2009, with trade as a percentage of GDP dropping to a still-high 49 percent in 2009, and the import-to-GDP ratio decreasing to 22 percent in 2009. The World Bank, http://data.worldbank.org. See also Nicholas R. Lardy, "The Transition to Consumption-Driven Growth in China," draft chapter for *China's Rise: Challenges and Opportunities* (Washington, D.C.: Peterson Institute for International Economics, 2008); C. Fred Bergsten, Bates Gill, Nicholas R. Lardy, and Derek J. Mitchell, *The Balance Sheet: What the World Needs to Know Now About China* (New York: Perseus Books, 2006); Michael R. Chambers, "Framing the Problem: China's Threat Environment and International Obligations," in *Right Sizing the People's Liberation Army: Exploring the Contours of China's Military*, edited by Roy Kamphausen and Andrew Scobell (Carlisle, Pa.: Strategic Studies Institute of the U.S. Army War College, 2007), 70.

2. Edward Wong and Michael Wines, "An Unsure China Steps Onto the Global Stage," *New York Times*, April 1, 2009, www.nytimes.com/2009/04/02/world/asia/02china.html. The authors state: "Three years ago, China did not have a single bank among the world's top 20, measured by market capitalization. Today the top three are Chinese." Also see Michael Pettis, "*The G20 Meetings: No Common Framework, No Consensus*," Policy Brief 79 (Washington, D.C.: Carnegie Endowment for International Peace, May 2009), 1–11, http://carnegieendowment.org/files/g20_consensus.pdf.

3. Ministry of Commerce of the People's Republic of China, "China FTA Network," http://fta.mofcom.gov.cn/english/index.shtml. I am indebted to Rachel Esplin Odell for her assistance in developing the summary regarding FTAs presented in this paragraph.

4. Ralph A. Cossa et al., "The United States and the Asia-Pacific Region: Security Strategy for the Obama Administration, 2008," Asia-Pacific Strategy Project, February 2009. As the authors state: "When fully implemented, the China–ASEAN FTA will be the world's third-largest trade agreement, after the European Union and the North American Free Trade Area (NAFTA)." Also see Dick K. Nanto, "East Asian Regional Architecture:

New Economic and Security Arrangements and U.S. Policy," CRS Report for Congress, January 4, 2008. This report examines in some detail China's attempt to establish a large network of FTAs with its trading partners.

5. For example, a recent study argues that China's trading behavior exhibited what the authors called a "Dalai Lama effect," where China did indeed follow up on threats to use economic sanctions to punish countries whose leaders met with the Dalai Lama. Andreas Fuchs and Nils-Hendrik Klann, *Paying a Visit: The Dalai Lama Effect on International Trade*, Research Paper 113 (Göttingen: Center for European Governance and Economic Development, University of Göttingen, 2010), www.uni-goettingen.de/de/document/download/24062d6f430a7c77ab7b1a54407ac843.pdf/113_Fuchs.pdf.

6. See Fred C. Bergsten, "A Partnership of Equals," *Foreign Affairs*, vol. 87, no. 4 (July–August 2008): 57–69; and Wong and Wines, "An Unsure China."

7. For a leading example, see Evan Feigenbaum, "America Risks Being Left Behind in Asia," *Financial Times*, November 11, 2009. Feigenbaum writes: "For more than a decade, Americans have mostly watched from the sidelines as Asians organise themselves into an alphabet soup of new trade pacts and regional institutions. The near-term costs are apparent as FTAs proliferate across the region. But over the longer term, U.S. strategic interests, credibility and influence are likely to suffer unless it acts to shape these trends."

8. Stockholm International Peace Research Institute, Military Expenditures Database, http://milexdata.sipri.org. The SIPRI figures for 2010 are reported in constant 2009 U.S. dollars. China's official military budget in 2010 was about $78 billion, rising 12.7 percent (in real terms) to $91.5 billion in 2011. See "China's defense budget to grow 7.5% in 2010: spokesman," Xinhua, March 4, 2010, www.chinadaily.com.cn/china/2010-03/04/content_9537753.htm; "China's defense budget to grow 12.7 pct in 2011: spokesman," Xinhua, March 4, 2011, http://news.xinhuanet.com/english2010/china/2011-03/04/c_13761030.htm.

9. Barry Naughton, "Understanding the Chinese Stimulus Package," *China Leadership Monitor*, no. 28 (Spring 2009): 377; Gideon Rachman, "Asia Rides High—for the Moment," *Financial Times*, September 29, 2008; David Barboza, "China Passes Japan as Second-Largest Economy," *New York Times*, August 15, 2010; U.S. Central Intelligence Agency, *CIA World Factbook* (Washington, D.C.: U.S. Government Printing Office, various years), https://www.cia.gov/library/publications/the-world-factbook; Wu Jiao, "France Welcomes China with Massive Deals," *China Daily*, November 5, 2010.

10. This processing trade is often characterized by a triangular pattern of exports, where intermediate goods are exported between countries and the product is processed further at each stage. For example, Japan or South Korea may produce a high-tech electronics component such as a semiconductor and then transport it to China, where it is assembled together with other components into a final product, before being reexported to the United States. This triangular pattern has become increasingly complex as firms seek greater economies of scale. See Indermit Gill and Homi Kharas with Deepak Bhattasal et al., *An East Asian Renaissance: Ideas for Economic Growth* (Washington, D.C.: World Bank, 2007); Shimelse Ali, Uri Dadush, "The Rise of Trade in Intermediates: Policy Implications," International Economic Bulletin, Carnegie Endowment for International Peace, February 10, 2011, http://carnegieendowment.org/

publications/index.cfm?fa=view&id=42578&prog=zgp&proj=zie; Uri Dadush, Shimelse Ali, and Rachel Esplin Odell, *Is Protectionism Dying?* Carnegie Paper 121 (Washington, D.C.: Carnegie Endowment for International Peace, April 2011).

China is serving as the hub of this increased Asian economic integration. The PRC is now the largest trade partner of Japan, South Korea, India, Bangladesh, Australia, and ASEAN. Eight of China's top ten trading partners are Asian economies, including Japan, Hong Kong, South Korea, and Taiwan in the top five after the United States. Trade between China and Asia reached $1.57 trillion in 2010 (according to China customs data), an increase of 473 percent from 2000. In 2010, China's trade with Japan reached nearly $300 billion (three and a half times its 2000 level); trade with South Korea surpassed $200 billion (six times its 2000 level); and trade with Taiwan reached $145 billion (nearly five times its 2000 level). Similarly, the top sources of non-financial FDI in China in 2009 were Hong Kong, Taiwan, Japan, Singapore, the United States, and South Korea (in that order); People's Republic of China General Administration of Customs, China's Customs Statistics; European Union Directorate General for Trade, "EU Bilateral Trade and Trade with the World," country statistics reports, January 2011, http://trade.ec.europa. eu/doclib; U.S. China Business Council, "U.S.-China Trade Statistics and China's World Trade Statistics," www.uschina.org/statistics/tradetable.html; U.S. China Business Council, "Foreign Direct Investment in China," www.uschina.org/statistics/fdi_cumulative. html. See also Cossa et al., "United States and the Asia-Pacific Region"; Bergsten at al., *Balance Sheet,* 84; Erik Britton and Christopher T. Mark Sr., *The China Effect: Assessing the Impact on the U.S. Economy of Trade and Investment with China,* (Washington, D.C.: China Business Forum, 2006) 3, www.chinabusinessforum.org/pdf/the-china-effect. pdf; Shambaugh, "China Engages Asia: Reshaping the Regional Order," *International Security,* vol. 29, no. 3 (Winter 2004–5): 79, 83–84. I am indebted to Rachel Esplin Odell for her assistance in developing this footnote and related text.

11. On a related note, the U.S. trade deficit with China—$273 billion in 2010—is often used as evidence of the unsustainable imbalances between China and the United States. However, since China serves as the location of final assembly for many goods whose components (and hence, in large part, monetary values) are actually produced or generated elsewhere in East Asia, as described above, a focus on the United States–China bilateral trade deficit as a purely bilateral problem is a somewhat inflated metric. The WTO estimates that if the U.S. trade deficit with China were calculated on an added-value basis or domestic content basis, it would be 21 or 40 percent lower (respectively). Andreas Maurer and Christophe Degain, "Globalization and trade flows: what you see is not what you get!" Staff Working Paper, World Trade Organization, no. ERSD-2010-12 (June 22, 2010), www.wto.org/english/res_e/reser_e/ersd201012_e. pdf; U.S. Census Bureau, Foreign Trade Division, Data Dissemination Branch, "Trade in Goods (Imports, Exports and Trade Balance) with China," March 10, 2011, www.census. gov/foreign-trade/balance/c5700.html#2010.

12. State Administration of Foreign Exchange, People's Republic of China, www.safe.gov. cn; "Major Foreign Holders of Treasury Securities," U.S. Treasury Department, www. treasury.gov/resource-center/data-chart-center/tic/Documents/mfh.txt.

13. Zachary Karabell, "Why Beijing Wants a Strong Dollar," *Wall Street Journal,* May 28, 2009, http://online.wsj.com/article/SB124347392809361019.html. Karabell states: "Any action taken by China to imperil the economic stability of the U.S. would be an act of mutually-assured destruction." Also see Kenneth Lieberthal, "The U.S.-China Agenda

Goes Global," *Current History*, vol. 108, no. 719 (September 2009): 243–49. Lieberthal states: "China is caught in what might be called a 'dollar trap.' It holds so many dollars that if it tries to sell enough of them to make a serious impact on its exposure, the sale itself will weaken the dollar and increase the value of the currencies China is purchasing instead. China in that case would lose a great deal of money simply by trying to reduce its dollar exposure. If, on the other hand, China holds onto its dollars, then U.S. treasuries provide a source of debt that is deep, flexible, and secure (except for the exchange rate risk)—a very desirable set of qualities in a time of uncertainty."

14. Kathrin Hille, "China Backs Washington Recovery Plan," *Financial Times*, June 3, 2009; Michael Wines, Keith Bradsher, and Mark Landler, "China's Leader Says He Is 'Worried' Over U.S. Treasuries," *New York Times*, March 13, 2009, www.nytimes.com/2009/03/14/world/asia/14china.html.

15. See Geoff Dyer, David Pilling, and Henny Sender, "China: A Strategy to Straddle the Planet," *Financial Times*, January 17, 2011, www.ft.com/cms/s/0/b852a826-2272-11e0-b6a2-00144feab49a.html; Charles Wolf Jr., "China's Next Buying Spree: Foreign Companies," *Wall Street Journal*, January 24, 2011, http://online.wsj.com/article/SB10001424052748704754304576095880533686442.html. And economists such as Pieter Bottelier assert that China is engaged in a deliberate effort to reduce dependence on Western consumer markets while strengthening economic/financial relations with the rest of emerging Asia, Africa, and Latin America. He adds that this undertaking is bolstered by China's renewed economic self-confidence and reduced admiration for the U.S. following the global financial crisis; personal correspondence.

16. George Parker and Guy Dinmore, "China Attacks Dollar's Dominance," *Financial Times*, July 9, 2009, www.ft.com/cms/s/0/81f3125a-6cae-11de-af56-00144feabdc0.html; Andrew Batson, "China Takes Aim at Dollar," *Wall Street Journal*, March 24, 2009, http://online.wsj.com/article/SB123780272456212885.html; Sean O'Grady, "Dollar's Status Under Attack from China," *Independent* (London), March 24, 2009, www.independent.co.uk/news/business/news/dollars-status-under-attack-from-china-1652683.html; Jamil Anderlini, "China Wants to Oust Dollar as International Reserve Currency," *Financial Times*, March 24, 2009, www.ft.com/cms/s/0/be359094-1812-11de-8c9d-0000779fd2ac.html; Wines, Bradsher, and Landler, "China's Leader Says He Is 'Worried' "; Nouriel Roubini, "The Chinese Proposal for a New Global Super Currency," *RGE Monitor*, June 26, 2009, www.rgemonitor.com/roubini-monitor/257169/the_chinese_proposal_for_a_new_global_super_currency; Nouriel Roubini, "The Almighty Renminbi?" *New York Times*, May 13, 2009. Roubini points out that "the renminbi is far from ready to achieve reserve currency status. China would first have to ease restrictions on money entering and leaving the country, make its currency fully convertible for such transactions, continue its domestic financial reforms and make its bond markets more liquid."

17. Wang Xiaotian, "Yuan trade barriers coming down," *China Daily*, January 29, 2011; Pieter Bottelier, "Yuan in the Ascendancy," *Asia Times*, May 29, 2009, www.atimes.com/atimes/China_Business/KE29Cb02.html. Some analysts fear that such efforts will undermine the function of the U.S. dollar as a reserve currency. However, its major impact has been on the dollar as a transaction currency. See Russell Hsiao, "Is Renminbi becoming Asia's Currency and Decoupling from the West?" *China Brief*, vol. 9, no. 21 (October 22, 2009).

18. Dov S. Zakheim, "Security Challenges from the Crisis," testimony before the House Committee on Armed Services in Washington, delivered March 11, 2009, www.isn.ethz.

ch/isn/Current-Affairs/Security-Watch/Detail/?ots591=4888CAA0-B3DB-1461-98B9-E20E7B9C13D4&lng=en&id=98001; Geoff Dyer, "China's Dollar Dilemma," *Financial Times*, February 22 2009; Julian Delasantellis, "U.S. Fed's Move Is the Bigger Problem," *Asia Times*, March 21, 2009, www.atimes.com/atimes/Global_Economy/KC21Dj03.html; W. Joseph Stroupe, "Dollar Crisis in the Making: The Not-So-Safe Haven," *Asia Times*, March 17, 2009, www.atimes.com/atimes/China_Business/KC17Cb02.html. Also see Roubini, "Chinese Proposal." Roubini writes that U.S. creditors "are already diversifying into gold, into resources (as China purchases mines and energy, mineral and commodity resources all over the world) and into shorter-term maturity U.S. Treasuries that have less market risk than longer term Treasuries." Also see Richard McGregor, "Countries and Companies Queue at Beijing Cash Point," *Financial Times*, January 27, 2010. McGregor writes: "The Chinese capital is the first port of call for countries and companies that need money. China has a huge stock of surplus cash, with $2,400 billion (€1,702 billion, £1,486 billion) in foreign exchange reserves, amassed by a decade of largely fixed-exchange rates, swelling trade surpluses, and capital inflows. China has both the need to diversify the way it invests those funds, reducing their reliance on U.S. Treasuries, and also an interest in leveraging the influence the money brings to its own rising diplomatic ambitions."

19. U.S. Chamber of Commerce, "Issues of Importance to American Business in the U.S.-China Commercial Relations," September 2007; China's Foreign Exchange Reserves," *Economist*. October 26, 2006. Also see Morris Goldstein and Nicholas R. Lardy, "China's Currency Needs to Rise Further," *Financial Times*, July 22, 2008, www.iie.com/publications/opeds/oped.cfm?ResearchID=978.

20. See Andrew Batson, "China Rises on Power of Stimulus," *Wall Street Journal*, July 16, 2009, http://online.wsj.com/article/SB124768125855446621.html. This point is discussed further below. Also see Christian Caryl, "Why Bow to China?" *Newsweek*, May 16, 2009, www.newsweek.com/id/197899/page/1.

21. "China Moves to Center Stage," *Economist*, October 30, 2008; Edward Wong, "Booming, China Faults U.S. Policy on the Economy," *New York Times*, June 17, 2008, www.nytimes.com/2008/06/17/world/asia/17china.html?pagewanted=1&_r=1&fta=y; Gideon Rachman, "Asia Rides High—for the Moment," *Financial Times*, September 29, 2008. This issue is discussed in greater detail below.

22. See David Pilling, "Vice-Premier Defends Chinese Policy," *Financial Times*, January 28, 2010. Pilling writes: "Vice-premier Li Keqiang resolutely defended China's record in pursuing balanced growth, implicitly rejecting criticism that Beijing had not done enough to mend its export-led model. "China's contribution to the world's economic recovery is obvious," he said, adding that "its 8.7 percent growth in output last year came in spite of falling exports that shaved nearly 4 percent off the headline rate. Growing domestic demand, both through government-led investment and consumption, contributed more than 12.5 percent to the growth in gross domestic product. . . . While promoting growth, we spared no effort in rebalancing the structure of the economy."

23. To enhance domestic consumption, the Chinese authorities are working to improve consumption-facilitating infrastructure and promote nonmortgage consumer financing in the near term, expand and strengthen the social safety net and other public services over the medium term, and rebalance the economy and raise the share of household

income in national income over the long run. See Qing Wang and Steven Zhang, "China's Under-Consumption Over-Stated," Morgan Stanley *Global Economic Forum*, September 15, 2009, www.morganstanley.com/views/gef/archive/2009/20090915-Tue. html#anchore2873f99-a1f4-11de-b417-0db96b986471.

24. Krishna Guha and Geoff Dyer, "China Dismisses Focus on Global Imbalances," *Financial Times*, September 18, 2009; Kevin Brown and Geoff Dyer, "Hu Defends China's Role in Global Recovery," *New York Times*, November 13, 2009. Also, Liu Mingkang, China's chief banking regulator, charged that the U.S. Federal Reserve is fueling "speculative investments" and endangering global recovery through loose monetary policy involving a weak dollar and low interest rates. See Geoff Dyer and Kevin Brown, "China Says Fed Policy Threatens Global Recovery," *Financial Times*, November 15, 2009. The authors state: "Mr Liu's unusually blunt remarks underscore how China—the largest U.S. creditor because of its massive holdings of Treasury bonds—has become a trenchant critic of monetary and fiscal policy in the U.S." For China's criticisms of U.S. quantitative easing, see "China vows to collar U.S. over monetary policies," *Shanghai Daily*, November 9, 2010, http://english.peopledaily.com.cn/90001/90778/90859/7192749.html;Liu Hong, "Global reserve currencies come with responsibilities," Xinhua, November 4, 2010, http://news.xinhuanet.com/english2010/indepth/2010-11/04/c_13591391.htm.

25. "Is China Still a Developing Nation? No Doubt," *China Daily*, January 30, 2010; "G20 Supplants G8, China Bids Farewell to 'Free Ride' Era," Nanfang Zhoumo Commentary, September 29, 2009; Ma Ning, "Who Is the Biggest Winner at the G20 Summit?" *Beijing Qingnian Bao Online*, September 28, 2009, in OSC CPP20090928710012. The author points out that the increase in China's voting power in the IMF is marginal, and that the developed countries still hold the real power. Also see Keith Bradsher, "China to Shun West's Finance Sector," *New York Times*, December 3, 2008; Elizabeth C. Economy and Adam Segal, "In China, Stimulus and Questions about Global Financial Governance," Council on Foreign Relations, November 13, 2008, www.cfr.org/publication/17742/in_china_stimulus_and_questions_about_global_financial_governance.html; and National Intelligence Council, *Global Trends 2025: A Transformed World* (Washington, D.C.: National Intelligence Council, 2008).

26. Evan Medeiros, *China's International Behavior: Activism, Opportunism, and Diversification* (Santa Monica, Calif.: RAND Corporation, 2006). As Medeiros states: "Beginning early in this decade, not only did China's GDP growth accelerate (from 8 percent in 2002 to 12 percent in 2007) but the resource intensity of GDP growth increased as well (measured in terms of the amount of resource inputs used for each dollar of GDP output). This trend required that China go abroad in search of resources to fuel continued growth, and not just oil and natural gas."

27. International Energy Agency, *World Energy Outlook 2010*, Executive Summary, www. worldenergyoutlook.org/docs/weo2010/WEO2010_ES_English.pdf; Jenny Barchfield, "China surpasses U.S. as world's top energy consumer," Associated Press, July 21, 2010, www.usatoday.com/tech/science/environment/2010-07-21-china-energy_N.htm; Clifford Krauss, "In Global Forecast, China Looms Large as Energy User and Maker of Green Power," *New York Times*, November 9, 2010, www.nytimes.com/2010/11/10/ business/global/10oil.html?_r=1; Elisabeth Rosenthal, "China Increases Lead as Biggest Carbon Dioxide Emitter," *New York Times*, June 14, 2008, www.nytimes. com/2008/06/14/world/asia/14china.html?_r=2; Chris Buckley, "China says it is

world's top greenhouse gas emitter," Reuters, November 23, 2010, www.reuters.com/article/2010/11/23/us-climate-cancun-china-idUSTRE6AM1NG20101123.

28. China's largest suppliers of petroleum include Angola, Saudi Arabia, Iran, Russia, Oman, Sudan, and Venezuela.

29. See IEA, *World Energy Outlook 2010*; Julie Jiang and Jonathan Sinton, *Overseas Investments by China's National Oil Companies*, International Energy Agency, February 2011, www.iea.org/papers/2011/overseas_china.pdf; "China conducts lower-than-expected increase in gasoline, diesel prices," Xinhua, February 19, 2011, http://news.xinhuanet.com/english2010/china/2011-02/19/c_13740044.htm. Also see Britton and Mark, *China Effect*, 4; David D. Hale, "Commodities, China, and American Foreign Policy," *International Economy*, vol. 20, no. 3 (Summer 2006): 16; Sascha Müller-Kraenner, *China's and India's Emerging Energy Foreign Policy* (Bonn: German Development Institute, 2008), www.die-gdi.de/cms-homepage/openwebcms3.nsf/(yndk_contentbykey)/anes-7hjaz8/$file/dppercent2015.2008.pdf.

30. Erica Downs, *China*, Brookings Foreign Policy Studies, Energy Security Series (Washington, D.C.: Brookings Institution, 2006), 16; Downs states that "China's energy projects and agenda are often driven by corporate interests of China's energy firms rather than by the national interests of the Chinese state." Also see Erica Downs, *China's Quest for Energy Security* (Santa Monica, Calif.: RAND Corporation, 2000); Kenneth Lieberthal and Mikkal Herberg, "China's Search for Energy Security: Implications for U.S. Policy," *NBR Analysis* 17, no. 1 (April 2006): 13; David Zweig and Bi Jianhai, "China's Global Hunt for Energy," *Foreign Affairs*, October 2005; Xiong Guang Kai, "The Role of Energy," *International Strategic Studies*, vol. 3 (2007): 8. Lieberthal and Herberg point to "a more active, energy-centric form of commercial diplomacy by Beijing's leaders within the key energy exporting regions, combined with widening campaign by China's three major NOC—CNPC, Sinopec, and CNOOC—to secure equity investments in oil and gas fields abroad (i.e., physical control over oil supplies) and a diversified slate of long-term crude and liquefied natural gas (LNG) supply contracts from a broad range of exporters to meet future needs." Also see Jeffrey A. Bader, "The Energy Future: China and the U.S.: What the United States Ought to Do," paper presented at a conference on China energy, February 8, 2006; Wenran Jiang, "China's Global Quest for Energy Security," *Canadian Foreign Policy*, vol. 13, no. 2 (2006); Daniel Yergin, "Ensuring Energy Security," *Foreign Affairs*, vol. 85, no. 2 (March–April 2006); and Zha Daojiong, "China's Energy Security: Domestic and International Issues," *Survival*, vol. 48, no. 1 (March 1, 2006).

31. Wan Zhihong, "Wen Heads 'Super Ministry' for Energy," *China Daily*, January 28, 2010. An overarching government agency has been set up to take charge of the country's energy policy for better coordination in formulating strategy and planning development. Premier Wen Jiabao will head the agency, called the National Energy Commission (NEC), and Vice-Premier Li Keqiang will be the deputy, the State Council, or the Cabinet, announced yesterday. The commission will be responsible for drafting national energy development plans, reviewing energy security, and coordinating international cooperation, it said yesterday. The NEC has twenty-one members, including ministers from various organizations such as the National Development and Reform Commission and the Ministry of Finance, as well as a representative from the central bank.

32. Peter Yuan Cai, "China's New National Energy Commission," East Asia Forum, blog posting, March 12, 2010, www.eastasiaforum.org/2010/03/12/chinas-new-national-energy-commission.

33. Charles W. Freeman Jr., "China and the Global Resource Balance," remarks to the Summer Roundtable of the Pacific Pension Institute, Victoria, July 25, 2007; Chambers, "Framing the Problem," 72.

34. See Poten & Partners, "China's Bright Horizon," Poten Tanker Market Opinions, February 19, 2010, www.poten.com/Document.aspx?id=15125&filename=China's percent20Bright percent20Horizon percent20(February-19-2010).pdf; "China's Largest Oil Tanker Set to Sail," *China Daily*, January 14, 2010. For its overall market size, China's tanker fleet is relatively small, with eighteen VLCCs, most of them among the oldest in the world's tanker fleets. Beijing plans to build a fleet of 75 tankers by 2012, with an eventual goal of providing a 90-tanker fleet by 2015, capable of carrying 50 percent of the nation's energy imports. See Daniel H. Rosen and Trevor Houser, "China Energy: A Guide for the Perplexed," paper from China Balance Sheet, Joint Project of Center for Strategic and International Studies and Peterson Institute for International Economics, May 2007; also see Andrew Erickson and Gabe Collins, "Beijing's Energy Security Strategy: The Significance of a Chinese State-Owned Tanker Fleet," *Orbis*, vol. 51, no. 4 (Fall 2007): 665–84.

35. For good overviews of the scale and impact of Sino-African relations, see Chris Alden, Daniel Large, and Ricardo Soares De Oliveira, eds., *China Returns to Africa: A Rising Power and a Continent Embrace* (New York: Columbia University Press, 2008); and Deborah Brautigam, *The Dragon's Gift: The Real Story of China in Africa* (New York: Oxford University Press, 2009). For a Chinese perspective, see Zhao Jinfu, "The Role of Africa in China's Rise," *Contemporary International Relations*, vol. 19, no. 4 (July–August 2009): 20–31. Also see Associated Press, "Glance at China-Africa Relations," March 23, 2009, www.google.com/hostednews/ap/article/ALeqM5i9FyFIVCp0wNH4nph9741vqe_NwD973PKI80; Bernt Berger and Uwe Wissenbach, "EU–China–Africa Trilateral Development Cooperation: Common Challenges and New Directions," Deutsches Institut für Entwicklungspolitik, 2007, 1–27, www.ec-an.eu/files/bergerweissenbach_0.pdf; Stephanie Hanson, *China, Africa, and Oil* (New York: Council on Foreign Relations, 2008), www.cfr.org/publication/9557/china_africa_and_oil.html; Chris Alden, "South Africa and China: Forging Africa's Strategic Partnership," *China Brief*, no. 13 (June 24, 2008), www.jamestown.org/single/?no_cache=1&tx_ttnewsswords=8fd5893941d69d0be3f378 576261ae3e&tx_ttnewsall_the_words=us percent20influence percent20asia&tx_ttnewscategories_1=8&tx_ttnewspointer=1&tx_ttnewstt_news=5001&tx_ttn ewsbackPid=7&cHash=9c0d457a7a; Elizabeth C. Economy, "China in Africa: Implications for U.S. Policy," testimony before the Senate Foreign Relations Committee, Washington, June 4, 2008, http://foreign.senate.gov/testimony/2008/EconomyTestimony080604a.pdf; Robert I. Rotberg, "China's Mixed Role in Africa," *Boston Globe*, June 23, 2007, www.boston.com/news/globe/editorial_opinion/oped/articles/2007/06/23/chinas_mixed_role_in_africa.

36. U.S. Energy Information Administration (EIA), *Country Analysis Brief: China, Oil* (Washington, D.C.: U.S. Government Printing Office, November 2010), www.eia.doe.gov/cabs/China/Oil.html; Steve A. Yetiv and Chunlong Lu, "China, Global Energy, and

the Middle East," *Middle East Journal*, vol. 61, no. 2 (April 2007): 199–218; John Garver, Flynt Leverett, and Hilary Mann Leverett, *Moving (Slightly) Closer to Iran: China's Shifting Calculus for Managing Its 'Persian Gulf Dilemma,' "* Asia-Pacific Policy Papers Series (Washington, D.C.: Edwin O. Reischauer Center for East Asian Studies, Paul H. Nitze School of Advanced International Studies, Johns Hopkins University, 2009); Jon B. Alterman and John W. Garver, *The Vital Triangle: China, United States, and Middle East* (Washington D.C.: Center for Strategic and International Studies, 2008); Brookings Institution, *"The Rise of China: Beijing's Role in the Middle East,"* conference proceedings (Washington, D.C.: Brookings Institution, 2008), www.brookings.edu/events/2008/0626_middle_east.aspx; Harsh V. Pant, "Saudi Arabia Woos China and India," *Middle East Quarterly*, vol. 8, no. 4 (Fall 2006): 45–52, www.meforum.org/1019/saudi-arabia-woos-china-and-india; M. Ghafouri, "China's Policy in the Persian Gulf," *Middle East Policy*, vol. 16 (2009): 80–92; FACTS Global Energy, 2009, www.eia.doe.gov/emeu/cabs/China/Oil.html; "China's Oil Security and Its Middle East Oil Strategy," *Shijie jingji yanjiu* (World Economic Studies), no. 1 (2001): 19–22; Ben Simpfendorfer, "China Rediscovers the Middle East," *Telegraph* (London), August 28, 2009, www.telegraph.co.uk/finance/china-business/6093541/China-rediscovers-the-Middle-East.html.

37. EU DG Trade, "EU Bilateral Trade"; Simon Romero and Alexei Barrionuevo, "Deal by Deal, China Expands Its Influence in Latin America," *New York Times*, April 15, 2009, www.nytimes.com/2009/04/16/world/16chinaloan.html?_r=1&ref=global-home; Evan Ellis, "China's Maturing Relationship with Latin America," *China Brief*, vol. 9, no. 6 (March 18, 2009), www.jamestown.org/programs/chinabrief/single/?tx_ttnewstt_news=34723&tx_ttnewsbackPid=414&no_cache=1; Hugo Restall, "China's Latin Economic Gambit," *Wall Street Journal*, August 24, 2009, http://online.wsj.com/article/SB10001424052970203706604574368602807031942.html: "At a time when capital is in short supply, especially in emerging markets, Chinese institutions can make a critical difference in financing new projects." Also see William Ratliff, "An Assessment of China's Deepening Ties to Latin America," *China Brief*, vol. 8, no. 11 (June 6, 2008); Wu Hongying, "Has Latin America Become China's Backyard?" *Contemporary International Relations*, vol. 19, no. 3 (May–June 2009): 16–26; Mohan Malik, "China's Growing Involvement in Latin America," Power and Interest News Report, June 11, 2006, www.pinr.com/report.php?ac=view_report&report_id=508&language_id=1; Craig Timberg, "In Africa, China Trade Brings Growth, Unease," *Washington Post*, June 13, 2006, www.washingtonpost.com/wp-dyn/content/article/2006/06/12/AR2006061201506.html; Alex Villarreal, "Clinton Says U.S. to Counter Chinese, Iranian and Russian Influence in Latin America," Voice of America, May 2, 2009, www.voanews.com/english/2009-05-02-voa2.cfm; Cynthia Watson, "Enter the Dragon? China's Presence in Latin America," Woodrow Wilson International Center for Scholars, February 21, 2007, www.wilsoncenter.org/index.cfm?fuseaction=events.event_summary&event_id=224457; Gonzalo S. Paz, "Rising China's 'Offensive' in Latin America and the U.S. Reaction," *Asian Perspectives*, vol. 30, no. 4 (2006): 110.

38. Edward Wong, "China Quietly Extends Footprints Into Central Asia," *New York Times*, January 2, 2011, www.nytimes.com/2011/01/03/world/asia/03china.html?pagewanted=1; "China to enhance natural gas imports from Central Asia," *Global Times*, September 19, 2010, www.china.org.cn/business/2010-09/19/content_20962907.htm; "China's Investments in Central Asian Energy," Reuters, December 14, 2009; Sébastien Peyrouse, "Economic Aspects of the Chinese–Central Asia Rapprochement," Central Asia–Caucasus

Institute and Silk Road Studies Program Paper, September 2007, www.silkroadstudies. org/new/docs/Silkroadpapers/2007/0709China-Central_Asia.pdf; Sadykzhan Ibraimov, "China–Central Asia Trade Relations: Economic and Social Patterns," *China and Eurasia Forum Quarterly*, vol. 7, no. 1 (2009): 47–59; Hak Yin Li and Zhengxu Wang, "Assessing China's Influence in Central Asia: A Dominant Regional Power?" University of Nottingham China Policy Institute, Briefing Series, no. 53 (July 2009), www.nottingham. ac.uk/cpi/documents/briefings/briefing-53-central-asia.pdf; Ablat Khodzhaev, "The Central Asian Policy of the People's Republic of China," *China and Eurasia Forum Quarterly*, vol. 7, no. 1 (2009): 9–28; Thrassy N. Marketos, "China's Energy Needs and the Shanghai Cooperation Organization in the Post 9/11 Period," *Defensor Pacis* (Defense Analyses Institute), August 17, 2008, www.rieas.gr/index.php?option=com_content&view=article&i d=724&catid=25&Itemid=72; and Gaël Raballand and Agnès Andrésy, "Why Should Trade between Central Asia and China Continue to Expand?" *Asia Europe Journal*, vol. 5, no. 2 (June 2007): 235–52; Rajan Menon, "The New Great Game in Central Asia," *Survival*, vol. 45, no. 2 (Summer 2003): 187–204.

39. European Union Directorate General for Trade, "ASEAN Trade Statistics—EU Bilateral Trade and Trade with the World," January 18, 2011, http://trade.ec.europa.eu/doclib/ docs/2006/september/tradoc_113471.pdf; "ASEAN surpasses Japan as China's 3rd largest trading partner," *People's Daily Online*, June 18, 2010, http://english.peopledaily. com.cn/90001/90778/90861/7030353.html "ASEAN, China to work on deepening strategic cooperation," *People's Daily Online*, March 3, 2011, http://english.peopledaily. com.cn/90001/90776/90883/7306353.html; Ding Ying, "FTA Driving ASEAN Growth," *Beijing Review*, no. 4, January 22, 2011, www.bjreview.com.cn/world/txt/2011-01/23/ content_327879.htm; International Monetary Fund Direction of Trade Statistics, www2.imfstatistics.org/DOT; "Backgrounder: Development of China–ASEAN Trade Relations," Xinhua, December 28, 2009; Wang Xinyuan, "China–ASEAN Ink Investment Agreement," *Global Times*, August 17, 2009; Zhao Jianglin, "ASEAN–China Trade Relations: 15 Years of Development and Prospects," paper presented at International Conference on ASEAN–China Trade Relations: 15 Years Development and Prospects, Hanoi, December 6–8, 2007, http://iaps.cass.cn/English/articles/showcontent. asp?id=1131; "China Rolls Out Aid Package for ASEAN," Xinhua, April 12, 2009, www. chinadaily.com.cn/china/2009-04/12/content_7669717.htm.

40. Gill and Kharas, *An East Asian Renaissance*; Edward J. Lincoln, "Comments on China as a Regional Player," paper presented at the China and the World Economy Workshop, The Atlantic Council of the United States, January 2006, www.acus.org/docs/0601-Comments_China_Regional_Player.pdf. I am indebted to Rachel Esplin Odell for drawing my attention to the increasingly positive aspects of Sino-ASEAN economic relations.

41. These noneconomic consequences of Chinese involvement are discussed in other chapters.

42. See James B. Steinberg, "Administration's Vision of the U.S.-China Relationship," keynote address at meeting of Center for a New American Security, Washington, September 24, 2009. Steinberg states: "Resource competition is another area of concern. With its rapid growth and large population, China's demand for resources, whether oil, gas, or minerals, is surging, but resource mercantilism is not the appropriate response. China's moves in that direction have raised legitimate concern not only in the United States, but also among our other partners and among resource-rich developing nations. The problem is not just that China's mercantilist approach disrupts markets; it also leads China to problematic engagement with actors

like Iran, Sudan, Burma, and Zimbabwe, and undermines the perception of China as a country interested in contributing to regional stability and humanitarian goals." For an earlier statement of U.S. concern over this issue, see Robert B. Zoellick, "Whither China: From Membership to Responsibility?" remarks to the National Committee on U.S.-China Relations, New York City, September 21, 2005, www.ncuscr.org/files/2005Gala_RobertZoellick_Whither_China1.pdf. Also see Medeiros, *China's International Behavior*, 172; Daniel P. Mulhollan, *China's Foreign Policy and "Soft Power" in South America, Asia, and Africa*, report for Congressional Research Service (Washington, D.C.: U.S. Government Printing Office, 2008); Daniel Yergin, "Ensuring Energy Security," *Foreign Affairs*, vol. 85, no. 2 (March–April 2006); Jill Shankleman, *Going Global: Chinese Oil and Mining Companies and the Governance of Resource Wealth* (Washington, D.C.: Woodrow Wilson International Center for Scholars, 2009); Restall, "China's Latin Economic Gambit"; Villarreal, "Clinton Says U.S. to Counter Chinese."

43. Thomas Lum, Christopher M. Blanchard, et al., "Comparing Global Influence: China's and U.S. Diplomacy, Foreign Aid, Trade, and Investment in the Developing World," Congressional Research Service, August 15, 2008, www.fas.org/sgp/crs/row/RL34620.pdf. However, China's level of economic assistance to Latin America, Central Asia, and the Middle East remains limited. Also see Phillip C. Saunders, *China's Global Activism: Strategy, Drivers, and Tools*, Occasional Paper 4 (Washington, D.C.: National Defense University Press, 2006); and Thomas J. Christensen, "China in Africa: Implications for U.S. Policy," testimony before the Senate Foreign Relations Committee, Washington, June 5, 2008, www.state.gov/p/eap/rls/rm/2008/06/105556.htm. And see U.S. Agency for International Development, "Report to Congress on Assistance by the People's Republic of China to Governments and Entities in Latin America and Africa, 2009," www.usaid.gov/press/congressional/2009/cr_china_7071f3.pdf. The report states that expert estimates of China's official development assistance to Latin America and Africa vary widely, from as low as $970 million in 2005 to as high as $25 billion in 2007. See also, "China's Foreign Aid," Information Office of the State Council, People's Republic of China, April 2011.

44. Brautigam, *Dragon's Gift*; NYU Wagner School, *Understanding Chinese Foreign Aid: A Look at China's Development Assistance to Africa, Southeast Asia, and Latin America*, April 25, 2008, cited in Thomas Lum et al., "China's Foreign Aid Activities in Africa, Latin America, and Southeast Asia," CRS Report for Congress, February 25, 2009, www.fas.org/sgp/crs/row/R40361.pdf; Chinese government's website, www.china.org.cn/english/features/China-Africa/81869.htm; Daniel Large, "Beyond 'Dragon in the Bush': The Study of China-Africa Relations, *African Affairs*, vol. 107, no. 426 (2008): 45–61; Stephen Morrison, James Swan, Bates Gill, Sun Baohong, and Mark Bellamy, "China's Expanding Role in Africa: Implications for the United States," paper presented at Center for Strategic and International Studies, Washington, February 8, 2007; Freeman, "China and the Global Resource Balance."

45. Lum et al., "China's Foreign Aid Activities"; Mulhollan, *China's Foreign Policy*.

46. Brautigam, *Dragon's Gift*. Brautigam explains, "China's aid is not huge; the traditional donors give far more aid to Africa. China's export credits are much larger than its aid, but not as large as commonly believed." I am indebted to Rachel Esplin Odell for her assistance in developing the presentation on China's foreign aid presented in the preceding paragraphs.

47. See Bergsten, "Partnership." Also see Malik, "China's Growing Involvement"; Timberg, "In Africa"; Economy, "China in Africa"; Rotberg, "China's Mixed Role"; Mulhollan, *China's Foreign Policy*. See also "China's Foreign Aid," Information Office of the State Council.

48. Sharon LaFraniere and John Grobler, "Uneasy Engagement: China Spreads Aid in Africa, with a Catch," *New York Times*, September 22, 2009; Lydia Polgreen and Howard W. French, "China's Largess in Africa Isn't Free," *International Herald Tribune*, August 20, 2007, www.iht.com/articles/2007/08/20/asia/zambia.php?page=1; Michael Wines, "China's Influence in Africa Arouses Some Resistance," *New York Times*, February 10, 2007, www.nytimes.com/2007/02/10/world/africa/10assess.html; Barbara Hogenboom, "Latin America and the Rise of China: Possibilities and Obstacles for Development," paper presented at McCulloch Center for Global Initiatives, Mount Holyoke College, South Hadley, Mass., March 2008, www.mtholyoke.edu/global/assets/ CGI/Hogenboom_paper_March_2008.pdf; and R. Evan Ellis, "U.S. National Security Implications of Chinese Involvement in Latin America," Strategic Studies Institute, June 2005, www.strategicstudiesinstitute.army.mil/pdffiles/PUB606.pdf; Stephanie Hanson, "China, Africa, and Oil," Council on Foreign Relations, June 6, 2008, www.cfr. org/publication/9557/china_africa_and_oil.html.

49. Zoellick, "Whither China?"

50. For an account of China's integration into the global economy leading up to its entry into the WTO, see Nicholas R. Lardy, *Integrating China into the Global Economy* (Washington, D.C.: Brookings Institution Press, 2002); for specific details on U.S.-China economic negotiations leading up to China's entry into the WTO, see Andrew Mertha, *The Politics of Piracy: Intellectual Property in Contemporary China* (Ithaca, N.Y.: Cornell University Press, 2005).

51. This is from interviews. Despite sharp rhetoric directed at China at the onset of the Bush administration, involving the designation of Beijing as a "strategic competitor," senior Bush officials recognized that China must be brought fully into the international economic order. Such U.S. support was intended in part to counterbalance the potentially confrontational actions being taken in the military arena, outlined above.

52. James A. Kelly, "The Future of U.S.-China Relations," testimony before the Senate Foreign Relations Committee, Subcommittee on East Asian and Pacific Affairs, Washington, May 1, 2001; Colin L. Powell, "Briefing on Trip to East Asia," remarks to the press en route to Canberra, July 29, 2001, www.state.gov/secretary/former/ powell/remarks/2001/4347.htm; Christopher R. Hill, "Emergence of China in the Asia-Pacific: Economic and Security Consequences for the U.S.," testimony before the Senate Foreign Relations Committee, Subcommittee on East Asian and Pacific Affairs, Washington, June 7, 2005, http://merln.ndu.edu/archivepdf/china/State/47334.pdf.

53. These included congressional opposition to the granting of permanent most-favored-nation status to China (largely emerging as a result of the appearance at the time of a congressional report containing misleading and faulty accusations of Chinese spying and theft of U.S. nuclear and other secrets), along with the need to retain vital labor union support. See David M. Lampton, *Same Bed, Different Dreams: Managing U.S.-China Relations, 1989–2000* (Berkeley: University of California Press, 2001), 58.

54. This is from interviews. Also see Jeffrey L. Gertler, "What China's WTO Accession Is All About," WTO Secretariat, December 14, 2002, http://siteresources.worldbank.org/ intranettrade/resources/gertler.pdf; Office of the U.S. Trade Representative, "U.S. and

China Reach Consensus on China's Accession to WTO," June 9, 2001, http://ustraderep.
gov/Document_Library/Press_Releases/2001/June/US_China_Reach_Consensus_on_
China's_Accession_to_WTO.html.

55. As one interviewee stated, "The WTO accession was a watershed moment for American
foreign policy because it confirmed in a very concrete manner that the U.S. is an
advocate of a prosperous, responsible China."

56. The Office of the U.S. Trade Representative's 2006 Report to Congress on China's WTO
Compliance stated that China had attained a mixed record. It acknowledged that China
had taken steps to reform its economy in accordance with its WTO obligations, but it
said much more progress needed to be made in developing China's industrial policies,
improving import and export restrictions, reversing discriminatory regulations and
prohibited subsidies, protecting intellectual property rights, and limiting government
intervention in the market. Office of the U.S. Trade Representative, *2006 Report to Congress
on China's WTO Compliance* (Washington, D.C.: Office of the U.S. Trade Representative,
2006), www.ustr.gov/assets/Document_Library/Reports_Publications/2006/asset_upload_
file688_10223.pdf; Robert L. Zoellick, "U.S.-China Relations," testimony before the House
Committee on International Relations, Washington, May 10, 2006, prepared materials;
and U.S. State Department website, www.state.gov/documents/organization/66187.pdf;
Thomas J. Christensen, "China's Role in the World: Is China a Responsible Stakeholder?"
remarks before the U.S.-China Economic and Security Review Commission, Washington,
August 3, 2006; U.S. State Department website, www.state.gov/p/eap/rls/rm/69899.htm;
China Business Forum, "The Prospects for U.S.-China Services Trade and Investment,"
December 2006, 8, www.chinabusinessforum.org/pdf/us-china-services-trade.pdf;
and Wayne M. Morrison, "China–U.S. Trade Issues," Congressional Research Service,
Washington, March 7, 2008, 1–31.

57. Christensen, "China's Role."

58. World Trade Organization Dispute Settlement Gateway, www.wto.org/english/tratop_e/
dispu_e/dispu_e.htm.

59. Randall G. Shriver, "The Effects and Consequences of an Emerging China," testimony
before the Subcommittee on East Asia and the Pacific, Senate Foreign Relations
Committee, Washington, March 19, 2003, U.S. State Department website, www.state.
gov/p/eap/rls/rm/2003/18879.htm; and "Background Briefing on President's Meeting
with Chinese Premier Wen," U.S. State Department website, December 9, 2003,
www.state.gov/p/eap/rls/rm/2003/27182.htm; Hill, "Emergence of China"; Zoellick,
"Whither China?"; "Issues of Importance to American Business in the U.S.-China
Commercial Relations," U.S. Chamber of Commerce Report, September 2007. For
comments on China's sovereign wealth fund, see Hearing before the Subcommittee on
Asia, the Pacific and the Global, Environment of the House Foreign Affairs Committee,
March 27, 2007, Washington.

60. Jacqui Goddard, "Tainted Drywall from China Is Driving Owners from Their Homes,"
Christian Science Monitor, April 4, 2009, www.csmonitor.com/2009/0404/p99s01-
usgn.html; Morrison, "China–U.S. Trade Issues"; Toni Johnson, "And Now, Food
Security, Too," Council on Foreign Relations, Daily Analysis, July 11, 2007, www.cfr.
org/publication/13775/and_now_food_security_too.html; Christopher P. Twomey,
"Missing Strategic Opportunity in U.S. China Policy Since 9/11," *Asian Survey*, vol. 47
no. 4 (July–August 2007): 536–59; David McCormick, "Rebalancing the U.S.-China

Economic Relationship," paper presented at Council on Foreign Relations, New York, January 30, 2008, www.cfr.org/publication/15386/rebalancing_the_uschina_economic_relationship_rush_transcript_federal_news_service.html; Gideon Rose's conference call with Elizabeth Economy, Council on Foreign Relations, New York, September 6, 2007, www.cfr.org/publication/14163/conference_call_with_elizabeth_economy.html.

61. See Daniel Dombey, "Congress Letter Urges Action on Renminbi," *Financial Times*, March 15, 2010. In line with such accusations, a 2008 report by the Economic Policy Institute found that the "U.S. trade deficit with China cost 2.3 million American jobs between 2001 and 2007. . . . Even when they found new jobs, workers displaced by job loss to China saw their earnings decrease by an average of $8,146 each year because the new jobs paid less." See Andrea Hopkins, "U.S.-China Trade Has Cost 2.3 Million U.S. jobs: Report," July 30, 2008, www.reuters.com/article/politicsNews/idUSN2935619520080730. In addition, in May 2005, the U.S. Treasury Department released a report stating that China's currency peg "is a substantial distortion to world markets." For a summary of U.S. charges against China in these areas and the Chinese response, see Morrison, "China–U.S. Trade Issues." For a more recent, similar argument from a non-U.S. government analyst, see Paul Krugman, "Chinese New Year," *New York Times*, January 1, 2010; and Paul Krugman, "World Out of Balance," *New York Times*, November 16, 2009.

62. David McCormick, "Rebalancing the U.S.-China Economic Relationship," paper presented at the Council on Foreign Relations, New York, January 30, 2008, www.cfr.org/publication/15386/rebalancing_the_uschina_economic_relationship_rush_transcript_federal_news_service.html. Also see Elizabeth Price, Greg Hitt, and Andrew Batson, "U.S. Case Against China in WTO Shows New Mood, Bush Answers Calls for Tougher Actions, Risks Further Tension," *Wall Street Journal Asia*, February 5, 2007; Lee Hudson Teslik's interview with Henry M. Paulson, Council on Foreign Relations, New York, June 14, 2007, www.cfr.org/publication/13598/paulson_says_chinas_currency_doesnt_reflect_reality.html?breadcrumb= percent2Fregion percent2F271 percent2Fchina.

63. "China Import Surge Casts Obama Tariff as Phony War," Bloomberg News, September 17, 2009. Tom Barkley, "U.S. Files WTO Case Versus China Over Brand Promotion Policy," Dow Jones Newswires, December 19, 2008. This article cites a news release by the Office of the U.S. Trade Representative office stating that "the promotion of Chinese-branded merchandise appear to use export subsidies, which would violate WTO trade rules, and to form part of a protectionist industrial policy." Also see "U.S. Files WTO Case Against China 'Famous Brands' Aid," *Forbes*, December 19, 2008, www.forbes.com/feeds/afx/2008/12/19/afx5845071.html.

64. WTO Dispute Settlement Gateway; Covington & Burling LLP, International Trade & Finance, Clean Energy & Climate Industry Group, "Potential U.S.-China Trade Dispute Over China's Clean Energy Policies," e-alert, September 30, 2010, www.cov.com/files/Publication/8eb69594-88ec-4c82-aa91-76dd3ef035b0/Presentation/PublicationAttachment/306d7e27-a18b-4f26-9975-7b6674ea2e83/Potential percent 20US-China percent20Trade percent20Dispute percent20Over percent20China's percent20Clean percent20Energy percent20Policies.pdf. I am indebted to Rachel Esplin Odell for her assistance in developing the information presented in this paragraph.

65. For example, see David Leonhardt, "The Real Problem With China," *New York Times*, January 11, 2011, www.nytimes.com/2011/01/12/business/economy/12leonhardt.html.

66. As indicated in chapter 3, under the Obama administration, the SED was folded into the Senior Dialogue directed by the State Department, to become part of a combined Strategic and Economic Dialogue (S&ED) jointly overseen by the U.S. secretary of state and secretary of the Treasury (currently Hillary Clinton and Timothy Geithner).

67. During Hu Jintao's January 2011 visit to Washington, China and the United States reiterated their commitment of "building a comprehensive and mutually beneficial economic partnership." Specifically, both parties agreed to strengthen macroeconomic communication and cooperation. Washington agreed to focus on its deficit and ensure fiscal sustainability. For its part, Beijing agreed to increase domestic demand, promote private investment in service sectors, and allow more freedom in market and resource allocation. See Office of the Press Secretary, White House, "U.S.-China Joint Statement," January 17, 2011, www.whitehouse.gov/the-press-office/us-china-joint-statement.

68. Office of Public Affairs, U.S. Department of Commerce, "Commerce Secretary Gary Locke and USTR [U.S. trade representative] Ronald Kirk Convene 20th Session of U.S.-China Joint Commission on Commerce and Trade in Hangzhou, China," October 21, 2009, www.commerce.gov/news/press-releases/2009/10/21/commerce-secretary-gary-locke-and-ustr-ronald-kirk-convene-20th-sessi.

69. For examples, see Office of the U.S. Trade Representative, "U.S.-China Joint Commission on Commerce and Trade Fact Sheet," October 29, 2009, www.ustr.gov/about-us/press-office/fact-sheets/2009/october/us-china-joint-commission-commerce-and-trade; U.S. Department of Commerce, "The U.S.-China Joint Commission on Commerce and Trade (JCCT) Fact Sheet," December 11, 2007, http://2001-2009.commerce.gov/NewsRoom/PressReleases_FactSheets/PROD01_004907. The December 2010 JCCT, held in the run-up to President Hu Jintao's state visit in January 2011, was praised as a particularly successful event in which key agreements were reached on IPR, indigenous innovation, and government procurement. See U.S. Department of Commerce, "21st U.S.-China Joint Commission on Commerce and Trade Fact Sheet," December 15, 2010, www.commerce.gov/node/12467. See also Douglas H. Paal, "Calming the Storm in U.S.-China Relations," Video Q&A, Carnegie Endowment for International Peace, January 11, 2011, www.carnegieendowment.org/publications/index.cfm?fa=view&id=42274; remarks by Myron Brilliant, "China's Unbalanced Growth: Vice or Virtue?," event transcript, Carnegie Endowment for International Peace, January 13, 2011, http://carnegieendowment.org/files/1217carnegie-chinaseconomicgrowth_-%20TRANSCRIP1.pdf; remarks by Douglas Paal, "U.S.-China Relations at a Crossroads: Briefing on Hu Jintao's State Visit," event transcript, Carnegie Endowment for International Peace, December 16, 2010, www.carnegieendowment.org/files/briefing_on_hu_jintao_visit.pdf. The author is indebted to Rachel Esplin Odell for providing the information and analysis of the JCCT and its relationship to the SED and S&ED.

70. Thomas J. Christensen, "The State of U.S.-China Diplomacy," remarks before the U.S. China Economic and Security Review Commission, delivered by John Norris, Washington, February 2, 2007; and U.S. State Department website, www.state.gov/p/eap/rls/rm/2007/79866.htm.

71. Henry Paulson Jr., "Meeting the Challenge: A Partnership on Energy and the Environment," remarks before the Chinese Academy of Sciences, Beijing, April 2, 2008, www.ustreas.gov/press/releases/hp903.htm.

72. U.S. Department of the Treasury, "U.S. Fact Sheet: First Cabinet-level Meeting of Economic Track of U.S.-China Strategic and Economic Dialogue," July 28, 2009, www.treasury.gov/initiatives/Documents/SEDfactsheet072809.pdf.

73. U.S. Department of the Treasury, "Second Meeting of the U.S.-China Strategic & Economic Dialogue," Fact Sheet—Economic Track, May 25, 2010, www.ustreas.gov/press/releases/tg717.htm; Morrison, "China–U.S. Trade Issues"; David Loevinger, "U.S.-China Relations: Maximizing the Effectiveness of the Strategic and Economic Dialogue," testimony for the House Foreign Affairs Committee, Subcommittee on Asia, the Pacific and the Global Environment, September 10, 2009; U.S. Department of the Treasury, "The First U.S.-China Strategic and Economic Dialogue Economic Track Joint Fact Sheet," July 28, 2009, www.treasury.gov/press-center/press-releases/Pages/tg240.aspx. For an overview of the SAED's purposes, see Hillary Clinton and Timothy Geithner, "A New Strategic and Economic Dialogue with China," Wall Street Journal, July 27, 2009, http://online.wsj.com/article/SB10001424052970204886304574308753825396372.html. Also see Subhash Kapila, "United States–China Strategic and Economic Dialogue (May 2010) Reviewed," South Asia Analysis, Paper 3833, May 28, 2010, www.southasiaanalysis.org/percent5Cpapers39 percent5Cpaper3833.html.

74. The dialogue involves as many as fifteen Chinese ministries and five Cabinet-level agencies of the U.S. government. U.S. Department of the Treasury, "Fact Sheet: U.S.-China Strategic and Economic Dialogue," July 28, 2009, http://treasury.gov/press/releases/reports/sed percent20fact percent20sheet.pdf.

75. These included a Ten-Year Energy and Environment Framework that established a working group and subordinate joint task force groups, for the areas of electricity, air, water, transportation, and conservation of forest and wetland ecosystems; Chinese agreement to consider voluntary participation in the joint actions of the International Energy Agency (IEA) during times of oil disruption and to "strengthen collaboration with the IEA on areas such as global energy markets, energy efficiency, and clean energy technology"; an agreement to negotiate a new treaty to ban discriminatory practices that obstruct foreign investments in both nations; and a consensus to place "U.S. Department of Health and Human Services/Food and Drug Administration personnel at the U.S. Embassy and Consulates General in China and agreed to work out detailed arrangements. This followed several earlier agreements in the area of health and safety that were negotiated in 2007. Washington and Beijing have also established many SED "working groups" to pursue a variety of economics-related issues, such as trade barriers to environmental goods, energy emergencies, and forest management. See "U.S. Fact Sheet: Fourth Cabinet-Level Meeting of the U.S.-China Strategic Economic Dialogue." U.S. Treasury Department. June 18, 2008; Morrison, "China–U.S. Trade Issues"; Bonnie Glaser, "Chock-Full of Dialogue: SED, Human Rights, and Security," Comparative Connections, vol. 10, no. 2 (July 2008); and Steven R. Weisman, "U.S. and China Agree to Ease Foreign Investment," New York Times, June 19, 2008, www.nytimes.com/2008/06/19/business/worldbusiness/19trade.html?partner=rssnyt&emc=rss.

76. U.S. Department of State, "Joint Press Release on the First Round of the U.S.-China Strategic and Economic Dialogue," July 28, 2009, www.state.gov/secretary/rm/2009a/july/126599.htm.

77. Weisman, "U.S. and China Agree."

78. See, in particular, Office of the United States Trade Representative, *2009 Report to Congress on China's WTO Compliance* (Washington, D.C.: Office of the U.S. Trade Representative, 2009), www.ustr.gov/webfm_send/1572. Also see Daniel Griswold, "Americans Reaping Benefits of U.S. Membership in WTO," *Washington Times*, January 5, 2010; and Alan Rappeport, "New Duties Slapped on Chinese Imports," *Financial Times*, December 31, 2009.

79. Some U.S. bills submitted in the Congress accuse Beijing of economic malfeasance, call for consultation, and then mandate submission of the case to the WTO if bilateral discussions fail to produce results. See Morrison, "China–U.S. Trade Issues"; Barkley, "U.S. Files WTO Case"; William New, "U.S. Says China to Sign Bilateral Cooperation Deals on IP Enforcement," September 17, 2008, www.ip-watch.org/weblog/index. php?p=1230; Weisman, "U.S. and China Agree; and U.S. State Department, "United States Launches Negotiations of an Investment Treaty with China," June 20, 2008, www.state.gov/e/eeb/rls/fs/2008/106132.htm. Some observers argue that, even though the WTO mechanism has helped resolve many trade disputes, it could also be used as a tool to highlight trade tensions and express a sense of unfairness in bilateral trade. See Andrew Beatty, "U.S. Takes Two China Trade Cases to WTO," Agence France-Presse, September 15, 2010.

80. WTO Dispute Settlement Gateway; John W. Miller, "Trade Body Rules in Beijing's Favor," *Wall Street Journal*, March 12, 2011; Doug Palmer, "U.S. Claims Win in WTO Piracy Case Versus China," Reuters, October 9, 2008; Michael Geist, "Why the U.S. Lost Its WTO IP Complaint Against China. Badly." January 27, 2009, www.michaelgeist.ca/ content/view/3645/125/; and Stan Abrams, "U.S.-China WTO IP Dispute IV—Final Thoughts," February 17, 2009, www.chinahearsay.com/us-china-wto-ip-dispute-iv-final-thoughts. China also utilized a complaint against the United States in the WTO over a congressional ban on Chinese poultry imports (Section 727 of the Omnibus Appropriations Act, known as the "DeLauro Amendment") to pressure the United States to remove the offending measure. Although the WTO expert panel ultimately ruled in China's favor, Congress allowed the measure to expire before the ruling was even issued. See Jennifer M. Freedman, "U.S. Ban on Chinese Poultry Imports Violates Global Trade Rules, WTO Says," Bloomberg News, September 29, 2010; Elliot J. Feldman, "China's Status as a Non-Market Economy," *China–U.S. Trade Law*, September 21, 2010, www.chinaustradelawblog.com/articles/trade-disputes/wto. See also Dan Neumann, "As 2010 Begins, U.S.-China WTO Disputes Stand at Distinct Stages," *Inside US–China Trade*, vol. 10, no. 1 (January 6, 2010). Jamil Anderlini, "Beijing Rejects Allegations of Protectionism," *Financial Times*, June 24, 2009, www.ft.com/cms/s/0/b70f1d52-60d4-11de-aa12-00144feabdc0.html; Geoff Dyer, "China Hits Out at US in Fresh Trade Spat," *Financial Times*, November 7, 2009; Art Pine, "Trade Restraint?" *National Journal.com–CongressDaily*, December 14, 2009, www.nationaljournal.com/congressdaily/cwa_20091214_8009.php. I am indebted to Rachel Esplin Odell for her assistance in preparing the information and analysis presented in this paragraph.

81. David Shambaugh, *China's Communist Party: Atrophy and Adaptation* (Berkeley: University of California Press, 2008); Yang Dali, *Remaking the Chinese Leviathan: Market Transition and the Politics of Governance in China* (Stanford, Calif.: Stanford University Press, 2004).

82. Heiligendamm Dialogue Process, "Concluding Report of the Heiligendamm Process," presented at the L'Aquila G8 Summit, July 9, 2009, www.g8italia2009.it/static/

G8_Allegato/06_Annex_1__HDP_Concluding.pdf; "G8 Hokkaido Toyako Summit Leaders Declaration." G8 Hokkaido Summit, July 8, 2008, www.g8summit.go.jp/eng/ doc/doc080714__en.html.

83. Communiqué, G-20 Meeting of Finance Ministers and Central Bank Governors, Paris, February 18–19, 2011, www.g20.org/Documents2011/02/COMMUNIQUE-G20_ MGM%20_18-19_February_2011.pdf; "G20 sceptics wait for shift in behavior," *Financial Times*, February 20, 2011, www.ft.com/cms/s/0/1b5a9a62-3d23-11e0-bbff-00144feabdc0. html#ixzz1EoUIWmEe; Gabriele Steinhauser and Greg Keller, "G-20 reach compromise deal on imbalances," Associated Press, February 19, 2011, www.businessweek.com/ap/ financialnews/D9LG1HB00.htm; "The Pittsburgh Summit: Key Accomplishments," Pittsburgh G-20 Summit, September 24–25, 2009, www.pittsburghsummit.gov/ resources/129665.htm; Edmund L. Andrews, "Leaders of G-20 Vow to Reshape Global Economy," *New York Times*, September 26, 2009; Annys Shin and Michael D. Shear, "Reflecting New Global Economic Order, More Expansive G-20 to Replace G-8," *Washington Post*, September 25, 2009; Wong and Wines, "An Unsure China"; Michael Pettis, "*The G20 Meetings: No Common Framework, No Consensus*," Policy Brief 79 (Washington, D.C.: Carnegie Endowment for International Peace, 2009), 1–11, www. carnegieendowment.org/files/g20_consensus.pdf. As Pettis argues, while Washington largely blames export-oriented, trade-surplus, low-consumption and high-savings nations like China for creating global financial imbalances, Europe (and to some extent China) cites inadequate government control over financial markets, while China blames U.S. overconsumption and deficit spending.

84. Mark Landler, "China Shows Little Patience for US Currency Pressure," *New York Times*, February 4, 2010; Alan Beattie, Geoff Dyer, and Chris Giles, "China Tees Up G20 Showdown with U.S.," *Financial Times*, November 5, 2010, www.ft.com/cms/ s/0/03567a28-e8a3-11df-a383-00144feab49a.html#axzz15TlT1oqF.

85. Robert G. Sutter, *The United States in Asia* (Lanham, Md.: Rowman & Littlefield, 2008); 14th APEC Economic Leaders' Meeting Ha Noi Declaration, Hanoi, November 18–19, 2006, www.apec.org/apec/leaders__declarations/2006.html; Governments of Australia, China, South Korea, and New Zealand, "Further Analytical Study on the Likely Economic Impact of an FTAAP," October 2009, Asia-Pacific Economic Cooperation, 2009/CSOM/R/010, http://aimp.apec.org/Documents/2009/SOM/CSOM-R/09_ csom_r_010.pdf; George Manzano and Myrene Bedaño, *Revisiting Sectoral Liberalization: An Alternative to the FTAAP? Implications on the Philippines*, Discussion Paper 2009-13 (Manila: Philippine Institute for Development Studies, 2009), http://dirp3.pids.gov. ph/ris/dps/pidsdps0913.pdf; Donald Weatherbee, "Strategic Dimensions of Economic Interdependence in Southeast Asia," in *Strategic Asia 2006–2007: Trade, Interdependence, and Security*, edited by Ashley Tellis and Michael Wills (Seattle: National Bureau of Asian Research, 2006), 282–300. As another historical note, ASEAN+3 established the East Asia Vision Group in 1998 and tasked it with developing ways of strengthening East Asian regionalism. The group's 2001 report is available at www.mofa.go.jp/region/ asia-paci/report2001.pdf. An East Asian Study Group was established that same year, and it submitted a report of its own the following year, which is available at www. aseansec.org/viewpdf.asp?file=/pdf/easg.pdf.

86. Office of the United States Trade Representative, "Trans-Pacific Partners and United States Launch FTA Negotiations," September 22, 2008, www.ustraderep.gov/

Document_Library/Press_Releases/2008/September/Trans-Pacific_Partners_United_
States_Launch_FTA_Negotiations.html.

87. The TPP is conceived as a high-standard, broad-based, Asia-Pacific-wide trade pact. TPP negotiations currently include nine countries from the Asia-Pacific Rim: Australia, Brunei, Chile, Malaysia, New Zealand, Peru, Singapore, Vietnam, and the United States. As of April 2011, six rounds of negotiations had already taken place in 2010 and 2011, with a seventh round scheduled for June 2011 in Singapore. See the United States Trade Representative Trans-Pacific Partnership website, www.ustr.gov/tpp. In the view of some observers, the TPP could thus provide the basis for a future FTA for the entire Asia-Pacific that includes the United States. This information is from interviews. Also see Mary Swire, "Obama's Green Light For Trans-Pacific Partnership Talks, Tax-News.com, Hong Kong, November 18, 2009. Former U.S. Trade Representative Clayton Yeutter has argued that the TPP could serve as a model for future plurilateral trade negotiation efforts, especially if multilateral WTO negotiations continue to stagnate. Remarks by Clayton Yeutter, "U.S. Trade Agenda 2011: Moving Forward?" event transcript, Center for Strategic and International Studies, March 3, 2011, http://csis.org/files/attachments/110303_moving_forward_transcript.pdf.

88. Jong-hyun Choi, minister for economic affairs, Embassy of the Republic of Korea in the United States, "KORUS FTA: Action or Inaction?" www.nbr.org/downloads/pdfs/NBR/Choi-KORUS-FTA.pdf. See also Laura M. Baughman and Joseph F. François, "Failure to Implement the U.S.–Korea Free Trade Agreement: The Cost for American Workers and Companies," U.S.–Korea Business Council, November 2009. The U.S.-Korea Business Council report estimates that failure to ratify KORUS would lead to "a decline of $35.1 billion in U.S. exports of goods and services to the world and U.S. national output failing to grow by $40.4 billion" with a loss of 345,017 U.S. jobs.

   After a prolonged period of inaction (the KORUS FTA was originally signed on June 30, 2007), the Obama administration renegotiated certain elements of the agreement related to trade in automobiles in early December 2010. President Obama then called for ratification of the KORUS FTA in his January 2011 State of the Union address. President Barack Obama, "Remarks by the President at the Announcement of a U.S.–Korea Free Trade Agreement," White House Office of the Press Secretary, December 4, 2010, www.whitehouse.gov/the-press-office/2010/12/04/remarks-president-announcement a us korea-free-trade-agreement; President Barack Obama, State of the Union Address, January 25, 2011, www.whitehouse.gov/the-press-office/2011/01/25/remarks-president-state-union-address. Observers hope that Obama's emphasis on the issue, combined with an influx of Republican members of Congress as a result of the Republican victory in the 2010 midterm elections, will facilitate movement on the agreement in 2011. I am indebted to Rachel Esplin Odell for her assistance in developing the information and analysis presented in this paragraph.

89. See Yeutter, "U.S. Trade Agenda 2011: Moving Forward?"

90. As Fareed Zakaria has observed, the financial crisis is causing the "delegitimization of American power." See Fareed Zakaria, "The Age of Bloomberg," *Newsweek*, October 4, 2008, www.newsweek.com/id/162272?from=rss. For similar assessments, see David Rothkopf, "9/11 Was Big, This Is Bigger," *Washington Post*, October 5, 2008; and John Gray, "A Shattering Moment in America's Fall from Power," *Guardian*, September 28, 2008, www.guardian.co.uk/commentisfree/2008/sep/28/usforeign policy.useconomicgrowth.

91. "Sustaining Economic Growth in China," in C. Fred Bergsten, Charles Freeman, Nicholas R. Lardy, and Derek J. Mitchell, *China's Rise: Challenges and Opportunities* (Washington, D.C.: Peterson Institute for International Economics and Center for Strategic and International Studies, 2008), 105–36. The authors state: "China now is the second largest contributor to global economic imbalances, after only the United States, which has the world's largest current account deficit. China's successful transition to a pattern of growth driven more by domestic consumption demand necessarily entails a reduction in China's national saving rate relative to its investment rate. That, in turn, would reduce China's current account surplus. . . . This evidence suggests that transition toward more consumption-driven growth in China will require more vigorous government policy action than we have seen to date . . ." Also see Pettis, "*G20 Meetings.*"

92. Albert Keidel, *China's Economic Rise: Fact and Fiction*, Policy Brief 61 (Washington, D.C.: Carnegie Endowment for International Peace, 2008), 1–15.

93. See Thomas Christensen, testimony on U.S.-China Relations before the Subcommittee on Asia, the Pacific, and the Global Environment of the House Foreign Affairs Committee, Washington, March 27, 2007. Christensen stated that, while the United States supports Chinese development assistance to Africa and Latin America, it also desires greater coordination of aid, loan, and investment programs, "so that China is more in line with efforts by the international community, including—or especially international organizations like the World Bank." This topic is discussed further below. In May 2006, Thomas A. Shannon Jr., assistant secretary of state for Western Hemisphere affairs, held the first-ever talks with his Chinese counterpart on China's role in Latin America. See Mohan Malik, "China's Growing Involvement."

94. For example, see U.S. Agency for International Development, "Report to Congress." The report states: "Although the PRC clearly is engaged in providing foreign assistance to countries in Africa and Latin America, the exact amount of the assistance as well as the details about its specific programs remain unclear. The Chinese government does not release official data about its foreign assistance, and limited information about its foreign assistance activities is available via press releases and news reports. Information is also difficult to interpret because China does not use the internationally accepted definition of "official development assistance.""

95. Thomas J. Christensen, deputy assistant secretary of state for East Asian and Pacific affairs, "The State of U.S.-China Diplomacy," statement before the U.S.-China Economic and Security Review Commission, February 2, 2007.

96. As indicated above, Chinese economic officials are more inclined to push back against U.S. criticism and rebuke Americans on the handling of both national and international economic issues. Edward Wong, "Booming, China Faults U.S. Policy on the Economy," *New York Times*, June 17, 2008, www.nytimes.com/2008/06/17/world/asia/17china.html?pagewanted=1&_r=1&fta=y; Bashir Goth, "Time to Share the Top Spot, America." *PostGlobal*, October 3, 2008, http://newsweek.washingtonpost.com/postglobal/bashir_goth/2008/10/time_to_share_the_top_spot_ame.html.

97. As Thomas Friedman has stated, the United States is "going to need foreigners and sovereign wealth funds from China, Asia, Europe and the Middle East more than ever to survive this crisis—and they are going to need the U.S. to be healthy as well. In the process, we are going to become even more intertwined and dependent on the rest of the world." See Thomas Friedman, "Swedish Spoken Here," *New*

York Times, October 4, 2008, www.nytimes.com/2008/10/05/opinion/05friedman. html?partner=rssnyt&emc=rss. For a more recent statement, see Minxin Pei, "The Tension Is Overrated," *International Herald Tribune*, February 16, 2010. Pei writes: "The two countries are now so economically intertwined that a major disruption in their political relationship could severely damage their respective economic interests, a price neither wants to pay. Economic interdependence also means that neither China nor the U.S. can hurt the other without harming itself." Also see Michael Mastanduno, "Rivals or Partners? Globalization and U.S.-China Relations," *Harvard International Review*, vol. 39, no. 3 (Fall 2007): 42–46.

98. Hillary Rodham Clinton, "Closing Remarks for U.S.-China Strategic and Economic Dialogue," Washington, July 28, 2009, www.state.gov/secretary/rm/2009a/july/ 126599.htm; U.S. Department of State, Joint Press Release on the First Round of the U.S.-China Strategic and Economic Dialogue, July 28, 2009, www.state.gov/ secretary/rm/2009a/july/126599.htm; Thomas J. Christensen, "The State of U.S.-China Diplomacy," remarks before the U.S.-China Economic and Security Review Commission (delivered by John Norris), Washington, D.C. (February 2, 2007), www. state.gov/p/eap/rls/rm/2007/79866.htm.

99. I am indebted to Albert Keidel for this insight.

100. Chad P. Bown, "U.S.-China Trade Conflicts and the Future of the WTO," *Fletcher Forum of World Affairs*, vol.33, no.1 (Winter–Spring 2009).

101. Shambaugh, *China's Communist Party*; Yang, *Remaking the Chinese Leviathan*.

102. Recent public opinion survey data suggest that economic relations with China are a matter of great concern to the American people. According to a January 2011 poll conducted by the Pew Research Center, 53 percent of Americans believe it is "very important" to "get tougher with China on economic and trade issues," while another 32 percent believe it is "somewhat important." This may stem from perceptions of China's growing economic might vis-à-vis the United States: 47 percent of poll respondents identified China as the world's leading economic power, while only 31 percent identified the United States as such (despite the fact that U.S. GDP in 2010 was still two-and-a-half times that of China). Moreover, a solid majority (60 percent) of those surveyed view China as a greater economic threat than military threat. Pew Research Center, "Strengthen Ties with China, But Get Tough on Trade," January 12, 2011, http://pewresearch.org/pubs/1855/ china-poll-americans-want-closer-ties-but-tougher-trade-policy.

A 2010 survey conducted by the Chicago Council on Global Affairs produced similar results, finding that 63 percent of Americans believe China practices unfair trade, 51 percent view U.S. debt to China as a "critical" threat to U.S. interests, and a large majority (71 percent) are somewhat or very concerned about China's undervalued currency. The Chicago Council on Global Affairs, "Global Views 2010: Constrained Internationalism: Adapting to New Realities—Results of a 2010 National Survey of Public Opinion" (Chicago: Chicago Council on Global Affairs, 2010).

103. This is from interviews with current and former U.S. officials.

104. Sutter, *United States in Asia*. As Sutter points out that "Chinese trade figures were exaggerated because of double counting associated with processing trade. Such double counting was estimated to account for 30 percent of China's trade with Southeast

Asia. . . . While Chinese investment abroad grew fairly rapidly, it did so from a low base, amounting to $16 billion for Chinese investment to the entire world in 2006."

105. China's economic activity is totally overshadowed by that of the United States, which carried on $560 billion of trade with Latin America in 2007. Although nearly one-quarter of China's FDI goes to Latin America, the amount only totaled $22 billion in 2007, which is almost insignificant when compared with the United States' $350 billion invested in the region. Nonetheless, for some observers, China is probably poised to be a much more important player in Latin American over the coming decade. See Daniel P. Erikson, "The New Challenge: China and the Western Hemisphere," testimony before the House Committee on Foreign Affairs, Subcommittee on the Western Hemisphere, Washington, June 11, 2008, http://foreignaffairs.house.gov/110/eri061108.htm.

106. See Evan Feigenbaum and Robert A. Manning, *The United States in the New Asia*, Council Special Report 50 (New York: Council on Foreign Relations, 2009). The authors write: "For so many reasons, the nature of American engagement in Asia will shape the region's future. But it is essential to adapt U.S. policy to the contours of change in Asia if the United States wishes to remain vital and relevant there. A generation hence, in 2030, the United States could find its firms at a competitive disadvantage in a part of the world that will constitute about half of the global economy. Already we see, for example, South Korea moving ahead on an FTA with the European Union as the Korea–U.S. Free Trade Agreement languishes in Washington. And that is not the end of the story. The United States could find an Asia much less willing to accommodate its interests, and particularly its commercial, economic, and financial interests. Without vigorous engagement, especially multilateral trade engagement and liberalization, American credibility and influence will wane. Others will fill the vacuum." Also see Feigenbaum, "America Risks Being Left Behind," where he writes: "China, Japan and South Korea plan to move towards a free-trade agreement. If Japanese and Korean companies enjoy tariff-free access to China while U.S. companies face the current average most-favoured nation rate of 9 percent, Americans will lose substantial sales in an import market worth well over $1,000 billion (668 billion, £604 billion). They will lose elsewhere, too, as these three countries move toward tariff reduction with Southeast Asia."

107. For a particularly strong argument against China's image as a supposed "rogue donor" to Africa or an unrepentant supporter of authoritarian governments, see Brautigam, *Dragon's Gift*. The author argues that many Western fears about China in Africa are misinformed and alarmist. Economically, China's aid to Africa is actually not as substantial as commonly believed, and many of China's worst practices are emulative of those in the West. The author argues that China is using its investment to develop opportunities for its business generally, not just to access natural resources. More important, even though much of China's investment in Africa threatens indigenous African companies, it also provides employment to Africans and creates strong special economic zones that will attract further outside investment. In fact, Brautigam argues that, in focusing primarily on infrastructure projects (and thereby emulating the Japanese aid model), China is providing a service to Africa that is desperately needed and neglected by Western aid donors. On the political front, the author argues that Beijing "is moving away from old alliances (Mugabe in Zimbabwe) and stepping into an unaccustomed role as a mediator in Sudan," as well as aiding in antipiracy efforts near Somalia. Although Chinese companies have traditionally had little regard for labor

and environmental standards, they are allegedly learning the need for corporate social responsibility in order to be globally competitive.

108. For example, in February 2007, Assistant Secretary of State for African Affairs James Swan stated that "the United States does not regard China's emerging interest in Africa as a security threat. . . . China has important interests in Africa which include access to resources and markets and the pursuit of diplomatic allies. None of these is inherently threatening to U.S. interests. U.S. policy is not to curtail China's involvement in Africa, but to seek cooperation where possible; moderate negative influences in some key areas, especially governance and human rights; and continue efforts to nudge China toward becoming a responsible international stakeholder." See Jon W Walker, "China, U.S. and Africa: Competition or Cooperation?" United States Air Force, March 15, 2008, www.dtic.mil/cgi bin/GetTRDoc?AD=ADA481365&Location=U2 &doc=GetTRDoc.pdf. In 2005, the U.S. principal deputy assistant secretary of state for African affairs, Michael Ranneberger, told the House Africa Subcommittee that China's increasing economic engagement across Sub-Saharan Africa "should not be read as a threat to U.S. economic and political interests in Africa. . . . In fact, he said, it can help to advance U.S. goals in Africa to the extent that it increases prosperity and stability on the continent, thus contributing to increased respect for human rights and individual freedoms. See Jim Fisher-Thompson, "China No Threat to United States in Africa, U.S. Official Says," July 28, 2005, www.globalsecurity.org/wmd/library/ news/china/2005/china-050729-usia01.htm. Also see Economy, "China in Africa"; Rotberg, "China's Mixed Role in Africa"; Mulhollan, *China's Foreign Policy*; and Jamie Heine, "China's Claim in Latin America: So Far, a Partner Not a Threat," Council on Hemispheric Affairs, July 25, 2008, www.coha.org/2008/07/china percentE2 percent80 percent99s-claim-in-latin-america-so-far-a-partner-not-a-threat.

109. Bergsten et al., *Balance Sheet*.

110. Most mainstream economists and economic organizations concluded in mid-2009 that the global economic recession had hit bottom and was gradually abating, due largely to massive fiscal stimulus programs implemented in the major developed and developing economics, including China. However, the recovery was widely regarded as fragile and the effects of the downturn long-lasting, involving relatively high unemployment rates and unused productive capacity (in at least the developing economies) for years to come. See Matthew Saltmarsh, "A Glimmer of Cheer for Developed Economies," *International Herald Tribune*, June 24, 2009; Sarah O'Connor and Kiran Stacey, "Fed Sees an End to U.S. Recession but No Let-Up in Unemployment," *Financial Times*, July 16, 2009; Louis Uchitelle and Jack Healy, "Job Losses Slow, Signaling Momentum for a Recovery," *New York Times*, August 8, 2009; Neil Irwin and Annys Shin, "In Jobless Rate Dip, a Partial Picture," *Washington Post*, August 8, 2009; and Chris Giles, " 'Jobless Recovery' Predicted to Last," *Financial Times*, October 2, 2009.

111. China Forecast," Economist Intelligence Unit, March 11, 2009, www.economist.com/ countries/china/profile.cfm?folder=Profile-Forecast; Dominique Strauss-Kahn, in a Briefing of Asia Press, February 2, 2009, www.imf.org/external/np/tr/2009/tr020209. htm; Jamil Anderlini, "Data Signal Growing Signs of Recovery for Beijing," *Financial Times*, April 14, 2009; China's Stimulus Policies Are Key for Growth in 2009 and an Opportunity for More Rebalancing, Says World Bank Update," World Bank, November 25, 2008, http://web.worldbank.org/wbsite/external/countries/eastasiapacificext/chin aextn/0,,contentMDK:21989619~pagePK:1497618~piPK:217854~theSitePK:318950,00.

html; Jim Yardley, "After 30 Years of Reform, Economic Perils on China's Path," *International Herald Tribune*, December 19, 2008; CNN, "Chinese Manufacturing in Steep Decline," November 3, 2008, http://money.cnn.com/2008/11/03/news/ international/china_manufacturing.ap/index.htm.

112. Michael Pettis, "Chinese Job Market Demographics: 3 Implications," March 13, 2008, http://seekingalpha.com/article/68395-chinese-job-market-demographics-3-implications; Nouriel Roubini, "The Outlook for China's Economy," *Forbes*, April 9, 2009, www.forbes.com/2009/04/08/china-economy-yuan-exports-opinions-columnists-nouriel-roubini.html; Jayshree Bajoria, "Financial Crisis May Worsen Poverty in China, India," Backgrounder, Council on Foreign Relations, November 20, 2008, www.cfr.org/ publication/17812/financial_crisis_may_worsen_poverty_in_china_india.html; "Pres. Hu: Economic Downturn Deepens," Reuters, December 1, 2008; "Suddenly Vulnerable," *Economist*, December 11, 2008; CNN, "Chinese Manufacturing"; Yardley, "After 30 Years of Reform"; Joseph Fewsmith, "Social Order in the Wake of Economic Crisis," *China Leadership Monitor*, no. 28 (Spring 2009); Hugo Restall, "China Enters a Period of Eruptions," *Far Eastern Economic Review*, July 10, 2009.

113. Chen Yongrong, "China's economy expands faster in 2010, tightening fears grow," Xinhua, January 20, 2011, http://news.xinhuanet.com/english2010/china/2011-01/20/c_13699250.htm; Pieter Bottelier, "China: Ahead of the Pack," *International Economic Bulletin*, January 2010; Edward Wong, "China on Path to Become Second-Largest Economy," *New York Times*, January 21, 2010; William H. Overholt, "China in the Global Financial Crisis: Rising Influence, Rising Challenges," *Washington Quarterly*, vol. 33, no. 1 (January 2010): 21–24; Kathrin Hille, "China's Economic Recovery Broadens," *Financial Times*, November 1, 2009; Keith Bradsher, "Recession Elsewhere, but It's Booming in China," *New York Times*, December 10, 2009; "China's Growth Accelerates to 8.9 Percent in 3Q," *China Daily*, October 22, 2009; Ted Plafker, "A Year Later, China's Stimulus Package Bears Fruit," *New York Times*, October 23, 2009; Krishna Guha, "Economies Rise but Politicians Cautious," *Financial Times*, September 1, 2009; Jamil Anderlini, "Data Signal Growing Signs of Recovery for Beijing," *Financial Times*, April 14, 2009; Geoff Dyer and Justine Lau, "China's Economic Recovery Gains Pace," *Financial Times*, September 11, 2009. Naughton, "Understanding the Chinese Stimulus Package"; Martin Wolf, "Wheel of Fortune Turns as China Outdoes West," *Financial Times*, September 14, 2009; Pieter Bottelier, "China's Astonishing Rebound Is for Real, but Prospects Remain Uncertain, *International Economic Bulletin*, September 2009; Albert Keidel, "Reversing the Global Slowdown," *Far Eastern Economic Review*, November 13, 2008, www.feer.com/economics/2008/november/Reversing-the-Global-Slowdown; Albert Keidel, "China and the Global Financial Crisis," based on a luncheon speech delivered at meeting of U.S.-China Business Council, Washington, October 16, 2008; Nipa Piboontanasawat and Kevin Hamlin, "China's Economy to Recover Strongly, Central Bank Adviser Says," Bloomberg, March 25, 2009, www.bloomberg.com/apps/ news?pid=20601080&sid=amFhSMVmyUUA&refer=asia. For the details of the Chinese stimulus package, see Economy and Segal, "In China, Stimulus and Questions." The authors state: "On November 9th, they announced a major stimulus package of 4 trillion yuan (about $586 billion). The funds are slated for investment over the next two years in a number of sectors, including low-income housing, rural infrastructure, water, electricity, transportation, the environment, technological innovation, and earthquake reconstruction. The government has also abolished the credit ceiling on commercial bank lending in the hopes of spurring falling investment levels."

114. David Barboza, "China Passes Japan as Second-Largest Economy," *New York Times*, August 15, 2010.

115. Remarks by Vivek Arora, "Rebalancing Growth in Asia: Economic Dimensions for China," Carnegie Endowment for International Peace, March 9, 2011, www. carnegieendowment.org/events/?fa=eventDetail&id=3183; Kevin Brown and Justine Lau, "Chinese Demand Drives Regional Recovery," *Financial Times*, January 7, 2010; Bottelier, "China: Ahead of the Pack": "China has also significantly contributed to the global economic recovery. In 2009, its trade surplus narrowed by about one-third (to $196 billion), and its contribution to global economic growth was about 50 percent. If there are no serious domestic stumbles and growth in the major OECD countries remains subdued, as expected, China's contribution to global growth in 2010 will again be disproportionately large." Also see Nelson D. Schwartz and Matthew Saltmarsh, "Developing World Seen as Engine for Recovery," *New York Times*, June 24, 2009. World Bank officials predicted in April 2009 that China's economy would show signs of recovery by midyear, and that such recovery would likely assist stabilization and recovery in Asia. See Shamim Adam and Kevin Hamlin, "China's Recovery to Aid Asian Growth, World Bank Says," Bloomberg, April 7, 2009, www.bloomberg.com/apps/news?pid=20601087&sid=aZ1nppC0mNeg&refer=home.

116. See Vivek Arora and Roberto Cardarelli, eds., *Rebalancing Growth in Asia: Economic Dimensions for China* (Washington, D.C.: International Monetary Fund, 2011); Yukon Huang, "China's Unbalanced Growth Has Served It Well," *Financial Times*, October 7, 2010, www.ft.com/cms/s/0/7dd52f82-d247-11df-8fbe-00144feabdc0.html. Huang argues that, while China has no incentive to abandon its unbalanced growth approach, the bigger concerns are the sustainability of the investment-driven economy and the environmental and social implications of its current economic development. Also see Kevin Brown, "ADB Warns on China's Long-Term Growth," *Financial Times*, September 28, 2010, www.ft.com/cms/s/0/7d660492-cad4-11df-bf36-00144feab49a.html; David Barboza, "As China Rolls Ahead, Fear Follows," *New York Times*, December 12, 2010, www.nytimes.com/2010/12/13/business/global/13yuan.html; Geoff Dyer, "No One Home," *Financial Times*, February 22, 2010; Kevin Brown, "ADB Warns of Inflation Risk for China and India," *Financial Times*, January 16, 2010; Victor Shih, "Looming Problem of Local Debt in China—1.6 Trillion Dollars and Rising," Elite Chinese Politics and Political Economy Blog posting, February 10, 2010, http://chinesepolitics.blogspot.com/2010/02/looming-problem-of-local-debt-in-china.html; Chris Giles, "Rebound Faces Fresh Risks, IMF Cautions," *Financial Times*, January 27, 2010; Victor Shih, "China's 8,000 Credit Risks," *Wall Street Journal Asia*, February 8, 2010, http://online.wsj.com/article/SB10001424052748703427704575052062978995460.html; William H. Overholt, "China in the Global Financial Crisis"; Rana Foroohar, "Everything You Know About China Is Wrong," *Newsweek*, October 17, 2009; Michael Pettis, "Brace for a Lower Decade of Chinese Growth," *Financial Times Online*, July 29, 2009, www.ft.com/cms/s/0/50179048-779f-11de-9713-00144feabdc0.html; Michael Pettis, *Sharing the Pain: The Global Struggle Over Savings*, Policy Brief 84 (Washington, D.C.: Carnegie Endowment for International Peace, 2009), www.carnegieendowment.org/files/global_struggle_savings.pdf. Pettis points to a long list of policies and structural problems that have supposedly led to wide and divergent growth rates between production and consumption, and thereby created and sustain China's large trade surplus. These include: an undervalued currency; excessively low interest rates; a large spread between

the deposit rate and the lending rate; sluggish wage growth, unraveling social safety nets over the past two decades; weak environmental restrictions; and other direct manufacturing subsidies, including controlled land and energy prices. Also see Michael Pettis, "China's Consumption Conundrum," *Wall Street Journal*, May 12, 2009, http://online.wsj.com/article/SB124207141833407823.html. Pettis writes: "With China unable to rely on the U.S. to consume the gap between China's own consumption and its output, China will face GDP growth that is likely to be rigidly limited by the growth in domestic consumption. . . . To rebalance an economy with excess capacity and to continue growing, China needs domestic consumption to grow much faster than domestic production for many years." Additional sources include Richard McGregor, "Beijing Risks Passing on a Poisoned Chalice," *Financial Times*, August 9, 2009, www.ft.com/cms/s/0/17cd01c0-84f9-11de-9a64-00144feabdc0.html; "China's Banks Are an Accident Waiting to Happen to Every One of Us," *Telegraph* (London), June 28, 2009, www.telegraph.co.uk/finance/comment/ambroseevans_pritchard/5675198/Chinas-banks-are-an-accident-waiting-to-happen-to-every-one-of-us.html; and David Shear, Derek Chollet, and David Loevinger, "Briefing on the U.S.-China Strategic and Economic Dialogue," U.S. Department of State Teleconference Briefing, Washington, July 27, 2009, www.state.gov/r/pa/prs/ps/2009/july/126525.htm. Dave Loevinger states, "If China's going to grow, it's not going to be able to grow by exporting to the U.S., and as far as we can tell, to the rest of the world. China is going to have to promote more homegrown consumption-led growth."

117. Michael Pettis is one of the major voices behind this concern. He writes: "As the U.S. rebalances its economy toward higher savings rates, China has no choice but to rebalance toward higher consumption rates. This can happen either because of a sharp pick-up in consumption growth or, more likely, a sharp slowdown in GDP growth. I worry that China will find it difficult to generate the kind of consumption growth that will take up some of the American slack, and we may be locked into a period during which the world adjusts by growing more slowly." See Michael Pettis, "Saving the World, Without U.S. Consumers—How Beijing Suppresses Spending," *New York Times*, Room for Debate Blog, September 24, 2009, http://roomfordebate.blogs.nytimes.com/2009/09/24/saving-the-world-without-us-consumers. Also see Pettis, *Sharing the Pain*, where he writes: "Ultimately the accelerating infrastructure investment that is needed to keep employment high is not only unsustainable, but it also does not resolve underconsumption in the medium term. It merely pushes the problem forward for a few years. What's more, the Chinese stimulus package has poured credit into increasingly questionable projects and will almost certainly increase the direct and indirect subsidies to investment and manufacturing." Also see Pettis, *G20 Meetings*; and Pettis, "China's Consumption Conundrum." For other similar pessimistic assessments of the Chinese economy, see Nouriel Roubini, "Outlook for China's Economy in 2009 and Beyond," *RGE Monitor*, April 2009, http://newsweek.washingtonpost.com/postglobal/pomfretschina/RGE percent20on percent20China.pdf; and Stephen S. Roach, "Manchurian Paradox," *National Interest*, April 27, 2009, www.nationalinterest.org/Article.aspx?id=21316. Roach states: "China needs to get far more serious in funding a social safety net—especially social security and pensions—if it is to reduce the excesses of fear-driven precautionary saving and foster a more broadly based consumer culture."

118. Martin Wolf, "Why China Must Do More to Rebalance Its Economy," *Financial Times*, September 23, 2009; Roubini, "Outlook for China's Economy," *Forbes*. Roubini writes:

"The world where the U.S. was the consumer of first and last resort—spending more than its income and running an ever larger current account deficit—and where China was the producer of first and last resort, spending less than its income and running ever larger current account surpluses, is changing." Also see Roubini, "Outlook for China's Economy in 2009 and Beyond," *RGE Monitor*; Nouriel Roubini, "The U.S. Financial System Is Effectively Insolvent," *Forbes*, March 5, 2009, www.forbes.com/2009/03/04/global-recession-insolvent-opinions-columnists-roubini-economy.html?321; Brad Setser, "Case Closed: A Savings Glut, Not an Investment Drought," April 13, 2008, *Follow the Money*, Council on Foreign Relations blog, http://blogs.cfr.org/setser/2008/04/13/case-closed-a-savings-glut-not-an-investment-drought; and Jörg Bibow, *The International Monetary (Non-)Order and the "Global Capital Flows Paradox,"* Working Paper 531 (Annandale-on-Hudson, N.Y.: Levy Economics Institute of Bard College and Skidmore College, 2008). Pettis's solution to this problem is a global compact between surplus and deficit countries: "In order to make the transition workable and avoid trade friction, the world's major economies must engineer a joint program of fiscal expansion. The trade-deficit countries should expand moderately so as to slow down the adjustment period and to give maximum traction to fiscal expansion on the part of the trade-surplus countries. China must be given at least three or four years to make concerted efforts to boost domestic demand to the point where global imbalances are more manageable." See Michael Pettis, "China's Great Demand Challenge," *Far Eastern Economic Review*, January–February 2009.

119. Janamitra Devan, Micah Rowland, and Jonathan Woetzel, "A Consumer Paradigm for China," *McKinsey Quarterly*, no. 4 (2009): 36–49.

120. See Michael Pettis, "China Faces a Difficult Economic Transition," Carnegie Commentary, August 25, 2010, www.carnegieendowment.org/publications/index.cfm?fa=view&id=41431; Michael Pettis, "Is China Turning Japanese?" *Foreign Policy*, August 19, 2010; Michael Pettis, "Chinese Consumption and the Japanese 'Sorpasso,'" *China Financial Markets*, August 10, 2010, www.carnegieendowment.org/publications/index.cfm?fa=view&id=41397.

121. The Twelfth Five Year Plan approved by China's National People's Congress in March 2011 places a strong emphasis on these priorities. Prime Sarmiento, "China's 12th Five-Year Plan seen to boost domestic consumption," Xinhua, March 3, 2011, http://news.xinhuanet.com/english2010/china/2011-03/03/c_13760001.htm; Shen Hong and Aaron Back, "China Stresses Stability Amid Further Growth," *Wall Street Journal*, March 6, 2010.

122. See remarks by Pieter Bottelier, "Rebalancing Growth in Asia: Economic Dimensions for China," Carnegie Endowment for International Peace, March 9, 2011, www.carnegieendowment.org/events/?fa=eventDetail&id=3183; Sam Jones, Alexandra Stevenson, and Robert Cookson, "Bulls and Bears Battle Over China's 'Miracle,'" *Financial Times*, October 15, 2010, www.ft.com/cms/s/0/de86f09a-d882-11df-8e05-00144feabdc0.html; Albert Keidel, "Imbalances Are Overstated," *China Economic Quarterly*, vol. 13, no. 4 (December 2009); Keith Bradsher, "In Downturn, China Sees Path to Growth," *New York Times*, March 16, 2009, www.nytimes.com/2009/03/17/business/worldbusiness/17compete.html?_r=1&hp; Keidel, "Reversing the Global Slowdown"; Keidel, "China and the Global Financial Crisis"; Nipa Piboontanasawat and Kevin Hamlin, "China's Economy to Recover Strongly, Central Bank Adviser Says," Bloomberg News, March 25, 2009, www.bloomberg.com/apps/news?pid=20601

080&sid=amFhSMVmyUUA&refer=asia; Zhiwu Chen, "Economic Crisis Could Push Reform in China," YaleGlobal, November12, 2008, http://yaleglobal.yale.edu/display. article?id=11596. For an impressionistic, and largely optimistic, assessment of China's ability to recover from the current recession, see James Fallows, "China's Way Forward," *Atlantic Monthly*, April 2009, www.theatlantic.com/doc/200904/chinese-innovation.

123. Remarks by Pieter Bottelier, "Rebalancing Growth in Asia: Economic Dimensions for China," Carnegie Endowment for International Peace, March 9, 2011, www. carnegieendowment.org/events/?fa=eventDetail&id=3183; Pieter Bottelier, "China and the International Financial Crisis," in *Strategic Asia 2009–10: Economic Meltdown and Geopolitical Stability*, edited by Ashley J. Tellis, Andrew Marble, and Travis Tanner (Seattle: National Bureau of Asian Research, 2009); Albert Keidel, "Global Imbalances and China," paper presented at the international conference "Towards a New Economic Multilateralism," Shanghai, April 20–21, 2009, sponsored by the Friedrich Ebert Stiftung of Berlin and the Shanghai Institutes for International Studies; Albert Keidel, "The Global Financial Crisis: Lessons for the United States and China," speech for the U.S.-China Business Council, Washington, October 16, 2008, www.carnegieendowment. org/files/Luncheon_Talk_Keidel.pdf; Keidel, "Imbalances Are Overstated"; Keidel, "Reversing the Global Slowdown"; Keidel, "China and the Global Financial Crisis." For reinforcing arguments that the U.S.-China imbalance is primarily "demand-driven" (that is, by the United States), see Roya Wolverson, "Confronting the China–U.S. Economic Imbalance," Council on Foreign Relations Backgrounder, November 16, 2009, www.cfr.org/publication/20758#p5; John Ross, "New U.S. and China Trade Figures Show Error In Martin Wolf's Analysis Of Global Imbalances," iStockAnalyst. com, February 11, 2010, www.istockanalyst.com/article/viewarticle/articleid/3857592; and Joseph W. Gruber and Steven B. Kamin, "Explaining the Global Pattern of Current Account Imbalances," *Journal of International Money and Finance*, no. 26 (2007): 502.

124. Keidel insists that long-term consumption rates in China would be higher if economic growth continues to be driven primarily by more productive infrastructure and public goods investment, rather than by simply increasing the consumption share in GDP at the expense of the investment share. In other words, a higher saving and investment rate means faster growth for everything in the economy, not only investment but consumption as well. He adds that, despite supposed overinvestment, China's incremental capital output ratio—the economic return for each dollar of increase in the nation's capital stock—remains comparable to that of India. See Keidel, "Imbalances Are Overstated." Analysts such as Michael Pettis directly reject the notion of building infrastructure as a way to increase domestic consumption by arguing that China is now nearing the point where it can no longer absorb high levels of inefficient infrastructure investment; as a result, economic returns will start to shrink. According to Pettis, the basic cause of China's low consumption level is low household income (relative to GDP), resulting from a combination of low wages, undervalued currency, and most important, the artificially low interest rate that transfers between 5 and 10 percent of China's GDP from households to producers per year. This pattern of "financial repression," if unchanged, will keep household income and thus domestic consumption low, according to Pettis. Moreover, he argues that spending on infrastructure will do nothing to help this situation, and may in fact hinder necessary rebalancing. For a representative article, see: Michael Pettis, "Bad Loans Could Take Their Toll on China's Growth," *Financial Times*, April 21, 2010. I am indebted to Tiffany Ng for bringing this argument to my attention.

125. See Qing Wang and Steven Zhang, "China's Under-Consumption Over-Stated," Morgan Stanley Global Economic Forum, September 15, 2009, www.morganstanley.com/views/gef/archive/2009/20090915-Tue.html#anchore2873f99-a1f4-11de-b417-0db96b986471. The authors state: "While the domestic dimension of China's under-consumption—namely consumption growth having lagged investment and export growth in China—is a valid observation, the absolute level of growth of China's personal consumption is remarkably strong in a global context. The incremental contribution of Chinese consumers in USD terms to the global consumption of tradable goods started to exceed that of the U.S. in 2007. . . . Going forward, the incremental contribution of Chinese consumers to global consumption demand will probably begin to consistently exceed that for U.S. consumers even in terms of overall consumption." For an analysis of different possible trajectories for the growth of Chinese consumption rates over the next fifteen years, based on a base case (no new action to raise consumption), a policy case (full implementation of proconsumption measures already announced), and a stretch case (a push beyond the current agenda to implement broad changes in the economy's structure), see Janamitra Devan, Micah Rowland, and Jonathan Woetzel, "A Consumer Paradigm for China," McKinsey Global Institute, August 2009. In the base case, China's consumption would rise to 39 percent of GDP, a gain of just 3 percentage points above the current level, leaving the country heavily dependent on exports and government-led spending for continued growth. In the policy scenario, consumption could account for as much as 45 percent of GDP, still well below levels in other major economies. If China's leaders committed themselves to the more aggressive program of comprehensive reform envisioned in the stretch scenario, however, they could raise private consumption above 50 percent of GDP by 2025. The last trajectory would bring China's consumption rate into line with those in the developed nations of Europe and Asia.

126. Hillary Rodham Clinton, "Closing Remarks for U.S.-China Strategic and Economic Dialogue," Washington, July 28, 2009, www.state.gov/secretary/rm/2009a/july/126599. htm; Dexter Roberts and Pete Engardio, "China's Economy: Behind All the Hype," *BusinessWeek*, October 22, 2009. The authors state: "In separate papers published this autumn, the U.S.-China Business Council and the European Chamber of Commerce in China both identified rising protectionism and economic nationalism as pressing concerns for foreign companies doing business in the mainland." Pettis, *G20 Meetings*. Pettis writes: "Because it is virtually impossible for China to raise domestic demand quickly enough to compensate for the severe drop in U.S. consumption, protectionism threatens to harm China more than it would harm any other major country." Tinge of Protectionism Caps Asian Advance," *Forbes*, March 18, 2009, www.forbes. com/2009/03/18/briefing-asia-closing-markets-equity-coke.html; Robert McMahon, "No End of Free Trade," *Newsweek*, December 4, 2008, www.newsweek.com/id/172072/page/1. Frank Bajak, "APEC Leaders: Trade Protectionism Is Road to Ruin," *Guardian*, November 23, 2009, www.guardian.co.uk/uslatest/story/0,,-8067325,00.html; Nelson D. Schwartz, "World Leaders Wary of U.S. Economic Measures," *New York Times*, February 1, 2009, www.nytimes.com/2009/02/02/business/worldbusiness/02global.html?fta=y; Tim Weber, "Davos Finds No Answers to Crisis," BBC, February 1, 2009, http://news.bbc.co.uk/2/hi/business/davos/7863684.stm; Jonathan Weisman, "Obama, in Canada, Warns Against Protectionism," *Wall Street Journal*, February 20, 2009, http://online.wsj.com/article/SB123504260038621641.html; "China's Hu Urges Obama to Resist Protectionism," Agence France-Presse, January 1, 2009; Keidel, "China and the Global

Financial Crisis"; Chen Deming, "Protectionism Doesn't Pay," *Wall Street Journal Asia*, February 20, 2009, http://online.wsj.com/article/SB123506269775323999.html; Mark Landler, "Trade Barriers Rise as the Recession's Grip Tightens," *New York Times*, March 23, 2009; and Fallows, "China's Way Forward." Fallows states that "China's government is unlikely to rely on outright Smoot-Hawley–style tariffs. Instead it could increase subsidies to exporters; it could try to push the RMB's value back down, after three years of letting the currency rise; it could encourage manufacturers to restrain wages; it could impose indirect barriers to imports, as with its recent pressure on China's airlines to cancel outstanding orders for Boeing and Airbus airplanes. By early this year, China's government was in fact doing every one of these things. . . . The worst would be for China to start a trade war that makes things even harder for itself."

127. Robert Cookson and Michael Mackenzie, "Beijing's Rebalancing Raises Fears for Treasuries," *Financial Times*, February 19, 2010; Wayne M. Morrison and Marc Labonte, "China's Holdings of U.S. Securities: Implications for the U.S. Economy," U.S. Congressional Research Service, May 19, 2008; Pacific Economic Cooperation Council, "Impact of the Global Financial Crisis on the Asia Pacific Region and Economic Outlook," in *State of the Region Report 2008–2009* (Singapore: Pacific Economic Cooperation Council, 2008), www.pecc.org/sotr/papers/SOTR-2008-Economic-Outlook.pdf; Robert Peston, "How Long Will China Finance America?" BBC, July 15, 2009, www.bbc.co.uk/blogs/thereporters/robertpeston/2009/07/how_long_will_china_finance_am.html; Agence France-Presse, "China Calls for Reform of Global Monetary System," April 26, 2009; Wines, Bradsher, and Landler, "China's Leader Says He Is 'Worried' "; Julian Delasantellis, "U.S. Fed's Move Is the Bigger Problem," *Asia Times*, March 21, 2009, www.atimes.com/atimes/Global_Economy/KC21Dj03.html; Keith Bradsher, "China to Shun West's Finance Sector," *New York Times*, December 3, 2008; Glenn Somerville and Zhou Xin, "China Urges U.S. to Do All It Can to Tame Crisis," Reuters, December 4, 2008; Brad Setser and Nouriel Roubini, "How Scary Is the Deficit?" *Foreign Affairs*, vol. 84, no. 4, July/August 2005.

128. Brad Setser and Nouriel Roubini, "How Scary Is the Deficit?" *Foreign Affairs*, vol. 84, no. 4, July/August 2005; Pacific Economic Cooperation Council, "Impact of the Global Financial Crisis"; Somerville and Zhou, "China Urges U.S. to Do All It Can."

129. Daniel W. Drezner, "Political, Diplomatic, and Security Implications of U.S. Debt to China," testimony before the U.S.-China Economic and Security Review Commission, hearing on U.S. Debt to China: Implications and Repercussions, Washington, February 25, 2010, www.uscc.gov/hearings/2010hearings/written_testimonies/10_02_25_wrt/10_02_25_drezner_statement.php; Simon Johnson, "Panel I: China's Lending Activities and the U.S. Debt," testimony before the U.S.-China Economic & Security Review Commission, hearing on "U.S. Debt to China: Implications and Repercussions," Washington, February 25, 2010, www.uscc.gov/hearings/2010hearings/written_testimonies/10_02_25_wrt/10_02_25_johnson_statement.pdf; Wayne M. Morrison and Marc Labonte, "China's Holdings of U.S. Securities: Implications for the U.S. Economy," U.S. Congressional Research Service, May 19, 2008; James Fallows, "The $1.4 Trillion Question," *Atlantic Monthly*, January–February 2008, www.theatlantic.com/doc/200801/fallows-chinese-dollars; and Frank Langfitt, "China's Effect on Dollar Reflects Growing Influence," NPR, November 8, 2007, www.npr.org/templates/story/story.php?storyId=16126258. Langfitt writes, citing Nick Lardy: "If China were to dump

dollars, it would hurt the U.S. currency. But because China is now so linked to the American and global economies, Nicholas Lardy says, it would pay a price for doing so. China depends on American consumers to buy its exports. 'It has a very strong interest in high economic growth in the United States because that's what generates our demand for imported goods, which is what generates the demand for China's exports,' Lardy says. 'China, for the last couple of years, has been the third-largest trading economy on the globe,' he says. 'They have the world's largest foreign exchange reserves; they are participating in all of the international financial institutions, which they were absent from.' And that integration has benefits for the United States. Cheap Chinese exports have helped keep inflation low, and China's purchase of treasury bonds has helped finance American debt."

130. Dune Lawrence and Kevin Hamlin, "China to Keep Buying Treasuries, Top Official Says," Bloomberg, March 23, 2009, www.bloomberg.com/apps/news?pid=20601087&si d=aUTIiOnyg6LQ&refer=home.

131. Zhou Xiaochuan, "Reform the International Monetary System," People's Bank of China, March 23, 2009, www.pbc.gov.cn/publish/english/956/2009/ 20091229104425550619706/20091229104425550619706_.html.

132. Ibid.; Elaine Kurtenback, "China Challenges U.S. Global Financial Leadership," *Washington Post*, May 27, 2009, www.washingtonpost.com/wp-dyn/content/article/ 2009/03/27/AR2009032701363.html?nav=rss_business/industries; Agence France-Press, "China Calls for Reform." Non-Chinese observers have also called for a need to create an alternative reserve currency using a multi-currency framework and IMF-based SDRs. See Jeffrey Garten, "We Must Get Ready for a Weak-Dollar World," *Financial Times*, November 30, 2009, www.ft.com/cms/s/0/d7c5b756-dd14-11de-ad60-00144feabdc0.html.

133. Kurtenback, "China Challenges U.S."

134. Indeed, even though China's exchange rate appreciated significantly during the period 2005–2008, the trade imbalance with the U.S. continued to grow rapidly, in part because over 60 percent of the value of China's exports to the U.S. consist of components imported from other nations. This suggests the need to examine a wide range of exchange rates (not just the U.S.-China rate) in order to assess the impact of a change in the bilateral rate; correspondence with Ken Lieberthal.

135. Niall Ferguson and Moritz Schularick, "The Great Wallop," *New York Times*, November 16, 2009; Yardley, "After 30 Years of Reform."

136. Albert Keidel, "The Global Economic Crisis and China's Response," paper delivered at Conference on "China Faces the Future," sponsored by Brookings Institution and the Institute of International Relations at National Chengchi University, Washington, July 14–15, 2009, www.brookings.edu/~/media/Files/events/2009/0714_china/0715_china_ keidel_paper.pdf.

137. Belinda Cao and Patricia Lui, "Yuan Gains on Signs China's Central Bank Prefers Appreciation," Bloomberg, June 30, 2010; Bettina Wassener, "China Lets Its Currency Hit a New High Against the Dollar Just Ahead of a G-20 Meeting," *New York Times*, June 25, 2010. This article cites Bill Belchere, global economist at Mirae Asset in Hong Kong, stating that frictions over the currency issue were unlikely to dissipate. "Unless China allows the renminbi to move much more aggressively than we anticipate, global

trade imbalances, which are already re-emerging, will continue to worsen," Belchere wrote. "This will heighten trade tensions and intensify volatility in global debt and foreign exchange markets." Also see William Pesek, "China Turns Tables on AAA Debt Time-Bomb Nations," Bloomberg, June 20, 2010. Pesek states: "It's wrong to conclude China was browbeaten into acting. Yes, the step means Chinese officials can breathe easier arriving in Toronto for next weekend's Group of 20 meeting. Yet a rising yuan will make it easier to tame asset bubbles and reduce inflation risks. It also increases the purchasing power for the nation's 1.3 billion people. Efforts to kick China's addiction to exports are now underway."

138. Timothy Geithner, U.S. Secretary of the Treasury, "The Path Ahead for the U.S.-China Economic Relationship," Remarks at Johns Hopkins University's School for Advanced International Studies, January 12, 2011, www.treasury.gov/press-center/press-releases/Pages/tg1019.aspx; Michael Casey, "Q&A: Peterson Institute's Bergsten on China's Currency," Wall Street Journal, February 18, 2011.

139. See Yukon Huang, "China's Currency Change Isn't Necessarily a Win for the United States," Q&A, Carnegie Endowment for International Peace, June 25, 2010, www.carnegieendowment.org/publications/index.cfm?fa=view&id=41065#rebalance. Huang argues that appreciation of the renminbi by itself probably will not alter the U.S. trade position, and some would argue that the United States may come out worse in the process—the cost of its imports will be higher, the cost of U.S. final products will rise, consumption may be hurt in the process, and there may even be a small decline in real wages in the United States because prices will go up, but earnings will not go up as much. So, the outcomes that may come from this in terms of its impact on U.S. welfare are potentially more negative than positive. I am indebted to Rachel Esplin Odell for this summary.

140. Martin Wolf, "Why China's Exchange Rate Policy Concerns Us," Financial Times, December 8, 2009. Wolf writes: "For the external deficit countries, the concern is how to lower fiscal deficits without tipping their economies back into recession. That will be impossible unless they are either able to get their private sectors spending and borrowing as before, or they enjoy rapid expansion in net exports. Of the two, the latter is the safer route to health. But that in turn, will only happen if surplus countries expand demand faster than potential output. China is the most important single player in this game."

141. Allison Jackson, "China Expected to Appreciate Yuan," Agence France-Presse, January 17, 2010; Euromonitor International, "Chinese Consumers in 2020: A Look into the Future," March 11, 2009, www.euromonitor.com/Chinese_consumers_in_2020_A_look_into_the_future. "By the year 2020, China will have a population of more than 1.4 billion people that will make up a significant portion in the world's consumer market. The annual disposable income of Chinese consumers is forecasted to increase to 65.4 billion yuan (US$9.57 billion) by 2020 compared with 15 billion yuan (US$2.19) in 2008." Somerville and Zhou, "China Urges U.S. to Do All It Can"; David D. Hale and Lyric Hughes Hale, "Reconsidering Revaluation," Foreign Affairs, vol. 87, no. 1 (January–February 2008); Keidel, "China and the Global Financial Crisis"; Setser and Roubini, "How Scary Is the Deficit?"; National Intelligence Council, Mapping the Global Future, Report of the National Intelligence Council's 2020 Project (Washington, D.C.: National Intelligence Council, 2004): "Rapidly rising income levels for a growing middle class will combine to mean a huge consumption explosion, which is already evident."

142. Bettina Wassener, "World Bank Lowers Growth Forecast for China," *International Herald Tribune*, March 18, 2009, www.iht.com/articles/2009/03/18/business/yuan.php; Pacific Economic Cooperation Council, "Impact of the Global Financial Crisis"; Wang Yong, "Domestic Demand and Continued Reform: China's Search for a New Model," *Global Asia*, vol. 3, no. 4 (Winter 2008): 24–28; and Keidel, "China and the Global Financial Crisis." Some economists argue that Beijing's growth stimulus policies will actually hurt domestic consumption in the long run. See Michael Pettis, "Is China Turning Japanese?" *Foreign Policy*, August 19, 2010.

143. U.S.-China Business Council, "U.S. Congressional District Exports to China: 2000–2009 111th Congress," Executive Summary, 2010, www.uschina.org/public/exports/2000_2009/files/US_Cong_Dist_Export_Summary.pdf; International Trade Administration, U.S. Department of Commerce, "Global Patterns of U.S. Merchandise Trade," TradeStats Express, 2010, http://tse.export.gov/TSE/TSEReports.aspx?DATA=NTD; U.S.-China Business Council, "U.S.-China Trade in Context," 2008, www.uschina.org/public/documents/2008/04/us-china_trade_in_context_2008.pdf; Keidel, "China and the Global Financial Crisis." Keidel, *China's Economic Rise*. Chinese citizens are rapidly gaining purchasing power and will become a giant market. Wayne M. Morrison, "China–U.S. Trade Issues," Congressional Research Service, July 29, 2010, www.fas.org/sgp/crs/row/RL33536.pdf.

144. After a decline in growth of 2.6 percent in 2009, the U.S. GDP growth rate in 2010 rebounded to around 2.8 percent, according to the CIA World Factbook, "United States," https://www.cia.gov/library/publications/the-world-factbook/geos/us.html. Most economists are projecting around a 2.5–3 percent GDP growth rate for the United States in 2011 (but not 1 or 2 percent). Chinese GDP growth was 10 percent in 2010. And most observers (barring the bearish Michael Pettis) do not foresee Chinese growth dropping to as low as 5 or 6 percent in the next three to five years, though it may decline to 7 or 8 percent. (The World Bank predicts 8.7 percent Chinese GDP growth in 2011, and 8.4 percent in 2012. See Hu Yuanyuan, "China's GDP growth forecast to slow down: WB," *China Daily*, January 14, 2011, http://news.xinhuanet.com/english2010/china/2011-01/14/c_13690152.htm). Also see Keidel, "China and the Global Financial Crisis"; Keidel, *China's Economic Rise*; Fareed Zakaria, "Wanted: A New Grand Strategy," *Newsweek*, November 29, 2008.

145. Ashley J. Tellis, "The Economic Crisis and the Future of U.S. Power," in *Strategic Asia 2009–10: Economic Meltdown and Geopolitical Stability*, edited by Ashley J. Tellis, Andrew Marble, and Travis Tanner (Seattle: National Bureau of Asian Research, 2009). Tellis states: "Sustaining U.S. hegemony over the long run will require engineering a controlled global adjustment of the international economic system that does not put the U.S. at an inordinate economic and geopolitical disadvantage."

146. National Intelligence Council, *Global Trends 2025*. "By 2025, international migration's human capital and technological transfer effects will begin to favor the most stable Asian and Latin American countries." Mercy Kuo, Andrew D. Marble, David M. Lampton, Cheng Li, Pieter Bottelier, and Fenggang Yang, "Roundtable: China in the Year 2020," *Asia Policy*, July 2007, no. 4, 1–52.

147. See, in particular, Alastair Iain Johnston, "Is China Rising?" (with Sheena Chestnut) in *Is China Changing the Rules of the Game?* edited by Eva Paus, Penelope Prime, and Jon Western (New York: Palgrave Macmillan 2009). The authors state that "China's power

as a proportion of U.S. power is increasing, but the absolute advantage in capabilities favoring America continues to widen. China and the U.S. have not yet reached the tipping point indicating the beginning of rising Chinese power. This pattern holds for a wide range of standard indicators that one might use to measure power capabilities—economic (GDP), military (military spending), and scientific-technological metrics." Until around 2015–2016, the size of the U.S. economy actually increases relative to China's; that is, the absolute difference between the U.S. and Chinese economies increases in the U.S. favor. After that point, only then does the Chinese economy begin to close the gap and catch up to the size of the United States, eventually equaling the U.S. economy in about 2033–2035.

148. Pieter Bottelier, "The Financial Crisis and Sino-American Relations," *Asia Policy*, no. 9 (January 2010): 121–31. Bottelier writes: The global economic crisis "will almost certainly accelerate China's economic and political rise and enhance its prestige in the developing world. . . . It is also likely that China will be more inclined to exercise global leadership in economic/financial arenas. . . . China now prides itself on not having followed US advice to accelerate financial sector reform and opening." Clyde Prestowitz, " 'Chindia' Levels the Playing Field," *Current History*, vol. 105, no. 690 (April 2006): 148–49. Paul Kennedy, "American Power Is on the Wane," *Wall Street Journal*, January 14, 2009. Kennedy argues that "the U.S. is going to take a bigger hit than any other country in the coming years for a few reasons. First, the U.S. budget and trade deficit is huge and will continue to grow rapidly. Second, and related, the U.S. will ultimately be dependent on foreign investors and other countries to cover the debt. Third, while US growth stagnates, China and India will continue to grow quickly, shifting relative global power. Fourth, amidst economic downturn, the U.S. will suffer from trying to sustain its tremendous overseas commitments and deployments—'imperial overstretch.'" Leslie H. Gelb, "Necessity, Choice, and Common Sense," *Foreign Affairs*, vol. 88, no. 3 (May–June 2009): 56–72: "The United States is in danger of becoming merely first among major powers and heading to a level somewhere between its current still-exalted position and that of China today. . . . The bases of the United States' international power are the country's economic competitiveness and its political cohesion, and there should be little doubt at this point that both are in decline."

149. Minxin Pei, "Think Again: Asia's Rise," *Foreign Policy*, July–August 2009, 32–36. Roberts and Engardio, "China's Economy"; National Intelligence Council, *Global Trends 2025*. "Although we believe chances are good that China and India will continue to rise, their ascent is not guaranteed and will require overcoming high economic and social hurdles. Because of this, both countries are likely to remain inwardly focused and per capita wealth will lag substantially behind Western economies throughout the period to 2025 and beyond. Individuals in these emerging economic powerhouses are likely to feel still poor in relation to Westerners even though their collective GDP increasingly will outdistance those of individual Western states." Alan Wheatley, "Age Wave to Come Crashing Soon Over China's Economy," Reuters, April 27, 2009, www.reuters.com/article/reutersEdge/idustre53q18h20090427. According to the UN, China's working-age population will peak in 2015 and plunge by 23 percent by 2050. By then, there will be 438 million Chinese aged 60 or over, or 61 for every 100 adults of working age, up from just 16 in 2005. A recent Center for Strategic and International Studies report, cited in this story, concludes that by the 2030s, the shrinkage of China's working-age population will be lopping 0.7 points a year off growth, while the shortage

of females will reduce consumption and place ever greater burdens on China's old-age support system, requiring major expenditures on a national, fully portable system of funded retirement accounts. Ian Johnson, "China Faces a Grad Glut After Boom at Colleges," *Wall Street Journal*, April 28, 2009, http://online.wsj.com/article/SB124087181303261033.html.

150. G. John Ikenberry, "The Rise of China and the Future of the West: Can the Liberal System Survive?" *Foreign Affairs*, vol. 87, no. 1 (January–February 2008). Ikenberry adds that "if China intends to rise up and challenge the existing order, it has a much more daunting task than simply confronting the United States."

151. For a recent discussion of this trend, see James Kynge, "Central Plot of China–U.S. Ties Faces Off-Stage Challenge," *Financial Times*, January 8, 2010. Kynge cite a recent upsurge in China's trade with Southeast Asia and the "newly-rising economies" of Brazil, Africa, and India. He writes: "Although Chinese trade with these places has historically been limited, it has grown so fast in the past five years that a robust performance in 2010 may be enough to offset any moderate weakness in China's trade with the U.S." The operative phrase here is "may be." It remains unclear to what degree Chinese economic diversification will significantly affect China's policies toward the U.S. But it certainly is an important issue that bears close watching.

152. Courtney Lakroix, "Burkle Hosts Symposium," *Daily Bruin*, February 2, 2009, www.international.ucla.edu/article.asp?parentid=104230; Frank Langfitt, "China's Effect on Dollar Reflects Growing Influence," NPR, November 8, 2007, www.npr.org/templates/story/story.php?storyId=16126258; UCLA Asian American Studies Center, "Impact of China's Economic Growth on the United States," 2008, www.aasc.ucla.edu/uschina/econ_whatsahead.shtml#two.

153. According to the IEA, this occurred in the first half of 2007; China officially claims that it occurred in 2009. International Energy Agency, "World Energy Outlook 2007: Fact Sheet - China," www.iea.org/papers/2007/fs_china.pdf; Yu Hongyan, "China becomes a net coal importer in 2009," *China Daily*, February 23, 2010, www.chinadaily.com.cn/bizchina/2010-02/23/content_9490004.htm.

154. IEA, *World Energy Outlook 2010*; Krauss, "In Global Forecast, China Looms Large"; U.S. EIA, *Country Analysis Brief: China, Oil*; Bo Kong, "Assessing China's Energy Security," presentation at Center for Strategic and International Studies, October 26, 2010, http://csis.org/files/attachments/102610_Bkong_0.pdf. Also see Daniel H. Rosen and Trevor Houser, *China Energy: A Guide for the Perplexed*, Joint Project by the Center for Strategic Studies and the Peterson Institute for International Economics, May 2007, 1–49; Michael T. Klare, "Fueling the Dragon: China's Strategic Energy Dilemma," *Current History*, vol. 105, no. 690 (April 2006): 180–85; Bradley A. Thayer, "Confronting China: An Evaluation of Options for the United States," *Comparative Strategy*, vol. 24, no. 1 (January–March 2005): 71–98; Downs, *China*; Lee Geng, "The Saudis Take a Chinese Wife," *Energy Tribune*, November 3, 2008, www.energytribune.com/articles.cfm?aid=1007; and David Shambaugh, "Beijing's Thrust into Latin America," *International Herald Tribune*, November 20, 2008.

155. Andrew Erickson, Gabe Collins, "Beijing's Energy Security Strategy: The Significance of a Chinese State-Owned Tanker Fleet," *Orbis*, vol. 51, no. 4 (Fall 2007): 665–84; David Zweig and Bi Jianhai, "China's Global Hunt for Energy," *Foreign Affairs*, vol. 84, no. 5 (September–October 2005); National Intelligence Council, *Global Trends 2025*;

Larry Wortzel and Admiral Joseph W. Prueher, "Agenda 2008: A New Look at the U.S.-China Relationship," Center for the Study of the Presidency. For a recent story on Chinese acquisitions of overseas holdings in the energy and other sectors, described as part of a disturbing attempt to "lock up" supplies of such resources, see Ariana Eunjung Cha, "China Gains Key Assets in Spate of Purchases," *Washington Post*, March 17, 2009. Also see David Pilling, "China Flexes New Economic Muscle at Sea," *Financial Times*, April 22, 2009, www.ft.com/cms/s/0/c467c848-2f63-11de-a8f6-00144feabdc0.html; Chris Alden, "South Africa and China: Forging Africa's Strategic Partnership," *China Brief*, no. 13 (June 24, 2008), www.jamestown.org/programs/chinabrief/single/?tx_ttnews%5Btt_news%5D=5001&tx_ttnews%5BbackPid%5D=168&no_cache=1. According to a 2008 report done by the National Intelligence Council, "China will continue to seek to buttress its market power by cultivating political relationships designed to safeguard its access to oil and gas. Beijing's ties with Saudi Arabia will strengthen, as the Kingdom is the only supplier capable of responding in a big way to China's petroleum thirst. . . . Sub-Saharan Africa will continue to be a major supplier of oil, gas, and metals to world markets and increasingly will attract the attention of Asian states seeking access to commodities, including China and India." National Intelligence Council, *Global Trends 2025*. Regarding rare earth elements, see Ambrose Evans-Pritchard, "World Faces Hi-Tech Crunch as China Eyes Ban on Rare Metal Exports," Telegraph (London), August 24, 2009; and "Worries Mount Over China's 'Rare Earth' Export Ban," EurActiv Network, June 9, 2010. Rare earth elements are used in the manufacturing of wind turbines, electronic consumer goods, nanotechnologies, batteries for electric cars, and various military applications. China produces more than 90 percent of existing supplies of such materials and is reportedly considering banning all exports, in response to growing domestic demand.

156. For a discussion of the challenges involved in protecting energy supply lines, see Michael D. Swaine, Andrew N. D. Yang, Evan S. Medeiros, and Oriana Skylar Mastro, eds., *Assessing the Threat: The Chinese Military and Taiwan's Security* (Washington, D.C.: Carnegie Endowment for International Peace, 2007).

157. Conversation with Erica Downs. For further analysis of the role that Chinese companies play in shaping China's energy policies, see Bo Kong, *China's International Petroleum Policy* (Santa Barbara, Calif.: Praeger Security International, 2010); Bo Kong, "China's Energy Decision-Making: Becoming more like the United States?" *Journal of Contemporary China*, vol. 18, no. 62 (2009): 789–812.

158. Jeffrey Herbst and Greg Mills, "Commodity Flux and China's Africa Strategy," *China Brief* 9, no. 2 (January 22, 2009), www.jamestown.org/programs/chinabrief/single/?tx_ttnewstt_news=34388&tx_ttnewsbackPid=414&no_cache=1; Ellis, "China's Maturing Relationship. Ellis states: "In the short to medium term, the recession is likely to severely strain China's relationship with Latin America. The PRC is likely to reduce its purchase of primary products from Latin America, while simultaneously seeking to boost its sale of goods there to compensate for lost sales to its traditional customers in the United States and Europe. This will exacerbate the existing trade deficit. The diminishing benefits of the PRC as a customer of Latin American goods, in combination with heightened competition from China as a major seller—as Latin American producers teeter on the edge of solvency—is likely to strengthen political forces with the social constituency in the region critical of trade with China."

159. Alex Vines, Lillian Wong, et al., *Thirst for African Oil: Asian National Oil Companies in Nigeria and Angola* (London: Chatham House, 2009). According to Erica Downs, some of the most attractive blocks in Nigeria and Angola lie deep in the Gulf of Guinea and none of the Asian oil corporations (including China) have deepwater drilling capabilities. In addition, although both Angola and Nigeria are working to diversify the number of foreign entities, neither country intends to let China play a dominant role. Private correspondence.

160. The United States accounted for 33.5 percent of Venezuela's foreign trade in 2009; China only accounted for 6.8 percent. European Union Directorate General for Trade, "Venezuela Trade Statistics EU Bilateral Trade and Trade with the World," January 18, 2011, http://trade.ec.europa.eu/doclib/docs/2006/september/tradoc_113462.pdf. See also Ratliff, "An Assessment of China's Deepening Ties"; J. F. Hornbeck and Marisabel Cid, "U.S.-Latin America Trade: Recent Trends," Congressional Research Service, July 18, 2008, http://fas.org/sgp/crs/row/98-840.pdf.

161. Conversation with Erica Downs; Downs, China, 16; Kenneth Lieberthal and Mikkal Herberg, "China's Search for Energy Security: Implications for U.S. Policy," *NBR Analysis*, vol. 17, no. 1 (April 2006); Institute for National Strategic Studies, "Project on the Next East Asia Security Strategy: Workshop #4 Summary," September 2008, 1–19. As this draft report states: "There is no particular advantage to China in bilateral energy relationships or alliances unless the Chinese feel excluded from the world energy market. . . . China is most concerned with stability in Middle East. Demand shock isn't a problem because there is a price mechanism to allow adjustments. China probably sees supply shocks as the most dangerous. The best way to avoid shocks is through cooperation."

162. Erica S. Downs, "Who's Afraid of China's Oil Companies?" in *Energy Security: Economics, Politics, Strategies, and Implications*, edited by Carlos Pascual and Jonathan Elkind (Washington, D.C.: Brookings Institution Press, 2009), 88–89.

163. Stephanie Hanson, "China, Africa, and Oil," *Council on Foreign Relations*, June, 2008, www.cfr.org/publication/9557/china_africa_and_oil.html. Also see Stephanie Kleine-Ahlbrandt and Andrew Small, "China's New Dictatorship Diplomacy," *Foreign Affairs*, January–February 2008, www.foreignaffairs.com/articles/63045/stephanie-kleine-ahlbrandt-and-andrew-small/chinas-new-dictatorship-diplomacy. The authors state: "Beijing's recent handling of the situation in Sudan shows that it is learning the limitations of noninterference, however much that principle remains part of its official rhetoric. China has found noninterference increasingly unhelpful as it learns the perils of tacitly entrusting its business interests to repressive governments."

164. See Erica S. Downs and Jeffrey A. Bader, "Oil-Hungry China Belongs at Big Table," Brookings Institution, September 8, 2006, www.brookings.edu/opinions/2006/0908china_bader.aspx. Concerning the issue of rare earth elements, Beijing has vigorously denied that it intends to ban the export of such materials. Instead, it is apparently attempting to gain greater control over their production and distribution primarily in order to counter the high level of illegal smuggling that plagues this industry in China. Beijing is also considering creating a strategic reserve of certain rare earth elements to reduce price fluctuations and shortages. One Western consulting source has stated outright that reports of Beijing's intent to ban or severely restrict the export of rare earth elements in order to maximize domestic use are "unfounded."

See Damien Ma and Divvya Reddy, *China: Rare Earth Supplies Won't Be Rare in Near Term*, Eurasia Group Note, October 15, 2009. Moreover, both Western countries and China are moving to secure new sources of rare earths, with some companies opening or reopening mines in California, Canada, South Africa, and Greenland. And at least one source asserts that estimates of likely long-term supplies of these materials will prove sufficient to meet projected global demand. See Marc Humphries, "Rare Earth Elements: the Global Supply Chain," CRS Report for Congress, Washington, September 30, 2010, www.fas.org/sgp/crs/natsec/R41347.pdf. Also see Cathy Proctor, "Molycorp gets OK for rare-earths processing plant," *Denver Business Journal*, December 13, 2010; Cahal Milmo, "Concern as China Clamps Down on Rare Earth Exports," *Independent* (London), January 2, 2010. In other words, the situation is not necessarily as grave or threatening as some reports suggest, and China's policy is apparently not driven by a "mercantilist" impulse.

165. Conversation with Erica Downs; Lieberthal and Herberg, "China's Search for Energy Security"; Klare, "Fueling the Dragon," 180–85; Twomey, "Missing Strategic Opportunity"; Müller-Kraenner, *China's and India's Emerging Energy Foreign Policy*. David Shambaugh, "Beijing's Thrust into Latin America," *International Herald Tribune*, November 20, 2008.

166. Beijing also resists such approaches because they are viewed as in many cases ineffective and a threat to the principle of national sovereignty, as discussed in chapter 8 and elsewhere in this study.

167. David Pierson, "Libyan strife exposes China's risks in global quest for oil," *Los Angeles Times*, March 9, 2011, www.latimes.com/business/la-fi-china-oil-20110310,0,6747704. story; Larry Wortzel and Admiral Joseph W. Prueher, "Agenda 2008: A New Look at the U.S.-China Relationship," Center for the Study of the Presidency, sent in an email to Michael Swaine, February 24, 2009; Henry Meyer and Ellen Pinchuk, "Russia Has Contacted Obama Aides to Pursue Iran Nuclear Deal," Bloomberg, November 26, 2008, www.bloomberg.com/apps/news?pid=20601085&sid=aMVpq97zAFIo&refer=europe; Lee Geng, "The Saudis Take a Chinese Wife."

CHAPTER 6

1. I am deeply indebted to Evan Medeiros for his assistance in the preparation of parts of the analysis of WMD proliferation contained in this chapter.

2. For a solid, general overview of Bush counterterrorism policies in East Asia, see Bronson Percival, "Countering Terrorism in East Asia," in *America's Role in Asia: Asian and American Views*, Michael Armacost, J. Stapleton Roy, Han Sung-Joo, Tommy Koh, C. Raja Mohan, project chairs (San Francisco: Asia Foundation, 2008), 243–51.

3. A wide variety of U.S. and Chinese agencies have participated in this dialogue, including, on the U.S. side, representatives from the State Department, Treasury Department, Department of Justice, Department of Defense, Department of Homeland Security, Department of Energy, Federal Bureau of Investigation, and National Counterterrorism Center. The Chinese delegation has included representatives from the Ministry of Foreign Affairs; Ministry of State Security; Ministry of Public Security; Ministry of National Defense; People's Bank of China; General Administration of

Quality, Supervision, Inspection, and Quarantine Supervision; General Administration of Customs and Inspections; and General Administration of Civil Aviation of China.

4. Renato Cruz De Castro, "U.S. War on Terror in East Asia: The Perils of Preemptive Defense in Waging a War of the Third Kind," *Asian Affairs*, vol. 31, no. 4 (2005): 212–31. Also see Shirley A. Kan, "U.S.-China Counterterrorism Cooperation: Issues for U.S. Policy," CRS Report for Congress, July 15, 2010, www.fas.org/sgp/crs/terror/RL33001.pdf.

5. Charlie Savage, "Obama's War on Terror May Resemble Bush's in Some Areas," *New York Times*, February 18, 2009; David E. Sanger, "Obama After Bush: Leading by Second Thought," *New York Times*, May 16, 2009; Jack Goldsmith, "The Cheney Fallacy," *New Republic*, May 18, 2009, www.tnr.com/article/politics/the-cheney-fallacy?id=1e733cac-c273-48e5-9140-80443ed1f5c2&p=1. Goldsmith writes: "The [Obama] administration has copied most of the Bush [counterterrorism] program, has expanded some of it, and has narrowed only a bit. Almost all of the Obama changes have been at the level of packaging, argumentation, symbol, and rhetoric." Obama officials do not accept such a judgment, of course. They emphasize that their policies place a greater emphasis on working with other nations and (especially multinational organizations such as the UN) to combat terrorism, and on dealing with the underlying political and other grievances that terrorists use to build support around the world. See Daniel Benjamin, "International Counterterrorism Policy in the Obama Administration: Developing a Strategy for the Future," remarks at the International Peace Institute, New York, March 1, 2010, www.state.gov/s/ct/rls/rm/2010/137865.htm.

6. Andrew Small, "China's Caution on Afghanistan–Pakistan," *Washington Quarterly*, vol. 33, no. 3 (July 2010): 81–97, www.twq.com/10july/docs/10jul_Small.pdf; Bureau of Public Affairs; Office of the Spokesman, U.S. Department of State, "Joint Press Release on the First Round of the U.S.-China Strategic and Economic Dialogue," Washington, D.C., July 28, 2009, www.state.gov/r/pa/prs/ps/2009/july/126596.htm; Kan, "U.S.-China Counterterrorism Cooperation," 31–33.

7. Personal correspondence with Evan Medeiros. Also see Michael D. Swaine, "China and the 'AfPak' Issue," *China Leadership Monitor*, no. 31 (Winter 2010), www.hoover.org/publications/clm/issues/84429922.html.

8. For further detail, see Evan S. Medeiros, *Reluctant Restraint: The Evolution of China's Nonproliferation Policies and Practices, 1980–2004* (Stanford, Calif.: Stanford University Press, 2007).

9. The Bush approach and its consequences are detailed in the conclusion by Medeiros, *Reluctant Restraint*, 240–65. The term "entities" is employed by the U.S. government to describe the targeted organizations because of the uncertainty of their status as independent commercial enterprises versus government-directed agencies.

10. See John R. Bolton, undersecretary of state for arms control and international security, "Coordinating Allied Approaches to China," U.S. Department of State, remarks co-sponsored by the Tokyo American Center and the Japan Institute for International Affairs, Tokyo, Japan, February 7, 2005, http://2001-2009.state.gov/t/us/rm/41938. htm. Also see Shirley A. Kan, "China and Proliferation of Weapons of Mass Destruction and Missiles: Policy Issues," CRS Report for Congress, March 3, 2011, www.fas.org/sgp/crs/nuke/RL31555.pdf; John Bolton, undersecretary of state for arms control and international security, "Press Conference on U.S.-China Security Dialogue," U.S.

Department of State, July 28, 2003, http://2001-2009.state.gov/t/us/rm/22917.htm; and personal correspondence with Evan Medeiros.

11. In addition, 14 of these entities are sanctioned as "persons who commit, threaten to commit, or support terrorism"; 59 of these entities are sanctioned as significant foreign narcotics traffickers; five are sanctioned for obstructing democracy in Belarus, and one is a former Iraqi official now in Beijing sanctioned as a member of Saddam Hussein's regime. See Office of Foreign Assets Control, U.S. Department of the Treasury, "Specially Designated Nationals and Blocked Persons," April 4, 2011, www.treasury.gov/ofac/downloads/t11sdn.pdf; and Office of Foreign Assets Control, U.S. Department of the Treasury, "SDN List by Country," www.treasury.gov/ofac/downloads/ctrylst.txt.

12. Both administrations have also sought to convince or compel Beijing to reduce or end its sale of conventional weapons to both Iran and North Korea. See Kan, "U.S.-China Counterterrorism Cooperation," 34–36.

13. The PSI emerged in response to a U.S. concern that existing laws and treaties designed to severely reduce or end global WMD proliferation had failed, and that the threat posed by such proliferation had increased markedly, in light of the discovery of the A. Q. Khan illicit nuclear trade network, the worsening North Korea nuclear crisis, and the emergence of more capable nonstate terrorist organizations interested in acquiring weapons of mass destruction. The PSI embodies a set of principles and activities—agreed to by more than 15 core nations (including the United States, Russia, Japan, France, Germany, and the United Kingdom) and supported by more than 60 other states—that is aimed at interdicting the transfer via air, land, or sea of WMD, their delivery systems, and related materials to and from nation-states and nonstate actors of proliferation concern. Most notably, the PSI enhances law enforcement cooperation and intelligence sharing among states and provides a basis for permitting the interception and search of suspect naval vessels in international waters. The PSI is a voluntary political commitment—not a formal treaty-based organization—that is to be activated when a particular need arises and is supposedly consistent with national legal authorities and relevant international law and frameworks. See Mark J. Valencia, *The Proliferation Security Initiative: Making Waves in Asia*, Adelphi Paper 376 (London: International Institute for Strategic Studies, 2005); Mark J. Valencia, "The Proliferation Security Initiative: A Glass Half-Full," *Arms Control Today*, vol. 37, no. 5 (2007): 17–21; "The Proliferation Security Initiative (PSI) At a Glance," *Arms Control Today*, October 2007, www.armscontrol.org/factsheets/PSI.asp; and John R. Bolton, undersecretary of state for arms control and international security, "International Security Issues, Arms Control Matters, and Nonproliferation," U.S. Department of State, February 16, 2004, http://2001-2009.state.gov/t/us/rm/29723.htm.

14. Kurt M. Campbell, "Press Availability in Beijing, China," remarks in Beijing, October 14, 2009, www.state.gov/p/eap/rls/rm/2009/10/130578.htm; John J. Norris, "China's Military and Security Activities Abroad," testimony before the U.S.-China Economic and Security Review Commission, Washington, D.C., March 4, 2009; Robert Burns, "Analysis: Obama Suggests Sanctions for Iran," *Washington Post*, July 10, 2009, www.washingtonpost.com/wp-dyn/content/article/2009/07/10/AR2009071002863.html; Daniel Dombey, James Blitz, and Harvey Morris, "China and Russia Face Pressure on Iran," *Financial Times*, November 30, 2009; Mark Landler, "Clinton Warns China on Iran Sanctions," *New York Times*, January 30, 2010; Paul Richter, "Clinton Warns

China to Stay the Course on Iran Nuclear Sanctions," *Los Angeles Times*, January 30, 2010; Helene Cooper and William J. Broad, "Russia and China Endorse Agency's Rebuke of Iran," *New York Times*, November 28, 2009; Glenn Kessler and Joby Warrick, "Latest U.N. Censure of Iran May Start More Confrontational Phase," *Washington Post*, November 28, 2009; Anthony Kuhn, "China Forced to Find Balance Between U.S., Iran," *NPR Morning Edition*, March 1, 2010. Washington has attempted to persuade China to back more punitive efforts against Iran by suggesting that a nuclear-armed Tehran might prompt an Israeli military strike or a nuclear arms race in the Persian Gulf, either of which could threaten China's political and commercial interests in the region. It has also suggested that China could face diplomatic isolation on the issue.

15. For example, see "Unserious on Iran Sanctions," *Wall Street Journal*, April 4, 2011, http://online.wsj.com/article/SB10001424052748703712504576236203773433900. html?mod=googlenews_wsj, 11; Josh Rogin, "Senators accuse China of violating sanctions against Iran," The Cable, *Foreign Policy*, January 18, 2011, http://thecable. foreignpolicy.com/posts/2011/01/18/senators_accuse_china_of_violating_sanctions_ against_iran; Christian Oliver, "U.S. Tells China Not to Exploit Sanctions on Iran," *Financial Times*, August 2, 2010, www.ft.com/cms/s/0/0253d046-9e28-11df-b377-00144feab49a.html; and Jason Dean, "U.S. Officials Head to Beijing to Ease Tensions," *Wall Street Journal*, September 3, 2010, http://online.wsj.com/article/SB10001424052748 703431604575467442190815072.html?mod=WSJ_World_MIDDLENews.

16. Ambassador Susan F. Burk, "Toward a Successful NPT Review Conference," remarks at the Carnegie Endowment for International Peace, Washington, D.C., March 31, 2010, www.state.gov/t/isn/rls/rm/139347.htm; Kingston Reif and Madeleine Foley, "Factsheet on the Fissile Material Cutoff Treaty (FMCT)," Center for Arms Control and Non-Proliferation, July 15, 2009, www.armscontrolcenter.org/policy/nuclearweapons/ articles/071509_factsheet_fmct; Office of the Press Secretary, White House, "Key Facts about the New START Treaty," March 26, 2009, www.whitehouse.gov/the-press-office/ key-facts-about-new-start-treaty; Barack Obama, "A New Beginning," speech at Cairo University in Cairo, June 4, 2009, www.whitehouse.gov/the_press_office/Remarks-by-the-President-at-Cairo-University-6-04-09; Office of the Press Secretary, "Remarks by President Barack Obama," speech at Hradcany Square in Prague, April 5, 2009, www. whitehouse.gov/the_press_office/Remarks-By-President-Barack-Obama-In-Prague-As-Delivered; Ellen Tauscher, "Arms Control and International Security," remarks to the U.S. Strategic Command Deterrence Symposium in Omaha, July 30, 2009, www. state.gov/t/us/126862.htm; U.S. Department of Defense, *Nuclear Posture Review Report* (Washington, D.C.: U.S. Government Printing Office, 2010), www.defense.gov/npr/ docs/2010%20Nuclear%20Posture%20Review%20Report.pdf. On Obama's remarks regarding the PSI, see Office of the Press Secretary, "Remarks by President Barack Obama," Hradcany Square in Prague. In July 2009, the Group of Eight released a statement endorsing Obama's vision for a strengthened PSI. See "L'Aquila Statement on Non-Proliferation," G8 Summit 2009, L'Aquila, Italy, July 8, 2009, www.g8italia2009.it/ static/G8_Allegato/2._LAquila_Statent_on_Non_proliferation.pdf.

17. Dong-Joon Jo and Erik Gartzke, "Determinants of Nuclear Weapons Proliferation," *Journal of Conflict Resolution*, vol. 51, no. 1 (2007): 167–94, http://dss.ucsd.edu/~egartzke/ publications/jo_gartzke_jcr_07.pdf. The authors state: "Ironically, our research implies that United States hegemony has the potential to encourage nuclear proliferation. The United States appears much more willing to intervene in contests that previously

would have invited opposition from the Soviet Union. States in the developing world can no longer look to the nuclear umbrella of the Soviet Union to protect them. The lack of a nuclear defender increases the willingness to proliferate, provided that a state possesses a nuclear program." For Chinese views highly critical of Bush policies in this area, see Yang Danpin and Jiang Liangguo, "Impacts of Iraq War on World Pattern," *Foreign Affairs* (Chinese People's Institute of Foreign Affairs), no. 68 (November 30, 2005), www.cpifa.org/en/Html/20051130142440-1.html; Hu Yumin, "Nuclear Weapon Issue Under the New Circumstances," *Foreign Affairs*, no. 83 (December 23, 2008), www.cpifa.org/en/Html/20081223232741-1.html; Jia Qingguo, "Unipolarity: Implications for China, the U.S. and the World," *International Review* (Shanghai Institutes for International Studies), Spring 2008, 29–44, www.siis.org.cn/Sh_Yj_Cms/Mgz/200801/200862418418SGL4.DOC; Jian Junbo, "A Clash of Civilization? Norms and Sino-EU Relations," *International Review*, Winter 2008, 53–84, www.siis.org.cn/Sh_Yj_Cms/Mgz/200804/2009326155417UX41.PDF; and Wang Yusheng, "One Tries to Manipulate World, the Other Wants Sovereign Democracy—Some Comments on Issue of the U.S. Turning to Focus Its Strike and Pressure on Russia," *Foreign Affairs*, no. 84 (December 23, 2008), www.cpifa.org/en/Html/20081223234040-1.html.

18. See, for example, George Perkovich, "The Road to Zero Nukes," *Guardian*, April 6, 2009, http://carnegieendowment.org/npp/publications/index.cfm?fa=view&id=22945&prog=zgp&proj=znpp; Sharon Squassoni, "Grading Progress on 13 Steps Toward Nuclear Disarmament," Policy Outlook, Carnegie Endowment for International Peace, May 2009, 1–10, http://carnegieendowment.org/files/13_steps.pdf; and People's Republic of China, "Arms Control and Disarmament: China's National Defense in 2008," 2008, www.china.org.cn/government/whitepaper/2009-01/21/content_17162787.htm. This official PRC report states: "China holds that all nuclear-weapon states should make an unequivocal commitment to the thorough destruction of nuclear weapons, undertake to stop research into and development of new types of nuclear weapons, and reduce the role of nuclear weapons in their national security policy. The two countries possessing the largest nuclear arsenals bear special and primary responsibility for nuclear disarmament. They should earnestly comply with the relevant agreements already concluded, and further drastically reduce their nuclear arsenals in a verifiable and irreversible manner, so as to create the necessary conditions for the participation of other nuclear-weapon states in the process of nuclear disarmament. . . . China maintains that the global missile defense program will be detrimental to strategic balance and stability, undermine international and regional security, and have a negative impact on the process of nuclear disarmament. China pays close attention to this issue."

19. See Office of the Press Secretary, "Remarks by President Barack Obama," Hradcany Square in Prague; and Hillary Rodham Clinton, "Remarks at the United States Institute of Peace," Washington, D.C., October 21, 2009. The NPR states: "The United States will not conduct nuclear testing and will pursue ratification and entry into force of the Comprehensive Nuclear Test Ban Treaty. . . . The United States will not develop new nuclear warheads. Life Extension Programs (LEPs) will use only nuclear components based on previously tested designs, and will not support new military missions or provide for new military capabilities. . . . The United States will not use or threaten to use nuclear weapons against non-nuclear-weapons states that are party to the NPT and in compliance with their nuclear nonproliferation obligations." See U.S. Department of Defense, *Nuclear Posture Review Report*.

20. See Swaine, "China and the 'AfPak' Issue"; Small, "China's Caution on Afghanistan—Pakistan"; Michael Swaine, "China: Exploiting a Strategic Opening," in *Strategic Asia 2004–05: Confronting Terrorism in the Pursuit of Power*, edited by Ashley J. Tellis and Michael Wills (Seattle: National Bureau of Asian Research, 2004), 67–101; and Office of the Coordinator for Counterterrorism, U.S. State Department, "Chapter 2. Country Reports: East Asia and Pacific Overview," *Country Reports on Terrorism 2007*, April 30, 2008, www.state.gov/s/ct/rls/crt/2007/103706.htm. Also see Kan, "U.S.-China Counterterrorism Cooperation"; and David M. Lampton and Richard Daniel Ewing, *The U.S.-China Relationship Facing International Security Crises: Three Case Studies in Post-9/11 Bilateral Relations* (Washington: Nixon Center, 2003). According to Lampton and Ewing (p. 2), China has three stakes in the global war on terrorism: (1) terrorism opens up a window of cooperation for Beijing and Washington; (2) terrorism poses a threat to trade and global economic performance; and (3) China is concerned that its separatists could be radicalized by external groups.

For a scholarly Chinese assessment of the value of the Shanghai Cooperation Organization to China in combating terrorism, see Pan Guang, "A Chinese Perspective on the Shanghai Cooperation Organization," in *The Shanghai Cooperation Organization as a Regional Security Institution*, SIPRI Policy Paper 17, edited by Alyson J. K. Bailes, Pál Dunay, Pan Guang, and Mikhail Troitskiy (Stockholm: Stockholm International Peace Research Institute, 2007), 45–58, http://books.sipri.org/files/PP/SIPRIPP17. pdf. Pan states: "The SCO provides a good framework for China to cooperate closely in combating terrorism, extremism, separatism and various other cross-border criminal forces. The primary target of the Chinese antiterrorism campaign is the East Turkestan Islamic Movement (ETIM), which advocates the independence of Xinjiang and is said to be supported by Osama bin Laden. From the Chinese perspective, it is of particular importance that China has been able, in the SCO framework, to count on the support of the other nine member and observer states in its campaign against ETIM."

For more information on the Global Initiative to Combat Nuclear Terrorism and China's involvement in it, see Office of the Coordinator for Counterterrorism, U.S. Department of State, "Chapter 4. The Global Challenge of WMD Terrorism," *Country Reports on Terrorism 2008*, April 30, 2009, www.state.gov/s/ct/rls/crt/2008/122437.htm; and Ministry of Foreign Affairs of the People's Republic of China, "Global Initiative to Combat Nuclear Terrorism," February 29, 2008, www.mfa.gov.cn/eng/wjb/zzjg/jks/kjlc/hwt/t410731.htm. For a Chinese perspective on nuclear terrorism, see Zou Yunhua, "Preventing Nuclear Terrorism: A View from China," *Nonproliferation Review*, vol. 13, no. 2 (July 2006): 253–73. China has also updated its export controls on nuclear technology. See Paul Kerr, "China Updates Nuclear Export Regulations," *Arms Control Today*, January–February 2007, www.armscontrol.org/2007_01-02/ChinaUpdate.

21. According to the Financial Action Task Force, as cited in Office of the Coordinator for Counterterrorism, U.S. State Department, "Chapter 2. Country Reports: East Asia and Pacific Overview," *Country Reports on Terrorism 2009*, August 5, 2010, www.state.gov/s/ct/rls/crt/2009/140884.htm.

22. The Financial Crimes Enforcement Network, which was established by the Department of the Treasury in 1990 to provide a government-wide multisource financial intelligence and analysis network, became a part of Treasury's Office of Terrorism and Financial Intelligence in 2004. See Financial Crimes Enforcement Network, U.S. Department

of the Treasury, "What We Do," www.fincen.gov/about_fincen/wwd. Also see Office of Public Affairs, U.S. Department of the Treasury, "Bush Administration Announces Creation of New Office in Ramped Up Effort to Fight the Financial War on Terror," press release JS-1219, March 8, 2004, www.ustreas.gov/press/releases/js1219.htm.

23. China is also a member of the Eurasian Group, a regional body similar to the Financial Action Task Force whose members include China, Russia, and several Central Asian states. Office of the Coordinator for Counterterrorism, U.S. State Department, "Chapter 2. Country Reports: East Asia and Pacific Overview," *Country Reports on Terrorism 2009*; Financial Action Task Force, "About the FATF," www.fatf-gafi.org/pages/0,3417,en_32250379_32236836_1_1_1_1,00.html; "China adopts anti-money laundering law," Xinhua, October 31, 2006, www.chinadaily.com.cn/china/2006-10/31/content_721316.htm.

24. Office of the Coordinator for Counterterrorism, U.S. State Department, "Chapter 2. Country Reports: East Asia and Pacific Overview," *Country Reports on Terrorism 2007*.

25. Kan, "U.S.-China Counterterrorism Cooperation," 27–29. Kan also notes that, as part of the Megaports Initiative, in 2005 Beijing signed an agreement with Washington to install equipment at China's ports in order to detect nuclear and other radioactive material that might be used for nuclear weapons and "dirty bombs."

26. Kan, "U.S.-China Counterterrorism Cooperation," 27–28.

27. In truth, according to one well-placed former Bush official, the Bush administration was concerned that Beijing might react negatively to "the fact that American had [initially—author's note] won a stunning military victory in a country where it shouldn't have been able to win, close to their own borders."

28. Small, "China's Caution on Afghanistan—Pakistan." See also Tiffany Ng, "China's Role in Shaping the Future of Afghanistan," Policy Outlook, Carnegie Endowment for International Peace, September 1, 2010, www.carnegieendowment.org/files/china_role_afghanistan.pdf; Russell Hsiao, Glen E. Howard, "China Builds Closer Ties to Afghanistan through Wakhan Corridor," *China Brief*, vol. 10, no. 1 (January 7, 2010), www.jamestown.org/single/?no_cache=1&tx_ttnews%5Btt_news%5D=35879.

29. For a detailed discussion of China's interests and policies toward Pakistan and Afghanistan, see Swaine, "China and the 'AfPak' Issue."

30. For an overview of common Chinese criticisms of U.S. counterterrorism policies— including overemphasis on military means, interference in other states' affairs, and selective treatment of terrorists (such as the Uyghurs at Guantánamo)—see Yang Qingchuan, "New Policy, Old Problem," Xinhua, December 2, 2009, OSC CPP20091202062004. Also see Kan, "U.S.-China Counterterrorism Cooperation"; Memorial Institute for the Prevention of Terrorism, "Patterns of Global Terrorism, China: 2006 Overview," Terrorism Knowledge Base, www.tkb.org/MorePatterns.jsp?countryCd=CH&year=2006; Lampton and Ewing, "U.S.-China Relationship," 2; Bates Gill and Melissa Murphy, "China's Evolving Approach to Counterterrorism," *Harvard Asia Quarterly*, vol. 9, nos. 1–2 (Winter–Spring 2005): 21–32, www.csis.org/media/csis/press/050815_counterterrorism.pdf; Jing-Dong Yuan, "China and the Shanghai Cooperation Organization: Anti-Terrorism and Beijing's Central Asian Policy," *Politologiske Studier*, vol. 6, no. 2 (September 2003); Joshua Kurlantzick, "China's Dubious Role in the War on Terror," *Current History*, vol. 102, no. 668 (December 2003); Aaron

Friedberg, "11 September and the Future of Sino-American Relations," *Survival*, vol. 44, no. 1 (Spring 2002): 33–50; and Cruz De Castro, "U.S. War on Terror."

31. A report from Human Rights Watch states that "after the September 11, 2001 attacks in the United States, China began to portray its security campaigns in Xinjiang as a contribution to the global war on terror." See Human Rights Watch, "'We Are Afraid to Even Look for Them:' Enforced Disappearances in the Wake of Xinjiang's Protests," *China Report*, October 2009. An earlier report by the same organization stated that China's counterterrorism laws are too often used as "new weapons against old political foes, [and permit the] systematic violation of terrorist suspects' due process rights, and tightening of controls on refugees and migrants." See Human Rights Watch, *In the Name of Counterterrorism: Human Rights Abuses Worldwide*, Human Rights Watch Briefing Paper for the 59th Session of the United Nations Commission on Human Rights, March 25, 2003. For a discussion of congressional actions and concerns, also see Kan, "U.S.-China Counterterrorism Cooperation"; and Martin I. Wayne, "Five Lessons from China's War on Terror," *Joint Force Quarterly*, fourth quarter 2007, 42–47. The author writes: "While China has kept its counterinsurgency actions in Xinjiang secret for fear of 'internationalizing' the conflict, Chinese leaders are now seeking to gain international acceptance for their counterinsurgency campaign as part of the larger war on terror."

32. See Bureau of Democracy, Human Rights, and Labor, U.S. Department of State, *2009 Human Rights Report: China* (Washington, D.C.: U.S. Government Printing Office, 2010); and Congressional-Executive Commission on China (CECC), *Congressional-Executive Commission on China Annual Report 2009*, edited by 111th Congress (Washington, D.C.: U.S. Government Printing Office, 2009). The CECC report states: The "Authorities in the Xinjiang Uyghur Autonomous Region (XUAR) continued in the past year to use the criminal justice system as a weapon for punishing dissent and penalizing peaceful expressions of ethnic identity and religious activity deemed 'extremist' or 'separatist'" (p. 253). For an expression of U.S. official concern on this issue, see Gretchen Birkle, acting principal deputy assistant secretary of state for democracy, human rights, and labor, "China's Human Rights Record and Falun Gong," testimony before the House Committee on International Relations, Subcommittee on Africa, Global Human Rights, and International Operations, Washington, D.C., July 21, 2005. Birkle states: "The government also has at times used the global war on terror as a pretext for cracking down on Uyghur Muslims who peacefully expressed dissent or sought to practice their faith, and on independent Muslim religious leaders. Where there are genuine terrorist activities, the U.S. certainly supports measures to address them, but where the evidence is lacking, the U.S. calls on China to not equate disagreement with terror. China must draw a bright line between legitimate non-violent dissent and terrorism."

33. For a discussion of the difficulties confronting Washington in addressing Beijing's handling of domestic terrorist activities, see Kan, "U.S.-China Counterterrorism Cooperation." Kan explains that since designating ETIM a terrorist group in 2002, Washington "has refused to designate any other PRC-targeted and 'East Turkistan' or Uighur-related organization as a 'terrorist organization.' . . . In the 110th Congress, the House passed H.Res. 497 (Ros-Lehtinen), nothing that the PRC has manipulated the campaign against terrorists to increase cultural and religious oppression of the Muslim Uighur people" (p. 6, 10). Also see Amy Chang, "Chinese Counterterrorism Policies: Minimizing Mounting Privacy Concerns," Policy Memorandum (Roosevelt Institution,

December 1, 2007), 1–5, http://rooseveltinstitution.org/policy/_file/_chinese_ counterterrorism_policies.pdf.

34. Center for Nonproliferation Studies, Monterey Institute of International Studies, "Prepared Statement by Leonard S. Spector, Jing-dong Yuan, and Phillip C. Saunders, for the Hearing on China's Proliferation Policies and Practices, Before the U.S.-China Economic and Security Review Commission," July 24, 2003, http://cns.miis.edu/ research/congress/testim/testlsp.htm.

35. Swaine, "China: Exploiting a Strategic Opening." Also see Information Office of the State Council of the People's Republic of China, "China's Non-proliferation Policy and Measures," white paper, December 3, 2003, www.caea.gov.cn/n602670/n621894/ n621899/36297.html; and Medeiros, *Reluctant Restraint*.

36. See Cristina Hansell and William C. Potter, eds., *Engaging China and Russia on Nuclear Disarmament*, Occasional Paper 15 (Monterey, Calif.: James Martin Center for Nonproliferation Studies, 2009), http://cns.miis.edu/opapers/op15/op15.pdf; Department of Arms Control, Ministry of Foreign Affairs of the People's Republic of China, "China's Non-Proliferation Policy and Measures," May 27, 2010, www.mfa.gov. cn/eng/wjb/zzjg/jks/kjlc/fkswt/t410729.htm; Jing-Dong Yuan, "China's Proliferation and the Impact of Trade Policy on Defense Industries in the United States and China," testimony before the U.S.-China Economic and Security Commission, Washington, D.C., July 12, 2007, www.uscc.gov/pressreleases/2007/testimony/Yuan.pdf; Scarlet Kim and Alex Bollfrass, "Arms Control and Proliferation Profile: China," Fact Sheet, Arms Control Association, November 2007, www.armscontrol.org/factsheets/chinaprofile; and Ann Kent, *Beyond Compliance: China, International Organizations and Global Security* (Stanford, Calif.: Stanford University Press, 2007). Also see Center for Nonproliferation Studies, Monterey Institute of International Studies, "Prepared Statement." For a succinct statement of China's arms control and disarmament positions, see People's Republic of China, "Arms Control and Disarmament." Also see Xia Liping, "Nuclear Non-Proliferation: A Chinese Perspective," FES Briefing Paper 8 (Bonn: Friedrich Ebert Stiftung, 2008), 1–9, http://library.fes.de/pdf-files/iez/global/05653.pdf.

37. See Evan S. Medeiros, *Chasing the Dragon: Assessing China's System of Export Controls for WMD-Related Goods and Technologies* (Santa Monica, Cal.: RAND, 2005), www.rand. org/content/dam/rand/pubs/monographs/2005/RAND_MG353.pdf; Evan S. Medeiros, "The Changing Character of China's WMD Proliferation Activities," paper presented at "China and Weapons of Mass Destruction: Implications for the United States," conference sponsored by the National Intelligence Council and Federal Research Division, November 5, 1999, www.fas.org/irp/nic/china_wmd.html. Also see Kenneth W. Allen, "Key Indicators of Changes in Chinese Development and Proliferation of Weapons of Mass Destruction," paper presented at "China and Weapons of Mass Destruction: Implications for the United States," conference sponsored by the National Intelligence Council and Federal Research Division, November 5, 1999, www.fas.org/ irp/nic/china_wmd.html.

38. Kim and Bollfrass, "Arms Control"; Denny Roy, "Going Straight, but Somewhat Late: China and Nuclear Nonproliferation," Asia-Pacific Center for Strategic Studies, February 2006; Niels Aadal Rasmussen, "Chinese Missile Technology Control: Regime or No Regime?" Danish Institute for International Studies, February 2007; Kan, "China and Proliferation of Weapons of Mass Destruction." Kan points out that

some of these Chinese steps forward came in advance of major United States–China leadership summits. Also see Patricia McNerney, principal deputy assistant secretary of state for international security and nonproliferation, "China's Nonproliferation Practices," statement before the U.S.-China Economic and Security Review Commission, Washington, D.C., May 20, 2008, www.uscc.gov/hearings/2008hearings/written_testimonies/08_05_20_wrts/08_05_20_mcnerney_statement.php; Paula A. DeSutter, "China's Record of Proliferation Activities," testimony before the U.S.-China Commission, Washington, D.C., July 24, 2003; Stephanie Lieggie, "China's White Paper on Nonproliferation: Export Controls Hit the Big Time," East Asia Nonproliferation Program, Center for Nonproliferation Studies, Monterey Institute of International Studies, December 2003, www.nti.org/e_research/c3_36a.html; Information Office of the State Council of the PRC, "China's Non-proliferation Policy and Measures"; Embassy of the People's Republic of China in the United States, "China Issues White Paper on Arms Control," September 1, 2005, www.china-embassy.org/eng/gyzg/t209697.htm; and Department of Arms Control, Ministry of Foreign Affairs of the People's Republic of China, "China's Endeavors for Arms Control, Disarmament and Non-Proliferation," white paper, September 1, 2005, www.mfa.gov.cn/eng/wjb/zzjg/jks/jkxw/t209613.htm.

39. Department of Arms Control, Ministry of Foreign Affairs of the PRC, "China's Non-Proliferation Policy and Measures," May 27, 2010.

40. Department of Arms Control, Ministry of Foreign Affairs of the People's Republic of China, "The Proliferation Security Initiative," April 7, 2011, www.mfa.gov.cn/eng/wjb/zzjg/jks/kjlc/fkswt/t410725.htm.

41. Department of Arms Control, Ministry of Foreign Affairs of the PRC, "The Proliferation Security Initiative."

42. Lee Michael Katz, "Counterproliferation Program Gains Traction, But Results Remain a Mystery," Global Security Newswire, December 10, 2010, http://gsn.nti.org/gsn/nw_20101208_8526.php; "China Warns of Illegalities in U.S.-Backed Non-Proliferation Plan," Agence France-Presse, December 4, 2003; Andreas Persbo, "The Proliferation Security Initiative: Dead in the Water or Steaming Ahead?" BASIC Notes, December 12, 2003, www.basicint.org/pubs/Notes/BN031212.htm; U.S. Department of State, "International Security Issues, Arms Control Matters, and Nonproliferation," February 16, 2004, www.state.gov/t/us/rm/29723.htm. Also see Gu Guoliang, "Analysis on Proliferation Security Initiative," American Studies Quarterly (Shanghai), vol. 3 (2004).

43. I am especially indebted to Tiffany Ng for her assistance in preparing parts of this section.

44. Medeiros, "Changing Character"; Cooper and Broad, "Russia and China"; Glenn Kessler and Joby Warrick, "Latest U.N. Censure of Iran May Start More Confrontational Phase," Washington Post, November 28, 2009; Dombey, Blitz, and Morris, "China and Russia."

45. Michael D. Swaine, "Beijing's Tightrope Walk on Iran," China Leadership Monitor, no. 33 (June 28, 2010), www.hoover.org/publications/china-leadership-monitor/article/35436.

46. See Kuhn, "China Forced to Find Balance"; Andrew Jacobs, "China Opposes Iran Sanctions Sought by U.S.," New York Times, September 25, 2009; M. K. Bhadrakumar, "Beijing Cautions U.S. Over Iran," Asia Times, June 20, 2009, www.atimes.com/atimes/Middle_East/KF20Ak03.html; Xiong Zhenyan and Wu Zhenhui, "Chinese Foreign

Ministry Spokesman Reiterates the Need to Resolve the Iran Nuclear Issue Through Dialogue and Talks," Xinhua, March 4, 2010, OSC CPP20100304004008; "China Calls for More Diplomatic Efforts on Iran Nuclear Issue," Xinhua, January 26, 2010, OSC CPP20100126968250; Lisa Schlein, "China: Iran Sanctions 'Counterproductive,'" Voice of America, March 17, 2010; Bridget Johnson, "China Not on board with Sanctions to Tackle Iran Nuclear Issue," Posting, Blog Briefing Room, *Hill*, March 7, 2010, http:// thehill.com/blogs/blog-briefing-room/news/85361-china-not-on-board-with-sanctions-to-tackle-iran-nuke-issue; Neil MacFarquhar, "China Agrees to Consider Steps on Iran," *New York Times*, March 31, 2010; and Andrew Quinn and Chris Buckley, "U.S. Sees China Progress on Iran Sanctions Drive," Reuters, April 1, 2010.

47. "Unserious on Iran Sanctions," *Wall Street Journal*; Josh Rogin, "Senators accuse China."

48. See Swaine, "Beijing's Tightrope Walk on Iran"; Kuhn, "China Forced to Find Balance"; John Garver, Flynt Leverett, and Hilary Mann Leverett, "Moving (Slightly) Closer to Iran: China's Shifting Calculus for Managing its 'Persian Gulf Dilemma,'" Edwin O. Reischauer Center for East Asian Studies, Asia-Pacific Policy Papers Series, October 2009; Kevin Larkin, "China Risk: Bursting with Energy: Sino-Iranian Relations—Issues, Interests and Insights," *Political and Security Risk in China*, vol. 2, no. 4 (April 16, 2009); Jon B. Alterman and John W. Garver, *The Vital Triangle: China, the United States, and the Middle East* (Washington, D.C.: CSIS Press, 2008); China's Oil Security and Its Middle East Oil Strategy," *Shijie jingji yanjiu* (World Economic Studies), no. 1 (2001): 19–22; Yetiv and Lu, "China, Global Energy, and the Middle East," *Middle East Journal*, 2007; and Brookings Institution, "The Rise of China: Beijing's Role in the Middle East," 2008, www.brookings.edu/events/2008/0626_middle_east.aspx. For a good assessment of how China views Iran, see Shulong Chu, "Iran's Nuclear Act and U.S.-China Relations: The View from Beijing," *China Brief*, vol. 7, no. 23 (December 13, 2007), www.jamestown.org/ single/?no_cache=1&tx_ttnews[tt_news]=4612. As one former official interviewed by the author stated, summing up the situation regarding Iran: "We're upset that they're signing new energy deals with Iran, and we feel like they could be much stronger on condemning Iran for sponsoring terrorism and building weapons, but they're doing more than they have in the past."

49. I am especially indebted to Tiffany Ng for her assistance in preparing parts of this section.

50. This resolution leveled sanctions on Pyongyang to prevent the supply of: major conventional weapons as well as items that could contribute to the North Korea's nuclear, missile, or other WMD programs; luxury goods; transfers of funds for such WMD programs; travel by people responsible for those programs; and inspection of overseas cargo suspected of involvement in WMD proliferation. See UN Security Council, "Security Council Imposes Sanctions on Iran for Failure to Halt Uranium Enrichment, Unanimously Adopting Resolution 1737 (2006)," December 23, 2006, www. un.org/News/Press/docs/2006/sc8928.doc.htm. Also see Kan, "China and Proliferation of Weapons of Mass Destruction"; McNerney, "China's Nonproliferation Practices"; IAEA Board of Governors, *Implementation of the NPT Safeguards Agreement in the Islamic Republic of Iran*, Report by the Director-General (Vienna: International Atomic Energy Agency), www.iaea.org/Publications/Documents/Board/2006/gov2006-15.pdf; Stephanie Kleine-Ahlbrandt and Andrew Small, "China's New Dictatorship Diplomacy; Is Beijing Parting with Pariahs?" *Foreign Affairs*, vol. 87, no. 1 (January–February 2008): 38–56; and Zhu Feng, "China Policy on the North Korean Nuclear Crisis," International

Security Program, Center for Strategic and International Studies, 2004; "Wen Jiabao Says Resolving the Korean Peninsula and Iran Nuclear Issues Requires Incessant Diplomatic Efforts," Xinhua, September 6, 2006, OSC CPP20060906063004; "PRC FM Spokesman: China Will Not Attend Talks in NY on DPRK Nuclear Program," Agence France-Presse, September 19, 2006, OSC CPP20060919150024.

51. Wang Yudan and Xu Song, "Foreign Ministry Spokesperson: Pressure and Sanctions Not Conducive to Non-Nuclearization of Korean Peninsula," Xinhua, April 9, 2009, OSC CPP20090409136015. Also see Zhang Haizhou, "U.S. Seeks China's Support in Stance Against DPRK," *China Daily Online*, June 4, 2009, OSC CPP20090604968061.

52. "Foreign Ministry Spokesman Qin Gang Issues Statement on Adoption of Resolution No. 1874 by UN Security Council on DPRK Nuclear Test Issue," Xinhua, June 12, 2009, OSC CPP20090612354001. Regarding sanctions, Qin Gang stated: "China is of the view that, as a sovereign country and a member of the United Nations, the DPRK's sovereignty, territorial integrity, and reasonable security concern and development interests should be respected. . . . Imposing sanctions is not the purpose of the UN Security Council's move and political and diplomatic channels are the only correct way to settle the relevant issues on the Korean Peninsula."

53. Ibid. For further details on the Chinese calculus toward North Korea, and unofficial Chinese debates over the issue, see Michael D. Swaine, "China's North Korea Dilemma," *China Leadership Monitor*, no. 30 (Fall 2009), www.hoover.org/publications/clm/issues/70534792.html.

54. For example, see Edward N. Luttwak, "Why North Korea Survives," *Wall Street Journal*, November 30, 2010; Victor D. Cha, "Five Myths About North Korea," *Washington Post*, December 10, 2010; and "An Act of Extortion," Editorial, *Wall Street Journal*, November 24, 2010.

55. For a discussion of the compromise statement on the *Cheonan's* sinking issued by the U.N. Security Council in July 2010, and the contrasting Chinese and U.S./South Korean views that led to it, see Chico Harlan and Colum Lynch, "U.N. Security Council Condemns Sinking of South Korean Warship," *Washington Post*, July 10, 2010. Also see "Greetings, Comrades: What Lies Behind the Dear Leader's Latest Trip to China?" *Economist*, September 2, 2010, www.economist.com/node/16945299; and Jason Dean, "U.S. Officials Head to Beijing to Ease Tensions," *Wall Street Journal*, September 3, 2010, http://online.wsj.com/article/SB10001424052748703431604575467442190815072.html?mod=WSJ_World_MIDDLENews. These issues are also discussed in chapters 2 and 4.

56. See Mark Landler, "China's North Korea Shift Helps U.S. Relations," *New York Times*, December 23, 2010; Mark Landler, "Obama Urges China to Check North Koreans," *New York Times*, December 6, 2010; Martin Fackler, "China Seeks New Talks to Ease Korean Tensions," *New York Times*, November 28, 2010; Martin Fackler, "U.S. and South Korea Begin Joint Naval Exercises," *New York Times*, November 27, 2010; John Pomfret, "U.S. to Stage Exercises with South Korea; Few Good Options for Dealing with North," *Washington Post*, November 24, 2010; Siegfried S. Hecker, "A Return Trip to North Korea's Yongbyon Nuclear Complex," Center for International Security and Cooperation, Stanford University, November 20, 2010, http://iis-db.stanford.edu/pubs/23035/HeckerYongbyon.pdf; and Office of the Press Secretary, White House, "Readout of the President's Call with President Hu of China," December 6, 2010, www.

whitehouse.gov/the-press-office/2010/12/06/readout-president-s-call-with-president-hu-china. See chapter 2 for further discussion of these events.

57. See Kan, "China and Proliferation of Weapons of Mass Destruction." Also see Swaine, "China's North Korea Dilemma," for an evaluation of some of the sharpest criticisms of Chinese policies toward Pyongyang.

58. See Center for Nonproliferation Studies, Monterey Institute of International Studies, "China's Nuclear Exports" and "Nuclear Nonproliferation Treaty (NPT)," http://cns. miis.edu. These sources also point out that China continues to state that it does not view nonproliferation as an end in itself but rather as a means to the ultimate objective of the complete prohibition and destruction of nuclear weapons.

59. The only unambiguous example of deliberate Chinese involvement in the transfer of nuclear, biological, or chemical weapons of mass destruction for national policy ends began in the post-Mao era and served much narrower regional strategic interests—that is, the creation of a strategic counterweight to India in South Asia—and to deter possible Soviet coercion, through the transfer of nuclear-weapons-related designs, technology, and equipment to Pakistan. For an excellent overview of China's nuclear-weapons assistance to Pakistan see Medeiros, "Changing Character," esp. 3–5.

60. Colum Lynch, "Chinese Firm Indicted in Sales to Iran," *Washington Post*, April 8, 2009, www.washingtonpost.com/wp-dyn/content/article/2009/04/07/AR2009040704010. html; McNerney, "China's Nonproliferation Practices." NcNerney stated: "This effort is, of course, only in its early stages. We need to ensure that these entities actually perform as they have pledged. We need to make sure they do not simply spin-off their proliferation-related activity to subsidiaries or sister companies so that the problem remains under another guise. And, these companies need to demonstrate that they are committed to the path of good corporate citizenship over the long haul. However, the possible impact of success would be dramatic. To have a commitment from a company such as NORINCO, a firm that has been sanctioned seven times since 2001, to get out of the proliferation business is a very positive development and one that could serve as an example to other Chinese companies. I am guardedly optimistic that our efforts can bring about meaningful results."

61. U.S. Department of the Treasury, "Treasury Lifts Sanctions on Chinese Firm," press release HP-1042, June 19, 2008, http://treas.tpaq.treasury.gov/press/releases/hp1042. htm; James Mulvenon and Rebecca Samm Tyroler-Cooper, "China's Defense Industry on the Path of Reform," Center for Intelligence Research and Analysis report prepared for the U.S.-China Economic and Security Review Commission, October 2009, www. uscc.gov/researchpapers/2009/DGIReportonPRCDefenseIndustry—FinalVersion_ withUSCCseal_02Nov2009_2_.pdf.

62. Kan, "China and Proliferation of Weapons of Mass Destruction," ii.

63. See Jing-dong Yuan, "China's Proliferation and the Impact of Trade Policy on Defense Industries in the United States and China," testimony before the U.S.-China Economic and Security Commission, July 12, 2007, 1–12, www.uscc.gov/pressreleases/2007/ testimony/Yuan.pdf. Yuan states: "Incapacity, insufficient infrastructure, and lack of outreach to some extent explain the existing gap between Chinese nonproliferation policy and commitments on the one hand, and continued violation of certain Chinese entities of domestic rules and regulations. To some extent, China's ongoing economic transition from a centrally planned economy to a market-based economy, coupled

with growing decentralization and increasing participation of foreign-owned, joint-venture-type, and private economic entities in international trade pose significant challenges for government monitoring and enforcement. While most of these entities are law-biding, there are some, driven by commercial interests, either bypass or deliberately violate Chinese export control regulations." Also see Anupam Srivastava, "China's Export Controls: Can Beijing's Actions Match Its Words?" *Arms Control Today*, November 2005, www.armscontrol.org/act/2005_11/NOV-China. For a far more critical assessment of Chinese proliferation behavior, see "Pyongyang's Accomplice," editorial, *Wall Street Journal*, December 7, 2010. The editorial states: "In 2002, CIA Director George Tenet said the proliferation activities of Chinese firms were at times 'condoned by the [Chinese] government.' And as recently as this year, Secretary of State Hillary Clinton asked Beijing to prevent the sale by Chinese companies of ballistic-missile components and chemical-weapons' precursors. . . . A November 2007 memo signed by then secretary of state Condoleezza Rice complains that shipments of North Korean ballistic missile jet vanes 'frequently transit Beijing on regularly scheduled flights' but that the Chinese had failed to act on specific information provided by the United States and despite a direct appeal by President Bush to Chinese paramount leader Hu Jintao."

64. Kan, "China and Proliferation of Weapons of Mass Destruction." Kan states: "In November 2004, the DCI told Congress in a 'Section 721 report' that, in the second half of 2003, PRC entities helped Pakistan to advance toward serial production of solid-fuel SRBMs (previously identified as the Shaheen-1, Abdali, and Ghaznavi) and supported Pakistan's development of solid-fuel MRBMs (previously noted as the Shaheen-2 MRBM). The intelligence community's 'Section 721 Report' for 2010 reported that PRC entities, that could include state-owned entities, continued to supply missile-related items to Pakistan. . . . In May 2006, diplomatic sources revealed that Iran had used uranium hexafluoride gas (UF6) from China to accelerate Iran's uranium enrichment program" (p. 9, 12).

65. McNerney, "China's Nonproliferation Practices." McNerney stated in her testimony that "an area of potential concern is possible additional Chinese support for Pakistan's civil nuclear program. . . . These are: the Karachi nuclear power plant; Chasma nuclear power plants 1 and 2; and Parr research reactors 1 and 2. Recently, Pakistan has expressed interest in increasing domestic nuclear power generation and has made overtures to China for support. This is something we continue to watch closely to ensure both that China abides by its commitments to the NSG and to ensure that ongoing Chinese cooperation with Pakistan does not support Pakistan's un-safeguarded nuclear weapons program." In addition, Kan states that "China's past and persisting connections to Pakistan's nuclear program raised questions about whether China was involved in or had knowledge about the long-time efforts, publicly confirmed in early 2004, of Abdul Qadeer Khan, the former head of Pakistan's nuclear weapon program, in selling uranium enrichment technology to Iran, North Korea, and Libya." See Kan, "China and Proliferation of Weapons of Mass Destruction," 6. In early 2008, Director of National Intelligence J. Michael McConnell claimed that PRC arms sales are "destabilizing" in the Middle East and that missile sales to Iran are a "threat to U.S. forces in the Persian Gulf." J. Michael McConnell, director of national intelligence, "Annual Threat Assessment of the Director of National Intelligence for the Senate Select Committee on Intelligence," February 5, 2008, http://intelligence.senate.gov/080205/mcconnell.pdf, 31.

66. Farhan Bokhari, James Lamont, and Geoff Dyer, "China plans fifth nuclear reactor for Pakistan," *Financial Times*, November 8, 2010, www.ft.com/cms/s/0/087cce10-eada-11df-b28d-00144feab49a.html#axzz1ImStt2dQ; "Pakistani Reactor Project Advances Despite Japan Crisis," Global Security Newswire, March 24, 2011, www.globalsecuritynewswire. org/gsn/nw_20110324_9375.php; Glenn Kessler, "Washington Objects to China–Pakistan Nuclear Deal," *Washington Post*, June 14, 2010, www.washingtonpost.com/wp-dyn/content/article/2010/06/14/AR2010061404680.html; Mark Hibbs, "China Can't Break the Rules," *New York Times*, August 20, 2010, www.nytimes.com/2010/08/21/opinion/21iht-edhibbs.html; Ashley J. Tellis, "Stop the Sino-Pak Nuclear Pact," *Wall Street Journal*, August 16, 2010, http://online.wsj.com/article/SB10001424052748704868604575432941374803392.html?mod=googlenews_wsj.

67. Mark Hibbs, "Pakistan Deal Signals China's Growing Nuclear Assertiveness," Nuclear Energy Brief, Carnegie Endowment for International Peace, April 27, 2010, www.carnegieendowment.org/publications/?fa=view&id=40685; "Pakistani Reactor Project Advances," Global Security Newswire.

68. Mark Hibbs, "What the China–Pakistan Nuclear Agreement Means," *Foreign Policy*, June 4, 2010, www.foreignpolicy.com/articles/2010/06/04/the_breach; Hibbs, "Pakistan Deal Signals"; Hibbs, "China Can't Break the Rules"; Bokhari, Lamont, and Dyer, "China plans fifth nuclear reactor"; Chris Buckley, "China pushes ahead Pakistan nuclear plant expansion," Reuters, March 24, 2011, http://in.reuters.com/article/2011/03/24/idINIndia-55836220110324.

69. Kan, "China and Proliferation of Weapons of Mass Destruction." Also see "China Gearing up to Export HQ-9 Anti-Air Missiles," *Defense Industry Daily*, March 8, 2009, www.defenseindustrydaily.com/China-Gearing-up-to-Export-HQ-9-Anti-Air-Missiles-05319. For a general assessment of China's conventional arms exports, see Richard A. Bitzinger, "China's Re-emergence as an Arms Dealer: The Return of the King?" *China Brief*, vol. 9, no. 14 (July 9, 2009). The author writes: "China is now, on average, the world's fifth-largest arms exporter, after the traditional leading suppliers: the United States, Russia, France, and the United Kingdom. Nearly all of China's arms transfers are to developing countries. . . . China's largest markets are in Asia, the Middle East, and particularly Africa." However, Bitzinger adds: "While China delivered $1.2 billion worth of arms to the developing world in 2007 to capture the number-three position, the number-one-ranked United States exported more than six times as much, or $7.6 billon, while Russia (number two), exported $4.6 billion, nearly four times as much as China. . . . China is still extremely constrained when it comes to potential customers, the types of arms they may want to buy, and the types of arms it can sell." Moreover, according to data from the Stockholm International Peace Research Institute provided by Bates Gill, during the period 2004–2008, China ranked twelfth globally in arms exports, a reduction from the period 2003–2007.

70. According to Shirley Kan, "the PRC did not deny its arms sales to Iran and indeed conveyed a sense of 'business as usual.' In 2007, when questioned by reporters about PRC arms sales to Iran that were found in Afghanistan (and Iraq), the PRC Foreign Ministry characterized its arms sales as 'normal' military trade and cooperation with other countries. The ministry stated China's position that its arms sales were beyond reproach and responsible because China follows these 'principles' for arms exports: they are for legitimate self-defense; they do not undermine international peace and stability; they do not interfere in the internal affairs of the recipients; and they are

exported only to sovereign countries. In addition, the Foreign Ministry claimed that China stipulated another condition: no re-transfer to a third party without PRC permission. The ministry also argued that China complied with international laws and United Nations Security Council (UNSC) resolutions. . . . Moreover, the Secretary of Defense reported to Congress in March 2009 that China's weapons supplied to Iran were then transferred to terrorist organizations in Iraq and Afghanistan, where U.S. troops fought." Kan, "U.S.-China Counterterrorism Cooperation," 35–36.

71. McNerney, "China's Nonproliferation Practices." For a report on a possible Chinese sale of an air defense system that concerns U.S. officials, see "Iran to Procure Chinese Defense System," *Jerusalem Post*, March 10, 2009.

72. Simon Roughneen, "Wikileaks Cables Reveal Burma Arms Deals," *Irrawaddy*, March 15, 2011, www.irrawaddy.org/article.php?art_id=20947, Cynthia Watson, "China's Arms Sales to Latin America: Another Arrow in the Quiver," *China Brief*, vol. 10, no. 4 (February 18, 2010), www.jamestown.org/programs/chinabrief/single/?tx_ttnews% 5Btt_news%5D=360538tx_ttnews%5BbackPid%5D=4148no_cache=1.

73. See, for example, Peter W. Rodman, "China's Military Modernization and Export Controls," testimony before the U.S.-China Economic and Security Review Commission, Washington, D.C., March 16, 2006, www.uscc.gov/hearings/2006hearings/transcripts/march16_17/rodman_prepared.pdf.

74. During 2009, Chinese companies signed several investment agreements to develop upstream oil resources in Iran, despite the threat of secondary sanctions from the United States. See Flynt Leverett and Hillary Mann Leverett, "China Moves Strategically While the U.S. Remains Stuck on Iran," posting, Race for Iran blog, February 10, 2010; and Garver, Leverett, and Leverett, "Moving (Slightly) Closer to Iran." For Tehran's strong interest in developing relations with China and Russia, as part of its overall effort to undermine international pressure on its nuclear program, see Mohsen M. Milani, "Tehran's Take," *Foreign Affairs*, vol. 88, no. 4 (July–August 2009): 46–54.

75. Leverett and Leverett, "China Moves Strategically"; Milani, "Tehran's Take"; Kevin Slaten, "China's Bigger Role in Pakistan, Afghanistan," *South China Morning Post*, February 12, 2009, www.carnegieendowment.org/publications/index.cfm?fa=view&id=22735&prog=zch,zgp&proj=zsa; "China, Iran Sign Biggest Oil & Gas Deal," *China Daily*, October 31, 2004, www.chinadaily.com.cn/english/doc/2004-10/31/content_387140.html; Wang Ying and Dinakar Sethuraman, "China, Iran Sign $2 Billion Oil Production Agreement," Bloomberg, December 10, 2007, www.bloomberg.com/apps/news?pid=20601080&sid=akKRGh8SSyMI&refer=asia; Nader Habibi, "The Cost of Economic Sanctions on Major Exporters to Iran," *Payvand's Iran News*, May 5, 2006, www.payvand.com/news/06/may/1046.html; "Iran, China Set Target of $200b in Trade," *Tehran Times*, September 25, 2008, www.tehrantimes.com/index_View.asp?code=178638; "China Signs Trade Pact with Pakistan," *China Daily*, November 25, 2006, www.chinadaily.com.cn/china/2006-11/25/content_742616.htm; "China, Pak Vow to Enhance Cooperation in Energy, Defence," OutlookIndia, April 11, 2008, www.outlookindia.com/pti_news.asp?id=561737; David Montero, "China, Pakistan Team Up on Energy," *Christian Science Monitor*, April 13, 2007, www.csmonitor.com/2007/0413/p06s01-wosc.htm; Jim Yardley, "Sanctions Don't Dent N. Korea-China Trade," *New York Times*, October 27, 2006, www.nytimes.com/2006/10/27/world/asia/27border.html?n=Top/News/World/Countries%20and%20Territories/China; Ting-i Tsai, "North Korean-China Trade Hotter Than Kimchi," *Asia Times*, October 6, 2007, www.atimes.com/atimes/China_

Business/IJ06Cb01.html; Jason Strother, "North Korea-China Trade Increases," Voice of America, October 7, 2008, www.voanews.com/english/2008-10-07-voa20.cfm.

76. For a good overview of China's mixed, but increasingly important, role in the U.S. diplomatic calculus vis-à-vis Iran and North Korea, see Steven Lee Myers, "Look Who's Mr. Fixit for a Fraught Age," *New York Times*, October 7, 2007, www.nytimes.com/2007/10/07/weekinreview/07myer.html. After resisting joining the PSI for several years, South Korea reversed course and decided to participate in May 2009, following Pyongyang's second nuclear-weapons test. See Lee Chi-dong, "S. Korea Joins PSI After N. Korea's Nuke Test," Yonhap, May 26, 2009.

77. Jing-Dong Yuan, "China's Proliferation and the Impact of Trade Policy on Defense Industries in the United States and China," testimony before the U.S.-China Economic and Security Commission, Washington, D.C., July 12, 2007, www.uscc.gov/pressreleases/2007/testimony/Yuan.pdf.

78. See Swaine, "China: Exploiting a Strategic Opening."

79. Cruz De Castro, "U.S. War on Terror."

80. For a recent summary of the nonmilitary aspects of Obama's counterterrorism strategy, see Daniel Benjamin, office of the Coordinator for Counterterrorism, "International Counterterrorism Policy in the Obama Administration: Developing a Strategy for the Future," remarks before the International Peace Institute, New York, March 1, 2010. Benjamin states: "First, we are focused on building political will through consistent diplomatic engagement with counterparts and senior leaders for common counterterrorism objectives. . . . Second, we are committed to addressing the state insufficiency that allows terrorists to operate freely by promoting effective civilian law enforcement, good governance and the rule of law. . . . Third, we are working with partners, including with UN agencies such as UNDP, UNICEF, and UNESCO, to help countries confront . . . the political, social, and economic conditions that terrorists try to exploit to win over new recruits. . . . Fourth, we are ratcheting up our efforts to resolve longstanding political and other conflicts that fuel the grievances that violent extremists can latch on to. . . . Fifth, and at the heart of the Obama Administration's approach, is to identify the drivers of radicalization and identify how to address them most effectively. . . . Finally, our approach recognizes that our counterterrorism efforts can best succeed when they make central respect for human rights and the rule of law."

81. Center for Nonproliferation Studies, Monterey Institute of International Studies, "Prepared Statement."

82. A similar point is made by Medeiros, *Reluctant Restraint*. Also see Srivastava, "China's Export Controls." The author states: "Enforcement is presently the weakest link in China's export control system. A wide disparity exists between the dictates of established Chinese law and the capacity of the Chinese state to consistently enforce them. For China, this is a significant challenge. Overcoming it will require both political will and a massive injection of physical, technical, and financial resources. Given China's checkered track record of controlling trade in sensitive goods and technologies, the international community is likely to use effective enforcement as the ultimate criterion for assessing Beijing's commitment to nonproliferation." Although more than five years old, Srivastava's conclusion remains relevant to some extent.

83. It is unclear as of this writing (April 2011) whether the crisis at Japan's Fukushima nuclear power plant caused by the earthquake and tsunami of the previous March will fundamentally undermine the increased emphasis on nuclear energy.

84. Although this danger has arguably declined as a result of the Obama administration's enunciation of a revised U.S. nuclear strategy designed to limit the use and testing of nuclear weapons, it nonetheless continues to exist as a general proposition.

85. See Sam Nunn, "Remarks before the Bulletin of the Atomic Scientists Symposium," January 13, 2010, www.nti.org/c_press/speech_Nunn_Bulletin_of_Atomic_ Scientists_011310.pdf; William C. Potter, "The Impact of U.S. Export Controls on National Security, Science and Technological Leadership," testimony before the U.S. House of Representatives Committee on Foreign Affairs, Palo Alto, Calif., January 15, 2010, http://cns.miis.edu/testimony/pdfs/potter_william_testimony_100115.pdf; Council on Foreign Relations, ed., *U.S. Nuclear Weapons Policy*, Independent Task Force Report 62 (New York: Council on Foreign Relations, 2009), www.cfr.org/content/publications/ attachments/Nuclear_Weapons_TFR62.pdf; Commission on the Prevention of Weapons of Mass Destruction Proliferation and Terrorism, *World at Risk: The Report of the Commission on the Prevention of WMD Proliferation and Terrorism* (Washington, D.C.: Commission on the Prevention of Weapons of Mass Destruction Proliferation and Terrorism, 2008), www.scribd.com/doc/8574914/World-at-Risk-The-Report-of-the-Commission-on-the-Prevention-of-WMD-Proliferation-and-Terrorism-Full-Report; Charles D. Ferguson, "U.S. Nuclear Weapons Policy," in *U.S. Nuclear Weapons Policy*, ed. Council on Foreign Relations; Hans M. Kristensen, "China Defense White Paper Describes Nuclear Escalation," posting, FAS Strategic Security Blog, January 23, 2009, www.fas.org/blog/ssp/2009/01/chinapaper.php; Pierre Goldschmidt, *Concrete Steps to Improve the Nonproliferation Regime*, Carnegie Paper 100 (Washington, D.C.: Carnegie Endowment for International Peace, 2009), 1–47, http://carnegieendowment.org/ files/improve_nonpro_regime.pdf; Pierre Goldschmidt, "Saving the NPT and the Nonproliferation Regime in an Era of Nuclear Renaissance," testimony before the House Foreign Affairs Subcommittee on Terrorism, Nonproliferation, and Trade, July 24, 2008, 1 16, http://carnegieendowment.org/files/goldschmidt_testimony_7-24-2008.pdf; Dong-Joon Jo and Erik Gartzke, "Determinants of Nuclear Weapons Proliferation," *Journal of Conflict Resolution*, vol. 51, no. 1 (2007): 167–94, http://dss.ucsd.edu/~egartzke/ publications/jo_gartzke_jcr_07.pdf; George Perkovich, "The End of the Nonproliferation Regime?" *Current History*, vol. 105, no. 694 (November 2006): 355–62, www. currenthistory.com/pdf_org_files/105_694_355.pdf; Office of the Coordinator for Counterterrorism, U.S. Department of State, "Chapter 1. Strategic Assessment," *Country Reports on Terrorism 2008*, April 30, 2009, www.state.gov/s/ct/rls/crt/2008/122411.htm; Office of the Coordinator for Counterterrorism, U.S. Department of State, "Chapter 4. The Global Challenge of WMD Terrorism," *Country Reports on Terrorism 2008*; Lora Saalman, "How Chinese Analysts View Arms Control, Disarmament, and Nuclear Deterrence after the Cold War," in *Engaging China and Russia*, edited by Cristina Hansell and William C. Potter, James Martin Center for Nonproliferation Studies Occasional Paper 15, April 2009, 47–71; Pavel S. Zolotarev, "The Prospect of Universal Complete Nuclear Disarmament," in Hansell and Potter, eds., *Engaging China and Russia*, 103–12; Ralf Trapp, "Getting Advances in Science and Technology and the Chemical Weapons Convention," in *2008 Chemical Weapons Convention Review Conference: A Collection of Articles, Essays, and Interviews on Tackling the Threats Posed by Chemical Weapons*

(Washington, D.C.: Arms Control Association, 2008), 17–20, www.armscontrol.org/pdf/CWC2008_READERWEB.pdf; Australian Department of Defence, "Defending Australia in the Asia Pacific Century: Force 2030," 2009, 1–130; and National Intelligence Council, "The Terrorist Threat to the U.S. Homeland," July 2007, http://media.npr.org/documents/2007/jul/20070717_nie.pdf.

86. Lewis A. Dunn, "Reshaping Strategic Relationships: Expanding the Arms Control Toolbox," *Arms Control Today*, vol. 39, no. 5 (May 2009), www.armscontrol.org/act/2009_5/Dunn.

87. Gareth Evans, "Getting to Zero: An Interview with International Nuclear Non-Proliferation and Disarmament Commission Co-Chair Gareth Evans," *Arms Control Today*, vol. 39, no. 4 (April 2009), www.armscontrol.org/act/2009_4/Evans#14; Rebecca Johnson, "Enhanced Prospects for 2010: An Analysis of the Third PrepCom and the Outlook for the 2010 NPT Review Conference," *Arms Control Today*, vol. 39, no. 6 (June 2009), www.armscontrol.org/act/2009_6/Johnson; and Pavel Podvig and Hui Zhang, "Russian and Chinese Responses to U.S. Military Plans in Space," American Academy of Arts and Sciences, 2008, www.amacad.org/publications/militarySpace.pdf.

88. Gill and Murphy, "China's Evolving Approach." Though this source is from 2005, the point it makes remains relevant.

89. Shi Weicheng, "Has American nuclear strategy really changed?" *Zhongguo Wang*, April 15, 2010, OSC CPP20100415787004; "CNS Experts Welcome Release of Nuclear Posture Review," press release, James Martin Center for Nonproliferation Studies, Monterey Institute of International Studies, April 6, 2010, http://cns.miis.edu/activities/pdfs/100408_pr_npr.pdf. This source states: "Although this Nuclear Posture Review is certainly much better than either of the two previous ones, thanks in no small measure to the timely and direct intervention of President Obama, it still suggests that the United States will continue to rely to a significant degree on nuclear weapons for the foreseeable future. It is also not clear that the new positive moves by the United States will be matched by some of the other nuclear-weapon states." Also see Saalman, "How Chinese Analysts View Arms Control, Disarmament." The author states: "Drastically drawing down nuclear weapons numbers, committing to the NFU principle, renouncing tactical nuclear weapons research, and ceasing missile defense pursuits are all frequently mentioned as behavior that Chinese analysts await from both the United States and Russia, in particular on the part of the United States. . . . Until some or all of these concerns are addressed through dialogue or action, Chinese analysts are loathe to even mention China's role in the process, much less advocate its active participation in global disarmament." Also see Kristensen, "China Defense White Paper"; Hansell and Potter, eds., *Engaging China and Russia*; and Hu, "Nuclear Weapon Issue."

90. For a similar assessment, see Pan Zhenqiang, "Abolishing Nuclear Weapons: Why Not Outlaw Them First?" in *Abolishing Nuclear Weapons: A Debate*, edited by George Perkovich and James M. Acton (Washington, D.C.: Carnegie Endowment for International Peace, 2010), 249–63. The authors write: "Many treatments of the nuclear disarmament challenge assume that after the United States and Russia reduce their arsenals to 1,000 each, China would join. Yet, there is no evidence for this assumption." Also see George Perkovich and James M. Acton, "Beyond U.S.–Russia Arms Control: Multilateral Reductions and the 'Low Numbers' Problem," Carnegie Endowment for International Peace, Abolition Debate Series, part 4 of 8, April 14, 2010, www.carnegieendowment.org/publications/index.cfm?fa=view&id=40601; Christopher P. Twomey, "Chinese–U.S.

Strategic Affairs: Dangerous Dynamism," *Arms Control Today*, January/February 2009, www.armscontrol.org/act/2009_01-02/china_us_dangerous_dynamism. The author states: "The Chinese are not currently interested in discussing traditional bilateral arms control agreements for two reasons: doing so suggests an equating of the contemporary Chinese–U.S. relationship with the Cold War standoff between the Soviet Union and the United States and the U.S. arsenal remains much larger than China's." However, the author adds: "It is wrong to expect such views to hold in perpetuity," which is probably true. Finally, see Ferguson, "U.S. Nuclear Weapons Policy."

91. Kristensen, "China Defense White Paper."

92. Perkovich, "Road to Zero Nukes." Also see Perkovich, "End of the Nonproliferation Regime?"

93. See Evans, "Getting to Zero." Evans states: "It would be pretty significant for the United States to say that the sole purpose of nuclear weapons is to deter other people from using them. It would play very much into global perceptions that the United States is really getting serious about winding back the centrality and salience of nuclear weapons. That would be relevant in terms of getting buy-in by others on the disarmament side of the house, but also to the nonproliferation side."

94. Fred Kaplan, "Nuclear Dreams and Nightmares: Obama's New and Old Policy on the Bomb," Slate, April 6, 2010, www.slate.com/toolbar.aspx?action=print&id=2249961.

95. McNerney, "China's Nonproliferation Practices."

96. Steven X. Li, "Implications of China's Growing Military Diplomatic Clout for the United States: Cooperation, Competition or Conflict?" Naval Postgraduate School, March 2009, 1–92, www.dtic.mil/cgi-bin/GetTRDoc?AD=ADA496887&Location=U2&doc=GetTRDoc.pdf.

97. One fairly recent area of limited cooperation consists of China's membership in the recently formed eleven-member "Friends of Democratic Pakistan," which also includes the United States. The group was formed in September 2008 and has pledged to lend collective support to Pakistan in consolidating its democratic institutions, the rule of law, good governance, socioeconomic advancement, economic reform, and progress in meeting the challenge of terrorism. See Lisa Curtis, "China's Military and Security Relationship with Pakistan," testimony before the U.S.-China Economic and Security Review Commission, May 20, 2009, www.heritage.org/research/asiaandthepacific/tst052609a.cfm. For a recent report that addresses the challenges and opportunities for future cooperation, see Bruce Riedel and Pavneet Singh, *U.S.-China Relations: Seeking Strategic Convergence in Pakistan*, Foreign Policy Paper 18 (Washington, D.C.: Brookings Institution, 2010), www.brookings.edu/papers/2010/0112_us_china_relations_riedel.aspx.

98. See Curtis, "China's Military and Security Relationship with Pakistan." Curtis states: "Security concerns about Pakistan could move the Chinese in the direction of working more closely with the international community to help stabilize the country. . . . China's apparent growing concern over Islamist extremism in Pakistan may provide opportunities for Washington to work more closely with Beijing in encouraging more effective Pakistani counterterrorism policies. Pakistan's reliance on both the U.S. and China for aid and diplomatic support means that coordinated approaches from Washington and Beijing provide the best chance for impacting Pakistani policies in a way that encourages regional stability." Also see Paul Richter, "U.S. Appeals to China to Help Stabilize Pakistan," *Los Angeles Times*, May 25, 2009; Paul Richter, "U.S. Calls on

China to Help Pakistan Fight Militants," *Los Angeles Times*, May 26, 2009, www.smh. com.au/world/us-calls-on-china-to-help-pakistan-fight-militants-20090525-bksv.html. Richter writes: "The Obama Administration has appealed to China to provide training and even military equipment to help Pakistan counter a growing militant threat, U.S. officials said. The proposal is part of a broad U.S. push to enlist key allies of Pakistan in an effort to stabilise the country. . . . [Holbrooke] has visited China and Saudi Arabia, another key ally, in recent weeks as part of the effort. . . . Chinese officials are concerned about the militant threat to its west, fearing it could destabilise the region and threaten China's growing economic presence in Pakistan. . . . A senior U.S. official, while acknowledging China's hesitation to become more deeply involved, said: 'You can see that they're thinking about it.' "

99. Shamim-ur-Rehman, "China Vows Support for Efforts to Boost Security," *Dawn* (Karachi), October 14, 2009; "Pakistan and China Vow to Fight Terror Together," *Daily Times* (Karachi), October 14, 2009; and "Pakistan, China Fighting Militancy Together— Official," Reuters, June 12, 2009, www.alertnet.org/thenews/newsdesk/PEK348351.htm.

100. Ministry of Foreign Affairs, "Statement of the Ministry of Foreign Affairs of the People's Republic of China," May 25, 2009, www.fmprc.gov.cn/eng/zxxx/t564432.htm. "To realize non-nuclearization on the peninsula, oppose nuclear proliferation, and maintain peace and stability in Northeast Asia has been the Chinese government's unswerving, consistent position. China strongly demands [yao qiu] that the DPRK abide by the non-nuclearization commitments, stop related actions that may lead to further deterioration of the situation, and return again to the track of the Six-Party Talks." According to Alan Romberg, "Americans have expressed confidence that if a suspect ship refuses to be inspected on the high seas, and if it is then directed to port for inspection but refuses, and if it then ends up in a Chinese port, Beijing will, in accordance with 1874, refuse to refuel and resupply it." Alan D. Romberg, "China and North Korea," June 19, 2009, unpublished essay sent to the author.

101. Romberg, "China and North Korea"; Liao Lei and Li Zhongfa, "Qin Gang Says That the Chinese Side Is Willing to Make Incessant Efforts to Help the Korean Peninsula Nuclear Issue Return to the Track of Dialogue," Xinhua, June 25, 2009; Gu Zhenqiu, Bai Jie, and Wang Xiangjiang, "New UN Resolution Not All About Sanctions Against DPRK," Xinhua, June 12, 2009, http://news.xinhuanet.com/english/2009-06/13/content_11536115.htm.

102. Confidental U.S. government cables leaked by the website Wikileaks in 2010 suggest that some Chinese officials may already be open (or resigned) to a scenario of Korean reunification. They also confirm that Chinese officials are highly frustrated with North Korea's actions, as a PRC leader in one instance referred to Kim Jong Il as a "spoiled child." See "Lips, Teeth and Spitting the Dummy," *Economist*, December 2, 2010.

103. Swaine, "China's North Korea Dilemma"; correspondence with Jonathan Pollack, June 2009; Bonnie Glaser, Scott Snyder, and John S. Park (Center for Strategic and International Studies and U.S. Institute of Peace), "Keeping an Eye on an Unruly Neighbor: Chinese Views of Economic Reform and Stability in North Korea," USIP Working Paper, www.usip.org/files/resources/Jan2008.pdf (January 2008). Also see Qin Gang (Foreign Ministry spokesperson), "Statement on the Adoption of the UN Security Council Resolution 1874 on the DPRK Nuclear Test," June 13, 2009, www.fmprc.gov.cn/eng/xwfw/s2510/t567565.htm; Liao and Li, "Qin Gang Says"; "Diplomacy to Ease

DPRK Tensions," *China Daily*, April 10, 2009, www.chinadaily.com.cn/china/2009-04/10/content_7663907.htm; "FM Holds Phone Talks with U.S., Russian, Japanese, S. Korean Counterparts," Xinhua, April 6, 2009, http://chinadaily.cn/Word/2009-04/06/content_7651307.htm; Wang and Xu, "Foreign Ministry Spokesperson."

104. Regarding the last point, several scholars who interviewed People's Liberation Army (PLA) and civilian analysts in Beijing have stated that the Chinese leadership are probably becoming more receptive to discussing future North Korean "instability" contingencies with U.S. officials, or with American scholars. See Glaser, Snyder, and Park, "Keeping an Eye on an Unruly Neighbor." The authors state: "There is apparent new willingness among Chinese institute analysts and PLA researchers to discuss the warning signs of instability in North Korea and how China might respond if the situation gets out of control and threatens Chinese interests. It is difficult to determine whether this willingness only applies to 'academic discussions' or extends to more formal venues between the U.S. and Chinese militaries or intelligence agencies."

105. David E. Sanger, "Despite Crisis, Policy on Iran Is Engagement," *New York Times*, July 5, 2009, www.nytimes.com/2009/07/06/world/middleeast/06policy.html.

106. Bruce Stokes, "China: A Rival but Not an Adversary," *National Journal*, May 9, 2009, www.nationaljournal.com/njmagazine/nj_20090509_8101.php. "China continues to do a thriving business with Iran, and Beijing shows little interest in participating in tougher international sanctions to get Tehran to curb its nuclear weapons program." Also see Bhadrakumar, "Beijing Cautions U.S."; Jian Junbo, "China Doesn't Want Iran Unstable," July 1, 2009, www.atimes.com/atimes/China/KG01Ad01.html. Beijing quickly endorsed the results of the Iranian election. See "China Hopes for Stability, Solidarity in Post-Election Iran," Xinhua, June 23, 2009, http://news.xinhuanet.com/english/2009-06/23/content_11588865.htm; and "Iranian President Criticizes Unipolar World Order at SCO Summit in Russia," Xinhua, June 16, 2009, http://news.xinhuanet.com/english/2009-06/16/content_11553050.htm.

107. Milani, "Tehran's Take." The author states: "The second component of Iran's strategy to undermine the United States' containment measures is to move closer to states that could counterbalance the United States. Iran has signed major economic and military agreements with China and Russia. It sees these two countries as natural allies, since they oppose the United States' unilateralism and its efforts to isolate Iran and have only reluctantly backed the sanctions against Iran."

108. Garver, Leverett, and Leverett, "Moving (Slightly) Closer to Iran." As indicated above, the authors convincingly show the depths of Beijing's dilemma in dealing with Iran.

109. Jinghao Zhou, "Does China's Rise Threaten the United States?" *Asian Perspective*, vol. 32, no. 3 (2008): 171–82, www.asianperspective.org/articles/v32n3-g.pdf.

110. According to Erica Downs, Chinese national oil companies have been signing new contracts with the Iranian national oil corporation, apparently to achieve a privileged position vis-à-vis their international competitors. However, according to Downs, it is very possible that the Chinese NOCs will only "lay claim to certain projects and then try to slow walk them, in hopes of delaying making substantial investments until the nuclear issue is resolved." Chinese companies did this with some success in Iraq. Private conversation with Erica Downs.

111. Garver, Leverett, and Leverett basically agree with this assessment. See Garver, Leverett, and Leverett, "Moving (Slightly) Closer to Iran." For confirmatory Chinese

statements, see Ministry of Foreign Affairs, "Foreign Ministry Spokesperson Qin Gang's Regular Press Conference on June 16, 2009," June 16, 2009, http://de.china-embassy. org/det/fyrth/t568126.htm; Ministry of Foreign Affairs, "China Calls for Resolving Iranian Nuclear Issue Through Negotiations," June 16, 2009, http://bn.china-embassy. org/eng/zgxw/t567884.htm; and Ministry of Foreign Affairs, "Vice Foreign Minister Wang Guangya Meets with Iran's Foreign Ministry Spokesman Qashqavi," June 4, 2009, www.fmcoprc.gov.hk/eng/zgwjsw/t566266.htm.

112. The 2010 SCO summit targeted the "three evil forces" of terrorism, separatism, and extremism, along with drug trafficking, weapon smuggling, and cross-border crimes. It also addressed economic cooperation. In 2009, the SCO defense ministers approved a plan for antiterrorism exercises coordinated by the SCO Regional Anti-Terrorism Structure in Tashkent. At the 2009 heads-of-state meeting, the SCO adopted the SCO Convention on Counter-Terrorism, as well as a plan for SCO counterterrorism efforts in 2010–2012. See Hai Yang, "Building a Bright Future with Coherent Effort," Xinhua Commentary, June 11, 2010, OSC CPP20100611968272; and A. Lukin, "Overview of Russia's SCO Presidency," *International Affairs: A Russian Journal of World Politics, Diplomacy, and International Relations*, vol. 55, no. 6 (2009): 58–71. See chapter 3 for more information on the SCO.

113. Ines F. Ruiz Palmer, "China's Perceptions of Post-Soviet Russia and Central Asia: The Evolving Role of the Shanghai Cooperation Organization," *International Review* (Shanghai Institutes for International Studies), Winter 2008, 103, www.siis.org.cn/Sh_ Yj_Cms/Mgz/200804/2009326155541IDOB.PDF. Also see Pan, "Chinese Perspective," 55–56. Pan states that "cooperation must be stepped up in finalizing the SCO list of the names of wanted terrorists and terrorist groups and in regularizing joint antiterrorist exercises. The Central Asian Nuclear Weapon Free-Zone (CANWFZ) programme should be carried forward, so that the region no longer risks a nuclear arms race and the proliferation of weapons of mass destruction."

114. See Alyson J. K. Bailes and Pál Dunay, "The Shanghai Cooperation Organization as a Regional Security Institution," in *Shanghai Cooperation Organization*, ed. Bailes et al., 1–27; and Chien-Peng Chung, "China's Policies Toward the SCO and ARF," in *Rise of China*, edited by Hsin-Huang Michael Hsiao and Cheng-yi Lin (London: Taylor & Francis, 2009), 168–88.

115. Lukin, "Overview"; Open Source Center, "OSC Analysis: SCO Members Emphasize Organization's Growing Economic, Security Roles," June 22, 2009, OSC CPF20090622554001.

116. McNerney, "China's Nonproliferation Practices"; Chang, "Chinese Counterterrorism Policies."

117. James R. Holmes, "Military Culture and Chinese Export Controls," *Nonproliferation Review*, vol. 12, no. 3 (November 2005): 473–502. Holmes states: "Guanxi continues to give the PLA an outsized say in arms and dual-use export decisions. . . . The project of improving China's nonproliferation policy will involve modifying conditional compliance—moving weapons-related exports into the purely civilian domain while biasing the PLA's culture against exports that breach China's export control laws and regulations."

118. Interviews with past U.S. government officials.

119. Bates Gill, "China's Changing Approach to Nonproliferation," in *Combating Weapons of Mass Destruction*, edited by Nathan E. Busch and Daniel H. Joyner (Athens: University of Georgia Press, 2009), 245–62. The authors add that "other low-level proliferation may also occur between China and North Korea, and the third-party phenomenon [in which sensitive Chinese exports are passed on from the original recipient to a third party] will no doubt continue to cloud China's proliferation record for the foreseeable future" (p. 258).

120. Gill and Murphy, "China's Evolving Approach."

121. For a good example, see Wayne, "Five Lessons." Wayne states: "While China's political evolution appears glacial to outside observers, a key reason Xinjiang's insurgency has been greatly reduced in scope and scale is the positive pull-factor of relative freedom and increased living standards, with the promise of more radiating out from eastern China into the west and from the big cities into the countryside" (p. 43). He adds: "In Xinjiang, China has purchased time with a firm hand accompanied by the promise of a great and prosperous future, the next national challenge is to reform local governance before corrupt and capricious officials discredit and undercut the entire Chinese project." Also see Chang, "Chinese Counterterrorism Policies."

CHAPTER 7

1. For an excellent overview of these threats in the environmental area, see Elizabeth Economy, "Asia's Environmental Crisis: Why the U.S. Should Care and What It Should Do," in *America's Role in Asia: Asian and American Views*, Michael Armacost, J. Stapleton Roy, Han Sung-Joo, Tommy Koh, C. Raja Mohan, project chairs (San Francisco: Asia Foundation, 2008), 146. In the area of pandemic disease, see "Pandemic Preparedness," World Health Organization, www.who.int/csr/disease/influenza/pandemic/en. Also see Australian Department of Defence, "Defending Australia in the Asia Pacific Century: Force 2030," 2009. This report states: "The Government . . . considered new security risks that might arise from the potential impact of climate change and resource security issues, involving future tensions over the supply of energy, food and water. These issues are likely to exacerbate already significant population, infrastructure and governance problems in developing countries, straining their capacity to adapt."

2. As Kenneth Lieberthal writes, with regard to climate change: "The centrality of climate change in Sino-U.S. relations is growing rapidly for four reasons. First, President Obama's view of the issue is the opposite of President Bush's. For Obama, shifting to a low-carbon economy—both domestically and globally—must be one of America's most important goals, and the government has a serious role to play in this project. . . . Second, the Chinese government has greatly increased its own attention to climate change in the past two years. . . . Third, the scientific community's understanding of the speed, scope, and consequences of climate change is improving rapidly. . . . Fourth, a meeting is scheduled for Copenhagen in December 2009 to adopt a new climate framework agreement as a successor to the Kyoto Protocol." See Kenneth Lieberthal, "The China-U.S. Relationship Goes Global," *Current History*, vol. 108, no. 719 (September 2009): 243–49. With regard to global pandemics, many observers have stressed the growing importance of China to the management of global health issues (and especially global diseases) due to its large and rapidly developing population, its role in health

innovation, its contribution to the control and spread of global health risks, and its more active involvement in global health institutions and efforts. For a discussion of these factors, see Qide Han et al., "China and Global Health," *Lancet*, vol. 372, no. 9648 (October 25, 2008): 1439.

3. In recent years, an increasing number of Americans have come to doubt the reality of global climate change. See Barry G. Rabe and Christopher P. Borick, "The Climate of Belief: American Public Opinion on Climate Change," Issues in Governance Studies no. 31, Brookings Institution (January 2010).

4. For example, from 1950 to 2002, China's carbon dioxide emissions (CO2) from fossil sources reportedly accounted for only 9.33 percent of the global total in the same period, and in 2004, its per capita emissions of CO2 from fossil sources was 3.65 tons, which is 87 percent of the world average and 33 percent of that of countries that belong to the Organization for Economic Cooperation and Development countries. See Ma Kai, "China Is Shouldering Its Climate Change Burden," *Financial Times*, June 3, 2007, http://us.ft.com/ftgateway/superpage.ft?news_id=fto060320071359458633; and Richard McGregor, "China Urges Rich Nations to Lead on Climate," *Financial Times*, June 4, 2007, http://us.ft.com/ftgateway/superpage.ft?news_id=fto060420070808278703. For similar data appearing after Copenhagen, see "China Active in Fight Against Global Warming," Xinhua, December 17, 2009; and World Resources Institute, Climate Analysis Indicators Tool, version 6.0, Washington, D.C., 2009, as cited in CoveringCopenhagen.com, http://coveringcopenhagen.com/countries/china.

5. Chris Buckley, "China Says It Is World's Top Greenhouse Gas Emitter," Reuters, November 23, 2010, http://af.reuters.com/article/energyOilNews/idAFTOE6AM02N20101123; John Vidal and David Adam, "China Overtakes U.S. as World's Biggest CO2 Emitter," *Energy Bulletin*, June 19, 2008, www.energybulletin.net/node/31156. Worldwide coal consumption has risen as much in the last three years as it had in the previous 23 years. See Keith Bradsher, "China to Pass U.S. in 2009 in Emissions," *New York Times*, November 7, 2006, www.nytimes.com/2006/11/07/business/worldbusiness/07pollute. html?partner=rssnyt&emc=rss; and "Recession, Oil Price Halve CO2 Emission Rise-Report," Reuters, June 25, 2009, http://in.reuters.com/article/oilRpt/idINLP104575020090625.

6. For example, the Asia–Pacific Partnership on Clean Development and Climate, established in 2006, is a public-private partnership of six nations—Australia, China, India, Japan, the Republic of Korea, and the United States—engaged in exploring "new mechanisms to meet national pollution reduction, energy security and climate change goals in ways that reduce poverty and promote economic development." See Judith E. Ayres, "China's Energy Consumption and Opportunities for U.S.-China Cooperation to Address the Effects of China's Energy Use," testimony before the U.S.-China Economic and Security Review Commission, Washington, D.C., June 14, 2007, www. uscc.gov/hearings/2007hearings/written_testimonies/07_06_14_15wrts/07_06_14_ ayres_statement.pdf. The Methane to Markets Partnership, launched in 2004, includes 18 national governments and nearly 200 private sector companies that aim to "help overcome the financial, regulatory, and technical barriers to coal mine methane (CMM) recovery projects. Such projects capture methane, improve safety of mines, and provide a clean energy source for communities surrounding mines. There are currently thirty CMM projects in China." See Jennifer L. Turner, "China's Energy Consumption and Opportunities for U.S.-China Cooperation to Address the Effects of China's Energy

Use," testimony before the U.S.-China Economic and Security Review Commission, Washington, D.C., June 14, 2007, www.uscc.gov/hearings/2007hearings/written_testimo nies/07_06_14_15wrts/07_06_14_turner_statement.pdf.

7. Thomas J. Christensen, "The State of U.S.-China Diplomacy," remarks before the U.S.-China Economic and Security Review Commission, delivered by John Norris, Washington, D.C., February 2, 2007, http://2001–2009.state.gov/p/eap/rls/ rm/2007/79866.htm.

8. Cheryl Pellerin, "U.S., China Move Forward on Environment, Energy Issues," U.S. Department of State, May 24, 2007, www.america.gov/st/washfile-english/2007/May/ 20070524155301lcnirellep9.307498e-02.html.

9. U.S. Department of State, "U.S., China to Partner for Better Global Environment," April 7, 2006, www.america.gov/st/washfile-english/2006/April/20060407121541lcnirel lep0.6696894.html.

10 Ayres, "China's Energy Consumption," In addition, in April 2006, a bilateral U.S.– Chinese initiative established a state-of-the-art air quality forecasting and public notification system in Shanghai that is successfully used in more than 300 cities in the United States.

11. The establishment of the Ministry of Environmental Protection in spring 2008 reflects the higher priority that the Chinese government places on the issue of environmental degradation. See Yang Xi, "SEPA Gets Stronger," China.org.cn, March 10, 2008, www. china.org.cn/environment/news/2008-03/10/content_12143406.htm.

12. As Elizabeth Economy states: "The central government sets the country's agenda, but it does not control all aspects of its implementation. In fact, local officials rarely heed Beijing's environmental mandates, preferring to concentrate their energies and resources on further economic growth." Elizabeth C. Economy, "The Great Leap Backward," *International Herald Tribune*, August 24, 2007, www.iht.com/ articles/2007/08/24/opinion/edeconomy.php.

13. This undertaking is funded by the Asian Development Bank. Turner, "China's Energy Consumption."

14. U.S.-China Joint Economic Research Group, "U.S.-China Joint Economic Study: Summary for Policymakers," U.S.-China Strategic Economic Dialogue, December 2007, www.epa.gov/airmarkt/international/china/JES_Summary.pdf; Paul E. Simons, deputy assistant secretary of state for energy, sanctions, and commodities, "Energy and National Security," statement before the Committee on Government Reform of the U.S. House of Representatives, May 16, 2006, http://2001–2009.state.gov/e/eeb/ rls/rm/2006/66625.htm; Condoleezza Rice, "International Affairs Budget for FY 2008," February 8, 2007, http://2001–2009.state.gov/secretary/rm/2007/feb/80259. htm; Turner, "China's Energy Consumption"; Ayres, "China's Energy Consumption"; Pellerin, "U.S., China Move Forward"; Thomas Christensen, testimony before the Subcommittee on Asia, the Pacific, and the Global Environment of the House Foreign Affairs Committee, "U.S.-China Relations," March 27, 2007, Washington, D.C.; Paula J. Dobriansky, "Asia–Pacific Partnership on Clean Development and Climate (APP)," remarks to the GLOBE Washington Legislators Forum, February 15, 2007, http://2001– 2009.state.gov/g/rls/rm/80897.htm; Henry Paulson Jr., "Meeting the Challenge: A Partnership on Energy and the Environment," remarks before the Chinese Academy of Sciences, Beijing, April 2, 2008.

15. For further details regarding the activities of specific nongovernmental organizations, see Carnegie Endowment for International Peace, "U.S.-China Climate Change Cooperation," panel discussion, March 18, 2009, www.carnegieendowment.org/files/xie-cantwell_transcript1.pdf. Also see Turner, "China's Energy Consumption"; and Andrzej Zwaniecki, "China Environmental Problems Tackled with U.S. Help: Pollutants Crossing National Borders, Experts Say," July 10, 2007, www.america.gov/st/washfile-english/2007/July/20070710163214saikceinawz0.1669275.html.

16. See Common Challenge (partnership of Asia Society, Pew Center for Global Climate Change, and Initiative for U.S.-China Cooperation on Energy and Climate), "Collaborative Response: A Roadmap for U.S.-China Cooperation on Energy and Climate Change," January 2009, www.pewclimate.org/docUploads/US-China-Roadmap-Feb09.pdf. This report states: "Too often, . . . cooperation has been miscellaneous and episodic rather than sustained. It has also been undermined by insufficient funding, shifting policy priorities, and failure to significantly 'scale-up' promising projects." Also see Kelly Sims Gallagher, "China's Energy Consumption and Opportunities for U.S.-China Cooperation to Address the Effects of China's Energy Use," testimony before the U.S.-China Economic and Security Review Commission, June 15, 2007, www.uscc.gov/hearings/2007hearings/written_testimonies/07_06_14_15wrts/07_06_14_gallagher_statement.php.

17. For example, see George W Bush, "Remarks Following a Meeting with President Hu Jintao of China in Sydney," *Weekly Compilation of Presidential Documents*, vol. 43, no. 36 (September 2007): 1181. At this event, Bush and Hu both asserted their common interest in combating climate change and affirmed that the issue should be appropriately tackled through stronger international cooperation. Also see Office of the Press Secretary, White House, "President Bush Delivers State of the Union," January 28, 2008, www.whitehouse.gov/news/releases/2008/01/20080128-13.html.

18. For example, in the international arena, during the Obama administration, the G-20 Pittsburgh Summit involved commitments by the United States, China, and other powers to phase out inefficient fossil fuel subsidies, increase oil market transparency and oversight, and increase investments in clean technologies. See "The Pittsburgh Summit: Acting on our Global Energy and Climate Change Challenges," in *Pittsburgh G20 Summit Factsheet*, September 2009, www.pittsburghsummit.gov/resources/129661.htm. Also, the nations belonging to the Asia-Pacific Partnership on Clean Development and Climate established eight public–private sector task forces covering the areas of aluminum, steel, cement, coal mining, buildings and appliances, power generation and transmission, the cleaner use of fossil energy, and renewable energy and distributed generation. See Asia-Pacific Partnership on Clean Development and Climate, "Shanghai Communiqué," Third Ministerial Meeting, Shanghai, October 27, 2009, www.asiapacificpartnership.org/pdf/shanghai/Shanghai_Communique.pdf.

19. See Office of the Press Secretary, White House, "Declaration of the Leaders of the Major Economies Forum on Energy and Climate," July 9, 2009, www.whitehouse.gov/the_press_office/Declaration-of-the-Leaders-the-Major-Economies-Forum-on-Energy-and-Climate.

20. Neil MacFarquhar, "U.S. and China Vow Action on Climate but Cite Needs," *New York Times*, September 23, 2009.

21. Charles Babington and Jennifer Loven, "Obama Raced Clock, Chaos, Comedy for Climate Deal," Associated Press, December 19, 2009. Also see Deborah Zabarenko and

Jeff Mason, "U.S. Pledges to Make Up for Lost Time in Climate Fight," Reuters, April 27, 2009. The authors write: "Environmentalists see a U.S. commitment to cut emissions as essential to a global pact and welcome Obama's desire to lead after what they view as eight years of lost time under Bush." For a summary of results of the Copenhagen Climate Summit, see Elliot Diringer, "Summary: Copenhagen Climate Summit," Pew Center on Global Climate Change, December 2009, www.pewclimate.org/international/copenhagen-climate-summit-summary. Diringer explains that the Copenhagen Accord includes "an aspirational goal of limiting global temperature increase to 2 degrees Celsius; a process for countries to enter their specific mitigation pledges by January 31, 2010; broad terms for the reporting and verification of countries' actions; a collective commitment by developed countries for $30 billion in 'new and additional' resources in 2010–2012 to help developing countries reduce emissions, preserve forests, and adapt to climate change; and a goal of mobilizing $100 billion a year in public and private finance by 2020 to address developing county needs. The accord also calls for the establishment of a Copenhagen Green Climate Fund, a high-level panel to examine ways of meeting the 2020 finance goal, a new Technology Mechanism, and a mechanism to channel incentives for reduced deforestation."

22. See Bureau of Public Affairs, "Memorandum of Understanding on Enhancing Cooperation on Climate Change, Energy and the Environment at the U.S.-China Strategic and Economic Dialogue," July 28, 2009, www.state.gov/r/pa/prs/ps/2009/july/126597.htm. Also see U.S. Department of Treasury, "Joint Press Release on the First Round of the U.S.-China Strategic and Economic Dialogue," Press Release TG-242, July 28, 2009, www.ustreas.gov/press/releases/tg242.htm.

23. U.S. Department of Energy, "U.S.-China Clean Energy Research Center Announced," July 15, 2009, www.energy.gov/news2009/7640.htm; U.S. Department of Energy, "Secretary Chu Announces $37.5 Million Available for Joint U.S.-China Clean Energy Research," press release, April 28, 2010, www.energy.gov/news/8804.htm. In recent years, the DOE has played a major role within the U.S. government in addressing climate and energy issues with China, having established a dedicated office on Asian issues that focuses primarily on the PRC. DOE currently manages twelve agreements with China on a wide variety of energy sciences and technologies. These include building and industrial energy efficiency, clean vehicles, renewable energy, nuclear energy and science, and biological and environmental research. See U.S. Department of Energy, "U.S.-China Clean Energy Research Center Announced."

24. U.S. Department of Energy, "U.S.-China Clean Energy Announcements," press release, November 17, 2009, www.energy.gov/news2009/8292.htm; Office of the Press Secretary, White House, "U.S.-China Joint Statement," Beijing, November 17, 2009, www.whitehouse.gov/the-press-office/us-china-joint-statement.

25. See U.S. Department of Energy, "Secretary Chu Announces $37.5 Million Available."

26. Office of the Spokesman, U.S. Department of State, "U.S.-China Strategic and Economic Dialogue 2010 Outcomes of the Strategic Track," May 25, 2010, www.state.gov/r/pa/prs/ps/2010/05/142180.htm.

27. Darius Dixon, "Amid Trade Tensions, U.S. Creates More Clean Tech Research Partnerships with China," *New York Times*, September 14, 2010, www.nytimes.com/cwire/2010/09/14/14climatewire-amid-trade-tensions-us-creates-more-clean-te-79928.html. These various objectives and venues of cooperation were also lauded in the U.S.-China

Joint Statement released after Hu Jintao's state visit in January 2011, which affirmed that "the two sides view climate change and energy security as two of the greatest challenges of our time" and expressed their agreement "to continue their close consultations on action to address" climate- and energy-related issues. See U.S.-China Joint Statement, January 19, 2011, Washington, D.C., www.whitehouse.gov/the-press-office/2011/01/19/us-china-joint-statement.

28. One observer has characterized the above-summarized agreements reached at Copenhagen as "merely the repackaging of old and toothless promises," while others described them as "a mixed bag," consisting largely of "a political agreement forged by major emitters to curb greenhouse gases, to help developing nations build clean-energy economies and to send money flowing to cushion the effects of climate change on vulnerable states." See Charles Babington and Jennifer Loven, "Obama Raced Clock"; and Andrew C. Revkin and John M. Broder, "A Grudging Accord in Climate Talks," *New York Times*, December 20, 2009. As explained in the text, the Copenhagen Accord was a mere twelve-paragraph statement of intentions, not a binding pledge. And, as Revkin and Broder, state, "even if countries live up to their commitments on emissions, a stark gap remains—measured in tens of billions of tons of projected flows of CO_2—between nations' combined pledges and what would be required to reliably avert the risks of disruptive changes in rainfall and drought, ecosystems and polar ice cover from global warming, scientists say. The chances of success substantially hinge on whether Mr. Obama can fulfill his promises to reduce American greenhouse gas emissions and raise tens of billions of dollars to help other countries deal with global warming. That in turn depends in large part on whether Congress takes action on a bill that puts a price on carbon and devotes a large part of the proceeds to foreign aid. And that is no sure thing."

29. Commenting on the United States' lack of movement on cap-and-trade legislation in 2010, Michael Levi of the Council on Foreign Relations stated, "The failure of the Senate to act was a huge blow to the U.S. negotiating team. . . . This fits into a broader perception of the U.S. political system being unable to deliver on some fairly basic areas that matter to the rest of the world. That underlying force is going to make life difficult for the U.S. in the world." Moreover, Barbara Finamore, China program director at the Natural Resources Defense Council, explained that "in international negotiations, the failure of the U.S. Senate [to pass climate change legislation] provided an opportunity for China to be much more aggressive in the negotiations." Coral Davenport, "Balance of Power," *National Journal*, November 18, 2010, www2.nationaljournal.com/member/magazine/u-s-china-tensions-could-doom-cancun-climate-talks-20101118?print=true. See also Kim Chipman and Mathew Carr, "China's Cap and Trade to Come Within Five Years, Professor Stern Predicts," Bloomberg, December 6, 2010, www.bloomberg.com/news/2010-12-06/china-s-cap-and-trade-to-come-within-five-years-professor-stern-predicts.html.

30. See Lieberthal, "China-U.S. Relationship." Lieberthal concludes: "Each side, therefore, wants the other to do more—partly in order to create a better environment for advancing its own efforts to restrain carbon emissions. This presents a natural environment in which to foster cooperation, but it also presents another arena in which failure to achieve cooperation might increase mutual suspicion and tension." Also see Kenneth Lieberthal and David Sandalow, *Overcoming Obstacles to U.S.-China Cooperation on Climate Change*, John L. Thornton China Center Monograph 1 (Washington, D.C.: Brookings Institution, 2009), www.brookings.edu/~/media/Files/rc/reports/2009/01_climate_change_lieberthal_sandalow/01_climate_change_lieberthal_sandalow.pdf;

Harvey Morris, Fiona Harvey, and Geoff Dyer, "China Makes Energy Efficiency Pledge," *Financial Times*, September 22, 2009; "Seven Questions: Can Climate Change Be Stopped?," interview with Eileen Claussen, June 2007, www.foreignpolicy.com/story/cms.php?story_id=3848; Elisabeth Rosenthal, "U.N. Chief Seeks More Climate Change Leadership," *New York Times*, November 18, 2007, www.nytimes.com/2007/11/18/science/earth/18climatenew.html?pagewanted=1&_r=1&ref=science; "Gore: U.S., China Must Lead Fight Against 'Planetary Emergency,' " CNN, December 10, 2007, http://edition.cnn.com/2007/WORLD/europe/12/10/gore.nobel/index.html; Orville Schell, "The U.S. and China: Common Ground on Climate," Yale Environment, August 18, 2008, http://e360.yale.edu/content/feature.msp?id=2043; and Zabarenko and Mason, "U.S. Pledges."

31. "Climate change limits unfair but necessary," *Global Times*, December 13, 2010, http://opinion.globaltimes.cn/foreign-view/2010-12/601126_2.html; Chris Buckley, "China Calls U.S. a Pig in the Mirror on Climate Change," Reuters, October 9, 2010, http://af.reuters.com/article/worldNews/idAFTRE6980NX20101009; David Stanway, "China Says Rich/Poor Divide Still Dogs Climate Pack Talks," Reuters, September 13, 2010, www.reuters.com/article/idUSTRE68C0RS20100913; Thomas Homer-Dixon, "Disaster at the Top of the World," *New York Times*, August 22, 2010, www.nytimes.com/2010/08/23/opinion/23homer-dixon.html?_r=1; Fiona Harvey, "Public Backing for Deep China Emission Cuts," *Financial Times*, October 18, 2009; Lieberthal, "China-U.S. Relationship." Also see John M. Broder and Jonathan Ansfield, "China and U.S. Seek a Truce on Greenhouse Gases," *New York Times*, June 7, 2009. The authors remark: "The Chinese continue to resist mandatory ceilings on their emissions and are making financial and environmental demands on the United States that are political roadblocks. The United States, despite optimistic words from the White House and Congress, has yet to enact any binding targets on greenhouse gas emissions. The energy bill now before Congress proposes emissions targets that are far short of what China and other nations say they expect of the United States. Compounding the difficulty is the fact that both countries are struggling economically and the Chinese and American publics appear far more interested in jobs than in tackling environmental problems, a task that would necessarily be costly."

32. As Lieberthal states: "No progress is likely to be made on cooperation if each side makes the other side's capitulation on these issues a condition for moving forward." Lieberthal, "China U.S. Relationship." I should add that the basic failure of the huge, international Copenhagen conference probably means that major progress toward more meaningful international climate change accords will likely depend in the future on cooperation among a much smaller group of major carbon emitting nations led by the United States, China, and a few others. See Revkin and Broder, "Grudging Accord"; and Kenneth Lieberthal, "Climate Change and China's Global Responsibilities," Brookings Institution, Up Front Blog, December 23, 2009, www.brookings.edu/opinions/2009/1222_china_climate_lieberthal.aspx. Lieberthal writes: "The effort to deal with climate change possibly will now revert to some combination of national, bilateral and regional initiatives, along with negotiations among the group of major greenhouse gas emitters (about fifteen countries account for over 90 percent of global emissions). This latter set of negotiations may take place in the G-20, the Major Economies Forum, or some other body particularly constituted for this task."

33. Lieberthal and Sandalow, *Overcoming Obstacles*. The authors write: "China's bottom line on this set of issues is quite clear, at least in principle. Beijing sees an imperative to

reduce carbon emissions per unit of GDP but does not believe it can credibly commit to reduce total levels of carbon emissions in the coming few years, given its goal of achieving sustained rapid increases in GDP itself. More broadly, China is extremely reluctant to accept binding international legal obligations that it fears it will not be able to meet. It therefore prefers to keep formal obligations below the level it believes can be achieved and then to reap the prestige of exceeding its commitments, rather than risk international embarrassment over unmet targets. China does, though, recognize that developing countries must begin to accept real fixed obligations." Also see Carnegie Endowment for International Peace, "U.S.-China Climate Change Cooperation."

34. Judy Hua and Tom Miles, "China Unveils 2015 Energy and Power Expansion Plans," Reuters, January 6, 2011, http://in.reuters.com/article/idINIndia-53967920110106.

35. The National Energy Administration is designed to strengthen the centralized management of energy sectors and deal with the growing energy challenge both at home and abroad. The new institution contains nine departments, with more than 100 personnel. Its main responsibilities include drafting energy development strategies, proposing advice for energy reforms, implementing the management of energy sectors, and putting forward policies to expand energy exploration and deepen international cooperation. See "China National Energy Administration Commences Operation," *China Daily*, July 30, 2008, www.chinadaily.net/bizchina/2008-07/30/content_6889843.htm.

36. "Guojia fazhan gaige wei deng liu bumen zuzhi kaizhan quanguo jieneng jian pai dianli jiage da jiancha du cha gongzuo" (Six Energy Saving Sector Organizations Conduct Nationwide Inspection of Supervisory Work on the Electricity Price), Zhonghua Renmin Gongheguo Guojia Fazhan he Gaige Weiyuanhui (People's Republic of China National Development and Reform Commission), June 30, 2010, www.ndrc.gov.cn/xwfb/t20100630_357909.htm.

37. Pew Charitable Trusts, "Who's Winning the Clean Energy Race? 2010 Edition: G-20 Investment Powering Forward," Clean Energy Program, March 29, 2011, www.pewenvironment.org/uploadedFiles/PEG/Publications/Report/G-20Report-LOWRes-FINAL.pdf; Zhang Qi, "$30b Set Aside for Green Stimulus to Double Alternative Fuel Use," *China Daily*, May 25, 2009; Rujun Shen and Jacqueline Wong, "Update 1: China Solar Set to be 5 Times 2020 Target," Reuters, May 5, 2009, www.reuters.com/article/marketsNews/idAFSHA5375020090505?rpc=44&pageNumber=1&virtualBrandChannel=0.

38. China's stated targets for total nuclear power production by 2020 range from 66 to 86 gigawatts. As of April 1, 2011, the World Nuclear Association reported that China was constructing 27 reactors, with 50 additional reactors planned (expected to begin operations in eight to ten years), and 110 proposed. After the nuclear disaster at Japan's Fukushima nuclear plant in early 2011, China appeared to partially scale back its nuclear power production targets; however, Chinese officials also reaffirmed their commitment to nuclear power, and it did not appear at the time of this writing that Beijing would abandon its plans to build dozens of additional nuclear reactors. "World Nuclear Power Reactors & Uranium Requirements," World Nuclear Association, April 1, 2011, www.world-nuclear.org/info/reactors.html; World Nuclear Association, "Nuclear Power in China," April 2011, www.world-nuclear.org/info/inf63.html; "China to Cut Nuclear Goal After Japan Reactor Crisis, Bloomberg, April 1, 2011, www.bloomberg.com/news/2011-04-01/china-to-cut-nuclear-goal-after-

japan-reactor-crisis-correct-.html; Justin Bergman, "After Japan, Will China Scale Back Its Nuclear Ambitions?" *Time*, March 28, 2011, www.time.com/time/world/article/0,8599,2061368,00.html#ixzz1JEC05pGI; "China can guarantee nuclear power plants safety: official," Xinhua, March 27, 2011, http://usa.chinadaily.com.cn/china/2011-03/27/content_12232552.htm; Didi Kirsten Tatlow, "Panic May Slow Nuclear Energy in China," *New York Times*, March 23, 2011, www.nytimes.com/2011/03/24/world/asia/24iht-letter24.html, Guowuyuan yanjiu shi (State Council Research Office), " 'Liaowang': Heli bawo hedian fazhan de guimo he jiezou ('Outlook': Reasonably Grasp the Scale and Pace of Nuclear Power Development)," *Liaowang*, January 10, 2011, www.lwgcw.com/NewsShow.aspx?newsId=17866; and Mark Hibbs, "Pakistan Deal Signals China's Growing Nuclear Assertiveness," Nuclear Energy Brief (Washington, D.C.: Carnegie Endowment for International Peace, 2010), www.carnegieendowment.org/publications/index.cfm?fa=view&id=40685.

39. Pew Charitable Trusts, "Who's Winning the Clean Energy Race? 2010 Edition"; Eric Martinot, "Renewable Energy in China," Renewable Energy Information, January 20, 2011, www.martinot.info/china.htm#targets; Todd Woody, "China Leads in Clean Energy Investments," Green Blog, *New York Times*, March 29, 2010, http://green.blogs.nytimes.com/2010/03/29/china-leads-in-renewable-investments; Pew Charitable Trusts, "Who's Winning the Clean Energy Race? 2010 Edition," Michael Wines, "China and U.S. Try to Speed Global Climate Strategy," *New York Times*, October 23, 2009. Wines states: "Chinese and American experts alike agreed that willingness to collaborate on climate-change issues, from sharing research to launching joint business ventures, has grown dramatically in the last year. The vice chairman of China's National Energy Administration, Wu Yin, said the relationship with Washington on clean energy issues 'has been elevated to a new level.'"

China is not only making positive investments in green technology, but also creating tougher legislation to cut emissions and increase efficiency—which create further incentives for even more green investment. See Natalie Matthews, "Energy Security, Clean Energy, Climate Change and the U.S.-China Relationship," Event Summary of remarks by David Sandalow, assistant secretary of energy for policy and international affairs, at the Nixon Center, April 27, 2010, www.nixoncenter.org/index.cfm?action=showpage&page=David-Sandalow 2010. Also see Kenneth Lieberthal, "Challenges and Opportunities for U.S.-China Cooperation on Climate Change," written testimony for the Senate Foreign Relations Committee Hearing on "Challenges and Opportunities for U.S.-China Cooperation on Climate Change," June 4, 2009, http://foreign.senate.gov/testimony/2009/LieberthalTestimony090604a.pdf. Lieberthal provides further details on the various policy initiatives China is undertaking to reduce greenhouse gas emissions. Also see Carnegie Endowment for International Peace, "U.S.-China Climate Change Cooperation"; William Chandler, *Breaking the Suicide Pact: U.S.-China Cooperation on Climate Change*, Policy Brief 57 (Washington, D.C.: Carnegie Endowment for International Peace, 2008), www.carnegieendowment.org/files/pb57_chandler_final2.pdf; William Chandler and Holly Gwin, *Financing Energy Efficiency in China* (Washington, D.C.: Carnegie Endowment for International Peace, 2008), www.carnegieendowment.org/files/chandler_clean_energy_final.pdf; and Bradsher, "China to Pass U.S."

40. Jonathan Watts, "China Ready for Post-Kyoto Deal on Climate Change," *Guardian*, May 6, 2009, www.guardian.co.uk/environment/2009/may/06/china-seeks-climate-

change-deal. The author states that Su Wei, a senior Chinese climate negotiator, told the Guardian that "the U.S. had made a 'substantive change' under the Obama administration." Su stated: "'The message we have got is that the current U.S. administration takes climate change seriously, that it recognises its historical responsibility and that it has the capacity to help developing countries address climate change." The *Guardian* article went on to state, "China wants developed nations to commit to more ambitious reduction targets, to share low-carbon technology and to set up a UN fund that would buy related intellectual property rights for use across the world. Beijing's position is complicated by the fact that it already owns a large share of the patents for wind and solar energy in developed nations."

41. See Neil MacFarquhar, "U.S. and China Vow Action on Climate but Cite Needs," *New York Times*, September 23, 2009. Subsequent to this announcement, Beijing stated that the "notable margin" mentioned by Hu would amount to a reduction in "carbon intensity" of 40 to 45 percent below 2005 levels, measured in terms of the amount of CO2 emitted per unit of GDP. See Edward Wong and Keith Bradsher, "China Joins U.S. in Pledge of Hard Targets on Emissions," *New York Times*, November 27, 2009.

42. "China Develops 5-Trillion-Yuan Alternative Energy Plan," *People's Daily*, July 22, 2010, http://english.peopledaily.com.cn/90001/90778/90862/7076933.html. The plan encompasses a comprehensive breadth of sectors that fall under the so-called new energy concept. These include not just renewable energies such as wind, solar and biomass but also energy efficiency, nuclear, a smart (and strong) grid, transportation, unconventional natural gas, and the more efficient use of fossil fuels.

43. Dinakar Sethuraman, "China Considers Rules for Domestic Carbon Trading Proposal, Official Says," Bloomberg, October 28, 2010, www.bloomberg.com/news/2010-10-28/china-considers-rules-for-domestic-carbon-trading-proposal-official-says.html; and Kim Chipman and Mathew Carr, "China's Cap and Trade to Come Within Five Years, Professor Stern Predicts," Bloomberg, December 6, 2010, www.bloomberg.com/news/2010-12-06/china-s-cap-and-trade-to-come-within-five-years-professor-stern-predicts.html. Nicholas Stern of the London School of Economics and Political Science predicts that China will have an operational carbon trading market by 2015. The precise nature and extent of this market is still unclear, but China is consulting with European Union officials to implement a cap-and-trade mechanism similar to that of the EU in eight of China's cities, according to Jos Delbeke, head of the European Commission's climate unit.

44. Rob Bradley, "Green Energy Policy in China," testimony before the U.S.-China Economic and Security Review Commission, Washington, D.C., April 8, 2010, www.uscc.gov/hearings/2010hearings/written_testimonies/10_04_08_wrt/10_04_08_bradley_statement.php. Bradley argues that these commitments "will require China to adopt a suite of policies that go significantly beyond its current efforts to measure and curb energy use and emissions."

45. Arthur Max, "U.S., China Close in on Accord on Key Climate Issue," Associated Press, December 2, 2010, www.chinadaily.com.cn/china/2010cancunclimate/2010-12/02/content_11642406.htm; John M. Broder, "U.S. and China Narrow Differences at Climate Talks in Cancún," *New York Times*, December 7, 2010, www.nytimes.com/2010/12/08/science/earth/08climate.html?_r=1.

46. Susanne Stahl, Angel Hsu, and Yupu Zhao, "Game Change or No Change? What to Make of China in Cancún," Yale Center for Environmental Law and Policy,

December 15, 2010, http://environment.yale.edu/envirocenter/post/game-change-or-no-change-what-to-make-of-china-in-cancun.

47. Edward Wong and Keith Bradsher, "China Joins U.S. in Pledge of Hard Targets on Emissions," *New York Times*, November 27, 2009.

48. I am indebted to Kenneth Lieberthal for these observations.

49. "Climate Change Limits Unfair but Necessary," *Global Times*, December 13, 2010, http://opinion.globaltimes.cn/foreign-view/2010-12/601126_2.html; William Bleisch, "China 'Unfairly Seen as Eco-Villain,'" Viewpoint, BBC News, June 16, 2009, http://news.bbc.co.uk/2/hi/science/nature/8100988; Sewell Chan and Keith Bradsher, "U.S. to Investigate China's Clean Energy Subsidies," *New York Times*, October 15, 2010, www.nytimes.com/2010/10/16/business/16wind.html. For the Chinese view on alleged U.S. hypocrisy, see "U.S. Move on Clean Energy Ironic," *China Daily*, October 22, 2010, www.chinadaily.com.cn/opinion/2010-10/22/content_11443534.htm. This article states: "Since the U.S. government decided to provide $25.2 billion in subsidies to its renewable energy industries last year, it has no right to start an investigation into those granted by China."

50. Broder and Ansfield, "China and U.S. Seek a Truce." The authors state: "As a measure of how far apart the two nations are, China says the United States should reduce its greenhouse gas emissions by 40 percent below 1990 levels by 2020. The bill before Congress, which could be further weakened, now calls for less than a 4 percent reduction over that period. . . . Beijing insists it will not sacrifice China's economy to meet the demands of outsiders, particularly those in the developed world that are responsible for the vast majority of human-caused CO_2 already in the atmosphere." Also see Vidal and Adam, "China Overtakes U.S."; "China Unveils Climate Change Plan," BBC, June 4, 2007, http://news.bbc.co.uk/2/hi/asia-pacific/6717671.stm; and Sascha Müller-Kraenner, "China's and India's Emerging Energy Foreign Policy," German Development Institute, 2008, www.die-gdi.de/CMS-Homepage/openwebcms3.nsf/(ynDK_contentByKey)/ANES-7HJAZ8/$FILE/DP percent2015.2008.pdf. The principle of "common but differentiated responsibility" was reaffirmed by Hu Jintao during an address to the UN General Assembly. See "Full Text of Hu Jintao's Speech at the General Debate of the 64th Session of the UN General Assembly," Xinhua, September 23, 2009.

51. See Jennifer L. Turner, "China's Green Energy and Environmental Policies," testimony before the U.S.-China Economic and Security Review Commission, Washington, D.C., April 8, 2010, www.uscc.gov/hearings/2010hearings/written_testimonies/10_04_08_wrt/10_04_08_turner_statement.pdf. Turner cites some sobering statistics about China's grim situation regarding environmental pollution: "[1] Air pollution from cars and coal plague all Chinese cities and an estimated 750,000 people die early each year from respiratory illnesses. [2] Over 700 million of China's rural population still has inadequate access to necessary infrastructure for safe water and energy. [3] China's Ministry of Health has stated that 190 million people in China drink water that is making them sick. [4] Hazardous wastes are poorly regulated and information on the extent of the problem is unclear. [5] Growing water scarcity in north China has forced agriculture to become 40% reliant on groundwater, which threatens China's goal of food self-sufficiency, for the north produces more than 50% of the nation's wheat and 33% of its maize. [6] 40 percent of China's waterways are the lowest quality levels of IV to V+ and 60,000, mainly rural children, die from diarrhea associated with dirty water each year." Also see "China Unveils Climate Change Plan," BBC, June 4, 2007.

52. Jim Efstathiou Jr., "China Spurns Pledges in Climate-Change Accord, U.S.'s Stern Says," Bloomberg, October 8, 2010, www.bloomberg.com/news/2010-10-08/ china-spurns-pledges-in-cancun-climate-change-accord-u-s-s-stern-says.html; Angel Hsu, "Of Pigs and Mirrors" The breakdown of the U.S.-China Dialogue in Tianjin,"guest post in "Account of the Tianjin Climate Talks" by Damien Ma, *Atlantic*, October 15, 2010, www.theatlantic.com/international/archive/2010/10/ account-of-the-tianjin-climate-talks/64649.

53. Stahl, Hsu, and Zhao, "Game Change"; KPMG, "Post-Cancún: What It Means," January 13, 2011, www.kpmg.com/Global/en/IssuesAndInsights/ArticlesPublications/kpmg-cop16-cancun/Pages/post-cancun-what-it-means.aspx. In addition to the agreements on emissions reporting, the Cancún conference's chief accomplishments were to establish a "Green Climate Fund" to channel assistance from developed to developing nations to deal with the effects of climate change, as well as other mitigation-oriented measures. Though many of these commitments lacked specifics, and countries failed to reach agreement on any sort of binding limit on greenhouse gas emissions, Cancún was nonetheless praised for making modest steps that would keep the troubled United Nations Framework Convention on Climate Change process alive. See Adam Vaughan, "Cancún Climate Agreements at a Glance," *Guardian*, December 13, 2010, www.guardian. co.uk/environment/2010/dec/13/cancun-climate-agreement; John Vidal, "Does the Cancún Agreement Show Climate Leadership?" *Guardian*, December 13, 2010, www. guardian.co.uk/environment/2010/dec/13/climate-leadership-cancun. Also see John M. Broder, "Climate Talks in Cancún End with Modest Deal on Emissions," *New York Times*, December 11, 2010, www.nytimes.com/2010/12/12/science/earth/12climate.html?_r=1.

54. Whereas the 1918–1919 pandemic caused 40 to 50 million deaths worldwide, according to current epidemiological models, a pandemic today would result in 2 to 7.4 million deaths globally. The two measures that are most effective in preventing a pandemic are (1) improving health infrastructure for pandemic planning in countries and (2) strengthening coordination between national and international actors to enhance global preparedness. See World Health Organization, "Pandemic Preparedness," www. who.int/csr/disease/influenza/pandemic/en.

55. "Swine Flu Found on China Mainland," BBC, May 11, 2009, http://news.bbc.co.uk/2/hi/ asia-pacific/8043189.stm; Jim Yardley, "After Its Epidemic Arrival, SARS Vanishes," *New York Times*, May 15, 2005, May 15, 2005, www.nytimes.com/2005/05/15/health/15sars. html; "Chinese Scientists Say SARS Efforts Stymied by Organizational Obstacles," summary of a story appearing in *China Youth Daily*, Yale Global Online, May 26, 2003, http://yaleglobal.yale.edu/display.article?id=1745; "China's Latest SARS Outbreak Has Been Contained, but Biosafety Concerns Remain—Update 7," World Health Organization, May 18, 2004, www.who.int/csr/don/2004_05_18a/en/index.html; Carin Zissis, "The Potential Avian Flu Pandemic," Council on Foreign Relations, November 21, 2006, www.cfr.org/publication/12061; Emma Chanlett-Avery, "Foreign Countries' Response to the Avian Influenza (H5N1) Virus: Current Status," Congressional Research Service, February 5, 2007, http://assets.opencrs.com/rpts/RL33871_20070205. pdf. As Chenlett-Avery states: "China's poor public health infrastructure and the Communist government's traditional lack of transparency have made international health specialists particularly concerned that China could become the origin of an H5N1 global flu pandemic. Observers are closely watching to see if China's record of withholding information and specimens from the SARS epidemic will be repeated with

H5N1 outbreaks. Some question Beijing's ability to deal responsibly with public health concerns while trying to maintain political control."

56. The IPAPI was developed in concert with the World Health Organization to "align nations around a series of key goals including: elevating the issue of avian influenza on national agendas; coordinating efforts among donors and affected nations; mobilizing and leveraging resources; increasing transparency in disease reporting; improving surveillance; and building local capacity to identify, contain, and respond to an influenza pandemic." U.S. Department of State, "National Strategy for Pandemic Influenza Implementation Plan One Year Summary," July 17, 2007, www.state.gov/g/avianflu/88567.htm. Also see U.S. Department of Health and Human Services, "Appendix H: International Partnership on Avian and Pandemic Influenza," "HHS Pandemic Influenza Plan," November 2005, www.hhs.gov/pandemicflu/plan/pdf/AppH.pdf; and "International Partnership on Avian and Pandemic Influenza," U.S. Department of Health and Human Services, "HHS Strategic Plan," Appendix, 2005, www.hhs.gov/pandemicflu/plan/appendixh.html.

57. See International Partnership on Avian and Pandemic Influenza, "The IMCAPI Process," paper presented at International Ministerial Conference on Animal and Pandemic Influenza: The Way Forward, Hanoi, April 19–21, 2010, www.imcapi-hanoi-2010.org/imcapi-process/en; and U.S. Department of State, "U.S. Joins Health and Agriculture Ministers at International Meeting in Hanoi to Address Ongoing Pandemic Preparedness," press release, April 19, 2010, www.state.gov/r/pa/prs/ps/2010/04/140477.htm.

58. This program, associated with the U.S. Centers for Disease Control and Prevention (CDC), is a network of international centers of excellence "dedicated to the surveillance of emerging infectious diseases, outbreak detection, identification, tracking, and response, as well as the provision of training programs for field epidemiology and laboratory scientists." "National Strategy for Pandemic Influenza Implementation Plan One Year Summary," U.S. Department of State, July 17, 2007, www.state.gov/g/avianflu/88567.htm.

59. "United States and China Announce Joint Initiative to Combat Avian Flu," *American Journal of International Law*, vol. 100, no. 2 (April 2006): 468–70.

60. "Global Disease Detection-CDC in China," Center for Disease Control and Prevention, www.cdc.gov/globalhealth/GDD/china.htm. The CDC's principal partners in China are the Ministry of Health, the Chinese Center for Disease Control and Prevention, and the World Health Organization.

61. Jon M. Huntsman, "U.S.-China Cooperation for a Healthy World," *Global Times*, April 6, 2010, http://opinion.globaltimes.cn/commentary/2010-04/519431.html; Elaine Kurtenbach, "China and U.S. Open Disease Study Center in Shanghai," Huffington Post, June 29, 2010, www.huffingtonpost.com/2010/06/30/china-and-us-open-disease_n_630604.html.

62. U.S. Department of State, "National Strategy for Pandemic Influenza Implementation Plan One Year Summary," July 17, 2007, www.state.gov/g/avianflu/88567.htm.

63. U.S. Department of Treasury, "The First U.S.-China Strategic and Economic Dialogue Economic Track Joint Fact Sheet," July 28, 2009, www.ustreas.gov/press/releases/tg240.htm; Nina Hachigian and Winny Chen, "President Obama's Progressive China Policy," Center for American Progress, May 21, 2010, www.americanprogress.org/

issues/2010/05/progressive_china_policy.html; "China, U.S. to Stage More Inter-Agency Talks," *China Daily* online, August 5, 2009, www.chinadaily.com.cn/world/2009-08/05/content_8529116.htm.

64. "U.S.-China Joint Statement," November 17, 2009.

65. See "China, U.S. to Enhance Collaboration in Public Health," Xinhua, June 22, 2010. According to this article, the topics addressed by the forum "included the challenges, progress, reform, and achievements of the two health care systems, health financing and insurance, disease control and public health services, and medical services and hospital management."

66. Xiaoqing Liu and Bates Gill, *China's Response to HIV/AIDS and U.S.-China Collaboration* (Washington, D.C.: Center for Strategic and International Studies, 2007), 6.

67. Huntsman, "U.S.-China Cooperation."

68. See Laurie Garrett, "Issues Facing of Maternal and Child Health," prepared statement before the Senate Subcommittee on State, Foreign Operations and Related Programs, Council on Foreign Relations, April 18, 2007, www.cfr.org/publication/13130. Garrett stated that, "Under the Global War on Terror 2007 supplemental, the president requests $161 million, in addition to the general budget of $100 million, for pandemic influenza surveillance and control, through USAID."

69. Kaiser Family Foundation, "Policy Brief: The U.S. Global Health Initiative: Overview & Budget Analysis," December 2009, www.kff.org/globalhealth/upload/8009.pdf.

70. Tiaji Salaam-Blyther, "The 2009 Influenza Pandemic: U.S. Reponses to Global Human Cases," Congressional Research Service, June 23, 2009.

71. The initial Republican proposal for the Fiscal Year 2011 budget, for example, would have reduced government spending on global health and childhood survival programs by $784 million from 2010 levels, while Obama's proposed FY 2011 budget would have increased such spending by a similar amount. Josh Rogin, "Obama cuts foreign assistance to several countries in new budget request," The Cable, *Foreign Policy*, February 14, 2011, http://thecable.foreignpolicy.com/posts/2011/02/14/obama_cuts_foreign_assistance_to_several_countries_in_new_budget_request; Kaiser Family Foundation, "House Republicans Release CR Proposing To Cut $100B From FY11 Budget," Kaiser Daily Global Health Policy Report, February 14, 2011, http://globalhealth.kff.org/Daily-Reports/2011/February/14/GH-021411-FY11-Budget.aspx; Kaiser Family Foundation, "Reaching the GHI's $63 Billion Funding Goal: Current and Proposed GHI Funding," February 25, 2011, http://facts.kff.org/chart.aspx?ch=1453.

72. Joan Kaufman, "Infectious Disease Challenges in China," in *China's Capacity to Manage Infectious Diseases: Global Implications*, edited by Charles W. Freeman III (Washington, D.C.: Center for Strategic and International Studies, 2009), 3–16; Nan-Shan Zhong and Guang-Qiao Zeng, "Pandemic Planning in China: Applying Lessons from Severe Acute Respiratory Syndrome," Respirology, vol. 13, no. s1 (March 2008): s33–s35; "Pandemics: Working Together for an Effective and Equitable Response," paper presented at Pacific Health Summit, National Bureau of Asian Research, Seattle, 2007.

73. Lu Chuanzhong, "China Adopts, Defends Strict Quarantine Amid Flu Threat," Xinhua, May 6, 2009.

74. Huang Yanzhong, "*China's Reaction to H1N1 Pandemic Flu*," East Asian Institute Background Brief 498 (Singapore: East Asian Institute at National University of

Singapore, 2010), www.eai.nus.edu.sg/BB498.pdf; Hans Troedsson, "Tale of Sars, H1N1: Once Burned, Twice Shy," *China Daily*, May 21, 2009.

75. Nina Hachigian and Mona Sutphen, "Strategic Collaboration: How the United States Can Thrive as Other Powers Rise," *Washington Quarterly*, vol. 31, no. 4 (Autumn 2008); State Key Laboratory of Virology (Bingdu xue guojia zhongdian shiyan shi), www.virology.chinalab.gov.cn; State Key Laboratory for Infectious Disease Prevention and Control (Chuanran bing yufang kongzhi guojia zhongdian shiyan shi), http://sklid.cn.

76. Zissis, "Potential Avian Flu Pandemic"; Chanlett-Avery, "Foreign Countries' Response." According to Chanlett-Avery, international observers will look for indications that Chan has autonomy from Beijing, especially because China has been criticized for withholding information and specimens about infectious diseases from the World Health Organization.

77. Yanzhong Huang, "China's New Health Diplomacy," in *China's Capacity*, ed. Freeman, 86–93.

78. "Pandemics: Working Together."

79. Ann Marie Kimball, "When the Flu Comes: Political and Economic Risks of Pandemic Disease in Asia," in *Strategic Asia 2006–2007: Trade, Interdependence, and Security*, edited by Ashley Tellis and Michael Wills (Seattle: National Bureau of Asian Research, 2006).

80. ASEAN Secretariat, "'Full Marks' for ASEAN in Common Defense Against Influenza A (H1N1)," press release, Bangkok, May 8, 2009, www.aseansec.org/22553.htm; ASEAN Secretariat, "Chairman's Statement of the 12th ASEAN-China Summit," Cha-am Hua Hin, Thailand, October 24, 2009, www.aseansec.org/23606.htm.

81. Huang, *China's Reaction*; J. Stephen Morrison, "The Prospects for Engaging China with Global Health Issues," in *China's Capacity*, ed. Freeman, 93–96; Kaufman, "Infectious Disease Challenges"; Zongchao Peng, "Preparing for the Real Storm During the Calm: A Comparison of the Crisis Preparation Strategies for Pandemic Influenza in China and the U.S.," *Journal of Homeland Security and Emergency Management*, vol. 5, no. 1 (2008). Also see World Bank, "Avian Flu: China," 2008.

82. Drew Thompson, "China's Health Care Reform Redux," in *China's Capacity*, ed. Freeman, 59–82.

83. "HFMD Outbreaks Expose Weak Link in China's Health System," Xinhua, April 24, 2010.

84. In November 2006, Beijing officials publicly rebuked Hong Kong–based scientists who had conducted research on the Mainland on the spread of H5N1, a strain of avian flu. See Chanlett-Avery, "Foreign Countries' Response."

85. Yanzhong, "China's New Health Diplomacy."

86. Morrison, "Prospects."

87. Kimball, "When the Flu Comes."

88. Yanzhong, "China's New Health Diplomacy."

89. Gallagher, "China's Energy Consumption."

90. I am indebted to Kenneth Lieberthal for this observation, made in a personal correspondence. Lieberthal writes: "When Todd negotiates with Xie, Todd does so without the set of domestic responsibilities (or domestic clout) that Xie brings to the table. This makes the negotiation far more difficult."

91. As Lieberthal states: "Neither side sufficiently understands the structure and processes of the other. Relatively few in Washington appreciate the relations up and down the Chinese political hierarchy (or that the environmental protection law puts enforcement in the hands of local, not national, leaders). Washington therefore tends to assign malignant perfidy to China's record of failure to achieve rigorous implementation when commitments run against the economic interests of local leaders. China does not understand that when the U.S. adopts a law or rule we actually implement it (given the number of folks who take the government to court if we do not). Beijing therefore discounts our regulatory and legal commitments (if you will, they tend to think we will get about the same percentage implementation as they do), and they are therefore very skeptical of our commitments."

92. See Chandler, *Breaking the Suicide Pact*.

93. Bradley, "Green Energy Policy."

94. Ibid.

95. Economy, "Asia's Environmental Crisis," 6.

96. For example, see Joe Amon, "Chinese Corruption Is Hazardous to Your Health," *Wall Street Journal*, May 13, 2010.

97. See Energy Information Administration, U.S. Department of Energy, *International Energy Outlook 2010* (Washington, D.C.: U.S. Government Printing Office, 2010), chap. 8, "Energy-Related Carbon Dioxide Emissions," www.eia.doe.gov/oiaf/ieo/emissions. html. See also Harry Harding, "China Risk," Eurasia Group, June 2006. This report states allocates environmental crises in China as events with a "high probability and potentially severe impact." And see National Intelligence Council, *Global Trends 2025: A Transformed World* (Washington, D.C.: National Intelligence Council, 2008): "If a pandemic disease emerges, it probably will first occur in an area marked by high population density and close association between humans and animals, such as many areas of China and Southeast Asia, where human populations live in close proximity to livestock." See Daniel H. Rosen and Trevor Houser, *China Energy: A Guide for the Perplexed* (Washington, D.C.: Center for Strategic Studies and Peterson Institute for International Economics, 2007), www.petersoninstitute.org/publications/papers/rosen0507.pdf, 1–49: "The inability of China's energy policy to address the environmental affects [sic] of its energy markets has caused a dramatic deterioration in the quality of the country's air and water. Some of this pollution stays inside China's borders and some doesn't. The impact of the share that doesn't is growing rapidly, and addressing it has become a critical component of any regional and global environmental initiatives" (also find more detail on 33–34). Also see Lieberthal and Sandalow, *Overcoming Obstacles*; Lieberthal, "China–U.S. Relationship"; and Joshua Busby, "Under What Conditions Could Climate Change Pose a Threat to U.S. National Security?" in *Global Climate Change: National Security Implications*, edited by Carolyn Pumphrey (Carlisle, Pa,: Strategic Studies Institute, 2008), 142–54.

98. See Energy Information Administration, U.S. Department of Energy, *International Energy Outlook 2010*, chap. 8; Energy Information Administration, U.S. Department of Energy, "China," Country Analysis Briefs, November 2010, www.eia.doe.gov/cabs/china/Full.html; Rosen and Houser, *China Energy*; and Kelly Sims Gallagher, "Key Opportunities for U.S.-China Cooperation on Coal and CCS," John L. Thornton China Center at Brookings, December 2009, www.brookings.edu/~/media/Files/rc/

papers/2010/0108_us_china_coal_gallagher/0108_us_china_coal_gallagher.pdf. Also see Institute for National Strategic Studies, "Project on the Next East Asia Security Strategy: Workshop #4 Summary," September 2008, 1–19. The report states: "China's economy was still 4–5 times more energy intensive than in the countries that belong to the Organization for Economic Cooperation and Development in 2000. Recent growth of heavy industry and infrastructure has driven energy consumption and intensity upwards, changing China's energy consumption and emissions forecast drastically. China depends on coal for nearly 70 percent of its energy. . . . Industry consumes 70 percent of energy." Also see Edward S. Steinfeld, Richard K. Lester, and Edward A. Cunningham, "Greener Plants, Grayer Skies? A Report from the Front Lines of China's Energy Sector," Massachusetts Institute of Technology Industrial Performance Center, August 2008; National Intelligence Council, *Global Trends 2025*; and World Resources Institute, "December 2008 Monthly Update: China's Future in an Energy-Constrained World," *EarthTrends*, January 1, 2008, http://earthtrends.wri.org/updates/node/274.

99. See chapter 5 for additional discussion of China's current and future energy usage.

100. World Resources Institute, "December 2008 Monthly Update." This update states: "Since China remains in the early stages of industrialization, now is a period in which much about the country's energy future is still open to influence. And the implications of this influence are substantial: while China has 300 million new consumers, there are 756 million more in the rest of the rapidly developing world. Policy precedents set with China in the next decade will likely shape the future landscape of sustainable development worldwide."

101. World Resources Institute, "Energy Consumption by Sector," data from IEA World Energy Balances 2009, www.chinafaqs.org/files/chinainfo/wri_Energy-Consumption-by-Sector.pdf. See also John Romankiewicz, "Deconstructing China's Energy Intensity: A Lesson in Fuzzy Math," *Green Leap Forward*, August 11, 2009, http://greenleapforward. com/2009/08/11/deconstructing-chinas-energy-intensity-a-lesson-in-fuzzy-math. As Romankiewicz explains, China's energy intensity decreased significantly from the early 1980s to 2000; however, it rose again from 2001 to 2005, accompanying China's rapid industrial growth during that period. In 2005, the central government announced as part of its Eleventh Year Guideline a renewed emphasis on reducing energy intensity. Since then, energy intensity has declined in China due to such measures as factory consolidation; however, there is disagreement over how much it has decreased. The Natural Resources Defense Council claimed a 10 percent decline in energy intensity from 2006 to 2008, but Romankiewicz calculates that it was likely closer to 7.7 percent based on data from China's own National Bureau of Statistics.

102. See Deborah Seligsohn and Kelly Levin, "China's Carbon Intensity Goal: A Guide for the Perplexed," paper presented at ChinaFAQs: Network for Climate and Energy Information, convened by World Resources Institute, April 20, 2010, www.chinafaqs. org/library/chinafaqs-chinas-carbon-intensity-goal-guide-perplexed. The authors state: "It is difficult to project precisely what impact the carbon intensity goal will have on absolute emissions, since at the same intensity, emissions can vary depending on the GDP growth rate. If China's economy grows quickly, absolute emissions could grow at a higher rate and still be within the 40–45 percent intensity target. Conversely, a slower growth rate would require lower absolute emissions growth to stay within the same intensity goal." Also see International Energy Agency, "World Energy Outlook 2010," in *Global Energy Trends* (Paris: International Energy Agency, 2010), 90, www.

oecd-ilibrary.org/energy/world-energy-outlook-2010_weo-2010-en; Carlo Carraro and Massimo Tavoni, "Looking Ahead from Copenhagen: How Challenging Is the Chinese Carbon Intensity Target?" VoxEU.org, January 5, 2010, www.voxeu.org/ index.php?q=node/4449; and Michael A. Levi, "Assessing China's Carbon-Cutting Proposal," Expert Brief, Council on Foreign Relations, November 30, 2009, www.cfr.org/ publication/20862.

103. Xie Zhenhua, vice chairman of China's national development and reform commission and China's top climate negotiator has stated: "I think China and the U.S. could find a lot of common ground on the issue of climate change. . . . In terms of specific cooperation areas—clean coal, carbon capture and storage, increasing energy efficiency, and use of renewable energy—these areas have the most potential. In addition to the central government's collaborative efforts, we should also explore collaboration between states and provinces." Carnegie Endowment for International Peace, "U.S.-China Climate Change Cooperation." Also see Broder and Ansfield, "China and U.S. Seek a Truce"; Müller-Kraenner, "China's and India's Emerging Energy Foreign Policy"; Lieberthal and Sandalow, *Overcoming Obstacles*; Chandler and Gwin, *Financing Energy Efficiency*; Chandler, *Breaking the Suicide Pact*; and Rosen and Houser, *China Energy*. Carbon capture and sequestration, the only feasible means of large-scale carbon mitigation at these plants, is a viable technology that still needs significant amounts of research and development before it can be widely commercialized. A recent study by the Massachusetts Institute of Technology outlines the need for several integrated projects to demonstrate the feasibility of carbon capture and sequestration in a variety of countries and geological settings. Massachusetts Institute of Technology, "The Future of Coal" (2007), http://web.mit.edu/coal/The_Future_of_Coal.pdf, cited in C. Fred Bergsten, Charles Freeman, Nicholas R. Lardy, and Derek J. Mitchell, *China's Rise: Challenges and Opportunities* (Washington, D.C.: Peterson Institute for International Economics and Center for Strategic and International Studies, 2008), 161. Bergsten et al. state: "We believe this should be a priority area of cooperation between the United States and China."

104. "Carnegie Endowment for International Peace, "U.S.-China Climate Change Cooperation." For a similar assessment, also see U.S. Department of Energy, "Secretary Chu Announces $37.5 Million Available."

105. Chandler and Gwin, *Financing Energy Efficiency*. The authors state that China's "financial system . . . is inherently biased against clean energy investing. . . . Annual investment in coal-fired electric power in China outstrips clean energy investment by a ratio of perhaps 10 to 1." Also see Rosen and Houser, *China Energy*; and Lieberthal and Sandalow, *Overcoming Obstacles*. Finally, citing a report by the independent lobbyist organization The Climate Group, Foster states that the litmus test for Beijing's progress in addressing the growing climate change challenge "will be how soon after 2020 China can start to reduce absolute emissions and hit the global target of emitting two tons of CO2 per capita by 2050—compared with 5.1 tons in China today, 8.6 tons in Europe and 19.4 tons in the US." See Peter Foster, "Is China Really Going Green?" *Daily Telegraph*, May 3, 2009, www.telegraph.co.uk/news/worldnews/asia/china/5258622/Is-China-really-going-green.html.

106. Rosen and Houser, *China Energy*.

107. This is, of course, a questionable assumption. But without such a positive shift in public attitudes, it is difficult to see how significant progress can be achieved in advancing

Sino-U.S. cooperation in this important policy area. For more positive takes on the prospects for cooperation on this issue provided in 2008 and 2009, see Chandler, *Breaking the Suicide Pact*. Chandler states that, despite major problems, "opportunities to profitably increase energy efficiency are large and growing, and domestic support in each country for limiting energy use is growing." Also see Steinfeld, Lester, and Cunningham, "Greener Plants, Grayer Skies?"; Carnegie Endowment for International Peace, "U.S.-China Climate Change Cooperation"; and Foster, "Is China Really Going Green?" Foster opines:" China's leaders now realise that for long-term growth to be sustainable they will have to both reduce power usage by finding greater efficiencies and boost the amount of renewable energy entering the national grid.' The desire to take a greener path is not confined to China's all-powerful government. Activists say there is growing grass-roots support for change among the Chinese public, spurred by a growing realisation that ordinary people are paying a heavy price for China's old 'dirty' development model."

108. Energy Information Administration, U.S. Department of Energy. "Graphic Data: Energy-Related Carbon Dioxide Emissions," figures 112 and 113, in *International Energy Outlook 2010*, www.eia.doe.gov/oiaf/ieo/graphic_data_emissions.html; Rosen and Houser, *China Energy*.

109. See Gillian Wong, "China Lectures U.S. on Climate Change; 'Do More,'" Associated Press, March 10, 2010. Wong reports: "China's top climate change negotiator, Xie Zhenhua, acknowledged the current U.S. administration's greater stress on greenhouse gas reductions, but said its pledges still fall short of expectations. 'So we hope the United States will do more. . . . We hope the United States will not shift the responsibility for taking more active action to other countries,' Xie told a news conference on the sidelines of China's annual legislative session." For a similar statement by Xie delivered one year earlier, see Carnegie Endowment for International Peace, "U.S.-China Climate Change Cooperation."

110. See Carl Hulse and David M. Herszenhorn, "Democrats Call Off Climate Bill Effort," *New York Times*, July 22, 2010, www.nytimes.com/2010/07/23/us/politics/23cong.html?_r=1&ref=science; John M. Broder, "Graham Pulls Support for Major Senate Climate Bill," *New York Times*, April 24, 2010; and Richard Cowan and Timothy Gardner, "Outlook for Climate Bill in U.S. Congress," Reuters, April 26, 2010, www.reuters.com/article/idUSTRE63P47Y20100426. Also see Joseph J. Schatz, "Deal Reached on Trade-in Program for Cars and Trucks," *Congressional Quarterly*, May 5, 2009, www.cqpolitics.com/wmspage.cfm?docID=news-000003110355; Kent Garber, "In Climate Change Debate, It's All about Jobs," *U.S. News & World Report*, April 28, 2009, www.usnews.com/articles/news/politics/2009/04/28/in-climate-change-debate-its-all-about-jobs.html; and John M. Broder, "Democrats Unveil Climate Bill," *New York Times*, March 31, 2009, www.nytimes.com/2009/04/01/us/politics/01energycnd.html?ref=earth.

111. Environmental Defense Fund, "Overview: Court Rules 5–4 in Massachusetts Versus EPA," May 12, 2009, www.edf.org/article.cfm?contentID=5623; "Supreme Court Says EPA Can Regulate Greenhouse Gases," PBS, April 2, 2007, www.pbs.org/newshour/bb/law/jan-june07/scotus_04-02.html. The Proposed Endangerment and Cause or Contribute Findings for Greenhouse Gases under the Clean Air Act was signed on April 17, 2009. On April 24, 2009, the proposed rule was published in the *Federal Register* (www.regulations.gov), under Docket ID EPA-HQ-OAR-2009-0171, http://epa.gov/climatechange/endangerment.html.

112. Internally, some Chinese climate change policy advisers have reportedly argued in a recent study that Beijing should set firm, quantified targets to limit overall greenhouse gas emissions so they will peak around 2030. This report supposedly "marks a high-level public departure from China's reluctance to spell out a proposed peak and date for it." See Chris Buckley, "China Study Urges Greenhouse Gas Caps, Peak in 2030," Reuters, August 17, 2009, www.reuters.com/article/2009/08/17/us-china-climate-idUSTRE57G0C520090817. In addition, outside analysts point to China's desire to portray itself as a responsible power, along with a host of other internal and external economic, political, and social factors pushing Beijing toward clearer, firmer commitments. These include a recognized need for massive restructuring in the energy field to ensure long-term economic growth and energy security; growing popular demand for substantial efforts to reduce pollution; and a strong desire to place China in the forefront of those nations developing innovative, clean technologies. See Anna Korppoo and Linda Jakobson, eds., *Towards a New Climate Regime? Views of China, India, Japan, Russia and the United States on the Road to Copenhagen* (Helsinki: Finnish Institute of International Affairs, 2009). There is also growing pressure for Chinese companies to adhere to Western environmental sustainability standards and regulations. See David Hathaway, *Strategies for Decreasing the Carbon Footprint of Chinese Companies and Meeting Global Sustainability Challenges*, China Environment Series 10 (Washington, D.C.: Woodrow Wilson International Center for Scholars, 2009), 120–23. The author states: "As the supply chain for most Western companies, Chinese companies will face increasing pressure to meet more stringent Western environmental sustainability standards and regulations. For example, many global electronics and [information technology] product firms are rolling out increasingly comprehensive sustainability programs among their supply chain manufacturers."

113. Rosen and Houser, *China Energy*.

114. Jeffery K. Taubenberger and David M. Morens, "Influenza: The Once and Future Pandemic," *Public Health Reports*, vol. 125, supp. 3 (2010), www.publichealthreports.org/archives/issueopen.cfm?articleID=2436. The authors add: "Understanding and predicting pandemic emergence is a difficult challenge that we are far from being able to meet in 2010." Also see Anna Mulrine, "Nuclear Terrorism, Pakistan, China, a Pandemic: Predicting the Next 9-11," *U.S. News & World Report*, March 20, 2009, www.usnews.com/articles/opinion/2009/03/20/nuclear-terrorism-pakistan-china-a-pandemic-predicting-the-next-9-11.html?PageNr=1; and "China Bird Flu Not Pandemic, But Be Prepared: UN," Agence France-Presse, February 18, 2009, www.google.com/hostednews/afp/article/ALeqM5gBOSyGD-LcNECKS2hoGggyQhNMBg. See "Watching Nervously," *Economist*, April 30, 2009, www.economist.com/opinion/displaystory.cfm?story_id=13576483: "A study published in the Lancet in 2006 used data from Spanish flu to predict that a modern pandemic of equivalent virulence would kill 62m people, with 96 percent of those deaths in low- and middle-income countries. Another study, by the World Bank, has estimated that such a pandemic could leave perhaps 70m dead." And see "The Butcher's Bill," *Economist*, April 30, 2009, www.economist.com/opinion/displaystory.cfm?story_id=13576491: "In 2006 Warwick McKibbin and Alexandra Sidorenko found in a study for the Lowy Institute for International Policy in Sydney that even a mild pandemic could shave 0.8 percent off world GDP. For the worst possibility they considered, the drop would be a staggering 12.6 percent." Finally, see Larry Brilliant, "The Age of Pandemics," *Wall Street Journal*, May 2, 2009, http://online.wsj.com/article/SB124121965740478983.html.

115. Brilliant, "Age of Pandemics"; Andrew S. Erickson, "Combating a Truly Collective Threat: Sino-American Military Cooperation Against Avian Influenza," *Global Health Governance*, vol. 1, no. 1 (January 2007).

116. Kaufman, "Infectious Disease Challenges." Also see Thompson, "China's Health Care Reform Redux"; and Frederik Balfour, "Is China Covering Up a New Bird Flu?" *BusinessWeek*, February 3, 2009, www.businessweek.com/globalbiz/blog/eyeonasia/archives/2009/02/is_china_coveri.html.

CHAPTER 8

1. For an overview of the goals and guiding principles of U.S. policy in advancing human rights and democracy in China, see David Kramer, assistant secretary of state for democracy, human rights, and labor, "Human Rights, Democracy, and the U.S. Relationship With China," remarks at Beijing Foreign Affairs University, Beijing, May 25, 2008, http://2001-2009.state.gov/g/drl/rls/rm/2008/105202.htm.

2. Gretchen Birkle, acting principal deputy assistant secretary of state for democracy, human rights, and labor, "China's Human Rights Record and Falun Gong," testimony before the House Committee on International Relations, Subcommittee on Africa, Global Human Rights, and International Operations, Washington, D.C., July 21, 2005. Also see George W. Bush, *The National Security Strategy of the United States of America* (Washington, D.C.: White House, 2006). That document links human rights in China with both market-led economic development and Beijing's status as a responsible international entity and law-abiding nation. It states: "Ultimately, China's leaders must see that they cannot let their population increasingly experience the freedoms to buy, sell, and produce, while denying them the rights to assemble, speak, and worship. Only by allowing the Chinese people to enjoy these basic freedoms and universal rights can China honor its own constitution and international commitments and reach its full potential. Our strategy seeks to encourage China to make the right strategic choices for its people, while we hedge against other possibilities."

3. Bonnie Glaser, "U.S.-China Relations: Chock-full of Dialogue: SED, Human Rights, and Security," *Comparative Connections*, vol. 10, no. 2 (July 2008): 31–46. For some analysts, the agreement to return to formal talks was seen as a gesture designed to appeal to public opinion abroad as China prepared to host the 2008 Olympics. See Edward Cody, "U.S. Reopens Talks with Chinese on Rights," *Washington Post*, May 28, 2008, www.washingtonpost.com/wp-dyn/content/article/2008/05/27/AR2008052701055.html. Although probably true to some extent, Beijing might have also agreed to resume the dialogue as part of an understanding reached with Washington in which it was removed from the list of the world's most systematic human rights violators in the 2007 Department of State Country Reports on Human Rights Practices.

4. U.S. Department of State, "East Asia and Pacific," in *Supporting Human Rights and Democracy: The U.S. Record 2006*, April 5, 2007, www.state.gov/g/drl/rls/shrd/2006/80587.htm.

5. Ibid. Also see Birkle, "China's Human Rights Record"; and Cody, "U.S. Reopens Talks."

6. U.S. Department of State, "East Asia and Pacific"; Birkle, "China's Human Rights Record."

7. Thomas Lum and Hannah Fischer, "Human Rights in China: Trends and Policy Implications," CRS Report for Congress, January 15, 2010, www.fas.org/sgp/crs/row/RL34729.pdf, 32.

8. Richard Boucher, State Department spokesman, "U.N. Commission on Human Rights China Resolution," press statement, Washington, D.C., March 22, 2004, http://2001-2009.state.gov/r/pa/prs/ps/2004/30650.htm.

9. Lum and Fischer, "Human Rights," 2010.

10. Ibid, 32–33. In addition, the Global Online Freedom Act of 2009 (H.R. 2271) was introduced in May 2009 to establish an Office of Global Internet Freedom in the Department of State. According to Lum and Fischer, "The act also would prohibit U.S. companies that provide Internet services in countries that restrict the free flow of information from providing personal user information to the governments of such countries and assisting such governments in the censorship of information." The proposed legislation was referred to the House Energy and Commerce Committee, but was not passed prior to the end of the 111th session of Congress. See "H.R. 2271: Global Online Freedom Act of 2009," 111th Congress 2009–2010, Govtrack.us, www.govtrack.us/congress/bill.xpd?bill=h111-2271. Similar legislation had previously been introduced in the 110th Congress as the Global Online Freedom Act of 2007. "H.R. 275: Global Online Freedom Act of 2007," 110th Congress 1st session, http://thomas.loc.gov/home/gpoxmlc110/h275_ih.xml

11. Dan Levin, "New Scrutiny on Censorship Issues for U.S. Companies in China," *New York Times*, March 1, 2010. Also see Robert Faris, "Information Technology and Freedom of Expression in China," written statement prepared for U.S.-China Economic and Security Review Commission Hearing on China's Media and Information Controls: The Impact in China and the United States," Washington, D.C., September 28, 2009, www.uscc.gov/hearings/2009hearings/hr09_09_10.php.

12. Lum and Fischer, "Human Rights," 2010, 36. The CEEC's website is at www.cecc.gov.

13. See Thomas J. Christensen, "China in Africa: Implications for U.S. Policy," testimony before the Senate Foreign Relations Committee, Washington, D.C., June 5, 2008, http://2001-2009.state.gov/p/eap/rls/rm/2008/06/105556.htm; Bureau of Public Affairs, U.S. Department of State, "The United States' Response to the Darfur Crisis," Fact Sheet, September 11, 2008, http://2001-2009.state.gov/r/pa/scp/2008/109902.htm; African Affairs, U.S. Department of State, "U.S. Response to the Situation in Darfur," Fact Sheet, April 23, 2008, http://2001-2009.state.gov/p/af/rls/fs/2008/103967.htm; Scot Marciel, deputy assistant secretary of state for East Asian and Pacific affairs, "The Way Forward in Burma," Foreign Press Center briefing, Washington, D.C., November 8, 2007, http://2002-2009-fpc.state.gov/94771.htm; and Bureau of East Asian and Pacific Affairs, U.S. Department of State, "Conditions in Burma and U.S. Policy Toward Burma for the Period September 28, 2005–March 27, 2006," May 18, 2006, released to Congress on April 17, 2006, http://2001-2009.state.gov/p/eap/rls/rpt/66449.htm. Also see Matt Spetalnick, "Bush urges China to use clout with Sudan on Darfur," Reuters, August 11, 2008, www.reuters.com/articlePrint?articleId=USN1030195920080811; and "U.S. Envoy to Sudan Critical of China," Reuters, February 8, 2007, www.alertnet.org/thenews/newsdesk/N08441844.htm.

14. Richard Boucher, "China: Human Rights Deterioration (Question Taken)," daily press briefing by Office of the Spokesman, U.S. Department of State, Washington, D.C., July 2, 2003, http://2001-2009.state.gov/r/pa/prs/dpb/2003/22196.htm#china.

15. For example, see Fred Hiatt, "Editorial: Constancy on China," *Washington Post*, May 26, 2003; and Glenn Kessler, "U.S. Opts Not to Censure China, Russia on Human Rights," *Washington Post*, April 12, 2003.

16. See "Statement of Dr. William F. Schulz Executive Director, Amnesty International USA," in *Amnesty International Annual Report*, May 25, 2005, www.amnestyusa.org/annualreport/statement.html. Schulz stated: "How far from that moral high ground the US government has fallen: Its descent into torture and ill treatment includes beatings, prolonged restraint in painful positions, hooding and the use of dogs at Abu Ghraib, Guantánamo Bay and Bagram Air Base and 'rendering' detainees to countries that practice torture." Also see Nicholas Kristof, "Repression by China, and by Us," *New York Times*, June 7, 2007. For sources on the UNHRC, see Luisa Blanchfield, "The United Nations Human Rights Council: Issues for Congress," Congressional Research Service Report for Congress, June 1, 2009, www.fas.org/sgp/crs/row/RL33608.pdf. The UNHRC replaced the UN Commission on Human Rights (UNCHR), as part of an overall effort at UN reform. The Bush administration reportedly withdrew its support for the UNHRC because it believed that the UNHRC would not adequately correct the deficiencies of its predecessor with regard to human rights issues. The UNCHR had been criticized because its members at times included perceived human rights abusers, and the Bush administration asserted that the UNHRC lacked the mechanisms for "maintaining credible membership." Nonetheless, the fact that 170 countries voted in favor of the creation of the UNHRC while the Bush administration was one of only four countries opposing it conveyed a lack of support for human rights to many observers.

17. Michael H. Posner, assistant secretary of state for democracy, human rights, and labor, "Briefing on the U.S.-China Human Rights Dialogue," U.S. Department of State, Washington, D.C., May 14, 2010, www.state.gov/r/pa/prs/ps/2010/05/141899.htm; Andrew Quinn, "U.S., China to Resume Human Rights Dialogue in May," Reuters, April 22, 2010. According to this report, the dialogue would address religious rights, the rule of law, and Internet freedom, reflecting several recent issues of concern to the United States (see below). The meeting was originally scheduled for February but had to be rescheduled because "the timing was not right," according to State Department spokesman P. J. Crowley.

18. Blanchfield, "United Nations Human Rights Council." Conversely, the Obama administration expressed concern over the "repeated and unbalanced" criticisms of Israel made by the UNHRC.

19. Lum and Fischer, "Human Rights," 2010, 36.

20. Hillary Rodham Clinton, "Remarks on Internet Freedom," Newseum, Washington, D.C., January 21, 2010, www.state.gov/secretary/rm/2010/01/135519.htm.

21. Hillary Rodham Clinton, "Working Toward Change in Perceptions of U.S. Engagement Around the World," Roundtable with Traveling Press, Seoul, February 20, 2009, www.state.gov/secretary/rm/2009a/02/119430.htm; Hillary Rodham Clinton, "Toward a Deeper and Broader Relationship with China," remarks with Chinese foreign minister Yang Jiechi, Beijing, February 21, 2009, www.state.gov/secretary/rm/2009a/02/119432.htm; Bret Stephens, "Does Obama Believe in Human Rights?" *Wall Street Journal*, October 19, 2009, http://online.wsj.com/article/SB10001424052748704500604574481341183751038.html.

22. See Jeffrey Bader, "Obama Goes to Asia: Understanding the President's Trip," remarks at the Brookings Institution, Washington, D.C., November 6, 2009. Bader was appointed as the Asia director within the National Security Council in January 2009.

23. George Packer, "Rights and Wrongs," *New Yorker*, May 17, 2010, www.newyorker.com/talk/comment/2010/05/17/100517taco_talk_packer.

24. See Office of the Press Secretary, White House, "U.S.-China Joint Statement," Beijing, November 17, 2009, www.whitehouse.gov/the-press-office/us-china-joint-statement. The statement included the following: "The United States and China underlined that each country and its people have the right to choose their own path, and all countries should respect each other's choice of a development model. Both sides recognized that the United States and China have differences on the issue of human rights. Addressing these differences in the spirit of equality and mutual respect, as well as promoting and protecting human rights consistent with international human rights instruments, the two sides agreed to hold the next round of the official human rights dialogue in Washington, D.C., by the end of February 2010." Also see "Obama's Soft Approach on Human Rights," Room for Debate Blog, *New York Times*, November 18, 2009, http://roomfordebate.blogs.nytimes.com/2009/11/18/obamas-soft-approach-on-human-rights.

25. "Obama's Soft Approach on Human Rights."

26. Office of the Press Secretary, White House, "Statement by the President on the Awarding of the Nobel Peace Prize to Liu Xiaobo," October 8, 2010, www.whitehouse.gov/the-press-office/2010/10/08/statement-president-awarding-nobel-peace-prize-liu-xiaobo; and Office of the Press Secretary, White House, "Statement from the Press Secretary on the President's Meeting with His Holiness the XIV Dalai Lama," February 18, 2010, www.whitehouse.gov/the-press-office/statement-press-secretary-presidents-meeting-with-his-holiness-xiv-dalai-lama.

27. Clinton, "Remarks on Internet Freedom."

28. Hillary Rodham Clinton, "Inaugural Richard C. Holbrooke Lecture on a Broad Vision of U.S.-China Relations in the 21st Century," Benjamin Franklin Room, Washington, D.C., January 14, 2011, www.state.gov/secretary/rm/2011/01/154653.htm. In this speech just before President Hu Jintao's 2011 state visit, Clinton insisted that human rights were "a matter that remains at the heart of American diplomacy" and reaffirmed America's commitment to speak out against China's oppression of political and religious activists. She called upon China to uphold its commitment to respect universal human rights as a founding member of the United Nations and denied that such calls were violations of China's sovereignty. She also highlighted the benefits that would come to China from political reform, a strengthened rule of law, and a more robust civil society.

29. Michael Wines, "Subtle Signs of Progress in U.S.–China Relations," *New York Times*, January 19, 2011, www.nytimes.com/2011/01/20/world/asia/20assess.html?_r=1&nl=tod aysheadlines&emc=tha22.

30. Office of the Press Secretary, White House, U.S.–China Joint Statement, January 19, 2011, www.whitehouse.gov/the-press-office/2011/01/19/us-china-joint-statement. The language in this U.S.-China Joint Statement was slightly strengthened from the November 2009 statement to clarify that "the promotion of human rights and democracy is an important part" of America's foreign policy. See also Jesse Lee, "President Obama Welcomes President Hu of China to the White House," White House Blog, January 19, 2011, www.whitehouse.gov/blog/2011/01/19/president-obama-welcomes-president-hu-china-white-house. In his welcome address, Obama stated, "History shows that societies are more harmonious, nations are more successful, and the world is more just, when the rights and responsibilities of all nations and all

people are upheld, including the universal rights of every human being." See also Helene Cooper, Sheryl Gay Stolberg, and Mark Landler, "Obama Pushes Hu on Rights but Stresses Ties to China," *New York Times*, January 19, 2011; and Office of the Press Secretary, White House, "Press Conference with President Obama and President Hu of the People's Republic of China," January 19, 2011. When asked about human rights concerns in this joint press conference with President Hu, Obama explained that although human rights are a serious concern and an occasional source of tension between the United States and China, "what I believed is the same thing that I think seven previous Presidents have believed, which is, is that we can engage and discuss these issues in a frank and candid way, focus on those areas where we agree, while acknowledging there are going to be areas where we disagree."

31. In an address in Shanghai in April 2011, Huntsman highlighted the central role that human rights advocacy plays in Washington's relationship with Beijing, while acknowledging that China holds different views and emphasizing the importance of maintaining cooperative ties despite those differences. Ambassador Jon M. Huntsman, Jr., "Remarks by Ambassador Jon M. Huntsman Jr. at the Barnett-Oksenberg Lecture," Shanghai, China, April 6, 2011, http://shanghai.usembassy-china.org. cn/040611ambassador.html. He stated: "Too often, divisions dominate our discourse and sap our ability to work together. Of course, it is natural for two great countries to have differences, and our differences on some issues are profound and well-known. It should come as no surprise, for example, that the United States will continue to champion respect for universal human rights, which is a fundamental extension of the American experience and a bedrock of our world view." He specifically mentioned the plights of Feng Xue, Liu Xiaobo, Chen Guangcheng, and Ai Weiwei, before continuing: "The United States will never stop supporting human rights because we believe in the fundamental struggle for human dignity and justice wherever it may occur. We do so not because we oppose China but, on the contrary, because we value our relationship. President Hu and Premier Wen have both acknowledged the universality of human rights. By speaking out candidly, we hope eventually to narrow and bridge this critical gap and move our relationship forward." See also David Barboza, "Departing U.S. Envoy Criticizes China on Human Rights," *New York Times*, April 6, 2011, www.nytimes. com/2011/04/07/world/asia/07china.html?ref=china. I am indebted to Rachel Esplin Odell for this footnote.

32. As noted below, in the wake of the widespread Middle Eastern uprisings occurring in 2011 and an online call for peaceful protests—a "Jasmine revolution"—in several major cities in China, the PRC government reportedly imposed "the largest crackdown on dissent in over a decade—one that differs ominously in scope, tactics and aims from previous campaigns." Nicholas Bequelin, "Crackdown in China," *International Herald Tribune*, April 7, 2011, www.nytimes.com/2011/04/08/opinion/08iht-edbequelin08. html?ref=china. See also Tania Branigan, "China's Human Rights Crackdown: Interactive Guide," *Guardian*, April 13, 2011, www.guardian.co.uk/world/china-human-rights-crackdown-interactive; Chris Buckley, "Exclusive: China Crackdown Driven by Fears of a Broad Conspiracy," Reuters, April 12, 2011, www.reuters.com/ article/2011/04/12/us-china-politics-crackdown-idUSTRE73B3DF20110412; Jeremy Page, "China's Crackdown Signals Shift," *Wall Street Journal*, April 11, 2011, http://online. wsj.com/article/SB10001424052748704366104576254630352511472.html. See below for a greater discussion of this crackdown.

This tough approach actually began years earlier. It was evident in the run-up to the 2008 Beijing Olympics and especially in the following year. As one human rights organization stated, "In 2009 the Chinese government continued to impose restrictions put in place for the 2008 Olympics, fearing unrest around a series of 'sensitive' anniversaries including the 20th anniversary of the Tiananmen massacre and the 60th anniversary of the founding of the People's Republic of China." See Human Rights Watch, "China: Events of 2009," in *World Report 2010* (New York: Human Rights Watch, 2010), www.hrw.org/en/node/87491.

As Iain Johnston has noted, articles that use the term "preserving stability" (weiwen, 维稳) in the *People's Daily*, an official PRC news outlet, have skyrocketed in recent years, from fewer than ten articles per year in the years up to 2005, to eleven articles in 2007, to more than 40 articles in 2008, more than 80 in 2009, and nearly 180 in 2010. This may reflect the Chinese Communist Party's growing concerns about domestic dissent and subversion. Personal correspondence and unpublished graphical data.

33. As Human Rights Watch states, "A variety of vaguely defined crimes including 'inciting subversion,' 'leaking state secrets,' and 'disrupting social order' provide the government with wide legal remit to stifle critics." See Human Rights Watch, "China Events in 2007," in *World Report 2008* (New York: Human Rights Watch, 2008), 260.

34. See Bureau of Democracy, Human Rights, and Labor, U.S. Department of State, "2009 Human Rights Report: China (includes Tibet, Hong Kong, and Macau)," 2009 Country Reports on Human Rights Practices, March 11, 2010, www.state.gov/g/drl/rls/hrrpt/2009/eap/135989.htm; Congressional-Executive Commission on China, *Congressional-Executive Commission on China Annual Report 2010*, edited by 111th Congress (Washington, D.C.: U.S. Government Printing Office, 2010), www.cecc.gov/pages/annualRpt/annualRpt10/CECCannRpt2010.pdf; Human Rights Watch, "China: Events of 2009"; Bureau of Democracy, Human Rights, and Labor, U.S. Department of State, "China (includes Tibet, Hong Kong, and Macau)," 2007 Country Reports on Human Rights Practices, March 11, 2008, www.state.gov/g/drl/rls/hrrpt/2007/100518.htm; and Congressional-Executive Commission on China, *Congressional-Executive Commission on China Annual Report 2007*, edited by 111th Congress (Washington, D.C.: U.S. Government Printing Office, 2007). For the Chinese government's more positive view of its own record, see "Section III: Legal Systems of Respecting and Safeguarding Human Rights," in *China's Efforts and Achievements in Promoting the Rule of Law*, edited by Information Office of the State Council of the People's Republic of China (Beijing: Information Office of the State Council of the People's Republic of China, 2008), www.china.org.cn/government/news/2008-02/28/content_11025486.htm.

35. Lum and Fischer, "Human Rights," 2010, 25; David Stanway, "Beijing Strikes at Dissidents," *Guardian*, January 4, 2009, www.guardian.co.uk/world/2009/jan/04/china-human-rights-charter-08.

36. Donald Clarke, "Lawyers and the State in China: Recent Developments," testimony before the Congressional-Executive Commission on China, Washington, D.C., October 7, 2009, www.cecc.gov/pages/hearings/2009/20091007/dclarke100709.pdf.

37. See Austin Ramzy, "In China, the Crackdown on Activists Continues," *Time*, November 8, 2010; Keith B. Richburg, "China Crackdown on Dissidents Continues Despite Citizen's Nobel Peace Prize," *Washington Post*, October 28, 2010; "China Warns States Not to Support Nobel dissident," CNN, November 5, 2010, www.bbc.co.uk/news/world-

asia-pacific-11701725; "China Warns Western Envoys Off Nobel Ceremony: Diplomats," Agence France-Presse, November 5, 2010, http://news.yahoo.com/s/afp/20101105/wl_asia_afp/nobelpeacechinanorwaydiplomacy; Michael Wines, "China Assails Nobel Peace Prize as 'Card' of West," *New York Times*, November 5, 2010, www.nytimes.com/2010/11/06/world/asia/06nobel.html?_r=1&scp=3&sq=nobel%20prize%20china&st=cse; Gillian Wong, "China's Monitoring of Activists Surges Post-Nobel," *Washington Post*, November 11, 2010, www.washingtonpost.com/wp-dyn/content/article/2010/11/11/AR2010111102238.html; and Peter Ford, "Chinese Authorities Silence Friends of Liu Xiaobo in Extensive Roundup," *Christian Science Monitor*, December 9, 2010. As a result of China's aggressive diplomatic campaign, nineteen countries in addition to China boycotted the ceremony. See "Who's Staying Away from Nobel Ceremony?" Agence France-Presse, December 9, 2010, http://timesofindia.indiatimes.com/world/europe/Whos-staying-away-from-Nobel-ceremony/articleshow/7072455.cms#ixzz1BVJPl0h5.

38. See Douglas H. Paal, "China Reacts to Middle East Unrest," Asia Pacific Brief, Carnegie Endowment for International Peace, February 28, 2011, http://carnegieendowment.org/publications/index.cfm?fa=view&id=42797; Page, "China's Crackdown Signals Shift"; Bequelin, "Crackdown in China"; Branigan, "China's Human Rights Crackdown"; Buckley, "China Crackdown Driven by Fears"; James Fallows, "The Chinese Crackdown: Arrogance? Or Insecurity?" *Atlantic*, April 13, 2011, www.theatlantic.com/international/archive/2011/04/the-chinese-crackdown-arrogance-or-insecurity/237234; Anita Chang, "China Tries to Stamp Out 'Jasmine Revolution,'" Associated Press, February 20, 2011, http://news.yahoo.com/s/ap/20110220/ap_on_re_as/as_china_jasmine_revolution. Prior to his being detained incommunicado in April 2011 for purported "economic crimes," Ai Weiwei's Shanghai studio had been destroyed by local authorities, and he had been placed under house arrest for a period of time. See Edward Wong, "Chinese Defend Detention of Artist on Grounds of 'Economic Crimes,'" *New York Times*, April 7, 2011, www.nytimes.com/2011/04/08/world/asia/08china.html; Edward Wong, "Chinese Authorities Raze an Artist's Studio," *New York Times*, January 12, 2011, www.nytimes.com/2011/01/13/world/asia/13china.html?scp=1&sq=ai%20weiwei&st=cse. I am indebted to Rachel Esplin Odell for providing the information contained in this paragraph and the preceding one.

39. Clinton, "Inaugural Richard C. Holbrooke Lecture"; Huntsman, "Remarks at Barnett-Oksenberg Lecture"; Posner, "Briefing on the U.S.-China Human Rights Dialogue"; Peter Ford, "Gao Zhisheng: One Year Later, China Still Mum on Missing Lawyer," *Christian Science Monitor*, February 4, 2010; Peter Ford, "China's Blind Activist Lawyer, Chen Guangcheng, Released from Prison," *Christian Science Monitor*, September 9, 2010; Charles Hutzler, "Missing Chinese Lawyer Told of Abuse," Associated Press, January 10, 2011, www.bloomberg.com/news/2011-01-10/ap-exclusive-missing-chinese-lawyer-told-of-abuse.html; Shaun Tandon, "Wife of China Dissident Speaks Out on Abuse," Agence France-Presse, January 18, 2011; Charles Hutzler, "Xue Feng, American Geologist, Held And Mistreated By China," Huffington Post, November 19, 2009, www.huffingtonpost.com/2009/11/19/xue-feng-american-geologi_n_363521.html; Andrew Jacobs, "China Upholds Conviction of American Geologist," *New York Times*, February 18, 2011, www.nytimes.com/2011/02/19/world/asia/19beijing.html. There appears to be at least some leeway in the repressive behavior of the Chinese government for some very-well-known bloggers with large popular followings, such as Han Han. See "Han Han: China's

Rebel Blogger," CNN Tech, June 3, 2010, http://articles.cnn.com/2010-06-03/tech/han.han.china_1_chinese-government-han-han-china?_s=PM:TECH.

40. Lum and Fischer, "Human Rights," 2010; Andrew Jacobs, "Trial in China Signals New Limits on Dissent," *New York Times*, December 24, 2009. This story quotes John Kamm, the founder of the Dui Hua Foundation, a group that advocates for human rights and works behind the scenes to free Chinese political prisoners, as stating, in reference to the trial of Liu Xiaobo: "Many people see this trial as a tipping point. . . . The government seems to be getting tougher and more unyielding." Also, according to Jacobs, "Legal scholars say they worry that top party leaders seem less amenable to building an impartial legal system and allowing people to exercise the political rights in China's Constitution, which could mean that intellectuals and civic groups have less room to operate." Also see Cara Anna, "Chinese Court Upholds Prominent Scholar's 11-Year Punishment," Associated Press, February 12, 2010; and Andrew Jacobs, "China's Defiance Stirs Fears for Missing Dissident," *New York Times*, February 3, 2010. According to Jacobs, "John Kamm . . . said that during three decades working in China he had rarely seen such a hard line toward dissidents—and unbridled defiance against pressure from abroad."

41. Richburg, "China's Crackdown." The author states: "The Chinese government . . . has intensified a subtle but steady tightening over the country's freewheeling civil society sector, with some nonprofit groups saying they are feeling increasingly harassed, targeted by tax investigations and subjected to new restrictions on receiving donations from abroad." Also see Edward Wong, "China Tightens Grip on Muslims in the Northwest," *International Herald Tribune*, October 19, 2008, www.iht.com/articles/2008/10/19/news/xinjiang.php?page=1. As indicated above, China has almost certainly also used the global war on terrorism to justify and deepen efforts to suppress domestic dissidents, especially in western areas such as Xinjiang. See Congressional-Executive Commission on China, *Congressional-Executive Commission on China Annual Report 2007*, 14.

42. Bureau of Democracy, Human Rights, and Labor, U.S. Department of State, "2009 Human Rights Report: China (includes Tibet, Hong Kong, and Macau)"; Lum and Fischer, "Human Rights," 2010; Edward Cody, "Fallout from Tibet Is Test for China's Rulers," *Washington Post*, March 28, 2008; Maureen Fan, "Nearly 1,000 in Lhasa, Provinces Are Said to Have Surrendered," *Washington Post*, March 27, 2008; Jane MacArtney, "China Imposes Lockdown After Protesters Kill Police Officer," *Times* (London), March 26, 2008; David Barboza, "660 Held in Tibetan Uprising, China Says," *New York Times*, March 27, 2008; and Gillian Wong, "China Sticks to Hard Line in Talks on Tibet," Associated Press, February 1, 2010.

43. Human Rights Watch, "China Events in 2007," 262.

44. Thomas Lum and Hannah Fischer, "Human Rights in China: Trends and Policy Implications," CRS Report for Congress, July 13, 2009, http://fpc.state.gov/documents/organization/128378.pdf. This report states that "from August to October 2007, when the CCP held its 17th Party Congress, PRC authorities reportedly carried out dozens of arrests, beatings, and abductions of petitioners, activists for human, housing, and land rights, lawyers, and Christian leaders in what some observers called the 'worst crackdown in five years.' Prior to the Olympics, the PRC government also detained 44 dissident writers and launched what one NGO leader referred to as a 'systematic crackdown on the voices of civil society,' including some prominent Chinese NGOs" (p. 9).

45. For example, see Human Rights Watch, "China: Beijing Relocations Put Migrants at Risk," March 31, 2010; and "China Razes Uyghur Homes," Radio Free Asia, July 13, 2010.

46. Christopher Bodeen, "Beijing Tightens Controls over Foreign Media," Associated Press, March 6, 2011, www.salon.com/wires/world/2011/03/06/D9LPQHQO0_as_china_protest_calls/index.html; "China's Press Freedoms Extended," BBC News, October 19, 2008, http://news.bbc.co.uk/1/hi/world/asia-pacific/7675306.stm. Also see Cody, "U.S. Reopens Talks."

47. Bureau of Democracy, Human Rights, and Labor, U.S. Department of State, "2009 Human Rights Report: China (includes Tibet, Hong Kong, and Macau)"; Michael Bristow, "China Defends Screening Software," BBC, June 9, 2009, http://news.bbc.co.uk/2/hi/asia-pacific/8091044.stm; Phelim Kine, "Leaning on the Dragon," *New York Times*, July 6, 2009, www.nytimes.com/2009/07/07/opinion/07iht-edkine.html?_r=1&scp=1&sq=phelim%20kine&st=cse; Lum and Fischer, "Human Rights," 2010.

48. In an apparent compromise, Google subsequently stopped automatically redirecting users to its Hong Kong site by providing them with the option of doing so. As a result, Google's license to operate in China was renewed in July 2010, but the Chinese site is partially blocked. See Keith Richburg, "Google Compromise Pays Off with Renewal of License in China," *Washington Post*, July 10, 2010. Another, apparently much larger, China-based computer hacking attack also took place in 2009, according to Canadian researchers. This electronic spy network, named GhostNet, allegedly infiltrated more than 1,000 computers in the offices of more than 100 foreign governments, including foreign ministries and embassies. See "Major Cyber Spy Network Uncovered," BBC News, March 29, 2009. The report states: "The Canadian researchers said that was no conclusive evidence that China's government was behind it, and Beijing denied involvement. But a separate report from the University of Cambridge said they believed that the Chinese government was behind the intrusions they analyzed against the Dalai Lama."

49. Paal, "China Reacts to Middle East Unrest"; Fallows, "The Chinese Crackdown"; Sharon Lafraniere and David Barboza, "China Tightens Censorship of Electronic Communications," *New York Times*, March 21, 2011, www.nytimes.com/2011/03/22/world/asia/22china.html; Chris Buckley, "China Steps Up Defense of Internet Controls," Reuters, January 25, 2010. As quoted in this Reuters news story, China's State Council Information Office asserted that Beijing "bans using the Internet to subvert state power and wreck national unity, to incite ethnic hatred and division, to promote cults and to distribute content that is pornographic, salacious, violent or terrorist." The story also cites comments on the central government's website by an unnamed government spokesperson that "China has an ample legal basis for punishing such harmful content, and there is no room for doubting this. This is completely different from so-called restriction of Internet freedom." Also see "Report: China's Web Industry Plugs into Social Networking," *People's Daily*, July 8, 2010; and Jamil Anderlini, "China's 'Twitters' Targeted by Internet Police," *Financial Times*, July 14, 2010.

50. Michael Wines, Sharon LaFraniere, and Jonathan Ansfield, "China's Censors Tackle and Trip Over the Internet," *New York Times*, April 7, 2010. Also see Lum and Fischer, "Human Rights," 2009. This source states that Beijing has successfully "employed a variety of 'hard' and 'soft' techniques and approaches to control online content and behavior, including electronic filtering, regulation of Internet Service Providers, monitoring of Internet cafes, and intimidation through the arrests of high profile 'cyber dissidents' " (pp. 25–26).

51. Christopher Walker and Sarah Cook, "China's Commercialization of Censorship," *Far Eastern Economic Review*, May 2, 2009, www.feer.com/politics/2009/may56/Chinas-Commercialization-of-Censorship.

52. U.S. Department of State, Bureau of East Asian and Pacific Affairs, "Background Note: China," August 5, 2010, www.state.gov/r/pa/ei/bgn/18902.htm.

53. See Keith Bradsher, "China Releases Human Rights Plan," *New York Times*, April 13, 2009, www.nytimes.com/2009/04/14/world/asia/14china.html?ref=global-home. Beijing's official Human Rights Plan "promises the right to a fair trial, the right to participate in government decisions and the right to learn about and question government policies. It calls for measures to discourage torture, such as requiring interrogation rooms to be designed to physically separate interrogators from the accused, and for measures to protect detainees from other abuse, from inadequate sanitation to the denial of medical care. There are also specific protections for children, women, senior citizens, ethnic minorities and people with disabilities."

54. For example, see Paul Mooney, "Legal Activist Fosters Public Interest in China Courts," *National*, October 22, 2008. Also see Jim Yardley, "A Judge Tests China's Courts, Making History," *New York Times*, November 28, 2005, www.nytimes.com/2005/11/28/international/asia/28judge.html.

55. Scott McDonald, "China May Drop Death Penalty for Economic Crimes," Associated Press, August 23, 2010; Amnesty International, "Proposed China Death Penalty Reforms May Have No Great Impact on Executions," August 22, 2010, www.amnesty.org/en/news-and-updates/proposed-china-death-penalty-reforms-may-have-no-great-impact-executions-2010-08-23.

56. Ann Florini and Yeling Tan, "Transparent Warriors," *Foreign Policy Online*, July 9, 2009, http://experts.foreignpolicy.com/posts/2009/07/09/transparent_warriors. The authors state: "One year in, the regulations are actively being used by citizens addressing grievances in land requisition, by environmental groups monitoring corporate standards, and by lawyers and public intellectuals scrutinizing everything from government toll collection to budget spending."

57. Marina Svensson, *Debating Human Rights in China: A Conceptual and Political History* (Lanham, Md.: Rowman & Littlefield, 2002), 309.

58. During the George W. Bush administration, the United States had no direct ability to counter such actions because it did not have a seat on the UNHRC, due to the fact that the president initiated a boycott of the organization. Under Obama, the United States has resumed its seat.

59. Pitman B. Potter, "China and the International Legal System: Challenges of Participation," *China Quarterly*, no. 191 (September 2007): 699–715.

60. Moisés Naím, "Rogue Aid," *Foreign Policy*, no. 159 (March–April 2007): 96–97.

61. "Are Human Rights Higher Than Sovereignty?" *People's Daily*, March 17, 2006; Human Rights Watch, "China Events in 2007," 270; Congressional-Executive Commission on China, *Congressional-Executive Commission on China Annual Report 2007*, 4–5; Jacques deLisle, "Into Africa: China's Quest for Resources and Influence," Foreign Policy Research Institute E-Notes, February 2007, www.fpri.org/enotes/200702.delisle.intoafricachinasquest.html. For examples of Chinese explanations, see "China's Influence on Darfur Should Not Be Overestimated, Says Envoy," Xinhua, March 7, 2008;

"China Plays Constructive Role in World Peace, Stability: Foreign Ministry," Xinhua, March 4, 2008; and "Talks, Not Sanctions, Way to Resolve Darfur Crisis: People's Daily," Xinhua, July 28, 2004.

62. Moisés Naím, "What Is a GONGO?" *Foreign Policy*, no. 160 (May–June 2007): 96–105. Also see the website of the China Society for Human Rights Studies, www.china humanrights.org.

63. See Douglas H. Paal, "China: Mugged by Reality in Libya, Again," Asia Pacific Brief, Carnegie Endowment for International Peace, April 11, 2011, http://carnegie endowment.org/publications/index.cfm?fa=view&id=43554; Michael Swaine, "China: Exploiting a Strategic Opening," in *Strategic Asia 2004–05: Confronting Terrorism in the Pursuit of Power*, edited by Ashley J. Tellis and Michael Wills (Seattle: National Bureau of Asian Research, 2004), 67–101; Robert Sutter, "China's Regional Strategy and America," in *Power Shift: China and Asia's New Dynamics*, edited by David Shambaugh (Berkeley: University of California Press, 2005), 290; Bates Gill, *Rising Star: China's New Security Diplomacy* (Washington, D.C.: Brookings Institution Press, 2007), 12–13; David Shambaugh, "China Engages Asia: Reshaping the Regional Order," *International Security*, vol. 29, no. 3 (Winter 2004–2005): 64–99; Susan L. Craig, *Chinese Perceptions of Traditional and Nontraditional Security Threats* (Carlisle, Pa.: Strategic Studies Institute, 2007); Gao Zugui, "Major Non-Traditional Security Threats in the Asia-Pacific Region: China's Perspective," in *A Collection of Papers of the International Symposium on Non-Traditional Security: Challenges and Responses* (Beijing: China Institute for International Strategic Studies, 2005), 336; Zhou Shengxian, "Implement the Spirit of 17th Party Congress on Environmental Protection," speech at the National Environment Conference, January 22, 2008; Banning Garrett and Jonathan Adams, *U.S.-China Cooperation on the Problem of Failing States and Transnational Threats*, Special Report 126 (Washington, D.C.: U.S. Institute for Peace Press, 2004); and Banning Garrett, "U.S.-China Relations in the Era of Globalization and Terror: A Framework for Analysis," *Journal of Contemporary China*, vol. 15, no. 48 (August 2006): 389–415.

64. China supported the referral of Libya to the International Criminal Court, voted in favor of UN Security Resolution 1970 imposing strict sanctions on Libya, and abstained on UN Security Resolution 1973 authorizing enforcement of a "no-fly zone" in Libya, thus enabling it to be adopted. (Since China has veto power as a permanent member of the UN Security Council, a nay vote by China would have resulted in the resolution's failure to pass.) Some analysts point to China's growing economic ties as a major driver of this shift: China has substantial economic interests in Libya—dozens of PRC companies and 36,000 Chinese laborers in Libya were working on over 50 projects in the railroad and petroleum sectors, and China reportedly sustained losses of over $18 billion as a result of the Libyan conflict. Moreover, Beijing also has important economic ties with member states of the Arab League and African Union—both of which had actively supported Resolution 1973. See Paal, "China: Mugged by Reality in Libya, Again"; Brian Spegele, "China Takes New Tack in Libya Vote," *Wall Street Journal*, March 20, 2011, http://online.wsj.com/article/SB10001424052748703292304576212431833887 422.html; Jason Dean, "China's Vote On Libya Signals Possible Shift," *Wall Street Journal*, February 28, 2011, http://online.wsj.com/article/SB10001424052748703934045761707 93783265986.html.

However, other observers deny that the PRC's behavior on Libya marked a significant departure from past actions, pointing to China's rare use of its veto power, particularly when no other state is wielding it, and its long-held desire to avoid isolation in the international community and on the UN Security Council. These observers also emphasize that China has at times past been willing to compromise its principles of noninterference when it perceived them as essential to its national interests—for example, when it abstained on a U.S.-sponsored UN Security Council resolution authorizing the invasion of Iraq in 1990 in an effort to escape its post-Tiananmen international isolation. See Yun Sun, "China's Acquiescence on UNSCR 1973: No Big Deal," PacNet #20, Pacific Forum CSIS, March 31, 2011, https://csis.org/files/publication/pac1120.pdf; Frank Ching, "China's Role Continues to Evolve," *China Post*, April 6, 2011, www.chinapost.com.tw/commentary/the-china-post/frank-ching/2011/04/06/297553/Chinas-role.htm. The latter article points to both continuity and change in China's foreign policy stances as evident in its actions toward Libya and argues that China's vote in favor of sanctions and its endorsement of Libya's referral to the ICC were actually more noteworthy than its abstention from Resolution 1973 authorizing a "no-fly zone." Ching concludes: "China's role in the world continues to heighten and its principle of non-interference in other countries' internal affairs continues to evolve."

It is also important to note that China has subsequently strongly criticized the military actions undertaken by U.S. and NATO forces in Libya. See "Hu: Use of Force No Solution to Problems Like Libyan Issue," Xinhua, March 30, 2011, www.china.org.cn/world/libya_air_strike/2011-03/30/content_22258604.htm; "Explanation of Vote by Ambassador Li Baodong after Adoption of Security Council Resolution on Libya," Permanent Mission of the People's Republic of China to the UN, March 17, 2011, www.china-un.org/eng/gdxw/t807544.htm; "Ambassador Li Baodong Chairs Security Council Meeting on Libya," Permanent Mission of the People's Republic of China to the UN, March 25, 2011, www.china-un.org/eng/hyyfy/t809816.htm; "Foreign Ministry Spokesperson Jiang Yu's Regular Press Conference on March 22, 2011," Ministry of Foreign Affairs of the People's Republic of China, March 23, 2011, www.fmprc.gov.cn/eng/xwfw/s2510/t809578.htm. Through these formal declarations, China repeatedly expressed its opposition to "the use of force in international relations" and "the abuse of force that can cause more civilian casualties and a bigger humanitarian crisis," and called for "an immediate ceasefire and a peaceful settlement of the issue." I am indebted to Rachel Esplin Odell for this footnote.

65. See United Nations Department of Peacekeeping Operations, "UN Peacekeeping Background Note," DPI/2429/Rev.10, January 2011, www.un.org/en/peacekeeping/documents/backgroundnote.pdf; State Council of the People's Republic of China, *China's National Defense in 2010* (Beijing: Information Office of the State Council of the People's Republic of China, March 2011), http://news.xinhuanet.com/english2010/china/2011-03/31/c_13806851.htm; Chin-Hao Huang, "China's Military and Security Activities Abroad," testimony before the U.S.-China Economic and Security Review Commission, Washington, D.C., March 4, 2009; Michael R. Chambers, "Framing the Problem: China's Threat Environment and International Obligations," in *Right Sizing the People's Liberation Army: Exploring the Contours of China's Military*, edited by Roy Kamphausen and Andrew Scobell (Carlisle, Pa.: Strategic Studies Institute, 2007), 19–67; Nicholas Fiorenza, "China Bolsters Peacekeeping Commitment," *Jane's Defence Weekly*, February 21, 2007; and Stephen Morrison, James Swan, Bates Gill, Sun Baohong, and Mark Bellamy, "China's Expanding Role in Africa: Implications for the United States," paper presented at Center for Strategic and International Studies, Washington, D.C., February 8, 2007.

66. Ann Kent, "China's International Socialization: The Role of International Organization," *Global Governance*, vol. 8, no. 3 (July–September 2002): 343–64. Kent summarizes the history of China's involvement in international human rights organizations in the following manner: "First, China chose to join human rights bodies and to ratify treaties, like the UN Convention Against Torture (CAT), whose norms did not appear to coincide with the values of the Chinese leadership. China became a member of the UN Human Rights Commission in 1981 and of the UN Sub-Commission on the Prevention of Discrimination and Protection of Minorities in 1984. China also acceded to other core human rights treaties: the Convention on the Elimination of All Forms of Discrimination Against Women in 1980, the Convention on the Elimination of Racial Discrimination in 1981, and the Convention on the Rights of the Child in 1992. Although for many years China avoided signing the International Covenant on Civil and Political Rights (ICCPR) and the International Covenant on Economic, Social, and Cultural Rights (ICESCR), it signed the ICESCR in October 1997 and the ICCPR in October 1998. Finally, in March 2001, China ratified the ICESCR. Its accession was doubtlessly influenced by its desire to assume its rightful place on the world stage as well as to have an input into negotiating treaties. Yet these developments mark China's greatest formal advance in human rights since 1949, even if the practical implementation of its treaty obligations remains deficient. China has also allowed continued reporting to the UN Human Rights Commission on the condition of human rights in Hong Kong."

67. Ibid. Kent explains that as a result of its participation in international legal institutions, "China introduced a plethora of new laws that appeared to move away from the previous emphasis on security and state-oriented goals to a greater concern with the rights of the individual. They included the new Prison Law and the State Compensation Law (1994); the PRC Law on Judges, the PRC Law on Procurators, and the People's Police Law (1995); the Lawyers' Law (1996); and major amendments to the Criminal Procedure Law (1996) and the Criminal Law (1997)." See also Ann E. Kent, *Beyond Compliance: China, International Organizations, and Global Security* (Stanford, Calif.: Stanford University Press, 2007).

68. Cherie Canning, "Pursuit of the Pariah: Iran, Sudan and Myanmar in China's Energy Security Strategy," *Security Challenges*, vol. 3, no. 1 (February 2007): 47–63. Another example is South Africa. In July 2008, "China and Russia vetoed a U.S.-sponsored U.N. Security Council resolution that proposed worldwide sanctions against Zimbabwean President Robert Mugabe, accusing him of trampling Zimbabweans' democratic rights and ruining the once prosperous nation's economy." See "Glance at China–Africa Relations," Associated Press, March 23, 2009.

69. See Andrew Natsios, special envoy to Sudan, "Planning for Peace in Darfur," remarks to the Center for Strategic and International Studies, U.S. Department of State, September 19, 2007, http://2001-2009.state.gov/p/af/ci/su/remarks/remarks2007/92958.htm; John D. Negroponte, deputy secretary of state, Adam Szubin, director of Office of Foreign Assets Control, Treasury Department, and Andrew Natsios, special envoy to Sudan, "Remarks on Darfur and Sanctions," U.S. Department of State, May 29, 2007, http://2001-2009.state.gov/s/d/2007/85716.htm; and James Swan, deputy assistant secretary of state for African affairs, "Civil War and Genocide in Darfur: Chinese and Saharan Dimensions," remarks at the American Enterprise Institute, U.S. Department of State, May 3, 2007, http://2001-2009.state.gov/p/af/rls/rm/84401.htm. Also see

Deborah Brautigam, *The Dragon's Gift: The Real Story of China in Africa* (New York: Oxford University Press, 2009).

70. Geoff Dyer, "Beijing and Troubled Nations: Signals of a Shift," *Financial Times*, January 20, 2011, www.ft.com/cms/s/0/426c3912-24c8-11e0-a919-00144feab49a. html#axzz1BaExZF00; Donata Hardenberg, "China: A Force for Peace in Sudan?" Al Jazeera, January 11, 2011, http://english.aljazeera.net/indepth/features/2011/01/20111910357773378.html.

71. International Crisis Group, "China's Myanmar Strategy: Elections, Ethnic Politics and Economics," Crisis Group Asia Briefing no. 112, September 21, 2010, www.crisisgroup. org/~/media/Files/asia/north-east-asia/B112%20Chinas%20Myanmar%20Strategy%20%20Elections%20Ethnic%20Politics%20and%20Economics.ashx; Dyer, "Beijing and Troubled Nations"; Stephanie Kleine-Ahlbrandt and Andrew Small, "China's New Dictatorship Diplomacy," *Foreign Affairs*, vol. 78, no. 1 (January–February 2008): 38–56; Andrew Small, "China's Changing Policies Towards Rogue States," testimony before the U.S.–China Economic and Security Review Commission, Washington, D.C., March 18, 2008, www.uscc.gov/hearings/2008hearings/written_testimonies/08_03_18_wrts/08_03_18_small_statement.pdf; Scot Marciel, deputy assistant secretary for East Asian and Pacific affairs, "Crisis in Burma: Can the U.S. Bring About a Peaceful Resolution?" testimony before Subcommittee on Asia, the Pacific, and the Global Environment, House Foreign Affairs Committee, U.S. Department of State, October 17, 2007, http://2001-2009.state.gov/p/eap/rls/rm/2007/93649.htm; and President George W. Bush, "President Bush Discusses Sanctions on Burma," U.S. Department of State, October 19, 2007, http://2001-2009.state.gov/p/eap/rls/rm/2007/93754.htm.

72. See, for example, Sophie Richardson, "Challenges for a 'Responsible Power,' " in *World Report: 2008—Events of 2007* (New York: Human Rights Watch, 2008), 25–35. The author adds, however, that "it is too soon to tell whether China's greater support for human rights issues in some cases constitute a shift away from the traditional policy of non-interference, or whether they are idiosyncratic changes made in response to intense international pressure." For a general discussion of China's gradual shift toward greater support for issues related to international human rights, see Guoli Liu, ed., *Chinese Foreign Policy in Transition* (Edison, N.J.: Aldine Transaction, 2004), 375–76.

73. For example, see Joshua Kurlantzick and Perry Link, "China: Resilient, Sophisticated Authoritarianism," in *Undermining Democracy: 21st Century Authoritarians* (Washington, D.C.: Freedom House, 2009), 13–28; Robert Kagan, "End of Dreams, Return of History," *Policy Review*, August–September 2007, www.hoover.org/publications/policyreview/8552512.html; and Naazneen Barma and Ely Ratner, "China's Illiberal Challenge," *Democracy*, Fall 2006. See also Edward Friedman, testimony before the U.S.-China Economic and Security Review Commission, Washington, D.C., March 18, 2008, www.uscc.gov/hearings/2008hearings/written_testimonies/08_03_18_wrts/08_03_18_friedman_statement.php. Friedman states: "Whereas the rise of the European Union . . . seemed to establish a link between prosperity and freedom, a rising China has broken that linkage and tried to establish a link instead between authoritarianism and development. This triumph of the CCP over the EU is manifest in Beijing's negation of conditionality and good governance regimes in Africa. Authoritarians, because of the rise of China and its global power, can now by-pass the forums established by the democracies and shop for money, loans, aid, weapons, and investment in the forums built by the authoritarian People's Republic of China."

74. See, for example, William Ratliff, "An Assessment of China's Deepening Ties to Latin America," *China Brief*, vol. 8, no. 11 (June 6, 2008). The author writes: "China's preference lies with governments that succeed, and thus their relations have developed most rapidly and smoothly with Chile, and secondarily with Brazil."

75. James F. Paradise, "China and International Harmony: The Role of Confucius Institutes in Bolstering Beijing's Soft Power," *Asian Survey*, vol. 49, no. 4 (July–August 2009).

76. Kerry Dumbaugh, "China–U.S. Relations: Current Issues and Implications for U.S. Policy," CRS Report for Congress, October 9, 2009, www.fas.org/sgp/crs/row/R40457. pdf.

77. For example, see Thomas Friedman, "Going Long Liberty in China," *New York Times*, October 16, 2010.

78. Homi Kharas and Geoffrey Gertz, "The New Global Middle Class: A Cross-Over from West to East," Wolfensohn Center for Development at Brookings, March 2010, www. brookings.edu/~/media/Files/rc/papers/2010/03_china_middle_class_kharas/ 03_china_middle_class_kharas.pdf; Cheng Li, "Democracy Gaining Momentum in China," *San Francisco Chronicle*, June 4, 2009, www.sfgate.com/cgi-bin/article.cgi?f=/ c/a/2009/06/03/EDU91807CR.DTL; Richard Gundey, "Bruce Gilley Discusses His New Book, China's Democratic Future," UCLA International Institute, March 4, 2004, www.international.ucla.edu/article.asp?parentid=8710; Bruce Gilley, *China's Democratic Future: How It Will Happen and Where It Will Lead* (New York: Columbia University Press, 2004); and John L. Thornton, "Long Time Coming: The Prospects for Democracy in China," *Foreign Affairs*, vol. 87, no. 1 (January–February 2008): 2–22.

79. China Factfile, "Mass Media," Gov.cn (Chinese government's official Web portal), http:// english.gov.cn/2006-02/08/content_182637.htm.

80. Jayshree Bajoria, interview with Cheng Li, in "Tiananmen Square and Two Chinas," Council of Foreign Relations, June 2, 2009, www.cfr.org/publication/19544/tiananmen_ square_and_two_chinas.html.

81. For example, Wen Jiabao has become symbolic of more liberal-leaning Chinese elites. In a now-famous interview with Fareed Zakaria (which was reportedly censored in some Chinese news sources), Wen called for continued democratic reform and an enhanced rule of law. He discussed the need for freedom of speech, stating that China "must create conditions to let [people] criticize the work of the government." See Fareed Zakaria, "Interview with Wen Jiabao," CNN Global Public Square, October 3, 2010, transcript at http://edition.cnn.com/TRANSCRIPTS/1010/03/fzgps.01.html.

82. Yijiang Ding, *Chinese Democracy After Tiananmen* (New York: Columbia University Press, 2002). Also see Cheng, "Democracy Gaining Momentum"; he states: "This rapidly growing and economically empowered group is better equipped to seek political participation than the Chinese citizens of 20 years ago and more likely to be successful. . . . Premier Wen Jiabao consistently advocates for the universal values of democracy. He has defined democracy in largely the same way as many in the West would, noting the importance of elections, judicial independence and supervision based on checks and balances." And see Gundey, "Bruce Gilley Discusses His New Book"; Gilley, *China's Democratic Future*; Minxin Pei, Zhang Guoyan, Pei Fei, and Chen Lixin (Carnegie Beijing and Shanghai Academy of Social Sciences), "China's Evolving Legal System," Carnegie Issue Brief, February 2009, www.carnegieendowment.org/files/ China_Legal_System_Full_Text2.pdf; and Thornton, "Long Time Coming." Thornton

cites a senior Communist Party official as stating that "now the debate in China is no longer about whether to have democracy, . . . but about when and how."

83. One area where some analysts see notable backsliding is in the advancement of the rule of law, particularly regarding human rights and high-level corruption. See Louisa Lim, "Rights Lawyers in China Face Growing Threats," NPR, May 3, 2009, www.npr.org/templates/story/story.php?storyId=103733164.

84. Gundey, "Bruce Gilley Discusses His New Book"; Geoff Dyer, "Little Leaps Forward?" *Financial Times*, May 27, 2009, www.ft.com/cms/s/0/dbd43930-4aed-11de-87c2-00144feabdc0.html; Arthur N. Waldron, testimony before the House National Security Committee on Security Challenges: China, Washington, D.C., March 20, 1996, www.fas.org/spp/starwars/congress/1996_h/wald0320.htm; Thornton, "Long Time Coming"; Suisheng Zhao, ed., *The Prospects for a Democratic China* (London: Routledge, 2000).

85. For some recent examples, see André Laliberté and Marc Lanteigne, eds., *The Chinese Party-State in the Twenty-First Century: Adaptation and the Reinvention of Legitimacy* (New York: Routledge, 2007); Suisheng Zhao, ed., *Debating Political Reform in China* (Armonk, N.Y.: M. E. Sharpe, 2006); Gilley, *China's Democratic Future*; Leong H. Liew and Shaoguang Wang, eds., *Nationalism, Democracy, and National Integration in China* (London: RoutledgeCurzon, 2004); Yijiang Ding, *Chinese Democracy After Tiananmen* (New York: Columbia University Press, 2002); Marina Svensson, *Debating Human Rights in China: A Conceptual and Political History* (Lanham, Md.: Rowman & Littlefield, 2002); and Ming Wan, *Human Rights in Chinese Foreign Relations: Defining and Defending National Interests* (Philadelphia: University of Pennsylvania Press, 2001).

86. Francis Fukuyama, "For China, Stability Comes Before Democracy," *Yomiuri Shimbun*, January 13, 2008, www.yomiuri.co.jp/dy/world/20080113TDY08001.htm. Fukuyama states: "Were China to democratize today, the political consequences would likely threaten middle-class prosperity, if not political stability in general."

87. Tania Branigan, "Young, Gifted and Red: The Communist Party's Quiet Revolution," *Guardian*, May 20, 2009, www.guardian.co.uk/world/2009/may/20/china-changing-communist-party.

88. See, for example, Guobin Yang, *The Power of the Internet in China: Citizen Activism Online* (New York: Columbia University Press, 2009). Also see Rebecca MacKinnon, "Google and Internet Control in China," testimony prepared for Congressional-Executive Commission on China, March 24, 2010, www.cecc.gov/pages/hearings/2010/20100324/mackinnonTestimony.pdf.

89. See Laliberté and Lanteigne, *The Chinese Party-State in the Twenty-First Century*.

90. Interviews with former and current U.S. officials.

91. See Peter Hays Gries, *China's New Nationalism: Pride, Politics, and Diplomacy* (Berkeley: University of California Press, 2004), 4–8; Jayshree Bajoria, "Nationalism in China," Council on Foreign Relations, April 23, 2008, www.cfr.org/publication/16079/nationalism_in_china.html; Denny Roy, "China's Democratised Foreign Policy," *Survival*, vol. 51, no. 2 (April–May 2009): 25–40; Branigan, "Young, Gifted and Red"; Kathrin Hille, "New Generation Puts Jobs Over Democracy," *Financial Times*, May 22, 2009, www.ft.com/cms/s/0/6e12edda-4668-11de-803f-00144feabdc0.html; Dyer, "Little Leaps Forward?"; David Shambaugh, *China's Communist Party: Atrophy and Adaptation* (Berkeley: University of California Press, 2008); Walker and Cook,

"China's Commercialization"; Economist Intelligence Unit, "Cracking Down on Dissent," January 7, 2009, www.economist.com/agenda/displaystory.cfm?story_id=12884302&fsrc=rss; and Andrew J. Nathan, "Authoritarian Resilience," *Journal of Democracy*, vol. 14, no. 1 (January 2003): 6–17.

92. For a thorough overview of these problems and issues, see Shambaugh, *China's Communist Party*.

93. David Pilling, "China's Success Outstrips Democracy for Now," *Financial Times*, June 3, 2009, www.ft.com/cms/s/0/167fd91e-506f-11de-9530-00144feabdc0.html. Piling writes: "If there were elections tomorrow, . . . the Communist party would probably win by a landslide. . . . As a result of the effective combination of governance reforms and co-opting the rich and the middle class, few analysts believe the party will face a serious threat over the next decade."

94. Thornton, "Long Time Coming." Thornton states: "Top officials stress that the CCP's leadership must be preserved. Although they see a role for elections, particularly at the local level, they assert that a 'deliberative' form of politics that allows individual citizens and groups to add their views to the decision-making process is more appropriate for China than open, multiparty competition for national power. . . . Chinese leaders do not welcome the latitude of freedom of speech, press, or assembly taken for granted in the West." Also see Hille, "New Generation"; Yun-han Chu, Larry Diamond, Andrew J. Nathan, and Doh Chull Shin, "Asia's Challenged Democracies," *Washington Quarterly*, vol. 32, no. 1 (January 2009): 143–57; David M. Lampton and James Mann, "What's Your China Fantasy?" *Foreign Policy*, May 2007, www.forcignpolicy.com/story/cms.php?story_id=3837&page=0; Jayshree Bajoria, interview with six experts, in "Tiananmen Square and Two Chinas"; and Fukuyama, "For China, Stability."

95. For example, see Zhengxu Wang, "Public Support for Democracy in China," *Journal of Contemporary China*, vol. 16, no. 53 (November 2007): 561–79. Zhengxu states: "It is clear that public support for democracy is high in China. Public opinion surveys show that more than 90% of Chinese citizens believe that having a democracy is good."

96. Roy, "China's Democratised Foreign Policy."

97. Chu et al., "Asia's Challenged Democracies." This study, based on an Asian-wide survey of popular attitudes toward government, also showed that Chinese citizens were often far more likely to trust their own political institutions than did those of many other Asian nations. The authors write: "We found high levels of trust in four central-level political institutions: the national government, the National People's Congress (national legislature), the Chinese Communist Party, and the People's Liberation Army. The percentage of respondents claiming that they did not trust any one of these institutions ranged from 6 to 8 percent, which is by far the lowest levels of distrust for any institutions in the East Asian countries that were surveyed. . . . These findings suggest that citizens do not always draw the same stark contrast between democratic and authoritarian regimes that political scientists do. Many Chinese perceive their country to be more democratic than do citizens in many truly democratic societies in the region. Chinese citizens appear to trust their political institutions more than citizens in the other societies that were surveyed." Also see Joseph Kahn, "In China, Talk of Democracy Is Simply That," *New York Times*, April 20, 2007, www.nytimes.com/2007/04/20/world/asia/20china.html.

98. Branigan, "Young, Gifted and Red." She states: "The Asian Barometer study of political attitudes, the most comprehensive to date, came up with some surprising findings. In Mainland China, 53.8 percent believed a democratic system was preferable. . . . To the confusion of some Western observers, Hu's speech to the last party congress used the D-word more than 60 times." See also Francis Fukuyama, "Is China Next?" *Wall Street Journal*, March 12, 2011, http://online.wsj.com/article/SB10001424052748703560404576188981829658442.html. As Fukuyama writes, "A majority of Chinese also believe that democracy is the best form of government, but in a curious twist, they think that China is already democratic and profess to be satisfied with this state of affairs. This translates into a relatively low degree of support for any short-term transition to genuine liberal democracy. Indeed, there is some reason to believe that the middle class in China may fear multiparty democracy in the short run, because it would unleash huge demands for redistribution precisely from those who have been left behind."

99. As Chu et al. state: "Pro-engagement optimists in the West are right to say that the forces of socioeconomic modernization and cultural globalization are spreading the abstract idea of democracy in China. Yet, they are wrong to assume that this attitudinal change creates an imminent threat to the authoritarian regime. Instead, for now the regime has persuaded its citizens that the current system is as democratic as they want it to be." Chu et al, "Asia's Challenged Democracies."

100. Fukuyama, "For China, Stability." Fukuyama states: "There is no mechanical linkage between wealth and democracy. In particular, the role of the middle classes in promoting democratic political participation is not inevitable, and in the Chinese case works to frustrate the emergence of greater democracy."

101. Shambaugh does point to the dangers inherent in the regime's focus on good government and rising living standards as a potential source of rapidly rising expectations that could turn to frustration and opposition if not adequately met, and to growing demands for autonomous political channels to express public views. But there is little hard and sustained evidence that China's citizens are expressing such sentiments or making such demands in significant numbers. In fact, he states: "If managed carefully, the CCP can adapt and respond effectively to the rising demands placed upon it by society." Shambaugh, *China's Communist Party*. Shambaugh's argument is similar to the general argument regarding the reliance of authoritarian regimes on so-called "performance legitimacy" to maintain power, and the dangers that could ensue if such performance falters, given the fact that, in such regimes, discontent cannot be expressed through democratic means. See Marc F. Plattner, "Democracy's Competitive Edge: Why Authoritarian Economies Could Have More to Fear From the Crisis," *Washington Post*, January 13, 2009; Gideon Rachman, "Chinese Views of the Crisis," *Financial Times*, February 25, 2009, http://blogs.ft.com/rachmanblog/2009/02/chinese-views-of-the-crisis/#more-528; and Zhang Wei-Wei, "Eight Ideas Behind China's Success," *New York Times*, September 30, 2009.

102. See Lampton remarks in "What's Your China Fantasy?" by Lampton and Mann. Also see Cheng Li, ed., *China's Changing Political Landscape: Prospects for Democracy* (Washington, D.C.: Brookings Institution Press, 2008); Cheng Li, "China in the Year 2020: Three Political Scenarios," *Asia Policy*, no. 4 (July 2007): 17–29; Cheng Li, "The New Bipartisanship within the Chinese Communist Party," *Orbis*, Summer 2005, 387–400; and Shambaugh, *China's Communist Party*. Shambaugh states: "I deeply doubt that Western-style democracy is going to come to China—either as a result of elite-

led tutelage or via mass demands from below. I also have serious doubts about Cheng Li's prediction that inner-party 'bipartisanship' can evolve into contested elections by rival factions. However, . . . this is not to rule out the possibility of the creation of competitive constituencies within a one-party system—along the lines of the Singaporean or Hong Kong models. This is consistent with a corporatist system."

103. For example, see Minxin Pei, *China's Trapped Transition: The Limits of Developmental Autocracy* (Cambridge, Mass.: Harvard University Press, 2006).

104. Kathryn Jean Lopez, "Getting Our Act Together: Frank Gaffney on War Footing," *National Review*, January 12, 2006, www.nationalreview.com/interrogatory/gaffney200601120826.asp.

105. Gordon G. Chang, *The Coming Collapse of China* (New York: Random House, 2001). Shambaugh, *China's Communist Party*, discusses several variants of the pessimistic, "regime collapse or steady disintegration" viewpoint and dismisses them all: "Despite the various stresses and strains on the party-state, particularly in rural areas, the chances of system meltdown and regime collapse seem remote. . . . Despite its atrophy, I see the CCP as a reasonably strong and resilient institution." For a nuanced analysis of several different scenarios regarding China's political future, as well as the factors influencing it, see "A Dragon of Many Colours," *Economist*, October 22, 2009.

106. For example, see Ming, *Human Rights*. The European Union in particular lacks influence in pressuring China to reform its human rights policy due to the absence of collective, coherent EU foreign policy in this area. See David Shambaugh, Eberhard Sandschneider, and Hong Zhou, eds., *China–Europe Relations: Perceptions, Policies, and Prospects* (New York: Routledge, 2007); Reuben Yik-Pern Wong, *The Europeanization of French Foreign Policy: France and the EU in East Asia*, French Politics, Society, and Culture Series (New York: Palgrave Macmillan, 2006); and "EU and China: the Summit of Discourtesy," *Economist*, November 27, 2008, www.economist.com/node/12708134.

107. As George Perkovich states, "To the extent that Moscow's and Beijing's own actions may violate international norms of human rights, for example, they do not want to strengthen precedents for sanctions or other punitive actions against violators of norms." George Perkovich, "The End of the Nonproliferation Regime?" *Current History*, November 2006, http://carnegieendowment.org/files/perkovich_current_history.pdf.

108. For example, see Kurlantzick and Link, "China."

109. Kleine-Ahlbrandt and Small, "China's New Dictatorship Diplomacy"

110. Harry Harding, "China Rediscovers Ethics in Foreign Policy," Carnegie Ethics Online, January 6, 2009, www.cceia.org/resources/articles_papers_reports/0013.html.

111. Ibid.

112. Kleine-Ahlbrandt and Small, "China's New Dictatorship Diplomacy," 39. See also Richardson, "Challenges"; and Brautigam, *Dragon's Gift*.

CHAPTER 9

1. The vast majority of these interview subjects are listed in the appendix. A few subjects requested that their names not be listed. Most of these officials and experts have long and extensive experience in dealing with China in a variety of policy areas. Others have

either broader policy backgrounds that include interactions with Chinese and other foreign officials or possess specialized knowledge in managing policy in one particular area of United States–China relations.

2. Other findings from these interviews have been incorporated into the analysis presented throughout this study.

3. For a similar point, see David Lampton, *Same Bed, Different Dreams: Managing U.S.-China Relations, 1989–2000* (Berkeley: University of California Press, 2001), 355. Lampton states: "People count because of the values they hold, the priorities they pursue, their propensity to take risks, and their tenacity or lack thereof. Individuals also count, especially in America, because money, the ability to mobilize talent, and vision are not monopolized by the government."

4. As one respondent stated: "At the top during the Clinton administration everyone got along well. During the Bush administration it was reversed; at the lower levels officials got along and the top had more trouble."

5. One respondent also pointed out that, even when he was in office, Armitage's ability to implement his strategy was to some extent obstructed by personal differences that existed between himself and Defense Secretary Donald Rumsfeld.

6. As one respondent stated, "It is very hard to run the process smoothly and obtain coordinated results if some individuals want total freedom of action and others want to produce agreements that require discipline and compromise."

7. As William J. Olson writes: "The modern U.S. Government is a maze of bureaucratic structures, overlapping agency responsibilities, redundant assignments, conflicting authorities, and institutional objectives. These have grown over time in response, perhaps, to parochial logic and immediate need but rarely in response to one another or in a consistent logic that applies across the breadth of government. This piecemeal evolution means piecemeal execution and a welter of activities resistant to logical analysis or coherent coordination. What was not arrived at by a logical process is likely to resist logical solutions." See William J. Olson, "Interagency Coordination: The Normal Accident or the Essence of Indecision," in *Affairs of State: The Interagency and National Security* (Carlisle, Pa.: Strategic Studies Institute, 2008), 215. Also see Clayton K. S. Chun and Frank L. Jones, "Learning to Play the Game: The National Security Policymaking Process," in *Affairs of State*, 210.

8. For a confirmation of this observation, see Council on Foreign Relations, *U.S.–China Relations: An Affirmative Agenda, Responsible Course*, Independent Task Force Report 59 (Carla A. Hills and Dennis C. Blair, chairs; Frank Sampson Jannuzi, project director) (New York: Council on Foreign Relations, 2007). This report states: "It is not unusual for assessments of China within the U.S. government or even within one administration to differ, sometimes radically. China defies easy definition. And different parts of the U.S. government often prioritize U.S. interests with China differently, leading some officials to see and note progress while others witness none. . . . Such divergent public views of China reflect both contending policy views within the administration and the diversity of China itself. However, they detract from the effectiveness of U.S. policy toward China."

9. One respondent with considerable experience within both defense and foreign policy circles remarked that "the truth is that it is like two torpedoes racing off on separate courses. They're not well integrated, it isn't well understood how they play. In our minds we talk about 'if we engage then we're also prepared' but we don't recognize how the two

relate to each other in our minds and the minds of the Chinese. Additionally, we don't know how to calibrate effectively between the two."

10. According to a few experienced respondents, such differences in outlook have been reinforced at times by personal issues and the timing of senior personnel rotations. For example, as one respondent stated, "A PACOM commander who is in place when a new civilian Pentagon leadership takes office is usually very stubborn in defending his policies, while a new PACOM commander is more likely to endorse an existing administration's policies."

11. The contrast in emphasis between cooperation and hedging/competition is of course only relative, because the missions of most agencies contain elements of both. As one respondent stated, "The key challenge is to be nimble enough to maneuver between responsibilities and balance them, both within and between agencies."

12. Supposed examples of such actions include the high level of secrecy that allegedly marked the normalization of bilateral relations in 1979, and the "overselling" of the World Trade Organization agreement as a mechanism for rapidly advancing democratization and reducing the U.S. trade deficit with China.

13. In fact, at least one respondent disagreed vehemently with the notion that Congress was angered by the secrecy employed by the executive branch during the normalization process. The interviewee stated that key members were briefed before secret negotiations had begun and that they had informed the administration that normalization should proceed, even though several of them might denounce the action publicly.

14. Despite its important role in coordinating the inter-agency process and providing substantive policy recommendations to the president, the NSC is probably not significantly involved in providing national security information to Congress. See Richard A. Best Jr., "The National Security Council: An Organizational Assessment," Congressional Research Service, January 20, 2011, www.fas.org/sgp/crs/natsec/RL30840.pdf.

15. As one respondent stated: "The executive branch doesn't like restrictions. It wants the president to have the full range of incentives and disincentives to bring to bear on China. And it has responsibility for managing the overall relationship with China, while the Congress does not."

16. Moreover, in the 2010 midterm elections, China figured prominently in dozens of campaign advertisements from both parties, mostly highlighting China's economic challenge as evidence of the need for America to change its direction (a message that President Obama also prominently included in his 2011 State of the Union Address). See Naftali Bendavid, "China-Bashing Gains Bipartisan Support," *Wall Street Journal*, October 8, 2010; David W. Chen, "China Emerges as a Scapegoat in Campaign Ads," *New York Times*, October 9, 2010; Adam Hanft, "Ad Attacks on China Cross the Line," Salon.com, October 12, 2010, www.salon.com/news/feature/2010/10/12/ad_attacks_on_china; Nin-Hai Tseng, "Parsing the Short-Sighted, China-Bashing Midterm Ads," Fortune.com, October 29, 2010; and Office of the Press Secretary, White House, "Remarks by the President in State of Union Address," United States Capitol, Washington, D.C., January 25, 2011, www.whitehouse.gov/the-press-office/2011/01/25/remarks-president-state-union-address.

17. Among the broader public, 48 percent of Democrats believe that it is "very important for the U.S. to do more to promote human rights in China," whereas

only 33 percent of Republicans feel the same. This divergence is also evident on the question of U.S. promotion of better environmental policies in China (43 percent of Democrats compared with 34 percent of Republicans). See Pew Research Center for the People and the Press, "Strengthen Ties with China, But Get Tough on Trade," January 12, 2011, http://pewresearch.org/pubs/1855/china-poll-americans-want-closer-ties-but-tougher-trade-policy.

18. See Ileana Ros-Lehtinen (R-Fla., chair of House Foreign Affairs Committee), "Statement at Briefing on China," U.S. House Foreign Affairs Committee, January 19, 2011, http://foreignaffairs.house.gov/press_display.asp?id=1688. In her statement on U.S. China policy, Ros-Lehtinen declared that the newly elected, Republican-controlled House was "determined to take back America's economy and . . . committed to a foreign policy that stands with our allies and holds accountable those who threaten our Nation's security interests." Moreover, among the broader public, Republicans are slightly more likely than Democrats to view China as an adversary (24 percent compared with 19 percent), and Democrats are more likely than Republicans to agree that it is "very important for the U.S. to build a stronger relationship with China" (62 percent compared with 54 percent). Republicans who identify with the Tea Party movement (which first became prominent in 2009 and exerted considerable influence in the 2010 midterm elections) generally harbor the most hard-line anti-China attitudes. For example, 33 percent of Tea Party Republicans view China as an adversary, compared with 17 percent of other Republicans (and 19 percent of Democrats). See Pew Research Center for the People and the Press, "Strengthen Ties with China."

19. See John Kerry (D-Mass., chair of Senate Foreign Relations Committee), "Chairman Kerry Delivers A Speech on U.S.-China Relations," U.S. Senate Committee on Foreign Relations, December 7, 2010, http://foreign.senate.gov/press/chair/release/?id=d7caf3fb-b946-4ffb-ade8-fce5008b5b6b. In his speech, Kerry acknowledged concerning aspects of China's rise but insisted that "it is critical that we not allow speculation about China's ambitions to degenerate into fear-mongering and demagoguery."

20. I am indebted to Rachel Esplin Odell for her invaluable assistance in preparing this section.

21. For a detailed discussion of how the Clinton administration managed the debate over linkage of China's most-favored-nation status with its human rights record—a measure opposed by the U.S. business community, see Jean A. Garrison, "A Tale of Three Engagements: Clinton and the Struggle to Balance Competing Interests," chap. 7 in *Making China Policy: From Nixon to G. W. Bush* (Boulder, Colo.: Lynne Rienner, 2005).

22. One prominent example from past China policy was the decision made by George H. W. Bush in the summer of 1992 to sell 150 F-16s to Taiwan to build support from pro-Taiwan Texans in the 1992 presidential elections. See Garrison, "Salvaging U.S.-China Relations: G. H. W. Bush and the Aftermath of Tiananmen Square," chap. 6 in *Making China Policy.*

23. In total, 40 percent of Americans believe it is "very important" to promote human rights in China, as revealed in a January 2011 opinion survey. See Pew Research Center for the People and the Press, "Strengthen Ties with China." The partisan differences and similarities on human rights are discussed in an endnote above.

24. For a somewhat similar but generally more dismissive viewpoint, see Robert Suettinger, *Beyond Tiananmen: The Politics of U.S.-China Relations 1989–2000* (Washington, D.C.: Brookings Institution Press, 2003), 427. Suettinger asserts that, while interest groups

"can provide effective and important inputs to the policy process," largely by defining or framing issues for public discussion and providing factual information to Congress and the executive branch, "they exert only minor influence in the actual deliberation and decision process for important policy matters." He concludes that "the influence of interest groups on important policy choices is marginal—and manageable." This author would not go quite that far. As indicated, the influence of groups seems to be more variable and at times more important than such a statement suggests.

25. See Chicago Council on Global Affairs, *Global Views 2010: Constrained Internationalism— Adapting to New Realities; Results of a 2010 National Survey of Public Opinion* (Chicago: Chicago Council on Global Affairs, 2010), www.thechicagocouncil.org/UserFiles/File/ POS_Topline%20Reports/POS%202010/Global%20Views%202010.pdf. The poll states that 68 percent of the American public favors a policy of cooperation and engagement with China rather than an attempt to work actively to limit the growth of China's power. This is an increase of four points in favor of cooperation and engagement since 2008. At the same time, Americans also place a strong emphasis on the need to work with allies such as Japan and South Korea to maintain stability in Asia. See also "Pew Research Center for the People and the Press, "Strengthen Ties with China." This study generally confirmed the findings of the Chicago Council poll, which included the fact that 60 percent of Americans "see China's economic strength as a greater threat than its military strength." That said, 58 percent of survey respondents said "it is very important to build a stronger relationship between the U.S. and China," and only 22 percent view China as an adversary. General attitudes in favor of engagement with China are long-standing. See WorldPublicOpinion.org, "General Engagement with China, Americans and the World Digest—China," August 2008, www.americans-world.org/digest/regional_issues/china/ china1.cfm.

26. Despite occasional spikes in public criticism of Chinese behavior, overall, congressional attitudes significantly diverge from the views of both ordinary citizens and nongovernmental elites with regard to China. A poll undertaken by the Committee of 100 in 2007 strongly suggested that congressional staff members hold a much lower opinion of China than the general public, opinion leaders, and business leaders. See Committee of 100, *Hope and Fear: Full Report of C-100's Survey on American and Chinese Attitudes Toward Each Other* (New York: Committee of 100, 2008), http://survey. committee100.org/2007/files/C100SurveyFullReport.pdf.

27. Robert Suettinger confirms this finding when he writes of U.S. policy toward China: "The influence of interest groups on important policy choices is marginal—and manageable— in comparison with bureaucratic interests, the actions of China and Taiwan, and the president's understanding of America's national interests." See Suettinger, *Beyond Tiananmen*.

28. Olson outlines some of the reasons why policy coordination is so extremely difficult in the U.S. policymaking process: "Different parts of the coordination environment, embassies, for example, may have a very different sense of policy urgency and policy reality than does Washington, or some critical component thereof. Reporting up and down the chain takes time, decisions on courses of action take time, bringing together capabilities to respond, should action be called for, takes time. Circumstances may not be forgiving of these needs—all of which are inherent in the need to coordinate and more and better coordination is likely to increase the lag time. Since the demands such situations levy are situation-specific, there are some real limits to what more and better

coordination can do to improve things and, given the timing problem, these very efforts may make matters worse." See Olson, "Interagency Coordination," 215.

29. The statutory members of the NSC are the president, vice president, and the secretaries of state, energy, and defense. The chairman of the Joint Chiefs of Staff and the director of national intelligence are statutory advisers to the NSC. Other senior U.S. officials can also be invited to attend NSC meetings at various times and under different administrations, including, for example, the chief of staff to the president, the counsel to the president, the secretary of the Treasury, the secretary of homeland security, the secretary of commerce, the U.S. representative to the United Nations, the U.S. trade representative, the assistant to the president for economic policy, the assistant to the president for homeland security, the attorney general, and the director of the Office of Management and Budget. See Alan G. Whittaker, Frederick C. Smith, and Elizabeth McKune, *The National Security Policy Process: The National Security Council and Interagency System*, Research Report, 2010 Annual Update (Washington, D.C.: Industrial College of the Armed Forces, National Defense University, U.S. Department of Defense, October 8, 2010), www.ndu.edu/icaf/outreach/publications/ nspp/docs/icaf-nsc-policy-process-report-10-2010.pdf.

30. As Whittaker states: "The President alone decides national security policy, but the National Security Advisor is responsible for ensuring that the President has all the necessary information, that a full range of policy options have been identified, that the prospects and risks of each option have been evaluated, that legal and funding considerations have been addressed, that potential difficulties in implementation have been identified, and that all NSC principals have been included in the policy development and recommendation process. . . . The National Security Advisor is not a statutory member [of the NSC], but traditionally is responsible for determining the agenda in consultation with the other regular attendees of the NSC, ensuring that the necessary papers are prepared, recording NSC deliberations, and disseminating Presidential decisions." Hence, the NSA's "primary roles are to advise the President, advance the President's national security policy agenda, and oversee the effective operation of the interagency system. . . . Because the statutory National Security Council historically has met infrequently and has had little direct contact with the staff level components of the Executive Branch as a body, the NSC staff is commonly referred to (incorrectly) as 'the NSC.' Thus, when people in the Executive Branch agencies or Legislative Branch talk about calling or working with the NSC, they nearly always are referring to the National Security Staff." See Whittaker et al., *National Security Policy Process*.

31. Interviews. There is also reportedly a so-called "sub"-PCC on China that "tries" to meet three or four times a year, according to one respondent. See also Whittaker et al., *National Security Policy Process*.

32. According to one respondent, during recent administrations, the China policymaking process also contained its own informal, small working groups, sometimes consisting largely of like-minded officials at the NSC and the State Department.

33. For a general summary of these features, see Chun and Jones, "Learning to Play the Game," 171.

34. This contrasting viewpoint probably reflects a larger difference in viewpoint among some policy figures over the extent to which China specialists within and near the government emphasize the need to maintain cooperation with Beijing over the need to more strongly assert U.S. interests.

35. See Lampton, *Same Bed, Different Dreams*, 307–9. As Lampton states: "Even though functional concerns are legitimate and important, unless the geographic bureaus play integrative roles, foreign policy is likely to be increasingly chaotic or simply to become the responsibility of the White House, where the capacity for policy coherence is greater and presidential commitment more easily obtained.

36. As one respondent added: "There are too many career people in State who just don't have the ability to look at the big picture. If administrators can't look at the big picture, you often can't rely on lower-level people to substitute for them."

37. This type of problem has created tensions between the State or Defense departments on the one hand and the NSC on the other, according to this source, given the smaller staff, more comprehensive outlook, and "results-oriented" perspective of the latter agency.

38. In this regard, one respondent stated that "the order to 'engage and hedge' is great because it can justify just about everything an agency wants to do."

39. As one informant stated, the policymaking process can "get stuck" because top leaders are too busy or simply will not focus or make decisions in a timely manner.

40. For example, broader strategic issues such as the overall long-term goals of U.S. policy regarding China's position in Asia, the U.S. role in the region, the balance to strike between hedging and cooperating with Beijing, and so on are rarely reexamined or adjusted on the strategic level. As one particularly pessimistic former official added, policy work "was sometimes like drinking through a fire hose; it was from one issue to the next. So in that context, how do you hold a conversation on the next six months, or on an overarching strategy? Trying to move a large U.S. strategy is just rhetoric. It is trying to call chaos a strategy."

41. "What we have now is merely the coordination of responses to events, not long-term strategy." As noted above, it is also due, according to a few respondents, to the simple fact that senior officials rarely have the time or inclination to address broader and longer-term strategic issues. They usually only do so when a particular event demands it.

42. As one interviewee stated: "You can be dominant without being overwhelming. You don't have to be unilaterally dominant. You can be dominant in conjunction with other Asian countries." Another former senior official remarked: "We're the most powerful nation on earth, the one with the strongest ideals and the greatest economy. For the United States to deal with the Chinese from a position that's not what we are would be inexplicable. We don't have to go to the Chinese and tell them that we're the biggest guys on the block—they know that full well."

43. As one former very senior national security official stated, "[the Chinese] can see the most benign moves by the U.S. as having ulterior motives to harm China. The legacy of the past is very powerful."

44. Interview. As one proponent of this viewpoint stated, "Militarily, we need to maintain capabilities sufficient to deter Chinese hegemonic thinking. Diplomatically, we need to maintain relationships in the region that give regional countries alternatives to excessive deference to China, and we need to pursue a relationship with China that makes cooperation more attractive and more beneficial to China than unconstrained strategic rivalry. . . . It requires active U.S. engagement in the region in ways that demonstrate to regional countries that our policies are compatible with their interests and take their views into account."

45. In this regard, several respondents stressed the overriding importance for the Chinese of domestic factors and the overall objective of economic growth and political stability, as identified in chapter 1. In other words, for many interviewees, it is important for U.S. decisionmakers to accurately grasp the domestic political, economic, and social context within which Chinese leaders view foreign policy issues.

46. Some respondents stressed that U.S. officials often had to work hard to remove Chinese fears of U.S. motives and actions regarding a specific policy issue and to convince them that they would benefit from adopting a particular stance. One respondent even added that the Chinese spend a lot of time "arguing against something that wasn't actual U.S. policy." Another added that the Chinese are inclined to see many issues involving the United States in "zero-sum" terms. Nonetheless, the notion of "vesting" Beijing in a course of action that serves U.S. interests by influencing their perceptions before they adopt troublesome behavior was stressed as absolutely critical by some very knowledgeable respondents. One former official expressed this as "engaging them in a process where you can help them get to where they want to be." Another former senior official stressed the importance of communicating disagreements with Beijing privately whenever possible while emphasizing areas of cooperation.

47. As Frank Lavin has stated: "In China's closed political system, no official depends on popular reelection as the reward for pursuing sound policies, so little incentive exists to risk even prudent policy changes. An overwhelming institutional bias exists in favor of the status quo." See Franklin L. Lavin, "Negotiating with the Chinese," *Foreign Affairs*, vol. 73, no. 4 (July–August 1994): 16–22.

48. One respondent referred to this as "inserting talking points into the Chinese system."

49. One former military officer stated: "I've never had the Chinese not follow through on something when a good personal relationship exists."

50. This is also an example of a case in which the U.S. government effectively "played" the internal Chinese bureaucracy to serve its interests. See below for more on this tactic.

51. Washington has also at times engaged in a fairly regular dialogue with Taipei, largely via the respective national security councils of both governments, that has reportedly exerted significant beneficial influence over Taiwan's behavior.

52. See Richard H. Solomon, *Chinese Political Negotiating Behavior, 1967–84* (Santa Monica, Calif.: RAND Corporation, 1995); and Lucian W. Pye, *Chinese Negotiating Style: Commercial Approaches and Cultural Principles* (Westport, Conn.: Quorum Books, 1992). Also see John L. Graham and N. Mark Lam, "Negotiating in China," excerpted from *Harvard Business Review*, October 2003, http://hbswk.hbs.edu/archive/3714.html.

53. One U.S. official with extensive experience stated that "the Chinese don't lie to you directly and will tell you the truth as they see it, so what they say is important."

54. At the same time, a few well-informed interviewees also believe that attempts to use the military-to-military relationship primarily to obtain intelligence or to intimidate or deter the PLA, for example, by brandishing large quantities of sophisticated weapons, can often backfire by simply spurring Beijing to increase its defense efforts and tighten its controls over information. This topic is discussed in greater detail in chapter 4.

55. While acknowledging the need to obtain some level of reciprocity from the Chinese side in military-to-military interactions, most of those respondents who addressed this issue also averred that strict reciprocity was unrealistic and should not be a goal of U.S. policy.

56. As one interviewee stated, "If you want the Chinese to do something that's not in their interest, you have to give them something or do something that makes it be in their interest."

57. In other words, the United States managed to credibly replace one set of Chinese interests in selling arms to Tehran (relations with Iran plus economic benefits) with another, more important set of interests (relations with the United States).

58. As one respondent stated, "You basically close all the doors that you do not want Beijing to walk through, and leave wide open the door that you want them to choose."

59. A variant of this tactic mentioned by a few interviewees was to *threaten* to take away something of value if China were pressuring the United States or not approaching an issue in a spirit of reciprocity.

60. Economics-related issues are more amenable to this approach in part because, as one respondent stated, the executive branch cannot credibly claim to enjoy dominant authority because Congress has the lead constitutionally on trade and economics issues.

61. Indeed, at times, Beijing has seemed to broach the possibility of "linking" PRC cooperation on an important issue such as the denuclearization of North Korean with certain U.S. concessions regarding Taiwan. Such feelers have been consistently rejected by Washington, according to respondents.

62. As one interviewee stated, "In my experience, we're not good at horse trading because Washington leaks so easily. We're not usually good at orchestrating a grand bargain. We're not the Chinese; we are a much more open system and are not as capable of pulling it off."

63. One individual was quite categorical in this regard, stating that "the notion that you can pressure China on human rights is an illusion; you have no leverage. You cannot effectively pressure or shame them on human rights issues."

64. Some respondents also made the point that sanctions in general are losing their effectiveness or utility because there are fewer issues in previously sanctioned areas such as weapons nonproliferation about which the United States and China disagree.

65. For a detailed discussion of the importance of international status for China's leaders, see Evan S. Medeiros, *China's International Behavior: Activism, Opportunism, Diversification*, report prepared for the U.S. Air Force (Santa Monica, Calif.: RAND Corporation, 2009).

66. Similarly, the Chinese are often more inclined to accept a policy suggestion if some kind of precedent for it can be offered, according to one respondent.

67. Clinton also pleased the Chinese by uttering the famous "three no's" regarding U.S. policy toward Taiwan during his visit to China, that is, that the United States does not support an independent Taiwan, will oppose Taiwan's entry into organizations that require sovereign statehood for admission, and does not support a policy of "one China, one Taiwan." This clarification of the U.S. position had been agreed upon between the two sides before Clinton's trip.

68. Rumsfeld took this position because the formal signing of a comprehensive military-to-military program (developed at the operational level by the two sides) was supposedly inconsistent with the broader policy decision he had made to advance the U.S.-PRC military-to-military relationship only on a case-by-case basis.

69. This is similar to arguments made by Iain Johnston. He identifies "social influence" (which includes both shaming and back patting) as one of three mechanisms (along with "mimicking" and "persuasion") whereby China has been socialized into the acceptance of international norms and treaties. See Alastair Iain Johnston, *Social States: China in International Institutions, 1980–2000* (Princeton, N.J.: Princeton University Press, 2008).

CHAPTER 10

1. As Thomas Christensen and other analysts have observed, the effective management or resolution of these issues requires policymakers in many countries to recognize that, in many ways, a more "assertive" China is essential to the advancement of global and U.S. interests. As Christensen states: "The United States and its diplomatic partners should promote . . . an assertive China—without which Washington will face greater difficulty in addressing pressing global challenges such as nuclear proliferation, climate change, and global economic instability. China has become far too big to stand on the sidelines— let alone to stand in the way—while others attempt to resolve these issues." See Thomas J. Christensen, "The Advantages of an Assertive China," *Foreign Affairs*, vol. 90, no. 2 (March/April 2011): 54–67.

2. For a recent confirmation of such Chinese debates, and an affirmation of the need for Beijing to avoid identifying the United States as a major threat to China, see Wang Jisi, "China's Search for a Grand Strategy: A Rising Great Power Finds Its Way," *Foreign Affairs*, vol. 90, no. 2 (March/April 2011). Wang states: "It would be imprudent of Beijing to identify any one country as a major threat and invoke the need to keep it at bay as an organizing principle of Chinese foreign policy—unless the United States, or another great power, truly did regard China as its main adversary and so forced China to respond in kind."

3. For a similar argument, see Wang, "China's Search for a Grand Strategy."

4. Johnston argues that Chinese balancing against U.S. hegemony is "hesitant, low-key, and inconsistent." He offers several specific points to support this argument: first, China's military expenditures as a percentage of gross domestic product do not appear to have reached the levels that would indicate that the Chinese economy has become militarized and mobilized to counterbalance U.S. military power. Second, China is not working hard to construct an anti-U.S. alliance or to undermine U.S. alliances globally or regionally. Specifically, it is not balancing against a possible United States–Japan–South Korea trilateral security structure and has not explicitly opposed the existence of the United States–Japan alliance. See Alastair Iain Johnston, "Is China a Status Quo Power?" *International Security*, vol. 27, no. 4 (Spring 2003): 5–56. The summary of PRC policies offered in chapters 2 through 4 largely confirm that such behavior has continued in recent years.

5. Clear examples of such behavior, as indicated in chapters 5 through 8, include China's expanding membership in a wide variety of international organizations in many functional areas discussed in those chapters; its continued support for the major nonproliferation regimes, as evidenced by its formal statements and votes in favor of sanctions regarding the North Korea and Iran nuclear issues; its continued efforts to adapt to and work within the structure and process of the WTO and other international economic regimes and to resist protectionism and other threats to a free trade system;

its deepening involvement in accepted international practices regarding the detection and management of potential and actual pandemics; its attempts to work with other countries to develop a common approach to combating climate change; and its continued participation in most of the major international human rights regimes and agreements (despite a clear failure to implement many such agreements). In addition, the summary of Chinese policy behavior in chapter 3 also suggests that, at least, Beijing's growing involvement in multilateral activities or forums reflects a greater willingness to utilize such peaceful interactions rather than to rely on purely bilateral contacts or coercion to attain its ends.

6. See Alastair Iain Johnston, *Social States: China in International Institutions, 1980–2000* (Princeton, N.J.: Princeton University Press, 2008). Johnston writes, "In sum, it is not a stretch to characterize Chinese diplomacy since the 1990s as being, in relative terms, more status quo oriented than at any period since 1949. That is, China has joined most international institutions that regulate interstate behavior. Inside the institutions, it generally has not tried to undermine the functioning or purposes of these institutions." Another leading scholar of China's approach to international norms, Ann Kent, makes essentially the same point. She writes: "In recent years, China scholars have emphasized the role of international regimes and international organizations in promoting China's national goals and interests. Participation has had the effect of protecting and extending China's sovereignty, projecting and enhancing its international status, maintaining its strategic independence, preserving an external environment conducive to its own developmental goals, and promoting internal developmental aims through foreign investment, expanded trade, technology transfer, and development assistance." See Ann Kent, "China's International Socialization: The Role of International Organization," *Global Governance*, vol. 8, no. 3 (July–September 2002): 343–64. See also Ann E. Kent, *Beyond Compliance: China, International Organizations, and Global Security* (Stanford, Calif.: Stanford University Press, 2007).

7. Kent summarizes the major compromises on its "fierce defense of sovereignty" that Beijing has made in such areas as: human rights (for example, subjecting China to the norms and mechanisms of international human rights regimes in general and the jurisdiction of UN human right bodies, as well as its support for UN actions in favor of humanitarian intervention in East Timor and the creation of an international human rights tribunal in Yugoslavia); free trade (for example, accepting significant limits to the PRC government's control over major economic and financial activities as part of its accession to the WTO); arms control and nonproliferation (for example, accepting new limits on nuclear testing and the overseas transfer of WMD technologies and materials), and even regarding issues relating to territorial security (for example, concluding an agreement to work toward a formal code of conduct among claimants to territories in the South China Sea that limits the ability of each party to assert control over the disputed areas). She concludes: "When national interests and the principle of absolute sovereignty are seen to coincide, China makes a theoretical statement about the absolute nature of sovereignty. But in general, China's power is enhanced by its preparedness to negotiate its sovereignty rather than to impose blanket vetoes." See Kent, "China's International Socialization."

8. As Kent writes: "For liberal democracies, cooperative behavior and acceptance of interdependence are not as costly, because such behavior normally coheres with domestically observed standards and goals. In China's case, international cooperation

and interdependence often conflict with the perceived needs of domestic stability, with the authority of party leaders, and with the norms of domestic culture." The latter norms in general rely on "ethics rather than on law, on moral consensus rather than on judicial procedure, and on benevolent government rather than on checks and balances." Ibid.

9. Also see Kent, "China's International Socialization." She writes: "Beijing also uses its seats on the UN Security Council and Human Rights Commission and its membership in other international human rights regimes to push a restrictive interpretation of international norms and treaties, stressing the importance of economic development, social stability, and collective rights over individual political rights."

10. Ibid.

11. As an example, Kent cites China's lack of support for reforms of the UN Security Council that would increase access by any nations (including developing nations) to the veto.

12. This observation is also supported by Johnston. He writes: "The most obviously persistent revisionist preferences in Chinese foreign policy today pertain mostly to territorial disputes." Johnston, "Is China a Status Quo Power?" Also see Johnston, *Social States*.

13. For examples of such arguments, see Doug Bandow, "The China Syndrome," *National Interest*, October 19, 2009; and Michael Mandelbaum, *The Frugal Superpower: America's Global Leadership in a Cash-Strapped Era* (New York: PublicAffairs, 2010). Whether the resulting U.S. military position should ideally consist of a clear level of predominance that extends up to China's maritime borders (that is, across the Western Pacific) is not made clear by Mandelbaum. This is a critical point however, as discussed below.

14. John J. Mearsheimer, "Imperial by Design," *National Interest*, December 16, 2010, http://nationalinterest.org/article/imperial-by-design-4576. Although Mearsheimer describes his approach as offshore balancing, it actually seems closer to the concept of "selective engagement." Also see John Mearsheimer, "The Gathering Storm: China's Challenge to U.S. Power in Asia," transcript of Fourth Annual Michael Hintze Lecture on International Security, August 4, 2010, www.usyd.edu.au/news/84.html?newsstoryid=5351; and John J. Mearsheimer, "China's Unpeaceful Rise," *Current History*, vol. 105, no. 690 (April 2006): 160–62.

15. For a similar assessment, see Jonathan Kirshner, "The Tragedy of Offensive Realism: Classical Realism and the Rise of China," *European Journal of International Relations*, vol. 20, no. 10 (October 2010): 1–23. "In sum, a full-blown confrontation with China along the lines suggested by offensive realism would be a self-mutilating geopolitical gesture that would damage the U.S., undermine its international political influence, and result in an angry and unstable China—and that is if it worked."

16. John J. Mearsheimer, *The Tragedy of Great Power Politics* (New York: W. W. Norton, 2001); "Offshore Balancing or International Institutions? The Way Forward for U.S. Foreign Policy," debate at Watson Institute for International Studies at Brown University between G. John Ikenberry and Stephen Walt, hosted by Christopher Lydon, *Brown Journal of World Affairs*, vol. 14, no. 1 (Fall–Winter 2007): 13–23.

17. See Christopher Layne, *The Peace of Illusions: American Grand Strategy from 1940 to the Present* (Ithaca, N.Y.: Cornell University Press, 2006). Also see Barry R. Posen, "A Grand Strategy of Restraint and Renewal," testimony before the Subcommittee on Oversight and Investigations, U.S. House Armed Services Committee, July 15, 2008; Barry R. Posen,

"The Case for Restraint," *American Interest*, vol. 3, no 2 (November–December 2007), www.the-american-interest.com/ai2/article.cfm?Id=331&MId=16; and Barry R. Posen, "Command of the Commons: The Military Foundation of U.S. Hegemony," *International Security*, vol. 28, no. 1 (Summer 2003): 5–46. Posen tends to avoid using the term "offshore balancing" to describe his approach, preferring instead "restraint" or "selective engagement" combined with "command of the commons." The latter means U.S. dominance in the sea, air, and space, but not necessarily forward basing. The argument amounts to a version of offshore balancing, however, with many of the attributes described above.

Another analyst who seems to adopt many elements of an offshore balancing approach for the United States in Asia (without specifically endorsing such a strategy) is Charles Glaser. Although a self-defined "optimistic realist" who argues that the United States should not be overly concerned about China's rise, Glaser nonetheless opines that "the United States should consider backing away from its commitment to Taiwan" in order to "remove the most obvious and contentious flash point between the United States and China and smooth the way for better relations between them in the decades to come." He also seems to advocate examining "the question of just how essential regional alliances in the Pacific are to U.S. security." See Charles Glaser, "Will China's Rise Lead to War?" *Foreign Affairs*, vol. 90, no. 2 (March/April 2011).

18. One proponent of offshore balancing who seems to recognize the above pitfalls is Lyle Goldstein. He advocates a less extreme or theoretical and more nuanced or "cautious and relaxed" variant of the approach that includes not only highly focused (or "directed") hedging activities centered on long-range submarine deployments (in place of aircraft carriers and highly aggressive concepts such as the "air-sea" battle strategy), but also much greater levels of security cooperation between Beijing and Washington. The latter, according to Goldstein, should be facilitated by U.S. reductions in the level of overt intelligence-collection activities along China's coastline, a shift from U.S. sea-control to sea-denial capabilities in maritime Asia, and a gradual reduction in U.S. arms sales to Taiwan. See Lyle J. Goldstein, "Resetting the U.S.-China Security Relationship," *Survival*, vol. 53, no. 2 (April–May 2011): 89–116.

19. Jonathan Holslag, *Trapped Giant: China's Military Rise*, Adelphi Paper (London: International Institute for Strategic Studies, 2010). Holslag argues that such a structure of "inclusive balancing" could help Washington "avoid the high costs of traditional containment or confrontation, while reassuring its traditional allies. For China, coordination with the other powers would be vital in reducing the burden of securing its growing interests abroad, tempering the suspicion of its rise and raising the costs for the others—particularly India and Japan—to resort to an aggressive unilateral military build-up." Also see G. John Ikenberry and Anne-Marie Slaughter (codirectors, Forging a World of Liberty Under Law: U.S. National Security in the 21st Century), "Final Paper of the Princeton Project on National Security," Woodrow Wilson School of Public and International Affairs, Princeton University, September 27, 2006, www.princeton. edu/~ppns/report/FinalReport.pdf; and Peter Van Ness, "Designing A Mechanism for Multilateral Security Cooperation in Northeast Asia," *Asian Perspective*, vol. 32, no. 4 (2008): 107–26.

Although focusing his attention on the notion of a Northeast Asia security cooperation mechanism derived from the Six Party Talks, much of Van Ness's analysis applies to even larger structures. He states: "A major advantage of a multilateral agreement, compared with a bilateral agreement, is that all of the parties have a stake in the commitments that have been made, so that if one party should fail to honor its commitments, all of the other five would have cause to pressure it to comply. This is what is meant by the idea of trust in the process. . . . governments should focus on their absolute gains from cooperating with each other, rather than relative gains, and work to maintain transparency and consistency in order to earn the confidence of the other partners. It will be important for them to take a long-term perspective and to identify opportunities for substantial material benefits for all parties. Reciprocity is a key. The six governments should be encouraged to meet cooperation with cooperation, but they should also include in their institution-building penalties for defection or a failure to fulfill commitments."

20. For a similar argument favoring a cooperative security structure, in this instance described as "integration," see Richard N. Haass, "The Palmerstonian Moment," *National Interest*, January 2, 2008, http://nationalinterest.org/article/the-palmerstonian-moment-1918?page=2. Haass writes: "A policy of integration would aim to create a cooperative relationship among the world's mid-level and major powers, built on a common commitment to promoting certain principles and outcomes. It would seek to translate this commitment into effective and lasting arrangements and actions wherever and whenever possible."

21. As suggested above, some of Lyle Goldstein's ideas provide at least partial answers to these questions. He advocates significant changes in U.S. military deployments and strategies in maritime Asia that could potentially provide a means of transitioning away from "an obsession with . . . maintaining military superiority," thus perhaps permitting a lessened reliance on existing U.S. bilateral security alliances. See Goldstein, "Resetting the U.S.-China Security Relationship."

22. The 2002 Declaration on the Conduct of Parties in the South China Sea incorporates elements of the latter requirement, albeit on a more limited scale. More importantly, that declaration is not legally binding.

23. Holslag, *Trapped Giant*.

24. For a similar argument from a leading Chinese expert on Sino-U.S. relations, see Wang Jisi, "It Will Be Difficult to Avoid a Major Strategic Trial of Strength Between China and the United States," *Guoji Xianqu Daobao Online*, August 9, 2010, OSC CPP20100830671002. Wang writes: "The power of the two nations is relatively converging, but the difference in cognition reflected by public opinion is actually widening. . . . The discrepancy in the cognition of the two sides regarding major international issues is expanding instead of narrowing." Also see "Strategic Analysis of Sino-U.S. Relations," interviews with Yang Shilong with Wu Baiyi; Huang Renwei; and Xu Tao, *Liaowang*, no. 36 (September 6, 2010): 10–14, OSC CPP20100910704005. Wu Baiyi states: "The facts have shown that the United States has never made proper psychological preparations for China's strong and rapid development, and it cannot resolve the contradictory preoccupation of both leading globalization and being unable to accept China's might. . . . As far as China is concerned, we too have not made various preparations for in-depth coexistence with the United States."

25. Van Ness ("Designing A Mechanism") argues that the participants in this process do not necessarily need to trust one another deeply, especially since such a level of trust is

infeasible. Rather, he argues that they just need to be able to trust the process, at least initially. This could prove much more feasible, he believes, as long as any cooperative security mechanism is structured using certain guarantees and material rewards. However, one must ask: On what basis are such guarantees and mutual rewards to be made entirely credible? This will likely bring the process back to the need to establish some significant levels of mutual trust early on.

26. Ikenberry and Slaughter, "Final Paper of the Princeton Project." The U.S.-PRC military-to-military relationship should constitute a critical element of such cooperative interactions. See below for a detailed discussion of that issue.

27. As suggested above, Lyle Goldstein offers some extremely interesting ways for U.S. policymakers to reduce the tensions generated by such sensitive issues. These include a transition away from "sea-control" to "sea-denial" capabilities (involving a lessened reliance on forward-deployed aircraft carriers in favor of submarines), gradual reductions in U.S. arms sales to Taiwan as part of broader confidence-building measures, and an overall reduction in overt intelligence-gathering activities along China's periphery. Moreover, Goldstein argues that, in return for the latter U.S. concession, Washington "could very reasonably expect China to offer tangible increases in transparency." See Goldstein, "Resetting the US-China Security Relationship."

28. See Henry A. Kissinger, "Avoiding a U.S.-China cold war," *Washington Post*, January 14, 2011, www.washingtonpost.com/wp-dyn/content/article/2011/01/13/AR2011011304832. html.

29. Carla A. Hills, Dennis C. Blair, and Frank Sampson Jannuzi, *U.S.-China Relations: An Affirmative Agenda, a Responsible Course* (New York: Council on Foreign Relations, 2007).

30. Obviously, this analysis assumes several things: first, that China will maintain high growth rates and increase its military and economic capacities to both threaten and pull Taiwan, respectively; second, that China will steadily increase its ability to pose a very credible challenge to U.S. air and naval power along its periphery; third, that Chinese nationalism will place growing pressure on China's leaders to make substantial *political* progress in the cross Strait situation; and fourth, that it is unlikely that current cross-Strait trends will evolve to produce an enduring, stable modus vivendi on their own before increases in PLA deployments relevant to Taiwan precipitate significant U.S. arms sales and hence severe crises in the bilateral relationship. All of these assumptions are highly credible, given existing trends.

31. One possible approach would be for Washington to offer to suspend all significant arms sales and defense assistance to Taiwan and reassert publicly the validity of the 1982 communiqué (in which the United States pledged to reduce arms sales to Taiwan as and if tensions across the Strait declined) in return for Beijing (1) destroying the short-range ballistic missiles it has deployed along China's coastline facing Taiwan; (2) suspending further production of such missiles indefinitely, along with any military maneuvers or exercises involving amphibious attacks or other Taiwan-related operations; and (3) pledging to enter into political talks with Taipei based on the 1992 consensus. Under such an agreement, Taipei would be free to bolster its own defenses, using its own means, while engaging in talks with Beijing. And Washington would also be free to continue to maintain or increase its deployments in the region. And the U.S. commitment to a peaceful, uncoerced resolution of the Taiwan problem would remain. Beijing might accept such an agreement, viewing it (whether accurate or not) as an

opportunity for maneuvering Taiwan into a situation in which it would gradually accept some form of political association. Equally important, Taipei might also do so, viewing such an agreement as a basis for arriving, at least, at some sort of interim solution that would reduce China's military threat to Taiwan while opening the door to a long-term modus vivendi on the basis of something other than a PRC-designed One China formula. As noted above, Lyle Goldstein advocates something similar to this notion, albeit in more general terms. See Goldstein, "Resetting the US-China Security Relationship."

32. Some of these deployments would obviously cause concern, but both sides would need to recognize that such capabilities remain necessary for other reasons. Agreements regarding notification of movement could be considered.

33. Chicago Council on Global Affairs, *Global Views 2010: Constrained Internationalism—Adapting to New Realities; Results of a 2010 National Survey of Public Opinion* (Chicago: Chicago Council on Global Affairs, 2010), www.thechicagocouncil.org/UserFiles/File/POS_Topline%20Reports/POS%202010/Global%20Views%202010.pdf.

34. In other words, as described in chapter 2, Washington should maintain policies and deployments that deter offensive actions by Beijing and reassure Taipei of U.S. commitments to prevent the use of force, while also opposing any efforts by Taipei to establish de jure "independence," thus reassuring Beijing that Washington will not support any unilateral attempt to permanently separate the island from mainland China.

35. For a strong exposition of this argument, see Charles W. Freeman, "The United States, China and the New Global Geometry," Middle East Policy Council, speech delivered at the Johns Hopkins University–Nanjing University Center for Chinese and American Studies, Nanjing, November 10, 2010, http://mepc.org/articles-commentary/speeches/united-states-china-and-new-global-geometry.

36. For a similar recommendation, albeit couched more broadly, see Wang, "China's Search for a Grand Strategy."

37. See Van Ness, "Designing a Mechanism."

38. This possibility is highlighted by many analysts. For a particularly notable example, see Thomas P. M. Barnett, "Big-War Thinking in a Small-War Era: The Rise of the Air-Sea Battle Concept," *China Security*, vol. 6, no. 3 (October 2010): 3–11. Barnett specifically criticizes the so-called air-sea battle concept noted in chapter 4 as a means of sustaining U.S. military predominance in the Western Pacific. For Barnett, that concept (based on the United States' acquiring a wide range of potentially costly and threatening forces designed in large part to thoroughly negate China's offshore antiaccess and area denial capabilities), if allowed to dominate the U.S. response to China's rise, will feed Chinese insecurities, encourage an unhealthy arms race, and thereby greatly undermine efforts at cooperation.

39. Goldstein adds, correctly: "Selective port visits and simple joint exercises have formed the limit of navy-to-navy engagement to date, but this limited engagement is hardly adequate to the task. At a minimum, Washington and Beijing should consider establishing academic and educational exchanges between military academies, war colleges and similar institutions. Additional future steps could include pre-notification and observation of exercises, facility visits and bilateral strategic dialogues. The Chinese navy and maritime services must not be viewed as comparable with the services of other countries that the US Navy engages with now and then. Rather, efforts to nurture a cooperative relationship must reflect the conviction of the current president and

secretary of state that there is no more important bilateral relationship." See Goldstein, "Resetting the US-China Security Relationship."

40. As Feigenbaum and Manning state, "With Asians unlikely to embrace the United States as a member of ASEAN Plus Three, the United States needs . . . to take intra-Asian trade liberalization efforts more seriously; . . . otherwise, U.S. economic losses will mount." Also see Evan Feigenbaum and Robert A. Manning, *The United States in the New Asia*, Council Special Report 50 (New York: Council on Foreign Relations, 2009). Feigenbaum adds, in a separate article, that without such greater activism, "China is most likely to fill the vacuum created by an American failure to lead on regional and global trade." Evan Feigenbaum, "America Risks Being Left Behind in Asia," *Financial Times*, November 11, 2009. See also Evan A. Feigenbaum, "Why America No Longer Gets Asia," *Washington Quarterly*, Spring 2011, www.twq.com/11spring/docs/11spring_Feigenbaum.pdf.

41. C. Fred Bergsten, Bates Gill, Nicholas R. Lardy, and Derek Mitchell, *China: The Balance Sheet—What the World Needs to Know Now About the Emerging Superpower* (New York: PublicAffairs, 2006); Hills, Blair, and Jannuzi, *U.S.–China Relations*.

42. David D. Hale and Lyric Hughes Hale, "Reconsidering Revaluation," *Foreign Affairs*, January–February 2008.

43. Robert E. Scott and Daniel J. Ikenson, "Should the Next U.S. President Adopt a Tougher Stance on Trade Policy with China?" Council on Foreign Relations, April 4, 2008, www.cfr.org/china/should-next-us-president-adopt-tougher-stance-trade-policy-china/p15888.

44. As Lampton states, "Economic interdependence is the most powerful integrative force available to reduce mutual strategic mistrust. . . . Job creation through foreign investment can lower the temperature in bilateral relations—if it is responsible investment compliant with national laws." See David Lampton, *Power Constrained: Sources of Mutual Strategic Suspicion in U.S.–China Relations*, NBR Analysis 93 (Seattle: National Bureau of Asian Research, 2010), www.nbr.org/publications/analysis/pdf/2010_U.S._China.pdf.

45. Bates Gill, Chin-Hao Huang, and J. Stephen Morrison, "China's Expanding Role in Africa: Implications for the United States," Center for Strategic and International Studies, www.csis.org/component/option,com_csis_pubs/task,view/id,3714/typ.

46. A recent example of the successful application of such factors occurred during the run-up to Hu Jintao's state visit to Washington, D.C., in January 2011. The visit to Beijing in September 2010 by then-deputy national security adviser Thomas Donilon and then-national economic adviser Lawrence Summers initiated a series of senior-level, face-to-face meetings with Chinese officials that eventually laid the foundation for a significant improvement in the bilateral relationship and a successful state visit. Issues of "face," a proper understanding of protocol, and a systematic and well-prepared discussion of U.S. and Chinese interests were all essential to the resulting outcome. See Douglas Paal, "China: Hu's State Visit an Opportunity," Asia Pacific Brief, Carnegie Endowment for International Peace, Washington, D.C., December 28, 2010.

BIBLIOGRAPHY

BOOKS, CHAPTERS IN BOOKS, AND PAMPHLETS

Alden, Chris, Daniel Large, and Ricardo Soares De Oliveira, eds. *China Returns to Africa: A Rising Power and a Continent Embrace.* New York: Columbia University Press, 2008.

Alterman, Jon B., and John W. Garver. *The Vital Triangle: China, United States, and Middle East.* Washington, D.C.: Center for Strategic and International Studies, 2008.

Armitage, Richard L., and Joseph S. Nye. *The U.S.-Japan Alliance: Getting Asia Right Through 2020.* Washington, D.C.: Center for Strategic and International Studies, 2007.

Arora, Vivek, and Roberto Cardarelli, eds. *Rebalancing Growth in Asia: Economic Dimensions for China.* Washington, D.C.: International Monetary Fund, 2011.

Austin, Greg. *China's Ocean Frontier: International Law, Military Force, and National Development.* Sydney: Allen & Unwin, 1998.

Bacevich, Andrew J. *The Limits of Power: The End of American Exceptionalism.* New York: Metropolitan Books, 2008.

Barnett, A. Doak. *China's Economy in Global Perspective.* Washington, D.C.: Brookings Institution Press, 1981.

———. *U.S. Arms Sales: The China-Taiwan Tangle.* Washington, D.C.: Brookings Institution Press, 1982.

———. *U.S.-China Relations: Time for a New Beginning—Again.* Pamphlet Based on James and Margaret Loe Memorial Lecture. Washington, D.C.: School for Advanced International Studies, Johns Hopkins University, 1994.

Bergsten, C. Fred, Charles Freeman, Nicholas R. Lardy, and Derek J. Mitchell. *China's Rise: Challenges and Opportunities.* Washington, D.C.: Peterson Institute for International Economics and Center for Strategic and International Studies, 2008.

Bergsten, C. Fred, Bates Gill, Nicholas R. Lardy, and Derek J. Mitchell. *The Balance Sheet: What the World Needs to Know Now About China.* New York: Perseus Books, 2006.

Bhagwati, Jagdish. *In Defense of Globalization.* New York: Oxford University Press, 2004.

Blair, Dennis C. "Military Power Projection in Asia." In *Strategic Asia 2008–09: Challenges and Choices,* edited by Ashley J. Tellis, Mercy Kuo, et al. Seattle: National Bureau of Asian Research, 2008.

Blasko, Dennis J. *The Chinese Army Today: Tradition and Transformation for the 21st Century.* London: Routledge, 2006.

Bottelier, Pieter. "China and the International Financial Crisis." In *Strategic Asia 2009–10: Economic Meltdown and Geopolitical Stability,* edited by Ashley J. Tellis, Andrew Marble, and Travis Tanner. Seattle: National Bureau of Asian Research, 2009.

Bouton, Marshall M., ed. *Global Views 2008: Anxious Americans Seek a New Direction in United States Foreign Policy: Results of a 2008 Survey of Public Opinion.* Chicago: Chicago Council on Global Affairs, 2008.

——. *Global Views 2010: Constrained Internationalism: Adapting to New Realities: Results of a 2010 National Survey of Public Opinion.* Chicago: Chicago Council on Global Affairs, 2010.

Brautigam, Deborah. *The Dragon's Gift: The Real Story of China in Africa.* New York: Oxford University Press, 2009.

Britton, Erik, and Christopher T. Mark, Sr. *The China Effect: Assessing the Impact on the U.S. Economy of Trade and Investment with China.* Washington, D.C.: China Business Forum, 2006.

Brooks, Linton. "The Sino-American Nuclear Balance: Its Future and Implications." In *China's Arrival: A Strategic Framework for a Global Relationship,* edited by Abraham Denmark and Nirav Patel. Washington, D.C.: Center for a New American Security, 2009.

Brown, Harold, et al. *Chinese Military Power: Report of an Independent Task Force.* New York: Council on Foreign Relations, 2003.

Busby, Joshua. "Under What Conditions Could Climate Change Pose a Threat to U.S. National Security?" In *Global Climate Change: National Security Implications,* edited by Carolyn Pumphrey. Carlisle, Pa.: Strategic Studies Institute, 2008.

Bush, Richard C. *Untying the Knot: Making Peace in the Taiwan Strait.* Washington, D.C.: Brookings Institution Press, 2005.

——. "The U.S. Policy of Dual Deterrence." In *If China Attacks Taiwan: Military Strategy, Politics, and Economics,* edited by Steve Tsang. New York: Routledge, 2006.

Bush, Richard C., and Michael E. O'Hanlon. *A War Like No Other: The Truth About China's Challenge to America.* New York: John Wiley & Sons, 2007.

Campbell, Kurt M., ed. *Climatic Cataclysm: The Foreign Policy and National Security Implications of Climate Change.* Washington, D.C.: Brookings Institution Press, 2008.

Chambers, Michael R. "Framing the Problem: China's Threat Environment and International Obligations." In *Right Sizing the People's Liberation Army: Exploring the Contours of China's Military,* edited by Roy Kamphausen and Andrew Scobell. Carlisle, Pa.: Strategic Studies Institute, 2007.

Chandler, William. *Breaking the Suicide Pact: U.S.-China Cooperation on Climate Change.* Policy Brief 57. Washington, D.C.: Carnegie Endowment for International Peace, 2008. www.carnegieendowment.org/files/pb57_chandler_final2.pdf.

Chandler, William, and Holly Gwin. *Financing Energy Efficiency in China.* Washington, D.C.: Carnegie Endowment for International Peace, 2008. www.carnegieendowment.org/files/chandler_clean_energy_final.pdf.

Chang, Gordon G. *The Coming Collapse of China.* New York: Random House, 2001.

Cheng, T. J. "China–Taiwan Economic Linkage: Between Insulation and Superconductivity." In *Dangerous Strait: The U.S., China, Taiwan Crisis,* edited by Nancy Bernkopf Tucker. New York: Columbia University Press, 2005.

Chestnut, Sheena, and Alastair Iain Johnston. "Is China Rising?" In *Global Giant: Is China Changing the Rules of the Game?* edited by Eva Paus, Penelope Prime, and Jon Western. New York: Palgrave Macmillan, 2009.

Christensen, Thomas J. *New Challenges and Opportunities in the Taiwan Strait: Defining America's Role.* New York: National Committee on U.S.-China Relations, 2003.

Christensen, Thomas J., and Michael A. Glosny. "China: Sources of Stability in U.S.-China Security Relations." In *Strategic Asia 2003–04: Fragility and Crisis,* edited by Richard Ellings, Aaron Friedberg, and Michael Wills. Seattle. National Bureau of Asian Research, 2003.

Chu, Yun-han. "The Evolution of Beijing's Policy Toward Taiwan During the Reform Era." In *China Rising: Power and Motivation in Chinese Foreign Policy,* edited by Yong Deng and Fei-ling Wang. Oxford: Rowman & Littlefield, 2005.

Chung, Jae Ho. *Between Ally and Partner: Korea–China Relations and the United States.* New York: Columbia University Press, 2007.

Cliff, Roger. "The Implications of Chinese Military Modernization for U.S. Force Posture in a Taiwan Conflict." In *Assessing the Threat: The Chinese Military and Taiwan's Security,* edited by Michael D. Swaine, Andrew N. D. Yang, Evan S. Medeiros, and Oriana Skylar Mastro. Washington, D.C.: Carnegie Endowment for International Peace, 2007.

Cliff, Roger, et al. *Entering the Dragon's Lair: Chinese Antiaccess Strategies and Their Implications for the United States.* Santa Monica, Calif.: RAND Corporation, 2007.

Cohen, Benjamin J. "Containing Backlash: Foreign Economic Policy in an Age of Globalization." In *Eagle Rules? Foreign Policy and American Primacy in the Twenty-First Century,* edited by Robert J. Lieber. Princeton, N.J.: Princeton University Press, 2002.

Cole, Bernard D. *The Great Wall at Sea: China's Navy Enters the Twenty-First Century.* Annapolis, Md.: Naval Institute Press, 2001.

——. "Right-Sizing the Navy: How Much Naval Force Will Beijing Deploy?" In *Right Sizing the People's Liberation Army: Exploring the Contours of China's Military,* edited by Roy Kamphausen and Andrew Scobell. Carlisle, Pa.: Strategic Studies Institute, 2007.

Committee of 100. *Hope and Fear: Full Report of C-100's Survey on American and Chinese Attitudes Toward Each Other.* New York: Committee of 100, 2008. http://survey.committee100.org/2007/files/C100SurveyFullReport.pdf.

Congressional-Executive Commission on China. *Congressional-Executive Commission on China Annual Report 2007,* edited by 111th Congress. Washington, D.C.: U.S. Government Printing Office, 2007.

——. *Congressional-Executive Commission on China Annual Report 2010,* edited by 111th Congress. Washington, D.C.: U.S. Government Printing Office, 2010. www.cecc.gov/pages/annualRpt/annualRpt10/CECCannRpt2010.pdf.

Copeland, Dale. "Economic Interdependence and the Future of U.S.-China Relations." In *International Relations Theory and the Asia-Pacific,* edited by G. John Ikenberry and Michael Mastundono. New York: Columbia University Press, 2003.

Cossa, Ralph A. "U.S.-Japan Relations: What Should Washington Do?" In *America's Role in Asia: Asian and American Views*, edited by Michael Armacost, J. Stapleton Roy, Han Sung-Joo, Tommy Koh, C. Raja Mohan. San Francisco: Asia Foundation, 2008.

Council on Foreign Relations. *Beginning the Journey: China, the United States, and the WTO*. Robert D. Hormats, chair; Elizabeth Economy and Kevin Nealer, project directors. New York: Council on Foreign Relations Press, 2001.

——. *U.S.-China Relations: An Affirmative Agenda, a Responsible Course*. Independent Task Force Report 59; Carla A. Hills and Dennis C. Blair, chairs; Frank Sampson Jannuzi, project director. New York: Council on Foreign Relations, 2007.

Cozad, Mark. "China's Regional Power Projection: Prospects for Future Missions in the South and East China Seas." In *Beyond the Strait: PLA Missions Other Than Taiwan*, edited by Roy Kamphausen, David Lai, and Andrew Scobell. Carlisle, Pa.: Strategic Studies Institute, 2009.

Craig, Susan L. *Chinese Perceptions of Traditional and Nontraditional Security Threats*. Carlisle, Pa.: Strategic Studies Institute, 2007.

Cummings, Bruce. *Parallax Visions: Making Sense of American-East Asian Relations on the Eve of the Twenty-First Century*. Durham, N.C.: Duke University Press, 1999.

Curtis, Gerald L., Ryosei Kokubun, and Wang Jisi, eds. *Getting the Triangle Straight: Managing China–Japan–US Relations*. New York: Japan Center for International Exchange, 2010.

Dadush, Uri, Shimelse Ali, and Rachel Esplin Odell. *Is Protectionism Dying?* Carnegie Paper 121. Washington, D.C.: Carnegie Endowment for International Peace, 2011.

Dent, Christopher M. *China, Japan and Regional Leadership in East Asia*. Northampton, Mass.: Edward Elgar, 2008.

Descisciolo, Dominic. "China's Space Development and Nuclear Strategy." In *China's Nuclear Force Modernization*, edited by Lyle J. Goldstein and Andrew S. Erickson. Naval War College Newport Papers 22. Newport: Naval War College, 2005.

Dessler, Andrew E., and Edward A. Parson. *The Science and Politics of Global Climate Change: A Guide to the Debate*. New York: Cambridge University Press, 2006.

Ding, Yijiang. *Chinese Democracy After Tiananmen*. New York: Columbia University Press, 2002.

Downs, Erica. *China*. Brookings Foreign Policy Studies, Energy Security Series. Washington, D.C.: Brookings Institution, 2006.

——. *China's Quest for Energy Security*. Santa Monica, Calif.: RAND Corporation, 2000.

——. "Who's Afraid of China's Oil Companies?" In *Energy Security: Economics, Politics, Strategies, and Implications*, edited by Carlos Pascual and Jonathan Elkind. Washington, D.C.: Brookings Institution Press, 2009.

Drohan, Thomas A. *American-Japanese Security Agreements, Past and Present*. Jefferson, N.C.: McFarland, 2007.

Economy, Elizabeth. "Asia's Environmental Crisis: Why the U.S. Should Care and What It Should Do." In *America's Role in Asia: Asian and American Views*, edited by Michael Armacost, J. Stapleton Roy, Han Sung-Joo, Tommy Koh, and C. Raja Mohan. San Francisco: Asia Foundation, 2008.

Economy, Elizabeth, and Michel Oksenberg, eds. *China Joins the World: Progress and Prospects*. New York: Council on Foreign Relations Press, 1999.

Edwards, R. Randle, Louis Henkin, and Andrew J. Nathan. *Human Rights in Contemporary China*. New York: Columbia University Press, 1986.

Erickson, Andrew S., Lyle J. Goldstein, and William S. Murray. *Chinese Mine Warfare: A PLA Navy 'Assassin's Mace' Capability*. Naval War College China Maritime Study. Newport: Naval War College, 2009.

Erickson, Andrew S., Lyle J. Goldstein, William S. Murray, and Andrew R. Wilson. *China's Future Nuclear Submarine Force*. Annapolis, Md.: Naval Institute Press, 2007.

Feigenbaum, Evan A., and Robert A. Manning. *The United States in the New Asia*. Council Special Report 50. New York: Council on Foreign Relations Press, 2009.

Ferguson, Charles D., William C. Potter, Amy Sands, Leonard S. Spector, and Fred L. Wehling, eds. *Four Faces of Nuclear Terrorism*. New York: Routledge, 2005.

Finkelstein, David. "China's New Concept of Security." In *The People's Liberation Army and China in Transition*, edited by Stephen J. Flanagan and Michael E. Marti. Washington, D.C.: Center for the Study of Chinese Military Affairs, 2003.

Finnegan, Michael. *Managing Unmet Expectations in the U.S.-Japan Alliance*.Special Report 17. Seattle: National Bureau of Asian Research, 2009.

Flannery, Tim. *The Weather Makers: How Man Is Changing the Climate and What It Means for Life on Earth*. New York: Atlantic Monthly Press, 2006.

Foot, Rosemary. *Rights Beyond Borders: The Global Community and the Struggle Over Human Rights in China*. Oxford. Oxford University Press, 2000.

Fouse, David, et al. *United States-China-Japan Working Group on Trilateral Confidence-and Security-Building Measures (CSBMs)*. Stanley Foundation Project Report. Muscatine, Iowa: Stanley Foundation, 2008.

Fravel, M. Taylor. *Strong Borders, Secure Nation: Cooperation and Conflict in China's Territorial Disputes*. Princeton, N.J.: Princeton University Press, 2008.

Frost, Ellen L. "America's Role in Engaging with Asia's New Regionalism." In *America's Role in Asia: Asian and American Views*, edited by Michael Armacost, J. Stapleton Roy, Han Sung-Joo, Tommy Koh, and C. Raja Mohan. San Francisco: Asia Foundation, 2008.

Fuchs, Andreas, and Nils-Hendrik Klann. *Paying a Visit: The Dalai Lama Effect on International Trade*. Research Paper 113. Göttingen: Center for European Governance and Economic Development, University of Göttingen, 2010. www.uni-goettingen.de/de/document/dow nload/24062d6f430a7c77ab7b1a54407ac843.pdf/113_Fuchs.pdf.

Funabashi, Yoichi, Michel Oksenberg, and Heinrich Weiss. *An Emerging China in a World of Interdependence*. New York: Trilateral Commission, 1994.

Fung, K. C., and Lawrence J. Lau. *The China-United States Bilateral Trade Balance: How Big Is It Really?* Stanford, Calif.: Asia-Pacific Research Center, 1996.

Gao Zugui. "Major Non Traditional Security Threats in the Asia-Pacific Region: China's Perspective." In *A Collection of Papers of the International Symposium on Non-Traditional Security: Challenges and Responses*. Beijing: China Institute for International Strategic Studies, 2005.

Garrett, Banning, and Jonathan Adams. *U.S.-China Cooperation on the Problem of Failing States and Transnational Threats*. Special Report 126. Washington, D.C.: U.S. Institute of Peace Press, 2004.

Garrison, Jean A. *Making China Policy: From Nixon to G. W. Bush*. Boulder, Colo.: Lynne Rienner, 2005.

Garver, John W. *Face Off: China, the United States, and Taiwan's Democratization*. Seattle: University of Washington Press, 1997.

———. *Protracted Contest: Sino-Indian Rivalry in the Twentieth Century*. Seattle: University of Washington Press, 2001.

Garver, John W., Flynt Leverett, and Hilary Mann Leverett. *Moving (Slightly) Closer to Iran: China's Shifting Calculus for Managing Its 'Persian Gulf Dilemma.'* Asia-Pacific Policy Papers Series. Washington, D.C.: Edwin O. Reischauer Center for East Asian Studies,

Paul H. Nitze School of Advanced International Studies, Johns Hopkins University, 2009.

Gill, Bates. "China's Changing Approach to Nonproliferation." In *Combating Weapons of Mass Destruction*, edited by Nathan E. Busch and Daniel H. Joyner. Athens: University of Georgia Press, 2009.

——. *Rising Star: China's New Security Diplomacy*. Washington, D.C.: Brookings Institution Press, 2007.

Gill, Bates, James Mulvenon, and Mark Stokes. "The Chinese Second Artillery Corps: Transition to Credible Deterrence." In *The People's Liberation Army as an Organization*, edited by James C. Mulvenon and Andrew N. D. Yang. Santa Monica, Calif.: RAND Corporation, 2002.

Gill, Bates, and Michael Schiffer. "A Rising China's Rising Responsibilities." In *Powers and Principles*, edited by Michael Schiffer and David Schorr. Lanham, Md.: Lexington Books, 2009.

Gill, Bates, et al. *Strategic Views on Asian Regionalism: Survey Results and Analysis*. Washington, D.C.: Center for Strategic and International Studies, 2009. www.csis.org/media/csis/pubs/090217_gill_stratviews_web.pdf.

Gilley, Bruce. *China's Democratic Future: How It Will Happen and Where It Will Lead*. New York: Columbia University Press, 2004.

Glaser, Bonnie S., Scott Snyder, and John S. Park. *Keeping an Eye on an Unruly Neighbor: Chinese Views of Economic Reform and Stability in North Korea*. Joint report by Center for Strategic and International Studies and U.S. Institute of Peace. Washington, D.C.: U.S. Institute of Peace Press, 2008.

Goldin, Ian. *Globalization for Development: Trade, Finance, Aid, Migration, and Policy*. New York: Palgrave Macmillan, 2007.

Goldstein, Avery. *Rising to the Challenge: China's Grand Strategy and International Security*. Stanford, Calif.: Stanford University Press, 2005.

Goldstein, Melvyn C. *The Snow Lion and the Dragon: Tibet, China and the Dalai Lama*. Berkeley: University of California Press, 1997.

Goldstein, Steven M., and Randall Schriver. "An Uncertain Relationship: The United States, Taiwan and the Taiwan Relations Act." In *Taiwan in the Twentieth Century*, edited by Richard Louis Edmonds and Steven Goldstein. Cambridge: Cambridge University Press, 2001.

Graham, Bob, and Jim Talent, eds. *World at Risk: The Report of the Commission on the Prevention of WMD Proliferation and Terrorism*. New York: Vintage Books, 2008.

Green, Michael J. "Organizing Asia: Politics, Trade, and the New Multilateralism." In *Global Forecast: the Top Security Challenges of 2008*. Washington, D.C.: Center for Strategic and International Studies, 2007.

Gries, Peter Hays. *China's New Nationalism: Pride, Politics, and Diplomacy*. Berkeley: University of California Press, 2004.

Hansell, Cristina, and William C. Potter, eds. *Engaging China and Russia on Nuclear Disarmament*. Occasional Paper 15. Monterey, Calif.: James Martin Center for Nonproliferation Studies, 2009. http://cns.miis.edu/opapers/op15/op15.pdf.

Harding, Harry. *A Fragile Relationship: The U.S. and China Since 1972*. New Haven, Conn.: Yale University Press, 1984.

Hathaway, David. *Strategies for Decreasing the Carbon Footprint of Chinese Companies and Meeting Global Sustainability Challenges*. China Environment Series 10. Washington, D.C.: Woodrow Wilson International Center for Scholars, 2009.

Holslag, Jonathan. *Trapped Giant: China's Military Rise.* Adelphi Paper. London: International Institute for Strategic Studies, 2010.

Hu, Weixing, Gerald Chan, and Daojiong Zha. *China's International Relations in the 21st Century: Dynamics of Paradigm Shifts.* Lanham, Md.: University Press of America, 2000.

Huang, Yanzhong. "China's New Health Diplomacy." In *China's Capacity to Manage Infectious Diseases: Global Implications,* edited by Charles W. Freeman III. Washington, D.C.: Center for Strategic and International Studies, 2009.

———. *China's Reaction to H1N1 Pandemic Flu.* East Asian Institute Background Brief 498. Singapore: East Asian Institute at National University of Singapore, 2010. www.eai.nus.edu.sg/BB498.pdf.

Hufbauer, Gary Clyde, Yee Wong, and Ketki Sheth. *U.S.-China Trade Disputes: Rising Tide, Rising Stakes.* Washington, D.C.: Institute for International Economics, 2006.

Hughes, Christopher W. "Japanese Military Modernization: In Search of a 'Normal' Security Role." In *Strategic Asia 2005–06: Military Modernization in an Era of Uncertainty,* edited by Ashley J. Tellis and Michael Wills. Seattle: National Bureau of Asian Research, 2005.

———. *Japan's Remilitarisation.* London: Routledge for International Institute for Strategic Studies, 2009.

Hughes, Christopher W., and Akiko Fukushima. "U.S.-Japan Security Relations: Toward Bilateralism Plus?" In *Beyond Bilateralism: U.S.-Japan Relations in the New Asia-Pacific,* edited by Ellis S. Krauss and T. J. Pempel. Stanford, Calif.: Stanford University Press, 2004.

Human Rights Watch. "China Events in 2007." In *World Report 2008.* New York: Human Rights Watch, 2008.

Information Office of the State Council of the People's Republic of China, ed. "Section III: Legal Systems of Respecting and Safeguarding Human Rights." In *China's Efforts and Achievements in Promoting the Rule of Law.* Beijing: Information Office of the State Council of the People's Republic of China, 2008. www.china.org.cn/government/news/2008-02/28/content_11025486.htm.

International Energy Agency. "World Energy Outlook 2010." In *Global Energy Trends.* Paris: International Energy Agency, 2010.

Jackson, Robert. *The Earth Remains Forever: Generations at a Crossroads.* Austin: University of Texas Press, 2002.

Johnston, Alastair Iain. "Is China Rising?" In *Is China Changing the Rules of the Game?* edited by Eva Paus, Penelope Prime, and Jon Western. New York: Palgrave Macmillan, 2009.

———. *Social States: China in International Institutions, 1980–2000.* Princeton, N.J.: Princeton University Press, 2008.

Johnston, Alastair Iain, and Robert S. Ross, eds. *New Directions in the Study of China's Foreign Policy.* Stanford, Calif.: Stanford University Press, 2006.

Kamphausen, Roy, David Lai, and Andrew Scobell, eds. *Beyond the Strait: PLA Missions Other Than Taiwan.* Carlisle, Pa.: Strategic Studies Institute, 2009.

———. *The PLA at Home and Abroad: Assessing the Operational Capabilities of China's Military.* Carlisle, Pa.: Strategic Studies Institute, 2010.

Kan, Shirley. *China and Proliferation of Weapons of Mass Destruction and Missiles: Policy Issues.* Congressional Research Service Report RL31555. Washington, D.C.: Library of Congress, 2006.

Kang, Harnit. *Maritime Issues in South China Sea: A Survey of Literature.* IPCS Special Report 76. New Delhi: Institute of Peace and Conflict Studies, 2009.

Kastner, Scott L. *Political Conflict and Economic Interdependence Across the Taiwan Strait and Beyond.* Studies in East Asian Security Series of the East-West Center. Stanford, Calif.: Stanford University Press, 2009.

Kaufman, Joan. "Infectious Disease Challenges in China." In *China's Capacity to Manage Infectious Diseases: Global Implications*, edited by Charles W. Freeman III. Washington, D.C.: Center for Strategic and International Studies, 2009.

Kawachi, Ichiro, and Sarah Wamala, eds. *Globalization and Health*. New York: Oxford University Press, 2006.

Keidel, Albert. *China's Economic Rise: Fact and Fiction*. Policy Brief 61. Washington, D.C.: Carnegie Endowment for International Peace, 2008.

Kennedy, Paul. "Global Challenges at the Beginning of the Twenty-First Century." In *Global Trends and Global Governance*, edited by Paul Kennedy, Dirk Messner, and Franz Nuscheler. London: Pluto Press, 2002.

Kent, Ann. *Beyond Compliance: China, International Organizations, and Global Security*. East-West Center Studies in Asian Security. Stanford, Calif.: Stanford University Press, 2007.

———. *China, the United Nations, and Human Rights*. Philadelphia: University of Pennsylvania Press, 1999.

Khalilzad, Zalmay, David Orletsky, Jonathan Pollack, Kevin Pollpeter, Angel Rabasa, David Shlapak, Abram Shulsky, and Ashley J. Tellis. *The United States and Asia: Toward a New U.S. Strategy and Force Posture*. Santa Monica, Calif.: RAND Corporation, 2001.

Khalilzad, Zalmay M., et al. *The United States and a Rising China: Strategic and Military Implications*. Santa Monica, Calif.: RAND Corporation, 1999.

Khanna, Parag. *The Second World: Empires and Influence in the New Global Order*. New York: Random House, 2008.

Kharas, Homi, with Deepak Bhattasal et al. *An East Asian Renaissance: Ideas for Economic Growth*. Washington, D.C.: World Bank, 2007.

Kimball, Ann Marie. "When the Flu Comes: Political and Economic Risks of Pandemic Disease in Asia." In *Strategic Asia 2006–07: Trade, Interdependence, and Security*, edited by Ashley Tellis and Michael Wills. Seattle: National Bureau of Asian Research, 2006.

Koh, Tommy. "The United States and Southeast Asia." In *America's Role in Asia: Asian and American Views*, edited by Michael Armacost, J. Stapleton Roy, Han Sung-Joo, Tommy Koh, and C. Raja Mohan. San Francisco: Asia Foundation, 2008.

Kong, Bo. *China's International Petroleum Policy*. Santa Barbara, Calif.: Praeger Security International, 2010.

Korppoo, Anna, and Linda Jakobson, eds. *Towards a New Climate Regime? Views of China, India, Japan, Russia and the United States on the Road to Copenhagen*. Helsinki: Finnish Institute of International Affairs, 2009.

Kugler, Richard L., and Ellen L. Frost, eds. *The Global Century: Globalization and National Security*. Washington, D.C.: National Defense University Press, 2001.

Kupchan, Charles A. *The End of an American Era: U.S. Foreign Policy and the Geopolitics of the Twenty-First Century*. New York: Alfred A. Knopf, 2002.

Kurlantzick, Joshua. *China's Charm: Implications of Chinese Soft Power*. Policy Brief 47. Washington, D.C.: Carnegie Endowment for International Peace, 2006.

———. *China's Charm Offensive: How China's Soft Power Is Transforming the World*. New Haven, Conn.: Yale University Press, 2007.

Kurlantzick, Joshua, and Perry Link. "China: Resilient, Sophisticated Authoritarianism." In *Undermining Democracy: 21st Century Authoritarians*. Washington, D.C.: Freedom House, 2009.

Laliberté, André, and Marc Lanteigne, eds. *The Chinese Party-State in the Twenty-First Century: Adaptation and the Reinvention of Legitimacy*. New York: Routledge, 2007.

Lampton, David M. *Power Constrained: Sources of Mutual Strategic Suspicion in U.S.-China Relations*. NBR Analysis 93. Seattle: National Bureau of Asian Research, 2010. www.nbr. org/publications/analysis/pdf/2010_U.S._China.pdf.

——. "A Precarious Balance." In *The Three Faces of Chinese Power: Might, Money, and Minds*, by David Lampton. Berkeley: University of California Press, 2008.

——. *Same Bed, Different Dreams: Managing U.S.-China Relations, 1989–2000*. Berkeley: University of California Press, 2001.

Lampton, David M., and Alfred Wilhelm, eds. *United States and China: Relations at a Crossroads*. Lanham, Md.: University Press of America, 1995.

Lardy, Nicholas. *Foreign Trade and Economic Reform in China*. New York: Cambridge University Press, 1992.

——. *Integrating China Into the Global Economy*. Washington, D.C.: Brookings Institution Press, 2002.

Lasater, Martin L. *The Taiwan Issue in Sino-American Strategic Relations*. Boulder, Colo.: Westview Press, 1984.

Lawson, Eugene, ed. *U.S.-China Trade: Problems and Prospects*. New York: Praeger, 1988.

Lewis, John Wilson, and Xue Litai. *China Builds the Bomb*. Stanford, Calif.: Stanford University Press, 1988.

Li, Cheng, ed. *China's Changing Political Landscape: Prospects for Democracy*. Washington, D.C.: Brookings Institution Press, 2008.

Lieberthal, Kenneth, and David Sandalow. *Overcoming Obstacles to U.S.-China Cooperation on Climate Change*. John L. Thornton China Center Monograph 1. Washington, D.C.: Brookings Institution, 2009. www.brookings.edu/~/media/Files/rc/reports/2009/01_climate_change_lieberthal_sandalow/01_climate_change_lieberthal_sandalow.pdf.

Liew, Leong H., and Shaoguang Wang, eds. *Nationalism, Democracy, and National Integration in China*. London: RoutledgeCurzon, 2004.

Lilley, James R., and Wendell I. Willkie II, eds. *Beyond MFN: Trade with China and American Interests*. Washington, D.C.: American Enterprise Institute, 1994.

Linden, Eugene. *The Winds of Change: Climate, Weather, and the Destruction of Civilizations*. New York: Simon & Schuster, 2006.

Liu, Guoli, ed. *Chinese Foreign Policy in Transition*. Edison, N.J.: Aldine Transaction, 2004.

Lo, Bobo. *Axis of Convenience: Moscow, Beijing, and the New Geopolitics*. Washington, D.C.: Brookings Institution Press, 2008.

Lord, Arthur. *Demystifying FTAs: A Comparative Analysis of American, Japanese, and Chinese Efforts to Shape the Future of Free Trade*. Asia Pacific Policy Papers Series 10. Washington, D.C.: Edwin O. Reischauer Center for East Asian Studies, Paul H. Nitze School of Advanced International Studies, Johns Hopkins University, 2010.

Lum, Thomas, and Hannah Fischer. "Human Rights in China: Trends and Policy Implications." Congressional Research Service Report for Congress, January 15, 2010, www.fas.org/sgp/crs/row/RL34729.pdf.

MacDonald, Bruce W. *China, Space Weapons, and U.S. Security*. Council Special Report 38. New York: Council on Foreign Relations, 2008.

Mandelbaum, Michael. *The Frugal Superpower: America's Global Leadership in a Cash-Strapped Era*. New York: PublicAffairs, 2010.

Manzano, George, and Myrene Bedaño. *Revisiting Sectoral Liberalization: An Alternative to the FTAAP? Implications on the Philippines*. Discussion Paper 2009-13. Manila: Philippine Institute for Development Studies, 2009. http://dirp3.pids.gov.ph/ris/dps/pidsdps0913. pdf.

McChesney, Robert W. *Communication Revolution: Critical Junctures and the Future of Media.* New York: New Press, 2007.

McConnaughy, Christopher. "China's Undersea Nuclear Deterrent: Will the U.S. Navy Be Ready?" In *China's Nuclear Force Modernization,* edited by Lyle J. Goldstein and Andrew S. Erickson. Naval War College Newport Papers 22. Newport: Naval War College, 2005.

McDevitt, Michael. "Alliance Relationships." In *America's Role in Asia: Asian and American Views,* edited by Michael Armacost, J. Stapleton Roy, Han Sung-Joo, Tommy Koh, and C. Raja Mohan. San Francisco: Asia Foundation, 2008.

——. "The Strategic and Operational Context Driving PLA Navy Building." In *Right Sizing the People's Liberation Army: Exploring the Contours of China's Military,* edited by Roy Kamphausen and Andrew Scobell. Carlisle, Pa.: Strategic Studies Institute, 2007.

McDevitt, Michael, et al. *Sino-Japanese Rivalry: Implications for U.S. Policy.* Washington, D.C.: Center for Naval Analyses, 2009.

Medeiros, Evan S. *Chasing the Dragon: Assessing China's System of Export Controls for WMD-Related Goods and Technologies.* Santa Monica, Cal.: RAND Corporation, 2005. www.rand.org/content/dam/rand/pubs/monographs/2005/RAND_MG353.pdf.

——. *China's International Behavior: Activism, Opportunism, and Diversification.* Santa Monica, Calif.: RAND Corporation, 2006.

——. *Reluctant Restraint: The Evolution of China's Nonproliferation Policies and Practices, 1980–2000.* Stanford, Calif.: Stanford University Press, 2007.

Medeiros, Evan S., Roger Cliff, Keith Crane, and James C. Mulvenon. *A New Direction for China's Defense Industry.* Santa Monica, Calif.: RAND Corporation, 2005.

Medeiros, Evan S., et al. *Pacific Currents: The Responses of U.S. Allies and Security Partners in East Asia to China's Rise.* Santa Monica, Calif.: RAND Corporation, 2008.

Mertha, Andrew. *The Politics of Piracy: Intellectual Property in Contemporary China.* Ithaca, N.Y.: Cornell University Press, 2005.

Micklethwait, John, and Adrian Wooldridge. *A Future Perfect: The Challenge and Promise of Globalization.* Toronto: Random House, 2003.

Mitchell, Derek. "Reduce, Maintain, Enhance: U.S. Force Structure Changes in the Asia-Pacific Region." In *America's Role in Asia: Asian and American Views,* edited by Michael Armacost, J. Stapleton Roy, Han Sung-Joo, Tommy Koh, and C. Raja Mohan. San Francisco: Asia Foundation, 2008.

Mitchell, Derek, and Yuki Tatsumi. "U.S. Domestic Foreign Policy Process and Its Impact on China Policy." In *An Alliance for Engagement: Building Cooperation in Security Relations with China,* edited by Benjamin L. Self and Jeffrey W. Thompson. Washington, D.C.: Henry L. Stimson Center, 2002.

Mittelman, James. *The Globalization Syndrome: Transformation and Resistance.* Princeton, N.J.: Princeton University Press, 2000.

Mochizuki, Michael M. "China–Japan Relations: Downward Spiral or a New Equilibrium?" In *Power Shift: China and Asia's New Dynamics,* edited by David Shambaugh. Berkeley: University of California Press, 2003.

——. "Japan's Long Transition: The Politics of Recalibrating Grand Strategy." In *Domestic Political Change and Grand Strategy,* edited by Ashley J. Tellis and Michael Wills. Seattle: National Bureau of Asian Research, 2007.

Morrison, J. Stephen. "The Prospects for Engaging China with Global Health Issues." In *China's Capacity to Manage Infectious Diseases: Global Implications,* edited by Charles W. Freeman III. Washington, D.C.: Center for Strategic and International Studies, 2009.

Morrison, Wayne. *China–U.S. Trade Issues.* Congressional Research Service Issue Brief
IB91121. Washington, D.C.: Library of Congress, 2006.

Müller-Kraenner, Sascha. *China's and India's Emerging Energy Foreign Policy.* Discussion
Paper 15. Bonn: German Development Institute, 2008. www.die-gdi.de/CMS-Homepage/
openwebcms3.nsf/(ynDK_contentByKey)/ANES-7HJAZ8/$FILE/DP%2015.
2008.pdf.

Nanto, Dick. *East Asian Regional Architecture: New Economic and Security Arrangements and
US Policy.* Congressional Research Service Report 33653. Washington, D.C.: Library of
Congress, 2006.

Nathan, Andrew J., and Robert J. Ross. *The Great Wall and the Empty Fortress: China's Search for
Security.* New York: W. W. Norton, 1997.

National Intelligence Council. *Global Trends 2025: A Transformed World.* Washington, D.C.:
National Intelligence Council, 2008.

———. *Mapping the Global Future.* Report of the National Intelligence Council's 2020 Project.
Washington, D.C.: National Intelligence Council, 2004.

Pacific Economic Cooperation Council. "Impact of the Global Financial Crisis on the
Asia Pacific Region and Economic Outlook." In *State of the Region Report 2008–2009.*
Singapore: Pacific Economic Cooperation Council, 2008. www.pecc.org/sotr/papers/
SOTR-2008-Economic-Outlook.pdf.

Pan, Esther, ed. *China's Soft Power Initiative.* New York: Council on Foreign Relations, 2006.
www.cfr.org/china/chinas-soft-power-initiative/p10715.

Pan Guang. "A Chinese Perspective on the Shanghai Cooperation Organization." In *The
Shanghai Cooperation Organization as a Regional Security Institution,* edited by Alyson J. K.
Bailes, Pál Dunay, Pan Guang, and Mikhail Troitskiy. SIPRI Policy Paper 17. Stockholm:
Stockholm International Peace Research Institute, 2007. http://books.sipri.org/files/PP/
SIPRIPP17.pdf.

Pan Zhenqiang. "Abolishing Nuclear Weapons: Why Not Outlaw Them First?" In *Abolishing
Nuclear Weapons: A Debate,* edited by George Perkovich and James M. Acton. Washington,
D.C.: Carnegie Endowment for International Peace, 2010.

Pei, Minxin. *China's Trapped Transition: The Limits of Developmental Autocracy.* Cambridge,
Mass.: Harvard University Press, 2006.

Pei, Minxin, Zhang Guoyan, Pei Fei, and Chen Lixin. "China's Evolving Legal System."
Carnegie Issue Brief, February 2009, www.carnegieendowment.org/files/China_Legal
System_Full_Text2.pdf.

Pempel, T. J. "Japan: Divided Government, Diminished Resources." In *Strategic Asia 2008–09:
Challenges and Choices,* edited by Ashley J. Tellis, Mercy Kuo, and Andrew Marble. Seattle:
National Bureau of Asian Research, 2008.

———. "What the President-Elect Should Know About Japan." In *Challenges and Choices,
Strategic Asia 2008–09,* edited by Ashley J. Tellis, Mercy Kuo, and Andrew Marble. Seattle:
National Bureau of Asian Research, 2008.

Percival, Bronson. "Countering Terrorism in East Asia." In *America's Role in Asia: Asian and
American Views,* edited by Michael Armacost, J. Stapleton Roy, Han Sung-Joo, Tommy
Koh, and C. Raja Mohan. San Francisco: Asia Foundation, 2008.

Pettis, Michael. "*The G20 Meetings: No Common Framework, No Consensus.*" Policy Brief 79.
Washington, D.C.: Carnegie Endowment for International Peace, 2009.

Pollack, Henry N. *Uncertain Science . . . Uncertain World.* New York: Cambridge University
Press, 2003.

Pollack, Jonathan D. "The Korean Peninsula in U.S. Strategy: Policy Issues for the Next President." In *Strategic Asia 2008–09: Challenges and Choices*, edited by Ashley J. Tellis, Mercy Kuo, and Andrew Marble. Seattle: National Bureau of Asian Research, 2008.

———. "The Strategic Futures and Military Capabilities of the Two Koreas." In *Strategic Asia 2005–06: Military Modernization in an Era of Uncertainty*, edited by Ashley J. Tellis and Michael Wills. Seattle: National Bureau of Asian Research, 2005.

———. "The Transformation of the Asian Security Order: Assessing China's Impact." In *Power Shift: China and Asia's New Dynamics*, edited by David Shambaugh. Berkeley: University of California Press, 2005.

Price, Monroe E. *Media and Sovereignty: The Global Information Revolution and its Challenge to State Power.* Cambridge, Mass.: MIT Press, 2002.

Przystup, James J. "The United States, Australia, and the Search for Order in East Asia and Beyond." In *The Other Special Relationship: The United States and Australia at the Start of the 21st Century*, edited by Jeffrey D. McCausland, Douglas T. Stuart, William Tow, and Michael Wesley. Carlisle, Pa.: Strategic Studies Institute, 2007.

Puska, Susan M. "Rough but Ready Force Projection: An Assessment of Recent PLA Training." In *China's Growing Military Power: Perspectives on Security, Ballistic Missiles, and Conventional Capabilities*, edited by Andrew Scobell and Larry M. Wortzel. Carlisle, Pa.: Strategic Studies Institute, 2002.

Pye, Lucian W. *Chinese Negotiating Style: Commercial Approaches and Cultural Principles.* Westport, Conn.: Quorum Books, 1992.

Richardson, Sophie. "Challenges for a 'Responsible Power.' " In *World Report: 2008—Events of 2007.* New York: Human Rights Watch, 2008.

Riedel, Bruce, and Pavneet Singh. *U.S.-China Relations: Seeking Strategic Convergence in Pakistan.* Foreign Policy Paper 18. Washington, D.C.: Brookings Institution, 2010. www.brookings.edu/papers/2010/0112_us_china_relations_riedel.aspx.

Rigger, Shelley. *Taiwan's Rising Rationalism: Generations, Politics, and "Taiwanese Nationalism."* Policy Study 26. Washington, D.C.: East-West Center, 2006. www.eastwestcenter.org/fileadmin/stored/pdfs/PS026.pdf.

Romberg, Alan D. *Rein In at the Brink of the Precipice: American Policy Toward Taiwan and U.S.-PRC Relations.* Washington, D.C.: Henry L. Stimson Center, 2003.

Rosen, Daniel H., and Trevor Houser. *China Energy: A Guide for the Perplexed.* Washington, D.C.: Center for Strategic Studies and Peterson Institute for International Economics, 2007. www.petersoninstitute.org/publications/papers/rosen0507.pdf.

Ross, Robert S. *After the Cold War: Domestic Factors and U.S.-China Relations.* Armonk, N.Y.: M. E. Sharpe, 1998.

———. "China." In *Fighting Chance: Global Trends and Shocks in the National Security Environment*, edited by Neyla Arnas. Washington, D.C.: National Defense University Press, 2009.

———. *Negotiating Cooperation: The United States and China, 1969–1989.* Stanford, Calif.: Stanford University Press, 1995.

Ross, Robert, and Zhu Feng, eds. *China's Ascent: Power, Security, and the Future of International Politics.* Ithaca, N.Y.: Cornell University Press, 2008.

Rothkopf, David J. "Foreign Policy in the Information Age." In *The Global Century: Globalization and National Security*, edited by Richard L. Kugler and Ellen L. Frost. Washington, D.C.: National Defense University Press, 2001.

Saikia, Jaideep, and Ekaterina Stepanova, eds. *Terrorism: Patterns of Internationalization.* Thousand Oaks, Calif.: Sage, 2009.

Samuels, Richard J. *Securing Japan: Tokyo's Grand Strategy and the Future of East Asia*. Ithaca, N.Y.: Cornell University Press, 2007.

Santoro, Michael A. *Profits and Principles: Global Capitalism and Human Rights in China*. Ithaca, N.Y.: Cornell University Press, 2000.

Saunders, Phillip C. *China's Global Activism: Strategy, Drivers, and Tools*. Occasional Paper 4. Washington, D.C.: National Defense University Press, 2006.

Schofield, Clive, and Ian Storey. *The South China Sea Dispute: Increasing Stakes and Rising Tensions*. Washington, D.C.: Jamestown Foundation, 2009.

Shambaugh, David. *China's Communist Party: Atrophy and Adaptation*. Berkeley: University of California Press, 2008.

——. "China's Military Modernization: Making Steady and Surprising Progress." In *Strategic Asia 2005–06: Military Modernization in an Era of Uncertainty*, edited by Ashley J. Tellis and Michael Wills. Seattle: National Bureau of Asian Research, 2005.

——. *Modernizing China's Military: Progress, Problems, and Prospects*. Berkeley: University of California Press, 2002.

——, ed. *Power Shift: China and Asia's New Dynamics*. Berkeley: University of California Press, 2005.

Shambaugh, David, Eberhard Sandschneider, and Hong Zhou, eds. *China–Europe Relations: Perceptions, Policies, and Prospects*. New York: Routledge, 2007.

Shankleman, Jill. *Going Global: Chinese Oil and Mining Companies and the Governance of Resource Wealth*. Washington, D.C.: Woodrow Wilson International Center for Scholars, 2009.

Shinn, James, ed. *Weaving the Net: Conditional Engagement With China*. New York: Council on Foreign Relations Press, 1996.

Shirk, Susan. *China: Fragile Superpower—How China's Internal Politics Could Derail Its Peaceful Rise*. New York: Oxford University Press, 2007.

Shlapak, David, David Orletsky, and Barry Wilson. *Dire Strait? Military Aspects of the China-Taiwan Confrontation and Options for U.S. Policy*. Santa Monica, Calif.: RAND Corporation, 2000.

Shlapak, David A., David T. Orletsky, et al. *A Question of Balance: Political Context and Military Aspects of the China–Taiwan Dispute*. Santa Monica, Calif.: RAND Corporation, 2009.

Smith, Paul J. ed. *Human Smuggling: Chinese Migrant Trafficking and the Challenge to America's Immigration Tradition*. Washington, D.C.: Center for Strategic and International Studies, 1997.

Solomon, Richard H. *Chinese Political Negotiating Behavior, 1967–84*. Santa Monica, Calif.: RAND Corporation, 1995.

State Council of the People's Republic of China. *China's National Defense in 2008*. Beijing: Information Office of the State Council of the People's Republic of China, 2009.

——. *China's National Defense in 2010*. Beijing: Information Office of the State Council of the People's Republic of China, 2011. http://news.xinhuanet.com/english2010/china/2011-03/31/c_13806851.htm.

Stiglitz, Joseph E. *Globalization and Its Discontents*. New York: W. W. Norton, 2003.

Stokes, Mark. *China's Strategic Modernization: Implications for the United States*. Carlisle, Pa.: Strategic Studies Institute, 1999.

Suettinger, Robert L. *Beyond Tiananmen: The Politics of U.S.-China Relations 1989–2000*. Washington, D.C.: Brookings Institution Press, 2003.

Sutter, Robert. *China's Rise: Implications for U.S. Leadership in Asia*. Washington, D.C.: East-West Center, 2006.

——. "China's Regional Strategy and America." In *Power Shift: China and Asia's New Dynamics*, edited by David Shambaugh. Berkeley: University of California Press, 2005.

———. *Chinese Foreign Relations: Power and Policy Since the Cold War.* Lanham, Md.: Rowman & Littlefield, 2008.

———. *Chinese Policy Priorities and Their Implications for the United States.* Lanham, Md.: Rowman & Littlefield, 2000.

———. *The United States in Asia.* Lanham, Md.: Rowman & Littlefield, 2008.

———. *U.S.-Chinese Relations: Perilous Past, Pragmatic Present.* Lanham, Md.: Rowman & Littlefield, 2010.

———. *U.S. Policy Toward China: An Introduction to the Role of Interest Groups.* Lanham, Md.: Rowman & Littlefield, 1998.

Svensson, Marina. *Debating Human Rights in China: A Conceptual and Political History.* Lanham, Md.: Rowman & Littlefield, 2002.

Swaine, Michael D. "China: Exploiting a Strategic Opening." In *Strategic Asia 2004–05: Confronting Terrorism in the Pursuit of Power,* edited by Ashley J. Tellis and Michael Wills. Seattle: National Bureau of Asian Research, 2004.

———. "China's Regional Military Posture." In *Power Shift: China and Asia's New Dynamics,* edited by David Shambaugh. Berkeley: University of California Press, 2005.

———. "Managing Relations with the United States." In *Presidential Politics in Taiwan: The Administration of Chen Shui-bian,* edited by Steven M. Goldstein and Julian Chang. Norwalk, Conn.: East Bridge, 2008.

Swaine, Michael D., and Alastair I. Johnston. "China and Arms Control Institutions." In *China Joins the World: Progress and Prospects,* edited by Elizabeth Economy and Michel Oksenberg. New York: Council on Foreign Relations, 1999.

Swaine, Michael D., and Roy D. Kamphausen. "Military Modernization in Taiwan." In *Strategic Asia 2005–06: Military Modernization in an Era of Uncertainty,* edited by Ashley J. Tellis and Michael Wills. Seattle: National Bureau of Asian Research, 2005.

Swaine, Michael D., and Ashley J. Tellis. *Interpreting China's Grand Strategy: Past, Present, and Future.* Santa Monica, Calif.: RAND Corporation, 2000.

Swaine, Michael D., and Zhang Tuosheng, with Danielle F. S. Cohen, eds. *Managing Sino-American Crises: Case Studies and Analysis.* Washington, D.C.: Carnegie Endowment for International Peace, 2006.

Swaine, Michael D., Andrew N. D. Yang, Evan S. Medeiros, and Oriana Skylar Mastro, eds. *Assessing the Threat: The Chinese Military and Taiwan's Security.* Washington, D.C.: Carnegie Endowment for International Peace, 2007.

Tangredi, Sam. *Futures of War: Towards a Consensus View of the Future Security Environment.* Newport: Alidade Press, 2008.

Tanner, Murray Scot. *Chinese Economic Coercion Against Taiwan: A Tricky Weapon to Use.* Santa Monica, Calif.: RAND Corporation, 2007.

Tay, Simon. *Asia Alone: The Dangerous Post-Crisis Divide from America.* New York: John Wiley & Sons, 2010.

Tellis, Ashley J. "The Economic Crisis and the Future of U.S. Power." In *Strategic Asia 2009–10: Economic Meltdown and Geopolitical Stability,* edited by Ashley J. Tellis, Andrew Marble, and Travis Tanner. Seattle: National Bureau of Asian Research, 2009.

———. *India as a New Global Power: An Action Agenda for the United States.* Washington, D.C.: Carnegie Endowment for International Peace, 2005.

———. "Preserving Hegemony: The Strategic Tasks Facing the United States." In *Strategic Asia 2008–09: Challenges and Choices,* edited by Ashley J. Tellis, Mercy Kuo, and Andrew Marble. Seattle: National Bureau of Asian Research, 2008.

———. "What Should We Expect from India as a Strategic Partner?" In *Gauging U.S. Indian Strategic Cooperation*, edited by Henry Sokolski. Carlisle, Pa: Strategic Studies Institute, 2007.

Thompson, Drew. "China's Health Care Reform Redux." In *China's Capacity to Manage Infectious Diseases: Global Implications*, edited by Charles W. Freeman III. Washington, D.C.: Center for Strategic and International Studies, 2009.

Tian, John Q. *Government, Business, and the Politics of Interdependence and Conflict Across the Taiwan Strait*. New York: Palgrave Macmillan, 2006.

Tibet Information Network and Human Rights Watch–Asia. *Cutting Off the Serpent's Head: Tightening Control in Tibet, 1994–1995*. New York: Human Rights Watch, 1996.

Till, Geoffrey. *Asia Rising and the Maritime Decline of the West: A Review of the Issues: IQPC/Asia Rising*. RSIS Working Paper 205. Singapore: Rajaratnam School of International Studies, 2010. www.rsis.edu.sg/publications/Working_papers.html.

Tkacik, John J., ed. *Rethinking "One China."* Washington, D.C.: Heritage Foundation, 2004.

Tucker, Nancy Bernkopf, ed. *Dangerous Strait: The U.S., China, Taiwan Crisis*. New York: Columbia University Press, 2005.

U.S. Department of Defense. *Annual Report to Congress: Military Power of the People's Republic of China 2009*. Washington, D.C.: U.S. Government Printing Office, 2009. www.defenselink. mil/pubs/pdfs/China_Military_Power_Report_2009.pdf.

———. *Annual Report to Congress: Military and Security Developments Involving the People's Republic of China 2010*. Washington, D.C.: U.S. Government Printing Office, 2010. www. defense.gov/pubs/pdfs/2010_CMPR_Final.pdf.

U.S. Department of State. "East Asia and Pacific." In *Supporting Human Rights and Democracy: The U.S. Record 2006*, April 5, 2007, www.state.gov/g/drl/rls/shrd/2006/80587.htm.

U.S. Institute of Peace. *"Trialogue": U.S.-Japan-China Relations and Asian-Pacific Stability*. Special Report 37. Washington, D.C.: U.S. Institute of Peace Press, 1998. www.usip.org/ pubs/specialreports/early/trilat/sr_trilat.html.

Valencia, Mark J. *China and the South China Seas Dispute*. Adelphi Paper. London: International Institute for Strategic Studies, 1995.

———. *The Proliferation Security Initiative: Making Waves in Asia*. Adelphi Paper 376. London: International Institute for Strategic Studies, 2005.

Vogel, Ezra F., ed. *Living with China: U.S.-China Relations in the Twenty-First Century*. New York: W. W. Norton, 1997.

Wan, Ming. *Human Rights in Chinese Foreign Relations: Defining and Defending National Interests*. Philadelphia: University of Pennsylvania Press, 2001.

Wanandi, Jusuf. "China and Asia-Pacific Regionalism." In *The Rise of China and a Changing East Asian Order*, edited by Kokubun Ryosei and Wang Jisi. Tokyo: Asia-Pacific Agenda Project, 2004.

Wanandi, Jusuf, and Tadashi Yamamoto. "The Strategic Rationale for East Community Building." In *East Asia at a Crossroads*, edited by Jusuf Wanandi and Tadashi Yamamoto. Tokyo: Japan Center for International Exchange, 2008.

Wang Jisi. *China's Changing Role in Asia*. Atlantic Council Occasional Paper. Washington, D.C.: Atlantic Council of the United States, 2004.

Weatherbee, Donald. "Strategic Dimensions of Economic Interdependence in Southeast Asia." In *Strategic Asia 2006–07: Trade, Interdependence, and Security*, edited by Ashley Tellis and Michael Wills. Seattle: National Bureau of Asian Research, 2006.

Webster, Frank. *Culture and Politics in the Information Age: A New Politics?* New York: Routledge, 2001.

Wolf, Martin. *Why Globalization Works.* New Haven, Conn.: Yale University Press, 2005.

Wortzel, Larry M. *China's Nuclear Forces: Operations, Training, Doctrine, Command, Control, and Campaign Planning.* Carlisle, Pa.: Strategic Studies Institute, 2007.

——. "PLA 'Joint' Operational Contingencies in South Asia, Central Asia, and Korea." In *Beyond the Strait: PLA Missions Other Than Taiwan,* edited by Roy Kamphausen, David Lai, and Andrew Scobell. Carlisle, Pa.: Strategic Studies Institute, 2009.

Xia Liping. *Nuclear Non-Proliferation: A Chinese Perspective.* FES Briefing Paper 8. Bonn: Friedrich Ebert Stiftung, 2008. http://library.fes.de/pdf-files/iez/global/05653.pdf.

Yahuda, Michael. "The Limits of Economic Interdependence: Sino-Japanese Relations." In *New Directions in the Study of China's Foreign Policy,* edited by Alastair Iain Johnston and Robert S. Ross. Stanford, Calif.: Stanford University Press, 2006.

Yan Xuetong, Wang Zaibang, Li Zhongcheng, and Hou Roushi. *Zhongguojueqi: Guojihuanjingpinggu* (International Environment for China's Rise). Tianjin: Renmin chubanshe, 1998.

Yang, Dali. *Remaking the Chinese Leviathan: Market Transition and the Politics of Governance in China.* Stanford, Calif.: Stanford University Press, 2004.

Yang, Guobin. *The Power of the Internet in China: Citizen Activism Online.* New York: Columbia University Press, 2009.

Zedillo, Ernesto. *Global Warming: Looking Beyond Kyoto.* Washington, D.C.: Brookings Institution Press, 2008.

Zhang Yunling and Tang Shiping. "China's Regional Trade and Investment Profile." In *Power Shift: China and Asia's New Dynamics,* edited by David Shambaugh. Berkeley: University of California Press, 2005.

Zhao, Suisheng, ed. *Debating Political Reform in China.* Armonk, N.Y.: M. E. Sharpe, 2006.

——. *China-U.S. Relations Transformed: Perspectives and Strategic Interactions.* New York: Routledge, 2008.

——. *The Prospects for a Democratic China.* London: Routledge, 2000.

JOURNAL ARTICLES AND OPINION ESSAYS

Abramowitz, Morton, and Stephen Bosworth. "America Confronts the Asian Century." *Current History,* vol. 105, no. 690 (April 2006): 147–52.

Barma, Naazneen, and Ely Ratner. "China's Illiberal Challenge." *Democracy,* Fall 2006.

Beeson, Mark, and Hidetaka Yoshimatsu. "Asia's Odd Men Out: Australia, Japan, and the Politics of Regionalism." *International Relations of the Asia-Pacific,* no. 7 (March 2007): 227–50.

Bergsten, C. Fred. "A Partnership of Equals." *Foreign Affairs,* vol. 87, no. 4 (July–August 2008): 57–69.

Bitzinger, Richard A. "Reforming China's Defense Industry: Progress in Spite of Itself?" *Korean Journal of Defense Analysis,* vol. 19, no. 3 (Fall 2007): 99–118.

Blazejewski, Kenneth S. "Space Weaponization and U.S.-China Relations." *Strategic Studies Quarterly,* Spring 2008, 33–55.

Bottelier, Pieter. "The Financial Crisis and Sino-American Relations." *Asia Policy*, no. 9 (January 2010): 121-31.

Bown, Chad P. "U.S.-China Trade Conflicts and the Future of the WTO." *Fletcher Forum of World Affairs*, vol. 33, no. 1 (Winter–Spring 2009): 27–48.

Brown, David G. "China–Taiwan Relations: Moving Relations Toward a New Level." *Comparative Connections*, vol. 11, no. 2 (July 2009), http://csis.org/files/publication/0902qchina_taiwan.pdf.

Buszynski, Leszek. "Sino-Japanese Relations: Interdependence, Rivalry and Regional Security." *Contemporary Southeast Asia: A Journal of International and Strategic Affairs*, vol. 31, no. 1 (2009): 143-71.

Calder, Kent E. "China and Japan's Simmering Rivalry." *Foreign Affairs*, vol. 85, no. 2 (March–April 2006). 129–39.

Canning, Cherie. "Pursuit of the Pariah: Iran, Sudan and Myanmar in China's Energy Security Strategy." *Security Challenges*, vol. 3, no. 1 (February 2007): 47–63.

Carpenter, Ted Galen. "Wild Card: A Democratic Taiwan." *China Security*, vol. 4, No. 1 (Winter 2008): 40–58.

Cha, Victor. "Winning Asia: Washington's Untold Success Story." *Foreign Affairs*, vol. 86, no. 6 (November–December 2007).

Cheng, Joseph Y. S., and Zhang Wankun. "Patterns and Dynamics of China's International Strategic Behavior." *Journal of Contemporary China*, vol. 11, no. 31 (May 2002): 259.

Christensen, Thomas J. "The Advantages of an Assertive China." *Foreign Affairs*, vol. 90, no. 2 (March–April 2011): 54–67.

———. "China, the U.S.-Japan Alliance, and the Security Dilemma in East Asia." *International Security*, vol. 23, no. 4 (Spring 1999): 49–80.

———. "Fostering Stability or Creating a Monster?" *International Security*, vol. 31, no. 1 (Summer 2006): 81–126.

———. "Posing Problems Without Catching Up: China's Rise and Challenges for U.S. Security Policy." *International Security*, vol. 25 no. 4 (Spring 2001): 5–40.

Chu Shulong. "The East Asia Summit: Looking for an Identity." *Brookings Northeast Asia Commentary*, no. 6 (February 2007), www.brookings.edu/opinions/2007/02northeastasia_chu.aspx.

Chu Shulong and Guo Yuli. "Change: Mainland's Taiwan Policy." *China Security*, vol. 4, no. 1 (Winter 2008): 127–33.

Chu, Yun-han. "Taiwan's National Identity Politics and the Prospect of Cross-Strait Relations." *Asian Survey*, vol. 44, no. 4 (2004): 484–512.

Chu, Yun-han, Larry Diamond, Andrew J. Nathan, and Doh Chull Shin. "Asia's Challenged Democracies." *Washington Quarterly*, vol. 32, no. 1 (January 2009): 143–57.

Cook, Malcolm. "The United States and the East Asia Summit: Finding the Proper Home." *Contemporary Southeast Asia*, vol. 30, no. 2 (August 2008): 293–312.

Cruz De Castro, Renato. "U.S. War on Terror in East Asia: The Perils of Preemptive Defense in Waging a War of the Third Kind." *Asian Affairs: An American Review*, vol. 31, no. 4 (2005): 212–31.

Dai Bingguo. "Stick to the Path of Peaceful Development." *Beijing Review*, December 21, 2010.

Deng, Yong. "Hegemon on the Offensive: Chinese Perspectives on U.S. Global Strategy." *Political Science Quarterly*, vol. 116, no. 3 (Fall 2001): 343–67.

Deng, Yong, and Thomas G. Moore. "China Views Globalization: Toward a New Great-Power Politics?" *Washington Quarterly*, vol. 27, no. 3 (2004).

Devan, Janamitra, Micah Rowland, and Jonathan Woetzel. "A Consumer Paradigm for China." *McKinsey Quarterly*, no. 4 (2009): 36–49.

Donnelly, Eric. "The United States–China EP-3 Incident: Legality and Realpolitik." *Journal of Conflict and Security Law*, vol. 9, no. 1 (2004): 25–42.

Dowd, Alan W. "Declinism." *Policy Review*, August–September 2007, 83–98.

Easley, Leif-Eric, Tetsuo Kotani, and Aki Mori. "Electing a New Japanese Security Policy? Examining Foreign Policy Visions Within the Democratic Party of Japan." *Asia Policy* (National Bureau of Asian Research), no. 9 (January 2010).

Erickson, Andrew S. "Assessing the New U.S. Maritime Strategy: A Window into Chinese Thinking." *Naval War College Review*, vol. 61, no. 4 (Autumn 2008): 35–71.

———. "Combating a Truly Collective Threat: Sino-American Military Cooperation Against Avian Influenza." *Global Health Governance*, vol. 1, no. 1 (January 2007).

Erickson, Andrew S., and Gabe Collins. "Beijing's Energy Security Strategy: The Significance of a Chinese State-Owned Tanker Fleet." *Orbis: A Journal of World Affairs*, vol. 51, no. 4 (Fall 2007): 665–84.

Erickson, Andrew S., and David D. Yang. "Using the Land to Control the Sea? Chinese Analysts Consider the Antiship Ballistic Missile." *Naval War College Review*, vol. 62, no. 4 (Autumn 2009): 53–86.

Fallows, James. "The Chinese Crackdown: Arrogance? Or Insecurity?" *Atlantic*, April 13, 2011, www.theatlantic.com/international/archive/2011/04/ the-chinese-crackdown-arrogance-or-insecurity/237234.

Ferguson, Niall. "An Empire at Risk." *Newsweek*, November 28, 2009.

Fewsmith, Joseph. "Social Order in the Wake of Economic Crisis." *China Leadership Monitor*, no. 28 (Spring 2009).

Fravel, M. Taylor. "Power Shifts and Escalation: Explaining China's Use of Force in Territorial Disputes." *International Security*, vol. 32, no. 3 (2007).

———. "Securing Borders: China's Doctrine and Force Structure for Frontier Defense." *Journal of Strategic Studies*, vol. 30, nos. 4–5 (August–October 2007): 705–37.

Friedberg, Aaron L. "Asia Rising." *American Interest*, vol. 6, no. 3 (Winter 2009): 53–61.

———. "The Future of U.S.-China Relations: Is Conflict Inevitable?" *International Security*, vol. 30, no. 2 (2005): 7–45.

Frost, Ellen L., James J. Przystup, and Phillip C. Saunders. "China's Rising Influence in Asia: Implications for U.S. Policy." *Strategic Forum*, no. 231 (April 2008): 1–8.

Garrett, Banning. "U.S.-China Relations in the Era of Globalization and Terror: A Framework for Analysis." *Journal of Contemporary China*, vol. 15 no. 48 (August 2006): 389–415.

Garver, John W. "The China–India–U.S. Triangle: Strategic Relations in the Post–Cold War Era." *NBR Analysis*, vol. 13, no. 5 (October 2002).

Gelb, Leslie H. "Necessity, Choice, and Common Sense." *Foreign Affairs*, vol. 88, no. 3 (May–June 2009): 56–72.

Ghafouri, M. "China's Policy in the Persian Gulf." *Middle East Policy*, vol. 16 (2009): 80–92.

Gill, Bates, and Melissa Murphy. "China's Evolving Approach to Counterterrorism." *Harvard Asia Quarterly*, vol. 9, nos. 1–2 (Winter–Spring 2005).

Giragosian, Richard. "The Strategic Central Asian Arena." *China and Eurasia Forum Quarterly*, vol. 4, no. 1 (2006): 133–53.

Glaser, Bonnie S. "China's Policy in the Wake of the Second DPRK Nuclear Test." *China Security*, vol. 5, no. 2 (2009): 1–11.

———. "Chock-Full of Dialogue: SED, Human Rights, and Security." *Comparative Connections*, vol. 10, no. 2 (July 2008).

——. "Obama–Hu Summit: Success or Disappointment?" *Comparative Connections*, vol. 11, no. 4 (January 2010), http://csis.org/files/publication/0904qus_china.pdf.

Godement, François. "The United States and Asia in 2009: Public Diplomacy and Strategic Continuity." *Asian Survey*, vol. 50, no. 1 (January–February 2010): 8–24.

Gold, Thomas B. "Taiwan in 2008: My Kingdom for a Horse." *Asian Survey*, vol. 49, no. 1 (January–February 2009): 88–97.

Goldstein, Lyle J., and William Murray. "Undersea Dragons: China's Maturing Submarine Force." *International Security*, vol. 28, no. 4 (Spring 2004): 161–96.

Goldstein, Steven M. "China and Taiwan: Signs of Change in Cross-Strait Relations." *China Security*, vol. 5, no. 1 (Winter 2009): 67–72.

Graham, John L., and N. Mark Lam. "Negotiating in China." *Harvard Business Review*, October 2003, http://hbswk.hbs.edu/archive/3714.html.

Green, Michael. "American Aims: Realism Still Prevails Over Community Idealism." *Global Asia*, vol. 5, no. 1 (Spring 2010): 32–36.

Griffin, Christopher, and Michael Auslin. "Time for Trilateralism?" *AEI Outlook*, March 2008.

Gu Guoliang. "Analysis on Proliferation Security Initiative." *American Studies Quarterly* (Shanghai), vol. 3 (2004).

Hachigian, Nina, and Mona Sutphen. "Strategic Collaboration: How the United States Can Thrive as Other Powers Rise." *Washington Quarterly*, vol. 31, no. 4 (Autumn 2008).

Hale, David D. "Commodities, China, and American Foreign Policy." *International Economy*, vol. 20, no. 3 (Summer 2006).

Han Qide, et al. "China and Global Health." *Lancet*, vol. 372, no. 9648 (October 25, 2008).

Heginbotham, Eric, and Christopher P. Twomey. "America's Bismarckian Asia Policy." *Current History*, vol. 104, no. 683 (September 2005).

Huang, Yasheng. "Rethinking the Beijing Consensus." *Asia Policy*, no. 11 (January 2011): 1–26.

Ibraimov, Sadykzhan. "China–Central Asia Trade Relations: Economic and Social Patterns." *China and Eurasia Forum Quarterly*, vol. 7, no. 1 (2009): 47–59.

Ikenberry, G. John. "The Rise of China and the Future of the West: Can the Liberal System Survive?" *Foreign Affairs*, vol. 87, no. 1 (January–February 2008).

Jervis, Robert. "Cooperation Under the Security Dilemma." *World Politics*, vol. 30, no. 2 (January 1978): 167–74.

Jia Qingguo. "The Impact of 9/11 on Sino-U.S. Relations: A Preliminary Assessment." *International Relations of the Asia Pacific*, vol. 3, no. 2 (August 2003): 159–77.

——. "Learning to Live with the Hegemon." *Journal of Contemporary China*, vol. 14, no. (August 2005): 395–407.

——. "Unipolarity: Implications for China, the U.S. and the World." *International Review* (Shanghai Institutes for International Studies), Spring 2008, 29–44, www.siis.org.cn/Sh_Yj_Cms/Mgz/200801/200862418418SGL4.doc.

Jian Junbo. "A Clash of Civilization? Norms and Sino-EU Relations." *International Review*, Winter 2008, 53–84, www.siis.org.cn/Sh_Yj_Cms/Mgz/200804/2009326155417UX41.pdf.

Jiang, Wenran. "China's Global Quest for Energy Security." *Canadian Foreign Policy*, vol. 13, no. 2 (2006).

Johnston, Alastair Iain. "China's New 'Old Thinking: The Concept of Limited Deterrence." *International Security*, vol. 20, no. 3 (Winter 1995–1996).

——. "Is China a Status Quo Power?" *International Security*, vol. 27, no. 4 (Spring 2003): 5–56.

Kagan, Robert. "End of Dreams, Return of History." *Policy Review*, August–September 2007, www.hoover.org/publications/policyreview/8552512.html.

Kaplan, Robert D. "Center Stage for the 21st Century: Power Plays in the Indian Ocean." *Foreign Affairs*, March–April 2009.

Kastner, Scott L. "Bridge Over Troubled Water?" *International Security* 33, no. 4 (Spring 2009).

Keidel, Albert. "Imbalances Are Overstated." *China Economic Quarterly*, vol. 13, no. 4 (December 2009).

Kent, Ann. "China's International Socialization: The Role of International Organization." *Global Governance*, vol. 8, no. 3 (July–September 2002): 343–64.

Khodzhaev, Ablat. "The Central Asian Policy of the People's Republic of China." *China and Eurasia Forum Quarterly*, vol. 7, no. 1 (2009): 9–28.

Kirshner, Jonathan. "The Tragedy of Offensive Realism: Classical Realism and the Rise of China." *European Journal of International Relations*, vol. 20, no. 10 (October 2010): 1–23.

Kissinger, Henry A. "Avoiding a U.S.-China Cold War." *Washington Post*, January 14, 2011.

Klare, Michael T. "Fueling the Dragon: China's Strategic Energy Dilemma." *Current History*, vol. 105, no. 690 (April 2006): 180–85.

Klein, Brian P., and Kenneth Neil Cukier. "Tamed Tigers, Distressed Dragon." *Foreign Affairs*, vol. 88, no. 4 (July–August 2009): 8–16.

Kleine-Ahlbrandt, Stephanie, and Andrew Small. "China's New Dictatorship Diplomacy: Is Beijing Parting with Pariahs?" *Foreign Affairs*, January–February 2008.

Kleiner, Juergen. "A Fragile Relationship: The United States and the Republic of Korea." *Diplomacy and Statecraft*, vol. 17, no. 2 (June 2006): 215–35.

Koll, Jesper. "Why I'm Bullish on Japan." *Far Eastern Economic Review*, March 26, 2009, www.feer.com/economics/2009/march58/Bullish-on-Japan.

Kong, Bo. "China's Energy Decision-Making: Becoming More Like the United States?" *Journal of Contemporary China*, vol. 18, no. 62 (2009): 789–812.

Koo, M. G. "The Senkaku/Diaoyu Dispute and Sino-Japanese Political-Economic Relations: Cold Politics and Hot Economics?" *Pacific Review*, vol. 22, no. 2 (2009): 205–32.

Kulacki, Gregory. "A Space Race with China." *Harvard Asia Pacific Review*, Spring 2008, 12–15.

Kuo, Mercy, Andrew D. Marble, David M. Lampton, Cheng Li, Pieter Bottelier, and Fenggang Yang. "Roundtable: China in the Year 2020." *Asia Policy*, no. 4 (July 2007): 1–52.

Kuppuswamy, C. S. *East Asia Summit: Was It Just a Get-Together?* South Asia Analysis Group Paper 1648, December 19, 2005, www.southasiaanalysis.org/%5Cpapers17%5Cpaper1648.html.

Kurlantzick, Joshua. "China's Dubious Role in the War on Terror." *Current History*, vol. 102, no. 668 (December 2003).

———. "Pax Asia-Pacifica? East Asian Integration and Its Implications for the United States." *Washington Quarterly*, vol. 30, no. 3 (Summer 2007): 67–77.

Lampton, David M., and James Mann. "What's Your China Fantasy?" *Foreign Policy*, May 2007, www.foreignpolicy.com/story/cms.php?story_id=3837&page=0.

Larkin, Kevin. "China Risk: Bursting with Energy: Sino-Iranian Relations—Issues, Interests and Insights." *Political and Security Risk in China*, vol. 2, no. 4 (April 16, 2009).

Li, Cheng. "China in the Year 2020: Three Political Scenarios." *Asia Policy*, no. 4 (July 2007): 17–29.

———. "The New Bipartisanship within the Chinese Communist Party." *Orbis*, Summer 2005, 387–400.

Li Keqiang. "The World Should Not Fear a Growing China." *Financial Times*, January 9, 2011.

Li, Nan. "The Evolution of China's Naval Strategy and Capabilities: From 'Near Coast' and 'Near Seas' to 'Far Seas.' " *Asian Security*, vol. 5 (May 2009): 144–69.

Lieberthal, Kenneth. "The U.S.-China Agenda Goes Global." *Current History*, September 2009, 243–49.

Lieberthal, Kenneth, and Mikkal Herberg. "China's Search for Energy Security: Implications for U.S. Policy." *NBR Analysis* 17, no. 1 (April 2006).

Liu Long. "Russia's Revival and Sino-Russia Relations." *International Strategic Studies*, vol. 3 (2007).

Lu Jianren. "Stepping Up." *Beijing Review*, December 24, 2009, www.bjreview.com.cn/quotes/txt/2009-12/18/content_238581.htm.

Mastanduno, Michael. "Rivals or Partners? Globalization and U.S.-China Relations." *Harvard International Review*, vol. 39, no. 3 (Fall 2007): 42–46.

Mauzy, Diane K., and Brian L. Job. "U.S. Policy in Southeast Asia: Limited Re-engagement after Years of Benign Neglect." *Asian Survey*, vol. 47, no. 4 (August 2007): 622–41.

McDevitt, Michael. "Asian Military Modernisation: Key Areas of Concern—Address to the IISS-JIIA Tokyo Conference." *Adelphi Series*, vol. 48, nos. 400–401 (October 2008): 125–32.

Mearsheimer, John J. "China's Unpeaceful Rise." *Current History*, vol. 105, no. 690 (April 2006): 160–62.

Medcalf, Rory. "Chinese Ghost Story." *Diplomat* (Lowy Institute for International Policy), February–March 2008, 16–18.

Medeiros, Evan S. "China's International Behavior: Activism, Opportunism, and Diversification." *Joint Forces Quarterly*, 4th quarter, 2007, 34–41.

———. "Is Beijing Ready for Global Leadership?" *Current History*, vol. 108, no. 719 (September 2009): 250–56.

———. "Strategic Hedging and the Future of Asia-Pacific Stability." *Washington Quarterly*, vol. 29, no. 1 (Winter 2005–2006): 145–67.

Menon, Rajan. "The Limits of Chinese–Russian Partnership." *Survival*, vol. 51, no. 3 (June–July 2009): 99–130.

———. "The New Great Game in Central Asia." *Survival*, vol. 45, no. 2 (Summer 2003): 187–204.

Metzler, P. Gregory. "China in Space: Implications for U.S. Military Strategy." *Joint Forces Quarterly*, 4th quarter, 2007, 96–98.

Naím, Moisés. "The Five Wars of Globalization." *Foreign Policy*, January–February 2003, 36–41.

———. "Rogue Aid." *Foreign Policy*, no. 159 (March–April 2007): 96–97.

———. "What Is a GONGO?" *Foreign Policy*, no. 160 (May–June 2007): 96–105.

Nathan, Andrew J. "Authoritarian Resilience." *Journal of Democracy*, vol. 14, no. 1 (January 2003): 6–17.

Naughton, Barry. "Understanding the Chinese Stimulus Package." *China Leadership Monitor*, no. 28 (Spring 2009).

Ni Jianmin. "China's Peaceful Development and Harmonious World." *China Strategic Review*, vol. 3 (2006): 3–4.

Niu Xinchun and Liu Quan. "China–U.S. Relations Facing with New Opportunities for Development." *Peace and Development*, no. 3 (June 2009): 73–80.

Norris, Robert S., and Hans M. Kristensen. "Chinese Nuclear Forces, 2008." *Bulletin of the Atomic Scientists*, July–August 2008, 42–45.

Nye, Joseph S., Jr. "The Future of American Power: Dominance and Decline in Perspective." *Foreign Affairs*, vol. 89, no. 6 (November–December 2010): 2–12.

Oresman, Matthew. "Reassessing the Fleeting Potential for U.S.-China Cooperation in Central Asia." *China and Eurasia Forum Quarterly*, vol. 6, no. 2 (2008): 5–13.

Overholt, William H. "China in the Global Financial Crisis: Rising Influence, Rising Challenges." *Washington Quarterly*, vol. 33, no. 1 (January 2010): 21–24.

Paal, Douglas. "China: Hu's State Visit an Opportunity." Asia Pacific Brief, Carnegie Endowment for International Peace, December 28, 2010.

———. "China: Mugged by Reality in Libya, Again." Asia Pacific Brief, Carnegie Endowment for International Peace, April 11, 2011, http://carnegieendowment.org/publications/index.cfm?fa=view&id=43554.

———. "China Reacts to Middle East Unrest." Asia Pacific Brief, Carnegie Endowment for International Peace, February 28, 2011, http://carnegieendowment.org/publications/index.cfm?fa=view&id=42797.

Pak, Jin H. "China's Pragmatic Rise and U.S. Interests in East Asia." *Military Review*, vol. 87, no. 6 (November–December 2007).

Pant, Harsh V. "Saudi Arabia Woos China and India." *Middle East Quarterly*, vol. 8, no. 4 (Fall 2006): 45–52, www.meforum.org/1019/saudi-arabia-woos-china-and-india.

Paradise, James F. "China and International Harmony: The Role of Confucius Institutes in Bolstering Beijing's Soft Power." *Asian Survey*, vol. 49, no. 4 (July–August 2009).

Pedrozo, Raul. "Close Encounters at Sea: The USNS Impeccable Incident." *Naval War College Review*, vol. 62, no. 3 (Summer 2009).

———. "Responding to Ms. Zhang's Talking Points on the EEZ." *Chinese Journal of International Law*, vol. 10, no. 1 (2011): 207–23.

Pei, Minxin. "Think Again: Asia's Rise." *Foreign Policy*, July–August 2009, 32–36.

Peng Zongchao. "Preparing for the Real Storm During the Calm: A Comparison of the Crisis Preparation Strategies for Pandemic Influenza in China and the U.S." *Journal of Homeland Security and Emergency Management*, vol. 5, no. 1 (2008).

Perkovich, George. "The End of the Nonproliferation Regime?" *Current History*, November 2006, http://carnegieendowment.org/files/perkovich_current_history.pdf.

Pettis, Michael. "Is China Turning Japanese?" *Foreign Policy*, August 19, 2010.

Pollack, Joshua. "Emerging Strategic Dilemmas in U.S.-Chinese Relations." *Bulletin of the Atomic Scientists*, July–August 2009, 53–63.

Posen, Barry R. "Command of the Commons: The Military Foundation of U.S. Hegemony." *International Security*, vol. 28, no. 1 (Summer 2003).

Potter, Pitman B. "China and the International Legal System: Challenges of Participation." *China Quarterly*, no. 191 (September 2007): 699–715.

Prestowitz, Clyde. "'Chindia' Levels the Playing Field." *Current History*, vol. 105, no. 690 (April 2006): 148–49.

Przystup, James J. "Japan–China Relations: Gyoza, Beans, and Aircraft Carriers." *CSIS Comparative Connections*, vol. 10, no. 4 (January 2009).

———. "Japan–China Relations: New Year, Old Problems, Hope for Wen." *Comparative Connections*, vol. 9, no. 1 (April 2007): 117–32.

———. "The United States and the Asia-Pacific Region: National Interests and Strategic Imperatives." *Strategic Forum*, no. 239 (April 2009): 1–5.

Przystup, James J., and Phillip C. Saunders. "China's Rising Influence in Asia: Implications for U.S. Policy." *Strategic Forum*, no. 231 (April 2008).

———. "Visions of Order: Japan and China in U.S. Strategy." *Strategic Forum*, no. 220 (June 2006).

Raballand, Gaël, and Agnès Andrésy. "Why Should Trade between Central Asia and China Continue to Expand?" *Asia Europe Journal*, vol. 5, no. 2 (June 2007): 235–52.

Rabe, Barry G., and Christopher P. Borick. "The Climate of Belief: American Public Opinion on Climate Change." *Issues in Governance Studies* (Brookings Institution) no. 31 (January 2010).

Ren Xiao and Travis Tanner. "Roundtable: Chinese Foreign Policy and Domestic Decisionmaking." *Asia Policy*, no. 10 (July 2010): 43–101.

Rice, Condoleezza. "Our Asia Strategy." *Wall Street Journal*, October 24, 2003.

Rigger, Shelley. "Taiwan's Presidential and Legislative Elections." *Orbis*, vol. 52, no. 4 (September 2008): 689–700. www.fpri.org/orbis/5204/rigger.taiwanelections.pdf.

Ren Xiaofeng and Cheng Xizhong. "A Chinese Perspective." *Marine Policy*, vol. 29, no. 2 (2005): 139–46.

Roehrig, Terence. "Restructuring the U.S. Military Presence in Korea: Implications for Korean Security and the U.S.-ROK Alliance." *Academic Paper Series on Korea*, vol. 1, 2008, www.keia.org/Publications/OnKorea/2008/08Roehrig.pdf.

Ross, Robert S. "Assessing the China Threat." *National Interest*, Fall 2005, 81–87.

———. "China's Naval Nationalism: Sources, Prospects, and the U.S. Response." *International Security*, vol. 34, no. 2 (Fall 2009): 46–81.

———. "The Stability of Deterrence in the Taiwan Strait." *National Interest*, Fall 2001, 67–68.

Roubini, Nouriel. "The Chinese Proposal for a New Global Super Currency." *RGE Monitor*, June 26, 2009, www.rgemonitor.com/roubini-monitor/257169/the_chinese_proposal_for_a_new_global_super_currency.

Roy, Denny. "China's Democratised Foreign Policy." *Survival*, vol. 51, no. 2 (April–May 2009): 25–40.

Rozman, Gilbert, and Shin-wha Lee. "Unraveling the Japan–South Korea 'Virtual Alliance': Populism and Historical Revisionism in the Face of Conflicting Regional Strategies." *Asian Survey*, vol. 46, no. 5 (September–October 2006): 761–84.

Saunders, Phillip C., and Erik R. Quam. "China's Air Force Modernization." *Joint Forces Quarterly*, 4th quarter, 2007, 28–33.

Scobell, Andrew, Roy Kamphausen, Ellis Joffe, Michael R. Chambers, David M. Finkelstein, Cortez A. Cooper III, Dennis J. Blasko, Bernard D. Cole, Michael McDevitt, Phillip C. Saunders, Erik Quam, and Larry Wortzel. "Roundtable: Sizing the Chinese Military." *Asia Policy*, no. 4 (July 2007): 53–105.

Shambaugh, David. "China Engages Asia: Reshaping the Regional Order." *International Security*, vol. 29, no. 3 (Winter 2004–5): 79, 83–84.

———. "A New China Requires a New U.S. Strategy." *Current History*, September 2010, 219–26.

Shen Dingli. "North Korea's Strategic Significance to China." *China Security*, Autumn 2006, 19–34, www.wsichina.org/cs4_2.pdf.

Small, Andrew. "China's Caution on Afghanistan—Pakistan." *Washington Quarterly*, vol. 33, no. 3 (July 2010): 81–97, www.twq.com/10july/docs/10jul_Small.pdf.

Smith, Paul J. "China–Japan Relations and the Future Geopolitics of East Asia." *Asian Affairs: An American Review*, vol. 35, no. 4 (Winter 2009): 230–56.

Snyder, Scott. "China–Korea Relations: Strategic Maneuvers for the 'Sandwich Economy.' " *Comparative Connections*, vol. 9, no. 2 (July 2007): 121–26.

Snyder, Scott, and See-won Byun. "China–Korea Relations: China Embraces South and North, but Differently." *Comparative Connections*, vol. 11, no. 4 (January 2010), http://csis.org/files/publication/0904qchina_korea.pdf.

———. "China–Korea Relations: China's Nuclear North Korea Fever." *Comparative Connections*, vol. 11, no. 3 (October 2009), http://csis.org/files/publication/0903qchina_korea.pdf.

Song, Yann-Huei. "Declarations and Statements with Respect to the 1982 UNCLOS: Potential Legal Disputes Between the United States and China after U.S. Accession to the Convention." *Ocean Development and International Law*, vol. 36 (2005): 261–89.

Sutter, Robert. "Asia in the Balance: America and China's 'Peaceful Rise.' " *Current History*, September 2004, 284–89.

——. "Trust Our Resiliency." *Asia Policy*, no. 7 (January 2009): 12–14.

Sutter, Robert, and Chin-Hao Huang. "China–Southeast Asia Relations: China Reassures Neighbors, Wary of US Intention." *Comparative Connections*, vol. 12, no. 4 (January 2011), http://csis.org/files/publication/1004qchina_seasia.pdf.

——. "China–Southeast Asia Relations: Myanmar, South China Sea Issues." *Comparative Connections*, vol. 11, no. 3 (October 2009), http://csis.org/files/publication/0903qchina_seasia.pdf.

——. "China–Southeast Asia Relations: Trade Agreement Registers China's Prominence." *Comparative Connections*, vol. 12, no. 1 (April 2010), http://csis.org/files/publication/1001qchina_seasia.pdf.

Swaine, Michael D. "Beijing's Tightrope Walk on Iran." *China Leadership Monitor*, no. 33 (Summer 2010).

——. "China and the 'AfPak' Issue." *China Leadership Monitor*, no. 31 (Winter 2010), www.hoover.org/publications/clm/issues/84429922.html.

——. "China's Assertive Behavior, Part One: On 'Core Interests.' " *China Leadership Monitor*, no. 34 (Winter 2011), http://media.hoover.org/sites/default/files/documents/CLM34MS.pdf.

——. "China's North Korea Dilemma." *China Leadership Monitor*, no. 30 (Fall 2009), http://media.hoover.org/documents/CLM30MS.pdf.

——. "Perceptions of an Assertive China." *China Leadership Monitor*, no. 32 (May 11, 2010), www.hoover.org/publications/china-leadership-monitor/article/35436.

——. "Trouble in Taiwan." *Foreign Affairs*, vol. 83, no. 2 (March–April 2004).

Swaine, Michael D., with Loren H. Runyon. "Ballistic Missiles and Missile Defense in Asia." *NBR Analysis*, vol. 13, no. 3 (June 2002).

Tanaka, Hitoshi. "Defining Normalcy: The Future Course of Japan's Foreign Policy." *East Asia Insights* (Japan Center for International Exchange), vol. 3, no. 1 (January 2008), www.jcie.org/researchpdfs/EAI/3-1.pdf.

——. "Japan Under the DPJ." *East Asia Insights*, vol. 4, no. 3 (September 2009).

Taubenberger, Jeffery K., and David M. Morens. "Influenza: The Once and Future Pandemic." *Public Health Reports*, vol. 125, supp. 3 (2010), www.publichealthreports.org/archives/issueopen.cfm?articleID=2436.

Tellis, Ashley J. "China's Military Space Strategy." *Survival*, vol. 49, no. 3 (Autumn 2007): 41–72.

Thayer, Bradley A. "Confronting China: An Evaluation of Options for the United States." *Comparative Strategy*, vol. 24, no. 1 (January–March 2005): 71–98.

Thornton, John L. "Long Time Coming: The Prospects for Democracy in China." *Foreign Affairs*, vol. 87, no. 1 (January–February 2008): 2–22.

Tucker, Nancy Bernkopf. "If Taiwan Chooses Unification, Should the United States Care?" *Washington Quarterly*, vol. 25, no. 3 (2002): 15–28.

Twining, Daniel. "America's Grand Design in Asia." *Washington Quarterly*, vol. 30, no. 3 (Summer 2007): 79–94.

Twomey, Christopher P. "Missing Strategic Opportunity in U.S. China Policy Since 9/11." *Asian Survey*, vol. 47, no. 4 (July–August 2007).

Vakil, Sanam. "Iran: Balancing East Against West." *Washington Quarterly*, vol. 29, no. 4 (Autumn 2006): 51–65.

Van Ness, Peter. "Designing A Mechanism for Multilateral Security Cooperation in Northeast Asia." *Asian Perspective*, vol. 32, no. 4 (2008): 107–26.

Wachman, Alan M. "Old Thinking Dominates 'New Thinking.' " *China Security*, vol. 5, no. 1 (Winter 2009): 73–79.

Waldron, Arthur. "How Would Democracy Change China?" *Orbis: A Journal of World Affairs*, vol. 48, no. 2 (Spring 2004): 247–61.

Wang Chuanxing. "On China's Foreign Policy." *Contemporary International Relations*, vol. 19, no. 4 (July–August 2009): 85–94.

Wang, Fei-Ling. "Preservation, Prosperity and Power: What Motivates China's Foreign Policy?" *Journal of Contemporary China*, vol. 14, no. 45 (November 2005): 669–94.

Wang Jiacheng. "Chinese Energy Security: Demand and Supply." *China Strategic Review*, vol. 11 (2005),

Wang Jisi. "China's Search for a Grand Strategy: A Rising Great Power Finds Its Way." *Foreign Affairs*, vol. 90, no. 2 (March–April 2011).

——. "China's Search for Stability with America." *Foreign Affairs*, vol. 84, no. 5 (September–October 2005): 39–48.

——. "The Role of the United States as a Global and Pacific Power: A View from China." *Pacific Review*, vol. 10, no. 1 (1997): 1–18.

Wang, Qing, and Steven Zhang. "China's Under-Consumption Over-Stated." *Global Economic Forum* (Morgan Stanley), September 15, 2009, www.morganstanley.com/views/gef/archive/2009/20090915-Tue.html#anchore2873f99-a1f4-11de-b417-0db96b986471.

Wang Yizhou. "China's Diplomacy: Ten Features." *Contemporary International Relations*, vol. 19, no. 1 (January–February 2009): 45–64.

——. "China's Path: Learning and Growing." *Global Asia*, vol. 5, no. 1 (Spring 2010): 12–16.

——. "Mianxiangershiyishiji de zhongguowaijiao: Sanzhongxuqiu de xunqiujiqipingheng" (Chinese diplomacy in the twenty-first century: Achieving and balancing three needs). *Zhanlue yu Guanli* (Strategy and Management), no. 6 (1999): 18–27.

Wang Yusheng. "One Tries to Manipulate World, the Other Wants Sovereign Democracy—Some Comments on Issue of the U.S. Turning to Focus Its Strike and Pressure on Russia." *Foreign Affairs*, no. 84 (December 23, 2008), www.cpifa.org/en/Html/20081223234040-1.html.

Wang Zaibang. "China and Global Governance." *Contemporary International Relations*, vol. 17, no. 2 (March–April 2007).

Wang, Zhengxu. "Public Support for Democracy in China." *Journal of Contemporary China*, vol. 16, no. 53 (November 2007): 561–79.

Wayne, Martin I. "Five Lessons from China's War on Terror." *Joint Force Quarterly*, 4th quarter, 2007, 42–47.

Weitz, Richard. "Averting a New Great Game in Central Asia." *Washington Quarterly*, vol. 29, no. 3 (Summer 2006): 155–67.

Wenger, Andreas. "U.S. Foreign Policy Under Bush: Balance Sheet and Outlook." *Center for Security Studies Analyses in Security Policy*, vol. 41, no. 3 (October 2008).

Wiegand, Krista. "China's Strategy in the Senkaku/Diaoyu Islands Dispute: Issue Linkage and Coercive Diplomacy." *Asian Security*, vol. 5, no. 2 (2009): 170–93.

Wohlforth, William C. "The Stability of a Unipolar World." *International Security*, vol. 24, no. 1 (Summer 1999): 5–41.

Womack, Brantly. "China and Southeast Asia: Asymmetry, Leadership and Normalcy." *Pacific Affairs*, vol. 76, no. 3 (Winter 2003–2004): 529–48.

Wu Hongying. "Has Latin America Become China's Backyard?" *Contemporary International Relations*, vol. 19, no. 3 (May–June 2009): 16–26.

Xiong Guangkai. "The Role of Energy." *International Strategic Studies*, vol. 3 (2007).

Xu Shiquan. "New Perspectives on the Chinese Mainland's Policy Toward Taiwan." *American Foreign Policy Interests*, vol. 28 (2006): 379–80.

Xu Tao. "The Course and Prospect for Shanghai Cooperation Organization's Regional Security Cooperation." *China Strategic Review*, no. 6 (2006).

Yan Wei. "Cementing Military Bonds." *Beijing Review*, vol. 51, no. 6 (February 7, 2008).

Yan Xuetong. "The Rise of China in Chinese Eyes." *Journal of Contemporary China*, vol. 10, no. 26 (2001): 33–39.

Yergin, Daniel. "Ensuring Energy Security." *Foreign Affairs*, vol. 85, issue 2 (March–April 2006.

Yetiv, Steve A., and Chunlong Lu. "China, Global Energy, and the Middle East." *Middle East Journal*, vol. 61, no. 2 (April 2007): 199–218.

Yoshihide, Soeya. "Taiwan in Japan's Security Considerations." *China Quarterly*, vol. 165 (March 2001): 141–44.

Yuan, Jing-dong. "The Dragon and the Elephant: Chinese–Indian Relations in the 21st Century." *Washington Quarterly*, vol. 30, no. 3 (Summer 2007): 131–44.

Zakaria, Fareed. "The Future of American Power." *Foreign Affairs*, vol. 87, no. 3 (May–June 2008).

Zha Daojiong. "China's Energy Security: Domestic and International Issues." *Survival*, vol. 48, no. 1 (March 1, 2006).

Zhang Ge and Liu Runyuan. "Sino-Indian Relations Entering a New Stage of Comprehensive Development." *International Strategic Studies*, vol. 3 (2005).

Zhao Jinfu. "The Role of Africa in China's Rise." *Contemporary International Relations*, vol. 19, no. 4 (July–August 2009): 20–31.

Zheng Bijian. "China's 'Peaceful Rise' to Great-Power Status." *Foreign Affairs*, vol. 84, no. 5 (September–October 2005): 18.

———. "China's Road for Peaceful Development and Revival of China's Civilization." *China Strategic Review*, vol. 9 (2006): 3.

Zhong, Nan-Shan, and Guang-Qiao Zeng. "Pandemic Planning in China: Applying Lessons from Severe Acute Respiratory Syndrome." Respirology, vol. 13, no. s1 (March 2008): s33–s35.

Zweig, David, and Bi Jianhai. "China's Global Hunt for Energy." *Foreign Affairs*, October 2005.

INDEX

Asia
    alliance of democracies in, 84
    China's economic behavior in,
        207–8
    China's strategic intentions in, 178–79
    critical allies in, 357–59
    inside-out approach to, 56–57
    military interactions in, 121–22
    relationships with, 9–10
    U.S. economic involvement in, 202–3
    U.S. global power structure and, 22–23
    U.S. military presence in, 151–53
Asia Cooperation Dialogue, 123
Asian Development Bank, 139, 184, 188
Asian powers
    China's bilateral relations with, 33–34
    objectives with, 26
    political and security relations with,
        357–65
    relations among, 12, 338
    U.S. policies toward China and, 53–54
Asia-Pacific Economic Cooperation
    (APEC), 123
    Bush, George W., and, 116
    Energy Working Forum, 257
    Japan and, 65
    Obama and, 119
    protectionism and, 212
    trade agreements and, 140
    U.S. involvement in, 202–3
Asia-Pacific Partnership on Clean
    Development and Climate, 257
Association of Southeast Asian Nations
    (ASEAN), 4, 6, 23, 184, 202–3, 207,
    365–66
    Bush, George W., and, 116–17
    Chinese involvement in, 126
    Declaration of Conduct, 123
    Defense Ministers Meeting-Plus, 121
    Japan and, 65
    Obama and, 118–19
    pandemics and, 269–70
    Regional Forum, 366
    territorial disputes within, 27, 164
    trade between China and, 124, 191
Astana Declaration, 120
Australia, 64
Australia Group, 235

Authoritarianism, 2
    Beijing Consensus and, 136–37
    mercantilism and, 30–31
    soft, 299
Avian influenza, 118, 266, 268–69

Ballistic Missile Defense Review, 154
Bank lending, Chinese, 209
Beijing Consensus, 134–39, 295
Beijing University, 259
Bergsten, Fred, 140
Bern Process meetings, 283
Bilateral dialogues, 115, 131–34
    demands of, 207
    S&ED and, 367
    strategic, 354–56, 370–71
    U.S. environmental policy and, 258
Biofuels, 258, 263
Biological Weapons Convention, 40
Blair, Dennis, 121
Bond market, 211
Bosworth, Stephen, 228–29
Bown, Chad, 206
Bradley, Rob, 272
Brautigam, Deborah, 192–93
Brazil, 190
Broadcasting Board of Governors, 284
Brookings Institution, 259
Brunei, 117
Bureaucratic coordination, 310–11
Burma, 132, 285, 294–95
Burns, William, 106
Bush, George H. W., 153, 329
Bush, George W., 14, 26, 55
    approach to counterterrorism of, 242
    ASEAN and, 116–17
    bilateral discussions with China and,
      131–32
    climate change and, 259–60
    counterproliferation efforts of, 227–28
    counterterrorism efforts of, 225–26
    democracy promotion policies of,
      282–86
    direct dialogues and, 329
    economic polices toward China of,
      194–95
    environmental policies of, 257–59
    HIV/AIDS and, 267

RMB and, 214
tainted, 74, 196–97
U.S., 215–216
ExxonMobil, 220

Facebook, 291
Falun Gong, 290
Family planning, coercive, 284
Far sea defense, 160
FDI. *See* Foreign direct investment
Federal Bureau of Investigation, 232
Feigenbaum, Evan, 140
Financial Action Task Force, 231
Financial Crimes Enforcement Network, 231
Financial deregulation, 211
Financial groupings, 201–3
Financial Intelligence Unit, 231
Financial services, 195
Financial systems, 4, 199
Fiscal stimulus, Chinese, 209
Fissile Material Cut-Off Treaty, 229, 245
Five Principles of Peaceful Coexistence,
    33, 346
Foreign direct investment (FDI), 4, 186
Foreign investment
    Heiligendamm Process and, 201–2
    intra-Asian, 134–35
    S&ED and, 199
Framework for Ten-Year Cooperation on
    Energy and Environment, 259
Fravel, Taylor, 174
Free Trade Agreement of the Asia-Pacific
    (FTAAP), 203
Free trade agreements (FTAs), 184–85,
    202–3, 207–8
FTAAP. *See* Free Trade Agreement of the
    Asia-Pacific
FTAs. *See* Free trade agreements
Fukuda, Yasuo, 73–74
Fulbright Scholarship, 284

G-8. *See* Group of Eight
G-20. *See* Group of Twenty
Gaddafi, Muammar, 293
Gambari, Ibrahim, 295
Gao Zhisheng, 290
Gates, Robert
    ASEAN and, 121

defense reprioritization and, 171–72
India and, 105
military-to-military relations and,
    168
U.S.-Japan alliance and, 71
GDP. *See* Gross domestic product
Geithner, Timothy, 199–200, 207
Geneva Protocol, 40
Georgia, 109–12
Gill, Bates, 141
Giving "face," 334–35, 379
Global AIDS Program, 267
Global Disease Detection Center, 266
Global economic engagement, of China,
    184–93
Global financial crisis, 22, 39, 43, 203, 205
    IMF and, 141
    India and, 105
Global Fund to Fight AIDS, Tuberculosis
    and Malaria, 267
Global Initiative to Combat Nuclear
    Terrorism, 229, 231
Global interdependence, 5, 184–85,
    216–17
Global Internet Freedom Task Force, 286
Globalization
    domain diplomacy and, 33
    multilateral regional interactions and,
        345
    perception of, 196
    post-Westphalian norms and, 306
    U.S. policies toward China and, 24
Global Network Initiative, 284
Global rebalancing, 209–15
Global recession
    China's role in, 187–88
    Chinese fiscal stimulus and, 209
    effect on China of, 209–15
    G-20 and, 202
    intra-Asian trade and, 135
    recovery from, 19, 209–15, 356
    SED and, 199
    U.S. defense spending and, 170
Global reserve currency, 213
Global Summit on Nuclear Security, 229
Global warming. *See* Climate change
Goldstein, Lyle, 371
Google, 287, 291

Principals Committee, 319–20
reactive, short-term mindset of,
323–24
National Security Space Strategy, 154
National Security Strategy, 63
NATO. *See* North Atlantic Treaty
Organization
Natural Resources Defense Council, 259
NDPG. *See* National Defense Program
Guidelines
New Security Concept, 35, 37–38, 46, 122,
344, 346
New Security Policy Conference, 123
New START. *See* Strategic Arms Reduction
Treaty
New Zealand, 117
NFU concept. *See* No-first-use concept
NGOs. *See* Nongovernmental organizations
Nigeria, 218
9/11 terrorist attacks, 55, 116, 225
Nobel Peace Prize, 287, 289
No-first-use (NFU) concept, 166–67
Nongovernmental organizations (NGOs),
283, 293
Nonterrorist dissidents, 252
Nontraditional security threats, 12, 22–23,
26, 255, 338
APT and, 126
ARF and, 116
Chinese policy objectives and, 40–41
evaluation of, 271–73
future trends in, 273–77
U.S. policies toward China and, 24
NORINCO. *See* China North Industries
Corporation
Norms, 9–11, 345–47
North Atlantic Treaty Organization
(NATO), 109, 293
Northeast Asian peace and security
mechanism, 117
Northeast Asia Security Mechanism, 144
North Korea, 5, 16, 98–104. *See also* Korean
Peninsula
attempted denuclearization of, 118
Bush, George W., and, 9, 57
Chinese assistance, 227
Chinese containment strategies,
248–49

Chinese influence on, 223–24
Chinese policies toward, 101–2,
363–64
cooperative security structures and,
143, 352
developments in, 247–50
future trends in, 102–4
Japan and, 71
NDPG and, 64
Northeast Asia Security Mechanism
and, 144
nuclear crisis, 363–64
nuclear proliferation and, 17
offshore balancing and, 349
policy coordination regarding,
103–4
proliferation-relevant exports to, 234
refugees from, 80
Russia and, 110
Sino-South Korean relations and,
80–81
6PT and, 236–38
Sunshine Policy and, 77
uranium enrichment program of, 100
U.S. counterterrorism policies and, 226
U.S. negotiated settlement with, 69–70
U.S. policy failures with, 374
U.S. policy toward, 99–100, 102–4,
363–64
U.S. policy toward China and, 27
weapons tests of, 102, 118, 237
withdrawal from Nuclear Non-
Proliferation Treaty by, 101
NPR. *See* Nuclear Posture Review
NPT. *See* Nuclear Non-Proliferation Treaty
NSC. *See* National Security Council
NSG. *See* Nuclear Suppliers Group
Nuclear Emergency Support Team, 232
Nuclear Non-Proliferation Treaty (NPT),
22, 40, 229
CTBT ratification and, 246
India and, 240
Japan and, 69–70
noncompliance, 245
North Korea's withdrawal from, 101
Review Conference, 110
Nuclear Posture Review (NPR), 153,
229–30, 247

Public opinion, 318
    democracy and, 302
    economic development and, 372
    human rights and, 377
    of nontraditional security threat
        policies, 256
Putin, Vladimir, 110
Pye, Lucian, 330

Al-Qaeda, 231
Quadrennial Defense Review, 63, 103,
    172 73
Quintuple Alliance, 350

RAND Corporation, 159
Reagan, Ronald, 63
Recession. *See* Global recession
Reforestation, 263–64
Reform era, 2–3
Regionalism
    Asian economic, 139–41
    East Asian, 125–27
    political-security, 141–45
Religious freedom, 17–18, 41, 285, 288–90
Renminbi (RMB), 196, 200, 213–15. *See also*
    Currency valuation
Republicans, 314–16
Resources
    acquisition policies, 204
    disputes, 27
Respect, 334–35, 379
Responsible stakeholdership, 57–61, 132,
    195
Revised Defense Guidelines of 1997, 65
Rice, Condoleezza, 116–17, 321 22
Rim of the Pacific exercise (RIMPAC), 121
RIMPAC. *See* Rim of the Pacific exercise
RMB. *See* Renminbi
Roh Moo-hyun, 77
Roy, Denny, 302
Royal Dutch/Shell, 220
Rudd, Kevin, 78
Rumsfeld, Donald, 311, 335
Russia, 109–12
    arms sales to China, 111
    cooperative security structures and,
        350
    future challenges with, 364–65

future trends in, 112
SCO and, 119–20
territorial dispute between China
    and, 36
U.S. global power structure and, 23

Sanctions, 281
    against Chinese corporations, 239
    Chinese opposition to, 294
    against Iran, 235–36
    lack of support for, 250
    limits of, 333–34
    against North Korea, 101
    in U.S. counterproliferation policies, 228
    utility of, 240–41
SARS. *See* Severe acute respiratory
    syndrome
Saudi Arabia, 190, 249
Schwab, Susan C., 117
SCO. *See* Shanghai Cooperation
    Organization
Security
    architecture, 9
    China's growing significance in, 6
    Chinese national, 56
    cooperative, 30, 147, 350–54
    EAS and, 118
    Obama and, 60–61
    partisan difference in, 316
    policies, of China, 43 44
    regional balance of, 163–66
    regionalism, 141–45
    South Korea and, 78–79
Security alliances. *See also specific alliances*
    Chinese policy objectives and, 35 36
    New Security Concept and, 46
    U.S. multilateral, 22–23
Security Dialogue, 57–58, 131–32
SED. *See* Strategic Economic Dialogue
S&ED. *See* Strategic and Economic
    Dialogue
Selective engagement, 18, 327, 347–48
Senate Energy and Natural Resource
    Committee, 275
Senior Dialogue, 57–58, 131–33
Senkaku/Diaoyu Islands, 74–75, 143
SEPA. *See* China State Environmental
    Protection Administration

ABOUT THE AUTHOR

Michael D. Swaine is one of the most prominent American analysts in Chinese security studies. A specialist in Chinese defense and foreign policy, U.S.-China relations, and East Asian international relations, he has authored and edited more than ten monographs and many journal and book articles on subjects ranging from the role of the military in China's national security decision making to aspects of Sino-U.S. crisis management. Swaine also advises the U.S. government on Asian security issues and consults regularly with government officials and scholars in China, Japan, and other Asian nations.